Ivor Horton's
Beginning
Visual C++® 2008

Ivor Horton's
Beginning
Visual C++® 2008

Ivor Horton

WILEY

Wiley Publishing, Inc.

Ivor Horton's Beginning Visual C++® 2008

Published by
Wiley Publishing, Inc.
10475 Crosspoint Boulevard
Indianapolis, IN 46256
www.wiley.com

Copyright © 2008 by Ivor Horton

Published by Wiley Publishing, Inc., Indianapolis, Indiana

Published simultaneously in Canada

ISBN: 978-0-470-22590-5

Manufactured in the United States of America

10 9 8 7 6 5 4 3

Library of Congress Cataloging-in-Publication Data is available from the publisher.

For general information on our other products and services please contact our Customer Care Department within the United States at (800) 762-2974, outside the United States at (317) 572-3993 or fax (317) 572-4002.

Trademarks: Wiley, the Wiley logo, Wrox, the Wrox logo, Wrox Programmer to Programmer, and related trade dress are trademarks or registered trademarks of John Wiley & Sons, Inc. and/or its affiliates, in the United States and other countries, and may not be used without written permission. Visual C++ is a registered trademark of Microsoft Corporation in the United States and/or other countries. All other trademarks are the property of their respective owners. Wiley Publishing, Inc., is not associated with any product or vendor mentioned in this book.

Wiley also publishes its books in a variety of electronic formats. Some content that appears in print may not be available in electronic books.

About the Author

Ivor Horton graduated as a mathematician and was lured into information technology by promises of great rewards for very little work. In spite of the reality being usually a great deal of work for relatively modest rewards, he has continued to work with computers to the present day. He has been engaged at various times in programming, systems design, consultancy, and the management of the implementation of projects of considerable complexity.

Horton has many years of experience in the design and implementation of computer systems applied to engineering design and to manufacturing operations in a variety of industries. He has considerable experience developing occasionally useful applications in a wide variety of programming languages, and teaching primarily scientists and engineers to do likewise. He has been writing books on programming for more than 10 years now, and his currently published works include tutorials on C, C++, and Java. At the present time, when he is not writing programming books or providing advice to others, he spends his time fishing, traveling, and trying to speak better French.

Acknowledgments

I'd like to acknowledge the efforts and support of the John Wiley & Sons and Wrox Press editorial and production team in the production of this book, especially my development editor, Ed Connor, who has been there from way back at the beginning and has stayed through to the end. I'd also like to thank my technical editor, John Mueller, once again for doing such an outstanding job of reviewing the text and checking out all the examples in the book; his many constructive comments undoubtedly helped make the book a much better tutorial.

As always, the love and support of my wife, Eve, have been fundamental to making it possible for me to write this book. She has pandered to my every need throughout and has remained patient and cheerful in spite of the hours I spend locked away in my office and my intermittent grumblings about the workload I imposed upon myself.

Credits

Executive Editor
Robert Elliott

Development Editor
Ed Connor

Technical Editor
John Mueller

Copy Editor
Mildred Sanchez

Editorial Manager
Mary Beth Wakefield

Production Manager
Tim Tate

Vice President and Executive Group Publisher
Richard Swadley

Vice President and Executive Publisher
Joseph B. Wikert

Project Coordinator, Cover
Lynsey Stanford

Compositor
Laurie Stewart, Happenstance Type-O-Rama

Proofreaders
Jeremy Bagai
Sheilah Ledwidge
Carrie Hunter
Lee Ewert
Will DeRooy

Indexer
Jack Lewis

Contents

Contents

Contents

Contents

Contents

Contents

Contents

Contents

Contents

Contents

Contents

Contents

Contents

Introduction

Welcome to *Beginning Visual C++® 2008*. With this book you can become an effective C++ programmer. The latest development system from Microsoft, Visual Studio 2008, supports two distinct but closely related flavors of the C++ language; it fully supports the original ISO/ANSI standard C++, and you also get support for a new version of C++ called C++/CLI that was developed by Microsoft and is now an ECMA standard. These two versions of C++ are complementary and fulfill different roles. ISO/ANSI C++ is there for the development of high-performance applications that run natively on your computer whereas C++/CLI has been developed specifically for writing applications that target the .NET Framework. This book will teach you how to write applications in both versions of C++.

You get quite a lot of assistance from automatically generated code when writing ISO/ANSI C++ programs, but you still need to write a lot of C++ yourself. You need a solid understanding of object-oriented programming techniques, as well as a good appreciation of what's involved in programming for Windows. Although C++/CLI targets the .NET Framework, it also is the vehicle for the development of Windows Forms applications that you can develop with little or in some cases no explicit code writing. Of course, when you do have to add code to a Windows Forms application, even though it may be a very small proportion of the total, you still need an in-depth knowledge of the C++/CLI language. ISO/ANSI C++ remains the language of choice for many professionals, but the speed of development that C++/CLI and Windows Forms applications bring to the table make that essential, too. For this reason I cover both flavors of C++ in this book.

Whom This Book Is For

This book is aimed at teaching you how to write C++ applications for the Microsoft Windows operating system using Visual C++ 2008 or any edition of Visual Studio 2008. I make no assumptions about prior knowledge of any particular programming language. This tutorial is for you if:

❑   You have a little experience programming in some other language, such as BASIC for example, and you are keen to learn C++ and develop practical Microsoft Windows programming skills.

❑   You have some experience in C or C++, but not in a Microsoft Windows context and want to extend your skills to program for the Windows environment using the latest tools and technologies.

❑   You have some knowledge of C++ and you want to extend your C++ skills to include C++/CLI.

❑   You are a newcomer to programming and sufficiently keen to jump in the deep end with C++. To be successful you need to have at least a rough idea of how your computer works, including the way in which the memory is organized and how data and instructions are stored.

What This Book Covers

My objective with this book is to teach you the essentials of C++ programming using both of the technologies supported by Visual C++ 2008. The book provides a detailed tutorial on both flavors of the C++ language, on native ISO/ANSI C++ Windows application development using the Microsoft Foundation Classes (MFC), and on the development of C++/CLI Windows applications using Windows Forms.

Because of the importance and pervasiveness of database technology today, the book also includes introductions to the techniques you can use for accessing data sources in both MFC and Windows Forms applications. MFC applications are relatively coding-intensive compared to Windows Forms applications. This is because you create the latter using a highly developed design capability in Visual C++ 2008 that enables you to assemble the entire graphical user interface (GUI) for an application graphically and have all the code that creates it generated automatically. For this reason, there are more pages in the book devoted to MFC programming than to Windows Forms programming.

How This Book Is Structured

The contents of this book are structured as follows:

❏ Chapter 1 introduces you to the basic concepts you need to understand for programming in C++ for native applications and for .NET Framework applications, together with the main ideas embodied in the Visual C++ 2008 development environment. It describes how you use the capabilities of Visual C++ 2008 for creating the various kinds of C++ applications you learn about in the rest of the book.

❏ Chapters 2 to 9 are dedicated to teaching you both versions of the C++ language. The content of each of the Chapters 2 through 9 is structured in a similar way; the first half of each chapter deals with ISO/ANSI C++ topics, and the second half deals with C++/CLI.

❏ Chapter 10 teaches you how you use the Standard Template Library (STL), which is a powerful and extensive set of tools for organizing and manipulating data in your native C++ programs. The STL is application-neutral so you will be able to apply it in a wide range of contexts. Chapter 10 also teaches you the STL/CLR, which is new in Visual C++ 2008. This is a version of the STL for C++/CLI applications.

❏ Chapter 11 introduces you to techniques for finding errors in your C++ programs.

❏ Chapter 12 discusses how Microsoft Windows applications are structured and describes and demonstrates the essential elements that are present in every Windows application. The chapter explains elementary examples of Windows applications using ISO/ANSI C++ and the Windows API and the MFC, as well as an example of a basic Windows Forms application in C++/CLI.

❏ Chapters 13 to 18 describe in detail the capabilities provided by the MFC for building a GUI and how you use the equivalent facilities in a program for the .NET Framework. You learn how you create and use common controls to build the graphical user interface for your application and how you handle the events that result from user interactions with your program. In the process, you create a substantial working application in native C++, and a program with essentially the same functionality in C++/CLI. In addition to the techniques you learn for building a GUI, the applications that you develop also show you how you print documents and how you save them on disk.

❑ Chapter 19 teaches you the essentials you need to know for creating your own libraries using MFC. You learn about the different kinds of libraries you can create, and you develop working examples of these that work with the application that you have evolved over the preceding six chapters.

❑ In Chapters 20 and 21, you learn about accessing data sources in an MFC application. You gain experience in accessing a database in read-only mode; then you learn the fundamental programming techniques for updating a database using MFC. The examples use the Northwind database that can be downloaded from the Web, but you can also apply the techniques described to your own data source.

❑ In Chapter 22 you work with Windows Forms and C++/CLI to build an example that teaches you how to create, customize, and use more Windows Forms controls in an application. You gain practical experience by building a second C++/CLI application incrementally throughout the chapter.

❑ Chapter 23 builds on the knowledge you gain in Chapter 22 and shows how the controls available for accessing data sources work, and how you customize them. You also learn how you can create an application for accessing a database with virtually no coding at all on your part.

All chapters include numerous working examples that demonstrate the programming techniques that are discussed. Every chapter concludes with a summary of the key points that were covered, and most chapters include a set of exercises at the end that you can attempt to apply what you have learned. Solutions to the exercises, together with all the code from the book, are available for download from the publisher's Web site (see the "Source Code" section later in this Introduction for more details).

The tutorial on the C++ language uses examples that are console programs with simple command-line input and output. This approach enables you to learn the various capabilities of C++ without getting bogged down in the complexities of Windows GUI programming. Programming for Windows is really only practicable after you have a thorough understanding of the programming language.

If you want to keep things as simple as possible, you can just learn ISO/ANSI C++ programming in the first instance. Each of the chapters that cover the C++ language (Chapters 2 to 9) first discusses particular aspects of the capabilities of ISO/ANSI C++, followed by the new features introduced by C++/CLI in the same context. The reason for organizing things this way is that C++/CLI is defined as an extension to the ISO/ANSI standard language, so an understanding of C++/CLI is predicated on knowledge of ISO/ANSI C++. Thus, you can just read the ISO/ANSI topics in each of Chapters 2 to 21 and ignore the C++/CLI sections that follow. You then can progress to Windows application development with ISO/ANSI C++ without having to keep the two versions of the language in mind. You can return to C++/CLI when you are comfortable with ISO/ANSI C++. Of course, you can also work straight through and add to your knowledge of both versions of the C++ language incrementally.

What You Need to Use This Book

To use this book you need any of Visual Studio 2008 Standard Edition, Visual Studio 2008 Professional Edition, or Visual Studio 2008 Team System. Note that Visual C++ Express 2008 is *not* sufficient because the MFC is not included.

Visual Studio 2008 requires Windows XP (x86 or x64) with Service Pack 2 or later, Windows Server 2003 with Service Pack 1 or later, or any edition of Windows Vista except Starter Edition. To install any of the three Visual Studio 2008 editions identified you need to have a 1.6 GHz processor with at least 384MB of memory (at least 768MB for Windows Vista) and at least 2.2GB of hard-disk space available. To install the full MSDN documentation that comes with the product you'll need an additional 1.8GB available on the installation drive.

The database examples in the book use the Northwind Traders database. You can find the download for this database by searching for "Northwind Traders" on http://msdn.microsoft.com. Of course, you can also adapt the examples to work with a database of your choice.

Most importantly, to get the most out of this book you need a willingness to learn, and a determination to master the most powerful programming tool for Windows applications presently available. You need the dedication to type in and work through all the examples and try out the exercises in the book. This sounds more difficult than it is, and I think you'll be surprised how much you can achieve in a relatively short period of time. Keep in mind that *everybody* who learns programming gets bogged down from time to time, but if you keep at it, things become clearer and you'll get there eventually. This book helps you to start experimenting on your own and, from there, to become a successful C++ programmer.

Using the Windows Classic Theme

If you're working in Windows Vista with Visual Studio 2008, you may have noticed that the view looks amazing. The transparency offered by the Aero Glass interface is quite breathtaking at first glance (and even many glances afterward). When you add in all of the visual effects that Vista has to offer, you might wonder why anyone would object to such a nice work environment. However, after a few hours of watching windows bursting forth and seeing the display dazzle your vision, you may prefer a setting that is less likely to cause eye fatigue. More importantly, you may notice a significant drop in your productivity because all of this eye candy robs your system of important processing cycles.

Eye candy is nice, but isn't it nicer to get home on time after a long day writing code? That's one reason why this book uses the Windows Classic theme to show Visual Studio 2008 windows. Another reason is that if you are still using Windows XP, the fancy Vista windows would not mean very much to you. The Windows Classic theme is common to both operating systems so it will fit with whatever operating system you are using, and it's definitely friendlier to your eyes than the Aero Glass interface.

If you are using Vista, I encourage you to try the various themes that Vista offers to see if they work for you. However, if you'd like to use the same theme in Vista as I have used for this book, then you can follow these steps to obtain it.

1. Right-click the Desktop and choose Personalize from the context menu. The Personalize window is shown in Figure I-1. This window provides access to all of the display settings you need to obtain the Windows Classic view.

2. Click Theme to display the Theme Settings dialog box shown in Figure I-2.

3. Choose Windows Classic in the Theme field and click OK. At this point, your display will begin looking very much like mine. Of course, you still have all of those special effects to consider. The next set of steps will get rid of the special effects.

4. Close the Personalize window.

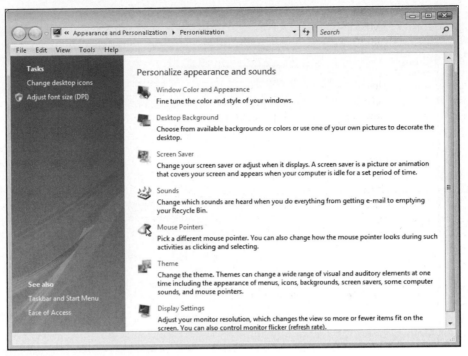

Figure I-1

Figure I-2

5. Open the System applet in the Control Panel to display the System window shown in Figure I-3.

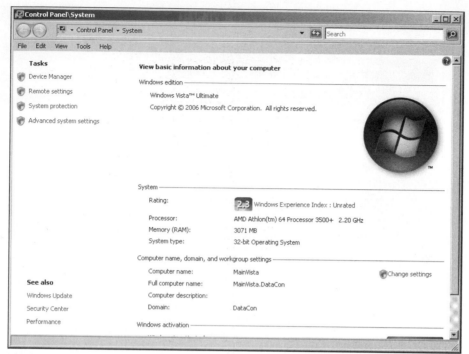

Figure I-3

6. Click Advanced System Settings to display the Advanced tab of the System Properties dialog box shown in Figure I-4.

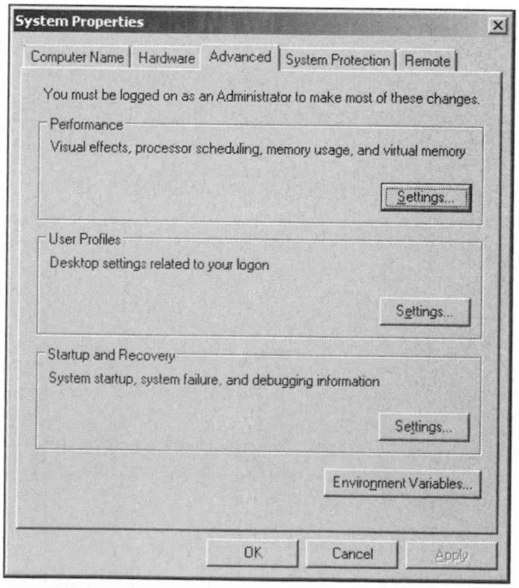

Figure I-4

7. Click Settings in the Performance area to display the Performance Options dialog box shown in Figure I-5.

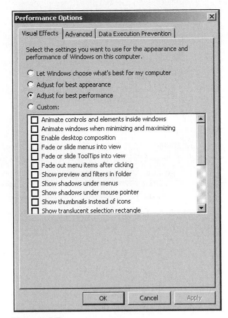

Figure I-5

8. Choose the Adjust for Best Performance option as shown in Figure I-5. Click OK twice to close both dialog boxes. At this point, your system is adjusted to provide the same view that I'm using and also for best graphic performance.

You may also want to use the Classic Start menu to make it easier to locate applications and to perform other tasks. To set your system up for the Classic Start menu, right-click the taskbar and choose Properties. Select the Start menu tab. Choose the Classic Start menu option, make any required customizations by clicking Customize, and click OK. You now have an optimal environment for working with Visual Studio.

Of course, if you are using Windows XP and you want your screen images to look like those in the book, you can use the Classic theme here, too. Just right-click on the Windows desktop, and select Properties from the pop-up menu to display the dialog shown in Figure I-6.

On the Themes tab in the Display Properties dialog, select Windows Classic from the drop-down list of themes. Click the OK button and you are in business.

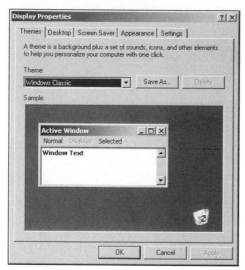

Figure I-6

Conventions

To help you get the most from the text and keep track of what's happening, a number of conventions are used throughout the book.

Try It Out

The *Try It Out* is an exercise involving a working example you should create, compile, and execute, following the text in the book. Output from a working example is shown in a monospaced font like this:

```
Here is output from the example.
Here is more output!
```

How It Works

After each Try It Out, the code you've typed is explained in detail in a How It Works section.

> **Boxes like this one hold important, not-to-be forgotten information that is directly relevant to the surrounding text.**

Notes, tips, hints, tricks, and asides to the current discussion are offset and placed in italics like this.

As for styles in the text:

❑ New terms and important words appear in **bold** when first introduced.

❑ Keyboard strokes are shown like this: Ctrl+A.

❑   File names, URLs, and code within the text appear like so: `persistence.properties`.

❑   Code is presented in two different ways:

```
Monofont type with no highlighting is used for code that you have seen before or
for code that was created automatically for you.
Gray highlighting is used to show code that's new or modified.
```

Source Code

As you work through the examples in this book, you may choose either to type in all the code manually or to use the source code files that accompany the book. All of the source code used in this book is available for download at `http://www.wrox.com`. At the site, simply locate the book's title (either by using the Search box or by using one of the title lists) and click the Download Code link on the book's detail page to obtain all the source code for the book.

While just using the downloaded code is an option, I strongly recommend that you type the code for examples manually and only turn to the code download as a last resort. This will not only be very effective in helping you learn and remember the language syntax, but will also give you valuable experience in making and hopefully correcting mistakes in your code.

> *Because many books have similar titles, you may find it easiest to search by ISBN; this book's ISBN is 978-0-470-22590-5.*

After you download the code, just decompress it with your favorite compression tool. Alternatively, you can go to the main Wrox code download page at `http://www.wrox.com/dynamic/books/download.aspx` to see the code available for this book and all other Wrox books.

Errata

We make every effort to ensure that there are no errors in the text or in the code. However, no one is perfect, and mistakes do occur. If you find an error in one of our books, like a spelling mistake or faulty piece of code, we would be very grateful for your feedback. By sending in errata you may save another reader hours of frustration, and at the same time you will be helping us provide even higher quality information.

To find the errata page for this book, go to `http://www.wrox.com` and locate the title using the Search box or one of the title lists. Then, on the book details page, click the Book Errata link. On this page you can view all errata that has been submitted for this book and posted by Wrox editors. A complete book list including links to each book's errata is also available at `www.wrox.com/misc-pages/booklist.shtml`.

If you don't spot "your" error on the Book Errata page, go to `www.wrox.com/contact/techsupport.shtml` and complete the form there to send us the error you have found. We'll check the information and, if appropriate, post a message to the book's errata page and fix the problem in subsequent editions of the book.

p2p.wrox.com

For author and peer discussion, join the P2P forums at p2p.wrox.com. The forums are a Web-based system for you to post messages relating to Wrox books and related technologies and interact with other readers and technology users. The forums offer a subscription feature to e-mail you topics of interest of your choosing when new posts are made to the forums. Wrox authors, editors, other industry experts, and your fellow readers are present on these forums.

At http://p2p.wrox.com you will find a number of different forums that will help you not only as you read this book, but also as you develop your own applications. To join the forums, just follow these steps:

1. Go to p2p.wrox.com and click the Register link.

2. Read the terms of use and click Agree.

3. Complete the required information to join as well as any optional information you wish to provide and click Submit.

4. You will receive an e-mail with information describing how to verify your account and complete the joining process.

   You can read messages in the forums without joining P2P but in order to post your own messages, you must join.

After you join, you can post new messages and respond to messages other users post. You can read messages at any time on the Web. If you would like to have new messages from a particular forum e-mailed to you, click the Subscribe to this Forum icon by the forum name in the forum listing.

For more information about how to use the Wrox P2P, be sure to read the P2P FAQs for answers to questions about how the forum software works as well as many common questions specific to P2P and Wrox books. To read the FAQs, click the FAQ link on any P2P page.

Programming with Visual C++ 2008

Windows programming isn't difficult. In fact, Microsoft Visual C++ 2008 makes it remarkably easy, as you'll see throughout the course of this book. There's just one obstacle in your path: Before you get to the specifics of Windows programming, you have to be thoroughly familiar with the capabilities of the C++ programming language, particularly the object-oriented aspects of the language. Object-oriented techniques are central to the effectiveness of all the tools that are provided by Visual C++ 2008 for Windows programming, so it's essential that you gain a good understanding of them. That's exactly what this book provides.

This chapter gives you an overview of the essential concepts involved in programming applications in C++. You'll take a rapid tour of the Integrated Development Environment (IDE) that comes with Visual C++ 2008. The IDE is straightforward and generally intuitive in its operation, so you'll be able to pick up most of it as you go along. The best approach to getting familiar with it is to work through the process of creating, compiling, and executing a simple program. By the end of this chapter, you will have learned:

❑ What the principal components of Visual C++ 2008 are

❑ What the .NET Framework consists of and the advantages it offers

❑ What solutions and projects are and how you create them

❑ About console programs

❑ How to create and edit a program

❑ How to compile, link, and execute C++ console programs

❑ How to create and execute basic Windows programs

So power up your PC, start Windows, load the mighty Visual C++ 2008, and begin your journey.

The .NET Framework

The .NET Framework is a central concept in Visual C++ 2008 as well as in all the other .NET development products from Microsoft. The .NET Framework consists of two elements: the **Common Language Runtime** (CLR) in which your application executes, and a set of libraries called the .NET Framework class libraries. The .NET Framework class libraries provide the functional support your code will need when executing with the CLR, regardless of the programming language used, so .NET programs written in C++, C#, or any of the other languages that support the .NET Framework all use the same .NET libraries.

There are two fundamentally different kinds of C++ applications you can develop with Visual C++ 2008. You can write applications that natively execute on your computer. These applications will be referred to as **native C++ programs**. You write native C++ programs in the version of C++ that is defined by the ISO/ANSI (International Standards Organization/American National Standards Institute) language standard. You can also write applications to run under the control of the CLR in an extended version of C++ called **C++/CLI**. These programs will be referred to as **CLR programs**, or **C++/CLI programs**.

The .NET Framework is not strictly part of Visual C++ 2008 but rather a component of the Windows operating system that makes it easier to build software applications and Web services. The .NET Framework offers substantial advantages in code reliability and security, as well as the ability to integrate your C++ code with code written in over 20 other programming languages that target the .NET Framework. A slight disadvantage of targeting the .NET Framework is that there is a small performance penalty, but you won't notice this in the majority of circumstances.

The Common Language Runtime (CLR)

The CLR is a standardized environment for the execution of programs written in a wide range of high-level languages including Visual Basic, C#, and of course C++. The specification of the CLR is now embodied in the European Computer Manufacturers Association (ECMA) standard for the **Common Language Infrastructure** (CLI), ECMA-335, and also in the equivalent ISO standard, ISO/IEC 23271, so the CLR is an implementation of this standard. You can see why C++ for the CLR is referred to as C++/CLI — it's C++ for the Common Language Infrastructure, so you are likely to see C++/CLI compilers on other operating systems that implement the CLI.

> Note that information on all ECMA standards is available from www.ecma-international.org and ECMA-335 is currently available as a free download.

The CLI is essentially a specification for a **virtual machine** environment that enables applications written in diverse high-level programming languages to be executed in different system environments without changing or recompiling the original source code. The CLI specifies a standard **intermediate** language for the virtual machine to which the high-level language source code is compiled. With the .NET Framework, this intermediate language is referred to as **Microsoft Intermediate Language** (**MSIL**). Code in the intermediate language is ultimately mapped to machine code by a just-in-time (JIT) compiler when you execute a program. Of course, code in the CLI intermediate language can be executed within any other environment that has a CLI implementation.

The CLI also defines a common set of data types called the **Common Type System** (**CTS**) that should be used for programs written in any programming language targeting a CLI implementation. The CTS specifies how data types are used within the CLR and includes a set of predefined types. You may also define your own data types, and these must be defined in a particular way to be consistent with the CLR, as you'll see. Having a standardized type system for representing data allows components written in different programming languages to handle data in a uniform way and makes it possible to integrate components written in different languages into a single application.

Data security and program reliability is greatly enhanced by the CLR, in part because dynamic memory allocation and release for data is fully automatic but also because the MSIL code for a program is comprehensively checked and validated before the program executes. The CLR is just one implementation of the CLI specification that executes under Microsoft Windows on a PC; there will undoubtedly be other implementations of the CLI for other operating system environments and hardware platforms. You'll sometimes find that the terms CLI and CLR are used interchangeably, although it should be evident that they are not the same thing. The CLI is a standard specification; the CLR is Microsoft's implementation of the CLI.

Writing C++ Applications

You have tremendous flexibility in the types of applications and program components that you can develop with Visual C++ 2008. As noted earlier in this chapter, you have two basic options for Windows applications: You can write code that executes with the CLR, and you can also write code that compiles directly to machine code and thus executes natively. For window-based applications targeting the CLR, you use Windows Forms as the base for the GUI provided by the .NET Framework libraries. Using Windows Forms enables rapid GUI development because you assemble the GUI graphically from standard components and have the code generated completely automatically. You then just need to customize the code that has been generated to provide the functionality you require.

For natively executing code, you have several ways to go. One possibility is to use the Microsoft Foundation Classes (MFC) for programming the graphical user interface for your Windows application. The MFC encapsulates the Windows operating system Application Programming Interface (API) for GUI creation and control and greatly eases the process of program development. The Windows API originated long before the C++ language arrived on the scene so it has none of the object-oriented characteristics that would be expected if it were written today; however, you are not obliged to use the MFC. If you want the ultimate in performance, you can write your C++ code to access the Windows API directly.

C++ code that executes with the CLR is described as **managed C++** because data and code are managed by the CLR. In CLR programs, the release of memory that you have allocated dynamically for storing data is taken care of automatically, thus eliminating a common source of error in native C++ applications. C++ code that executes outside of the CLR is sometimes described by Microsoft as **unmanaged C++** because the CLR is not involved in its execution. With unmanaged C++ you must take care of all aspects of allocating and releasing memory during execution of your program yourself, and you also forego the enhanced security provided by the CLR. You'll also see unmanaged C++ referred to as **native C++** because it compiles directly to native machine code.

Figure 1-1 shows the basic options you have for developing C++ applications.

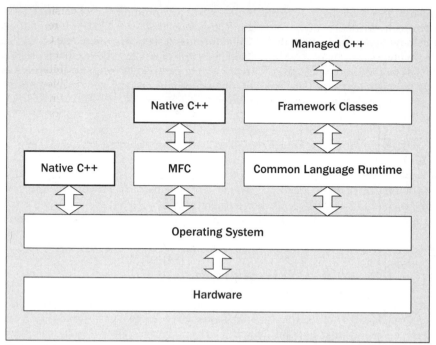

Figure 1-1

Figure 1-1 is not the whole story. An application can consist partly of managed C++ and partly of native C++, so you are not obliged to stick to one environment or the other. Of course, you do lose out somewhat by mixing the code, so you would choose to follow this approach only when necessary, such as when you want to convert an existing native C++ application to run with the CLR. You obviously won't get the benefits inherent in managed C++ in the native C++ code, and there can also be appreciable overhead involved in communications between the managed and unmanaged code components. The ability to mix managed and unmanaged code can be invaluable, however, when you need to develop or extend existing unmanaged code but also want to obtain the advantages of using the CLR. Of course, for new applications you should decide whether you want to create a managed C++ application or a native C++ application at the outset.

Learning Windows Programming

There are always two basic aspects to interactive applications executing under Windows: You need code to create the Graphical User Interface (the GUI) with which the user interacts, and you need code to process these interactions to provide the functionality of the application. Visual C++ 2008 provides you with a great deal of assistance in both aspects of Windows application development. As you'll see later in this chapter, you can create a working Windows program with a GUI without writing any code yourself at all. All the basic code to create the GUI can be generated automatically by Visual C++ 2008; however, it's essential to understand how this automatically generated code works because you need to extend and modify it to make it do what you want, and to do that you need a comprehensive understanding of C++.

For this reason, you'll first learn C++ — both the native C++ and C++/CLI versions of the language — without getting involved in Windows programming considerations. After you're comfortable with C++, you'll learn how you develop fully-fledged Windows applications using native C++ and C++/CLI. This means that while you are learning C++, you'll be working with programs that just involve command line input and output. By sticking to this rather limited input and output capability, you'll be able to concentrate of the specifics of how the C++ language works and avoid the inevitable complications involved in GUI building and control. After you become comfortable with C++, you'll find that it's an easy and natural progression to applying C++ to the development of Windows application programs.

Learning C++

Visual C++ 2008 fully supports two versions of C++ defined by two separate standards:

❑   The ISO/ANSI C++ standard is for implementing native applications — unmanaged C++. This version of C++ is supported on the majority of computer platforms.

❑   The C++/CLI standard is designed specifically for writing programs that target the CLR and is an extension to the ISO/ANSI C++.

Chapters 2 through 9 of this book teach you the C++ language. Because C++/CLI is an extension of ISO/ANSI C++, the first part of each chapter introduces elements of the ISO/ANSI C++ language; the second part explains the additional features that C++/CLI introduces.

Writing programs in C++/CLI allows you to take full advantage of the capabilities of the .NET Framework, something that is not possible with programs written in ISO/ANSI C++. Although C++/CLI is an extension of ISO/ANSI C++, to be able to execute your program fully with the CLR means that it must conform to the requirements of the CLR. This implies that there are some features of ISO/ANSI C++ that you cannot use in your CLR programs. One example of this that you might deduce from what I have said up to now is that the dynamic memory allocation and release facilities offered by ISO/ANSI C++ are not compatible with the CLR; you must use the CLR mechanism for memory management and this implies that you must use C++/CLI classes, not native C++ classes.

The C++ Standards

The ISO/ANSI standard is defined by the document ISO/IEC 14882 that is published by the American National Standards Institute (ANSI). ISO/ANSI standard C++ is the well-established version of C++ that has been around since 1998 and is supported by compilers on the majority of computer hardware platforms and operating systems. Programs that you write in ISO/ANSI C++ can be ported from one system environment to another reasonably easily, although the library functions that a program uses — particularly those related to building a graphical user interface — are a major determinant of how easy or difficult it will be. ISO/ANSI standard C++ has been the first choice of many professional program developers because it is so widely supported, and because it is one of the most powerful programming languages available today.

The ISO/ANSI standard for C++ can be purchased from www.iso.org.

C++/CLI is a version of C++ that extends the ISO/ANSI standard for C++ to better support the Common Language Infrastructure (CLI) that is defined by the standard ECMA-355. The first draft of this standard appeared in 2003 and was developed from an initial technical specification that was produced by Microsoft to support the execution of C++ programs with the .NET Framework. Thus both the CLI and C++/CLI were originated by Microsoft in support of the .NET Framework. Of course, standardizing the CLI and C++/CLI greatly increases the likelihood of implementations in environments other than Windows. It's important to appreciate that although C++/CLI is an extension of ISO/ANSI C++, there are features of ISO/ANSI C++ that you must not use when you want your program to execute fully under the control of the CLR. You'll learn what these are as you progress through the book.

The CLR offers substantial advantages over the native environment. By targeting your C++ programs at the CLR, your programs will be more secure and not prone to the potential errors you can make when using the full power of ISO/ANSI C++. The CLR also removes the incompatibilities introduced by various high-level languages by standardizing the target environment to which they are compiled and thus permits modules written in C++ to be combined with modules written in other languages such as C# or Visual Basic.

Attributes

Attributes are an advanced feature of programming with C++/CLI that allow you to add descriptive declarations to your code. At the simplest level, you can use attributes to annotate particular programming elements in your program but there's more to attributes than just additional descriptive data. Attributes can affect how your code behaves at run time by modifying the way the code is compiled or by causing extra code to be generated that supports additional capabilities. A range of standard attributes is available for C++/CLI and it is also possible to create your own.

A detailed discussion of attributes is beyond the scope of this book but I mention them here because you will make use of attributes in one or two places in the book, particularly in Chapter 18 where you learn how to write objects to a file.

Console Applications

As well as developing Windows applications, Visual C++ 2008 also allows you to write, compile, and test C++ programs that have none of the baggage required for Windows programs — that is, applications that are essentially character-based, command-line programs. These programs are called **console applications** in Visual C++ 2008 because you communicate with them through the keyboard and the screen in character mode.

Writing console applications might seem as though you are being sidetracked from the main objective of Windows programming, but when it comes to learning C++ (which you do need to do before embarking on Windows-specific programming), it's the best way to proceed. There's a lot of code in even a simple Windows program, and it's very important not to be distracted by the complexities of Windows when learning the ins and outs of C++. Therefore, in the early chapters of the book where you are concerned with how C++ works, you'll spend time walking with a few lightweight console applications before you get to run with the heavyweight sacks of code in the world of Windows.

While you're learning C++, you'll be able to concentrate on the language features without worrying about the environment in which you're operating. With the console applications that you'll write, you have only a text interface, but this will be quite sufficient for understanding all of C++ because there's no graphical capability within the definition of the language. Naturally, I will provide extensive coverage of graphical user interface programming when you come to write programs specifically for Windows using Microsoft Foundation Classes (MFC) in native C++ applications and Windows Forms with the CLR.

There are two distinct kinds of console applications and you'll be using both. **Win32 console applications** compile to native code, and you'll be using these to try out the capabilities of ISO/ANSI C++. **CLR console applications** target the CLR so you'll be using these when you are working with the features of C++/CLI.

Windows Programming Concepts

Our approach to Windows programming is to use all the tools that Visual C++ 2008 provides. The project creation facilities that are provided with Visual C++ 2008 can generate skeleton code for a wide variety of native C++ application programs automatically, including basic Windows programs. For Windows applications that you develop for the CLR you get even more automatic code generation. You can create complete applications using Windows Forms that only require a small amount of customizing code to be written by you and sometimes no additional code at all. Creating a project is the starting point for all applications and components that you develop with Visual C++ 2008, and to get a flavor of how this works, you'll look at the mechanics of creating some examples, including an outline Windows program, later in this chapter.

A Windows program, whether a native C++ program or a program written for the CLR, has a different structure from that of the typical console program you execute from the command line, and it's more complicated. In a console program, you can get input from the keyboard and write output back to the command line directly, whereas a Windows program can access the input and output facilities of the computer only by way of functions supplied by the host environment; no direct access to the hardware resources is permitted. Because several programs can be active at one time under Windows, Windows has to determine which application a given raw input such as a mouse click or the pressing of a key on the keyboard is destined for and signal the program concerned accordingly. Thus the Windows operating system has primary control of all communications with the user.

Also, the nature of the interface between a user and a Windows application is such that a wide range of different inputs is usually possible at any given time. A user may select any of a number of menu options, click a toolbar button, or click the mouse somewhere in the application window. A well-designed Windows application has to be prepared to deal with any of the possible types of input at any time because there is no way of knowing in advance which type of input is going to occur. These user actions are received by the operating system in the first instance and are all regarded by Windows as **events**. An event that originates with the user interface for your application will typically result in a particular piece of your program code being executed. How program execution proceeds is therefore determined by the sequence of user actions. Programs that operate in this way are referred to as **event-driven programs** and are different from traditional procedural programs that have a single order of execution. Input to a procedural program is controlled by the program code and can occur only when the program permits it; therefore, a Windows program consists primarily of pieces of code that respond to events caused by the action of the user, or by Windows itself. This sort of program structure is illustrated in Figure 1-2.

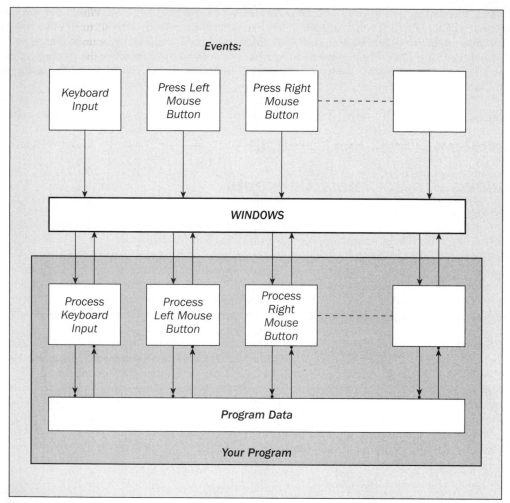

Figure 1-2

Each square block in Figure 1-2 represents a piece of code written specifically to deal with a particular event. The program may appear to be somewhat fragmented because of the number of disjointed blocks of code, but the primary factor welding the program into a whole is the Windows operating system itself. You can think of your program as customizing Windows to provide a particular set of capabilities.

Of course, the modules servicing various external events, such as selecting a menu or clicking the mouse, all typically have access to a common set of application-specific data in a particular program. This application data contains information that relates to what the program is about — for example, blocks of text in an editor or player scoring records in a program aimed at tracking how your baseball team is doing — as well as information about some of the events that have occurred during execution of the program. This shared collection of data allows various parts of the program that look independent to communicate and operate in a coordinated and integrated fashion. I will go into this in much more detail later in the book.

Even an elementary Windows program involves several lines of code, and with Windows programs that are generated by the Application Wizards that come with Visual C++ 2008, "several" turns out to be "many." To simplify process of understanding how C++ works, you need a context that is as uncomplicated as possible. Fortunately, Visual C++ 2008 comes with an environment that is ready-made for the purpose.

What Is the Integrated Development Environment?

The Integrated Development Environment (IDE) that comes with Visual C++ 2008 is a completely self-contained environment for creating, compiling, linking, and testing your C++ programs. It also happens to be a great environment in which to learn C++ (particularly when combined with a great book).

Visual C++ 2008 incorporates a range of fully integrated tools designed to make the whole process of writing C++ programs easy. You will see something of these in this chapter, but rather than grind through a boring litany of features and options in the abstract, first take a look at the basics to get a view of how the IDE works and then pick up the rest in context as you go along.

Components of the System

The fundamental parts of Visual C++ 2008, provided as part of the IDE, are the editor, the compiler, the linker, and the libraries. These are the basic tools that are essential to writing and executing a C++ program. Their functions are as follows.

The Editor

The editor provides an interactive environment for you to create and edit C++ source code. As well as the usual facilities, such as cut and paste, which you are certainly already familiar with, the editor also provides color cues to differentiate between various language elements. The editor automatically recognizes fundamental words in the C++ language and assigns a color to them according to what they are. This not only helps to make your code more readable but also provides a clear indicator of when you make errors in keying such words.

The Compiler

The compiler converts your source code into **object code**, and detects and reports errors in the compilation process. The compiler can detect a wide range of errors that are due to invalid or unrecognized program code, as well as structural errors, where, for example, part of a program can never be executed. The object code output from the compiler is stored in files called **object files**. There are two types of object code that the compiler produces. These object codes usually have names with the extension .obj.

The Linker

The linker combines the various modules generated by the compiler from source code files, adds required code modules from program libraries supplied as part of C++, and welds everything into an executable whole. The linker can also detect and report errors — for example, if part of your program is missing or a non-existent library component is referenced.

The Libraries

A **library** is simply a collection of pre-written routines that supports and extends the C++ language by providing standard professionally produced code units that you can incorporate into your programs to carry out common operations. The operations that are implemented by routines in the various libraries provided by Visual C++ 2008 greatly enhance productivity by saving you the effort of writing and testing the code for such operations yourself. I have already mentioned the .NET Framework library, and there are a number of others — too many to enumerate here — but I'll mention the most important ones.

The **Standard C++ Library** defines a basic set of routines common to all ISO/ANSI C++ compilers. It contains a wide range of routines including numerical functions such as calculating square roots and evaluating trigonometrical functions, character and string processing routines such as classifying characters and comparing character strings, and many others. You'll get to know quite a number of these as you develop your knowledge of ISO/ANSI C++. There are also libraries that support the C++/CLI extensions to ISO/ANSI C++.

Native window-based applications are supported by a library called the **Microsoft Foundation Classes** (MFC). The MFC greatly reduces the effort needed to build the graphical user interface for an application. You'll see a lot more of the MFC when you finish exploring the nuances of the C++ language. Another library contains a set of facilities called **Windows Forms** that are roughly the equivalent of the MFC for window-based applications that are executed with the .NET Framework. You'll be seeing how you make use of Windows Forms to develop applications, too.

Using the IDE

All program development and execution in this book is performed from within the IDE. When you start Visual C++ 2008, notice an application window similar to that shown in Figure 1-3.

Figure 1-3 shows the Visual Studio 2008 windows using the Classic theme. If you are not using the Windows Classic theme, your window will look different, especially if you have Windows Vista installed. All the screen images in the book use the Windows Classic theme for commonality between Vista and XP, and if you want to make the windows display the same on your machine, follow the instructions in the "Using the Windows Classic Theme" section in the Introduction.

The window to the left in Figure 1-3 is the **Solution Explorer window**, the top-right window presently showing the Start page is the **Editor window**, and the tab visible in the window at the bottom is the **Code Definition window**. The Solution Explorer window enables you to navigate through your program files and display their contents in the Editor window and to add new files to your program. The Solution Explorer window has an additional tab (only three are shown in Figure 1-3) that displays the **Resource View** for your application, and you can select which tabs are to be displayed from the View menu. The Editor window is where you enter and modify source code and other components of your application. The Code Definition window displays the definition of a symbol selected in the Editor window. There are two tabs displayed alongside the Code Definition tab, the Call Browser window that enables you to search your code for function calls, and the Output window that displays messages that result from compiling and linking your program.

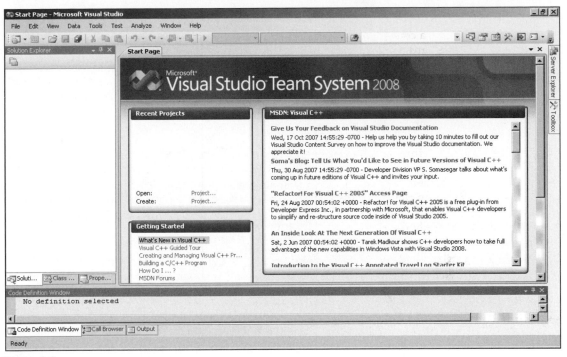

Figure 1-3

Toolbar Options

You can choose which toolbars are displayed in your Visual C++ window by right-clicking in the toolbar area. A pop-up menu with a list of toolbars (Figure 1-4) appears, and the toolbars that are currently displayed have check marks alongside.

This is where you decide which toolbars are visible at any one time. You can make your set of toolbars the same as those shown in Figure 1-3 by making sure the Build, Class Designer, Debug, Standard, and View Designer menu items are checked. Clicking in the gray area to the left of a toolbar checks it if it is unchecked and results in it being displayed; clicking a check mark hides the corresponding toolbar.

You don't need to clutter up the application window with all the toolbars you think you might need at some time. Some toolbars appear automatically when required, so you'll probably find that the default toolbar selections are perfectly adequate most of the time. As you develop your applications, from time to time you might think it would be more convenient to have access to toolbars that aren't displayed. You can change the set of toolbars that are visible whenever it suits you by right-clicking in the toolbar area and choosing from the context menu.

Figure 1-4

Similar to many other Windows applications, the toolbars that make up Visual C++ 2008 come complete with tooltips. Just let the mouse pointer linger over a toolbar button for a second or two and a white label displays the function of that button.

Dockable Toolbars

A **dockable** toolbar is one that you can drag around with the mouse to position at a convenient place in the window. When it is placed in any of the four borders of the application, it is said to be *docked* and looks similar to the toolbars you see at the top of the application window. The toolbar on the upper line of toolbar buttons that contains the disk icons and the text box to the right of a pair of binoculars is the Standard toolbar. You can drag this away from the toolbar by placing the cursor on it and dragging it with the mouse while you hold down the left mouse button. It then appears as a separate window you can position anywhere.

If you drag any dockable toolbar away from its docked position, it looks like the Standard toolbar you see in Figure 1-5, enclosed in a little window — with a different caption. In this state, it is called a **floating toolbar**. All the toolbars that you see in Figure 1-3 are dockable and can be floating, so you can experiment with dragging any of them around. You can position them in docked positions where they revert to their normal toolbar appearance. You can dock a dockable toolbar at any side of the main window.

Figure 1-5

You'll become familiar with many of the toolbar icons that Visual C++ 2008 uses from other Windows applications, but you may not appreciate exactly what these icons do in the context of Visual C++, so I'll describe them as we use them.

Because you'll use a new project for every program you develop, looking at what exactly a project is and understanding how the mechanism for defining a project works is a good place to start finding out about Visual C++ 2008.

Documentation

There will be plenty of occasions when you'll want to find out more information about Visual C++ 2008. The **Microsoft Development Network (MSDN) Library** provides comprehensive reference material on all the capabilities on Visual C++ 2008 and more besides. When you install Visual C++ 2008 onto your machine, there is an option to install part or all of the MSDN documentation. If you have the disk space available I strongly recommend that you install the MSDN Library.

Press the F1 function to browse the MSDN Library. The Help menu also provides various routes into the documentation. As well as offering reference documentation, the MSDN Library is a useful tool when dealing with errors in your code, as you'll see later in this chapter.

Projects and Solutions

A **project** is a container for all the things that make up a program of some kind — it might be a console program, a window-based program, or some other kind of program — and it usually consists of one or more source files containing your code plus possibly other files containing auxiliary data. All the files for a project are stored in **the project folder** and detailed information about the project is stored in an XML file with the extension .vcproj that is also in the project folder. The project folder also contains other folders that are used to store the output from compiling and linking your project.

The idea of a **solution** is expressed by its name, in that it is a mechanism for bringing together all the programs and other resources that represent a solution to a particular data processing problem. For example, a distributed order entry system for a business operation might be composed of several different programs that could each be developed as a project within a single solution; therefore, a **solution** is a folder in which all the information relating to one or more projects is stored, so one or more project folders are subfolders of the solution folder. Information about the projects in a solution is stored in two files with the extensions .sln and .suo. When you create a project, a new solution is created automatically unless you elect to add the project to an existing solution.

When you create a project along with a solution, you can add further projects to the same solution. You can add any kind of project to an existing solution, but you would usually add only a project that was related in some way to the existing project or projects in the solution. Generally, unless you have a good reason to do otherwise, each of your projects should have its own solution. Each example you create with this book will be a single project within its own solution.

Defining a Project

The first step in writing a Visual C++ 2008 program is to create a project for it using the `File > New > Project` menu option from the main menu or you can press `Ctrl+Shift+N`; you can also simply click Project... adjacent to Create: in the Recent Projects pane. As well as containing files that define all the code and any other data that goes to make up your program, the project XML file in the project folder also records the Visual C++ 2008 options you're using. Although you don't need to concern yourself with the project file — it is entirely maintained by the IDE — you can browse it if you want to see what the contents are, but take care not to modify it accidentally.

That's enough introductory stuff for the moment. It's time to get your hands dirty.

Try It Out   **Creating a Project for a Win32 Console Application**

You'll now take a look at creating a project for a console application. First select `File > New > Project` or use one of the other possibilities mentioned earlier to bring up the New Project dialog box, shown in Figure 1-6.

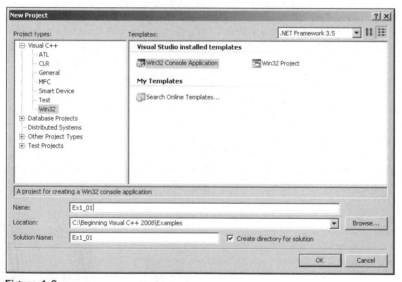

Figure 1-6

The left pane in the New Project dialog box displays the types of projects you can create; in this case, click `Win32`. This also identifies an Application Wizard that creates the initial contents for the project. The right pane displays a list of templates available for the project type you have selected in the left pane. The template you select is used by the Application Wizard when creating the files that make up the project. In the next dialog box, you have an opportunity to customize the files that are created when you click the OK button in this dialog box. For most of the type/template options, a basic set of program source modules are created automatically.

You can now enter a suitable name for your project by typing into the Name: edit box — for example, you could call this one Ex1_01, or you can choose your own project name. Visual C++ 2008 supports long file names, so you have a lot of flexibility. The name of the solution folder appears in the bottom edit box and, by default, the solution folder has the same name as the project. You can change this if you want. The dialog box also allows you to modify the location for the solution that contains your project — this appears in the Location: edit box. If you simply enter a name for your project, the solution folder is automatically set to a folder with that name, with the path shown in the Location: edit box. By default the solution folder is created for you if it doesn't already exist. If you want to specify a different path for the solution folder, just enter it in the Location: edit box. Alternatively, you can use the Browse button to select another path for your solution. Clicking the OK button displays the Win32 Application Wizard dialog box shown in Figure 1-7.

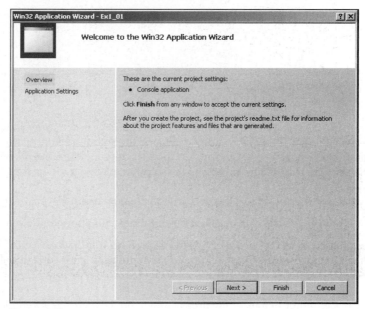

Figure 1-7

This dialog box explains the settings currently in effect. If you click the Finish button, the wizard creates all the project files based on this. In this case you can click Application Settings on the left to display the Application Settings page of the wizard shown in Figure 1-8.

The Application Settings page allows you to choose options that you want to apply to the project. For most of the projects you'll be creating when you are learning the C++ language, you select the Empty project checkbox, but here you can leave things as they are and click the Finish button. The Application Wizard then creates the project with all the default files.

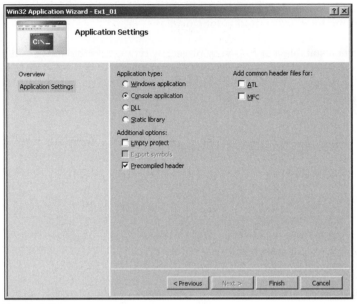

Figure 1-8

The project folder will have the name that you supplied as the project name and will hold all the files making up the project definition. If you didn't change it, the solution folder has the same name as the project folder and contains the project folder plus the files defining the contents of the solution. If you use Windows Explorer to inspect the contents of the solution folder, you'll see that it contains three files:

❑   A file with the extension .sln that records information about the projects in the solution.

❑   A file with the extension .suo in which user options that apply to the solution will be recorded.

❑   A file with the extension .ncb that records data about **Intellisense** for the solution. Intellisense is the facility that provides auto-completion and prompting for code in the Editor window as you enter it.

If you use Windows Explorer to look in the project folder, notice there are seven files initially, including a file with the name ReadMe.txt that contains a summary of the contents of the files that have been created for the project. The project you have created will automatically open in Visual C++ 2008 with the left pane as in Figure 1-9. I have increased the width of this pane so that you can see the complete names on the tabs.

The **Solution Explorer** tab presents a view of all the projects in the current solution and the files they contain — here there is just one project of course. You can display the contents of any file as an additional tab in the Editor pane just by double-clicking in name in the Solution Explorer tab. In the Replace with Editor pane you can switch instantly between any of the files that have been displayed just by clicking on the appropriate tab.

Figure 1-9

The **Class View** tab displays the classes defined in your project and also shows the contents of each class. You don't have any classes in this application, so the view is empty. When we discuss classes, you will see that you can use the Class View tab to move around the code relating to the definition and implementation of all your application classes quickly and easily.

The **Property Manager** tab shows the properties that have been set for the Debug and Release versions of your project. I'll explain these versions a little later in this chapter. You can change any of the properties shown by right-clicking a property and selecting Properties from the context menu; this displays a dialog box where you can set the project property. You can also press Alt+F7 to display the properties dialog box at any time; I'll also discuss this in more detail when we go into the Debug and Release versions of a program.

The **Resource View** shows the dialog boxes, icons, menus toolbars, and other resources that are used by the program. Because this is a console program, no resources are used; however, when you start writing Windows applications, you'll see a lot of things here. Through this tab you can edit or add to the resources available to the project.

Like most elements of the Visual C++ 2008 IDE, the Solution Explorer and other tabs provide context-sensitive pop-up menus when you right-click items displayed in the tab and in some cases in the empty space in the tab, too. If you find that the Solution Explorer pane gets in your way when writing code, you can hide it by clicking the Autohide icon. To redisplay it, click the name tab on the left of the IDE window.

Modifying the Source Code

The Application Wizard generates a complete Win32 console program that you can compile and execute. Unfortunately, the program doesn't do anything as it stands, so to make it a little more interesting you need to change it. If it is not already visible in the Editor pane, double-click Ex1_01.cpp in the Solution

Explorer pane. This file is the main source file for the program that the Application Wizard generated and it looks like that shown in Figure 1-10.

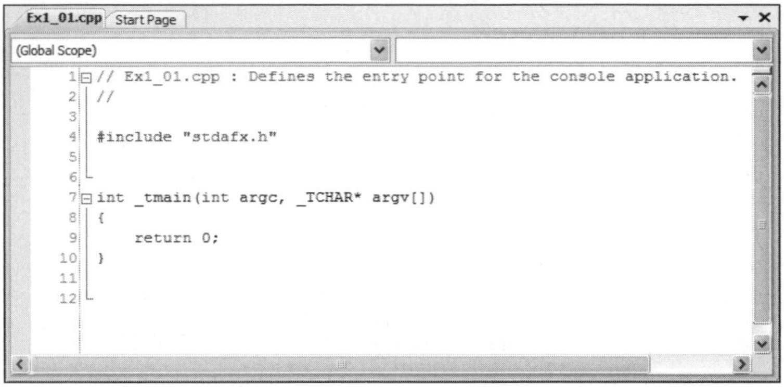

Figure 1-10

If the line numbers are not displayed on your system, select `Tools > Options` from the main menu to display the Options dialog box. If you extend the C/C++ option in the TextEditor subtree in the right pane and select General from the extended tree, you can select Line Numbers in the right pane of the dialog box. I'll first give you a rough guide to what this code in Figure 1-10 does, and you'll see more on all of these later.

The first two lines are just comments. Anything following "`//`" in a line is ignored by the compiler. When you want to add descriptive comments in a line, precede your text by "`//`".

Line 4 is an `#include` directive that adds the contents of the file `stdafx.h` to this file in place of this `#include` directive. This is the standard way of adding the contents of `.h` source files to a `.cpp` source file a in a C++ program.

Line 7 is the first line of the executable code in this file and the beginning of the function `_tmain()`. A function is simply a named unit of executable code in a C++ program; every C++ program consists of at least one — and usually many more — functions.

Lines 8 and 10 contain left and right braces, respectively, that enclose all the executable code in the function `_tmain()`. The executable code is, therefore, just the single line 10 and all this does is end the program.

Now you can add the following two lines of code in the Editor window:

```
// Ex1_01.cpp : Defines the entry point for the console application.
//

#include "stdafx.h"
#include <iostream>
```

```
int _tmain(int argc, _TCHAR* argv[])
{
   std::cout << "Hello world!\n";
   return 0;
}
```

The unshaded lines are the ones generated for you. The new lines you should add are shown shaded. To introduce each new line, place the cursor at the end on the text on the preceding line and press Enter to create an empty line in which you can type the new code. Make sure it is exactly as shown in the preceding example; otherwise, the program may not compile.

The first new line is an #include directive that adds the contents of one of the standard libraries for ISO/ANSI C++ to the source file. The <iostream> library defines facilities for basic I/O operations, and the one you are using in the second line that you added writes output to the command line. std::cout is the name of the standard output stream and you write the string "Hello world!\n" to std::cout in the second addition statement. Whatever appears between the pair of double quote characters is written to the command line.

Building the Solution

To build the solution, press F7 or select the Build > Build Solution menu item. Alternatively, you can click the toolbar button corresponding to this menu item. The toolbar buttons for the Build menu may not display, but you can easily fix this by right-clicking in the toolbar area and selecting the Build toolbar from those in the list. The program should then compile successfully. If there are errors, ensure that you didn't make an error while entering the new code, so check the two new lines very carefully.

Files Created by Building a Console Application

After the example has been built without error, take a look in the project folder by using Windows Explorer to see a new subfolder to the solution folder Ex1_01 called Debug. This folder contains the output of the build you just performed on the project. Notice that this folder contains three files.

Other than the .exe file, which is your program in executable form, you don't need to know much about what's in these files. In case you're curious, however, the .ilk file is used by the linker when you rebuild your project. It enables the linker to incrementally link the object files produced from the modified source code into the existing .exe file. This avoids the need to re-link everything each time you change your program, and the .pdb file contains debugging information that is used when you execute the program in debug mode. In this mode, you can dynamically inspect information that is generated during program execution.

There's a Debug subdirectory to the Ex1_01 project file, too. This contains ten more files that were created during the build process and you can see what kind of information they contain from the Type description in Windows Explorer.

Debug and Release Versions of Your Program

You can set a range of options for a project through the `Project > Ex1_01 Properties` menu item. These options determine how your source code is processed during the compile and link stages. The set of options that produces a particular executable version of your program is called a **configuration**. When you create a new project workspace, Visual C++ 2008 automatically creates configurations for producing two versions of your application. One version, called the `Debug` version, includes information that helps you debug the program. With the `Debug` version of your program you can step through the code when things go wrong, checking on the data values in the program. The other, called the `Release` version, has no debug information included and has the code optimization options for the compiler turned on to provide you with the most efficient executable module. These two configurations are sufficient for your needs throughout this book, but when you need to add other configurations for an application, you can do so through the `Build > Configuration Manager` menu. Note that this menu item won't appear if you haven't got a project loaded. This is obviously not a problem, but might be confusing if you're just browsing through the menus to see what's there.

You can choose which configuration of your program to work with by selecting the configuration from the `Active solution configuration` drop-down list in the `Configuration Manager` dialog box, as shown in Figure 1-11.

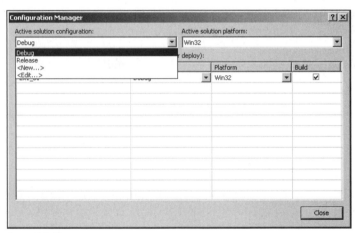

Figure 1-11

Select the configuration you want to work with from the list and then click the `Close` button. While you're developing an application, you'll work with the debug configuration. After your application has been tested using the debug configuration and appears to be working correctly, you typically rebuild the program as a release version; this produces optimized code without the debug and trace capability, so the program runs faster and occupies less memory.

Executing the Program

After you have successfully compiled the solution, you can execute your program by pressing `Ctrl+F5`. You should see the window shown in Figure 1-12.

Figure 1-12

As you see, you get the text that was between the double quotes written to the command line. The "\n" that appeared at the end of the text string is a special sequence called an **escape sequence** that denotes a newline character. Escape sequences are used to represent characters in a text string that you cannot enter directly from the keyboard.

Try It Out   Creating an Empty Console Project

The previous project contained a certain amount of excess baggage that you don't need when working with simple C++ language examples. The precompiled headers option chosen by default resulted in the stdafx.h file being created in the project. This is a mechanism for making the compilation process more efficient when there are a lot of files in a program but this won't be necessary for many of our examples. In these instances you start with an empty project to which you can add your own source files. You can see how this works by creating a new project in a new solution for a Win32 console program with the name Ex1_02. After you have entered the project name and clicked the OK button, click Applications Settings on the left side (right below Overview) of the dialog box that follows. You can then select Empty project from the additional options, as Figure 1-13 shows.

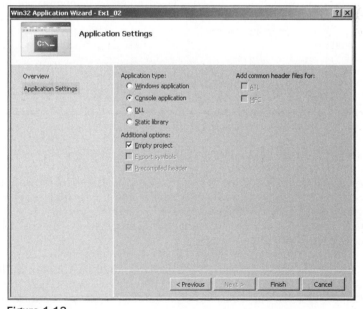

Figure 1-13

When you click the Finish button, the project is created as before, but this time without any source files.

Next you add a new source file to the project. Right-click the Solution Explorer pane and then select Add > New Item from the context menu. A dialog box displays; click Code in the left pane, and C++ File(.cpp) in the right pane. Enter the file name as Ex1_02, as shown in Figure 1-14.

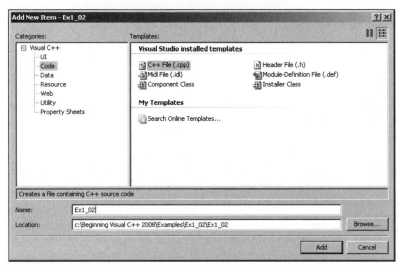

Figure 1-14

When you click the Add button, the new file is added to the project and is displayed in the Editor window. Of course, the file is empty so nothing will be displayed; enter the following code in the Editor window:

```
// Ex1_02.cpp A simple console program
#include <iostream>                       // Basic input and output library

int main()
{
  std::cout << "This is a simple program that outputs some text." << std::endl;
  std::cout << "You can output more lines of text" << std::endl;
  std::cout << "just by repeating the output statement like this." << std::endl;
  return 0;                               // Return to the operating system
}
```

Note the automatic indenting that occurs as you type the code. C++ uses indenting to make programs more readable, and the editor automatically indents each line of code that you enter, based on what was in the previous line. You can also see the syntax color highlighting in action as you type. Some elements of the program are shown in different colors as the editor automatically assigns colors to language elements depending on what they are.

The preceding code is the complete program. You probably noticed a couple of differences compared to the code generated by the Application Wizard in the previous example. There's no #include directive for the stdafx.h file. You don't have this file as part of the project here because you are not using the precompiled headers facility. The name of the function here is main; before it was _tmain. In fact all ISO/ANSI C++ programs start execution in a function called main(). Microsoft also provides for this function to be called wmain when Unicode characters are used and the name _tmain is defined to be either main or wmain, depending on whether or not the program is going to use Unicode characters. For the previous example, the name _tmain is defined behind the scenes to be main. You use the name main in all the ISO/ANSI C++ examples.

The output statements are a little different. The first statement in main() is:

```
std::cout << "This is a simple program that outputs some text." << std::endl;
```

You have two occurrences of the << operator, and each one sends whatever follows to std::cout, which is the standard output stream. First the string between double quotes is sent to the stream and then std::endl where std::endl is defined in the standard library as a newline character. Earlier you used the escape sequence \n for a newline character within a string between double quotes. You could have written the preceding statement as:

```
std::cout << "This is a simple program that outputs some text.\n";
```

I should explain why the line is shaded, where the previous line of code is not. Where I repeat a line of code for explanation purposes I show it unshaded. The preceding line of code is new and does not appear earlier so I have shown it shaded.

You can now build this project in the same way as the previous example. Note that any open source files in the Editor pane are saved automatically if you have not already saved them. When you have compiled the program successfully, press Ctrl+F5 to execute it. The window shown in Figure 1-15 displays.

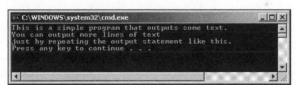

Figure 1-15

Dealing with Errors

Of course, if you didn't type the program correctly, you get errors reported. To show how this works, you could deliberately introduce an error into the program. If you already have errors of your own, you can use those to perform this exercise. Go back to the Editor pane and delete the semicolon at the end of the second-to-last line between the braces (line 8); then rebuild the source file. The Output pane at the bottom of the application window includes the error message:

```
C2143: syntax error : missing ';' before 'return'
```

Every error message during compilation has an error number that you can look up in the documentation. Here, the problem is obvious; however, in more obscure cases, the documentation may help you figure out what is causing the error. To get the documentation on an error, click the line in the Output pane that contains the error number and then press F1. A new window displays containing further information about the error. You can try it with this simple error, if you like.

When you have corrected the error, you can then rebuild the project. The build operation works efficiently because the project definition keeps track of the status of the files making up the project. During a normal build, Visual C++ 2008 recompiles only the files that have changed since the program was last compiled or built. This means that if your project has several source files and you've edited only one of the files since the project was last built, only that file is recompiled before linking to create a new .exe file.

You'll also use CLR console programs, so the next section shows you what a CLR console project looks like.

Try It Out   Creating a CLR Console Project

Press Ctrl+Shift+N to display the New Project dialog box; then select the project type as CLR and the template as CLR Console Application, as shown in Figure 1-16.

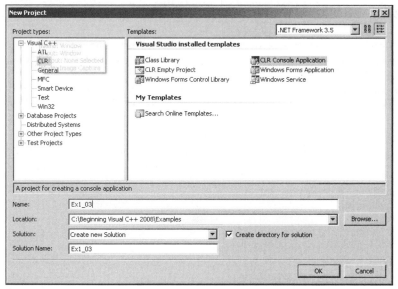

Figure 1-16

Enter the name as Ex1_03. When you click the OK button, the files for the project are created. There are no options for a CLR console project, so you always start with the same set of files in a project with this template. If you want an empty project — something you won't need with this book — there's a separate template for this.

If you look at the Solution Explorer pane shown in Figure 1-17, you see there are some extra files compared to a Win32 console project.

There are a couple of files in the virtual Resource Files folder. The .ico file stores an icon for the application that is displayed when the program is minimized; the .rc file records the resources for the application — just the icon in this case.

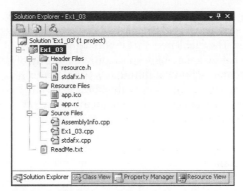

Figure 1-17

There is also a file with the name `AssemblyInfo.cpp`. Every CLR program consists of one or more **assemblies** where an assembly is a collection of code and resources that form a functional unit. An assembly also contains extensive data for the CLR; there are specifications of the data types that are being used, versioning information about the code, and information that determines if the contents of the assembly can be accessed from another assembly. In short, an assembly is a fundamental building block in all CLR programs.

If the source code in the `Ex1_03.cpp` file is not displayed in the Editor window, double-click the file name in the Solution Explorer pane. It should look like Figure 1-18.

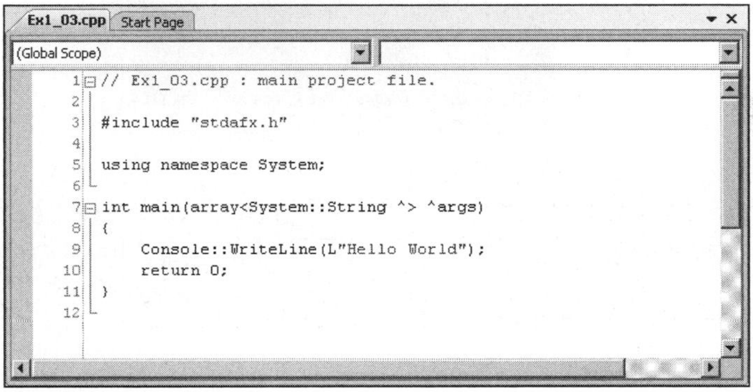

```
// Ex1_03.cpp : main project file.

#include "stdafx.h"

using namespace System;

int main(array<System::String ^> ^args)
{
    Console::WriteLine(L"Hello World");
    return 0;
}
```

Figure 1-18

It has the same `#include` directive as the default native C++ console program because CLR programs use precompiled headers for efficiency. The next line is new:

```
using namespace System;
```

The .NET library facilities are all defined within a **namespace**, and all the standard sort of stuff you are likely to use is in a namespace with the name `System`. This statement indicates the program code that follows uses the `System` namespace, but what exactly is a namespace?

A namespace is a very simple concept. Within your program code and within the code that forms the .NET libraries, names have to be given to lots of things — data types, variables, and blocks of code called functions all have to have names. The problem is that if you happen to invent a name that is already used in the library, there's potential for confusion. A namespace provides a way of getting around this problem. All the names in the library code that is defined within the `System` namespace are implicitly prefixed with the namespace name. So, a name such as `String` in the library is really `System::String`. This means that if you have inadvertently used the name `String` for something in your code, you can use `System::String` to refer `String` from the .NET library.

The two colons — `::` — are an operator called the scope resolution operator. Here the scope resolution operator separates the namespace name `System` from the type name `String`. You have seen this in the native C++ examples earlier in this chapter with `std::cout` and `std::endl`. This is the same story — `std` is the namespace name for native C++ libraries, and `cout` and `endl` are the names that have been defined within the `std` namespace to represent the standard output stream and the newline character, respectively.

In fact, the `using namespace` statement in the example allows you to use any name from the `System` namespace without having to use the namespace name as a prefix. If you did end up with a name conflict between a name you have defined and a name in the library, you could resolve the problem by removing the `using namespace` statement and explicitly qualifying the name from the library with the namespace name. You learn more about namespaces in Chapter 2.

You can compile and execute the program by pressing `Ctrl+F5`. The output is as shown in Figure 1-19.

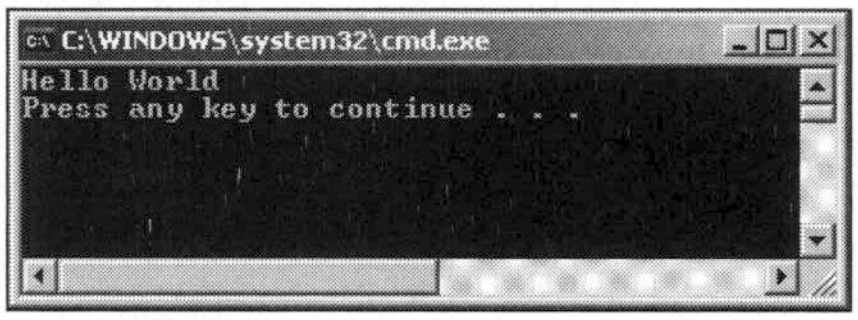

Figure 1-19

The output is similar to that from the first example. This output is produced by the line:

```
Console::WriteLine(L"Hello World");
```

This uses a .NET library function to write the information between the double quotes to the command line, so this is the CLR equivalent of the native C++ statement that you added to Ex1_01:

```
std::cout << "Hello world!\n";
```

It is more immediately apparent what the CLR statement does than the native C++ statement.

Setting Options in Visual C++ 2008

There are two sets of options you can set. You can set options that apply to the tools provided by Visual C++ 2008, which apply in every project context. Also, you can set options that are specific to a project and determine how the project code is to be processed when it is compiled and linked. Options are set through the Options dialog box that's displayed when you select `Tools > Options` from the main menu. The Options dialog box is shown in Figure 1-20.

Clicking the plus sign (+) for any of the items in the left pane displays a list of subtopics. Figure 1-20 shows the options for the `General` subtopic under `Projects and Solutions`. The right pane displays the options you can set for the topic you have selected in the left pane. You should concern yourself with only a few of these at this time, but you'll find it useful to spend a little time browsing the range of options available to you. Clicking the Help button (with the ?) at the top right of the dialog box displays an explanation of the current options.

You probably want to choose a path to use as a default when you create a new project, and you can do this through the first option shown in Figure 1-20. Just set the path to the location where you want your projects and solutions stored.

You can set options that apply to every C++ project by selecting the `Projects and Solutions > VC++ Project Settings` topic in the left pane. You can also set options specific to the current project through the `Project > Properties` menu item in the main menu. This menu item label is tailored to reflect the name of the current project.

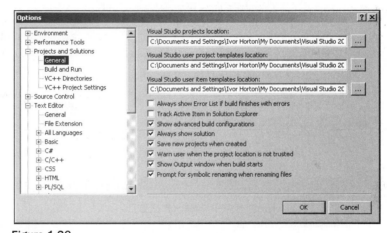

Figure 1-20

Creating and Executing Windows Applications

Just to show how easy it's going to be, you can now create two working Windows applications. You'll create a native C++ application using MFC and then you'll create a Windows Forms application that runs with the CLR. I'll defer discussion of the programs that you generate until I've covered the necessary ground for you to understand it in detail. You will see, though, that the processes are straightforward.

Creating an MFC Application

To start with, if an existing project is active — as indicated by the project name appearing in the title bar of the Visual C++ 2008 main window — you can select `Close Solution` from the `File` menu. Alternatively, you can create a new project and have the current solution closed automatically.

To create the Windows program select `New > Project` from the `File` menu or press `Ctrl+Shift+N`; then choose the project type as *MFC* and select `MFC Application` as the project template. You can then enter the project name as `Ex1_04`, as shown in Figure 1-21.

When you click the OK button, the MFC Application Wizard dialog box is displayed. The dialog box has a range of options that let you choose which features you'd like to have included in your application. These are identified by the items in the list on the right of the dialog box, as Figure 1-22 shows. You'll get to use many of these in examples later on.

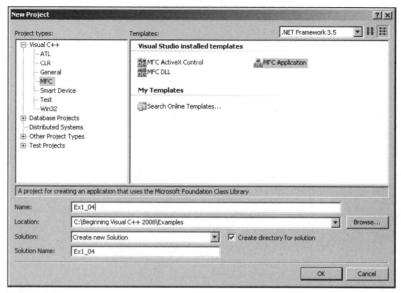

Figure 1-21

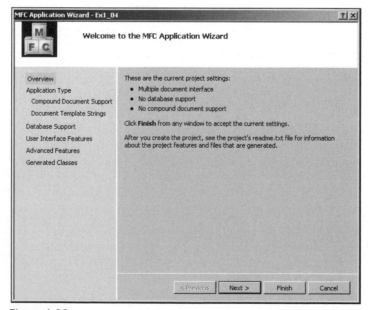

Figure 1-22

You can ignore all these options in this instance and just accept the default settings, so click the `Finish` button to create the project with the default settings. The Solution Explorer pane in the IDE window looks like Figure 1-23.

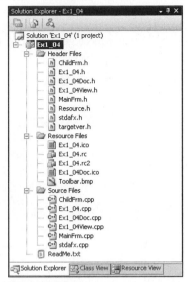

Figure 1-23

Note that I have hidden the Property Manager tab by right-clicking it and selecting Hide, so it doesn't appear in Figure 1-23. The list shows a large number of files that have been created. You need plenty of space on your hard drive when writing Windows programs! The files with the extension `.cpp` contain executable C++ source code, and the `.h` files contain C++ code consisting of definitions that are used by the executable code. The `.ico` files contain icons. The files are grouped into the subfolders you can see for ease of access. These aren't real folders, though, and they won't appear in the project folder on your disk.

If you now take a look at the `Ex1_04` solution folder using Windows Explorer or whatever else you may have handy for looking at the files on your hard disk, notice that you have generated a total of 26 files. Three of these are in the solution folder, a further 19 are in the project folder and four more are in a subfolder, `res`, to the project folder. The files in the `res` subfolder contain the resources used by the program — such as the menus and icons used in the program. You get all this as a result of just entering the name you want to assign to the project. You can see why, with so many files and file names being created automatically, a separate directory for each project becomes more than just a good idea.

One of the files in the `Ex1_04` project directory is `ReadMe.txt`, and this provides an explanation of the purpose of each of the files that the MFC Application Wizard has generated. You can take a look at it if you want, using Notepad, WordPad, or even the Visual C++ 2008 editor. To view it in the Editor window, double-click it in the Solution Explorer pane.

Building and Executing the MFC Application

Before you can execute the program, you have to build the project — meaning, compile the source code and link the program modules. You do this in exactly the same way that you did with the console application example. To save time, press Ctrl+F5 to get the project built and then executed in a single operation.

After the project has been built, the Output window indicates that there are no errors and the executable starts running. The window for the program you've generated is shown in Figure 1-24.

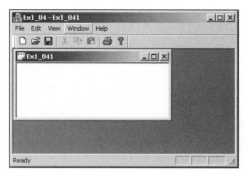

Figure 1-24

As you see, the window is complete with menus and a toolbar. Although there is no specific functionality in the program — that's what you need to add to make it *your* program — all the menus work. You can try them out. You can even create further windows by selecting New from the File menu.

I think you'll agree that creating a Windows program with the MFC Application Wizard hasn't stressed too many brain cells. You'll need to get a few more ticking away when you come to developing the basic program you have here into a program that does something more interesting, but it won't be that hard. Certainly, for many people, writing a serious Windows program the old-fashioned way, without the aid of Visual C++ 2008, required at least a couple of months on a fish diet before making the attempt. That's why so many programmers used to eat sushi. That's all gone now with Visual C++ 2008. You never know, however, what's around the corner in programming technology. If you like sushi, it's best to continue with it to be on the safe side.

Creating a Windows Forms Application

This is a job for another Application Wizard. So create yet another new project, but this time select the type as CLR in the left pane of the New Project dialog box and the template as Windows Forms Application. You can then enter the project name as Ex1_05, as shown in Figure 1-25.

There are no options to choose from in this case, so click the OK button to create the project.

The Solution Explorer pane in Figure 1-26 shows the files that have been generated for this project.

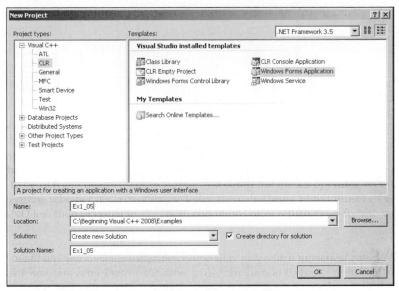

Figure 1-25

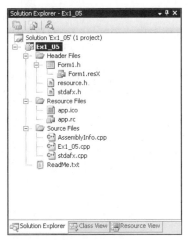

Figure 1-26

There are considerably fewer files in this project — if you look in the directories, you'll see there are a total of 15 including the solution files. One reason for this is the initial GUI is much simpler than the native C++ application using MFC. The Windows Forms application has no menus or toolbars, and there is only one window. Of course, you can add all these things quite easily, but the wizard for a Windows Forms application does not assume you want them from the start.

The Editor window looks rather different as Figure 1-27 shows.

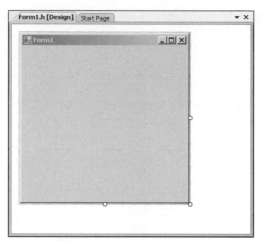

Figure 1-27

The `Editor` window shows an image of the application window rather than code. The reason for this is that developing the GUI for a Windows Forms is oriented towards a graphical design approach rather than a coding approach. You add GUI components to the application window by dragging or placing them there graphically, and Visual C++ 2008 automatically generates the code to display them. If you press `Ctrl+Alt+X` or select `View > Toolbox`, you'll see an additional window displayed showing a list of GUI components as in Figure 1-28.

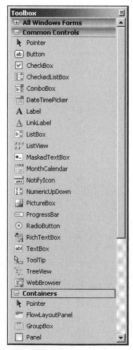

Figure 1-28

The `Toolbox` window presents a list of standard components that you can add to a Windows Forms application. You can try adding some buttons to the window for Ex1_05. Click `Button` in the `Toolbox` window list and then click in the client area of the Ex1_05 application window that is displayed in the Editor window where you want the button to be placed. You can adjust the size of the button by dragging its borders, and you can reposition the button by dragging it around. You can also change the caption just by typing — try entering `Start` on the keyboard and then press `Enter`. The caption changes and along the way another window displays, showing the properties for the button. I won't go into these now, but essentially these are the specifications that affect the appearance of the button, and you can change these to suit your application. Try adding another button with the caption Stop, for example. The Editor window will look like Figure 1-29.

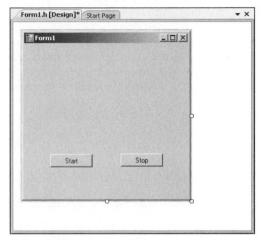

Figure 1-29

You can graphically edit any of the GUI components at any time, and the code adjusts automatically. Try adding a few other components in the same way and then compile and execute the example by pressing `Ctrl+F5`. The application window displays in all its glory. Couldn't be easier, could it?

Summary

In this chapter, you have run through the basic mechanics of using Visual C++ 2008 to create applications of various kinds. You created and executed native and CLR console programs, and with the help of the Application Wizards, you created an MFC-based Windows program and a Windows Forms program that executes with the CLR.

The points from this chapter that you should keep in mind are:

❑ The Common Language Runtime (CLR) is the Microsoft implementation of the Common Language Infrastructure (CLI) standard.

❑ The .NET Framework comprises the CLR plus the .NET libraries that support applications targeting the CLR.

❑ Native C++ applications are written the ISO/ANSI C++ language.

❑ Programs written in the C++/CLI language execute with the CLR.

❑ Attributes can provide additional information to the compiler to instruct it to modify or extend particular programming elements in a program.

❑ A solution is a container for one or more projects that form a solution to an information-processing problem of some kind.

❑ A project is a container for the code and resource elements that make up a functional unit in a program.

❑ An assembly is a fundamental unit in a CLR program. All CLR programs are made up of one or more assemblies.

Starting with the next chapter, you'll use console applications extensively throughout the first half of the book. All the examples illustrating how C++ language elements are used are executed using either Win32 or CLR console applications. You will return to the Application Wizard for MFC-based programs and Windows Forms applications as soon as you have finished delving into the secrets of C++.

Data, Variables, and Calculations

In this chapter, you'll get down to the essentials of programming in C++. By the end of the chapter you'll be able to write a simple C++ program of the traditional form: input-process-output. As I said in the previous chapter, I'll first discuss the ANSI/ISO C++ language features and then cover any additional or different aspects of the C++/CLI language.

As you explore aspects of the language using working examples, you'll have an opportunity to get some additional practice with the Visual C++ Development Environment. You should create a project for each of the examples before you build and execute them. Remember that when you are defining projects in this chapter and the following chapters through to Chapter 11, they are all console applications.

In this chapter you will learn about:

- ❑ C++ program structure
- ❑ Namespaces
- ❑ Variables in C++
- ❑ Defining variables and constants
- ❑ Basic input from the keyboard and output to the screen
- ❑ Performing arithmetic calculations
- ❑ Casting operands
- ❑ Variable scope

The Structure of a C++ Program

Programs that will run as console applications under Visual C++ 2008 are programs that read data from the command line and output the results to the command line. To avoid having to dig into the complexities of creating and managing application windows before you have enough knowledge to understand how they work, all the examples that you'll write to understand how the C++ language works will be console programs, either Win32 console programs or .NET console programs. This will enable you to focus entirely on the C++ language in the first instance; once you have mastered that, you'll be ready to deal with creating and managing application windows. You'll first look at how console programs are structured.

A program in C++ consists of one or more **functions**. In Chapter 1, you saw an example that was a Win32 console program consisting simply of the function main(), where main is the name of the function. Every ANSI/ISO standard C++ program contains the function main(), and all C++ programs of any size consist of several functions — the main() function where execution of the program starts, plus a number of other functions. A function is simply a self-contained block of code with a unique name that you invoke for execution by using the name of the function. As you saw in Chapter 1, a Win32 console program that is generated by the Application Wizard has a main function with the name _tmain. This is a programming device to allow the name to be main or wmain depending on whether or not the program is using Unicode characters. The names wmain and _tmain are Microsoft-specific. The name for the main function conforming to the ISO/ANSI standard for C++ is main. I'll use the name main for all our ISO/ANSI C++ examples because this is the most portable option. If you only intend to compile your code with Microsoft Visual C++, then it is advantageous to use the Microsoft-specific names for main.

A typical command line program might be structured as shown in Figure 2-1.

Figure 2-1 illustrates that execution of the program shown starts at the beginning of the function main(). From main(), execution transfers to a function input_names(), which returns execution to the position immediately following the point where it was called in main(). The sort_names() function is then called from main(), and, once control returns to main(), the final function output_names() is called. Eventually, once output has been completed, execution returns once again to main() and the program ends.

Of course, different programs may have radically different functional structures, but they all start execution at the beginning of main(). The principal advantage of having a program broken up into functions is that you can write and test each piece separately. There is a further advantage in that functions written to perform a particular task can be re-used in other programs. The libraries that come with C++ provide a lot of standard functions that you can use in your programs. They can save you a great deal of work.

You'll see more about creating and using functions in Chapter 5.

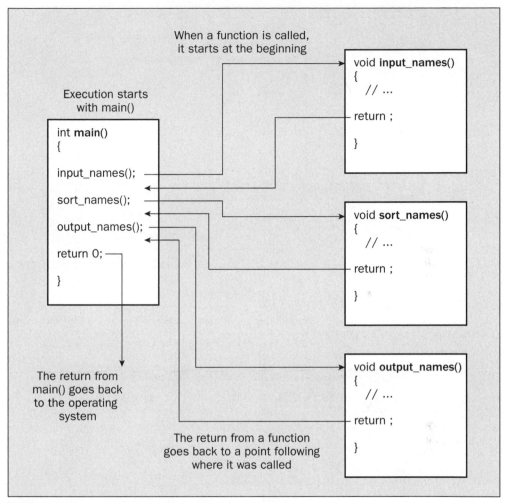

Figure 2-1

Try It Out A Simple Program

A simple example can help you to understand the elements of a program a little better. Start by creating a new project — you can use the Ctrl+Shift+N key combination as a shortcut for this. When the dialog shown in Figure 2-2 appears, select Win32 as the project type and Win32 Console Application as the template. You can name the project Ex2_01.

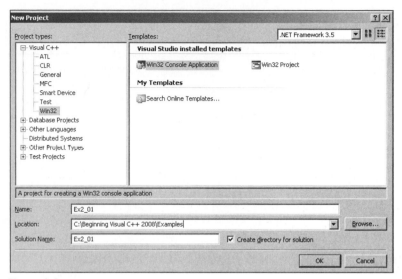

Figure 2-2

If you click the OK button, you'll see a new dialog in the form shown in Figure 2-3 that shows an overview of what the Application Wizard will generate.

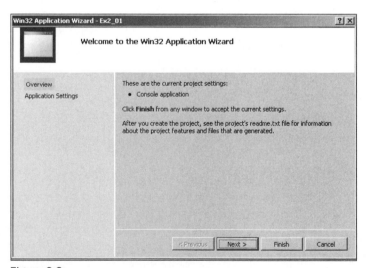

Figure 2-3

If you now click Application Settings on the left of this dialog, you'll see further options for a Win32 application displayed, as shown in Figure 2-4.

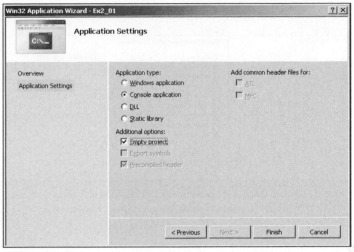

Figure 2-4

The default setting is a Console application that will include a file containing a default version of main(), but you'll start from the most basic project structure, so choose Empty project from the set of additional options and click the Finish button. Now you have a project created, but it contains no files at all. You can see what the project contains from the Solution Explorer pane on the left of the Visual C++ 2008 main window, as shown in Figure 2-5.

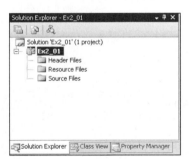

Figure 2-5

You'll start by adding a new source file to the project, so right-click Source Files in the Solution Explorer pane and select the Add > New Item . . . menu option. The Add New Item dialog, similar to that shown in Figure 2-6, displays.

Make sure the C++ File(.cpp) template is highlighted by clicking on it and enter the file name, as shown in Figure 2-6. The file will automatically be given the extension .cpp, so you don't have to enter the extension. There is no problem having the name of the file the same as the name of the project. The project file will have the extension .vcproj so that will differentiate it from the source file.

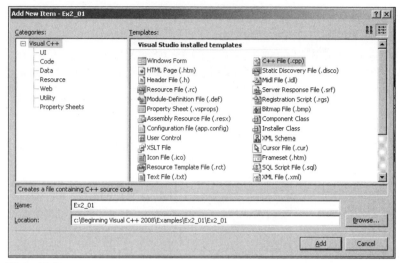

Figure 2-6

Click the Add button to create the file. You can then type the following code in the Editor pane of the IDE window:

```cpp
// Ex2_01.cpp
// A Simple Example of a Program
#include <iostream>

using std::cout;
using std::endl;

int main()
{
    int apples, oranges;                   // Declare two integer variables
    int fruit;                             // ...then another one

    apples = 5; oranges = 6;               // Set initial values
    fruit = apples + oranges;              // Get the total fruit

    cout << endl;                          // Start output on a new line
    cout << "Oranges are not the only fruit... " << endl
         << "- and we have " << fruit << " fruits in all.";
    cout << endl;                          // Output a new line character

    return 0;                              // Exit the program
}
```

The preceding example is intended to illustrate some of the ways in which you can write C++ statements and is not a model of good programming style.

Since the file is identified by its extension as a file containing C++ code, the keywords in the code that the editor recognizes will be colored to identify them. You will be able to see if you have entered Int where you should have entered int, because Int will not have the color used to highlight keywords in your source code.

If you look at the Solution Explorer pane for your new project, you'll see the newly created source file. Solution Explorer will always show all the files in a project. If you click on the Class View tab at the bottom of the Solution Explorer pane the Class View will be displayed. This consists of two panes, the upper pane showing global functions and macros within the project (and classes when you get to create a project involving classes) and the lower pane presently empty. The main() function will appear in the lower pane if you select Global Functions and Variables in the upper Class View pane; this is shown in Figure 2-7. I'll consider what this means in more detail later, but essentially **globals** are functions and/or variables that are accessible from anywhere in the program.

Figure 2-7

The third tab in Class View is labeled Property Manager and if you click on this and extend the items in the tree that is displayed by clicking the + signs, it will look like Figure 2-8.

Figure 2-8

This shows the two possible versions you can build, the Debug version for testing and the Release version when your program has been tested. The properties for each version of the project are shown, and double-clicking on any of them will display a dialog showing the Property Pages where you can change properties if necessary.

You have three ways to compile and link the program; you can select the Build Ex2_01 menu item from the Build menu, you can press the F7 function key, or you can select the appropriate toolbar button — you can identify what a toolbar button does by hovering the mouse cursor over it. If there is no toolbar button that shows the tooltip `Build Ex2_01` when the cursor is over it, then the Build toolbar is not currently displayed. You can remedy this by right-clicking on an empty part of the toolbar area and selecting Build from the list of toolbars that is displayed. It's a very long list and you will probably want to choose different sets of toolbars to be displayed, depending on what you are doing.

Assuming the build operation was successful you can execute the program by pressing the `Ctrl+F5` keys or by selecting `Start Without Debugging` from the `Debug` menu. You should get the following output in a command line window:

```
Oranges are not the only fruit...
- and we have 11 fruits in all.
Press any key to continue . . .
```

The first two lines were produced by the program, and the last line indicates how you can end the execution and close the command line window. I won't show this last line of output from other console examples but it's always there.

Program Comments

The first two lines in the program are **comments**. Comments are an important part of any program, but they're not executable code — they are there simply to help the human reader. All comments are ignored by the compiler. On any line of code, two successive slashes `//` that are not contained within a text string (you'll see what text strings are later) indicate that the rest of the line is a comment.

You can see that several lines of the program contain comments as well as program statements. You can also use an alternative form of comment bounded by `/*` and `*/`. For example, the first line of the program could have been written:

```
/*    Ex2_01.cpp    */
```

The comment using `//` covers only the portion of the line following the two successive slashes, whereas the `/*...*/` form defines whatever is enclosed between the `/*` and the `*/` as a comment and can span several lines. For example, you could write:

```
/*
    Ex2_01.cpp
    A Simple Program Example
*/
```

All four lines are comments. If you want to highlight some particular comment lines, you can always embellish them with a frame of some description:

```
/******************************
 *   Ex2-01.cpp               *
 *   A Simple Program Example *
 ******************************/
```

As a rule, you should always comment your programs comprehensively. The comments should be sufficient for another programmer or you at a later date to understand the purpose of any particular piece of code and how it works. I will often use comments in examples to explain in more detail than you would in a production program.

The #include Directive — Header Files

Following the comments, you have an #include directive:

```
#include <iostream>
```

This is called a **directive** because it directs the compiler to do something — in this case to insert the contents of the file <iostream> into the program source file before compilation. The <iostream> file is called a **header file** because it's usually brought in at the beginning of a program file. The <iostream> header file contains definitions that are necessary for you to be able to use C++ input and output statements. If you didn't include the contents of <iostream> into the program, it wouldn't compile because you use output statements in the program that depend on some of the definitions in this file. There are many different header files provided by Visual C++ that cover a wide range of capabilities. You'll be seeing more of them as you progress through the language facilities.

An #include statement is one of several **preprocessor directives** and I'll be introducing other preprocessor directives as you need them throughout the book. The Visual C++ editor recognizes preprocessor directives and highlights them in blue in your edit window. Preprocessor directives are commands executed by the preprocessor phase of the compiler that executes before your code is compiled into object code, and preprocessor directives generally act on your source code in some way before it is compiled. They all start with the # character.

Namespaces and the Using Declaration

As you saw in Chapter 1, the **standard library** is an extensive set of routines that have been written to carry many common tasks: for example, dealing with input and output, performing basic mathematical calculations. Since there are a very large number of these routines as well as other kinds of things that have names, it is quite possible that you might accidentally use the same name as one of the names defined in the standard library for your own purposes. A **namespace** is a mechanism in C++ for avoiding problems that can arise when duplicate names are used in a program for different things, and it does this by associating a given set of names such as those from the standard library with a sort of family name, which is the namespace name.

Every name that is defined in code that appears within a namespace also has the namespace name associated with it. All the standard library facilities for ISO/ANSI C++ are defined within a namespace with the name std, so every item from this standard library that you can access in your program has its own name, plus the namespace name, std, as a qualifier. The names cout and endl are defined within the standard library so their full names are std::cout and std::endl, and you saw these in action in Chapter 1. The two colons that separate the namespace name from the name of an entity form an operator called the **scope resolution operator**, and I'll discuss other uses for this operator later on in the book. Using the full names in the program will tend to make the code look a bit cluttered, so it would be nice to be able to use their simple names, unqualified by the namespace name, std. The two lines in our program that follow the #include directive for <iostream> make this possible:

```
using std::cout;
using std::endl;
```

These are **using declarations** that tell the compiler that you intend to use the names cout and endl from the namespace std without specifying the namespace name. The compiler will now assume that wherever you use the name cout in the source file subsequent to the first using declaration, you mean the cout that is defined in the standard library. The name cout represents the standard output stream that by default corresponds to the command line and the name endl represents the newline character.

You'll learn more about namespaces, including how you define your own namespaces, a little later this chapter.

The main() Function

The function main() in the example consists of the function header defining it as main() plus everything from the first opening curly brace ({) to the corresponding closing curly brace (}). The braces enclose the executable statements in the function, which are referred to collectively as the **body** of the function.

As you'll see, all functions consist of a header that defines (amongst other things) the function name, followed by the function body that consists of a number of program statements enclosed between a pair of braces. The body of a function may contain no statements at all, in which case it doesn't do anything.

A function that doesn't do anything may seem somewhat superfluous, but when you're writing a large program, you may map out the complete program structure in functions initially but omit the code for many of the functions leaving them with empty or minimal bodies. Doing this means that you can compile and execute the whole program with all its functions at any time and add detailed coding for the functions incrementally.

Program Statements

The program statements making up the function body of main() are each terminated with a *semicolon*. It's the semicolon that marks the end of a statement, not the end of the line. Consequently a statement can be spread over several lines when this makes the code easier to follow and several statements can appear in a single line. The program statement is the basic unit in defining what a program does. This is a bit like a sentence in a paragraph of text, where each sentence stands by itself in expressing an action or an idea, but relates to and combines with the other sentences in the paragraph in expressing a more general idea. A statement is a self-contained definition of an action that the computer is to carry out, but that can be combined with other statements to define a more complex action or calculation.

The action of a function is always expressed by a number of statements, each ending with a semicolon. Take a quick look at each of the statements in the example just written, just to get a general feel for how it works. I will discuss each type of statement more fully later in this chapter.

The first statement in the body of the main() function is:

```
int apples, oranges;            // Declare two integer variables
```

This statement declares two variables, apples and oranges. A **variable** is just a named bit of computer memory that you can use to store data, and a statement that introduces the names of one or more variables is called a **variable declaration**. The keyword int in the preceding statement indicates that the variables with the names apples and oranges are to store values that are whole numbers, or integers. Whenever you introduce the name of a variable into a program, you always specify what kind of data it will store, and this is called the type of the variable.

The next statement declares another integer variable, `fruit`:

```
    int fruit;                                    // ...then another one
```

While you can declare several variables in the same statement, as you did in the preceding statement for `apples` and `oranges`, it is generally a good idea to declare each variable in a separate statement on its own line as this enables you to comment them individually to explain how you intend to use them.

The next line in the example is:

```
   apples = 5; oranges = 6;         // Set initial values
```

This line contains two statements, each terminated by a semicolon. I put this here just to demonstrate that you can put more than one statement in a line. While it isn't obligatory, it's generally good programming practice to write only one statement on a line as it makes the code easier to understand. Good programming practice is about adopting approaches to coding that make your code easy to follow, and minimize the likelihood of errors.

The two statements in the preceding line store the values 5 and 6 in the variables `apples` and `oranges`, respectively. These statements are called **assignment statements** because they assign a new value to a variable and the = is the assignment operator.

The next statement is:

```
   fruit = apples + oranges;        // Get the total fruit
```

This is also an assignment statement but is a little different because you have an **arithmetic expression** to the right of the assignment operator. This statement adds together the values stored in the variables `apples` and `oranges` and stores the result in the variable `fruit`.

The next three statements are:

```
   cout << endl;                    // Start output on a new line
   cout << "Oranges are not the only fruit... " << endl
        << "- and we have " << fruit << " fruits in all.";
   cout << endl;                    // Start output on a new line
```

These are all **output statements**. The first statement is the first line here, and it sends a newline character, denoted by the word `endl`, to the command line on the screen. In C++, a source of input or a destination for output is referred to as a **stream**. The name `cout` specifies the "standard" output stream, and the operator << indicates that what appears to the right of the operator is to be sent to the output stream, `cout`. The << operator "points" in the direction that the data flows — from the variable or string that appears on the right of the operator to the output destination on the left. Thus in the first statement the value represented by the name `endl` — which represents a newline character — is sent to the stream identified by the name `cout` — and data transferred to `cout` is written to the command line.

The meaning of the name `cout` and the operator << are defined in the standard library header file `<iostream>`, which you added to the program code by means of the `#include` directive at the beginning of the program. cout is a name in the standard library and therefore is within the namespace std. Without the using directive it would not be recognized unless you used its fully qualified name, which is std::cout, as I mentioned earlier. Because cout has been defined to represent the standard output stream, you shouldn't use the name cout for other purposes so you can't use it as the name of a variable in your program for example. Obviously, using the same name for different things is likely to cause confusion.

The second output statement of the three is spread over two lines:

```
cout << "Oranges are not the only fruit... " << endl
     << "- and we have " << fruit << " fruits in all.";
```

As I said earlier, you can spread each statement in a program over as many lines as you wish if it helps to make the code clearer. The end of a statement is always signaled by a semicolon, not the end of a line. Successive lines are read and combined into a single statement by the compiler until it finds the semicolon that defines the end of the statement. Of course, this means that if you forget to put a semicolon at the end of a statement, the compiler will assume the next line is part of the same statement and join them together. This usually results in something the compiler cannot understand, so you'll get an error message.

The statement sends the text string "Oranges are not the only fruit... " to the command line, followed by another newline character (endl), then another text string, "- and we have ", followed by the value stored in the variable fruit, then finally another text string, " fruits in all.". There is no problem stringing together a sequence of things that you want to output in this way. The statement executes from left to right, with each item being sent to cout in turn. Note that each item to be sent to cout is preceded by its own << operator.

The third and last output statement just sends another newline character to the screen, and the three statements produce the output from the program that you see.

The last statement in the program is:

```
return 0;                        // Exit the program
```

This terminates execution of the main() function, which stops execution of the program. Control returns to the operating system, and the 0 is a return code that tells the operating system that the application terminated successfully after completing its task. I'll discuss all of these statements in more detail later on.

The statements in a program are executed in the sequence in which they are written, unless a statement specifically causes the natural sequence to be altered. In Chapter 3, you'll look at statements that alter the sequence of execution.

Whitespace

Whitespace is the term used in C++ to describe blanks, tabs, newline characters, form feed characters, and comments. Whitespace serves to separate one part of a statement from another and enables the compiler to identify where one element in a statement, such as int, ends and the next element begins. Otherwise, whitespace is ignored and has no effect.

Look at this statement for example:

```
    int fruit;                     // ...then another one
```

There must be at least one whitespace character (usually a space) between `int` and `fruit` for the compiler to be able to distinguish them but if you add more whitespace characters they will be ignored. The content of the line following the semicolon is all whitespace and is therefore ignored.

On the other hand, look at this statement:

```
    fruit = apples + oranges;      // Get the total fruit
```

No whitespace characters are necessary between `fruit` and `=`, or between `=` and `apples`, although you are free to include some if you wish. This is because the `=` is not alphabetic or numeric, so the compiler can separate it from its surroundings. Similarly, no whitespace characters are necessary on either side of the `+` sign but you can include some if you want to aid the readability of your code.

As I said, apart from its use as a separator between elements in a statement that might otherwise be confused, whitespace is ignored by the compiler (except, of course, in a string of characters between quotes). You can therefore include as much whitespace as you like to make your program more readable, as you did when you spread an output statement in the last example over several lines. Remember that in C++ the end of a statement is wherever the semicolon occurs.

Statement Blocks

You can enclose several statements between a pair of braces, in which case they become a **block**, or a **compound statement**. The body of a function is an example of a block. Such a compound statement can be thought of as a single statement (as you'll see when you look at the decision-making possibilities in C++ in Chapter 3). In fact, wherever you can put a single statement in C++, you could equally well put a block of statements between braces. As a consequence, blocks can be placed inside other blocks. In fact, blocks can be nested, one within another, to any depth.

*A statement block also has important effects on variables, but I will defer discussion of this until later in this chapter when I discuss something called **variable scope**.*

Automatically Generated Console Programs

In the last example you opted to produce the project as an empty project with no source files, and then you added the source file subsequently. If you just allow the Application Wizard to generate the project as you did in Chapter 1, the project will contain several files, and you should explore their contents in a little more depth. Create a new Win32 console project with the name `Ex2_01A` and this time just allow the Application Wizard to finish without choosing to set any of the options in the `Application Settings` dialog. The project will have three files containing code: the `Ex2_01A.cpp` and `stdafx.cpp` source files, and the `stdafx.h` header file. This is to provide for basic capability that you might need in a console program and represents a working program as it stands, which does nothing. If you have a project open, you can close it by selecting the `File > Close Solution` item on the main menu. You can create a new project with an existing project open, in which case the old project will be closed automatically unless you elect to add it to the same solution.

First of all, the contents of `Ex2_01A.cpp` will be:

```
// Ex2_01A.cpp : Defines the entry point for the console application.
//

#include "stdafx.h"

int _tmain(int argc, _TCHAR* argv[])
{
  return 0;
}
```

This is decidedly different from the previous example. There is an `#include` directive for the `stdafx.h` header file that was not in the previous version, and the function where execution starts is called `_tmain()`, not `main()`.

The Application Wizard has generated the `stdafx.h` header file as part of the project, and if you take a look at the code in there, you'll see there are two further `#include` directives for standard library header files `stdio.h` and `tchar.h`. The old-style header `stdio.h` is for standard I/O and was used before the current ISO/ANSI standard for C++; this covers the same functionality as the `<iostream>` header. `tchar.h` is a Microsoft-specific header file defining text functions. The idea is that `stdafx.h` should define a set of standard system include files for your project — you would add `#include` directives for any other system headers that you need in this file. While you are learning ISO/ANSI C++, you won't be using either of the headers that appear in `stdafx.h`, which is one reason for not using the default file generation capability provided by the Application Wizard.

As I already explained, Visual C++ 2008 supports `wmain()` as an alternative to `main()` when you are writing a program that's using Unicode characters — `wmain()` being a Microsoft-specific command that is not part of ISO/ANSI C++. In support of that, the `tchar.h` header defines the name `_tmain` so that it will normally be replaced by `main`, but will be replaced by `wmain` if the symbol `_UNICODE` is defined. Thus to identify a program as using UNICODE you would add the following statement to the beginning of the `stdafx.h` header file:

```
#define _UNICODE
```

Now that I've explained all that, I'll stick to plain old `main()` for our ISO/ANSI C++ examples that are console applications because this option is standard C++ and therefore the most portable coding approach.

Defining Variables

A fundamental objective in all computer programs is to manipulate some data and get some answers. An essential element in this process is having a piece of memory that you can call your own, that you can refer to using a meaningful name, and where you can store an item of data. Each individual piece of memory so specified is called a **variable**.

As you already know, each variable will store a particular kind of data, and the type of data that can be stored is fixed when you define the variable in your program. One variable might store whole numbers (that is, integers), in which case you couldn't use it to store numbers with fractional values. The value that each variable contains at any point is determined by the statements in your program, and of course, its value will usually change many times as the program calculation progresses.

The next section looks first at the rules for naming a variable when you introduce it into a program.

Naming Variables

The name you give to a variable is called an **identifier**, or more conveniently a **variable name**. Variable names can include the letters A–z (upper- or lowercase), the digits 0–9, and the underscore character. No other characters are allowed, and if you happen to use some other character, you will typically get an error message when you try to compile the program. Variable names must also begin with either a letter or an underscore. Names are usually chosen to indicate the kind of information to be stored.

Because variable names in Visual C++ 2008 can be up to 2048 characters long, you have a reasonable amount of flexibility in what you call your variables. In fact, as well as variables, there are quite a few other things that have names in C++ and they too can have names of up to 2048 characters, with the same definition rules as a variable name. Using names of the maximum length allowed can make your programs a little difficult to read, and unless you have amazing keyboard skills, they are the very devil to type in. A more serious consideration is that not all compilers support such long names. If you anticipate compiling your code in other environments, it's a good idea to limit names to a maximum of 31 characters; this will usually be adequate for devising meaningful names and will avoid problems of compiler name length constraints in most instances.

Although you can use variable names that begin with an underscore, for example _this and _that, this is best avoided because of potential clashes with standard system variables that have the same form. You should also avoid using names starting with a double underscore for the same reason.

Examples of good variable names are:

- ❑ price
- ❑ discount
- ❑ pShape
- ❑ value_
- ❑ COUNT

8_Ball, 7Up, and 6_pack are not legal. Neither is Hash! or Mary-Ann. This last example is a common mistake, although Mary_Ann with an underscore in place of the hyphen would be quite acceptable. Of course, Mary Ann would not be, because blanks are not allowed in variable names. Note that the variable names republican and Republican are quite different, as names are case-sensitive so upper- and lower-case letters are differentiated. Of course, whitespace characters in general cannot appear within a name, and if you inadvertently include whitespace characters, you will have two or more names instead of one, which will usually cause the compiler to complain.

A convention that is often adopted in C++ is to reserve names beginning with a capital letter for naming classes and use names beginning with a lowercase letter for variables. I'll discuss classes in Chapter 8.

Keywords in C++

There are reserved words in C++ called **keywords** that have special significance within the language. They will be highlighted with a particular color by the Visual C++ 2008 editor as you enter your program — in my system the default color is blue. If a keyword you type does not appear highlighted, then you have entered the keyword incorrectly. Incidentally, if you don't like the default colors used by the text editor, you can change them by selecting `Options` from the `Tools` menu and making changes when you select `Environment/Fonts and Colors` in the dialog.

Remember that keywords, like the rest of the C++ language, are case-sensitive. For example, the program that you entered earlier in the chapter contained the keywords `int` and `return`; if you write `Int` or `Return`, these are not keywords and therefore will not be recognized as such. You will see many more as you progress through the book. You must ensure that the names you choose for entities in your program, such as variables, are not the same as any of the keywords in C++. A complete list of the keywords used in Visual C++ 2008 appears in Appendix A.

Declaring Variables

As you saw earlier, a variable **declaration** is a program statement that specifies the name of a variable of a given type. For example:

```
int value;
```

This declares a variable with the name `value` that can store integers. The type of data that can be stored in the variable `value` is specified by the keyword `int`, so you can only use `value` to store data of type `int`. Because `int` is a keyword, you can't use `int` as a name for one of your variables.

Note that a variable declaration always ends with a semicolon.

A single declaration can specify the names of several variables but, as I have said, it is generally better to declare variables in individual statements, one per line. I'll deviate from this from time to time in this book, but only in the interests of not spreading code over too many pages.

In order to store data (for example, the value of an integer), you not only need to have defined the name of the variable, you also need to have associated a piece of the computer's memory with the variable name. This process is called variable **definition**. In C++, a variable declaration is also a definition (except in a few special cases, which we shall come across during the book). In the course of a single statement, we introduce the variable name, and also tie it to an appropriately sized piece of memory.

So, the statement

```
int value;
```

is both a declaration and a definition. You use the variable *name* `value` that you have declared, to access the piece of the computer's *memory* that you have defined and that can store a single value of type `int`.

You use the term declaration when you introduce a name into your program, with information on what the name will be used for. The term definition refers to the allotment of computer memory to the name. In the case of variables, you can declare and define in a single statement, as in the preceding line. The reason for this apparently pedantic differentiation between a declaration and a definition is that you will meet statements that are declarations but not definitions.

You must declare a variable at some point between the beginning of your program and when the variable is used for the first time. In C++, it is good practice to declare variables close to their first point of use.

Initial Values for Variables

When you declare a variable, you can also assign an initial value to it. A variable declaration that assigns an initial value to a variable is called an **initialization**. To initialize a variable when you declare it, you just need to write an equals sign followed by the initializing value after the variable name. You can write the following statements to give each of the variables an initial value:

```
int value = 0;
int count = 10;
int number = 5;
```

In this case, value will have the value 0, count will have the value 10, and number will have the value 5.

There is another way of writing the initial value for a variable in C++ called **functional notation**. Instead of an equals sign and the value, you can simply write the value in parentheses following the variable name. So you could rewrite the previous declarations as:

```
int value(0);
int count(10);
int number(5);
```

Generally it's a good idea to use either one notation or the other consistently when you are initializing variables. However, I'll use one notation in some examples and the other notation in others so you get used to seeing both of them in working code.

If you don't supply an initial value for a variable, then it will usually contain whatever garbage was left in the memory location it occupies by the previous program you ran (there is an exception to this that you will meet later in this chapter). Wherever possible, you should initialize your variables when you declare them. If your variables start out with known values, it makes it easier to work out what is happening when things go wrong. And one thing you can be sure of — things *will* go wrong.

Fundamental Data Types

The sort of information that a variable can hold is determined by its **data type**. All data and variables in your program must be of some defined type. ISO/ANSI standard C++ provides you with a range of **fundamental data types**, specified by particular keywords. Fundamental data types are so called because they store values of types that represent fundamental data in your computer, essentially numerical values, which also includes characters because a character is represented by a numerical character code. You have already seen the keyword int for defining integer variables. C++/CLI also defines fundamental data types that are not part of ISO/ANSI C++, and I'll go into those a little later in this chapter.

As part of the object-oriented aspects of the language, you can also create your own data types, as you'll see later, and of course the various libraries that you have at your disposal with Visual C++ 2008 also define further data types. For the moment, explore the elementary numerical data types that ISO/ANSI C++ provides. The fundamental types fall into three categories: types that store integers, types that store non-integral values — which are called floating-point types — and the `void` type that specifies an empty set of values or no type.

Integer Variables

As I have said, integer variables are variables that can have only values that are whole numbers. The number of players in a football team is an integer, at least at the beginning of the game. You already know that you can declare integer variables using the keyword `int`. Variables of type `int` occupy 4 bytes in memory and can store both positive and negative integer values. The upper and lower limits for the values of a variable of type `int` correspond to the maximum and minimum signed binary numbers, which can be represented by 32 bits. The upper limit for a variable of type `int` is $2^{31}-1$ which is 2,147,483,647, and the lower limit is $-(2^{31})$, which is −2,147,483,648. Here's an example of defining a variable of type `int`:

```
int toeCount = 10;
```

In Visual C++ 2008, the keyword `short` also defines an integer variable, this time occupying two bytes. The keyword `short` is equivalent to `short int`, and you could define two variables of type `short` with the following statements:

```
short feetPerPerson = 2;
short int feetPerYard = 3;
```

Both variables are of the same type here because `short` means exactly the same as `short int`. I used both forms of the type name to show them in use, but it would be best to stick to one representation of the type in your programs and `short` is used most often.

C++ also provides another integer type, `long`, which can also be written as `long int`. Here's how you declare variables of type `long`:

```
long bigNumber = 1000000L;
long largeValue = 0L;
```

Of course, you could also use functional notation when specifying the initial values:

```
long bigNumber(1000000L);
long largeValue(0L);
```

These statements declare the variables `bigNumber` and `largeValue` with initial values `1000000` and `0`, respectively. The letter `L` appended to the end of the literals specifies that they are integers of type `long`. You can also use the small letter `l` for the same purpose, but it has the disadvantage that it is easily confused with the numeral `1`. Integer literals without an `L` appended are of type `int`.

You must not include commas when writing large numeric values in a program. In text you might write the number 12,345, but in your program code you must write this as 12345.

Integer variables declared as `long` in Visual C++ 2008 occupy 4 bytes and can have values from −2,147,483,648 to 2,147,483,647. This is the same range as for variables declared as `int`.

With other C++ compilers, variables of type long *(which is the same as type* long int*) may not be the same as type* int, *so if you expect your programs to be compiled in other environments, don't assume that* long *and* int *are equivalent. For truly portable code, you should not even assume that an* int *is 4 bytes (for example, under older 16-bit versions of Visual C++ a variable of type* int *was 2 bytes).*

Character Data Types

The char data type serves a dual purpose. It specifies a one-byte variable that you can use to store integers within a given range or to store the code for a single **ASCII** character, which is the **A**merican **S**tandard **C**ode for **I**nformation **I**nterchange. The codes in the ASCII character set appears in Appendix B. You can declare a char variable with this statement:

```
char letter = 'A';
```

Or you could write this as:

```
char letter('A');
```

This declares the variable with the name letter and initializes it with the constant 'A'. Note that you specify a value that is a single character between single quotes, rather than the double quotes used previously for defining a string of characters to be displayed. A string of characters is a series of values of type char that are grouped together into a single entity called an **array**. I'll discuss arrays and how strings are handled in C++ in Chapter 4.

Because the character 'A' is represented in ASCII by the decimal value 65, you could have written the statement as:

```
char letter = 65;              // Equivalent to A
```

This produces the same result as the previous statement. The range of integers that can be stored in a variable of type char with Visual C++ is from –128 to 127.

Note that the ISO/ANSI C++ standard does not require that type char *should represent signed 1-byte integers. It is the compiler implementer's choice as to whether type* char *represents signed integers in the range –128 to +127 or unsigned integers in the range 0 to 255. You need to keep this in mind if you are porting your C++ code to a different environment.*

The type wchar_t is so called because it is a **w**ide **char**acter type, and variables of this type store 2-byte character codes with values in the range from 0 to 65,535. Here's an example of defining a variable of type wchar_t:

```
wchar_t letter = L'Z';         // A variable storing a 16-bit character code
```

This defines a variable, letter, that is initialized with the 16-bit code for the letter Z. The L preceding the character constant, 'Z', tells the compiler that this is a 16-bit character code value. A wchar_t variable stores Unicode code values.

You could have used functional notation here, too:

```
wchar_t letter(L'Z');        // A variable storing a 16-bit character code
```

You can also use hexadecimal constants to initialize char variables (and other integer types), and it is obviously going to be easier to use this notation when character codes are available as hexadecimal values. A hexadecimal number is written using the standard representation for hexadecimal digits: 0 to 9, and A to F (or a to f) for digits with values from 10 to 15. It's also preceded by 0x (or 0X) to distinguish it from a decimal value. Thus, to get exactly the same result again, you could rewrite the last statement as follows:

```
wchar_t letter(0x5A);        // A variable storing a 16-bit character code
```

Don't write decimal integer values with a leading zero. The compiler will interpret such values as octal (base 8), so a value written as 065 will be equivalent to 53 in normal decimal notation.

Notice that Windows XP provides a Character Map utility that enables you to locate characters from any of the fonts available to Windows. It will show the character code in hexadecimal and tell you the keystroke to use for entering the character. You'll find the Character map utility if you click on the Start button and look in the System Tools folder that is within the Accessories folder.

Integer Type Modifiers

Variables of the integral types char, int, short, or long store signed integer values by default, so you can use these types to store either positive or negative values. This is because these types are assumed to have the default **type modifier** signed. So, wherever you wrote int or long you could have written signed int or signed long, respectively.

You can also use the signed keyword by itself to specify the type of a variable, in which case it means signed int. For example:

```
signed value = -5;           // Equivalent to signed int
```

This usage is not particularly common, and I prefer to use int, which makes it more obvious what is meant.

The range of values that can be stored in a variable of type char is from –128 to +127, which is the same as the range of values you can store in a variable of type signed char. In spite of this, type char and type signed char are different types, so you should not make the mistake of assuming they are the same.

If you are sure that you don't need to store negative values in a variable (for example, if you were recording the number of miles you drive in a week), then you can specify a variable as unsigned:

```
unsigned long mileage = 0UL;
```

Here, the minimum value that can be stored in the variable mileage is zero, and the maximum value is 4,294,967,295 (that's $2^{32}-1$). Compare this to the range of –2,147,483,648 to 2,147,483,647 for a signed long. The bit that is used in a signed variable to determine the sign of the value is used in an unsigned variable as part of the numeric value instead. Consequently, an unsigned variable has a larger range of positive values, but it can't represent a negative value. Note how a U (or u) is appended to unsigned constants. In the preceding example I also have L appended to indicate that the constant is long. You can use either upper- or lowercase for U and L, and the sequence is unimportant. However, it's a good idea to adopt a consistent way of specifying such values.

You can also use unsigned by itself as the type specification for a variable, in which case you are specifying the variable to be of type unsigned int.

Remember, both signed *and* unsigned *are keywords, so you can't use them as variable names.*

The Boolean Type

Boolean variables are variables that can have only two values: a value called true and a value called false. The type for a logical variable is bool, named after George Boole, who developed Boolean algebra, and type bool is regarded as an integer type. Boolean variables are also referred to as **logical variables**. Variables of type bool are used to store the results of tests that can be either true or false, such as whether one value is equal to another.

You could declare the name of a variable of type bool with the statement:

```
bool testResult;
```

Of course, you can also initialize variables of type bool when you declare them:

```
bool colorIsRed = true;
```

Or like this:

```
bool colorIsRed(true);
```

You will find that the values TRUE *and* FALSE *are used quite extensively with variables of numeric type, and particularly of type* int. *This is a hangover from the time before variables of type* bool *were implemented in C++ when variables of type* int *were typically used to represent logical values. In this case a zero value is treated as false and a non-zero value as true. The symbols* TRUE *and* FALSE *are still used within the MFC where they represent a non-zero integer value and 0, respectively. Note that* TRUE *and* FALSE *— written with capital letters — are not keywords in C++; they are just symbols defined within the MFC. Note also that* TRUE *and* FALSE *are not legal* bool *values, so don't confuse* true *with* TRUE.

Floating-Point Types

Values that aren't integral are stored as **floating-point** numbers. A floating-point number can be expressed as a decimal value such as 112.5, or with an exponent such as 1.125E2 where the decimal part is multiplied by the power of 10 specified after the E (for Exponent). Our example is, therefore, 1.125×10^2, which is 112.5.

> **A floating-point constant must contain a decimal point, or an exponent, or both. If you write a numerical value with neither, you have an integer.**

You can specify a floating-point variable using the keyword `double`, as in this statement:

```
double in_to_mm = 25.4;
```

A variable of type `double` occupies 8 bytes of memory and stores values accurate to approximately 15 decimal digits. The range of values stored is much wider than that indicated by the 15 digits accuracy, being from 1.7×10^{-308} to 1.7×10^{308}, positive and negative.

If you don't need 15 digits precision, and you don't need the massive range of values provided by `double` variables, you can opt to use the keyword `float` to declare floating-point variables occupying 4 bytes. For example:

```
float pi = 3.14159f;
```

This statement defines a variable `pi` with the initial value 3.14159. The `f` at the end of the constant specifies that it is of type `float`. Without the `f`, the constant would have been of type `double`. Variables that you declare as `float` have approximately 7 decimal digits of precision and can have values from 3.4×10^{-38} to 3.4×10^{38}, positive and negative.

The ISO/ANSI standard for C++ also defines the `long double` floating-point type, which in Visual C++ 2008 is implemented with the same range and precision as type `double`. With some compilers `long double` corresponds to a 16-byte floating-point value with a much greater range and precision than type `double`.

Fundamental Types in ISO/ANSI C++

The following table contains a summary of all the fundamental types in ISO/ANSI C++ and the range of values that are supported for these in Visual C++ 2008.

Type	Size in Bytes	Range of Values
`bool`	1	`true` or `false`
`char`	1	By default the same as type `signed char`: –128 to +127 Optionally you can make `char` the same range as type `unsigned char`.
`signed char`	1	–128 to +127
`unsigned char`	1	0 to 255
`wchar_t`	2	0 to 65,535
`short`	2	–32,768 to +32,767
`unsigned short`	2	0 to 65,535
`int`	4	–2,147,483,648 to 2,147,483,647
`unsigned int`	4	0 to 4,294,967,295

Type	Size in Bytes	Range of Values
long	4	–2,147,483,648 to 2,147,483,647
unsigned long	4	0 to 4,294,967,295
float	4	±3.4×10$^{\pm38}$ with approximately 7 digits accuracy
double	8	±1.7×10$^{\pm308}$ with approximately 15 digits accuracy
long double	8	±1.7×10$^{\pm308}$ with approximately 15 digits accuracy

Literals

I have already used lots of explicit values to initialize variables and in C++, fixed values of any kind are referred to as **literals**. A literal is a value of a specific type so values such as 23, 3.14159, 9.5f, and true are examples of literals of type int, type double, type float, and type bool, respectively. The literal "Samuel Beckett" is an example of a literal that is a string, but I'll defer discussion of exactly what type this is until Chapter 4. Here's a summary of how you write literals of various types.

Type	Examples of Literals
char, signed char, or unsigned char	'A', 'Z', '8', '*'
wchar_t	L'A', L'Z', L'8', L'*'
int	-77, 65, 12345, 0x9FE
unsigned int	10U, 64000u
long	-77L, 65L, 12345l
unsigned long	5UL, 999999999UL, 25ul, 35Ul
float	3.14f, 34.506F
double	1.414, 2.71828
long double	1.414L, 2.71828l
bool	true, false

You can't specify a literal to be of type short or unsigned short, but the compiler will accept initial values that are literals of type int for variables of these types provided the value of the literal is within the range of the variable type.

You will often need to use literals in calculations within a program, for example, conversion values such as 12 for feet into inches or 25.4 for inches to millimeters, or a string to specify an error message. However, you should avoid using numeric literals within programs explicitly where their significance is not obvious. It is not necessarily apparent to everyone that when you use the value 2.54, it is the number of centimeters in an inch. It is better to declare a variable with a fixed value corresponding to your literal instead — you might name the variable inchesToCentimeters, for example. Then wherever you use inchesToCentimeters in your code, it will be quite obvious what it is. You will see how to fix the value of a variable a little later on in this chapter.

Defining Synonyms for Data Types

The typedef keyword enables you to define your own type name for an existing type. Using typedef, you could define the type name BigOnes as equivalent to the standard long int type with the declaration:

```
typedef long int BigOnes;          // Defining BigOnes as a type name
```

This defines BigOnes as an alternative type specifier for long int, so you could declare a variable mynum as long int with the declaration:

```
BigOnes mynum = 0L;                // Define a long int variable
```

There's no difference between this declaration and the one using the built-in type name. You could equally well use

```
long int mynum = 0L;               // Define a long int variable
```

for exactly the same result. In fact, if you define your own type name such as BigOnes, you can use both type specifiers within the same program for declaring different variables that will end up as having the same type.

Since typedef only defines a synonym for an existing type, it may appear to be a bit superficial, but it is not at all. You'll see later that it fulfills a very useful role in enabling you to simplify more complex declarations by defining a single name that represents a somewhat convoluted type specification, and this can make your code much more readable.

Variables with Specific Sets of Values

You will sometimes be faced with the need for variables that have a limited set of possible values that can be usefully referred to by labels — the days of the week, for example, or months of the year. There is a specific facility in C++ to handle this situation, called an **enumeration**. Take one of the examples I have just mentioned — a variable that can assume values corresponding to days of the week. You can define this as follows:

```
enum Week{Mon, Tues, Wed, Thurs, Fri, Sat, Sun} thisWeek;
```

This declares an enumeration type with the name Week and the variable thisWeek, which is an instance of the enumeration type Week that can assume only the constant values specified between the braces. If you try to assign to thisWeek anything other than one of the set of values specified, it will cause an error. The symbolic names listed between the braces are known as **enumerators**. In fact, each of the names of the days will be automatically defined as representing a fixed integer value. The first name in the list, Mon, will have the value 0, Tues will be 1, and so on.

You could assign one of the enumeration constants as the value of the variable thisWeek like this:

```
thisWeek = Thurs;
```

Note that you do not need to qualify the enumeration constant with the name of the enumeration. The value of thisWeek will be 3 because the symbolic constants that an enumeration defines are assigned values of type int by default in sequence starting with 0.

By default, each successive enumerator is one larger than the value of the previous one, but if you would prefer the implicit numbering to start at a different value, you can just write:

```
enum Week {Mon = 1, Tues, Wed, Thurs, Fri, Sat, Sun} thisWeek;
```

Now the enumeration constants will be equivalent to 1 through 7. The enumerators don't even need to have unique values. You could define Mon and Tues as both having the value 1, for example, with the statement:

```
enum Week {Mon = 1, Tues = 1, Wed, Thurs, Fri, Sat, Sun} thisWeek;
```

As the type of the variable thisWeek is type int, it will occupy four bytes, as will all variables that are of an enumeration type.

Note that you are *not* allowed to use functional notation for initializing enumerators. You must use the assignment operator as in the examples you have seen.

Having defined the form of an enumeration, you can define another variable thus:

```
enum Week nextWeek;
```

This defines a variable nextWeek as an enumeration that can assume the values previously specified. You can also omit the enum keyword in declaring a variable, so, instead of the previous statement, you could write:

```
Week next_week;
```

If you wish, you can assign specific values to all the enumerators. For example, you could define this enumeration:

```
enum Punctuation {Comma = ',', Exclamation = '!', Question = '?'} things;
```

Here you have defined the possible values for the variable things as the numerical equivalents of the appropriate symbols. If you look in the ASCII table in Appendix B, you will see that the symbols are 44, 33 and 63, respectively, in decimal. As you can see, the values assigned don't have to be in ascending order. If you don't specify all the values explicitly, each enumerator will be assigned a value incrementing by 1 from the last specified value, as in our second Week example.

You can omit the enumeration type if you don't need to define other variables of this type later. For example:

```
enum {Mon, Tues, Wed, Thurs, Fri, Sat, Sun} thisWeek, nextWeek, lastWeek;
```

Here you have three variables declared that can assume values from Mon to Sun. Because the enumeration type is not specified, you cannot refer to it. Note that you cannot define other variables for this enumeration *at all*, because you would not be permitted to repeat the definition. Doing so would imply that you were redefining values for Mon to Sun, and this isn't allowed.

Basic Input/Output Operations

Here, you will only look at enough of native C++ input and output to get you through learning about C++. It's not that it's difficult — quite the opposite in fact — but for Windows programming you won't need it at all. C++ input/output revolves around the notion of a data stream, where you can insert data into an output stream or extract data from an input stream. You have already seen that the ISO/ANSI C++ standard output stream to the command line on the screen is referred to as cout. The complementary input stream from the keyboard is referred to as cin.

Input from the Keyboard

You obtain input from the keyboard through the stream cin, using the extractor operator for a stream >>. To read two integer values from the keyboard into integer variables num1 and num2, you can write this statement:

```
cin >> num1 >> num2;
```

The **extraction operator**, >>, "points" in the direction that data flows — in this case, from cin to each of the two variables in turn. Any leading whitespace is skipped, and the first integer value you key in is read into num1. This is because the input statement executes from left to right. Any whitespace following num1 is ignored and the second integer value that you enter is read into num2. There has to be some whitespace between successive values though, so that they can be differentiated. The stream input operation ends when you press the *Enter* key, and execution then continues with the next statement. Of course, errors can arise if you key in the wrong data, but I will assume that you always get it right!

Floating-point values are read from the keyboard in exactly the same way as integers and, of course, you can mix the two. The stream input and operations automatically deal with variables and data of any of the fundamental types. For example, in the statements,

```
int num1 = 0, num2 = 0;
double factor = 0.0;
cin >> num1 >> factor >> num2;
```

the last line will read an integer into num1, then a floating-point value into factor and, finally, an integer into num2.

Output to the Command Line

You have already seen output to the command line, but I want to revisit it anyway. Writing information to the display operates in a complementary fashion to input. As you have seen, the stream is called cout, and you use the insertion operator, << to transfer data to the output stream. This operator also "points" in the direction of data movement. You have already used this operator to output a text string between quotes. I can demonstrate the process of outputting the value of a variable with a simple program.

Try It Out   **Output to the Command Line**

I'll assume that you've got the hang of creating a new empty project by adding a new source file to the project and building it into an executable. Here's the code that you need to put in the source file once you have created the `Ex2_02` project:

```
// Ex2_02.cpp
// Exercising output
#include <iostream>

using std::cout;
using std::endl;

int main()
{
   int num1 = 1234, num2 = 5678;
   cout << endl;                         // Start on a new line
   cout << num1 << num2;                 // Output two values
   cout << endl;                         // End on a new line
   return 0;                             // Exit program
}
```

How It Works

The first statement in the body of `main()` declares and initializes two integer variables, `num1` and `num2`. This is followed by two output statements, the first of which moves the screen cursor position to a new line. Because output statements execute from left to right, the second output statement displays the value of `num1` followed by the value of `num2`.

When you compile and execute this, you will get the output:

```
12345678
```

The output is correct, but it's not exactly helpful. You really need the two output values to be separated by at least one space. The default for stream output is to just output the digits in the output value, which doesn't provide for spacing successive output values out nicely so they can be differentiated. As it is, you have no way to tell where the first number ends and the second number begins.

Formatting the Output

You can fix the problem of there being no spaces between items of data quite easily, though, just by outputting a space between the two values. You can do this by replacing the following line in your original program:

```
cout << num1 << num2;                    // Output two values
```

Just substitute the statement:

```
cout << num1 << ' ' << num2;             // Output two values
```

Of course, if you had several rows of output that you wanted to align in columns, you would need some extra capability because you do not know how many digits there will be in each value. You can take care of this situation by using what is called a **manipulator**. A manipulator modifies the way in which data output to (or input from) a stream is handled.

Manipulators are defined in the header file <iomanip>, so you need to add an #include directive for it. The manipulator that you'll use is setw(n), which will output the value that follows right-justified in a field n spaces wide, so setw(6) causes the next output value to be presented in a field with a width of six spaces. Let's see it working.

Try It Out   **Using Manipulators**

To get something more like the output you want, you can change the program to the following:

```
// Ex2_03.cpp
// Exercising output
#include <iostream>
#include <iomanip>

using std::cout;
using std::endl;
using std::setw;

int main()
{
    int num1 = 1234, num2 = 5678;
    cout << endl;                            // Start on a new line
    cout << setw(6) << num1 << setw(6) << num2;  // Output two values
    cout << endl;                            // Start on a new line
    return 0;                                // Exit program
}
```

How It Works

The changes from the last example are the addition of the #include directive for the <iomanip> header file, the addition of a using declaration for the setw name from the std namespace, and the insertion of the setw() manipulator in the output stream preceding each value so that the output values are presented in a field six characters wide. Now you get nice neat output where you can actually separate the two values:

```
  1234  5678
```

Note that the setw() manipulator works only for the single output value immediately following its insertion into the stream. You have to insert the manipulator into the stream immediately preceding each value that you want to output within a given field width. If you put only one setw(), it would apply to the first value to be output after it was inserted. Any following value would be output in the default manner. You could try this out by deleting the second setw(6) and its insertion operator in the example.

Escape Sequences

When you write a character string between double quotes, you can include special characters called **escape sequences** in the string They are called escape sequences because they allow characters to be included in a string that otherwise could not be represented by escaping from the default interpretation of the characters. An escape sequence starts with a backslash character, \, and the backslash character cues the compiler to interpret the character that follows in a special way. For example, a tab character is written as \t, so the t is understood by the compiler to represent a tab in the string, and not the letter t. Look at these two output statements:

```
cout << endl << "This is output.";
cout << endl << "\tThis is output after a tab.";
```

They will produce these lines:

```
This is output.
        This is output after a tab.
```

The \t in the second output statement causes the output text to be indented to the first tab position.

In fact, instead of using endl you could use the escape sequence for the newline character, \n, in each string, so you could rewrite the preceding statements as follows:

```
cout << "\nThis is output.";
cout << "\n\tThis is output after a tab.";
```

Here are some escape sequences that may be particularly useful:

Escape Sequence	What It Does
\a	sounds a beep
\n	newline
\'	single quote
\\	backslash
\b	backspace
\t	tab
\"	double quote
\?	question mark

Obviously, if you want to be able to include a backslash or a double quote as a character to appear in a string, you must use the appropriate escape sequences to represent them. Otherwise, the backslash would be interpreted as the start of another escape sequence, and the double quote would indicate the end of the character string.

You can also use characters specified by escape sequences in the initialization of variables of type `char`. For example:

```
char Tab = '\t';                // Initialize with tab character
```

Because a character literal is delimited by single quote characters, you must use an escape sequence to specify a character literal that is a single quote, thus ' \ ' '.

Try It Out   Using Escape Sequences

Here's a program that uses some of the escape sequences in the table in the previous section:

```cpp
// Ex2_04.cpp
// Using escape sequences
#include <iostream>
#include <iomanip>

using std::cout;

int main()
{
    char newline = '\n';                         // Newline escape sequence
    cout << newline;                             // Start on a new line
    cout << "\"We\'ll make our escapes in sequence\", he said.";
    cout << "\n\tThe program\'s over, it\'s time take make a beep beep.\a\a";
    cout << newline;                             // Start on a new line
    return 0;                                     // Exit program
}
```

If you compile and execute this example it will produce the following output:

```
"We'll make our escapes in sequence", he said.
        The program's over, it's time take make a beep beep.
```

How It Works

The first line in `main()` defines the variable `newline` and initializes it with a character defined by the escape sequence for a new line. You can then use `newline` instead of `endl` from the standard library.

After writing `newline` to `cout` you output a string that uses the escape sequences for a double quote (\ ") and a single quote (\ '). You don't have to use the escape sequence for a single quote here because the string is delimited by double quotes and the compile would recognize a single quote character as just that, and not a delimiter. You must use the escape sequences for the double quotes in the string though. The string starts with a newline escape sequence followed by a tab escape sequence, so the output line is indented by the tab distance. The string also ends with two instances of the escape sequence for a beep, so you should hear a double beep from your PC's speaker.

Calculating in C++

This is where you actually start doing something with the data that you enter. You know how to carry out simple input and output; now you are beginning the bit in the middle, the "processing" part of a C++ program. Almost all of the computational aspects of C++ are fairly intuitive, so you should slice through this like a hot knife through butter.

The Assignment Statement

You have already seen examples of the assignment statement. A typical assignment statement looks like this:

```
whole = part1 + part2 + part3;
```

The assignment statement enables you to calculate the value of an expression which appears on the right-hand side of the equals sign, in this case the sum of part1, part2, and part3, and store the result in the variable specified on the left-hand side, in this case the variable with the name whole. In this statement, the whole is exactly the sum of its parts, and no more.

Note how the statement, as always, ends with a semicolon.

You can also write repeated assignments such as:

```
a = b = 2;
```

This is equivalent to assigning the value 2 to b and then assigning the value of b to a, so both variables will end up storing the value 2.

Understanding Lvalues and Rvalues

An **lvalue** is something that refers to an address in memory, and is so called because any expression that results in an lvalue can appear on the left of the equals sign in an assignment statement. Most variables are lvalues, because they specify a place in memory. However, as you'll see, there are variables that aren't lvalues and can't appear on the left of an assignment because their values have been defined as constant.

The variables a and b that appear in the preceding paragraph are lvalues, whereas the result of evaluating the expression a+b would not be, because its result doesn't determine an address in memory where a value might be stored. The result of an expression that is not an lvalue is referred to as an **rvalue**.

Lvalues will pop up at various times throughout the book, sometimes where you least expect them, so keep the idea in mind.

Arithmetic Operations

The basic arithmetic operators you have at your disposal are addition, subtraction, multiplication, and division, represented by the symbols +, -, *, and /, respectively. These operate generally as you would expect, with the exception of division which has a slight aberration when working with integer variables or constants, as you'll see. You can write statements such as the following:

```
netPay = hours * rate - deductions;
```

Here, the product of `hours` and `rate` will be calculated and then `deductions` subtracted from the value produced. The multiply and divide operators are executed before addition and subtraction, as you would expect. I will discuss the order of execution of the various operators in expressions more fully later in this chapter. The overall result of evaluating the expression `hours * rate - deductions` will be stored in the variable `netPay`.

The minus sign used in the last statement has two operands — it subtracts the value of its right operand from the value of its left operand. This is called a *binary* operation because two values are involved. The minus sign can also be used with one operand to change the sign of the value to which it is applied, in which case it is called a *unary* minus. You could write this:

```
int a = 0;
int b = -5;
a = -b;                       // Changes the sign of the operand
```

Here, a will be assigned the value +5 because the unary minus changes the sign of the value of the operand b.

Note that an assignment is not the equivalent of the equations you saw in high school algebra. It specifies an action to be carried out rather than a statement of fact. The expression to the right of the assignment operator is evaluated and the result is stored in the lvalue — typically a variable — that appears on the left.

Look at this statement:

```
number = number + 1;
```

This means "add 1 to the current value stored in `number` and then store the result back in `number`." As a normal algebraic statement it wouldn't make sense.

Exercising Basic Arithmetic

You can exercise basic arithmetic in C++ by calculating how many standard rolls of wallpaper are needed to paper a room. The following example does this:

```
// Ex2_05.cpp
// Calculating how many rolls of wallpaper are required for a room
#include <iostream>

using std::cout;
using std::cin;
using std::endl;

int main()
{
    double height = 0.0, width = 0.0, length = 0.0; // Room dimensions
    double perimeter = 0.0;                         // Room perimeter

    const double rollwidth = 21.0;                  // Standard roll width
```

```
    const double rolllength = 12.0*33.0;            // Standard roll length(33ft.)

    int strips_per_roll = 0;                        // Number of strips in a roll
    int strips_reqd = 0;                            // Number of strips needed
    int nrolls = 0;                                 // Total number of rolls

    cout << endl                                    // Start a new line
        << "Enter the height of the room in inches: ";
    cin >> height;

    cout  << endl                                   // Start a new line
        << "Now enter the length and width in inches: ";
    cin >> length >> width;

    strips_per_roll = rolllength / height;          // Get number of strips per roll
    perimeter = 2.0*(length + width);               // Calculate room perimeter
    strips_reqd = perimeter / rollwidth;            // Get total strips required
    nrolls = strips_reqd / strips_per_roll;         // Calculate number of rolls

    cout << endl
        << "For your room you need " << nrolls << " rolls of wallpaper."
        << endl;

    return 0;
}
```

Unless you are more adept than I am at typing, chances are there will be a few errors when you compile this for the first time. Once you have fixed the typos, it will compile and run just fine. You'll get a couple of warning messages from the compiler. Don't worry about them — the compiler is just making sure you understand what's going on. I'll explain the reason for the warning messages in a moment.

How It Works

One thing needs to be clear at the outset — I assume no responsibility for you running out of wallpaper as a result of using this program! As you'll see, all errors in the estimate of the number of rolls required are due to the way C++ works and to the wastage that inevitably occurs when you hang your own wallpaper — usually 50 percent +!

I'll work through the statements in this example in sequence, picking out the interesting, novel, or even exciting features. The statements down to the start of the body of main() are familiar territory by now, so I will take those for granted.

A couple of general points about the layout of the program are worth noting. First, the statements in the body of main() are indented to make the extent of the body easier to see, and second, various groups of statements are separated by a blank line to indicate that they are functional groups. Indenting statements is a fundamental technique in laying out program code in C++. You will see that this is applied universally to provide visual cues to help you identify the various logical blocks in a program.

The const Modifier

You have a block of declarations for the variables used in the program right at the beginning of the body of main(). These statements are also fairly familiar, but there are two that contain some new features:

```
    const double rollwidth = 21.0;                  // Standard roll width
    const double rolllength = 12.0*33.0;             // Standard roll length(33ft.)
```

They both start out with a new keyword: `const`. This is a **type modifier** that indicates that the variables are not just of type `double`, but are also constants. Because you effectively tell the compiler that these are constants, the compiler will check for any statements that attempt to change the values of these variables, and if it finds any, it will generate an error message. A variable declared as `const` is not an lvalue and, therefore, can't legally be placed on the left of an assignment operation.

You could check this out by adding, anywhere after the declaration of `rollwidth`, a statement such as:

```
rollwidth = 0;
```

You will find the program no longer compiles, returning `'error C2166: l-value specifies const object'`.

It can be very useful to define constants that you use in a program by means of `const` variable types, particularly when you use the same constant several times in a program. For one thing, it is much better than sprinkling literals throughout your program that may not have blindingly obvious meanings; with the value 42 in a program you could be referring to the meaning of life, the universe, and everything, but if you use a `const` variable with the name `myAge` that has a value of 42, it becomes obvious that you are not. For another thing, if you need to change the value of a `const` variable that you are using, you will need to change its definition only in a source file to ensure that the change automatically appears throughout. You'll see this technique used quite often.

Constant Expressions

The `const` variable `rolllength` is also initialized with an arithmetic expression (`12.0*33.0`). Being able to use constant expressions to initialize variables saves having to work out the value yourself. It can also be more meaningful, as it is in this case because 33 feet times 12 inches is a much clearer expression of what the value represents than simply writing 396. The compiler will generally evaluate constant expressions accurately, whereas if you do it yourself, depending on the complexity of the expression and your ability to number-crunch, there is a finite probability that it may be wrong.

You can use any expression that can be calculated as a constant at compile time, including `const` objects that you have already defined. So, for instance, if it was useful in the program to do so, you could declare the area of a standard roll of wallpaper as:

```
const double rollarea = rollwidth*rolllength;
```

This statement would need to be placed after the declarations for the two `const` variables used in the initialization of `rollarea` because all the variables that appear in a constant expression must be known to the compiler at the point in the source file where the constant expression appears.

Program Input

After declaring some integer variables, the next four statements in the program handle input from the keyboard:

```
cout << endl                                // Start a new line
     << "Enter the height of the room in inches: ";
cin >> height;

cout << endl                                // Start a new line
```

```
                    << "Now enter the length and width in inches: ";
   cin >> length >> width;
```

Here you have written text to `cout` to prompt for the input required and then read the input from the keyboard using `cin`, which is the standard input stream. You first obtain the value for the room `height` and then read the `length` and `width` successively. In a practical program, you would need to check for errors and possibly make sure that the values that are read are sensible, but you don't have enough knowledge to do that yet!

Calculating the Result

You have four statements involved in calculating the number of standard rolls of wallpaper required for the size of room given:

```
strips_per_roll = rolllength / height;        // Get number of strips in a roll
perimeter = 2.0*(length + width);             // Calculate room perimeter
strips_reqd = perimeter / rollwidth;          // Get total strips required
nrolls = strips_reqd / strips_per_roll;       // Calculate number of rolls
```

The first statement calculates the number of strips of paper with a length corresponding to the height of the room that you can get from a standard roll, by dividing one into the other. So, if the room is 8 feet high, you divide 96 into 396, which would produce the floating-point result 4.125. There is a subtlety here, however. The variable where you store the result, `strips_per_roll`, was declared as `int`, so it can store only integer values. Consequently, any floating-point value to be stored as an integer is rounded down to the nearest integer, 4 in this case, and this value is stored. This is actually the result that you want here because, although they may fit under a window or over a door, fractions of a strip are best ignored when estimating.

The conversion of a value from one type to another is called **casting**. This particular example is called an **implicit cast**, because the code doesn't explicitly state that a cast is needed, and the compiler has to work it out for itself. The two warnings you got during compilation were issued because the implicit casts that were inserted implied information could be lost due to the conversion from one type to another.

You should beware when using implicit casts. Compilers do not always supply a warning that an implicit cast is being made, and if you are assigning a value of one type to a variable of a type with a lesser range of values, then there is always a danger that you will lose information. If there are implicit casts in your program that you have included accidentally, then they may represent bugs that may be difficult to locate.

Where such an assignment is unavoidable, you can specify the conversion explicitly to demonstrate that it is no accident and that you really meant to do it. You do this by making an **explicit cast** of the value on the right of the assignment to `int`, so the statement would become:

```
strips_per_roll = static_cast<int>(rolllength / height);   // Get number of strips
                                                           // in a roll
```

The addition of `static_cast<int>` with the parentheses around the expression on the right tells the compiler explicitly that you want to convert the value of the expression to `int`. Although this means that you still lose the fractional part of the value, the compiler assumes that you know what you are doing and will not issue a warning. You'll see more about `static_cast<>()` and other types of explicit casting, later in this chapter.

Note how you calculate the perimeter of the room in the next statement. To multiply the sum of the `length` and the `width` by two, you enclose the expression summing the two variables between parentheses. This ensures that the addition is performed first and the result is multiplied by 2.0 to produce the correct value for the perimeter. You can use parentheses to make sure that a calculation is carried out in the order you require because expressions in parentheses are always evaluated first. Where there are nested parentheses, the expressions within the parentheses are evaluated in sequence, from the innermost to the outermost.

The third statement, calculating how many strips of paper are required to cover the room, uses the same effect that you observed in the first statement: The result is rounded down to the nearest integer because it is to be stored in the integer variable, `strips_reqd`. This is not what you need in practice. It would be best to round up for estimating, but you don't have enough knowledge of C++ to do this yet. Once you have read the next chapter, you can come back and fix it!

The last arithmetic statement calculates the number of rolls required by dividing the number of strips required (an integer) by the number of strips in a roll (also an integer). Because you are dividing one integer by another, the result has to be an integer, and any remainder is ignored. This would still be the case if the variable `nrolls` were floating point. The integer value resulting from the expression would be converted to floating-point form before it was stored in `nrolls`. The result that you obtain is essentially the same as if you had produced a floating-point result and rounded down to the nearest integer. Again, this is not what you want, so if you want to use this, you will need to fix it.

Displaying the Result

The result of the calculation is displayed by the following statement:

```
cout << endl
     << "For your room you need " << nrolls << " rolls of wallpaper."
     << endl;
```

This is a single output statement spread over three lines. It first outputs a newline character and then the text string `"For your room you need "`. This is followed by the value of the variable `nrolls` and finally the text string `" rolls of wallpaper."`. As you can see, output statements are very easy in C++.

Finally, the program ends when this statement is executed:

```
return 0;
```

The value zero here is a return value that, in this case, will be returned to the operating system. You will see more about return values in Chapter 5.

Calculating a Remainder

You saw in the last example that dividing one integer value by another produces an integer result that ignores any remainder, so that 11 divided by 4 gives the result 2. Because the remainder after division can be of great interest, particularly when you are dividing cookies amongst children, for example, C++

provides a special operator, %, for this. So you can write the following statements to handle the cookie-sharing problem:

```
int residue = 0, cookies = 19, children = 5;
residue = cookies % children;
```

The variable `residue` will end up with the value 4, the number left after dividing 19 by 5. To calculate how many cookies each child receives, you just need to use division, as in the statement:

```
each = cookies / children;
```

Modifying a Variable

It's often necessary to modify the existing value of a variable, such as by incrementing it or doubling it. You could increment a variable called `count` using the statement:

```
count = count + 5;
```

This simply adds 5 to the current value stored in `count` and stores the result back in `count`, so if `count` started out at 10, it would end up as 15.

You also have an alternative, shorthand way of writing the same thing in C++:

```
count += 5;
```

This says, "Take the value in `count`, add 5 to it, and store the result back in `count`." We can also use other operators with this notation. For example,

```
count *= 5;
```

has the effect of multiplying the current value of `count` by 5 and storing the result back in `count`. In general, you can write statements of the form,

```
lhs op= rhs;
```

lhs stands for any legal expression for the left-hand side of the statement and is usually (but not necessarily) a variable name. *rhs* stands for any legal expression on the right-hand side of the statement. *op* is any of the following operators:

+	−	*	/	%
<<	>>	&	^	|

You have already met the first five of these operators, and you'll see the others, which are the shift and logical operators, later in this chapter.

The general form of the statement is equivalent to this:

```
lhs = lhs op (rhs);
```

The parentheses around `rhs` imply that this expression is evaluated first, and the result becomes the right operand for `op`.

This means that you can write statements such as:

```
a /- b + c;
```

This will be identical in effect to this statement:

```
a = a/(b + c);
```

Thus, the value of a will be divided by the sum of b and c, and the result will be stored back in a.

The Increment and Decrement Operators

I will now introduce some unusual arithmetic operators called the **increment** and **decrement operators**, as you will find them to be quite an asset once you get further into applying C++ in earnest. These are unary operators that you use to increment or decrement the value stored in a variable that holds an integral value. For example, assuming the variable `count` is of type `int`, the following three statements all have exactly the same effect:

```
count = count + 1;          count += 1;          ++count;
```

They each increment the variable `count` by 1. The last form, using the increment operator, is clearly the most concise.

The increment operator not only changes the value of the variable to which you apply it, but also results in a value. Thus, using the increment operator to increase the value of a variable by 1 can also appear as part of a more complex expression. If incrementing a variable using the ++ operator, as in ++count, is contained within another expression, then the action of the operator is to *first* increment the value of the variable and *then* use the incremented value in the expression. For example, suppose `count` has the value 5, and you have defined a variable `total` of type `int`. Suppose you write the following statement:

```
total = ++count + 6;
```

This results in `count` being incremented to 6, and this result is added to 6, so `total` is assigned the value 12.

So far, you have written the increment operator, ++, in front of the variable to which it applies. This is called the **prefix** form of the increment operator. The increment operator also has a **postfix** form, where the operator is written *after* the variable to which it applies; the effect of this is slightly different. The variable to which the operator applies is incremented only *after* its value has been used in context. For example, reset `count` to the value 5 and rewrite the previous statement as:

```
total = count++ + 6;
```

Then `total` is assigned the value 11, because the initial value of `count` is used to evaluate the expression before the increment by 1 is applied. The preceding statement is equivalent to the two statements:

```
total = count + 6;
++count;
```

The clustering of '+' signs, in the example of the preceding postfix form, is likely to lead to confusion. Generally, it isn't a good idea to write the increment operator in the way that I have written it here. It would be clearer to write:

```
total = 6 + count++;
```

Where you have an expression such as a++ + b, or even a+++b, it becomes less obvious what is meant or what the compiler will do. They are actually the same, but in the second case you might really have meant a + ++b, which is different. It evaluates to one more than the other two expressions.

Exactly the same rules that I have discussed in relation to the increment operator apply to the decrement operator, --. For example, if `count` has the initial value 5, then the statement

```
total = --count + 6;
```

results in `total` having the value 10 assigned, whereas,

```
total = 6 + count--;
```

sets the value of `total` to 11. Both operators are usually applied to integers, particularly in the context of **loops**, as you will see in Chapter 3. You will see in later chapters that they can also be applied to other data types in C++, notably variables that store addresses.

Try It Out   The Comma Operator

The comma operator allows you to specify several expressions where normally only one might occur. This is best understood by looking at an example that demonstrates how it works:

```cpp
// Ex2_06.cpp
// Exercising the comma operator
#include <iostream>

using std::cout;
using std::endl;

int main()
{
   long num1(0L), num2(0L), num3(0L), num4(0L);

   num4 = (num1 = 10L, num2 = 20L, num3 = 30L);
   cout << endl
        << "The value of a series of expressions "
        << "is the value of the rightmost: "
        << num4;
   cout << endl;
```

```
        return 0;
    }
```

How It Works

If you compile and run this program you will get this output:

```
The value of a series of expressions is the value of the rightmost: 30
```

This is fairly self-explanatory. The first statement in main() creates four variables, num1 through num4, and initializes them to zero using functional notation. The variable num4 receives the value of the last of the series of three assignments, the value of an assignment being the value assigned to the left-hand side. The parentheses in the assignment for num4 are essential. You could try executing this without them to see the effect. Without the parentheses, the first expression separated by commas in the series will become:

```
num4 = num1 = 10L
```

So, num4 will have the value 10L.

Of course, the expressions separated by the comma operator don't have to be assignments. You could equally well write the following statements:

```
long num1(1L), num2(10L), num3(100L), num4(0L);
num4 = (++num1, ++num2, ++num3);
```

The effect of the assignment statement will be to increment the variables num1, num2, and num3 by 1, and to set num4 to the value of the last expression which will be 101L. This example is aimed at illustrating the effect of the comma operator and is not an example of how to write good code.

The Sequence of Calculation

So far, I haven't talked about how you arrive at the sequence of calculations involved in evaluating an expression. It generally corresponds to what you will have learned at school when dealing with basic arithmetic operators, but there are many other operators in C++. To understand what happens with these you need to look at the mechanism used in C++ to determine this sequence. It's referred to as **operator precedence**.

Operator Precedence

Operator precedence orders the operators in a priority sequence. In any expression, operators with the highest precedence are always executed first, followed by operators with the next highest precedence, and so on, down to those with the lowest precedence of all. The precedence of the operators in C++ is shown in the following table.

Operators	Associativity
`::`	Left
`()` `[]` `->` `.`	Left
`!` `~` `+(unary)` `-(unary)` `++` `--` `&(unary)` `*(unary)` `(typecast)` `static_cast` `const_cast` `dynamic_cast` `reinterpret_cast` `sizeof` `new` `delete typeid`	Right
`.*(unary)` `->*`	Left
`*` `/` `%`	Left
`+` `-`	Left
`<<` `>>`	Left
`<` `<=` `>` `>=`	Left
`==` `!=`	Left
`&`	Left
`^`	Left
`|`	Left
`&&`	Left
`||`	Left
`?:`(conditional operator)	Right
`=` `*=` `/=` `%=` `+=` `-=` `&=` `^=` `|=` `<<=` `>>=`	Right
`,`	Left

There are a lot of operators here that you haven't seen yet, but you will know them all by the end of the book. Rather than spreading them around, I have put all the C++ operators in the precedence table so that you can always refer back to it if you are uncertain about the precedence of one operator relative to another.

Operators with the highest precedence appear at the top of the table. All the operators that appear in the same cell in the table have equal precedence. If there are no parentheses in an expression, operators with equal precedence are executed in a sequence determined by their **associativity**. Thus, if the associativity is "left," the left-most operator in an expression is executed first, progressing through the expression to the right-most. This means that an expression such as a + b + c + d is executed as though it was written (((a + b) + c) + d) because binary + is left-associative.

Note that where an operator has a unary (working with one operand) and a binary (working with two operands) form, the unary form is always of a higher precedence and is, therefore, executed first.

> You can always override the precedence of operators by using parentheses. Because there are so many operators in C++, it's sometimes hard to be sure what takes precedence over what. It is a good idea to insert parentheses to make sure. A further plus is that parentheses often make the code much easier to read.

Variable Types and Casting

Calculations in C++ can be carried out only between values of the same type. When you write an expression involving variables or constants of different types, for each operation to be performed the compiler has to convert the type of one of the operands to match that of the other. This conversion process is called **casting**. For example, if you want to add a `double` value to a value of an integer type, the integer value is first converted to `double`, after which the addition is carried out. Of course, the variable that contains the value to be cast is itself not changed. The compiler will store the converted value in a temporary memory location, which will be discarded when the calculation is finished.

There are rules that govern the selection of the operand to be converted in any operation. Any expression to be calculated breaks down into a series of operations between two operands. For example, the expression 2*3-4+5 amounts to the series 2*3 resulting in 6, 6-4 resulting in 2, and finally 2+5 resulting in 7. Thus, the rules for casting operands where necessary need to be defined only in terms of decisions about pairs of operands. So, for any pair of operands of different types, the following rules are checked in the order that they are written. When one applies, that rule is used.

Rules for Casting Operands

1. If either operand is of type `long double`, the other is converted to `long double`.

2. If either operand is of type `double`, the other is converted to `double`.

3. If either operand is of type `float`, the other is converted to `float`.

4. Any operand of type `char`, `signed char`, `unsigned char`, `short`, or `unsigned short` is converted to type `int`.

5. An enumeration type is converted to the first of `int`, `unsigned int`, `long`, or `unsigned long` that accommodates the range of the enumerators.

6. If either operand is of type `unsigned long`, the other is converted to `unsigned long`.

7. If one operand is of type `long` and the other is of type `unsigned int`, then both operands are converted to type `unsigned long`.

8. If either operand is of type `long`, the other is converted to type `long`.

This looks and reads as though it is incredibly complicated, but the basic principle is to always convert the value that has the type that is of a more limited range to the type of the other value. This maximizes the likelihood of being able to accommodate the result. You could try these rules on a hypothetical expression to see how they work. Suppose that you have a sequence of variable declarations as follows:

```
double value = 31.0;
int count = 16;
float many = 2.0f;
char num = 4;
```

Also suppose that you have the following rather arbitrary arithmetic statement:

```
value = (value - count)*(count - num)/many + num/many;
```

You can now work out what casts the compiler will apply in the execution of the statement.

The first operation is to calculate (value - count). Rule 1 doesn't apply but Rule 2 does, so the value of count is converted to double and the double result 15.0 is calculated.

Next (count - num) must be evaluated, and here the first rule in sequence that applies is Rule 4, so num is converted from char to int and the result 12 is produced as a value of type int.

The next calculation is the product of the first two results, a double 15.0 and an int 12. Rule 2 applies here, and the 12 is converted to 12.0 as double, and the double result 180.0 is produced.

This result now has to be divided by many, so Rule 2 applies again, and the value of many is converted to double before generating the double result 90.0.

The expression num/many is calculated next, and here Rule 3 applies to produce the float value 2.0f after converting the type of num from char to float.

Lastly, the double value 90.0 is added to the float value 2.0f for which Rule 2 applies, so after converting the 2.0f to 2.0 as double, the final result of 92.0 is stored in value.

In spite of the preceding sequence reading a bit like *The Auctioneer's Song*, you should get the general idea.

Casts in Assignment Statements

As you saw in example Ex2_05.cpp earlier in this chapter, you can cause an implicit cast by writing an expression on the right-hand side of an assignment that is of a different type from the variable on the left-hand side. This can cause values to be changed and information to be lost. For instance, if you assign a float or double value to a variable of type int or a long, the fractional part of the float or double will be lost and just the integer part will be stored. (You may lose even more information if your floating-point variable exceeds the range of values available for the integer type concerned.)

For example, after executing the following code fragment,

```
int number = 0;
float decimal = 2.5f;
number = decimal;
```

the value of `number` will be 2. Note the `f` at the end of the constant 2.5f. This indicates to the compiler that this constant is single precision floating point. Without the `f`, the default would have been type `double`. Any constant containing a decimal point is floating point. If you don't want it to be double precision, you need to append the `f`. A capital letter `F` would do the job just as well.

Explicit Casts

With mixed expressions involving the basic types, your compiler automatically arranges casting where necessary, but you can also force a conversion from one type to another by using an **explicit cast**. To cast the value of an expression to a given type, you write the cast in the form:

```
static_cast<the_type_to_convert_to>(expression)
```

The keyword `static_cast` reflects the fact that the cast is checked statically — that is, when your program is compiled. No further checks are made when you execute the program to see if this cast is safe to apply. Later, when you get to deal with classes, you will meet `dynamic_cast`, where the conversion is checked dynamically — that is, when the program is executing. There are also two other kinds of cast — `const_cast` for removing the `const`-ness of an expression and `reinterpret_cast`, which is an unconditional cast — but I'll say no more about these here.

The effect of the `static_cast` operation is to convert the value that results from evaluating *expression* to the type that you specify between the angled brackets. The *expression* can be anything from a single variable to a complex expression involving lots of nested parentheses.

Here's a specific example of the use of `static_cast<>()`:

```
double value1 = 10.5;
double value2 = 15.5;
int whole_number = static_cast<int>(value1) + static_cast<int>(value2);
```

The initializing value for the variable `whole_number` is the sum of the integral parts of `value1` and `value2`, so they are each explicitly cast to type `int`. The variable `whole_number` will therefore have the initial value 25. The casts do *not* affect the values stored in `value1` and `value2`, which will remain as 10.5 and 15.5, respectively. The values 10 and 15 produced by the casts are just stored temporarily for use in the calculation and then discarded. Although both casts cause a loss of information in the calculation, the compiler will always assume that you know what you are doing when you specify a cast explicitly.

Also, as I described in `Ex2_05.cpp` relating to assignments involving different types, you can always make it clear that you know the cast is necessary by making it explicit:

```
strips_per_roll = static_cast<int>(rolllength / height);     //Get number of strips
                                                             // in a roll
```

You can write an explicit cast for a numerical value to any numeric type, but you should be conscious of the possibility of losing information. If you cast a value of type `float` or `double` to type `long`, for example, you will lose the fractional part of the value when it is converted, so if the value started out as less than 1.0, the result will be 0. If you cast a value of type `double` to type `float`, you will lose accuracy because a `float` variable has only 7 digits precision, whereas `double` variables maintain 15. Even casting between integer types provides the potential for losing data, depending on the values involved. For example, the value of an integer of type `long` can exceed the maximum that you can store in a variable of type `short`, so casting from a `long` value to a `short` may lose information.

In general, you should avoid casting as far as possible. If you find that you need a lot of casts in your program, the overall design of your program may well be at fault. You need to look at the structure of the program and the ways in which you have chosen data types to see whether you can eliminate, or at least reduce, the number of casts in your program.

Old-Style Casts

Prior to the introduction of `static_cast<>()` (and the other casts: `const_cast<>()`, `dynamic_cast<>()`, and `reinterpret_cast<>()`, which I'll discuss later in the book) into C++, an explicit cast of the result of an expression to another type was written as:

```
(the_type_to_convert_to)expression
```

The result of *expression* is cast to the type between the parentheses. For example, the statement to calculate `strips_per_roll` in the previous example could be written:

```
strips_per_roll = (int)(rolllength / height);        //Get number of strips in a roll
```

Essentially, there are four different kinds of casts, and the old-style casting syntax covers them all. Because of this, code using the old-style casts is more error prone — it is not always clear what you intended, and you may not get the result you expected. Although you will still see the old style of casting used extensively (it's still part of the language and you will see it in MFC code for historical reasons), I strongly recommend that you stick to using only the new casts in your code.

The Bitwise Operators

The bitwise operators treat their operands as a series of individual bits rather than a numerical value. They work only with integer variables or integer constants as operands, so only data types `short`, `int`, `long`, `signed char`, and `char`, as well as the unsigned variants of these, can be used. The bitwise operators are useful in programming hardware devices, where the status of a device is often represented as a series of individual flags (that is, each bit of a byte may signify the status of a different aspect of the device), or for any situation where you might want to pack a set of on-off flags into a single variable. You will see them in action when you look at input/output in detail, where single bits are used to control various options in the way data is handled.

There are six bitwise operators:

& bitwise AND	| bitwise OR	^ bitwise exclusive OR
~ bitwise NOT	>> shift right	<< shift left

The next sections take a look at how each of them works.

The Bitwise AND

The bitwise AND, &, is a binary operator that combines corresponding bits in its operands in a particular way. If both corresponding bits are 1, the result is a 1 bit, and if either or both bits are 0, the result is a 0 bit.

The effect of a particular binary operator is often shown using what is called a **truth table**. This shows, for various possible combinations of operands, what the result is. The truth table for & is as follows:

Bitwise AND	0	1
0	0	0
1	0	1

For each row and column combination, the result of & combining the two is the entry at the intersection of the row and column. You can see how this works in an example:

```
char letter1 = 'A', letter2 = 'Z', result = 0;
result = letter1 & letter2;
```

You need to look at the bit patterns to see what happens. The letters `'A'` and `'Z'` correspond to hexadecimal values 0x41 and 0x5A, respectively (see Appendix B for ASCII codes). The way in which the bitwise AND operates on these two values is shown in Figure 2-9.

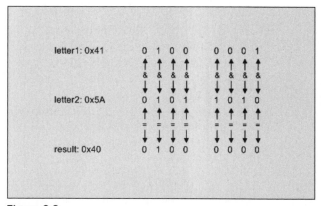

Figure 2-9

You can confirm this by looking at how corresponding bits combine with & in the truth table. After the assignment, `result` will have the value 0x40, which corresponds to the character '@'.

Because the & produces zero if *either* bit is zero, you can use this operator to make sure that unwanted bits are set to 0 in a variable. You achieve this by creating what is called a "mask" and combining with the original variable using &. You create the mask by specifying a value that has 1 where you want to keep a bit, and 0 where you want to set a bit to zero. The result of ANDing the mask with another integer will be 0 bits where the mask bit is 0, and the same value as the original bit in the variable where the mask bit is 1. Suppose you have a variable letter of type char where, for the purposes of illustration, you want to eliminate the high order 4 bits, but keep the low order 4 bits. This is easily done by setting up a mask as 0x0F and combining it with the value of letter using & like this:

```
letter = letter & 0x0F;
```

or, more concisely:

```
letter &= 0x0F;
```

If letter started out as 0x41, it would end up as 0x01 as a result of either of these statements. This operation is shown in Figure 2-10.

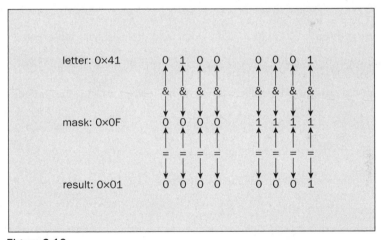

Figure 2-10

The 0 bits in the mask cause corresponding bits in letter to be set to 0, and the 1 bits in the mask cause corresponding bits in letter to be kept as they are.

Similarly, you can use a mask of 0xF0 to keep the 4 high order bits, and zero the 4 low order bits. Therefore, this statement,

```
letter &= 0xF0;
```

will result in the value of letter being changed from 0x41 to 0x40.

The Bitwise OR

The bitwise OR, |, sometimes called the **inclusive OR**, combines corresponding bits such that the result is a 1 if either operand bit is a 1, and 0 if both operand bits are 0. The truth table for the bitwise OR is:

Bitwise OR	0	1
0	0	1
1	1	1

You can exercise this with an example of how you could set individual flags packed into a variable of type int. Suppose that you have a variable called `style` of type `short` that contains 16 individual 1-bit flags. Suppose further that you are interested in setting individual flags in the variable `style`. One way of doing this is by defining values that you can combine with the OR operator to set particular bits on. To use in setting the rightmost bit, you can define:

```
short vredraw = 0x01;
```

For use in setting the second-to-rightmost bit, you could define the variable `hredraw` as:

```
short hredraw = 0x02;
```

So you could set the rightmost two bits in the variable `style` to 1 with the statement:

```
style = hredraw | vredraw;
```

The effect of this statement is illustrated in Figure 2-11.

Because the OR operation results in 1 if either of two bits is a 1, ORing the two variables together produces a result with both bits set on.

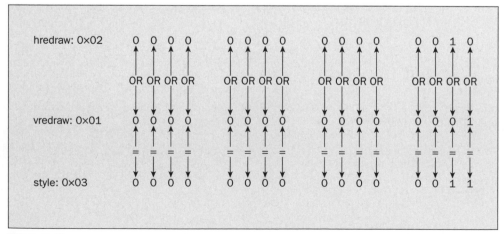

Figure 2-11

A very common requirement is to be able to set flags in a variable without altering any of the others which may have been set elsewhere. You can do this quite easily with a statement such as:

```
style |= hredraw | vredraw;
```

This statement will set the two rightmost bits of the variable `style` to 1, leaving the others at whatever they were before the execution of this statement.

The Bitwise Exclusive OR

The **exclusive OR**, ^, is so called because it operates similarly to the inclusive OR but produces 0 when both operand bits are 1. Therefore, its truth table is as follows:

Bitwise EOR	0	1
0	0	1
1	1	0

Using the same variable values that we used with the AND, you can look at the result of the following statement:

```
result = letter1 ^ letter2;
```

This operation can be represented as:

`letter1` 0100 0001

`letter2` 0101 1010

EORed together produce:

`result` 0001 1011

The variable `result` is set to 0x1B, or 27 in decimal notation.

The ^ operator has a rather surprising property. Suppose that you have two `char` variables, `first` with the value `'A'`, and `last` with the value `'Z'`, corresponding to binary values 0100 0001 and 0101 1010. If you write the statements

```
first ^= last;          // Result first is 0001 1011
last ^= first;          // Result last is 0100 0001
first ^= last;          // Result first is 0101 1010
```

the result of these is that `first` and `last` have exchanged values without using any intermediate memory location. This works with any integer values.

The Bitwise NOT

The bitwise NOT, ~, takes a single operand for which it inverts the bits: 1 becomes 0, and 0 becomes 1. Thus, if you execute the statement

```
result = ~letter1;
```

if `letter1` is 0100 0001, the variable `result` will have the value 1011 1110, which is 0xBE, or 190 as a decimal value.

The Bitwise Shift Operators

These operators shift the value of an integer variable a specified number of bits to the left or right. The operator >> is for shifts to the right, while << is the operator for shifts to the left. Bits that "fall off" either end of the variable are lost. Figure 2-12 shows the effect of shifting the 2-byte variable left and right, with the initial value shown.

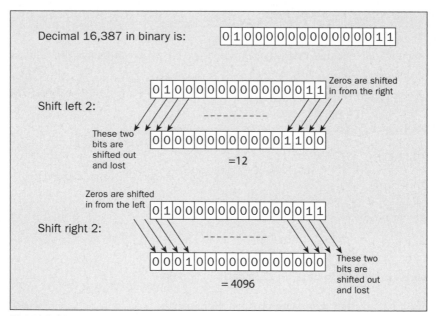

Figure 2-12

You declare and initialize a variable called `number` with the statement:

```
unsigned short number = 16387U;
```

As you saw earlier in this chapter, you write unsigned integer literals with a letter U or u appended to the number. You can shift the contents of this variable to the left with the statement:

```
number <<= 2;              // Shift left two bit positions
```

The left operand of the shift operator is the value to be shifted, and the number of bit positions that the value is to be shifted is specified by the right operand. The illustration shows the effect of the operation. As you can see, shifting the value 16,387 two positions to the left produces the value 12. The rather drastic change in the value is the result of losing the high order bit when it is shifted out.

You can also shift the value to the right. Let's reset the value of number to its initial value of 16,387. Then you can write:

```
number >>= 2;                    // Shift right two bit positions
```

This shifts the value 16,387 two positions to the right, storing the value 4,096. Shifting right two bits is effectively dividing the value by 4 (without remainder). This is also shown in the illustration.

As long as bits are not lost, shifting n bits to the left is equivalent to multiplying the value by 2, n times. In other words, it is equivalent to multiplying by 2^n. Similarly, shifting right n bits is equivalent to dividing by 2^n. But beware: as you saw with the left shift of the variable number, if significant bits are lost, the result is nothing like what you would expect. However, this is no different from the multiply operation. If you multiplied the 2-byte number by 4 you would get the same result, so shifting left and multiply are still equivalent. The problem of accuracy arises because the value of the result of the multiplication is outside the range of a 2-byte integer.

You might imagine that confusion could arise between the operators that you have been using for input and output and the shift operators. As far as the compiler is concerned, the meaning will always be clear from the context. If it isn't, the compiler will generate a message, but you need to be careful. For example, if you want to output the result of shifting a variable number left by 2 bits, you could write the following statement:

```
cout << (number << 2);
```

Here, the parentheses are essential. Without them, the shift operator will be interpreted by the compiler as a stream operator, so you won't get the result that you intended; the output will be the value of number followed by the value 2.

In the main, the right shift operation is similar to the left shift. For example, suppose the variable number has the value 24, and you execute the following statement:

```
number >>= 2;
```

This will result in number having the value 6, effectively dividing the original value by 4. However, the right shift operates in a special way with signed integer types that are negative (that is, the sign bit, which is the leftmost bit, is 1). In this case, the sign bit is propagated to the right. For example, declare and initialize a variable number of type char with the value -104 in decimal:

```
char number = -104;              // Binary representation is 1001 1000
```

Now you can shift it right 2 bits with the operation:

```
number >>= 2;                    // Result 1110 0110
```

The decimal value of the result is -26, as the sign bit is repeated. With operations on `unsigned` integer types, of course, the sign bit is not repeated and zeros appear.

You may be wondering how the shift operators, << and >>, can be the same as the operators used with the standard streams for input and output. These operators can have different meanings in the two contexts because `cin` *and* `cout` *are stream objects, and because they are objects it is possible to redefine the meaning of operators in context by a process called **operator overloading**. Thus the >> operator has been redefined for input stream objects such as* `cin` *so you can use it in the way you have seen. The << operator has also been redefined for use with output stream objects such as* `cout`*. You will learn about operator overloading in Chapter 8.*

Understanding Storage Duration and Scope

All variables have a finite lifetime when your program executes. They come into existence from the point at which you declare them and then, at some point, they disappear — at the latest, when your program terminates. How long a particular variable lasts is determined by a property called its **storage duration**. There are three different kinds of storage duration that a variable can have:

- ❏ Automatic storage duration
- ❏ Static storage duration
- ❏ Dynamic storage duration

Which of these a variable will have depends on how you create it. I will defer discussion of variables with dynamic storage duration until Chapter 4, but you will be exploring the characteristics of the other two in this chapter.

Another property that variables have is **scope**. The scope of a variable is simply that part of your program over which the variable name is valid. Within a variable's scope you can legally refer to it, either to set its value or to use it in an expression. Outside of the scope of a variable, you cannot refer to its name — any attempt to do so will cause a compiler error. Note that a variable may still *exist* outside of its scope, even though you cannot refer to it by name. You will see examples of this situation a little later in this discussion.

All of the variables that you have declared up to now have had **automatic storage duration**, and are therefore called **automatic variables**. Let's take a closer look at these first.

Automatic Variables

The variables that you have declared so far have been **automatic** declared within a block — that is, within the extent of a pair of braces. These are called **automatic** variables and are said to have **local scope** or **block scope**. An automatic variable is "in scope" from the point at which it is declared until the end of the block containing its declaration. The space that an automatic variable occupies is allocated automatically in a memory area called the **stack** that is set aside specifically for this purpose. The default size for the stack is 1MB, which is adequate for most purposes, but if it should turn out to be insufficient, you can increase the size of the stack by setting the `/STACK` option for the project to a value of your choosing.

An automatic variable is "born" when it is defined and space for it is allocated on the stack, and it automatically ceases to exist at the end of the block containing the definition of the variable. This will be at the closing brace matching the first opening brace that precedes the declaration of the variable. Every time the block of statements containing a declaration for an automatic variable is executed, the variable is created anew, and if you specified an initial value for the automatic variable, it will be reinitialized each time it is created. When an automatic variable dies, its memory on the stack will be freed for use by other automatic variables.

There is a keyword, `auto`, which you can use to specify automatic variables, but it is rarely used since it is implied by default. What follows is an example of what I've discussed so far about scope.

Try It Out   **Automatic Variables**

I can demonstrate the effect of scope on automatic variables with the following example:

```
// Ex2_07.cpp
// Demonstrating variable scope
#include <iostream>

using std::cout;
using std::endl;

int main()
{                                        // Function scope starts here
   int count1 = 10;
   int count3 = 50;
   cout << endl
        << "Value of outer count1 = " << count1
        << endl;

   {                                     // New scope starts here...
      int count1 = 20;                   // This hides the outer count1
      int count2 = 30;
      cout << "Value of inner count1 = " << count1
           << endl;
      count1 += 3;                       // This affects the inner count1
      count3 += count2;
   }                                     // ...and ends here

   cout << "Value of outer count1 = " << count1
        << endl
        << "Value of outer count3 = " << count3
        << endl;

   // cout << count2 << endl;            // uncomment to get an error

   return 0;
}                                        // Function scope ends here
```

The output from this example will be:

```
Value of outer count1 = 10
Value of inner count1 = 20
Value of outer count1 = 10
Value of outer count3 = 80
```

How It Works

The first two statements declare and define two integer variables, `count1` and `count3`, with initial values of 10 and 50, respectively. Both these variables exist from this point to the closing brace at the end of the program. The scope of these variables also extends to the closing brace at the end of `main()`.

> *Remember that the lifetime and scope of a variable are two different things. It's important not to get these two ideas confused. The lifetime is the period during execution from when the variable is first created to when it is destroyed and the memory it occupies is freed for other uses. The scope of a variable is the region of program code over which the variable may be accessed.*

Following the variable definitions, the value of `count1` is output to produce the first of the lines shown above. There is then a second brace, which starts a new block. Two variables, `count1` and `count2`, are defined within this block, with values 20 and 30 respectively. The `count1` declared here is *different* from the first `count1`. The first `count1` still exists, but its name is masked by the second `count1`. Any use of the name `count1` following the declaration within the inner block refers to the `count1` declared within that block.

> *I used a duplicate of the variable name `count1` here only to illustrate what happens. Although this code is legal, it isn't a good approach to programming in general. In a real-world programming environment it would be confusing, and if you use duplicate names it makes it very easy to hide variables defined in an outer scope accidentally.*

The value shown in the second output line shows that within the inner block, you are using the `count1` in the inner scope — that is, inside the innermost braces:

```
cout << "Value of inner count1 = " << count1
     << endl;
```

Had you still been using the outer `count1`, then this would display the value 10. The variable `count1` is then incremented by the statement:

```
count1 += 3;                // This affects the inner count1
```

The increment applies to the variable in the inner scope, since the outer one is still hidden. However, `count3`, which was defined in the outer scope, is incremented in the next statement without any problem:

```
count3 += count2;
```

This shows that the variables that were declared at the beginning of the outer scope are accessible from within the inner scope. (Note that if `count3` had been declared *after* the second of the inner pair of braces, then it would still be within the outer scope, but in that case `count3` would not exist when the above statement is executed.)

After the brace ending the inner scope, `count2` and the inner `count1` cease to exist. The variables `count1` and `count3` are still there in the outer scope and the values displayed show that `count3` was indeed incremented in the inner scope.

If you uncomment the line

```
// cout << count2 << endl;         // uncomment to get an error
```

the program will no longer compile correctly because it attempts to output a non-existent variable. You will get an error message something like,

```
c:\microsoft visual studio\myprojects\Ex2_07\Ex2_07.cpp(29) : error C2065: 'count2'
: undeclared identifier
```

This is because count2 is out of scope at this point.

Positioning Variable Declarations

You have great flexibility in where you place the declarations for your variables. The most important aspect to consider is what scope the variables need to have. Beyond that, you should generally place a declaration close to where the variable is to be first used in a program. You should write your programs with a view to making them as easy as possible for another programmer to understand, and declaring a variable at its first point of use can be helpful in achieving that.

It is possible to place declarations for variables outside of all of the functions that make up a program. The next section looks what effect that has on the variables concerned.

Global Variables

Variables that are declared outside of all blocks and classes (I will discuss classes later in the book) are called **globals** and have **global scope** (which is also called **global namespace scope** or **file scope**). This means that they are accessible throughout all the functions in the file, following the point at which they are declared. If you declare them at the very top of your program, they will be accessible from anywhere in the file.

Globals also have **static storage duration** by default. Global variables with static storage duration will exist from the start of execution of the program until execution of the program ends. If you do not specify an initial value for a global variable, it will be initialized with 0 by default. Initialization of global variables takes place before the execution of main() begins, so they are always ready to be used within any code that is within the variable's scope.

Figure 2-13 shows the contents of a source file, Example.cpp, and the arrows indicate the scope of each of the variables.

The variable value1, which appears at the beginning of the file, is declared at global scope, as is value4, which appears after the function main(). The scope of each global variable extends from the point at which it is defined to the end of the file. Even though value4 exists when execution starts, it cannot be referred to in main() because main() is not within the variable's scope. For main() to use value4, you would need to move its declaration to the beginning of the file. Both value1 and value4 will be initialized with 0 by default, which is not the case for the automatic variables. Note that the local variable called value1 in function() hides the global variable of the same name.

Since global variables continue to exist for as long as the program is running, this might raise the question in your mind, "Why not make all variables global and avoid this messing about with local variables that disappear?" This sounds very attractive at first, but as with the Sirens of mythology, there are serious side effects that completely outweigh any advantages you may gain.

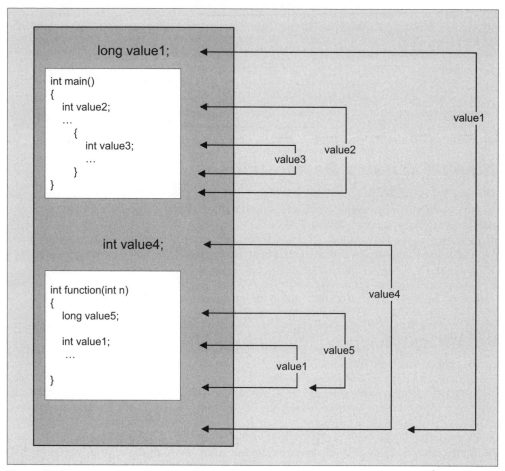

Figure 2-13

Real programs are generally composed of a large number of statements, a significant number of functions, and a great many variables. Declaring all variables at the global scope greatly magnifies the possibility of accidental erroneous modification of a variable, as well as making the job of naming them sensibly quite intractable. They will also occupy memory for the duration of program execution. By keeping variables local to a function or a block, you can be sure they have almost complete protection from external effects, they will only exist and occupy memory from the point at which they are defined to the end of the enclosing block, and the whole development process becomes much easier to manage.

If you take a look at the Class View pane on the right of the IDE window for any of the examples that you have created so far and extend the class tree for the project by clicking on the +, you will see an entry called Global Functions and Variables. If you click on this, you will see a list of everything in your program that has global scope. This will include all the global functions, as well as any global variables that you have declared.

The Scope Resolution Operator

As you have seen, a global variable can be hidden by a local variable with the same name. However, it's still possible to get at the global variable by using the **scope resolution operator** (::), which you saw in Chapter 1 when I was discussing namespaces. I can demonstrate how this works with a revised version of the last example:

```
// Ex2_08.cpp
// Demonstrating variable scope
#include <iostream>

using std::cout;
using std::endl;

int count1 = 100;                               // Global version of count1

int main()
{                                               // Function scope starts here
    int count1 = 10;
    int count3 = 50;
    cout << endl
        << "Value of outer count1 = " << count1
        << endl;
    cout << "Value of global count1 = " << ::count1        // From outer block
        << endl;

    {                                   // New scope starts here...
        int count1 = 20;               //This hides the outer count1
        int count2 = 30;
        cout << "Value of inner count1 = " << count1
            << endl;
        cout << "Value of global count1 = " << ::count1        // From inner block
            << endl;

        count1 += 3;                   // This affects the inner count1
        count3 += count2;
    }                                  // ...and ends here.

    cout << "Value of outer count1 = " << count1
        << endl
        << "Value of outer count3 = " << count3
        << endl;

    //cout << count2 << endl;          // uncomment to get an error
    return 0;
}                                               // Function scope ends here
```

If you compile and run this example, you'll get the following output:

```
Value of outer count1 = 10
Value of global count1 = 100
Value of inner count1 = 20
Value of global count1 = 100
Value of outer count1 = 10
Value of outer count3 = 80
```

How It Works

The shaded lines of code indicate the changes I have made to the previous example; I just need to discuss the effects of those. The declaration of count1 prior to the definition of the function main() is global, so in principle it is available anywhere through the function main(). This global variable is initialized with the value of 100:

```
int count1 = 100;                          // Global version of count1
```

However, you have two other variables called count1, which are defined within main(), so throughout the program the global count1 is hidden by the local count1 variables. The first new output statement is:

```
cout << "Value of global count1 = " << ::count1          // From outer block
     << endl;
```

This uses the scope resolution operator (::) to make it clear to the compiler that you want to reference the global variable count1, *not* the local one. You can see that this works from the value displayed in the output.

In the inner block, the global count1 is hidden behind *two* variables called count1: the inner count1 and the outer count1. We can see the global scope resolution operator doing its stuff within the inner block, as you can see from the output generated by the statement we have added there:

```
cout << "Value of global count1 = " << ::count1          // From inner block
     << endl;
```

This outputs the value 100, as before — the long arm of the scope resolution operator used in this fashion always reaches a global variable.

> *You have seen earlier that you can refer to a name in the std namespace by qualifying the name with the namespace name, such as with std::cout or std::endl. The compiler searches the namespace that has the name specified by the left operand of the scope resolution operator for the name that you specify as the right operand. In the preceding example, you are using the scope resolution operator to search the global namespace for the variable count1. By not specifying a namespace name in front of the operator, you are telling the compiler to search the global namespace for the name that follows it.*

You'll see a lot more of this operator when you get to explore object-oriented programming in Chapter 9 where it is used extensively.

Static Variables

It's conceivable that you might want to have a variable that's defined and accessible locally, but which also continues to exist after exiting the block in which it is declared. In other words, you need to declare a variable within a block scope, but to give it **static storage duration**. The static specifier provides you with the means of doing this, and the need for this will become more apparent when we come to deal with functions in Chapter 5.

In fact, a static variable will continue to exist for the life of a program even though it is declared within a block and available only from within that block (or its sub-blocks). It still has block scope, but it has static storage duration. To declare a static integer variable called count you would write:

```
static int count;
```

If you don't provide an initial value for a static variable when you declare it, then it will be initialized for you. The variable count declared here will be initialized with 0. The default initial value for a static variable is always 0, converted to the type applicable to the variable. Remember that this is *not* the case with automatic variables.

If you don't initialize your automatic variables, they will contain junk values left over from the program that last used the memory they occupy.

Namespaces

I have mentioned namespaces several times, so it's time you got a better idea of what they are about. They are not used in the libraries supporting MFC, but the libraries that support the CLR and Windows forms use namespaces extensively, and of course the ANSI C++ standard library does, too.

You know already that all the names used in the ISO/ANSI C++ standard library are defined in a namespace with the name std. This means that all the names used in the standard library have an additional qualifying name, std, so cout for example is really std::cout. You can see fully qualified names in use with this trivial example:

```cpp
// Ex2_09.cpp
// Demonstrating namespace names
#include <iostream>

  int value = 0;

int main()
{
  std::cout << "enter an integer: ";
  std::cin  >> value;
  std::cout << "\nYou entered " << value
            << std:: endl;
  return 0;
}
```

The declaration for the variable `value` is outside of the definition of `main()`. This declaration is said to be at `global namespace scope`, because the variable declaration does not appear within a namespace. The variable is accessible from anywhere within `main()` as well as from within any other function definitions that you might have in the same source file. I have put the declaration for `value` outside of `main()` just so I can demonstrate in the next section how it could be in a namespace.

Note the absence of `using` declarations for `cout` and `endl`. It isn't necessary in this case because you are fully qualifying the names you are using from the namespace `std`. It would be silly to do so, but you could use `cout` as the name of the integer variable here, and there would be no confusion because `cout` by itself is different from `std::cout`. Thus namespaces provide a way to separate the names used in one part of a program from those used in another. This is invaluable with large projects involving several teams of programmers working on different parts of the program. Each team can have its own namespace name, and worries about two teams accidentally using the same name for different functions disappear.

Look at this line of code:

```
using namespace std;
```

This statement is a **using directive**.

The effect of this is to import all the names from the `std` namespace into the source file so you can refer to anything that is defined in this namespace without qualifying the name in your program. Thus you can write the name `cout` instead of `std::cout` and `endl` instead of `std::endl`. The downside of this blanket `using` directive is that it effectively negates the primary reason for using a namespace — that is, preventing accidental name clashes. There are two ways to access names from a namespace without negating its intended effect. One way is to qualify each name explicitly with the namespace name; unfortunately, this tends to make the code very verbose and reduce its readability. The other possibility that I mentioned early on in this chapter is to introduce just the names that you use in your code with using declarations, like this for example:

```
using std::cout;        // Allows cout usage without qualification
using std::endl;        // Allows endl usage without qualification
```

These statements are called **using declarations**. Each statement introduces a single name from the specified namespace and allows it to be used unqualified within the program code that follows. This provides a much better way of importing names from a namespace as you only import the names that you actually use in your program. Because Microsoft has set the precedent of importing all names from the `System` namespace with C+/CLI code, I will continue with that in the C++/CLI examples. In general I recommend that you use `using` declarations in your own code rather than `using` directives when you are writing programs of any significant size.

Of course, you can define your own namespace that has a name that you choose. The next section shows how that's done.

Declaring a Namespace

You use the keyword `namespace` to declare a namespace — like this:

```
namespace myStuff
{
```

```
        // Code that I want to have in the namespace myStuff...
    }
```

This defines a namespace with the name myStuff. All name declarations in the code between the braces will be defined within the myStuff namespace, so to access any such name from a point outside this namespace, the name must be qualified by the namespace name, myStuff, or have a using declaration that identifies that the name is from the myStuff namespace.

You can't declare a namespace inside a function. It's intended to be used the other way round; you use a namespace to contain functions, global variables, and other named entities such as classes in your program. You must not put the definition of main() in a namespace, though. The function main() is where execution starts and it must always be at global namespace scope, otherwise the compiler won't recognize it.

You could put the variable value in the previous example in a namespace:

```
// Ex2_10.cpp
// Declaring a namespace
#include <iostream>

namespace myStuff
{
   int value = 0;
}

int main()
{
   std::cout << "enter an integer: ";
   std::cin  >> myStuff::value;
   std::cout << "\nYou entered " << myStuff::value
             << std:: endl;
   return 0;
}
```

The myStuff namespace defines a scope, and everything within the namespace scope is qualified with the namespace name. To refer to a name declared within a namespace from outside, you must qualify it with the namespace name. Inside the namespace scope any of the names declared within it can be referred to without qualification — they are all part of the same family. Now you must qualify the name value with myStuff, the name of our namespace. If not, the program will not compile. The function main() now refers to names in two different namespaces, and in general you can have as many namespaces in your program as you need. You could remove the need to qualify value by adding a using directive:

```
// Ex2_11.cpp
// Using a using directive
#include <iostream>

namespace myStuff
{
   int value = 0;
}

using namespace myStuff;              // Make all the names in myStuff available

int main()
```

```
  {
    std::cout << "enter an integer: ";
    std::cin  >> value;
    std::cout << "\nYou entered " << value
              << std:: endl;
    return 0;
  }
```

You could also have a using directive for std as well, so you wouldn't need to qualify standard library names either, but as I said, this defeats the whole purpose of namespaces. Generally, if you use namespaces in your program, you should not add using directives all over your program; otherwise, you might as well not bother with namespaces in the first place. Having said that, I will add a using directive for std in some of our examples to keep the code less cluttered and easier for you to read. When you are starting out with a new programming language, you can do without clutter, no matter how useful it is in practice.

Multiple Namespaces

A real-world program is likely to involve multiple namespaces. You can have multiple declarations of a namespace with a given name and the contents of all namespace blocks with a given name are within the same namespace. For example, you might have a program file with two namespaces:

```
namespace sortStuff
{
   // Everything in here is within sortStuff namespace
}
```

```
namespace calculateStuff
{
  // Everything in here is within calculateStuff namespace
  // To refer to names from sortStuff they must be qualified
}
```

```
namespace sortStuff
{
  // This is a continuation of the namespace sortStuff
  // so from here you can refer to names in the first sortStuff namespace
  // without qualifying the names
}
```

A second declaration of a namespace with a given name is just a continuation of the first, so you can reference names in the first namespace block from the second without having to qualify them. They are all in the same namespace. Of course, you would not usually organize a source file in this way deliberately, but it can arise quite naturally with header files that you include into a program. For example, you might have something like this:

```
#include <iostream>        // Contents are in namespace std
#include "myheader.h"      // Contents are in namespace myStuff
#include <string>          // Contents are in namespace std
```

```
// and so on...
```

Here, `<iostream>` and `string` are ISO/ANSI C++ standard library headers, and `myheader.h` represents a header file that contains our program code. You have a situation with the namespaces that is an exact parallel of the previous illustration.

This has given you a basic idea of how namespaces work. There is a lot more to namespaces than I have discussed here, but if you grasp this bit you should be able to find out more about it without difficulty, if the need arises.

Note that the two forms of `#include` *directive in the previous code fragment cause the compiler to search for the file in different ways. When you specify the file to be included between angled brackets, you are indicating to the compiler that it should search for the file along the path specified by the* `/I` *compiler option, and failing that along the path specified by the* `INCLUDE` *environment variable. These paths locate the C+ library files, which is why this form is reserved for library headers. The* `INCLUDE` *environment variable points to the folder holding the library header and the* `/I` *option allows an additional directory containing library headers to be specified. When the file name is between double quotes, the compiler will search the folder that contains the file in which the* `#include` *directive appears. If the file is not found it will search in any directories that* `#include` *the current file. If that fails to find the file it will search the library directories.*

C++/CLI Programming

C++/CLI provides a number of extensions and additional capabilities to what I have discussed in this chapter up to now. I'll first summarize these additional capabilities before going into details. The additional C++/CLI capabilities are:

❑　All of the ISO/ANSI fundamental data types can be used as I have described in a C++/CLI program, but they have some extra properties in certain contexts that I'll come to.

❑　C++/CLI provides its own mechanism for keyboard input and output to the command line in a console program.

❑　C++/CLI introduces the `safe_cast` operator that ensures that a cast operation results in verifiable code being generated.

❑　C++/CLI provides an alternative enumeration capability that is class-based and offers more flexibility than the ISO/ANSI C++ `enum` declaration you have seen.

You'll learn more about CLR reference class types beginning in Chapter 4, but because I have introduced global variables for native C++ I'll mention now that variables of CLR reference class types cannot be global variables.

I want to begin by looking at fundamental data types in C++/CLI.

C++/CLI Specific: Fundamental Data Types

You can and should use the ISO/ANSI C++ fundamental data type names in your C++/CLI programs, and with arithmetic operations they work exactly as you have seen in native C++. In addition C++/CLI defines two additional integer types:

Type	Size(bytes)	Range of Values
long long	8	From 9,223,372,036,854,775,808 to 9,223,372,036,854,775,807
unsigned long long	8	From 0 to 18,446,744,073,709,551,615

To specify literals of type long long you append LL or lowercase ll to the integer value. For example:

```
long long big = 123456789LL;
```

A literal of type unsigned long long you append ULL or ull to the integer value:

```
unsigned long long huge = 999999999999999ULL;
```

Although all the operations with fundamental types you have seen work in the same way in C++/CLI, the fundamental type names in a C++/CLI program have a different meaning and introduce additional capabilities in certain situations. A fundamental type in a C++/CLI program is a value class type and can behave either as an ordinary value or as an object if the circumstances require it.

Within the C++/CLI language, each ISO/ANSI fundamental type name maps to a **value class type** that is defined in the System namespace. Thus in a C++/CLI program the ISO/ANSI fundamental type names are shorthand for the associated value class type. This enables the value of a fundamental type to be treated simply as a value or be automatically converted to an object of its associated value class type when necessary. The fundamental types, the memory they occupy, and the corresponding value class types are shown in the following table:

Fundamental Type	Size(bytes)	CLI Value Class
bool	1	System::Boolean
char	1	System::SByte
signed char	1	System::SByte
unsigned char	1	System::Byte
short	2	System::Int16
unsigned short	2	System::UInt16
int	4	System::Int32

Fundamental Type	Size(bytes)	CLI Value Class
unsigned int	4	System::UInt32
long	4	System::Int32
unsigned long	4	System::UInt32
long long	8	System::Int64
unsigned long long	8	System::UInt64
float	4	System::Single
double	8	System::Double
long double	8	System::Double
wchar_t	2	System::Char

By default, type char is equivalent to signed char so the associated value class type is System::SByte. Note that you can change the default for char to unsigned char by setting the compiler option /J, in which case the associated value class type will be System::Byte. System is the root namespace name in which the C++/CLI value class types are defined. There are many other types defined within the System namespace, such as the type String for representing strings that you'll meet in Chapter 4. C++/CLI also defines the System::Decimal value class type within the System namespace and variables of type Decimal store exact decimal values with 28 decimal digits precision.

As I said, the value class type associated with each fundamental type name adds important additional capabilities for such variables in C++/CLI. When necessary, the compiler will arrange for automatic conversions from the original value to an object of a value class type and vice versa; these processes are referred to as **boxing** and **unboxing**, respectively. This allows a variable of any of these types to behave as a simple value or as an object, depending on the circumstances. You'll learn more about how and when this happens in Chapter 9.

Because the ISO/ANSI C++ fundamental type names are aliases for the value class type names in a C++/CLI program, in principle you can use either in your C++/CLI code. For example, you already know you can write statements creating integer and floating-point variables like this:

```
int count = 10;
double value = 2.5;
```

You could use the value class names that correspond with the fundamental type names and have the program compile without any problem, like this:

```
System::Int32 count = 10;
System::Double value = 2.5;
```

Note that this is not exactly the same as using the fundamental type names such as int and double in your code, rather than the value class names System::Int32 and System::Double. The reason is that the mapping between fundamental type names and value class types I have described applies to the Visual C++ 2008 compiler; other compilers are not obliged to implement the same mapping. Type long in Visual C++ 2008 maps to type Int32, but it is quite possible that it could map to type Int64 on some other implementation. On the other hand, the representations of the value class type that are equivalents to the fundamental native C++ types are fixed; for example, type System::Int32 will always be a 32-bit signed integer on any C++/CLI implementation.

Having data of the fundamental types being represented by objects of a value class type is an important feature of C++/CLI. In ISO/ANSI C++ fundamental types and class types are quite different, whereas in C++/CLR all data is stored as objects of a class type, either as a value class type or as a reference class type. You'll learn about reference class types in Chapter 7.

Next, you'll try a CLR console program.

Try It Out   A Fruity CLR Console Program

Create a new project and select the project type as CLR and the template as CLR Console Application. You can then enter the project name as Ex2_12, as shown in Figure 2-14.

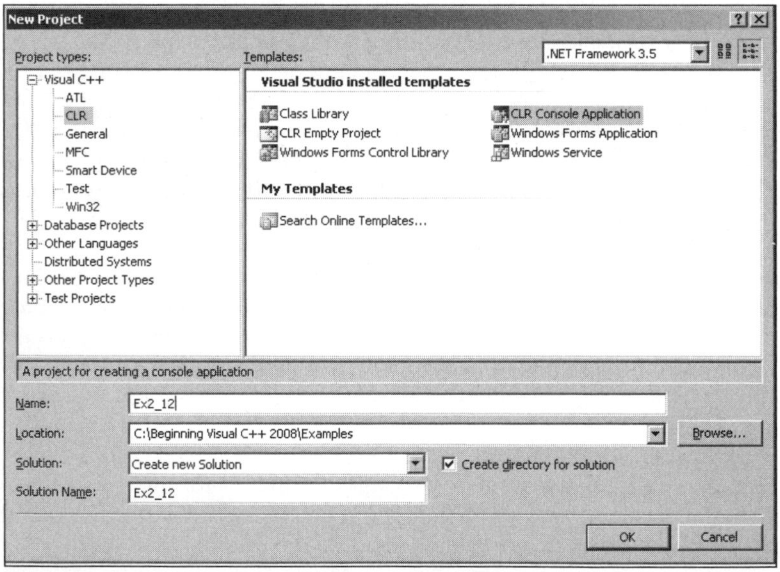

Figure 2-14

When you click on the OK button, the Application Wizard will generate the project containing the following code:

```
// Ex2_12.cpp : main project file.

#include "stdafx.h"
```

```
using namespace System;

int main(array<System::String ^> ^args)
{
    Console::WriteLine(L"Hello World");
    return 0;
}
```

I'm sure you noticed the extra stuff between the parentheses following `main`. This is concerned with passing values to the function `main()` when you initiate execution of the program from the command line, and you'll learn more about this when you explore functions in detail. If you compile and execute the default project it will write `"Hello World"` to the command line. Now, you'll convert this program to a CLR version of `Ex2_02` so you can see how similar it is. To do this you can modify the code in `Ex2_12.cpp` as follows:

```
// Ex2_12.cpp : main project file.
#include "stdafx.h"

using namespace System;

int main(array<System::String ^> ^args)
{
    int apples, oranges;                 // Declare two integer variables
    int fruit;                           // ...then another one

    apples = 5; oranges = 6;             // Set initial values
    fruit = apples + oranges;            // Get the total fruit

    Console::WriteLine(L"\nOranges are not the only fruit...");
    Console::Write(L"- and we have ");
    Console::Write(fruit);
    Console::Write(L" fruits in all.\n");
    return 0;
}
```

The new lines are shown shaded and those in the lower block replace the two lines in the automatically generated version of `main()`. You can now compile and execute the project. The program should produce the following output:

```
Oranges are not the only fruit...
- and we have 11 fruits in all.
```

How It Works

The only significant difference is in how the output is produced. The definitions for the variables and the computation are the same. Although you are using the same type names as in the ISO/ANSI C++ version of the example, the effect is not the same. The variables `apples`, `oranges`, and `fruit` will be of the C++/CLI type, `System::Int32`, that is specified by type `int`, and they have some additional capabilities compared to the ISO/ANSI type. The variables here can act as objects in some circumstances or as simple values as they do here. If you want to confirm that `Int32` is the same as `int` in this case, you could replace the `int` type name with `Int32` and recompile the example. It should work in exactly the same way.

Evidently the following line of code produces the first line of output:

```
Console::WriteLine(L"\nOranges are not the only fruit...");
```

The `WriteLine()` function is a C++/CLI function that is defined in the `Console` class in the `System` namespace. You'll learn about classes in detail in Chapter 6, but for now the `Console` class represents the standard input and output streams that correspond to the keyboard and the command line in a command line window. Thus the `WriteLine()` function writes whatever is between the parentheses following the function name to the command line and then writes a newline character to move the cursor to the next line ready for the next output operation. Thus the preceding statement writes the text `"\nOranges are not the only fruit..."` between the double quotes to the command line. The `L` that precedes the string indicates that it is a wide-character string where each character occupies two bytes.

The `Write()` function in the `Console` class is essentially the same as the `WriteLine()` function, the only difference being that it does not automatically write a newline character following the output that you specify. You can therefore use the `Write()` function when you want to write two or more items of data to the same line in individual output statements.

Values that you place between the parentheses that follow the name of a function are called **arguments**. Depending on how a function was written, it will accept zero, one, or more arguments when it is called. When you need to supply more than one argument they must be separated by commas. There's more to the output functions in the `Console` class, so I want to explore `Write()` and `WriteLine()` in a little more depth.

C++/CLI Output to the Command Line

You saw in the previous example how you can use the `Console::Write()` and `Console::WriteLine()` methods to write a string or other items of data to the command line. You can put a variable of any of the types you have seen between the parentheses following the function name and the value will be written to the command line. For example, you could write the following statements to output information about a number of packages:

```
int packageCount = 25;                      // Number of packages
Console::Write(L"There are ");              // Write string - no newline
Console::Write(packageCount);               // Write value -no newline
Console::WriteLine(L" packages.");          // Write string followed by newline
```

Executing these statements will produce the output:

```
There are 25 packages.
```

The output is all on the same line because the first two output statements use the `Write()` function, which does not output a newline character after writing the data. The last statement uses the `WriteLine()` function, which does write a newline after the output so any subsequent output will be on the next line.

It looks a bit of a laborious process having to use three statements to write one line of output, and it will be no surprise to you that there is a better way. That capability is bound up with formatting the output to the command line in a .NET Framework program so you'll explore that a little next.

C++/CLI Specific — Formatting the Output

Both the `Console::Write()` and `Console::WriteLine()` functions have a facility for you to control the format of the output, and the mechanism works in exactly the same way with both. The easiest way to understand it is through some examples. First look at how you can get the output that was produced by the three output statements in the previous section with a single statement:

```
int packageCount = 25;
Console::WriteLine(L"There are {0} packages.", packageCount);
```

The second statement here will output the same output as you saw in the previous section. The first argument to the `Console::WriteLine()` function here is the string `L"There are {0} packages."`, and the bit that determines that the value of the second should be placed in the string is `"{0}"`. The braces enclose a format string that applies to the second argument to the function although in this instance the format string is about as simple as it could get, being just a zero. The arguments that follow the first argument to the `Console::WriteLine()` function are numbered in sequence starting with zero, like this:

```
referenced by:                    0   1   2   etc.
Console::WriteLine("Format string", arg2, arg3, arg4,... );
```

Thus the zero between the braces in the previous code fragment indicates that the value of the `packageCount` argument should replace the `{0}` in the string that is to be written to the command line.

If you want to output the weight as well as the number of packages, you could write this:

```
int packageCount = 25;
double packageWeight = 7.5;
Console::WriteLine(L"There are {0} packages weighing {1} pounds.",
                                        packageCount, packageWeight);
```

The output statement now has three arguments, and the second and third arguments are referenced by 0 and 1, respectively, between the braces. So, this will produce the output:

```
There are 25 packages weighing 7.5 pounds.
```

You could also write the statement with the last two arguments in reverse sequence, like this:

```
Console::WriteLine(L"There are {1} packages weighing {0} pounds.",
                                        packageWeight, packageCount);
```

The `packageWeight` variable is now referenced by 0 and `packageCount` by 1 in the format string, and the output will be the same as previously.

You also have the possibility to specify how the data is to be presented on the command line. Suppose that you wanted the floating-point value `packageWeight` to be output with two places of decimals. You could do that with the following statement:

```
Console::WriteLine(L"There are {0} packages weighing {1:F2} pounds.",
                                        packageCount, packageWeight);
```

In the substring `{1:F2}`, the colon separates the index value, 1, that identifies the argument to be selected from the format specification that follows, F2. The F in the format specification indicates that the output should be in the form "±ddd.dd…" (where *d* represents a digit) and the 2 indicates that you want to have two decimal places after the point. The output produced by the statement will be:

```
There are 25 packages weighing 7.50 pounds.
```

In general you can write the format specification in the form `{n,w : Axx}` where the *n* is an index value selecting the argument following the format string, *w* is an optional field width specification, the *A* is a single letter specifying how the value should be formatted, and the *xx* is an optional one or two digits specifying the precision for the value. The field width specification is a signed integer. The value will be right-justified in the field if *w* is positive and left-justified when it is negative. If the value occupies less than the number of positions specified by *w* the output is padded with spaces; if the value requires more positions than that specified by *w* the width specification is ignored. Here's another example:

```
Console::WriteLine(L"Packages:{0,3} Weight: {1,5:F2} pounds.",
                                    packageCount, packageWeight);
```

The package count is output with a field width of 3 and the weight in a field width of 5, so the output will be:

```
Packages:  25 Weight:  7.50 pounds.
```

There are other format specifiers that enable you to present various types of data in different ways. Here are some of the most useful format specifications:

Format Specifier	Description
C or c	Outputs the value as a currency amount.
D or d	Outputs an integer as a decimal value. If you specify the precision to be more than the number of digits the number will be padded with zeroes to the left.
E or e	Outputs a floating-point value in scientific notation, that is, with an exponent. The precision value will indicate the number of digits to be output following the decimal point.
F or f	Outputs a floating-point value as a fixed-point number of the form ±dddd.dd. . . .
G or g	Outputs the value in the most compact form depending on the type of the value and whether you have specified the precision. If you don't specify the precision, a default precision value will be used.
N or n	Outputs the value as a fixed-point decimal value using comma separators between each group of three digits when necessary.
X or x	Output an integer as a hexadecimal value. Upper or lowercase hexadecimal digits will be output depending on whether you specify X or x.

That gives you enough of a toehold in output to continue with more C++/CLI examples. Now, you'll take a quick look at some of this in action.

Formatted Output

Here's an example that calculates the price of a carpet in order to demonstrate output in a CLR console program:

```
// Ex2_13.cpp : main project file.
// Calculating the price of a carpet
#include "stdafx.h"

using namespace System;

int main(array<System::String ^> ^args)
{
  double carpetPriceSqYd = 27.95;
  double roomWidth = 13.5;                 // In feet
  double roomLength = 24.75;               // In feet
  const int feetPerYard = 3;
  double roomWidthYds = roomWidth/feetPerYard;
  double roomLengthYds = roomLength/feetPerYard;
  double carpetPrice = roomWidthYds*roomLengthYds*carpetPriceSqYd;

  Console::WriteLine(L"Room size is {0:F2} yards by {1:F2} yards",
                             roomLengthYds, roomWidthYds);
  Console::WriteLine(L"Room area is {0:F2} square yards",
                             roomLengthYds*roomWidthYds);
  Console::WriteLine(L"Carpet price is ${0:F2}", carpetPrice);
  return 0;
}
```

The output should be:

```
Room size is 8.25 yards by 4.50 yards
Room area is 37.13 square yards
Carpet price is $1037.64
```

How It Works

The dimensions of the room are specified in feet whereas the carpet is priced per square yard so you have defined a constant, feetPerYard, to use in the conversion from feet to yards. In the expression to convert each dimension you are dividing a value of type double by a value of type int. The compiler will insert code to convert the value of type int to type double before carrying out the multiplication. After converting the room dimensions to yards you calculate the price of the carpet by multiplying the dimensions in yards to obtain the area in square yards and multiplying that by the price per square yard.

The output statements use the F2 format specification to limit the output values to two decimal places. Without this there would be more decimal places in the output that would be inappropriate, especially for the price. You could try removing the format specification to see the difference.

Note that the statement to output the area has an arithmetic expression as the second argument to the `WriteLine()` function. The compiler will arrange to first evaluate the expression, and then the result will be passed as the actual argument to the function. In general you can always use an expression as an argument to a function as long as the result of evaluating the expression is of a type that is consistent with the function parameter type.

C++/CLI Input from the Keyboard

The keyboard input capabilities that you have with a .NET Framework console program are somewhat limited. You can read a complete line of input as a string using the `Console::ReadLine()` function, or you can read a single character using the `Console::Read()` function. You can also read which key was pressed using the `Console::ReadKey()` function.

You would use the `Console::ReadLine()` function like this:

```
String^ line = Console::ReadLine();
```

This reads a complete line of input text that is terminated when you press the `Enter` key. The variable `line` is of type `String^` and stores a reference to the string that results from executing the `Console::ReadLine()` function; the little hat character, `^`, following the type name, `String`, indicates that this is a **handle** that references an object of type `String`. You'll learn more about type `String` and handles for `String` objects in Chapter 4.

A statement that reads a single character from the keyboard looks like this:

```
char ch = Console::Read();
```

With the `Read()` function you could read input data character by character and then analyze the characters read and convert the input to a corresponding numeric value.

The `Console::ReadKey()` function returns the key that was pressed as an object of type `ConsoleKeyInfo`, which is a value class type defined in the `System` namespace. Here's a statement to read a key press:

```
ConsoleKeyInfo keyPress = Console::ReadKey(true);
```

The argument `true` to the `ReadKey()` function results in the key press not being displayed on the command line. An argument value of `false` (or omitting the argument) will cause the character corresponding the key pressed being displayed. The result of executing the function will be stored in `keyPress`. To identify the character corresponding to the key (or keys) pressed, you use the expression `keyPress.KeyChar`. Thus you could output a message relating to a key press with the following statement:

```
Console::WriteLine(L"The key press corresponds to the character: {0}",
                                                keyPress.KeyChar);
```

The key that was pressed is identified by the expression `keyPress.Key`. This expression refers to a value of a C++/CLI enumeration (which you'll learn about very soon) that identifies the key that was pressed. There's more to the `ConsoleKeyInfo` objects than I have described. You'll meet them again later in the book.

While not having formatted input in a C++/CLI console program is a slight inconvenience while you are learning, in practice this is a minor limitation. Virtually all the real-world programs you are likely to write will receive input through components of a window so you won't typically have the need to read data from the command line. However, if you do, the value classes that are the equivalents of the fundamental types can help.

Reading numerical values from the command line will involve using some facilities that I have not yet discussed. You'll learn about these later in the book so I'll gloss over some of the detail at this point.

If you read a string containing an integer value using the `Console::ReadLine()` function, the `Parse()` function in the `Int32` class will convert it to a 32-bit integer for you. Here's how you might read an integer using that:

```
Console::Write(L"Enter an integer: ");
int value = Int32::Parse(Console::ReadLine());
Console::WriteLine(L"You entered {0}", value);
```

The first statement just prompts for the input that is required, and the second statement reads the input. The string that the `Console::ReadLine()` function returns is passed as the argument to the `Parse()` function that belongs to the `Int32` class. This will convert the string to a 32-bit integer and store it in `value`. The last statement outputs the value to show that all is well. Of course, if you enter something that is not an integer, disaster will surely follow.

The other value classes that correspond to native C++ fundamental types also define a `Parse()` function so for example, when you want to read a floating-point value from the keyboard, you can pass the string that `Console::ReadLine()` returns to the `Double::Parse()` function. The result will be a value of type `double`.

Using safe_cast

The `safe_cast` operation is for explicit casts in the CLR environment. In most instances you can use `static_cast` to cast from one type to another in a C++/CLI program without problems, but because there are exceptions that will result in an error message, it is better to use `safe_cast`. You use `safe_cast` in exactly the same way as `static_cast`. For example:

```
double value1 = 10.5;
double value2 = 15.5;
int whole_number = safe_cast<int>(value1) + safe_cast<int>(value2);
```

The last statement casts each of the values of type `double` to type `int` before adding them together and storing the result in `whole_number`.

C++/CLI Enumerations

Enumerations in a C++/CLI program are significantly different from those in an ISO/ANSI C++ program. For a start you define an enumeration in C++/CLI like this:

```
enum class Suit{Clubs, Diamonds, Hearts, Spades};
```

This defines an enumeration type, Suit, and variables of type Suit can be assigned only one of the values defined by the enumeration — Hearts, Clubs, Diamonds, or Spades. When you refer to the constants in a C++/CLI enumeration you must always qualify the constant you are using with the enumeration type name. For example:

```
Suit suit = Suit::Clubs;
```

This statement assigns the value Clubs from the Suit enumeration to the variable with the name suit. The :: operator that separates the type name, Suit, from the name of the enumeration constant, Clubs, is the scope resolution operator that you have seen before, and it indicates that Clubs exists within the scope of the Suit enumeration.

Note the use of the word class in the definition of the enumeration, following the enum keyword. This does not appear in the definition of an ISO/ANSI C++ enumeration as you saw earlier, and it identifies the enumeration as C++/CLI. In fact the two words combined, enum class, are a keyword in C++/CLI that is different from the two keywords, enum and class. The use of the enum class keyword gives a clue to another difference from an ISO/ANSI C++ enumeration; the constants here that are defined within the enumeration — Hearts, Clubs, and so on — are *objects*, not simply values of a fundamental type as in the ISO/ANSI C++ version. In fact by default they are objects of type Int32, so they each encapsulate a 32-bit integer value; however, you must cast a constant to the fundamental type int before attempting to use it as such.

You can use enum struct *instead of* enum class *when you define an enumeration. These are equivalent so it comes down to personal choice as to which you use. I will use* enum class *throughout.*

Because a C++/CLI enumeration is a class type, you cannot define it locally, within a function for example, so if you want to define such an enumeration for use in main(), for example, you would define it at global scope.

This is easy to see with an example.

Try It Out   Defining a C++/CLI Enumeration

Here's a very simple example using an enumeration:

```
// Ex2_14.cpp : main project file.
// Defining and using a C++/CLI enumeration.
#include "stdafx.h"

using namespace System;

// Define the enumeration at global scope
enum class Suit{Clubs, Diamonds, Hearts, Spades};

int main(array<System::String ^> ^args)
{
    Suit suit = Suit::Clubs;
    int value = safe_cast<int>(suit);
    Console::WriteLine(L"Suit is {0} and the value is {1} ", suit, value);
    suit = Suit::Diamonds;
```

```
    value = safe_cast<int>(suit);
    Console::WriteLine(L"Suit is {0} and the value is {1} ", suit, value);
    suit = Suit::Hearts;
    value = safe_cast<int>(suit);
    Console::WriteLine(L"Suit is {0} and the value is {1} ", suit, value);
    suit = Suit::Spades;
    value = safe_cast<int>(suit);
    Console::WriteLine(L"Suit is {0} and the value is {1} ", suit, value);
    return 0;
}
```

This example will produce the following output:

```
Suit is Clubs and the value is 0
Suit is Diamonds and the value is 1
Suit is Hearts and the value is 2
Suit is Spades and the value is 3
```

How It Works

Because it is a class type, the `Suit` enumeration cannot be defined within the function `main()`, so its definition appears before the definition of `main()` and is therefore defined at global scope. The example defines a variable, `suit`, of type `Suit` and allocates the value `Suit::Clubs` to it initially with the statement:

```
Suit suit = Suit::Clubs;
```

The qualification of the constant name `Clubs` with the type name `Suit` is essential; without it `Clubs` would not be recognized by the compiler.

If you look at the output, the value of suit is displayed as the name of the corresponding constant — `"Clubs"` in the first instance. This is quite different from what happens with native enums. To obtain the constant value that corresponds to the object in a C++/CLI enum, you must explicitly cast the value to the underlying type, type `int` in this instance:

```
value = safe_cast<int>(suit);
```

You can see from the output that the enumeration constants have been assigned values starting from 0. In fact you can change the type that is used for the enumeration constants. The next section looks at how that's done.

Specifying a Type for Enumeration Constants

The constants in a C++/CLI enumeration can be any of the following types:

short	int	long	long long	signed char	char
unsigned short	unsigned int	unsigned long	unsigned long long	unsigned char	bool

To specify the type for the constants in an enumeration, you write the type after the enumeration type name, but separated from it by a colon, just as with the native C++ `enum`. For example, to specify the enumeration constant type as `char`, you could write:

```
enum class Face : char {Ace, Two, Three, Four, Five, Six, Seven,
                        Eight, Nine, Ten, Jack, Queen, King};
```

The constants in this enumeration will be of type `System::Sbyte` and the underlying fundamental type will be type `char`. The first constant will correspond to code value 0 by default, and the subsequent values will be assigned in sequence. To get at the underlying value you must explicitly cast the value to the type.

Specifying Values for Enumeration Constants

You don't have to accept the default for the underlying values. You can explicitly assign values to any or all of the constants defined by an enumeration. For example:

```
enum class Face : char {Ace = 1, Two, Three, Four, Five, Six, Seven,
                        Eight, Nine, Ten, Jack, Queen, King};
```

This will result in `Ace` having the value 1, `Two` having the value 2, an so on with `King` having the value 13. If you wanted the values to reflect the relative face card values with `Ace` high, you could write the enumeration as:

```
enum class Face : char {Ace = 14, Two = 2, Three, Four, Five, Six, Seven,
                        Eight, Nine, Ten, Jack, Queen, King};
```

In this case `Two` will have the value 2, and successive constants will have values in sequence so `King` will still be 13. `Ace` will be 14, the value you have explicitly assigned.

The values you assign to enumeration constants do not have to be unique. This provides the possibility of using the values of the constants to convey some additional property. For example:

```
enum class WeekDays : bool { Mon =true, Tues = true, Wed = true,
                        Thurs = true, Fri = true, Sat = false, Sun = false };
```

This defines the enumeration `WeekDays` where the enumeration constants are of type `bool`. The underlying values have been assigned to identify which represent work days as opposed to rest days. In the particular case of enumerators of type `bool`, you must supply all enumerators with explicit values.

Operations on Enumeration Constants

You can increment or decrement variables of an enum type using `++` or `--`, providing the enumeration constants are of an integral type other than `bool`. For example, consider this fragment using the `Face` type from the previous section:

```
Face card = Face::Ten;
++card;
Console::WriteLine(L"Card is {0}", card);
```

Here you initialize the `card` variable to `Face::Ten` and then increment it. The output from the last statement will be:

```
Card is Jack
```

Incrementing or decrementing an enum variable does not involve any validation of the result, so it is up to you to ensure that the result corresponds to one of the enumerators so that it makes sense.

You can also use the + or – operators with enum values:

```
card = card - Face::Two;
```

This is not a very likely statement in practice but the effect is to reduce the value of `card` by 2 because that is the value of `Face::Two`. Note that you cannot write:

```
card = card - 2;                          // Wrong! Will not compile.
```

This will not compile because the operands for the subtraction operator are of different types and there is no automatic conversion here. To make this work you must use a cast:

```
card = card - safe_cast<Face>(2);         //OK!
```

Casting the integer to type `Face` allows `card` to be decremented by 2.

You can also use the bitwise operators ^, |, &, and ~ with enum values but these are typically used with enums that represent flags, which I'll discuss in the next section. As with the arithmetic operations, the enum type must have enumeration constants of an integral type other than bool.

Finally you can compare enum values using the relational operators:

```
== != < <= > >=
```

I'll be discussing the relational operators in the next chapter. For now these operators compare two operands and result in a value of type `bool`. This allows you to use expressions such as `card ==` `Face::Eight`, which will result in the value `true` if `card` is equal to `Face::Eight`.

Using Enumerators as Flags

It is possible to use an enumeration in quite a different way from what you have seen up to now. You can define an enumeration such that the enumeration constants represent **flags** or **status bits** for something. Most hardware storage devices use status bits to indicate the status of the device before or after an I/O operation for example and you can also use status bits or flags in your programs to record events of one kind or another.

Defining an enumeration to represent flags involves using an attribute. Attributes are additional information that you add to program statements to instruct the compiler to modify the code in some way or to insert code. This is rather an advanced topic for this book so I won't discuss attributes in general but I'll make an exception in this case. Here's an example of an `enum` defining flags:

```
[Flags] enum class FlagBits{ Ready = 1, ReadMode = 2, WriteMode = 4,
                                       EOF = 8, Disabled = 16};
```

The `[Flags]` part of this statement is the attribute and it tells the compiler that the enumeration constants are single bit values; note the choice of explicit values for the constants. It also tells the compiler to treat a variable of type `FlagBits` as a collection of flag bits rather than a single value, for example:

```
FlagBits status = FlagBits::Ready | FlagBits::ReadMode | FlagBits::EOF;
```

111

The status variable will have the value

```
0000 0000 0000 0000 0000 0000 0000 1011
```

with bits set to 1 corresponding to the enumerations constants that have been ORed together. This corresponds to the decimal value 11. If you now output the value of status with the following statement:

```
Console::WriteLine(L"Current status: {0}", status);
```

the output will be:

```
Current status: Ready, ReadMode, EOF
```

The conversion of the value of status to a string is not considering status as an integer value, but as a collection of bits, and the output is the names of the flags that have been set in the variable separated by commas.

To reset one of the bits in a FlagBits variable, you use the bitwise operators. Here's how you could switch off the Ready bit in status:

```
status = status & ~ FlagBits::Ready;
```

The expression ~FlagBits::Ready results in a value with all bits set to 1 except the bit corresponding to FlagBits::Ready. When you AND this with status only the FlagBits::Ready bit in status will be set to 0; all other bits in status will be left at their original setting.

Note that the op= operators are not defined for enum values so you cannot write:

```
status &= ~ FlagBits::Ready;              // Wrong! Will not compile.
```

Native Enumerations in a C++/CLI Program

You can use the same syntax as native C++ enumerations in a C++/CLI program and they will behave the same as they do in a native C++ program. The syntax for native C++ enums is extended in a C++/CLI program to allow you to specify the type for the enumeration constants explicitly. I recommend that you stick to C++/CLI enums in your code, unless you have a good reason to do otherwise.

Summary

In this chapter, I have covered the basics of computation in C++. You have learned about all of the elementary types of data provided for in the language, and all the operators that manipulate these types directly. The essentials of what I have discussed up to now are as follows:

❑   A program in C++ consists of at least one function called main().

❑   The executable part of a function is made up of statements contained between braces.

❑   A statement in C++ is terminated by a semicolon.

❑ Named objects in C++, such as variables or functions, can have names that consist of a sequence of letters and digits, the first of which is a letter, and where an underscore is considered to be a letter. Upper and lower case letters are distinguished.

❑ All the objects, such as variables, that you name in your program must not have a name that coincides with any of the reserved words in C++. The full set of reserved words in C++ appears in Appendix A.

❑ All constants and variables in C++ are of a given type. The fundamental types in ISO/ANSI C++ are char, signed char, unsigned char, wchar_t, short, unsigned short, int, unsigned int, long, unsigned long, bool, float, double, and long double. C++/CLI also defines the types long long and unsigned long long.

❑ The name and type of a variable is defined in a declaration statement ending with a semicolon. Variables may also be given initial values in a declaration.

❑ You can protect the value of a variable of a basic type by using the modifier const. This will prevent direct modification of the variable within the program and give you compiler errors everywhere that a constant's value is altered.

❑ By default, a variable is automatic, which means that it exists only from the point at which it is declared to the end of the scope in which it is defined, indicated by the corresponding closing brace after its declaration.

❑ A variable may be declared as static, in which case it continues to exist for the life of the program. It can be accessed only within the scope in which it was defined.

❑ Variables can be declared outside of all blocks within a program, in which case they have global namespace scope. Variables with global namespace scope are accessible throughout a program, except where a local variable exists with the same name as the global variable. Even then, they can still be reached by using the scope resolution operator.

❑ A namespace defines a scope where each of the names declared within it are qualified by the namespace name. Referring to names from outside a namespace requires the names to be qualified.

❑ The ISO/ANSI C++ Standard Library contains functions and operators that you can use in your program. They are contained in the namespace std. The root namespace for C++/CLI libraries has the name System. Individual objects in a namespace can be accessed by using namespace name to qualify the object name by using the scope resolution operator, or you can supply a using declaration for a name from the namespace.

❑ An lvalue is an object that can appear on the left-hand side of an assignment. Non-const variables are examples of lvalues.

❑ You can mix different types of variables and constants in an expression, but they will be automatically converted to a common type where necessary. Conversion of the type of the right-hand side of an assignment to that of the left-hand side will also be made where necessary. This can cause loss of information when the left-hand side type can't contain the same information as the right-hand side: double converted to int, or long converted to short, for example.

❑ You can explicitly cast the value of an expression to another type. You should always make an explicit cast to convert a value when the conversion may lose information. There are also situations where you need to specify an explicit cast in order to produce the result that you want.

❑ The keyword typedef allows you to define synonyms for other types.

Although I have discussed all the fundamental types, don't be misled into thinking that's all there is. There are more complex types based on the basic set as you'll see, and eventually you will be creating original types of your own.

From this chapter you can see there are three coding strategies you can adopt when writing a C++/CLI program:

❑ You should use the fundamental type names for variables but keep in mind that they are really synonyms for the value class type names in a C++/CLI program. The significance of this will be more apparent when you learn more about classes.

❑ You should use `safe_cast` and not `static_cast` in your C++/CLI code. The difference will be much more important in the context of casting class objects, but if you get into the habit of using `safe_cast`, generally you can be sure you will avoid problems.

❑ You should use `enum class` to declare enumeration types in C++/CLI.

Exercises

1. Write an ISO/ANSI C++ program that asks the user to enter a number and then prints it out, using an integer as a local variable.

2. Write a program which reads an integer value from the keyboard into a variable of type `int`, and uses one of the bitwise operators (i.e. not the % operator!) to determine the positive remainder when divided by 8. For example, 29 = (3x8)+5 and -14 = (-2x8)+2 have positive remainder 5 and 2 respectively when divided by 8.

3. Fully parenthesize the following expressions, in order to show the precedence and associativity:

   ```
   1 + 2 + 3 + 4

   16 * 4 / 2 * 3

   a > b? a: c > d? e: f

   a & b && c & d
   ```

4. Create a program that will calculate the aspect ratio of your computer screen, given the width and height in pixels, using the following statements:

   ```
   int width = 1280;
   int height = 1024;

   double aspect = width / height;
   ```

   When you output the result, what answer will you get? Is it satisfactory — and if not, how could you modify the code, without adding any more variables?

5. (Advanced) Without running it, can you work out what value the following code is going to output, and why?

```
unsigned s = 555;

int i = (s >> 4) & ~(~0 << 3);
cout << i;
```

6. Write a C++/CLI console program that uses an enumeration to identify months in the year with the values associated with the months running from 1 to 12. The program should output each enumeration constants and its underlying value.

7. Write a C++/CLI program that will calculate the areas of three rooms to the nearest number of whole square feet that have the following dimensions in feet:

Room1: 10.5 by 17.6 Room2: 12.7 by 18.9 Room3: 16.3 by 15.4

The program should also calculate and output the average area of the three rooms and the total area; in each case the result should be to the nearest whole number of square feet.

Decisions and Loops

In this chapter, you will look at how to add decision-making capabilities to your C++ programs. You'll also learn how to make your programs repeat a set of actions until a specific condition is met. This will enable you to handle variable amounts of input, as well as make validity checks on the data that you read in. You will also be able to write programs that can adapt their actions depending on the input data and to deal with problems where logic is fundamental to the solution. By the end of this chapter, you will have learned:

- ❑ How to compare data values
- ❑ How to alter the sequence of program execution based on the result
- ❑ How to apply logical operators and expressions
- ❑ How to deal with multiple choice situations
- ❑ How to write and use loops in your programs

I'll start with one of the most powerful and fundamental tools in programming: the ability to compare variables and expressions with other variables and expressions and, based on the outcome, execute one set of statements or another.

Comparing Values

Unless you want to make decisions on a whim, you need a mechanism for comparing things. This involves some new operators called **relational operators**. Because all information in your computer is ultimately represented by numerical values (in the last chapter you saw how character information is represented by numeric codes), comparing numerical values is the essence of practically all decision making. You have six fundamental operators for comparing two values available:

<	less than	<=	less than or equal to
>	greater than	>=	greater than or equal to
==	equal to	!=	not equal to

The "equal to" comparison operator has two successive '=' signs. This is not the same as the assignment operator, which consists only of a single '=' sign. It's a common mistake to use the assignment operator instead of the comparison operator, so watch out for this potential cause of confusion.

Each of these operators compares the values of two operands and returns one of the two possible values of type `bool`: `true` if the comparison is true, or `false` if it is not. You can see how this works by having a look at a few simple examples of comparisons. Suppose you have created integer variables i and j with the values 10 and –5, respectively. The expressions,

```
i > j     i != j     j > -8     i <= j + 15
```

all return the value `true`.

Further assume that you have defined the following variables:

```
char first = 'A', last = 'Z';
```

Here are some examples of comparisons using these character variables:

```
first == 65    first < last    'E' <= first    first != last
```

All four expressions involve comparing ASCII code values. The first expression returns `true` because `first` was initialized with `'A'`, which is the equivalent of decimal 65. The second expression checks whether the value of `first`, which is `'A'`, is less than the value of `last`, which is `'Z'`. If you check the ASCII codes for these characters in Appendix B, notice that the capital letters are represented by an ascending sequence of numerical values from 65 to 90, 65 representing `'A'` and 90 representing `'Z'`, so this comparison also returns the value `true`. The third expression returns the value `false` because `'E'` is greater than the value of `first`. The last expression returns `true` because `'A'` is definitely not equal to `'Z'`.

Consider some slightly more complicated numerical comparisons. With variables defined by the statements

```
int i = -10, j = 20;
double x = 1.5, y = -0.25E-10;
```

take a look at the following:

```
-1 < y      j < (10 - i)     2.0*x >= (3 + y)
```

As you can see, you can use expressions that result in a numerical value as operands in comparisons. If you check with the precedence table for operators that you saw in Chapter 2, you see that none of the parentheses are strictly necessary, but they do help to make the expressions clearer. The first comparison is true and so returns the `bool` value `true`. The variable `y` has a very small negative value, -0.000000000025, and so is greater than -1. The second comparison returns the value `false`. The expression `10 - i` has the value 20 which is the same as `j`. The third expression returns `true` because the expression `3 + y` is slightly less than 3.

You can use relational operators to compare values of any of the fundamental types, or of the enumeration types as I mentioned in Chapter 2, so all you need now is a practical way of using the results of a comparison to modify the behavior of a program.

The if Statement

The basic `if` statement allows your program to execute a single statement, or a block of statements enclosed within braces, if a given condition expression evaluates to the value `true`, or skip the statement or block of statements if the condition evaluates to `false`. This is illustrated in Figure 3-1.

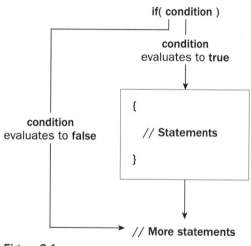

Figure 3-1

A simple example of an `if` statement is:

```
if(letter == 'A')
    cout << "The first capital, alphabetically speaking.";
```

The condition to be tested appears in parentheses immediately following the keyword, `if`, and this is followed by the statement to be executed when the condition is `true`. Note the position of the semicolon here. It goes after the statement *following* the `if` and the condition between parentheses; there shouldn't be a semicolon after the condition in parentheses because the two lines essentially make up a single statement. You also can see how the statement following the `if` is indented, to indicate that it is only executed when the `if` condition returns the value `true`. The indentation is not necessary for the program to execute, but it helps you to recognize the relationship between the `if` condition and the statement that depends on it. The output statement in the code fragment is executed only if the variable `letter` has the value `'A'`.

You could extend this example to change the value of `letter` if it contains the value `'A'`:

```
if(letter == 'A')
{
    cout << "The first capital, alphabetically speaking.";
    letter = 'a';
}
```

The block of statements that is controlled by the `if` statement is delimited by the curly braces. Here you execute the statements in the block only if the condition (`letter -- 'A'`) evaluates to `true`. Without the braces, only the first statement would be the subject of the `if`, and the statement assigning the value `'a'` to `letter` would always be executed. Note that there is a semicolon after each of the statements in the block, not after the closing brace at the end of the block. There can be as many statements as you like within the block. Now, as a result of `letter` having the value `'A'`, you change its value to `'a'` after outputting the same message as before. If the condition returns `false`, neither of these statements is executed.

Nested if Statements

The statement to be executed when the condition in an `if` statement is true can also be an `if`. This arrangement is called a **nested** `if`. The condition for the inner `if` is only tested if the condition for the outer `if` is `true`. An `if` that is nested inside another can also contain a nested `if`. You can generally continue nesting `if`s one inside the other like this for as long as you know what you are doing.

Try It Out   Using Nested Ifs

The following is the nested `if` with a working example.

```
// Ex3_01.cpp
// A nested if demonstration
#include <iostream>

using std::cin;
using std::cout;
using std::endl;

int main()
{
    char letter = 0;                        // Store input in here

    cout << endl
         << "Enter a letter: ";             // Prompt for the input
    cin >> letter;                          // then read a character

    if(letter >= 'A')                       // Test for 'A' or larger
       if(letter <= 'Z')                    // Test for 'Z' or smaller
       {
          cout << endl
               << "You entered a capital letter."
               << endl;
          return 0;
       }
```

```
      if(letter >= 'a')                    // Test for 'a' or larger
         if(letter <= 'z')                 // Test for 'z' or smaller
         {
            cout << endl
                 << "You entered a small letter."
                 << endl;
            return 0;
         }

      cout << endl << "You did not enter a letter." << endl;
      return 0;
}
```

How It Works

This program starts with the usual comment lines; then the `#include` statement for the header file supporting input/output and the `using` declarations for `cin`, `cout`, and `endl` that are the `std` namespace. The first action in the body of `main()` is to prompt for a letter to be entered. This is stored in the `char` variable with the name `letter`.

The `if` statement that follows the input checks whether the character entered is `'A'` or larger. Because the ASCII codes for lowercase letters (97 to 122) are greater than those for uppercase letters (65 to 90), entering a lowercase letter causes the program to execute the first `if` block, as `(letter >= 'A')` returns `true` for all letters. In this case, the nested `if`, which checks for an input of `'Z'` or less, is executed. If it is `'Z'` or less, you know that you have a capital letter, the message is displayed, and you are done, so you execute a `return` statement to end the program. Both statements are enclosed between braces, so they are both executed when the nested `if` condition returns `true`.

The next `if` checks whether the character entered is lowercase, using essentially the same mechanism as the first `if`, displays a message and returns.

If the character entered is not a letter, the output statement following the last `if` block is executed. This displays a message to the effect that the character entered was not a letter. The `return` is then executed.

You can see that the relationship between the nested `if`s and the output statement is much easier to follow because of the indentation applied to each.

A typical output from this example is:

```
Enter a letter: T
You entered a capital letter.
```

You could easily arrange to change uppercase to lowercase by adding just one extra statement to the `if`, checking for uppercase:

```
      if(letter >= 'A')                    // Test for 'A' or larger
         if(letter <= 'Z')                 // Test for 'Z' or smaller
         {
            cout << endl
                 << "You entered a capital letter.";
                 << endl;
            letter += 'a' - 'A';            // Convert to lowercase
            return 0;
         }
```

This involves adding one additional statement. This statement for converting from uppercase to lowercase increments the `letter` variable by the value `'a'` - `'A'`. It works because the ASCII codes for `'A'` to `'Z'` and `'a'` to `'z'` are two groups of consecutive numerical codes, decimal 65 to 90 and 97 to 122 respectively, so the expression `'a'` - `'A'` represents the value to be added to an uppercase letter to get the equivalent lowercase letter and corresponds to 97 - 65, which is 32. Thus , if you add 32 to the code value for `'K'`, which is 75, you get 107, which is the code value for `'k'`.

You could equally well use the equivalent ASCII values for the letters here, but by using the letters you've ensured that this code would work on computers where the characters were not ASCII, as long as both the upper- and lowercase sets are represented by a contiguous sequence of numeric values.

There is an ISO/ANSI C++ library function to convert letters to uppercase, so you don't normally need to program for this yourself. It has the name `toupper()` *and appears in the standard library file* `<ctype>`. *You will see more about standard library facilities when you get to look specifically at how functions are written.*

The Extended if Statement

The `if` statement that you have been using so far executes a statement if the condition specified returns `true`. Program execution then continues with the next statement in sequence. You also have a version of the `if` that allows one statement to be executed if the condition returns `true`, and a different statement to be executed if the condition returns `false`. Execution then continues with the next statement in sequence. As you saw in Chapter 2, a block of statements can always replace a single statement, so this also applies to these `if`s.

Try It Out   Extending the If

Here's an extended `if` example.

```
// Ex3_02.cpp
// Using the extended if
#include <iostream>

using std::cin;
using std::cout;
using std::endl;

int main()
{
   long number = 0;                 // Store input here
   cout << endl
        << "Enter an integer number less than 2 billion: ";
   cin >> number;

   if(number % 2L)                  // Test remainder after division by 2
      cout << endl                  // Here if remainder 1
```

```
                  << "Your number is odd." << endl;
    else
       cout << endl                  // Here if remainder 0
             << "Your number is even." << endl;

    return 0;
}
```

Typical output from this program is:

```
Enter an integer less than 2 billion: 123456
Your number is even,
```

How It Works

After reading the input value into number, the value is tested by taking the remainder after division by two (using the remainder operator % that you saw in the last chapter) and using that as the condition for the if. In this case, the condition of the if statement returns an integer, not a Boolean. The if statement interprets a non-zero value returned by the condition as true, and interprets zero as false. In other words, the condition expression for the if statement

```
(number % 2L)
```

is equivalent to

```
(number % 2L != 0)
```

If the remainder is 1, the condition is true, and the statement immediately following the if is executed. If the remainder is 0, the condition is false, and the statement following the else keyword is executed. It's obvious here what the if expression is doing, but with more complicated expressions it's better to add the extra few characters needed for the comparison with zero to ensure that the code is easily understood.

> In an if statement, *the condition can be an expression that results in a value of any of the fundamental data types that you saw in Chapter 2. When the condition expression evaluates to a numerical value rather than the bool value required by the if statement, the compiler inserts an automatic cast of the result of the expression to type* bool. *A non-zero value that is cast to type* bool *results in* true, *and a zero value results in* false.

Because the remainder from the division of an integer by two can only be one or zero, I have commented the code to indicate this fact. After either outcome, the return statement is executed to end the program.

> The else *keyword is written without a semicolon, similar to the if part of the statement. Again, indentation is used as a visible indicator of the relationship between various statements. You can clearly see which statement is executed for a true or non-zero result, and which for a false or zero result. You should always indent the statements in your programs to show their logical structure.*

The if-else combination provides a choice between two options. The general logic of the if-else is shown in Figure 3-2.

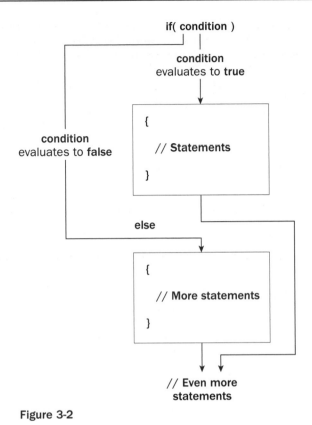

Figure 3-2

The arrows in the diagram indicate the sequence in which statements are executed, depending on whether the if condition returns true or false.

Nested if-else Statements

As you have seen, you can nest if statements within if statements. You can also nest if-else statements within ifs, ifs within if-else statements, and if-else statements within if-else statements. This provides considerable room for confusion, so take a look at a few examples. The following is an example of an if-else nested within an if.

```
if(coffee == 'y')
    if(donuts == 'y')
        cout << "We have coffee and donuts.";
    else
        cout << "We have coffee, but not donuts";
```

The test for `donuts` is executed only if the result of the test for `coffee` returns `true`, so the messages reflect the correct situation in each case; however, it is easy to get this confused. If you write much the same thing with incorrect indentation, you can be trapped into the wrong conclusion:

```
if(coffee == 'y')
    if(donuts == 'y')
        cout << "We have coffee and donuts.";
    else                                    // This else is indented incorrectly
        cout << "We have no coffee...";     // Wrong!
```

The mistake is easy to see here, but with more complicated `if` structures you need to keep in mind the rule about which `if` owns which `else`.

> An `else` *always belongs to the nearest preceding* `if` *that is not already spoken for by another* `else`.

Whenever things look a bit complicated, you can apply this rule to sort things out. When you are writing your own programs you can always use braces to make the situation clearer. It isn't really necessary in such a simple case, but you could write the last example as follows:

```
if(coffee == 'y')
{
    if(donuts == 'y')
        cout << "We have coffee and donuts.";
    else
        cout << "We have coffee, but not donuts";
}
```

and it should be absolutely clear. Now that you know the rules, understanding the case of an `if` nested within an `if-else` becomes easy.

```
if(coffee == 'y')
{
    if(donuts == 'y')
        cout << "We have coffee and donuts.";
}
else
    if(tea == 'y')
        cout << "We have tea, but not coffee";
```

Here the braces are essential. If you leave them out, the `else` would belong to the second `if`, which is looking out for `donuts`. In this kind of situation, it is easy to forget to include them and create an error that may be hard to find. A program with this kind of error compiles fine and even produces the right results some of the time.

If you removed the braces in this example, you get the correct results only as long as `coffee` and `donuts` are both equal to `'y'` so that the `if(tea == 'y')` check wouldn't be executed.

Here you'll look at `if-else` statements nested in `if-else` statements. This can get very messy, even with just one level of nesting.

```cpp
if(coffee == 'y')
   if(donuts == 'y')
      cout << "We have coffee and donuts.";
   else
      cout << "We have coffee, but not donuts";
else
   if(tea == 'y')
      cout << "We have no coffee, but we have tea, and maybe donuts...";
   else
      cout << "No tea or coffee, but maybe donuts...";
```

The logic here doesn't look quite so obvious, even with the correct indentation. No braces are necessary, as the rule you saw earlier verifies that this is correct, but it would look a bit clearer if you included them.

```cpp
if(coffee == 'y')
{
   if(donuts == 'y')
      cout << "We have coffee and donuts.";
   else
      cout << "We have coffee, but not donuts";
}
else
{
   if(tea == 'y')
      cout << "We have no coffee, but we have tea, and maybe donuts...";
   else
      cout << "No tea or coffee, but maybe donuts...";
}
```

There are much better ways of dealing with this kind of logic in a program. If you put enough nested `if`s together, you can almost guarantee a mistake somewhere. The following section will help to simplify things.

Logical Operators and Expressions

As you have just seen, using `if`s where you have two or more related conditions can be a bit cumbersome. We have tried our `iffy` talents on looking for coffee and donuts, but in practice you may want to check much more complex conditions.

Logical operators provide a neat and simple solution. Using logical operators, you can combine a series of comparisons into a single logical expression, so you end up needing just one `if`, virtually regardless of the complexity of the set of conditions, as long as the decision ultimately boils down to a choice between two possibilities — true or false.

You have just three logical operators:

&&	Logical AND
||	Logical OR
!	Logical negation (NOT)

Logical AND

You would use the AND operator, &&, where you have two conditions that must both be true for a true result. You want to be rich *and* healthy. For example, you could use the && operator when you are testing a character to determine whether it's an uppercase letter; the value being tested must be both greater than or equal to 'A' AND less than or equal to 'Z'. Both conditions must return true for the value to be a capital letter.

> *As before, the conditions you combine using logical operators may return numerical values. Remember that in this case a non-zero value casts to the value true; zero casts to false.*

Taking the example of a value stored in a char variable letter, you could replace the test using two ifs for one that uses only a single if and the && operator:

```
if((letter >= 'A') && (letter <= 'Z'))
    cout << "This is a capital letter.";
```

The parentheses inside the expression that is the if condition ensure that there is no doubt that the comparison operations are executed first, which makes the statement clearer. Here, the output statement is executed only if *both* of the conditions that are combined by the && operator are true.

Just as with binary operators in the last chapter, you can represent the effect of a particular logical operator using a truth table. The truth table for && is as follows:

&&	false	true
false	false	false
true	false	true

The row headings of the left and the column headings at the top represent the value of the logical expressions to be combined by the operator &&. Thus, to determine the result of combining a true condition with a false condition, select the row with true at the left and the column with false at the top and look at the intersection of the row and column for the result (false). Actually, you don't really need a truth table because it's very simple; the && operation results in the value true only if both operands are true.

Logical OR

The OR operator, ||, applies when you have two conditions and you want a true result if either or both of them are true. For example, you might be considered creditworthy for a loan from the bank if your income was at least $100,000 a year, or you had $1,000,000 in cash. This could be tested using the following if.

```
if((income >= 100000.00) || (capital >= 1000000.00))
    cout << "How much would you like to borrow, Sir (grovel, grovel)?";
```

The ingratiating response emerges when either or both of the conditions are true. (A better response might be, "Why do you *want* to borrow?" It's strange how banks lend you money only if you don't need it.)

You can also construct a truth table for the || operator:

||	false	true
false	false	true
true	true	true

The result here can also be stated very simply: you only get a false result with the || operator when both operands are false.

Logical NOT

The third logical operator, !, takes one operand of type bool and inverts its value. So if the value of a variable test is true, !test is false; and if test is false, !test is true. To take the example of a simple expression, if x has the value 10, the expression

```
!(x > 5)
```

is false, because x > 5 is true.

You could also apply the ! operator in an expression that was a favorite of Charles Dickens:

```
!(income > expenditure)
```

If this expression is true, the result is misery, at least as soon as the bank starts bouncing your checks.

Finally, you can apply the ! operator to other basic data types. Suppose you have a variable, rate, that is of type float and has the value 3.2. For some reason you might want to test to verify that the value of rate is non-zero, in which case you could use the expression:

```
!(rate)
```

The value 3.2 is non-zero and thus converts to the bool value true so the result of this expression is false.

Try It Out   **Combining Logical Operators**

You can combine conditional expressions and logical operators to any degree that you feel comfortable with. For example, you could construct a test for whether a variable contained a letter just using a single `if`. Let's write it as a working example:

```cpp
// Ex3_03.cpp
// Testing for a letter using logical operators
#include <iostream>

using std::cin;
using std::cout;
using std::endl;

int main()
{
   char letter = 0;                                       // Store input in here

   cout << endl
        << "Enter a character: ";
   cin >> letter;

   if(((letter >= 'A') && (letter <= 'Z')) ||
      ((letter >= 'a') && (letter <= 'z')))               // Test for alphabetic
      cout << endl
           << "You entered a letter." << endl;
   else
      cout << endl
           << "You didn't enter a letter." << endl;

   return 0;
}
```

How It Works

This example starts out in the same way as `Ex3_01.cpp` by reading a character after a prompt for input. The interesting part of the program is in the `if` statement condition. This consists of two logical expressions combined with the `||` (OR) operator, so that if either is `true`, the condition returns `true` and the message

You entered a letter.

is displayed. If both logical expressions are `false`, the `else` statement is executed, which displays the message

You didn't enter a letter.

Each of the logical expressions combines a pair of comparisons with the operator `&&` (AND), so both comparisons must return `true` if the logical expression is to be `true`. The first logical expression returns `true` if the input is an uppercase letter, and the second returns `true` if the input is a lowercase letter.

The Conditional Operator

The `conditional operator` is sometimes called the **ternary operator** because it involves three operands. It is best understood by looking at an example. Suppose you have two variables, a and b, and you want to assign the maximum of a and b to a third variable c. You can do this with the following statement:

```
c = a > b ? a : b;            // Set c to the maximum of a or b
```

The first operand for the conditional operator must be an expression that results in a `bool` value, true or false, and in this case it is a > b. If this expression returns `true`, the second operand — in this case a — is selected as the value resulting from the operation. If the first argument returns `false`, the third operand — in this case b — is selected as the value that results from the operation. Thus, the result of the conditional expression a > b ? a : b is a if a is greater than b, and b otherwise. This value is stored in c as a result of the assignment operation. The use of the conditional operator in this assignment statement is equivalent to the `if` statement:

```
if(a > b)
   c = a;
else
   c = b;
```

The conditional operator can be written generally as:

```
condition ? expression1 : expression2
```

If the *condition* evaluates as `true`, the result is the value of *expression1*, and if it evaluates to `false`, the result is the value of *expression2*.

Try It Out   **Using the Conditional Operator with Output**

A common use of the conditional operator is to control output, depending on the result of an expression or the value of a variable. You can vary a message by selecting one text string or another, depending on the condition specified.

```cpp
// Ex3_04.cpp
// The conditional operator selecting output
#include <iostream>

using std::cout;
using std::endl;

int main()
{
   int nCakes = 1;              // Count of number of cakes

   cout << endl
        << "We have " << nCakes << " cake" << ((nCakes > 1) ? "s." : ".")
        << endl;
```

```
    ++nCakes;

    cout << endl
        << "We have " << nCakes << " cake" << ((nCakes > 1) ? "s." : ".")
        << endl;
    return 0;
}
```

The output from this program is:

```
We have 1 cake.
We have 2 cakes.
```

How It Works

You first initialize the nCakes variable with the value 1; then you have an output statement that shows the number of cakes. The part that uses the conditional operator simply tests the variable to determine whether you have a singular cake or several cakes:

```
((nCakes>1) ? "s." : ".")
```

This expression evaluates to "s." if nCakes is greater than 1, or "." otherwise. This enables you to use the same output statement for any number of cakes and get grammatically correct output. You show this in the example by incrementing the nCakes variable and repeating the output statement.

There are many other situations where you can apply this sort of mechanism; selecting between "is" and "are", for example.

The switch Statement

The switch statement enables you to select from multiple choices based on a set of fixed values for a given expression. It operates like a physical rotary switch in that you can select one of a fixed number of choices; some makes of washing machine provide a means of choosing an operation for processing your laundry in this way. There are a given number of possible positions for the switch, such as cotton, wool, synthetic fiber, and so on, and you can select any one of them by turning the knob to point to the option you want.

In the switch statement, the selection is determined by the value of an expression that you specify. You define the possible switch positions by one or more **case values**, a particular one being selected if the value of the switch expression is the same as the particular case value. There is one case value for each possible choice in the switch and all the case values must be distinct.

If the value of the switch expression does not match any of the case values, the switch automatically selects the default case. You can, if you want, specify the code for the default case, as you will do below; otherwise, the default is to do nothing.

You can examine how the `switch` statement works with the following example.

```cpp
// Ex3_05.cpp
// Using the switch statement
#include <iostream>

using std::cin;
using std::cout;
using std::endl;

int main()
{
   int choice = 0;                        // Store selection value here

   cout << endl
        << "Your electronic recipe book is at your service." << endl
        << "You can choose from the following delicious dishes: "
        << endl
        << endl << "1 Boiled eggs"
        << endl << "2 Fried eggs"
        << endl << "3 Scrambled eggs"
        << endl << "4 Coddled eggs"
        << endl << endl << "Enter your selection number: ";
   cin >> choice;

   switch(choice)
   {
      case 1: cout << endl << "Boil some eggs." << endl;
            break;
      case 2: cout << endl << "Fry some eggs." << endl;
            break;
      case 3: cout << endl << "Scramble some eggs." << endl;
            break;
      case 4: cout << endl << "Coddle some eggs." << endl;
            break;
      default: cout << endl <<"You entered a wrong number, try raw eggs."
                  << endl;
   }

   return 0;
}
```

How It Works

After defining your options in the stream output statement and reading a selection number into the variable `choice`, the `switch` statement is executed with the condition specified as simply `choice` in parentheses, immediately following the keyword `switch`. The possible options in the `switch` are enclosed between braces and are each identified by a **case label**. A case label is the keyword `case`, followed by the value of `choice` that corresponds to this option, and terminated by a colon.

As you can see, the statements to be executed for a particular `case` are written following the colon at the end of the case label, and are terminated by a `break` statement. The `break` transfers execution to the statement after the `switch`. The `break` isn't mandatory, but if you don't include it, execution continues with the statements for the case that follows, which isn't usually what you want. You can demonstrate this by removing the `break` statements from this example and seeing what happens.

If the value of `choice` doesn't correspond with any of the case values specified, the statements preceded by the `default` label are executed. A `default` case isn't essential. In its absence, if the value of the test expression doesn't correspond to any of the cases, the `switch` is exited and the program continues with the next statement after the `switch`.

Try It Out   **Sharing a Case**

Each of the expressions that you specify to identify the cases must be constant so that the value can be determined at compile time, and must evaluate to a unique integer value. The reason that no two case constants can be the same is that the compiler would have no way of knowing which case statement should be executed for that particular value; however, different cases don't need to have a unique action. Several cases can share the same action, as shown here.

```cpp
// Ex3_06.cpp
// Multiple case actions
#include <iostream>

using std::cin;
using std::cout;
using std::endl;

int main()
{
   char letter = 0;
   cout << endl
        << "Enter a small letter: ";
   cin >> letter;

   switch(letter*(letter >= 'a' && letter <= 'z'))
   {
      case 'a':
      case 'e':
      case 'i':
      case 'o':
      case 'u': cout << endl << "You entered a vowel.";
               break;

      case 0: cout << endl << "That is not a small letter.";
               break;

      default: cout << endl << "You entered a consonant.";
   }

   cout << endl;
   return 0;
}
```

How It Works

In this example, you have a more complex expression in the `switch`. If the character entered isn't a lower-case letter, the expression

```
(letter >= 'a' && letter <= 'z')
```

results in the value `false`; otherwise it evaluates to `true`. Because `letter` is multiplied by this expression, the value of the logical expression is cast to an integer — 0 if the logical expression is false and 1 if it is true. Thus the `switch` expression evaluates to 0 if a lowercase letter was not entered and to the value of `letter` if it was. The statements following the case label `case 0` are executed whenever the character code stored in `letter` does not represent a lowercase case letter.

If a lowercase letter was entered, the `switch` expression evaluates to the same value as `letter` so for all values corresponding to vowels, the output statement following the sequence of case labels that have case values that are vowels. The same statement executes for any vowel because when any of these case labels is chosen successive statements are executed until the `break` statement is reached. You can see that a single action can be taken for a number of different cases by writing each of the case labels one after the other before the statements to be executed. If a lowercase letter that is a consonant is entered as program input, the `default` case label statement is executed.

Unconditional Branching

The `if` statement provides you with the flexibility to choose to execute one set of statements or another, depending on a specified condition, so the statement execution sequence is varied depending on the values of the data in the program. The `goto` statement, in contrast, is a blunt instrument. It enables you to branch to a specified program statement unconditionally. The statement to be branched to must be identified by a statement label which is an identifier defined according to the same rules as a variable name. This is followed by a colon and placed before the statement requiring labeling. Here is an example of a labeled statement.

```
myLabel: cout << "myLabel branch has been activated" << endl;
```

This statement has the label `myLabel`, and an unconditional branch to this statement would be written as follows:

```
goto myLabel;
```

Whenever possible, you should avoid using `goto`s in your program. They tend to encourage convoluted code that can be extremely difficult to follow.

Because the `goto` is theoretically unnecessary in a program — there's always an alternative approach to using `goto` — a significant cadre of programmers say you should never use it. I don't subscribe to such an extreme view. It is a legal statement after all, and there are occasions when it can be convenient such as when you must exit from a deeply nested set of loops (you learn about loops in the next section). I do, however, recommend that you only use it where you can see an obvious advantage over other options that are available; otherwise, you may end up with convoluted error-prone code that is hard to understand and even harder to maintain.

Repeating a Block of Statements

The capability to repeat a group of statements is fundamental to most applications. Without this capability, an organization would need to modify the payroll program every time an extra employee was hired, and you would need to reload Halo 2 every time you wanted to play another game. So let's first understand how a loop works.

What Is a Loop?

A loop executes a sequence of statements until a particular condition is true (or false). You can actually write a loop with the C++ statements that you have met so far. You just need an if and the dreaded goto. Look at the following example.

```cpp
// Ex3_07.cpp
// Creating a loop with an if and a goto
#include <iostream>

using std::cin;
using std::cout;
using std::endl;

int main()
{
   int i = 0, sum = 0;
   const int max = 10;

   i = 1;
loop:
   sum += i;                  // Add current value of i to sum
   if(++i <= max)
      goto loop;              // Go back to loop until i = 11

   cout << endl
        << "sum = " << sum
        << endl
        << "i = " << i
        << endl;
   return 0;
}
```

This example accumulates the sum of integers from 1 to 10. The first time through the sequence of statements, i is 1 and is added to sum which starts out as zero. In the if, i is incremented to 2 and, as long as it is less than or equal to max, the unconditional branch to loop occurs and the value of i, now 2, is added to sum. This continues with i being incremented and added to sum each time, until finally, when i is incremented to 11 in the if, the branch back is not executed. If you run this example, you get the following output:

```
sum = 55
i = 11
```

This shows quite clearly how the loop works; however, it uses a goto and introduces a label into the program, both of which you should avoid if possible. You can achieve the same thing, and more, with the next statement, which is specifically for writing a loop.

Try It Out   Using the for Loop

You can rewrite the last example using what is known as a `for` loop.

```cpp
// Ex3_08.cpp
// Summing integers with a for loop
#include <iostream>

using std::cin;
using std::cout;
using std::endl;

int main()
{
   int i = 0, sum = 0;
   const int max = 10;

   for(i = 1; i <= max; i++)            // Loop specification
      sum += i;                         // Loop statement

   cout << endl
        << "sum = " << sum
        << endl
        << "i = " << i
        << endl;
   return 0;
}
```

How It Works

If you compile and run this, you get exactly the same output as the previous example, but the code is much simpler here. The conditions determining the operation of the loop appear in parentheses after the keyword `for`. There are three expressions that appear within the parentheses separated by semicolons:

❑   The first expression executes once at the outset and sets the initial conditions for the loop. In this case, it sets `i` to 1.

❑   The second expression is a logical expression that determines whether the loop statement (or block of statements) should continue to be executed. If the second expression is `true`, the loop continues to execute; when it is false, the loop ends and execution continues with the statement that follows the loop. In this case the loop statement on the following line is executed as long as `i` is less than or equal to `max`.

❑   The third expression is evaluated after the loop statement (or block of statements) executes, and in this case increments `i` each iteration. After this expression has been evaluated the second expression is evaluated once more to see whether the loop should continue.

Actually, this loop is not *exactly* the same as the version in Ex3_07.cpp. You can demonstrate this if you set the value of `max` to 0 in both programs and run them again; then, you will find that the value of `sum` is 1 in Ex3_07.cpp and 0 in Ex3_08.cpp, and the value of `i` differs too. The reason for this is that the `if` version of the program always executes the loop at least once because you don't check the condition until the end. The `for` loop doesn't do this, because the condition is actually checked at the beginning.

The general form of the for loop is:

```
for (initializing_expression ; test_expression ; increment_expression)
    loop_statement;
```

Of course, *loop_statement* can be a single statement or a block of statements between braces. The sequence of events in executing the for loop is shown in Figure 3-3.

As I have said, the loop statement shown in Figure 3-3 can also be a block of statements. The expressions controlling the for loop are very flexible. You can even write two or more expressions separated by the comma operator for each control expression. This gives you a lot of scope in what you can do with a for loop.

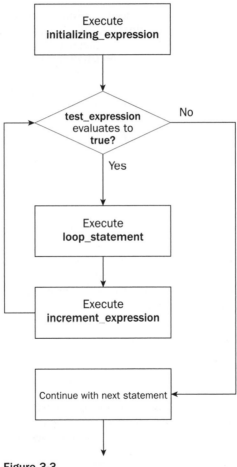

Figure 3-3

Variations on the for Loop

Most of the time, the expressions in a for loop are used in a fairly standard way: the first for initializing one or more loop counters, the second to test if the loop should continue, and the third to increment or decrement one or more loop counters. You are not obliged to use these expressions in this way, however, and quite a few variations are possible.

The initialization expression in a for loop can also include a declaration for a loop variable. In the previous example you could have written the loop to include the declaration for the loop counter i in the first control expression.

```
for(int i = 1; i <= max; i++)        // Loop specification
    sum += i;                        // Loop statement
```

Naturally, the original declaration for i would need to be omitted in the program. If you make this change to the last example, you will find that it now does not compile because the loop variable, i, ceases to exist after the loop so you cannot refer to it in the output statement. A loop has a scope which extends from the for expression to the end of the body of the loop, which of course can be a block of code between braces, as well as just a single statement. The counter i is now declared within the loop scope, so you cannot refer to it in the output statement because this is outside the scope of the loop. By default the C++ compiler enforces the ISO/ANSI C++ standard by insisting that a variable defined within a loop condition cannot be reference outside the loop. If you need to use the value in the counter after the loop has executed, you must declare the counter variable *outside* the scope of the loop.

You can omit the initialization expression altogether from the loop. If you initialize i appropriately in the declaration statement for it, you can write the loop as:

```
int i = 1;
for(; i <= max; i++)                 // Loop specification
    sum += i;                        // Loop statement
```

You still need the semicolon that separates the initialization expression from the test condition for the loop. In fact, both semicolons must always be present regardless of whether any or all of the control expressions are omitted. If you omit the first semicolon, the compiler is unable to decide which expression has been omitted or even which semicolon is missing.

The loop statement can be empty. For example, you could place the loop statement in for loop from the previous example inside the increment expression; in this case the loop becomes

```
for(i = 1; i <= max; sum += i++);    // The whole loop
```

You still need the semicolon after the closing parentheses, to indicate that the loop statement is now empty. If you omit this, the statement immediately following this line is interpreted as the loop statement. Sometimes you'll see the empty loop statement written on a separate line like the following:

```
for(i = 1; i <= max; sum += i++)     // The whole loop
    ;
```

Try It Out — Using Multiple Counters

You can use the comma operator to include multiple counters in a `for` loop. You can see this in operation in the following program.

```cpp
// Ex3_09.cpp
// Using multiple counters to show powers of 2
#include <iostream>
#include <iomanip>

using std::cin;
using std::cout;
using std::endl;
using std::setw;

int main()
{
    long i = 0, power = 0;
    const int max = 10;

    for(i = 0, power = 1; i <= max; i++, power += power)
        cout << endl
             << setw(10) << i << setw(10) << power;      // Loop statement

    cout << endl;
    return 0;
}
```

How It Works

You initialize two variables in the initialization section of the `for` loop, separated by the comma operator, and increment each of them in the increment section. Clearly, you can put as many expressions as you like in each position.

> You can even specify multiple conditions, separated by commas, in second expression that represents the test part of the for loop that determines whether it should continue; but only the right-most condition affects when the loop ends.

Note that the assignments defining the initial values for `i` and `power` are expressions, not statements. A statement always ends with a semicolon.

For each increment of `i`, the value of the variable `power` is doubled by adding it to itself. This produces the powers of two that we are looking for and so the program produces the following output.

```
         0         1
         1         2
         2         4
         3         8
         4        16
```

```
 5        32
 6        64
 7       128
 8       256
 9       512
10      1024
```

The setw() manipulator that you saw in the previous chapter is used to align the output nicely. You have included <iomanip> header file and added a using declaration for the name in the std namespace so you can use setw() without qualifying the name.

Try It Out   **The Indefinite for Loop**

If you omit the second control expression that specifies the test condition for a for loop, the value is assumed to be true, so the loop continues indefinitely unless you provide some other means of exiting from it. In fact, if you like, you can omit all the expressions in the parentheses after for. This may not seem to be useful; in fact, however, quite the reverse is true. You will often come across situations where you want to execute a loop a number of times, but you do not know in advance how many iterations you will need. Have a look at the following:

```cpp
// Ex3_10.cpp
// Using an infinite for loop to compute an average
#include <iostream>

using std::cin;
using std::cout;
using std::endl;

int main()
{
    double value = 0.0;              // Value entered stored here
    double sum = 0.0;                // Total of values accumulated here
    int i = 0;                       // Count of number of values
    char indicator = 'n';            // Continue or not?

    for(;;)                          // Infinite loop
    {
      cout << endl
          << "Enter a value: ";
      cin >> value;                  // Read a value
      ++i;                           // Increment count
      sum += value;                  // Add current input to total

      cout << endl
          << "Do you want to enter another value (enter n to end)? ";
      cin >> indicator;              // Read indicator
      if ((indicator == 'n') || (indicator == 'N'))
        break;                       // Exit from loop
    }
```

```
        cout << endl
            << "The average of the " << i
            << " values you entered is " << sum/i << "."
            << endl;
    return 0;
}
```

How It Works

This program computes the average of an arbitrary number of values. After each value is entered, you need to indicate whether you want to enter another value, by entering a single character y or n. Typical output from executing this example is:

```
Enter a value: 10

Do you want to enter another value (enter n to end)? y

Enter a value: 20

Do you want to enter another value (enter n to end)? y

Enter a value: 30

Do you want to enter another value (enter n to end)? n

The average of the 3 values you entered is 20.
```

After declaring and initializing the variables that you're going to use, you start a `for` loop with no expressions specified, so there is no provision for ending it here. The block immediately following is the subject of the loop that is to be repeated.

The loop block performs three basic actions:

❑   It reads a value

❑   It adds the value read from `cin` to sum

❑   It checks whether you want to continue to enter values

The first action within the block is to prompt you for input and then read a value into the variable `value`. The value that you enter is added to `sum` and the count of the number of values, i, is incremented. After accumulating the value in `sum`, you are asked if you want to enter another value and prompted to enter `'n'` if you have finished. The character that you enter is stored in the variable `indicator` for testing against `'n'` or `'N'` in the `if` statement. If neither is found, the loop continues; otherwise, a `break` is executed. The effect of `break` in a loop is similar to its effect in the context of the `switch` statement. In this instance, it exits the loop immediately by transferring control to the statement following the closing brace of the loop block.

Finally, you output the count of the number of values entered and their average, which is calculated by dividing `sum` by i. Of course, i is promoted to type `double` before the calculation, as you remember from the casting discussion in Chapter 2.

Using the continue Statement

There is another statement, besides break, used to affect the operation of a loop: the continue statement. This is written simply as:

```
continue;
```

Executing continue within a loop starts the next loop iteration immediately, skipping over any statements remaining in the current iteration. I can demonstrate how this works with the following code:

```cpp
#include <iostream>

using std::cin;
using std::cout;
using std::endl;

int main()
{
   int i = 0, value = 0, product = 1;

   for(i = 1; i <= 10; i++)
   {
     cout << "Enter an integer: ";
     cin >> value;

     if(value == 0)                   // If value is zero
         continue;                    // skip to next iteration

     product *= value;
   }

   cout << "Product (ignoring zeros): " << product
        << endl;

   return 0;                          // Exit from loop
}
```

This loop reads 10 values with the intention of producing the product of the values entered. The if checks each value entered, and if it is zero, the continue statement skips to the next iteration. This is so that you don't end up with a zero product if one of the values is zero. Obviously, if a zero value occurred on the last iteration, the loop would end. There are clearly other ways of achieving the same result, but continue provides a very useful capability, particularly with complex loops where you may need to skip to the end of the current iteration from various points in the loop.

The effect of the break and continue statements on the logic of a for loop is illustrated in Figure 3-4.

Obviously, in a real situation, you would use the break and continue statements with some condition-testing logic to determine when the loop should be exited, or when an iteration of the loop should be skipped. You can also use the break and continue statements with the other kinds of loop, which I'll discuss later on in this chapter, where they work in exactly the same way.

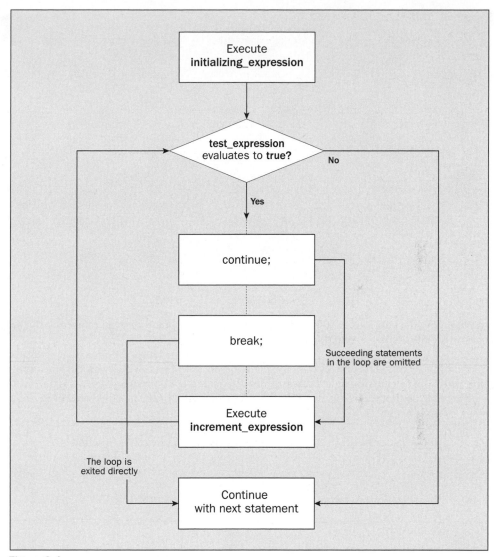

Figure 3-4

Try It Out   Using Other Types in Loops

So far, you have only used integers to count loop iterations. You are in no way restricted as to what type of variable you use to count iterations. Look at the following example:

```
// Ex3_11.cpp
// Display ASCII codes for alphabetic characters
#include <iostream>
#include <iomanip>
```

```
using std::cout;
using std::endl;
using std::hex;
using std::dec;
using std::setw;

int main()
{
    for(char capital = 'A', small = 'a'; capital <= 'Z'; capital++, small++)
        cout << endl
             << "\t" << capital                              // Output capital as a character
             << hex << setw(10) << static_cast<int>(capital)    // and as hexadecimal
             << dec << setw(10) << static_cast<int>(capital)    // and as decimal
             << "    " << small                              // Output small as a character
             << hex << setw(10) << static_cast<int>(small)      // and as hexadecimal
             << dec << setw(10) << static_cast<int>(small);     // and as decimal

    cout << endl;
    return 0;
}
```

How It Works

You have using declarations for the names of some new manipulators that are used in the program to affect how the output is presented.

The loop in this example is controlled by the char variable capital, which you declare along with the variable small in the initializing expression. You also increment both variables in the third control expression for the loop so that the value of capital varies from 'A' to 'Z', and the value of small correspondingly varies from 'a' to 'z'.

The loop contains just one output statement spread over seven lines. The first line is:

```
cout << endl
```

This starts a new line on the screen.

The next three lines are:

```
             << "\t" << capital                              // Output capital as a character
             << hex << setw(10) << static_cast<int>(capital)    // and as hexadecimal
             << dec << setw(10) << static_cast<int>(capital)    // and as decimal
```

On each iteration, after outputting a tab character, the value of capital is displayed three times: as a character, as a hexadecimal value, and as a decimal value.

When you insert the manipulator hex into the cout stream, this causes subsequent data values to be displayed as hexadecimal values rather than the default decimal representation for integer values so the second output of capital is as a hexadecimal representation of the character code.

You then insert the dec manipulator into the stream to cause succeeding values to be output as decimal once more. By default a variable of type char is interpreted by the stream as a character, not a numerical value. You get the char variable `capital` to output as a numerical value by casting its value to type `int`, using the `static_cast<>()` operator that you saw in the previous chapter in the discussion following the Try It Out – Exercising Basic Arithmetic example.

The value of `small` is output in a similar way by the next three lines of the output statement:

```
<< "    " << small                              // Output small as a character
<< hex << setw(10) << static_cast<int>(small)    // and as hexadecimal
<< dec << setw(10) << static_cast<int>(small);   // and as decimal
```

As a result, the program generates the following output:

A	41	65	a	61	97
B	42	66	b	62	98
C	43	67	c	63	99
D	44	68	d	64	100
E	45	69	e	65	101
F	46	70	f	66	102
G	47	71	g	67	103
H	48	72	h	68	104
I	49	73	i	69	105
J	4a	74	j	6a	106
K	4b	75	k	6b	107
L	4c	76	l	6c	108
M	4d	77	m	6d	109
N	4e	78	n	6e	110
O	4f	79	o	6f	111
P	50	80	p	70	112
Q	51	81	q	71	113
R	52	82	r	72	114
S	53	83	s	73	115
T	54	84	t	74	116
U	55	85	u	75	117
V	56	86	v	76	118
W	57	87	w	77	119
X	58	88	x	78	120
Y	59	89	y	79	121
Z	5a	90	z	7a	122

Floating-Point Loop Counters

You can also use a floating-point value as a loop counter. Here's an example of a `for` loop with this kind of counter:

```
double a = 0.3, b = 2.5;
for(double x = 0.0; x <= 2.0; x += 0.25)
    cout << "\n\tx = " << x
         << "\ta*x + b = " << a*x + b;
```

This code fragment calculates the value of a*x+b for values of x from 0.0 to 2.0 in steps of 0.25; however, you need to take care when using a floating-point counter in a loop. Many decimal values cannot be represented exactly in binary floating-point form, so discrepancies can build up with accumulative values. This means that you should not code a `for` loop such that ending the loop depends on a floating-point loop counter reaching a precise value. For example, the following poorly designed loop never ends.

```
for(double x = 0.0 ; x != 1.0 ; x += 0.2)
   cout << x;
```

The intention with this loop is to output the value of x as it varies from 0.0 to 1.0; however, 0.2 has no exact representation as a binary floating-point value so the value of x is never exactly 1. Thus the second loop control expression is always `false` and so the loop continues indefinitely.

The while Loop

A second kind of loop in C++ is the `while` loop. Where the `for` loop is primarily used to repeat a statement or a block for a prescribed number of iterations, the `while` loop is used to execute a statement or block of statements as long as a specified condition is `true`. The general form of the `while` loop is:

```
while(condition)
   loop_statement;
```

Here *loop_statement* is executed repeatedly as long as the *condition* expression has the value `true`. After the condition becomes `false`, the program continues with the statement following the loop. As always, a block of statements between braces could replace the single *loop_statement*.

The logic of the `while` loop can be represented, as shown in Figure 3-5.

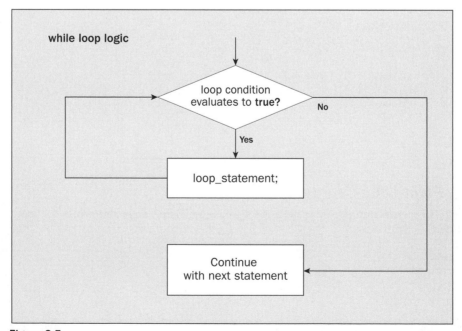

Figure 3-5

Try It Out   ### Using the while Loop

You could rewrite the earlier example that computes averages (Ex3_10.cpp) to use the while loop.

```cpp
// Ex3_12.cpp
// Using a while loop to compute an average
#include <iostream>

using std::cin;
using std::cout;
using std::endl;

int main()
{
    double value = 0.0;          // Value entered stored here
    double sum = 0.0;            // Total of values accumulated here
    int i = 0;                   // Count of number of values
    char indicator = 'y';        // Continue or not?

    while(indicator == 'y')      // Loop as long as y is entered
    {
        cout << endl
             << "Enter a value: ";
        cin >> value;            // Read a value
        ++i;                     // Increment count
        sum += value;            // Add current input to total

        cout << endl
             << "Do you want to enter another value (enter n to end)? ";
        cin >> indicator;        // Read indicator
    }

    cout << endl
         << "The average of the " << i
         << " values you entered is " << sum/i << "."
         << endl;
    return 0;
}
```

How It Works

For the same input, this version of the program produces the same output as before. One statement has been updated, and another has been added — they are highlighted in the previous code. The for loop statement has been replaced by the while statement, and the test for indicator in the if has been deleted, as this function is performed by the while condition. You have to initialize indicator with 'y' in place of the 'n' which appeared previously — otherwise the while loop terminates immediately. As long as the condition in the while returns true, the loop continues.

You can put any expression resulting in true or false as a while loop condition. The example would be a better program if the loop condition were extended to allow 'Y' to be entered to continue the loop as well as 'y'. You could modify the while to the following to do the trick.

```cpp
while((indicator == 'y') || (indicator == 'Y'))
```

You can also create a `while` loop that potentially executes indefinitely by using a condition that is always `true`. This can be written as follows:

```
while(true)
{
    ...
}
```

You could also write the loop control expression as the integer value 1, which would be converted to the `bool` value `true`. Naturally, the same requirement applies here as in the case of the infinite `for` loop: namely, that you must provide some way of exiting the loop within the loop block. You'll see other ways to use the `while` loop in Chapter 4.

The do-while Loop

The `do-while` loop is similar to the `while` loop in that the loop continues as long as the specified loop condition remains `true`. The main difference is that the condition is checked at the end of the loop — which contrasts with the `while` loop and the `for` loop where the condition is checked at the beginning of the loop. Consequently, the `do-while` loop statement is *always* executed at least once. The general form of the `do-while` loop is:

```
do
{
    loop_statements;
}while(condition);
```

The logic of this form of loop is shown in Figure 3-6.

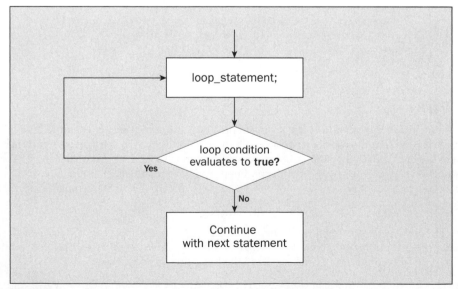

Figure 3-6

You could replace the `while` loop in the last version of the program to calculate an average with a `do-while` loop:

```
do
{
   cout << endl
        << "Enter a value: ";
   cin >> value;               // Read a value
   ++i;                        // Increment count
   sum += value;               // Add current input to total

   cout << "Do you want to enter another value (enter n to end)?";
   cin >> indicator;           // Read indicator
} while((indicator == 'y') || (indicator == 'Y'));
```

There's little to choose between the two versions of the loop, except that this version doesn't depend on the initial value set in `indicator` for correct operation. As long as you want to enter at least one value, which is not unreasonable for the calculation in question, this version of the loop is preferable.

Nested Loops

You can nest one loop inside another. In Chapter 4, the usual application of this will become more apparent — it's typically applied to repeating actions at different levels of classification. An example might be calculating the total marks for each student in a class and then repeating the process for each class in a school.

Try It Out   **Nested Loops**

You can see the effects of nesting one loop inside another by calculating the values of a simple formula. A factorial of an integer is the product of all the integers from 1 to the integer in question; so the factorial of 3, for example, is 1 times 2 times 3, which is 6. The following program computes the factorial of integers that you enter (until you've had enough):

```cpp
// Ex3_13.cpp
// Demonstrating nested loops to compute factorials
#include <iostream>

using std::cin;
using std::cout;
using std::endl;

int main()
{
   char indicator = 'n';
   long value = 0,
        factorial = 0;

   do
   {
      cout << endl
           << "Enter an integer value: ";
      cin >> value;
```

```
        factorial = 1;
        for(int i = 2; i <= value; i++)
            factorial *= i;

        cout << "Factorial " << value << " is " << factorial;
        cout << endl
            << "Do you want to enter another value (y or n)? ";
        cin >> indicator;
    } while((indicator == 'y') || (indicator == 'Y'));

    return 0;
}
```

If you compile and execute this example, the typical output produced is:

```
Enter an integer value: 5
Factorial 5 is 120
Do you want to enter another value (y or n)? y

Enter an integer value: 10
Factorial 10 is 3628800
Do you want to enter another value (y or n)? y

Enter an integer value: 13
Factorial 13 is 1932053504
Do you want to enter another value (y or n)? y

Enter an integer value: 22
Factorial 22 is -522715136
Do you want to enter another value (y or n)? n
```

How It Works

Factorial values grow very fast. In fact, 12 is the largest input value for which this example produces a correct result. The factorial of 13 is actually 6,227,020,800, not 1,932,053,504 as the program tells you. If you run it with even larger input values, leading digits are lost in the result stored in the variable `factorial`, and you may well get negative values for the factorial as you do when you ask for the factorial of 22.

This situation doesn't cause any error messages, so it is of paramount importance that you are sure that the values you're dealing with in a program can be contained in the permitted range of the type of variable you're using. You also need to consider the effects of incorrect input values. Errors of this kind, which occur silently, can be very hard to find.

The outer of the two nested loops is the `do-while` loop, which controls when the program ends. As long as you keep entering y or Y at the prompt, the program continues to calculate factorial values. The factorial for the integer entered is calculated in the inner `for` loop. This is executed `value` times to multiply the variable `factorial` (with an initial value of 1) with successive integers from 2 to `value`.

Try It Out   Another Nested Loop

Nested loops can be a little confusing, so let's try another example. This program generates a multiplication table of a given size.

```cpp
// Ex3_14.cpp
// Using nested loops to generate a multiplication table
#include <iostream>
#include <iomanip>

using std::cout;
using std::endl;
using std::setw;

int main()
{
   const int size = 12;                 // Size of table
   int i = 0, j = 0;                    // Loop counters

   cout << endl                         // Output table title
        << size << " by " << size
        << " Multiplication Table" << endl << endl;

   cout << endl << "    |";

   for(i = 1; i <= size; i++)           // Loop to output column headings
      cout << setw(3) << i << "  ";

   cout << endl;                        // Newline for underlines

   for(i = 0; i <= size; i++)
      cout << "_____";                  // Underline each heading

   for(i = 1; i <= size; i++)           // Outer loop for rows
   {
      cout << endl
           << setw(3) << i << " |";     // Output row label
      for(j = 1; j <= size; j++)            // Inner loop for the rest of the row
         cout << setw(3) << i*j << "  ";    // End of inner loop
   }                                    // End of outer loop
   cout << endl;

   return 0;
}
```

The output from this example is:

```
12 by 12 Multiplication Table

    |  1    2    3    4    5    6    7    8    9   10   11   12
 _____
  1 |  1    2    3    4    5    6    7    8    9   10   11   12
  2 |  2    4    6    8   10   12   14   16   18   20   22   24
  3 |  3    6    9   12   15   18   21   24   27   30   33   36
  4 |  4    8   12   16   20   24   28   32   36   40   44   48
  5 |  5   10   15   20   25   30   35   40   45   50   55   60
  6 |  6   12   18   24   30   36   42   48   54   60   66   72
  7 |  7   14   21   28   35   42   49   56   63   70   77   84
  8 |  8   16   24   32   40   48   56   64   72   80   88   96
  9 |  9   18   27   36   45   54   63   72   81   90   99  108
 10 | 10   20   30   40   50   60   70   80   90  100  110  120
 11 | 11   22   33   44   55   66   77   88   99  110  121  132
 12 | 12   24   36   48   60   72   84   96  108  120  132  144
```

How It Works

The table title is produced by the first output statement in the program. The next output statement, combined with the loop following it, generates the column headings. Each column is five characters wide, so the heading value is displayed in a field width of three specified by the setw(3) manipulator, followed by two blanks. The output statement preceding the loop outputs four spaces and a vertical bar above the first column which contains the row headings. A series of underline characters is then displayed beneath the column headings.

The nested loop generates the main table contents. The outer loop repeats once for each row, so i is the row number. The output statement

```
cout << endl
     << setw(3) << i << " |";    // Output row label
```

goes to a new line for the start of a row and then outputs the row heading given by the value of i in a field width of three, followed by a space and a vertical bar.

A row of values is generated by the inner loop:

```
for(j = 1; j <= size; j++)           // Inner loop for the rest of the row
   cout << setw(3) << i*j << "  ";    // End of inner loop
```

This loop outputs values i*j corresponding to the product of the current row value i, and each of the column values in turn by varying j from 1 to size. So for each iteration of the outer loop, the inner loop executes size iterations. The values are positioned in the same way as the column headings.

When the outer loop is completed, the return is executed to end the program.

___

C++/CLI Programming

Everything I have discussed in this chapter applies equally well in a C++/CLI program. Just to illustrate the point we can look at some examples of CLR console programs that demonstrate some of what you have learned so far in this chapter. The following is a CLR program that's a slight variation on Ex3_01.

Try It Out   **A CLR Program Using Nested if Statements**

Create a CLR console program with the default code and modify the `main()` function like this:

```
// Ex3_15.cpp : main project file.

#include "stdafx.h"

using namespace System;

int main(array<System::String ^> ^args)
{
  wchar_t letter;                        // Corresponds to the C++/CLI Char type
  Console::Write(L"Enter a letter: ");
  letter = Console::Read();

  if(letter >= 'A')                      // Test for 'A' or larger
    if(letter <= 'Z')                    // Test for 'Z' or smaller
    {
      Console::WriteLine(L"You entered a capital letter.");
      return 0;
    }

  if(letter >= 'a')                      // Test for 'a' or larger
    if(letter <= 'z')                    // Test for 'z' or smaller
    {
      Console::WriteLine(L"You entered a small letter.");
      return 0;
    }

  Console::WriteLine(L"You did not enter a letter.");
    return 0;
}
```

As always, the shaded lines are the new code you should add.

How It Works

The logic is exactly the same as in the Ex3_01 example — in fact all the statements are the same except for those producing the output and the declaration of `letter`. I changed the type to wchar_t because type System::Char has some extra facilities that I'll mention. The `Console::Read()` function reads a single character from the keyboard. Because you use the `Console::Write()` function to output the initial prompt there is no newline character issued so you can enter the letter on the same line as the prompt.

The .NET Framework provides its own functions for converting character codes to upper- or lowercase within the Char class. These are the functions `Char::ToUpper()` and `Char::ToLower()` and you put the character to be converted between the parentheses as the argument to the function. For example:

```
wchar_t uppcaseLetter = Char::ToUpper(letter);
```

Of course, you could store the result of the conversion back in the original variable, similar to the following:

```
letter = Char::ToUpper(letter);
```

The Char class also provides `IsUpper()` and `IsLower()` functions that test whether a letter is upper- or lowercase. You pass the letter to be tested as the argument to the function and the function returns a `bool` value as a result. You could use these to code the `main()` function quite differently.

```
wchar_t letter;                        // Corresponds to the C++/CLI Char type
Console::Write(L"Enter a letter: ");
letter = Console::Read();
wchar_t upper = Char::ToUpper(letter);
if(upper >= 'A' && upper <= 'Z')        // Test for between 'A' and 'Z'
  Console::WriteLine(L"You entered a {0} letter.",
                     Char::IsUpper(letter) ? "capital" : "small");
else
  Console::WriteLine(L"You did not enter a letter.");
return 0;
```

This simplifies the code considerably. After converting a letter to uppercase, you test the uppercase value to check whether it's `'A'` to `'Z'`. If it is, you output a message that depends on the result of the conditional operator expression that forms the second argument to the `WriteLine()` function. The conditional operator expression evaluates to `"capital"` if letter is uppercase and `"small"` if it is not, and this result is inserted in the output as determined by the position of the format string {0}.

Try another CLR example that uses the `Console::ReadKey()` function in a loop and explores the `ConsoleKeyInfo` class a little more.

Try It Out   **Reading Key Presses**

Create a CLR console program and add the following code to `main()`:

```
// Ex3_16.cpp : main project file.
// Testing key presses in a loop.

#include "stdafx.h"
using namespace System;

int main(array<System::String ^> ^args)
{
   Console::WriteLine(L"Press a key combination - press Escape to quit.");
```

```
    ConsoleKeyInfo keyPress;

    do
    {
      keyPress = Console::ReadKey(true);
      Console::Write(L"You pressed");
      if(safe_cast<int>(keyPress.Modifiers)>0)
        Console::Write(L" {0},", keyPress.Modifiers);
      Console::WriteLine(L" {0} which is the {1} character",
                                      keyPress.Key, keyPress.KeyChar);

    }while(keyPress.Key != ConsoleKey::Escape);
    return 0;
}
```

The following is some sample output from this program:

```
Press a key combination - press Escape to quit.
You pressed Shift, B which is the B character
You pressed Shift, Control, N which is the ? character
You pressed Shift, Control, Oem1 which is the   character
You pressed Oem1 which is the ; character
You pressed Oem3 which is the ' character
You pressed Shift, Oem3 which is the @ character
You pressed Shift, Oem7 which is the ~ character
You pressed Shift, Oem6 which is the } character
You pressed D3 which is the 3 character
You pressed Shift, D3 which is the ? character
You pressed Shift, D5 which is the % character
You pressed Oem8 which is the ` character
You pressed Escape which is the ? character
```

Of course, there are key combinations that do not represent a displayable character so in these cases there is no character in the output. The program also ends if you press Ctrl+C because the operating system recognizes this as the command to end the program.

How It Works

Key presses are tested in the do-while loop and this loop continues until the Escape key is pressed. Within the loop the Console::ReadKey() function is called and the result is stored in the variable keyPress, which is of type ConsoleKeyInfo. The ConsoleKeyInfo class has three properties that you can access to help identify the key or keys that were pressed — the Key property identifies the key that was pressed, the KeyChar property represents the Unicode character code for the key, and the Modifiers property is a bitwise combination of ConsoleModifiers constants that represent the Shift, Alt, and Ctrl keys. ConsoleModifiers is an enumeration that is defined in the System library and the constants defined in the enumeration have the names Alt, Shift, and Control.

As you can see from the arguments to the WriteLine() function in the last output statement, to access a property for an object you place the property name following the object name, separated by a period; the period is referred to as the **member access** operator. To access the KeyChar property for the object keyPress, you write keyPress.KeyChar.

The operation of the program is very simple. Within the loop you call the `ReadKey()` function to read a key press and the result is stored in the variable `keyPress`. Next you write the initial part of the output to the command line using the `Write()` function; because no newline is written in this case, the next output statement writes to the same line. You then test whether the `Modifiers` property is greater than zero. If it is, modifier keys were pressed and you output them; otherwise, you skip the output for modifier keys. You will probably remember that a C++/CLI enumeration constant is an object that you must explicitly cast to an integer type before you can use it as a numerical value — hence the cast to type `int` in the `if` expression.

The output of the `Modifiers` value is interesting. As you can see from the output, when more than one modifier key was pressed, you get all the modifier keys from the single output statement. This is because the `Modifiers` enumeration is defined with bit flags. As you saw in Chapter 2, this allows a variable of the enumeration type to consist of several flags ORed together, and the individual flags recognized and output by the `Write()` or `WriteLine()` functions.

The loop continues as long as the condition `keyPress.Key != ConsoleKey::Escape` is true. It is `false` when the `keyPress.Key` property is equal to `ConsoleKey::Escape`, which is when the Escape key is pressed.

The for each Loop

All the loop statements I have discussed apply equally well to C++/CLI programs and the C++/CLI language provides you with the luxury of an additional kind of loop called the `for each` loop. This loop is specifically for iterating through all the objects in a particular kind of set of objects and because you haven't learned about these yet, I'll just introduce the `for each` loop briefly here, and elaborate on it some more a bit later in the book.

One thing that you do know a little about is a `String` object which represents a set of characters, so you can use a `for each` loop to iterate through all the characters in a string. Let's try an example of that.

Try It Out   Using a for each Loop to Access the Characters in a String

Create a new CLR console program project with the name Ex3_17 and modify the code to the following:

```
// Ex3_17.cpp : main project file.
// Analyzing a string using a for each loop

#include "stdafx.h"
using namespace System;


int main(array<System::String ^> ^args)
{
    int vowels = 0;
    int consonants = 0;
    String^ proverb = L"A nod is as good as a wink to a blind horse.";
```

```
      for each(wchar_t ch in proverb)
      {
        if(Char::IsLetter(ch))
        {
          ch = Char::ToLower(ch);        // Convert to lowercase
          switch(ch)
          {
          case 'a': case 'e': case 'i':
          case 'o': case 'u':
            ++vowels;
            break;
          default:
            ++consonants;
            break;
          }
        }
      }

    Console::WriteLine(proverb);
    Console::WriteLine(L"The proverb contains {0} vowels and {1} consonants.",
                                                  vowels, consonants);

    return 0;
}
```

This example produces the following output:

```
A nod is as good as a wink to a blind horse.
The proverb contains 14 vowels and 18 consonants.
```

How It Works

The program counts the number of vowels and consonants in the string referenced by the `proverb` variable. The program does this by iterating over each character in the string using a `for each` loop. You first define two variables used to accumulate the total number of vowels and the total number of consonants.

```
int vowels = 0;
int consonants = 0;
```

Under the covers, both are of the C++/CLI `Int32` type, which stores a 32-bit integer.

Next you define the string to analyze.

```
String^ proverb = L"A nod is as good as a wink to a blind horse.";
```

The `proverb` variable is of type `String^` that is described as type "handle to `String`"; a handle is used to store the location of an object on the garbage-collected heap that is managed by the CLR. You'll learn more about handles and type `String^` when we get into C++/CLI class types; for now, just take it that this is the type you use for C++/CLI variables that store strings.

The for each loop that iterates over the characters in the string referenced by proverb is of this form:

```
for each(wchar_t ch in proverb)
{
  // Process the current character stored in ch…
}
```

The characters in the proverb string are Unicode characters so you use a variable of type wchar_t (equivalent to type Char) to store them. The loop successively stores characters from the proverb string in the loop variable ch, which is of the C++/CLI type Char. This variable is local to the loop — in other words, it exists only within the loop block. On the first iteration ch contains the first character from the string, on the second iteration it contains the second character, on the third iteration the third character, and so on until all the characters have been processed and the loop ends.

Within the loop you determine whether the character is a letter in the if expression:

```
if(Char::IsLetter(ch))
```

The Char::IsLetter() function returns the value true if the argument — ch in this case — is a letter, and false otherwise. Thus the block following the if only executes if ch contains a letter. This is necessary because you don't want punctuation characters to be processed as though they were letters.

Having established that ch is indeed a letter you convert it to lowercase with the following statement:

```
ch = Char::ToLower(ch);      // Convert to lowercase
```

This uses the Char::ToLower() function from the .NET Framework library, which returns the lowercase equivalent of the argument — ch in this case. If the argument is already lowercase, the function just returns the same character code. By converting the character to lowercase, you avoid having to test subsequently for both upper- and lowercase vowels.

You determine whether ch contains a vowel or a consonant within the switch statement.

```
switch(ch)
{
case 'a': case 'e': case 'i':
case 'o': case 'u':
  ++vowels;
  break;
default:
  ++consonants;
  break;
}
```

For any of the five cases where ch is a vowel, you increment the value stored in vowels; otherwise, you increment the value stored in consonants. This switch is executed for each character in proverb so when the loop finishes, vowels contain the number of vowels in the string and consonants contain the number of consonants. You then output the result with the following statements:

```
Console::WriteLine(proverb);
Console::WriteLine(L"The proverb contains {0} vowels and {1} consonants.",
                                                     vowels, consonants);
```

In the last statement, the value of vowels replaces the "{0}" in the string and the value of consonants replaces the "{1}". This is because the arguments that follow the first format string argument are referenced by index values starting from 0.

Summary

In this chapter, you learned all of the essential mechanisms for making decisions in C++ programs. You have also gone through all the facilities for repeating a group of statements. The essentials of what I've discussed are as follows:

❑ The basic decision-making capability is based on the set of relational operators, which allow expressions to be tested and compared, and yield a `bool` value as the result — `true` or `false`.

❑ You can also make decisions based on conditions that return non-`bool` values. Any non-zero value is cast to `true` when a condition is tested; zero casts to `false`.

❑ The primary decision-making capability in C++ is provided by the `if` statement. Further flexibility is provided by the `switch` statement, and by the conditional operator.

❑ There are three basic methods provided in ISO/ANSI C++ for repeating a block of statements: the `for` loop, the `while` loop and the `do-while` loop. The `for` loop allows the loop to repeat a given number of times. The `while` loop allows a loop to continue as long as a specified condition returns `true`. Finally, `do-while` executes the loop at least once and allows continuation of the loop as long as a specified condition returns `true`.

❑ C++/CLI has the `for each` loop statement in addition to the three loop statements defined in ISO/ANSI C++.

❑ Any kind of loop may be nested within any other kind of loop.

❑ The keyword `continue` allows you to skip the remainder of the current iteration in a loop and go straight to the next iteration.

❑ The keyword `break` provides an immediate exit from a loop. It also provides an exit from a `switch` at the end of the statements for a `case`.

Exercises

You can download the source code for the examples in the book and the solutions to the following exercises from http://www.wrox.com.

1. Write a program that reads numbers from `cin` and then sums them, stopping when 0 has been entered. Construct three versions of this program, using the `while`, `do-while`, and `for` loops.

2. Write an ISO/ANSI C++ program to read characters from the keyboard and count the vowels. Stop counting when a Q (or a q) is encountered. Use a combination of an indefinite loop to get the characters, and a `switch` statement to count them.

3. Write a program to print out the multiplication tables from 2 to 12 in columns.

4. Imagine that in a program you want to set a 'file open mode' variable based on two attributes: the file type, which can be text or binary, and the way in which you want to open the file to read or write it or append data to it. Using the bitwise operators (& and |) and a set of flags, devise a method to allow a single integer variable to be set to any combination of the two attributes. Write a program that sets such a variable and then decodes it, printing out its setting, for all possible combinations of the attributes.

5. Repeat Ex3_2 as a C++/CLI program — you can use Console::ReadKey() to read characters from the keyboard.

6. Write a CLR console program that defines a string (as type String^) and then analyzes the characters in the string to discover the number of uppercase letters, the number of lowercase letters, the number of non-alphabetic characters, and the total number of characters in the string.

Arrays, Strings, and Pointers

So far, you have covered all the fundamental data types of consequence and you have a basic knowledge of how to perform calculations and make decisions in a program. This chapter is about broadening the application of the basic programming techniques that you have learned so far, from using single items of data to working with whole collections of data items. In this chapter, you will learn about:

❑   Arrays and how you use them

❑   How to declare and initialize arrays of different types

❑   How to declare and use multidimensional arrays

❑   Pointers and how you use them

❑   How to declare and initialize pointers of different types

❑   The relationship between arrays and pointers

❑   References, how they are declared, and some initial ideas on their uses

❑   How to allocate memory for variables dynamically in a native C++ program

❑   How dynamic memory allocation works in a Common Language Runtime (CLR) program

❑   Tracking handles and tracking references and why you need them in a CLR program

❑   How to work with strings and arrays in C++/CLI programs

❑   What interior pointers are and how you can create and use them

In this chapter you'll be using objects more extensively although you have not yet explored the details of how they are created so don't worry if everything is not completely clear. You'll learn about classes and objects in detail starting in Chapter 7.

Handling Multiple Data Values of the Same Type

You already know how to declare and initialize variables of various types that each holds a single item of information; I'll refer to single items of data as **data elements**. You know how to create a single character in a variable of type char or type wchar_t, a single integer in a variable of type short, type int, type long, or a single floating point number in a variable of type float or of type double. The most obvious extension to these ideas is to be able to reference several data elements of a particular type with a single variable name. This would enable you to handle applications of a much broader scope.

Here's an example of where you might need this. Suppose that you needed to write a payroll program. Using a separately named variable for each individual's pay, their tax liability, and so on, would be an uphill task to say the least. A much more convenient way to handle such a problem would be to reference an employee by some kind of generic name — employeeName to take an imaginative example — and to have other generic names for the kinds of data related to each employee, such as pay, tax, and so on. Of course, you would also need some means of picking out a particular employee from the whole bunch, together with the data from the generic variables associated with them. This kind of requirement arises with any collection of like entities that you want to handle in your program, whether they're baseball players or battleships. Naturally, C++ provides you with a way to deal with this.

Arrays

The basis for the solution to all of these problems is provided by the **array** in ISO/ANSI C++. An array is simply a number of memory locations called **array elements** or simply **elements**, each of which can store an item of data of the same given data type and which are all referenced through the same variable name. The employee names in a payroll program could be stored in one array, the pay for each employee in another, and the tax due for each employee could be stored in a third array.

Individual items in an array are specified by an index value which is simply an integer representing the sequence number of the elements in the array, the first having the sequence number 0, the second 1, and so on. You can also envisage the index value of an array element as being an offset from the first element in an array. The first element has an offset of 0 and therefore an index of 0, and an index value of 3 will refer to the fourth element of an array. For the payroll, you could arrange the arrays so that if an employee's name was stored in the employeeName array at a given index value, then the arrays pay and tax would store the associated data on pay and tax for the same employee in the array positions referenced by the same index value.

The basic structure of an array is illustrated in Figure 4-1.

Figure 4-1 shows an array. The name height has six elements, each storing a different value. These might be the heights of the members of a family, for instance, recorded to the nearest inch. Because there are six elements, the index values run from 0 through 5. To refer to a particular element, you write the array name, followed by the index value of the particular element between square brackets. The third element is referred to as height[2], for example. If you think of the index as being the offset from the first element, it's easy to see that the index value for the fourth element will be 3, for example.

The amount of memory required to store each element is determined by its type, and all the elements of an array are stored in a contiguous block of memory.

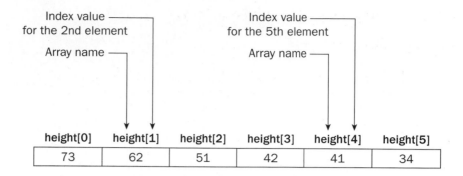

The **height** array has 6 elements.

Figure 4-1

Declaring Arrays

You declare an array in essentially the same way as you declared the variables that you have seen up to now, the only difference being that the number of elements in the array is specified between square brackets immediately following the array name. For example, you could declare the integer array `height`, shown in the previous figure, with the following declaration statement:

```
long height[6];
```

Because each `long` value occupies 4 bytes in memory, the whole array requires 24 bytes. Arrays can be of any size, subject to the constraints imposed by the amount of memory in the computer on which your program is running.

You can declare arrays to be of any type. For example, to declare arrays intended to store the capacity and power output of a series of engines, you could write the following:

```
double cubic_inches[10];      // Engine size
double horsepower[10];        // Engine power output
```

If auto mechanics are your thing, this would enable you to store the cubic capacity and power output of up to 10 engines, referenced by index values from 0 to 9. As you have seen before with other variables, you can declare multiple arrays of a given type in a single statement, but in practice it is almost always better to declare variables in separate statements.

Try It Out   Using Arrays

As a basis for an exercise in using arrays, imagine that you have kept a record of both the amount of gasoline you have bought for the car and the odometer reading on each occasion. You can write a program to analyze this data to see how the gas consumption looks on each occasion that you bought gas:

```
// Ex4_01.cpp
// Calculating gas mileage
#include <iostream>
```

```
#include <iomanip>

using std::cin;
using std::cout;
using std::endl;
using std::setw;

int main()
{
    const int MAX = 20;                     // Maximum number of values
    double gas[ MAX ];                      // Gas quantity in gallons
    long miles[ MAX ];                      // Odometer readings
    int count = 0;                          // Loop counter
    char indicator = 'y';                   // Input indicator

    while( (indicator == 'y' || indicator == 'Y') && count < MAX )
    {
        cout << endl
            << "Enter gas quantity: ";
        cin >> gas[count];                  // Read gas quantity
        cout << "Enter odometer reading: ";
        cin >> miles[count];                // Read odometer value

        ++count;
        cout << "Do you want to enter another(y or n)? ";
        cin >> indicator;
    }

    if(count <= 1)                          // count = 1 after 1 entry completed
    {                                       // ... we need at least 2
        cout << endl
            << "Sorry - at least two readings are necessary.";
        return 0;
    }

    // Output results from 2nd entry to last entry
    for(int i = 1; i < count; i++)
    cout << endl
        << setw(2) << i << "."              // Output sequence number
        << "Gas purchased = " << gas[i] << " gallons" // Output gas
        << " resulted in "                  // Output miles per gallon
        << (miles[i] - miles[i - 1])/gas[i] << " miles per gallon.";

    cout << endl;
    return 0;
}
```

The program assumes that you fill the tank each time so the gas bought was the amount consumed by driving the distance recorded. Here's an example of the output produced by this example:

```
Enter gas quantity: 12.8
Enter odometer reading: 25832
Do you want to enter another(y or n)? y
```

```
Enter gas quantity: 14.9
Enter odometer reading: 26337
Do you want to enter another(y or n)? y

Enter gas quantity: 11.8
Enter odometer reading: 26598
Do you want to enter another(y or n)? n

 1.Gas purchased = 14.9 gallons resulted in 33.8926 miles per gallon.
 2.Gas purchased = 11.8 gallons resulted in 22.1186 miles per gallon.
```

How It Works

Because you need to take the difference between two odometer readings to calculate the miles covered for the gas used, you use the odometer reading only from the first pair of input values — you ignore the gas bought in the first instance as that would have been consumed during miles driven earlier.

During the second period shown in the output, the traffic must have been really bad — or maybe the parking brake was always on.

The dimensions of the two arrays gas and miles used to store the input data are determined by the value of the constant with the name MAX. By changing the value of MAX, you can change the program to accommodate a different maximum number of input values. This technique is commonly used to make a program flexible in the amount of information that it can handle. Of course, all the program code must be written to take account of the array dimensions, or of any other parameters being specified by const variables. This presents little difficulty in practice, however, so there's no reason why you should not adopt this approach. You'll also see later how to allocate memory for storing data as the program executes, so that you don't need to fix the amount of memory allocated for data storage in advance.

Entering the Data

The data values are read in the while loop. Because the loop variable count can run from 0 to MAX - 1, we haven't allowed the user of our program to enter more values than the array can handle. You initialize the variables count and indicator to 0 and 'y' respectively, so that the while loop is entered at least once. There's a prompt for each input value required and the value is read into the appropriate array element. The element used to store a particular value is determined by the variable count, which is 0 for the first input. The array element is specified in the cin statement by using count as an index, and count is then incremented ready for the next value.

After you enter each value, the program prompts for confirmation that another value is to be entered. The character entered is read into the variable indicator and then tested in the loop condition. The loop will terminate unless 'y' or 'Y' is entered and the variable count is less than the specified maximum value, MAX.

After the input loop ends (by whatever means), the value of count contains one more than the index value of the last element entered in each array. (Remember, you increment it after you enter each new element). This is checked in order to verify that at least two pairs of values were entered. If this wasn't the case, the program ends with a suitable message because two odometer values are necessary to calculate a mileage value.

Producing the Results

The output is generated in the `for` loop. The control variable i runs from 1 to count-1, allowing mileage to be calculated as the difference between the current element, `miles[i]` and the previous element, `miles[i - 1]`. Note that an index value can be any expression evaluating to an integer that represents a legal index for the array in question, which is an index value from 0 to one less than the number of elements in the array.

If the value of an index expression lies outside of the range corresponding to legitimate array elements, you will reference a spurious data location that may contain other data, garbage, or even program code. If the reference to such an element appears in an expression, you will use some arbitrary data value in the calculation, which certainly produces a result that you did not intend. If you are storing a result in an array element using an illegal index value, you will overwrite whatever happens to be in that location. When this is part of your program code, the results are catastrophic. If you use illegal index values, there are no warnings produced either by the compiler or at runtime. The only way to guard against this is to code your program to prevent it happening.

The output is generated by a single `cout` statement for all values entered, except for the first. A line number is also generated for each line of output using the loop control variable i. The miles per gallon are calculated directly in the output statement. You can use array elements in exactly the same way as any other variables in an expression.

Initializing Arrays

To initialize an array in its declaration, you put the initializing values separated by commas between braces, and you place the set of initial values following an equals sign after the array name. Here's an example of how you can declare and initialize an array:

```
int cubic_inches[5] = { 200, 250, 300, 350, 400 };
```

The array has the name `cubic_inches` and has five elements that each store a value of type int. The values in the initializing list between the braces correspond to successive index values of the array, so in this case `cubic_inches[0]` has the value 200, `cubic_inches[1]` the value 250, `cubic_inches[2]` the value 300, and so on.

You must not specify more initializing values than there are elements in the array, but you can include fewer. If there *are* fewer, the values are assigned to successive elements, starting with the first element — which is the one corresponding to the index value 0. The array elements for which you didn't provide an initial value are initialized with zero. This isn't the same as supplying no initializing list. Without an initializing list, the array elements contain junk values. Also, if you include an initializing list, there must be at least one initializing value in it; otherwise the compiler generates an error message. I can illustrate this with the following rather limited example.

Try It Out Initializing an Array

```
// Ex4_02.cpp
// Demonstrating array initialization
#include <iostream>
#include <iomanip>
```

```
using std::cout;
using std::endl;
using std::setw;

int main()
{
   int value[5] = { 1, 2, 3 };
   int junk [5];

   cout << endl;
   for(int i = 0; i < 5; i++)
      cout << setw(12) << value[i];

   cout << endl;
   for(int i = 0; i < 5; i++)
      cout << setw(12) << junk[i];

   cout << endl;
   return 0;
}
```

In this example, you declare two arrays, the first of which, value, you initialize in part, and the second, junk, you don't initialize at all. The program generates two lines of output, which on my computer look like this:

```
           1           2           3           0           0
 -858993460  -858993460  -858993460  -858993460  -858993460
```

The second line (corresponding to values of junk[0] to junk[4]) may well be different on your computer.

How It Works

The first three values of the array value are the initializing values and the last two have the default value of 0. In the case of junk, all the values are spurious because you didn't provide any initial values at all. The array elements contain whatever values were left there by the program that last used these memory locations.

A convenient way to initialize a whole array to zero is simply to specify a single initializing value as 0. For example:

```
long data[100] = {0};        // Initialize all elements to zero
```

This statement declares the array data, with all one hundred elements initialized with 0. The first element is initialized by the value you have between the braces and the remaining elements are initialized to zero because you omitted values for these.

You can also omit the dimension of an array of numeric type, providing you supply initializing values. The number of elements in the array is determined by the number of initializing values you specify. For example, the array declaration

```
int value[] = { 2, 3, 4 };
```

defines an array with three elements that have the initial values 2, 3, and 4.

Character Arrays and String Handling

An array of type char is called a **character array** and is generally used to store a character string. A character string is a sequence of characters with a special character appended to indicate the end of the string. The string terminating character indicates the end of the string and this character is defined by the escape sequence '\0', and is sometimes referred to as a **null character**, being a byte with all bits as zero. A string of this form is often referred to as a C-style string because defining a string in this way was introduced in the C language from which C++ was developed by Bjarne Stroustrup (you can find his home page at www.research.att.com/~bs/). This is not the only representation of a string that you can use — you'll meet others later in the book. In particular, C++/CLI programs use a different representation of a string and the MFC defines a CString class to represent strings.

The representation of a C-style string in memory is shown in Figure 4-2.

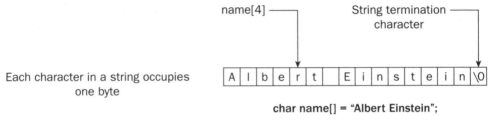

Figure 4-2

Figure 4-2 illustrates how a string looks in memory and shows a form of declaration for a string that I'll get to in a moment.

> *Each character in the string occupies one byte, so together with the terminating null character, a string requires a number of bytes that is one greater than the number of characters contained in the string.*

You can declare a character array and initialize it with a string literal. For example:

```
char movie_star[15] = "Marilyn Monroe";
```

Note that the terminating '\0' is supplied automatically by the compiler. If you include one explicitly in the string literal, you end up with two of them. You must, however, allow for the terminating null in the number of elements that you allot to the array.

You can let the compiler work out the length of an initialized array for you, as you saw in Figure 4-1. Here's another example:

```
char president[] = "Ulysses Grant";
```

Because the dimension is unspecified, the compiler allocates space for enough elements to hold the initializing string, plus the terminating null character. In this case it allocates 14 elements for the array president. Of course, if you want to use this array later for storing a different string, its length (including the terminating null character) must not exceed 14 bytes. In general, it is your responsibility to ensure that the array is large enough for any string you might subsequently want to store.

You can also create strings that comprise Unicode characters, the characters in the string being of type wchar_t. Here's a statement that creates a Unicode string:

```
wchar_t president[] = L"Ulysses Grant";
```

The L prefix indicates that the string literal is a wide character string, so each character in the string, including the terminating null character, will occupy two bytes. Of course, indexing the string references characters, not bytes, so president[2] corresponds to the character L'y'.

String Input

The <iostream> header file contains definitions of a number of functions for reading characters from the keyboard. The one that you'll look at here is the function getline(), which reads a sequence of characters entered through the keyboard and stores it in a character array as a string terminated by \0. You typically use the getline() function statements like this:

```
const int MAX = 80;          // Maximum string length including \0
char name[MAX];              // Array to store a string
cin.getline(name, MAX, '\n'); // Read input line as a string
```

These statements first declare a char array name with MAX elements and then read characters from cin using the function getline(). The source of the data, cin, is written as shown, with a period separating it from the function name. The period indicates that the getline() function you are calling is the one belonging to the cin object. The significance of the arguments to the getline() function is shown in Figure 4-3.

Because the last argument to the getline() function is '\n' (newline or end line character) and the second argument is MAX, characters are read from cin until the '\n' character is read, or when MAX - 1 characters have been read, whichever occurs first. The maximum number of characters read is MAX - 1 rather than MAX to allow for the '\0' character to be appended to the sequence of characters stored in the array. The '\n' character is generated when you press the *Return* key on your keyboard and is therefore usually the most convenient character to end input. You can, however, specify something else by changing the last argument. The '\n' isn't stored in the input array name, but as I said, a '\0' is added at the end of the input string in the array.

You will learn more about this form of syntax when classes are discussed later on. Meanwhile, you'll just take it for granted and use it in an example.

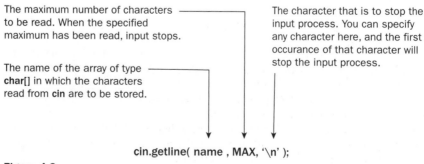

The maximum number of characters to be read. When the specified maximum has been read, input stops.

The character that is to stop the input process. You can specify any character here, and the first occurance of that character will stop the input process.

The name of the array of type **char[]** in which the characters read from **cin** are to be stored.

cin.getline(name , MAX, '\n');

Figure 4-3

Programming with Strings

You now have enough knowledge to write a simple program to read a string and then count how many characters it contains.

```cpp
// Ex4_03.cpp
// Counting string characters
#include <iostream>
using std::cin;
using std::cout;
using std::endl;

int main()
{
   const int MAX = 80;                  // Maximum array dimension
   char buffer[MAX];                    // Input buffer
   int count = 0;                       // Character count

   cout << "Enter a string of less than 80 characters:\n";
   cin.getline(buffer, MAX, '\n');      // Read a string until \n

   while(buffer[count] != '\0')         // Increment count as long as
      count++;                          // the current character is not null

   cout << endl
        << "The string \"" << buffer
        << "\" has " << count << " characters.";
   cout << endl;
   return 0;
}
```

Typical output from this program is as follows:

```
Enter a string of less than 80 characters:
Radiation fades your genes
The string "Radiation fades your genes" has 26 characters.
```

How It Works

This program declares a character array `buffer` and reads a character string into the array from the keyboard after displaying a prompt for the input. Reading from the keyboard ends when the user presses *Return*, or when `MAX-1` characters have been read.

A `while` loop is used to count the number of characters read. The loop continues as long as the current character referenced with `buffer[count]` is not `'\0'`. This sort of checking on the current character while stepping through an array is a common technique in native C++. The only action in the loop is to increment `count` for each non-null character.

There is a library function, `strlen()` that will do what this loop does and you'll learn about it later in this chapter.

Finally in the example, the string and the character count is displayed with a single output statement. Note the use of the escape character ' \ " ' to output a double quote.

Multidimensional Arrays

The arrays that you have defined so far with one index are referred to as **one-dimensional** arrays. An array can also have more than one index value, in which case it is called a **multidimensional** array. Suppose you have a field in which you are growing bean plants in rows of 10, and the field contains 12 such rows (so there are 120 plants in all). You could declare an array to record the weight of beans produced by each plant using the following statement:

```
double beans[12][10];
```

This declares the two-dimensional array `beans`, the first index being the row number, and the second index the number within the row. To refer to any particular element requires two indices. For example, you could set the value of the element reflecting the fifth plant in the third row with the following statement:

```
beans[2][4] = 10.7;
```

Remember that the index values start from zero, so the row index value is 2 and the index for the fifth plant within the row is 4.

Being a successful bean farmer, you might have several identical fields planted with beans in the same pattern. Assuming that you have eight fields, you could use a three-dimensional array to record data about these, declared thus:

```
double beans[8][12][10];
```

This records production for all of the plants in each of the fields, the leftmost index referencing a particular field. If you ever get to bean farming on an international scale, you are able to use a four-dimensional array, with the extra dimension designating the country. Assuming that you're as good a salesman as you are a farmer, growing this quantity of beans to keep up with the demand may well start to affect the ozone layer.

Arrays are stored in memory such that the rightmost index value varies most rapidly. Thus the array `data[3][4]` is three one-dimensional arrays of four elements each. The arrangement of this array is illustrated in Figure 4-4.

The elements of the array are stored in a contiguous block of memory, as indicated by the arrows in Figure 4-4. The first index selects a particular row within the array and the second index selects an element within the row.

Note that a two-dimensional array in native C++ is really a one-dimensional array of one-dimensional arrays. A native C++ array with three dimensions is actually a one-dimensional array of elements where each element is a one-dimensional array of one-dimensional arrays. This is not something you need to worry about most of the time, but as you will see later, C++/CLI arrays are not the same as this. It also implies that for the array in Figure 4-4 the expressions data[0], data[1], and data[2], represent one-dimensional arrays.

The array elements are stored in contiguous locations in memory.

Figure 4-4

Initializing Multidimensional Arrays

To initialize a multidimensional array, you use an extension of the method used for a one-dimensional array. For example, you can initialize a two-dimensional array, data, with the following declaration:

```
long data[2][4] = {
                    { 1,  2,  3,  5 },
                    { 7, 11, 13, 17 }
                  };
```

Thus, the initializing values for each row of the array are contained within their own pair of braces. Because there are four elements in each row, there are four initializing values in each group, and because there are two rows, there are two groups between braces, each group of initializing values being separated from the next by a comma.

You can omit initializing values in any row, in which case the remaining array elements in the row are zero. For example:

```
long data[2][4] = {
                    { 1,  2,  3      },
                    { 7, 11          }
                  };
```

I have spaced out the initializing values to show where values have been omitted. The elements data[0][3], data[1][2], and data[1][3] have no initializing values and are therefore zero.

If you wanted to initialize the whole array with zeros you could simply write:

```
long data[2][4] = {0};
```

If you are initializing arrays with even more dimensions, remember that you need as many nested braces for groups of initializing values as there are dimensions in the array.

Try It Out   ## Storing Multiple Strings

You can use a single two-dimensional array to store several C-style strings. You can see how this works with an example:

```
// Ex4_04.cpp
// Storing strings in an array.
#include <iostream>
using std::cout;
using std::cin;
using std::endl;

int main()
{
   char stars[6][80] = { "Robert Redford",
                         "Hopalong Cassidy",
                         "Lassie",
                         "Slim Pickens",
                         "Boris Karloff",
                         "Oliver Hardy"
                        };
   int dice = 0;

   cout << endl
        << " Pick a lucky star!"
        << " Enter a number between 1 and 6: ";
   cin >> dice;

   if(dice >= 1 && dice <= 6)                    // Check input validity
      cout << endl                               // Output star name
           << "Your lucky star is " << stars[dice - 1];
   else
      cout << endl                               // Invalid input
           << "Sorry, you haven't got a lucky star.";

   cout << endl;
   return 0;
}
```

How It Works

Apart from its incredible inherent entertainment value, the main point of interest in this example is the declaration of the array `stars`. It is a two-dimensional array of elements of type `char` that can hold up to six strings, each of which can be up to 80 characters long (including the terminating null character that is automatically added by the compiler). The initializing strings for the array are enclosed between braces and separated by commas.

One disadvantage of using arrays in this way is the memory that is almost invariably left unused. All of the strings are fewer than 80 characters and the surplus elements in each row of the array are wasted.

You can also let the compiler work out how many strings you have by omitting the first array dimension and declaring it as follows:

```
char stars[][80] = { "Robert Redford",
                     "Hopalong Cassidy",
                     "Lassie",
                     "Slim Pickens",
                     "Boris Karloff",
                     "Oliver Hardy"
                   };
```

This causes the compiler to define the first dimension to accommodate the number of initializing strings that you have specified. Because you have six, the result is exactly the same, but it avoids the possibility of an error. Here you can't omit both array dimensions. With an array of two or more dimensions the rightmost dimension must always be defined.

Note the semicolon at the end of the declaration. It's easy to forget it when there are initializing values for an array.

Where you need to reference a string for output in the following statement, you need only specify the first index value:

```
cout << endl                             // Output star name
     << "Your lucky star is " << stars[dice - 1];
```

A single index value selects a particular 80-element sub-array, and the output operation displays the contents up to the terminating null character. The index is specified as `dice - 1` as the `dice` values are from 1 to 6, whereas the index values clearly need to be from 0 to 5.

Indirect Data Access

The variables that you have dealt with so far provide you with the ability to name a memory location in which you can store data of a particular type. The contents of a variable are either entered from an external source, such as the keyboard, or calculated from other values that are entered. There is another kind of variable in C++ that does not store data that you normally enter or calculate, but greatly extends the power and flexibility of your programs. This kind of variable is called a **pointer**.

What Is a Pointer?

Each memory location that you use to store a data value has an address. The address provides the means for your PC hardware to reference a particular data item. A pointer is a variable that stores an address of another variable of a particular type. A pointer has a variable name just like any other variable and also has a type that designates what kind of variables its contents refer to. Note that the type of a pointer variable includes the fact that it's a pointer. A variable that is a pointer that can contain addresses of locations in memory containing values of type `int`, is of type 'pointer to `int`'.

Declaring Pointers

The declaration for a pointer is similar to that of an ordinary variable, except that the pointer name has an asterisk in front of it to indicate that it's a variable that is a pointer. For example, to declare a pointer pnumber of type long, you could use the following statement:

```
long* pnumber;
```

This declaration has been written with the asterisk close to the type name. If you want, you can also write it as:

```
long *pnumber;
```

The compiler won't mind at all; however, the type of the variable pnumber is 'pointer to long', which is often indicated by placing the asterisk close to the type name. Whichever way you choose to write a pointer type, be consistent.

You can mix declarations of ordinary variables and pointers in the same statement. For example:

```
long* pnumber, number = 99;
```

This declares the pointer pnumber of type 'pointer to long' as before, and also declares the variable number, of type long. On balance, it's probably better to declare pointers separately from other variables; otherwise, the statement can appear misleading as to the type of the variables declared, particularly if you prefer to place the * adjacent to the type name. The following statements certainly look clearer and putting declarations on separate lines enables you to add comments for them individually, making for a program that is easier to read.

```
long number = 99;      // Declaration and initialization of long variable
long* pnumber;         // Declaration of variable of type pointer to long
```

It's a common convention in C++ to use variable names beginning with p to denote pointers. This makes it easier to see which variables in a program are pointers, which in turn can make a program easier to follow.

Let's take an example to see how this works, without worrying about what it's for. I will get to how you use pointers very shortly. Suppose you have the long integer variable number because you declared it above containing the value 99. You also have the pointer, pnumber, of type pointer to long, which you could use to store the address of the variable number. But how do you obtain the address of a variable?

The Address-Of Operator

What you need is the **address-of operator**, &. This is a unary operator that obtains the address of a variable. It's also called the reference operator, for reasons I will discuss later in this chapter. To set up the pointer that I have just discussed, you could write this assignment statement:

```
pnumber = &number;            // Store address of number in pnumber
```

The result of this operation is illustrated in Figure 4-5.

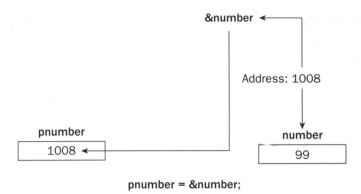

pnumber = &number;

Figure 4-5

You can use the operator & to obtain the address of any variable, but you need a pointer of the appropriate type to store it. If you want to store the address of a double variable for example, the pointer must have been declared as type double*, which is type 'pointer to double'.

Using Pointers

Taking the address of a variable and storing it in a pointer is all very well, but the really interesting aspect is how you can use it. Fundamental to using a pointer is accessing the data value in the variable to which a pointer points. This is done using the **indirection operator**, *.

The Indirection Operator

You use the **indirection operator**, *, with a pointer to access the contents of the variable that it points to. The name 'indirection operator' stems from the fact that the data is accessed indirectly. It is also called the dereference operator, and the process of accessing the data in the variable pointed to by a pointer is termed **de-referencing** the pointer.

One aspect of this operator that can seem confusing is the fact that you now have several different uses for the same symbol, *. It is the multiply operator, it also serves as the indirection operator, and it is used in the declaration of a pointer. Each time you use *, the compiler is able to distinguish its meaning by the context. When you multiply two variables, A*B for instance, there's no meaningful interpretation of this expression for anything other than a multiply operation.

Why Use Pointers?

A question that usually springs to mind at this point is, "Why use pointers at all?" After all, taking the address of a variable you already know and sticking it in a pointer so that you can dereference it seems like an overhead you can do without. There are several reasons why pointers are important.

As you will see shortly, you can use pointer notation to operate on data stored in an array, which often executes faster than if you use array notation. Also, when you get to define your own functions later in the book, you will see that pointers are used extensively for enabling access within a function to large blocks of data, such as arrays, that are defined outside the function. Most importantly, however, you will also see later that you can allocate space for variables dynamically, that is, during program execution. This sort of capability allows your program to adjust its use of memory depending on the input to the program. Because you don't know in advance how many variables you are going to create dynamically, a primary way you have for doing this is by using pointers — so make sure you get the hang of this bit.

Using Pointers

You can try out various aspects of pointer operations with an example:

```cpp
//Ex4_05.cpp
// Exercising pointers
#include <iostream>
using std::cout;
using std::endl;
using std::hex;
using std::dec;

int main()
{
   long* pnumber = NULL;               // Pointer declaration & initialization
   long number1 = 55, number2 = 99;

   pnumber = &number1;                 // Store address in pointer
   *pnumber += 11;                     // Increment number1 by 11
   cout << endl
        << "number1 = " << number1
        << "    &number1 = " << hex << pnumber;

   pnumber = &number2;                 // Change pointer to address of number2
   number1 = *pnumber*10;              // 10 times number2

   cout << endl
        << "number1 = " << dec << number1
        << "    pnumber = " << hex << pnumber
        << "    *pnumber = " << dec << *pnumber;

   cout << endl;
   return 0;
}
```

On my computer, this example generates the following output:

```
number1 = 66    &number1 = 0012FEC8
number1 = 990   pnumber = 0012FEBC    *pnumber = 99
```

How It Works

There is no input to this example. All operations are carried out with the initializing values for the variables. After storing the address of number1 in the pointer pnumber, the value of number1 is incremented indirectly through the pointer in this statement:

```cpp
   *pnumber += 11;                             // Increment number1 by 11
```

Note that when you first declared the pointer pnumber, *you initialized it to NULL. I'll discuss pointer initialization in the next section.*

The indirection operator determines that you are adding 11 to the contents of the variable pointed to by `pnumber`, which is `number1`. If you forgot the `*` in this statement, you would be attempting to add 11 to the address stored in the pointer.

The values of `number1`, and the address of `number1` that is stored in `pnumber`, are displayed. You use the `hex` manipulator to generate the address output in hexadecimal notation.

You can obtain the value of ordinary integer variables as hexadecimal output by using the manipulator `hex`. You send it to the output stream in the same way that you have applied `endl`, with the result that all following output is in hexadecimal notation. If you want the following output to be decimal, you need to use the manipulator `dec` in the next output statement to switch the output back to decimal mode again.

After the first line of output, the contents of `pnumber` are set to the address of `number2`. The variable `number1` is then changed to the value of 10 times `number2`:

```
number1 = *pnumber*10;                    // 10 times number2
```

This is calculated by accessing the contents of `number2` indirectly through the pointer. The second line of output shows the results of these calculations.

The address values you see in your output may well be different from those shown in the output here since they reflect where the program is loaded in memory, which depends on how your operating system is configured. The `0x` prefixing the address values indicates that they are hexadecimal numbers. Note that the addresses `&number1` and `pnumber` (when it contains `&number2`) differ by four bytes. This shows that `number1` and `number2` occupy adjacent memory locations, as each variable of type `long` occupies four bytes. The output demonstrates that everything is working as you would expect.

Initializing Pointers

Using pointers that aren't initialized is extremely hazardous. You can easily overwrite random areas of memory through an uninitialized pointer. The resulting damage just depends on how unlucky you are, so it's more than just a good idea to initialize your pointers. It's very easy to initialize a pointer to the address of a variable that has already been defined. Here you can see that I have initialized the pointer `pnumber` with the address of the variable `number` just by using the operator `&` with the variable name:

```
int number = 0;                // Initialized integer variable
int* pnumber = &number;        // Initialized pointer
```

When initializing a pointer with the address of another variable, remember that the variable must already have been declared prior to the pointer declaration.

Of course, you may not want to initialize a pointer with the address of a specific variable when you declare it. In this case, you can initialize it with the pointer equivalent of zero. For this, Visual C++ provides the symbol `NULL` that is already defined as 0, so you can declare and initialize a pointer using the following statement, rather like you did in the last example:

```
int* pnumber = NULL;           // Pointer not pointing to anything
```

This ensures that the pointer doesn't contain an address that will be accepted as valid and provides the pointer with a value that you can check in an `if` statement, such as:

```
if(pnumber == NULL)
    cout << endl << "pnumber is null.";
```

Of course, you can also initialize a pointer explicitly with 0, which also ensures that it is assigned a value that doesn't point to anything. No object can be allocated the address 0, so in effect 0 used as an address indicates that the pointer has no target. In spite of it being arguably somewhat less legible, if you expect to run your code with other compilers, it is preferable to use 0 as an initializing value for a pointer that you want to be null. I'll use 0 rather than NULL in ISO/ANSI C++ examples.

> *This is also more consistent with the current 'good practice' in ISO/ANSI C++, the argument being that if you have an object with a name in C++, it should have a type; however, NULL does not have a type — it's an alias for 0. As you'll see later in this chapter, things are a little different in C++/CLI.*

To use 0 as the initializing value for a pointer you simply write:

```
int* pnumber = 0;                   // Pointer not pointing to anything
```

To check whether a pointer contains a valid address, you could use the statement:

```
if(pnumber == 0)
    cout << endl << "pnumber is null.";
```

Equally well, you could use the statement:

```
if(!pnumber)
    cout << endl << "pnumber is null.";
```

This statement does exactly the same as the previous example.

Of course, you can also use the form:

```
if(pnumber != 0)
    // Pointer is valid, so do something useful
```

> *The address pointed to by the NULL pointer contains a junk value. You should never attempt to dereference a null pointer, because it will cause your program to end immediately.*

Pointers to char

A pointer of type `char*` has the interesting property that it can be initialized with a string literal. For example, you can declare and initialize such a pointer with the statement:

```
char* proverb = "A miss is as good as a mile.";
```

This looks similar to initializing a `char` array, but it's slightly different. This creates a string literal (actually an array of type `const char`) with the character string appearing between the quotes and terminating with /0, and stores the address of the literal in the pointer `proverb`. The address of the literal will be the address of its first character. This is shown in Figure 4-6.

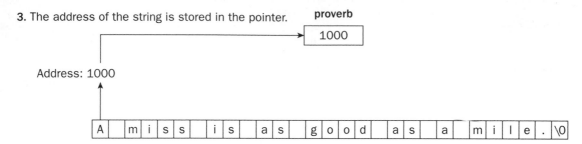

1. The pointer **proverb** is created.

3. The address of the string is stored in the pointer.

proverb

1000

Address: 1000

| A | | m | i | s | s | | i | s | | a | s | | g | o | o | d | | a | s | | a | | m | i | l | e | . | \0 |

2. The constant string is created, terminated with \0.

Figure 4-6

Try It Out   **Lucky Stars With Pointers**

You could rewrite the lucky stars example using pointers instead of an array to see how that would work:

```cpp
// Ex4_06.cpp
// Initializing pointers with strings
#include <iostream>
using std::cin;
using std::cout;
using std::endl;

int main()
{
   char* pstr1 = "Robert Redford";
   char* pstr2 = "Hopalong Cassidy";
   char* pstr3 = "Lassie";
   char* pstr4 = "Slim Pickens";
   char* pstr5 = "Boris Karloff";
   char* pstr6 = "Oliver Hardy";
   char* pstr  = "Your lucky star is ";

   int dice = 0;

   cout << endl
        << " Pick a lucky star!"
        << " Enter a number between 1 and 6: ";
   cin >> dice;

   cout << endl;
   switch(dice)
   {
      case 1: cout << pstr << pstr1;
              break;

      case 2: cout << pstr << pstr2;
              break;
```

```
        case 3: cout << pstr << pstr3;
                break;

        case 4: cout << pstr << pstr4;
                break;

        case 5: cout << pstr << pstr5;
                break;

        case 6: cout << pstr << pstr6;
                break;

        default: cout << "Sorry, you haven't got a lucky star.";
    }

    cout << endl;
    return 0;
}
```

How It Works

The array in Ex4_04.cpp has been replaced by the six pointers, pstr1 to pstr6, each initialized with a name. You also have declared an additional pointer, pstr, initialized with the phrase that you want to use at the start of a normal output line. Because you have discrete pointers, it is easier to use a switch statement to select the appropriate output message than to use an if as you did in the original version. Any incorrect values entered are all taken care of by the default option of the switch.

Outputting the string pointed to by a pointer couldn't be easier. As you can see, you simply write the pointer name. It may cross your mind at this point that in Ex4_05.cpp you wrote a pointer name in the output statement and the address that it contained was displayed. Why is it different here? The answer is in the way the output operation views a pointer of type 'pointer to char'. It treats a pointer of this type in a special way in that it regards it as a string (which is an array of char), and so outputs the string itself, rather than its address.

Using pointers in the example has eliminated the waste of memory that occurred with the array version of this program, but the program seems a little long-winded now — there must be a better way. Indeed there is — using an array of pointers.

Try It Out   Arrays of Pointers

With an array of pointers of type char, each element can point to an independent string, and the lengths of each of the strings can be different. You can declare an array of pointers in the same way that you declare a normal array. Let's go straight to rewriting the previous example using a pointer array:

```
// Ex4_07.cpp
// Initializing pointers with strings
#include <iostream>
using std::cin;
using std::cout;
using std::endl;
```

```
int main()
{
   char* pstr[] =  { "Robert Redford",        // Initializing a pointer array
                     "Hopalong Cassidy",
                     "Lassie",
                     "Slim Pickens",
                     "Boris Karloff",
                     "Oliver Hardy"
                   };
   char* pstart = "Your lucky star is ";

   int dice = 0;

   cout << endl
        << " Pick a lucky star!"
        << " Enter a number between 1 and 6: ";
   cin >> dice;

   cout << endl;
   if(dice >= 1 && dice <= 6)                  // Check input validity
      cout << pstart << pstr[dice - 1];        // Output star name

   else
      cout << "Sorry, you haven't got a lucky star."; // Invalid input

   cout << endl;
   return 0;
}
```

How It Works

In this case, you are nearly getting the best of all possible worlds. You have a one-dimensional array of pointers to type char declared such that the compiler works out what the dimension should be from the number of initializing strings. The memory usage that results from this is illustrated in Figure 4-7.

Compared to using a 'normal' array, the pointer array normally carries less overhead in terms of space. With an array, you would need to make each row the length of the longest string, and six rows of seventeen bytes each is 102 bytes, so by using a pointer array you have saved a whole -1 bytes! What's gone wrong? The simple truth is that for this small number of relatively short strings, the size of the extra array of pointers is significant. You *would* make savings if you were dealing with more strings that were longer and had more variable lengths.

Space saving isn't the only advantage that you get by using pointers. In a lot of circumstances you save time too. Think of what happens if you want to move "Oliver Hardy" to the first position and "Robert Redford" to the end. With the pointer array as above you just need to swap the pointers — the strings themselves stay where they are. If you had stored these simply as strings, as you did in Ex4_04.cpp, a great deal of copying would be necessary — you need to copy the whole string "Robert Redford" to a temporary location while you copied "Oliver Hardy" in its place, and then you need to copy "Robert Redford" to the end position. This requires significantly more computer time to execute.

Because you are using pstr as the name of the array, the variable holding the start of the output message needs to be different; it is called pstart. You select the string that you want to output by means of a very simple if statement, similar to that of the original version of the example. You either display a star selection or a suitable message if the user enters an invalid value.

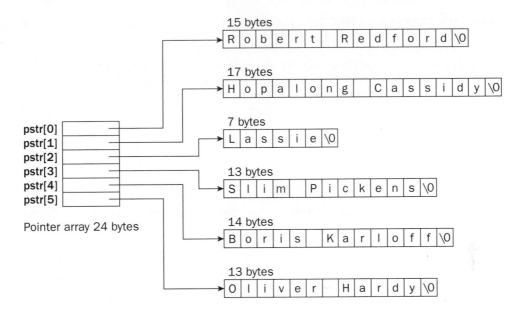

Figure 4-7

One weakness of the way the program is written is that the code assumes there are six options, even though the compiler is allocating the space for the pointer array from the number of initializing strings that you supply. So if you add a string to the list, you have to alter other parts of the program to take account of this. It would be nice to be able to add strings and have the program automatically adapt to however many strings there are.

The sizeof Operator

A new operator can help us here. The sizeof operator produces an integer value of type size_t that gives the number of bytes occupied by its operand where size_t is a type defined by the standard library. Many standard library functions return a value of type size_t and the size_t type is defined within the standard library using a typedef statement to be equivalent to one of the fundamental types, usually unsigned int. The reason for using size_t rather than a fundamental type directly is that it allows flexibility in what the actual type is in different C++ implementations. The C++ standard permits the range of values accommodated by a fundamental type to vary to make the best of a given hardware architecture, and size_t can be defined to be the equivalent of the most suitable fundamental type in the current machine environment.

Look at this statement that refers to the variable dice from the previous example:

```
cout << sizeof dice;
```

The value of the expression `sizeof dice` is 4 because `dice` was declared as type `int` and therefore occupies 4 bytes. Thus this statement outputs the value 4.

The `sizeof` operator can be applied to an element in an array or to the whole array. When the operator is applied to an array name by itself, it produces the number of bytes occupied by the whole array, whereas when it is applied to a single element with the appropriate index value or values, it results in the number of bytes occupied by that element. Thus, in the last example, you could output the number of elements in the `pstr` array with the expression:

```
cout << (sizeof pstr)/(sizeof pstr[0]);
```

The expression `(sizeof pstr)/(sizeof pstr[0])` divides the number of bytes occupied by the whole pointer array by the number of bytes occupied by the first element of the array. Because each element in the array occupies the same amount of memory, the result is the number of elements in the array.

> Remember that `pstr` is an array of pointers — using the `sizeof` operator on the array or on individual elements will not tell us anything about the memory occupied by the text strings.

You can also apply the `sizeof` operator to a type name rather than a variable, in which case the result is the number of bytes occupied by a variable of that type. In this case the type name should be enclosed between parentheses. For example, after executing the statement,

```
size_t long_size = sizeof(long);
```

the variable `long_size` will have the value 4. The variable `long_size` is declared to be of type `size_t` to match the type of the value produced by the `sizeof` operator. Using a different integer type for `long_size` may result in a warning message from the compiler.

Try It Out   Using the sizeof Operator

You can amend the last example to use the `sizeof` operator so that the code automatically adapts to an arbitrary number of string values from which to select:

```cpp
// Ex4_08.cpp
// Flexible array management using sizeof
#include <iostream>
using std::cin;
using std::cout;
using std::endl;

int main()
{
    char* pstr[] = { "Robert Redford",        // Initializing a pointer array
                     "Hopalong Cassidy",
                     "Lassie",
                     "Slim Pickens",
                     "Boris Karloff",
                     "Oliver Hardy"
                   };
    char* pstart = "Your lucky star is ";
```

```
    int count = (sizeof pstr)/(sizeof pstr[0]);   // Number of array elements

    int dice = 0;

    cout << endl
        << " Pick a lucky star!"
        << " Enter a number between 1 and " << count << ": ";
    cin >> dice;

    cout << endl;
    if(dice >= 1 && dice <= count)                 // Check input validity
        cout << pstart << pstr[dice - 1];          // Output star name
    else
        cout << "Sorry, you haven't got a lucky star."; // Invalid input

    cout << endl;
    return 0;
}
```

How It Works

As you can see, the changes required in the example are very simple. You just calculate the number of elements in the pointer array `pstr` and store the result in `count`. Then, wherever the total number of elements in the array was referenced as 6, you just use the variable `count`. You could now just add a few more names to the list of lucky stars and everything affected in the program is adjusted automatically.

Constant Pointers and Pointers to Constants

The array `pstr` in the last example is clearly not intended to be modified in the program, and nor are the strings being pointed to, nor the variable `count`. It would be a good idea to ensure that these didn't get modified by mistake in the program. You could very easily protect the variable `count` from accidental modification by writing this:

```
const int count = (sizeof pstr)/(sizeof pstr[0]);
```

However, the array of pointers deserves closer examination. You declared the array like this:

```
char* pstr[] = { "Robert Redford",    // Initializing a pointer array
                 "Hopalong Cassidy",
                 "Lassie",
                 "Slim Pickens",
                 "Boris Karloff",
                 "Oliver Hardy"
               };
```

Each pointer in the array is initialized with the address of a string literal, "Robert Redford", "Hopalong Cassidy", and so on. The type of a string literal is 'array of const char' so you are storing the address of a const array in a non-const pointer. The reason the compiler allows us to use a string literal to initialize an element of an array of char* is for reasons of backward compatibility with existing code.

If you try to alter the character array with a statement like this:

```
*pstr[0] = "Stan Laurel";
```

the program does not compile.

If you were to reset one of the elements of the array to point to a character using a statement like this:

```
*pstr[0] = 'X';
```

the program compiles but crashes when this statement is executed.

You don't really want to have unexpected behavior like the program crashing at run time, and you can prevent it. A far better way of writing the declaration is as follows:

```
const char* pstr[] = { "Robert Redford",      // Array of pointers
                       "Hopalong Cassidy",    // to constants
                       "Lassie",
                       "Slim Pickens",
                       "Boris Karloff",
                       "Oliver Hardy"
                     };
```

In this case, there is no ambiguity about the const-ness of the strings pointed to by the elements of the pointer array. If you now attempt to change these strings, the compiler flags this as an error at compile time.

However, you could still legally write this statement:

```
pstr[0] = pstr[1];
```

Those lucky individuals due to be awarded Mr. Redford would get Mr. Cassidy instead because both pointers now point to the same name. Note that this isn't changing the values of the objects pointed to by the pointer array element — it is changing the value of the pointer stored in pstr[0]. You should therefore inhibit this kind of change as well because some people may reckon that good old Hoppy may not have the same sex appeal as Robert. You can do this with the following statement:

```
// Array of constant pointers to constants
const char* const pstr[] = { "Robert Redford",
                             "Hopalong Cassidy",
                             "Lassie",
                             "Slim Pickens",
                             "Boris Karloff",
                             "Oliver Hardy"
                           };
```

To summarize, you can distinguish three situations relating to const, pointers and the objects to which they point:

❑   A pointer to a constant object

❑   A constant pointer to an object

❑   A constant pointer to a constant object

In the first situation, the object pointed to cannot be modified, but you can set the pointer to point to something else:

```
const char* pstring = "Some text";
```

In the second, the address stored in the pointer can't be changed, but the object pointed to can be:

```
char* const pstring = "Some text";
```

Finally, in the third situation, both the pointer and the object pointed to have been defined as constant and, therefore, neither can be changed:

```
const char* const pstring = "Some text";
```

Of course, all this applies to pointers to any type. A pointer to type char is used here purely for illustrative purposes.

Pointers and Arrays

Array names can behave like pointers under some circumstances. In most situations, if you use the name of a one-dimensional array by itself, it is automatically converted to a pointer to the first element of the array. Note that this is not the case when the array name is used as the operand of the `sizeof` operator.

If you have these declarations,

```
double* pdata;
double data[5];
```

you can write this assignment:

```
pdata = data;        // Initialize pointer with the array address
```

This is assigning the address of the first element of the array `data` to the pointer `pdata`. Using the array name by itself refers to the address of the array. If you use the array name `data` with an index value, it refers to the contents of the element corresponding to that index value. So, if you want to store the address of that element in the pointer, you have to use the address-of operator:

```
pdata = &data[1];
```

Here, the pointer `pdata` contains the address of the second element of the array.

Pointer Arithmetic

You can perform arithmetic operations with pointers. You are limited to addition and subtraction in terms of arithmetic, but you can also perform comparisons of pointer values to produce a logical result. Arithmetic with a pointer implicitly assumes that the pointer points to an array, and that the arithmetic operation is on the address contained in the pointer. For the pointer `pdata` for example, you could assign the address of the third element of the array `data` to a pointer with this statement:

```
pdata = &data[2];
```

In this case, the expression `pdata+1` would refer to the address of `data[3]`, the fourth element of the `data` array, so you could make the pointer point to this element by writing this statement:

```
pdata += 1;          // Increment pdata to the next element
```

This statement increments the address contained in `pdata` by the number of bytes occupied by one element of the array `data`. In general, the expression `pdata+n`, where n can be any expression resulting in an integer, adds `n*sizeof(double)` to the address contained in the pointer `pdata` because it was declared to be of type pointer to `double`. This is illustrated in Figure 4-8.

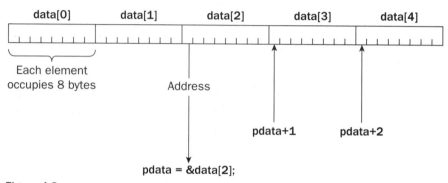

double data[5];

Figure 4-8

In other words, incrementing or decrementing a pointer works in terms of the type of the object pointed to. Increasing a pointer to `long` by one changes its contents to the next `long` address and so increments the address by four. Similarly, incrementing a pointer to `short` by one increments the address by two. The more common notation for incrementing a pointer is using the increment operator. For example:

```
pdata++;             // Increment pdata to the next element
```

This is equivalent to (and more common than) the `+=` form. However, I used the preceding `+=` form to make it clear that although the increment value is actually specified as one, the effect is usually an increment greater than one, except in the case of a pointer to type `char`.

> *The address resulting from an arithmetic operation on a pointer can be a value ranging from the address of the first element of the array to the address that is one beyond the last element. Outside of these limits, the behavior of the pointer is undefined.*

You can, of course, dereference a pointer on which you have performed arithmetic (there wouldn't be much point to it otherwise). For example, assuming that `pdata` is still pointing to `data[2]`, this statement,

```
*(pdata + 1) = *(pdata + 2);
```

is equivalent to this:

```
data[3] = data[4];
```

When you want to dereference a pointer after incrementing the address it contains, the parentheses are necessary because the precedence of the indirection operator is higher than that of the arithmetic operators, + or −. If you write the expression *pdata + 1, instead of *(pdata + 1), this adds one to the value stored at the address contained in pdata, which is equivalent to executing data[2] + 1. Because this isn't an lvalue, its use in the previous assignment statement causes the compiler to generate an error message.

You can use an array name as though it were a pointer for addressing elements of an array. If you have the same one-dimensional array as before, declared as

```
long data[5];
```

using pointer notation, you can refer to the element data[3] for example as *(data + 3). This kind of notation can be applied generally so that, corresponding to the elements data[0], data[1], data[2], you can write *data, *(data + 1), *(data+2), and so on.

Try It Out   **Array Names as Pointers**

You could exercise this aspect of array addressing with a program to calculate prime numbers (a prime number is divisible only by itself and one).

```
// Ex4_09.cpp
// Calculating primes
#include <iostream>
#include <iomanip>
using std::cout;
using std::endl;
using std::setw;

int main()
{
    const int MAX = 100;             // Number of primes required
    long primes[MAX] = { 2,3,5 };    // First three primes defined
    long trial = 5;                  // Candidate prime
    int count = 3;                   // Count of primes found
    int found = 0;                   // Indicates when a prime is found

    do
    {
        trial += 2;                         // Next value for checking
        found = 0;                          // Set found indicator

        for(int i = 0; i < count; i++)      // Try division by existing primes
        {
            found = (trial % *(primes + i)) == 0;// True for exact division
                if(found)                        // If division is exact
                    break;                       // it's not a prime
        }

        if (found == 0)                     // We got one...
```

```
        *(primes + count++) = trial;   // ...so save it in primes array
   }while(count < MAX);

   // Output primes 5 to a line
   for(int i = 0; i < MAX; i++)
   {
      if(i % 5 == 0)                    // New line on 1st, and every 5th line
         cout << endl;
      cout << setw(10) << *(primes + i);
   }
   cout << endl;

   return 0;
}
```

If you compile and execute this example, you should get the following output:

2	3	5	7	11
13	17	19	23	29
31	37	41	43	47
53	59	61	67	71
73	79	83	89	97
101	103	107	109	113
127	131	137	139	149
151	157	163	167	173
179	181	191	193	197
199	211	223	227	229
233	239	241	251	257
263	269	271	277	281
283	293	307	311	313
317	331	337	347	349
353	359	367	373	379
383	389	397	401	409
419	421	431	433	439
443	449	457	461	463
467	479	487	491	499
503	509	521	523	541

How It Works

You have the usual `#include` statements for the `<iostream>` header file for input and output and for `<iomanip>` because you will use a stream manipulator to set the field width for output.

You use the constant `MAX` to define the number of primes that you want the program to produce. The `primes` array, which stores the results, has the first three primes already defined to start the process off. All the work is done in two loops: the outer `do-while` loop, which picks the next value to be checked and adds the value to the `primes` array if it is prime, and the inner `for` loop that actually checks the value to see whether it's prime or not.

The algorithm in the `for` loop is very simple and is based on the fact that if a number is not a prime, it must be divisible by one of the primes found so far — all of which are less than the number in question because all numbers are either prime or a product of primes. In fact, only division by primes less than or equal to the square root of the number in question need to be checked, so this example isn't as efficient as it might be.

```
found = (trial % *(primes + i)) == 0;   // True for exact division
```

This statement sets the variable found to be 1 if there's no remainder from dividing the value in trial by the current prime *(primes + i) (remember that this is equivalent to primes[i]), and 0 otherwise. The if statement causes the for loop to be terminated if found has the value 1 because the candidate in trial can't be a prime in that case.

After the for loop ends (for whatever reason), it's necessary to decide whether or not the value in trial was prime. This is indicated by the value in the indicator variable found.

```
*(primes + count++) = trial;   // ...so save it in primes array
```

If trial *does* contain a prime, this statement stores the value in primes[count] and then increments count through the postfix increment operator.

After MAX number of primes have been found, they are output with a field width of 10 characters, 5 to a line, as a result of this statement:

```
if(i % 5 == 0)                 // New line on 1st, and every 5th line
    cout << endl;
```

This starts a new line when i has the values 0, 5, 10, and so on.

Try It Out   Counting Characters Revisited

To see how handling strings works in pointer notation, you could produce a version of the program you looked at earlier for counting the characters in a string:

```cpp
// Ex4_10.cpp
// Counting string characters using a pointer
#include <iostream>
using std::cin;
using std::cout;
using std::endl;

int main()
{
   const int MAX = 80;                  // Maximum array dimension
   char buffer[MAX];                    // Input buffer
   char* pbuffer = buffer;              // Pointer to array buffer

   cout << endl                         // Prompt for input
        << "Enter a string of less than "
        << MAX << " characters:"
        << endl;

   cin.getline(buffer, MAX, '\n');      // Read a string until \n

   while(*pbuffer)                      // Continue until \0
      pbuffer++;
```

```
        cout << endl
            << "The string \"" << buffer
            << "\" has " << pbuffer - buffer << " characters.";
        cout << endl;

    return 0;
}
```

Here's an example of typical output from this example:

```
Enter a string of less than 80 characters:
The tigers of wrath are wiser than the horses of instruction.
The string "The tigers of wrath are wiser than the horses of instruction." has 61
characters.
```

How It Works

Here the program operates using the pointer `pbuffer` rather than the array name `buffer`. You don't need the `count` variable because the pointer is incremented in the `while` loop until '\0' is found. When the '\0' character is found, `pbuffer` will contain the address of that position in the string. The count of the number of characters in the string entered is therefore the difference between the address stored in the pointer `pbuffer` and the address of the beginning of the array denoted by `buffer`.

You could also have incremented the pointer in the loop by writing the loop like this:

```
    while(*pbuffer++);                          // Continue until \0
```

Now the loop contains no statements, only the test condition. This would work adequately, except for the fact that the pointer would be incremented after '\0' was encountered, so the address would be one more than the last position in the string. You would therefore need to express the count of the number of characters in the string as `pbuffer - buffer - 1`.

Note that you can't use the array name here in the same way that you have used the pointer. The expression `buffer++` is strictly illegal because you can't modify the address value that an array name represents. Even though you can use an array name in an expression as though it is a pointer, it isn't a pointer, because the address value that it represents is fixed.

Using Pointers with Multidimensional Arrays

Using a pointer to store the address of a one-dimensional array is relatively straightforward, but with multidimensional arrays, things can get a little complicated. If you don't intend to do this, you can skip this section as it's a little obscure; however, if you have previous experience with C, this section is worth a glance.

If you have to use a pointer with multidimensional arrays, you need to keep clear in your mind what is happening. By way of illustration, you can use an array `beans`, declared as follows:

```
    double beans[3][4];
```

You can declare and assign a value to the pointer pbeans as follows:

```
double* pbeans;
pbeans = &beans[0][0];
```

Here you are setting the pointer to the address of the first element of the array, which is of type double. You could also set the pointer to the address of the first row in the array with the statement:

```
pbeans = beans[0];
```

This is equivalent to using the name of a one-dimensional array, which is replaced by its address. You used this in the earlier discussion; however, because beans is a two-dimensional array, you cannot set an address in the pointer with the following statement:

```
pbeans = beans;            // Will cause an error!!
```

The problem is one of type. The type of the pointer you have defined is double*, but the array is of type double[3][4]. A pointer to store the address of this array must be of type double*[4]. C++ associates the dimensions of the array with its type and the statement above is only legal if the pointer has been declared with the dimension required. This is done with a slightly more complicated notation than you have seen so far:

```
double (*pbeans)[4];
```

The parentheses here are essential; otherwise, you would be declaring an array of pointers. Now the previous statement is legal, but this pointer can only be used to store addresses of an array with the dimensions shown.

Pointer Notation with Multidimensional Arrays

You can use pointer notation with an array name to reference elements of the array. You can reference each element of the array beans that you declared earlier, which had three rows of four elements, in two ways:

- ❏ Using the array name with two index values.
- ❏ Using the array name in pointer notation

Therefore, the following two statements are equivalent:

```
beans[i][j]
*(*(beans + i) + j)
```

Let's look at how these work. The first line uses normal array indexing to refer to the element with offset j in row i of the array.

You can determine the meaning of the second line by working from the inside, outwards. beans refers to the address of the first row of the array, so beans + i refers to row i of the array. The expression *(beans + i) is the address of the first element of row i, so *(beans + i) + j is the address of the element in row i with offset j. The whole expression therefore refers to the value of that element.

If you really want to be obscure — and it isn't recommended that you should be — the following two statements, where you have mixed array and pointer notation, are also legal references to the same element of the array:

```
*(beans[i] + j)
(*(beans + i))[j]
```

There is yet another aspect to the use of pointers that is really the most important of all: the ability to allocate memory for variables dynamically. You'll look into that next.

Dynamic Memory Allocation

Working with a fixed set of variables in a program can be very restrictive. The need often arises within an application to decide the amount of space to be allocated for storing different types of variables at execution time, depending on the input data for the program. With one set of data it may be appropriate to use a large integer array in a program, whereas with a different set of input data, a large floating-point array may be required. Any program that involves reading and processing a number of data items that is not known in advance can take advantage of the ability to allocate memory to store the data at run time. For example, if you need to implement a program to store information about the students in a class, the number of students is not fixed and their names will vary in length so to deal with the data most efficiently, you'll want to allocate space dynamically at execution time.

Obviously, because any dynamically allocated variables can't have been defined at compile time, they can't be named in your source program. When they are created, they are identified by their address in memory, which is contained within a pointer. With the power of pointers and the dynamic memory management tools in Visual C++ 2008, writing your programs to have this kind of flexibility is quick and easy.

The Free Store, Alias the Heap

In most instances, when your program is executed, there is unused memory in your computer. This unused memory is called the heap in C++, or sometimes the **free store**. You can allocate space within the free store for a new variable of a given type using a special operator in C++ that returns the address of the space allocated. This operator is new, and it's complemented by the operator delete, which de-allocates memory previously allocated by new.

You can allocate space in the free store for some variables in one part of a program, and then release the allocated space and return it to the free store after you have finished with the variables concerned. This makes the memory available for reuse by other dynamically allocated variables, later in the same program.

You would want to use memory from the free store whenever you need to allocate memory for items that can only be determined at runtime. One example of this might be allocating memory to hold a string entered by the user of your application. There is no way you can know in advance how large this string needs to be, so you would allocate the memory for the string at run time, using the new operator. Later, you'll look at an example of using the free store to dynamically allocate memory for an array, where the dimensions of the array are determined by the user at run time.

This can be a very powerful technique; it enables you to use memory very efficiently, and in many cases, it results in programs that can handle much larger problems, involving considerably more data than otherwise might be possible.

The new and delete Operators

Suppose that you need space for a `double` variable. You can define a pointer to type `double` and then request that the memory be allocated at execution time. You can do this using the operator `new` with the following statements:

```
double* pvalue = NULL;    // Pointer initialized with null
pvalue = new double;      // Request memory for a double variable
```

This is a good moment to recall that *all pointers should be initialized*. Using memory dynamically typically involves a number of pointers floating around, so it's important that they should not contain spurious values. You should try to arrange that if a pointer doesn't contain a legal address value, it is set to 0.

The `new` operator in the second line of code above should return the address of the memory in the free store allocated to a `double` variable, and this address is stored in the pointer `pvalue`. You can then use this pointer to reference the variable using the indirection operator as you have seen. For example:

```
*pvalue = 9999.0;
```

Of course, the memory may not have been allocated because the free store had been used up, or because the free store is fragmented by previous usage, meaning that there isn't a sufficient number of contiguous bytes to accommodate the variable for which you want to obtain space. You don't have to worry too much about this, however. With ANSI standard C++, the `new` operator will *throw an exception* if the memory cannot be allocated for any reason, which terminates your program. Exceptions are a mechanism for signaling errors in C++ and you learn about these in Chapter 6.

You can also initialize a variable created by `new`. Taking the example of the `double` variable that was allocated by new and the address stored in `pvalue`, you could have set the value to 999.0 as it was created with this statement:

```
pvalue = new double(999.0);    // Allocate a double and initialize it
```

When you no longer need a variable that has been dynamically allocated, you can free up the memory that it occupies in the free store with the `delete` operator:

```
delete pvalue;                 // Release memory pointed to by pvalue
```

This ensures that the memory can be used subsequently by another variable. If you don't use `delete`, and subsequently store a different address value in the pointer `pvalue`, it will be impossible to free up the memory or to use the variable that it contains because access to the address is lost. In this situation, you have what is referred to as a memory leak, especially when this situation recurs in your program.

Allocating Memory Dynamically for Arrays

Allocating memory for an array dynamically is very straightforward. If you wanted to allocate an array of type `char`, assuming `pstr` is a pointer to `char`, you could write the following statement:

```
pstr = new char[20];       // Allocate a string of twenty characters
```

This allocates space for a `char` array of 20 characters and stores its address in `pstr`.

To remove the array that you have just created in the free store, you must use the `delete` operator. The statement would look like this:

```
delete [] pstr;          // Delete array pointed to by pstr
```

Note the use of square brackets to indicate that what you are deleting is an array. When removing arrays from the free store, you should always include the square brackets or the results are unpredictable. Note also that you do not specify any dimensions here, simply `[]`.

Of course, the `pstr` pointer now contains the address of memory that may already have been allocated for some other purpose so it certainly should not be used. When you use the delete operator to discard some memory that you previously allocated, you should always reset the pointer to 0, like this:

```
pstr = 0;                // Set pointer to null
```

Try It Out   Using Free Store

You can see how dynamic memory allocation works in practice by rewriting the program that calculates an arbitrary number of primes, this time using memory in the free store to store them.

```cpp
// Ex4_11.cpp
// Calculating primes using dynamic memory allocation
#include <iostream>
#include <iomanip>
using std::cin;
using std::cout;
using std::endl;
using std::setw;

int main()
{
   long* pprime = 0;            // Pointer to prime array
   long trial = 5;              // Candidate prime
   int count = 3;               // Count of primes found
   int found = 0;               // Indicates when a prime is found
   int max = 0;                 // Number of primes required

   cout << endl
        << "Enter the number of primes you would like (at least 4): ";
   cin >> max;                  // Number of primes required

   if(max < 4)                  // Test the user input, if less than 4
      max = 4;                  // ensure it is at least 4

   pprime = new long[max];

   *pprime = 2;                 // Insert three
   *(pprime + 1) = 3;           // seed primes
   *(pprime + 2) = 5;

   do
   {
      trial += 2;                                    // Next value for checking
```

```
        found = 0;                                  // Set found indicator

        for(int i = 0; i < count; i++)              // Division by existing primes
        {
            found =(trial % *(pprime + i)) == 0;// True for exact division
            if(found)                               // If division is exact
                break;                              // it's not a prime
        }

        if (found == 0)                             // We got one...
            *(pprime + count++) = trial;   // ...so save it in primes array
    } while(count < max);

    // Output primes 5 to a line
    for(int i = 0; i < max; i++)
    {
        if(i % 5 == 0)                              // New line on 1st, and every 5th line
            cout << endl;
        cout << setw(10) << *(pprime + i);
    }

    delete [] pprime;                               // Free up memory
    pprime = 0;                                     // and reset the pointer
    cout << endl;
    return 0;
}
```

Here's an example of the output from this program:

```
Enter the number of primes you would like (at least 4): 20
          2          3          5          7         11
         13         17         19         23         29
         31         37         41         43         47
         53         59         61         67         71
```

How It Works

In fact, the program is similar to the previous version. After receiving the number of primes required in the int variable max, you allocate an array of that size in the free store using the operator new. Note that you have made sure that max can be no less than 4. This is because the program requires space to be allocated in the free store for at least the three seed primes, plus one new one. You specify the size of the array that is required by putting the variable max between the square brackets following the array type specification:

```
pprime = new long[max];
```

You store the address of the memory area that is allocated by new in the pointer pprime. The program would terminate at this point if the memory could not be allocated.

After the memory that stores the prime values has been successfully allocated, the first three array elements are set to the values of the first three primes:

```
*pprime = 2;                    // Insert three
```

```
*(pprime + 1) = 3;              // seed primes
*(pprime + 2) = 5;
```

You are using the dereference operator to access the first three elements of the array. As you saw earlier, the parentheses in the second and third statements are because the precedence of the * operators is higher than that of the + operator.

You can't specify initial values for elements of an array that you allocate dynamically. You have to use explicit assignment statements if you want to set initial values for elements of the array.

The calculation of the prime numbers is exactly as before; the only change is that the name of the pointer you have here, pprime, is substituted for the array name, primes, that you used in the previous version. Equally, the output process is the same. Acquiring space dynamically is really not a problem at all. After it has been allocated, it in no way affects how the computation is written.

After you finish with the array, you remove it from the free store using the delete operator, remembering to include the square brackets to indicate that it is an array you are deleting.

```
delete [] pprime;               // Free up memory
```

Although it's not essential here, you also set the pointer to 0:

```
pprime = 0;                                  // and reset the pointer
```

All memory allocated in the free store is released when your program ends, but it is good to get into the habit of resetting pointers to 0 when they no longer point to valid memory areas.

Dynamic Allocation of Multidimensional Arrays

Allocating memory in the free store for a multidimensional array involves using the new operator in a slightly more complicated form than that for a one-dimensional array. Assuming that you have already declared the pointer pbeans appropriately, to obtain the space for the array beans[3][4] that you used earlier in this chapter, you could write this:

```
pbeans = new double [3][4];      // Allocate memory for a 3x4 array
```

You just specify both array dimensions between square brackets after the type name for the array elements.

Allocating space for a three-dimensional array simply requires that you specify the extra dimension with new, as in this example:

```
pBigArray = new double [5][10][10]; // Allocate memory for a 5x10x10 array
```

However many dimensions there are in the array that has been created, to destroy it and release the memory back to the free store you write the following:

```
delete [] pBigArray;             // Release memory for array
```

You always use just one pair of square brackets following the delete operator, regardless of the dimensionality of the array with which you are working.

You have already seen that you can use a variable as the specification of the dimension of a one-dimensional array to be allocated by new. This extends to two or more dimensions but with the restriction that only the leftmost dimension may be specified by a variable. All the other dimensions must be constants or constant expressions. So you could write this:

```
pBigArray = new double[max][10][10];
```

where max is a variable; however, specifying a variable for any dimension other than the left most causes an error message to be generated by the compiler.

Using References

A **reference** appears to be similar to a pointer in many respects, which is why I'm introducing it here, but it really isn't the same thing at all. The real importance of references becomes apparent only when you get to explore their use with functions, particularly in the context of object-oriented programming. Don't be misled by its simplicity and what might seem to be a trivial concept. As you will see later, references provide some extraordinarily powerful facilities and in some contexts enable you to achieve results that would be impossible without using them.

What Is a Reference?

A reference is an alias for another variable. It has a name that can be used in place of the original variable name. Because it is an alias and not a pointer, the variable for which it is an alias has to be specified when the reference is declared, and unlike a pointer, a reference can't be altered to represent another variable.

Declaring and Initializing References

Suppose that you have declared a variable as follows:

```
long number = 0;
```

You can declare a reference for this variable using the following declaration statement:

```
long& rnumber = number;      // Declare a reference to variable number
```

The ampersand following the type name long and preceding the variable name rnumber, indicates that a reference is being declared and the variable name it represents, number, is specified as the initializing value following the equals sign; therefore, the variable rnumber is of type 'reference to long'. You can now use the reference in place of the original variable name. For example, this statement,

```
rnumber += 10;
```

has the effect of incrementing the variable number by 10.

Let's contrast the reference rnumber with the pointer pnumber, declared in this statement:

```
long* pnumber = &number;        // Initialize a pointer with an address
```

This declares the pointer pnumber, and initializes it with the address of the variable number. This then allows the variable number to be incremented with a statement such as:

```
*pnumber += 10;                 // Increment number through a pointer
```

There is a significant distinction between using a pointer and using a reference. The pointer needs to be dereferenced and whatever address it contains is used to access the variable to participate in the expression. With a reference, there is no need for de-referencing. In some ways, a reference is like a pointer that has already been dereferenced, although it can't be changed to reference another variable. The reference is the complete equivalent of the variable for which it is a reference. A reference may seem like just an alternative notation for a given variable, and here it certainly appears to behave like that. However, you'll see when I discuss functions in C++ that this is not quite true and that it can provide some very impressive extra capabilities.

Native C++ Library Functions for Strings

The standard library provides the <cstring> header that contains functions that operate on null-terminated strings. These are a set of functions that are specified to the C++ standard. There are also alternatives to some of these that are not standard, but which provide a more secure implementation of the function than the original versions. In general I'll mention both where they exist in the <cstring> header but I'll use the more secure versions in examples. Let's explore some of the most useful functions provided by the <cstring> header.

> Note that the <string> standard header for native C++ defines the string and wstring classes that represent character strings. The string class represents strings of characters of type char and the wstring class represents strings of characters of type wchar_t. Both are defined in the <string> header as template classes that are instances of the basic_string<T> class template. A class template is a parameterized class (with parameter T in this case) that you can use to create new classes to handle different types of data. I won't be discussing templates and the string and wstring classes until Chapter 8, but I thought I'd mention them here because there have some features in common with the functions provided by the String type that you'll be using in C++/CLI programs later in this chapter. If you are really interested to see how they compare, you could always have a quick look at the section in Chapter 8 that has the same title as this section. It should be reasonably easy to follow at this point, even without knowledge of templates and classes.

Finding the Length of a Null-Terminated String

The strlen() function returns the length of the argument string of type char* as a value of type size_t. The type size_t is an implementation defined type that corresponds to an unsigned integer type that is used generally to represent the lengths of sequences of various kinds. The wcslen() function does the same thing for strings of type wchar_t*.

Here's how you use the `strlen()` function:

```
char * str("A miss is as good as a mile.");
cout << "The string contains " <<  strlen(str) << " characters." << endl;
```

The output produced when this fragment executes is:

```
The string contains 28 characters.
```

As you can see from the output, the length value that is returned does not include the terminating null. It is important to keep this in mind, especially when you are using the length of one string to create another of the same length.

Both `strlen()` and `wcslen()` find the length by looking for the null at the end. If there isn't one, the functions will happily continue beyond the end of the string checking throughout memory in the hope of finding a null. For this reason these functions represent a security risk when you are working with data from an untrusted external source. In this situation you can use the `strnlen()` and `wcsnlen()` functions, both of which require a second argument that specifies the length of the buffer in which the string specified by the first argument is stored.

Joining Null-Terminated Strings

The `strcat()` function concatenates two null-terminated strings. The string specified by the second argument is appended to the string specified by the first argument. Here's an example of how you might use it:

```
char str1[30]= "Many hands";
char* str2(" make light work.");
strcat(str1, str2);
cout << str1 << endl;
```

Note that the first string is stored in the array `str1` of 30 characters, which is far more than the length of the initializing string, `"Many hands"`. The string specified by the first argument must have sufficient space to accommodate the two strings when they are joined. If it doesn't, disaster will surely result because the function will then try to overwrite the area beyond the end of the first string.

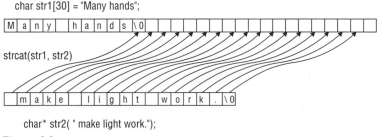

Figure 4-9

As Figure 4-9 shows, the first character of the string specified by the second argument overwrites the terminating null of the first argument and all the remaining characters of the second string are copied across, including the terminating null. Thus the output from the fragment will be:

```
Many hands make light work.
```

The `strcat()` function returns the pointer that is the first argument so you could combine the last two statements in the fragment above into one:

```
cout << strcat(str1, str2) << endl;
```

The `wcscat()` function concatenates wide-character strings but otherwise works exactly the same as the `strcat()` function.

With the `strncat()` function you can append part of one null-terminated string to another. The first two arguments are the destination and source strings respectively, and the third argument is a count of the number of characters from the source string that are to be appended. With the strings as defined in Figure 4-9, here's an example of using `strncat()`:

```
cout << strncat(str1, str2, 11) << endl;
```

After executing this statement, `str1` contains the string `"Many hands make light"`. The operation appends 11 characters from `str2` to `str1`, overwriting the terminating `'\0'` in `str1`, and then appends a final `'\0'` character. The `wcsncat()` provides the same capability as `strncat()` but for wide-character strings.

All the functions for concatenating strings that I have introduced up to now rely on finding the terminating nulls in the strings to work properly so they are also insecure when it comes to dealing with untrusted data. The `strcat_s()`, `wcscat_s()`, `strncat_s()`, and `wcsncat_s()` functions in `<cstring>` provide secure alternatives. Just to take one example, here's how you could use `strcat_s()` to carry out the operation shown in Figure 4-9:

```
const size_t count = 30;
char str1[count]= "Many hands";
char* str2(" make light work.");

errno_t error = strcat_s(str1, count, str2);

if(error == 0)
  cout << " Strings joined successfully." << endl;

else if(error == EINVAL)
  cout << "Error" Source or destination string is NULL." << endl;

else if(error == ERANGE)
  cout << " Error! Destination string too small." << endl;
```

For convenience I defined the array size as the constant, `count`. The first argument to `strcat_s()` is the destination string to which the source string specified by the third argument is to be appended. The second argument is the total number of bytes available at the destination. The function returns an integer value of type errno_t to indicate how things went. The error return value will be zero if the operation is successful, EINVAL if the source or destination is NULL, or ERANGE if destination length is too small. In the event of an error occurring, the destination will be left unchanged. The error code values EINVAL and ERANGE are defined in the <cerrno> header so you need an #include directive for this as well as for <cstring> to compile the fragment above correctly. Of course, you are not obliged to test for the error codes that the function might return and if you don't, you won't need the #include directive for <cerrno>.

Copying Null-Terminated Strings

The standard library function, strcpy(), copies a string from a source location to a destination. The first argument is a pointer to the destination location and the second argument is a pointer to the source string; both arguments are of type char*. The function returns a pointer to the destination string. Here's an example of how you use it:

```
const size_t LENGTH = 22;
const char source[LENGTH] ="The more the merrier!";
char destination[LENGTH];
cout << "The destination string is: " << strcpy(destination, source) << endl;
```

The source string and the destination buffer can each accommodate a string containing 21 characters plus the terminating null. You copy the source string to destination in the last statement. The output statement makes use of the fact that the strcpy() function returns a pointer to the destination string so the output is:

```
The destination string is: The more the merrier!
```

You must ensure that the destination string has sufficient space to accommodate the source string. If you don't, something will get overwritten in memory and disaster is the likely result.

The strcpy_s() function is a more secure version of strcpy(). It requires an extra argument between the destination and source arguments that specifies the size of the destination string buffer. The strcpy_s() function returns an integer value of type errno_t that indicates whether an error occurred. Here's how you might use this function:

```
const size_t LENGTH = 22;
const char source[LENGTH] ="The more the merrier!";
char destination[LENGTH];

errno_t error = strcpy_s(destination, length, source);

if(error == EINVAL)
  cout << "Error. The source or the destination is NULL." << endl;
else if(error == ERANGE)
   cout << "Error. The destination is too small." << endl;
else
   cout << "The destination string is: " << destination << endl;
```

You need to include the <cstring> and <cerrno> headers for this to compile. The strcpy_s() function verifies that the source and destination are not NULL and that the destination buffer has sufficient space to accommodate the source string. When either or both the source and destination are NULL, the function returns the value EINVAL. If the destination buffer is too small, the function returns ERANGE. If the copy is successful, the return value is 0.

You have analogous wide-character versions of these copy functions; these are wcscpy() and wcscpy_s().

Comparing Null-Terminated Strings

The strcmp() function compares two null-terminated strings that you specify by arguments that are pointers of type char*. The function returns a value of type int that is -1, 0, or 1 depending on whether the string pointed to by the first argument is less than, equal to, or greater than the string pointed to by the second argument. Here's an example:

```
char* str1("Jill");
char* str2("Jacko");
char* comp[] = { "less than ", "equal to ", "greater than "};
cout << str1 << " is " << comp[strcmp(str1, str2) + 1] << str2 << '.' << endl;
```

This fragment compares the strings str1 and str2. The comp array contains the three strings you may want to use in the output and the return value from the strcmp() function is used to select from this array. By adding 1 to the value strcmp() returns, you conveniently get 0, 1, or 2 so you can use this to select the appropriate phrase from comp.

Comparing the strings works by comparing the character codes of successive pairs of corresponding characters. The first pair of characters that are different determines whether the first string is less than or greater than the second string. Two strings are equal if they contain the same number of characters and corresponding characters are identical. Of course, the output is:

```
Jill is greater than Jacko.
```

The wstrcmp() function is the wide-character string equivalent of strcmp().

Searching Null-Terminated Strings

The strspn() function searches a string for the first character that is *not* contained in a given set and returns the index of the character found. The first argument is a pointer to the string to be searched and the second argument is a pointer to a string containing the set of characters. You could search for the first character that is not a vowel like this:

```
char* str = "I agree with everything.";
char* vowels = "aeiouAEIOU ";
size_t index = strspn(str, vowels);
cout << "The first character that is not a vowel is '" << str[index]
     << "' at position " << index << endl;
```

This searches str for the first character that is not in vowels. Note that I included a space in the vowels set so a space will be ignored so far as the search is concerned. The output from this fragment is:

```
The first character that is not a vowel is 'g' at position 3
```

Another way of looking at the value the `strspn()` function returns is that it represents the length of the substring starting from the first character in the first argument string that consists entirely of characters in the second argument string. In the example it is the first three characters `"I a"`.

The `wcsspn()` function is the wide-character string equivalent of `strspn()`.

The `strstr()` functions return a pointer to the position in the first argument of a substring specified by the second argument. Here's a fragment that shows this in action:

```
char* str = "I agree with everything.";
char* substring = "ever";
char* psubstr = strstr(str, substring);

if(!psubstr)
  cout << "\"" << substring << "\" not found in \"" << str << "\"" << endl;
else
  cout << "The first occurrence of \"" << substring
       << "\" in \"" << str << "\" is at position "
       << psubstr-str << endl;
```

The third statement calls the `strstr()` function to search `str` for the first occurrence of substring. The function returns a pointer to the position of the substring if it is found or NULL when it is not found. The `if` statement outputs a message depending on whether or not `substring` was found in `str`. The expression `psubstr-str` gives the index position of the first character in the substring. The output produced by this fragment is:

```
The first occurrence of "ever" in "I agree with everything." is at position 13
```

Try It Out   Searching Null-Terminated Strings

This example searches a given string to determine the number of occurrences of a given substring. Here's the code:

```
//Ex4_12.cpp
// Searching a string
#include <iostream>
#include <cstring>
using std::cout;
using std::endl;
using std::strlen;
using std::strstr;

int main()
{
  char* str = "Smith, where Jones had had \"had had\" had had \"had\"."
                     "\n\"Had had\" had had the examiners' approval.";
  char* word = "had";
  cout << "The string to be searched is: "
       << endl << str << endl;

  int count = 0;                // Number of occurrences of word in str
  char* pstr = str;             // Pointer to search start position
  char* found = 0;              // Pointer to occurrence of word in str
```

```
  while(true)
  {
    found = strstr(pstr, word);
    if(!found)
      break;
    ++count;
    pstr = found+strlen(word);      // Set next search start as 1 past the word found
  }

  cout << "\"" << word << "\" was found "
       << count << " times in the string." << endl;
  return 0;
}
```

The output from this example is:

```
The string to be searched is: Smith, where Jones had had "had had" had had "had".
"Had had" had had the examiners' approval.
"had" was found 10 times in the string.
```

How It Works

All the action takes place in the indefinite while loop:

```
  while(true)
  {
    found = strstr(pstr, word);
    if(!found)
      break;
    ++count;
    pstr = found+strlen(word);      // Set next search start as 1 past the word found
  }
```

The first step is to search the string for word starting at position pstr, which initially is the beginning of the string. You store the address that strstr() returns in found; this will be null if word was not found in str so the if statement ends the loop in that case.

If found is not null, you increment the count of the number of occurrences of word and update the pstr pointer so it points to one character past the word instance that was found in str. This will be the starting point for the search on the next loop iteration.

From the output you can see that word was found ten times in str. Of course "Had" doesn't count because it starts with an uppercase letter.

C++/CLI Programming

Dynamic memory allocation works differently with the CLR, and the CLR maintains its own memory heap that is independent of the native C++ heap. The CLR automatically deletes memory that you allocate on the CLR heap when it is no longer required, so you do not need to use the delete operator in a program written for the CLR. The CLR may also compact heap memory to avoid fragmentation from time to time. Thus at a stroke, the CLR greatly reduces the possibility of memory leaks and memory fragmentation. The management and clean-up of the heap that the CLR provides is described as **garbage collection** — the garbage being your discarded variables and objects, and the heap that is managed by the CLR is called the **garbage-collected heap**. You use the gcnew operator instead of new to allocate memory in a C++/CLI, program and the 'gc' prefix is a cue to the fact that you are allocating memory on the garbage-collected heap and not the native C++ heap where all the housekeeping is down to you.

The CLR garbage collector is able to delete objects and release the memory that they occupy when they are no longer required. An obvious question arises: How does the garbage collector know when an object on the heap is no longer required? The answer is quite simple; the CLR keeps track of every variable that references each object in the heap and when there are no variables containing the address of a given object, the object can no longer be referred to in a program and therefore can be deleted.

Because the garbage collection process can involve compacting of the heap memory area to remove fragmented unused blocks of memory, the addresses of data item that you have stored in the heap can change. Consequently you cannot use ordinary native C++ pointers with the garbage-collected heap because if the location of the data pointed to changes, the pointer will no longer be valid. You need a way to access objects on the heap that enables the address to be updated when the garbage collector relocates the data item in the heap. This capability is provided in two ways: by a **tracking handle** (also referred to simply as a **handle**) that is analogous to a pointer in native C++ and by a tracking reference that provides the equivalent of a native C++ reference in a CLR program.

Tracking Handles

A tracking handle has similarities to a native C++ pointer but there are significant differences, too. A tracking handle does store an address, and the address it contains is automatically updated by the garbage collector if the object it references is moved during compaction of the heap. However, you cannot perform address arithmetic with a tracking handle as you can with a native pointer, and casting of a tracking handle is not permitted.

You use tracking handles to reference objects created in the CLR heap. All objects that are reference class types are stored in the heap and therefore the variables you create to refer to such objects must be tracking handles. For instance, the String class type is a reference class type so variables that reference String objects must be tracking handles. The memory for value class types is allocated on the stack by default, but you can choose to store values in the heap by using the gcnew operator. This is also a good time to remind you of a point I mentioned in Chapter 2 — that variables allocated on the CLR heap, which includes all CLR reference types, cannot be declared at global scope.

Declaring Tracking Handles

You specify a handle for a type by placing the ^ symbol (commonly referred to as a 'hat') following the type name. For example, here's how you could declare a tracking handle with the name proverb that can store the address of a String object:

```
String^ proverb;
```

This defines the variable proverb to be a tracking handle of type String^. When you declare a handle it is automatically initialized with null, so it will not refer to anything. To explicitly set a handle to null you use the keyword nullptr like this:

```
proverb = nullptr;                    // Set handle to null
```

Note that you cannot use 0 to represent null here, as you can with native pointers. If you initialize a handle with 0, the value 0 is converted to the type of object that the handle references and the address of this new object is stored in the handle.

Of course, you can initialize a handle explicitly when you declare it. Here's another statement that defines a handle to a String object:

```
String^ saying = L"I used to think I was indecisive but now I'm not so sure";
```

This statement creates a String object on the heap that contains the string on the right of the assignment; the address of the new object is stored in saying. Note that the type of the string literal is const wchar_t*, not type String. The way the String class has been defined makes it possible for such a literal to be used to create an object of type String.

Here's how you could create a handle for a value type:

```
int^ value = 99;
```

This statement creates the handle value of type int^ and the value it points to on the heap is initialized to 99. Remember that you have created a kind of pointer so value cannot participate in arithmetic operations without dereferencing it. To dereference a tracking handle, you use the * operator in the same way as for native pointers. For example, here is a statement that uses the value pointed to by a tracking handle in an arithmetic operation:

```
int result = 2*(*value)+15;
```

The expression *value between the parentheses accesses the integer stored at the address held in the tracking handle so the variable result is set to 213.

Note that when you use a handle on the left of an assignment, there's no need to explicitly dereference it to store a result; the compiler takes care of it for you. For example:

```
int^ result = 0;
result = 2*(*value)+15;
```

Here you first create the handle result that points to a value 0 on the heap. Note that this results in a warning from the compiler because it deduces that you might intend to initialize the handle to null and this is not the way to do that. Because result appears on the left of an assignment in the next statement and the right hand side produces a value, the compiler is able to determine that result must be dereferenced to store the value. Of course, you could write it explicitly like this:

```
*result = 2*(*value)+15;
```

Note that this works only if result has actually been defined. If result has only been declared, when you execute the code you get a runtime error. For example:

```
int^ result;                    // Declaration but no definition
*result = 2*(*value)+15;        // Error message - unhandled exception
```

Because you are dereferencing `result` in the second statement, you are implying that the object pointed to already exists. Because this is not the case you get a runtime error. The first statement is a declaration of the handle, `result`, and this is set to null by default and you cannot dereference a null handle. If you *don't* explicitly dereference `result` in the second statement, everything works as it should because the result of the expression on the right of the assignment is a value class type and its address is stored in `result`.

CLR Arrays

CLR arrays are different from the native C++ arrays. Memory for a CLR array is allocated on the garbage-collected heap, but there's more to it than that. CLR arrays have built-in functionality that you don't get with native C++ arrays, as you'll see shortly. You specify an array variable type using the keyword `array`. You must also specify the type for the array elements between angled brackets following the `array` keyword, so the general form the type of for a variable to reference a one-dimensional array is `array<element_type>^`. Because a CLR array is created on the heap, an array variable is always a tracking handle. Here's an example of a declaration for an array variable:

```
array<int>^ data;
```

The array variable, `data`, can store a reference to any one-dimensional array of elements of type `int`.

You can create a CLR array using the `gcnew` operator at the same time you declare the array variable:

```
array<int>^ data = gcnew array<int>(100);   // Create an array to store 100 integers
```

This statement creates a one-dimensional array with the name `data` — note that an array variable is a tracking handle, so you must not forget the hat following the element type specification between the angled brackets. The number of elements appears between parentheses following the array type specification so this array contains 100 elements each of which can store a value of type `int`.

Similar to native C++ arrays, CLR array elements are indexed from zero so you could set values for the elements in the `data` array like this:

```
for(int i = 0 ; i<100 ; i++)
   data[i] = 2*(i+1);
```

This loop sets the values of the elements to 2, 4, 6, and so on up to 200. Elements in a CLR array are objects so here you are storing objects of type `Int32` in the array. Of course, these behave like ordinary integers in arithmetic expressions so the fact that they are objects is transparent in such situations.

In the previous loop, the number of elements appears in the loop as a literal value. It would be better to use the `Length` property of the array that records the number of elements, like this:

```
for(int i = 0 ; i < data->Length ; i++)
   data[i] = 2*(i+1);
```

To access the `Length` property, you use the `->` operator because `data` is a tracking handle and works like a pointer. The `Length` property records the number of values as a 32-bit integer value. If you need it, you can get the array length as a 64-bit value through the `LongLength` property.

You can also iterate over all the elements in an array using the `for each` loop:

```
array<int>^ values = { 3, 5, 6, 8, 6};
for each(int item in values)
{
  item = 2*item + 1;
  Console::Write("{0,5}",item);
}
```

Within the loop, `item` references each of the elements in the `values` array in turn. The first statement in the body of the loop replaces the current element's value by twice the value plus 1. The second statement in the loop outputs the new value right-justified in a field width of five characters so the output produced by this code fragment is:

```
    7   11   13   17   13
```

An array variable can store the address of any array of the same rank (the rank being the number of dimensions, which in the case of the data array is 1) and element type. For example:

```
data = gcnew array<int>(45);
```

This statement creates a new one-dimensional array of 45 elements of type `int` and stores its address in `data`. The original array is discarded.

You can also create an array from a set of initial values for the elements:

```
array<double>^ samples = { 3.4, 2.3, 6.8, 1.2, 5.5, 4.9. 7.4, 1.6};
```

The size of the array is determined by the number of initial values between the braces, in this case eight, and the values are assigned to the elements in sequence.

Of course, the elements in an array can be of any type, so you can easily create an array of strings:

```
array<String^>^ names = { "Jack", "Jane", "Joe", "Jessica", "Jim", "Joanna"};
```

The elements of this array are initialized with the strings that appear between the braces, and the number of strings determines the number of elements in the array. `String` objects are created on the CLR heap so the element type is a tracking handle type, `String^`.

If you declare the array variable without initializing it, you must explicitly create the array if you want to use a list of initial values. For example:

```
array<String^>^ names;                   // Declare the array variable
names = gcnew array<String^>{ "Jack", "Jane", "Joe", "Jessica", "Jim", "Joanna"};
```

The second statement creates the array and initializes it with the strings between the braces. Without the explicit `gcnew` definition the statement will not compile.

You can use the static `Clear()` function that is defined in the `Array` class to set any sequence of numeric elements in an array to zero. You call a static function using the class name and you'll learn more about such functions when you explore classes in detail. Here's an example of how you could use the `Clear()` function:

```
Array::Clear(samples, 0, samples->Length);          // Set all elements to zero
```

The first argument to `Clear()` is the array that is to be cleared, the second argument is the index for the first element to be cleared, and the third argument is the number of elements to be cleared. Thus this example sets all the elements of the `samples` array to 0.0. If you apply the `Clear()` function to an array of tracking handles such as `String^`, the elements are set to null, and if you apply it to an array of `bool` elements they are set to `false`.

It's time to let a CLR array loose in an example.

Try It Out   Using a CLR Array

In this example, you generate an array containing random values and then find the maximum value. Here's the code:

```
// Ex4_13.cpp : main project file.


// Using a CLR array
#include "stdafx.h"

using namespace System;

int main(array<System::String ^> ^args)
{
   array<double>^ samples = gcnew array<double>(50);

   // Generate random element values
   Random^ generator = gcnew Random;
   for(int i = 0 ; i< samples->Length ; i++)
     samples[i] = 100.0*generator->NextDouble();

   // Output the samples
   Console::WriteLine(L"The array contains the following values:");
   for(int i = 0 ; i< samples->Length ; i++)
   {
     Console::Write(L"{0,10:F2}", samples[i]);
     if((i+1)%5 == 0)
       Console::WriteLine();
   }

   // Find the maximum value
   double max = 0;
   for each(double sample in samples)
     if(max < sample)
       max = sample;

   Console::WriteLine(L"The maximum value in the array is {0:F2}", max);
   return 0;
}
```

Typical output from this example looks like this:

```
The array contains the following values:
    30.38     73.93     29.82     93.00        78.14
    89.53     75.87      5.98     45.29        89.83
     5.25     53.86     11.40      3.34        83.39
    69.94     82.43     43.05     32.87        59.50
    58.89     96.69     34.67     18.81        72.99
    89.60     25.53     34.00     97.35        55.26
    52.64     90.85     10.35     46.14        82.03
    55.46     93.26     92.96     85.11        10.55
    50.50      8.10     29.32     82.98        76.48
    83.94     56.95     15.04     21.94        24.81
The maximum value in the array is 97.35
```

How It Works

You first create an array that stores 50 values of type `double`:

```
array<double>^ samples = gcnew array<double>(50);
```

The array variable, `samples`, must be a tracking handle because CLR arrays are created on the garbage-collected heap.

You populate the array with pseudo-random values of type `double` with the following statements:

```
Random^ generator = gcnew Random;
for(int i = 0 ; i< samples->Length ; i++)
   samples[i] = 100.0*generator->NextDouble();
```

The first statement creates an object of type `Random` on the CLR heap. A `Random` object has functions that will generate pseudo-random values. Here you use the `NextDouble()` function in the loop, which returns a random value of type `double` that lies between 0.0 and 1.0. By multiplying this by 100.0 you get a value between 0.0 and 100.0. The `for` loop stores a random value in each element of the samples array.

A `Random` object also has a `Next()` function that returns a random non-negative value of type `int`. If you supply an integer argument when you call the `Next()` function, it will return a random non-negative integer less than the argument value. You can also supply two integer arguments that represent the minimum and maximum values for the random integer to be returned.

The next loop outputs the contents of the array five elements to a line:

```
Console::WriteLine(L"The array contains the following values:");
for(int i = 0 ; i< samples->Length ; i++)
{
  Console::Write(L"{0,10:F2}", samples[i]);
  if((i+1)%5 == 0)
    Console::WriteLine();
}
```

Within the loop you write the value each element with a field width of 10 and 2 decimal places. Specifying the field width ensures the values align in columns. You also write a newline character to the output whenever the expression `(i+1)%5` is zero, which is after every fifth element value so you get five to a line in the output.

Finally you figure out what the maximum element value is:

```
double max = 0;
for each(double sample in samples)
  if(max < sample)
    max = sample;
```

This uses a `for each` loop just to show that you can. The loop compares `max` with each element value in turn and whenever the element is greater than the current value in `max`, `max` is set to that value so you end up with the maximum element value in `max`.

You could use a `for` loop here if you also wanted to record the index position of the maximum element as well as its value — for example:

```
double max = 0;
int index = 0;
for (int i = 0 ; i < samples->Length ; i++)
  if(max < samples[i])
  {
    max = samples[i];
    index = i;
  }
```

Sorting One-Dimensional Arrays

The `Array` class in the `System` namespace defines a `Sort()` function that sorts the elements of a one-dimensional array so that they are in ascending order. To sort an array you just pass the array handle to the `Sort()` function. Here's an example:

```
array<int>^ samples = { 27, 3, 54, 11, 18, 2, 16};
Array::Sort(samples);                           // Sort the array elements

for each(int value in samples)                  // Output the array elements
  Console::Write(L"{0, 8}", value);
Console::WriteLine();
```

The call to the `Sort()` function rearranges the values of the elements in the samples array so they are in ascending sequence. The result of executing this code fragment is:

```
    2    3    11    16    18    27    54
```

You can also sort a range of elements in an array by supplying two more arguments to the `Sort()` function specifying the index for the first element of those to be sorted and the number of elements to be sorted. For example:

```
array<int>^ samples = { 27, 3, 54, 11, 18, 2, 16};
Array::Sort(samples, 2, 3);                      // Sort elements 2 to 4
```

This statement sorts the three elements in the samples array that begin at index position 2. After executing these statements, the elements in the array will have the values:

```
27   3   11   18   54   2   16
```

The are several other versions of the `Sort()` function that you can find if you consult the documentation but I'll introduce one other that is particularly useful. This version presumes you have two arrays that are associated so that the elements in the first array represent keys to the corresponding elements in the second array. For example, you might store names of people in one array and the weights of the individuals in a second array. The `Sort()` function sorts the array of `names` in ascending sequence and also rearrange the elements of the `weights` array so the weights still match the appropriate person. Let's try it in an example.

Try It Out   **Sorting Two Associated Arrays**

This example creates an array of names and stores the weights of each person in the corresponding element of a second array. It then sorts both arrays in a single operation. Here's the code:

```
// Ex4_14.cpp : main project file.
// Sorting an array of keys(the names) and an array of objects(the weights)

#include "stdafx.h"

using namespace System;

int main(array<System::String ^> ^args)
{
  array<String^>^ names = { "Jill", "Ted", "Mary", "Eve", "Bill", "Al"};
  array<int>^ weights = { 103, 168, 128, 115, 180, 176};

  Array::Sort( names,weights);                    // Sort the arrays
  for each(String^ name in names)                 // Output the names
    Console::Write(L"{0, 10}", name);
  Console::WriteLine();

  for each(int weight in weights)                 // Output the weights
    Console::Write(L"{0, 10}", weight);
  Console::WriteLine();
    return 0;
}
```

The output from this program is:

```
    Al      Bill       Eve      Jill      Mary       Ted
   176       180       115       103       128       168
```

How It Works

The values in the `weights` array correspond to the weight of the person at the same index position in the names array. The `Sort()` function you call here sorts both arrays using the first array argument — names in this instance — to determine the order of both arrays. You can see from that output that after sorting everyone still has his or her correct weight recorded in the corresponding element of the weights array.

Searching One-Dimensional Arrays

The `Array` class also provides functions that search the elements of a one-dimensional array. Versions of the `BinarySearch()` function uses a binary search algorithm to find the index position of a given element in the entire array, or from a given range of elements. The binary search algorithm requires that the elements are ordered if it is to work, so you need to sort the elements before searching an array.

Here's how you could search an entire array:

```
array<int>^ values = { 23, 45, 68, 94, 123, 127, 150, 203, 299};
int toBeFound = 127;
int position = Array::BinarySearch(values, toBeFound);
if(position<0)
  Console::WriteLine(L"{0} was not found.", toBeFound);
else
  Console::WriteLine(L"{0} was found at index position {1}.", toBeFound, position);
```

The value to be found is stored in the `toBeFound` variable. The first argument to the `BinarySearch()` function is the handle of the array to be searched and the second argument specifies what you are looking for. The result of the search is returned by the `BinarySearch()` function as a value of type `int`. If the second argument to the function is found in the array specified by the first argument, its index position is returned; otherwise a negative integer is returned. Thus you must test the value returned to determine whether or not the search target was found. Because the values in the `values` array are already in ascending sequence there is no need to sort the array before searching it. This code fragment would produce the output:

```
127 was found at index position 5.
```

To search a given range of elements in an array you use a version of the `BinarySearch()` function that accepts four arguments. The first argument is the handle of the array to be searched, the second argument is the index position of the element where the search should start, the third argument is the number of elements to be searched, and the fourth argument is what you are looking for. Here's how you might use that:

```
array<int>^ values = { 23, 45, 68, 94, 123, 127, 150, 203, 299};
int toBeFound = 127;
int position = Array::BinarySearch(values, 3, 6, toBeFound);
```

This searches the values array from the fourth array element through to the last. As with the previous version of `BinarySearch()`, the function returns the index position found or a negative integer if the search fails.

Let's try a searching example.

Try It Out   Searching Arrays

This is a variation on the previous example with a search operation added:

```
// Ex4_15.cpp : main project file.
// Searching an array

#include "stdafx.h"
```

```
using namespace System;

int main(array<System::String ^> ^args)
{
  array<String^>^ names = { "Jill", "Ted", "Mary", "Eve", "Bill",
                            "Al",   "Ned", "Zoe",  "Dan", "Jean"};
  array<int>^ weights = { 103, 168, 128, 115, 180,
                          176, 209, 98,  190, 130 };
  array<String^>^ toBeFound = {"Bill", "Eve", "Al", "Fred"};

  Array::Sort( names, weights);                    // Sort the arrays

  int result = 0;                                  // Stores search result
  for each(String^ name in toBeFound)              // Search to find weights
  {
    result = Array::BinarySearch(names, name);     // Search names array

    if(result<0)                                   // Check the result
      Console::WriteLine(L"{0} was not found.", name);
    else
      Console::WriteLine(L"{0} weighs {1} lbs.", name, weights[result]);
  }
  return 0;
}
```

This program produces the output:

```
Bill weighs 180 lbs.
Eve weighs 115 lbs.
Al weighs 176 lbs.
Fred was not found.
```

How It Works

You create two associated arrays — an array of names and an array of corresponding weights in pounds. You also create the toBeFound array that contains the names of the people for whom you'd like to know their weights.

You sort the names and weights arrays using the names array to determine the order. You then search the names array for each name in the toBeFound array in a for each loop. The loop variable, name, is assigned each of the names in the toBeFound array in turn. Within the loop, you search for the current name with the statement:

```
result = Array::BinarySearch(names, name);    // Search names array
```

This returns the index of the element from names that contains name or a negative integer if the name is not found. You then test the result and produce the output in the if statement:

```
if(result<0)                                   // Check the result
  Console::WriteLine(L"{0} was not found.", name);
else
  Console::WriteLine(L"{0} weighs {1} lbs.", name, weights[result]);
```

Because the ordering of the `weights` array was determined by the ordering of the `names` array, you are able to index the `weights` array with `result`, the index position in the `names` array where `name` was found. You can see from the output that `"Fred"` was not found in the `names` array.

When the binary search operation fails, the value returned is not just any old negative value. It is in fact the bitwise complement of the index position of the first element that is greater than the object you are searching for, or the bitwise complement of the `Length` property of the array if no element is greater than the object sought. Knowing this you can use the `BinarySearch()` function to work out where you should insert a new object in an array and still maintain the order of the elements. Suppose you wanted to insert `"Fred"` in the `names` array. You can find the index position where it should be inserted with these statements:

```
array<String^>^ names = { "Jill", "Ted", "Mary", "Eve", "Bill",
                          "Al",   "Ned", "Zoe",  "Dan", "Jean"};
Array::Sort(names);                      // Sort the array
String^ name = L"Fred";
int position = Array::BinarySearch(names, name);
if(position<0)                           // If it is negative
  position = ~position;                  // flip the bits to get the insert index
```

If the result of the search is negative, flipping all the bits gives you the index position of where the new name should be inserted. If the result is positive, the new name is identical to the name at this position, so you can use the result as the new position directly.

You can now copy the `names` array into a new array that has one more element and use the position value to insert `name` at the appropriate place:

```
array<String^>^ newNames = gcnew array<String^>(names->Length+1);

// Copy elements from names to newNames
for(int i = 0 ; i<position ; i++)
  newNames[i] = names[i];

newNames[position] = name;                        // Copy the new element

if(position<names->Length)                        // If any elements remain in names
  for(int i = position ; i<names->Length ; i++)
    newNames[i+1] = names[i];                      // copy them to newNames
```

This creates a new array with a length one greater than the old array. You then copy all the elements from the old to the new up to index position `position-1`. You then copy the new name followed by the remaining elements from the old array. To discard the old array, you would just write:

```
names = nullptr;
```

Multidimensional Arrays

You can create arrays that have two or more dimensions; the maximum number of dimensions an array can have is 32, which should accommodate most situations. You specify the number of dimensions that your array has between the angled brackets immediately following the element type and separated from it by a comma. The dimension of an array is 1 by default, which is why you did not need to specify up to now. Here's how you can create a two-dimensional array of integer elements:

```
array<int, 2>^ values = gcnew array<int, 2>(4, 5);
```

This statement creates a two-dimensional array with four rows and five columns so it has a total of 20 elements. To access an element of a multidimensional array you specify a set of index values, one for each dimension; these are place between square brackets separated by commas following the array name. Here's how you could set values for the elements of a two-dimensional array of integers:

```
int nrows = 4;
int ncols = 5;
array<int, 2>^ values = gcnew array<int, 2>(nrows, ncols);
for(int i = 0 ; i<nrows ; i++)
  for(int j = 0 ; j<ncols ; j++)
    values[i,j] = (i+1)*(j+1);
```

The nested loop iterates over all the elements of the array. The outer loop iterates over the rows and the inner loop iterates over every element in the current row. As you see, each element is set to a value that is given by the expression $(i+1)*(j+1)$ so elements in the first row will be set to 1,2,3,4,5; elements in the second row will be 2,4,6,8,10; and so on through to the last row which will be 4,6,12,16,20.

I'm sure you will have noticed that the notation for accessing an element of a two-dimensional array here is different from the notation used for native C++ arrays. This is no accident. A C++/CLI array is not an array of arrays like a native C++ array; it is a true two-dimensional array. You cannot use a single index with a two-dimensional C++/CLI array, because this has no meaning; the array is a two-dimensional array of elements, not an array of arrays. As I said earlier, the dimensionality of an array is referred to as its **rank**, so the rank of the values array in the previous fragment is 2. Of course you can also define C++/CLI arrays of rank 3 or more, up to an array of rank 32. In contrast, native C++ arrays are actually always of rank 1 because native C++ arrays of two or more dimensions are really arrays of arrays. As you'll see later, you can also define arrays of arrays in C++/CLI.

Let's put a multidimensional array to use in an example.

Try It Out   Using a Multidimensional Array

This CLR console example creates a 12x12 multiplication table in a two-dimensional array:

```
// Ex4_16.cpp : main project file.
// Using a two-dimensional array

#include "stdafx.h"

using namespace System;

int main(array<System::String ^> ^args)
{
  const int SIZE = 12;
  array<int, 2>^ products = gcnew array<int, 2>(SIZE,SIZE);

  for (int i = 0 ; i < SIZE ; i++)
    for(int j = 0 ; j < SIZE ; j++)
      products[i,j] = (i+1)*(j+1);
```

```
Console::WriteLine(L"Here is the {0} times table:",  SIZE);

// Write horizontal divider line
for(int i = 0 ; i <= SIZE ; i++)
  Console::Write(L"_____");
Console::WriteLine();              // Write newline

// Write top line of table
Console::Write(L"    |");
for(int i = 1 ; i <= SIZE ; i++)
  Console::Write(L"{0,3} |", i);
Console::WriteLine();              // Write newline

// Write horizontal divider line with verticals
for(int i = 0 ; i <= SIZE ; i++)
  Console::Write(L"____|");
Console::WriteLine();              // Write newline

// Write remaining lines
for(int i = 0 ; i<SIZE ; i++)
{
  Console::Write(L"{0,3} |", i+1);
  for(int j = 0 ; j<SIZE ; j++)
    Console::Write(L"{0,3} |", products[i,j]);

  Console::WriteLine();            // Write newline
}

// Write horizontal divider line
for(int i = 0 ; i <= SIZE ; i++)
  Console::Write(L"_____");
Console::WriteLine();              // Write newline

  return 0;
}
```

This example should produce the following output:

```
Here is the 12 times table:

    |  1 |  2 |  3 |  4 |  5 |  6 |  7 |  8 |  9 | 10 | 11 | 12 |
____|____|____|____|____|____|____|____|____|____|____|____|____|
  1 |  1 |  2 |  3 |  4 |  5 |  6 |  7 |  8 |  9 | 10 | 11 | 12 |
  2 |  2 |  4 |  6 |  8 | 10 | 12 | 14 | 16 | 18 | 20 | 22 | 24 |
  3 |  3 |  6 |  9 | 12 | 15 | 18 | 21 | 24 | 27 | 30 | 33 | 36 |
  4 |  4 |  8 | 12 | 16 | 20 | 24 | 28 | 32 | 36 | 40 | 44 | 48 |
  5 |  5 | 10 | 15 | 20 | 25 | 30 | 35 | 40 | 45 | 50 | 55 | 60 |
  6 |  6 | 12 | 18 | 24 | 30 | 36 | 42 | 48 | 54 | 60 | 66 | 72 |
  7 |  7 | 14 | 21 | 28 | 35 | 42 | 49 | 56 | 63 | 70 | 77 | 84 |
  8 |  8 | 16 | 24 | 32 | 40 | 48 | 56 | 64 | 72 | 80 | 88 | 96 |
  9 |  9 | 18 | 27 | 36 | 45 | 54 | 63 | 72 | 81 | 90 | 99 |108 |
 10 | 10 | 20 | 30 | 40 | 50 | 60 | 70 | 80 | 90 |100 |110 |120 |
 11 | 11 | 22 | 33 | 44 | 55 | 66 | 77 | 88 | 99 |110 |121 |132 |
 12 | 12 | 24 | 36 | 48 | 60 | 72 | 84 | 96 |108 |120 |132 |144 |
```

219

How It Works

It looks like a lot of code, but most of it is concerned with making the output pretty. You create the two-dimensional array with the following statements:

```
const int SIZE = 12;
array<int, 2>^ products = gcnew array<int, 2>(SIZE,SIZE);
```

The first line defines a constant integer value that specifies the number of elements in each array dimension. The second line defines an array of rank 2 that has 12 rows of 12 elements. This array stores the products in the 12 × 12 table.

You set the values of the elements in the products array in a nested loop:

```
for (int i = 0 ; i < SIZE ; i++)
  for(int j = 0 ; j < SIZE ; j++)
    products[i,j] = (i+1)*(j+1);
```

The outer loop iterates over the rows, and the inner loop iterates over the columns. The value of each element is the product of the row and column index values after they are incremented by 1. The rest of the code in main() is concerned solely with generating output.

After writing the initial table heading, you create a row of bars to mark the top of the table like this:

```
for(int i = 0 ; i <= SIZE ; i++)
  Console::Write(L"_____");
Console::WriteLine();                 // Write newline
```

Each iteration of the loop writes five horizontal bar characters. Note that the upper limit for the loop is inclusive, so you write 13 sets of five bars to allow for the row labels in the table plus the 12 columns.

Next you write the row of column labels for the table with another loop:

```
// Write top line of table
Console::Write(L"    |");
for(int i = 1 ; i <= SIZE ; i++)
  Console::Write(L"{0,3} |", i);
Console::WriteLine();                 // Write newline
```

You have to write the space over the row label position separately because that is a special case with no output value. Each of the column labels is written in the loop. You then write a newline character ready for the row outputs that follow.

The row outputs are written in a nested loop:

```
for(int i = 0 ; i<SIZE ; i++)
{
  Console::Write(L"{0,3} |", i+1);
  for(int j = 0 ; j<SIZE ; j++)
    Console::Write(L"{0,3} |", products[i,j]);

  Console::WriteLine();               // Write newline
}
```

The outer loop iterates over the rows and the code inside the outer loop writes a complete row, including the row label on the left. The inner loop writes the values from the `products` array that correspond to the ith row, with the values separated by vertical bars.

The remaining code writes more horizontal bars to finish off the bottom of the table.

Arrays of Arrays

Array elements can be of any type, so you can create arrays where the elements are tracking handles that reference arrays. This gives you the possibility of creating so-called **jagged arrays** because each handle referencing an array can have a different number of elements. This is most easily understood by looking at an example. Suppose you want to store the names of children in a class grouped by the grade they scored, where there are five classifications corresponding to grades A, B, C, D, and E. You could first create an array of five elements where each element stores an array of names. Here's the statement that will do that:

```
array< array< String^ >^ >^ grades = gcnew array< array< String^ >^ >(5);
```

Don't let all the hats confuse you — it's simpler than it looks. The array variable, `grades`, is a handle of type `array<type>^`. Each element in the array is also a handle to an array, so the type of the array elements is of the same form — `array<type>^` so this has to go between the angled brackets in the original array type specification, which results in `array< array<type>^ >^`. The elements stored in the array are also handles to `String` objects so you must replace type in the last expression by `String^`; thus you end up with the array type being `array< array< String^ >^ >^`.

With the array of arrays worked out, you can now create the arrays of names. Here's an example of what that might look like:

```
grades[0] = gcnew array<String^>{"Louise", "Jack"};                       // Grade A
grades[1] = gcnew array<String^>{"Bill", "Mary", "Ben", "Joan"};          // Grade B
grades[2] = gcnew array<String^>{"Jill", "Will", "Phil"};                 // Grade C
grades[3] = gcnew array<String^>{"Ned", "Fred", "Ted", "Jed", "Ed"};      // Grade D
grades[4] = gcnew array<String^>{"Dan", "Ann"};                           // Grade E
```

The expression `grades[n]` accesses the nth element of the grades array, and of course this is a handle to an array of `String^` handles in each case. Thus each of the five statements creates an array of `String` object handles and stores the address in one of the elements of the `grades` array. As you see, the arrays of strings vary in length, so clearly you can manage a set of arrays with arbitrary lengths in this way.

You could create and initialize the whole array of arrays in a single statement:

```
array< array< String^ >^ >^ grades = gcnew array< array< String^ >^ >
     {
         gcnew array<String^>{"Louise", "Jack"},                        // Grade A
         gcnew array<String^>{"Bill", "Mary", "Ben", "Joan"},           // Grade B
         gcnew array<String^>{"Jill", "Will", "Phil"},                  // Grade C
         gcnew array<String^>{"Ned", "Fred", "Ted", "Jed", "Ed"},       // Grade D
         gcnew array<String^>{"Dan", "Ann"}                             // Grade E
     };
```

The initial values for the elements are between the braces.

Let's put this in a working example that demonstrates how you can process arrays of arrays.

Try It Out   Using an Array of Arrays

Create a CLR console program project and modify it as follows:

```cpp
// Ex4_17.cpp : main project file.
// Using an array of arrays

#include "stdafx.h"

using namespace System;

int main(array<System::String ^> ^args)
{
  array< array< String^ >^ >^ grades = gcnew array< array< String^ >^ >
        {
            gcnew array<String^>{"Louise", "Jack"},                  // Grade A
            gcnew array<String^>{"Bill", "Mary", "Ben", "Joan"},     // Grade B
            gcnew array<String^>{"Jill", "Will", "Phil"},            // Grade C
            gcnew array<String^>{"Ned", "Fred", "Ted", "Jed", "Ed"}, // Grade D
            gcnew array<String^>{"Dan", "Ann"}                       // Grade E
        };

  wchar_t gradeLetter = 'A';

  for each(array< String^ >^ grade in grades)
  {
    Console::WriteLine(L"Students with Grade {0}:", gradeLetter++);

    for each( String^ student in grade)
      Console::Write(L"{0,12}",student);            // Output the current name

    Console::WriteLine();                           // Write a newline
  }
  return 0;
}
```

This example produces the following output:

```
Students with Grade A:
      Louise        Jack
Students with Grade B:
        Bill        Mary         Ben        Joan
Students with Grade C:
        Jill        Will        Phil
Students with Grade D:
         Ned        Fred         Ted         Jed          Ed
Students with Grade E:
         Dan         Ann
```

How It Works

The array definition is exactly as you saw in the previous section. Next you define the `gradeLetter` variable as type `wchar_t` with the initial value `'A'`. This is to be used to present the grade classification in the output.

The students and their grades are listed by the nested loops. The outer `for each` loop iterates over the elements in the grades array:

```
for each(array< String^ >^ grade in grades)
{
  // Process students in the current grade...
}
```

The loop variable, `grade`, is of type `array< String^ >^` because that's the element type in the `grades` array. The variable `grade` references each of the arrays of `String^` handles in turn, so first time around the loop references the array of grade A student names, second time around it references grade B student names, and so on until the last loop iteration when it references the grade E student names.

On each iteration of the outer loop, you execute the following code:

```
Console::WriteLine(L"Students with Grade {0}:", gradeLetter++);

for each( String^ student in grade)
  Console::Write(L"{0,12}",student);              // Output the current name

Console::WriteLine();                             // Write a newline
```

The first statement writes a line that includes the current value of `gradeLetter`, which starts out as `'A'`. The statement also increments `gradeLetter` so it will be, `'B'`, `'C'`, `'D'`, and `'E'` successively on subsequent iterations of the outer loop.

Next you have the inner `for each` loop that iterates over each of the names in the current grade array in turn. The output statement uses the `Console::Write()` function so all the names appear on the same line. The names are presented right-justified in the output in a field width of 12, so the names in the lines of output are aligned. After the loop, the `WriteLine()` just writes a newline to the output so the next grade output starts on a new line.

You could have used a `for` loop for the inner loop:

```
for (int i = 0 ; i < grade->Length ; i++)
  Console::Write(L"{0,12}",grade[i]);            // Output the current name
```

The loop is constrained by the `Length` property of the current array of names that is referenced by the `grade` variable.

You could also have used a `for` loop for the outer loop as well, in which case the inner loop needs to be changed further and the nested loop looks like this:

```
for (int j = 0 ; j < grades->Length ; j++)
{
  Console::WriteLine(L"Students with Grade {0}:", gradeLetter+j);
  for (int i = 0 ; i < grades[j]->Length ; i++)
    Console::Write(L"{0,12}",grades[j][i]);           // Output the current name
  Console::WriteLine();
}
```

Now `grades[j]` references the `j`th array of names so the expression `grades[j][i]` references the `i`th name in the `j`th array of names.

Strings

You have already seen that the String class type that is defined in the System namespace represents a string in C++/CLI — in fact a string consists of Unicode characters. To be more precise it represents a string consisting of a sequence of characters of type System::Char. You get a huge amount of powerful functionality with String class objects so it makes string processing very easy. Let's start at the beginning with string creation.

You can create a String object like this:

```
System::String^ saying = L"Many hands make light work.";
```

The variable, saying, is a tracking handle that references the String object that is initialized with the string that appears on the right of the =. You must always use a tracking handle to store a reference to a String object. The string literal here is a wide character string because it has the prefix L. If you omit the L prefix, you have a string literal containing 8-bit characters, but the compiler ensures it is converted to a wide-character string.

You can access individual characters in a string by using a subscript just like an array, and the first character in the string has an index value of 0. Here's how you could output the third character in the string saying:

```
Console::WriteLine(L"The third character in the string is {0}", saying[2]);
```

Note that you can only retrieve a character from a string using an index value; you cannot update the string in this way. String objects are immutable and therefore cannot be modified.

You can obtain the number of characters in a string by accessing its Length property. You could output the length of saying with this statement:

```
Console::WriteLine(L"The string has {0} characters.", saying->Length);
```

Because saying is a tracking handle — which as you know is a kind of pointer — you must use the -> operator to access the Length property (or any other member of the object). You'll learn more about properties when you get to investigate C++/CLI classes in detail.

Joining Strings

You can use the + operator to join strings to form a new String object. Here's an example:

```
String^ name1 = L"Beth";
String^ name2 = L"Betty";
String^ name3 = name1 + L" and " + name2;
```

After executing these statements, name3 contains the string "Beth and Betty". Note how you can use the + operator to join String objects with string literals. You can also join String objects with numerical values or bool values and have the values converted automatically to a string before the join operation. The following statements illustrate this:

```
String^ str = L"Value: ";
String^ str1 = str + 2.5;                    // Result is new string "Value: 2.5"
```

```
String^ str2 = str + 25;              // Result is new string L"Value: 25"
String^ str3 = str + true;            // Result is new string L"Value: True"
```

You can also join a string and a character, but the result depends on the type of character:

```
char ch = 'Z';
wchar_t wch = L'Z';
String^ str4 = str + ch;              // Result is new string L"Value: 90"
String^ str5 = str + wch;             // Result is new string L"Value: Z"
```

The comments show the results of the operations. A character of type char is treated as a numerical value so you get the character code value joined to the string. The wchar_t character is of the same type as the characters in the String object (type Char) so the character is appended to the string.

Don't forget that String objects are immutable; once created, they cannot be changed. This means that *all* operations that apparently modify String objects always result in new String objects being created.

The String class also defines a Join() function that you use when you want to join a series of strings stored in an array into a single string with separators between the original strings. Here's how you could join names together in a single string with the names separated by commas:

```
array<String^>^ names = { L"Jill", L"Ted", L"Mary", L"Eve", L"Bill"};
String^ separator = L", ";
String^ joined = String::Join(separator, names);
```

After executing these statements, joined references the string L"Jill, Ted, Mary, Eve, Bill". The separator string has been inserted between each of the original strings in the names array. Of course, the separator string can be anything you like — it could be L" and ", for example, which results in the string L"Jill and Ted and Mary and Eve and Bill".

Let's try a full example of working with String objects.

Try It Out   Working with Strings

Suppose you have an array of integer values that you want to output aligned in columns. You want the values aligned but you want the columns to be just sufficiently wide to accommodate the largest value in the array with a space between columns. This program does that.

```
// Ex4_18.cpp : main project file.
// Creating a custom format string

#include "stdafx.h"

using namespace System;

int main(array<System::String ^> ^args)
{
  array<int>^ values = { 2, 456, 23, -46, 34211, 456, 5609, 112098,
    234, -76504, 341, 6788, -909121, 99, 10};
  String^ formatStr1 = L"{0,"           // 1st half of format string
  String^ formatStr2 = L"}";            // 2nd half of format string
```

225

```
    String^ number;                         // Stores a number as a string

    // Find the length of the maximum length value string
    int maxLength = 0;                      // Holds the maximum length found
    for each(int value in values)
    {
      number = L"" + value;                 // Create string from value
      if(maxLength<number->Length)
        maxLength = number->Length;
    }

    // Create the format string to be used for output
    String^ format = formatStr1 + (maxLength+1) + formatStr2;

    // Output the values
    int numberPerLine = 3;
    for(int i = 0 ; i< values->Length ; i++)
    {
      Console::Write(format, values[i]);
      if((i+1)%numberPerLine == 0)
        Console::WriteLine();
    }
    return 0;
}
```

The output from this program is:

```
      2     456      23
    -46   34211     456
   5609  112098     234
 -76504     341    6788
-909121      99      10
```

How It Works

The objective of this program is to create a format string to align the output of integers from the values array in columns with a width sufficient to accommodate the maximum length string representation of the integers. You create the format string initially in two parts:

```
String^ formatStr1 = L"{0,";            // 1st half of format string
String^ formatStr2 = L"}";              // 2nd half of format string
```

These two strings are the beginning and end of the format string you ultimately require. You need to work out the length of the maximum-length number string, and sandwich that value between formatStr1 and formatStr2 to form the complete format string.

You find the length you require with the following code:

```
int maxLength = 0;                      // Holds the maximum length found
for each(int value in values)
{
  number = "" + value;                  // Create string from value
  if(maxLength<number->Length)
    maxLength = number->Length;
}
```

Within the loop you convert each number from the array to its `String` representation by joining it to an empty string. You compare the `Length` property of each string to `maxLength`, and if it's greater than the current value of `maxLength`, it becomes the new maximum length.

Creating the format string is simple:

```
String^ format = formatStr1 + (maxLength+1) + formatStr2;
```

You need to add 1 to `maxLength` to allow one additional space in the field when the maximum length string is displayed. Placing the expression `maxLength+1` between parentheses ensures that it is evaluated as an arithmetic operation before the string joining operations are executed.

Finally you use the `format` string in the code to output values from the array:

```
int numberPerLine = 3;
for(int i = 0 ; i< values->Length ; i++)
{
  Console::Write(format, values[i]);
  if((i+1)%numberPerLine == 0)
    Console::WriteLine();
}
```

The output statement in the loop uses `format` as the string for output. With the `maxLength` plugged into the `format` string, the output is in columns that are one greater than the maximum length output value. The `numberPerLine` variable determines how many values appear on a line so the loop is quite general in that you can vary the number of columns by changing the value of `numberPerLine`.

Modifying Strings

The most common requirement for trimming a string is to trim spaces from both the beginning and the end. The `Trim()` function for a string object does that:

```
String^ str = {L"  Handsome is as handsome does...    "};
String^ newStr = str->Trim();
```

The `Trim()` function in the second statement removes any spaces from the beginning and end of `str` and returns the result as a new `String` object stored in `newStr`. Of course, if you did not want to retain the original string, you could store the result back in `str`.

There's another version of the `Trim()` function that allows you to specify the characters that are to be removed from the start and end of the string. This function is very flexible because you have more than one way of specifying the characters to be removed. You can specify the characters in an array and pass the array handle as the argument to the function:

```
String^ toBeTrimmed = L"wool wool sheep sheep wool wool wool";
array<wchar_t>^ notWanted = {L'w',L'o',L'l',L' '};
Console::WriteLine(toBeTrimmed->Trim(notWanted));
```

Here you have a string, `toBeTrimmed`, that consists of sheep covered in wool. The array of characters to be trimmed from the string is defined by the `notWanted` array so passing that to the `Trim()` function for the string removes any of the characters in the array from both ends of the string. Remember, `String` objects are immutable so the original string is not being changed in any way — a new string is created and returned by the `Trim()` operation. Executing this code fragment produces the output:

```
sheep sheep
```

If you happen to specify the character literals without the `L` prefix, they will be of type `char` (which corresponds to the `SByte` value class type); however, the compiler arranges that they are converted to type `wchar_t`.

You can also specify the characters that the `Trim()` function is to remove explicitly as arguments, so you could write the last line of the previous fragment as:

```
Console::WriteLine(toBeTrimmed->Trim(L'w', L'o', L'l', L' '));
```

This produces the same output as the previous version of the statement. You can have as many arguments of type `wchar_t` as you like, but if there are a lot of characters to be specified an array is the best approach.

If you want to trim only one end of a string, you can use the `TrimEnd()` or `TrimStart()` functions. These come in the same variety of versions as the `Trim()` function so without arguments you trim spaces, with an array argument you trim the characters in the array, and with explicit `wchar_t` arguments those characters are removed.

The inverse of trimming a string is padding it at either end with spaces or other characters. You have `PadLeft()` and `PadRight()` functions that pad a string at the left or right end respectively. The primary use for these functions is in formatting output where you want to place strings either left- or right-justified in a fixed width field. The simpler versions of the `PadLeft()` and `PadRight()` functions accept a single argument specifying the length of the string that is to result from the operation. For example:

```
String^ value = L"3.142";
String^ leftPadded = value->PadLeft(10);      // Result is L"     3.142"
String^ rightPadded = value->PadRight(10);    // Result is L"3.142     "
```

If the length you specify as the argument is less than or equal to the length of the original string, either function returns a new `String` object that is identical to the original.

To pad a string with a character other than a space, you specify the padding character as the second argument to the `PadLeft()` or `PadRight()` functions. Here are a couple of examples of this:

```
String^ value = L"3.142";
String^ leftPadded = value->PadLeft(10, L'*');   // Result is L"*****3.142"
String^ rightPadded = value->PadRight(10, L'#'); // Result is L"3.142#####"
```

Of course, with all these examples, you could store the result back in the handle referencing the original string, which would discard the original string.

The `String` class also has the `ToUpper()` and `ToLower()` functions to convert an entire string to upper- or lowercase. Here's how that works:

```
String^ proverb = L"Many hands make light work.";
String^ upper = proverb->ToUpper();     // Result L"MANY HANDS MAKE LIGHT WORK."
```

The `ToUpper()` function returns a new string that is the original string converted to uppercase.

You use the `Insert()` function to insert a string at a given position in an existing string. Here's an example of doing that:

```
String^ proverb = L"Many hands make light work.";
String^ newProverb = proverb->Insert(5, L"deck ");
```

The function inserts the string specified by the second argument starting at the index position in the old string specified by the first argument. The result of this operation is a new string containing:

```
Many deck hands make light work.
```

You can also replace all occurrences of a given character in a string with another character or all occurrences of a given substring with another substring. Here's a fragment that shows both possibilities:

```
String^ proverb = L"Many hands make light work.";
Console::WriteLine(proverb->Replace(L' ', L'*');
Console::WriteLine(proverb->Replace(L"Many hands", L"Pressing switch"));
```

Executing this code fragment produces the output:

```
Many*hands*make*light*work.
Pressing switch make light work.
```

The first argument to the `Replace()` function specifies the character or substring to be replaced and the second argument specifies the replacement.

Comparing Strings

You can compare two `String` objects using the `Compare()` function in the `String` class. The function returns an integer that is less than zero, equal to zero, or greater than zero, depending on whether the first argument is less than, equal to, or greater than the second argument. Here's an example:

```
String^ him(L"Jacko");
String^ her(L"Jillo");
int result = String::Compare(him, her);
if(result < 0)
  Console::WriteLine(L"{0} is less than {1}.", him, her);
else if(result > 0)
  Console::WriteLine(L"{0} is greater than {1}.", him, her);
else
  Console::WriteLine(L"{0} is equal to {1}.", him, her);
```

You store the integer that the `Compare()` function returns in `result` and use that in the `if` statement to decide the appropriate output. Executing this fragment produces the output:

```
Jacko is less than Jillo.
```

There's another version of `Compare()` that requires a third argument of type `bool`. If the third argument is `true`, then the strings referenced by the first two arguments are compared ignoring case; if the third argument is `false` then the behavior is the same as the previous version of `Compare()`.

Searching Strings

Perhaps the simplest search operation is to test whether a string starts or ends with a given substring. The StartsWith() and EndsWith() functions do that. You supply a handle to the substring you are looking for as the argument to either function, and the function returns a bool value that indicates whether or not the substring is present. Here's a fragment showing how you might use the StartsWith() function:

```
String^ sentence = L"Hide, the cow's outside.";
if(sentence->StartsWith(L"Hide"))
    Console::WriteLine(L"The sentence starts with 'Hide'.");
```

Executing this fragment results in the output:

```
The sentence starts with 'Hide'.
```

Of course, you could also apply the EndsWith() function to the sentence string:

```
Console::WriteLine(L"The sentence does{0} end with 'outside'.",
                        sentence->EndsWith(L"outside") ? L"" : L" not");
```

The result of the conditional operator expression is inserted in the output string. This is an empty string if EndsWith() returns true and " not" if it returns false. In this instance the function returns false (because of the period at the end of the sentence string).

The IndexOf() function searches a string for the first occurrence of a specified character or a substring and returns the index if it is present or -1 if it is not found. You specify the character or the substring you are looking for as the argument to the function. For example:

```
String^ sentence = L"Hide, the cow's outside.";
int ePosition = sentence->IndexOf(L'e');          // Returns 3
int thePosition = sentence->IndexOf(L"the");      // Returns 6
```

The first search is for the letter 'e' and the second is for the word "the". The values returned by the IndexOf() function are indicated in the comments.

More typically you will want to find all occurrences of a given character or substring and another version of the IndexOf() function is designed to be used repeatedly to enable you to do that. In this case you supply a second argument specifying the index position where the search is to start. Here's an example of how you might use the function in this way:

```
int index = 0;
int count = 0;
while((index = words->IndexOf(word,index)) >= 0)
{
    index += word->Length;
    ++count;
}
Console::WriteLine(L"'{0}' was found {1} times in:\n{2}", word, count, words);
```

This fragment counts the number of occurrences of "wool" in the words string. The search operation appears in the while loop condition and the result is stored in index. The loop continues as long as index is non-negative so when IndexOf() returns -1 the loop ends. Within the loop body, the value of `index` is incremented by the length of `word`, which moves the index position to the character following the instance of `word` that was found, ready for the search on the next iteration. The count variable is incremented within the loop so when the loop ends it has accumulated the total number of occurrences of `word` in `words`. Executing the fragment results in the following output:

```
'wool' was found 5 times in:
wool wool sheep sheep wool wool wool
```

The `LastIndexOf()` function is similar to the `IndexOf()` function except that it searches backwards through the string from the end or from a specified index position. Here's how the operation performed by the previous fragment could be performed using the `LastIndexOf()` function:

```
int index = words->Length - 1;
int count = 0;
while(index >= 0 && (index = words->LastIndexOf(word,index)) >= 0)
{
  --index;
  ++count;
}
```

With the `word` and `words` strings the same as before, this fragment produces the same output. Because `LastIndexOf()` searches backwards, the starting index is the last character in the string, which is `words->Length-1`. When an occurrence of `word` is found, you must now decrement `index` by 1 so that the next backward search starts at the character preceding the current occurrence of `word`. If `word` occurs right at the beginning of `words` — at index position 0 — decrementing `index` results in –1, which is not a legal argument to the `LastIndexOf()` function because the search starting position must always be within the string. The addition check for a negative value of `index` in the loop condition prevents this from happening; if the left operand of the `&&` operator is `false`, the right operand is not evaluated.

The last search function I want to mention is `IndexOfAny()` that searches a string for the first occurrence of any character in the array of type `array<wchar_t>` that you supply as the argument. Similar to the `IndexOf()` function, the `IndexOfAny()` function comes in versions that search from the beginning of a string or from a specified index position. Let's try a full working example of using the `IndexOfAny()` function.

Try It Out Searching for Any of a Set of Characters

This example searches a string for punctuation characters:

```cpp
// Ex4_19.cpp : main project file.
// Searching for punctuation

#include "stdafx.h"

using namespace System;

int main(array<System::String ^> ^args)
{
  array<wchar_t>^ punctuation = {L'"', L'\'', L'.', L',', L':', L';', L'!', L'?'};
  String^ sentence = L"\"It's chilly in here\", the boy's mother said coldly.";

  // Create array of space characters same length as sentence
```

```
array<wchar_t>^ indicators = gcnew array<wchar_t>(sentence->Length){L' '};

int index = 0;                          // Index of character found
int count = 0;                          // Count of punctuation characters
while((index = sentence->IndexOfAny(punctuation, index)) >= 0)
{
  indicators[index] = L'^';             // Set marker
  ++index;                              // Increment to next character
  ++count;                              // Increase the count
}
Console::WriteLine(L"There are {0} punctuation characters in the string:",
                                                                    count);
Console::WriteLine(L"\n{0}\n{1}", sentence, gcnew String(indicators));
return 0;
}
```

This example should produce the following output:

```
There are 6 punctuation characters in the string:

"It's chilly in here", the boy's mother said coldly.
 ^  ^                  ^^          ^                ^
```

How It Works

You first create an array containing the characters to be found and the string to be searched:

```
array<wchar_t>^ punctuation = {L'"', L'\'', L'.', L',', L':', L';', L'!', L'?'};
String^ sentence = L"\"It's chilly in here\", the boy's mother said coldly.";
```

Note that you must specify a single quote character using an escape sequence because a single quote is a delimiter in a character literal. You can use a double quote explicitly in a character literal because there's no risk of it being interpreted as a delimiter in this context.

Next you define an array of characters with the elements initialized to a space character:

```
array<wchar_t>^ indicators = gcnew array<wchar_t>(sentence->Length){L' '};
```

This array has as many elements as the sentence string has characters. You'll be using this array in the output to mark where punctuation characters occur in the sentence string. You'll just change the appropriate array element to '^' whenever a punctuation character is found. Note how a single initializer between the braces following the array specification can be used to initialize all the elements in the array.

The search takes place in the while loop:

```
while((index = sentence->IndexOfAny(punctuation, index)) >= 0)
{
  indicators[index] = L'^';             // Set marker
  ++index;                              // Increment to next character
  ++count;                              // Increase the count
}
```

The loop condition is essentially the same as you have seen in earlier code fragments. Within the loop body you update the `indicators` array element at position `index` to be a `'^'` character before incrementing index ready for the next iteration. When the loop ends, `count` contains the number of punctuation characters that were found, and `indicators` will contain `'^'` characters at the positions in sentence where such characters were found.

The output is produced by the statements:

```
Console::WriteLine(L"There are {0} punctuation characters in the string:",
                                                                      count);
Console::WriteLine(L"\n{0}\n{1}" sentence, gcnew String(indicators));
```

The second statement creates a new `String` object on the heap from the indicators array by passing the array to the `String` class **constructor**. A class constructor is a function that will create a class object when it is called. You'll learn more about constructors when you get into defining your own classes.

Tracking References

A tracking reference provides a similar capability to a native C++ reference in that it represents an alias for something on the CLR heap. You can create tracking references to value types on the stack and to handles in the garbage-collected heap; the tracking references themselves are always created on the stack. A tracking reference is automatically updated if the object referenced is moved by the garbage collector.

You define a tracking reference using the `%` operator. For example, here's how you could create a tracking reference to a value type:

```
int value = 10;
int% trackValue = value;
```

The second statement defines `stackValue` to be a tracking reference to the variable `value`, which has been created on the stack. You can now modify `value` using `stackValue`:

```
trackValue *= 5;
Console::WriteLine(value);
```

Because `trackValue` is an alias for `value`, the second statement outputs 50.

Interior Pointers

Although you cannot perform arithmetic on the address in a tracking handle, C++/CLI does provide a form of pointer with which it is possible to apply arithmetic operations; it's called an **interior pointer** and is defined using the keyword `interior_ptr`. The address stored in an interior pointer can be updated automatically by the CLR garbage collection when necessary. An interior pointer is always an automatic variable that is local to a function.

Here's how you could define an interior point containing the address of the first element in an array:

```
array<double>^ data = {1.5, 3.5, 6.7, 4.2, 2.1};
interior_ptr<double> pstart = &data[0];
```

You specify the type of object pointed to by the interior pointer between angled brackets following the `interior_ptr` keyword. In the second statement here you initialize the pointer with the address of the first element in the array using the `&` operator, just as you would with a native C++ pointer. If you do not provide an initial value for an interior pointer, it is initialized with `nullptr` by default. An array is always allocated on the CLR heap so here's a situation where the garbage collector may adjust the address contained in an interior pointer.

There are constraints on the type specification for an interior pointer. An interior pointer can contain the address of a value class object on the stack or the address of a handle to an object on the CLR heap; it cannot contain the address of a whole object on the CLR heap. An interior pointer can also point to a native class object or a native pointer.

You can also use an interior pointer to hold the address of a value class object that is part of an object on the heap, such as an element of a CLR array. This way you can create an interior pointer that can store the address of a tracking handle to a `System::String` object but you cannot create an interior pointer to store the address of the `String` object itself. For example:

```
interior_ptr<String^> pstr1;      // OK - pointer to a handle
interior_ptr<String> pstr2;       // Will not compile - pointer to a String object
```

All the arithmetic operations that you can apply to a native C++ pointer you can also apply to an interior pointer. You can increment and decrement an interior pointer to change the address it contains to refer to the following or preceding data item. You can also add or subtract integer values and compare interior points. Let's put together an example that does some of that.

Try It Out   Creating and Using Interior Pointers

This example exercises interior pointers with numerical values and strings:

```
// Ex4_20.cpp : main project file.
// Creating and using interior pointers

#include "stdafx.h"

using namespace System;

int main(array<System::String ^> ^args)
{
   // Access array elements through a pointer
   array<double>^ data = {1.5, 3.5, 6.7, 4.2, 2.1};
   interior_ptr<double> pstart = &data[0];
   interior_ptr<double> pend = &data[data->Length - 1];
   double sum = 0.0;
   while(pstart <= pend)
     sum += *pstart++;

   Console::WriteLine(L"Total of data array elements = {0}\n", sum);

   // Just to show we can - access strings through an interior pointer
   array<String^>^ strings = { L"Land ahoy!",
                               L"Splice the mainbrace!",
                               L"Shiver me timbers!",
```

```
                                  L"Never throw into the wind!"
                     };

   for(interior_ptr<String^> pstrings = &strings[0] ;
            pstrings-&strings[0] < strings->Length ; ++pstrings)
     Console::WriteLine(*pstrings);

   return 0;
}
```

The output from this example is:

```
Total of data array elements = 18
Land ahoy!
Splice the mainbrace!
Shiver me timbers!
Never throw into the wind!
```

How It Works

After creating the `data` array of elements of type `double`, you define two interior pointers:

```
interior_ptr<double> pstart = &data[0];
interior_ptr<double> pend = &data[data->Length - 1];
```

The first statement creates `pstart` as a pointer to type `double` and initializes it with the address of the first element in the array, `data[0]`. The interior pointer, `pend`, is initialized with the address of the last element in the array, `data[data->Length - 1]`. Because `data->Length` is the number of elements in the array, subtracting 1 from this value produces the index for the last element.

The `while` loop accumulates the sum of the elements in the array:

```
while(pstart <= pend)
   sum += *pstart++;
```

The loop continues as long as the interior pointer, `pstart`, contains an address that is not greater than the address in `pend`. You could equally well have expressed the loop condition as `!pstart > pend`.

Within the loop, `pstart` starts out containing the address of the first array element. The value of the first element is obtained by dereferencing the pointer with the expression `*pstart` and the result of this is added to `sum`. The address in the pointer is then incremented using the `++` operator. On the last loop iteration, `pstart` contains the address of the last element which is the same as the address value that `pend` contains, so incrementing `pstart` makes the loop condition `false` because `pstart` is then greater than `pend`. After the loop ends the value of `sum` is written out so you can confirm that the `while` loop is working as it should.

Next you create an array of four strings:

```
array<String^>^ strings = { L"Land ahoy!",
                            L"Splice the mainbrace!",
                            L"Shiver me timbers!",
```

```
                          L"Never throw into the wind!"
                  };
```

The `for` loop then outputs each string to the command line:

```
    for(interior_ptr<String^> pstrings = &strings[0] ;
             pstrings-&strings[0] < strings->Length ; ++pstrings)
      Console::WriteLine(*pstrings);
```

The first expression in the `for` loop condition declares the interior pointer, `pstrings`, and initializes it with the address of the first element in the `strings` array. The second expression determines whether the for loop continues:

```
    pstrings-&strings[0] < strings->Length
```

As long as `pstrings` contains the address of a valid array element, the difference between the address in `pstrings` and the address of the first element in the array is less than the number of elements in the array, given by the expression `strings->Length`. Thus when this difference equals the length of the array, the loop ends. You can see from the output that everything works as expected.

The most frequent use of an interior pointer is to reference objects that are part of a CLR heap object, and you'll see more about this later in the book.

Summary

You are now familiar with all of the basic types of values in C++, how to create and use arrays of those types, and how to create and use pointers. You have also been introduced to the idea of a reference. However, we have not exhausted all of these topics. I'll come back to the topics of arrays, pointers, and references later in the book. The important points discussed in this chapter relating to native C++ programming are:

❑   An array allows you to manage a number of variables of the same type using a single name. Each dimension of an array is defined between square brackets following the array name in the declaration of the array.

❑   Each dimension of an array is indexed starting from zero. Thus the fifth element of a one-dimensional array has the index value 4.

❑   Arrays can be initialized by placing the initializing values between curly braces in the declaration.

❑   A pointer is a variable that contains the address of another variable. A pointer is declared as a 'pointer to *type*' and may only be assigned addresses of variables of the given type.

❑ A pointer can point to a constant object. Such a pointer can be reassigned to another object. A pointer may also be defined as `const`, in which case it can't be reassigned.

❑ A reference is an alias for another variable, and can be used in the same places as the variable it references. A reference must be initialized in its declaration.

❑ A reference can't be reassigned to another variable.

❑ The operator `sizeof` returns the number of bytes occupied by the object specified as its argument. Its argument may be a variable or a type name between parentheses.

❑ The operator `new` allocates memory dynamically in the free store in a native C++ application. When memory has been assigned as requested, it returns a pointer to the beginning of the memory area provided. If memory cannot be assigned for any reason, an exception is thrown that by default causes the program to terminate.

The pointer mechanism is sometimes a bit confusing because it can operate at different levels within the same program. Sometimes it is operating as an address, and at other times it can be operating with the value stored at an address. It's very important that you feel at ease with the way pointers are used, so if you find that they are in any way unclear, try them out with a few examples of your own until you feel confident about applying them.

The key points that you learned about in relation to programming for the CLR are:

❑ In CLR program, you allocate memory of the garbage-collected heap using the `gcnew` operator.

❑ Reference class objects in general and `String` objects in particular are always allocated on the CLR heap.

❑ You use `String` objects when working with strings in a CLR program.

❑ The CLR has its own array types with more functionality that native array types.

❑ CLR arrays are created on the CLR heap.

❑ A tracking handle is a form of pointer used to reference variables defined on the CLR heap. A tracking handle is automatically updated if what it refers to is relocated in the heap by the garbage collector.

❑ Variable that reference objects and arrays on the heap are always tracking handles.

❑ A tracking reference is similar to a native reference except that the address it contains is automatically updated if the object referenced is moved by the garbage collector.

❑ An interior pointer is a C++/CLI pointer type to which you can apply the same operation as a native pointer.

❑ The address contained in an interior pointer can be modified using arithmetic operations and still maintain an address correctly even when referring to something stored in the CLR heap.

Exercises

You can download the source code for the examples in the book and the solutions to the following exercises from www.wrox.com.

1. Write a native C++ program that allows an unlimited number of values to be entered and stored in an array allocated in the free store. The program should then output the values five to a line followed by the average of the values entered. The initial array size should be five elements. The program should create a new array with five additional elements when necessary and copy values from the old array to the new.

2. Repeat the previous exercise but use pointer notation throughout instead of arrays.

3. Declare a character array, and initialize it to a suitable string. Use a loop to change every other character to uppercase.

Hint: In the ASCII character set, values for uppercase characters are 32 less than their lowercase counterparts.

4. Write a C++/CLI program that creates an array with a random number of elements of type int. The array should have from 10 to 20 elements. Set the array elements to random values between 100 and 1000. Output the elements five to a line in ascending sequence without sorting the array; for example find the smallest element and output that, then the next smallest, and so on.

5. Write a C++/CLI program that will generate a random integer greater than 10,000. Output the integer and then output the digits in the integer in words. For example, if the integer generated were 345678, then the output should be:

```
The value is 345678
three four five six seven eight
```

6. Write a C++/CLI program that creates an array containing the following strings:

```
"Madam I'm Adam."
"Don't cry for me, Marge and Tina."
"Lid off a daffodil."
"Red lost soldier."
"Cigar? Toss it in a can. It is so tragic."
```

The program should examine each string in turn, output the string and indicate whether it is or is not a palindrome (that is, the same sequence of letters reading backward or forward, ignoring spaces and punctuation).

Introducing Structure into Your Programs

Up to now, you haven't really been able to structure your program code in a modular fashion because you have only been able to construct a program as a single function, `main()`; but you *have* been using library functions of various kinds as well as functions belonging to objects. Whenever you write a C++ program, you should have a modular structure in mind from the outset and, as you'll see, a good understanding of how to implement functions is essential to object-oriented programming in C++. In this chapter, you'll learn:

- ❑ How to declare and write your own C++ functions
- ❑ How function arguments are defined and used
- ❑ How arrays can be passed to and from a function
- ❑ What pass-by-value means
- ❑ How to pass pointers to functions
- ❑ How to use references as function arguments, and what pass-by-reference means
- ❑ How the `const` modifier affects function arguments
- ❑ How to return values from a function
- ❑ How recursion can be used

There's quite a lot to structuring your C++ programs, so to avoid indigestion, you won't try to swallow the whole thing in one gulp. After you have chewed over and gotten the full flavor of these morsels, you'll move on to the next chapter, where you will get further into the meat of the topic.

Understanding Functions

First take a look at the broad principles of how a function works. A function is a self-contained block of code with a specific purpose. A function has a name that both identifies it and is used to call it for execution in a program. The name of a function is global but is not necessarily unique in C++, as you'll see in the next chapter; however, functions that perform different actions should generally have different names.

The name of a function is governed by the same rules as those for a variable. A function name is, therefore, a sequence of letters and digits, the first of which is a letter, where an underscore (_) counts as a letter. The name of a function should generally reflect what it does, so for example, you might call a function that counts beans `count_beans()`.

You pass information to a function by means of **arguments** specified when you invoke it. These arguments need to correspond with **parameters** that appear in the definition of the function. The arguments that you specify replace the parameters used in the definition of the function when the function executes. The code in the function then executes as though it was written using your argument values. Figure 5-1 illustrates the relationship between arguments in the function call and the parameters specified in the definition of the function.

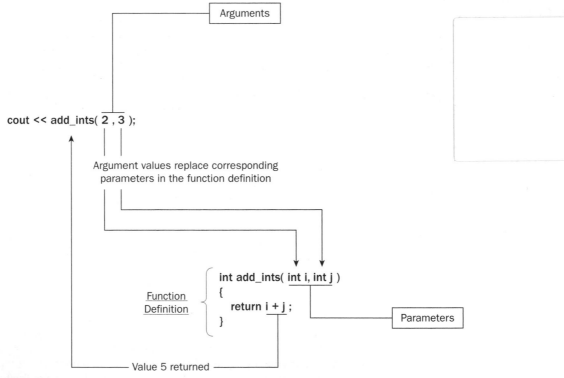

Figure 5-1

In this example, the function returns the sum of the two arguments passed to it. In general, a function returns either a single value to the point in the program where it was called, or nothing at all, depending on how the function is defined. You might think that returning a single value from a function is a constraint, but the single value returned can be a pointer that might contain the address of an array, for example. You will see more about how data is returned from a function a little later in this chapter.

Why Do You Need Functions?

One major advantage that a function offers is that it can be executed as many times as necessary from different points in a program. Without the ability to package a block of code into a function, programs would end up being much larger because you would typically need to replicate the same code at various points in them. But the real reason that you need functions is to break up a program into easily manageable chunks for development and testing; small blocks of code are easier to understand than large blocks of code.

Imagine a really big program — let's say a million lines of code. A program of this size would be virtually impossible to write without functions. Functions enable you to segment a program so that you can write the code piecemeal, and test each piece independently before bringing it together with the other pieces. It also allows the work to be divided among members of a programming team, with each team member taking responsibility for a tightly specified piece of the program, with a well-defined functional interface to the rest of the code.

Structure of a Function

As you have seen when writing the function `main()`, a function consists of a **function header** that identifies the function, followed by the **body** of the function between curly braces containing the executable code for the function. Let's look at an example. You could write a function to raise a value to a given power, that is, to compute the result of multiplying the value x by itself n times, which is x^n:

```
// Function to calculate x to the power n, with n greater than or equal to 0
double power(double x, int n)          // Function header
{                                      // Function body starts here...
   double result = 1.0;                // Result stored here
   for(int i = 1; i <= n; i++)
     result *= x;

   return result;
}                                      // ...and ends here
```

The Function Header

Let's first examine the function header in this example. The following is the first line of the function.

```
double power(double x, int n)          // Function header
```

It consists of three parts:

❑ The type of the **return value** (`double` in this case)

❑ The name of the function (`power` in this case)

❑ The parameters of the function enclosed between parentheses (x and n in this case, of types double and int respectively)

The return value is returned to the calling function when the function is executed, so when the function is called, it results in a value of type `double` in the expression in which it appears.

Our function has two parameters: x, the value to be raised to a given power which is of type `double`, and the value of the power, n, which is of type `int`. The computation that the function performs is written using these parameter variables together with another variable, `result`, declared in the body of the function. The parameter names and any variables defined in the body of the function are local to the function.

Note that no semicolon is required at the end of the function header or after the closing brace for the function body.

The General Form of a Function Header

The general form of a function header can be written as follows:

```
return_type function_name(parameter_list)
```

The *return_type* can be any legal type. If the function does not return a value, the return type is specified by the keyword `void`. The keyword `void` is also used to indicate the absence of parameters, so a function that has no parameters and doesn't return a value would have the following function header.

```
void my_function(void)
```

An empty parameter list also indicates that a function takes no arguments, so you could omit the keyword `void` between the parentheses like:

```
void my_function()
```

A function with a return type specified as void should not be used in an expression in the calling program. Because it doesn't return a value, it can't sensibly be part of an expression, so using it in this way causes the compiler to generate an error message.

The Function Body

The desired computation in a function is performed by the statements in the function body following the function header. The first of these in our example declares a variable `result` that is initialized with the value 1.0. The variable `result` is local to the function, as are all automatic variables declared within the function body. This means that the variable `result` ceases to exist after the function has completed execution. What might immediately strike you is that if `result` ceases to exist on completing execution of the function, how is it returned? The answer is that a copy of the value being returned is made automatically, and this copy is available to the return point in the program.

The calculation is performed in the `for` loop. A loop control variable `i` is declared in the `for` loop which assumes successive values from 1 to n. The variable `result` is multiplied by x once for each loop iteration, so this occurs n times to generate the required value. If n is 0, the statement in the loop won't be executed at all because the loop continuation condition immediately fails, and so `result` is left as 1.0.

As I've said, the parameters and all the variables declared within the body of a function are local to the function. There is nothing to prevent you from using the same names for variables in other functions for quite different purposes. Indeed, it's just as well this is so because it would be extremely difficult to ensure variables names were always unique within a program containing a large number of functions, particularly if the functions were not all written by the same person.

The scope of variables declared within a function is determined in the same way that I have already discussed. A variable is created at the point at which it is defined and ceases to exist at the end of the block containing it. There is one type of variable that is an exception to this — variables declared as `static`. I'll discuss static variables a little later in this chapter.

Be careful about masking global variables with local variables of the same name. You first met this situation back in Chapter 2 where you saw how you could use the scope resolution operator : : *to access global variables.*

The return Statement

The `return` statement returns the value of `result` to the point where the function was called. The general form of the return statement is

```
return expression;
```

where `expression` must evaluate to a value of the type specified in the function header for the return value. The expression can be any expression you want, as long as you end up with a value of the required type. It can include function calls — even a call of the same function in which it appears, as you'll see later in this chapter.

If the type of return value has been specified as `void`, there must be no expression appearing in the `return` statement. It must be written simply as:

```
return;
```

Using a Function

At the point at which you use a function in a program, the compiler must know something about it to compile the function call. It needs enough information to be able to identify the function, and to verify that you are using it correctly. Unless the definition of the function that you intend to use appears earlier in the same source file, you must declare the function using a statement called a **function prototype**.

Function Prototypes

A prototype of a function provides the basic information that the compiler needs to check that you are using a function correctly. It specifies the parameters to be passed to the function, the function name, and the type of the return value — basically, it contains the same information as appears in the function header, with the addition of a semicolon. Clearly, the number of parameters and their types must be the same in the function prototype as they are in the function header in the definition of the function.

The prototypes for the functions that you call from within another function must appear before the statements doing the calling and are usually placed at the beginning of the program source file. The header files that you've been including for standard library functions contain the prototypes of the functions provided by the library, amongst other things.

For the `power()` function example, you could write the prototype as:

```
double power(double value, int index);
```

Don't forget that a semicolon is required at the end of a function prototype. Without it, you get error messages from the compiler.

Note that I have specified names for the parameters in the function prototype that are different from those I used in the function header when I defined the function. This is just to indicate that it's possible. Most often, the same names are used in the prototype and in the function header in the definition of the function, but this doesn't *have* to be so. You can use longer more expressive parameter names in the function prototype to aid understanding of the significance of the parameters and then use shorter parameter names in the function definition where the longer names would make the code in the body of the function less readable.

If you like, you can even omit the names altogether in the prototype, and just write:

```
double power(double, int);
```

This provides enough information for the compiler to do its job; however, it's better practice to use some meaningful name in a prototype because it aids readability and, in some cases, makes all the difference between clear code and confusing code. If you have a function with two parameters of the same type (suppose our index was also of type `double` in the function `power()`, for example), the use of suitable names indicates which parameter appears first and which second.

Try It Out   Using a Function

You can see how all this goes together in an example exercising the `power()` function.

```cpp
// Ex5_01.cpp
// Declaring, defining, and using a function
#include <iostream>
using std::cout;
using std::endl;

double power(double x, int n);      // Function prototype

int main(void)
{
   int index = 3;                   // Raise to this power
   double x = 3.0;                  // Different x from that in function power
   double y = 0.0;

   y = power(5.0, 3);               // Passing constants as arguments
   cout << endl
        << "5.0 cubed = " << y;

   cout << endl
        << "3.0 cubed = "
        << power(3.0, index);       // Outputting return value

   x = power(x, power(2.0, 2.0));   // Using a function as an argument
   cout << endl                     // with auto conversion of 2nd parameter
        << "x = " << x;

   cout << endl;
   return 0;
}

// Function to compute positive integral powers of a double value
// First argument is value, second argument is power index
double power(double x, int n)
```

```
{                                       // Function body starts here...
   double result = 1.0;                 // Result stored here
   for(int i = 1; i <= n; i++)
      result *= x;
   return result;
}                                       // ...and ends here
```

This program shows some of the ways in which you can use the function power(), specifying the arguments to the function in a variety of ways. If you run this example, you get the following output:

```
5.0 cubed = 125
3.0 cubed = 27
x = 81
```

How It Works

After the usual #include statement for input/output and the using declarations, you have the prototype for the function power(). If you were to delete this and try recompiling the program, the compiler wouldn't be able to process the calls to the function in main() and would instead generate a whole series of error messages:

```
error C3861: 'power': identifier not found
```

and the error message:

```
error C2365: 'power' : redefinition; previous definition was 'formerly unknown
identifier'
```

In a change from previous examples, I've used the new keyword void in the function main() where the parameter list would usually appear to indicate that no parameters are to be supplied. Previously, I left the parentheses enclosing the parameter list empty, which is also interpreted in C++ as indicating that there are no parameters; but it's better to specify the fact by using the keyword void. As you saw, the keyword void can also be used as the return type for a function to indicate that no value is returned. If you specify the return type of a function as void, you must not place a value in any return statement within the function; otherwise, you get an error message from the compiler.

You gathered from some of the previous examples that using a function is very simple. To use the function power() to calculate 5.0^3 and store the result in a variable y in our example, you have the following statement:

```
y = power(5.0, 3);
```

The values 5.0 and 3 here are the arguments to the function. They happen to be constants, but you can use any expression as an argument, as long as a value of the correct type is ultimately produced. The arguments to the power() function substitute for the parameters x and n, which were used in the definition of the function. The computation is performed using these values and then a copy of the result, 125, is returned to the calling function, main(), which is then stored in y. You can think of the function as having this value in the statement or expression in which it appears. You then output the value of y:

```
cout << endl
     << "5.0 cubed = " << y;
```

The next call of the function is used within the output statement:

```
cout << endl
    << "3.0 cubed = "
    << power(3.0, index);          // Outputting return value
```

Here, the value returned by the function is transferred directly to the output stream. Because you haven't stored the returned value anywhere, it is otherwise unavailable to you. The first argument in the call of the function here is a constant; the second argument is a variable.

The function power() is used next in this statement:

```
x = power(x, power(2.0, 2.0));     // Using a function as an argument
```

Here the power() function is called twice. The first call to the function is the rightmost in the expression, and the result supplies the value for the second argument to the leftmost call. Although the arguments in the sub-expression power(2.0, 2.0) are both specified as the double literal 2.0, the function is actually called with the first argument as 2.0 and the second argument as the integer literal, 2. The compiler converts the double value specified for the second argument to type int because it knows from the function prototype (shown again below) that the type of the second parameter has been specified as int.

```
double power(double x, int n);     // Function prototype
```

The double result 4.0 is returned by the first call to the power() function, and after conversion to type int, the value 4 is passed as the second argument in the next call of the function, with x as the first argument. Because x has the value 3.0, the value of 3.0^4 is computed and the result, 81.0, stored in x. This sequence of events is illustrated in Figure 5-2.

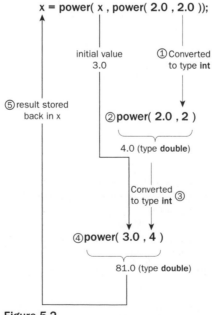

Figure 5-2

This statement involves two implicit conversions from type `double` to type `int` that were inserted by the compiler. There's a possible loss of data when converting from type `double` to type `int` so the compiler issues warning message when this occurs, even though the compiler has itself inserted this conversion. Generally relying on automatic conversions where there is potential for data loss is a dangerous programming practice, and it is not at all obvious from the code that this conversion is intended. It is far better to be explicit in your code by using the `static_cast` operator when necessary. The statement in the example is much better written as:

```
x = power(x, static_cast<int>(power(2.0, 2)));
```

Coding the statement like this avoids both the compiler warning messages that the original version caused. Using a static cast does not remove the possibility of losing data in the conversion of data from one type to another. Because you specified it though, it is clear that this is what you intended, recognizing that data loss might occur.

Passing Arguments to a Function

It's very important to understand how arguments are passed to a function, as it affects how you write functions and how they ultimately operate. There are also a number of pitfalls to be avoided, so we'll look at the mechanism for this quite closely.

The arguments you specify when a function is called should usually correspond in type and sequence to the parameters appearing in the definition of the function. As you saw in the last example, if the type of an argument specified in a function call doesn't correspond with the type of parameter in the function definition, (where possible) it converts to the required type, obeying the same rules as those for casting operands that were discussed in Chapter 2. If this proves not to be possible, you get an error message from the compiler; however, even if the conversion is possible and the code compiles, it could well result in the loss of data (for example from type `long` to type `short`) and should therefore be avoided.

There are two mechanisms used generally in C++ to pass arguments to functions. The first mechanism applies when you specify the parameters in the function definition as ordinary variables (*not* references). This is called the **pass-by-value** method of transferring data to a function so let's look into that first of all.

The Pass-by-value Mechanism

With this mechanism, the variables or constants that you specify as arguments are not passed to a function at all. Instead, copies of the arguments are created and these copies are used as the values to be transferred. Figure 5-3 shows this in a diagram using the example of our `power()` function.

Each time you call the function `power()`, the compiler arranges for copies of the arguments that you specify to be stored in a temporary location in memory. During execution of the functions, all references to the function parameters are mapped to these temporary copies of the arguments.

```
int index = 2;
double value = 10.0;
double result = power(value, index);
```

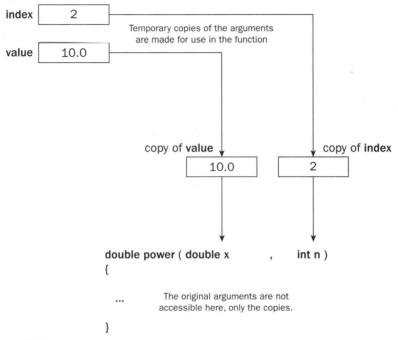

Figure 5-3

Passing-by-value

One consequence of the pass-by-value mechanism is that a function can't directly modify the arguments passed. You can demonstrate this by deliberately trying to do so in an example:

```
// Ex5_02.cpp
// A futile attempt to modify caller arguments
#include <iostream>
using std::cout;
using std::endl;

int incr10(int num);              // Function prototype

int main(void)
{
   int num = 3;

   cout << endl
        << "incr10(num) = " << incr10(num)
        << endl
```

```
                    << "num = " << num;
   cout << endl;
   return 0;
}

// Function to increment a variable by 10
int incr10(int num)                 // Using the same name might help...
{
   num += 10;                       // Increment the caller argument - hopefully

   return num;                      // Return the incremented value
}
```

Of course, this program is doomed to failure. If you run it, you get this output:

```
incr10(num) = 13
num = 3
```

How It Works

The output confirms that the original value of num remains untouched. The incrementing occurred on the copy of num that was generated and was eventually discarded on exiting from the function.

Clearly, the pass-by-value mechanism provides you with a high degree of protection from having your caller arguments mauled by a rogue function, but it is conceivable that you might actually want to arrange to modify caller arguments. Of course, there is a way to do this. Didn't you just know that pointers would turn out to be incredibly useful?

Pointers as Arguments to a Function

When you use a pointer as an argument, the pass-by-value mechanism still operates as before; however, a pointer is an address of another variable, and if you take a copy of this address, the copy still points to the same variable. This is how specifying a pointer as a parameter enables your function to get at a caller argument.

Try It Out   **Pass-by-pointer**

You can change the last example to use a pointer to demonstrate the effect:

```
// Ex5_03.cpp
// A successful attempt to modify caller arguments
#include <iostream>
using std::cout;
using std::endl;

int incr10(int* num);                // Function prototype

int main(void)
{
```

```
    int num = 3;

    int* pnum = &num;                    // Pointer to num

    cout << endl
        << "Address passed = " << pnum;

    int result = incr10(pnum);
    cout << endl
        << "incr10(pnum) = " << result;

    cout << endl
        << "num = " << num;

    cout << endl;
    return 0;
}

// Function to increment a variable by 10
int incr10(int* num)                     // Function with pointer argument
{
    cout << endl
        << "Address received = " << num;

    *num += 10;                          // Increment the caller argument
                                         //  - confidently
    return *num;                         // Return the incremented value
}
```

The output from this example is:

```
Address passed = 0012FF6C
Address received = 0012FF6C
incr10(pnum) = 13
num = 13
```

The address values produced by your computer may be different from those shown above, but the two values should be identical to each other.

How It Works

In this example, the principal alterations from the previous version relate to passing a pointer, pnum, in place of the original variable, num. The prototype for the function now has the parameter type specified as a pointer to int, and the main() function has the pointer pnum declared and initialized with the address of num. The function main(), and the function incr10(), output the address sent and the address received respectively, to verify that the same address is indeed being used in both places. Because the incr10() function is writing to cout, you now call it before the output statement and store the return value in result:

```
    int result = incr10(pnum);
    cout << endl
        << "incr10(pnum) = " << result;
```

This ensures proper sequencing of the output. The output shows that this time the variable num has been incremented and has a value that's now identical to that returned by the function.

In the rewritten version of the function incr10(), both the statement incrementing the value passed to the function and the return statement now de-reference the pointer to use the value stored.

Passing Arrays to a Function

You can also pass an array to a function, but in this case the array is not copied, even though a pass-by-value method of passing arguments still applies. The array name is converted to a pointer, and a copy of the pointer to the beginning of the array is passed by value to the function. This is quite advantageous because copying large arrays is very time consuming. As you may have worked out, however, elements of the array may be changed within a function and thus an array is the only type that cannot be passed by value.

Try It Out   **Passing Arrays**

You can illustrate the ins and outs of this by writing a function to compute the average of a number of values passed to a function in an array.

```cpp
// Ex5_04.cpp
// Passing an array to a function
#include <iostream>
using std::cout;
using std::endl;

double average(double array[], int count);        //Function prototype

int main(void)
{
   double values[] = { 1.0, 2.0, 3.0, 4.0, 5.0, 6.0, 7.0, 8.0, 9.0, 10.0 };

   cout << endl
        << "Average = "
        << average(values, (sizeof values)/(sizeof values[0]));

   cout << endl;
   return 0;
}

// Function to compute an average
double average(double array[], int count)
{
   double sum = 0.0;                      // Accumulate total in here
   for(int i = 0; i < count; i++)
     sum += array[i];                     // Sum array elements

   return sum/count;                      // Return average
}
```

The program produces the following output:

```
Average = 5.5
```

How It Works

The `average()` function is designed to work with an array of any length. As you can see from the prototype, it accepts two arguments: the array and a count of the number of elements. Because you want it to work with arrays of arbitrary length, the array parameter appears without a dimension specified.

The function is called in `main()` in this statement,

```
cout << endl
     << "Average = "
     << average(values, (sizeof values)/(sizeof values[0]));
```

The function is called with the first argument as the array name, `values`, and the second argument as an expression that evaluates to the number of elements in the array.

You'll recall this expression, using the operator `sizeof`, *from when you looked at arrays in Chapter 4.*

Within the body of the function, the computation is expressed in the way you would expect. There's no significant difference between this and the way you would write the same computation if you implemented it directly in `main()`.

The output confirms that everything works as we anticipated.

Try It Out **Using Pointer Notation When Passing Arrays**

You haven't exhausted all the possibilities here. As you determined at the outset, the array name is passed as a pointer — to be precise, as a copy of a pointer — so within the function you are not obliged to work with the data as an array at all. You could modify the function in the example to work with pointer notation throughout, in spite of the fact that you are using an array.

```
// Ex5_05.cpp
// Handling an array in a function as a pointer
#include <iostream>
using std::cout;
using std::endl;

double average(double* array, int count);        //Function prototype

int main(void)
{
    double values[] = { 1.0, 2.0, 3.0, 4.0, 5.0, 6.0, 7.0, 8.0, 9.0, 10.0 };

    cout << endl
         << "Average = "
         << average(values, (sizeof values)/(sizeof values[0]));
```

```
      cout << endl;
      return 0;
   }

   // Function to compute an average
   double average(double* array, int count)
   {
      double sum = 0.0;                        // Accumulate total in here
      for(int i = 0; i < count; i++)
         sum += *array++;                      // Sum array elements

      return sum/count;                        // Return average
   }
```

The output is exactly the same as in the previous example.

How It Works

As you can see, the program needed very few changes to make it work with the array as a pointer. The prototype and the function header have been changed, although neither change is absolutely necessary. If you change both back to the original version with the first parameter specified as a `double` array and leave the function body written in terms of a pointer, it works just as well. The most interesting aspect of this version is the body of the `for` loop statement:

```
      sum += *array++;                         // Sum array elements
```

Here you apparently break the rule about not being able to modify an address specified as an array name because you are incrementing the address stored in `array`. In fact, you aren't breaking the rule at all. Remember that the pass-by-value mechanism makes a copy of the original array address and passes that to the function, so you are just modifying the copy here — the original array address is quite unaffected. As a result, whenever you pass a one-dimensional array to a function, you are free to treat the value passed as a pointer in every sense, and change the address in any way that you want.

Passing Multidimensional Arrays to a Function

Passing a multidimensional array to a function is quite straightforward. The following statement declares a two dimensional array, `beans`:

```
   double beans[2][4];
```

You could then write the prototype of a hypothetical function, `yield()`, like this:

```
   double yield(double beans[2][4]);
```

You may be wondering how the compiler can know that this is defining an array of the dimensions shown as an argument, and not a single array element. The answer is simple — you can't write a single array element as a parameter in a function definition or prototype, although you can pass one as an argument when you call a function. For a parameter accepting a single element of an array as an argument, the parameter would have just a variable name. The array context doesn't apply.

When you are defining a multi-dimensional array as a parameter, you can also omit the first dimension value. Of course, the function needs some way of knowing the extent of the first dimension. For example, you could write this:

```
double yield(double beans[][4], int index);
```

Here, the second parameter would provide the necessary information about the first dimension. The function can operate with a two-dimensional array with the value for the first dimension specified by the second argument to the function and with the second dimension fixed at 4.

Try It Out   Passing Multidimensional Arrays

You define such a function in the following example:

```cpp
// Ex5_06.cpp
// Passing a two-dimensional array to a function
#include <iostream>
using std::cout;
using std::endl;

double yield(double array[][4], int n);

int main(void)
{
   double beans[3][4] =  {    { 1.0,  2.0,  3.0,  4.0 },
                              { 5.0,  6.0,  7.0,  8.0 },
                              { 9.0, 10.0, 11.0, 12.0 }    };

   cout << endl
        << "Yield = " << yield(beans, sizeof beans/sizeof beans[0]);

   cout << endl;
   return 0;
}

// Function to compute total yield
double yield(double beans[][4], int count)
{
   double sum = 0.0;
   for(int i = 0; i < count; i++)         // Loop through number of rows
      for(int j = 0; j < 4; j++)          // Loop through elements in a row
         sum += beans[i][j];
   return sum;
}
```

The output from this example is:

```
Yield = 78
```

How It Works

I have used different names for the parameters in the function header from those in the prototype, just to remind you that this is possible — but in this case, it doesn't really improve the program at all. The first parameter is defined as an array of an arbitrary number of rows, each row having four elements.

You actually call the function using the array beans with three rows. The second argument is specified by dividing the total size of the array in bytes by the size of the first row. This evaluates to the number of rows in the array.

The computation in the function is simply a nested for loop with the inner loop summing elements of a single row and the outer loop repeating this for each row.

Using a pointer in a function rather than a multidimensional array as an argument doesn't really apply particularly well in this example. When the array is passed, it passes an address value which points to an array of four elements (a row). This doesn't lend itself to an easy pointer operation within the function. You would need to modify the statement in the nested for loop to the following:

```
sum += *(*(beans + i) + j);
```

So the computation is probably clearer in array notation.

References as Arguments to a Function

We now come to the second of the two mechanisms for passing arguments to a function. Specifying a parameter to a function as a reference changes the method of passing data for that parameter. The method used is not pass-by-value, where an argument is copied before being transferred to the function, but **pass-by-reference** where the parameter acts as an alias for the argument passed. This eliminates any copying and allows the function to access the caller argument directly. It also means that the de-referencing, which is required when passing and using a pointer to a value, is also unnecessary.

Try It Out   Pass-by-reference

Let's go back to a revised version of a very simple example, Ex5_03.cpp, to see how it would work using reference parameters:

```cpp
// Ex5_07.cpp
// Using a reference to modify caller arguments
#include <iostream>
using std::cout;
using std::endl;

int incr10(int& num);                  // Function prototype

int main(void)
{
   int num = 3;
   int value = 6;

   int result = incr10(num);
   cout << endl
        << "incr10(num) = " << result;

   cout << endl
        << "num = " << num;
```

```
        result = incr10(value);
        cout << endl
            << "incr10(value) = " << result;

    cout << endl
            << "value = " << value;

    cout << endl;
    return 0;
}

// Function to increment a variable by 10
int incr10(int& num)                    // Function with reference argument
{
    cout << endl
            << "Value received = " << num;

    num += 10;                          // Increment the caller argument
                                        //   - confidently
    return num;                         // Return the incremented value
}
```

This program produces the output:

```
Value received = 3
incr10(num) = 13
num = 13
Value received = 6
incr10(value) = 16
value = 16
```

How It Works

You should find the way this works quite remarkable. This is essentially the same as Ex5_03.cpp, except that the function uses a reference as a parameter. The prototype has been changed to reflect this. When the function is called, the argument is specified just as though it was a pass-by-value operation, so it's used in the same way as the earlier version. The argument value isn't passed to the function. The function parameter is *initialized* with the address of the argument, so whenever the parameter num is used in the function, it accesses the caller argument directly.

Just to reassure you that there's nothing fishy about the use of the identifier num in main() as well as in the function, the function is called a second time with the variable value as the argument. At first sight, this may give you the impression that it contradicts what I said was a basic property of a reference — that after declared and initialized, it couldn't be reassigned to another variable. The reason it isn't contradictory is that a reference as a function parameter is created and initialized each time the function is called and is destroyed when the function ends, so you get a completely new reference created each time you use the function.

Within the function, the value received from the calling program is displayed onscreen. Although the statement is essentially the same as the one used to output the address stored in a pointer, because num is now a reference, you obtain the data value rather than the address.

This clearly demonstrates the difference between a reference and a pointer. A reference is an alias for another variable, and therefore can be used as an alternative way of referring to it. It is equivalent to using the original variable name.

The output shows that the function incr10() is directly modifying the variable passed as a caller argument.

You will find that if you try to use a numeric value, such as 20, as an argument to incr10(), the compiler outputs an error message. This is because the compiler recognizes that a reference parameter can be modified within a function, and the last thing you want is to have your constants changing value now and again. This would introduce a kind of excitement into your programs that you could probably do without.

This security is all very well, but if the function didn't modify the value, you wouldn't want the compiler to create all these error messages every time you pass a reference argument that was a constant. Surely there ought to be some way to accommodate this? As Ollie would have said, 'There most certainly is, Stanley!'

Use of the const Modifier

You can apply the const modifier to a parameter to a function to tell the compiler that you don't intend to modify it in any way. This causes the compiler to check that your code indeed does not modify the argument, and there are no error messages when you use a constant argument.

Try It Out   Passing a const

You can modify the previous program to show how the const modifier changes the situation.

```cpp
// Ex5_08.cpp
// Using a reference to modify caller arguments

#include <iostream>
using std::cout;
using std::endl;

int incr10(const int& num);        // Function prototype

int main(void)
{
    const int num = 3;             // Declared const to test for temporary creation
    int value = 6;

    int result = incr10(num);
    cout << endl
         << "incr10(num) = " << result;

    cout << endl
         << "num = " << num;

    result = incr10(value);
    cout << endl
```

```
              << "incr10(value) = " << result;

    cout << endl
         << "value = " << value;

    cout << endl;
    return 0;
}

// Function to increment a variable by 10
int incr10(const int& num)          // Function with const reference argument
{
    cout << endl
         << "Value received = " << num;

//    num += 10;                     // this statement would now be illegal
    return num+10;                  // Return the incremented value
}
```

The output when you execute this is:

```
Value received = 3
incr10(num) = 13
num = 3
Value received = 6
incr10(value) = 16
value = 6
```

How It Works

You declare the variable num in main() as const to show that when the parameter to the function incr10() is declared as const, you no longer get a compiler message when passing a const object.

It has also been necessary to comment out the statement that increments num in the function incr10(). If you uncomment this line, you'll find the program no longer compiles because the compiler won't allow num to appear on the left side of an assignment. When you specified num as const in the function header and prototype, you promised not to modify it, so the compiler checks that you kept your word.

Everything works as before, except that the variables in main() are no longer changed in the function.

By using reference arguments, you now have the best of both worlds. On one hand, you can write a function that can access caller arguments directly, and avoid the copying that is implicit in the pass-by-value mechanism. On the other hand, where you don't intend to modify an argument, you can get all the protection against accidental modification you need by using a const modifier with a reference.

Arguments to main()

You can define main() with no parameters (or better, with the parameter list as void) or you can specify a parameter list that allows the main() function to obtain values from the command line from the execute command for the program. Values passed from the command line as arguments to main() are always interpreted as strings. If you want to get data into `main()` from the command line, you must define it like this:

```
int main(int argc, char* argv[])
{
  // Code for main()...
}
```

The first parameter is the count of the number of strings found on the command line including the program name, and the second parameter is an array that contains pointers to these strings plus an additional element that is null. Thus `argc` is always at least 1 because you at least must enter the name of the program. The number of arguments received depends on what you enter on the command line to execute the program. For example, suppose that you execute the `DoThat` program with the command:

```
DoThat.exe
```

There is just the name of the .exe file for the program so `argc` is 1 and the `argv` array contains two elements — `argv[0]` pointing to the string `"DoThat.exe"` and `argv[1]` that contains null.

Suppose you enter this on the command line:

```
DoThat or else "my friend" 999.9
```

Now `argc` is 5 and `argv` contains six elements, the last element being 0 and the first five pointing to the strings:

```
"DoThat"   "or"   "else" "my friend"   "999.9"
```

You can see from this that if you want to have a string that includes spaces received as a single string you must enclose it between double quotes. You can also see that numerical values are read as strings so if you want conversion to the numerical value that is up to you.

Let's see it working.

Try It Out   Receiving Command-Line Arguments

This program just lists the arguments it receives from the command line.

```
// Ex5_09.cpp
// Reading command line arguments
#include <iostream>
using std::cout;
using std::endl;

int main(int argc, char* argv[])
{
  cout << endl << "argc = " << argc << endl;
  cout << "Command line arguments received are:" << endl;
  for(int i = 0 ; i <argc ; i++)
    cout << "argument " << (i+1) << ": " << argv[i] << endl;
  return 0;
}
```

You have two choices when entering the command-line arguments. After you build the example in the IDE, you can open a command window at the folder containing the `.exe` file and then enter the program name followed by the command-line arguments. Alternatively, you can specify the command-line arguments in the IDE before you execute the program. Just open the project properties window by selecting `Project > Properties` from the main menu and then extend the `Configuration Properties` tree in the left pane by clicking the plus sign (+). Click the `Debugging` folder to see where you can enter command line values in the right pane.

I enter the following in the command window with the current directory containing the `.exe` file for the program:

```
Ex5_09 trying multiple "argument values" 4.5 0.0
```

Here is the output from resulting from my input:

```
argc = 6
Command line arguments received are:
argument 1: Ex5_09
argument 2: trying
argument 3: multiple
argument 4: argument values
argument 5: 4.5
argument 6: 0.0
```

How It Works

The program first outputs the value of `argc` and then the values of each argument from the `argv` array in the `for` loop. You can see from the output that the first argument value is the program name. `"argument values"` is treated as a single argument because of the enclosing double quotes.

You could make use of the fact that the last element in `argv` is null and code the output of the command-line argument values like this:

```
int i = 0;
while(argv[i] != 0)
  cout << "argument " << (i+1) << ": " << argv[i++] << endl;
```

The `while` loop ends when `argv[argc]` is reached because that element is null.

Accepting a Variable Number of Function Arguments

You can define a function so that it allows any number of arguments to be passed to it. You indicate that a variable number of arguments can be supplied when a function is called by placing an ellipsis (which is three periods, . . .) at the end of the parameter list in the function definition. For example:

```
int sumValues(int first,...)
{
```

```
    //Code for the function
}
```

There must be at least one ordinary parameter, but you can have more. The ellipsis must always be placed at the end of the parameter list.

Obviously there is no information about the type or number of arguments in the variable list, so your code must figure out what is passed to the function when it is called. The native C++ library defines `va_start`, `va_arg`, and `va_end` macros in the `<cstdarg>` header to help you do this. It's easiest to show how these are used with an example.

Try It Out   Receiving a Variable Number of Arguments

This program uses a function that just sums the values of a variable number of arguments passed to it.

```cpp
// Ex5_10.cpp
// Handling a variable number of arguments
#include <iostream>
#include <cstdarg>
using std::cout;
using std::endl;

int sum(int count, ...)
{
  if(count <= 0)
    return 0;

  va_list arg_ptr;                      // Declare argument list pointer
  va_start(arg_ptr, count);             // Set arg_ptr to 1st optional argument

  int sum =0;
  for(int i = 0 ; i<count ; i++)
    sum += va_arg(arg_ptr, int);        // Add int value from arg_ptr and increment

  va_end(arg_ptr);                      // Reset the pointer to null
  return sum;
}

int main(int argc, char* argv[])
{
  cout << sum(6, 2, 4, 6, 8, 10, 12) << endl;
  cout << sum(9, 11, 22, 33, 44, 55, 66, 77, 66, 99) << endl;
}
```

This example produces the following output:

```
42
473
```

How It Works

The main() function calls the sum() function in the two output statements, in the first instance with seven arguments and in the second with ten arguments. The first argument in each case specifies the number of arguments that follow. It's important not to forget this because if you omit the first count argument, the result will be rubbish.

The sum() function has a single normal parameter of type int that represents the count of the number of arguments that follow. The ellipsis in the parameter list indicates an arbitrary number of arguments can be passed. Basically you have two ways of determining how many arguments there are when the function is called — you can require that the number of arguments is specified by a fixed parameter as in the case of sum(), or you can require that the last argument has a special marker value that you can check for and recognize.

To start processing the variable argument list you declare a pointer of type va_list:

```
va_list arg_ptr;                        // Declare argument list pointer
```

The va_list type is defined in the <cstdarg> header file and the pointer is used to point to each argument in turn.

The va_start macro is used to initialize arg_ptr so that it points to the first argument in the list:

```
va_start(arg_ptr, count);               // Set arg_ptr to 1st optional argument
```

The second argument to the macro is the name of the fixed parameter that precedes the ellipsis in the parameter, and this is used by the macro to determine where the first variable argument is.

You retrieve the values of the arguments in the list in the for loop:

```
int sum =0;
for(int i = 0 ; i<count ; i++)
   sum += va_arg(arg_ptr, int);         // Add int value from arg_ptr and increment
```

The va_arg macro returns the value of the argument at the location specified by arg_ptr and increments arg_ptr to point to the next argument value. The second argument to the va_arg macro is the argument type, and this determines the value that you get as well as how arg_ptr increments so if this is not correct you get chaos; the program probably executes, but the values you retrieve are rubbish and arg_ptr is incremented incorrectly to access more rubbish.

When you are finished retrieving argument values, you reset arg_ptr with the statement:

```
va_end(arg_ptr);                        // Reset the pointer to null
```

The va_end macro resets the pointer of type va_list that you pass as the argument to it to null. It's a good idea to always do this because after processing the arguments arg_ptr points to a location that does not contain valid data.

Returning Values from a Function

All the example functions that you have created have returned a single value. Is it possible to return anything other than a single value? Well, not directly, but as I said earlier, the single value returned needn't be a numeric value; it could also be an address, which provides the key to returning any amount of data. You simply use a pointer. Unfortunately, this also is where the pitfalls start, so you need to keep your wits about you for the adventure ahead.

Returning a Pointer

Returning a pointer value is easy. A pointer value is just an address, so if you want to return the address of some variable value, you can just write the following:

```
    return &value;                    // Returning an address
```

As long as the function header and function prototype indicate the return type appropriately, you have no problem — or at least no apparent problem. Assuming that the variable value is of type double, the prototype of a function called treble, which might contain the above return statement, could be as follows:

```
    double* treble(double data);
```

I have defined the parameter list arbitrarily here.

So let's look at a function that returns a pointer. It's only fair that I warn you in advance — this function doesn't work, but it is educational. Let's assume that you need a function that returns a pointer to a memory location containing three times its argument value. Our first attempt to implement such a function might look like this:

```
// Function to treble a value - mark 1
double* treble(double data)
{
    double result = 0.0;

    result = 3.0*data;
    return &result;
}
```

Try It Out   **Returning a Bad Pointer**

You could create a little test program to see what happens (remember that the treble function won't work as expected):

```
// Ex5_11.cpp
#include <iostream>
using std::cout;
using std::endl;

double* treble(double);                      // Function prototype
```

```
int main(void)
{
   double num = 5.0;                    // Test value
   double* ptr = 0;                     // Pointer to returned value

   ptr = treble(num);

   cout << endl
        << "Three times num = " << 3.0*num;

   cout << endl
        << "Result = " << *ptr;         // Display 3*num

   cout << endl;
   return 0;
}

// Function to treble a value - mark 1
double* treble(double data)
{
   double result = 0.0;

   result = 3.0*data;
   return &result;
}
```

There's a hint that everything is not as it should be because compiling this program results in a warning from the compiler:

```
warning C4172: returning address of local variable or temporary
```

The output that I got from executing the program was:

```
Three times num = 15
Result = 4.10416e-230
```

How It Works (or Why It Doesn't)

The function main() calls the function treble() and stores the address returned in the pointer ptr, which should point to a value which is three times the argument, num. You then display the result of computing three times num, followed by the value at the address returned from the function.

Clearly, the second line of output doesn't reflect the correct value of 15, but where's the error? Well, it's not exactly a secret because the compiler gives fair warning of the problem. The error arises because the variable result in the function treble() is created when the function begins execution, and is destroyed on exiting from the function — so the memory that the pointer is pointing to no longer contains the original variable value. The memory previously allocated to result becomes available for other purposes, and here it has evidently been used for something else.

A Cast Iron Rule for Returning Addresses

There is an absolutely cast iron rule for returning addresses:

Never ever return the address of a local automatic variable from a function.

You obviously can't use a function that doesn't work, so what can you do to rectify that? You could use a reference parameter and modify the original variable, but that's not what you set out to do. You are trying to return a pointer to some useful data so that, ultimately, you can return more than a single item of data. One answer lies in dynamic memory allocation (you saw this in action in the last chapter). With the operator new, you can create a new variable in the free store that continues to exist until it is eventually destroyed by delete — or until the program ends. With this approach, the function looks like this:

```
// Function to treble a value - mark 2
double* treble(double data)
{
    double* result = new double(0.0);
    *result = 3.0*data;
    return result;
}
```

Rather than declaring result as of type double, you now declare it to be of type double* and store in it the address returned by the operator new. Because the result is a pointer, the rest of the function is changed to reflect this, and the address contained in the result is finally returned to the calling program. You could exercise this version by replacing the function in the last working example with this version.

You need to remember that with dynamic memory allocation from within a native C++ function such as this, more memory is allocated each time the function is called. The onus is on the calling program to delete the memory when it's no longer required. It's easy to forget to do this in practice, with the result that the free store is gradually eaten up until, at some point, it is exhausted and the program fails. As mentioned before, this sort of problem is referred to as a **memory leak**.

Here you can see how the function would be used. The only necessary change to the original code is to use delete to free the memory as soon as you have finished with the pointer returned by the treble() function.

```
#include <iostream>

using std::cout;
using std::endl;

double* treble(double);              // Function prototype

int main(void)
{
    double num = 5.0;                // Test value
    double* ptr = 0;                 // Pointer to returned value

    ptr = treble(num);

    cout << endl
```

```
              << "Three times num = " << 3.0*num;

    cout << endl
         << "Result = " << *ptr;        // Display 3*num
    delete ptr;                         // Don't forget to free the memory

    cout << endl;
    return 0;
}

// Function to treble a value - mark 2
double* treble(double data)
{
    double* result = new double(0.0);
    *result = 3.0*data;
    return result;
}
```

Returning a Reference

You can also return a reference from a function. This is just as fraught with potential errors as returning a pointer, so you need to take care with this too. Because a reference has no existence in its own right (it's always an alias for something else), you must be sure that the object that it refers to still exists after the function completes execution. It's very easy to forget this when you use references in a function because they appear to be just like ordinary variables.

References as return types are of primary significance in the context of object-oriented programming. As you will see later in the book, they enable you to do things that would be impossible without them. (This particularly applies to "operator overloading," which I'll come to in Chapter 8). The principal characteristic of a reference-type return value is that it's an lvalue. This means that you can use the result of a function that returns a reference on the left side of an assignment statement.

Try It Out   Returning a Reference

Next, look at one example that illustrates the use of reference return types, and also demonstrates how a function can be used on the left of an assignment operation when it returns an lvalue. This example assumes that you have an array containing a mixed set of values. Whenever you want to insert a new value into the array, you want to replace the element with the lowest value.

```
// Ex5_12.cpp
// Returning a reference
#include <iostream>
#include <iomanip>
using std::cout;
using std::endl;
using std::setw;

double& lowest(double values[], int length); // Prototype of function
                                              // returning a reference

int main(void)
{
```

```
    double array[] = { 3.0, 10.0, 1.5, 15.0, 2.7, 23.0,
                       4.5, 12.0, 6.8, 13.5, 2.1, 14.0 };
    int len = sizeof array/sizeof array[0];   // Initialize to number
                                              // of elements

    cout << endl;
    for(int i = 0; i < len; i++)
       cout << setw(6) << array[i];

    lowest(array, len) = 6.9;                 // Change lowest to 6.9
    lowest(array, len) = 7.9;                 // Change lowest to 7.9

    cout << endl;
    for(int i = 0; i < len; i++)
       cout << setw(6) << array[i];

    cout << endl;
    return 0;
}

double& lowest(double a[], int len)
{
    int j = 0;                                // Index of lowest element
    for(int i = 1; i < len; i++)
       if(a[j] > a[i])                        // Test for a lower value...
          j = i;                              // ...if so update j
    return a[j];                              // Return reference to lowest
                                              // element
}
```

The output from this example is:

```
3    10   1.5    15   2.7    23   4.5    12   6.8  13.5   2.1    14
3    10   6.9    15   2.7    23   4.5    12   6.8  13.5   7.9    14
```

How It Works

Let's first take a look at how the function is implemented. The prototype for the function lowest() uses double& as the specification of the return type, which is therefore of type 'reference to double'. You write a reference type return value in exactly the same way as you have already seen for variable declarations, appending the & to the data type. The function has two parameters specified — a one-dimensional array of type double and a parameter of type int that specifies the length of the array.

The body of the function has a straightforward for loop to determine which element of the array passed contains the lowest value. The index, j, of the array element with the lowest value is arbitrarily set to 0 at the outset, and then modified within the loop if the current element, a[i], is less than a[j]. Thus, on exit from the loop, j contains the index value corresponding to the array element with the lowest value. The return statement is as follows:

```
    return a[j];                    // Return reference to lowest element
```

In spite of the fact that this looks identical to the statement that would return a value, because the return type was declared as a reference, this returns a reference to the array element a[j] rather than the value that the element contains. The address of a[j] is used to initialize the reference to be returned. This reference is created by the compiler because the return type was declared as a reference.

Don't confuse returning &a[j] with returning a reference. If you write &a[j] as the return value, you are specifying the address of a[j], which is a *pointer*. If you do this after having specified the return type as a *reference*, you get an error message from the compiler. Specifically, you get this:

```
error C2440: 'return' : cannot convert from 'double *__w64 ' to 'double &'
```

The function main(), which exercises the lowest() function, is very simple. An array of type double is declared and initialized with 12 arbitrary values, and an int variable len is initialized to the length of the array. The initial values in the array are output for comparison purposes.

> *Again, the program uses the stream manipulator* setw() *to space the values uniformly, requiring the* #include *directive for* <iomanip>.

The function main() then calls the function lowest() on the left side of an assignment to change the lowest value in the array. This is done twice to show that it does actually work and is not an accident. The contents of the array are then output to the display again, with the same field width as before, so corresponding values line up.

As you can see from the output with the first call to lowest(), the third element of the array, array[2], contained the lowest value, so the function returned a reference to it and its value was changed to 6.9. Similarly, on the second call, array[10] was changed to 7.9. This demonstrates quite clearly that returning a reference allows the use of the function on the left side of an assignment statement. The effect is as if the variable specified in the return statement appeared on the left of the assignment.

Of course, if you want to, you can also use it on the right side of an assignment, or in any other suitable expression. If you had two arrays, X and Y, with the number of array elements specified by lenx and leny respectively, you could set the lowest element in the array x to twice the lowest element in the array y with this statement:

```
lowest(x, lenx) = 2.0*lowest(y, leny);
```

This statement would call your lowest() function twice — once with arguments y and leny in the expression on the right side of the assignment and once with arguments x and lenx to obtain the address where the result of the right-hand expression is to be stored.

A Teflon-Coated Rule: Returning References

A similar rule to the one concerning the return of a pointer from a function also applies to returning references:

> *Never ever return a reference to a local variable from a function.*

I'll leave the topic of returning a reference from a function for now, but I haven't finished with it yet. I will come back to it again in the context of user-defined types and object-oriented programming, when you will unearth a few more magical things that you can do with references.

Static Variables in a Function

There are some things you can't do with automatic variables within a function. You can't count how many times a function is called, for example, because you can't accumulate a value from one call to the next. There's more than one way to get around this if you need to. For instance, you could use a reference parameter to update a count in the calling program, but this wouldn't help if the function was called from lots of different places within a program. You could use a global variable that you incremented from within the function, but globals are risky things to use, as they can be accessed from anywhere in a program, which makes it very easy to change them accidentally.

Global variables are also risky in applications that have multiple threads of execution that access them, and you must take special care to manage how the globals are accessed from different threads. The basic problem that has to be addressed when more than one thread can access a global variable is that one thread can change the value of a global variable while another thread is working with it. The best solution in such circumstances is to avoid the use of global variables altogether.

To create a variable whose value persists from one call of a function to the next, you can declare a variable within a function as `static`. You use exactly the same form of declaration for a `static` variable that you saw in Chapter 2. For example, to declare a variable `count` as `static` you could use this statement:

```
static int count = 0;
```

This also initializes the variable to zero.

Initialization of a static variable within a function only occurs the first time that the function is called. In fact, on the first call of a function, the static variable is created and initialized. It then continues to exist for the duration of program execution, and whatever value it contains when the function is exited is available when the function is next called.

Try It Out   Using Static Variables in Functions

You can demonstrate how a static variable behaves in a function with the following simple example:

```cpp
// Ex5_13.cpp
// Using a static variable within a function
#include <iostream>
using std::cout;
using std::endl;

void record(void);        // Function prototype, no arguments or return value

int main(void)
{
   record();

   for(int i = 0; i <= 3; i++)
      record();

   cout << endl;
   return 0;
```

```
   }

   // A function that records how often it is called
   void record(void)
   {
      static int count = 0;
      cout << endl
          << "This is the " << ++count;
      if((count > 3) && (count < 21))          // All this....
         cout <<"th";
      else
         switch(count%10)                      // is just to get...
         {
            case 1: cout << "st";
                    break;
            case 2: cout << "nd";
                    break;
            case 3: cout << "rd";
                    break;
            default: cout << "th";             // the right ending for...
         }                                     // 1st, 2nd, 3rd, 4th, etc.
      cout << " time I have been called";
      return;
   }
```

Our function here serves only to record the fact that it was called. If you build and execute it, you get this output:

```
This is the 1st time I have been called
This is the 2nd time I have been called
This is the 3rd time I have been called
This is the 4th time I have been called
This is the 5th time I have been called
```

How It Works

You initialize the static variable count with 0 and increment it in the first output statement in the function. Because the increment operation is prefixed, the incremented value is displayed by the output statement. It will be 1 on the first call, 2 on the second, and so on. Because the variable count is static, it continues to exist and retain its value from one call of the function to the next.

The remainder of the function is concerned with working out when 'st', 'nd', 'rd', or 'th' should be appended to the value of count that is displayed. It's surprisingly irregular. (I guess 101 should be 101st rather than 101th, shouldn't it?)

> Note the return statement. Because the return type of the function is void, to include a value would cause a compiler error. You don't actually need to put a return statement in this particular case as running off the closing brace for the body of the function is equivalent to the return statement without a value. The program would compile and run without error even if you didn't include the return.

Recursive Function Calls

When a function contains a call to itself it's referred to as a **recursive function**. A recursive function call can also be indirect, where a function `fun1` calls a function `fun2`, which in turn calls `fun1`.

Recursion may seem to be a recipe for an indefinite loop, and if you aren't careful it certainly can be. An indefinite loop will lock up your machine and require *Ctrl+Alt+Del* to end the program, which is always a nuisance. A prerequisite for avoiding an indefinite loop is that the function contains some means of stopping the process.

Unless you have come across the technique before, the sort of things to which recursion may be applied may not be obvious. In physics and mathematics there are many things that can be thought of as involving recursion. A simple example is the factorial of an integer which for a given integer N, is the product 1x2x3...xN. This is very often the example given to show recursion in operation. Recursion can also be applied to the analysis of programs during the compilation process; however, you will look at something even simpler.

Try It Out   A Recursive Function

At the start of this chapter (see `Ex5_01.cpp`), you produced a function to compute the integral power of a value, that is, to compute x^n. This is equivalent to x multiplied by itself n times. You can implement this as a recursive function as an elementary illustration of recursion in action. You can also improve the implementation of the function to deal with negative index values, where x^{-n} is equivalent to $1/x^n$.

```
// Ex5_14.cpp (based on Ex5_01.cpp)
// A recursive version of x to the power n
#include <iostream>
using std::cout;
using std::endl;

double power(double x, int n);     // Function prototype

int main(void)
{
  double x = 2.0;                  // Different x from that in function power
  double result = 0.0;

  // Calculate x raised to powers -3 to +3 inclusive
  for(int index = -3 ; index<=3 ; index++)
    cout << x << " to the power " << index << " is " << power(x, index)<< endl;

  return 0;
}

// Recursive function to compute integral powers of a double value
// First argument is value, second argument is power index
double power(double x, int n)
{
    if(n < 0)
```

```
      {
         x = 1.0/x;
         n = -n;
      }
      if(n > 0)
         return x*power(x, n-1);
      else
         return 1.0;
   }
```

The output from this program is:

```
2 to the power -3 is 0.125
2 to the power -2 is 0.25
2 to the power -1 is 0.5
2 to the power 0 is 1
2 to the power 1 is 2
2 to the power 2 is 4
2 to the power 3 is 8
```

How It Works

The function now supports positive and negative powers of x, so the first action is to check whether the value for the power that x is to be raised to, n, is negative:

```
if(n < 0)
{
    x = 1.0/x;
    n = -n;
}
```

Supporting negative powers is easy; it just uses the fact that x^{-n} can be evaluated as $(1/x)^n$. Thus if n is negative, you set x to be 1.0/x and change the sign of n so it's positive.

The next if statement decides whether or not the power() function should call itself once more:

```
if(n > 0)
    return x*power(x, n-1);
else
    return 1.0;
```

The if statement provides for the value 1.0 being returned if n is zero, and in all other cases it returns the result of the expression, x*power(x, n-1). This causes a further call to the function power() with the index value reduced by 1. Thus the else clause in the if statement provides the essential mechanism necessary to avoid an indefinite sequence of recursive function calls.

Clearly, within the function power(), if the value of n is other than zero, a further call to the function power() occurs. In fact, for any given value of n other than 0, the function calls itself n times, ignoring the sign of n. The mechanism is illustrated in Figure 5-4, where the value 3 for the index argument is assumed.

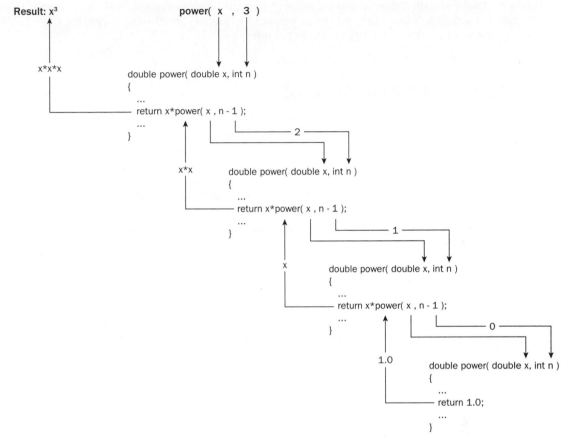

Figure 5-4

As you see, the power() function is called a total of four times to generate x^3, three of the calls being recursive where the function is calling itself.

Using Recursion

Unless you have a problem that particularly lends itself to using recursive functions, or if you have no obvious alternative, it's generally better to use a different approach, such as a loop. This is much more efficient than using recursive function calls. Think about what happens with our last example to evaluate a simple product, x*x*...x, n times. On each call, the compiler generates copies of the two arguments to the function, and also has to keep track of the location to return to when each return is executed. It's also necessary to arrange to save the contents of various registers in your computer so that they can be used within the function power(), and of course these need to be restored to their original state at each return from the function. With a quite modest depth of recursive call, the overhead can be considerably greater than if you use a loop.

This is not to say you should never use recursion. Where the problem suggests the use of recursive function calls as a solution, it can be an immensely powerful technique, greatly simplifying the code. You'll see an example where this is the case in the next chapter.

C++/CLI Programming

For the most part, functions in a C++/CLI program work in exactly the same way as in a native program. Of course, you deal in handles and tracking references when programming for the CLR, not native pointers and references, and that introduces some differences. There are a few other things that are a little different, so let's itemize them.

❑ Function parameters and return values in a CLR program can be value class types, tracking handles, tracking references, and interior pointers.

❑ When a parameter is an array there no need to have a separate parameter for the size of the array because C++/CLI arrays have the size built into the Length property.

❑ You cannot do address arithmetic with array parameters in a C++/CLI program as you can in a native C++ program so you must always use array indexing.

❑ Returning a handle to memory you have allocated on the CLR heap is not a problem because the garbage collector takes care of releasing the memory when it is no longer in use.

❑ The mechanism for accepting a variable number of arguments in C++/CLI is different from the native C++ mechanism.

❑ Accessing command line arguments in main() in a C++/CLI program is also different from the native C++ mechanism.

Let's look at the last two differences in more detail.

Functions Accepting a Variable Number of Arguments

The C++/CLI language provides for a variable number of arguments by allowing you to specify the parameter list as an array with the array specification preceded by an ellipsis. Here's an example of a function with this parameter list:

```
int sum(... array<int>^ args)
{
  // Code for sum
}
```

The sum() function here accepts any number of arguments of type int. To process the arguments you just access the elements of the array args. Because it is a CLR array, the number of elements is recorded as its Length property, so you have no problem determining the number of arguments in the body of the function. This mechanism is also an improvement over the native C++ mechanism you saw earlier because it is type-safe. The arguments clearly have to be of type int to be accepted by this function. Let's try a variation on Ex5_10 to see the CLR mechanism working.

Try It Out   **A Variable Number of Function Arguments**

Here's the code for this CLR project.

```
// Ex5_15.cpp : main project file.
// Passing a variable number of arguments to a function

#include "stdafx.h"

using namespace System;

double sum(... array<double>^ args)
{
  double sum = 0.0;
  for each(double arg in args)
    sum += arg;
  return sum;
}

int main(array<System::String ^> ^args)
{
  Console::WriteLine(sum(2.0, 4.0, 6.0, 8.0, 10.0, 12.0));
  Console::WriteLine(sum(1.1, 2.2, 3.3, 4.4, 5.5, 6.6, 7.7, 8.8, 9.9));
  return 0;
}
```

This example produces the following output:

```
42
49.5
```

How It Works

The sum() function here has been implemented to accept arguments of type double. The ellipsis preceding the array parameter tells the compiler to expect an arbitrary number of arguments and the argument values should be stored in an array of elements of type double. Of course, without the ellipsis, the function would expect just one argument when it was called that was a tracking handle for an array.

Compared to the native version in Ex5_10 the definition of the sum() function is remarkably simple. All the problems associated with the type and the number of arguments have disappeared in the C++/CLI version. The sum is accumulated in a simple for each loop that iterates over all the elements in the array.

Arguments to main()

You can see from the previous example that there is only one parameter to the main() function in a C++/CLI program and it is an array of elements of type String^. Accessing and processing command-line arguments in a C++/CLI program boils down to just accessing the elements in the array parameter. You can try it out.

Try It Out   Accessing Command-Line Arguments

Here's a C++/CLI version of Ex5_09.

```
// Ex5_16.cpp : main project file.
// Receiving multiple command liner arguments.

#include "stdafx.h"

using namespace System;

int main(array<System::String ^> ^args)
{
  Console::WriteLine(L"There were {0} command line arguments.",
    args->Length);
  Console::WriteLine(L"Command line arguments received are:");
    int i = 1;
  for each(String^ str in args)
    Console::WriteLine(L"Argument {0}: {1}", i++, str);

    return 0;
}
```

You can enter the command-line arguments in the command window or through the project properties window as described earlier in the chapter. I entered the following on the command line:

```
Ex5_16 trying multiple "argument values" 4.5 0.0
```

I got the following output:

```
There were 5 command line arguments.
Command line arguments received are:
Argument 1: trying
Argument 2: multiple
Argument 3: argument values
Argument 4: 4.5
Argument 5: 0.0
```

How It Works

From the output, you can see that one difference between this and the native C++ version is that you don't get the program name passed to main() as an argument — not really a great disadvantage, really a positive feature in most circumstances. Accessing the command-line arguments is now a trivial exercise involving just iterating through the elements in the args array.

Summary

In this chapter, you learned about the basics of program structure. You should have a good grasp of how functions are defined, how data can be passed to a function, and how results are returned to a calling program. Functions are fundamental to programming in C++, so everything you do from here on will involve using multiple functions in a program. The key points that you should keep in mind about writing your own functions are these:

❑ Functions should be compact units of code with a well-defined purpose. A typical program will consist of a large number of small functions, rather than a small number of large functions.

❑ Always provide a function prototype for each function defined in your program, positioned before you call that function.

❑ Passing values to a function using a reference can avoid the copying implicit in the call-by-value transfer of arguments. Parameters that are not modified in a function should be specified as const.

❑ When returning a reference or a pointer from a native C++ function, ensure that the object being returned has the correct scope. Never return a pointer or a reference to an object that is local to a native C++ function.

❑ In a C++/CLI program there is no problem with returning a handle to memory that has been allocated dynamically because the garbage collector takes care of deleting it when it is no longer required.

❑ When you pass a C++/CLI array to a function, there is no need for another parameter for the length of the array, as the number of elements is available in the function body as the Length property for the array.

The use of references as arguments is a very important concept, so make sure you are confident about using them. You'll see a lot more about references as arguments to functions when you look into object-oriented programming.

Exercises

You can download the source code for the examples in the book and the solutions to the following exercises from www.wrox.com.

1. The **factorial** of 4 (written as 4!) is 4*3*2*1 = 24, and 3! is 3*2*1 = 6, so it follows that 4! = 4*3!, or more generally:

fact(n) = n*fact(n - 1)

The limiting case is when n is 1, in which case 1! = 1. Write a recursive function that calculates factorials, and test it.

2. Write a function that swaps two integers, using pointers as arguments. Write a program that uses this function and test that it works correctly.

3. The trigonometry functions (`sin()`, `cos()`, and `tan()`) in the standard <cmath> library take arguments in radians. Write three equivalent functions, called `sind()`, `cosd()`, and `tand()`, which take arguments in degrees. All arguments and return values should be type `double`.

4. Write a native C++ program that reads a number (an integer) and a name (less than 15 characters) from the keyboard. Design the program so that the data entry is done in one function, and the output in another. Keep the data in the main program. The program should end when zero is entered for the number. Think about how you are going to pass the data between functions — by value, by pointer, or by reference?

5. (Advanced) Write a function that, when passed a string consisting of words separated by single spaces, returns the first word; calling it again with an argument of NULL returns the second word, and so on, until the string has been processed completely, when NULL is returned. This is a simplified version of the way the native C++ run-time library routine `strtok()` works. So, when passed the string **'one two three'**, the function returns you **'one'**, then **'two'**, and finally **'three'**. Passing it a new string results in the current string being discarded before the function starts on the new string.

More about Program Structure

In the previous chapter, you learned about the basics of defining functions and the various ways in which data can be passed to a function. You also saw how results are returned to a calling program.

In this chapter, you will explore the further aspects of how functions can be put to good use, including:

- ❑ What a pointer to a function is
- ❑ How to define and use pointers to functions
- ❑ How to define and use arrays of pointers to functions
- ❑ What an exception is and how to write exception handlers that deal with them
- ❑ How to write multiple functions with a single name to handle different kinds of data automatically
- ❑ What function templates are and how you define and use them
- ❑ How to write a substantial native C++ program example using several functions
- ❑ What generic functions are in C++/CLI
- ❑ How to write a substantial C++/CLI program example using several functions

Pointers to Functions

A pointer stores an address value that, up to now, has been the address of another variable with the same basic type as the pointer. This has provided considerable flexibility in allowing you to use different variables at different times through a single pointer. A pointer can also point to the address of a function. This enables you to call a function through a pointer, which will be the function at the address that was last assigned to the pointer.

Obviously, a pointer to a function must contain the memory address of the function that you want to call. To work properly, however, the pointer must also maintain information about the parameter list for the function it points to, as well as the return type. Therefore, when you declare a pointer to a function, you have to specify the parameter types and the return type of the functions that it can point to, in addition to the name of the pointer. Clearly, this is going to restrict what you can store in a particular pointer to a function. If you have declared a pointer to functions that accept one argument of type int and return a value of type double, you can only store the address of a function that has exactly the same form. If you want to store the address of a function that accepts two arguments of type int and returns type char, you must define another pointer with these characteristics.

Declaring Pointers to Functions

You can declare a pointer pfun that you can use to point to functions that take two arguments, of type char* and int, and return a value of type double. The declaration would be as follows:

```
double (*pfun)(char*, int);            // Pointer to function declaration
```

At first you may find that the parentheses make this look a little weird. This statement declares a pointer with the name pfun that can point to functions that accept two arguments of type pointer to char and of type int, and return a value of type double. The parentheses around the pointer name, pfun, and the asterisk are necessary; without them, the statement would be a function declaration rather than a pointer declaration. In this case, it would look like this:

```
double *pfun(char*, int);              // Prototype for a function
                                       // returning type double*
```

This statement is a prototype for a function pfun() that has two parameters, and returns a pointer to a double value. Because you intended to declare a pointer, this is clearly not what you want at the moment.

The general form of a declaration of a pointer to a function looks like this:

```
return_type (*pointer_name)(list_of_parameter_types);
```

The pointer can only point to functions with the same return_type *and* list_of_parameter_types *specified in the declaration.*

This shows that the declaration of a pointer to a function consists of three components:

❑   The return type of the functions that can be pointed to

❑   The pointer name preceded by an asterisk to indicate it is a pointer

❑   The parameter types of the functions that can be pointed to

If you attempt to assign a function to a pointer that does not conform to the types in the pointer declaration, the compiler generates an error message.

You can initialize a pointer to a function with the name of a function within the declaration of the pointer. The following is an example of this:

```
long sum(long num1, long num2);        // Function prototype
long (*pfun)(long, long) = sum;        // Pointer to function points to sum()
```

In general you can set the `pfun` pointer that you declared here to point to any function that accepts two arguments of type `long` and returns a value of type `long`. In the first instance you initialized it with the address of the `sum()` function that has the prototype given by the first statement.

Of course, you can also initialize a pointer to a function by using an assignment statement. Assuming the pointer `pfun` has been declared as above, you could set the value of the pointer to a different function with these statements:

```
long product(long, long);              // Function prototype
...
pfun = product;                        // Set pointer to function product()
```

As with pointers to variables, you must ensure that a pointer to a function is initialized before you use it to call a function. Without initialization, catastrophic failure of your program is guaranteed.

Try It Out   Pointers to Functions

To get a proper feel for these newfangled pointers and how they perform in action, try one out in a program.

```cpp
// Ex6_01.cpp
// Exercising pointers to functions
#include <iostream>
using std::cout;
using std::endl;

long sum(long a, long b);              // Function prototype
long product(long a, long b);          // Function prototype

int main(void)
{
  long (*pdo_it)(long, long);          // Pointer to function declaration

  pdo_it = product;
  cout << endl
       << "3*5 = " << pdo_it(3, 5);    // Call product thru a pointer

  pdo_it = sum;                        // Reassign pointer to sum()
  cout << endl
       << "3*(4 + 5) + 6 = "
       << pdo_it(product(3, pdo_it(4, 5)), 6);   // Call thru a pointer,
                                                 // twice

  cout << endl;
```

```
    return 0;
}

// Function to multiply two values
long product(long a, long b)
{
    return a*b;
}

// Function to add two values
long sum(long a, long b)
{
    return a + b;
}
```

This example produces the output:

```
3*5 = 15
3*(4 + 5) + 6 = 33
```

How It Works

This is hardly a useful program, but it does show very simply how a pointer to a function is declared, assigned a value, and subsequently used to call a function.

After the usual preamble, you declare a pointer to a function, pdo_it, which can point to either of the other two functions that you have defined, sum() or product(). The pointer is given the address of the function product() in this assignment statement:

```
pdo_it = product;
```

You just supply the name of the function as the initial value for the pointer and no parentheses or other adornments are required. The function name is automatically converted to an address, which is stored in the pointer.

The function product() is called indirectly through the pointer pdo_it in the output statement.

```
cout << endl
     << "3*5 = " << pdo_it(3, 5);          // Call product thru a pointer
```

You use the name of the pointer just as if it was a function name, followed by the arguments between parentheses exactly as they would appear if you were using the original function name directly.

Just to show that you can do it, you change the pointer to point to the function sum().

```
pdo_it = sum;                              // Reassign pointer to sum()
```

You then use it again in a ludicrously convoluted expression to do some simple arithmetic:

```
cout << endl
     << "3*(4 + 5) + 6 = "
     << pdo_it(product(3, pdo_it(4, 5)), 6);  // Call thru a pointer,
                                              // twice
```

This shows that a pointer to a function can be used in exactly the same way as the function that it points to. The sequence of actions in the expression is shown in Figure 6-1.

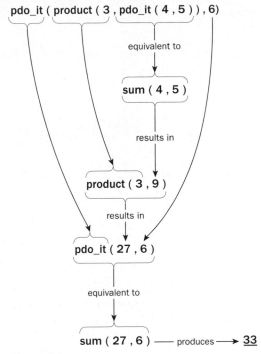

Figure 6-1

A Pointer to a Function as an Argument

Because 'pointer to a function' is a perfectly reasonable type, a function can also have a parameter that is a pointer to a function. The function can then call the function pointed to by the argument. Because the pointer can be made to point at different functions in different circumstances, this allows the particular function that is to be called from inside a function to be determined in the calling program. In this case, you can pass a function explicitly as an argument.

Try It Out   **Passing a Function Pointer**

You can look at this with an example. Suppose you need a function that processes an array of numbers by producing the sum of the squares of each of the numbers on some occasions, and the sum of the cubes on other occasions. One way of achieving this is by using a pointer to a function as an argument.

```
// Ex6_02.cpp
// A pointer to a function as an argument
```

```
#include <iostream>
using std::cout;
using std::endl;

// Function prototypes
double squared(double);
double cubed(double);
double sumarray(double array[], int len, double (*pfun)(double));

int main(void)
{
  double array[] = { 1.5, 2.5, 3.5, 4.5, 5.5, 6.5, 7.5 };
  int len = sizeof array/sizeof array[0];

  cout << endl
       << "Sum of squares = "
       << sumarray(array, len, squared);

  cout << endl
       << "Sum of cubes = "
       << sumarray(array, len, cubed);

  cout << endl;
  return 0;
}

// Function for a square of a value
double squared(double x)
{
  return x*x;
}

// Function for a cube of a value
double cubed(double x)
{
  return x*x*x;
}

// Function to sum functions of array elements
double sumarray(double array[], int len, double (*pfun)(double))
{
  double total = 0.0;                      // Accumulate total in here

  for(int i = 0; i < len; i++)
    total += pfun(array[i]);

  return total;
}
```

If you compile and run this code, you should see the following output:

```
Sum of squares = 169.75
Sum of cubes = 1015.88
```

How It Works

The first statement of interest is the prototype for the function `sumarray()`. Its third parameter is a pointer to a function that has a parameter of type `double`, and returns a value of type `double`.

```
double sumarray(double array[], int len, double (*pfun)(double));
```

The function `sumarray()` processes each element of the array passed as its first argument with whatever function is pointed to by its third argument. The function then returns the sum of the processed array elements.

You call the function `sumarray()` twice in `main()`, the first time with the function name `squared` as the third argument, and the second time using `cubed`. In each case, the address corresponding to the function name that you use as the argument is substituted for the function pointer in the body of the function `sumarray()`, so the appropriate function is called within the `for` loop.

There are obviously easier ways of achieving what this example does, but using a pointer to a function provides you with a lot of generality. You could pass any function to `sumarray()` that you care to define as long as it takes one `double` argument and returns a value of type `double`.

Arrays of Pointers to Functions

In the same way as with regular pointers, you can declare an array of pointers to functions. You can also initialize them in the declaration. Here is an example of declaring an array of pointers.

```
double sum(double, double);                             // Function prototype
double product(double, double);                         // Function prototype
double difference(double, double);                      // Function prototype
double (*pfun[3])(double,double) =
                 { sum, product, difference };          // Array of function pointers
```

Each of the elements in the array is initialized by the corresponding function address appearing in the initializing list between braces. To call the function `product()` using the second element of the pointer array, you would write:

```
pfun[1](2.5, 3.5);
```

The square brackets that select the function pointer array element appear immediately after the array name and before the arguments to the function being called. Of course, you can place a function call through an element of a function pointer array in any appropriate expression that the original function might legitimately appear in, and the index value selecting the pointer can be any expression producing a valid index value.

Initializing Function Parameters

With all the functions you have used up to now, you have had to take care to provide an argument corresponding to each parameter in a function call. It can be quite handy to be able to omit one or more arguments in a function call and have some default values for the arguments that you leave out supplied automatically. You can arrange this by initializing the parameters to a function in its prototype.

For example, suppose that you write a function to display a message, where the message to be displayed is passed as an argument. Here is the definition of such a function:

```
void showit(const char message[])
{
  cout << endl
       << message;
  return;
}
```

You can initialize the parameter to this function by specifying the initializing string value in the function prototype, as follows:

```
void showit(const char message[] = "Something is wrong.");
```

Here, the parameter message is initialized with the string literal shown. Once you initialize a parameter to a function in the prototype, if you leave out that argument when you call the function, the initializing value is used in the call.

Try It Out   Omitting Function Arguments

Leaving out the function argument when you call the function executes it with the default value. If you supply the argument, it replaces the default value. You can use the showit() function to output a variety of messages.

```
// Ex6_03.cpp
// Omitting function arguments
#include <iostream>
using std::cout;
using std::endl;

void showit(const char message[] = "Something is wrong.");

int main(void)
{
  const char mymess[] = "The end of the world is nigh.";

  showit();                                  // Display the basic message
  showit("Something is terribly wrong!");    // Display an alternative
  showit();                                  // Display the default again
  showit(mymess);                            // Display a predefined message

  cout << endl;
  return 0;
}

void showit(const char message[])
{
  cout << endl
       << message;
  return;
}
```

If you execute this example, it produces the following apocalyptic output:

```
Something is wrong.
Something is terribly wrong!
Something is wrong.
The end of the world is nigh.
```

How It Works

As you can see, you get the default message specified in the function prototype whenever the argument is left out; otherwise, the function behaves normally.

If you have a function with several arguments, you can provide initial values for as many of them as you like. If you want to omit more than one argument to take advantage of a default value, all arguments to the right of the leftmost argument that you omit must also be left out. For example, suppose you have this function:

```
int do_it(long arg1 = 10, long arg2 = 20, long arg3 = 30, long arg4 = 40);
```

and you want to omit one argument in a call to it. You can omit only the last one, arg4. If you want to omit arg3, you must also omit arg4. If you omit arg2, arg3 and arg4 must also be omitted, and if you want to use the default value for arg1, you have to omit all of the arguments in the function call.

You can conclude from this that you need to put the arguments which have default values in the function prototype together in sequence at the end of the parameter list, with the argument most likely to be omitted appearing last.

Exceptions

If you've had a go at the exercises that appear at the end of the previous chapters, you've more than likely come across compiler errors and warnings, as well as errors that occur while the program is running. **Exceptions** are a way of flagging errors or unexpected conditions that occur in your C++ programs, and you already know that the new operator throws an exception if the memory you request cannot be allocated.

So far, you have typically handled error conditions in your programs by using an if statement to test some expression, and then executing some specific code to deal with the error. C++ also provides another, more general mechanism for handling errors that allows you to separate the code that deals with these conditions from the code that executes when such conditions do not arise. It is important to realize that exceptions are not intended to be used as an alternative to the normal data checking and validating that you might do in a program. The code that is generated when you use exceptions carries quite a bit of overhead with it, so exceptions are really intended to be applied in the context of exceptional, near catastrophic conditions that might arise, but are not normally expected to occur in the normal course of events. An error reading from a disk might be something that you use exceptions for. An invalid data item being entered is not a good candidate for using exceptions.

The exception mechanism uses three new keywords:

- `try` — identifies a code block in which an exception can occur
- `throw` — causes an exception condition to be originated
- `catch` — identifies a block of code in which the exception is handled

In the following Try It Out, you can see how they work in practice.

Try It Out   Throwing and Catching Exceptions

You can easily see how exception handling operates by working through an example. Let's use a very simple context for this. Suppose that you are required to write a program that calculates the time it takes in minutes to make a part on a machine. The number of parts made in each hour is recorded, but you must keep in mind that the machine breaks down regularly and may not make any parts.

You could code this using exception handling as follows:

```cpp
// Ex6_04.cpp  Using exception handling
#include <iostream>
using std::cout;
using std::endl;

int main(void)
{
  int counts[] = {34, 54, 0, 27, 0, 10, 0};
  int time = 60;                          // One hour in minutes

  for(int i = 0 ; i < sizeof counts/sizeof counts[0] ; i++)
    try
    {
      cout << endl
           << "Hour " << i+1;

      if(counts[i] == 0)
        throw "Zero count - calculation not possible.";

      cout << " minutes per item: "
           << static_cast<double>(time)/counts[i];
    }
    catch(const char aMessage[])
    {
      cout << endl
           << aMessage
           << endl;
    }
  return 0;
}
```

If you run this example, the output is:

```
Hour 1 minutes per item: 1.76471
Hour 2 minutes per item: 1.11111
```

```
Hour 3
Zero count - calculation not possible.

Hour 4 minutes per item: 2.22222
Hour 5
Zero count - calculation not possible.

Hour 6 minutes per item: 6
Hour 7
Zero count - calculation not possible.
```

How It Works

The code in the `try` block is executed in the normal sequence. The `try` block serves to define where an exception can be raised. You can see from the output that when an exception is thrown, the sequence of execution continues with the `catch` block and after the code in the catch block has been executed, execution continues with the next loop iteration. Of course, when no exception is thrown, the `catch` block is not executed. Both the `try` block and the `catch` block are regarded as a single unit by the compiler, so they both form the `for` loop block and the loop continues after an exception is thrown.

The division is carried out in the output statement that follows the `if` statement checking the divisor. When a `throw` statement is executed, control passes immediately to the first statement in the `catch` block, so the statement that performs the division is bypassed when an exception is thrown. After the statement in the `catch` block executes, the loop continues with the next iteration if there is one.

Throwing Exceptions

Exceptions can be thrown anywhere within a `try` block, and the operand of the `throw` statements determines a type for the exception — the exception thrown in the example is a string literal and therefore of type `const char[]`. The operand following the `throw` keyword can be any expression, and the type of the result of the expression determines the type of exception thrown.

Exceptions can also be thrown in functions called from within a `try` block and caught by a `catch` block following the `try` block. You could add a function to the previous example to demonstrate this, with the definition:

```
void testThrow(void)
{
  throw " Zero count - calculation not possible.";
}
```

You place a call to this function in the previous example in place of the throw statement:

```
if(counts[i] == 0)
  testThrow();                   // Call a function that throws an exception
```

The exception is thrown by the `testThrow()` function and caught by the `catch` block whenever the array element is zero, so the output is the same as before. Don't forget the function prototype if you add the definition of `testThrow()` to the end of the source code.

Catching Exceptions

The `catch` block following the `try` block in our example catches any exception of type `const char[]`. This is determined by the parameter specification that appears in parentheses following the keyword `catch`. You must supply at least one `catch` block for a `try` block, and the `catch` blocks must immediately follow the `try` block. A `catch` block catches all exceptions (of the correct type) that occur anywhere in the code in the immediately preceding `try` block, including those thrown in any functions called directly or indirectly within the `try` block.

If you want to specify that a `catch` block is to handle any exception thrown in a `try` block, you must put an ellipsis (. . .) between the parentheses enclosing the exception declaration:

```
catch (...)
{
   // code to handle any exception
}
```

This `catch` block must appear last if you have other `catch` blocks defined for the `try` block.

Try It Out   Nested try Blocks

You can nest `try` blocks one within another. With this situation, if an exception is thrown from within an inner `try` block that is not followed by a `catch` block corresponding to the type of exception thrown, the catch handlers for the outer `try` block are searched. You can demonstrate this with the following example:

```cpp
// Ex6_05.cpp
// Nested try blocks
#include <iostream>
using std::cin;
using std::cout;
using std::endl;

int main(void)
{
  int height = 0;
  const double inchesToMeters = 0.0254;
  char ch = 'y';

  try                                         // Outer try block
  {
    while(ch == 'y'||ch =='Y')
    {
      cout << "Enter a height in inches: ";
      cin >> height;                          // Read the height to be converted

      try                                     // Defines try block in which
      {                                       // exceptions may be thrown
        if(height > 100)
          throw "Height exceeds maximum";     // Exception thrown
        if(height < 9)
          throw height;                       // Exception thrown
```

```
        cout << static_cast<double>(height)*inchesToMeters
            << " meters"
            << endl;

    }
    catch(const char aMessage[])               // start of catch block which
    {                                          // catches exceptions of type
      cout << aMessage << endl;                // const char[]
    }
    cout << "Do you want to continue(y or n)?";
    cin >> ch;
  }
}
catch(int badHeight)
{
  cout << badHeight << " inches is below minimum" << endl;
}
return 0;
}
```

How It Works

Here there is a `try` block enclosing the `while` loop and an inner try block in which two different types of exception may be thrown. The exception of type `const char[]` is caught by the `catch` block for the inner `try` block, but the exception of type `int` has no catch handler associated with the inner `try` block; therefore, the `catch` handler in the outer try block is executed. In this case, the program ends immediately because the statement following the `catch` block is a `return`.

Exception Handling in the MFC

This is a good point to raise the question of MFC and exceptions because they are used to some extent. If you browse the documentation that came with Visual C++ 2008, you may come across TRY, THROW, and CATCH in the index. These are macros defined within MFC that were created before the exception handling was implemented in the C++ language. They mimic the operation of `try`, `throw`, and `catch` in the C++ language, but the language facilities for exception handling really render these obsolete so you should not use them. They are, however, still there for two reasons. There are large numbers of programs still around that use these macros, and it is important to ensure that as far as possible old code still compiles. Also, most of the MFC that throws exceptions was implemented in terms of these macros. In any event, any new programs should use the `try`, `throw`, and `catch` keywords in C++ because they work with the MFC.

There is one slight anomaly you need to keep in mind when you use MFC functions that throw exceptions. The MFC functions that throw exceptions generally throw exceptions of class types — you will find out about class types before you get to use the MFC. Even though the exception that an MFC function throws is of a given class type — CDBException say — you need to catch the exception as a pointer, not as the type of the exception. So with the exception thrown being of type CDBException, the type that appears as the `catch` block parameter is CBDException*. You will see examples of functions that throw exceptions of type CDBException where this is the case in Chapter 21.

Handling Memory Allocation Errors

When you used the operator new to allocate memory for our variables (as you saw in Chapters 4 and 5), you ignored the possibility that the memory might not be allocated. If the memory isn't allocated, an exception is thrown that results in the termination of the program. Ignoring this exception is quite acceptable in most situations because having no memory left is usually a terminal condition for a program that you can usually do nothing about. However, there can be circumstances where you might be able to do something about it if you had the chance or you might want to report the problem in your own way. In this situation, you can catch the exception that the new operator throws. Let's contrive an example to show this happening.

Try It Out   Catching an Exception Thrown by the new Operator

The exception that the new operator throws when memory cannot be allocated is of type bad_alloc. bad_alloc is a class type defined in the <new> standard header file, so you'll need an #include directive for that. Here's the code:

```cpp
// Ex6_06.cpp
// Catching an exception thrown by new
#include<new>                        // For bad_alloc type
#include<iostream>
using std::bad_alloc;
using std::cout;
using std::endl;

int main( )
{
  char* pdata = 0;
  size_t count = ~static_cast<size_t>(0)/2;
  try
  {
    pdata = new char[count];
    cout << "Memory allocated." << endl;
  }
  catch(bad_alloc &ex)
  {
    cout << "Memory allocation failed." << endl
         << "The information from the exception object is: "
         << ex.what() << endl;
  }
  delete[] pdata;
  return 0;
}
```

On my machine this example produces the following output:

```
Memory allocation failed.
The information from the exception object is: bad allocation
```

If you are in the fortunate position of having many gigabytes of memory in your computer, you may not get the exception thrown.

How It Works

The example allocates memory dynamically for an array of type `char[]` where the length is specified by the `count` variable that you define as:

```
size_t count = ~static_cast<size_t>(0)/2;
```

The size of an array is an integer of type `size_t` so you declare `count` to be of this type. The value for `count` is generated by a somewhat complicated expression. The value 0 is type `int` so the value produced by the expression `static_cast<size_t>(0)` is a zero of type `size_t`. Applying the ~ operator to this flips all the bits so you then have a `size_t` value with all the bits as 1, which corresponds to the maximum value you can represent as `size_t` because `size_t` is an unsigned type. This value exceeds the maximum amount of memory that the `new` operator can allocate in one go so you divide by 2 to bring it within the bounds of what is possible. This is still a very large value so unless your machine is exceptionally well endowed with memory, the allocation request will fail.

The allocation of the memory takes place in the `try` block. If the allocation succeeds you'll see a message to that effect but if as you expect it fails, an exception of type `bad_alloc` will be thrown by the new operator. This causes the code in the `catch` block to be executed. Calling the `what()` function for the `bad_alloc` object reference ex returns a string describing the problem that caused the exception and you see the result of this call in the output. Most exception classes implement the `what()` function to provide a string describing why the exception was thrown.

To handle out-of-memory situations with some positive effect, clearly you must have some means of returning memory to the free store. In most practical cases, this involves some serious work on the program to manage memory so it is not often undertaken.

Function Overloading

Suppose you have written a function that determines the maximum value in an array of values of type `double`:

```
// Function to generate the maximum value in an array of type double
double maxdouble(double array[], int len)
{
   double max = array[0];

   for(int i = 1; i < len; i++)
      if(max < array[i])
         max = array[i];

   return max;
}
```

You now want to create a function that produces the maximum value from an array of type `long`, so you write another function similar to the first, with this prototype:

```
long maxlong(long array[], int len);
```

You have chosen the function name to reflect the particular task in hand, which is OK for two functions, but you may also need the same function for several other types of argument. It seems a pity that you have to keep inventing names. Ideally, you would use the same function name max() regardless of the argument type, and have the appropriate version executed. It probably won't be any surprise to you that you can indeed do this, and the C++ mechanism that makes it possible is called **function overloading**.

What Is Function Overloading?

Function overloading allows you to use the same function name for defining several functions as long as they each have different parameter lists. When the function is called, the compiler chooses the correct version for the job based on the list of arguments you supply. Obviously, the compiler must always be able to decide unequivocally which function should be selected in any particular instance of a function call, so the parameter list for each function in a set of overloaded functions must be unique. Following on from the max() function example, you could create overloaded functions with the following prototypes:

```
int max(int array[], int len);            // Prototypes for
long max(long array[], int len);          // a set of overloaded
double max(double array[], int len);      // functions
```

These functions share a common name, but have a different parameter list. In general, overloaded functions can be differentiated by having corresponding parameters of different types, or by having a different number of parameters.

Note that a different return type does not distinguish a function adequately. You can't add the following function to the previous set:

```
double max(long array[], int len);      // Not valid overloading
```

The reason is that this function would be indistinguishable from the function that has this prototype:

```
long max(long array[], int len);
```

If you define functions like this, it causes the compiler to complain with the following error:

```
error C2556: 'double max(long [],int)' : overloaded function differs only by return
type from 'long max(long [],int)'
```

and the program does not compile. This may seem slightly unreasonable, until you remember that you can write statements such as these:

```
long numbers[] = {1, 2, 3, 3, 6, 7, 11, 50, 40};
int len = sizeof numbers/sizeof numbers[0];
max(numbers, len);
```

The fact that the call for the max() function doesn't make much sense here because you discard the result does not make it illegal. If the return type were permitted as a distinguishing feature, the compiler would be unable to decide whether to choose the version with a long return type or a double return type in the instance of the preceding code. For this reason the return type is not considered to be a differentiating feature of overloaded functions.

In fact every function — not just overloaded functions — is said to have a **signature**, where the signature of a function is determined by its name and its parameter list. All functions in a program must have unique signatures; otherwise the program does not compile.

Try It Out   **Using Overloaded Functions**

You can exercise the overloading capability with the function max() that you have already defined. Try an example that includes the three versions for int, long and double arrays.

```cpp
// Ex6_07.cpp
// Using overloaded functions
#include <iostream>
using std::cout;
using std::endl;

int max(int array[], int len);              // Prototypes for
long max(long array[], int len);            // a set of overloaded
double max(double array[], int len);        // functions

int main(void)
{
    int small[] = {1, 24, 34, 22};
    long medium[] = {23, 245, 123, 1, 234, 2345};
    double large[] = {23.0, 1.4, 2.456, 345.5, 12.0, 21.0};

    int lensmall = sizeof small/sizeof small[0];
    int lenmedium = sizeof medium/sizeof medium[0];
    int lenlarge = sizeof large/sizeof large[0];

    cout << endl << max(small, lensmall);
    cout << endl << max(medium, lenmedium);
    cout << endl << max(large, lenlarge);

    cout << endl;
    return 0;
}

// Maximum of ints
int max(int x[], int len)
{
    int max = x[0];
    for(int i = 1; i < len; i++)
        if(max < x[i])
            max = x[i];
    return max;
}

// Maximum of longs
long max(long x[], int len)
{
    long max = x[0];
    for(int i = 1; i < len; i++)
        if(max < x[i])
```

```
        max = x[i];
    return max;
}

// Maximum of doubles
double max(double x[], int len)
{
    double max = x[0];
    for(int i = 1; i < len; i++)
        if(max < x[i])
            max = x[i];
    return max;
}
```

The example works as you would expect and produces this output:

```
34
2345
345.5
```

How It Works

You have three prototypes for the three overloaded versions of the function max(). In each of the three output statements, the appropriate version of the function max() is selected by the compiler based on the argument list types. This works because each of the versions of the max() function has a unique signature because its parameter list is different from that of the other max() functions.

When to Overload Functions

Function overloading provides you with the means of ensuring that a function name describes the function being performed and is not confused by extraneous information such as the type of data being processed. This is akin to what happens with basic operations in C++. To add two numbers you use the same operator, regardless of the types of the operands. Our overloaded function max() has the same name, regardless of the type of data being processed. This helps to make the code more readable and makes these functions easier to use.

The intent of function overloading is clear: to enable the same operation to be performed with different operands using a single function name. So, whenever you have a series of functions that do essentially the same thing, but with different types of arguments, you should overload them and use a common function name.

Function Templates

The last example was somewhat tedious in that you had to repeat essentially the same code for each function, but with different variable and parameter types. However, there is a way of avoiding this. You have the possibility of creating a recipe that will enable the compiler to automatically generate functions with various parameter types. The code defining the recipe for generating a particular group of functions is called a **function template**.

A function template has one or more **type parameters**, and you generate a particular function by supplying a concrete type argument for each of the template's parameters. Thus the functions generated by a function template all have the same basic code, but customized by the type arguments that you supply. You can see how this works in practice by defining a function template for the function max() in the previous example.

Using a Function Template

You can define a template for the function max() as follows:

```
template<class T> T max(T x[], int len)
{
    T max = x[0];
    for(int i = 1; i < len; i++)
        if(max < x[i])
            max = x[i];
    return max;
}
```

The template keyword identifies this as a template definition. The angled brackets following the template keyword enclose the type parameters that are used to create a particular instance of the function separated by commas; in this instance you have just one type parameter, T. The keyword class before the T indicates that the T is the type parameter for this template, class being the generic term for type. Later in the book you will see that defining a class is essentially defining your own data type. Consequently, you have fundamental types in C++, such as type int and type char, and you also have the types that you define yourself. Note that you can use the keyword typename instead of class to identify the parameters in a function template, in which case the template definition would look like this:

```
template<typename T> T max(T x[], int len)
{
    T max = x[0];
    for(int i = 1; i < len; i++)
        if(max < x[i])
            max = x[i];
    return max;
}
```

Some programmers prefer to use the typename keyword as the class keyword tends to connote a user-defined type, whereas typename is more neutral and therefore is more readily understood to imply fundamental types as well as user-defined types. In practice you'll see both keywords used widely.

Wherever T appears in the definition of a function template, it is replaced by the specific type argument, such as long, that you supply when you create an instance of the template. If you try this out manually by plugging in long in place of T in the template, you'll see that this generates a perfectly satisfactory function for calculating the maximum value from an array of type long:

```
long max(long x[], int len)
{
    long max = x[0];
    for(int i = 1; i < len; i++)
        if(max < x[i])
```

```
        max = x[i];
    return max;
}
```

The creation of a particular function instance is referred to as **instantiation**.

Each time you use the function max() in your program, the compiler checks to see if a function corresponding to the type of arguments that you have used in the function call already exists. If the function required does not exist, the compiler creates one by substituting the argument type that you have used in your function call in place of the parameter T throughout the source code in the corresponding template definition. You could exercise the template for max() function with the same main() function that you used in the previous example.

Try It Out   Using a Function Template

Here's a version of the previous example modified to use a template for the max() function:

```
// Ex6_08.cpp
// Using function templates

#include <iostream>
using std::cout;
using std::endl;

// Template for function to compute the maximum element of an array
template<typename T> T max(T x[], int len)
{
    T max = x[0];
    for(int i = 1; i < len; i++)
        if(max < x[i])
            max = x[i];
    return max;
}

int main(void)
{
    int small[] = { 1, 24, 34, 22};
    long medium[] = { 23, 245, 123, 1, 234, 2345};
    double large[] = { 23.0, 1.4, 2.456, 345.5, 12.0, 21.0};

    int lensmall = sizeof small/sizeof small[0];
    int lenmedium = sizeof medium/sizeof medium[0];
    int lenlarge = sizeof large/sizeof large[0];

    cout << endl << max(small, lensmall);
    cout << endl << max(medium, lenmedium);
    cout << endl << max(large, lenlarge);

    cout << endl;
    return 0;
}
```

If you run this program, it produces exactly the same output as the previous example.

How It Works

For each of the statements outputting the maximum value in an array, a new version of `max()` is instantiated using the template. Of course, if you add another statement calling the function `max()` with one of the types used previously, no new version of the code is generated.

Note that using a template doesn't reduce the size of your compiled program in any way. The compiler generates a version of the source code for each function that you require. In fact, using templates can generally *increase* the size of your program, as functions can be created automatically even though an existing version might satisfactorily be used by casting the argument accordingly. You can force the creation of particular instances of a template by explicitly including a declaration for it. For example, if you wanted to ensure that an instance of the template for the function `max()` was created corresponding to the type `float`, you could place the following declaration after the definition of the template:

```
float max(float, int);
```

This forces the creation of this version of the function template. It does not have much value in the case of our program example, but it can be useful when you know that several versions of a template function might be generated, but you want to force the generation of a subset that you plan to use with arguments cast to the appropriate type where necessary.

An Example Using Functions

You have covered a lot of ground in C++ up to now and a lot on functions in this chapter alone. After wading through a varied menu of language capabilities, it's not always easy to see how they relate to one another. Now would be a good point to see how some of this goes together to produce something with more meat than a simple demonstration program.

Let's work through a more realistic example to see how a problem can be broken down into functions. The process involves defining the problem to be solved, analyzing the problem to see how it can be implemented in C++, and finally writing the code. The approach here is aimed at illustrating how various functions go together to make up the final result, rather than providing a tutorial on how to develop a program.

Implementing a Calculator

Suppose you need a program that acts as a calculator; not one of these fancy devices with lots of buttons and gizmos designed for those who are easily pleased, but one for people who know where they are going, arithmetically speaking. You can really go for it and enter a calculation from the keyboard as a single arithmetic expression, and have the answer displayed immediately. An example of the sort of thing that you might enter is:

```
2*3.14159*12.6*12.6 / 2 + 25.2*25.2
```

To avoid unnecessary complications for the moment, you won't allow parentheses in the expression and the whole computation must be entered in a single line; however, to allow the user to make the input look attractive, you *will* allow spaces to be placed anywhere. The expression entered may contain the operators multiply, divide, add, and subtract represented by *, /, + and – respectively, and the expression entered will be evaluated with normal arithmetic rules, so that multiplication and division take precedence over addition and subtraction.

The program should allow as many successive calculations to be performed as required, and should terminate if an empty line is entered. It should also have helpful and friendly error messages.

Analyzing the Problem

A good place to start is with the input. The program reads in an arithmetic expression of any length on a single line, which can be any construction within the terms given. Because nothing is fixed about the elements making up the expression, you have to read it as a string of characters and then work out within the program how it's made up. You can decide arbitrarily that you will handle a string of up to 80 characters, so you could store it in an array declared within these statements:

```
const int MAX = 80;              // Maximum expression length including '\0'
char buffer[MAX];                // Input area for expression to be evaluated
```

To change the maximum length of the string processed by the program, you will only need to alter the initial value of MAX.

You need to understand the basic structure of the information that appears in the input string, so let's break it down step-by-step.

You will want to make sure that the input is as uncluttered as possible when you are processing it, so before you start analyzing the input string, you will get rid of any spaces in it. You can call the function that will do this eatspaces(). This function can work by stepping through the input buffer — which is the array buffer[] — and shuffling characters up to overwrite any spaces. This process uses two indexes to the buffer array, i and j, which start out at the beginning of the buffer; in general, you'll store element j at position i. As you progress through the array elements, each time you find a space you increment j but not i, so the space at position i gets overwritten by the next character you find at index position j that is not a space. Figure 6-2 illustrates the logic of this.

This process is one of copying the contents of the array buffer[] to itself, excluding any spaces. Figure 6-2 shows the **buffer** array before and after the copying process and the arrows indicate which characters are copied and the position to which each character is copied.

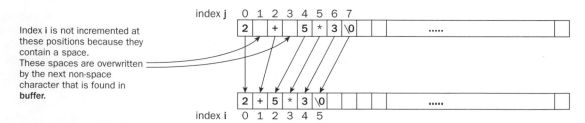

Figure 6-2

When you have removed spaces from the input you are ready to evaluate the expression. You define the function `expr()` which returns the value that results from evaluating the whole expression in the input buffer. To decide what goes on inside the `expr()` function, you need to look into the structure of the input in more detail. The add and subtract operators have the lowest precedence and so are evaluated last. You can think of the input string as comprising one or more **terms** connected by operators, which can be either the operator + or the operator –. You can refer to either operator as an `addop`. With this terminology, you can represent the general form of the input expression like this:

```
expression: term addop term ... addop term
```

The expression contains at least one `term` and can have an arbitrary number of following `addop term` combinations. In fact, assuming that you have removed all the blanks, there are only three legal possibilities for the character that follows each `term`:

❑   The next character is `'\0'`, so you are at the end of the string.

❑   The next character is `'-'`, in which case you should subtract the next `term` from the value accrued for the expression up to this point.

❑   The next character is `'+'`, in which case you should add the value of the next `term` to the value of the expression accumulated so far.

If anything else follows a `term`, the string is not what you expect, so you'll display an error message and exit from the program. Figure 6-3 illustrates the structure of a sample expression.

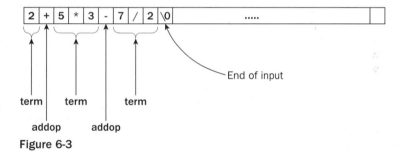

Figure 6-3

Next, you need a more detailed and precise definition of a `term`. A `term` is simply a series of numbers connected by either the operator * or the operator /. Therefore, a `term` (in general) looks like this:

```
term: number multop number ... multop number
```

`multop` represents either a multiply or a divide operator. You could define a function `term()` to return the value of a term. This needs to scan the string to a number first and then to look for a `multop` followed by another number. If a character is found that isn't a `multop`, the `term()` function assumes that it is an `addop` and returns the value that has been found up to that point.

The last thing you need to figure out before writing the program is how you recognize a number. To minimize the complexity of the code, you'll only recognize unsigned numbers; therefore, a number consists of a series of digits that may be optionally followed by a decimal point and some more digits. To determine the value of a number you step through the buffer looking for digits. If you find anything that isn't a digit, you check whether it's a decimal point. If it's not a decimal point it has nothing to do with a number, so you return what you have got. If you find a decimal point, you look for more digits. As soon as you find anything that's not a digit, you have the complete number and you return that. Imaginatively, you'll call the function to recognize a number and return its value `number()`. Figure 6-4 shows an example of how an expression breaks down into terms and numbers.

You now have enough understanding of the problem to write some code. You can work through the functions you need and then write a `main()` function to tie them all together. The first and perhaps easiest function to write is `eatspaces()`, which is going to eliminate the blanks from the input string.

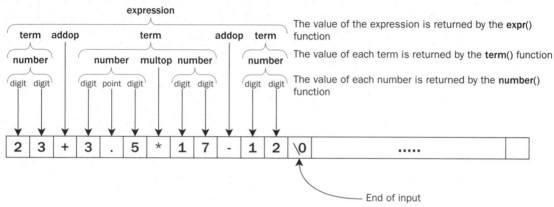

Figure 6-4

Eliminating Blanks from a String

You can write the prototype for the `eatspaces()` function as follows:

```
void eatspaces(char* str);          // Function to eliminate blanks
```

The function doesn't need to return any value because the blanks can be eliminated from the string *in situ*, modifying the original string directly through the pointer that is passed as the argument. The process for eliminating blanks is a very simple one. You copy the string to itself, overwriting any spaces as you saw earlier in this chapter.

You can define the function to do this as follows:

```
// Function to eliminate spaces from a string
void eatspaces(char* str)
{
  int i = 0;                              // 'Copy to' index to string
  int j = 0;                              // 'Copy from' index to string

  while((*(str + i) = *(str + j++)) != '\0')   // Loop while character is not \0
    if(*(str + i) != ' ')                       // Increment i as long as
      i++;                                       // character is not a space
  return;
}
```

How the Function Functions

All the action is in the `while` loop. The loop condition copies the string by moving the character at position j to the character at position i and then increments j to the next character. If the character copied was `'\0'`, you have reached the end of the string and you're done.

The only action in the loop statement is to increment i to the next character if the last character copied was not a blank. If it *is* a blank, i is not be incremented and the blank can therefore be overwritten by the character copied on the next iteration.

That wasn't hard, was it? Next, you can try writing the function that returns the result of evaluating the expression.

Evaluating an Expression

The `expr()` function returns the value of the expression specified in the string that is supplied as an argument, so you can write its prototype as follows:

```
double expr(char* str);              // Function evaluating an expression
```

The function declared here accepts a string as an argument and returns the result as type `double`. Based on the structure for an expression that you worked out earlier, you can draw a logic diagram for the process of evaluating an expression as shown in Figure 6-5.

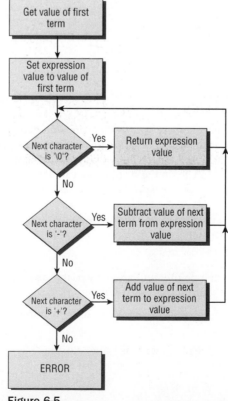

Figure 6-5

Using this basic definition of the logic, you can now write the function:

```cpp
// Function to evaluate an arithmetic expression
double expr(char* str)
{
   double value = 0.0;                   // Store result here
   int index = 0;                        // Keeps track of current character position

   value = term(str, index);            // Get first term

   for(;;)                               // Indefinite loop, all exits inside
   {
     switch(*(str + index++))           // Choose action based on current character
     {
       case '\0':                        // We're at the end of the string
         return value;                   // so return what we have got

       case '+':                         // + found so add in the
         value += term(str, index);      // next term
         break;

       case '-':                         // - found so subtract
         value -= term(str, index);      // the next term
         break;

       default:                          // If we reach here the string
         cout << endl                    // is junk
             << "Arrrgh!*#!! There's an error"
             << endl;
         exit(1);
     }
   }
}
```

How the Function Functions

Considering this function is analyzing any arithmetic expression that you care to throw at it (as long as it uses our operator subset), it's not a lot of code. You define a variable index of type int, which keeps track of the current position in the string where you are working, and you initialize it to 0, which corresponds to the index position of the first character in the string. You also define a variable value of type double in which you'll accumulate the value of the expression that is passed to the function in the char array str.

Because an expression must have at least one term, the first action in the function is to get the value of the first term by calling the function term(), which you have yet to write. This actually places three requirements on the function term():

1. It should accept a char* pointer and an int variable as parameters, the second parameter being an index to the first character of the term in the string supplied.

2. It should update the index value passed to position it at the character following the last character of the term found.

3. It should return the value of the term as type double.

The rest of the program is an indefinite `for` loop. Within the loop, the action is determined by a `switch` statement, which is controlled by the current character in the string. If it is a `'+'`, you call the `term()` function to get the value of the next term in the expression and add it to the variable `value`. If it is a `'-'`, you subtract the value returned by `term()` from the variable `value`. If it is a `'\0'`, you are at the end of the string, so you return the current contents of the variable `value` to the calling program. If it is any other character, it shouldn't be there, so after remonstrating with the user you end the program!

As long as either a `'+'` or a `'-'` is found, the loop continues. Each call to `term()` moves the value of the `index` variable to the character following the term that was evaluated, and this should be should be either another `'+'` or `'-'`, or the end of string character `'\0'`. Thus, the function either terminates normally when `'\0'` is reached, or abnormally by calling `exit()`. You need to remember the `#include` directive for `<cstdlib>` header file that provides the definition of the function `exit()` when you come to put the whole program together.

You also could also analyze an arithmetic expression using a recursive function. If you think about the definition of an expression slightly differently, you could specify it as being either a term, or a term followed by an expression. The definition here is recursive (i.e. the definition involves the item being defined), and this approach is very common in defining programming language structures. This definition provides just as much flexibility as the first, but using it as the base concept, you could arrive at a recursive version of `expr()` instead of using a loop as you did in the implementation above. You might want to try this alternative approach as an exercise after you have completed the first version.

Getting the Value of a Term

The `term()` function returns a value for a term as type `double` and receives two arguments: the string being analyzed and an index to the current position in the string. There are other ways of doing this, but this arrangement is quite straightforward. You can, therefore, write the prototype of the function `term()` as follows:

```
double term(char* str, int& index);        // Function analyzing a term
```

You have specified the second parameter as a reference. This is because you want the function to be able to modify the value of the variable `index` in the calling program to position it at the character following the last character of the term found in the input string. You could return `index` as a value, but then you would need to return the value of the term in some other way, so this arrangement seems quite natural.

The logic for analyzing a term is going to be similar in structure to that for an expression. A term is a number, potentially followed by one or more combinations of a multiply or a divide operator and another number. You can write the definition of the `term()` function as follows:

```
// Function to get the value of a term
double term(char* str, int& index)
{
  double value = 0.0;                  // Somewhere to accumulate
                                       // the result

  value = number(str, index);          // Get the first number in the term

  // Loop as long as we have a good operator
  while((*(str + index) == '*') || (*(str + index) == '/'))
```

```
    {
        if(*(str + index) == '*')          // If it's multiply,
            value *= number(str, ++index);  // multiply by next number

        if(*(str + index) == '/')          // If it's divide,
            value /= number(str, ++index);  // divide by next number
    }
    return value;                          // We've finished, so return what
                                           // we've got
}
```

How the Function Functions

You first declare a local `double` variable, `value`, in which you'll accumulate the value of the current term. Because a term must contain at least one number, the first action in the function is to obtain the value of the first number by calling the `number()` function and storing the result in `value`. You implicitly assume that the function `number()` accepts the string and an index to a position in the string as arguments, and returns the value of the number found. Because the `number()` function must also update the index to the string to the position after the number that was found, you'll again specify the second parameter as a reference when you come to define that function.

The rest of the `term()` function is a `while` loop that continues as long as the next character is `'*'` or `'/'`. Within the loop, if the character found at the current position is `'*'`, you increment the variable `index` to position it at the beginning of the next number, call the function `number()` to get the value of the next number, and then multiply the contents of `value` by the value returned. In a similar manner, if the current character is `'/'`, you increment the `index` variable and divide the contents of `value` by the value returned from `number()`. Because the function `number()` automatically alters the value of the variable index to the character following the number found, `index` is already set to select the next available character in the string on the next iteration.

The loop terminates when a character other than a multiply or divide operator is found, whereupon the current value of the term accumulated in the variable `value` is returned to the calling program.

The last analytical function that you require is `number()`, which determines the numerical value of any number appearing in the string.

Analyzing a Number

Based on the way you have used the `number()` function within the `term()` function, you need to declare it with this prototype:

```
double number(char* str, int& index);    // Function to recognize a number
```

The specification of the second parameter as a reference allows the function to update the argument in the calling program directly, which is what you require.

You can make use of a function provided in a standard C++ library here. The <cctype> header file provides definitions for a range of functions for testing single characters. These functions return values of type `int` where nonzero values correspond to `true` and zero corresponds to `false`. Four of these functions are shown in the following table:

Functions	Description
`int isalpha(int c)`	Returns **nonzero** if the argument is alphabetic, **0** otherwise.
`int isupper(int c)`	Returns **nonzero** if the argument is an upper case letter, **0** otherwise.
`int islower(int c)`	Returns **nonzero** if the argument is a lower case letter, **0** otherwise.
`int isdigit(int c)`	Returns **nonzero** if the argument is a digit, **0** otherwise.

A number of other functions are provided by <cctype>, but I won't grind through all the detail. If you're interested, you can look them up in the Visual C++ 2008 Help. A search on "is routines" should find them.

You only need the last of the functions shown above in the program. Remember that `isdigit()` is testing a character, such as the character `'9'` (ASCII character 57 in decimal notation) for instance, not a numeric 9, because the input is a string.

You can define the function `number()` as follows:

```
// Function to recognize a number in a string
double number(char* str, int& index)
{
  double value = 0.0;                    // Store the resulting value

  while(isdigit(*(str + index)))         // Loop accumulating leading digits
    value = 10*value + (*(str + index++) - '0');

                                         // Not a digit when we get to here
  if(*(str + index) != '.')              // so check for decimal point
    return value;                        // and if not, return value

  double factor = 1.0;                   // Factor for decimal places
  while(isdigit(*(str + (++index))))     // Loop as long as we have digits
  {
    factor *= 0.1;                       // Decrease factor by factor of 10
    value = value + (*(str + index) - '0')*factor;   // Add decimal place
  }

  return value;                          // On loop exit we are done
}
```

How the Function Functions

You declare the local variable `value` as type `double` that holds the value of the number that is found. You initialize it with 0.0 because you add in the digit values as you go along.

As the number in the string is a series of digits as ASCII characters, the function steps through the string accumulating the value of the number digit by digit. This occurs in two phases — the first phase accumulates digits before the decimal point; then if you find a decimal point, the second phase accumulates the digits after it.

The first step is in the `while` loop that continues as long as the current character selected by the variable `index` is a digit. The value of the digit is extracted and added to the variable `value` in the loop statement:

```
value = 10*value + (*(str + index++) - '0');
```

The way this is constructed bears a closer examination. A digit character has an ASCII value between 48, corresponding to the digit 0, and 57 corresponding to the digit 9. Thus, if you subtract the ASCII code for '0' from the code for a digit, you convert it to its equivalent numeric digit value from 0 to 9. You have parentheses around the subexpression `*(str + index++) - '0'`; these are not essential, but they do make what's going on a little clearer. The contents of the variable `value` are multiplied by 10 to shift the value one decimal place to the left before adding in the digit value because you'll find digits from left to right — that is, the most significant digit first. This process is illustrated in Figure 6-6.

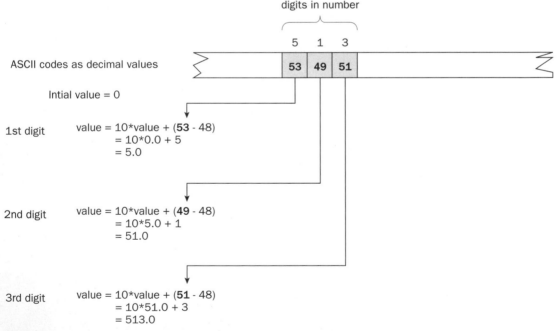

Figure 6-6

As soon as you come across something other than a digit, it is either a decimal point or something else. If it's not a decimal point, you've finished, so you return the current contents of the variable `value` to the calling program. If it is a decimal point, you accumulate the digits corresponding to the fractional part of the number in the second loop. In this loop, you use the `factor` variable, which has the initial value 1.0, to set the decimal place for the current digit, and consequently `factor` is multiplied by 0.1 for each digit found. Thus, the first digit after the decimal point is multiplied by 0.1, the second by 0.01, the third by 0.001, and so on. This process is illustrated in Figure 6-7.

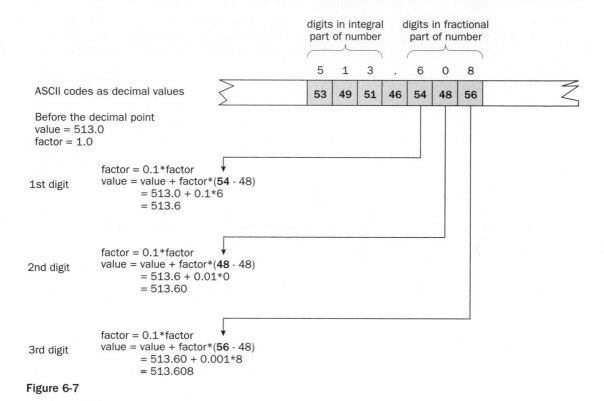

Figure 6-7

As soon as you find a non-digit character you are done, so after the second loop you return the value of the variable `value`. You almost have the whole thing now. You just need a `main()` function to read the input and drive the process.

Putting the Program Together

You can collect the `#include` statements together and assemble the function prototypes at the beginning of the program for all the functions used in this program:

```cpp
// Ex6_09.cpp
// A program to implement a calculator

#include <iostream>                       // For stream input/output
#include <cstdlib>                        // For the exit() function
#include <cctype>                         // For the isdigit() function
using std::cin;
using std::cout;
using std::endl;

void eatspaces(char* str);                // Function to eliminate blanks
double expr(char* str);                   // Function evaluating an expression
double term(char* str, int& index);       // Function analyzing a term
double number(char* str, int& index);     // Function to recognize a number
```

```
const int MAX = 80;                    // Maximum expression length,
                                       // including '\0'
```

You have also defined a global variable MAX, which is the maximum number of characters in the expression processed by the program (including the terminating '\0' character.

Now you can add the definition of the main() function and your program is complete. The main() function should read a string and exit if it is empty; otherwise, call the function expr() to evaluate the input and display the result. This process should repeat indefinitely. That doesn't sound too difficult, so let's give it a try.

```
int main()
{
  char buffer[MAX] = {0};     // Input area for expression to be evaluated

  cout << endl
       << "Welcome to your friendly calculator."
       << endl
       << "Enter an expression, or an empty line to quit."
       << endl;

  for(;;)
  {
    cin.getline(buffer, sizeof buffer);     // Read an input line
    eatspaces(buffer);                      // Remove blanks from input

    if(!buffer[0])                          // Empty line ends calculator
      return 0;

    cout << "\t= " << expr(buffer)          // Output value of expression
         << endl << endl;
  }
}
```

How the Function Functions

In main(), you set up the char array buffer to accept an expression up to 80 characters long (including the string termination character). The expression is read within the indefinite for loop using the getline() input function and after obtaining the input, spaces are removed from the string by calling the function eatspaces().

All the other things that the function main() provides for are within the loop. They are to check for an empty string, which consists of just the null character, '\0', in which case the program ends, and to output the value of the string produced by the function expr().

After you type all the functions, you should get output similar to the following:

```
2 * 35
        = 70
2/3 + 3/4 + 4/5 + 5/6 + 6/7
        = 3.90714
```

```
1 + 2.5 + 2.5*2.5 + 2.5*2.5*2.5
       = 25.375
```

You can enter as many calculations as you like, and when you are fed up with it, just press *Enter* to end the program.

Extending the Program

Now that you have got a working calculator, you can start to think about extending it. Wouldn't it be nice to be able to handle parentheses in an expression? It can't be that difficult, can it? Let's give it a try.

Think about the relationship between something in parentheses that might appear in an expression and the kind of expression analysis that you have made so far. Look at an example of the kind of expression you want to handle:

```
2*(3 + 4) / 6 - (5 + 6) / (7 + 8)
```

Notice that the expressions in parentheses always form part of a `term` in your original parlance. Whatever sort of computation you come up with, this is always true. In fact, if you could substitute the value of the expressions within parentheses back into the original string, you would have something that you can already deal with. This indicates a possible approach to handling parentheses. You might be able to treat an expression in parentheses as just another number, and modify the function `number()` to sort out the value of whatever appears between the parentheses.

That sounds like a good idea, but 'sorting out' the expression in parentheses requires a bit of thought: the clue to success is in the terminology used here. An expression that appears within parentheses is a perfectly good example of a full-blown expression, and you already have the `expr()` function that will return the value of an expression. If you can get the `number()` function to work out what the contents of the parentheses are and extract those from the string, you could pass the substring that results to the `expr()` function, so recursion would really simplify the problem. What's more, you don't need to worry about nested parentheses. Because any set of parentheses contains what you have defined as an expression, they are taken care of automatically. Recursion wins again.

Take a stab at rewriting the `number()` function to recognize an expression between parentheses.

```cpp
// Function to recognize an expression in parentheses
// or a number in a string
double number(char* str, int& index)
{
  double value = 0.0;                  // Store the resulting value

  if(*(str + index) == '(')            // Start of parentheses
  {
    char* psubstr = 0;                 // Pointer for substring
    psubstr = extract(str, ++index);   // Extract substring in brackets
    value = expr(psubstr);             // Get the value of the substring
    delete[]psubstr;                   // Clean up the free store
    return value;                      // Return substring value
  }

  while(isdigit(*(str + index)))       // Loop accumulating leading digits
```

```
      value = 10*value + (*(str + index++) - 48);
                                        // Not a digit when we get to here
   if(*(str + index)!= '.')            // so check for decimal point
      return value;                    // and if not, return value

   double factor = 1.0;                // Factor for decimal places
   while(isdigit(*(str + (++index))))  // Loop as long as we have digits
   {
      factor *= 0.1;                   // Decrease factor by factor of 10
      value = value + (*(str + index) - 48)*factor;  // Add decimal place
   }
   return value;                       // On loop exit we are done
}
```

This is not yet complete, because you still need the `extract()` function, but you'll fix that in a moment.

How the Function Functions

Look how little has changed to support parentheses. I suppose it is a bit of a cheat because you use a function (`extract()`) that you haven't written yet, but for one extra function you get as many levels of nested parentheses as you want. This really is icing on the cake, and it's all down to the magic of recursion!

The first thing that the function `number()` does now is to test for a left parenthesis. If it finds one, it calls another function, `extract()` to extract the substring between the parentheses from the original string. The address of this new substring is stored in the pointer `psubstr`, so you then apply the `expr()` function to the substring by passing this pointer as an argument. The result is stored in `value`, and after releasing the memory allocated on the free store in the function `extract()` (as you will eventually implement it), you return the value obtained for the substring as though it were a regular number. Of course, if there is no left parenthesis to start with, the function `number()` continues exactly as before.

Extracting a Substring

You now need to write the function `extract()`. It's not difficult, but it's also not trivial. The main complication comes from the fact that the expression within parentheses may also contain other sets of parentheses, so you can't just go looking for the first right parenthesis you can find. You must watch out for more left parentheses as well, and for every one you find, ignore the corresponding right parenthesis. You can do this by maintaining a count of left parentheses as you go along, adding one to the count for each left parenthesis you find. If the left parenthesis count is not zero, you subtract one for each right parenthesis. Of course, if the left parenthesis count is zero and you find a right parenthesis, you're at the end of the substring. The mechanism for extracting a parenthesized substring is illustrated in Figure 6-8.

Because the string you extract here contains subexpressions enclosed within parentheses, eventually `extract()` is called again to deal with those.

The function `extract()` also needs to allocate memory for the substring and return a pointer to it. Of course, the index to the current position in the original string must end up selecting the character following the substring, so the parameter for that should be specified as a reference. The prototype of `extract()`, therefore, is as follows:

```
char* extract(char* str, int& index); //Function to extract a substring
```

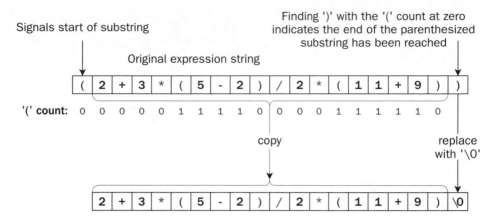

Figure 6-8

You can now have a shot at the definition of the function.

```cpp
// Function to extract a substring between parentheses
// (requires <cstring> header file)
char* extract(char* str, int& index)
{
  char buffer[MAX];                    // Temporary space for substring
  char* pstr = 0;                      // Pointer to new string for return
  int numL = 0;                        // Count of left parentheses found
  int bufindex = index;                // Save starting value for index

  do
  {
    buffer[index - bufindex] = *(str + index);
    switch(buffer[index - bufindex])
    {
      case ')':
        if(numL == 0)
        {
          buffer[index - bufindex] = '\0';  // Replace ')' with '\0'
          ++index;
          pstr = new char[index - bufindex];
          if(!pstr)
          {
            cout << "Memory allocation failed,"
                 << " program terminated.";
            exit(1);
          }
          strcpy_s(pstr, index-bufindex, buffer); // Copy substring to new memory
          return pstr;                  // Return substring in new memory
        }
        else
```

```
            numL--;                    // Reduce count of '(' to be matched
            break;

        case '(':
            numL++;                    // Increase count of '(' to be
                                       // matched
            break;
        }
    } while(*(str + index++) != '\0');  // Loop - don't overrun end of string

    cout << "Ran off the end of the expression, must be bad input."
         << endl;
    exit(1);
    return pstr;
}
```

How the Function Functions

You declare a char array to temporarily hold the substring. You don't know how long the substring will be, but it can't be more than MAX characters. You can't return the address of buffer to the calling function because it is local and will be destroyed on exit from the function; therefore, you need to allocate some memory on the free store when you know how long the string is. You do this by declaring a variable pstr of type 'pointer to char', which you return by value when you have the substring safe and sound in the free store memory.

You declare a counter numL to keep track of left parentheses in the substring (as I discussed earlier). The initial value of index (when the function begins execution) is stored in the variable bufindex. You use this in combination with incremented values of index to index the array buffer.

The executable part of the function is basically one big do-while loop. The substring is copied from str to buffer one character on each loop iteration, with a check for left or right parentheses during each cycle. If a left parenthesis is found, numL is incremented, and if a right parenthesis is found and numL is non-zero, it is decremented. When you find a right parenthesis and numL is zero, you have found the end of the substring. The ')' in the substring in buffer is then replaced by '\0', and sufficient memory is obtained on the free store to hold the substring. The substring in buffer is then copied to the memory you obtained through the operator new by using the strcpy_s() function that is declared in the<cstring> header file; this is a safe version of the old strcpy() function that is declared in the same header. This function copies the string specified by the third argument, buffer, to the address specified by the first argument, pstr. The second argument is the length of the destination string, pstr.

If you fall through the bottom of the loop, it means that you hit the '\0' at the end of the expression in str without finding the complementary right bracket, so you display a message and terminate the program.

Running the Modified Program

After replacing the number() function in the old version of the program, adding the #include statement for <cstring>, and incorporating the prototype and the definition for the new extract() function you have just written, you're ready to roll with an all-singing, all-dancing calculator. If you have assembled all that without error, you can get output something like this:

```
Welcome to your friendly calculator.
Enter an expression, or an empty line to quit.
1/(1+1/(1+1/(1+1)))
        = 0.6
(1/2-1/3)*(1/3-1/4)*(1/4-1/5)
        = 0.000694444
3.5*(1.25-3/(1.333-2.1*1.6))-1
        = 8.55507
2,4-3.4
Arrrgh!*#!! There's an error
```

The friendly and informative error message in the last output line is due to the use of the comma instead of the decimal point in the expression above it, in what should be 2.4. As you can see, you get nested parentheses to any depth with a relatively simple extension of the program, all due to the amazing power of recursion.

C++/CLI Programming

Just about everything discussed so far in relation to functions for native C++ applies equally well to C++/CLI language code with the proviso that parameter types and return types will be fundamental types, which as you know are equivalent to value class types in a CLR program, tracking handle types, or tracking reference types. Because you cannot perform arithmetic on the address stored in a tracking handle, the coding techniques that I demonstrated for treating parameters that are native C++ arrays as pointers on which you can perform arithmetic operations do not apply to C++/CLI arrays. Many of the complications that can arise with arguments to native C++ functions disappear, but there is still the odd trap in C++/CLI for the unwary. A CLR version of the calculator can help you understand how functions look written in C++/CLI.

The throw and catch mechanism for exceptions works much the same in CLR programs as it does in native C++ programs, but there are some differences. The exceptions that you throw in a C++/CLI program must always be thrown using tracking handles. Consequently you should always be throwing exception objects and as far as possible you should avoid throwing literals, especially string literals. For example, consider this try-catch code:

```
try
{
  throw L"Catch me if you  can.";
}
catch(String^ ex)                      // The exception will not be caught by this
{
  Console::WriteLine(L"String^: {0}",ex);
}
```

The `catch` block cannot catch the object thrown here, because the `throw` statement throws an exception of type `const wchar_t*`, not of type `String^`. To catch the exception as thrown, the `catch` block needs to be:

```
try
{
  throw L"Catch me if you  can.";
}
catch(const wchar_t* ex)                 // OK. The exception thrown is of this type
{
  String^ exc = gcnew String(ex);
  Console::WriteLine(L"wchar_t:{0}", exc);
}
```

This `catch` block catches the exception because it now has the correct type.

To throw the exception so that it can be caught by the original catch block, you must change the code in the try block:

```
try
{
  throw gcnew String(L"Catch me if you  can.");
}
catch(String^ ex)                        // OK. Exception thrown is of this type
{
  Console::WriteLine(L"String^: {0}",ex);
}
```

Now the exception is a `String` object and is thrown as type `String^`, a handle that references the string.

You can use function templates in your C++/CLI programs, but you have an additional capability called **generic functions** that looks remarkably similar; however, there are significant differences.

Understanding Generic Functions

Although generic functions appear to do the same thing as function templates and therefore at first sight seem superfluous, generic functions work rather differently from template functions and the differences make them a valuable additional capability in CLR programs. When you use a function template, the compiler generates the source code for functions that you require from the template; this generated code is then compiled along with the rest of your program code. In some cases this can result in many functions being generated and the size of the execution module may be increased substantially. On the other hand a generic function specification is itself compiled, and when you call a function that matches the generic function specification, actual types are substituted for the type parameters at execution time. No extra code is generated at compile time and the code-bloat that can arise with template functions does not occur.

Some aspects of defining a generic function depend on a knowledge of stuff that comes in later chapters but it will all be clear eventually. I'll provide minimal explanations here of the things that are new and you'll learn the detail later in the book.

Defining Generic Functions

You define a generic function using type parameters that are replaced by actual types when the function is called. Here's an example of a generic function definition:

```
generic<typename T> where T:IComparable
T MaxElement(array<T>^ x)
{
  T max = x[0];
  for(int i = 1; i < x->Length; i++)
    if(max->CompareTo(x[i]) < 0)
      max = x[i];
  return max;
}
```

This generic function does the same job as the native C++ function template you saw earlier in this chapter. The `generic` keyword in the first line identifies what follows as a generic specification and the first line defines the type parameter for the function as `T`; the `typename` keyword between the angled brackets indicates that the `T` that follows is the name of a type parameter in the generic function, and that this type parameter is replaced by an actual type when the generic function is used. For a generic function with multiple type parameters, the parameter names go between the angled brackets, each preceded by the `typename` keyword and separated by commas.

The `where` keyword that follows the closing angled bracket introduces a `constraint` on the actual type that may be substituted for `T` when the generic function is used. This particular constraint says that any type that is to replace `T` in the generic function must implement the `IComparable` interface. You'll learn about interfaces later in the book, but for now I'll say that it implies that the type must define the `CompareTo()` function that allows two objects of the type to be compared. Without this constraint the compiler has no knowledge of what operations are possible for the type that is to replace `T` because until the generic function is used, this is completely unknown. With the constraint you can use the `CompareTo()` function to compare `max` with an element of the array. The `CompareTo()` function returns an integer value that is less than zero when the object for which it is called (`max` in this case) is less than the argument, zero if it equals the argument, and greater than zero if it is greater than the argument.

The second line specifies the generic function name `MaxElement`, its return type `T`, and its parameter list. This looks rather like an ordinary function header except that it involves the generic type parameter `T`. The return type for the generic function and the array element type that is part of the parameter type specification are both of type `T`, so both these types are determined when the generic function is used.

Using Generic Functions

The simplest way of calling a generic function is just to use it like any ordinary function. For example, you could use the generic `MaxElement()` from the previous section like this:

```
array<double>^ data = {1.5, 3.5, 6.7, 4.2, 2.1};
double maxData = MaxElement(data);
```

The compiler is able to deduce that the type argument to the generic function is `double` in this instance and generates the code to call the function accordingly. The function executes with instances of `T` in the function being replaced by `double`. As I said earlier, this is not like a template function; there is no creation of function instances at compile time. The compiled generic function is able to handle type argument substitutions when it is called.

Note that if you pass a string literal as an argument to a generic function, the compiler deduces that the type argument is String^, regardless of whether the string literal is a narrow string constant such as "Hello!" or a wide string constant such as L"Hello!".

It is possible that the compiler may not be able to deduce the type argument from a call of a generic function. In these instances you can specify the type argument(s) explicitly between angled brackets following the function name in the call. For example, you could write the call in the previous fragment as:

```
double maxData = MaxElement<double>(data);
```

With an explicit type argument specified there is no possibility of ambiguity.

There are limitations on what types you can supply as a type argument to a generic function. A type argument cannot be a native C++ class type, nor a native pointer or reference, nor a handle to a value class type such as int^. Thus only value class types such as int or double and tracking handles such as String^ are allowed (but not a handle to a value class type).

Let's try a working example.

Try It Out   Using a Generic Function

Here's an example that defines and uses three generic functions:

```
// Ex6_10.cpp : main project file.
// Defining and using generic functions

#include "stdafx.h"

using namespace System;

// Generic function to find the maximum element in an array
generic<typename T> where T:IComparable
T MaxElement(array<T>^ x)
{
  T max = x[0];
  for(int i = 1; i < x->Length; i++)
    if(max->CompareTo(x[i]) < 0)
      max = x[i];
  return max;
}

// Generic function to remove an element from an array
generic<typename T> where T:IComparable
array<T>^ RemoveElement(T element, array<T>^ data)
{
  array<T>^ newData = gcnew array<T>(data->Length - 1);
  int index = 0;                     // Index to elements in newData array
  bool found = false;                // Indicates that the element to remove was found
  for each(T item in data)
```

```
    {
      // Check for invalid index or element found
      if((!found) && item->CompareTo(element) == 0)
      {
        found = true;
        continue;
      }
      else
      {
        if(index == newData->Length)
        {
          Console::WriteLine(L"Element to remove not found");
          return data;
        }
        newData[index++] = item;
      }
    }
    return newData;
}
```

```
// Generic function to list an array
generic<typename T> where T:IComparable
void ListElements(array<T>^ data)
{
  for each(T item in data)
    Console::Write(L"{0,10}", item);
  Console::WriteLine();
}
```

```
int main(array<System::String ^> ^args)
{
  array<double>^ data = {1.5, 3.5, 6.7, 4.2, 2.1};
  Console::WriteLine(L"Array contains:");
  ListElements(data);
  Console::WriteLine(L"\nMaximum element = {0}\n", MaxElement(data));
  array<double>^ result = RemoveElement(MaxElement(data), data);
  Console::WriteLine(L" After removing maximum, array contains:");
  ListElements(result);

  array<int>^ numbers = {3, 12, 7, 0, 10,11};
  Console::WriteLine(L"\nArray contains:");
  ListElements(numbers);
  Console::WriteLine(L"\nMaximum element = {0}\n", MaxElement(numbers));
  Console::WriteLine(L"\nAfter removing maximum, array contains:");
  ListElements(RemoveElement(MaxElement(numbers), numbers));

  array<String^>^ strings = {L"Many", L"hands", L"make", L"light", L"work"};
  Console::WriteLine(L"\nArray contains:");
  ListElements(strings);
  Console::WriteLine(L"\nMaximum element = {0}\n", MaxElement(strings));
  Console::WriteLine(L"\nAfter removing maximum, array contains:");
  ListElements(RemoveElement(MaxElement(strings), strings));
  return 0;
}
```

The output from this example is:

```
Array contains:
      1.5        3.5        6.7        4.2        2.1

Maximum element = 6.7

 After removing maximum, array contains:
      1.5        3.5        4.2        2.1

Array contains:
        3         12          7          0         10         11

Maximum element = 12

After removing maximum, array contains:
        3          7          0         10         11

Array contains:
      Many      hands      make      light      work

Maximum element = work


After removing maximum, array contains:
      Many      hands      make      light
```

How It Works

The first generic function that this example defines is MaxElement(), which is identical to the one you saw in the preceding section that finds the maximum element in an array so I won't discuss it again.

The next generic function, RemoveElements(), removes the element passed as the first argument from the array specified by the second argument and the function returns a handle to the new array that results from the operation. You can see from the first two lines of the function definition that both parameter types and the return type involve the type parameter, T.

```
generic<typename T> where T:IComparable
array<T>^ RemoveElement(T element, array<T>^ data)
```

The constraint on T is the same as for the first generic function and implies that whatever type is used as the type argument must implement the CompareTo() function to allow objects of the type to be compared. The second parameter and the return type are both handles to an array of elements of type T. The first parameter is simply type T.

The function first creates an array to hold the result:

```
array<T>^ newData = gcnew array<T>(data->Length - 1);
```

The newData array is of the same type as the second argument — an array of elements of type T — but has one fewer elements because one element is to be removed from the original.

The elements are copied from the `data` array to the `newData` array in the `for` each loop:

```
int index = 0;                          // Index to elements in newData array
bool found = false;                     // Indicates that element to remove was found
for each(T item in data)
{
  // Check for invalid index or element found
  if((!found) && item->CompareTo(element) == 0)
  {
    found = true;
    continue;
  }
  else
  {
    if(index == newData->Length)
    {
      Console::WriteLine(L"Element to remove not found");
      return data;
    }
    newData[index++] = item;
  }
}
```

All elements are copied except the one identified by the first argument to the function. You use the `index` variable to select the next `newData` array element that is to receive the next element from the data array. Each element from `data` is copied unless it is equal to `element`, in which case `found` is set to `true` and the `continue` statement skips to the next iteration. It is quite possible that an array could have more than one element equal to the first argument and the `found` variable prevents subsequent elements that are the same as `element` from being skipped in the loop.

You also have a check for the index variable exceeding the legal limit for indexing elements in `newData`. This could arise if there is no element in the data array equal to the first argument to the function. In this eventuality, you just return the handle to the original array.

The third generic function just lists the elements from an array of type `array<T>`:

```
generic<typename T>
void ListElements(array<T>^ data)
{
  for each(T item in data)
    Console::Write(L"{0,10}", item);
  Console::WriteLine();
}
```

This is one of the few occasions where no constraint on the type parameter is needed. There is very little you can do with objects that are of a completely unknown type so typically generic function type parameters will have constraints. The operation of the function is very simple — each element from the array is written to the command line in an output field with a width of 10 in the `for` each loop. If you want, you could add a little sophistication by adding a parameter for the field width and creating the format string to be used as the first argument to the `Write()` function in the `Console` class. You could also add logic to the loop to write a specific number of elements per line based on the field width.

The `main()` function exercises these generic functions with type parameters of types `double`, `int`, and `String^`. Thus you can see that all three generic functions work with value types and handles. In the second and third examples, the generic functions are used in combination in a single statement. For example, look at this statement in the third sample use of the functions:

```
ListElements(RemoveElement(MaxElement(strings), strings));
```

The first argument to the `RemoveElement()` generic function is produced by the `MaxElement()` generic function call, so these generic functions can be used in the same way as equivalent ordinary functions.

The compiler is able to deduce the type argument in all instances where the generic functions are used but you could specify them explicitly if you wanted to. For example, you could write the previous statement like this:

```
ListElements(RemoveElement<String^>(MaxElement<String^>(strings), strings));
```

A Calculator Program for the CLR

Let's re-implement the calculator as a C++/CLI example. We'll assume the same program structure and hierarchy of functions as you saw for the native C++ program but the functions will be declared and defined as C++/CLI functions. A good starting point is the set of function prototypes at the beginning of the source file — I have used `Ex6_11` as the CLR project name:

```cpp
// Ex6_11.cpp : main project file.
// A CLR calculator supporting parentheses

#include "stdafx.h"
#include <cstdlib>                       // For exit()

using namespace System;
String^ eatspaces(String^ str);          // Function to eliminate blanks
double expr(String^ str);                // Function evaluating an expression
double term(String^ str, int^ index);    // Function analyzing a term
double number(String^ str, int^ index);  // Function to recognize a number
String^ extract(String^ str, int^ index);// Function to extract a substring
```

All the parameters are now handles; the string parameters are type `String^` and the index parameter that records the current position in the string is also a handle of type `int^`. Of course, a string is returned as a handle of type `String^`.

The `main()` function implementation looks like this:

```cpp
int main(array<System::String ^> ^args)
{
  String^ buffer;      // Input area for expression to be evaluated

  Console::WriteLine(L"Welcome to your friendly calculator.");
  Console::WriteLine(L"Enter an expression, or an empty line to quit.");
```

```
  for(;;)
  {
    buffer = eatspaces(Console::ReadLine());          // Read an input line

    if(String::IsNullOrEmpty(buffer))                 // Empty line ends calculator
      return 0;

    Console::WriteLine(L"  = {0}\n\n",expr(buffer));   // Output value of expression
  }
  return 0;
}
```

The function is a lot shorter and easier to read. Within the indefinite `for` loop you call the `String` class function, `IsNullOrEmpty()`. This function returns `true` if the string passed as the argument is null or of zero length so it does exactly what you want here.

Removing Spaces from the Input String

The function to remove spaces is also simpler and shorter:

```
// Function to eliminate spaces from a string
String^ eatspaces(String^ str)
{
  // Array to hold string without spaces
  array<wchar_t>^ chars = gcnew array<wchar_t>(str->Length);
  int length = 0;                          // Number of chars in array

  // Copy non-space characters to chars array
  for each(wchar_t ch in str)
    if(ch != ' ')
      chars[length++] = ch;

  // Return chars array as string
  return gcnew String(chars, 0, length);
}
```

You first create an array to accommodate the string when the spaces have been removed. This is an array of elements of type `wchar_t` because strings in C++/CLI are Unicode characters. The process for removing the spaces is very simple — you copy all the characters that are not spaces from the string `str` to the array, `chars`, keeping track of the number of characters copied in the `length` variable. You finally create a new `String` object using a `String` class constructor that creates the object from elements in an array. The first argument to the constructor is the array that is the source of characters for the string, the second argument is the index position for the first character from the array that forms the string, and the third argument is the total number of characters from the array that are to be used. The `String` class defines a range of constructors for creating strings in various ways.

Evaluating an Arithmetic Expression

You can implement the function to evaluate an expression like this:

```
// Function to evaluate an arithmetic expression
double expr(String^ str)
{
```

```
    int^ index = 0;                       // Keeps track of current character position

    double value = term(str, index);      // Get first term

    while(*index < str->Length)
    {
      switch(str[*index])                 // Choose action based on current character
      {
        case '+':                         // + found so
           ++(*index);                    // increment index and add
           value += term(str, index);     // the next term
           break;

        case '-':                         // - found so
            ++(*index);                   // decrement index and add
          value -= term(str, index);      // the next term
          break;

        default:                          // If we reach here the string is junk
          Console::WriteLine(L"Arrrgh!*#!! There's an error.\n");
          exit(1);
      }
    }
    return value;
}
```

The index variable is declared as a handle because you want to pass it to the term() function and allow the term() function to modify the original variable. If you declared index simply as type int, the term() function would receive a copy of the value and could not refer to the original variable to change it.

The declaration of index results in a warning message from the compiler because the statement relies on autoboxing of the value 0 to produce the Int32 value class object that the handle references, and the warning is because people often write the statement like this but intend to initialize the handle to null. Of course, to do this you must use nullptr as the initial value in place of 0. If you want to eliminate the warning, you could rewrite the statement as:

```
  int^ index = gcnew int(0);
```

This statement uses a constructor explicitly to create the object and initialize it with 0 so there's no warning from the compiler.

After processing the initial term by calling the term() function, the while loop steps through the string looking for + or - operators followed by another term. The switch statement identifies and processes the operators. If you have been using native C++ for a while, you might be tempted to write the case statements in the switch a little differently — for example:

```
    // Incorrect code!! Does not work!!
    case '+':                          // + found so
      value += term(str, ++(*index));  // increment index & add the next term
      break;
```

Of course, this would typically be written without the first comment. This code is wrong, but why is it wrong? The term() function expects a handle in type int^ as the second argument and that is what is supplied here although maybe not as you expect. The compiler arranges for the expression ++(*index) to be evaluated and the result stored in a temporary location. The expression indeed updates the value referenced by index, but the handle that is passed to the term() function is a handle to the temporary location holding the result of evaluating the expression, not the handle index. This handle is produced by autoboxing the value stored in the temporary location. When the term() function updates, the value referenced by the handle that is passed to it the temporary location is updated, not the location referenced by index; thus all the updates to the index position of the string made in the term() function are lost. If you expect a function to update a variable in the calling program, you must not use an expression as the function argument — you must always use the handle variable name.

Obtaining the Value of a Term

As in the native C++ version, the term() function steps through the string that is passed as the first argument, starting at the character position referenced by the second argument:

```
// Function to get the value of a term
double term(String^ str, int^ index)
{
  double value = number(str, index);        // Get the first number in the term

  // Loop as long as we have characters and a good operator
  while(*index < str->Length)
  {
    if(str[*index] == L'*')                  // If it's multiply,
    {
      ++(*index);                            // increment index and
      value *= number(str, index);           // multiply by next number
    }
    else if( str[*index] == L'/')            // If it's divide
    {
      ++(*index);                            // increment index and
      value /= number(str, index);           // divide by next number
    }
    else
      break;                                 // Exit the loop
  }
  // We've finished, so return what we've got
  return value;
}
```

After calling the number() function to get the value of the first number or parenthesized expression in a term, the function steps through the string in the while loop. The loop continues while there are still characters in the input string, as long as a * or / operator followed by another number or parenthesized expression is found.

Evaluating a Number

The number function extracts and evaluates a parenthesized expression if there is one; otherwise, it determines the value of the next number in the input:

```
// Function to recognize a number
double number(String^ str, int^ index)
{
  double value = 0.0;                         // Store for the resulting value
```

```
// Check for expression between parentheses
if(str[*index] == L'(' )                    // Start of parentheses
{
  ++(*index);
  String^ substr = extract(str, index);     // Extract substring in brackets
  return expr(substr);                       // Return substring value
}

// Loop accumulating leading digits
while((*index < str->Length) && Char::IsDigit(str, *index))
{
  value = 10.0*value + Char::GetNumericValue(str[(*index)]);
  ++(*index);
}

// Not a digit when we get to here
if((*index == str->Length) || str[*index] != '.')    // so check for decimal point
  return value;                                       // and if not, return value

double factor = 1.0;                        // Factor for decimal places
++(*index);                                 // Move to digit

// Loop as long as we have digits
while((*index < str->Length) && Char::IsDigit(str, *index))
{
  factor *= 0.1;                            // Decrease factor by factor of 10
  value = value + Char::GetNumericValue(str[*index])*factor; // Add decimal place
  ++(*index);
}

return value;                              // On loop exit we are done
}
```

As in the native C++ version, the extract() function is used to extract a parenthesized expression and the substring that results is passed to the expr() function to be evaluated. If there's no parenthesized expression — indicated by the absence of an opening parenthesis, the input is scanned for a number, which is a sequence of zero or more digits followed by an optional decimal point plus fractional digits. The IsDigit() function in the Char class returns true if a character is a digit and false otherwise. The character here is in the string passed as the first argument to the function at the index position specified by the second argument. There's another version if the IsDigit() function that accepts a single argument of type wchar_t so you could use this with the argument str[*index]. The GetNumericValue() function in the Char class returns the value of a Unicode digit character that you pass as the argument as a value of type double. There's another version of this function to which you can pass a string handle and an index position to specify the character.

Extracting a Parenthesized Substring

You can implement the `extract()` function that returns a parenthesized substring from the input like this:

```
// Function to extract a substring between parentheses
String^ extract(String^ str, int^ index)
{
  String^ substr;                        // Substring to return
  int numL = 0;                          // Count of left parentheses found
  int bufindex = *index;                 // Save starting value for index

  while(*index < str->Length)
  {
    switch(str[*index])
    {
      case ')':
        if(numL == 0)
        {
          array<wchar_t>^ substrChars = gcnew array<wchar_t>(*index - bufindex);
          str->CopyTo(bufindex, substrChars, 0, substrChars->Length);
          substr = gcnew String(substrChars);
          ++(*index);

          return substr;                 // Return substring in new memory
        }
        else
          numL--;                        // Reduce count of '(' to be matched
        break;

      case '(':
        numL++;                          // Tncrease count of '(' to be
                                         // matched
        break;
    }
    ++(*index);
  }

  Console::WriteLine(L"Ran off the end of the expression, must be bad input.");
  exit(1);
  return substr;
}
```

Again, the strategy is the same as the native C++ version, but the differences are in the details. To find the complementary right parenthesis the function keeps track of how many new left parentheses are found using the variable `numL`. The substring is extracted when a right parenthesis is found and the left parenthesis count in `numL` is zero. The substring is copied into the `substrChars` array using the `CopyTo()` function for the String object, str. The function copies characters beginning at the string index position speci-fied by the first argument into the array specified by the second argument; the third argument defines the starting element in the array to receive characters and the fourth argument is the number of charac-ters to be copied. You create the string that is returned as the result of the extraction by using the String class constructor that creates an object from all the elements in the array, substrChars, that is passed as the argument.

If you assemble all the functions in a CLR console project you'll have a C++/CLI implementation of the calculator running with the CLR. The output should be much the same as the native C++ version.

Summary

You now have a reasonably comprehensive knowledge of writing and using functions. You've used a pointer to a function in a practical context for handling out-of-memory conditions in the free store, and you have used overloading to implement a set of functions providing the same operation with different types of parameters. You'll see more about overloading functions in the following chapters.

The important bits that you learned in this chapter include:

❑ A pointer to a function stores the address of a function, plus information about the number and types of parameters and return type for a function.

❑ You can use a pointer to a function to store the address of any function with the appropriate return type, and number and types of parameters.

❑ You can use a pointer to a function to call the function at the address it contains. You can also pass a pointer to a function as a function argument.

❑ An exception is a way of signaling an error in a program so that the error handling code can be separated from the code for normal operations.

❑ You throw an exception with a statement that uses the keyword throw.

❑ Code that may throw exceptions should be placed in a try block, and the code to handle a par-ticular type of exception is placed in a catch block immediately following the try block. There can be several catch blocks following a try block, each catching a different type of exception.

❑ Overloaded functions are functions with the same name, but with different parameter lists.

❑ When you call an overloaded function, the function to be called is selected by the compiler based on the number and types of the arguments that you specify.

❑ A function template is a recipe for generating overloaded functions automatically.

❑ A function template has one or more arguments that are type variables. An instance of the func-tion template — that is, a function definition — is created by the compiler for each function call that corresponds to a unique set of type arguments for the template.

❑ You can force the compiler to create a particular instance from a function template by specifying the function you want in a prototype declaration.

You also got some experience of using several functions in a program by working through the calculator example. But remember that all the uses of functions up to now have been in the context of a traditional procedural approach to programming. When you come to look at object-oriented programming, you will still use functions extensively, but with a very different approach to program structure and to the design of a solution to a problem.

Exercises

You can download the source code for the examples in the book and the solutions to the following exercises from www.wrox.com.

1. Consider the following function:

```
int ascVal(size_t i, const char* p)
{
   // print the ASCII value of the char
   if (!p || i > strlen(p))
      return -1;
   else
      return p[i];
}
```

Write a program that will call this function through a pointer and verify that it works. You'll need an #include directive for the <cstring> header in your program to use the strlen() function.

2. Write a family of overloaded functions called equal(), which take two arguments of the same type, returning 1 if the arguments are equal, and 0 otherwise. Provide versions having char, int, double, and char* arguments. (Use the strcmp() function from the runtime library to test for equality of strings. If you don't know how to use strcmp(), search for it in the online help. You'll need an #include directive for the <cstring> header file in your program.) Write test code to verify that the correct versions are called.

3. At present, when the calculator hits an invalid input character, it prints an error message, but doesn't show you where the error was in the line. Write an error routine that prints out the input string, putting a caret (^) below the offending character, like this:

```
12 + 4,2*3
        ^
```

4. Add an exponentiation operator, ^, to the calculator, fitting it in alongside * and /. What are the limitations of implementing it in this way, and how can you overcome them?

5. (Advanced) Extend the calculator so it can handle trig and other math functions, allowing you to input expressions such as:

```
2 * sin(0.6)
```

The math library functions all work in radians; provide versions of the trigonometric functions so that the user can use degrees, for example:

```
2 * sind(30)
```

Defining Your Own Data Types

This chapter is about creating your own data types to suit your particular problem. It's also about creating objects, the building blocks of object-oriented programming. An object can seem a bit mysterious to the uninitiated but, as you will see in this chapter, an object can be just an instance of one of your own data types.

In this chapter, you will learn about:

- ❏   Structures and how they are used
- ❏   Classes and how they are used
- ❏   The basic components of a class and how you define class types
- ❏   Creating and using objects of a class
- ❏   Controlling access to members of a class
- ❏   Constructors and how to create them
- ❏   The default constructor
- ❏   References in the context of classes
- ❏   The copy constructor and how it is implemented
- ❏   How C++/CLI classes differ from native C++ classes
- ❏   Properties in a C++/CLI class and how you define and use them
- ❏   Literal fields and how you define and use them
- ❏   `initonly` fields and how you define and use them
- ❏   What a static constructor is

The struct in C++

A structure is a user-defined type that you define using the keyword `struct`, so it is often referred to as a struct. The `struct` originated back in the C language, and C++ incorporates and expands on the C `struct`. A `struct` in C++ is functionally replaceable by a class insofar as anything you can do with a `struct` you can also achieve by using a class; however, because Windows was written in C before C++ became widely used, the `struct` appears pervasively in Windows programming. It is also widely used today, so you really need to know something about `structs`. We'll first take a look at (C-style) `structs` in this chapter before exploring the more extensive capabilities offered by classes.

What Is a struct?

Almost all the variables that you have seen up to now have been able to store a single type of entity — a number of some kind, a character, or an array of elements of the same type. The real world is a bit more complicated than that, and just about any physical object you can think of needs several items of data to describe it even minimally. Think about the information that might be needed to describe something as simple as a book. You might consider title, author, publisher, date of publication, number of pages, price, topic or classification, and ISBN number just for starters, and you can probably come up with a few more without too much difficulty. You could specify separate variables to contain each of the parameters that you need to describe a book, but ideally you would want to have a single data type, BOOK say, which embodied all of these parameters. I'm sure you won't be surprised to hear that this is exactly what a `struct` can do for you.

Defining a struct

Let's stick with the notion of a book, and suppose that you just want to include the title, author, publisher, and year of publication within your definition of a book. You could declare a structure to accommodate this as follows:

```
struct BOOK
{
  char Title[80];
  char Author[80];
  char Publisher[80];
  int Year;
};
```

This doesn't define any variables, but it actually creates a new type for variables and the name of the type is BOOK. The keyword `struct` defines BOOK as such, and the elements making up an object of this type are defined within the braces. Note that each line defining an element in the `struct` is terminated by a semicolon, and that a semicolon also appears after the closing brace. The elements of a `struct` can be of any type, except the same type as the `struct` being defined. You couldn't have an element of type BOOK included in the structure definition for BOOK, for example. You may think this to be a limitation, but note that you could include a pointer to a variable of type BOOK, as you'll see a little later on.

The elements `Title`, `Author`, `Publisher`, and `Year` enclosed between the braces in the definition above may also be referred to as **members** or **fields** of the BOOK structure. Each object of type BOOK contains the members `Title`, `Author`, `Publisher`, and `Year`. You can now create variables of type `BOOK` in exactly the same way that you create variables of any other type:

```
BOOK Novel;                              // Declare variable Novel of type BOOK
```

This declares a variable with the name `Novel` that you can now use to store information about a book. All you need now is to understand how you get data into the various members that make up a variable of type `BOOK`.

Initializing a struct

The first way to get data into the members of a `struct` is to define initial values in the declaration. Suppose you wanted to initialize the variable `Novel` to contain the data for one of your favorite books, *Paneless Programming*, published in 1981 by the Gutter Press. This is a story of a guy performing heroic code development while living in an igloo, and as you probably know, inspired the famous Hollywood box office success, *Gone with the Window*. It was written by I.C. Fingers, who is also the author of that seminal three-volume work, *The Connoisseur's Guide to the Paper Clip*. With this wealth of information you can write the declaration for the variable `Novel` as:

```
BOOK Novel =
{
  "Paneless Programming",               // Initial value for Title
  "I.C. Fingers",                       // Initial value for Author
  "Gutter Press",                       // Initial value for Publisher
  1981                                  // Initial value for Year
};
```

The initializing values appear between braces, separated by commas, in much the same way that you defined initial values for members of an array. As with arrays, the sequence of initial values obviously needs to be the same as the sequence of the members of the `struct` in its definition. Each member of the structure `Novel` has the corresponding value assigned to it, as indicated in the comments.

Accessing the Members of a struct

To access individual members of a `struct`, you can use the **member selection operator**, which is a period; this is sometimes referred to as the **member access operator**. To refer to a particular member, you write the `struct` variable name, followed by a period, followed by the name of the member that you want to access. To change the `Year` member of the `Novel` structure, you could write:

```
Novel.Year = 1988;
```

This would set the value of the `Year` member to 1988. You can use a member of a structure in exactly the same way as any other variable of the same type as the member. To increment the member `Year` by two, for example, you can write:

```
Novel.Year += 2;
```

This increments the value of the `Year` member of the `struct`, just like any other variable.

Try It Out   Using structs

You can use another console application example to exercise a little further how referencing the members of a `struct` works. Suppose you want to write a program to deal with some of the things you might find in a yard, such as those illustrated in the professionally landscaped yard in Figure 7-1.

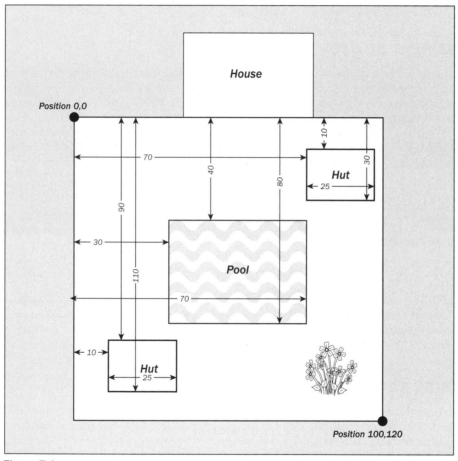

Figure 7-1

I have arbitrarily assigned the coordinates 0,0 to the top-left corner of the yard. The bottom-right corner has the coordinates 100,120. Thus, the first coordinate value is a measure of the horizontal position relative to the top-left corner, with values increasing from left to right, and the second coordinate is a measure of the vertical position from the same reference point, with values increasing from top to bottom. Figure 7-1 also shows the position of the pool and that of the two huts relative to the top-left corner of the yard. Because the yard, huts, and pool are all rectangular, you could define a `struct` type to represent any of these objects:

```
struct RECTANGLE
{
```

```
  int Left;                            // Top-left point
  int Top;                             // coordinate pair

  int Right;                           // Bottom-right point
  int Bottom;                          // coordinate pair
};
```

The first two members of the RECTANGLE structure type correspond to the coordinates of the top-left point of a rectangle, and the next two to the coordinates of the bottom-right point. You can use this in an elementary example dealing with the objects in the yard as follows:

```cpp
// Ex7_01.cpp
// Exercising structures in the yard
#include <iostream>
using std::cout;
using std::endl;

// Definition of a struct to represent rectangles
struct RECTANGLE
{
  int Left;                            // Top-left point
  int Top;                             // coordinate pair

  int Right;                           // Bottom-right point
  int Bottom;                          // coordinate pair
};

// Prototype of function to calculate the area of a rectangle
long Area(RECTANGLE& aRect);

// Prototype of a function to move a rectangle
void MoveRect(RECTANGLE& aRect, int x, int y);

int main(void)
{
  RECTANGLE Yard = { 0, 0, 100, 120 };
  RECTANGLE Pool = { 30, 40, 70, 80 };
  RECTANGLE Hut1, Hut2;

  Hut1.Left = 70;
  Hut1.Top = 10;
  Hut1.Right = Hut1.Left + 25;
  Hut1.Bottom = 30;

  Hut2 = Hut1;                         // Define Hut2 the same as Hut1
  MoveRect(Hut2, 10, 90);             // Now move it to the right position

  cout << endl
       << "Coordinates of Hut2 are "
       << Hut2.Left << "," << Hut2.Top << " and "
       << Hut2.Right << "," << Hut2.Bottom;

  cout << endl
       << "The area of the yard is "
       << Area(Yard);
```

```
        cout << endl
             << "The area of the pool is "
             << Area(Pool)
             << endl;

    return 0;
}

// Function to calculate the area of a rectangle
long Area(RECTANGLE& aRect)
{
    return (aRect.Right - aRect.Left)*(aRect.Bottom - aRect.Top);
}


// Function to Move a Rectangle
void MoveRect(RECTANGLE& aRect, int x, int y)
{
    int length = aRect.Right - aRect.Left;      // Get length of rectangle
    int width = aRect.Bottom - aRect.Top;       // Get width of rectangle

    aRect.Left = x;                             // Set top-left point
    aRect.Top = y;                              // to new position
    aRect.Right = x + length;                   // Get bottom-right point as
    aRect.Bottom = y + width;                   // increment from new position

    return;
}
```

The output from this example is:

```
Coordinates of Hut2 are 10,90 and 35,110
The area of the yard is 12000
The area of the pool is 1600
```

How It Works

Note that the `struct` definition appears at global scope in this example. You'll be able to see it in the Class View tab for the project. Putting the definition of the `struct` at global scope allows you to declare a variable of type `RECTANGLE` anywhere in the `.cpp` file. In a program with a more significant amount of code, such definitions would normally be stored in a `.h` file and then added to each `.cpp` file where necessary by using a `#include` directive.

You have defined two functions to process `RECTANGLE` objects. The function `Area()` calculates the area of the `RECTANGLE` object that you pass as a reference argument as the product of the length and the width, where the length is the difference between the horizontal positions of the defining points, and the width is the difference between the vertical positions of the defining points. By passing a reference, the code runs a little faster because the argument is not copied. The `MoveRect()` function modifies the defining points of a `RECTANGLE` object to position it at the coordinates x, y which are passed as arguments. The position of a `RECTANGLE` object is assumed to be the position of the `Left`, `Top` point. Because the `RECTANGLE` object is passed as a reference, the function is able to modify the members of the `RECTANGLE` object directly. After calculating the length and width of the RECTANGLE object passed, the Left and Top members are set to x and y respectively, and the new Right and Bottom members are calculated by incrementing x and y by the length and width of the original RECTANGLE object.

In the main() function, you initialize the Yard and Pool RECTANGLE variables with their coordinate positions, as shown in Figure 7-1. The variable Hut1 represents the hut at the top-right in the illustration and its members are set to the appropriate values using assignment statements. The variable Hut2, corresponding to the hut at the bottom-left of the yard, is first set to be the same as Hut1 in the assignment statement:

```
Hut2 = Hut1;                          // Define Hut2 the same as Hut1
```

This statement results in the values of the members of Hut1 being copied to the corresponding members of Hut2. You can only assign a struct of a given type to another of the same type. You can't increment a struct directly or use a struct in an arithmetic expression.

To alter the position of Hut2 to its place at the bottom-left of the yard, you call the MoveRect() function with the coordinates of the required position as arguments. This roundabout way of getting the coordinates of Hut2 is totally unnecessary and serves only to show how you can use a struct as an argument to a function.

IntelliSense Assistance with Structures

You've probably noticed that the editor in Visual C++ 2008 is quite intelligent — it knows the types of variables, for instance. This is because of the IntelliSense feature. If you hover the mouse cursor over a variable name in the editor window, it pops up a little box showing its definition. It also can help a lot with structures (and classes, as you will see) because not only does it know the types of ordinary variables, it also knows the members that belong to a variable of a particular structure type. If your computer is reasonably fast, as you type the member selection operator following a structure variable name, the editor pops a window showing the list of members. If you click one of the members, it shows the comment that appeared in the original definition of the structure, so you know what it is. This is shown in Figure 7-2 using a fragment of the previous example.

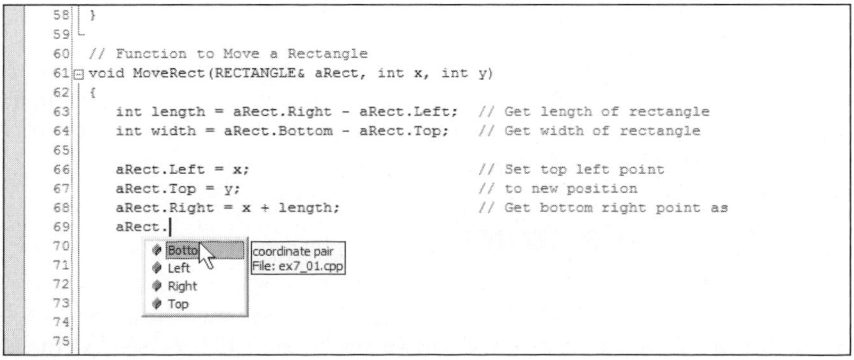

```
58   }
59
60   // Function to Move a Rectangle
61   void MoveRect(RECTANGLE& aRect, int x, int y)
62   {
63       int length = aRect.Right - aRect.Left;   // Get length of rectangle
64       int width = aRect.Bottom - aRect.Top;    // Get width of rectangle
65
66       aRect.Left = x;                          // Set top left point
67       aRect.Top = y;                           // to new position
68       aRect.Right = x + length;                // Get bottom right point as
69       aRect.
70           ● Botto       coordinate pair
71           ● Left        File: ex7_01.cpp
72           ● Right
73           ● Top
74
75
```

Figure 7-2

Now there's a real incentive to add comments, and to keep them short and to the point. If you double-click on a member in the list or press the Enter key when the item is highlighted, it is automatically inserted after the member selection operator, thus eliminating one source of typos in your code. Great, isn't it?

You can turn any or all of the IntelliSense features off if you want to via the Text Editor folder that you get to by clicking the Tools > Options menu item, but I guess the only reason you would want to is if your machine is too slow to make them useful. You can turn the statement-completion features on or off on the C/C++ editor page that you select in the right options pane. If you turn them off, you can still call them up when you want too, either through the Edit menu or through the keyboard. Pressing Ctrl+J, for example, pops up the members for an object under the cursor. The editor also shows the parameter list for a function when you are typing the code to call it — it pops up as soon as you enter the left parenthesis for the argument list. This is particularly helpful with library functions as its tough to remember the parameter list for all of them. Of course, the #include directive for the header file must already be there in the source code for this to work. Without it the editor has no idea what the library function is. You will see more things that the editor can help with as you learn more about classes.

After that interesting little diversion, let's get back to structures.

The struct RECT

Rectangles are used a great deal in Windows programs. For this reason, there is a RECT structure predefined in the header file windows.h. Its definition is essentially the same as the structure that you defined in the last example:

```
struct RECT
{
  int left;                          // Top-left point
  int top;                           // coordinate pair

  int right;                         // Bottom-right point
  int bottom;                        // coordinate pair
};
```

This struct is usually used to define rectangular areas on your display for a variety of purposes. Because RECT is used so extensively, windows.h also contains prototypes for a number of functions to manipulate and modify rectangles. For example, windows.h provides the function InflateRect() to increase the size of a rectangle and the function EqualRect() to compare two rectangles.

MFC also defines a class called CRect, which is the equivalent of a RECT structure. After you understand classes, you will be using this in preference to the RECT structure. The CRect class provides a very extensive range of functions for manipulating rectangles, and you will be using a number of these when you are writing Windows programs using MFC.

Using Pointers with a struct

As you might expect, you can create a pointer to a variable of a structure type. In fact, many of the functions declared in windows.h that work with RECT objects require pointers to a RECT as arguments because this avoids the copying of the whole structure when a RECT argument is passed to a function. To define a pointer to a RECT object for example, the declaration is what you might expect:

```
RECT* pRect = NULL;                  // Define a pointer to RECT
```

Assuming that you have defined a RECT object, aRect, you can set the pointer to the address of this variable in the normal way, using the address-of operator:

```
pRect = &aRect;                          // Set pointer to the address of aRect
```

As you saw when the idea of a struct was introduced, a struct can't contain a member of the same type as the struct being defined, but it can contain a pointer to a struct, including a pointer to a struct of the same type. For example, you could define a structure like this:

```
struct ListElement
{
  RECT aRect;                            // RECT member of structure
  ListElement* pNext;                    // Pointer to a list element
};
```

The first element of the ListElement structure is of type RECT, and the second element is a pointer to a structure of type ListElement — the same type as that being defined. (Remember that this element isn't of type ListElement, it's of type 'pointer to ListElement'.) This allows objects of type ListElement to be daisy-chained together, where each ListElement can contain the address of the next ListElement object in a chain, the last in the chain having the pointer as zero. This is illustrated in Figure 7-3.

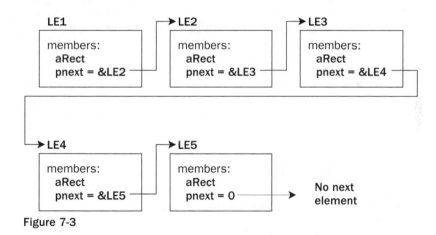

Figure 7-3

Each box in the diagram represents an object of type ListElement and the pNext member of each object stores the address of the next object in the chain, except for the last object where pNext is 0. This kind of arrangement is usually referred to as a **linked list**. It has the advantage that as long as you know the first element in the list, you can find all the others. This is particularly important when variables are created dynamically, since a linked list can be used to keep track of them all. Every time a new one is created, it's simply added to the end of the list by storing its address in the pNext member of the last object in the chain.

Accessing Structure Members through a Pointer

Consider the following statements:

```
RECT aRect = {0, 0, 100, 100};
RECT* pRect = &aRect;
```

The first declares and defines the aRect object to be of type RECT with the first pair of members initialized to (0, 0) and the second pair to (100, 100). The second statement declares pRect as a pointer to type RECT and initializes it with the address of aRect. You can now access the members of aRect through the pointer with a statement such as this:

```
(*pRect).Top += 10;                    // Increment the Top member by 10
```

The parentheses to dereference the pointer here are essential because the member access operator takes precedence over the dereferencing operator. Without the parentheses, you would be attempting to treat the pointer as a struct and to dereference the member, so the statement would not compile. After executing this statement, the Top member will have the value 10 and, of course, the remaining members will be unchanged.

The method that you used here to access the member of a struct through a pointer looks rather clumsy. Because this kind of operation crops up very frequently in C++, the language includes a special operator to enable you to express the same thing in a much more readable and intuitive form, so let's look at that next.

The Indirect Member Selection Operator

The **indirect member selection operator**, ->, is specifically for accessing members of a struct (or a class) through a pointer; this operator is also referred to as the **indirect member access operator**. The operator looks like a little arrow (->) and is formed from a minus sign (-) followed by the symbol for greater than (>). You could use it to rewrite the statement to access the Top member of aRect through the pointer pRect, as follows:

```
pRect->Top += 10;                      // Increment the Top member by 10
```

This is much more expressive of what is going on, isn't it? The indirect member selection operator is also used with classes, and you'll see a lot more of it throughout the rest of the book.

Data Types, Objects, Classes, and Instances

Before I get into the language, syntax, and programming techniques of classes, I'll start by considering how your existing knowledge relates to the concept of classes.

So far, you've learned that native C++ lets you create variables that can be any of a range of fundamental data types: int, long, double and so on. You have also seen how you can use the struct keyword to define a structure that you could then use as the type for a variable representing a composite of several other variables.

The variables of the fundamental types don't allow you to model real-world objects (or even imaginary objects) adequately. It's hard to model a box in terms of an int, for example; however, you can use the members of a struct to define a set of attributes for such an object. You could define variables, length, width, and height to represent the dimensions of the box and bind them together as members of a Box structure, as follows:

```
struct Box
{
```

```
      double length;
      double width;
      double height;
   };
```

With this definition of a new data type called Box, you define variables of this type just as you did with variables of the basic types. You can then create, manipulate, and destroy as many Box objects as you need to in your program. This means that you can model objects using structs and write your programs around them. So — that's object-oriented programming all wrapped up then?

Well, not quite. You see, object-oriented programming (OOP) is based on a number of foundations (famously *encapsulation*, *polymorphism*, and *inheritance*) and what you have seen so far doesn't quite fit the bill. Don't worry about what these terms mean for the moment — you'll explore that in the rest of this chapter and throughout the book.

The notion of a struct in C++ goes far beyond the original concept of struct in C — it incorporates the object-oriented notion of a **class**. This idea of classes, from which you can create your own data types and use them just like the native types, is fundamental to C++, and the new keyword class was introduced into the language to describe this concept. The keywords struct and class are almost identical in C++, except for the access control to the members, which you will find out more about later in this chapter. The keyword struct is maintained for backwards compatibility with C, but everything that you can do with a struct and more, you can achieve with a class.

Take a look at how you might define a class representing boxes:

```
class CBox
{
  public:
    double m_Length;
    double m_Width;
    double m_Height;
};
```

When you define CBox as a class you are essentially defining a new data type, similar to when you defined the Box structure. The only differences here are the use of the keyword class instead of struct, and the use of the keyword public followed by a colon that precedes the definition of the members of the class. The variables that you define as part of the class are called **data members** of the class, because they are variables that store data.

You have also called the class CBox instead of Box. You could have called the class Box, but the MFC adopts the convention of using the prefix C for all class names, so you might as well get used to it. MFC also prefixes data members of classes with m_ to distinguish them from other variables, so I'll use this convention, too. Remember though that in other contexts where you might use C++ and in C++/CLI in particular, this will not be the case; in some instances the convention for naming classes and their members may be different, and in others there may be no particular convention adopted for naming entities.

The public keyword is a clue as to the difference between a structure and a class. It just defines the members of the class as being generally accessible, in the same way as the members of a structure are. The members of a struct, however, are public by default. As you'll see a little later in the chapter, though, it's also possible to place restrictions on the accessibility of the class members.

You can declare a variable, `bigBox` say, which represents an instance of the `CBox` class type like this:

```
CBox bigBox;
```

This is exactly the same as declaring a variable for a `struct`, or indeed for any other variable type. After you have defined the class `CBox`, declarations for variables of this type are quite standard.

First Class

The notion of class was invented by an Englishman to keep the general population happy. It derives from the theory that people who knew their place and function in society would be much more secure and comfortable in life than those who did not. The famous Dane, Bjarne Stroustrup, who invented C++, undoubtedly acquired a deep knowledge of class concepts while at Cambridge University in England and appropriated the idea very successfully for use in his new language.

Class in C++ is similar to the English concept, in that each class usually has a very precise role and a permitted set of actions. However, it differs from the English idea because class in C++ has largely socialist overtones, concentrating on the importance of working classes. Indeed, in some ways it is the reverse of the English ideal, because, as you will see, working classes in C++ often live on the backs of classes that do nothing at all.

Operations on Classes

In C++ you can create new data types as classes to represent whatever kinds of objects you like. As you'll come to see, classes (and structures) aren't limited to just holding data; you can also define member functions or even operations that act between objects of your classes using the standard C++ operators. You can define the class `CBox`, for example, so that the following statements work and have the meanings you want them to have:

```
CBox box1;
CBox box2;

if(box1 > box2)            // Fill the larger box
  box1.fill();
else
  box2.fill();
```

You could also implement operations as part of the `CBox` class for adding, subtracting or even multiplying boxes — in fact, almost any operation to which you could ascribe a sensible meaning in the context of boxes.

I'm talking about incredibly powerful medicine here and it constitutes a major change in the approach that you can take to programming. Instead of breaking down a problem in terms of what are essentially computer-related data types (integer numbers, floating point numbers and so on) and then writing a program, you're going to be programming in terms of problem-related data types, in other words classes. These classes might be named `CEmployee`, or `CCowboy`, or `CCheese`, or `CChutney`, each defined specifically for the kind of problem that you want to solve, complete with the functions and operators that are necessary to manipulate instances of your new types.

Program design now starts with deciding what new application-specific data types you need to solve the problem in hand and writing the program in terms of operations on the specifics that the problem is concerned with, be it CCoffins or CCowpokes.

Terminology

I'll first summarize some of the terminology that I will be using when discussing classes in C++:

❑   A **class** is a user-defined data type.

❑   **Object-oriented programming** (OOP) is the programming style based on the idea of defining your own data types as classes.

❑   Declaring an object of a class type is sometimes referred to as **instantiation** because you are creating an **instance** of a class.

❑   Instances of a class are referred to as **objects**.

❑   The idea of an object containing the data implicit in its definition, together with the functions that operate on that data, is referred to as **encapsulation**.

When I get into the detail of object-oriented programming, it may seem a little complicated in places, but getting back to the basics of what you're doing can often help to make things clearer, so always keep in mind what objects are really about. They are about writing programs in terms of the objects that are specific to the domain of your problem. All the facilities around classes in C++ are there to make this as comprehensive and flexible as possible. Let's get down to the business of understanding classes.

Understanding Classes

A class is specification of a data type that you define. It can contain data elements that can either be variables of the basic types in C++, or of other user-defined types. The data elements of a class may be single data elements, arrays, pointers, arrays of pointers of almost any kind, or objects of other classes, so you have a lot of flexibility in what you can include in your data type. A class also can contain functions that operate on objects of the class by accessing the data elements that they include. So, a class combines both the definition of the elementary data that makes up an object and the means of manipulating the data that belongs to individual objects of the class.

The data and functions within a class are called **members** of the class. Oddly enough, the members of a class that are data items are called **data members** and the members that are functions are called **function members** or **member functions**. The member functions of a class are also sometimes referred to as **methods**; I will not use this term in this book but keep it in mind as you may see it used elsewhere. The data members are also referred to as **fields**, and this terminology is used with C++/CLI, so I will be using this terminology from time to time.

When you define a class, you define a blueprint for a data type. This doesn't actually define any data but it does define what the class name means, that is, what an object of the class will consist of and what operations can be performed on such an object. It's much the same as if you wrote a description of the basic type double. This wouldn't be an actual variable of type double, but a definition of how it's made up and how it operates. To create a variable of a basic data type, you need to use a declaration statement. It's exactly the same with classes, as you will see.

Defining a Class

Take a look again at the class example mentioned earlier — a class of boxes. You defined the CBox data type using the keyword class as follows:

```
class CBox
{
  public:
    double m_Length;                  // Length of a box in inches
    double m_Width;                   // Width of a box in inches
    double m_Height;                  // Height of a box in inches
};
```

The name of the class appears following the class keyword, and the three data members are defined between the curly braces. The data members are defined for the class using the declaration statements that you already know and love and the whole class definition is terminated with a semicolon. The names of all the members of a class are local to the class. You can therefore use the same names elsewhere in a program without causing any problems.

Access Control in a Class

The public keyword looks a bit like a label, but in fact it is more than that. It determines the access attributes of the members of the class that follow it. Specifying the data members as public means that these members of an object of the class can be accessed anywhere within the scope of the class object to which they belong. You can also specify the members of a class as private or protected. In fact, if you omit the access specification altogether, the members have the default attribute, private. (This is the only difference between a class and a struct in C++ — the default access specifier for a struct is public.) You will look into the effect of these keywords in a class definition a bit later.

Remember that all you have defined so far is a class, which is a data type. You haven't declared any objects of the class type. When I talk about accessing a class member, say m_Height, I'm talking about accessing the data member of a particular object, and that object needs to be defined somewhere.

Declaring Objects of a Class

You declare objects of a class with exactly the same sort of declaration that you use to declare objects of basic types, so you could declare objects of the CBox class type with these statements:

```
CBox box1;                           // Declare box1 of type CBox
CBox box2;                           // Declare box2 of type CBox
```

Both of the objects box1 and box2 will, of course, have their own data members. This is illustrated in Figure 7-4.

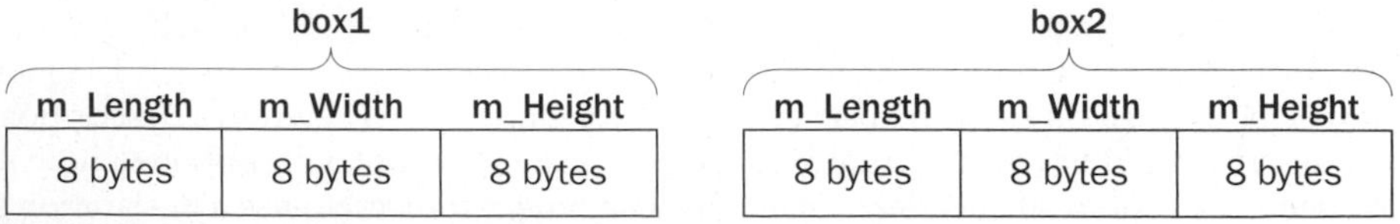

Figure 7-4

The object name box1 embodies the whole object, including its three data members. They are not initialized to anything, however — the data members of each object will simply contain junk values, so you need to look at how you can access them for the purpose of setting them to some specific values.

Accessing the Data Members of a Class

You can refer to the data members of objects of a class using the **direct member selection operator** that you used to access members of a struct. So, to set the value of the data member m_Height of the object box2 to, say, 18.0, you could write this assignment statement:

```
box2.m_Height = 18.0;                   // Setting the value of a data member
```

You can only access the data member in this way in a function that is outside the class because the m_Height member was specified as having public access. If it wasn't defined as public, this statement would not compile. You'll see more about this shortly.

Try It Out   Your First Use of Classes

Verify that you can use your class in the same way as the structure. Try it out in the following console application:

```cpp
// Ex7_02.cpp
// Creating and using boxes
#include <iostream>
using std::cout;
using std::endl;

class CBox                              // Class definition at global scope
{
  public:
    double m_Length;                    // Length of a box in inches
    double m_Width;                     // Width of a box in inches
    double m_Height;                    // Height of a box in inches
};

int main()
{
  CBox box1;                            // Declare box1 of type CBox
  CBox box2;                            // Declare box2 of type CBox

  double boxVolume = 0.0;              // Stores the volume of a box

  box1.m_Height = 18.0;                 // Define the values
  box1.m_Length = 78.0;                 // of the members of
  box1.m_Width = 24.0;                  // the object box1

  box2.m_Height = box1.m_Height - 10;   // Define box2
  box2.m_Length = box1.m_Length/2.0;    // members in
  box2.m_Width = 0.25*box1.m_Length;    // terms of box1

  // Calculate volume of box1
  boxVolume = box1.m_Height*box1.m_Length*box1.m_Width;
```

```
      cout << endl
          << "Volume of box1 = " << boxVolume;

      cout << endl
          << "box2 has sides which total "
          << box2.m_Height+ box2.m_Length+ box2.m_Width
          << " inches.";

      cout << endl                          // Display the size of a box in memory
          << "A CBox object occupies "
          << sizeof box1 << " bytes.";

      cout <<endl;
      return 0;
  }
```

As you type in the code for main(), you should see the editor prompting you with a list of member names whenever you enter a member selection operator following the name of a class object. You can then select the member you want from the list by double-clicking it. Hovering the mouse cursor for a moment over any of the variables in your code will result in the type being displayed.

How It Works

Back to console application examples again for the moment, so the project should be defined accordingly. Everything here works, as you would have expected from your experience with structures. The definition of the class appears outside of the function main() and, therefore, has global scope. This enables you to declare objects in any function in the program and causes the class to show up in the Class View tab once the program has been compiled.

You have declared two objects of type CBox within the function main(), box1 and box2. Of course, as with variables of the basic types, the objects box1 and box2 are local to main(). Objects of a class type obey the same rules with respect to scope as variables declared as one of the basic types (such as the variable boxVolume used in this example).

The first three assignment statements set the values of the data members of box1. You define the values of the data members of box2 in terms of the data members of box1 in the next three assignment statements.

You then have a statement that calculates the volume of box1 as the product of its three data members, and this value is output to the screen. Next, you output the sum of the data members of box2 by writing the expression for the sum of the data members directly in the output statement. The final action in the program is to output the number of bytes occupied by box1, which is produced by the operator sizeof.

If you run this program, you should get this output:

```
Volume of box1 = 33696
box2 has sides which total 66.5 inches.
A CBox object occupies 24 bytes.
```

The last line shows that the object `box1` occupies 24 bytes of memory, which is a result of having 3 data members of 8 bytes each. The statement that produced the last line of output could equally well have been written like this:

```
cout << endl                          // Display the size of a box in memory
     << "A CBox object occupies "
     << sizeof (CBox) << " bytes.";
```

Here, I have used the type name between parentheses, rather than a specific object name as the operand for the `sizeof` operator. You'll remember that this is standard syntax for the `sizeof` operator, as you saw in Chapter 4.

This example has demonstrated the mechanism for accessing the `public` data members of a class. It also shows that they can be used in exactly the same way as ordinary variables. You are now ready to break new ground by taking a look at member *functions* of a class.

Member Functions of a Class

A member function of a class is a function that has its definition or its prototype within the class definition. It operates on any object of the class of which it is a member, and has access to all the members of a class for that object.

Try It Out   **Adding a Member Function to CBox**

To see how you access the members of the class from within a function member, create an example extending the CBox class to include a member function that calculates the volume of the CBox object.

```
// Ex7_03.cpp
// Calculating the volume of a box with a member function
#include <iostream>
using std::cout;
using std::endl;

class CBox                            // Class definition at global scope
{
  public:
    double m_Length;                  // Length of a box in inches
    double m_Width;                   // Width of a box in inches
    double m_Height;                  // Height of a box in inches

    // Function to calculate the volume of a box
    double Volume()
    {
      return m_Length*m_Width*m_Height;
    }
};

int main()
{
```

```
    CBox box1;                              // Declare box1 of type CBox
    CBox box2;                              // Declare box2 of type CBox

    double boxVolume = 0.0;                 // Stores the volume of a box

    box1.m_Height = 18.0;                   // Define the values
    box1.m_Length = 78.0;                   // of the members of
    box1.m_Width = 24.0;                    // the object box1

    box2.m_Height = box1.m_Height - 10;     // Define box2
    box2.m_Length = box1.m_Length/2.0;      // members in
    box2.m_Width = 0.25*box1.m_Length;      // terms of box1

    boxVolume = box1.Volume();              // Calculate volume of box1
    cout << endl
        << "Volume of box1 = " << boxVolume;

    cout << endl
        << "Volume of box2 = "
        << box2.Volume();

    cout << endl
        << "A CBox object occupies "
        << sizeof box1 << " bytes.";

    cout << endl;
    return 0;
}
```

How It Works

The new code that you add to the CBox class definition is shaded. It's just the definition of the Volume() function, which is a member function of the class. It also has the same access attribute as the data members: public. This is because every class member that you declare following an access attribute will have that access attribute, until another access attribute is specified within the class definition. The Volume() function returns the volume of a CBox object as a value of type double. The expression in the return statement is just the product of the three data members of the class.

> *There's no need to qualify the names of the class members in any way when you access them in member functions. The unqualified member names automatically refer to the members of the object that is current when the member function is executed.*

The member function Volume() is used in the highlighted statements in main(), after initializing the data members (as in the first example). Using the same name for a variable in main() causes no conflict or problem. You can call a member function of a particular object by writing the name of the object to be processed, followed by a period, followed by the member function name. As noted previously, the function automatically accesses the data members of the object for which it was called, so the first use of Volume() calculates the volume of box1. Using only the name of a member will always refer to the member of the object for which the member function has been called.

The member function is used a second time directly in the output statement to produce the volume of box2. If you execute this example, it produces this output:

```
Volume of box1 = 33696
Volume of box2 = 6084
A CBox object occupies 24 bytes.
```

Note that the CBox object is still the same number of bytes. Adding a function member to a class doesn't affect the size of the objects. Obviously, a member function has to be stored in memory somewhere, but there's only one copy regardless of how many class objects you create, and the memory occupied by member functions isn't counted when the `sizeof` operator produces the number of bytes that an object occupies.

The names of the class data members in the member function automatically refer to the data members of the specific object used to call the function, and the function can only be called for a particular object of the class. In this case, this is done by using the direct member access operator with the name of an object.

If you try to call a member function without specifying an object name, your program will not compile.

Positioning a Member Function Definition

A member function definition need not be placed inside the class definition. If you want to put it outside the class definition, you need to put the prototype for the function inside the class. If you rewrite the previous class with the function definition outside, the class definition looks like this:

```
class CBox                              // Class definition at global scope
{
  public:
    double m_Length;                    // Length of a box in inches
    double m_Width;                     // Width of a box in inches
    double m_Height;                    // Height of a box in inches
    double Volume(void);                // Member function prototype
};
```

Now you need to write the function definition, but because it appears outside the definition of the class, there has to be some way of telling the compiler that the function belongs to the class CBox. This is done by prefixing the function name with the name of the class and separating the two with the **scope resolution operator**, `::`, which is formed from two successive colons. The function definition would now look like this:

```
// Function to calculate the volume of a box
double CBox::Volume()
{
  return m_Length*m_Width*m_Height;
}
```

It produces the same output as the last example; however, it isn't exactly the same program. In the second case, all calls to the function are treated in the way that you're already familiar with. However, when you define a function within the definition of the class, as in Ex7_03.cpp, the compiler implicitly treats the function as an **inline function**.

Inline Functions

With an inline function, the compiler tries to expand the code in the body of the function in place of a call to the function. This avoids much of the overhead of calling the function and, therefore, speeds up your code. This is illustrated in Figure 7-5.

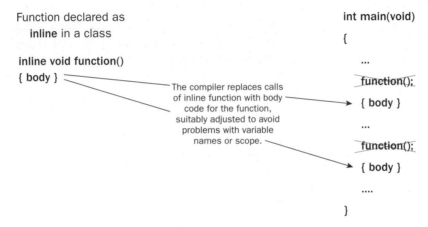

Figure 7-5

Of course, the compiler ensures that expanding a function inline doesn't cause any problems with variable names or scope.

The compiler may not always be able to insert the code for a function inline (such as with recursive functions or functions for which you have obtained an address), but generally it will work. It's best used for very short, simple functions, such as our function Volume() in the CBox class because such functions execute faster and inserting the body code does not significantly increase the size of the executable module.

With the function definition outside of the class definition, the compiler treats the function as a normal function and a call of the function will work in the usual way; however, it's also possible to tell the compiler that, if possible, you would like the function to be considered as inline. This is done by simply placing the keyword inline at the beginning of the function header. So, for this function, the definition would be as follows:

```
// Function to calculate the volume of a box
inline double CBox::Volume()
{
   return m_Length*m_Width*m_Height;
}
```

With this definition for the function, the program would be exactly the same as the original. This enables you to put the member function definitions outside of the class definition, if you so choose, and still retain the execution performance benefits of inlining.

You can apply the keyword `inline` to ordinary functions in your program that have nothing to do with classes and get the same effect. Remember, however, that it's best used for short, simple functions.

You now need to understand a little more about what happens when you declare an object of a class.

Class Constructors

In the previous program example, you declared the CBox objects, box1 and box2, and then laboriously worked through each of the data members for each object in order to assign an initial value to it. This is unsatisfactory from several points of view. First of all, it would be easy to overlook initializing a data member, particularly with a class that had many more data members than our CBox class. Initializing the data members of several objects of a complex class could involve pages of assignment statements. The final constraint on this approach arises when you get to defining data members of a class that don't have the attribute `public` — you won't be able to access them from outside the class anyway. There has to be a better way, and of course there is — it's known as the class **constructor**.

What Is a Constructor?

A class constructor is a special function in a class that is responsible for creating new objects when required. A constructor therefore provides the opportunity to initialize objects as they are created and to ensure that data members only contain valid values. A class may have several constructors enabling you to create objects in various ways.

You have no leeway in naming the constructors in a class — they always have the same name as the class in which they are defined. The function `CBox()`, for example, is a constructor for our class CBox. It also has no return type. It's wrong to specify a return type for a constructor; you must not even write it as `void`. The primary purpose of a class constructor is to assign initial values to the data elements of the class, and no return type for a constructor is necessary or permitted. If you inadvertently specify a return type for a constructor, the compiler will report it as an error with error number C2380.

Try It Out   **Adding a Constructor to the CBox class**

Let's extend our CBox class to incorporate a constructor.

```
// Ex7_04.cpp
// Using a constructor
#include <iostream>
using std::cout;
using std::endl;

class CBox                              // Class definition at global scope
{
```

```
  public:
    double m_Length;                // Length of a box in inches
    double m_Width;                 // Width of a box in inches
    double m_Height;                // Height of a box in inches

    // Constructor definition
    CBox(double lv, double bv, double hv)
    {
      cout << endl << "Constructor called.";
      m_Length = lv;                // Set values of
      m_Width = bv;                 // data members
      m_Height = hv;
    }

    // Function to calculate the volume of a box
    double Volume()
    {
      return m_Length* m_Width* m_Height;
    }
};

int main()
{
  CBox box1(78.0,24.0,18.0);        // Declare and initialize box1
  CBox cigarBox(8.0,5.0,1.0);       // Declare and initialize cigarBox

  double boxVolume = 0.0;           // Stores the volume of a box

  boxVolume = box1.Volume();        // Calculate volume of box1
  cout << endl
       << "Volume of box1 = " << boxVolume;

  cout << endl
       << "Volume of cigarBox = "
       << cigarBox.Volume();

  cout << endl;
  return 0;
}
```

How It Works

The CBox() constructor has been written with three parameters of type double, corresponding to the initial values for the m_Length, m_Width, and m_Height members of a CBox object. The first statement in the constructor outputs a message so that you can tell when it's been called. You wouldn't do this in production programs, but because it's very helpful in showing when a constructor is called, it's often used when testing a program. I'll use it regularly for the purposes of illustration. The code in the body of the constructor is very simple. It just assigns the arguments that you pass to the constructor when you call it to the corresponding data members. If necessary, you could also include checks that valid, non-negative arguments are supplied and, in a real context, you probably would want to do this, but our primary interest here is in seeing how the mechanism works.

Within main(), you declare the object box1 with initializing values for the data members m_Length, m_Width, and m_Height, in sequence. These are in parentheses following the object name. This uses the functional notation for initialization that, as you saw in Chapter 2, can also be applied to initializing ordinary variables of basic types. You also declare a second object of type CBox, called cigarBox, which also has initializing values.

The volume of box1 is calculated using the member function Volume() as in the previous example and is then displayed on the screen. You also display the value of the volume of cigarBox. The output from the example is:

```
Constructor called.
Constructor called.
Volume of box1 = 33696
Volume of cigarBox = 40
```

The first two lines are output from the two calls of the constructor CBox(), once for each object declared. The constructor that you have supplied in the class definition is automatically called when a CBox object is declared, so both CBox objects are initialized with the initializing values appearing in the declaration. These are passed to the constructor as arguments, in the sequence that they are written in the declaration. As you can see, the volume of box1 is the same as before and cigarBox has a volume looking suspiciously like the product of its dimensions, which is quite a relief.

The Default Constructor

Try modifying the last example by adding the declaration for box2 that you had previously in Ex7_03.cpp:

```
CBox box2;                                    // Declare box2 of type CBox
```

Here, you've left box2 without initializing values. When you rebuild this version of the program, you get the error message:

```
error C2512: 'CBox': no appropriate default constructor available
```

This means that the compiler is looking for a **default constructor** for box2 (also referred to as the **noarg** constructor because it doesn't require arguments when it is called) because you haven't supplied any initializing values for the data members. A default constructor is one that does not require any arguments to be supplied, which can be either a constructor that has no parameters specified in the constructor definition, or one whose arguments are all optional. Well, this statement was perfectly satisfactory in Ex7_02.cpp, so why doesn't it work now?

The answer is that the previous example used a default no-argument constructor that was supplied by the compiler, and the compiler provided this constructor because you didn't supply one. Because in this example you *did* supply a constructor, the compiler assumed that you were taking care of everything and didn't supply the default. So, if you still want to use declarations for CBox objects that aren't initialized, you have to include the default constructor yourself. What exactly does the default constructor look like? In the simplest case, it's just a constructor that accepts no arguments; it doesn't even need to do anything:

```
CBox()                    // Default constructor
{}                        // Totally devoid of statements
```

You can see such a constructor in action.

Try It Out   Supplying a Default Constructor

Let's add our version of the default constructor to the last example, along with the declaration for box2, plus the original assignments for the data members of box2. You must enlarge the default constructor just enough to show that it is called. Here is the next version of the program:

```cpp
// Ex7_05.cpp
// Supplying and using a default constructor
#include <iostream >
using std::cout;
using std::endl;

class CBox                              // Class definition at global scope
{
  public:
    double m_Length;                    // Length of a box in inches
    double m_Width;                     // Width of a box in inches
    double m_Height;                    // Height of a box in inches

    // Constructor definition
    CBox(double lv, double bv, double hv)
    {
      cout << endl << "Constructor called.";
      m_Length = lv;                    // Set values of
      m_Width = bv;                     // data members
      m_Height = hv;
    }

    // Default constructor definition
    CBox()
    {
      cout << endl << "Default constructor called.";
    }

    // Function to calculate the volume of a box
    double Volume()
    {
      return m_Length*m_Width*m_Height;
    }
};

int main()
{
  CBox box1(78.0,24.0,18.0);           // Declare and initialize box1
  CBox box2;                           // Declare box2 - no initial values
  CBox cigarBox(8.0, 5.0, 1.0);        // Declare and initialize cigarBox

  double boxVolume = 0.0;              // Stores the volume of a box

  boxVolume = box1.Volume();           // Calculate volume of box1
  cout << endl
       << "Volume of box1 = " << boxVolume;
```

```
        box2.m_Height = box1.m_Height - 10;   // Define box2
        box2.m_Length = box1.m_Length / 2.0;  // members in
        box2.m_Width = 0.25*box1.m_Length;    // terms of box1

    cout << endl
         << "Volume of box2 = "
         << box2.Volume();

    cout << endl
         << "Volume of cigarBox = "
         << cigarBox.Volume();

    cout << endl;
    return 0;
}
```

How It Works

Now that you have included your own version of the default constructor, there are no error messages from the compiler and everything works. The program produces this output:

```
Constructor called.
Default constructor called.
Constructor called.
Volume of box1 = 33696
Volume of box2 = 6084
Volume of cigarBox = 40
```

All that the default constructor does is display a message. Evidently, it was called when you declared the object box2. You also get the correct value for the volumes of all three CBox objects, so the rest of the program is working as it should.

One aspect of this example that you may have noticed is that you now know you can overload constructors just as you overloaded functions in Chapter 6. You have just executed an example with two constructors that differ only in their parameter list. One has three parameters of type double and the other has no parameters at all.

Assigning Default Parameter Values in a Class

When discussing functions, you saw how you could specify default values for the parameters to a function in the function prototype. You can also do this for class member functions, including constructors. If you put the definition of the member function inside the class definition, you can put the default values for the parameters in the function header. If you include only the prototype of a function in the class definition, the default parameter values should go in the prototype.

If you decided that the default size for a CBox object was a unit box with all sides of length 1, you could alter the class definition in the last example to this:

```
class CBox                          // Class definition at global scope
{
```

355

```
public:
  double m_Length;                  // Length of a box in inches
  double m_Width;                   // Width of a box in inches
  double m_Height;                  // Height of a box in inches

  // Constructor definition
  CBox(double lv = 1.0, double bv = 1.0, double hv = 1.0)
  {
    cout << endl << "Constructor called.";
    m_Length = lv;                    // Set values of
    m_Width = bv;                     // data members
    m_Height = hv;
  }

  // Default constructor definition
  CBox()
  {
    cout << endl << "Default constructor called.";
  }

  // Function to calculate the volume of a box
  double Volume()
  {
    return m_Length*m_Width*m_Height;
  }
};
```

If you make this change to the last example, what happens? You get another error message from the compiler, of course. Amongst a lot of other stuff, you get these useful comments from the compiler:

```
warning C4520: 'CBox': multiple default constructors specified
error C2668: 'CBox::CBox': ambiguous call to overloaded function
```

This means that the compiler can't work out which of the two constructors to call — the one for which you have set default values for the parameters or the constructor that doesn't accept any parameters. This is because the declaration of box2 requires a constructor without parameters and either constructor can now be called without parameters. The immediately obvious solution to this is to get rid of the constructor that accepts no parameters. This is actually beneficial. Without this constructor, any CBox object declared without being explicitly initialized will automatically have its members initialized to 1.

Try It Out   Supplying Default Values for Constructor Arguments

You can demonstrate this with the following simplified example:

```
// Ex7_06.cpp
// Supplying default values for constructor arguments
#include <iostream>
using std::cout;
using std::endl;

class CBox                                // Class definition at global scope
{
```

```
   public:
      double m_Length;                    // Length of a box in inches
      double m_Width;                     // Width of a box in inches
      double m_Height;                    // Height of a box in inches

      // Constructor definition
      CBox(double lv = 1.0, double bv = 1.0, double hv = 1.0)
      {
        cout << endl << "Constructor called.";
        m_Length = lv;                    // Set values of
        m_Width = bv;                     // data members
        m_Height = hv;
      }

      // Function to calculate the volume of a box
      double Volume()
      {
        return m_Length*m_Width*m_Height;
      }
};

int main()
{
  CBox box2;                              // Declare box2 - no initial values

  cout << endl
       << "Volume of box2 = "
       << box2.Volume();

  cout << endl;
  return 0;
}
```

How It Works

You only declare a single uninitialized CBox variable — box2 — because that's all you need for demonstration purposes. This version of the program produces the following output:

```
Constructor called.
Volume of box2 = 1
```

This shows that the constructor with default parameter values is doing its job of setting the values of objects that have no initializing values specified.

You should not assume from this that this is the only, or even the recommended, way of implementing the default constructor. There will be many occasions where you won't want to assign default values in this way, in which case you'll need to write a separate default constructor. There will even be times when you don't want to have a default constructor operating at all, even though you have defined another constructor. This would ensure that all declared objects of a class must have initializing values explicitly specified in their declaration.

Using an Initialization List in a Constructor

Previously, you initialized the members of an object in the class constructor using explicit assignment. You could also have used a different technique, using what is called an **initialization list**. I can demonstrate this with an alternative version of the constructor for the class CBox:

```
// Constructor definition using an initialization list
CBox(double lv = 1.0, double bv = 1.0, double hv = 1.0):
                          m_Length(lv), m_Width(bv), m_Height(hv)
{
  cout << endl << "Constructor called.";
}
```

The way this constructor definition is written assumes that it appears within the body of the class definition. Now the values of the data members are not set in assignment statements in the body of the constructor. As in a declaration, they are specified as initializing values using functional notation and appear in the initializing list as part of the function header. The member m_Length is initialized by the value of lv, for example. This can be more efficient than using assignments as you did in the previous version. If you substitute this version of the constructor in the previous example, you will see that it works just as well.

Note that the initializing list for the constructor is separated from the parameter list by a colon and each of the initializers is separated by a comma. This technique for initializing parameters in a constructor is important, because, as you will see later, it's the only way of setting values for certain types of data members of an object. The MFC also relies heavily on the initialization list technique.

Private Members of a Class

Having a constructor that sets the values of the data members of a class object but still admits the possibility of any part of a program being able to mess with what are essentially the guts of an object is almost a contradiction in terms. To draw an analogy, after you have arranged for a brilliant surgeon such as Dr. Kildare, whose skills were honed over years of training, to do things to your insides, letting the local plumber or bricklayer have a go hardly seems appropriate. You need some protection for your class data members.

You can get the security you need by using the keyword private when you define the class members. Class members that are private can, in general, be accessed only by member functions of a class. There's one exception, but we'll worry about that later. A normal function has no direct means of accessing the private members of a class. This is shown in Figure 7-6.

Having the possibility of specifying class members as private also enables you to separate the interface to the class from its internal implementation. The interface to a class is composed of the public members and the public member functions in particular because they can provide indirect access to all the members of a class, including the private members. By keeping the internals of a class private, you can later modify them to improve performance for example without necessitating modifications to the code that uses the class through its public interface. To keep data and function members of a class safe from unnecessary meddling, it's good practice to declare those that don't need to be exposed as private. Only make public what is essential to the use of your class.

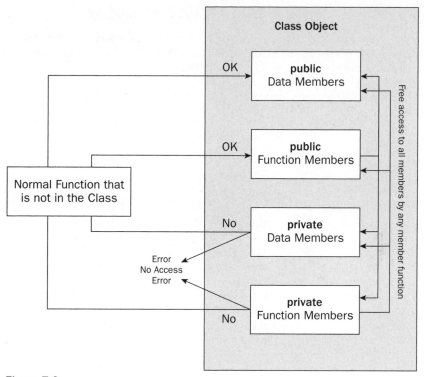

Figure 7-6

Try It Out   Private Data Members

You can rewrite the CBox class to make its data members `private`.

```cpp
// Ex7_07.cpp
// A class with private members
#include <iostream>
using std::cout;
using std::endl;

class CBox                              // Class definition at global scope
{
  public:
    // Constructor definition using an initialisation list
    CBox(double lv = 1.0, double bv = 1.0, double hv = 1.0):
                        m_Length(lv), m_Width(bv), m_Height(hv)
    {
      cout << endl << "Constructor called.";
    }

    // Function to calculate the volume of a box
```

```
    double Volume()
    {
      return m_Length*m_Width*m_Height;
    }

  private:
    double m_Length;                       // Length of a box in inches
    double m_Width;                        // Width of a box in inches
    double m_Height;                       // Height of a box in inches
};

int main()
{
  CBox match(2.2, 1.1, 0.5);              // Declare match box
  CBox box2;                             // Declare box2 - no initial values

  cout << endl
       << "Volume of match = "
       << match.Volume();

// Uncomment the following line to get an error
// box2.m_Length = 4.0;

  cout << endl
       << "Volume of box2 = "
       << box2.Volume();
  cout << endl;

  return 0;
}
```

How It Works

The definition of the CBox class now has two sections. The first is the public section containing the constructor and the member function Volume(). The second section is specified as private and contains the data members. Now the data members can only be accessed by the member functions of the class. You don't have to modify any of the member functions — they can access all the data members of the class anyway. If you uncomment the statement in the function main() that assigns a value to the m_Length member of the object box2, however, you'll get a compiler error message confirming that the data member is inaccessible. If you haven't already done so, take a look at the members of the CBox class in Class View; you'll see that the icon alongside each member indicates its accessibility; a small padlock in the icon shows when a member is private.

A point to remember is that using a constructor or a member function is now the only way to get a value into a private data member of an object. You have to make sure that all the ways in which you might want to set or modify private data members of a class are provided for through member functions.

You can also put functions into the private section of a class. In this case, they can only be called by other function members of the same class. If you put the function Volume() in the private section, you will get a compiler error from the statements that attempt to use it in the function main(). If you put the constructor in the private section, you won't be able to declare any objects of the class type.

The preceding example generates this output:

```
Constructor called.
Constructor called.
Volume of match = 1.21
Volume of box2 = 1
```

The output demonstrates that the class is still working satisfactorily, with its data members defined as having the access attribute `private`. The major difference is that they are now completely protected from unauthorized access and modification.

If you don't specify otherwise, the default access attribute that applies to members of a class is `private`. *You could, therefore, put all your private members at the beginning of the class definition and let them default to private by omitting the keyword. It's better, however, to take the trouble to explicitly state the access attribute in every case, so there can be no doubt about what you intend.*

Of course, you don't have to make all your data members `private`. If the application for your class requires it, you can have some data members defined as `private` and some as `public`. It all depends on what you're trying to do. If there's no reason to make members of a class `public`, it is better to make them `private` as it makes the class more secure. Ordinary functions won't be able to access any of the `private` members of your class.

Accessing private Class Members

On reflection, declaring the data members of a class as `private` is rather extreme. It's all very well protecting them from unauthorized modification, but that's no reason to keep their values a secret. What you need is a Freedom of Information Act for `private` members.

You don't have to start writing to your state senator to get it — it's already available to you. All that's necessary is to write a member function to return the value of a data member. Look at this member function for the class `CBox`:

```
inline double CBox::GetLength()
{
  return m_Length;
}
```

Just to show how it looks, this has been written as a member function definition, which is external to the class. I've specified it as `inline`, since we'll benefit from the speed increase without increasing the size of the code too much. Assuming that you have the declaration of the function in the `public` section of the class, you can use it by writing statements such as this:

```
int len = box2.GetLength();            // Obtain data member length
```

All you need to do is to write a similar function for each data member that you want to make available to the outside world, and their values can be accessed without prejudicing the security of the class. Of course, if you put the definitions for these functions within the class definition, they will be `inline` by default.

The friend Functions of a Class

There may be circumstances when, for one reason or another, you want certain selected functions which are not members of a class to, nonetheless, be able to access all the members of a class — a sort of elite group with special privileges. Such functions are called **friend functions** of a class and are defined using the keyword `friend`. You can either include the prototype of a friend function in the class definition, or you can include the whole function definition. Functions that are friends of a class and are defined within the class definition are also by default `inline`.

Friend functions are not members of the class, and therefore the access attributes do not apply to them. They are just ordinary global functions with special privileges.

Imagine that you want to implement a friend function in the CBox class to compute the surface area of a CBox object.

Try It Out   Using a friend to Calculate the Surface Area

You can see how a friend function works in the following example:

```
// Ex7_08.cpp
// Creating a friend function of a class
#include <iostream>
using std::cout;
using std::endl;

class CBox                              // Class definition at global scope
{
  public:

    // Constructor definition
    CBox(double lv = 1.0, double bv = 1.0, double hv = 1.0)
    {
      cout << endl << "Constructor called.";
      m_Length = lv;                    // Set values of
      m_Width = bv;                     // data members
      m_Height = hv;
    }

    // Function to calculate the volume of a box
    double Volume()
    {
      return m_Length*m_Width*m_Height;
    }

  private:
    double m_Length;                    // Length of a box in inches
    double m_Width;                     // Width of a box in inches
    double m_Height;                    // Height of a box in inches

    // Friend function
    friend double BoxSurface(CBox aBox);
```

```
};
```

```
// friend function to calculate the surface area of a Box object
double BoxSurface(CBox aBox)
{
  return 2.0*(aBox.m_Length*aBox.m_Width +
              aBox.m_Length*aBox.m_Height +
              aBox.m_Height*aBox.m_Width);
}
```

```
int main()
{
  CBox match(2.2, 1.1, 0.5);          // Declare match box
  CBox box2;                          // Declare box2 - no initial values

  cout << endl
       << "Volume of match = "
       << match.Volume();

  cout << endl
       << "Surface area of match = "
       << BoxSurface(match);

  cout << endl
       << "Volume of box2 = "
       << box2.Volume();

  cout << endl
       << "Surface area of box2 = "
       << BoxSurface(box2);

  cout << endl;
  return 0;
}
```

How It Works

You declare the function `BoxSurface()` as a friend of the `CBox` class by writing the function prototype with the keyword `friend` at the front. Since the `BoxSurface()` function itself is a global function, it makes no difference where you put the `friend` declaration within the definition of the class, but it's a good idea to be consistent when you position this sort of declaration. You can see that I have chosen to position ours after all the `public` and `private` members of the class. Remember that a `friend` function isn't a member of the class, so access attributes don't apply.

The definition of the function follows that of the class. Note that you specify access to the data members of the object within the definition of `BoxSurface()`, using the `CBox` object passed to the function as a parameter. Because a `friend` function isn't a class member, the data members can't be referenced just by their names. They each have to be qualified by the object name in exactly the same way as they might in an ordinary function, except, of course, that an ordinary function can't access the `private` members of a class. A `friend` function is the same as an ordinary function, except that it can access all the members of the class or classes for which it is a friend without restriction.

The example produces the following output:

```
Constructor called.
Constructor called.
Volume of match = 1.21
Surface area of match = 8.14
Volume of box2 = 1
Surface area of box2 = 6
```

This is exactly what you would expect. The friend function is computing the surface area of the CBox objects from the values of the private members.

Placing friend Function Definitions Inside the Class

You could have combined the definition of the function with its declaration as a friend of the CBox class within the class definition and the code would run as before. The function definition in the class would be:

```
friend double BoxSurface(CBox aBox)
{
  return 2.0*(aBox.m_Length*aBox.m_Width +
              aBox.m_Length*aBox.m_Height +
              aBox.m_Height*aBox.m_Width);
}
```

However, this has a number of disadvantages relating to the readability of the code. Although the function would still have global scope, this might not be obvious to readers of the code, because the function would be hidden in the body of the class definition.

The Default Copy Constructor

Suppose that you declare and initialize a CBox object box1 with this statement:

```
CBox box1(78.0, 24.0, 18.0);
```

You now want to create another CBox object, identical to the first. You would like to initialize the second CBox object with box1. Let's try it.

Try It Out   Copying Information Between Instances

The following example shows this in action:

```
// Ex7_09.cpp
// Initializing an object with an object of the same class
#include <iostream>
using std::cout;
using std::endl;

class CBox                              // Class definition at global scope
{
```

```cpp
  public:
    // Constructor definition
    CBox(double lv = 1.0, double bv = 1.0, double hv = 1.0)
    {
      cout << endl << "Constructor called.";
      m_Length = lv;                        // Set values of
      m_Width = bv;                         // data members
      m_Height = hv;
    }

    // Function to calculate the volume of a box
    double Volume()
    {
      return m_Length*m_Width*m_Height;
    }

  private:
    double m_Length;                        // Length of a box in inches
    double m_Width;                         // Width of a box in inches
    double m_Height;                        // Height of a box in inches
};

int main()
{
   CBox box1(78.0, 24.0, 18.0);
   CBox box2 = box1;                        // Initialize box2 with box1

   cout << endl
        << "box1 volume = " << box1.Volume()
        << endl
        << "box2 volume = " << box2.Volume();

   cout << endl;
   return 0;
}
```

This example produces the following output:

```
Constructor called.
box1 volume = 33696
box2 volume = 33696
```

How It Works

Clearly, the program is working as you would want, with both boxes having the same volume. However, as you can see from the output, our constructor was called only once for the creation of box1. The question is, how was box2 created? The mechanism is similar to the one that you experienced when you had no constructor defined and the compiler supplied a default constructor to allow an object to be created. In this case, the compiler generates a default version of what is referred to as a **copy constructor**.

A copy constructor does exactly what we're doing here — it creates an object of a class by initializing it with an existing object of the same class. The default version of the copy constructor creates the new object by copying the existing object, member by member.

This is fine for simple classes such as CBox, but for many classes — classes that have pointers or arrays as members for example — it won't work properly. Indeed, with such classes the default copy constructor can create serious errors in your program. In these cases, you must create your own class copy constructor. This requires a special approach that you'll look into more fully towards the end of this chapter and again in the next chapter.

The Pointer this

In the CBox class, you wrote the Volume() function in terms of the class member names in the definition of the class. Of course, every object of type CBox that you create contains these members so there has to be a mechanism for the function to refer to the members of the particular object for which the function is called.

When any member function executes, it automatically contains a hidden pointer with the name this, which points to the object used with the function call. Therefore, when the member m_Length is accessed in the Volume() function during execution, it's actually referring to this->m_Length, which is the fully specified reference to the object member that is being used. The compiler takes care of adding the necessary pointer name this to the member names in the function.

If you need to, you can use the pointer this explicitly within a member function. You might, for example, want to return a pointer to the current object.

Try It Out   **Explicit Use of this**

You could add a public function to the CBox class that compares the volume of two CBox objects.

```cpp
// Ex7_10.cpp
// Using the pointer this
#include <iostream>
using std::cout;
using std::endl;

class CBox                              // Class definition at global scope
{
  public:
    // Constructor definition
    CBox(double lv = 1.0, double bv = 1.0, double hv = 1.0)
    {
      cout << endl << "Constructor called.";
      m_Length = lv;                    // Set values of
      m_Width = bv;                     // data members
      m_Height = hv;
    }

    // Function to calculate the volume of a box
    double Volume()
    {
```

```
      return m_Length*m_Width*m_Height;
   }

   // Function to compare two boxes which returns true (1)
   // if the first is greater than the second, and false (0) otherwise
   int Compare(CBox xBox)
   {
     return this->Volume() > xBox.Volume();
   }

   private:
     double m_Length;                    // Length of a box in inches
     double m_Width;                     // Width of a box in inches
     double m_Height;                    // Height of a box in inches

};

int main()
{
   CBox match(2.2, 1.1, 0.5);           // Declare match box
   CBox cigar(8.0, 5.0,1.0);            // Declare cigar box

   if(cigar.Compare(match))
     cout << endl
          << "match is smaller than cigar";
   else
     cout << endl
          << "match is equal to or larger than cigar";

   cout << endl;
   return 0;
}
```

How It Works

The member function `Compare()` returns `true` if the prefixed `CBox` object in the function call has a greater volume than the `CBox` object specified as an argument, and `false` if it doesn't. In the `return` statements, the prefixed object is referred to through the pointer `this`, used with the indirect member access operator, `->`, that you saw earlier in this chapter.

> *Remember that you use the direct member access operator when accessing members through objects and the indirect member access operator when accessing members through pointers to objects.* `this` *is a pointer so you use the* `->` *operator.*

The `->` operator works the same for pointers to class objects as it did when you were dealing with a `struct`. Here, using the pointer `this` demonstrates that it exists and *does* work, but it's quite unnecessary to use it explicitly in this case. If you change the `return` statement in the `Compare()` function to be

```
   return Volume() > xBox.Volume();
```

you'll find that the program works just as well. Any references to unadorned member names are automatically assumed to be the members of the object pointed to by `this`.

You use the `Compare()` function in `main()` to check the relationship between the volumes of the objects `match` and `cigar`. The output from the program is:

```
Constructor called.
Constructor called.
match is smaller than cigar
```

This confirms that the `cigar` object is larger than the `match` object.

It also wasn't essential to define the `Compare()` function as a class member. You could just as well have written it as an ordinary function with the objects as arguments. Note that this isn't true of the function `Volume()`, because it needs to access the `private` data members of the class. Of course, if you implemented the `Compare()` function as an ordinary function, it wouldn't have access to the pointer `this`, but it would still be very simple:

```
// Comparing two CBox objects - ordinary function version
int Compare(CBox B1, CBox B2)
{
   return B1.Volume() > B2.Volume();
}
```

This has both objects as arguments and returns `true` if the volume of the first is greater than the last. You would use this function to perform the same function as in the last example with this statement:

```
if(Compare(cigar, match))
   cout << endl
        << "match is smaller than cigar";
else
   cout << endl
        << "match is equal to or larger than cigar";
```

If anything, this looks slightly better and easier to read than the original version; however, there's a much better way to do this, which you will learn about in the next chapter.

const Objects of a Class

The `Volume()` function that you defined for the `CBox` class does not alter the object for which it is called; neither does a function such as `getHeight()` that returns the value of the `m_Height` member. Likewise, the `Compare()` function in the previous example didn't change the class objects at all. This may seem at first sight to be a mildly interesting but largely irrelevant observation, but it isn't — it's quite important. Let's think about it.

You will undoubtedly want to create class objects that are fixed from time to time, just like values such as `pi` or `inchesPerFoot` that you might declare as `const double`. Suppose you wanted to define a `CBox` object as `const` — because it was a very important standard sized box, for instance. You might define it with the following statement:

```
const CBox standard(3.0, 5.0, 8.0);
```

Now that you have defined your standard box having dimensions 3 × 5 × 8, you don't want it messed about with. In particular, you don't want to allow the values stored in its data members to be altered. How can you be sure they won't be?

Well, you already are. If you declare an object of a class as const, the compiler will not allow any member function to be called for it that might alter it. You can demonstrate this quite easily by modifying the declaration for the object, cigar, in the previous example to:

```
const CBox cigar(8.0, 5.0,1.0);                 // Declare cigar box
```

If you try recompiling the program with this change, it won't compile. You see the error message:

```
error C2662: 'compare' : cannot convert 'this' pointer from 'const class CBox' to
'class CBox &'          Conversion loses qualifiers
```

This is produced for the if statement that calls the Compare() member of cigar. An object that you declare as const will always have a this pointer that is const, so the compiler will not allow any member function to be called that does not assume the this pointer that is passed to it is const. You need to find out how to make the this pointer in a member function const.

const Member Functions of a Class

To make the this pointer in a member function const, you must declare the function as const within the class definition. Take a look at how you do that with the Compare() member of CBox. The class definition needs to be modified to the following:

```
class CBox                                  // Class definition at global scope
{
  public:
    // Constructor definition
    CBox(double lv = 1.0, double bv = 1.0, double hv = 1.0)
    {
      cout << endl << "Constructor called.";
      m_Length = lv;                   // Set values of
      m_Width = bv;                    // data members
      m_Height = hv;
    }

    // Function to calculate the volume of a box
    double Volume()
    {
      return m_Length*m_Width*m_Height;
    }

    // Function to compare two boxes which returns true (1)
    // if the first is greater than the second, and false (0) otherwise
    int Compare(CBox xBox) const
    {
      return this->Volume() > xBox.Volume();
    }

  private:
```

```
      double m_Length;                     // Length of a box in inches
      double m_Width;                      // Width of a box in inches
      double m_Height;                     // Height of a box in inches
};
```

To specify that a member function is `const`, you just append the `const` keyword to the function header. Note that you can only do this with class member functions, not with ordinary global functions. Declaring a function as `const` is only meaningful in the case of a function that is a member of a class. The effect is to make the `this` pointer in the function `const`, which in turn means that you cannot write a data member of the class on the left of an assignment within the function definition; it will be flagged as an error by the compiler. A `const` member function cannot call a non-`const` member function of the same class, since this would potentially modify the object.

When you declare an object as `const`, the member functions that you call for it must be declared as `const`; otherwise the program will not compile.

Member Function Definitions Outside the Class

When the definition of a `const` member function appears outside the class, the header for the definition must have the keyword `const` added, just as the declaration within the class does. In fact, you should always declare all member functions that do not alter the class object for which they are called as `const`. With this in mind, the `CBox` class could be defined as:

```
class CBox                               // Class definition at global scope
{
  public:
    // Constructor
    CBox(double lv = 1.0, double bv = 1.0, double hv = 1.0);

    double Volume() const;               // Calculate the volume of a box
    int Compare(CBox xBox) const;        // Compare two boxes

  private:
    double m_Length;                     // Length of a box in inches
    double m_Width;                      // Width of a box in inches
    double m_Height;                     // Height of a box in inches
};
```

This assumes that all function members are defined separately, including the constructor. Both the `Volume()` and `Compare()` members have been declared as `const`. The `Volume()` function is now defined outside the class as:

```
double CBox::Volume() const
{
  return m_Length*m_Width*m_Height;
}
```

The `Compare()` function definition is:

```
int CBox::Compare(CBox xBox) const
{
```

```
        return this->Volume() > xBox.Volume();
    }
```

As you can see, the `const` modifier appears in both definitions. If you leave it out, the code will not compile. A function with a `const` modifier is a different function from one without, even though the name and parameters are exactly the same. Indeed you can have both `const` and non-`const` versions of a function in a class, and sometimes this can be very useful.

With the class declared as shown, the constructor also needs to be defined separately, like this:

```
CBox::CBox(double lv, double bv, double hv):
                m_Length(lv), m_Width(bv), m_Height(hv)
{
    cout << endl << "Constructor called.";
}
```

Arrays of Objects of a Class

You can declare an array of objects of a class in exactly the same way that you have declared an ordinary array where the elements were one of the built-in types. Each element of an array of class objects causes the default constructor to be called.

Try It Out   Arrays of Class Objects

We can use the class definition of CBox from the last example but modified to include a specific default constructor:

```
// Ex7_11.cpp
// Using an array of class objects
#include <iostream>
using std::cout;
using std::endl;

class CBox                            // Class definition at global scope
{
  public:
    // Constructor definition
    CBox(double lv, double bv = 1.0, double hv = 1.0)
    {
      cout << endl << "Constructor called.";
      m_Length = lv;                  // Set values of
      m_Width = bv;                   // data members
      m_Height = hv;
    }

    CBox()                            // Default constructor
    {
      cout << endl
          << "Default constructor called.";
      m_Length = m_Width = m_Height = 1.0;
```

```
        }

        // Function to calculate the volume of a box
        double Volume() const
        {
          return m_Length*m_Width*m_Height;
        }

      private:
        double m_Length;              // Length of a box in inches
        double m_Width;               // Width of a box in inches
        double m_Height;              // Height of a box in inches

};

int main()
{
  CBox boxes[5];                      // Array of CBox objects declared
  CBox cigar(8.0, 5.0, 1.0);          // Declare cigar box

  cout << endl
       << "Volume of boxes[3] = " << boxes[3].Volume()
       << endl
       << "Volume of cigar = " << cigar.Volume();

  cout << endl;
  return 0;
}
```

The program produces this output:

```
Default constructor called.
Default constructor called.
Default constructor called.
Default constructor called.
Default constructor called.
Constructor called.
Volume of boxes[3] = 1
Volume of cigar = 40
```

How It Works

You have modified the constructor-accepting arguments so that only two default values are supplied, and you have added a default constructor that initializes the data members to 1 after displaying a message that it was called. You are now able to see *which* constructor was called *when*. The constructors now have quite distinct parameter lists, so there's no possibility of the compiler confusing them.

You can see from the output that the default constructor was called five times, once for each element of the boxes array. The other constructor was called to create the cigar object. It's clear from the output that the default constructor initialization is working satisfactorily, as the volume of the array element is 1.

Static Members of a Class

Both data members and function members of a class can be declared as `static`. Because the context is a class definition, there's a little more to it than the effect of the `static` keyword outside of a class, so let's look at static data members.

Static Data Members of a Class

When you declare data members of a class to be `static`, the effect is that the static data members are defined only once and are shared between all objects of the class. Each object gets its own copies of each of the ordinary data members of a class, but only one instance of each static data member exists, regardless of how many class objects have been defined. Figure 7-7 illustrates this.

One use for a static data member is to count how many objects actually exist. You could add a static data member to the public section of the CBox class by adding the following statement to the previous class definition:

```
static int objectCount;                   // Count of objects in existence
```

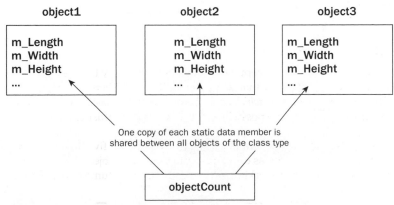

Class Definition

```
class CBox
{
    public:
        static int objectCount;

        ...
    private:
        double m_Length;
        double m_Width;
        double m_Height;
        ...
```

object1

m_Length
m_Width
m_Height
...

object2

m_Length
m_Width
m_Height
...

object3

m_Length
m_Width
m_Height
...

One copy of each static data member is
shared between all objects of the class type

objectCount

Figure 7-7

You now have a problem. How do you initialize the static data member?

You can't initialize the static data member in the class definition — that's simply a blueprint for an object, and initializing values are not allowed. You don't want to initialize it in a constructor because you want to increment it every time the constructor is called so the count of the number of objects created is accumulated. You can't initialize it in another member function because a member function is associated with an object, and you want it initialized before any object is created. The answer is to write the initialization of the static data member outside of the class definition with this statement:

```
int CBox::objectCount = 0;          // Initialize static member of class CBox
```

Notice that the static keyword is not included here; however, you do need to qualify the member name by using the class name and the scope resolution operator so that the compiler understands that you are referring to a static member of the class. Otherwise, you would simply create a global variable that had nothing to do with the class.

Try It Out   Counting Instances

Let's add the static data member and the object-counting capability to the last example.

```cpp
// Ex7_12.cpp
// Using a static data member in a class
#include <iostream>
using std::cout;
using std::endl;

class CBox                          // Class definition at global scope
{
  public:
    static int objectCount;         // Count of objects in existence

    // Constructor definition
    CBox(double lv, double bv = 1.0, double hv = 1.0)
    {
      cout << endl << "Constructor called.";
      m_Length = lv;                // Set values of
      m_Width = bv;                 // data members
      m_Height = hv;
      objectCount++;
    }

    CBox()                          // Default constructor
    {
      cout << endl
           << "Default constructor called.";
      m_Length = m_Width = m_Height = 1.0;
      objectCount++;
    }

    // Function to calculate the volume of a box
    double Volume() const
    {
```

```
        return m_Length*m_Width*m_Height;
    }

  private:
    double m_Length;              // Length of a box in inches
    double m_Width;               // Width of a box in inches
    double m_Height;              // Height of a box in inches
};

int CBox::objectCount = 0;        // Initialize static member of CBox class

int main()
{
  CBox boxes[5];                  // Array of CBox objects declared
  CBox cigar(8.0, 5.0, 1.0);      // Declare cigar box

  cout << endl << endl
       << "Number of objects (through class) = "
       << CBox::objectCount;

  cout << endl
       << "Number of objects (through object) = "
       << boxes[2].objectCount;

  cout << endl;
  return 0;
}
```

This example produces the following output:

```
Default constructor called.
Default constructor called.
Default constructor called.
Default constructor called.
Default constructor called.
Constructor called.
Number of objects (through class) = 6
Number of objects (through object) = 6
```

How It Works

This code shows that it doesn't matter how you refer to the static member ObjectCount (whether through the class itself or any of the objects of that class). The value is the same and it is equal to the number of objects of that class that have been created. The six objects are obviously the five elements of the Boxes array, plus the cigar object. It's interesting to note that static members of a class exist even though there may be no members of the class in existence. This is evidently the case, because you initialized the static member ObjectCount before any class objects were declared.

Static data members are automatically created when your program begins, and they will be initialized with 0 unless you initialize them with some other value. Thus you need only to initialize static data members of a class if you want them to start out with a value other than 0.

Static Function Members of a Class

By declaring a function member as static, you make it independent of any particular object of the class. Referencing members of the class from within a static function must be done using qualified names (as you would do with an ordinary global function accessing a public data member). The static member function has the advantage that it exists, and can be called, even if no objects of the class exist. In this case, only static data members can be used because they are the only ones that exist. Thus, you can call a static function member of a class to examine static data members, even when you do not know for certain that any objects of the class exist. You could, therefore, use a static member function to determine whether some objects of the class have been created or, indeed, how many have been created.

Of course, after the objects have been defined, a static member function can access private as well as public members of class objects. A static function might have this prototype:

```
static void Afunction(int n);
```

A static function can be called in relation to a particular object by a statement such as the following:

```
aBox.Afunction(10);
```

where aBox is an object of the class. The same function could also be called without reference to an object. In this case, the statement would take the following form,

```
CBox::Afunction(10);
```

where CBox is the class name. Using the class name and the scope resolution operator serves to tell the compiler to which class the function Afunction() belongs.

Pointers and References to Class Objects

Using pointers, and particularly references to class objects, is very important in object-oriented programming and in particular in the specification of function parameters. Class objects can involve considerable amounts of data, so using the pass-by-value mechanism by specifying parameters to a function to be objects can be very time-consuming and inefficient because each argument object will be copied. There are also some techniques involving the use of references that are essential to some operations with classes. As you'll see, you can't write a copy constructor without using a reference parameter.

Pointers to Class Objects

You declare a pointer to a class object in the same way that you declare other pointers. For example, a pointer to objects of the class CBox is declared in this statement:

```
CBox* pBox = 0;                    // Declare a pointer to CBox
```

You can now use this to store the address of a CBox object in an assignment in the usual way, using the address operator:

```
pBox = &cigar;                     // Store address of CBox object cigar in pBox
```

As you saw when you used the `this` pointer in the definition of the `Compare()` member function, you can call a function using a pointer to an object. You can call the function `Volume()` for the pointer `pBox` in a statement like this:

```
cout << pBox->Volume();              // Display volume of object pointed to by pBox
```

Again, this uses the indirect member selection operator. This is the typical notation used by most programmers for this kind of operation, *so from now on I'll use it universally.*

Try It Out   Pointers to Classes

Let's try exercising the indirect member access operator a little more. We will use the example `Ex7_10.cpp` as a base, but change it a little.

```cpp
// Ex7_13.cpp
// Exercising the indirect member access operator
#include <iostream>
using std::cout;
using std::endl;

class CBox                               // Class definition at global scope
{
  public:
    // Constructor definition
    CBox(double lv = 1.0, double bv = 1.0, double hv = 1.0)
    {
      cout << endl << "Constructor called.";
      m_Length = lv;                     // Set values of
      m_Width = bv;                      // data members
      m_Height = hv;
    }

    // Function to calculate the volume of a box
    double Volume() const
    {
      return m_Length*m_Width*m_Height;
    }

    // Function to compare two boxes which returns true (1)
    // if the first is greater that the second, and false (0) otherwise
    int Compare(CBox* pBox) const
    {
      return this->Volume() > pBox->Volume();
    }

  private:
    double m_Length;                     // Length of a box in inches
    double m_Width;                      // Width of a box in inches
    double m_Height;                     // Height of a box in inches
};

int main()
{
```

377

```
CBox boxes[5];                         // Array of CBox objects declared
CBox match(2.2, 1.1, 0.5);             // Declare match box
CBox cigar(8.0, 5.0, 1.0);             // Declare cigar Box
CBox* pB1 = &cigar;              // Initialize pointer to cigar object address
CBox* pB2 = 0;                         // Pointer to CBox initialized to null

cout << endl
    << "Address of cigar is " << pB1      // Display address
    << endl
    << "Volume of cigar is "
    << pB1->Volume();                      // Volume of object pointed to

pB2 = &match;
if(pB2->Compare(pB1))                      // Compare via pointers
  cout << endl
      << "match is greater than cigar";
else
  cout << endl
      << "match is less than or equal to cigar";

pB1 = boxes;                           // Set to address of array
boxes[2] = match;                      // Set 3rd element to match
cout << endl                           // Now access thru pointer
    << "Volume of boxes[2] is " << (pB1 + 2)->Volume();

cout << endl;
return 0;
}
```

If you run the example, the output looks something like that shown here:

```
Constructor called.
Constructor called.
Constructor called.
Constructor called.
Constructor called.
Constructor called.
Constructor called.
Address of cigar is 0012FE20
Volume of cigar is 40
match is less than or equal to cigar
Volume of boxes[2] is 1.21
```

Of course, the value of the address for the object cigar *may well be different on your PC.*

How It Works

The only change to the class definition isn't one of great substance. You have only modified the Compare()
function to accept a pointer to a CBox object as an argument, and now you know about const member
functions. You declare it as const because it doesn't alter the object. The function main() merely exercises
pointers to CBox type objects in various, rather arbitrary, ways.

Within the `main()` function you declare two pointers to `CBox` objects after declaring an array, `Boxes`, and the `CBox` objects `cigar` and `match`. The first, `pB1`, is initialized with the address of the object `cigar`, and the second, `pB2`, is initialized to `NULL`. All of this uses the pointer in exactly the same way you would when you're applying a pointer to a basic type. The fact that you are using a pointer to a type that you have defined yourself makes no difference.

You use `pB1` with the indirect member access operator to generate the volume of the object pointed to, and the result is displayed. You then assign the address of `match` to `pB2` and use both pointers in calling the compare function. Because the argument of the function `Compare()` is a pointer to a `CBox` object, the function uses the indirect member selection operator in calling the `Volume()` function for the object.

To demonstrate that you can use address arithmetic on the pointer `pB1` when using it to select the member function, you set `pB1` to the address of the first element of the array of type `CBox`, `boxes`. In this case, you select the third element of the array and calculate its volume. This is the same as the volume of `match`.

You can see from the output that there were seven calls of the constructor for `CBox` objects: five because of the array `Boxes`, plus one each for the objects `cigar` and `match`.

Overall, there's virtually no difference between using a pointer to a class object and using a pointer to a basic type, such as `double`.

References to Class Objects

References really come into their own when they are used with classes. As with pointers, there is virtually no difference between the way you declare and use references to class objects and the way in which we've already declared and used references to variables of basic types. To declare a reference to the object `cigar`, for instance, you would write this:

```
    CBox& rcigar = cigar;                    // Define reference to object cigar
```

To use a reference to calculate the volume of the object `cigar`, you would just use the reference name where the object name would otherwise appear:

```
    cout << rcigar.Volume();                 // Output volume of cigar thru a reference
```

As you may remember, a reference acts as an alias for the object it refers to, so the usage is exactly the same as using the original object name.

Implementing a Copy Constructor

The importance of references is really in the context of arguments and return values in functions, particularly class member functions. Let's return to the question of the copy constructor as a first toe in the water. For the moment, I'll sidestep the question of *when* you need to write your own copy constructor and concentrate on the problem of *how* you can write one. I'll use the `CBox` class just to make the discussion more concrete.

The copy constructor is a constructor that creates an object by initializing it with an existing object of the same class. It therefore needs to accept an object of the class as an argument. You might consider writing the prototype like this:

```
CBox(CBox initB);
```

Now consider what happens when this constructor is called. If you write this declaration:

```
CBox myBox = cigar;
```

this generates a call of the copy constructor as follows:

```
CBox::CBox(cigar);
```

This seems to be no problem, until you realize that the argument is passed by value. So, before the object `cigar` can be passed, the compiler needs to arrange to make a copy of it. Therefore, it calls the copy constructor to make a copy of the argument for the call of the copy constructor. Unfortunately, since it is passed by value, this call also needs a copy of its argument to be made, so the copy constructor is called, and so on and so on. You end up with an infinite number of calls to the copy constructor.

The solution, as I'm sure you have guessed, is to use a `const` reference parameter. You can write the prototype of the copy constructor like this:

```
CBox(const CBox& initB);
```

Now, the argument to the copy constructor doesn't need to be copied. It is used to initialize the reference parameter, so no copying takes place. As you remember from the discussion on references, if a parameter to a function is a reference, no copying of the argument occurs when the function is called. The function accesses the argument variable in the caller function directly. The `const` qualifier ensures that the argument can't be modified in the function.

> *This is another important use of the* `const` *qualifier. You should always declare a reference parameter of a function as* `const` *unless the function will modify it.*

You could implement the copy constructor as follows:

```
CBox::CBox(const CBox& initB)
{
  m_Length = initB.m_Length;
  m_Width = initB.m_Width;
  m_Height = initB.m_Height;
}
```

This definition of the copy constructor assumes that it appears outside of the class definition. The constructor name is therefore qualified with the class name using the scope resolution operator. Each data member of the object being created is initialized with the corresponding member of the object passed as an argument. Of course, you could equally well use the initialization list to set the values of the object.

This case is not an example of when you need to write a copy constructor. As you have seen, the default copy constructor works perfectly well with CBox objects. I will get to *why* and *when* you need to write your own copy constructor in the next chapter.

C++/CLI Programming

The C++/CLI programming language has its own `struct` and `class` types. In fact C++/CLI allows the definition of two different `struct` and `class` types that have different characteristics; `value struct` types and `value class` types, and `ref struct` types and `ref class` types. Each of the two word combinations, `value struct`, `ref struct`, `value class`, and `ref class`, is a keyword and distinct from the keywords `struct` and `class`; `value` and `ref` are not by themselves keywords. As in native C++, the only difference between a struct and a class in C++/CLI is that members of a struct are public by default whereas members of a class are private by default. One essential difference between value classes (or value structs) and reference classes (or ref structs) is that variables of value class types contain their own data whereas variables to access reference class types must be handles and therefore contain an address.

Note that member functions of C++/CLI classes cannot be declared as `const`. Another difference from native C++ is that the `this` pointer in a non-static function member of a value class type T is an interior pointer of type `interior_ptr<T>`, whereas the `this` pointer in a ref class type T is a handle of type `T^`. You need to keep this in mind when returning the `this` pointer from a C++/CLI function or storing it in a local variable. There are three other restrictions that apply to both value classes and reference classes:

❑ A value class or ref class cannot contain fields that are native C++ arrays or native C++ class types.

❑ Friend functions are not allowed.

❑ A value class or ref class cannot have members that are bit-fields.

You have already heard back in Chapter 4 that the fundamental type names such as type `int` and type `double` are shorthand for value class types in a CLR program. When you declare a data item of a value class type, memory for it will be allocated on the stack but you can create value class objects on the heap using the `gcnew` operator, in which case the variable that you use to access the value class object must be a handle. For example:

```
double pi = 3.142;           // pi is stored on the stack
int^ lucky = gcnew int(7);   // lucky is a handle and 7 is stored on the heap
double^ two = 2.0;           // two is a handle, and 2.0 is stored on the heap
```

You can use any of these variables in arithmetic expression but you must use the * operator to dereference the handle to access the value. For example:

```
Console::WriteLine(L"2pi = {0}", *two*pi);
```

Note that you could write the product as `pi**two` and get the right result but it is better to use parentheses in such instances and write `pi*(*two)`, as this makes the code clearer.

Defining Value Class Types

I won't discuss `value struct` types separately from `value class` types as the only difference is that the members of a `value struct` type are `public` by default whereas `value class` members are private by default. A value class is intended to be a relatively simple class type that provides the possibility for you to define new primitive types that can be used in a similar way to the fundamental types; however, you won't be in a position to do this fully until you learn about a topic called **operator overloading** in the next chapter. A variable of a value class type is created on the stack and stores the value directly, but as you have already seen, you can also use a tracking handle to reference a value class type stored on the CLR heap.

Take an example of a simple value class definition:

```
// Class representing a height
value class Height
{
private:
   // Records the height in feet and inches
   int feet;
   int inches;

public:
   // Create a height from inches value
   Height(int ins)
   {
      feet = ins/12;
      inches = ins%12;
   }

   // Create a height from feet and inches
   Height(int ft, int ins) : feet(ft), inches(ins){}
};
```

This defines a value class type with the name `Height`. It has two private fields that are both of type `int` that record a height in feet and inches. The class has two constructors — one to create a `Height` object from a number of inches supplied as the argument, and the other to create a `Height` object from both a feet and inches specification. The latter should really check that the number of inches supplied as an argument is less than 12, but I'll leave you to add that as a fine point. To create a variable of type `Height` you could write:

```
Height tall = Height(7, 8);          // Height is 7 feet 8 inches
```

This creates the variable, tall, containing a `Height` object representing 7 feet 8 inches; this object is created by calling the constructor with two parameters.

```
Height baseHeight;
```

This statement creates a variable, `baseHeight`, that will be automatically initialized to a height of zero. The `Height` class does not have a no-arg constructor specified and because it is a value class, you are not permitted to supply one in the class definition. There will be a no-arg constructor included automatically in a value class that will initialize all value type fields to the equivalent of zero and all fields that are handles to `nullptr` and you cannot override the implicit constructor with your own version. It's this default constructor that will be used to create the value of `baseHeight`.

There are a couple of other restrictions on what a value class can contain:

❑   You must not include a copy constructor in a value class definition.

❑   You cannot override the assignment operator in a value class (I'll discuss how you override operators in a class in Chapter 8).

Value class objects are always copied by just copying fields and the assignment of one value class object to another is done in the same way. Value classes are intended to be used to represent simple objects defined by a limited amount of data, so for objects that don't fit this specification or where the value class restrictions are problematical you should use `ref class` types to represent them.

Let's take the `Height` class for a test drive.

Try It Out   Defining and Using a Value Class Type

Here's the code to exercise the `Height` value class:

```cpp
// Ex7_14.cpp : main project file.
// Defining and using a value class type

#include "stdafx.h"

using namespace System;

// Class representing a height
value class Height
{
private:
  // Records the height in feet and inches
  int feet;
  int inches;

public:
  // Create a height from inches value
  Height(int ins)
  {
    feet = ins/12;
    inches = ins%12;
  }

  // Create a height from feet and inches
  Height(int ft, int ins) : feet(ft), inches(ins){}
};

int main(array<System::String ^> ^args)
{
  Height myHeight = Height(6,3);
  Height^ yourHeight = Height(70);
  Height hisHeight = *yourHeight;

  Console::WriteLine(L"My height is {0}", myHeight);
  Console::WriteLine(L"Your height is {0}", yourHeight);
  Console::WriteLine(L"His height is {0}", hisHeight);
  return 0;
}
```

Executing this program results in the following output:

```
My height is Height
Your height is Height
His height is Height
```

383

How It Works

Well, the output is a bit monotonous and perhaps less than we were hoping for, but let's come back to that a little later. In the `main()` function, you create three variables with the following statement:

```
Height myHeight = Height(6,3);
Height^ yourHeight = Height(70);
Height hisHeight = *yourHeight;
```

The first variable is of type `Height` so the object that represents a height of 6 feet 3 inches is allocated on the stack. The second variable is a handle of type `Height^` so the object representing a height of 5 feet 10 inches is created on the CLR heap. The third variable is another stack variable that is a copy of the object referenced by `yourHeight`. Because `yourHeight` is a handle, you have to dereference it to assign it to the `hisHeight` variable and the result is that `hisHeight` contains a duplicate of the object referenced by `yourHeight`. Variables of a value class type always contain a unique object so two such variables cannot reference the same object; assigning one variable of a value class type to another always involves copying. Of course, several handles can reference a single object and assigning the value of one handle to another simply copies the address (or `nullptr`) from one to the other so that both objects reference the same object.

The output is produced by the three calls of the `Console::WriteLine()` function. Unfortunately the output is not the values of the value class objects, but simply the class name. So how did this come about? It was optimistic to expect the values to be produced — after all, how is the compiler to know how they should be presented? `Height` objects contain two values — which one should be presented as the value? The class has to have a way to make the value available in this context.

The ToString() Function in a Class

Every C++/CLI class that you define has a `ToString()` function — I'll explain how this comes about in the next chapter when I discuss class inheritance — that returns a handle to a string that is supposed to represent the class object. The compiler arranges for the `ToString()` function for an object to be called whenever it recognizes that a string representation of an object is required and you can call it explicitly if necessary. For example, you could write this:

```
double pi = 3.142;
Console::WriteLine(pi.ToString());
```

This outputs the value of `pi` as a string and it is the `ToString()` function that is defined in the `System::Double` class that provides the string. Of course, you would get the same output without explicitly calling the `ToString()` function.

The default version of the `ToString()` function that you get in the `Height` class just outputs the class name because there is no way to know ahead of time what value should be returned as a string for an object of your class type. To get an appropriate value output by the `Console::WriteLine()` function in the previous example, you must add a `ToString()` function to the `Height` class that presents the value of an object in the form that you want.

Here's how the class looks with a `ToString()` function:

```
// Class representing a height
value class Height
```

```
{
private:
  // Records the height in feet and inches
  int feet;
  int inches;

public:
  // Create a height from inches value
  Height(int ins)
  {
    feet = ins/12;
    inches = ins%12;
  }

  // Create a height from feet and inches
  Height(int ft, int ins) : feet(ft), inches(ins){}

  // Create a string representation of the object
  virtual String^ ToString() override
  {
    return feet + L" feet "+ inches + L" inches";
  }
};
```

The combination of the `virtual` keyword before the return type for `ToString()` and the `override` keyword following the parameter list for the function indicates that this version of the `ToString()` function overrides the version of the function that is present in the class by default. You'll hear a lot more about this in Chapter 8. Our new version of the `ToString()` function now outputs a string expressing a height in feet and inches. If you add this function to the class definition in the previous example, you get the following output when you compile and execute the program:

```
My height is 6 feet 3 inches
Your height is 5 feet 10 inches
His height is 5 feet 10 inches
```

This is more like what you were expecting to get before. You can see from the output that the `WriteLine()` function quite happily deals with an object on the CLR heap that you reference through the `yourHeight` handle, as well as the `myHeight` and `hisHeight` objects that were created on the stack.

Literal Fields

The factor 12 that you use to convert from feet to inches and vice versa is a little troubling. It is an example of what is called a "magic number," where a person reading the code has to guess or deduce its significance and origin. In this case it's fairly obvious what the 12 is but there will be many instances where the origin of a numerical constant in a calculation is not so apparent. C++/CLI has a **literal field** facility for introducing named constants into a class that will solve the problem in this case. Here's how you can eliminate the magic number from the code in the single-argument constructor in the `Height` class:

```
value class Height
{
private:
  // Records the height in feet and inches
  int feet;
  int inches;
```

```
      literal int inchesPerFoot = 12;

  public:
    // Create a height from inches value
    Height(int ins)
    {
      feet = ins/ inchesPerFoot;
      inches = ins% inchesPerFoot;
    }

    // Create a height from feet and inches
    Height(int ft, int ins) : feet(ft), inches(ins){}

    // Create a string representation of the object
    virtual  String^ ToString() override
    {
      return feet + L" feet "+ inches + L" inches";
    }
};
```

Now the constructor uses the name `inchesPerFoot` instead of 12, so there is no doubt as to what is going on.

You can define the value of a literal field in terms of other literal fields as long as the names of the fields you are using to specify the value are defined first. For example:

```
value class Height
{
  // Other code...
  literal int inchesPerFoot = 12;
  literal double millimetersPerInch = 25.4;
  literal double millimetersPerFoot = inchesPerFoot*millimetersPerInch;

  // Other code...
};
```

Here you define the value for the literal field `millimetersPerFoot` as the product of the other two literal fields. If you were to move the definition of the `millimetersPerFoot` field so that it precedes either or both of the other two, the code would not compile.

A literal field can only be initialized with a value that is a constant integral value, an enum value, or a string; this obviously limits the possible types for a literal field to those you can initialize in this way.

Defining Reference Class Types

A reference class is comparable to a native C++ class in capabilities and does not have the restrictions that a value class has. Unlike a native C++ class, however, a reference class does not have a default copy constructor or a default assignment operator. If your class needs to support either of these operators, you must explicitly add a function for the capability — you'll see how in the next chapter.

You define a reference class using the `ref class` keyword — both words together separated by one or more spaces represent a single keyword. Here's the `CBox` class from the `Ex7_07` example redefined as a reference class.

```
ref class Box
{
  public:
    // No-arg constructor supplying default field values
    Box(): Length(1.0), Width(1.0), Height(1.0)
    {
      Console::WriteLine(L"No-arg constructor called.");
    }

    // Constructor definition using an initialisation list
    Box(double lv, double bv, double hv):
                          Length(lv), Width(bv), Height(hv)
    {
      Console::WriteLine(L"Constructor called.");
    }

    // Function to calculate the volume of a box
    double Volume()
    {
      return Length*Width*Height;
    }

  private:
    double Length;                 // Length of a box in inches
    double Width;                  // Width of a box in inches
    double Height;                 // Height of a box in inches
};
```

Note first that I have removed the `C` prefix for the class name and the `m_` prefix for member names because this notation is not recommended for C++/CLI classes. You cannot specify default values for function and constructor parameters in C++/CLI classes so you have to add a no-arg constructor to the `Box` class to fulfill this function. The no-arg constructor just initializes the three private fields with 1.0.

Try It Out   Using a Reference Class Type

Here's an example that uses the `Box` class that you saw in the previous section.

```
// Ex7_15.cpp : main project file.
// Using the Box reference class type

#include "stdafx.h"

using namespace System;

ref class Box
{
```

```
  public:
    // No-arg constructor supplying default field values
    Box(): Length(1.0), Width(1.0), Height(1.0)
    {
      Console::WriteLine(L"No-arg constructor called.");
    }

    // Constructor definition using an initialisation list
    Box(double lv, double bv, double hv):
                          Length(lv), Width(bv), Height(hv)
    {
      Console::WriteLine(L"Constructor called.");
    }

    // Function to calculate the volume of a box
    double Volume()
    {
      return Length*Width*Height;
    }

  private:
    double Length;                  // Length of a box in inches
    double Width;                   // Width of a box in inches
    double Height;                  // Height of a box in inches
};
```

```
int main(array<System::String ^> ^args)
{
  Box^ aBox;                              // Handle of type Box^
  Box^ newBox = gcnew Box(10, 15, 20);
  aBox = gcnew Box;                       // Initialize with default Box
  Console::WriteLine(L"Default box volume is {0}", aBox->Volume());
  Console::WriteLine(L"New box volume is {0}", newBox->Volume());
  return 0;
}
```

The output from this example is:

```
Constructor called.
No-arg constructor called.
Default box volume is 1
New box volume is 3000
```

How It Works

The first statement in `main()` creates a handle to a `Box` object.

```
Box^ aBox;                              // Handle of type Box^
```

No object is created by this statement, just the tracking handle, `aBox`. The `aBox` variable is initialized by default with `nullptr` so it does not point to anything yet. In contrast, a variable of a value class type always contains an object.

The next statement creates a handle to a new `Box` object.

```
Box^ newBox = gcnew Box(10, 15, 20);
```

The constructor accepting three arguments is called to create the `Box` object on the heap and the address is stored in the handle, `newBox`. As you know, objects of ref class types are always created on the CLR heap and are referenced generally using a handle.

You create a `Box` object by calling the no-arg constructor and store its address in `aBox`.

```
aBox = gcnew Box;                        // Initialize with default Box
```

This object has the `Length`, `Width`, and `Height` fields set to 1.0.

Finally you output the volumes of the two Box objects you have created.

```
Console::WriteLine(L"Default box volume is {0}", aBox->Volume());
Console::WriteLine(L"New box volume is {0}", newBox->Volume());
```

Because `aBox` and `newBox` are handles, you use the `->` operator to call the `Volume()` function for the objects to which they refer.

Defining a Copy Constructor for a Reference Class Type

You are unlikely to be doing it very often but if you do pass objects of a reference class type to a function by value, you must implement a public copy constructor; this situation can arise with the Standard Template Library implementation for the CLR, which you will learn about in Chapter 10. The parameter to the copy constructor must be a `const` reference, so you would define the copy constructor for the `Box` class like this:

```
Box(const Box% box) : Length(box.Length), Width(box.Width), Height(box.Height)
{}
```

In general, the form of the copy constructor for a ref class `T` that allows a `ref` type object of type `T` to be passed by value to a function is:

```
T(const T% t)
{
  if(*this != t)
  {
    // Code to make the copy...
  }
  return *this;
}
```

Occasionally you may also need to implement a copy constructor that takes an argument that is a handle. Here's how you could do that for the `Box` class:

```
Box(const Box^ box) : Length(box->Length), Width(box->Width), Height(box->Height)
{}
```

As you can see, there is little difference between this and the previous version.

Class Properties

A **property** is a member of either a value class or a reference class that you access as though it were a field, but it really isn't a field. The primary difference between a property and a field is that the name of a field refers to a storage location whereas the name of a property does not — it calls a function. A property has `get()` and `set()` accessor functions to retrieve and set its value respectively so when you use a property name to obtain its value, behind the scenes you are calling the `get()` function for the property and when you use the name of a property on the right of an assignment statement you are calling its `set()` function. If a property only provides a definition for the `get()` function, it is called a **read-only property** because the `set()` function is not available to set the property value. A property may just have the `set()` function defined for it, in which case it is described as a **write-only property**.

A class can contain two different kinds of properties: **scalar properties** and **indexed properties**. Scalar properties are a single value accessed using the property name whereas indexed properties are a set of values that you access using an index between square brackets following the property name. The `String` class has the scalar property, `Length`, that provides you with the number of characters in a string, and for a `String` object `str` you access the `Length` property using the expression `str>Length` because `str` is a handle. Of course, to access a property with the name `MyProp` for a value class object store in the variable `val`, you would use the expression `val.MyProp`, just like accessing a field. The `Length` property for a string is an example of a read-only property because no `set()` function is defined for it — you cannot set the length of a string as a `String` object is immutable. The `String` class also gives you access to individual characters in the string as indexed properties. For a string handle, `str`, you can access the third indexed property with the expression `str[2]`, which corresponds to the third character in the string.

Properties can be associated with, and specific to, a particular object, in which case the properties are described as instance properties. The `Length` property for a `String` object is an example of an instance property. You can also specify a property as `static`, in which case the property is associated with the class and the property value will be the same for all objects of the class type. Let's explore properties in a little more depth.

Defining Scalar Properties

As scalar property has a single value and you define a scalar property in a class using the `property` keyword. The `get()` function for a scalar property must have a return type that is the same as the property type and the `set()` function must have a parameter of the same type as the property. Here's an example of a property in the `Height` value class that you saw earlier.

```
value class Height
{
private:
  // Records the height in feet and inches
  int feet;
```

```
   int inches;
   literal int inchesPerFoot = 12;
   literal double inchesToMeters = 2.54/100;

public:
  // Create a height from inches value
  Height(int ins)
  {
    feet = ins / inchesPerFoot;
    inches = ins % inchesPerFoot;
  }

  // Create a height from feet and inches
  Height(int ft, int ins) : feet(ft), inches(ins){}

  // The height in meters as a property
  property double meters
  {
    // Returns the property value
    double get()
    {
      return inchesToMeters*(feet*inchesPerFoot+inches);
    }

    // You would define the set() function for the property here...
  }

  // Create a string representation of the object
  virtual  String^ ToString() override
  {
    return feet + L" feet "+ inches + L" inches";
  }
};
```

The Height class now contains a property with the name meters. The definition of the get function for the property appears between the braces following the property name. You would put the set() function for the property here too, if there were one. Note that there is no semicolon following the braces that enclose the get() and set() function definitions for a property. The get() function for the meters property makes use of a new literal class member, inchesToMeters, to convert the height in inches to meters. Accessing the meters property for an object of type Height makes the height available in meters. Here's how you could do that:

```
Height ht = Height(6, 8);               // Height of 6 feet 8 inches
Console::WriteLine(L"The height is {0} meters", ht.meters);
```

The second statement outputs the value of ht in meters using the expression ht.meters.

You are not obliged to define the get() and set() functions for a property inline; you can define them outside the class definition in a .cpp file. For example, you could specify the meters property in the Height class like this:

```
value class Height
{
```

```
  // Code as before...

public:
  // Code as before...
```

```
  // The height in meters
  property double meters
  {
    double get();                      // Returns the property value

    // You would define the set() function for the property here...
  }
```

```
  // Code as before...
};
```

The get() function for the meters property is now declared but not defined in the Height class, so a definition must be supplied outside the class definition. In the get() function definition in the Height.cpp file the function name must be qualified by the class name and the property name so the definition looks like this:

```
Height::meters::get()
{
  return inchesToMeters*(feet*inchesPerFoot+inches);
}
```

The Height qualifier indicates that this function definition belongs to the Height class and the meters qualifier indicates the function is for the meters property in the class.

Of course, you can define properties for a reference class. Here's an example:

```
ref class Weight
{
private:
  int lbs;
  int oz;

public:
  property int pounds
  {
    int get() { return lbs;  }
    void set(int value) {  lbs = value;  }
  }

  property int ounces
  {
    int get() { return oz;  }
    void set(int value) {  oz = value;  }
  }
};
```

Here the `pounds` and `ounces` properties are used to provide access to the values of the private fields, `lbs` and `oz`. You can set values for the properties of a `Weight` object and access them subsequently like this:

```
Weight^ wt = gcnew Weight;
wt->pounds = 162;
wt->ounces = 12;
Console::WriteLine(L"Weight is {0} lbs {1} oz.", wt->pounds, wt->ounces);
```

A variable accessing a `ref class` object is generally a handle so you must use the `->` operator to access properties of an object of a reference class type.

Trivial Scalar Properties

You can define a scalar property for a class without providing definitions for the `get()` and `set()` functions, in which case it is called a trivial scalar property. To specify a trivial scalar property you just omit the braces containing the `get()` and `set()` function definitions and end the property declaration with a semi-colon. Here's an example of a value class with trivial scalar properties:

```
value class Point
{
public:
  property int x;                           // Trivial property
  property int y;                           // Trivial property

  virtual String^ ToString() override
  {
    return L"(" + x + L"," + y + L")";      // Returns "(x,y)"
  }
};
```

Default `get()` and `set()` function definitions are supplied automatically for each trivial scalar property and these return the property value and set the property value to the argument of the type specified for the property. Private space is allocated to accommodate the property value behind the scenes.

Let's see some scalar properties working.

Try It Out   Using Scalar Properties

This example uses three classes, two value classes, and a ref class:

```
// Ex7_16.cpp : main project file.
// Using scalar properties

#include "stdafx.h"

using namespace System;

// Class defining a person's height
value class Height
{
```

```
private:
  // Records the height in feet and inches
  int feet;
  int inches;

  literal int inchesPerFoot = 12;
  literal double inchesToMeters = 2.54/100;

public:
  // Create a height from inches value
  Height(int ins)
  {
    feet = ins / inchesPerFoot;
    inches = ins % inchesPerFoot;
  }

  // Create a height from feet and inches
  Height(int ft, int ins) : feet(ft), inches(ins){}

  // The height in meters
  property double meters                              // Scalar property
  {
    // Returns the property value
    double get()
    {
      return inchesToMeters*(feet*inchesPerFoot+inches);
    }

    // You would define the set() function for the property here...
  }

  // Create a string representation of the object
  virtual  String^ ToString() override
  {
    return feet + L" feet "+ inches + L" inches";
  }
};
```

```
// Class defining a person's weight
value class Weight
{
private:
  int lbs;
  int oz;

  literal int ouncesPerPound = 16;
  literal double lbsToKg = 1.0/2.2;

public:
  Weight(int pounds, int ounces)
  {
    lbs = pounds;
    oz = ounces;
  }
```

```cpp
    property int pounds                              // Scalar property
    {
      int get() { return lbs;  }
      void set(int value) {  lbs = value;  }
    }

    property int ounces                              // Scalar property
    {
      int get() { return oz;  }
      void set(int value) {  oz = value;  }
    }

    property double kilograms                        // Scalar property
    {
      double get() { return lbsToKg*(lbs + oz/ouncesPerPound);   }
    }

    virtual String^ ToString() override
    { return lbs + L" pounds " + oz + L" ounces"; }
};
```

```cpp
// Class defining a person
ref class Person
{
private:
  Height ht;
  Weight wt;

public:
  property String^ Name;                             // Trivial scalar property
  Person(String^ name, Height h, Weight w) : ht(h), wt(w)
  {
    Name = name;
  }

  Height getHeight(){ return ht;   }
  Weight getWeight(){ return wt;   }
};
```

```cpp
int main(array<System::String ^> ^args)
{
  Weight hisWeight = Weight(185, 7);
  Height hisHeight = Height(6, 3);
  Person^ him = gcnew Person(L"Fred", hisHeight, hisWeight);

  Weight herWeight = Weight(105, 3);
  Height herHeight = Height(5, 2);
  Person^ her = gcnew Person(L"Freda", herHeight, herWeight);

  Console::WriteLine(L"She is {0}", her->Name);
  Console::WriteLine(L"Her weight is {0:F2} kilograms.",
                                          her->getWeight().kilograms);
  Console::WriteLine(L"Her height is {0} which is {1:F2} meters.",
                          her->getHeight(),her->getHeight().meters);
```

```
    Console::WriteLine(L"He is {0}", him->Name);
    Console::WriteLine(L"His weight is {0}.", him->getWeight());
    Console::WriteLine(L"His height is {0} which is {1:F2} meters.",
                                    him->getHeight(),him->getHeight().meters);

    return 0;
}
```

This example produces the following output:

```
She is Freda
Her weight is 47.73 kilograms.
Her height is 5 feet 2 inches which is 1.57 meters.
He is Fred
His weight is 185 pounds 7 ounces.
His height is 6 feet 3 inches which is 1.91 meters.
```

How It Works

The two value classes, Height and Weight, define the height and weight of a person. The Person class has fields of type Height and Weight to store the height and weight of a person and the name of a person is stored in the Name property, which is a trivial property because no explicit get() and set() functions have been defined for it; it therefore has the default get() and set() functions.

The first two statements in main() define Height and Weight objects and these are then used to define him:

```
Weight hisWeight = Weight(185, 7);
Height hisHeight = Height(6, 3);
Person^ him = gcnew Person(L"Fred", hisHeight, hisWeight);
```

Height and Weight are value classes so the variables of these types store the values directly. Person is a reference class so him is a handle. The first argument to the Person class constructor is a string literal so the compiler arranges for a String object to be created from this and the handle to this object is passed as the argument. The second and third arguments are the value class objects that you create in the first two statements. Of course, copies of these are passed as arguments because of the pass-by-value mechanism for function arguments. Within the Person class constructor, the assignment statement sets the value of the Name parameter and the values of the two fields, ht and wt, are set in the initialization list. The only way to set a property is through an implicit call of its set() function; a property cannot be initialized in the initializer list of a constructor.

There is a similar sequence of three statements to those for him that define her. With two Person objects created on the heap you first output information about her with these statements:

```
Console::WriteLine(L"She is {0}", her->Name);
Console::WriteLine(L"Her weight is {0:F2} kilograms.",
                                        her->getWeight().kilograms);
Console::WriteLine(L"Her height is {0} which is {1:F2} meters.",
                                her->getHeight(),her->getHeight().meters);
```

In the first statement, you access the Name property for the object referenced by the handle, her, with the expression her->Name; the result of executing this is a handle to the string that the property's get() value returns, so it is of type String^.

In the second statement, you access the kilograms property of the wt field for the object referenced by her with the expression her->getWeight().kilograms. The her->getWeight() part of this expression returns a copy of the wt field, and this is used to access the kilograms property; thus the value returned by the get() function for the kilograms property becomes the value of the second argument to the WriteLine() function.

In the third output statement, the second argument is the result of the expression, her>getHeight(), which returns a copy of ht. To produce the value of this in a form suitable for output the compiler arranges for the ToString() function for the object to be called, so the expression is equivalent to her>getHeight().ToString(), and in fact you could write it like this if you want. The third argument to the WriteLine() function is the meters property for the Height object that is returned by the getHeight() function the the Person object, her.

The last three output statements output information about the him object in a similar fashion to the her object. In this case the weight is produced by an implicit call of the ToString() function for the wt field in the him object.

Defining Indexed Properties

Indexed properties are a set of property values in a class that you access using an index between square brackets, just like accessing an array element. You have already made use of indexed properties for strings because the String class makes characters from the string available as indexed properties. As you have seen, if str is the handle to a String object then the expression str[4] accesses the fifth indexed property value, which corresponds to the fifth character in the string. A property that you access by placing an index in square brackets following the name of the variable referencing the object, this is an example of a **default indexed property**. An indexed property that has a property name is described as a **named indexed property**.

Here's a class containing a default indexed property:

```
ref class Name
{
  private:
    array<String^>^ Names;                // Stores names as array elements

public:
    Name(...array<String^>^ names) : Names(names) {}

    // Indexed property to return any name
    property String^ default[int]
    {
      // Retrieve indexed property value
      String^ get(int index)
      {
        if(index >= Names->Length)
          throw gcnew Exception(L"Index out of range");
        return Names[index];
      }
    }
};
```

The idea of the `Name` class is to store a person's name as an array of individual names. The constructor accepts an arbitrary number of arguments of type `String^` that are then stored in the `Names` field so a `Name` object can accommodate any number of names.

The indexed property here is a *default* indexed property because the name is specified by the `default` keyword. If you supplied a regular name in this position in the property specification it would be a named indexed property. The square brackets following the `default` keyword indicate that it is indeed an indexed property and the type they enclose — type `int` in this case — is the type of the index values that is to be used when retrieving values for the property. The type of the index does not have to be a numeric type and you can have more than one index parameter for accessing indexed property values.

For an indexed property accessed by a single index, the `get()` function must have a parameter specifying the index that is of the same type as that which appears between the square brackets following the property name. The `set()` function for such an indexed property must have two parameters: the first parameter is the index, and the second is the new value to be set for the property corresponding to the first parameter.

Let's see how indexed properties behave in practice.

Try It Out   **Using a Default Indexed Property**

Here's an example that makes use of a slightly extended version of the `Name` class:

```
// Ex7_17.cpp : main project file.
// Defining and using default indexed properties

#include "stdafx.h"

using namespace System;

ref class Name
{
  private:
  array<String^>^ Names;

public:
  Name(...array<String^>^ names) : Names(names) {}

  // Scalar property specifying number of names
  property int NameCount
  {
    int get() {return Names->Length; }
  }

  // Indexed property to return names
  property String^ default[int]
  {
    String^ get(int index)
    {
      if(index >= Names->Length)
```

```
            throw gcnew Exception(L"Index out of range");
          return Names[index];
      }
    }
};

int main(array<System::String ^> ^args)
{
  Name^ myName = gcnew Name(L"Ebenezer", L"Isaiah", L"Ezra", L"Inigo",
                                             L"Whelkwhistle");

  // List the names
  for(int i = 0 ; i < myName->NameCount ; i++)
    Console::WriteLine(L"Name {0} is  {1}", i+1, myName[i]);
  return 0;
}
```

This example produces the following output:

```
Name 1 is  Ebenezer
Name 2 is  Isaiah
Name 3 is  Ezra
Name 4 is  Inigo
Name 5 is  Whelkwhistle
```

How It Works

The Name class in the example is basically the same as in the previous section but with a scalar property with the name NameCount added that returns the number of names in the Name object. In main() you first create a Name object with five names:

```
Name^ myName = gcnew Name(L"Ebenezer", L"Isaiah", L"Ezra", L"Inigo",
                                             L"Whelkwhistle");
```

The parameter list for the constructor in the Name class starts with an ellipsis so it accepts any number of arguments. The arguments that are supplied when it is called will be stored in the elements of the names array, so initializing the Names field with names makes Names reference the names array. In the previous statement, you supply five arguments to the constructor, so the Names field in the object referenced by myName is an array with five elements.

You access the properties for myName in a for loop to list the names the object contains:

```
for(int i = 0 ; i < myName->NameCount ; i++)
  Console::WriteLine(L"Name {0} is  {1}", i+1, myName[i]);
```

You use the NameCount property value to control the for loop. Without this property you would not know how many names there are to be listed. Within the loop the last argument to the WriteLine() function accesses the ith indexed property. As you see, accessing the default indexed property just involves placing the index value in square brackets after the myName variable name. The output demonstrates that the indexed properties are working as expected.

The indexed property is read-only because the Name class only includes a get() function for the property. To allow properties to be changed you could add a definition for the set() function for the default indexed property like this:

```
ref class Name
{
  // Code as before...

  // Indexed property to return names
  property String^ default[int]
  {
    String^ get(int index)
    {
      if(index >= Names->Length)
        throw gcnew Exception(L"Index out of range");
      return Names[index];
    }

    void set(int index, String^ name)
    {
      if(index >= Names->Length)
        throw gcnew Exception(L"Index out of range");
      Names[index] = name;
    }
  }
};
```

You can now use the ability to set indexed properties by adding a statement in main() to set the last indexed property value:

```
Name^ myName = gcnew Name(L"Ebenezer", L"Isaiah", L"Ezra",
                                          L"Inigo", L"Whelkwhistle");
myName[myName->NameCount - 1] = L"Oberwurst";  // Change last indexed property

// List the names
for(int i = 0 ; i < myName->NameCount ; i++)
  Console::WriteLine(L"Name {0} is  {1}", i+1, myName[i]);
```

With this addition you'll see from the output for the new version of the program that the last name has indeed been updated by the statement assigning a new value to the property at index position myName>NameCount-1.

You could also try adding a named indexed property to the class:

```
ref class Name
{
  // Code as before...

  // Indexed property to return initials
  property wchar_t Initials[int]
  {
    wchar_t get(int index)
    {
```

```
        if(index >= Names->Length)
           throw gcnew Exception(L"Index out of range");
        return Names[index][0];
      }
   }
};
```

The indexed property has the name `Initials` because its function is to return the initial of a name specified by an index. You define a named indexed property in essentially the same way as a default indexed
property but with the property name replacing the default keyword.

If you recompile the program and execute it once more, you see the following output.

```
Name 1 is  Ebenezer
Name 2 is  Isaiah
Name 3 is  Ezra
Name 4 is  Inigo
Name 4 is  Oberwurst
The initials are: E.I.E.I.O.
```

The initials are produced by accessing the named indexed property in the `for` loop and the output
shows that they work as expected.

More Complex Indexed Properties

As mentioned, indexed properties can be defined so that more than one index is necessary to access a
value and the indexes need not be numeric. Here's an example of a class with such an indexed property:

```
enum class Day{Monday, Tuesday, Wednesday,Thursday, Friday, Saturday, Sunday};

// Class defining a shop
ref class Shop
{
public:
  property String^ Opening[Day, String^]              // Opening times
  {
    String^ get(Day day, String^ AmOrPm)
    {
      switch(day)
      {
        case Day::Saturday:                            // Saturday opening:
          if(AmOrPm == L"am")
            return L"9:00";                             //          morning is 9 am
          else
            return L"14:30";                            //          afternoon is 2:30 pm
          break;

        case Day::Sunday:                              // Saturday opening:
          return L"closed";                            //          closed all day
          break;
```

```
            default:
                if(AmOrPm == L"am")                 // Monday to Friday opening:
                    return L"9:30";                 //          morning is 9:30 am
                else
                    return L"14:00";                //          afternoon is 2 pm
                break;
            }
        }
    }
};
```

The class representing a shop has an indexed property specifying opening times. The first index is an enumeration value of type Day that identifies the day of the week and the second index is a handle to a string that determines whether it is morning or afternoon. You could output the Opening property value for a Shop object like this:

```
Shop^ shop = gcnew Shop;
Console::WriteLine(shop->Opening[Day::Saturday, L"pm"]);
```

The first statement creates the Shop object and the second displays the opening time for the shop for Saturday afternoon. As you see, you just place the two index values for the property between square brackets and separate them by a comma. The output from the second statement is the string "14:30". If you can dream up a reason why you need them, you could also define indexed properties with three or more indexes in a class.

Static Properties

Static properties are similar to static class members in that they are defined for the class and are the same for all objects of the class type. You define a static property by adding the static keyword in the definition of the property. Here's how you might define a static property in the Length class you saw earlier:

```
value class Length
{
  // Code as before...
public:
  static property String^ Units
  {
    String^ get() {  return L"feet and inches";  }
  }
};
```

This is a simple property that makes available the units assumed by the class as a string. You access a static property by qualifying the property name with the name of the class, just as you would any other static member of the class:

```
Console::WriteLine(L"Class units are {0}.", Length::Units);
```

Static class properties exist whether or not any objects of the class type have been created. This differs from instance properties, which are specific to each object of the class type. Of course, if you have defined a class object, you can access a static property using the variable name. If you have created a `Length` object with the name `len` for example, you could output the value of the static `Units` property with the statement:

```
Console::WriteLine(L"Class units are {0}.", len.Units);
```

For accessing a static property in a reference class through a handle to an object of that type you would use the `->` operator.

Reserved Property Names

Although properties are different from fields, the values for properties still have to be stored somewhere and the storage locations need to be identified somehow. Internally, properties have names created for the storage locations that are needed, and such names are reserved in a class that has properties so you must not use these names for other purposes.

If you define a scalar or named indexed property with the name NAME in a class, the names `get_NAME` and `set_NAME` are reserved in the class so you must not use them for other purposes. Both names are reserved regardless of whether or not you define the `get()` and `set()` functions for the property. When you define a default indexed property in a class, the names `get_Item` and `set_Item` are reserved. The possibility of there being reserved names that use underscore characters is a good reason for avoiding the use of the underscore character in your own names in a C++/CLI program.

initonly Fields

Literal fields are a convenient way of introducing constants into a class, but they have the limitation that their values must be defined when you compile the program. C++/CLI also provides `initonly` fields in a class that are constants that you can initialize in a constructor. Here's an example of an `initonly` field in a skeleton version of the `Length` class:

```
value class Length
{
private:
  int feet;
  int inches;

public:
  initonly int inchesPerFoot;                    // initonly field

  // Constructor
  Length(int ft, int ins) :
          feet(ft), inches(ins),                 // Initialize fields
          inchesPerFoot(12)                      // Initialize initonly field
  {}
};
```

Here the `initonly` field has the name `inchesPerFoot` and is initialized in the initializer list for the constructor. This is an example of a non-static `initonly` field and each object will have its own copy, just like the ordinary fields, `feet` and `inches`. Of course, the big difference between `initonly` fields and ordinary fields is that you cannot subsequently change the value of an `initonly` field — after it has been initialized, it is fixed for all time. Note that you must not specify an initial value for a non-static `initonly` field when you declare it; this implies that you *must* initialize all non-static `initonly` fields in a constructor.

You don't have to initialize non-static `initonly` fields in the constructor's initializer list — you could do it in the body of the constructor:

```
Length(int ft, int ins) :
        feet(ft), inches(ins),          // Initialize fields
{
  inchesPerFoot = 12;                   // Initialize initonly field
}
```

Now the field is initialized in the body of the constructor. You would typically pass the value for a non-static `initonly` field as an argument to the constructor rather than use an explicit literal as we have done here because the point of such fields is that their values are instance specific. If the value is known when you write the code you might as well use a literal field.

You can also define an `initonly` field in a class to be `static`, in which case it is shared between all members of the class, and if it is a public `initonly` field it's accessible by qualifying the field name with the class name. The `inchesPerFoot` field would make much more sense as a static `initonly` field — the value really isn't going to vary from one object to another. Here's a new version of the `Length` class with a static `initonly` field:

```
value class Length
{
private:
  int feet;
  int inches;

public:
  initonly static int inchesPerFoot = 12;       // Static initonly field

  // Constructor
  Length(int ft, int ins) :
          feet(ft), inches(ins)                  // Initialize fields
  {}
};
```

Now the `inchesPerFoot` field is static, and it has its value specified in the declaration rather than in the constructor initializer list. Indeed, you are not permitted to set values for static fields of any kind in the constructor. If you think about it, this makes sense because static fields are shared among all objects of the class and therefore setting values for such fields each time a constructor is called would conflict with this notion.

You now seem to be back with `initonly` fields only being initialized at compile time where literal fields could do the job anyway; however, you have another way to initialize static `initonly` fields at runtime — through a **static constructor**.

Static Constructors

A static constructor is a constructor that you declare using the `static` keyword and that you use to initialize static fields and static `initonly` fields. A static constructor has no parameters and cannot have an initializer list. A static constructor is always `private`, regardless of whether or not you put it in a public section of the class. You can define a static constructor for value classes and for reference classes. You cannot call a static constructor directly — it will be called automatically prior to the execution of a normal constructor. Any static fields that have initial values specified in their declarations will be initialized prior to the execution of the static constructor. Here's how you could initialize the `initonly` field in the `Length` class using a static constructor:

```
value class Length
{
private:
  int feet;
  int inches;

  // Static constructor
  static Length() { inchesPerFoot = 12; }

public:
  initonly static int inchesPerFoot;              // Static initonly field

  // Constructor
  Length(int ft, int ins) :
          feet(ft), inches(ins)                   // Initialize fields
  {}
}
```

This example of using a static constructor has no particular advantage over explicit initialization of `inchesPerFoot`, but bear in mind that the big difference is that the initialization is now occurring at runtime and the value could be acquired from an external source.

Summary

You now understand the basic ideas behind classes in C++. You're going to see more and more about using classes throughout the rest of the book. The key points to keep in mind from this chapter are:

❑ A **class** provides a means of defining your own data types. They can reflect whatever types of **objects** your particular problem requires.

❑ A class can contain **data members** and **function members**. The function members of a class always have free access to the data members of the same class. Data members of a C++/CLI class are referred to as **fields**.

❑ Objects of a class are created and initialized using functions called **constructors**. These are automatically called when an object declaration is encountered. Constructors may be overloaded to provide different ways of initializing an object.

❑   Classes in a C++/CLI program can be value classes or ref class.

❑   Variables of a value class type store data directly whereas variables referencing ref class objects are always handles.

❑   C++/CLI classes can have a static constructor defined that initializes the static members of a class.

❑   Members of a class can be specified as public, in which case they are freely accessible by any function in a program. Alternatively, they may be specified as private, in which case they may only be accessed by member functions or friend functions of the class.

❑   Members of a class can be defined as static. Only one instance of each static member of a class exists, which is shared amongst all instances of the class, no matter how many objects of the class are created.

❑   Every non-static object of a class contains the pointer this, which points to the current object for which the function was called.

❑   In non-static function members of a value class type, the this pointer is an interior pointer whereas in a ref class type it is a handle.

❑   A member function that is declared as const has a const this pointer, and therefore cannot modify data members of the class object for which it is called. It also cannot call another member function that is not const.

❑   You can only call const member functions for a class object declared as const.

❑   Function members of value classes and ref classes cannot be declared as const.

❑   Using references to class objects as arguments to function calls can avoid substantial overheads in passing complex objects to a function.

❑   A copy constructor, which is a constructor for an object initialized with an existing object of the same class, must have its parameter specified as a const reference.

❑   You cannot define a copy constructor in a value class because copying value class objects is always done by member-by-member copying.

Exercises

You can download the source code for the examples in the book and the solutions to the following exercises from www.wrox.com.

1.   Define a struct Sample that contains two integer data items. Write a program which declares two object of type Sample, called a and b. Set values for the data items that belong to a and then check that you can copy the values into b by simple assignment.

2.   Add a char* member to struct Sample in the previous exercise called sPtr. When you fill in the data for a, dynamically create a string buffer initialized with "Hello World!" and make a.sptr point to it. Copy a into b. What happens when you change the contents of the character buffer pointed to by a.sPtr and then output the contents of the string pointed to by b.sPtr? Explain what is happening. How would you get around this?

3. Create a function which takes a pointer to an object of type Sample as an argument, and which outputs the values of the members of any object Sample that is passed to it. Test this function by extending the program that you created for the previous exercise.

4. Define a class CRecord with two private data members that store a name up to 14 characters long and an integer item number. Define a getRecord() function member of the CRecord class that will set values for the data members by reading input from the keyboard and a putRecord() function member that outputs the values of the data members. Implement the getRecord() function so that a calling program can detect when a zero item number is entered. Test your CRecord class with a main() function that reads and outputs CRecord objects until a zero item number is entered.

5. Write a class called CTrace that you can use to show you at run time when code blocks have been entered and exited, by producing output like this:

```
function 'f1' entry
'if' block entry
'if' block exit
function 'f1' exit
```

6. Can you think of a way to automatically control the indentation in the last exercise, so that the output looks like this?

```
function 'f1' entry
    'if' block entry
    'if' block exit
function 'f1' exit
```

7. Define a class to represent a **push-down stack** of integers. A stack is a list of items that permits adding ('pushing') or removing ('popping') items only from one end and works on a last-in, first-out principle. For example, if the stack contained [10 4 16 20], pop() would return 10, and the stack would then contain [4 16 20]; a subsequent push(13) would leave the stack as [13 4 16 20]. You can't get at an item that is not at the top without first popping the ones above it. Your class should implement push() and pop() functions, plus a print() function so that you can check the stack contents. Store the list internally as an array, for now. Write a test program to verify the correct operation of your class.

8. What happens with your solution to the previous exercise if you try to pop() more items than you've pushed, or save more items than you have space for? Can you think of a robust way to trap this? Sometimes you might want to look at the number at the top of the stack without removing it; implement a peek() function to do this.

9. Repeat Ex7-4 but as a CLR console program using ref classes.

More on Classes

In this chapter, you will extend your knowledge of classes by understanding how you can make your class objects work more like the basic types in C++. You will learn:

- ❑ What a class destructor is and when and why it is necessary
- ❑ How to implement a class destructor
- ❑ How to allocate data members of a native C++ class in the free store and how to delete them when they are no longer required
- ❑ When you must write a copy constructor for a class
- ❑ What a union is and how it can be used
- ❑ How to make objects of your class work with C++ operators such as + or *
- ❑ What class templates are and how you define and use them
- ❑ How to use the standard `string` class for string operations in native C++ programs
- ❑ How to overload operators in C++/CLI classes

Class Destructors

Although this section heading refers to destructors, it's also about dynamic memory allocation. When you allocate memory in the free store for class members, you are invariably obliged to make use of a destructor, in addition to a constructor of course, and, as you'll see later in this chapter, using dynamically allocated class members will also require you to write your own copy constructor.

What Is a Destructor?

A **destructor** is a function that destroys an object when it is no longer required or when it goes out of scope. The class destructor is called automatically when an object goes out of scope. Destroying an object involves freeing the memory occupied by the data members of the object (except for static members which continue to exist even when there are no class objects in existence). The destructor for a class is a member function with the same name as the class, preceded by a tilde (~). The class destructor doesn't return a value and doesn't have parameters defined. For the CBox class, the prototype of the class destructor is:

```
~CBox();                    // Class destructor prototype
```

Because a destructor has no parameters, there can only ever be one destructor in a class.

It's an error to specify a return value or parameters for a destructor.

The Default Destructor

All the objects that you have been using up to now have been destroyed automatically by the **default destructor** for the class. The default destructor is always generated automatically by the compiler if you do not define your own class destructor. The default destructor doesn't delete objects or object members that have been allocated in the free store by the operator new. If space for class members has been allocated dynamically in a contructor, then you must define your own destructor that will explicitly use the delete operator to release the memory that has been allocated by the constructor using the operator new, just as you would with ordinary variables. You need some practice in writing destructors, so let's try it out.

Try It Out   A Simple Destructor

To get an appreciation of when the destructor for a class is called, you can include a destructor in the class CBox. Here's the definition of the example including the CBox class with a destructor:

```cpp
// Ex8_01.cpp
// Class with an explicit destructor
#include <iostream>
using std::cout;
using std::endl;

class CBox                       // Class definition at global scope
{
  public:
    // Destructor definition
    ~CBox()
    {
      cout << "Destructor called." << endl;
    }

    // Constructor definition
    CBox(double lv = 1.0, double wv = 1.0, double hv = 1.0):
                            m_Length(lv), m_Width(wv), m_Height(hv)
    {
      cout << endl << "Constructor called.";
    }

    // Function to calculate the volume of a box
    double Volume() const
    {
      return m_Length*m_Width*m_Height;
    }

    // Function to compare two boxes which returns true
```

```
     // if the first is greater that the second, and false otherwise
     int compare(CBox* pBox) const
     {
       return this->Volume()  >  pBox->Volume();
     }

   private:
     double m_Length;              // Length of a box in inches
     double m_Width;               // Width of a box in inches
     double m_Height;              // Height of a box in inches
};

// Function to demonstrate the CBox class destructor in action
int main()
{
   CBox boxes[5];                 // Array of CBox objects declared
   CBox cigar(8.0, 5.0, 1.0);  // Declare cigar box
   CBox match(2.2, 1.1, 0.5);  // Declare match box
   CBox* pB1 = &cigar;            // Initialize pointer to cigar object address
   CBox* pB2 = 0;                 // Pointer to CBox initialized to null

   cout << endl
        << "Volume of cigar is "
        << pB1->Volume();         // Volume of obj. pointed to

   pB2 = boxes;                   // Set to address of array
   boxes[2] = match;              // Set 3rd element to match
   cout << endl
        << "Volume of boxes[2] is "
        << (pB2 + 2)->Volume();   // Now access thru pointer

   cout << endl;
   return 0;
}
```

How It Works

The only thing that the CBox class destructor does is to display a message showing that it was called. The output is:

```
Constructor called.
Constructor called.
Constructor called.
Constructor called.
Constructor called.
Constructor called.
Constructor called.
Volume of cigar is 40
Volume of boxes[2] is 1.21
Destructor called.
Destructor called.
Destructor called.
Destructor called.
Destructor called.
Destructor called.
Destructor called.
```

You get one call of the destructor at the end of the program for each of the objects that exist at that time. For each constructor call that occurred, there's a matching destructor call. You don't need to call the destructor explicitly here. When an object of a class goes out of scope, the compiler will arrange for the destructor for the class to be called automatically. In our example, the destructor calls occur after main() has finished executing, so it's quite possible for an error in a destructor to cause a program to crash after main() has safely terminated.

Destructors and Dynamic Memory Allocation

You will find that you often want to allocate memory for class data members dynamically. You can use the operator new in a constructor to allocate memory for an object member. In such a case, you must assume responsibility for releasing the memory when the object is no longer required by providing a suitable destructor. Let's first define a simple class where we can do this.

Suppose you want to define a class where each object is a message of some description, for example, a text string. The class should be as memory efficient as possible so, rather than defining a data member as a char array big enough to hold the maximum length string that you might require, you'll allocate memory in the free store for the message when an object is created. Here's the class definition:

```
//Listing 08_01
class CMessage
{
  private:
    char* pmessage;                    // Pointer to object text string

  public:

    // Function to display a message
    void ShowIt() const
    {
      cout << endl << pmessage;
    }

    // Constructor definition
    CMessage(const char* text = "Default message")
    {
      pmessage = new char[strlen(text) + 1];   // Allocate space for text
      strcpy(pmessage, text);                  // Copy text to new memory
    }

    ~CMessage();                               // Destructor prototype
};
```

This class has only one data member defined, pmessage, which is a pointer to a text string. This is defined in the private section of the class, so that it can't be accessed from outside the class.

In the public section, you have the ShowIt() function that will output a CMessage object to the screen. You also have the definition of a constructor and you have the prototype for the class destructor, ~CMessage(), which I'll come to in a moment.

The constructor for the class requires a string as an argument, but if none is passed, it uses the default string that is specified for the parameter. The constructor obtains the length of the string supplied as the argument, excluding the terminating NULL, by using the library function strlen(). For the constructor to use this library function, there must be an #include statement for the <cstring> header file. The constructor determines the number of bytes of memory necessary to store the string in the free store by adding 1 to the value that the function strlen() returns.

> *Of course, if the memory allocation fails, an exception will be thrown that will terminate the program. If you want to manage such a failure to provide a more graceful end to the program, you would catch the exception within the constructor code. (See Chapter 6 for information on handling out-of-memory conditions.)*

Having obtained the memory for the string using the operator new, you use the strcpy() library function that is also declared in the <cstring> header file to copy the string supplied as the argument to the constructor into the memory allocated for it. The strcpy() function copies the string specified by the second pointer argument to the address contained in the first pointer argument.

You now need to write a class destructor that will free up the memory allocated for a message. If you don't provide a destructor for the class, there's no way to delete the memory allocated for an object. If you use this class as it stands in a program where a large number of CMessage objects are created, the free store will be gradually eaten away until the program fails. It's easy for this to occur in circumstances where it may not be obvious that it is happening. For example, if you create a temporary CMessage object in a function that is called many times in a program, you might assume that the objects are being destroyed at the return from the function. You'd be right about that, of course, but the free store memory will not be released. Thus for each call of the function, more of the free store will be occupied by memory for discarded CMessage objects.

The code for the CMessage class destructor is as follows:

```
// Listing 08_02
// Destructor to free memory allocated by new
CMessage::~CMessage()
{
  cout << "Destructor called."        // Just to track what happens
       << endl;
  delete[] pmessage;                  // Free memory assigned to pointer
}
```

Because you're defining the destructor outside of the class definition, you must qualify the name of the destructor with the class name, CMessage. All the destructor does is to first display a message so that you can see what's going on, and then use the delete operator to free the memory pointed to by the member pmessage. Note that you have to include the square brackets with delete because you're deleting an array (of type char).

Try It Out   Using the Message Class

You can exercise the CMessage class with a little example:

```
// Ex8_02.cpp
// Using a destructor to free memory
#include <iostream>            // For stream I/O
#include <cstring>             // For strlen() and strcpy()
using std::cout;
```

```
    using std::endl;

    // Put the CMessage class definition here (Listing 08_01)

    // Put the destructor definition here (Listing 08_02)

    int main()
    {
      // Declare object
      CMessage motto("A miss is as good as a mile.");

      // Dynamic object
      CMessage* pM = new CMessage("A cat can look at a queen.");

      motto.ShowIt();            // Display 1st message
      pM->ShowIt();              // Display 2nd message
      cout << endl;

      // delete pM;              // Manually delete object created with new
       return 0;
    }
```

Don't forget to replace the comments in the code with the CMessage class and destructor definitions from the previous section; it won't compile without this (the source code in the download contains all the code for the example).

How It Works

At the beginning of main(), you declare and define an initialized CMessage object, motto, in the usual manner. In the second declaration you define a pointer to a CMessage object, pM, and allocate memory for the CMessage object that is pointed to by using the operator new. The call to new invokes the CMessage class constructor, which has the effect of calling new again to allocate space for the message text pointed to by the data member pmessage. If you build and execute this example, it will produce the following output:

```
A miss is as good as a mile.
A cat can look at a queen.
Destructor called.
```

You have only one destructor call recorded in the output, even though you created two CMessage objects. I said earlier that the compiler doesn't take responsibility for objects created in the free store. The compiler arranged to call your destructor for the object motto because this is a normal automatic object, even though the memory for the data member was allocated in the free store by the constructor. The object pointed to by pM is different. You allocated memory for the *object* in the free store, so you have to use delete to remove it. You need to uncomment the following statement that appears just before the return statement in main():

```
    // delete pM;              // Manually delete object created with new
```

If you run the code now, it will produce this output:

```
A miss is as good as a mile.
A cat can look at a queen.
Destructor called.
Destructor called.
```

Now you get an extra call of your destructor. This is surprising in a way. Clearly, `delete` is only dealing with the memory allocated by the call to `new` in the function `main()`. It only freed the memory pointed to by pM. Because your pointer pM points to a `CMessage` object (for which a destructor has been defined), `delete` also calls your destructor to allow you to release the memory for the members of the object. So when you use `delete` for an object created dynamically with `new`, it will always call the destructor for the object before releasing the memory that the object occupies. This ensures that any memory allocated dynamically for members of the class will also be freed.

Implementing a Copy Constructor

When you allocate space for class members dynamically, there are demons lurking in the free store. For the `CMessage` class, the default copy constructor is woefully inadequate. Suppose you write these statements:

```
CMessage motto1("Radiation fades your genes.");
CMessage motto2(motto1);    // Calls the default copy constructor
```

The effect of the default copy constructor will be to copy the address that is stored in the pointer member of the class from `motto1` to `motto2` because the copying process implemented by the default copy constructor involves simply copying the values stored in the data members of the original object to the new object. Consequently, there will be only one text string shared between the two objects, as Figure 8-1 illustrates.

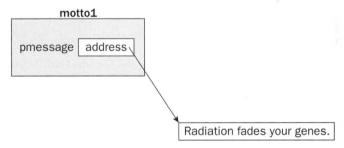

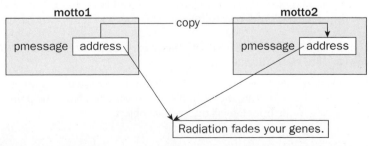

Figure 8-1

If the string is changed from either of the objects, it will be changed for the other object as well because both objects share the same string. If motto1 is destroyed, the pointer in motto2 will be pointing at a memory area that has been released, and may now be used for something else, so chaos will surely ensue. Of course, the same problem arises if motto2 is deleted; motto1 would then contain a member pointing to a nonexistent string.

The solution is to supply a class copy constructor to replace the default version. You could implement this in the public section of the class as follows:

```
CMessage(const CMessage& initM)          // Copy Constructor definition
{
  // Allocate space for text
  pmessage = new char[ strlen(initM.pmessage) + 1 ];

  // Copy text to new memory
  strcpy(pmessage, initM.pmessage);
}
```

Remember from the previous chapter that, to avoid an infinite spiral of calls to the copy constructor, the parameter must be specified as a const reference. This copy constructor first allocates enough memory to hold the string in the object initM, storing the address in the data member of the new object, and then copies the text string from the initializing object. Now, the new object will be identical to, but quite independent of, the old one.

Just because you don't initialize one CMessage class object with another, don't think that you're safe and need not bother with the copy constructor. Another monster lurks in the free store that can emerge to bite you when you least expect it. Consider the following statements:

```
CMessage thought("Eye awl weighs yews my spell checker.");
DisplayMessage(thought);     // Call a function to output a message
```

where the function DisplayMessage() is defined as:

```
void DisplayMessage(CMessage localMsg)
{
  cout << endl << "The message is: "
       << localMsg.ShowIt();
  return;
}
```

Looks simple enough doesn't it? What could be wrong with that? A catastrophic error, that's what! What the function DisplayMessage() does is actually irrelevant. The problem lies with the parameter. The parameter is a CMessage object so the argument in a call is passed by value. With the default copy constructor, the sequence of events is as follows:

1. The object thought is created with the space for the message "Eye awl weighs yews my spell checker" allocated in the free store.

2. The function DisplayMessage() is called and, because the argument is passed by value, a copy, localMsg, is made using the default copy constructor. Now the pointer in the copy points to the same string in the free store as the original object.

3. At the end of the function, the local object goes out of scope, so the destructor for the `CMessage` class is called. This deletes the local object (the copy) by deleting the memory pointed to by the pointer `pmessage`.

4. On return from the function `DisplayMessage()`, the pointer in the original object, `thought`, still points to the memory area that has just been deleted. Next time you try to use the original object (or even if you don't, since it will need to be deleted sooner or later) your program will behave in weird and mysterious ways.

Any call to a function that passes by value an object of a class that has a member defined dynamically will cause problems. So, out of this, you have an absolutely 100 percent, 24 carat golden rule:

> *If you allocate space for a member of a native C++ class dynamically, always implement a copy constructor.*

Sharing Memory Between Variables

As a relic of the days when 64KB was quite a lot of memory, you have a facility in C++ that allows more than one variable to share the same memory (but obviously not at the same time). This is called a **union**, and there are four basic ways in which you can use one:

❑ You can use it so that a variable A occupies a block of memory at one point in a program, which is later occupied by another variable B of a different type, because A is no longer required. I recommend that you don't do this. It's not worth the risk of error that is implicit in such an arrangement. You can achieve the same effect by allocating memory dynamically.

❑ Alternatively, you could have a situation in a program where a large array of data is required, but you don't know in advance of execution what the data type will be — it will be determined by the input data. I also recommend that you don't use unions in this case, since you can achieve the same result using a couple of pointers of different types and again allocating the memory dynamically.

❑ A third possible use for a union is one that you may need now and again — when you want to interpret the same data in two or more different ways. This could happen when you have a variable that is of type `long`, and you want to treat it as two values of type `short`. Windows will sometimes package two `short` values in a single parameter of type `long` passed to a function. Another instance arises when you want to treat a block of memory containing numeric data as a string of bytes, just to move it around.

❑ You can use a union as a means of passing an object or a data value around where you don't know in advance what its type is going to be. The union can provide for storing any one of the possible range of types that you might have.

Defining Unions

You define a union using the keyword `union`. It is best understood by taking an example of a definition:

```
union shareLD                // Sharing memory between long and double
{
  double dval;
  long lval;
};
```

This defines a union type shareLD that provides for the variables of type long and double to occupy the same memory. The union type name is usually referred to as a **tag name**. This statement is rather like a class definition, in that you haven't actually defined a union instance yet, so you don't have any variables at this point. Once the union type has been defined, you can define instances of a union in a declaration. For example:

```
shareLD myUnion;
```

This defined an instance of the union type, shareLD, that you defined previously. You could also have defined myUnion by including it in the union definition statement:

```
union shareLD                    // Sharing memory between long and double
{
  double dval;
  long lval;
} myUnion;
```

To refer to a member of the union, you use the direct member selection operator (the period) with the union instance name, just as you have done when accessing members of a class. So, you could set the long variable lval to 100 in the union instance MyUnion with this statement:

```
myUnion.lval = 100;              // Using a member of a union
```

Using a similar statement later in a program to initialize the double variable dval will overwrite lval. The basic problem with using a union to store different types of values in the same memory is that, because of the way a union works, you also need some means of determining which of the member values is current. This is usually achieved by maintaining another variable that acts as an indicator of the type of value stored.

A union is not limited to sharing between two variables. If you wish, you can share the same memory between several variables. The memory occupied by the union will be that which is required by its largest member. For example, suppose you define this union:

```
union shareDLF
{
  double dval;
  long lval;
  float fval;
} uinst = {1.5};
```

An instance of shareDLF will occupy 8 bytes, as illustrated in Figure 8-2.

In the example, you defined an instance of the union, uinst, as well as the tag name for the union. You also initialized the instance with the value 1.5.

You can only initialize the first member of the union when you declare an instance.

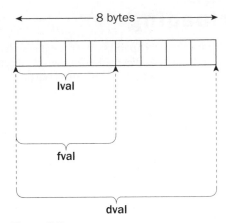

Figure 8-2

Anonymous Unions

You can define a union without a union type name, in which case an instance of the union is automatically declared. For example, suppose you define a union like this:

```
union
{
  char* pval;
  double dval;
  long lval;
};
```

This statement defines both a union with no name and an instance of the union with no name. Consequently, you can refer the variables that it contains just by their names, as they appear in the union definition, pval, dval, and lval. This can be more convenient than a normal union with a type name, but you need to be careful that you don't confuse the union members with ordinary variables. The members of the union will still share the same memory. As an illustration of how the anonymous union above works, to use the double member, you could write this statement:

```
dval = 99.5;                    // Using a member of an anonymous union
```

As you can see, there's nothing to distinguish the variable dval as a union member. If you need to use anonymous unions, you could use a naming convention to make the members more obvious and thus make your code a little less obscure.

Unions in Classes and Structures

You can include an instance of a union in a class or in a structure. If you intend to store different types of value at different times, this usually necessitates maintaining a class data member to indicate what kind of value is stored in the union. There isn't usually a great deal to be gained by using unions as class or struct members.

Operator Overloading

Operator overloading is a very important capability because it enables you to make standard C++ operators, such as +, -, * and so on, work with objects of your own data types. It allows you to write a function that redefines a particular operator so that it performs a particular action when it's used with objects of a class. For example, you could redefine the operator > so that, when it was used with objects of the class CBox that you saw earlier, it would return `true` if the first CBox argument had a greater volume than the second.

Operator overloading doesn't allow you to invent new operators, nor can you change the precedence of an operator, so your overloaded version of an operator will have the same priority in the sequence of evaluating an expression as the original base operator. The operator precedence table can be found in Chapter 2 of this book and in the MSDN Library.

Although you can't overload all the operators, the restrictions aren't particularly oppressive. These are the operators that you can't overload:

The scope resolution operator	::
The conditional operator	?:
The direct member selection operator	.
The size-of operator	sizeof
The de-reference pointer to class member operator	.*

Anything else is fair game, which gives you quite a bit of scope. Obviously, it's a good idea to ensure that your versions of the standard operators are reasonably consistent with their normal usage, or at least reasonably intuitive in their operation. It wouldn't be a very sensible approach to produce an overloaded + operator for a class that performed the equivalent of a multiply on class objects. The best way to understand how operator overloading works is to work through an example, so let's implement what I just referred to, the greater-than operator, >, for the CBox class.

Implementing an Overloaded Operator

To implement an overloaded operator for a class, you have to write a special function. Assuming that it is a member of the class CBox, the declaration for the function to overload the > operator within the class definition will be as follows:

```
class CBox
{
  public:
    bool operator>(CBox& aBox) const;  // Overloaded 'greater than'

  // Rest of the class definition...
};
```

The word `operator` here is a keyword. Combined with an operator symbol or name, in this case, `>`, it defines an operator function. The function name in this case is `operator>`. You can write an operator function with or without a space between the keyword `operator` and the operator itself, as long as there's no ambiguity. The ambiguity arises with operators with names rather than symbols such as `new` or `delete`. If you were to write `operatornew` and `operatordelete` without a space, they are legal names for ordinary functions, so for operator functions with these operators, you must leave a space between the keyword `operator` and the operator name itself. The strangest looking function name for an overloaded operator function is `operator()()`. This looks like a typing error but it is in fact a function that overloads the function call operator, `()`. Note that you declare the `operator>()` function as `const` because it doesn't modify the data members of the class.

With the `operator>()` operator function, the right operand of the operator will be defined by the function parameter. The left operand will be defined implicitly by the pointer `this`. So, if you have the following `if` statement:

```
if(box1 > box2)
   cout << endl << "box1 is greater than box2";
```

then the expression between the parentheses in the `if` will call our operator function, and is equivalent to this function call:

```
box1.operator>(box2);
```

The correspondence between the CBox objects in the expression and the operator function parameters is illustrated in Figure 8-3.

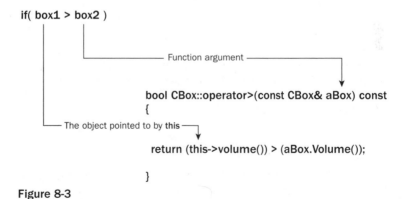

Figure 8-3

Let's look at how the code for the `operator>()` function works:

```
// Operator function for 'greater than' which
// compares volumes of CBox objects.
bool CBox::operator>(const CBox& aBox) const
{
  return this->Volume() > aBox.Volume();
}
```

You use a reference parameter to the function to avoid unnecessary copying when the function is called. Because the function does not alter the object for which it is called, you can declare it as const. If you don't do this, you cannot use the operator to compare const objects of type CBox at all.

The return expression uses the member function Volume() to calculate the volume of the CBox object pointed to by this, and compares the result with the volume of the object aBox using the basic operator >. The basic > operator returns a value of type int (not a type bool) and thus, 1 is returned if the CBox object pointed to by the pointer this has a larger volume than the object aBox passed as a reference argument, and 0 otherwise. The value that results from the comparison will be automatically converted to the return type of the operator function, type bool.

Try It Out   Operator Overloading

You can exercise the operator>() function with an example:

```
// Ex8_03.cpp
// Exercising the overloaded 'greater than' operator
#include <iostream>                        // For stream I/O
using std::cout;
using std::endl;

class CBox                                 // Class definition at global scope
{
  public:
    // Constructor definition
    CBox(double lv = 1.0, double wv = 1.0, double hv = 1.0):
                          m_Length(lv), m_Width(wv), m_Height(hv)
    {
      cout << endl << "Constructor called.";
    }

    // Function to calculate the volume of a box
    double Volume() const
    {
      return m_Length*m_Width*m_Height;
    }

    bool operator>(const CBox& aBox) const;  // Overloaded 'greater than'

    // Destructor definition
    ~CBox()
    {
      cout << "Destructor called." << endl;
    }

  private:
    double m_Length;                       // Length of a box in inches
    double m_Width;                        // Width of a box in inches
    double m_Height;                       // Height of a box in inches
};

// Operator function for 'greater than' that
// compares volumes of CBox objects.
```

```
bool CBox::operator>(const CBox& aBox) const
{
  return this->Volume() > aBox.Volume();
}

int main()
{
  CBox smallBox(4.0, 2.0, 1.0);
  CBox mediumBox(10.0, 4.0, 2.0);
  CBox bigBox(30.0, 20.0, 40.0);

  if(mediumBox > smallBox)
    cout << endl
         << "mediumBox is bigger than smallBox";

  if(mediumBox > bigBox)
    cout << endl
         << "mediumBox is bigger than bigBox";
  else
    cout << endl
         << "mediumBox is not bigger than bigBox";

  cout << endl;
  return 0;
}
```

How It Works

The prototype of the `operator>()` operator function appears in the `public` section of the class. As the function definition is outside the class definition, it won't default to `inline`. This is quite arbitrary. You could just as well have put the definition in place of the prototype in the class definition. In this case, you wouldn't need to qualify the function name with `CBox::` in front of it. As you'll remember, this is necessary when you define a function member outside the class definition because this tells the compiler that the function is a member of the `CBox` class.

The function `main()` has two `if` statements using the operator > with class members. These automatically invoke the overloaded operator function. If you wanted to get confirmation of this, you could add an output statement to the operator function. The output from this example is:

```
Constructor called.
Constructor called.
Constructor called.
mediumBox is bigger than smallBox
mediumBox is not bigger than bigBox
Destructor called.
Destructor called.
Destructor called.
```

The output demonstrates that the `if` statements work fine with our operator function, so being able to express the solution to `CBox` problems directly in terms of `CBox` objects is beginning to be a realistic proposition.

Implementing Full Support for a Comparison Operator

With the current version of the operator function `operator>()`, there are still a lot of things that you can't do. Specifying a problem solution in terms of CBox objects might well involve statements such as the following:

```
if(aBox > 20.0)
    // Do something...
```

Our function won't deal with that. If you try to use an expression comparing a CBox object with a numerical value, you'll get an error message. To support this capability, you would need to write another version of the `operator>()` function as an overloaded function.

You can quite easily support the type of expression that you've just seen. The declaration of the member function within the class would be:

```
// Compare a CBox object with a constant
bool operator>(const double& value) const;
```

This would appear in the definition of the class and the right operand for the > operator corresponds to the function parameter here. The CBox object that is the left operand will be passed as the implicit pointer `this`.

The implementation of this overloaded operator is also easy. It's just one statement in the body of the function:

```
// Function to compare a CBox object with a constant
bool CBox::operator>(const double& value) const
{
    return this->Volume() > value;
}
```

This couldn't be much simpler, could it? But you still have a problem using the > operator with CBox objects. You may well want to write statements such as this:

```
if(20.0 > aBox)
    // do something...
```

You might argue that this could be done by implementing the `operator<()` operator function that accepted a right argument of type `double` and rewriting the statement above to use it, which is quite true. Indeed, implementing the < operator is likely to be a requirement for comparing CBox objects anyway, but an implementation of support for an object type shouldn't artificially restrict the ways in which you can use the objects in an expression. The use of the objects should be as natural as possible. The problem is how to do it.

A member operator function always provides the left argument as the pointer `this`. Because the left argument, in this case, is of type `double`, you can't implement it as a member function. That leaves you with two choices: an ordinary function or a `friend` function. Because you don't need to access the `private` members of the class, it doesn't need to be a `friend` function, so you can implement the overloaded > operator with a left operand of type `double` as an ordinary function. The prototype, placed outside the class definition of course because it isn't a member, would need to be:

```
bool operator>(const double& value, const CBox& aBox);
```

The implementation would be this:

```
// Function comparing a constant with a CBox object
bool operator>(const double& value, const CBox& aBox)
{
   return value > aBox.Volume();
}
```

As you have seen already, an ordinary function (and a `friend` function too for that matter) accesses the members of an object by using the direct member selection operator and the object name. Of course, an ordinary function only has access to the public members. The member function `Volume()` is `public`, so there's no problem using it here.

If the class didn't have the `public` function `Volume()`, you could either declare the operator function a `friend` function that could access the `private` data members directly, or you could provide a set of member functions to return the values of the `private` data members and use those in an ordinary function to implement the comparison.

Try It Out   Complete Overloading of the > Operator

We can put all this together in an example to show how it works:

```
// Ex8_04.cpp
// Implementing a complete overloaded 'greater than' operator
#include <iostream>                          // For stream I/O
using std::cout;
using std::endl;

class CBox                                   // Class definition at global scope
{
  public:
    // Constructor definition
    CBox(double lv = 1.0, double wv = 1.0, double hv = 1.0):
                          m_Length(lv), m_Width(wv), m_Height(hv)
    {
      cout << endl << "Constructor called.";
    }

    // Function to calculate the volume of a box
    double Volume() const
    {
      return m_Length*m_Width*m_Height;
    }

    // Operator function for 'greater than' that
    // compares volumes of CBox objects.
    bool operator>(const CBox& aBox) const
    {
      return this->Volume() > aBox.Volume();
    }

    // Function to compare a CBox object with a constant
    bool operator>(const double& value) const
    {
```

```
            return this->Volume() > value;
      }

      // Destructor definition
      ~CBox()
      { cout << "Destructor called." << endl;}

   private:
      double m_Length;              // Length of a box in inches
      double m_Width;               // Width of a box in inches
      double m_Height;              // Height of a box in inches
};
```

```
int operator>(const double& value, const CBox& aBox); // Function prototype
```

```
int main()
{
  CBox smallBox(4.0, 2.0, 1.0);
  CBox mediumBox(10.0, 4.0, 2.0);

  if(mediumBox > smallBox)
    cout << endl
         << "mediumBox is bigger than smallBox";
```

```
  if(mediumBox > 50.0)
    cout << endl
         << "mediumBox capacity is more than 50";
  else
    cout << endl
         << "mediumBox capacity is not more than 50";

  if(10.0 > smallBox)
    cout << endl
         << "smallBox capacity is less than 10";
  else
    cout << endl
         << "smallBox capacity is not less than 10";
```

```
  cout << endl;
  return 0;
}
```

```
// Function comparing a constant with a CBox object
int operator>(const double& value, const CBox& aBox)
{
  return value > aBox.Volume();
}
```

How It Works

Note the position of the prototype for the ordinary function version of operator>(). It needs to follow the class definition, because it refers to a CBox object in the parameter list. If you place it before the class definition, the example will not compile.

There is a way to place it at the beginning of the program file following the #include statement: Use an **incomplete class declaration**. This would precede the prototype and would look like this:

```
class CBox;                                   // Incomplete class declaration
int operator>(const double& value, CBox& aBox);  // Function prototype
```

The incomplete class declaration identifies CBox to the compiler as a class and is sufficient to allow the compiler to process the prototype for the function properly, since the compiler now knows that CBox is a user-defined type to be specified later.

This mechanism is also essential in circumstances such as those where you have two classes, each of which has a pointer to an object of the other class as a member. They will each require the other to be declared first. It is only possible to resolve such an impasse through the use of an incomplete class declaration.

The output from the example is:

```
Constructor called.
Constructor called.
mediumBox is bigger than smallBox
mediumBox capacity is more than 50
smallBox capacity is less than 10
Destructor called.
Destructor called.
```

After the constructor messages due to the declarations of the objects smallBox and mediumBox, you have the output lines from the three if statements, each of which is working as you would expect. The first of these calls the operator function that is a class member and works with two CBox objects. The second calls the member function that has a parameter of type double. The expression in the third if statement calls the operator function that you have implemented as an ordinary function.

As it happens, you could have made both the operator functions that are class members ordinary functions, because they only need access to the member function Volume(), which is public.

Any comparison operator can be implemented in much the same way as you have implemented these. They would only differ in the minor details and the general approach to implementing them would be exactly the same.

Overloading the Assignment Operator

If you don't provide an overloaded assignment operator function for your class, the compiler will provide a default. The default version will simply provide a member-by-member copying process, similar to that of the default copy constructor. However, don't confuse the default copy constructor with the default assignment operator. The default copy constructor is called by a declaration of a class object that's initialized with an existing object of the same class, or by passing an object to a function by value. The default assignment operator, on the other hand, is called when the left side and the right side of an assignment statement are objects of the same class type.

For the CBox class, the default assignment operator works with no problem, but for any class which has space for members allocated dynamically, you need to look carefully at the requirements of the class in question. There may be considerable potential for chaos in your program if you leave the assignment operator out under these circumstances.

For a moment, let's return to the CMessage class that you used when I was talking about copy constructors. You'll remember it had a member, pmessage, that was a pointer to a string. Now consider the effect that the default assignment operator could have. Suppose you had two instances of the class, motto1 and motto2. You could try setting the members of motto2 equal to the members of motto1 using the default assignment operator, as follows:

```
motto2 = motto1;                    // Use default assignment operator
```

The effect of using the default assignment operator for this class is essentially the same as using the default copy constructor: disaster will result! Since each object will have a pointer to the same string, if the string is changed for one object, it's changed for both. There's also the problem that when one of the instances of the class is destroyed, its destructor will free the memory used for the string and the other object will be left with a pointer to memory that may now be used for something else.

What you need the assignment operator to do is to copy the text to a memory area owned by the destination object.

Fixing the Problem

You can fix this with your own assignment operator function, which we will assume is defined within the class definition:

```
// Overloaded assignment operator for CMessage objects
CMessage& operator=(const CMessage& aMess)
{
  // Release memory for 1st operand
  delete[] pmessage;
  pmessage = new char[ strlen(aMess.pmessage) + 1];

  // Copy 2nd operand string to 1st
  strcpy(this->pmessage, aMess.pmessage);

  // Return a reference to 1st operand
  return *this;
}
```

An assignment might seem very simple, but there's a couple of subtleties need further investigation. First of all, note that you return a *reference* from the assignment operator function. It may not be immediately apparent why this is so — after all, the function does complete the assignment operation entirely, and the object on the right of the assignment will be copied to that on the left. Superficially this would suggest that you don't need to return anything, but you need to consider in a little more depth how the operator might be used.

There's a possibility that you might need to use the result of an assignment operation on the right hand side of an expression. Consider a statement such as this:

```
motto1 = motto2 = motto3;
```

Because the assignment operator is right-associative, the assignment of motto3 to motto2 will be carried out first, so this will translate into the following statement:

```
motto1 = (motto2.operator=(motto3));
```

The result of the operator function call here is on the right of the equals sign, so the statement will finally become this:

```
motto1.operator=(motto2.operator=(motto3));
```

If this is to work, you certainly have to return something. The call of the operator=() function between the parentheses must return an object that can be used as an argument to the other operator=() function call. In this case a return type of either CMessage or CMessage& would do it, so a reference is not mandatory in this situation, but you must at least return a CMessage object.

However, consider the following example:

```
(motto1 = motto2) = motto3;
```

This is perfectly legitimate code — the parentheses serve to make sure the leftmost assignment is carried out first. This translates into the following statement:

```
(motto1.operator=(motto2)) = motto3;
```

When you express the remaining assignment operation as the explicit overloaded function call this ultimately becomes:

```
(motto1.operator=(motto2)).operator=(motto3);
```

Now you have a situation where the object returned from the operator=() function is used to call the operator=() function. If the return type is just CMessage, this will not be legal because a temporary copy of the original object is actually returned, and the compiler will not allow a member function call using a temporary object. In other words, the return value when the return type is CMessage is not an lvalue. The only way to ensure this sort of thing will compile and work correctly is to return a reference, which is an lvalue, so the only possible return type if want to allow fully flexible use of the assignment operator with your class objects is CMessage&.

Note that the native C++ language does not enforce any restrictions on the accepted parameter or return types for the assignment operator, but it makes sense to declare the operator in the way I have just described if you want your assignment operator functions to support normal C++ usage of assignment.

The second subtlety you need to keep in mind is that each object already has memory for a string allocated, so the first thing that the operator function has to do is to delete the memory allocated to the first object and reallocate sufficient memory to accommodate the string belonging to the second object. Once this is done, the string from the second object can be copied to the new memory now owned by the first.

There's still a defect in this operator function. What if you were to write the following statement?

```
motto1 = motto1;
```

Obviously, you wouldn't do anything as stupid as this directly, but it could easily be hidden behind a pointer, for instance, as in the following statement,

```
Motto1 = *pMess;
```

If the pointer `pMess` points to `motto1` you essentially have the preceding assignment statement. In this case, the operator function as it stands would delete the memory for `motto1`, allocate some more memory based on the length of the string that has already been deleted and try to copy the old memory which, by then, could well have been corrupted. You can fix this with a check for identical left and right operands at the beginning of the function, so now the definition of the `operator=()` function would become this:

```
// Overloaded assignment operator for CMessage objects
CMessage& operator=(const CMessage& aMess)
{
   if(this == &aMess)                    // Check addresses, if equal
     return *this;                       // return the 1st operand

   // Release memory for 1st operand
   delete[] pmessage;
   pmessage = new char[ strlen(aMess.pmessage) +1];

   // Copy 2nd operand string to 1st
   strcpy(this->pmessage, aMess.pmessage);

   // Return a reference to 1st operand
   return *this;
}
```

This code assumes that the function definition appears within the class definition.

<hr>

Try It Out   Overloading the Assignment Operator

Let's put this together in a working example. We'll add a function, called `Reset()`, to the class at the same time. This just resets the message to a string of asterisks.

```
// Ex8_05.cpp
// Overloaded copy operator perfection
#include <iostream>
#include <cstring>
using std::cout;
using std::endl;

class CMessage
{
  private:
    char* pmessage;                       // Pointer to object text string

  public:
    // Function to display a message
    void ShowIt() const
    {
      cout << endl << pmessage;
    }
```

```
    //Function to reset a message to *
    void Reset()
    {
      char* temp = pmessage;
      while(*temp)
        *(temp++) = '*';
    }
```

```
    // Overloaded assignment operator for CMessage objects
    CMessage& operator=(const CMessage& aMess)
    {
      if(this == &aMess)                 // Check addresses, if equal
        return *this;                    // return the 1st operand

      // Release memory for 1st operand
      delete[] pmessage;
      pmessage = new char[ strlen(aMess.pmessage) +1];

      // Copy 2nd operand string to 1st
      strcpy(this->pmessage, aMess.pmessage);

      // Return a reference to 1st operand
      return *this;
    }
```

```
    // Constructor definition
    CMessage(const char* text = "Default message")
    {
      pmessage = new char[ strlen(text) +1 ]; // Allocate space for text
      strcpy(pmessage, text);                 // Copy text to new memory
    }

    // Destructor to free memory allocated by new
    ~CMessage()
    {
      cout << "Destructor called."     // Just to track what happens
           << endl;
      delete[] pmessage;               // Free memory assigned to pointer
    }
};
```

```
int main()
{
  CMessage motto1("The devil takes care of his own");
  CMessage motto2;

  cout << "motto2 contains - ";
  motto2.ShowIt();
  cout << endl;

  motto2 = motto1;                          // Use new assignment operator

  cout << "motto2 contains - ";
  motto2.ShowIt();
```

```
        cout << endl;

        motto1.Reset();                         // Setting motto1 to * doesn't
                                                // affect motto2

        cout << "motto1 now contains - ";
        motto1.ShowIt();
        cout << endl;

        cout << "motto2 still contains - ";
        motto2.ShowIt();
        cout << endl;

        return 0;
}
```

You can see from the output of this program that everything works exactly as required, with no linking between the messages of the two objects, except where you explicitly set them equal:

```
motto2 contains -
Default message
motto2 contains -
The devil takes care of his own
motto1 now contains -
******************************
motto2 still contains -
The devil takes care of his own
Destructor called.
Destructor called.
```

So let's have another golden rule out of all of this:

> *Always implement an assignment operator if you allocate space dynamically for a data member of a class.*

Having implemented the assignment operator, what happens with operations such as +=? Well, they don't work unless you implement them. For each form of *op=* that you want to use with your class objects, you need to write another operator function.

Overloading the Addition Operator

Let's look at overloading the addition operator for our CBox class. This is interesting because it involves creating and returning a new object. The new object will be the sum (whatever you define that to mean) of the two CBox objects that are its operands.

So what do we want the sum of two boxes to mean? Well, there are quite a few legitimate possibilities but we'll keep it simple here. Let's define the sum of two CBox objects as a CBox object that is large enough to contain the other two boxes stacked on top of each other. You can do this by making the new object have an m_Length member that is the larger of the m_Length members of the objects being added, and an m_Width member derived in a similar way. The m_Height member will be the sum of the m_Height members of the two operand objects, so that the resultant CBox object can contain the other two CBox objects. This isn't necessarily an optimal solution, but it will be sufficient for our purposes. By altering the constructor, we'll also arrange that the m_Length member of a CBox object is always greater than or equal to the m_Width member.

Our version of the addition operation for boxes is easier to explain graphically, so it's illustrated in Figure 8-4.

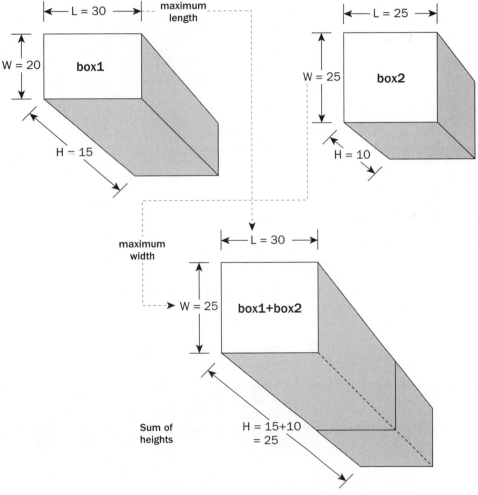

Figure 8-4

Because you need to get at the members of an object directly, you will make the operator+() a member function. The declaration of the function member within the class definition will be this:

```
CBox operator+(const CBox& aBox) const; // Function adding two CBox objects
```

You define the parameter as a reference to avoid unnecessary copying of the right argument when the function is called, and you make it a const reference because the function does not modify the argument. If you don't declare the parameter as a const reference, the compiler will not allow a const object to be passed to the function, so it would then not be possible for the right operand of + to be a const CBox object. You also declare the function as const as it doesn't change the object for which it is called. Without this, the left operand of + could not be a const CBox object.

The operator+() function definition would now be as follows:

```
// Function to add two CBox objects
CBox CBox::operator+(const CBox& aBox) const
{
  // New object has larger length and width, and sum of heights
  return CBox(m_Length > aBox.m_Length ? m_Length:aBox.m_Length,
          m_Width > aBox.m_Width ? m_Width:aBox.m_Width,
          m_Height + aBox.m_Height);
}
```

You construct a local CBox object from the current object (*this) and the object that is passed as the argument, aBox. Remember that the return process will make a temporary copy of the local object and that is what is passed back to the calling function, not the local object, which is discarded on return from the function.

Try It Out   Exercising Our Addition Operator

You'll be able to see how the overloaded addition operator in the CBox class works in this example:

```
// Ex8_06.cpp
// Adding CBox objects
#include <iostream>                          // For stream I/O
using std::cout;
using std::endl;

class CBox                                   // Class definition at global scope
{
  public:
    // Constructor definition
    CBox(double lv = 1.0, double wv = 1.0, double hv = 1.0): m_Height(hv)
    {
      m_Length = lv > wv? lv: wv;            // Ensure that
      m_Width = wv < lv? wv: lv;             // length >= width
    }

    // Function to calculate the volume of a box
    double Volume() const
```

```
    {
      return m_Length*m_Width*m_Height;
    }

    // Operator function for 'greater than' which
    // compares volumes of CBox objects.
    int CBox::operator>(const CBox& aBox) const
    {
      return this->Volume() > aBox.Volume();
    }

    // Function to compare a CBox object with a constant
    int operator>(const double& value) const
    {
      return Volume() > value;
    }

    // Function to add two CBox objects
    CBox operator+(const CBox& aBox) const
    {
      // New object has larger length & width, and sum of heights
      return CBox(m_Length > aBox.m_Length? m_Length:aBox.m_Length,
              m_Width > aBox.m_Width? m_Width:aBox.m_Width,
              m_Height + aBox.m_Height);
    }

    // Function to show the dimensions of a box
    void ShowBox() const
    {
      cout << m_Length << " "
           << m_Width  << " "
           << m_Height << endl;
    }

  private:
    double m_Length;                  // Length of a box in inches
    double m_Width;                   // Width of a box in inches
    double m_Height;                  // Height of a box in inches
};

int operator>(const double& value, const CBox& aBox); // Function prototype

int main()
{
  CBox smallBox(4.0, 2.0, 1.0);
  CBox mediumBox(10.0, 4.0, 2.0);
  CBox aBox;
  CBox bBox;

  aBox = smallBox + mediumBox;
  cout << "aBox dimensions are ";
  aBox.ShowBox();
```

```
      bBox = aBox + smallBox + mediumBox;
      cout << "bBox dimensions are ";
      bBox.ShowBox();

      return 0;
}
```

```
// Function comparing a constant with a CBox object
int operator>(const double& value, const CBox& aBox)
{
   return value > aBox.Volume();
}
```

You'll be using the CBox class definition again a few pages down the road in this chapter, so make a note that you'll want to return to this point in the book.

How It Works

In this example I have changed the CBox class members a little. I have deleted the destructor as it isn't necessary for this class, and I have modified the constructor to ensure that the m_Length member isn't less than the m_Width member. Knowing that the length of a box is always at least as big as the width makes the add operation a bit easier. I've also added the ShowBox() function to output the dimensions of a CBox object. Using this, we'll be able to verify that our overloaded add operation is working as we expect.

The output from this program is:

```
aBox dimensions are 10 4 3
bBox dimensions are 10 4 6
```

This seems to be consistent with the notion of adding CBox objects that we have defined and, as you can see, the function also works with multiple add operations in an expression. For the computation of bBox, the overloaded addition operator will be called twice.

You could equally well have implemented the add operation for the class as a friend function. Its prototype would then be this:

```
friend CBox operator+(const CBox& aBox, const CBox& bBox);
```

The process for producing the result would be much the same, except that you'd need to use the direct member selection operator to obtain the members for both the arguments to the function. It would work just as well as the first version of the operator function.

Overloading the Increment and Decrement Operators

I'll briefly introduce the mechanism for overloading the increment and decrement operators in a class because they have some special characteristics that make them different from other unary operators. You need a way to deal with the fact that the ++ and -- operators come in a prefix and postfix form, and the effect is different depending on whether the operator is applied in its prefix or postfix form. In native

C++ the overloaded operator is different for the prefix and postfix forms of the increment and decrement operators. Here's how they would be defined in a class with the name `Length` for example:

```cpp
class Length
{
  private:
    double len;                           // Length value for the class

  public:
    Length& operator++();                 // Prefix increment operator
    const Length operator++(int);         // Postfix increment operator

    Length& operator--();                 // Prefix decrement operator
    const Length operator--(int);         // Postfix decrement operator

  // rest of the class...

}
```

This simple class assumes a length is stored just as a value of type `double`. You would probably in reality make a length class more sophisticated than this but it will serve to illustrate how you overload the increment and decrement operators.

The primary way the prefix and postfix forms of the overloaded operators are differentiated is by the parameter list; for the prefix form there are no parameters and for the postfix form there is a parameter of type `int`. The parameter in the postfix operator function is only to distinguish it from the prefix form and is otherwise unused in the function implementation.

The prefix increment and decrement operators increment or decrement the operand before its value is used in an expression, so you just return a reference to the current object after it has been incremented or decremented. Here's how an implementation of the prefix `operator++()` function would look for the `Length` class:

```cpp
Length& Length::operator++()
{
  ++(this->len);
  return *this;
}
```

With the postfix forms, the operand is incremented after its current value is used in an expression. This is achieved by creating a new object that is a copy of the current object before incrementing the current object and returning the copy after the current object has been modified. Here's how you might implement the function to overload the postfix ++ operator for the `Length` class:

```cpp
const Length& Length::operator++(int)
{
  Length length = *this;                  // Copy the current object
  ++*this;                                // Increment the current object
  return length;                          // Return the original copy
}
```

After copying the current object, you increment it using the prefix ++ operator for the class. You then return the original unincremented copy of the current object. Declaring the return value as `const` prevents expressions such as `data++++` from compiling.

Class Templates

You saw back in Chapter 6 that you could define a function template that would automatically generate functions varying in the type of arguments accepted, or in the type of values returned. C++ has a similar mechanism for classes. A **class template** is not in itself a class, it's a sort of "recipe" for a class that will be used by the compiler to generate the code for a class. As you can see from Figure 8-5, it's like the function template — you determine the class that you want generated by specifying your choice of type for the parameter (T in this case) that appears between the angled brackets in the template. Doing this generates a particular class that is referred to as an **instance** of the class template. The process of creating a class from a template is described as **instantiating** the template.

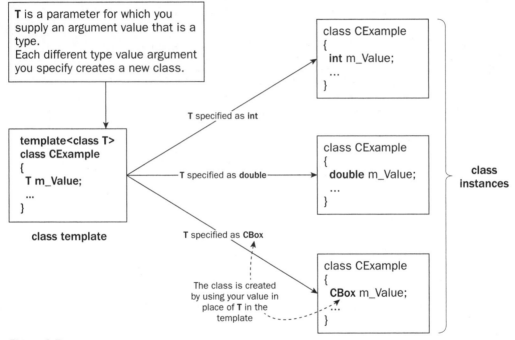

Figure 8-5

An appropriate class definition is generated when you instantiate an object of a template class for a particular type, so you can generate any number of different classes from one class template. You'll get a good idea of how this works in practice by looking at an example.

Defining a Class Template

I'll choose a simple example to illustrate how you define and use a class template, and I won't complicate things by worrying too much about possible errors that can arise if it's misused. Suppose you want to define classes that can store a number of data samples of some kind, and each class is to provide a Max() function to determine the maximum sample value of those stored. This function will be similar to the one you saw in the function template discussion in Chapter 6. You can define a class template, which will generate a class CSamples to store samples of whatever type you want:

```
template <class T>
class CSamples
{
  public:
    // Constructor definition to accept an array of samples
    CSamples(const T values[], int count)
    {
      m_Free = count < 100? count:100; // Don't exceed the array
      for(int i = 0; i < m_Free; i++)
        m_Values[i] = values[i];       // Store count number of samples
    }

    // Constructor to accept a single sample
    CSamples(const T& value)
    {
      m_Values[0] = value;             // Store the sample
      m_Free = 1;                      // Next is free
    }

    // Default constructor
    CSamples(){ m_Free = 0 }           // Nothing stored, so first is free

    // Function to add a sample
    bool Add(const T& value)
    {
      bool OK = m_Free < 100;          // Indicates there is a free place
      if(OK)
        m_Values[m_Free++] = value;    // OK true, so store the value
      return OK;
    }

    // Function to obtain maximum sample
    T Max() const
    {
      // Set first sample or 0 as maximum
      T theMax = m_Free ? m_Values[0] : 0;

      for(int i = 1; i < m_Free; i++)  // Check all the samples
        if(m_Values[i] > theMax)
          theMax = m_Values[i];        // Store any larger sample
      return theMax;
    }

  private:
    T m_Values[100];                   // Array to store samples
    int m_Free;                        // Index of free location in m_Values
};
```

To indicate that you are defining a template rather than a straightforward class, you insert the `template` keyword and the type parameter, `T`, between angled brackets, just before the `class` keyword and the class name, `CSamples`. This is essentially the same syntax that you used to define a function template back in Chapter 6. The parameter `T` is the type variable that will be replaced by a specific type when you declare a class object. Wherever the parameter `T` appears in the class definition, it will be replaced by the type that you specify in your object declaration; this creates a class definition corresponding to this type. You can specify any type (a basic data type or a class type), but it has to make sense in the context of the class template, of course. Any class type that you use to instantiate a class from a template must have all the operators defined that the member functions of the template will use with such objects. If your class hasn't implemented `operator>()`, for example, it will not work with the `CSamples` class template above. In general, you can specify multiple parameters in a class template if you need them. I'll come back to this possibility a little later in the chapter.

Getting back to the example, the type of the array in which the samples will be stored is specified as `T`. The array will therefore be an array of whatever type you specify for `T` when you declare a `CSamples` object. As you can see, you also use the type `T` in two of the constructors for the class, as well as in the `Add()` and `Max()` functions. Each of these occurrences will also be replaced when you instantiate a class object using the template.

The constructors support the creation of an empty object, an object with a single sample, and an object initialized with an array of samples. The `Add()` function allows samples to be added to an object one at a time. You could also overload this function to add an array of samples. The class template includes some elementary provision to prevent the capacity of the `m_Values` array being exceeded in the `Add()` function, and in the constructor that accepts an array of samples.

As I said earlier, in theory you can create objects of `CSamples` classes that will handle any data type: type `int`, type `double`, or any class type that you've defined. In practice, this doesn't mean it will necessarily compile and work as you expect. It all depends on what the template definition does, and usually a template will only work for a particular range of types. For example, the `Max()` function implicitly assumes that the > operator is available for whatever type is being processed. If it isn't, your program will not compile. Clearly, you'll usually be in the position of defining a template that works for some types but not others, but there's no way you can restrict what type is applied to a template.

Template Member Functions

You may want to place the definition of a class template member function outside of the template definition. The syntax for this isn't particularly obvious, so let's look at how you do it. You put the function declaration in the class template definition in the normal way. For instance:

```
template <class T>
class CSamples
{
   // Rest of the template definition...
   T Max() const;                // Function to obtain maximum sample
   // Rest of the template definition...
}
```

This declares the `Max()` function as a member of the class template but doesn't define it. You now need to create a separate function template for the definition of the member function. You must use the template class name plus the parameters in angled brackets to identify the class template to which the function template belongs:

```
template<class T>
T CSamples<T>::Max() const
{
  T theMax = m_Values[0];              // Set first sample as maximum

  for(int i = 1; i < m_Free; i++)      // Check all the samples
    if(m_Values[i] > theMax)
      theMax = m_Values[i];            // Store any larger sample
  return theMax;
}
```

You saw the syntax for a function template back in Chapter 6. Since this function template is for a member of the class template with the parameter T, the function template definition here should have the same parameters as the class template definition. There's just one in this case — T — but in general there can be several. If the class template had two or more parameters, then so would each template defining a member function.

Note how you only put the parameter name, T, along with the class name before the scope resolution operator. This is necessary — the parameters are fundamental to the identification of the class to which a function, produced from the template, belongs. The type will be CSamples<T> with whatever type you assign to T when you create an instance of the class template. Your type is plugged into the class template to generate the class definition, and into the function template to generate the definition for the Max() function for the class. Each class that's produced from the class template needs to have its own definition for the function Max().

Defining a constructor or a destructor outside of the class template definition is very similar. You could write the definition of the constructor that accepts an array of samples as:

```
template<class T>
CSamples<T>::CSamples(T values[], int count)
{
  m_Free = count < 100? count:100;     // Don't exceed the array

  for(int i = 0; i < m_Free; i++)
    m_Values[i] = values[i];           // Store count number of samples
}
```

The class to which the constructor belongs is specified in the template in the same way as for an ordinary member function. Note that the constructor name doesn't require the parameter specification — it is just CSamples, but it needs to be qualified by the class template type CSamples<T>. You only use the parameter with the class template name *preceding* the scope resolution operator.

Creating Objects from a Class Template

When you use a function defined by a function template, the compiler is able to generate the function from the types of the arguments used. The type parameter for the function template is implicitly defined by the specific use of a particular function. Class templates are a little different. To create an object based on a class template, you must always specify the type parameter following the class name in the declaration.

For example, to declare a CSamples<> object to handle samples of type double, you could write the declaration as:

```
CSamples<double> myData(10.0);
```

This defines an object of type CSamples<double> that can store samples of type double, and the object is created with one sample stored with the value 10.0.

Try It Out   Class Templating

You could create an object from the CSamples<> template that stores CBox objects. This will work because the CBox class implements the operator>() function to overload the greater-than operator. You could exercise the class template with the main() function in the following listing:

```cpp
// Ex8_07.cpp
// Using a class template
#include <iostream>
using std::cout;
using std::endl;

// Put the CBox class definition from Ex8_06.cpp here...

// CSamples class template definition
template <class T> class CSamples
{
  public:
    // Constructors
    CSamples(const T values[], int count);
    CSamples(const T& value);
    CSamples(){ m_Free = 0; }

    bool Add(const T& value);            // Insert a value
    T Max() const;                       // Calculate maximum

  private:
    T m_Values[100];                     // Array to store samples
    int m_Free;                          // Index of free location in m_Values
};

// Constructor template definition to accept an array of samples
template<class T> CSamples<T>::CSamples(const T values[], int count)
{
  m_Free = count < 100? count:100;       // Don't exceed the array
  for(int i = 0; i < m_Free; i++)
    m_Values[i] = values[i];             // Store count number of samples
}

// Constructor to accept a single sample
template<class T> CSamples<T>::CSamples(const T& value)
```

```
{
  m_Values[0] = value;                // Store the sample
  m_Free = 1;                         // Next is free
}

// Function to add a sample
template<class T> bool CSamples<T>::Add(const T& value)
{
  bool OK = m_Free < 100;             // Indicates there is a free place
  if(OK)
    m_Values[m_Free++] = value;       // OK true, so store the value
  return OK;
}

// Function to obtain maximum sample
template<class T> T CSamples<T>::Max() const
{
  T theMax = m_Free ? m_Values[0] : 0; // Set first sample or 0 as maximum
  for(int i = 1; i < m_Free; i++)      // Check all the samples
    if(m_Values[i] > theMax)
      theMax = m_Values[i];            // Store any larger sample
  return theMax;
}

int main()
{
  CBox boxes[] = {                           // Create an array of boxes
                  CBox(8.0, 5.0, 2.0),       // Initialize the boxes...
                  CBox(5.0, 4.0, 6.0),
                  CBox(4.0, 3.0, 3.0)
                 };

  // Create the CSamples object to hold CBox objects
  CSamples<CBox> myBoxes(boxes, sizeof boxes / sizeof CBox);

  CBox maxBox = myBoxes.Max();               // Get the biggest box
  cout << endl                               // and output its volume
       << "The biggest box has a volume of "
       << maxBox.Volume()
       << endl;
  return 0;
}
```

You should replace the comment with the CBox class definition from Ex8_06.cpp. You need not worry about the operator>() function that supports comparison of a CBox object with a value of type double as this example does not need it. With the exception of the default constructor, all the member functions of the template are defined by separate function templates, just to show you a complete example of how it's done.

In main() you create an array of three CBox objects and then use this array to initialize a CSamples object that can store CBox objects. The declaration of the CSamples object is basically the same as it would be for an ordinary class, but with the addition of the type parameter in angled brackets following the template class name.

The program will generate the following output:

```
The biggest box has a volume of 120
```

Note that when you create an instance of a class template, it does not follow that instances of the function templates for function members will also be created. The compiler will only create instances of templates for member functions that you actually call in your program. In fact, your function templates can even contain coding errors, and as long as you don't call the member function that the template generates, the compiler will not complain. You can test this out with the example. Try introducing a few errors into the template for the `Add()` member. The program will still compile and run because it doesn't call the `Add()` function.

You could try modifying the example and perhaps seeing what happens when you instantiate classes by using the template with various other types.

You might be surprised at what happens if you add some output statements to the class constructors. The constructor for the CBox *is being called 103 times! Look at what is happening in the* main() *function. First you create an array of three* CBox *objects, so that's three calls. You then create a* CSamples *object to hold them, but a* CSamples *object contains an array of 100 variables of type* CBox, *so you call the default constructor another 100 times, once for each element in the array. Of course, the* maxBox *object will be created by the default copy constructor that is supplied by the compiler.*

Class Templates with Multiple Parameters

Using multiple type parameters in a class template is a straightforward extension of the example using a single parameter that you have just seen. You can use each of the type parameters wherever you want in the template definition. For example, you could define a class template with two type parameters:

```
template<class T1, class T2>
class CExampleClass
{
  // Class data members

  private:
    T1 m_Value1;
    T2 m_Value2;

  // Rest of the template definition...
};
```

The types of the two class data members shown will be determined by the types you supply for the parameters when you instantiate an object.

The parameters in a class template aren't limited to types. You can also use parameters that require constants or constant expressions to be substituted in the class definition. In our `CSamples` template, we arbitrarily defined the `m_Values` array with 100 elements. You could, however, let the user of the template choose the size of the array when the object is instantiated, by defining the template as:

```
template <class T, int Size> class CSamples
{
```

```
    private:
      T m_Values[Size];            // Array to store samples
      int m_Free;                  // Index of free location in m_Values

    public:
      // Constructor definition to accept an array of samples
      CSamples(const T values[], int count)
      {
        m_Free = count < Size? count:Size; // Don't exceed the array

        for(int i = 0; i < m_Free; i++)
          m_Values[i] = values[i];         // Store count number of samples
      }

      // Constructor to accept a single sample
      CSamples(const T& value)
      {
        m_Values[0] = value;             // Store the sample
        m_Free = 1;                      // Next is free
      }

      // Default constructor
      CSamples()
      {
        m_Free = 0;                      // Nothing stored, so first is free
      }

      // Function to add a sample
      int Add(const T& value)
      {
        int OK = m_Free < Size;          // Indicates there is a free place
        if(OK)
          m_Values[m_Free++] = value;    // OK true, so store the value
        return OK;
      }

      // Function to obtain maximum sample
      T Max() const
      {
        // Set first sample or 0 as maximum
        T theMax = m_Free ? m_Values[0] : 0;

        for(int i = 1; i < m_Free; i++)  // Check all the samples
          if(m_Values[i] > theMax)
            theMax = m_Values[i];        // Store any larger sample
        return theMax;
      }
};
```

The value supplied for `Size` when you create an object will replace the appearance of the parameter throughout the template definition. Now you can declare the `CSamples` object from the previous example as:

```
CSamples<CBox, 3> MyBoxes(boxes, sizeof boxes/sizeof CBox);
```

Because you can supply *any* constant expression for the Size parameter, you could also have written this as:

```
CSamples<CBox, sizeof boxes/sizeof CBox>
                        MyBoxes(boxes, sizeof boxes/sizeof CBox);
```

The example is a poor use of a template though — the original version was much more usable. A consequence of making Size a template parameter is that instances of the template that store the same types of objects but have different size parameter values are totally different classes and cannot be mixed. For instance, an object of type CSamples<double, 10> cannot be used in an expression with an object of type CSamples<double, 20>.

You need to be careful with expressions that involve comparison operators when instantiating templates. Look at this statement:

```
CSamples<aType, x > y ? 10 : 20 > MyType();        // Wrong!
```

This will not compile correctly because the > preceding y in the expression will be interpreted as a right-angled bracket. Instead, you should write this statement as:

```
CSamples<aType, (x > y ? 10 : 20) > MyType();      // OK
```

The parentheses ensure that the expression for the second template argument doesn't get mixed up with the angled brackets.

Using Classes

I've touched on most of the basic aspects of defining a native C++ class, so maybe we should look at how a class might be used to solve a problem. I'll need to keep the problem simple in order to keep this book down to a reasonable number of pages, so we'll consider problems in which we can use an extended version of the CBox class.

The Idea of a Class Interface

The implementation of an extended CBox class should incorporate the notion of a **class interface**. You are going to provide a tool kit for anyone wanting to work with CBox objects so you need to assemble a set of functions that represents the interface to the world of boxes. Because the interface will represent the only way to deal with CBox objects, it needs to be defined to cover adequately the likely things one would want to do with a CBox object, and be implemented, as far as possible, in a manner that protects against misuse or accidental errors.

The first question that you need to consider in designing a class is the nature of the problem you intend to solve and, from that, determine the kind of functionality you need to provide in the class interface.

Defining the Problem

The principal function of a box is to contain objects of one kind or another so, in a word, the problem is **packaging**. We'll attempt to provide a class that eases packaging problems in general and then see how it might be used. We will assume that we'll always be working on packing CBox objects into other CBox objects since, if you want to pack candy in a box, you can always represent each of the pieces of candy as an idealized CBox object. The basic operations that you might want to provide in the CBox class include:

❑   Calculate the volume of a CBox. This is a fundamental characteristic of a CBox object and you have an implementation of this already.

❑   Compare the volumes of two CBox objects to determine which is the larger. You probably should support a complete set of comparison operators for CBox objects. You already have a version of the > operator.

❑   Compare the volume of a CBox object with a specified value and vice versa. You also have an implementation of this for the > operator, but you will also need to implement functions supporting the other comparison operators.

❑   Add two CBox objects to produce a new CBox object that will contain both the original objects. Thus, the result will be at least the sum of the volumes, but may be larger. You have a version of this already that overloads the + operator.

❑   Multiply a CBox object by an integer (and vice versa) to provide a new CBox object that will contain a specified number of the original objects. This is effectively designing a carton.

❑   Determine how many CBox objects of a given size can be packed in another CBox object of a given size. This is effectively division, so you could implement this by overloading the / operator.

❑   Determine the volume of space remaining in a CBox object after packing it with the maximum number of CBox objects of a given size.

I had better stop right there! There are undoubtedly other functions that would be very useful but, in the interest of saving trees, we'll consider the set to be complete, apart from ancillaries such as accessing dimensions, for example.

Implementing the CBox Class

You really need to consider the degree of error protection that you want to build into the CBox class. The basic class that you defined to illustrate various aspects of classes is a starting point, but you should also consider some points a little more deeply. The constructor is a little weak in that it doesn't ensure that the dimensions for a CBox are valid so perhaps the first thing you should do is to ensure that you always have valid objects. You could redefine the basic class as follows to do this:

```
class CBox                              // Class definition at global scope
{
  public:
    // Constructor definition
    CBox(double lv = 1.0, double wv = 1.0, double hv = 1.0)
    {
      lv = lv <= 0? 1.0: lv;            // Ensure positive
      wv = wv <= 0? 1.0: wv;            // dimensions for
      hv = hv <= 0? 1.0: hv;           // the object

      m_Length = lv > wv? lv: wv;       // Ensure that
      m_Width = wv < lv? wv: lv;       // length >= width
      m_Height = hv;
    }

    // Function to calculate the volume of a box
```

```
    double Volume() const
    {
      return m_Length*m_Width*m_Height;
    }

    // Function providing the length of a box
    double GetLength() const { return m_Length; }

    // Function providing the width of a box
    double GetWidth() const { return m_Width; }

    // Function providing the height of a box
    double GetHeight() const { return m_Height; }

  private:
    double m_Length;            // Length of a box in inches
    double m_Width;             // Width of a box in inches
    double m_Height;            // Height of a box in inches
};
```

The constructor is now secure because any dimension that the user of the class tries to set to a negative number or zero will be set to 1 in the constructor. You might also consider displaying a message for a negative or zero dimension because there's obviously an error when this occurs, and arbitrarily and silently setting a dimension to 1 might not be the best solution.

The default copy constructor is satisfactory for our class, because you have no dynamic memory allocation for data members, and the default assignment operator will also work as you would like. The default destructor also works perfectly well in this case so you don't need to define it. Perhaps now you should consider what is required to support comparisons of objects of our class.

Comparing CBox Objects

You should include support for the operators >, >=, ==, <, and <= so that they work with both operands as CBox objects, as well between a CBox object and a value of type double. You can implement these as ordinary global functions because they don't need to be member functions. You can write the functions that compare the volumes of two CBox objects in terms of the functions that compare the volume of a CBox object with a double value, so let's start with the latter. You can start by repeating the operator>() function that you had before:

```
// Function for testing if a constant is > a CBox object
int operator>(const double& value, const CBox& aBox)
{
  return value > aBox.Volume();
}
```

You can now write the operator<() function in a similar way:

```
// Function for testing if a constant is < CBox object
int operator<(const double& value, const CBox& aBox)
{
  return value < aBox.Volume();
}
```

You can code the implementations of the same operators with the arguments reversed in terms of the two functions you have just defined:

```
// Function for testing if CBox object is > a constant
int operator>(const CBox& aBox, const double& value)
{ return value < aBox; }

// Function for testing if CBox object is < a constant
int operator<(const CBox& aBox, const double& value)
{ return value > aBox; }
```

You just use the appropriate overloaded operator function that you wrote before, with the arguments from the call to the new function switched.

The functions implementing the >= and <= operators will be the same as the first two functions but with the <= operator replacing each use of <, and >= instead of >; there's little point in reproducing them at this stage. The `operator==()` functions are also very similar:

```
// Function for testing if constant is == the volume of a CBox object
int operator==(const double& value, const CBox& aBox)
{
    return value == aBox.Volume();
}

// Function for testing if CBox object is == a constant
int operator==(const CBox& aBox, const double& value)
{
    return value == aBox;
}
```

You now have a complete set of comparison operators for CBox objects. Keep in mind that these will also work with expressions, as long as the expressions result in objects of the required type, so you will be able to combine them with the use of other overloaded operators.

Combining CBox Objects

Now you come to the question of overloading the operators +, *, /, and %. I will take them in order. The add operation that you already have from Ex8_06.cpp has this prototype:

```
CBox operator+(const CBox& aBox);        // Function adding two CBox objects
```

Although the original implementation of this isn't an ideal solution, let's use it anyway to avoid overcomplicating the class. A better version would need to examine whether the operands had any faces with the same dimensions and if so, join along those faces, but coding that could get a bit messy. Of course, if this were a practical application, a better add operation could be developed later and substituted for the existing version, and any programs written using the original would still run without change. The separation of the interface to a class from its implementation is crucial to good C++ programming.

Notice that I conveniently forgot the subtraction operator. This is a judicious oversight to avoid the complications inherent in implementing this. If you're really enthusiastic about it, and you think it's a sensible idea, you can give it a try — but you need to decide what to do when the result has a negative volume. If you allow the concept, you need to resolve which box dimension or dimensions are to be negative, and how such a box is to be handled in subsequent operations.

The multiply operation is very easy. It represents the process of creating a box to contain n boxes, where n is the multiplier. The simplest solution would be to take the m_Length and m_Width of the object to be packed and multiply the height by n to get the new CBox object. You can make it a little cleverer by checking whether or not the multiplier is even and, if it is, stack the boxes side by side by doubling the m_Width value and only multiplying the m_Height value by half of n. This mechanism is illustrated in Figure 8-6.

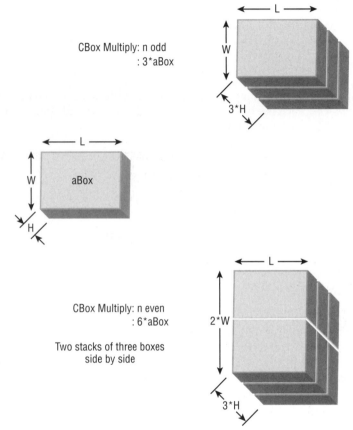

CBox Multiply: n odd
: 3*aBox

aBox

CBox Multiply: n even
: 6*aBox

Two stacks of three boxes
side by side

Figure 8-6

Of course, you don't need to check which is the larger of the length and width for the new object because the constructor will sort it out automatically. You can write the version of the operator*() function as a member function with the left operand as a CBox object:

```
// CBox multiply operator this*n
CBox operator*(int n) const
{
  if(n % 2)
    return CBox(m_Length, m_Width, n*m_Height);          // n odd
  else
    return CBox(m_Length, 2.0*m_Width, (n/2)*m_Height);  // n even
}
```

Here, you use the % operator to determine whether n is even or odd. If n is odd, the value of n % 2 is 1 and the if statement is true. If it's even, n % 2 is 0 and the statement is false.

You can now use the function you have just written in the implementation of the version with the left operand as an integer. You can write this as an ordinary non-member function:

```
// CBox multiply operator n*aBox
CBox operator*(int n, const CBox& aBox)
{
  return aBox*n;
}
```

This version of the multiply operation simply reverses the order of the operands so as to use the previous version of the function directly. That completes the set of arithmetic operators for CBox objects that you defined. You can finally look at the two analytical operator functions, operator/() and operator%().

Analyzing CBox Objects

As I have said, the division operation will determine how many CBox objects identical to that specified by the right operand can be contained in the CBox object specified by the left operand. To keep it relatively simple, assume that all the CBox objects are packed the right way up, that is, with the height dimensions vertical. Also assume that they are all packed the same way round, so that their length dimensions are aligned. Without these assumptions, it can get rather complicated.

The problem will then amount to determining how many of the right-operand objects can be placed in a single layer, and then deciding how many layers you can get inside the left-operand CBox.

You can code this as a member function like this:

```
int operator/(const CBox& aBox)
{
  int tc1 = 0;          // Temporary for number in horizontal plane this way
  int tc2 = 0;          // Temporary for number in a plane that way

  tc1 = static_cast<int>((m_Length / aBox.m_Length))*
        static_cast<int>((m_Width / aBox.m_Width));  // to fit this way
  tc2 = static_cast<int>((m_Length / aBox.m_Width))*
        static_cast<int>((m_Width / aBox.m_Length)); // and that way

  //Return best fit
  return static_cast<int>((m_Height/aBox.m_Height)*(tc1>tc2 ? tc1 : tc2));
}
```

This function first determines how many of the right-operand CBox objects can fit in a layer with their lengths aligned with the length dimension of the left-operand CBox. This is stored in tc1. You then calculate how many can fit in a layer with the lengths of the right-operand CBoxes lying in the width direction of the left-operand CBox. Finally you multiply the larger of tc1 and tc2 by the number of layers you can pack in, and return that value. This process is illustrated in Figure 8-7.

We look at two possibilities: fitting bBox into aBox with the length aligned with that of aBox, and then with the length of bBox aligned with the width of aBox. You can see from Figure 8-7 that the best packing results from rotating bBox so that the width divides into the length of aBox.

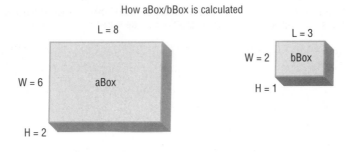

How aBox/bBox is calculated

There are two rectangular arrangements possible for fitting a
number of bBox objects within aBox, as shown below.

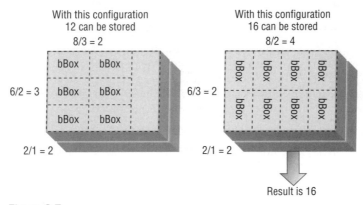

Figure 8-7

The other analytical operator function, `operator%()`, for obtaining the free volume in a packed `aBox`
is easier because you can use the operator you have just written to implement it. You can write it as an
ordinary global function because you don't need access to the `private` members of the class.

```
// Operator to return the free volume in a packed box
double operator%(const CBox& aBox, const CBox& bBox)
{
  return aBox.Volume() - ((aBox/bBox)*bBox.Volume());
}
```

This computation falls out very easily using existing class functions. The result is the volume of the big box,
`aBox`, minus the volume of the `bBox` boxes that can be stored in it. The number of `bBox` objects packed into
`aBox` is given by the expression `aBox/bBox`, which uses the previous overloaded operator. You multiply this
by the volume of `bBox` objects to get the volume to be subtracted from the volume of the large box, `aBox`.

That completes the class interface. Clearly, there are many more functions that might be required for a
production problem solver but, as an interesting working model demonstrating how you can produce
a class for solving a particular kind of problem, it will suffice. Now you can go ahead and try it out on a
real problem.

Try It Out A Multifile Project Using the CBox Class

Before you can actually start writing the code to *use* the CBox class and its overloaded operators, first you need to assemble the definition for the class into a coherent whole. You're going to take a rather different approach from what you've seen previously, in that you're going to write multiple files for the project. You're also going to start using the facilities that Visual C++ 2008 provides for creating and maintaining code for our classes. This will mean that you do rather less of the work, but it will also mean that the code will be slightly different in places.

Start by creating a new WIN32 project for a console application called Ex8_08 and check the Empty project application option. If you select the Class View tab, you'll see the window shown in Figure 8-8.

Figure 8-8

This shows a view of all the classes in a project but of course, there are none here for the moment. Although there are no classes defined — or anything else for that matter — Visual C++ 2008 has already made provision for including some. You can use Visual C++ 2008 to create a skeleton for our CBox class, and the files that relate to it too. Right-click Ex8_08 in Class View and select Add/Class... from the pop-up menu that appears. You can then select C++ from the class categories in the left pane of the Add Class dialog that is displayed and the C++ Class template in the right pane and press Enter. You will then be able to enter the name of the class that you want to create, CBox, in the Generic Class Wizard dialog, as shown in Figure 8-9.

The name of the file that's indicated on the dialog, Box.cpp, will be used to contain the **class implementation**, which consists of the definitions for the function members of the class. This is the executable code for the class. You can change the name of this file if you want, but Box.cpp looks like a good name for the file in this case. The class definition will be stored in a file called Box.h. This is the standard way of structuring a program. Code that consists of class definitions is stored in files with the extension .h, and code that defines functions is stored in files with the extension .cpp. Usually, each class definition goes in its own .h file, and each class implementation goes in its own .cpp file.

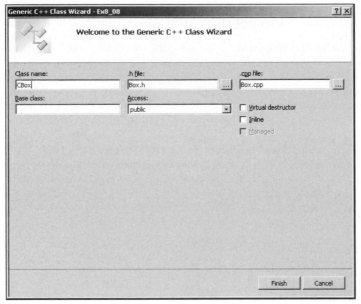

Figure 8-9

When you click the Finish button in the dialog two things happen:

1. A file Box.h is created containing a skeleton definition for the class CBox. This includes a no-argument constructor and a destructor.

2. A file Box.cpp is created containing a skeleton implementation for the functions in the class with definitions for the constructor and the destructor — both bodies are empty of course.

The editor pane displaying the code should be as shown in Figure 8-10. If it is not presently displayed, just double-click CBox in Class View, and it should appear.

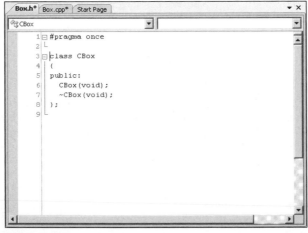

Figure 8-10

As you can see, above the pane containing the code listing for the class there are two controls. The left control displays the current class name, CBox, and clicking the button to the right of the class name will display the list of all the classes in the project. In general you can use this control to switch to another class by selecting it from the list, but here you have just one class defined. The control to the right relates to the members defined in the .cpp file for the current class, and clicking its button will display the members of the class. Selecting a member from the list will cause its code to be visible in the pane below.

Let's start developing the CBox class based on what Visual C++ has provided automatically for us.

Defining the CBox Class

If you click the + to the left of Ex8_08 in the Class View, the tree will be expanded and you will see that CBox is now defined for the project. All the classes in a project are displayed in this tree. You can view the source code supplied for the definition of a class by double-clicking the class name in the tree, or by using the controls above the pane displaying the code as I described in the previous section.

The CBox class definition that was generated starts with a preprocessor directive:

```
#pragma once
```

The effect of this is to prevent the file from being opened and included into the source code more than once by the compiler in a build. Typically a class definition will be included into several files in a project because each file that references the name of a particular class will need access to its definition. In some instances a header file may itself have #include directives for other header files. This can result in the possibility of the contents of a header file appearing more than once in the source code. Having more than one definition of a class in a build is not allowed and will be flagged as an error. Having the #pragma once directive at the start of every header file will ensure this cannot happen.

Note that #pragma once is a Microsoft-specific directive that may not be supported in other development environments. If you are developing code that you anticipate may need to be compiled in other environments you can use the following form of directive in a header file to achieve the same effect:

```
// Box.h header file
#ifndef BOX_H
#define BOX_H
// Code that must not be included more than once
// such as the CBox class definition
#endif
```

The important lines are shaded and correspond to directives that are supported by any ISO/ANSI C++ compiler. The lines following the #ifndef directive down to the #endif directive will be included in a build as long as the symbol BOX_H is not defined. The line following #ifndef defines the symbol BOX_H thus ensuring that the code in this header file will not be included a second time. Thus this has the same effect as placing the #pragma once directive at the beginning of a header file. Clearly the #pragma once directive is simpler and less cluttered so it's better to use that when you only expect to be using your code in the Visual C++ 2008 development environment. You will sometimes see the `#ifndef`/`#endif` combination written as:

```
#if !defined BOX_H
#define BOX_H
// Code that must not be included more than once
// such as the CBox class definition
#endif
```

The `Box.cpp` file that was generated by Class Wizard contains the following code:

```
#include "Box.h"

CBox::CBox(void)
{
}

CBox::~CBox(void)
{
}
```

The first line is an `#include` preprocessor directive that has the effect of including the contents of the `Box.h` file — the class definition — into this file, `Box.cpp`. This is necessary because the code in `Box.cpp` refers to the `CBox` class name and the class definition needs to be available to assign meaning to the name `CBox`.

Adding Data Members

First, you can add the private data members `m_Length`, `m_Width`, and `m_Height`. Right click `CBox` in Class View and select `Add/Add Variable...` from the pop-up menu. You can then specify the name, type, and access for the first data member that you want to add to the class in the `Add Member Variable Wizard` dialog.

The way you specify a new data member in this dialog is quite self-explanatory. If you specify a lower limit for a data member, you must also specify an upper limit. When you specify limits, the constructor definition in the `.cpp` file will be modified to add a default value for the data member corresponding to the lower limit. You can add a comment in the lower input field if you wish. When you click the OK button, the variable will be added to the class definition along with the comment if you have supplied one. You should repeat the process for the other two class data members, `m_Width` and `m_Height`. The class definition in `Box.h` will then be modified to look like this:

```
#pragma once

class CBox
{
public:
  CBox(void);
public:
  ~CBox(void);
private:
  // Length of a box in inches
```

```
    double m_Length;
    // Width of a box in inches
    double m_Width;
    // Height of a box in inches
    double m_Height;
};
```

Of course, you're quite free to enter the declarations for these members manually, directly into the code, if you want. You always have the choice of whether you use the automation provided by the IDE. You can also manually delete anything that was generated automatically, but don't forget that sometimes both the .h and .cpp file will need to be changed. It's a good idea to save all the files whenever you make manual changes as this will cause the information in Class View to be updated.

If you look in the Box.cpp file, you'll see that the Wizard has also added an initialization list to the constructor definition for the data members you have added, with each variable initialized to 0. You'll modify the constructor to do what you want next.

Defining the Constructor

You need to change the declaration of the no-arg constructor in the class definition so that it has arguments with default values, so modify it to:

```
CBox(double lv = 1.0, double wv = 1.0, double hv = 1.0);
```

Now you're ready to implement it. Open the Box.cpp file if it isn't open already and modify the constructor definition to:

```
CBox::CBox(double lv, double wv, double hv)
{
    lv = lv <= 0.0 ? 1.0 : lv;          // Ensure positive
    wv = wv <= 0.0 ? 1.0 : wv;          // dimensions for
    hv = hv <= 0.0 ? 1.0 : hv;          // the object

    m_Length = lv>wv ? lv : wv;         // Ensure that
    m_Width = wv<lv ? wv : lv;          // length >= width
    m_Height = hv;
}
```

Remember that the initializers for the parameters to a member function should only appear in the member declaration in the class definition, not in the definition of the function. If you put them in the function definition, your code will not compile. You've seen this code already, so I won't discuss it again. It would be a good idea to save the file at this point by clicking on the Save toolbar button. Get into the habit of saving the file you're editing before you switch to something else. If you need to edit the constructor again, you can get to it easily by either double-clicking its entry in the lower pane on the Class View tab or by selecting it from the right drop-down menu above the pane displaying the code.

You can also get to a member function's definition in a .cpp file or to its declaration in a .h file directly by right clicking its name in the Class View pane and selecting the appropriate item from the context menu that appears.

Adding Function Members

You need to add all the functions you saw earlier to the CBox class. Previously, you defined several function members within the class definition, so that these functions were automatically inline. You can achieve the same result by entering the code in the class definition for these functions manually, or you can use the Add Member Function Wizard.

You might think that you can define each inline function in the .cpp file, and add the keyword inline to the function definitions, but the problem here is that inline functions end up not being "real" functions. Because the code from the body of each function has to be inserted directly at the position it is called, the definitions of the functions need to be available when the file containing calls to the functions is compiled. If they're not, you'll get linker errors and your program will not run. If you want member functions to be inline, you *must* include the function definitions in the .h file for the class. They can be defined either within the class definition, or immediately following it in the .h file. You should put any global inline functions you need into a .h file, and #include that file into any .cpp file that uses them.

To add the GetHeight() function as inline, right-click CBox on the Class View tab and select Add/Add Function... from the context menu. You then can enter the data defining the function in the dialog that is displayed, as Figure 8-11 shows.

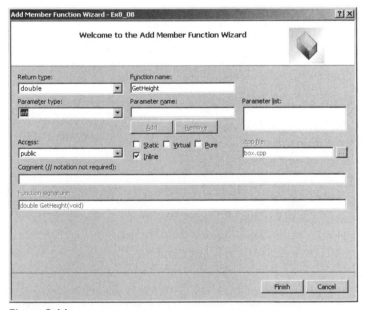

Figure 8-11

You can specify the return type to be double by selecting from the drop-down list, but you could equally well type it in. Obviously for a type that does not appear in the list you would just enter it from the keyboard. Selecting the inline checkbox ensures that GetHeight() will be created as an inline function. Note the other options to declare a function as static, virtual, or pure. As you know, a static member function exists independently of any objects of a class. You'll get to `virtual` and `pure virtual` functions in Chapter 9. The `GetHeight()` function has no parameters so nothing further needs to be added. Clicking the OK button will add the function definition to the class definition in `Box.h`. If you repeat this process for the `GetWidth()`, `GetLength()`, and `Volume()` member functions, the `CBox` class definition in `Box.h` will look like this:

```cpp
#pragma once

class CBox
{
public:
    CBox(double lv = 1.0, double wv = 1.0, double hv = 1.0);
    ~CBox(void);
private:
    // Length of a box in inches
    double m_Length;
    // Width of a box in inches
    double m_Width;
    // Height of a box in inches
    double m_Height;
public:
    double GetHeight(void)
    {
      return 0;
    }

    double GetWidth(void)
    {
      return 0;
    }

    double CBox::GetLength(void)
    {
      return 0;
    }

    // Calculate the volume of a box
    double Volume(void)
    {
      return 0;
    }
};
```

An additional public section has been added to the class definition that contains the inline function definitions. You need to modify each of the definitions to provide the correct return value and to declare the functions to be `const`. For example, the code for `GetHeight()` function should be changed to:

```cpp
double GetHeight(void) const
{
  return m_Height;
}
```

You can change the definitions of the `GetWidth()` and `GetLength()` functions in a similar way. The `Volume()` function definition should be changed to:

```
double Volume(void) const
{
  return m_Length*m_Width*m_Height;
}
```

You could enter the other non-inline member functions directly in the editor pane that shows the code, but of course you can also use the Add Member Function Wizard to do it, and the practice will be useful. Right-click `CBox` in the Class View tab and select the `Add/Add Function...` menu item from the context menu, as before. You can then enter the details of the first function you want to add in the dialog that appears, as Figure 8-12 shows.

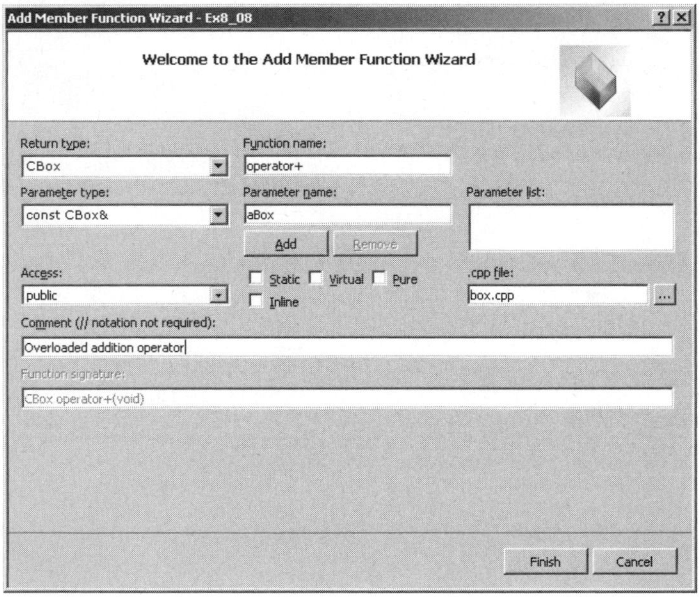

Figure 8-12

Here I have defined the `operator+()` function as `public` with a return type of `CBox`. The parameter type and name have also been entered in the appropriate fields. You must click the `Add` button to register the parameter as being in the parameter list before clicking the `Finish` button. This will also update the function signature shown at the bottom of the Add Member Function Wizard dialog. You could then enter details of another parameter if there were more than one and click Add once again to add it. I have also entered a comment in the dialog and the Wizard will insert this in both `Box.h` and `Box.cpp`. When you click `Finish`, the declaration for the function will be added to the class definition in the `Box.h` file, and a skeleton definition for the function will be added to the `Box.cpp` file. The function needs to be declared as `const` so you must add this keyword to the declaration of the `operator+()` function within the class definition, and to the definition of the function on `Box.cpp`. You must also add the code in the body of the function, like this:

```
CBox CBox::operator +(const CBox& aBox) const
{
```

```
    // New object has larger length and width of the two,
    // and sum of the two heights
    return CBox(m_Length > aBox.m_Length ? m_Length : aBox.m_Length,
                m_Width > aBox.m_Width ? m_Width : aBox.m_Width,
                m_Height + aBox.m_Height);
}
```

You need to repeat this process for the `operator*()` and `operator/()` functions that you saw earlier. When you have completed this, the class definition in `Box.h` will look something like this:

```
#pragma once

class CBox
{
public:
    CBox(double lv = 1.0, double wv = 1.0, double hv = 1.0);
    ~CBox(void);

private:
    // Length of a box in inches
    double m_Length;

    // Width of a box in inches
    double m_Width;

    // Height of a box in inches
    double m_Height;
public:

    double GetHeight(void) const
    {
        return m_Height;
    }
public:

    double GetWidth(void) const
    {
        return m_Width;
    }
public:

    double GetLength(void) const
    {
        return m_Length;
    }
public:

    double Volume(void) const
    {
        return m_Length*m_Width*m_Height;
    }
public:

    // Overloaded addition operator
    CBox operator+(const CBox& aBox) const;
```

```
public
  // Multiply a box by an integer
  CBox operator*(int n) const;
public:

  // Divide one box into another
  int operator/(const CBox& aBox) const;
};
```

You can edit or rearrange the code in any way that you want — as long as it's still correct of course. I have added a few empty lines to make the code a bit more readable.

The contents of the Box.cpp file ultimately look something like this:

```
#include ".\box.h"
```

```
CBox::CBox(double lv, double wv, double hv)
{
  lv = lv <= 0.0 ? 1.0 : lv;          // Ensure positive
  wv = wv <= 0.0 ? 1.0 : wv;          // dimensions for
  hv = hv <= 0.0 ? 1.0 : hv;          // the object

  m_Length = lv>wv ? lv : wv;         // Ensure that
  m_Width = wv<lv ? wv : lv;          // length >= width
  m_Height = hv;
}
```

```
CBox::~CBox(void)
{
}
```

```
// Overloaded addition operator
CBox CBox::operator+(const CBox& aBox) const
{
  // New object has larger length and width of the two,
  // and sum of the two heights
  return CBox(m_Length > aBox.m_Length ? m_Length : aBox.m_Length,
              m_Width > aBox.m_Width ? m_Width : aBox.m_Width,
              m_Height + aBox.m_Height);
}
```

```
// Multiply a box by an integer
CBox CBox::operator*(int n) const
{
  if(n%2)
    return CBox(m_Length, m_Width, n*m_Height);          // n odd
  else
    return CBox(m_Length, 2.0*m_Width, (n/2)*m_Height);  // n even
}
```

```
// Divide one box into another
int CBox::operator/(const CBox& aBox) const
{
```

```
        // Temporary for number in horizontal plane this way
        int tc1 = 0;
        // Temporary for number in a plane that way
        int tc2 = 0;

        tc1 = static_cast<int>((m_Length/aBox.m_Length))*
              static_cast<int>((m_Width/aBox.m_Width));      // to fit this way

        tc2 = static_cast<int>((m_Length/aBox.m_Width))*
              static_cast<int>((m_Width/aBox.m_Length));      // and that way

        //Return best fit
        return static_cast<int>((m_Height/aBox.m_Height))*(tc1>tc2 ? tc1 : tc2);
    }
```

The shaded lines are those that you should have modified or added manually.

The very short functions, particularly those that just return the value of a data member, have their definitions within the class definition so that they are `inline`. If you take a look at ClassView by clicking on the tab, and then click the + beside the CBox class name, you'll see that all the members of the class are shown in the lower pane.

This completes the CBox class, but you still need to define the global functions that implement operators to compare the volume of a CBox object with a numerical value.

Adding Global Functions

You need to create a `.cpp` file that will contain the definitions for the global functions supporting operations on CBox objects. The file also needs to be part of the project. Click the `Solution Explorer` tab to display it (you currently will have the `Class View` tab displayed) and right click the `Source Files` folder. Select `Add | New Item...` from the context menu to display the dialog. Choose the category as `Code` and the template as `C++ File (.cpp)` in the right pane of the dialog and enter the file name as `BoxOperators`.

You can now enter the following code in the editor pane:

```cpp
// BoxOperators.cpp
// CBox object operations that don't need to access private members
#include "Box.h"

// Function for testing if a constant is > a CBox object
bool operator>(const double& value, const CBox& aBox)
{ return value > aBox.Volume(); }

// Function for testing if a constant is < CBox object
bool operator<(const double& value, const CBox& aBox)
{ return value < aBox.Volume(); }

// Function for testing if CBox object is > a constant
bool operator>(const CBox& aBox, const double& value)
{ return value < aBox; }
```

```
// Function for testing if CBox object is < a constant
bool operator<( const CBox& aBox, const double& value)
{ return value > aBox; }

// Function for testing if a constant is >= a CBox object
bool operator>=(const double& value, const CBox& aBox)
{ return value >= aBox.Volume(); }

// Function for testing if a constant is <= CBox object
bool operator<=(const double& value, const CBox& aBox)
{ return value <= aBox.Volume(); }

// Function for testing if CBox object is >= a constant
bool operator>=( const CBox& aBox, const double& value)
{ return value <= aBox; }

// Function for testing if CBox object is <= a constant
bool operator<=( const CBox& aBox, const double& value)
{ return value >= aBox; }

// Function for testing if a constant is == CBox object
bool operator==(const double& value, const CBox& aBox)
{ return value == aBox.Volume(); }

// Function for testing if CBox object is == a constant
bool operator==(const CBox& aBox, const double& value)
{ return value == aBox; }

// CBox multiply operator n*aBox
CBox operator*(int n, const CBox& aBox)
{ return aBox * n; }

// Operator to return the free volume in a packed CBox
double operator%( const CBox& aBox, const CBox& bBox)
{ return aBox.Volume() - (aBox / bBox) * bBox.Volume(); }
```

You have an #include directive for Box.h because the functions refer to the CBox class. Save the file. When you have completed this, you can select the Class View tab. The Class View tab now includes a Global Functions and Variables folder that will contain all the functions you have just added.

You have seen definitions for all these functions earlier in the chapter, so I won't discuss their implementations again. When you want to use any of these functions in another .cpp file, you'll need to be sure that you declare all the functions that you use so the compiler will recognize them. You can achieve this by putting a set of declarations in a header file. Switch back to the Solution Explorer pane once more and right-click the Header Files folder name. Select Add | New Item... from the context menu to display the dialog, but this time select category as Code and the template to be Header File(.h) and enter the name as BoxOperators. After clicking the Add button an empty header file is added to the project, and you can add the following code in the editor window:

```
// BoxOperators.h - Declarations for global box operators
#pragma once

bool operator>(const double& value, const CBox& aBox);
bool operator<(const double& value, const CBox& aBox);
bool operator>(const CBox& aBox, const double& value);
```

```
bool operator<(const CBox& aBox, const double& value);
bool operator>=(const double& value, const CBox& aBox);
bool operator<=(const double& value, const CBox& aBox);
bool operator>=(const CBox& aBox, const double& value);
bool operator<=(const CBox& aBox, const double& value);
bool operator==(const double& value, const CBox& aBox);
bool operator==(const CBox& aBox, const double& value);
CBox operator*(int n, const CBox aBox);
double operator%(const CBox& aBox, const CBox& bBox);
```

The #pragma once directive ensures that the contents of the file will not be included more than once in a build. It's important to place this directive in all your own header files as it is easy to inadvertently attempt to include a header more than once. If you do end up with a header file included more than once into a source file, then you will have multiple definitions for the same thing in the source file and your code will not compile. You just need to add an #include directive for BoxOperators.h to any source file that makes use of any of these functions.

You're now ready to start applying these functions, along with the CBox class, to a specific problem in the world of boxes.

Using Our CBox Class

Suppose that you are packaging candies. The candies are on the big side, real jaw breakers, occupying an envelope 1.5 inches long by 1 inch wide by 1 inch high. You have access to a standard candy box that is 4.5 inches by 7 inches by 2 inches, and you want to know how many candies will fit in the box so that you can set the price. You also have a standard carton that is 2 feet 6 inches long, by 18 inches wide and 18 inches deep, and you want to know how many boxes of candy it can hold and how much space you're wasting when it has been filled.

In case the standard candy box isn't a good solution, you would also like to know what custom candy box would be suitable. You know that you can get a good price on boxes with a length from 3 inches to 7 inches, a width from 3 inches to 5 inches and a height from 1 inch to 2.5 inches, where each dimension can vary in steps of half an inch. You also know that you need to have at least 30 candies in a box, because this is the minimum quantity consumed by your largest customers at a sitting. Also, the candy box should not have empty space, because the complaints from customers who think they are being cheated goes up. Further, ideally you want to pack the standard carton completely so the candies don't rattle around. You don't want to be too stringent about this otherwise packing could become difficult, so let's say you have no wasted space if the free space in the packed carton is less than the volume of a single candy box.

With the CBox class, the problem becomes almost trivial; the solution is represented by the following main() function. Add a new C++ source file, Ex8_08.cpp, to the project through the context menu you get when you right-click Source Files in the Solution Explorer pane, as you've done before. You can then type in the code shown here:

```
// Ex8_08.cpp
// A sample packaging problem
#include <iostream>
#include "Box.h"
#include "BoxOperators.h"
using std::cout;
using std::endl;
```

```
int main()
{
   CBox candy(1.5, 1.0, 1.0);              // Candy definition
   CBox candyBox(7.0, 4.5, 2.0);           // Candy box definition
   CBox carton(30.0, 18.0, 18.0);          // Carton definition

   // Calculate candies per candy box
   int numCandies = candyBox/candy;

   // Calculate candy boxes per carton
   int numCboxes = carton/candyBox;

   // Calculate wasted carton space
   double space = carton%candyBox;

   cout << endl
        << "There are " << numCandies
        << " candies per candy box"
        << endl
        << "For the standard boxes there are " << numCboxes
        << " candy boxes per carton " << endl << "with "
        << space << " cubic inches wasted.";

   cout << endl << endl << "CUSTOM CANDY BOX ANALYSIS (No Waste)";

   // Try the whole range of custom candy boxes
   for(double length = 3.0 ; length <= 7.5 ; length += 0.5)
     for(double width = 3.0 ; width <= 5.0 ; width += 0.5)
       for(double height = 1.0 ; height <= 2.5 ; height += 0.5)
       {
          // Create new box each cycle
          CBox tryBox(length, width, height);

          if(carton%tryBox < tryBox.Volume() &&
                        tryBox % candy == 0.0 && tryBox/candy >= 30)
             cout << endl << endl
                  << "Trial Box L = " << tryBox.GetLength()
                  << " W = " << tryBox.GetWidth()
                  << " H = " << tryBox.GetHeight()
                  << endl
                  << "Trial Box contains " << tryBox / candy << " candies"
                  << " and a carton contains " << carton / tryBox
                  << " candy boxes.";
       }
   cout << endl;
   return 0;
}
```

Let's first look at how the program is structured. You have divided it into a number of files, which is common when writing in C++. You will be able to see them if you look at the Solution Explorer tab, which will look as shown in Figure 8-13.

Figure 8-13

The file `Ex8_08.cpp` contains the `main()` function and an `#include` directive for the file `BoxOperators.h` that contains the prototypes for the functions in `BoxOperators.cpp` (which aren't class members). It also has an `#include` directive for the definition of the class `CBox` in `Box.h`. A C++ console program is usually divided into a number of files that will each fall into one of three basic categories:

1. `.h` files containing library `#include` commands, global constants and variables, class definitions and function prototypes — in other words, everything except executable code. They also contain inline function definitions. Where a program has several class definitions, they are often placed in separate `.h` files.

2. `.cpp` files containing the executable code for the program, plus `#include` commands for all the definitions required by the executable code.

3. Another `.cpp` file containing the function `main()`.

The code in our `main()` function really doesn't need a lot of explanation — it's almost a direct expression of the definition of the problem in words, because the operators in the class interface perform problem-oriented actions on `CBox` objects.

The solution to the question of the use of standard boxes is in the declaration statements, which also compute the answers we require as initializing values. You then output these values with some explanatory comments.

The second part of the problem is solved using the three nested `for` loops iterating over the possible ranges of `m_Length`, `m_Width` and `m_Height` so that you evaluate all possible combinations. You could output them all as well, but because this would involve 200 combinations, of which you might only be interested in a few, you have an `if` statement which identifies the options that you're actually interested in. The `if` expression is only `true` if there's no space wasted in the carton *and* the current trial candy box has no wasted space *and* it contains at least 30 candies.

How It Works

Here's the output from this program:

```
There are 42 candies per candy box
For the standard boxes there are 144 candy boxes per carton
with 648 cubic inches wasted.

CUSTOM CANDY BOX ANALYSIS (No Waste)

Trial Box L = 5 W = 4.5 H = 2
Trial Box contains 30 candies and a carton contains 216 candy boxes.

Trial Box L = 5 W = 4.5 H = 2
Trial Box contains 30 candies and a carton contains 216 candy boxes.

Trial Box L = 6 W = 4.5 H = 2
Trial Box contains 36 candies and a carton contains 180 candy boxes.

Trial Box L = 6 W = 5 H = 2
Trial Box contains 40 candies and a carton contains 162 candy boxes.

Trial Box L = 7.5 W = 3 H = 2
Trial Box contains 30 candies and a carton contains 216 candy boxes.
```

You have a duplicate solution due to the fact that, in the nested loop, you evaluate boxes that have a length of 5 and a width of 4.5, as well as boxes that have a length of 4.5 and a width of 5. Because the CBox class constructor ensures that the length is not less than the width, these two are identical. You could include some additional logic to avoid presenting duplicates, but it hardly seems worth the effort. You could treat it as a small exercise if you like.

Organizing Your Program Code

In example Ex8_08, you distributed the code among several files for the first time. Not only is this common practice with C++ applications generally, but with Windows programming it is essential. The sheer volume of code involved in even the simplest program necessitates dividing it into workable chunks.

As I discussed in the previous section, there are basically two kinds of source code files in a C++ program, .h files and .cpp files. This is illustrated in Figure 8-14.

First of all, there's the executable code that corresponds to the definitions of the functions that make up the program. Second, there are definitions of various kinds that are necessary for the executable code to compile correctly. These are global constants and variables; data types that include classes, structures, and unions; and function prototypes. The executable source code is stored in files with the extension .cpp, and the definitions are stored in files with the extension .h.

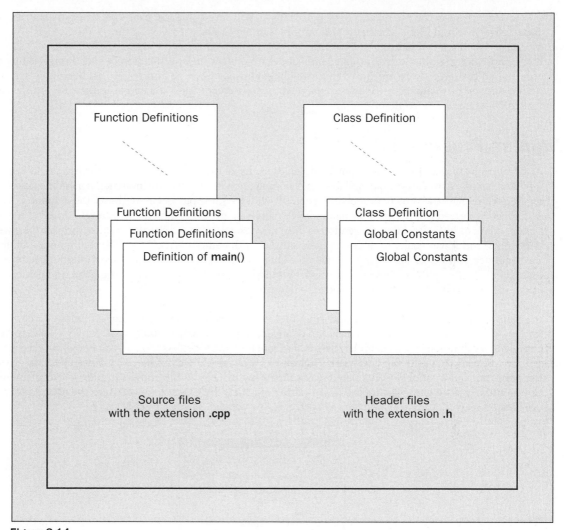

Figure 8-14

From time to time, you might want to use code from existing files in a new project. In this case you only have to add the .cpp files to the project, which you can do by using the Project | Add Existing Item... menu option, or by right-clicking either Source Files or Header Files in the Solution Explorer tab and selecting Add > Existing Item... from the context menu to add the file to your project. You don't need to add .h files to your project, although you can if you want them to be shown in the Solution Explorer pane immediately. The code from .h files will be added at the beginning of the .cpp files that require them as a result of the #include directives that you specify. You need #include directives for header files containing standard library functions and other standard definitions, as well as for your own header files. Visual C++ 2008 automatically keeps track of all these files, and enables you to view them in the `Solution Explorer` tab. As you saw in the last example, you can also view the class definitions and global constants and variables in the `Class View` tab.

In a Windows program, there are other kinds of definitions for the specification of such things as menus and toolbar buttons. These are stored in files with extensions like `.rc` and `.ico`. Just like `.h` files, these do not need to be explicitly added to a project as they are created and tracked automatically by Visual C++ 2008 when you need them.

Naming Program Files

As I have already said, for classes of any complexity, it's usual to store the class definition in a `.h` file with a filename based on the class name, and to store the implementation of the function members of the class that are defined outside the class definition in a `.cpp` file with the same name. On this basis, the definition of our CBox class appeared in a file with the name `Box.h`. Similarly, the class implementation was stored in the file `Box.cpp`. We didn't follow this convention in the earlier examples in the chapter because the examples were very short, and it was easier to reference the examples with names derived from the chapter number and the sequence number of the example within the chapter. With programs of any size though it becomes essential to structure the code in this way, so it would be a good idea to get into the habit of creating `.h` and `.cpp` files to hold your program code from now on.

Segmenting a C++ program into `.h` and `.cpp` files is a very convenient approach, as it makes it easy for you to find the definition or implementation of any class, particularly if you're working in a development environment that doesn't have all the tools that Visual C++ provides. As long as you know the class name, you can go directly to the file you want. This isn't a rigid rule, however. It's sometimes useful to group the definitions of a set of closely related classes together in a single file and assemble their implementations similarly. However you choose to structure your files, the Class View still displays all the individual classes, as well as all the members of each class, as you can see in Figure 8-15.

Figure 8-15

I adjusted the size of the Class View pane so all the elements in the project are visible. Here, you can see the details of the classes and globals for the last example. As I've mentioned before, double-clicking any of the entries in the tree will take you directly to the relevant source code.

Native C++ Library Classes for Strings

As I mentioned in Chapter 4, the `<string>` standard header defines the `string` and `wstring` classes that represent character strings. Both are defined in the `<string>` header as template classes that are instances of the `basic_string<T>` class template. The `string` class is defined as `basic_string<char>` and `wstring` is defined as `basic_string<wchar_t>`, so the `string` class represents strings of characters of type `char` and `wstring` represents strings of characters of type `wchar_t`.

These string types are much easier to use than null-terminated strings and bring with them a whole range of powerful functions. Because `string` and `wstring` are both instances of the same template, `basic_string<T>`, they provide the same functionality, so I'll only discuss the features and use in the context of the `string` type. The `wstring` type will work just the same except that the strings contain Unicode character codes and you must use the `L` prefix for string literals in your code.

Creating String Objects

Creating string objects is very easy but you have a lot of choices as to how you do it. Firstly, you can create and initialize a string object like this:

```
string sentence = "This sentence is false.";
```

The `sentence` object will be initialized with the string literal that appears to the right of the assignment operator. A string object has no terminating null character, so the string length is the number of characters in the string, 23 in this instance. You can discover the length of the string encapsulated by a string object at any time by calling its `length()` member function. For example:

```
cout << "The string is of length " << sentence.length() << endl;
```

Executing the statement produces the output:

```
The string is of length 23
```

Incidentally, you can output a string object to `stdout` in the same way as any other variable:

```
cout << sentence << endl;
```

This displays the `sentence` string on a line by itself. You can also read a character string into a string object like this:

```
cin >> sentence;
```

However, reading from `stdin` in this way ignores leading whitespace until a non-whitespace character is found and also terminates input when you enter a space following one or more non-whitespace characters. You will often want to read text into a string object that includes spaces and may span several lines. In this case the `getline()` function template that is defined in the `<string>` header is much more convenient. For example:

```
getline(cin, sentence, '*');
```

This function template is specifically for reading data from a stream into a string or `wstring` object. The first argument is the stream that is the source of input — it doesn't have to be `cin`; the second argument is the object that is to receive the input, and the third argument is the character that terminates reading. Here I have specified the terminating character as `'*'`, so this statement will read text from `cin`, including spaces, into `sentence`, until the end of input is indicated by an asterisk being read from the input stream.

Of course, you can also use functional notation to initialize a `string` object:

```
string sentence("This sentence is false.");
```

If you don't specify an initial string literal when you create a `string` object, the object will contain an empty string:

```
string astring;                         // Create an empty string
```

Calling the `length()` of the string `astring` will result in zero.

Another possibility is to initialize a string object with a single character repeated a specified number of times:

```
string bees(7, 'b');                    // String is "bbbbbbb"
```

The first argument to the constructor is the number of repetitions of the character specified by the second argument.

Finally you can initialize a string object with all or part of another string object. Here's an example of using another string object as an initializer:

```
string letters(bees);
```

The `letters` object will be initialized with the string contained in `bees`.

To select part of a string object as initializer you call the string contructor with three arguments, the first being the string object that is the source of the initializing string, the second is the index position of the first character to be selected, and the third argument is the number of characters to be selected. Here's an example:

```
string sentence("This sentence is false.");
string part(sentence, 5, 11);
```

The `part` object will be initialized with 11 characters from `sentence` beginning with the sixth character (the first character is at index position 0). Thus `part` will contain the string `"sentence is"`.

Of course, you can create arrays of string objects and initialize them using the usual notation. For example:

```
string animals[] = { "dog", "cat", "horse", "donkey", "lion"};
```

This creates an array of string objects that has five elements initialized with the string literals between the braces.

Concatenating Strings

Perhaps the most common operation with strings is joining two strings to form a single string. You can use the + operator to concatenate two string objects or a string object and a string literal. Here are some examples:

```
string sentence1("This sentence is false.");
string sentence2("Therefore the sentence above must be true!");
string combined;                    // Create an empty string
sentence1 = sentence1 + "\n";       // Append string containing newline
combined = sentence1 + sentence2;   // Join two strings
cout << combined << endl;           // Output the result
```

Executing these statements will result in the output:

```
This sentence is false.
Therefore the sentence above must be true!
```

The first three statements create string objects. The next statement appends the string literal "\n" to sentence1 and stores the result in sentence1. The next statement joins sentence1 and sentence2 and stores the result in combined. The last state outputs the string combined.

String concatenation using the + operator is possible because the string class implements operator+(). This implies that one of the operands must be a string object so you can't use the + operator to join two string literals. Keep in mind that each time you use the + operator to join two strings you are creating a new string object, which involves a certain amount of overhead. You'll see in the next section how you can modify and extend an existing string object and this may be a more efficient alternative in some cases because it does not involve creating new objects.

You can also use the + operator to join a character to a string object, so you could have written the third statement in the previous code fragment as:

```
sentence1 = sentence1 + '\n';       // Append newline character to string
```

The string class also implements operator+=() such that the right operand can be a string literal, a string object, or a single character. You could write the previous statement as:

```
sentence1 += '\n';
```

or as:

```
sentence1 += "\n";
```

There is a difference between using the += operator and using the + operator. As I said, the + operator creates a new string object containing the combined string. The += operator appends the string or character that is the right operand to the string object that is the left operand, so the string object is modified directly and no new object is created.

Let's exercise some of what I have described in an example.

Try It Out   Creating and Joining Strings

This is a simple example that reads names and ages from the keyboard and then lists what you entered. Here's the code:

```cpp
// Ex8_09.cpp
// Creating and joining string objects
#include <iostream>
#include <string>
using std::cin;
using std::cout;
using std::endl;
using std::string;
using std::getline;

// List names and ages
void listnames(string names[], string ages[], size_t count)
{
  size_t i = 0;
  cout << endl << "The names you entered are: " << endl;
  while(i<count && !names[i].empty()){
  cout << names[i] + " aged " + ages[i] + '.' << endl; i++;
}
}

int main()
{
  const size_t count = 100;
  string names[count];
  string ages[count];
  string firstname;
  string secondname;

  for(size_t i = 0 ; i<count ; i++)
  {
    cout << endl << "Enter a first name or press Enter to end: ";
    getline(cin, firstname, '\n');
    if(firstname.empty())
    {
      listnames(names, ages, i);
      cout << "Done!!" << endl;
      return 0;
    }

    cout << "Enter a second name: ";
    getline(cin, secondname, '\n');
```

```
        names[i] = firstname + ' ' + secondname;
        cout << "Enter " + firstname + "'s age: ";
        getline(cin, ages[i], '\n');
    }
    cout << "No space for more names." << endl;
    listnames(names, ages, count);
    return 0;
}
```

This example produces output similar to the following:

```
Enter a first name or press Enter to end: Marilyn
Enter a second name: Munroe
Enter Marilyn's age: 26

Enter a first name or press Enter to end: Tom
Enter a second name: Crews
Enter Tom's age: 45

Enter a first name or press Enter to end: Arnold
Enter a second name: Weisseneggar
Enter Arnold's age: 52

Enter a first name or press Enter to end:

The names you entered are:
Marilyn Munroe aged 26.
Tom Crews aged 45.
Arnold Weisseneggar aged 52.
Done!!
```

How It Works

The `listnames` function lists names and ages stored in arrays that are passed as the first two arguments. The third argument is a count of the number of elements in the array. Listing of the data occurs in a loop:

```
while(i<count && !names[i].empty())
    cout << names[i] + " aged " + ages[i++] + '.' << endl;
```

The loop condition is a belt and braces control mechanism in that it not only checks that the index i is less than the value of count that is passed as the third argument, but it also calls the empty() function for the current element to verify that it is not an empty string. The single statement in the body of the loop concatenates the current string in names[i] with the literal " aged ", the ages[i] string and the character '.' using the + operator and writes the resultant string to cout. The expression concatenating the strings is equivalent to:

```
((names[i].operator+(" aged ")).operator+(ages[i++])).operator+('.')
```

Each call of the operator+() function returns a string object that results from the operation, so three temporary string objects are created in evaluating this expression. Thus the expression demonstrates combining a string object with a string literal, a string object with another string object, and a string object with a character literal.

In `main()`, you first create two arrays of `string` objects of length `count` with the statements:

```
const size_t count = 100;
string names[count];
string ages[count];
```

The `names` and `ages` arrays will store names and corresponding age values that are entered from the keyboard.

Within the `for` loop in `main()` you read the first and second names separately using the `getline()` function template that is defined in the `<string>` header:

```
cout << endl << "Enter a first name or press Enter to end: ";
getline(cin, firstname, '\n');
if(firstname.empty())
{
  listnames(names, ages, i);
  cout << "Done!!" << endl;
  return 0;
}

cout << "Enter a second name: ";
getline(cin, secondname, '\n');
```

The `getline()` function allows an empty string to be read, something you cannot do using the `>>` operator with `cin`. The first argument to `getline()` is the stream that is the source of the input, the second argument is the destination for the input, and the third argument is the character that signals the end on the input operation. If you omit the third argument, entering `'\n'` will terminate the input process so you could have omitted it here. You use the ability to read an empty string here as you test for an empty string in `firstname` by calling its `empty()` function. An empty string signals the end of input so you call `listnames()` to output the data and end program execution.

When `firstname` is not empty, you continue with reading the second name into `secondname`, again using the `getline()` template function. You concatenate `firstname` and `secondname` using the `+` operator and store the result in `names[i]`, the currently unused element in the `names` array.

Finally in the loop you read a string for the age of the person and store the result in `ages[i]`. The `for` loop limits the number of entries to `count`, which corresponds to the number of elements in the arrays. If you fall through the end of the loop, the arrays are full so after displaying a message you output the data that was entered.

Accessing and Modifying Strings

You can access any character in a `string` object to read it or overwrite it by using the subscript operator, `[]`. Here's an example:

```
string sentence("Too many cooks spoil the broth.");
for(size_t i = 0; i<sentence.length(); i++)
if(sentence[i] == ' ')
  sentence[i] = '*';
```

This just inspects each character in the `sentence` string in turn to see if it is a space, and if it is, replaces the character with an asterisk.

You can use the `at()` member function to achieve the same result as the `[]` operator:

```
string sentence("Too many cooks spoil the broth.");
for(size_t i = 0; i<sentence.length(); i++)
if(sentence.at(i) == ' ')
  sentence.at(i) = '*';
```

This does exactly the same as the previous fragment, so what's the difference between using `[]` and using `at()`? Well, subscripting is faster than using the `at()` function, but the downside is the validity of the index is not checked. If the index is out of range, the result of using the subscript operator is undefined. The `at()` function on the other hand is a bit slower, but it does check the index and if it is not valid, the function will throw an `out_of_range` exception. You would use the `at()` function when there is the possibility of the index value being out of range, and in this situation you should put the code in a `try` block and handle the exception appropriately. If you are sure index out of range conditions cannot arise, then use the `[]` operator.

You can extract a part of an existing `string` object as a new `string` object. For example:

```
string sentence("Too many cooks spoil the broth.");
string substring = sentence.substr(4, 10);              // Extracts "many cooks"
```

The first argument to the `substr()` function is the first character of the substring to be extracted and the second argument is the count of the number of characters in the substring.

By using the `append()` function for a string object you can add one or more characters to the end of the string. This function comes in several versions; there are versions that append one or more of a given character, a string literal, or a `string` object to the object for which the function is called. For example:

```
string phrase("The higher");
string word("fewer");
phrase.append(1, ' ');                // Append one space
phrase.append("the ");                // Append a string literal
phrase.append(word);                  // Append a string object
phrase.append(2, '!');                // Append two exclamation marks
```

After executing this sequence, `phrase` will have been modified to `"The higher the fewer!!"`. With the version of `append()` with two arguments, the first argument is the count of the number of times the character specified by the second argument is to be appended. When you call `append()` the function returns a reference to the object for which it was called, so you could write the four `append()` calls above in a single statement:

```
phrase.append(1, ' ').append("the ").append(word).append(2, '!');
```

You can also use `append()` to append part of a string literal or part of a `string` object to an existing string:

```
string phrase("The more the merrier.");
string query("Any");
query.append(phrase, 3, 5).append(1, '?');
```

The result of executing these statements is that `query` will contain the string `"Any more?"`. In the last statement, the first call to the `append()` function has three arguments:

❏ The first argument, `phrase`, is the `string` object from which characters are to be extracted and appended to `query`.

❏ The second argument, 3, is the index position of the first character to be extracted.

❏ The third argument, 5, is the count of the total number of characters to be appended.

Thus the substring `" more"` is appended to `query` by this call. The second call for the `append()` function appends a question mark to `query`.

When you want to append a single character to a string object, you could use the `push_back()` function as an alternative to `append()`. Here's how you would use that:

```
query.push_back('*');
```

This appends an asterisk character to the end of the `query` string.

Sometimes adding characters to the end of a string just isn't enough. There will be occasions when you want to insert one or more characters at some position in the interior of a string. The various flavors of the `insert()` function will do that for you:

```
string saying("A horse");
string word("blind");
string sentence("He is as good as gold.");
string phrase("a wink too far");
saying.insert(1, " ");                          // Insert a space character
saying.insert(2, word);                         // Insert a string object
saying.insert(2, "nodding", 3);                 // Insert 3 characters of a string literal
saying.insert(5, sentence, 2, 15);              // Insert part of a string at position 5
saying.insert(20, phrase, 0, 9);                // Insert part of a string at position 20
saying.insert(29, " ").insert(30, "a poor do", 0, 2);
```

I'm sure you'll be interested to know that after executing the statements above, `saying` will contain the string `"A nod is as good as a wink to a blind horse"`. The parameters to the various versions of `insert()` are:

Function Prototype	Description
`string& insert(size_t index, const char* pstring)`	Inserts the null-terminated string `pstring` at position `index`.
`string& insert(size_t index, const string astring)`	Inserts the `string` object `astring` at position `index`.
`string& insert(size_t index, const char* pstring, size_t count)`	Inserts the first `count` characters from the null-terminated string `pstring` at position `index`.

Function Prototype	Description
`string& insert(size_t index, const string astring, size_t count)`	Inserts the first count characters from the string object astring at position index.
`string& insert(size_t index, const string astring, size_t start, size_t count)`	Inserts count characters from the string object astring beginning with the character at position start; the substring is inserted at position index.
`string& insert(size_t index, const char* pstring, size_t start, size_t count)`	Inserts count characters from the null-terminated string pstring beginning with the character at position start; the substring is inserted at position index.

In each of these versions of insert() a reference to the string object for which the function is called is returned; this allows you to chain calls together as in the last statement in the code fragment.

This is not the complete set of insert() functions but you can do everything you need with those in the table. The other versions use **iterators** as arguments and you'll learn about iterators in Chapter 10.

You can interchange the strings encapsulated by two string objects by calling the swap() member function. For example:

```
string phrase("The more the merrier.");
string query("Any");
query.swap(phrase);
```

This results in query containing the string "The more the merrier." and phrase containing the string "Any". Of course, executing phrase.swap(query) would have the same effect.

If you need to convert a string object to a null-terminated string, the c_str() function will do this. For example:

```
string phrase("The higher the fewer");
const char *pstring = phrase.c_str();
```

The c_str() function returns a pointer to a null-terminated string with the same contents as the string object.

You can also obtain the contents of a string object as an array of elements of type char by calling the data() member function. Note that the array contains just the characters from the string object without a terminating null.

You can replace part of a string object by calling its replace() member function. This also comes in several versions, as the following table shows.

Function Prototype	Description
```string& replace(size_t index, size_t count, const char* pstring)```	Replaces count characters starting at position index with the first count characters from pstring.
```string& replace(size_t index, size_t count, const string astring)```	Replaces count characters starting at position index with the first count characters from astring.
```string& replace(size_t index, size_t count1, const char* pstring, size_t count2)```	Replaces count1 characters starting at position index with up to count2 characters from pstring. This allows the replacement substring to be longer or shorter than the substring that is replaced.
```string& replace(size_t index1, size_t count1, const string astring, size_t index2, size_t count2)```	Replaces count1 characters starting at position index1 with count2 characters from astring starting at position index2.
```string& replace(size_t index, size_t count1, size_t count2, char ch)```	Replaces count1 characters starting at index with count2 occurrences of the character ch.

In each case a reference to the string object for which the function is called is returned.

Here's an example:

```
string proverb("A nod is as good as a wink to a blind horse");
string sentence("It's bath time!");
proverb.replace(38, 5, sentence, 5, 3);
```

This fragment uses the fifth version of the replace() function from the preceding table to substitute "bat" in place of "horse" in the string proverb.

Comparing Strings

You have a full complement of operators for comparing two string objects or comparing a string object with a string literal. Operator overloading has been implemented in the string class for the following operators:

```
==    !=    <    <=    >    >=
```

Here's an example of the use of these operators:

```
string dog1("St Bernard");
string dog2("Tibetan Mastiff");
```

```
if(dog1 < dog2)
  cout << "dog2 comes first!" << endl;
else if(dog1 > dog2)
  cout << "dog1 comes first!" << endl;
```

When you compare two strings, corresponding characters are compared until a pair of characters is found that differ, or the end of one or both strings is reached. When two corresponding characters are found to be different, the values of the character codes determine which string is less than the other. If no characters pairs are found to be different, the string with fewer characters is less than the other string. Two strings will be equal if they contain the same number of characters and corresponding characters are identical.

Try It Out   Comparing Strings

This example illustrates the use of the comparison operators by implementing an extremely inefficient sorting method. Here's the code:

```cpp
// Ex8_10.cpp
// Comparing and sorting words
#include <iostream>
#include <iomanip>
#include <string>
using std::cin;
using std::cout;
using std::endl;
using std::ios;
using std::setiosflags;
using std::setw;
using std::string;

string* sort(string* strings, size_t count)
{
  bool swapped = false;
  while(true)
  {
    for(size_t i = 0 ; i<count-1 ; i++)
    {
      if(strings[i] > strings[i+1])
      {
        swapped = true;
        strings[i].swap(strings[i+1]);
      }
    }
    if(!swapped)
      break;
    swapped = false;
  }
  return strings;
}

int main()
{
  const size_t maxstrings = 100;
  string strings[maxstrings];
```

```
    size_t nstrings = 0;
    size_t maxwidth = 0;

    // Read up to 100 words into the strings array
    while(nstrings < maxstrings)
    {
      cout << "Enter a word or press Enter to end: ";
      getline(cin, strings[nstrings]);
      if(maxwidth < strings[nstrings].length())
        maxwidth = strings[nstrings].length();
      if(strings[nstrings].empty())
        break;
      ++nstrings;
    }

    // Sort the input in ascending sequence
    sort(strings,nstrings);
    cout << endl
         << "In ascending sequence, the words you entered are:"
         << endl
         << setiosflags(ios::left);          // Left-justify the output
    for(size_t i = 0 ; i<nstrings ; i++)
    {
      if(i % 5 == 0)
        cout << endl;
      cout << setw(maxwidth+2) << strings[i];
    }
    cout << endl;
    return 0;
}
```

Here's some typical output from this example:

```
Enter a word or press Enter to end: loquacious
Enter a word or press Enter to end: transmogrify
Enter a word or press Enter to end: abstemious
Enter a word or press Enter to end: facetious
Enter a word or press Enter to end: xylophone
Enter a word or press Enter to end: megaphone
Enter a word or press Enter to end: chauvinist
Enter a word or press Enter to end:

In ascending sequence, the words you entered are:

abstemious    chauvinist    facetious    loquacious    megaphone
transmogrify  xylophone
```

How It Works

The most interesting part is the sort() function that accepts two arguments, the address of a string array and the count of the number of array elements.

The function implements the bubble sort, which works by scanning through the elements in sequences and comparing successive elements. All the work is done in the `while` loop:

```
bool swapped = false;
while(true)
{
  for(size_t i = 0 ; i<count-1 ; i++)
  {
    if(strings[i] > strings[i+1])
    {
      swapped = true;
      strings[i].swap(strings[i+1]);
    }
  }
  if(!swapped)
    break;
  swapped = false;
}
```

Successive elements in the `strings` array are compared using the > operator. If the first element is greater than the second in a pair, the elements are swapped. In this case the elements are interchanged by calling the `swap()` function for one `string` object with the second `string` object as argument. Comparing successive elements and swapping when necessary continues for the entire array of elements. This process is repeated until there is a pass through all the elements where no elements are swapped. The elements are then in ascending sequence. The `bool` variable `swapped` acts as an indicator for whether swapping occurs on any given pass. It is only set to `true` when two elements are swapped.

The `main()` function reads up to 100 words into the strings array in a loop:

```
while(nstrings < maxstrings)
{
  cout << "Enter a word or press Enter to end: ";
  getline(cin, strings[nstrings]);
  if(maxwidth < strings[nstrings].length())
    maxwidth = strings[nstrings].length();
  if(strings[nstrings].empty())
    break;
  ++nstrings;
}
```

The `getline()` function here reads characters from `cin` until `'\n'` is read. The input is stored in the `string` object specified by the second argument `strings[nstrings]`. Just pressing the `Enter` key will result in an `empty()` string so the loop is terminated when the `empty()` function for the last `string` object read returns `true`. The `maxwidth` variable is used to record the length of the longest string entered. This will be used later in the output process after the input has been sorted.

Calling the `sort()` function sorts the contents of the `strings` array in ascending sequence. The result is output in a loop:

```
cout << endl
     << "In ascending sequence, the words you entered are:"
```

```
            << endl
            << setiosflags(ios::left);          // Left-justify the output
    for(size_t i = 0 ; i<nstrings ; i++)
    {
      if(i % 5 == 0)
        cout << endl;
      cout << setw(maxwidth+2) << strings[i];
    }
```

This outputs each element in a field width of maxwidth+2 characters. Each word is left justified in the field because of the call to the setiosflags() manipulator with the argument ios::left. Unlike the setw() manipulator, the setiosflags() manipulator remains in effect until you reset it.

Searching Strings

You have four versions of the find() function that search a string object for a given character or sub-string and they are described in the following table.

Function	Description
size_t find(char ch, size_t offset=0)	Searches a string object for the character ch starting at index position offset. You can omit the second argument in which case the default value is 0.
size_t find(const char* pstr, size_t offset=0)	Searches a string object for the null-terminated string pstr starting at index position offset. You can omit the second argument in which case the default value is 0.

size_t find(const char* pstr,
         size_t offset,
         size_t count)
	Searches a string object for the first count characters of the null-terminated string pstr starting at index position offset.

size_t find(const string str, size_t offset=0)	Searches a string object for the string object str starting at index position offset. You can omit the second argument in which case the default value is 0.

In each case the find() function returns the index position where the character or first character of the substring was found. The function returns the value string::npos if the item was not found. This latter value is a constant defined in the string class that represents an illegal position in a string object; it is used generally to signal a search failure.

Here's a fragment showing some of the ways you might use the find() function:

```
    string phrase("So near and yet so far");
    string str("So near");
    cout << phrase.find(str) << endl;          // Outputs 0
```

```
cout << phrase.find("so far") << endl;     // Outputs 16
cout << phrase.find("so near") << endl;    // Outputs string::npos = 4294967295
```

The value of `string::npos` can vary with different C++ compiler implementations, so to test for it you should always use `string::npos` and not the explicit value.

Here's another example that scans the same string repeatedly searching for occurrences of a particular substring:

```
string str( "Smith, where Jones had had \"had had\", \"had had\" had."
            " \"Had had\" had had the examiners' approval.");
string substr("had");

cout << "The string to be searched is:"
     << endl << str << endl;
size_t offset = 0;
size_t count = 0;
size_t increment = substr.length();

while(true)
{
  offset = str.find(substr, offset);
  if(offset == string::npos)
    break;
  offset += increment;
  ++count;
}
cout << endl << " The string \"" << substr
     << "\" was found " << count << " times in the string above."
     << endl;
```

Here you search the string `str` to see how many times "had" appears. The search is done in the `while` loop where `offset` records the position found, and is also used as the start position for the search. The search starts at index position 0, the start of the string, and each time the substring is found, the new starting position for the next search is set to the found position plus the length of the substring. This ensures that the substring that was found is bypassed. Every time the substring is found, count is incremented. If `find()` returns `string::npos`, then the substring was not found and the search ends. Executing this fragment produces the output:

```
The string to be searched is:
Smith, where Jones had had "had had", "had had" had. "Had had" had had the
examiners' approval.

 The string "had" was found 10 times in the string above.
```

Of course, `"Had"` is not a match for the substring `"had"` so 10 is the correct result.

The `find_first_of()` and `find_last_of()` member functions search a `string` object for an occurrence of any character from a given set. You could search a string to find spaces or punctuation characters for example, which would allow you to break a string up into individual words. Both functions come in several flavors, as the following table shows.

Function	Description
`find_first_of(char ch, size_t offset = 0)`	Searches a `string` object for the first occurrence of the character, `ch`, starting at position `offset`, and returns the index position where the character is found as a value of type `size_t`. If you omit the second argument, the default value of `offset` is 0.
`find_first_of(char* pstr, size_t offset = 0)`	Searches a `string` object for the first occurrence of any character in the null-terminated string, `pstring`, starting at position `offset`, and returns the index position where the character is found as a value of type `size_t`. If you omit the second argument, the default value of `offset` is 0.
`find_first_of(char* pstr, size_t offset, size_t count)`	Searches a `string` object for the first occurrence of any character in the first `count` characters of the null-terminated string, `pstring`, starting at position `offset`, and returns the index position where the character is found as a value of type `size_t`.
`find_first_of(string str, size_t offset = 0)`	Searches a `string` object for the first occurrence of any character in the string, `pstring`, starting at position `offset`, and returns the index position where the character is found as a value of type `size_t`. If you omit the second argument, the default value of `offset` is 0.
`find_last_of(char ch, size_t offset=npos)`	Searches backward through a `string` object for the last occurrence of the character, `ch`, starting at position `offset`, and returns the index position where the character is found as a value of type `size_t`. If you omit the second argument, the default value of `offset` is `npos`, which is the end of the string.
`find_last_of(char* pstr, size_t offset=npos)`	Searches backward through a `string` object for the last occurrence of any character in the null-terminated string, `pstr`, starting at position `offset`, and returns the index position where the character is found as a value of type `size_t`. If you omit the second argument, the default value of `offset` is `npos`, which is the end of the string.
`find_last_of(char* pstr, size_t offset, size_t count)`	Searches backward through a `string` object for the last occurrence of any of the first `count` characters in the null-terminated string, `pstr`, starting at position `offset`, and returns the index position where the character is found as a value of type `size_t`.

Function	Description
`find_last_of(string str, size_t offset=npos)`	Searches backward through a `string` object for the last occurrence of any character in the string, `str`, starting at position `offset`, and returns the index position where the character is found as a value of type `size_t`. If you omit the second argument, the default value of `offset` is `npos`, which is the end of the string.

With all versions of the `find_first_of()` and `find_last_of()` functions, `string::npos` will be returned if no matching character is found.

With the same string as the last fragment, you could see what the `find_last_of()` function does with the same search string "had".

```
size_t count = 0;
size_t offset = string::npos;
while(true)
{
  offset = str.find_last_of(substr, offset);
  if(offset == string::npos)
    break;
  --offset;
  ++count;
}
cout << endl << " Characters from the string \"" << substr
     << "\" were found " << count << " times in the string above."
     << endl;
```

This time you are searching backward starting at index position, `string::npos`, the end of the string, because this is the default starting position. The output from this fragment is:

```
The string to be searched is:
Smith, where Jones had had "had had", "had had" had. "Had had" had had the
examiners' approval.

 Characters from the string "had" were found 38 times in the string above.
```

The result should not be a surprise. Remember you are searching for occurrences of *any* of the characters in "had" in the string `str`. There are 32 in the `"Had"` and `"had"` words, and 6 in the remaining words. Because you are searching backward through the string, you decrement `offset` within the loop when you find a character.

The last set of search facilities are versions of the `find_first_not_of()` and `find_last_not_of()` functions.

Function	Description
`find_first_ not_of(char ch,` `        size_t offset = 0)`	Searches a `string` object for the first occurrence of a character that is not the character, `ch`, starting at position `offset`. The function returns the index position where the character is found as a value of type `size_t`. If you omit the second argument, the default value of `offset` is 0.

`find_first_ not_of(`
 	
`        char* pstr,`
`        size_t offset = 0)`
	Searches a `string` object for the first occurrence of a character that is not in the null-terminated string, `pstring`, starting at position `offset`, and returns the index position where the character is found as a value of type `size_t`. If you omit the second argument, the default value of `offset` is 0.

`find_first_ not_of(`
 	
`        char* pstr,`
`        size_t offset,`
`        size_t count)`
	Searches a `string` object for the first occurrence of a character that is not in the first `count` characters of the null-terminated string, `pstring`, starting at position `offset`. The function returns the index position where the character is found as a value of type `size_t`.

`find_first_ not_of(`
 	
`        string str,`
`        size_t offset = 0)`
	Searches a `string` object for the first occurrence of any character that is not in the string, `pstring`, starting at position `offset`. The function returns the index position where the character is found as a value of type `size_t`. If you omit the second argument, the default value of `offset` is 0.

`find_last_ not_of(char ch,` `        size_t offset=npos)`	Searches backward through a `string` object for the last occurrence of a character that is not the character, `ch`, starting at position `offset`. The index position where the character is found is returned as a value of type `size_t`. If you omit the second argument, the default value of `offset` is `npos`, which is the end of the string.
`find_last_ not_of(char* pstr,` `        size_t offset=npos)`	Searches backward through a `string` object for the last occurrence of any character that is not in the null-terminated string, `pstr`, starting at position `offset`. The index position where the character is found is returned as a value of type `size_t`. If you omit the second argument, the default value of `offset` is `npos`, which is the end of the string.

`find_last_ not_of(char* pstr,`
`        size_t offset,`
 	
`        size_t count)`
	Searches backward through a `string` object for the last occurrence of a character that is not among the first `count` characters in the null-terminated string, `pstr`, starting at position `offset`. The function returns the index position where the character is found as a value of type `size_t`.

Function	Description
`find_last_not_of(string str, size_t offset=npos)`	Searches backward through a `string` object for the last occurrence of any character not in the string, `str`, starting at position `offset`. The function returns the index position where the character is found as a value of type `size_t`. If you omit the second argument, the default value of `offset` is `npos`, which is the end of the string.

As with previous search functions, `string::npos` will be returned if the search does not find a character. These functions have many uses, typically finding tokens in a string that may be separated by characters of various kinds. For example, text consists of words separated by spaces and punctuation characters, so you could use these functions to find the words in a block of text. Let's see that working in an example.

Try It Out   Sorting Words from Text

This example will read a block of text, and then extract the words and output them in ascending sequence. I'll use the somewhat inefficient bubble sort function that you saw in `Ex8_10` here. In Chapter 10 you will use a library function for sorting that would be much better, but you need to learn about some other stuff before you can use that. The program will also figure out how many times each word occurs and output the count for each word. Such an analysis is called a **collocation**. Here's the code:

```cpp
// Ex8_11.cpp
// Extracting words from text
#include <iostream>
#include <iomanip>
#include <string>
using std::cin;
using std::cout;
using std::endl;
using std::ios;
using std::setiosflags;
using std::resetiosflags;
using std::setw;
using std::string;

// Sort an array of string objects
string* sort(string* strings, size_t count)
{
  bool swapped = false;
  while(true)
  {
    for(size_t i = 0 ; i<count-1 ; i++)
    {
      if(strings[i] > strings[i+1])
      {
        swapped = true;
        strings[i].swap(strings[i+1]);
      }
    }
    if(!swapped)
```

```
      break;
    swapped = false;
  }
  return strings;
}

int main()
{
  const size_t maxwords(100);
  string words[maxwords];
  string text;
  string separators(" \".,:;!?()\n");
  size_t nwords = 0;
  size_t maxwidth = 0;

  cout << "Enter some text on as many lines as you wish."
    << endl << "Terminate the input with an asterisk:" << endl;

  getline(cin, text, '*');

  size_t start(0), end(0), offset(0);    // Record start & end of word & offset
  while(true)
  {
    // Find first character of a word
    start = text.find_first_not_of(separators, offset);  // Find non-separator
    if(start == string::npos)              // If we did not find it, we are done
      break;
    offset = start + 1;                    // Move past character found


    // Find first separator past end of current word
    end = text.find_first_of(separators,offset);        // Find separator
    if(end == string::npos)                // If it's the end of the string
    {                                      // current word is last in string
      offset = end;                        // We use offset to end loop later
      end = text.length();                 // Set end as 1 past last character
    }
    else
      offset = end + 1;                    // Move past character found

    words[nwords] = text.substr(start, end-start);       // Extract the word

    // Keep track of longest word
    if(maxwidth < words[nwords].length())
      maxwidth = words[nwords].length();

    if(offset == string::npos)             // If we reached the end of the string
      break;                               // We are done

    if(++nwords == maxwords)               // Check for array full
    {
      cout << endl << "Maximum number of words reached."
           << endl << "Processing what we have." << endl;
      break;
```

```
        }
    }

    sort(words, nwords);

    cout << endl
         << "In ascending sequence, the words in the text are:"
         << endl;

    size_t count(0);                               // Count of duplicate words
    // Output words and number of occurrences
    for(size_t i = 0 ; i<nwords ; i++)
    {
      if(count == 0)
        count = 1;
      if(i < nwords-2 && words[i] == words[i+1])
      {
        ++count;
        continue;
      }
      cout << setiosflags(ios::left)               // Output word left-justified
           << setw(maxwidth+2) << words[i];
      cout << resetiosflags(ios::right)            // and word count right-justified
           << setw(5) << count << endl;
      count = 0;
    }
    cout << endl;
    return 0;
}
```

Here's an example of some output from this program:

```
Enter some text on as many lines as you wish.
Terminate the input with an asterisk:
I sometimes think I'd rather crow
And be a rooster that to roost
And be a crow. But I dunno.

A rooster he can roost also,
Which don't seem fair when crows can't crow
Which may help some. Still I dunno.*

In ascending sequence, the words in the text are:
A          1
And        2
But        1
I          3
I'd        1
Still      1
Which      2
a          2
also       1
be         2
can        1
```

```
can't        1
crow         3
crows        1
don't        1
dunno        2
fair         1
he           1
help         1
may          1
rather       1
roost        2
rooster      2
seem         1
some         1
sometimes    1
that         1
think        1
to           1
when         1
```

How It Works

The input is read from `cin` using the `getline()` with the termination character specified as an asterisk. This allows an arbitrary number of lines of input to be entered. Individual words are extracted from the input in the string object `text` and stored in the `words` array. This is done in the `while` loop.

The first step in extracting a word from `text` is to find the index position of the first character of the word:

```
start = text.find_first_not_of(separators, offset);  // Find non-separator
if(start == string::npos)              // If we did not find it, we are done
   break;
offset = start + 1;                    // Move past character found
```

The `find_first_not_of()` function call returns the index position of the first character from the position `offset` that is not one of the characters in `separators`. You could use the `find_first_of()` function here to search for any of A to Z, a to z to achieve the same result. When the last word has been extracted, the search will reach the end of the string without finding a character so you test for this by comparing the value that was returned with `string::npos`. If it is the end of the string, all words have been extracted, so you exit the loop. In any other instance, you set offset at one past the character that was found.

The next search is for any separator character:

```
end = text.find_first_of(separators,offset);        // Find separator
if(end == string::npos)                // If it's the end of the string
{                                      // current word is last in string
   offset = end;                       // We use offset to end loop later
   end = text.length();                // Set end as 1 past last character
}
else
   offset = end + 1;                   // Move past character found
```

The search for any separator is from index position `offset`, which is one past the first character of the word, so usually you will find the separator that is one past the last character of the word. When the word is the last in the text and there is no separator following the last character of the word, the function will return `string::npos` so you deal with this situation by setting `end` to one past the last character in the string and setting `offset` to `string::npos`. The `offset` variable will be tested later in the loop after the current word has been extracted to determine whether the loop should end.

Extracting a word is easy:

```
words[nwords] = text.substr(start, end-start);        // Extract the word
```

The `substr()` function extracts `end-start` characters from `text`, starting with the character at `start`. The length of the word is `end-start` because `start` is the first character and `end` is one past the last character in the word.

The rest of the `while` loop body keeps track of the maximum word length in the way you have seen before, checks for the end-of-string condition, and checks whether the `words` array is full.

The words are output in a `for` loop that iterates over all the elements in the `words` array. The `if` statements in the loop deal with counting duplicate words:

```
if(count == 0)
  count = 1;
if(i < nwords-2 && words[i] == words[i+1])
{
  ++count;
  continue;
}
```

The `count` variable records the number of duplicate words so it is always a minimum of 1. At the end of the loop `count` is set to 0 when a word and its count is written out. This acts as an indicator that a new word count is starting, so when `count` is 0, the first `if` statement sets it to 1, otherwise it is left at its current value.

The second `if` statement checks if the next word is the same as the current word, and if it is, `count` is incremented and the rest of the current loop iteration is skipped. This mechanism accumulates the number of times a word is duplicated in `count`. The loop condition also checks that the index, `i`, is less than `nwords-2` because we don't want to check the next word when the current word is the last in the array. Thus we only output a word and its count when the next word is different, or the current word is the last in the array.

The last step in the `for` loop is to output a word and its count:

```
cout << setiosflags(ios::left)             // Output word left-justified
     << setw(maxwidth+2) << words[i];
cout << resetiosflags(ios::right)          // and word count right-justified
     << setw(5) << count << endl;
count = 0;
```

The output statement left-justifies the word in a field width that is two greater than the longest word. The count is output right-justified in a field width of five.

C++/CLI Programming

While you can define a destructor in a reference class in the same way as you do for native C++ classes, most of the time it is not necessary. However, I'll return to the topic of destructors for reference classes in the next chapter. You can also call delete for a handle to a reference class, but again, this is not normally necessary as the garbage collector will delete unwanted objects automatically.

C++/CLI classes support overloading of operators but there are some differences that you need to explore. First of all, let's consider some basic differences between operator overloading in C++/CLI classes and in native C++ classes. A couple of differences you have already heard about. You'll probably recall that you must not overload the assignment operator in your value classes because the process for the assignment of one value class object to another of the same type is already defined to be member-by-member copying and you cannot change this. I also mentioned that unlike native classes, a ref class does not have a default assignment operator — if you want the assignment operator to work with your ref class objects then you must implement the appropriate function. Another difference from native C++ classes is that functions that implement operator overloading in C++/CLI classes can be static members of a class as well as instance members. This means that you have the option of implementing binary operators in C++/CLI classes with static member functions with two parameters in addition to the possibilities you have seen in the context of native C++ for operator functions as instance functions with one parameter or non-member functions with two parameters. Similarly, in C++/CLI you have the additional possibility to implement a prefix unary operator as a static member function with no parameters. Finally, although in native C++ you can overload the new operator, you cannot overload the gcnew operator in a C++/CLI class.

Let's look into some of the specifics, starting with value classes.

Overloading Operators in Value Classes

Let's define a class to represent a length in feet and inches and use that as a base for demonstrating how operator overloading can be implemented for a value class. Addition seems like a good place to start so here's the Length value class, complete with the addition operator function:

```
value class Length
{
private:
  int feet;                          // Feet component
  int inches;                        // Inches component

public:
  static initonly int inchesPerFoot = 12;

  // Constructor
  Length(int ft, int ins) : feet(ft), inches(ins){ }

  // A length as a string
  virtual String^ ToString() override
  { return feet+L" feet " + inches + L" inches";  }

  // Addition operator
  Length operator+(Length len)
  {
    int inchTotal = inches+len.inches+inchesPerFoot*(feet+len.feet);
    return Length(inchTotal/inchesPerFoot, inchTotal%inchesPerFoot);
```

```
    }
};
```

The constant, `inchesPerFoot` is `static` so it will be directly available to static and non-static function members of the class. Declaring `inchesPerFoot` as `initonly` means that it cannot be modified so it can be a public member of the class. There's a `ToString()` function override defined for the class so you can write `Length` objects to the command line using the `Console::WriteLine()` function. The `operator+()` function implementation is very simple. The function returns a new `Length` object produced by combining the `feet` and `inches` component for the current object and the parameter, `len`. The calculation is done by combining the two lengths in inches and then computing the arguments to the `Length` class constructor for the new object from the value for the combined lengths in inches.

The following code fragment would exercise the new operator function for addition:

```
Length len1 = Length(6, 9);
Length len2 = Length(7, 8);
Console::WriteLine(L"{0} plus {1} is {2}", len1, len2, len1+len2);
```

The last argument to the `WriteLine()` function is the sum of two `Length` objects so this will invoke the `operator+()` function. The result will be a new `Length` object for which the compiler will arrange to call the `ToString()` function so the last statement is really the following:

```
Console::WriteLine(L"{0} plus {1} is {2}", len1, len2,
                                        len1.operator+(len2).ToString());
```

The execution of the code fragment will result in the following output:

```
6 feet 9 inches plus 7 feet 8 inches is 14 feet 5 inches
```

Of course, you could define the `operator+()` function as a static member of the `Length` class, like this:

```
static Length operator+(Length len1, Length len2)
{
   int inchTotal = len1.inches+len2.inches+inchesPerFoot*(len1.feet+len2.feet);
   return Length(inchTotal/inchesPerFoot, inchTotal%inchesPerFoot);
}
}
```

The parameters are the two `Length` objects to be added together to produce a new `Length` object. Because this is a static member of the class, the `operator+()` function is fully entitled to access the private members, `feet` and `inches`, of both the `Length` objects passed as arguments. Friend functions are not allowed in C++/CLI classes and an external function would not have access to private members of the class so you have no other possibilities for implementing the addition operator.

Because you are not working with areas multiplication for `Length` objects, it really only makes sense to provide for multiplying a `Length` object by a numerical value. You can implement multiply operator overloading as a static member of the class, but let's define the function outside the class. The class would look like this:

```
value class Length
{
private:
```

```
      int feet;
      int inches;

public:
   static initonly int inchesPerFoot = 12;

   // Constructor
   Length(int ft, int ins) : feet(ft), inches(ins){ }

   // A length as a string
   virtual String^ ToString() override
   { return feet+L" feet " + inches + L" inches";  }

   // Addition operator
   Length operator+(Length len)
   {
      int inchTotal = inches+len.inches+inchesPerFoot*(feet+len.feet);
      return Length(inchTotal/inchesPerFoot, inchTotal%inchesPerFoot);
   }

   static Length operator*(double x, Length len); // Pre-multiply by a double value
   static Length operator*(Length len, double x); // Post-multiply by a double value
};
```

The new function declarations in the class provide for overloaded * operator functions to pre- and post-multiply a `Length` object by a value of type `double`. The definition of the `operator*()` function outside the class for pre-multiplication would be:

```
Length Length::operator *(double x, Length len)
{
   int ins = safe_cast<int>(x*len.inches +x*len.feet*inchesPerFoot);
   return Length(ins/12, ins %12);
}
```

The post-multiplication version can now be implemented in terms of this:

```
Length Length::operator *(Length len, double x)
{ return operator*(x, len);  }
```

This just calls the pre-multiply version with the arguments reversed. You could exercise these functions with the following fragment:

```
double factor = 2.5;
Console::WriteLine(L"{0} times {1} is {2}", factor, len2, factor*len2);
Console::WriteLine(L"{1} times {0} is {2}", factor, len2, len2*factor);
```

Both lines of output from this code fragment should reflect the same result from multiplication — 19 feet 2 inches. The argument expression `factor*len2` is equivalent to:

```
Length::operator*(factor, len2).ToString()
```

The result of calling the static `operator*()` function is a new `Length` object and the `ToString()` function for that is called to produce the argument to the `WriteLine()` function. The expression `len2*factor` is similar but calls the `operator*()` function that has the parameters reversed. Although the `operator*()`

functions have been written to deal with a multiplier of type `double`, they will also work with integers. The compiler will automatically promote an integer values to type `double` when you use it in an expression such as `12*(len1+len2)`.

We could expand a little further on overloaded operators in the `Length` class with a working example.

Try It Out   **A Value Class with Overloaded Operators**

This example implements operator overloading for addition, multiplication and division for the Length class:

```
// Ex8_12.cpp : main project file.
// Overloading operators in the value class, Length
#include "stdafx.h"
using namespace System;
```

```
value class Length
{
private:
  int feet;
  int inches;

public:
  static initonly int inchesPerFoot = 12;

  // Constructor
  Length(int ft, int ins) : feet(ft), inches(ins){ }

  // A length as a string
  virtual String^ ToString() override
  { return feet+L" feet " + inches + L" inches";  }

  // Addition operator
  Length operator+(Length len)
  {
    int inchTotal = inches+len.inches+inchesPerFoot*(feet+len.feet);
    return Length(inchTotal/inchesPerFoot, inchTotal%inchesPerFoot);
  }

  // Division operator
  static Length operator/(Length len, double x)
  {
    int ins = safe_cast<int>((len.feet*inchesPerFoot + len.inches)/x);
    return Length(ins/inchesPerFoot, ins%inchesPerFoot);
  }

  static Length operator*(double x, Length len); // Pre-multiply by a double value
  static Length operator*(Length len, double x); // Post-multiply by a double value
};
```

```
Length Length::operator *(double x, Length len)
{
  int ins = safe_cast<int>(x*len.inches +x*len.feet*inchesPerFoot);
  return Length(ins/inchesPerFoot, ins%inchesPerFoot);
```

```
    }

    Length Length::operator *(Length len, double x)
    { return operator*(x, len);   }

    int main(array<System::String ^> ^args)
    {
      Length len1 = Length(6, 9);
      Length len2 = Length(7, 8);
      double factor = 2.5;

      Console::WriteLine(L"{0} plus {1} is {2}", len1, len2, len1+len2);
      Console::WriteLine(L"{0} times {1} is {2}", factor, len2, factor*len2);
      Console::WriteLine(L"{1} times {0} is {2}", factor, len2, len2*factor);
      Console::WriteLine(L"The sum of {0} and {1} divided by {2} is {3}",
                                    len1, len2, factor, (len1+len2)/factor);
      return 0;
    }
```

The output from the example is:

```
6 feet 9 inches plus 7 feet 8 inches is 14 feet 5 inches
2.5 times 7 feet 8 inches is 19 feet 2 inches
7 feet 8 inches times 2.5 is 19 feet 2 inches
The sum of 6 feet 9 inches and 7 feet 8 inches divided by 2.5 is 5 feet 9 inches
```

How It Works

The new operator overloading function in the Length class is for division and it allows division of a Length value by a value of type double. Dividing a double value by a Length object does not have an obvious meaning so there's no need to implement this version. The operator/() function is implemented as another static member of the class and the definition appears within the body of the class definition to contrast how that looks compared with the operator*() functions. You would normally define all these functions inside the class definition.

Of course, you could define the operator/() function as a non-static class member like this:

```
    Length operator/(double x)
    {
      int ins = safe_cast<int>((feet*inchesPerFoot + inches)/x);
      return Length(ins/inchesPerFoot, ins%inchesPerFoot);
    }
```

It now has one argument, which will be the right operand for the / operator. The left operand is the current object that is referenced by the this pointer (implicitly in this case).

The operators are exercised in the four output statements. Only the last one is new to you and this combines the use of the overloaded + operator for Length objects with the overloaded / operator. The last argument to the Console::WriteLine() function in the fourth output statement is (len1+len2)/factor which is equivalent to the expression:

```
    Length::operator/(len1.operator+(len2), factor) .ToString()
```

The first argument to the static `operator/()` function is the `Length` object that is returned by the `operator+()` function, and the second argument is the `factor` variable, which is the divisor. The `ToString()` function for the `Length` object returned by `operator/()` is called to produce the argument string that is passed to the `Console::WriteLine()` function.

It is possible that you might want the capability to divide one `Length` object by another and have a value of type `int` as the result. This would allow you to figure out how many 17 inch lengths you can cut from a piece of timber 12 feet 6 inches long for instance. You can implement this quite easily like this:

```
static int operator/(Length len1, Length len2)
{
  return
  (len1.feet*inchesPerFoot + len1.inches)/( len2.feet*inchesPerFoot + len2.inches);
}
```

This just returns the result of dividing the first length in inches by the second in inches.

To complete the set you could add a function to overload the `%` operator to tell you how much is left over. This could be implemented as:

```
static Length operator%(Length len1, Length len2)
{
  int ins = (len1.feet*inchesPerFoot + len1.inches)%
                              (len2.feet*inchesPerFoot + len2.inches);
  return Length(ins/inchesPerFoot, ins%inchesPerFoot);
}
```

You compute the residue in inches after dividing `len1` by `len2` and return it as a new `Length` object.

With all these operators you really can use your `Length` objects in arithmetic expressions. You can write statements such as:

```
Length len1 = Length(2,6);         // 2 feet 6 inches
Length len2 = Length(3,5);         // 3 feet 5 inches
Length len3 = Length(14,6);        // 14 feet 6 inches
Length total = 12*(len1 + len2 + len3) + (len3/Length(1,7))*len2;
```

The value of `total` will be 275 feet 9 inches. The last statement makes use of the assignment operator that comes with every value class as well as the `operator*()`, `operator+()`, and `operator/()` functions in the `Length` class. This operator overloading is not only powerful stuff, it really is easy isn't it?

Overloading the Increment and Decrement Operators

Overloading the increment and decrement operators is simpler in C++/CLI than in native C++. As long as you implement the operator function as a static class member, the same function will serve as both the prefix and postfix operator functions. Here's how you could implement the increment operator for the `Length` class:

```
value class Length
{
public:
```

```
// Code as before...
```

```
// Overloaded increment operator function - increment by 1 inch
static Length operator++(Length len)
{
  ++len.inches;
  len.feet += len.inches/len.inchesPerFoot;
  len.inches %= len.inchesPerFoot;
  return len;
}
};
```

This implementation of the `operator++()` function increments a length by 1 inch. The following code would exercise the function:

```
Length len = Length(1, 11);          // 1 foot 11 inches
Console::WriteLine(len++);
Console::WriteLine(++len);
```

Executing this fragment will produce the output:

```
1 feet 11 inches
2 feet 1 inches
```

Thus the prefix and postfix increment operations are working as they should using a single operator function in the `Length` class. This occurs because the compiler is able to determine whether to use the value of the operand in a surrounding expression before or after the operand has been incremented and compile the code accordingly.

Overloading Operators in Reference Classes

Overloading operators in a reference class is essentially the same as overloading operators in a value class, the primary difference being that parameters and return values are typically handles. Let's see how the `Length` class looks implemented as a reference class, then you'll be able to compare the two versions.

Try It Out   Overloaded Operators in a Reference Class

This example defines `Length` as a reference class with the same set of overloaded operators as the value class version:

```
// Ex8_13.cpp : main project file.
// Defining and using overloaded operator

#include "stdafx.h"
using namespace System;

ref class Length
{
private:
  int feet;
  int inches;
```

```
public:
  static initonly int inchesPerFoot = 12;

  // Constructor
  Length(int ft, int ins) : feet(ft), inches(ins){ }

  // A length as a string
  virtual String^ ToString() override
  { return feet+L" feet " + inches + L" inches";  }

  // Overloaded addition operator
  Length^ operator+(Length^ len)
  {
    int inchTotal = inches+len->inches+inchesPerFoot*(feet+len->feet);
    return gcnew Length(inchTotal/inchesPerFoot, inchTotal%inchesPerFoot);
  }

  // Overloaded divide operator - right operand type double
  static Length^ operator/(Length^ len, double x)
  {
    int ins = safe_cast<int>((len->feet*inchesPerFoot + len->inches)/x);
    return gcnew Length(ins/inchesPerFoot, ins%inchesPerFoot);
  }

  // Overloaded divide operator - both operands type Length
  static int operator/(Length^ len1, Length^ len2)
  {
    return (len1->feet*inchesPerFoot + len1->inches)/
                             (len2->feet*inchesPerFoot + len2->inches);
  }

  // Overloaded remainder operator
  static Length^ operator%(Length^ len1, Length^ len2)
  {
    int ins = (len1->feet*inchesPerFoot + len1->inches)%
                             (len2->feet*inchesPerFoot + len2->inches);
    return gcnew Length(ins/inchesPerFoot, ins%inchesPerFoot);
  }

  static Length^ operator*(double x, Length^ len); // Multiply - L operand double
  static Length^ operator*(Length^ len, double x); // Multiply - R operand double

  // Pre- and postfix increment operator
  static Length^ operator++(Length^ len)
  {
    Length^ temp = gcnew Length(len->feet, len->inches);
    ++temp->inches;
    temp->feet += temp->inches/temp->inchesPerFoot;
    temp->inches %= temp->inchesPerFoot;
    return temp;
  }
};

// Multiply operator implementation - left operand double
Length^ Length::operator*(double x, Length^ len)
{
```

```
    int ins = safe_cast<int>(x*len->inches +x*len->feet*inchesPerFoot);
    return gcnew Length(ins/inchesPerFoot, ins%inchesPerFoot);
}
```

```
// Multiply operator implementation - right operand double
Length^ Length::operator*(Length^ len, double x)
{ return operator*(x, len);  }
```

```
int main(array<System::String ^> ^args)
{
  Length^ len1 = gcnew Length(2,6);              // 2 feet 6 inches
  Length^ len2 = gcnew Length(3,5);              // 3 feet 5 inches
  Length^ len3 = gcnew Length(14,6);             // 14 feet 6 inches

  // Use +, * and / operators
  Length^ total = 12*(len1+len2+len3) + (len3/gcnew Length(1,7))*len2;
  Console::WriteLine(total);

  // Use remainder operator
  Console::WriteLine(
              L"{0} can be cut into {1} pieces {2} long with {3} left over.",
                                      len3, len3/len1, len1, len3%len1);
  Length^ len4 = gcnew Length(1, 11);            // 1 foot 11 inches

  // Use pre- and postfix increment operator
  Console::WriteLine(len4++);                    // Use postfix increment operator
  Console::WriteLine(++len4);                    // Use prefix increment operator
  Console::WriteLine(len4);                      // Final value of len4
  return 0;
}
```

This example will produce the following output:

```
275 feet 9 inches
14 feet 6 inches can be cut into 5 pieces 2 feet 6 inches long
with 2 feet 0 inches left over.
1 feet 11 inches
2 feet 1 inches
2 feet 1 inches
```

How It Works

Compared to a value class, there are differences in the parameter and return types for the overloaded operator functions, the use of the -> operator as a consequence of that, and objects of type Length are now created on the CLR heap using the gcnew keyword. In addition the overloaded increment operator function returns a temporary object and does not modify the original object using the reference argument.

It is important that you do not modify the original object when you are overloading the increment or decrement operator in a reference class because the code that the compiler generates relies on the object that is passed to the overload function being left unchanged. When the function is called for a postfix increment or decrement operation, the code that is generated uses the object in the expression in which it appears, and then stores the object that you return to replace the original. Apart from these changes the code is basically the same and the operator functions work just as effectively as in the previous example.

Implementing the Assignment Operator for Reference Types

There are relative few circumstances where you will need to implement the assignment operator for a reference type because you will typically use handles to refer to objects and the need for a copy constructor does not arise. However, if you use the Standard Template Library for the CLR that you will meet in Chapter 10, in some situations you will need to implement the assignment operator and the compiler will never supply one by default. The form of the function to overload the assignment operator in a reference class is very simple and is easily understood if you look at an example. Here's how the assignment operator would look for the Length class for instance:

```
Length% operator=(const Length% len)
{
  if(this != %len)
  {
    feet = len.feet;
    inches = len.inches;
  }
  return *this;
}
```

The function parameter is const because it will not be changed, and if you don't declare it as const, the argument will be passed by value and will cause the copy constructor to be called. The return type is also a reference because you always return the object pointed to by this. The if statement checks whether or not the argument and the current object are identical, and if they are, the function just returns *this, which will be the current object. If they are not, you copy each of the data members of len to the current object before returning it.

Summary

In this chapter you have learned the basics of how you can define classes and how you create and use class objects. You have also learned about how you can overload operators in a class to allow the operators to be applied to class objects.

The key points to keep in mind from this chapter are:

❑   Objects are created by functions called **constructors**. The primary role of a constructor is to set values for the data members (fields) for a class object.

❑   C++/CLI classes can also have a **static contructor** that initializes the static fields in a class.

❑   Objects are destroyed using functions called **destructors**. It is essential to define a destructor in native C++ classes to destroy objects which contain members that are allocated on the heap because the default constructor will not do this.

❑   The compiler will supply a default copy constructor for a native C++ class if you do not define one. The default copy constructor will not deal correctly with objects of classes that have data members allocated on the free store.

❑   When you define your own copy constructor in a native C++ class, you must use a reference parameter.

❏ You must not define a copy constructor in a value classes; copies of value class objects are always created by copying fields.

❏ No default copy constructor is supplied for a reference class although you can define your own when this is necessary.

❏ If you do not define an assignment operator for your native C++ class, the compiler will supply a default version. As with the copy constructor, the default assignment operator will not work correctly with classes that have data members allocated on the free store.

❏ You must not define the assignment operator in a value class. Assignment of value class objects is always done by copying fields.

❏ A default assignment operator is not provided for reference classes but you can define your own assignment operator function when necessary.

❏ It is essential that you provide a destructor, a copy constructor, and an assignment operator for native C++ classes that have members allocated by new.

❏ A union is a mechanism that allows two or more variables to occupy the same location in memory.

❏ C++/CLI classes can contain **literal fields** that define constants within a class. The can also contain **initonly fields** that cannot be modified once they have been initialized.

❏ Most basic operators can be overloaded to provide actions specific to objects of a class. You should only implement operator functions for your classes that are consistent with the normal interpretation of the basic operators.

❏ The string class in the standard library for native C++ provides a powerful and superior way to process strings in your programs.

❏ A class template is a pattern that you can use to create classes with the same structure, but which support different data types.

❏ You can define a class template that has multiple parameters, including parameters that can assume constant values rather than types.

❏ You should put definitions for your programs in .h files, and executable code — function definitions — in .cpp files. You can then incorporate .h files into your .cpp files by using #include directives.

Exercises

1. Define a native C++ class to represent an estimated integer, such as 'about 40'. These are integers whose value may be regarded as exact or estimated, so the class needs to have as data members a value and an 'estimation' flag. The state of the estimation flag affects arithmetic operations, so that '2 * about 40' is 'about 80'. The state of variables should be switchable between 'estimated' and 'exact'.

Provide one or more constructors for such a class. Overload the + operator so that these integers can be used in arithmetic expressions. Do you want the + operator to be a global or a member function? Do you need an assignment operator? Provide a Print() member function so that they can be printed out, using a leading 'E' to denote that the 'estimation' flag is set. Write a program to test the operation of your class, checking especially that the operation of the estimation flag is correct.

2. Implement a simple string class in native C++ that holds a `char*` and an integer length as `private` data members. Provide a constructor which takes an argument of type `const char*`, and implement the copy constructor, assignment operator and destructor functions. Verify that your class works. You will find it easiest to use the string functions from the `<cstring>` header file.

3. What other constructors might you want to supply for your string class? Make a list, and code them up.

4. (Advanced) Does your class correctly deal with cases such as this?

```
string s1;
...
s1 = s1;
```

   If not, how should it be modified?

5. (Advanced) Overload the + and += operators of your class for concatenating strings.

6. Modify the stack example from Exercise 7 in the previous chapter so that the size of the stack is specified in the constructor and dynamically allocated. What else will you need to add? Test the operation of your new class.

7. Define a `Box` ref class with the same functionality as the `CBox` class in Ex8_08.cpp and reimplement the example as a program for the CLR.

8. This exercise might be of use to someone working with sensitive documents. Write a native C++ program that uses the `string` class that is declared in the `<string>` header to read a text string of arbitrary length from the keyboard. The program should then prompt for entry of one or more words that appears in the input text. All occurrences of the chosen words in the input text, regardless of case, should be replaced with as many asterisks as there are letters in the word. Only whole words should be replaced so if the string is `"Our friend Wendy is at the end of the road."` and the chosen word is `"end"`, the result should be `"Our friend Wendy is at the *** of the road."`, not `"Our fri*** W***y is at the *** of the road."`.

Class Inheritance and Virtual Functions

In this chapter, you're going to look into a topic that lies at the heart of object-oriented programming: **class inheritance**. Simply put, inheritance is the means by which you can define a new class in terms of one you already have. This is fundamental to programming in C++ so it's important that you understand how inheritance works.

In this chapter, you will learn about:

- ❏   How inheritance fits into the idea of object-oriented programming
- ❏   Defining a new class in terms of an existing one
- ❏   The use of the `protected` keyword to define a new access specification for class members
- ❏   How a class can be a friend to another class
- ❏   Virtual functions and how you can use them
- ❏   Pure virtual functions
- ❏   Abstract classes
- ❏   Virtual destructors and when to use them

Basic Ideas of OOP

As you have seen, a class is a data type that you define to suit your own application requirements. Classes in object-oriented programming also define the objects to which your program relates. You program the solution to a problem in terms of the objects that are specific to the problem, using operations that work directly with those objects. You can define a class to represent something abstract, such as a complex number, which is a mathematical concept, or a truck, which is decidedly physical (especially if you run into one on the highway). So, as well as being a data type, a class can also be a definition of a set of real-world objects of a particular kind, at least to the degree necessary to solve a given problem.

You can think of a class as defining the characteristics of a particular group of things that are specified by a common set of parameters and share a common set of operations that may be performed on them. The operations that you can apply to objects of a given class type are defined by the class interface, which corresponds to the functions contained in the `public` section of the class definition. The CBox class that you used in the previous chapter is a good example — it defined a box in terms of its dimensions plus a set of public functions that you could apply to CBox objects to solve a problem.

Of course, there are many different kinds of boxes in the real world: There are cartons, coffins, candy boxes, and cereal boxes, to name but a few, and you will certainly be able to come up with many others. You can differentiate boxes by the kinds of things they hold, the materials with which they are made, and in a multitude of other ways, but even though there are many different kinds of boxes, they share some common characteristics — the essence of *boxiness* perhaps. Therefore you can still visualize all kinds of boxes as actually being related to one another, even though they have many differentiating features. You could define a particular kind of box as having the generic characteristics of all boxes — perhaps just a length, a width, and a height. You could then add some additional characteristics to the basic box type to differentiate a particular kind of box from the rest. You may also find that there are new things you can do with your specific kind of box that you can't do with other boxes.

It's also possible that some objects may be the result of combining a particular kind of box with some other type of object: a box of candy or a crate of beer, for example. To accommodate this you could define one kind of box as a generic box with basic boxiness characteristics and then specify another sort of box as a further specialization of that. Figure 9-1 illustrates an example of the kinds of relationships you might define between different sorts of boxes.

The boxes become more specialized as you move down the diagram and the arrows run from a given box type to the one on which it is based. Figure 9-1 defines three different kinds of boxes based on the generic type, CBox. It also defines beer crates as a further refinement of crates designed to hold bottles.

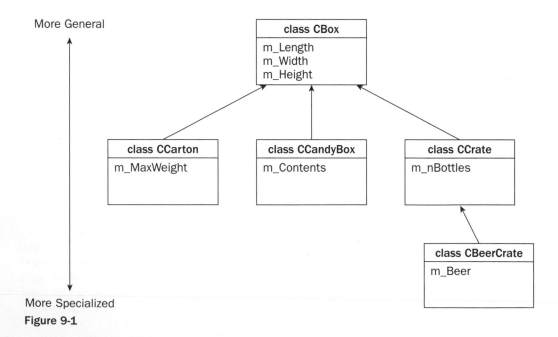

Figure 9-1

Thus a good way to approximate the real world relatively well using classes in C++ is through the ability to define classes that are interrelated. A candy box can be considered to be a box with all the characteristics of a basic box, plus a few characteristics of its own. This precisely illustrates the relationship between classes in C++ when one class is defined based on another. A more specialized class has all the characteristics of the class on which it is based, plus a few characteristics of its own that identify what makes it special. Let's look at how this works in practice.

Inheritance in Classes

When you define one class based on another, the former is referred to as a **derived class**. A derived class automatically contains all the data members of the class that you used to define it and, with some restrictions, the function members as well. The class is said to **inherit** the data members and function members of the class on which it is based.

The only members of a base class that are not inherited by a derived class are the destructor, the constructors, and any member functions overloading the assignment operator. All other function members, together with all the data members of a base class, are inherited by a derived class. Of course, the reason for certain base members not being inherited is that a derived class always has its own constructors and destructor. If the base class has an assignment operator, the derived class provides its own version. When I say these functions are not inherited, I mean that they don't exist as members of a derived class object. However, they still exist for the base class part of an object, as you will see.

What Is a Base Class?

A **base class** is any class that you use as a basis for defining another class. For example, if you define a class B directly in terms of a class A, A is said to be a **direct base class** of B. In Figure 9-1 the CCrate class is a direct base class of CBeerCrate. When a class such as CBeerCrate is defined in terms of another class CCrate, CBeerCrate is said to be derived from CCrate. Because CCrate is itself defined in terms of the class CBox, CBox is said to be an **indirect base class** of CBeerCrate. You'll see how this is expressed in the class definition in a moment. Figure 9-2 illustrates the way in which base class members are inherited in a derived class.

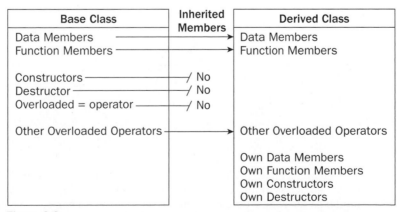

Figure 9-2

Just because member functions are inherited doesn't mean that you won't want to replace them in the derived class with new versions, and, of course, you can do that when necessary.

Deriving Classes from a Base Class

Let's go back to the original CBox class with `public` data members that you saw at the beginning of the previous chapter:

```
// Header file Box.h in project Ex9_01
#pragma once

class CBox
{
  public:
    double m_Length;
    double m_Width;
    double m_Height;

    CBox(double lv = 1.0, double wv = 1.0, double hv = 1.0):
                        m_Length(lv), m_Width(wv), m_Height(hv){}
};
```

Create a new empty WIN32 console project with the name Ex9_01 and save this code in a new header file in the project with the name Box.h. The #pragma once directive ensures the definition of CBox appears only once in a build. There's a constructor in the class so that you can initialize objects when you declare them. Suppose you now need another class of objects, CCandyBox, that are the same as CBox objects but also have another data member — a pointer to a text string — that identifies the contents of the box.

You can define CCandyBox as a derived class with the CBox class as the base class, as follows:

```
// Header file CandyBox.h in project Ex9_01
#pragma once
#include "Box.h"
class CCandyBox: CBox
{
  public:
    char* m_Contents;

    CCandyBox(char* str = "Candy")                // Constructor
    {
      m_Contents = new char[ strlen(str) + 1 ];
      strcpy_s(m_Contents, strlen(str) + 1, str);
    }

    ~CCandyBox()                                  // Destructor
    { delete[] m_Contents; };
};
```

Add this header file to the project Ex9_01. You need the #include directive for the Box.h header file because you refer to the CBox class in the code. If you were to leave this directive out, CBox would be unknown to the compiler so the code would not compile. The base class name, CBox, appears after the name of the derived class `CCandyBox` and is separated from it by a colon. In all other respects, it looks like a normal class definition. You have added the new member, `m_Contents`, and, because it is a pointer to a string, you need a constructor to initialize it and a destructor to release the memory for the string. You have also put a default value for the string describing the contents of a `CCandyBox` object in the constructor. Objects of the `CCandyBox` class type contain all the members of the base class, `CBox`, plus the additional data member, `m_Contents`.

Note the use of the `strcpy_s()` function that you first saw in Chapter 6. Here there are three arguments — the destination for the copy operation, the length of the destination buffer, and the source. If both arrays were static — that is, not allocated on the heap — you could omit the second argument and just supply the destination and source pointers. This is possible because the `strcpy_s()` function is also available as a template function that can infer the length of the destination string automatically. You can therefore call the function just with the destination and source strings as arguments when you are working with static strings.

Try It Out   Using a Derived Class

Now you'll see how the derived class works in an example. Add the following code to the `Ex9_01` project as the source file `Ex9_01.cpp`:

```cpp
// Ex9_01.cpp
// Using a derived class
#include <iostream>                   // For stream I/O
#include <cstring>                    // For strlen() and strcpy()
#include "CandyBox.h"                 // For CBox and CCandyBox
using std::cout;
using std::endl;

int main()
{
  CBox myBox(4.0, 3.0, 2.0);                   // Create CBox object
  CCandyBox myCandyBox;
  CCandyBox myMintBox("Wafer Thin Mints");     // Create CCandyBox object

  cout << endl
       << "myBox occupies " << sizeof myBox      // Show how much memory
       << " bytes" << endl                       // the objects require
       << "myCandyBox occupies " << sizeof myCandyBox
        << " bytes" << endl
       << "myMintBox occupies " << sizeof myMintBox
       << " bytes";

  cout << endl
       << "myBox length is " << myBox.m_Length;

  myBox.m_Length = 10.0;

  // myCandyBox.m_Length = 10.0;       // uncomment this for an error

  cout << endl;
  return 0;
}
```

How It Works

You have an `#include` directive for the `CandyBox.h` header here, and because you know that that contains an `#include` directive for `Box.h`, you don't need to add a directive to include `Box.h`. You could put an `#include` directive for `Box.h` in this file, in which case the `#pragma once` directive in `Box.h` would prevent its inclusion more than once. This is important because each class can only be defined once; two definitions for a class in the code would be an error.

After declaring a `CBox` object and two `CCandyBox` objects, you output the number of bytes that each object occupies. Let's look at the output:

```
myBox occupies 24 bytes
myCandyBox occupies 32 bytes
myMintBox occupies 32 bytes
myBox length is 4
```

The first line is what you would expect from the discussion in the previous chapter. A `CBox` object has three data members of type `double`, each of which is 8 bytes, making 24 bytes in all. Both the `CCandyBox` objects are the same size — 32 bytes. The length of the string doesn't affect the size of an object, as the memory to hold the string is allocated in the free store. The 32 bytes are made up of 24 bytes for the three `double` members inherited from the base class `CBox`, plus 4 bytes for the pointer member `m_Contents`, which makes 28 bytes. So where did the other four bytes come from? This is due to the compiler aligning members at addresses that are multiples of eight bytes. You should be able to demonstrate this by adding an extra member of type `int`, say, to the class `CCandyBox`. You will find that the size of a class object is still 32 bytes.

You also output the value of the `m_Length` member of the `CBox` object `myBox`. Even though you have no difficulty accessing this member of the `CBox` object, if you uncomment the following statement in the function `main()`,

```
// myCandyBox.m_Length = 10.0;      // uncomment this for an error
```

the program no longer compiles. The compiler generates the following message:

```
error C2247: 'CBox::m_Length' not accessible because 'CCandyBox' uses 'private' to
inherit from 'CBox'
```

It says quite clearly that the `m_Length` member from the base class is not accessible because `m_Length` has become `private` in the derived class. This is because there is a default access specifier of `private` for a base class when you define a derived class — it's as if the first line of the derived class definition had been

```
class CCandyBox: private CBox
```

There always has to be an access specification for a base class that determines the status of the inherited members in the derived class. If you omit the access specification for a base class, the compiler assumes that it's `private`. If you change the definition of the `CCandyBox` class in `CandyBox.h` to the following,

```
class CCandyBox: public CBox
{
  public:
```

```
    char* m_Contents;

    CCandyBox(char* str = "Candy")                    // Constructor
    {
      m_Contents = new char[ strlen(str) + 1 ];
      strcpy_s(m_Contents, strlen(str) + 1, str);
    }

    ~CCandyBox()                                       // Destructor
    { delete[] m_Contents; };
};
```

the m_Length member is inherited in the derived class as public and is accessible in the function main(). With the access specifier public for the base class, all the inherited members originally specified as public in the base class have the same access level in the derived class.

Access Control Under Inheritance

The whole question of the access of inherited members in a derived class needs to be looked at more closely. Consider the status of the private members of a base class in a derived class.

There was a good reason to choose the version of the class CBox with public data members in the previous example, rather than the later, more secure version with private data members. The reason was that although private data members of a base class are also members of a derived class, they remain private to the base class in the derived class so member functions added to the derived class cannot access them. They are only accessible in the derived class through function members of the base class that are not in the private section of the base class. You can demonstrate this very easily by changing all the CBox class data members to private and putting a Volume() function in the derived class CCandyBox, so that the class definition is as follows:

```
// Version of the classes that will not compile
class CBox
{
  public:
    CBox(double lv = 1.0, double wv = 1.0, double hv = 1.0):
    m_Length(lv), m_Width(wv), m_Height(hv){}

  private:
    double m_Length;
    double m_Width;
    double m_Height;
};
```

```
class CCandyBox: public CBox
{
  public:
    char* m_Contents;
```

```
    // Function to calculate the volume of a CCandyBox object
    double Volume() const              // Error - members not accessible
    { return m_Length*m_Width*m_Height; }

    CCandyBox(char* str = "Candy")     // Constructor
    {
      m_Contents = new char[ strlen(str) + 1 ];
      strcpy_s(m_Contents, strlen(str) + 1, str);
    }

    ~CCandyBox()                       // Destructor
    { delete[] m_Contents; }
};
```

A program using these classes does not compile. The function `Volume()` in the class `CCandyBox` attempts to access the `private` members of the base class, which is not legal so the compile will flag each instance with error number C2248.

Try It Out   Accessing Private Members of the Base Class

It is, however, legal to use the `Volume()` function in the base class, so if you move the definition of the function `Volume()` to the `public` section of the base class, `CBox`, not only will the program compile but you can use the function to obtain the volume of a `CCandyBox` object. Create a new WIN32 project, `Ex9_02`, with the `Box.h` contents as the following:

```
// Box.h in Ex9_02
#pragma once

class CBox
{
  public:
    CBox(double lv = 1.0, double wv = 1.0, double hv = 1.0):
                        m_Length(lv), m_Width(wv), m_Height(hv){}

    //Function to calculate the volume of a CBox object
    double Volume() const
    { return m_Length*m_Width*m_Height; }

  private:
    double m_Length;
    double m_Width;
    double m_Height;
};
```

The `CandyBox.h` header in the project contains:

```
// Header file CandyBox.h in project Ex9_02
#pragma once
#include "Box.h"
class CCandyBox: public CBox
{
  public:
```

```
      char* m_Contents;

      CCandyBox(char* str = "Candy")                // Constructor
      {
        m_Contents = new char[ strlen(str) + 1 ];
        strcpy_s(m_Contents, strlen(str) + 1, str);
      }

      ~CCandyBox()                                  // Destructor
      { delete[] m_Contents; };
    };
```

The `Ex9_02.cpp` file in the project contains:

```cpp
// Ex9_02.cpp
// Using a function inherited from a base class
#include <iostream>              // For stream I/O
#include <cstring>               // For strlen() and strcpy()
#include "CandyBox.h"            // For CBox and CCandyBox
using std::cout;
using std::endl;

int main()
{
  CBox myBox(4.0,3.0,2.0);                      // Create CBox object
  CCandyBox myCandyBox;
  CCandyBox myMintBox("Wafer Thin Mints");      // Create CCandyBox object

  cout << endl
       << "myBox occupies " << sizeof  myBox       // Show how much memory
       << " bytes" << endl                         // the objects require
       << "myCandyBox occupies " << sizeof myCandyBox
       << " bytes" << endl
       << "myMintBox occupies " << sizeof myMintBox
       << " bytes";
  cout << endl
       << "myMintBox volume is " << myMintBox.Volume(); // Get volume of a
                                                        // CCandyBox object
  cout << endl;
  return 0;
}
```

This example produces the following output:

```
myBox occupies 24 bytes
myCandyBox occupies 32 bytes
myMintBox occupies 32 bytes
myMintBox volume is 1
```

How It Works

The interesting additional output is the last line. This shows the value produced by the function `Volume()`, which is now in the `public` section of the base class. Within the derived class, it operates on the members of the derived class that are inherited from the base. It is a full member of the derived class, so it can be used freely with objects of the derived class.

The value for the volume of the derived class object is 1 because, in creating the CCandyBox object, the CBox() default constructor was called first to create the base class part of the object, and this sets default CBox dimensions to 1.

Constructor Operation in a Derived Class

Although I said the base class constructors are not inherited in a derived class, they still exist in the base class and are used for creating the base part of a derived class object. This is because creating the base class part of a derived class object is really the business of a base class constructor, not the derived class constructor. After all, you have seen that private members of a base class are inaccessible in a derived class object, even though they are inherited, so responsibility for these has to lie with the base class constructors.

The default base class constructor was called automatically in the last example to create the base part of the derived class object, but this doesn't have to be the case. You can arrange to call a particular base class constructor from the derived class constructor. This enables you to initialize the base class data members with a constructor other than the default, or indeed to choose to call a particular class constructor, depending on the data supplied to the derived class constructor.

Try It Out   **Calling Constructors**

You can see this in action through a modified version of the previous example. To make the class usable, you really need to provide a constructor for the derived class that allows you to specify the dimensions of the object. You can add an additional constructor in the derived class to do this, and call the base class constructor explicitly to set the values of the data members that are inherited from the base class.

In the Ex9_03 project, Box.h contains:

```
// Box.h in Ex9_03
#pragma once
#include <iostream>
using std::cout;
using std::endl;

class CBox
{
  public:
    // Base class constructor
    CBox(double lv = 1.0, double wv = 1.0, double hv = 1.0):
                    m_Length(lv), m_Width(wv), m_Height(hv)
    {  cout << endl << "CBox constructor called";  }

    //Function to calculate the volume of a CBox object
    double Volume() const
    { return m_Length*m_Width*m_Height; }

  private:
    double m_Length;
```

```
      double m_Width;
      double m_Height;
};
```

The `CandyBox.h` header file should contain:

```cpp
// CandyBox.h in Ex9_03
#pragma once
#include <iostream>
#include "Box.h"
using std::cout;
using std::endl;

class CCandyBox: public CBox
{
  public:
    char* m_Contents;

    // Constructor to set dimensions and contents
    // with explicit call of CBox constructor
    CCandyBox(double lv, double wv, double hv, char* str = "Candy")
                                                :CBox(lv, wv, hv)
    {
      cout << endl <<"CCandyBox constructor2 called";
      m_Contents = new char[ strlen(str) + 1 ];
      strcpy_s(m_Contents, strlen(str) + 1, str);
    }

    // Constructor to set contents
    // calls default CBox constructor automatically
    CCandyBox(char* str = "Candy")
    {
      cout << endl << "CCandyBox constructor1 called";
      m_Contents = new char[ strlen(str) + 1 ];
      strcpy_s(m_Contents, strlen(str) + 1, str);
    }

    ~CCandyBox()                                    // Destructor
    { delete[] m_Contents; }
};
```

The `#include` directive for the `<iostream>` header and the two using declarations are not strictly necessary here because `Box.h` contains the same code, but it does no harm to put them in. On the contrary, putting these statements in here also means that if you were to remove this code from `Box.h` because it was no longer required there, `CandyBox.h` still compiles.

The contents of `Ex9_03.cpp` is:

```cpp
// Ex9_03.cpp
// Calling a base constructor from a derived class constructor
#include <iostream>                 // For stream I/O
#include <cstring>                  // For strlen() and strcpy()
#include "CandyBox.h"               // For CBox and CCandyBox
using std::cout;
```

517

```
using std::endl;

int main()
{
  CBox myBox(4.0, 3.0, 2.0);
  CCandyBox myCandyBox;
  CCandyBox myMintBox(1.0, 2.0, 3.0, "Wafer Thin Mints");

  cout << endl
       << "myBox occupies " << sizeof  myBox       // Show how much memory
       << " bytes" << endl                         // the objects require
       << "myCandyBox occupies " << sizeof myCandyBox
       << " bytes" << endl
       << "myMintBox occupies " << sizeof myMintBox
       << " bytes";
  cout << endl
       << "myMintBox volume is "                   // Get volume of a
       << myMintBox.Volume();                      // CCandyBox object
  cout << endl;
  return 0;
}
```

How It Works

As well as adding the additional constructor in the derived class, you have added an output statement in each constructor so you know when either gets called. The explicit call of the constructor for the CBox class appears after a colon in the function header of the derived class constructor. You have perhaps noticed that the notation is exactly the same as what you have been using for initializing members in a constructor anyway:

```
// Calling the base class constructor
CCandyBox(double lv, double wv, double hv, char* str= "Candy"):
                                              CBox(lv, wv, hv)
{
...
}
```

This is perfectly consistent with what you are doing here because you are essentially initializing a CBox sub-object of the derived class object. In the first case, you are explicitly calling the default constructor for the double members m_Length, m_Width and m_Height in the initialization list. In the second instance, you are calling the constructor for CBox. This causes the specific CBox constructor you have chosen to be called before the CCandyBox constructor is executed.

If you build and run this example, it produces the following output:

```
CBox constructor called
CBox constructor called
CCandyBox constructor1 called
CBox constructor called
CCandyBox constructor2 called
myBox occupies 24 bytes
myCandyBox occupies 32 bytes
myMintBox occupies 32 bytes
myMintBox volume is 6
```

The calls to the constructors are explained in the following table:

Screen output	Object being constructed
CBox constructor called	`MyBox`
CBox constructor called	`MyCandyBox`
CCandyBox constructor1 called	`MyCandyBox`
CBox constructor called	`MyMintBox`
CCandyBox constructor2 called	`MyMintBox`

The first line of output is due to the CBox class constructor call, originating from the declaration of the CBox object, myBox. The second line of output arises from the automatic call of the base class constructor caused by the declaration of the CCandyBox object myCandyBox.

> *Notice how the base class constructor is always called before the derived class constructor. The base class is the foundation on which the derived class is built so the base class must be created first.*

The following line is due to your version of the default derived class constructor being called for the myCandyBox object. This constructor is invoked because the object is not initialized. The fourth line of output arises from the explicit identification of the CBox class constructor to be called in our new constructor for CCandyBox objects. The argument values specified for the dimensions of the CCandyBox object are passed to the base class constructor. Next comes the output from the new derived class constructor itself, so constructors are again called for the base class first, followed by the derived class.

It should be clear from what you have seen up to now that when a derived class constructor is executed, a base class constructor is always called to construct the base part of the derived class object. If you don't specify the base class constructor to be used, the compiler arranges for the default base class constructor to be called.

The last line in the table shows that the initialization of the base part of the myMintBox object is working as it should be, with the private members having been initialized by the CBox class constructor.

Having the private members of a base class only accessible to function members of the base class isn't always convenient. There will be many instances where you want to have private members of a base class that *can* be accessed from within the derived class. As you surely have anticipated by now, C++ provides a way to do this.

Declaring Class Members to Be Protected

In addition to the public and private access specifiers for members of a class, you can also declare members of a class as protected. Within the class, the protected keyword has the same effect as the private keyword: members of a class that are protected can only be accessed by member functions of the class, and by friend functions of the class (also by member functions of a class that is declared as a `friend` of the class — you will learn about `friend` classes later in this chapter). Using the `protected` keyword, you could redefine the `CBox` class as follows:

```cpp
// Box.h in Ex9_04
#pragma once
#include <iostream>
using std::cout;
using std::endl;

class CBox
{
  public:
    // Base class constructor
    CBox(double lv = 1.0, double wv = 1.0, double hv = 1.0):
                          m_Length(lv), m_Width(wv), m_Height(hv)
    {  cout << endl << "CBox constructor called";  }

    // CBox destructor - just to track calls
    ~CBox()
    { cout << "CBox destructor called" << endl; }

  protected:
    double m_Length;
    double m_Width;
    double m_Height;
};
```

Now the data members are still effectively `private`, in that they can't be accessed by ordinary global functions, but they'll still be accessible to member functions of a derived class.

Try It Out   Using Protected Members

You can demonstrate the use of `protected` data members by using this version of the class `CBox` to derive a new version of the class `CCandyBox`, which accesses the members of the base class through its own member function, `Volume()`:

```cpp
// CandyBox.h in Ex9_04
#pragma once
#include "Box.h"
#include <iostream>
using std::cout;
using std::endl;

class CCandyBox: public CBox
{
  public:
    char* m_Contents;

    // Derived class function to calculate volume
    double Volume() const
    { return m_Length*m_Width*m_Height; }
```

```
    // Constructor to set dimensions and contents
    // with explicit call of CBox constructor
    CCandyBox(double lv, double wv, double hv, char* str = "Candy")
                                    :CBox(lv, wv, hv)  // Constructor
    {
      cout << endl <<"CCandyBox constructor2 called";
      m_Contents = new char[ strlen(str) + 1 ];
      strcpy_s(m_Contents, strlen(str) + 1, str);
    }

    // Constructor to set contents
    // calls default CBox constructor automatically
    CCandyBox(char* str = "Candy")                  // Constructor
    {
      cout << endl << "CCandyBox constructor1 called";
      m_Contents = new char[ strlen(str) + 1 ];
      strcpy_s(m_Contents, strlen(str) + 1, str);
    }

    ~CCandyBox()                                    // Destructor
    {
      cout << "CCandyBox destructor called" << endl;
      delete[] m_Contents;
    }
};
```

The code for main() in Ex9_04.cpp is:

```
// Ex9_04.cpp
// Using the protected access specifier
#include <iostream>              // For stream I/O
#include <cstring>               // For strlen() and strcpy()
#include "CandyBox.h"            // For CBox and CCandyBox
using std::cout;
using std::endl;
```

```
int main()
{
  CCandyBox myCandyBox;
  CCandyBox myToffeeBox(2, 3, 4, "Stickjaw Toffee");

  cout << endl
       << "myCandyBox volume is " << myCandyBox.Volume()
       << endl
       << "myToffeeBox volume is " << myToffeeBox.Volume();

  // cout << endl << myToffeeBox.m_Length;  // Uncomment this for an error

  cout << endl;
  return 0;
}
```

How It Works

In this example you calculate the volumes of the two CCandyBox objects by invoking the Volume() function that is a member of the derived class. This function accesses the inherited members m_Length, m_Width, and m_Height to produce the result. The members are declared as protected in the base class and remain protected in the derived class. The program produces the output shown as follows:

```
CBox constructor called
CCandyBox constructor1 called
CBox constructor called
CCandyBox constructor2 called
myCandyBox volume is 1
myToffeeBox volume is 24
CCandyBox destructor called
CBox destructor called
CCandyBox destructor called
CBox destructor called
```

The output shows that the volume is being calculated properly for both CCandyBox objects. The first object has the default dimensions produced by calling the default CBox constructor, so the volume is 1, and the second object has the dimensions defined as initial values in its declaration.

The output also shows the sequence of constructor and destructor calls, and you can see how each derived class object is destroyed in two steps.

> Destructors for a derived class object are called in the reverse order to the constructors for the object. This is a general rule that always applies. Constructors are invoked starting with the base class constructor and then the derived class constructor, whereas the destructor for the derived class is called first when an object is destroyed, followed by the base class destructor.

You can demonstrate that the protected members of the base class remain protected in the derived class by uncommenting the statement preceding the return statement in the function main(). If you do this, you get the following error message from the compiler,

```
error C2248: 'm_Length': cannot access protected member declared in class 'CBox'
```

which indicates quite clearly that the member m_Length is inaccessible.

The Access Level of Inherited Class Members

You know that if you have no access specifier for the base class in the definition of a derived class, the default specification is private. This has the effect of causing the inherited public and protected members of the base class to become private in the derived class. The private members of the base class remain private to the base and therefore inaccessible to member functions of the derived class. In fact, they remain private to the base class regardless of how the base class is specified in the derived class definition.

You have also used public as the specifier for a base class. This leaves the members of the base class with the same access level in the derived class as they had in the base, so public members remain public and protected members remain protected.

The last possibility is that you declare a base class as `protected`. This has the effect of making the inherited `public` members of the base `protected` in the derived class. The `protected` (and `private`) inherited members retain their original access level in the derived class. This is summarized in Figure 9-3.

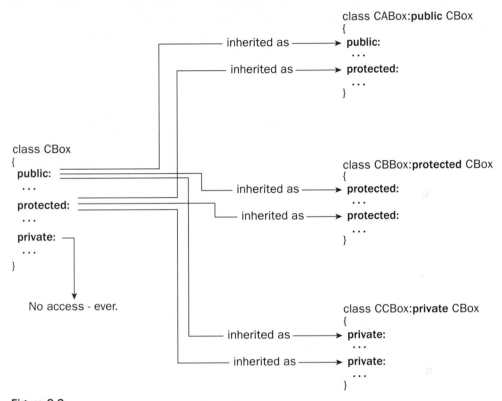

Figure 9-3

This may look a little complicated, but you can reduce it to the following three points about the inherited members of a derived class:

❑   Members of a base class that are declared as `private` are never accessible in a derived class.

❑   Defining a base class as `public` doesn't change the access level of its members in the derived class.

❑   Defining a base class as `protected` changes its `public` members to `protected` in the derived class.

Being able to change the access level of inherited members in a derived class gives you a degree of flexibility, but don't forget that you cannot relax the level specified in the base class; you can only make the access level more stringent. This suggests that your base classes need to have `public` members if you want to be able to vary the access level in derived classes. This may seem to run contrary to the idea of encapsulating data in a class in order to protect it from unauthorized access, but, as you'll see, it is often the case that you define base classes in such a manner that their only purpose is to act as a base for other classes, and they aren't intended to be used for instantiating objects in their own right.

The Copy Constructor in a Derived Class

Remember that the copy constructor is called automatically when you declare an object that is initialized with an object of the same class. Look at these statements:

```
CBox myBox(2.0, 3.0, 4.0);              // Calls constructor
CBox copyBox(myBox);                    // Calls copy constructor
```

The first statement calls the constructor that accepts three arguments of type `double`, and the second calls the copy constructor. If you don't supply your own copy constructor, the compiler supplies one that copies the initializing object member by member to the corresponding members of the new object. So that you can see what is going on during execution, you can add your own version of a copy constructor to the class `CBox`. You can then use this class as a base for defining the `CCandyBox` class.

```
// Box.h in Ex9_05
#pragma once
#include <iostream>
using std::cout;
using std::endl;

class CBox                     // Base class definition
{
  public:
    // Base class constructor
    CBox(double lv = 1.0, double wv = 1.0, double hv = 1.0):
                         m_Length(lv), m_Width(wv), m_Height(hv)
    { cout << endl << "CBox constructor called"; }

    // Copy constructor
    CBox(const CBox& initB)
    {
      cout << endl << "CBox copy constructor called";
      m_Length = initB.m_Length;
      m_Width = initB.m_Width;
      m_Height = initB.m_Height;
    }

    // CBox destructor - just to track calls
    ~CBox()
    { cout << "CBox destructor called" << endl; }

  protected:
    double m_Length;
    double m_Width;
    double m_Height;
};
```

Also recall that the copy constructor must have its parameter specified as a reference to avoid an infinite number of calls to itself, which would otherwise result from the need to copy an argument that is transferred by value. When the copy constructor in our example is invoked, it outputs a message to the screen, so you'll be able to see from the output when this is happening.

We will use the version of CCandyBox class from Ex9_04.cpp, shown again here:

```cpp
// CandyBox.h in Ex9_05
#pragma once
#include "Box.h"
#include <iostream>
using std::cout;
using std::endl;

class CCandyBox: public CBox
{
  public:
    char* m_Contents;

    // Derived class function to calculate volume
    double Volume() const
    { return m_Length*m_Width*m_Height; }

    // Constructor to set dimensions and contents
    // with explicit call of CBox constructor
    CCandyBox(double lv, double wv, double hv, char* str = "Candy")
                                       :CBox(lv, wv, hv)  // Constructor
    {
      cout << endl <<"CCandyBox constructor2 called";
      m_Contents = new char[ strlen(str) + 1 ];
      strcpy_s(m_Contents, strlen(str) + 1, str);
    }

    // Constructor to set contents
    // calls default CBox constructor automatically
    CCandyBox(char* str = "Candy")                      // Constructor
    {
      cout << endl << "CCandyBox constructor1 called";
      m_Contents = new char[ strlen(str) + 1 ];
      strcpy_s(m_Contents, strlen(str) + 1, str);
    }

    ~CCandyBox()                                        // Destructor
    {
      cout << "CCandyBox destructor called" << endl;
      delete[] m_Contents;
    }
};
```

This doesn't have a copy constructor added yet, so you'll be relying on the compiler-generated version.

<hr>

Try It Out   **The Copy Constructor in Derived Classes**

You can exercise the copy constructor that you have just defined with the following example:

```cpp
// Ex9_05.cpp
// Using a derived class copy constructor
#include <iostream>                    // For stream I/O
#include <cstring>                     // For strlen() and strcpy()
#include "CandyBox.h"                  // For CBox and CCandyBox
```

```
using std::cout;
using std::endl;

int main()
{
  CCandyBox chocBox(2.0, 3.0, 4.0, "Chockies");   // Declare and initialize
  CCandyBox chocolateBox(chocBox);                 // Use copy constructor

  cout << endl
       << "Volume of chocBox is " << chocBox.Volume()
       << endl
       << "Volume of chocolateBox is " << chocolateBox.Volume()
       << endl;

  return 0;
}
```

How It Works (or Why It Doesn't)

When you run the Debug version of this example, in addition to the expected output, you'll see the dialog shown in Figure 9-4 displayed.

Click Abort to clear the dialog box and you'll see the output in the console window that you might expect. The output shows that the compiler-generated copy constructor for the derived class automatically called the copy constructor for the base class.

However, as you've probably realized, all is not as it should be. In this particular case, the compiler-generated copy constructor causes problems because the memory pointed to by the m_Contents member of the derived class in the second object declared points to the same memory as the one in the first object. When one object is destroyed (when it goes out of scope at the end of main()), it releases the memory occupied by the text. When the second object is destroyed, the destructor attempts to release some memory that has already been freed by the destructor call for the previous object — and that's the reason for the error message in the dialog box.

The way to fix this is to supply a copy constructor for the derived class that allocates some additional memory for the new object.

Figure 9-4

Fixing the Copy Constructor Problem

You can do this by adding the following code for the copy constructor to the `public` section of the derived `CCandyBox` class in `Ex9_05`:

```
// Derived class copy constructor
CCandyBox(const CCandyBox& initCB)
{
  cout << endl << "CCandyBox copy constructor called";

  // Get new memory
  m_Contents = new char[ strlen(initCB.m_Contents) + 1 ];

  // Copy string
  strcpy_s(m_Contents, strlen(initCB.m_Contents) + 1, initCB.m_Contents);
}
```

You can now run this new version of the last example with the same function `main()` to see how the new copy constructor works.

How It Works

Now when you run the example, it behaves better and produces the following output:

```
CBox constructor called
CCandyBox constructor2 called
CBox constructor called
CCandyBox copy constructor called
Volume of chocBox is 24
Volume of chocolateBox is 1
CCandyBox destructor called
CBox destructor called
CCandyBox destructor called
CBox destructor called
```

However, there is still something wrong. The third line of output shows that the default constructor for the `CBox` part of the object `chocolateBox` is called, rather than the copy constructor. As a consequence, the object has the default dimensions rather than the dimensions of the initializing object, so the volume is incorrect. The reason for this is that when you write a constructor for an object of a derived class, you are responsible for ensuring that the members of the derived class object are properly initialized. This includes the inherited members.

The fix for this is to call the copy constructor for the base part of the class in the initialization list for the copy constructor for the `CCandyBox` class. The copy constructor then becomes:

```
// Derived class copy constructor
CCandyBox(const CCandyBox& initCB): CBox(initCB)
{
  cout << endl << "CCandyBox copy constructor called";

  // Get new memory
```

```
      m_Contents = new char[ strlen(initCB.m_Contents) + 1 ];

      // Copy string
      strcpy_s(m_Contents, strlen(initCB.m_Contents) + 1, initCB.m_Contents);
    }
```

Now the CBox class copy constructor is called with the initCB object. Only the base part of the object is passed to it, so everything works out. If you modify the last example by adding the base copy constructor call, the output is as follows:

```
CBox constructor called
CCandyBox constructor2 called
CBox copy constructor called
CCandyBox copy constructor called
Volume of chocBox is 24
Volume of chocolateBox is 24
CCandyBox destructor called
CBox destructor called
CCandyBox destructor called
CBox destructor called
```

The output shows that all the constructors and destructors are called in the correct sequence and the copy constructor for the CBox part of chocolateBox is called before the CCandyBox copy constructor. The volume of the object chocolateBox of the derived class is now the same as that of its initializing object, which is as it should be.

You have, therefore, another golden rule to remember:

If you write any kind of constructor for a derived class, you are responsible for the initialization of all members of the derived class object, including all its inherited members.

Class Members as Friends

You saw in Chapter 7 how a function can be declared as a friend of a class. This gives the friend function the privilege of free access to any of the class members. Of course, there is no reason why a friend function cannot be a member of another class.

Suppose you define a CBottle class to represent a bottle:

```
class CBottle
{
  public:
    CBottle(double height, double diameter)
    {
      m_Height = height;
      m_Diameter = diameter;
    }
```

```
    private:
      double m_Height;                    // Bottle height
      double m_Diameter;                  // Bottle diameter
};
```

You now need a class to represent the packaging for a dozen bottles that automatically has custom dimensions to accommodate a particular kind of bottle. You could define this as:

```
class CCarton
{
  public:
    CCarton(const CBottle& aBottle)
    {
      m_Height = aBottle.m_Height;        // Bottle height
      m_Length = 4.0*aBottle.m_Diameter;  // Four rows of ...
      m_Width = 3.0*aBottle.m_Diameter;   // ...three bottles
    }

  private:
    double m_Length;                      // Carton length
    double m_Width;                       // Carton width
    double m_Height;                      // Carton height
};
```

The constructor here sets the height to be the same as that of the bottle it is to accommodate, and the length and width are set based on the diameter of the bottle so that twelve fit in the box.

As you know by now, this won't work. The data members of the CBottle class are private, so the CCarton constructor cannot access them. As you also know, a friend declaration in the CBottle class fixes it:

```
class CBottle
{
  public:
    CBottle(double height, double diameter)
    {
      m_Height = height;
      m_Diameter = diameter;
    }

  private:
    double m_Height;                              // Bottle height
    double m_Diameter;                            // Bottle diameter
```

```
  // Let the carton constructor in
  friend CCarton::CCarton(const CBottle& aBottle);
};
```

The only difference between the friend declaration here and what you saw in Chapter 7 is that you must put the class name and the scope resolution operator with the friend function name to identify it. For this to compile correctly, the compiler needs to have information about the CCarton class constructor, so you would need to put an #include statement for the header file containing the CCarton class definition before the definition of the CBottle class.

Friend Classes

You can also allow all the function members of one class to have access to all the data members of another by declaring it as a **friend class**. You could define the CCarton class as a friend of the CBottle class by adding a friend declaration within the CBottle class definition:

```
friend CCarton;
```

With this declaration in the CBottle class, all function members of the CCarton class now have free access to all the data members of the CBottle class.

Limitations on Class Friendship

Class friendship is not reciprocated. Making the CCarton class a friend of the CBottle class does not mean that the CBottle class is a friend of the CCarton class. If you want this to be so, you must add a friend declaration for the CBottle class to the CCarton class.

Class friendship is also not inherited. If you define another class with CBottle as a base, members of the CCarton class will not have access to its data members, not even those inherited from CBottle.

Virtual Functions

Look more closely at the behavior of inherited member functions and their relationship with derived class member functions. You could add a function to the CBox class to output the volume of a CBox object. The simplified class then becomes:

```cpp
// Box.h in Ex9_06
#pragma once
#include <iostream>
using std::cout;
using std::endl;

class CBox                          // Base class
{
  public:

    // Function to show the volume of an object
    void ShowVolume() const
    {
      cout << endl
           << "CBox usable volume is " << Volume();
    }

    // Function to calculate the volume of a CBox object
    double Volume() const
    { return m_Length*m_Width*m_Height; }

    // Constructor
    CBox(double lv = 1.0, double wv = 1.0, double hv = 1.0)
                       :m_Length(lv), m_Width(wv), m_Height(hv) {}
```

```
  protected:
    double m_Length;
    double m_Width;
    double m_Height;
};
```

Now you can output the usable volume of a CBox object just by calling the ShowVolume() function for any object for which you require it. The constructor sets the data member values in the initialization list, so no statements are necessary in the body of the function. The data members are as before and are specified as protected, so they are accessible to the member functions of any derived class.

Suppose you want to derive a class for a different kind of box called CGlassBox, to hold glassware. The contents are fragile, and because packing material is added to protect them, the capacity of the box is less than the capacity of a basic CBox object. You therefore need a different Volume() function to account for this, so you add it to the derived class:

```
// GlassBox.h in Ex9_06
#pragma once
#include "Box.h"

class CGlassBox: public CBox            // Derived class
{
  public:
    // Function to calculate volume of a CGlassBox
    // allowing 15% for packing
    double Volume() const
    { return 0.85*m_Length*m_Width*m_Height; }

    // Constructor
    CGlassBox(double lv, double wv, double hv): CBox(lv, wv, hv){}
};
```

There could conceivably be other additional members of the derived class, but we'll keep it simple and concentrate on how the inherited functions work for the moment. The constructor for the derived class objects just calls the base class constructor in its initialization list to set the data member values. No statements are necessary in its body. You have included a new version of the Volume() function to replace the version from the base class, the idea being that you can get the inherited function ShowVolume() to call the derived class version of the member function Volume() when you call it for an object of the class CGlassBox.

Try It Out   **Using an Inherited Function**

Now see how your derived class works in practice. You can try this out very simply by creating an object of the base class and an object of the derived class with the same dimensions and then verifying that the correct volumes are being calculated. The main() function to do this is as follows:

```
// Ex9_06.cpp
// Behavior of inherited functions in a derived class
#include <iostream>
#include "GlassBox.h"                      // For CBox and CGlassBox
using std::cout;
using std::endl;
```

```
int main()
{
  CBox myBox(2.0, 3.0, 4.0);                // Declare a base box
  CGlassBox myGlassBox(2.0, 3.0, 4.0);      // Declare derived box - same size

  myBox.ShowVolume();                       // Display volume of base box
  myGlassBox.ShowVolume();                  // Display volume of derived box

  cout << endl;
  return 0;
}
```

How It Works

If you run this example, it produces the following output:

```
CBox usable volume is 24
CBox usable volume is 24
```

This isn't only dull and repetitive, but it's also disastrous. It isn't working the way you want at all, and the only interesting thing about it is why. Evidently, the fact that the second call is for an object of the derived class CGlassBox is not being taken into account. You can see this from the incorrect result for the volume in the output. The volume of a CGlassBox object should definitely be less than that of a basic CBox with the same dimensions.

The reason for the incorrect output is that the call of the Volume() function in the function ShowVolume() is being set once and for all by the compiler as the version defined in the base class. ShowVolume() is a base class function and when CBox is compiled the call to Volume() is resolved at that time to the base class Volume() function; the compiler has no knowledge of any other Volume() function. This is called **static resolution** of the function call since the function call is fixed before the program is executed. This is also sometimes called **early binding** because the particular Volume() function chosen is bound to the call from the function ShowVolume() during the compilation of the program.

What we were hoping for in this example was that the question of which Volume() function call to use in any given instance would be resolved when the program was executed. This sort of operation is referred to as **dynamic linkage**, or **late binding**. We want the actual version of the function Volume() called by ShowVolume() to be determined by the kind of object being processed, and not arbitrarily fixed by the compiler before the program is executed.

No doubt you'll be less than astonished that C++ does, in fact, provide you with a way to do this, because this whole discussion would have been futile otherwise! You need to use something called a **virtual function**.

What Is a Virtual Function?

A virtual function is a function in a base class that is declared using the keyword virtual. If you specify a function in a base class as virtual and there is another definition of the function in a derived class, it signals to the compiler that you don't want static linkage for this function. What you *do* want is the selection of the function to be called at any given point in the program to be based on the kind of object for which it is called.

Try It Out   Fixing the CGlassBox

To make this example work as originally hoped, you just need to add the keyword `virtual` to the definitions of the `Volume()` function in the two classes. You can try this in a new project, `Ex9_07`. Here's how the definition of `CBox` should be:

```
// Box.h in Ex9_07
#pragma once
#include <iostream>
using std::cout;
using std::endl;

class CBox                                  // Base class
{
  public:
    // Function to show the volume of an object
    void ShowVolume() const
    {
      cout << endl
           << "CBox usable volume is " << Volume();
    }

    // Function to calculate the volume of a CBox object
    virtual double Volume() const
    { return m_Length*m_Width*m_Height; }

    // Constructor
    CBox(double lv = 1.0, double wv = 1.0, double hv = 1.0)
                      :m_Length(lv), m_Width(wv), m_Height(hv) {}

  protected:
    double m_Length;
    double m_Width;
    double m_Height;
};
```

The `GlassBox.h` header file contents should be:

```
// GlassBox.h in Ex9_07
#pragma once
#include "Box.h"

class CGlassBox: public CBox              // Derived class
{
  public:
    // Function to calculate volume of a CGlassBox
    // allowing 15% for packing
```

```
      virtual double Volume() const
    { return 0.85*m_Length*m_Width*m_Height; }

    // Constructor
    CGlassBox(double lv, double wv, double hv): CBox(lv, wv, hv){}
};
```

The Ex9_07.cpp file version of main() is the same as for the previous example:

```
// Ex9_07.cpp (the same as Ex9_06.cpp)
// Using a virtual function
#include <iostream>
#include "GlassBox.h"                  // For CBox and CGlassBox
using std::cout;
using std::endl;

int main()
{
  CBox myBox(2.0, 3.0, 4.0);          // Declare a base box
  CGlassBox myGlassBox(2.0, 3.0, 4.0); // Declare derived box - same size

  myBox.ShowVolume();                  // Display volume of base box
  myGlassBox.ShowVolume();             // Display volume of derived box

  cout << endl;
  return 0;
}
```

How It Works

If you run this version of the program with just the little word virtual added to the definitions of Volume(), it produces this output:

```
CBox usable volume is 24
CBox usable volume is 20.4
```

This is now clearly doing what you wanted in the first place. The first call to the function ShowVolume() with the CBox object myBox calls the CBox class version of Volume(). The second call with the CGlassBox object myGlassBox calls the version defined in the derived class.

Note that although you have put the keyword virtual in the derived class definition of the function Volume(), it's not essential to do so. The definition of the base version of the function as virtual is sufficient. However, I recommend that you *do* specify the keyword for virtual functions in derived classes because it makes it clear to anyone reading the derived class definition that they are virtual functions and that they are selected dynamically.

For a function to behave as virtual, it must have the same name, parameter list, and return type in any derived class as the function has in the base class, and if the base class function is const, the derived class function must be, too. If you try to use different parameters or return types, or declare one as const and the other not, the virtual function mechanism won't work. The function operates with static linkage established and fixed at compile time.

The operation of virtual functions is an extraordinarily powerful mechanism. You may have heard the term **polymorphism** in relation to object-oriented programming, and this refers to the virtual function capability. Something that is polymorphic can appear in different guises, like a werewolf, or Dr. Jekyll, or a politician before and after an election for example. Calling a virtual function produces different effects depending on the kind of object for which it is being called.

> *Note that the* Volume() *function in the derived* CGlassBox *class actually hides the base class version from the view of derived class functions. If you wanted to call the base version of* Volume() *from a derived class function, you would need to use the scope resolution operator to refer to the function as* CBox::Volume().

Using Pointers to Class Objects

Using pointers with objects of a base class and of a derived class is an important technique. A pointer to a base class object can be assigned the address of a derived class object as well as that of the base. You can thus use a pointer of the type 'pointer to base' to obtain different behavior with virtual functions, depending on what kind of object the pointer is pointing to. You can see how this works more clearly by looking at an example.

Try It Out   **Pointers to Base and Derived Classes**

You'll use the same classes as in the previous example, but make a small modification to the function main() so that it uses a pointer to a base class object. Create the Ex9_08 project with Box.h and GlassBox.h header files the same as in the previous example. You can copy the Box.h and Glassbox.h files from the Ex9_07 project to this project folder. Adding an existing file to a project is quite easy; you right-click Ex9_08 in the Solution Explorer tab, select Add > New Item from the pop-up menu; then select a header file to add it to the project. When you have added the headers, modify Ex9_08.cpp to the following:

```
// Ex9_08.cpp
// Using a base class pointer to call a virtual function
#include <iostream>
#include "GlassBox.h"                    // For CBox and CGlassBox
using std::cout;
using std::endl;

int main()
{
  CBox myBox(2.0, 3.0, 4.0);             // Declare a base box
  CGlassBox myGlassBox(2.0, 3.0, 4.0);   // Declare derived box of same size
  CBox* pBox = 0;                 // Declare a pointer to base class objects
```

```
    pBox = &myBox;              // Set pointer to address of base object
    pBox->ShowVolume();         // Display volume of base box
    pBox = &myGlassBox;         // Set pointer to derived class object
    pBox->ShowVolume();         // Display volume of derived box

  cout << endl;
  return 0;
}
```

How It Works

The classes are the same as in example Ex9_07.cpp, but the function main() has been altered to use a pointer to call the function ShowVolume(). Because you are using a pointer, you use the indirect member selection operator, ->, to call the function. The function ShowVolume() is called twice, and both calls use the same pointer to base class objects, pBox. On the first occasion, the pointer contains the address of the base object, myBox, and on the occasion of the second call, it contains the address of the derived class object, myGlassBox.

The output produced is as follows:

```
CBox usable volume is 24
CBox usable volume is 20.4
```

This is exactly the same as that from the previous example where you used explicit objects in the function call.

You can conclude from this example that the virtual function mechanism works just as well through a pointer to a base class, with the specific function being selected based on the type of object being pointed to. This is illustrated in Figure 9-5.

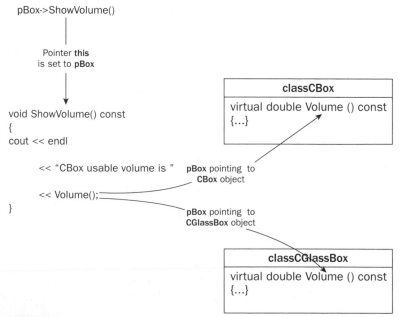

Figure 9-5

This means that, even when you don't know the precise type of the object pointed to by a base class pointer in a program (when a pointer is passed to a function as an argument, for example), the virtual function mechanism ensures that the correct function is called. This is an extraordinarily powerful capability, so make sure you understand it. Polymorphism is a fundamental mechanism in C++ that you will find yourself using again and again.

Using References with Virtual Functions

If you define a function with a reference to a base class as a parameter, you can pass an object of a derived class to it as an argument. When your function executes, the appropriate virtual function for the object passed is selected automatically. We could see this happening by modifying the function `main()` in the last example to call a function that has a reference as a parameter.

Try It Out   **Using References with Virtual Functions**

Let's move the call to `ShowVolume()` to a separate function and call that separate function from `main()`:

```
// Ex9_09.cpp
// Using a reference to call a virtual function
#include <iostream>
#include "GlassBox.h"                    // For CBox and CGlassBox
using std::cout;
using std::endl;

void Output(const CBox& aBox);           // Prototype of function

int main()
{
  CBox myBox(2.0, 3.0, 4.0);             // Declare a base box
  CGlassBox myGlassBox(2.0, 3.0, 4.0); // Declare derived box of same size

  Output(myBox);                         // Output volume of base class object
  Output(myGlassBox);                    // Output volume of derived class object

  cout << endl;
  return 0;
}

void Output(const CBox& aBox)
{
  aBox.ShowVolume();
}
```

`Box.h` and `GlassBox.h` for this example have the same contents as the previous example.

How It Works

The function `main()` now basically consists of two calls of the function `Output()`, the first with an object of the base class as an argument and the second with an object of the derived class. Because the parameter is a reference to the base class, `Output()` accepts objects of either class as an argument and the appropriate version of the virtual function Volume() is called, depending on the object that is initializing the reference.

The program produces exactly the same output as the previous example, demonstrating that the virtual function mechanism does indeed work through a reference parameter.

Incomplete Class Definitions

At the beginning of the previous example, you have the prototype declaration for the Output() function. To process this declaration the compiler needs to have access to the definition of the CBox class because the parameter is of type CBox&. In this case the definition of the CBox class is available at this point because you have an #include directive for GlassBox.h that has its own #include directive for Box.h.

However, there may be situations where you have such a declaration and the class definition cannot be included in this way, in which case you would need some other way to at least identify that the name CBox refers to a class type. In this situation you could provide an **incomplete definition** of the class CBox preceding the prototype of the output function. The statement that provides an incomplete definition of the CBox class is simply:

```
class CBox;
```

The statement just identifies that the name CBox refers to a class that is not defined at this point, but this is sufficient for the compiler know of that CBox is the name of a class, and this allows it to process the prototype of the function Output(). Without some indication that CBox is a class, the prototype causes an error message to be generated.

Pure Virtual Functions

It's possible that you'd want to include a virtual function in a base class so that it may be redefined in a derived class to suit the objects of that class, but that there is no meaningful definition you could give for the function in the base class.

For example, you could conceivably have a class CContainer, which could be used as a base for defining the CBox class, or a CBottle class, or even a CTeapot class. The CContainer class wouldn't have data members, but you might want to provide a virtual member function Volume() for any derived classes. Because the CContainer class has no data members, and therefore no dimensions, there is no sensible definition that you can write for the Volume() function. You can still define the class, however, including the member function Volume(), as follows:

```
// Container.h for Ex9_10
#pragma once
#include <iostream>
using std::cout;
using std::endl;

class CContainer            // Generic base class for specific containers
{
  public:
```

```
      // Function for calculating a volume - no content
      // This is defined as a 'pure' virtual function, signified by '= 0'
      virtual double Volume() const = 0;

      // Function to display a volume
      virtual void ShowVolume() const
      {
        cout << endl
             << "Volume is " << Volume();
      }
};
```

The statement for the virtual function `Volume()` defines it as having no content by placing the equals sign and zero in the function header. This is called a **pure virtual function**. Any class derived from this class must either define the `Volume()` function or redefine it as a pure virtual function. Because you have declared `Volume()` as const, its implementation in any derived class must also be const. Remember that const and non-const varieties of a function with the same name and parameter list are different functions. In other words you can overload a function using const.

The class also contains the function `ShowVolume()`, which displays the volume of objects of derived classes. Because this is declared as `virtual`, it can be replaced in a derived class, but if it isn't, the base class version that you see here is called.

Abstract Classes

A class containing a pure virtual function is called an **abstract class**. It's called abstract because you can't define objects of a class containing a pure virtual function. It exists only for the purpose of defining classes that are derived from it. If a class derived from an abstract class still defines a pure virtual function of the base as pure, it too is an abstract class.

You should not conclude, from the previous example of the `CContainer` class, that an abstract class can't have data members. An abstract class can have both data members and function members. The presence of a pure virtual function is the only condition that determines that a given class is abstract. In the same vein, an abstract class can have more than one pure virtual function. In this case, a derived class must have definitions for every pure virtual function in its base; otherwise, it too will be an abstract class. If you forget to make the derived class version of the `Volume()` function const, the derived class will still be abstract because it contains the pure virtual `Volume()` member function that is const, as well as the non-const `Volume()` function that you have defined.

Try It Out   An Abstract Class

You could implement a `CCan` class, representing beer or cola cans perhaps, together with the original `CBox` class and derive both from the `CContainer` class that you defined in the previous section. The definition of the `CBox` class as a subclass of `CContainer` is as follows:

```
// Box.h for Ex9_10
#pragma once
#include "Container.h"                   // For CContainer definition
#include <iostream>
using std::cout;
```

```
using std::endl;

class CBox: public CContainer         // Derived class
{
  public:

    // Function to show the volume of an object
    virtual void ShowVolume() const
    {
      cout << endl
           << "CBox usable volume is " << Volume();
    }

    // Function to calculate the volume of a CBox object
    virtual double Volume() const
    { return m_Length*m_Width*m_Height; }

    // Constructor
    CBox(double lv = 1.0, double wv = 1.0, double hv = 1.0)
                       :m_Length(lv), m_Width(wv), m_Height(hv){}

  protected:
    double m_Length;
    double m_Width;
    double m_Height;
};
```

The unshaded lines are the same as in the previous version of the CBox class. The CBox class is essentially as we had it in the previous example, except this time you have specified that it is derived from the CContainer class. The Volume() function is fully defined within this class (as it must be if this class is to be used to define objects). The only other option would be to specify it as a pure virtual function, since it is pure in the base class, but then we couldn't create CBox objects.

You could define the CCan class in the Can.h header file like this:

```
// Can.h for Ex9_10
#pragma once
#include "Container.h"              // For CContainer definition
extern const double PI;             // PI is defined elsewhere

class CCan: public CContainer
{
  public:
    // Function to calculate the volume of a can
    virtual double Volume() const
    { return 0.25*PI*m_Diameter*m_Diameter*m_Height; }

    // Constructor
    CCan(double hv = 4.0, double dv = 2.0): m_Height(hv), m_Diameter(dv){}

  protected:
    double m_Height;
    double m_Diameter;
};
```

The CCan class also defines a Volume() function based on the formula $h\pi r2$, where h is the height of a can and r is the radius of the cross-section of a can. The volume is calculated as the height multiplied by the area of the base. The expression in the function definition assumes a global constant PI is defined, so we have the extern statement indicating that PI is a global variable of type const double that is defined elsewhere — in this program it is defined in the Ex9_10.cpp file. Also notice that we redefined the ShowVolume() function in the CBox class, but not in the CCan class. You can see what effect this has when we get some program output.

You can exercise these classes with the following source file containing the main() function:

```cpp
// Ex9_10.cpp
// Using an abstract class
#include "Box.h"                     // For CBox and CContainer
#include "Can.h"                     // For CCan (and CContainer)
#include <iostream>                  // For stream I/O
using std::cout;
using std::endl;

const double PI= 3.14159265;         // Global definition for PI

int main(void)
{
  // Pointer to abstract base class
  // initialized with address of CBox object
  CContainer* pC1 = new CBox(2.0, 3.0, 4.0);

  // Pointer to abstract base class
  // initialized with address of CCan object
  CContainer* pC2 = new CCan(6.5, 3.0);

  pC1->ShowVolume();                 // Output the volumes of the two
  pC2->ShowVolume();                 // objects pointed to
  cout << endl;

  delete pC1;                        // Now clean up the free store
  delete pC2;                        // ....

  return 0;
}
```

How It Works

In this program, you declare two pointers to the base class, CContainer. Although you can't define CContainer objects (because CContainer is an abstract class), you can still define a pointer to a CContainer, which you can then use to store the address of a derived class object; in fact you can use it to store the address of any object whose type is a direct or indirect subclass of CContainer. The pointer pC1 is assigned the address of a CBox object created in the free store by the operator new. The second pointer is assigned the address of a CCan object in a similar manner.

Of course, because the derived class objects were created dynamically, you must use the delete operator to clean up the free store when you have finished with them. You learned about the delete *operator back in Chapter 4.*

The output produced by this example is as follows:

```
CBox usable volume is 24
Volume is 45.9458
```

Because you have defined `ShowVolume()` in the `CBox` class, the derived class version of the function is called for the `CBox` object. You did not define this function in the `CCan` class, so the base class version that the `CCan` class inherits is invoked for the `CCan` object. Because `Volume()` is a virtual function implemented in both derived classes (necessarily, because it is a pure virtual function in the base class), the call to it is resolved when the program is executed by selecting the version belonging to the class of the object being pointed to. Thus, for the pointer pC1, the version from the class `CBox` is called and, for the pointer pC2, the version in the class `CCan` is called. In each case, therefore, you obtain the correct result.

You could equally well have used just one pointer and assigned the address of the `CCan` object to it (after calling the `Volume()` function for the `CBox` object). A base class pointer can contain the address of *any* derived class object, even when several different classes are derived from the same base class, and so you can have automatic selection of the appropriate virtual function across a whole range of derived classes. Impressive stuff, isn't it?

Indirect Base Classes

At the beginning of this chapter, I said that a base class for a subclass could in turn be derived from another, 'more' base class. A small extension of the last example provides you with an illustration of this, as well as demonstrates the use of a virtual function across a second level of inheritance.

Try It Out   **More Than One Level of Inheritance**

All you need to do is add the class `CGlassBox` to the classes you have from the previous example. The relationship between the classes you now have is illustrated in Figure 9-6.

The class `CGlassBox` is derived from the `CBox` class exactly as before, but we omit the derived class version of `ShowVolume()` to show that the base class version still propagates through the derived classes. With the class hierarchy shown above, the class `CContainer` is an indirect base of the class `CGlassBox`, and a direct base of the classes `CBox` and `CCan`.

The `GlassBox.h` header file for the example contains:

```
// GlassBox.h for Ex9_11
#pragma once
#include "Box.h"                    // For CBox

class CGlassBox: public CBox        // Derived class
{
  public:

    // Function to calculate volume of a CGlassBox
    // allowing 15% for packing
    virtual double Volume() const
    { return 0.85*m_Length*m_Width*m_Height; }
```

```
        // Constructor
        CGlassBox(double lv, double wv, double hv): CBox(lv, wv, hv){}
};
```

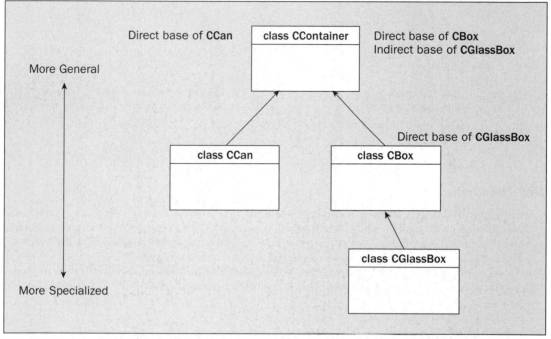

Figure 9-6

The `Container.h`, `Can.h`, and `Box.h` header files contain the same code as those in the previous example, `Ex9_10`.

The source file for new example, with an updated function `main()` to use the additional class in the hierarchy, is as follows:

```
// Ex9_11.cpp
// Using an abstract class with multiple levels of inheritance
#include "Box.h"                      // For CBox and CContainer
#include "Can.h"                      // For CCan (and CContainer)
#include "GlassBox.h"                 // For CGlassBox (and CBox and CContainer)
#include <iostream>                   // For stream I/O
using std::cout;
using std::endl;

const double PI = 3.14159265;                   // Global definition for PI

int main()
{
  // Pointer to abstract base class initialized with CBox object address
```

```
    CContainer* pC1 = new CBox(2.0, 3.0, 4.0);

    CCan myCan(6.5, 3.0);                    // Define CCan object
    CGlassBox myGlassBox(2.0, 3.0, 4.0);  // Define CGlassBox object

    pC1->ShowVolume();                       // Output the volume of CBox
    delete pC1;                              // Now clean up the free store

    // initialized with address of CCan object
    pC1 = &myCan;                            // Put myCan address in pointer
    pC1->ShowVolume();                       // Output the volume of CCan

    pC1 = &myGlassBox;                       // Put myGlassBox address in pointer
    pC1->ShowVolume();                       // Output the volume of CGlassBox

    cout << endl;
    return 0;
  }
```

How It Works

You have the three-level class hierarchy shown in Figure 9-6 with CContainer as an abstract base class because it contains the pure virtual function, Volume(). The main() function now calls the ShowVolume() function three times using the same pointer to the base class, but with the pointer containing the address of an object of a different class each time. Because ShowVolume() is not defined in any of the derived classes you have here, the base class version is called in each instance. A separate branch from the base CContainer defines the derived class CCan.

The example produces this output:

```
CBox usable volume is 24
Volume is 45.9458
CBox usable volume is 20.4
```

The output shows that one of the three different versions of the function Volume() is selected for execution according to the type of object involved.

Note that you must delete the CBox object from the free store before you assign another address value to the pointer. If you don't do this, you won't be able to clean up the free store, because you would have no record of the address of the original object. This is an easy mistake to make when reassigning pointers and using the free store.

Virtual Destructors

One problem that arises when dealing with objects of derived classes using a pointer to the base class is that the correct destructor may not be called. You can see this effect by modifying the last example.

Calling the Wrong Destructor

You just need to add a destructor to each of the classes in the example that outputs a message so that you can track which destructor is called when the objects are destroyed. The `Container.h` file for this example is:

```
// Container.h for Ex9_12
#pragma once
#include <iostream>
using std::cout;
using std::endl;

class CContainer          // Generic base class for specific containers
{
  public:
    // Destructor
    ~CContainer()
    { cout << "CContainer destructor called" << endl; }

    // Function for calculating a volume - no content
    // This is defined as a 'pure' virtual function, signified by '= 0'
    virtual double Volume() const = 0;

    // Function to display a volume
    virtual void ShowVolume() const
    {
      cout << endl
           << "Volume is " << Volume();
    }
};
```

The contents of `Can.h` in the example is:

```
// Can.h for Ex9_12
#pragma once
#include "Container.h"                    // For CContainer definition
extern const double PI;

class CCan: public CContainer
{
  public:
    // Destructor
    ~CCan()
    { cout << "CCan destructor called" << endl; }

    // Function to calculate the volume of a can
    virtual double Volume() const
    { return 0.25*PI*m_Diameter*m_Diameter*m_Height; }

    // Constructor
```

```
        CCan(double hv = 4.0, double dv = 2.0): m_Height(hv), m_Diameter(dv){}

   protected:
     double m_Height;
     double m_Diameter;
};
```

The contents of Box.h should be:

```
// Box.h for Ex9_12
#pragma once
#include "Container.h"                    // For CContainer definition
#include <iostream>
using std::cout;
using std::endl;

class CBox: public CContainer         // Derived class
{
  public:
    // Destructor
    ~CBox()
    { cout << "CBox destructor called" << endl; }

    // Function to show the volume of an object
    virtual void ShowVolume() const
    {
      cout << endl
          << "CBox usable volume is " << Volume();
    }

    // Function to calculate the volume of a CBox object
    virtual double Volume() const
    { return m_Length*m_Width*m_Height; }

    // Constructor
    CBox(double lv = 1.0, double wv = 1.0, double hv = 1.0)
                       :m_Length(lv), m_Width(wv), m_Height(hv){}

  protected:
    double m_Length;
    double m_Width;
    double m_Height;
};
```

The GlassBox.h header file should contain:

```
// GlassBox.h for Ex9_12
#pragma once
#include "Box.h"                          // For CBox

class CGlassBox: public CBox              // Derived class
```

```
{
  public:
    // Destructor
    ~CGlassBox()
    { cout << "CGlassBox destructor called" << endl; }


    // Function to calculate volume of a CGlassBox
    // allowing 15% for packing
    virtual double Volume() const
    { return 0.85*m_Length*m_Width*m_Height; }

    // Constructor
    CGlassBox(double lv, double wv, double hv): CBox(lv, wv, hv){}
};
```

Finally, the source file Ex9_12.cpp for the program should be as follows:

```
// Ex9_12.cpp
// Destructor calls with derived classes
// using objects via a base class pointer
#include "Box.h"                      // For CBox and CContainer
#include "Can.h"                      // For CCan (and CContainer)
#include "GlassBox.h"                 // For CGlassBox (and CBox and CContainer)
#include <iostream>                   // For stream I/O
using std::cout;
using std::endl;

const double PI = 3.14159265;         // Global definition for PI

int main()
{
  // Pointer to abstract base class initialized with CBox object address
  CContainer* pC1 = new CBox(2.0, 3.0, 4.0);

  CCan myCan(6.5, 3.0);               // Define CCan object
  CGlassBox myGlassBox(2.0, 3.0, 4.0); // Define CGlassBox object

  pC1->ShowVolume();                  // Output the volume of CBox
  cout << endl << "Delete CBox" << endl;
  delete pC1;                         // Now clean up the free store

  pC1 = new CGlassBox(4.0, 5.0, 6.0); // Create CGlassBox dynamically
  pC1->ShowVolume();                  // ...output its volume...
  cout << endl << "Delete CGlassBox" << endl;
  delete pC1;                         // ...and delete it

  pC1 = &myCan;                       // Get myCan address in pointer
  pC1->ShowVolume();                  // Output the volume of CCan

  pC1 = &myGlassBox;                  // Get myGlassBox address in pointer
```

```
    pC1->ShowVolume();                    // Output the volume of CGlassBox

    cout << endl;
    return 0;
}
```

How It Works

Apart from adding a destructor to each class that outputs a message to the effect that it was called, the only other change is a couple of additions to the function main(). There are additional statements to create a CGlassBox object dynamically, output its volume and then delete it. There is also a message displayed to indicate when the dynamically created CBox object is deleted. The output generated by this example is shown as follows:

```
CBox usable volume is 24
Delete CBox
CContainer destructor called

CBox usable volume is 102
Delete CGlassBox
CContainer destructor called

Volume is 45.9458
CBox usable volume is 20.4
CGlassBox destructor called
CBox destructor called
CContainer destructor called
CCan destructor called
CContainer destructor called
```

You can see from this that when you delete the CBox object pointed to by pC1, the destructor for the base class CContainer is called but there is no call of the CBox destructor recorded. Similarly, when the CGlassBox object that you added is deleted, again the destructor for the base class CContainer is called but not the CGlassBox or CBox destructors. For the other objects, the correct destructor calls occur with the derived class constructor being called first, followed by the base class constructor. For the first CGlassBox object created in a declaration, three destructors are called: first, the destructor for the derived class, followed by the direct base destructor and, finally, the indirect base destructor.

All the problems are with objects created in the free store. In both cases, the wrong destructor is called. The reason for this is that the linkage to the destructors is resolved statically, at compile time. For the automatic objects, there is no problem — the compiler knows what they are and arranges for the correct destructors to be called. With objects created dynamically and accessed through a pointer, things are different. The only information that the compiler has when the delete operation is executed is that the pointer type is a pointer to the base class. The type of object the pointer is actually pointing to is unknown to the compiler because this is determined when the program executes. The compiler therefore simply ensures that the delete operation is set up to call the base class destructor. In a real application, this can cause a lot of problems, with bits of objects left strewn around the free store and possibly more serious problems, depending on the nature of the objects involved.

The solution is simple. You need the calls to be resolved dynamically — as the program is executed. You can organize this by using **virtual destructors** in your classes. As I said when I first discussed virtual functions, it's sufficient to declare a base class function as virtual to ensure that all functions in any derived classes with the same name, parameter list, and return type are virtual as well. This applies to destructors just as it does to ordinary member functions. You need to add the keyword `virtual` to the definition of the destructor in the class `CContainer` in `Container.h` so that the class definition is as follows:

```
class CContainer                      // Generic base class for containers
{
   public:

      // Destructor
      virtual ~CContainer()
      { cout << "CContainer destructor called" << endl; }

      // Rest of the class as before
};
```

Now the destructors in all the derived classes are automatically virtual, even though you don't explicitly specify them as such. Of course, you're free to specify them as virtual if you want the code to be absolutely clear.

If you rerun the example with this modification, it produces the following output:

```
CBox usable volume is 24
Delete CBox
CBox destructor called
CContainer destructor called

CBox usable volume is 102
Delete CGlassBox
CGlassBox destructor called
CBox destructor called
CContainer destructor called

Volume is 45.9458
CBox usable volume is 20.4
CGlassBox destructor called
CBox destructor called
CContainer destructor called
CCan destructor called
CContainer destructor called
```

As you can see, all the objects are now destroyed with a proper sequence of destructor calls. Destroying the dynamic objects produces the same sequence of destructor calls as the automatic objects of the same type in the program.

The question may arise in your mind at this point, can constructors be declared as virtual? The answer is no — only destructors and other member functions.

It's a good idea always to declare your base class destructor as virtual as a matter of course when using inheritance. There is a small overhead in the execution of the class destructors, but you won't notice it in the majority of circumstances. Using virtual destructors ensures that your objects will be properly destroyed and avoids potential program crashes that might otherwise occur.

Casting Between Class Types

You have seen how you can store the address of a derived class object in a variable of a base class type so a variable of type CContainer* can store the address of a CBox object for example. So if you have an address stored in a pointer of type CContainer* can you cast it to type CBox*? Indeed you can and the dynamic_cast operator is specifically intended for this kind of operation. Here's how it works:

```
CContainer* pContainer = new CGlassBox(2.0, 3.0, 4.0);
CBox* pBox = dynamic_cast<CBox*>( pContainer);
CGlassBox* pGlassBox = dynamic_cast<CGlassBox*>( pContainer);
```

The first statement stores the address of the CGlassBox object created on the heap in a base class pointer of type CContainer*. The second statement casts pContainer up the class hierarchy to type CBox*. The third statement casts the address in pContainer to its actual type, CGlassBox*.

You can apply the dynamic_cast operator to references as well as pointers. The difference between dynamic_cast and static_cast is that the dynamic_cast operator checks the validity of a cast at run-time whereas the static_cast operator does not. If a dynamic_cast operation is not valid, the result is null. The compiler relies on the programmer for the validity of a static_cast operation so you should always use dynamic_cast for casting up and down a class hierarchy and check for a null result if you want to avoid abrupt termination of your program as a result of using a null pointer.

Nested Classes

You can put the definition of one class inside the definition of another, in which case you have defined a **nested class**. A nested class has the appearance of being a static member of the class that encloses it and is subject to the member access specifiers, just like any other member of the class. If you place the definition of a nested class in the private section of the class, the class can only be referenced from within the scope of the enclosing class. If you specify a nested class as public, the class is accessible from outside the enclosing class but the nested class name must be qualified by the outer class name in such circumstances.

A nested class has free access to all the static members of the enclosing class. All the instance members can be accessed through an object of the enclosing class type, or a pointer or reference to an object. The enclosing class can only access the public members of the nested class, but in a nested class that is private in the enclosing class the members are frequently declared as public to provide free access to the entire nested class from functions in the enclosing class.

A nested class is particularly useful when you want to define a type that is only to be used within another type, whereupon the nested class can be declared as private. Here's an example of that:

```
// A push-down stack to store Box objects
```

```
class CStack
{
private:
  // Defines items to store in the stack
  struct CItem
  {
    CBox* pBox;                           // Pointer to the object in this node
    CItem* pNext;                         // Pointer to next item in the stack or null

    // Constructor
    CItem(CBox* pB, CItem* pN): pBox(pB), pNext(pN){}
  };

  CItem* pTop;                            // Pointer to item that is at the top

public:
  // Push a Box object on to the stack
  void Push(CBox* pBox)
  {
    pTop = new CItem(pBox, pTop);         // Create new Item and make it the top
  }

  // Pop an  object off the stack
  CBox* Pop()
  {
    if(pTop == 0)                         // If.the stack is empty
      return 0;                           // return null

    CBox* pBox = pTop->pBox;              // Get box from item
    CItem* pTemp = pTop;                  // Save address of the top Item
    pTop = pTop->pNext;                   // Make next item the top
    delete pTemp;                         // Delete old top Item from the heap
    return pBox;
  }
};
```

The CStack class defines a push-down stack for storing CBox objects. To be absolutely precise it stores pointers to CBox objects so the objects pointed to are still the responsibility of the code making use of the Stack class. The nested struct, CItem, defines the items that are held in the stack. I chose to define Item as a nested struct rather than a nested class because members of a struct are public by default. You could define CItem as a class and then specify the members as public so they can be accessed from the functions in the CStack class. The stack is implemented as a set of CItem objects where each CItem object stores a pointer to a CBox object plus the address of the next CItem object down in the stack. The Push() function in the CStack class pushes a CBox object on to the top of the stack and the Pop() function pops an object off the top of the stack.

Pushing an object on to the stack involves creating a new CItem object that stores the address of the object to be stored plus the address of the previous item that was on the top of the stack — this is null the first time you push an object on to the stack. Popping an object off the stack returns the address of the object in the item, pTop. The top item is deleted and the next item becomes the item at the top of the stack. Let's see if it works.

Try It Out   Using a Nested Class

This example uses CContainer, CBox, and CGlassBox classes from Ex9_12 so create an empty
WIN32 console project, Ex9_13, and add the header files containing those class definitions to it. Then
add Stack.h to the project containing the definition of the CStack class from the previous section,
and add Ex9_13.cpp to the project with the following contents:

```cpp
// Ex9_13.cpp
// Using a nested class to define a stack
#include "Box.h"                         // For CBox and CContainer
#include "GlassBox.h"                    // For CGlassBox (and CBox and CContainer)
#include "Stack.h"                       // For the stack class with nested struct Item

#include <iostream>                      // For stream I/O
using std::cout;
using std::endl;

int main()
{
  CBox* pBoxes[] = { new CBox(2.0, 3.0, 4.0),
                     new CGlassBox(2.0, 3.0, 4.0),
                     new CBox(4.0, 5.0, 6.0),
                     new CGlassBox(4.0, 5.0, 6.0)
                   };

  cout << "The array of boxes have the following volumes:";
  for (int i = 0 ; i<4 ; i++)
    pBoxes[i]->ShowVolume();             // Output the volume of a box

  cout << endl << endl
       << "Now pushing the boxes on the stack..."
       << endl;

  CStack* pStack = new CStack;           // Create the stack
  for (int i = 0 ; i<4 ; i++)
    pStack->Push(pBoxes[i]);

  cout << "Popping the boxes off the stack presents them in reverse order:";
  for (int i = 0 ; i<4 ; i++)
    pStack->Pop()->ShowVolume();

  cout << endl;
  return 0;
}
```

The output from this example is:

```
The array of boxes have the following volumes:
CBox usable volume is 24
CBox usable volume is 20.4
CBox usable volume is 120
CBox usable volume is 102

Now pushing the boxes on the stack...
```

```
Popping the boxes off the stack presents them in reverse order:
CBox usable volume is 102
CBox usable volume is 120
CBox usable volume is 20.4
CBox usable volume is 24
```

How It Works

You create an array of pointers to CBox objects so each element in the array can store the address of a CBox object or an address of any type that is derived from CBox. The array is initialized with the adresses of four objects created on the heap:

```
CBox* pBoxes[] = { new CBox(2.0, 3.0, 4.0),
                   new CGlassBox(2.0, 3.0, 4.0),
                   new CBox(4.0, 5.0, 6.0),
                   new CGlassBox(4.0, 5.0, 6.0)
                 };
```

The objects are two CBox object and two CGlassBox objects with the same dimensions as the CBox objects.

After listing the volumes of the four objects, you create a CStack object and push the objects on to the stack in a for loop:

```
CStack* pStack = new CStack;        // Create the stack
for (int i = 0 ; i<4 ; i++)
  pStack->Push(pBoxes[i]);
```

Each element in the pBoxes array is pushed on to the stack by passing the array element as the argument to the Push() function for the CStack object. This results in the first element from the array being at the bottom of the stack and the last element at the top.

You pop the objects off the stack in another for loop:

```
for (int i = 0 ; i<4 ; i++)
  pStack->Pop()->ShowVolume();
```

The Pop() function returns the address of the element at the top of the stack and you use this to call the ShowVolume() function for the object. Because the last element was at the top of the stack, the loop lists the volumes of the objects in reverse order. From the output you can see that the CStack class does indeed implement a stack using a nested struct to define the items to be stored in the stack.

C++/CLI Programming

All C++/CLI classes, including classes that you define, are derived classes by default. This is because both value classes and reference classes have a standard class, System::Object, as a base class. This means that both value classes and reference classes inherit from the System::Object class and therefore have the capabilities of the System::Object class in common. Because the ToString() function is defined as a virtual function in System::Object, you can override it in your own classes and have the function called polymorphically when required. This is what you have been doing in previous chapters when you defined the ToString() function in a class.

Because `System::Object` is a base class for all C++/CLI classes, the handle type `System::Object^` fulfils a similar role to the `void*` type in native C++ in that it can be used to reference any type of object.

Boxing and Unboxing

The `System::Object` base class for all value class types is also responsible for enabling the boxing and unboxing of values of the fundamental types. Boxing a value type instance converts it to an object on the garbage-collected heap, so it will carry full type information along with the basic value. Unboxing is the reverse of boxing. The boxing/unboxing capability means that values of the fundamental types can behave as objects, but can participate in numerical operations without carrying the overhead of being objects. Values of the fundamental types are stored on the stack just as values for the purposes of normal operations and are only converted to an object on the heap that is referenced by a handle of type `System::Object^` when they need to behave as objects. For example, if you pass an unboxed value to a function with a parameter that is an appropriate value class type, the compiler will arrange for the value to be converted to an object on the heap; this is achieved by creating a new object on the heap containing the value. Thus you get **implicit boxing** and the argument value will be boxed automatically.

Of course, **explicit boxing** is also possible. You can force a value to be boxed by assigning it to a variable of type `Object^`. For example:

```
double value = 3.14159265;
Object^ boxedValue = value;
```

The second statement forces the boxing of `value` and the boxed representation is referenced by the handle `boxedValue`.

You can also force boxing of a value using `gcnew` to create a boxed value on the garbage-collected heap, for example:

```
long^ number = gcnew(999999L);
```

This statement implicitly boxes the value `999999L` and stores it on the heap in a location referenced by the handle `number`.

You can unbox a value type using the dereference operator, for example:

```
Console::WriteLine(*number);
```

The value pointed to by the handle `number` is unboxed and then passed as a value to the `WriteLine()` function.

Finally you can unbox a boxed value using `safe_cast`:

```
long n = safe_cast<long>(number);
```

This statement unboxes `number` and stores the value in n. Note that without the `safe_cast`, this statement will not compile because there is no implicit conversion in this situation.

Inheritance in C++/CLI Classes

Although value classes always have the `System::Object` class as a base, you cannot derive a value class from an existing class. To put it another way, when you define a value class you are not allowed to specify a base class. This implies that polymorphism in value classes is limited to the functions that are defined as virtual in the `System::Object` class. These are the virtual functions that all value classes inherit from `System::Object`:

Function	Description
`String^ ToString()`	Returns a `String` representation of an object and the implementation in the `System::Object` class returns the class name as a string. You would typically override this function in your own classes to return a string representation of the value of an object.
`bool Equals(Object^ obj)`	Compares the current object to `obj` and returns `true` if they are equal and `false` otherwise. Equal in this case means referential equality — that is the objects are one and the same. Typically you would override this function in your own classes to return `true` when the current object is the same value as the argument — in other words, when the fields are equal.
`int GetHashCode()`	Returns an integer that is a hash code for the current object. Hash codes are used as keys to store objects in a collection that stores `(key, object)` pairs. Objects are subsequently retrieved from such a collection by supplying the key that was used when the object was stored.

Of course, because `System::Object` is also a base class for reference classes you may want to override these functions in reference classes, too.

You can derive a reference class from an existing reference class in the same way as you define a derived class in native C++. Let's re-implement `Ex9_12` as a C++/CLI program as this also demonstrates nested classes in a CLR program. We can start by defining the `Container` class:

```
// Container.h for Ex9_14
#pragma once
using namespace System;

// Abstract base class for specific containers
ref class Container abstract
{
  public:
    // Function for calculating a volume - no content
    // This is defined as an 'abstract' virtual function,
    // indicated by the 'abstract' keyword
```

```
      virtual double Volume() abstract;

    // Function to display a volume
    virtual void ShowVolume()
    {
      Console::WriteLine(L"Volume is {0}", Volume());
    }
};
```

The first thing to note is the `abstract` keyword following the class name. If a C++/CLI class contains the native C++ equivalent of a pure virtual function, you must specify the class as abstract. You can, however, also specify a class as abstract that does not contain any abstract functions, which prevents you from creating objects of that class type. The `abstract` keyword also appears at the end of the `Volume()` function member declaration to indicate that it is be defined for this class. You could also add the `" = 0"` to the end of the member declaration for `Volume()` as you would for a native C++ member, but it is not required.

Both the `Volume()` and `ShowVolume()` functions are virtual here so they can be called polymorphically for objects of class types that are derived from `Container`.

You can define the `Box` class like this:

```
// Box.h for Ex9_14
#pragma once
#include "Container.h"                // For Container definition

ref class Box : Container            // Derived class
{
  public:
    // Function to show the volume of an object
    virtual void ShowVolume() override
    {
      Console::WriteLine(L"Box usable volume is {0}", Volume());
    }

    // Function to calculate the volume of a Box object
    virtual double Volume() override
    { return m_Length*m_Width*m_Height; }

    // Constructor
    Box() : m_Length(1.0), m_Width(1.0), m_Height(1.0){}

    // Constructor
    Box(double lv, double wv, double hv)
                          : m_Length(lv), m_Width(wv), m_Height(hv){}

  protected:
    double m_Length;
    double m_Width;
    double m_Height;
};
```

A base class for a ref class is always public and the `public` keyword is assumed by default. You can specify the base class explicitly as `public` but it is not necessary to do so. A base class to a ref class cannot be specified as anything other than `public`. Because you cannot supply default values for parameters as in

556

the native C++ version of the class, you define the no-arg constructor so that it initializes all three fields to 1.0. The Box class defines the Volume() function as an override to the inherited base class version. You must always specify the override keyword when you want to override a function in the base class. If the Box class did not implement the Volume() function, it would be abstract and you would need to specify it as such to compile the class successfully.

Here's how the GlassBox class definition looks:

```
// GlassBox.h for Ex9_14
#pragma once
#include "Box.h"                       // For Box

ref class GlassBox : Box              // Derived class
{
  public:
    // Function to calculate volume of a GlassBox
    // allowing 15% for packing
    virtual double Volume() override
    { return 0.85*m_Length*m_Width*m_Height; }

    // Constructor
    GlassBox(double lv, double wv, double hv): Box(lv, wv, hv){}
};
```

The base class is Box, which is public by default. The rest of the class is essentially the same as the original.

Here's the Stack class definition:

```
// Stack.h for Ex9_14
// A push-down stack to store objects of any ref class type
#pragma once

ref class Stack
{
private:
  // Defines items to store in the stack
  ref struct Item
  {
    Object^ Obj;                      // Handle for the object in this item
    Item^ Next;                       // Handle for next item in the stack or nullptr

    // Constructor
    Item(Object^ obj, Item^ next): Obj(obj), Next(next){}
  };

  Item^ Top;                          // Handle for item that is at the top
public:
  // Push an object on to the stack
  void Push(Object^ obj)
  {
    Top = gcnew Item(obj, Top);       // Create new item and make it the top
  }
```

```
    // Pop an  object off the stack
    Object^ Pop()
    {
      if(Top == nullptr)                 // If the stack is empty
        return nullptr;                  // return nullptr

      Object^ obj = Top->Obj;            // Get object from item
      Top = Top->Next;                   // Make next item the top
      return obj;
    }
};
```

The first difference to notice is that the function parameters and fields are now handles because you are dealing with ref class objects. The inner `struct`, `Item`, now stores a handle of type `Object^`, which allows objects of any CLR class type to be stored in the stack; this means either value class or ref class objects can be accommodated which is a significant improvement over the native C++ `CStack` class. You don't need to worry about deleting Item objects when the `Pop()` function is called, because the garbage collector takes care of that.

Here's a summary of the differences from native C++ that these classes have demonstrated:

❑   Only ref classes can be derived class types.

❑   A base class for a derived ref class is always `public`.

❑   A function that has no definition for a ref class is an abstract function and must be declared using the `abstract` keyword.

❑   A class that contains one or more abstract functions must be explicitly specified as abstract by placing the `abstract` keyword following the class name.

❑   A class that does not contain abstract functions can be specified as `abstract`, in which case instances of the class cannot be defined.

❑   You must explicitly use the `override` keyword when specifying a function that overrides a function inherited from the base class.

All you need to try out these classes is a CLR console project with a definition of `main()` so let's do it.

Try It Out   Using Derived Reference Classes

Create a CLR console program with the name `Ex9_14` and add the classes in the previous section to the project; then add the following contents to `Ex9_14.cpp`:

```
// Ex9_14.cpp : main project file.
// Using a nested class to define a stack

#include "stdafx.h"
#include "Box.h"                    // For Box and Container
#include "GlassBox.h"               // For GlassBox (and Box and Container)
#include "Stack.h"                  // For the stack class with nested struct Item
```

```
using namespace System;

int main(array<System::String ^> ^args)
{
   array<Box^>^ boxes = { gcnew Box(2.0, 3.0, 4.0),
                          gcnew GlassBox(2.0, 3.0, 4.0),
                          gcnew Box(4.0, 5.0, 6.0),
                          gcnew GlassBox(4.0, 5.0, 6.0)
                        };

   Console::WriteLine(L"The array of boxes have the following volumes:");
   for each(Box^ box in boxes)
     box->ShowVolume();            // Output the volume of a box

   Console::WriteLine(L"\nNow pushing the boxes on the stack...");

   Stack^ stack = gcnew Stack;         // Create the stack
   for each(Box^ box in boxes)
     stack->Push(box);

   Console::WriteLine(
            L"Popping the boxes off the stack presents them in reverse order:");
   Object^ item;
   while((item = stack->Pop()) != nullptr)
     safe_cast<Container^>(item)->ShowVolume();


   Console::WriteLine(L"\nNow pushing integers on to the stack:");
   for(int i = 2 ; i<=12 ; i += 2)
   {
     Console::Write(L"{0,5}",i);
     stack->Push(i);
   }

   Console::WriteLine(L"\n\nPopping integers off the stack produces:");
   while((item = stack->Pop()) != nullptr)
     Console::Write(L"{0,5}",item);

   Console::WriteLine();
   return 0;
}
```

The output from this example is:

```
The array of boxes have the following volumes:
Box usable volume is 24
Box usable volume is 20.4
Box usable volume is 120
Box usable volume is 102

Now pushing the boxes on the stack...
Popping the boxes off the stack presents them in reverse order:
Box usable volume is 102
```

```
Box usable volume is 120
Box usable volume is 20.4
Box usable volume is 24


Now pushing integers on to the stack:
    2    4    6    8    10    12

Popping integers off the stack produces:
    12    10    8    6    4    2
```

How It Works

You first create an array of handles to boxes:

```
array<Box^>^ boxes = { gcnew Box(2.0, 3.0, 4.0),
                       gcnew GlassBox(2.0, 3.0, 4.0),
                       gcnew Box(4.0, 5.0, 6.0),
                       gcnew GlassBox(4.0, 5.0, 6.0)
                     };
```

Because Box and GlassBox are ref classes, you create the objects on the CLR heap using gcnew. The addresses of the objects initialize the elements of the boxes array.

You then create a Stack object and push the strings on to the stack:

```
Stack^ stack = gcnew Stack;          // Create the stack
for each(Box^ box in boxes)
   stack->Push(box);
```

The parameter to the Push() function is of type Object^ so the function accepts any class type as the argument. The for each loop pushes each of the elements in the boxes array on to the stack.

Popping the elements off the stack occurs in a while loop:

```
Object^ item;
while((item = stack->Pop()) != nullptr)
   safe_cast<Container^>(item)->ShowVolume();
```

The loop condition stores the value returned from the Pop() function for the stack object in item, and compares it with nullptr. As long as item has not been set to nullptr, the statement that is the body of the while loop is executed. Within the loop you cast the handle stored in item to type Container^. The item variable is of type Object^, and because the Object class does not define the ShowVolume() function, you cannot call the ShowVolume() function using a handle of this type; to call a function poly-morphically, you must use a handle of a base class type that declares the function to be a virtual member. By casting the handle to type Container^ you are able to call the ShowVolume() function polymorphi-cally, so the function is selected for the ultimate class type of the object that the handle references. In this case you could have achieved the same result by casting item to type Box^. You use safe_cast here because you are casting up the class hierarchy and it's as well to use a checked cast operation in such cir-cumstances. The safe_cast operator checks the cast for validity and, if the conversion fails, the opera-tor throws an exception of type System::InvalidCastException. You could use dynamic_cast but it is better to use safe_cast in CLR programs.

Interface Classes

The definition of an interface class looks quite similar to the definition of a ref class but it is quite a different concept. An interface is a class that specifies a set of functions that are to be implemented by other classes to provide a standardized way of providing some specific functionality. Both value classes and ref classes can implement interfaces. An interface does not define any of its function members — these are defined by each class that implements the interface.

You have already met the `System::IComparable` interface in the context of generic functions where you specified the `IComparable` interface as a constraint. The `IComparable` interface specifies the `CompareTo()` function for comparing objects so all classes that implement this interface have the same mechanism for comparing objects. You specify an interface a class implements in the same way as a base class. For example, here's how you could make the `Box` class from the previous example implement the `System::IComparable` interface:

```
ref class Box : Container, IComparable            // Derived class
{
  public:
    // The function specified by IComparable interface
    virtual int CompareTo(Object^ obj)
    {
      if(Volume() < safe_cast<Box^>(obj)->Volume())
        return -1;
      else if(Volume() > safe_cast<Box^>(obj)->Volume())
        return 1;
      else
        return 0;
    }

  // Rest of the class as before...
};
```

The name of the interface follows the name of the base class, `Container`. If there were no base class, the interface name alone would appear here. A ref class can only have one base class but it can implement as many interfaces as you want. The class must define every function specified by each of the interfaces that it claims to implement. The `IComparable` interface only specifies one function but there can be as many functions in an interface as you want. The `Box` class now defines the `CompareTo()` function with the same signature as the `IComparable` interface specifies for the function. Because the parameter to the `CompareTo()` function is of type `Object^`, you have to cast it to type `Box^` before you can access members of the `Box` object it references.

Defining Interface Classes

You define an interface class using either of the keywords `interface class` or `interface struct`. Regardless of whether you use the `interface class` or the `interface struct` keyword to define an interface, all the members of an interface are always `public` by default and you cannot specify them to be otherwise. The members of an interface can be functions including operator functions, properties, static fields, and events, all of which you'll learn about later in this chapter. An interface can also specify a static constructor and can contain a nested class definition of any kind. In spite of all that potential diversity of members, most interfaces are relatively simple. Note that you can derive one interface from another in basically the same way as you use to derive one ref class from another. For example:

```
interface class IController : ITelevison, IRecorder
{
  // Members of IController...
};
```

The `IController` interface contains its own members, and it also inherits the members of the `ITelevision` and `IRecorder` interfaces. A class that implements the `IController` interface has to define the member functions from `IController`, `ITelevision`, and `IRecorder`.

You could use an interface instead of the `Container` base class in `Ex9_14`. Here's how the definition of this interface would look:

```
// IContainer.h for Ex9_15
#pragma once

interface class IContainer
{
  double Volume();                    // Function for calculating a volume
  void ShowVolume();                  // Function to display a volume
};
```

By convention the names of interfaces start with I in C++/CLI so the interface name is `IContainer`. It has two members: the `Volume()` function and the `ShowVolume()` function, which are public because members of an interface are always public. Both functions are effectively abstract because an interface never includes function definitions — indeed, you could add the `abstract` keyword to both here but it is not required. Instance functions in an interface definition can be specified as `virtual` and `abstract` but it is not necessary to do so as they are anyway.

Any class that implements the `IContainer` interface must implement both functions if the class is not to be abstract. Let's see how the `Box` class looks:

```
// Box.h for Ex9_15
#pragma once

#include "IContainer.h"                // For interface definition

using namespace System;

ref class Box : IContainer
{
  public:
    // Function to show the volume of an object
    virtual void ShowVolume()
    {
      Console::WriteLine(L"CBox usable volume is {0}", Volume());
    }

    // Function to calculate the volume of a Box object
    virtual double Volume()
```

```
          { return m_Length*m_Width*m_Height; }

          // Constructor
          Box() : m_Length(1.0), m_Width(1.0), m_Height(1.0){}

          // Constructor
          Box(double lv, double wv, double hv)
                              : m_Length(lv), m_Width(wv), m_Height(hv){}

      protected:
        double m_Length;
        double m_Width;
        double m_Height;
    };
```

The name of the interface goes after the colon in the first line of the class definition, just as if it were a base class. Of course, there could also be a base class, in which case the interface name would follow the base class name separated from it by a comma. A class can implement multiple interfaces in which case the names of the interfaces are separated by commas.

The Box class must implement both function members of the IContainer interface class; otherwise, it would be an abstract class and would need to be declared as such. The definitions for these functions in the Box class do not have the override keyword appended because you are not overriding existing function definitions here; you are implementing them for the first time.

The GlassBox class is derived from the Box class and therefore inherits the implementation of IContainer. The GlassBox class definition needs no changes at all to accommodate the introduction of the IContainer interface class.

The IContainer interface class has the same role as a base class in polymorphism. You can use a handle of type IContainer to store the address of an object of any class type that implements the interface. Thus a handle of type IContainer can be used to reference objects of type Box or type GlassBox and obtain polymorphic behavior when calling the functions that are members of the interface class. Let's try it.

Try It Out Implementing an Interface Class

Create the CLR console project Ex9_15 and add the IContainer.h and Box.h header files with the contents from the previous section. You should also add copies of the Stack.h and GlassBox.h header files from Ex9_14 to the project. Finally, modify the contents of Ex9_15.cpp to the following:

```
// Ex9_15.cpp : main project file.
// Implementing an interface class
#include "stdafx.h"
#include "Box.h"                    // For Box and IContainer
#include "GlassBox.h"               // For GlassBox (and Box and IContainer)
#include "Stack.h"                  // For the stack class with nested struct Item

using namespace System;

int main(array<System::String ^> ^args)
{
  array<IContainer^>^ containers = { gcnew Box(2.0, 3.0, 4.0),
```

```
                                                gcnew GlassBox(2.0, 3.0, 4.0),
                                                gcnew Box(4.0, 5.0, 6.0),
                                                gcnew GlassBox(4.0, 5.0, 6.0)
                                             };

     Console::WriteLine(L"The array of containers have the following volumes:");
     for each(IContainer^ container in containers)
       container->ShowVolume();                // Output the volume of a box

     Console::WriteLine(L"\nNow pushing the containers on the stack...");

     Stack^ stack = gcnew Stack;              // Create the stack
     for each(IContainer^ container in containers)
       stack->Push(container);


     Console::WriteLine(
             L"Popping the containers off the stack presents them in reverse order:");
     Object^ item;
     while((item = stack->Pop()) != nullptr)
       safe_cast<IContainer^>(item)->ShowVolume();

     Console::WriteLine();
     return 0;
}
```

This example produces the following output:

```
The array of containers have the following volumes:
CBox usable volume is 24
CBox usable volume is 20.4
CBox usable volume is 120
CBox usable volume is 102

Now pushing the containers on the stack...
Popping the containers off the stack presents them in reverse order:
CBox usable volume is 102
CBox usable volume is 120
CBox usable volume is 20.4
CBox usable volume is 24
```

How It Works

You create an array of elements of type IContainer^ and initialize the elements with the addresses of Box and GlassBox objects:

```
array<IContainer^>^ containers = { gcnew Box(2.0, 3.0, 4.0),
                                   gcnew GlassBox(2.0, 3.0, 4.0),
                                   gcnew Box(4.0, 5.0, 6.0),
                                   gcnew GlassBox(4.0, 5.0, 6.0)
                                 };
```

The Box and GlassBox classes implement the IContainer interface so you can store addresses of objects of these types in variables of type handle to IContainer. The advantage of doing this is that you'll be able to call the function members of the IContainer interface class polymorphically.

You list the volumes of the `Box` and `GlassBox` objects in a `for each` loop:

```
for each(IContainer^ container in containers)
  container->ShowVolume();                    // Output the volume of a box
```

The loop body shows polymorphism in action; the `ShowVolume()` function for the specific type of object referenced by `container` is called, as you can see from the output.

You push the elements of the containers array on to the stack in essentially the same way as the previous example. Popping the elements off the stack is also similar to the previous example:

```
Object^ item;
while((item = stack->Pop()) != nullptr)
  safe_cast<IContainer^>(item)->ShowVolume();
```

The loop body shows that you can cast a handle to an interface type using `safe_cast` in exactly the same way as you would cast to a ref class type. You are then able to use the handle to call the `ShowVolume()` function polymorphically.

Using interface classes is not only a useful way of defining sets of functions that represent standard class interfaces but also a powerful mechanism for applying polymorphism in your programs.

Classes and Assemblies

A C++/CLI application always resides in one or more assemblies so C++/CLI classes always reside in an assembly. The classes we have defined for each example up to now have all been contained in a single simple assembly that is the executable, but you can create assemblies that contain your own library classes. C++/CLI adds **visibility specifiers** for classes that determine whether a given class is accessible from outside the assembly in which it resides which is referred to as its `parent assembly`. In addition to the `public`, `private`, and `protected` member access specifiers that you have in native C++, C++/CLI has additional access specifiers for class members that determine from where they may be accessed in different assemblies.

Visibility Specifiers for Classes and Interfaces

You can specify the visibility of a non-nested class, interface, or enum as `private` or `public`. A public class is visible and accessible outside the assembly in which is resides whereas a private class is only accessible within its parent assembly. Classes, interfaces, and enum classes are private by default and therefore only visible within their parent assembly. To specify a class as public, you just use the `public` keyword, like this:

```
public interface class IContainer
{
  // Details of the interface...
};
```

The `IContainer` interface here is visible in an external assembly because you have defined it as public. If you omit the `public` keyword, the interface would be private by default and only usable within its parent assembly. You can specify a class, `enum`, or interface explicitly as `private` if you want, but it is not necessary.

Access Specifiers for Class and Interface Members

C++/CLI adds three more access specifiers for class members: `internal`, `public protected`, and `private protected`. The effects of these are described in the comments in the class definition:

```
public ref class MyClass        // Class visible outside assembly
{
public:
  // Members accessible from classes inside and outside the parent assembly

internal:
  // Members accessible from classes inside the parent assembly

public protected:
  // Members accessible in types derived from MyClass outside the parent assembly
  // and in any classes inside the parent assembly

private protected:
  // Members accessible in types derived from MyClass inside the parent assembly
};
```

Obviously the class must be public for the member access specifiers to allow access from outside the parent assembly. Where the access specifier involves two keywords such as `private protected` the less restrictive keyword applies inside the assembly and the more restrictive keyword applies outside the assembly. You can reverse the sequence of the keyword pairs so `protected private` has the same meaning as `private protected`.

To use some of these you need to create an application that consists of more than one assembly, so let's recreate `Ex9_15` as a class library assembly plus an application assembly that uses the class library.

Try It Out   **Creating a Class Library**

To create a class library you can first create a CLR project with the name `Ex9_16lib` using the `Class Library` template. The project contains a header file, `Ex9_16lib.h`, with the following content:

```
// Ex9_16lib.h

#pragma once

using namespace System;

namespace Ex9_16lib
{
  public ref class Class1
  {
    // TODO: Add your methods for this class here.
  };
}
```

A class library has its own namespace and here the namespace name is `Ex9_16lib` by default. You could change this name to something more suitable if you want. The names of the classes in the library are qualified by the namespace name so you need a `using` directive for the namespace name in any external source file that is accessing any of the classes in the library. The definitions of the classes that are to be in the library go between the braces for the namespace. There's a default ref class defined within the namespace, but you replace this with your own classes. Note that the Class1 class is public; all classes that are to be visible in another assembly must be specified as public.

Modify the contents of Ex9_16lib.h to:

```
// Ex9_16lib.h

#pragma once

using namespace System;

namespace Ex9_16lib
{
// IContainer.h for Ex9_16
public interface class IContainer
{
  virtual double Volume();          // Function for calculating a volume
  virtual void ShowVolume();        // Function to display a volume
};


// Box.h for Ex9_16
public ref class Box : IContainer
{
  public:
    // Function to show the volume of an object
    virtual void ShowVolume()
    {
      Console::WriteLine(L"CBox usable volume is {0}", Volume());
    }

    // Function to calculate the volume of a Box object
    virtual double Volume()
    { return m_Length*m_Width*m_Height; }

    // Constructor
    Box() : m_Length(1.0), m_Width(1.0), m_Height(1.0){}

    // Constructor
    Box(double lv, double wv, double hv)
                      : m_Length(lv), m_Width(wv), m_Height(hv){}

  public protected:
    double m_Length;
    double m_Width;
    double m_Height;
};

// Stack.h for Ex9_16
public ref class Stack
{
private:
```

```
   // Defines items to store in the stack
   ref struct Item
   {
     Object^ Obj;                     // Handle for the object in this item
     Item^ Next;                      // Handle for next item in the stack or nullptr

     // Constructor
     Item(Object^ obj, Item^ next): Obj(obj), Next(next){}
   };

   Item^ Top;                         // Handle for item that is at the top
 public:
   // Push an object on to the stack
   void Push(Object^ obj)
   {
     Top = gcnew Item(obj, Top);      // Create new item and make it the top
   }

   // Pop an  object off the stack
   Object^ Pop()
   {
     if(Top == nullptr)               // If the stack is empty
       return nullptr;                // return nullptr

     Object^ obj = Top->Obj;          // Get box from item
     Top = Top->Next;                 // Make next item the top
     return obj;
   }
 };
 }
```

The IContainer interface class, the Box class, and the Stack class are now in this library. The changes to the original definitions for these classes are shaded. Each class is now public, which makes them accessible from an external assembly. The fields in the Box class are public protected, which means that they are inherited in a derived class as protected fields but are public so far as classes within the parent assembly are concerned. You don't actually refer to these fields from other classes within the parent assembly so you could have left the fields in the Box class as protected in this case.

When you have built this project successfully, the assembly containing the class library is in a file Ex9_16lib.dll that is in the debug subdirectory to the project directory if you built a debug version of the project or in a release subdirectory if you built the release version. The .dll extension means that this is a **dynamic link library** or **DLL**. You now need another project that uses your class library.

Try It Out   **Using a Class Library**

Add a new CLR console project with the name Ex9_16 in its own solution as always. You can then modify Ex9_16.cpp as follows:

```
// Ex9_16.cpp : main project file.
// Using a class library in a separate assembly
```

```
#include "stdafx.h"
#include "GlassBox.h"
#using <Ex9_16lib.dll>

using namespace System;
using namespace Ex9_16lib;

int main(array<System::String ^> ^args)
{
  array<IContainer^>^ containers = { gcnew Box(2.0, 3.0, 4.0),
                                     gcnew GlassBox(2.0, 3.0, 4.0),
                                     gcnew Box(4.0, 5.0, 6.0),
                                     gcnew GlassBox(4.0, 5.0, 6.0)
                                   };

  Console::WriteLine(L"The array of containers have the following volumes:");
  for each(IContainer^ container in containers)
    container->ShowVolume();              // Output the volume of a box

  Console::WriteLine(L"\nNow pushing the containers on the stack...");

  Stack^ stack = gcnew Stack;             // Create the stack
  for each(IContainer^ container in containers)
    stack->Push(container);

  Console::WriteLine(
        L"Popping the containers off the stack presents them in reverse order:");
  Object^ item;
  while((item = stack->Pop()) != nullptr)
    safe_cast<IContainer^>(item)->ShowVolume();

  Console::WriteLine();
  return 0;
}
```

You also need to add the GlassBox.h header to the project with the same code as in Ex9_15 so you can copy the file to this project directory and then add it to the project by right-clicking Header Files in the Solution Explorer tab and selecting Add > Existing Item... from the context menu. Of course, the GlassBox class is derived from the Box class, so the compiler needs to know where to find the Box class definition. In this case it's in the library you created in the previous project, so add the following directive to the GlassBox.h header file after the #pragma once directive:

```
#using <Ex9_16lib.dll>
```

The Box class name is defined within the Ex9_16lib namespace, so you also need to add a using statement for that following the #using directive:

```
using namespace Ex9_16lib;
```

To enable the compiler to find the library, copy the Ex9_16lib.dll file from the Ex9_16lib project to the debug subdirectory to the Ex9_16 solution directory that contains the Ex9_16.exe file. You could specify the full path to the assembly in the #using directive, but it is more usual to put any class libraries that a project uses in the directory that contains the executable for an application. It's easy to get the directories muddled here. The Ex9_16lib.dll file is in the debug subdirectory to the Ex9_16lib *solution* directory, not the debug subdirectory to the Ex9_16lib project directory. You are copying the library file to the debug subdirectory of the Ex9_16 solution directory. Make sure you copy the .dll file to the correct directory or the library won't be found.

Because the classes in the external assembly are in their own namespace, you have a using directive for the Ex9_16lib namespace name. Without this you would have to qualify the IContainer, Box, and Stack names with the namespace name so you would write Ex9_16lib::Box instead of just Box for example.

The remainder of the code is exactly the same as in the main() function for Ex9_15; no changes are necessary because you are now using classes from an external assembly. If you execute the program, you'll see the output is the same as that from Ex9_15.

Functions Specified as new

You have seen how you use the override keyword to override a function in a base class. You can also specify a function in a derived class as new, in which case it hides the function in the base class that has the same signature and the new function does not participate in polymorphic behavior. To define the Volume() function as new in a class NewBox that is derived from Box you code it like this:

```
ref class NewBox : Box                    // Derived class
{
  public:
    // New function to calculate the volume of a NewBox object
    virtual double Volume() new
    { return 0.5*m_Length*m_Width*m_Height; }

    // Constructor
    NewBox(double lv, double wv, double hv): Box(lv, wv, hv){}
};
```

This version of the function hides the version of the Volume() function that is defined in Box, so if you call the Volume() function using a handle of type NewBox^ the new version is called. For example:

```
NewBox^ newBox = gcnew NewBox(2.0, 3.0,4.0);
Console::WriteLine(newBox->Volume());  // Output is 12
```

The result is 12 because the new Volume() function hides the polymorphic version that the NextBox class inherits from Box.

The new Volume() function is not a polymorphic function so for polymorphic calls using a handle to a base class type, the new version is not called. For example:

```
Box^ newBox = gcnew NewBox(2.0, 3.0,4.0);
Console::WriteLine(newBox->Volume());  // Output is 24
```

The only polymorphic `Volume()` function in the `NewBox` class is the one that is inherited from the `Box` class so that is the function that is called in this case.

Delegates and Events

An **event** is a member of a class that enables an object to signal when a particular event has occurred, and the signaling process for an event involves a **delegate** that provides the mechanism for responding to the event is some way. A mouse click is a typical example of an event and the object that originated the mouse click event would signal that the event has occurred by calling one or more functions that are responsible for dealing with the event; a delegate would provide the means to access the function that is to respond to the event. Let's look at delegates first and return to events a little later in this chapter.

The idea of a delegate is very simple — it's an object that can encapsulate one or more pointers to functions that have a given parameter list and return type. A function that a delegate points to will deal with a particular kind of event. Thus a delegate provides a similar facility in C++/CLI to a function pointer in native C++. Although the idea of a delegate is simple, however, the detail of creating and using delegates can get a little confusing so it's time to concentrate.

Declaring Delegates

The declaration for a delegate looks like a function prototype preceded by the `delegate` keyword but in reality it defines two things: the reference type name for a delegate object, and the parameter list and return type of the functions that can be associated with the delegate. A delegate reference type has the `System::Delegate` class as a base class so a delegate type always inherits the member of this class. The declaration for a delegate looks like a function prototype preceded by the `delegate` keyword but in reality it defines a reference type for the delegate, and the signature of the functions that can be associated with the delegate. Here's an example of a declaration for a delegate:

```
public delegate void Handler(int value);        // Delegate declaration
```

This defines a delegate reference type `Handler` where the `Handler` type is derived from `System::Delegate`. An object of type `Handler` can contain pointers to one or more functions that have a single parameter of type `int` and a return type that is `void`. The functions pointed to by a delegate can be instance functions or static functions.

Creating Delegates

Having defined the delegate type, you can now create delegate objects of this type. You have a choice of two constructors for a delegate: one that accepts a single argument and another that accepts two arguments.

The argument to the delegate constructor that accepts one argument must be a static function member of a class or a global function that has the return type and parameter list specified in the delegate declaration. Suppose you define a class with the name `HandlerClass` like this:

```
public ref class HandlerClass
{
public:
  static void Fun1(int m)
  { Console::WriteLine(L"Function1 called with value {0}", m); }
```

```
     static void Fun2(int m)
     { Console::WriteLine(L"Function2 called with value {0}", m); }

     void Fun3(int m)
     { Console::WriteLine(L"Function3 called with value {0}", m+value); }

     void Fun4(int m)
     { Console::WriteLine(L"Function3 called with value {0}", m+value); }

     HandlerClass():value(1){}

     HandlerClass(int m):value(m){}
   protected:
     int value;
   };
```

The class has four functions with a parameter of type int and a return type of void. Two of these are static functions and two are instance functions. It also has two constructors including a no-arg constructor. This class doesn't do much except produce output where you'll be able to determine which function was called and for instance functions what the object was.

You could create a Handler delegate like this:

```
   Handler^ handler = gcnew Handler(HandlerClass::Fun1);     // Delegate object
```

The handler object contains the address of the static function, Fun1, in the HandlerClass class. If you call the delegate, the HandlerClass::Fun1() function is called with the argument the same as you pass in the delegate call. You can write the delegate call like this:

```
   handler->Invoke(90);
```

This calls all the functions in the invocation list for the handler delegate. In this case there is just one function in the invocation list, HandlerClass::Fun1(), so the output is:

```
   Function1 called with value 90
```

You could also call the delegate with the following statement:

```
   handler(90);
```

This is shorthand for the previous statement that explicitly called the Invoke() function and this is the form of delegate call you see generally.

The + operator is overloaded for delegate types to combine the invocation lists for two delegates into a new delegate object. For example, you could apparently modify the invocation list for the handler delegate with this statement:

```
   handler += gcnew Handler(HandlerClass::Fun2);
```

The handler variable now references a delegate object with an invocation list containing two functions: Fun1 and Fun2. However, this is a new delegate object. The invocation list for a delegate cannot be changed so the + operator works in a similar way to the way it works with String objects — you always get a new object created. You could invoke the delegate again with this statement:

```
handler(80);
```

Now you get the output:

```
Function1 called with value 80
Function2 called with value 80
```

Both functions in the invocation list are called and they are called in the sequence in which they were added to the delegate object.

You can effectively remove an entry from the invocation list for a delegate by using the — operator:

```
handler -= gcnew Handler(HandlerClass::Fun1);
```

This creates a new delegate object that contains just HandlerClass::Fun2() in its invocation list. The effect of using the -= operator is to remove the functions that are in the invocation list on the right side (HandlerClass::Fun1) from the list for the handler and create a new object pointing to the functions that remain.

> *Note that the invocation list for a delegate must contain at least one function pointer. If you remove all the function pointers using the subtraction operator then the result will be nullptr.*

When you use the delegate constructor that has two parameters, the first argument is a reference to an object on the CLR heap and the second object is the address of an instance function for that object's type. Thus this constructor creates a delegate that contains a pointer to the instance function specified by the second argument for the object specified by the first argument. Here's how you can create such a delegate:

```
HandlerClass^ obj = gcnew HandlerClass;
Handler^ handler2 = gcnew Handler (obj, &HandlerClass::Fun3);
```

The first statement creates an object and the second statement creates a delegate pointing to the Fun3() function for the HandlerClass object obj. The delegate expects an argument of type int so you can invoke it with the statement:

```
handler2(70);
```

This results in Fun3() for obj being called with an argument value of 70, so the output is:

```
Function3 called with value 71
```

The value stored in the value field for obj is 1 because you create the object using the default constructor. The statement in the body of Fun3() adds the value field to the function argument — hence the 71 in the output.

Because they are both of the same type, you could combine the invocation list for handler with the list for the handler2 delegate:

```
Handler^ handler = gcnew Handler(HandlerClass::Fun1);    // Delegate object
```

```
handler += gcnew Handler(HandlerClass::Fun2);

HandlerClass^ obj = gcnew HandlerClass;
Handler^ handler2 = gcnew Handler (obj, &HandlerClass::Fun3);
handler += handler2;
```

Here you recreate `handler` to reference a delegate that contains pointers to the static `Fun1()` and `Fun2()` functions. You then create a new delegate referenced by `handler` that contains the static functions plus the `Fun3()` instance function for `obj`. You can now invoke the delegate with the statement:

```
handler(50);
```

This results in the following output:

```
Function1 called with value 50
Function2 called with value 50
Function3 called with value 51
```

As you see, invoking the delegate calls the two static functions plus the `Fun3()` member of `obj`, so you can combine static and non-static functions with a single invocation list for a delegate.

Let's put some of the fragments together in an example to make sure it does really work.

Try It Out   Creating and Calling Delegates

Here's a potpourri of what you have seen so far about delegates:

```
// Ex9_17.cpp : main project file.
// Creating and calling delegates

#include "stdafx.h"

using namespace System;

public ref class HandlerClass
{
public:
  static void Fun1(int m)
  { Console::WriteLine(L"Function1 called with value {0}", m); }

  static void Fun2(int m)
  { Console::WriteLine(L"Function2 called with value {0}", m); }

  void Fun3(int m)
  { Console::WriteLine(L"Function3 called with value {0}", m+value); }

  void Fun4(int m)
  { Console::WriteLine(L"Function3 called with value {0}", m+value); }

  HandlerClass():value(1){}

  HandlerClass(int m):value(m){}
```

```
  protected:
    int value;
  };
```

```
public delegate void Handler(int value);          // Delegate declaration
```

```
int main(array<System::String ^> ^args)
{
  Handler^ handler = gcnew Handler(HandlerClass::Fun1); // Delegate object
  Console::WriteLine(L"Delegate with one pointer to a static function:");
  handler->Invoke(90);

  handler += gcnew Handler(HandlerClass::Fun2);
  Console::WriteLine(L"\nDelegate with two pointers to static functions:");
  handler->Invoke(80);

  HandlerClass^ obj = gcnew HandlerClass;
  Handler^ handler2 = gcnew Handler (obj, &HandlerClass::Fun3);
  handler += handler2;
  Console::WriteLine(L"\nDelegate with three pointers to functions:");
  handler(70);

  Console::WriteLine(L"\nShortening the invocation list...");
  handler -= gcnew Handler(HandlerClass::Fun1);
  Console::WriteLine
          (L"\nDelegate with pointers to one static and one instance function:");
  handler(60);
}
```

This example produces the following output:

```
Delegate with one pointer to a static function:
Function1 called with value 90

Delegate with two pointers to static functions:
Function1 called with value 80
Function2 called with value 80

Delegate with three pointers to functions:
Function1 called with value 70
Function2 called with value 70
Function3 called with value 71

Shortening the invocation list...

Delegate with pointers to one static and one instance function:
Function2 called with value 60
Function3 called with value 61
```

How It Works

You saw all the operations that appear in main() in the previous section. You invoke a delegate using the Invoke() function explicitly and by just using the delegate handle followed by its argument list. You can see from the output that everything works as it should.

Although the example shows a delegate that can contain pointers to functions with a single argument, a delegate can point to functions with as many arguments as you want. For example, you could declare a delegate type like this:

```
delegate void MyHandler(double x, String^ description);
```

This statement declares the `MyHandler` delegate type that can only point to functions with a `void` return type and two parameters, the first of type `double` and the second of type `String^`.

Unbound Delegates

The delegates you have seen up to now have been examples of **bound** delegates. They are called bound delegates because they each have a fixed set of functions in their invocation list. You can also create unbound delegates; an unbound delegate points to an instance function with a given parameter list and return type for a given type of object. Thus the same delegate can invoke the instance function for any object of the specified type. Here's an example of declaring an unbound delegate:

```
public delegate void UBHandler(ThisClass^, int value);
```

The first argument specifies the type of the `this` pointer for which a delegate of type `UBHandler` can call an instance function; the function must have a single parameter of type `int` and a return type of `void`. Thus a delegate of type `UBHandler` can only call a function for an object of type `ThisClass` but for *any* object of that type. This may sound a bit restrictive but turns out to be quite useful; you could use the delegate to call a function for each element of type `ThisClass^` in an array for example.

You can create a delegate of type `UBHandler` like this:

```
UBHandler^ ubh = gcnew UBHandler(&ThisClass::Sum);
```

The argument to the constructor is the address of a function in the `ThisClass` class that has the required parameter list and return type.

Here's a definition for `ThisClass`:

```
public ref class ThisClass
{
public:
  void Sum(int n, String^ str)
  { Console::WriteLine(L"Sum result = {0}", value + n); }

  void Product(int n, String^ str)
  { Console::WriteLine(L"Product result = {0}", value*n); }

  ThisClass(double v) : value(v){}

private:
  double value;
};
```

The `Sum()` function is a public instance member of the `ThisClass` class, so invoking the `ubh` delegate will call the `Sum()` function for any object of this class type.

When you call an unbound delegate, the first argument is the object for which the functions in the invocation list are to be called, and the subsequent arguments are the arguments to those functions. Here's how you might call the `ubh` delegate:

```
ThisClass^ obj = gcnew ThisClass(99.0);
ubh(obj, 5);
```

The first argument is a handle to a `ThisClass` object that you created on the CLR heap by passing the value 99.0 to the class constructor. The second argument to the `ubh` call is 5, so it results in the `Sum()` function being called with an argument of 5 for the object referenced by `obj`.

You can combine unbound delegates using the + operator to create a delegate that calls multiple functions. Of course, all the functions must be compatible with the delegate, so for `ubh` they must be instance functions in the `ThisClass` class that have one parameter of type `int` and a `void` return type. Here's an example:

```
ubh += gcnew UBHandler(&ThisClass::Product);
```

Invoking the new delegate referenced by `ubh` calls both the `Sum()` and `Product()` functions for an object of type `ThisClass`. Let's see it in action.

Try It Out   Using an Unbound Delegate

This example uses the code fragments from the previous section to demonstrate the operation of an unbound delegate:

```
// Ex9_18.cpp : main project file.
// Using an unbound delegate

#include "stdafx.h"

using namespace System;

public ref class ThisClass
{
public:
  void Sum(int n)
  { Console::WriteLine(L"Sum result = {0} ", value+n); }

  void Product(int n)
  { Console::WriteLine(L"product result = {0} ", value*n); }

  ThisClass(double v) : value(v){}

private:
  double value;
```

```
  };

public delegate void UBHandler(ThisClass^, int value);

int main(array<System::String ^> ^args)
{
  array<ThisClass^>^ things = { gcnew ThisClass(5.0),gcnew ThisClass(10.0),
                                gcnew ThisClass(15.0),gcnew ThisClass(20.0),
                                gcnew ThisClass(25.0)
                              };

  UBHandler^ ubh = gcnew UBHandler(&ThisClass::Sum);  // Create a delegate object

  // Call the delegate for each things array element
  for each(ThisClass^ thing in things)
    ubh(thing, 3);

   ubh += gcnew UBHandler(&ThisClass::Product);  // Add a function to the delegate

  // Call the new delegate for each things array element
  for each(ThisClass^ thing in things)
    ubh(thing, 2);

  return 0;
}
```

This example produces the following output:

```
Sum result = 8
Sum result = 13
Sum result = 18
Sum result = 23
Sum result = 28
Sum result = 7
product result = 10
Sum result = 12
product result = 20
Sum result = 17
product result = 30
Sum result = 22
product result = 40
Sum result = 27
product result = 50
```

How It Works

The UBHandler delegate type is declared by the following statement.

```
public delegate void UBHandler(ThisClass^, int value);
```

UBHandler delegate objects are unbound delegates that can call instance functions for objects of type ThisClass as long as they have a single parameter of type int and a return type of void.

The `ThisClass` class definition in the example is the same as you saw in the previous section. It has two instance functions — `Sum()` and `Product()` — that have a parameter type of `int` and a return type of `void` so either or both may be called by a delegate of type `UBHandler`.

You create an array of handles to `ThisClass` objects in `main()` with the statement:

```
array<ThisClass^>^ things = { gcnew ThisClass(5.0),gcnew ThisClass(10.0),
                              gcnew ThisClass(15.0),gcnew ThisClass(20.0),
                              gcnew ThisClass(25.0)
                            };
```

The five objects in the initialization list each encapsulate a different value of type `double`, so for `Sum()` and `Product()` function calls the object involved will be easy to identify in the output.

You create a delegate object with the statement:

```
UBHandler^ ubh = gcnew UBHandler(&ThisClass::Sum);  // Create a delegate object
```

Invoking the delegate object referenced by the handle `ubh` calls the `Sum()` function for any object of type `ThisClass`, and you do this for each object in the `things` array:

```
for each(ThisClass^ thing in things)
  ubh(thing, 3);
```

The `for each` loop iterates over each element in the `things` array so in the loop body you call the delegate with an element from the array as the first argument. This causes the `Sum()` function to be called for the `thing` object with an argument of 3. Thus this loop produces the first five output lines.

Next you create a new delegate:

```
ubh += gcnew UBHandler(&ThisClass::Product);   // Add a function to the delegate
```

This statement creates a new `UBHandler` delegate that points to the `Product()` function and combines this with the existing delegate referenced by `ubh`. The result is another delegate that has pointers to both the `Sum()` and `Product()` functions in its invocation list.

The last loop calls the `ubh` delegate for each element in the `things` array with the argument value 2. The result will be that both `Sum()` and `Product()` will be called for each `ThisClass` object with the argument value 2, so the loop produces the next ten lines of output.

Although you have used unbound delegates in a very simple way, here they provide immense flexibility in your programs. You could pass an unbound delegate as an argument to a function, for example, to enable the same function to call different combinations of instance functions at different times so the delegate becomes a kind of function selector. The sequence in which functions are called by a delegate is the sequence that they appear in the invocation list so a delegate provides you with the means of controlling the sequence in which functions are called.

Creating Events

As I said earlier, the signaling of an event involves a delegate and the delegate contains pointers to the functions that are to be called when the event occurs. Most of the events you work with in your programs are events associated with controls such as buttons or menu items and these events arise from user interactions with your program, but you can also define and trigger events in your own program code.

An event is a member of a reference class that you define using the `event` keyword and a delegate class name:

```
public delegate void DoorHandler(String^ str);

// Class with an event member
public ref class Door
{
public:
  // An event that will call functions associated
  // with an DoorHandler delegate object
  event DoorHandler^ Knock;

  // Function to trigger events
  void TriggerEvents()
  {
    Knock("Fred");
    Knock("Jane");
  }
};
```

The `Door` class has an event member with the name `Knock` that corresponds to a delegate of type `DoorHandler`. `Knock` is an instance member of the class, but you can specify an event as a static class member using the `static` keyword. You can also declare an event to be `virtual`. When a `Knock` event is triggered, it can call functions with the parameter list and return type that are specified by the `DoorHandler` delegate.

The `Door` class also has a public function, `TriggerEvent()` that triggers two `Knock` events, each with different arguments. The arguments are passed to the functions that have been registered to receive notification of the `Knock` event. As you see, triggering an event is essentially the same as calling a delegate.

You could define a class that might handle `Knock` events like this:

```
public ref class AnswerDoor
{
public:
  void ImIn(String^ name)
  {
    Console::WriteLine(L"Come in {0}, it's open.",name);
  }

  void ImOut(String^ name)
  {
    Console::WriteLine(L"Go away {0}, I'm out.",name);
  }
};
```

The `AnswerDoor` class has two public function members that potentially could handle a `Knock` event because they both have the parameter list and return type identified in the declaration of the `DoorHandler` delegate.

Before you can register functions that are to receive notifications of `Knock` events, you need to create a `Door` object. You can create a `Door` object like this:

```
Door^ door = gcnew Door;
```

Now you can register a function to receive notification of the `Knock` event in the `Cap Door` object like this:

```
AnswerDoor^ answer = gcnew AnswerDoor;
door->Knock += gcnew DoorHandler(answer, &AnswerDoor::ImIn);
```

The first statement creates an object of type `AnswerDoor` — you need this because the `ImIn()` and `ImOut()` functions are not static class members. You then add an instance of the `DoorHandler` delegate type to the `Knock` member of `Cap Door`. This exactly parallels the process of adding function pointers to a delegate and you could add further handler functions to be called when a `Knock` event is triggered in the same way. We can see it operating in an example.

Try It Out   **Handling Events**

This example uses the classes from the preceding section to define, trigger, and handle events:

```
// Ex9_19.cpp : main project file.
// Defining, triggering and handling events.
#include "stdafx.h"

using namespace System;

public delegate void DoorHandler(String^ str);
```

```
// Class with an event member
public ref class Door
{
public:
  // An event that will call functions associated
  // with an DoorHandler delegate object
  event DoorHandler^ Knock;

  // Function to trigger events
  void TriggerEvents()
  {
    Knock(L"Fred");
    Knock(L"Jane");
  }
};
```

```
// Class defining handler functions for Knock events
public ref class AnswerDoor
{
public:
  void ImIn(String^ name)
```

```
    {
      Console::WriteLine(L"Come in {0}, it's open.",name);
    }

    void ImOut(String^ name)
    {
      Console::WriteLine(L"Go away {0}, I'm out.",name);
    }
};

int main(array<System::String ^> ^args)
{
    Door^ door = gcnew Door;
    AnswerDoor^ answer = gcnew AnswerDoor;

    // Add handler for Knock event member of door
    door->Knock += gcnew DoorHandler(answer, &AnswerDoor::ImIn);

    door->TriggerEvents();              // Trigger Knock events

    // Change the way a knock is dealt with
    door->Knock -= gcnew DoorHandler(answer, &AnswerDoor::ImIn);
    door->Knock += gcnew DoorHandler(answer, &AnswerDoor::ImOut);
    door->TriggerEvents();              // Trigger Knock events
    return 0;
}
```

Executing this example results in the following output:

```
Come in Fred, it's open.
Come in Jane, it's open.
Go away Fred, I'm out.
Go away Jane, I'm out.
```

How It Works

You first create two objects in `main()`:

```
Door^ door = gcnew Door;
AnswerDoor^ answer = gcnew AnswerDoor;
```

The `door` object has an event member, `Knock`, and the `answer` object has member functions that can be registered to be called for `Knock` events.

The next statement registers the `ImIn()` member of the `answer` object to receive notification of `Knock` events for the `door` object:

```
door->Knock += gcnew DoorHandler(answer, &AnswerDoor::ImIn);
```

If it made sense to do so, you could register other functions to be called when a `Knock` event is triggered.

The next statement calls the `TriggerEvents()` member of the `door` object:

```
door->TriggerEvents();                 // Trigger Knock events
```

This results in two `Knock` events, one with the argument `"Fred"` and the other with the argument `"Jane"`. The result is that the `ImIn()` function is called once for each event, which produces the first two lines of output.

Of course, you might want to respond differently to an event at different times, depending on the circumstances, and this is what the next three statements in `main()` demonstrate:

```
door->Knock -= gcnew DoorHandler(answer, &AnswerDoor::ImIn);
door->Knock += gcnew DoorHandler(answer, &AnswerDoor::ImOut);
door->TriggerEvents();              // Trigger Knock events
```

The first statement removes the pointer to the `ImIn()` function from the event and the second statement registers the `ImOut()` function for the `answer` object to receive event notifications. When the `Knock` events are triggered by the third statement, the `ImOut()` function is called so the results are a little different.

Destructors and Finalizers in Reference Classes

You can define a destructor for a reference class in the same way as you define a constructor for a native C++ class. The destructor for a reference class is called when the handle goes out of scope or the object is part of another object that is being destroyed. You can also apply the `delete` operator to a handle for a reference class object and that results in the destructor being called. The primary reason for implementing a destructor for a native C++ class is to deal with data members allocated on the heap, but obviously that doesn't apply to reference classes so there is less need to define a destructor in a ref class. You might do this when objects of the class are using other resources that are not managed by the garbage collector, such as files that need to be closed in an orderly fashion when an object is destroyed. You can also clean up such resources in another kind of class member called a **finalizer**.

A finalizer is a special kind of function member of a reference class that is called automatically by the garbage collector when destroying an object. Note that the finalizer is not called for a class object if the destructor was called explicitly or was called as a result of applying the `delete` operator to the object. In a derived class, finalizers are called in the same sequence as destructor calls would be, so the finalizer for the basest class is called first, followed by the finalizers for successive classes in the hierarchy with the finalizer for the most derived class being called last.

You define a finalizer in a class like this:

```
public ref class MyClass
{
  // Finalizer definition
  !MyClass()
  {
    // Code to clean-up when an object is destroyed...
  }

  // Rest of the class definition...
};
```

You define a finalizer function in a class in a similar way to a destructor, but with `!` instead of the `~` that you use preceding the class name for a destructor. Similar to a destructor, you must not supply a return type for a finalizer, and the access specifier for a finalizer will be ignored. You can see how destructors and finalizers operate with a little example.

Try It Out   **Finalizers and Destructors**

This example shows when destructors and finalizers get called in an application:

```cpp
// Ex9_20.cpp : main project file.
// Finalizers and destructors

#include "stdafx.h"

using namespace System;

ref class MyClass
{
public:
  // Constructor
  MyClass(int n) : value(n){}

  // Destructor
  ~MyClass()
  {
    Console::WriteLine("MyClass object({0}) destructor called.", value);
  }

  // Finalizer
  !MyClass()
  {
    Console::WriteLine("MyClass object({0}) finalizer called.", value);
  }
private:
  int value;
};

int main(array<System::String ^> ^args)
{
  MyClass^ obj1 = gcnew MyClass(1);
  MyClass^ obj2 = gcnew MyClass(2);
  MyClass^ obj3 = gcnew MyClass(3);
  delete obj1;
  obj2->~MyClass();

  Console::WriteLine(L"End Program");
  return 0;
}
```

The output from this example is:

```
MyClass object(1) destructor called.
MyClass object(2) destructor called.
End Program
MyClass object(3) finalizer called.
```

How It Works

The `MyClass` class has a constructor, a destructor, and a finalizer. The destructor and finalizer just write output to the command line so you know when each is called. You are also able to tell for which object the finalizer or destructor was called because they output the value of the `value` field.

In the `main()` function, you create three objects of type `MyClass` encapsulating values 1, 2, and 3 to distinguish them. You then apply the delete operator to `obj1` and then explicitly call the destructor for `obj2`. Making these calls results in the first two lines of the example output. This output is generated by the destructor calls for the objects that results from making the delete and explicit destructor calls.

The next line of output is produced by the statement preceding the return statement in `main()`, so the last line of output generated by the finalizer for `obj3` occurs after the end of `main()`. The output shows that constructors are called when you delete an object or call its destructor explicitly, the destructor for the object will be executed, and these operations also suppress the execution of the finalizers for the objects. The object referenced by `obj3` is destroyed by the garbage collector when the program ends so the finalizer gets called to clean up any non-managed resources.

Thus, if a class has a finalizer and a destructor, only one of these is called when the object is destroyed, the destructor is called if you programmatically destroy the object, and the finalizer is called if it dies naturally by going out of scope. You can also deduce from this that if you rely on a finalizer to clean up after your objects have been destroyed, you should not explicitly delete the objects.

If you comment out the statements in `main()` that destroy `obj1` and `obj2`, you will see that the finalizers for these objects are called by the garbage collector when the program ends. On the other hand, if you comment out the finalizer from `MyClass`, you will see that the destructor for obj3 does not get called by the garbage collector so no clean up occurs. You can conclude that if you want to be sure that unmanaged resources used by an object are taken care of regardless of how an object is terminated, you should implement both a destructor and a finalizer in the class.

Generic Classes

C++/CLI provides you with the capability for defining generic classes where a specific class is instantiated from the generic class type at run-time. You can define generic value classes, generic reference classes, generic interface classes, and generic delegates. You define a generic class using one or more type parameters in a similar way to generic functions that you saw in Chapter 6.

For example, here's how you could define a generic version of the `Stack` class you saw in `Ex9_14`:

```
// Stack.h for Ex9_21
// A generic pushdown stack

generic<typename T> ref class Stack
{
private:
  // Defines items to store in the stack
  ref struct Item
  {
```

```
        T Obj;                          // Handle for the object in this item
        Item^ Next;                     // Handle for next item in the stack or nullptr

        // Constructor
        Item(T obj, Item^ next): Obj(obj), Next(next){}
    };

    Item^ Top;                          // Handle for item that is at the top
public:
    // Push an object on to the stack
    void Push(T obj)
    {
        Top = gcnew Item(obj, Top);   // Create new item and make it the top
    }

    // Pop an  object off the stack
    T Pop()
    {
        if(Top == nullptr)              // If the stack is empty
            return T();                 // return null equivalent

        T obj = Top->Obj;               // Get object from item
        Top = Top->Next;                // Make next item the top
        return obj;
    }
};
```

The generic version of the class now has a type parameter, T. Note that you could use the class keyword instead of the typename keyword when specifying the parameter — there is no difference between them in this context. A type argument replaces T when the generic class type is used; T is replaced by the type argument through the definition of the class so a major advantage over the original version is that the generic class type is much safer without losing any of its flexibility. The Push() member of the original class accepts any handle, so you could happily push a mix of objects of type MyClass^, String^, or indeed any handle type onto the same stack, whereas an instance of the generic type accepts only objects of the type specified as the type argument of objects of a type that have the type argument as a base.

Look at the implementation of the Pop() function. The original version returned nullptr if the top item in the stack was null, but you can't return nullptr for a type parameter because the type argument could be a value type. The solution is to return T(), which is a no-arg constructor call for type T. This results in the equivalent of 0 for a value type and nullptr for a handle.

> Note that you can specify constraints on a generic class type parameter using the where keyword in the same way as you did for generic functions in Chapter 6.

You could create a stack from the Stack<> generic type that stores handles to Box objects like this:

```
Stack<Box^>^ stack = gcnew Stack<Box^>;
```

The type argument Box^ goes between the angled brackets and the statement creates a Stack<Box^> object on the CLR heap. This object allows handles of type Box^ to be pushed onto the stack as well as handles of any type that have Box as a direct or indirect base class. You can try this out with a revised version of Ex9_14.

Try It Out   **Using a Generic Class Type**

Create a new CLR console program with the name Ex9_21 and then copy the header files Container.h, Box.h, and GlassBox.h from Ex9_14 to the directory for this project. Add these headers to the project by right-clicking Header Files in the Solution Explorer tab and selecting Add > Existing Item from the context menu. You can then add a new header file, Stack.h, to the project and enter the generic Stack class definition that you saw in the previous section. Don't forget the #pragma once directive at the beginning of the file.

```cpp
// Ex9_21.cpp : main project file.
```

```cpp
// Using a nested class to define a stack

#include "stdafx.h"
#include "Box.h"                        // For Box and Container
#include "GlassBox.h"                   // For GlassBox (and Box and Container)
#include "Stack.h"                      // For the generic stack class

using namespace System;

int main(array<System::String ^> ^args)
{
  array<Box^>^ boxes = { gcnew Box(2.0, 3.0, 4.0),
                         gcnew GlassBox(2.0, 3.0, 4.0),
                         gcnew Box(4.0, 5.0, 6.0),
                         gcnew GlassBox(4.0, 5.0, 6.0)
                       };

  Console::WriteLine(L"The array of boxes have the following volumes:");
  for each(Box^ box in boxes)
    box->ShowVolume();                               // Output the volume of a box

  Console::WriteLine(L"\nNow pushing the boxes on the stack...");

  Stack<Box^>^ stack = gcnew Stack<Box^>;           // Create the stack
  for each(Box^ box in boxes)
    stack->Push(box);


  Console::WriteLine(
            L"Popping the boxes off the stack presents them in reverse order:");
  Box^ item;
  while((item = stack->Pop()) != nullptr)
    safe_cast<Container^>(item)->ShowVolume();

  // Try the generic Stack type storing integers
  Stack<int>^ numbers = gcnew Stack<int>;           // Create the stack
  Console::WriteLine(L"\nNow pushing integers on to the stack:");
  for(int i = 2 ; i<=12 ; i += 2)
  {
    Console::Write(L"{0,5}",i);
    numbers->Push(i);
  }
  int number;
```

```
        Console::WriteLine(L"\n\nPopping integers off the stack produces:");
        while((number = numbers->Pop()) != 0)
          Console::Write(L"{0,5}",number);

        Console::WriteLine();
        return 0;
}
```

This example produces the following output:

```
The array of boxes have the following volumes:
CBox usable volume is 24
CBox usable volume is 20.4
CBox usable volume is 120
CBox usable volume is 102

Now pushing the boxes on the stack...
Popping the boxes off the stack presents them in reverse order:
CBox usable volume is 102
CBox usable volume is 120
CBox usable volume is 20.4
CBox usable volume is 24

Now pushing integers on to the stack:
    2    4    6    8    10    12

Popping integers off the stack produces:
    12    10    8    6    4    2
```

How It Works

The stack to store Box object handles is defined in the statement:

```
Stack<Box^>^ stack = gcnew Stack<Box^>;        // Create the stack
```

The type parameter is Box^ so the stack stores handles to Box objects or handles to GlassBox objects. The code to push objects on to the stack and to pop them off again is exactly the same as in Ex9_14 and the output is the same, too. The difference here is that you could not push an object on to the stack if the type did not have Box as a direct or indirect base class so the generic type guarantees that all the objects are Box objects.

Storing integers now requires a new Stack<> object:

```
Stack<int>^ numbers = gcnew Stack<int>;        // Create the stack
```

The original version used the same non-generic Stack object to store Box object references and integers thus demonstrating how type safety was completely lacking in the operation of the stack. Here you specify the type argument for the generic class as the value type int, so only objects of this type are accepted by the Push() function.

The loops that pop objects off the stack demonstrate that returning T() in the Pop() function does indeed return 0 for type int and nullptr for the handle type Box^.

Generic Interface Classes

You can define generic interfaces in the same way as you define generic reference classes and a generic reference class can be defined in terms of a generic interface. To show how this works, you can define a generic interface that can be implemented by the generic class, Stack<>. Here's a definition for a generic interface:

```
// Interface for stack operations
generic<typename T> public interface class IStack
{
  void Push(T obj);        // Push an item on to the stack
  T Pop();
};
```

This interface has two functions identifying the push and pop operations for a stack.

The definition of the generic Stack<> class that implements the IStack<> generic interface is:

```
generic<typename T> ref class Stack : IStack<T>
{
private:
  // Defines items to store in the stack
  ref struct Item
  {
    T Obj;                       // Handle for the object in this item
    Item^ Next;                  // Handle for next item in the stack or nullptr

    // Constructor
    Item(T obj, Item^ next): Obj(obj), Next(next){}
  };

  Item^ Top;                     // Handle for item that is at the top

public:
  // Push an object on to the stack
  virtual void Push(T obj)
  {
    Top = gcnew Item(obj, Top);   // Create new item and make it the top
  }

  // Pop an  object off the stack
  virtual T Pop()
  {
    if(Top == nullptr)            // If the stack is empty
      return T();                 // return null equivalent

    T obj = Top->Obj;             // Get object from item
    Top = Top->Next;              // Make next item the top
    return obj;
  }
};
```

The changes from the previous generic Stack<> class definition are shaded. In the first line of the generic class definition the type parameter T is used as the type argument to the interface IStack so the type argument used for the Stack<> class instance also applies to the interface. The Push() and Pop() functions in the class now have to be specified as `virtual` because the functions are virtual in the interface. You could add a header file containing the `IStack` interface to the previous example and amend the generic `Stack<>` class definition to the example and recompile the program to see it operating with a generic interface.

Generic Collection Classes

A **collection class** is a class that organizes and stores objects in a particular way; a linked list and a stack are typical examples of collection classes. The `System::Collections::Generic` namespace contains a wide range of generic collection classes that implement strongly typed collections. The generic collection classes available include the following:

Type	Description
List<T>	Stores items of type T in a simple list that can grow in size automatically when necessary
LinkedList<T>	Stores items of type T in a doubly linked list
Stack<T>	Stores item of type T in a stack, which is a first-in last-out storage mechanism
Queue<T>	Stores items of type T in a queue, which is a first-in first-out storage mechanism
Dictionary<K,V>	Stores key/value pairs where the keys are of type K and the values are of type V

I won't go into details of all these, but I'll mention briefly just three that you are most likely to want to use in your programs. I'll use examples that store value types for simplicity, but of course the collection classes work just as well with reference types.

List<T> — A Generic List

`List<T>` defines a generic list that automatically increases in size when necessary. You can add items to a list using the `Add()` function and you can access items stored in a `List<T>` using an index, just like an array. Here's how you define a list to store values of type `int`:

```
List<int> numbers = gcnew List<int>;
```

This has a default capacity, but you could specify the capacity you require. Here's a definition of a list with a capacity of 500:

```
List<int> numbers = gcnew List<int>;
```

You can add objects to the list using the `Add()` functions:

```
for(int i = 0 ; i<1000 ; i++)
   numbers->Add( 2*i+1);
```

This adds 1000 integers to the numbers list. The list grows automatically if its capacity is less than 1000. When you want to insert an item in an existing list, you can use the `Insert()` function to insert the item specified by the second argument at the index position specified by the first argument. Items in a list are indexed from zero like an array.

You could sum the contents of the list like this:

```
int sum = 0;
for(int i = 0 ; i<numbers->Count ; i++)
   sum += numbers[i];
```

Count is a property that returns the current number of items in the list. The items in the list may be accessed through the default indexed property and you can get and set values in this way. Note that you cannot increase the capacity of a list using the default indexed property. If you use an index outside the current range of items in the list, an exception is thrown.

You could also sum the items in the list like this:

```
for each(int n in numbers)
   sum +=n;
```

You have a wide range of other functions you can apply to a list including functions for removing elements, and sorting and searching the contents of the list.

LinkedList<T> — A Generic Doubly Linked List

LinkedList<T> defines a linked list with forward and backward pointers so you can iterate through the list in either direction. You could define a linked list that stores floating-point values like this:

```
LinkedList<double>^ values = gcnew LinkedList<double>;
```

You could add values to the list like this:

```
for(int i = 0 ; i<1000 ; i++)
   values->AddLast(2.5*i);
```

The AddLast() function adds an item to the end of the list. You can add items to the beginning of the list by using the AddFirst() function. Alternatively, you can use the AddHead() and AddTail() functions to do the same things.

The Find() function returns a handle of type LinkedListNode<T>^ to a node in the list containing the value you pass as the argument to Find(). You could use this handle to insert a new value before or after the node that you found. For example:

```
LinkedListNode<double>^ node = values->Find(20.0);    // Find node containing 20.0
if(node != nullptr)
   values->AddBefore(node, 19.9);                // Insert 19.1 before node
```

The first statement finds the node containing the value 20.0. If it does not exist, the Find() function returns nullptr. The last statement executed if node is not null adds a new value of 19.9 before node. You could use the AddAfter() function to add a new value after a given node. Searching a linked list is relatively slow because it is necessary to iterate through the elements sequentially.

You could sum the items in the list like this:

```
double sumd = 0;
for each(double v in values)
  sumd += v;
```

The `for each` loop iterates through all the items in the list and accumulates the total in `sum`.

The `Count` property returns the number of items in the linked list and the `Head` and `Tail` properties return the values of the first and last items. The `First` and `Last` properties are alternatives to `Head` and `Tail`.

Dictionary<TKey, TValue> — A Generic Dictionary Storing Key/Value Pairs

The generic `Dictionary<>` collection class requires two type arguments; the first is the type for the key and the second is the type for the value associated with the key. A dictionary is especially useful when you have pairs of objects that you want to store where one object is a key to accessing the other object. A name and a phone number are an example of a key value pair that you might want to store in a dictionary because you would typically want to retrieve a phone number using a name as the key. Suppose you have defined `Name` and `PhoneNumber` classes to encapsulate names and phone numbers respectively. You can define a dictionary to store name/number pairs like this:

```
Dictionary<Name^, PhoneNumber^>^ phonebook = gcnew Dictionary<Name^, PhoneNumber^>;
```

The two type arguments are `Name^` and `PhoneNumber^` so the key is a handle for a name and the value is a handle for a phone number.

You can add an entry in the `phonebook` dictionary like this:

```
Name^ name = gcnew Name("Jim", "Jones");
PhoneNumber^ number = gcnew PhoneNumber(914, 316, 2233);
phonebook->Add(name, number);          // Add name/number pair to dictionary
```

To retrieve an entry in a dictionary you can use the default indexed property — for example:

```
try
{
  PhoneNumber^ theNumber = phonebook[name];
}
catch(KeyNotFoundFoundException^ knfe)
{
  Console::WriteLine(knfe);
}
```

You supply the key as the index value for the default indexed property, which in this case is a handle to a `Name` object. The value is returned if the key is present, or an exception of type `KeyNotFoundException` is thrown if the key is not found in the collection; therefore, whenever you are accessing a value for a key that may not be present, the code should be in a `try` block.

A `Dictionary<>` object has a `Keys` property that returns a collection containing the keys in the dictionary as well as a `Values` property that returns a collection containing the values. The `Count` property returns the number of key/value pairs in the dictionary.

Let's try some of these in a working example.

Try It Out   **Using Generic Collection Classes**

This example exercises the three collection classes you have seen:

```cpp
// Ex9_22.cpp : main project file.
// Using generic collection classes

#include "stdafx.h"

using namespace System;
using namespace System::Collections::Generic;     // For generic collections

// Class encapsulating a name
ref class Name
{
public:
  Name(String^ name1, String^ name2) : First(name1),Second(name2){}
  virtual String^ ToString() override{ return First + L" " + Second;}
private:
  String^ First;
  String^ Second;
};

// Class encapsulating a phone number
ref class PhoneNumber
{
public:
  PhoneNumber(int area, int local, int number):
      Area(area),Local(local), Number(number){}
  virtual String^ ToString() override
  { return Area + L" " + Local + L" " + Number; }

private:
  int Area;
  int Local;
  int Number;

};

int main(array<System::String ^> ^args)
{
  // Using List<T>
  Console::WriteLine(L"Creating a List<T> of integers:");
  List<int>^ numbers = gcnew List<int>;
  for(int i = 0 ; i<1000 ; i++)
    numbers->Add(2*i+1);

  // Sum the contents of the list
  int sum = 0;
  for(int i = 0 ; i<numbers->Count ; i++)
    sum += numbers[i];
  Console::WriteLine(L"Total = {0}", sum);

  // Using LinkedList<T>
  Console::WriteLine(L"\nCreating a LinkedList<T> of double values:");
```

```
LinkedList<double>^ values = gcnew LinkedList<double>;
for(int i = 0 ; i<1000 ; i++)
  values->AddTail(2.5*i);

double sumd = 0.0;
for each(double v in values)
  sumd += v;

Console::WriteLine(L"Total = {0}", sumd);

LinkedListNode<double>^ node = values->Find(20.0);    // Find node containing 20.0
values->AddBefore(node, 19.9);
values->AddAfter(values->Find(30.0), 30.1);

// Sum the contents of the linked list again
sumd = 0.0;
for each(double v in values)
  sumd += v;

Console::WriteLine(L"Total after adding values = {0}", sumd);

// Using Dictionary<K,V>
Console::WriteLine(L"\nCreating a Dictionary<K,V> of name/number pairs:");
Dictionary<Name^, PhoneNumber^>^ phonebook =
                                    gcnew Dictionary<Name^, PhoneNumber^>;

// Add name/number pairs to dictionary
Name^ name = gcnew Name("Jim", "Jones");
PhoneNumber^ number = gcnew PhoneNumber(914, 316, 2233);
phonebook->Add(name, number);
phonebook->Add(gcnew Name("Fred","Fong"), gcnew PhoneNumber(123,234,3456));
phonebook->Add(gcnew Name("Janet","Smith"), gcnew PhoneNumber(515,224,6864));

// List all numbers
Console::WriteLine(L"List all the numbers:");
for each(PhoneNumber^ number in phonebook->Values)
  Console::WriteLine(number);

// List names and numbers
Console::WriteLine(L"Access the keys to list all name/number pairs:");
for each(Name^ name in phonebook->Keys)
  Console::WriteLine(L"{0} : {1}", name, phonebook[name]);

    return 0;
}
```

The output from this example should be as follows:

```
Creating a List<T> of integers:
Total = 1000000
```

```
Creating a LinkedList<T> of double values:
Total = 1248750
Total after adding values = 1248800

Creating a Dictionary<K,V> of name/number pairs:
List all the numbers:
914 316 2233
123 234 3456
515 224 6864
Access the keys to list all name/number pairs:
Jim Jones : 914 316 2233
Fred Fong : 123 234 3456
Janet Smith : 515 224 6864
```

How It Works

Note the `using namespace` directive for the `System::Collections::Generic` namespace; this is essential when you want to use the generic collections classes without specifying fully qualified class names.

The first block of code in `main()` uses the `List<>` collection using the code from the previous section. It creates a class that stores integers in a list and then stores 1000 values in it. The loop that sums the contents of the list uses the default indexed property to retrieve the values. This could also be written as a `for each` loop. Don't forget — the default indexed property only accesses items already in the list. You can change the value of an existing item using the default indexed property, but you cannot add new items this way. To add an item to the end of the list, you use the `Add()` function; you can also use the `Insert()` function to insert an item at a given index position.

The next block of code in `main()` demonstrates the use of the `LinkedList<>` collection to sort values of type `double`. Values of type `double` are added to the end of the linked list using the `AddTail()` function in a `for` loop. You could equally well use the `AddLast()` function to do the same thing. Values are retrieved and summed in a `for each` loop. Note that there is no default indexed property for accessing items in a linked list. The code also shows the use of the `Find()` and `AddBefore()` and `AddAfter()` functions to add new elements at a specific position in the linked list.

The last block of code in `main()` shows a `Dictionary<>` collection being used to store phone numbers with names as keys. The `Name` and `Phone` number classes implement an override to the inherited `ToString()` function to enable the `Console::WriteLine()` function to output suitable representations of objects of these types. Three name/number pairs are added to the `phonebook` dictionary. The code then lists the numbers in the dictionary by using a `for each` loop to iterate over the values contained in the collection object that are returned by the `Values` property for `phonebook`. The last loop iterates over the names in the collection returned by the `Keys` property and uses the default indexed property for phonebook to access the values. No `try` block is necessary here because you are certain that all the keys in the `Keys` collection are present in the dictionary — if they are not, there's a serious problem with the implementation of the `Dictionary<>` generic class!

Summary

This chapter covered the principal ideas involved in using inheritance for native C++ classes and C++/CLI classes. The fundamentals that you should keep in mind are:

❑ A derived class inherits all the members of a base class except for constructors, the destructor, and the overloaded assignment operator.

❑ Members of a base class declared as `private` in the base class are not accessible in any derived class. To obtain the effect of the keyword `private` but allow access in a derived class, you should use the keyword `protected` in place of `private`.

❑ A base class can be specified for a derived class with the keyword `public`, `private`, or `protected`. If none is specified, the default is `private`. Depending on the keyword specified for a base, the access level of the inherited members may be modified.

❑ If you write a derived class constructor, you must arrange for data members of the base class to be initialized properly, as well as those of the derived class.

❑ A function in a base class may be declared as `virtual`. This allows other definitions of the function appearing in derived classes to be selected at execution time, depending on the type of object for which the function call is made.

❑ You should declare the destructor in a native C++ base class that contains a virtual function as `virtual`. This ensures correct selection of a destructor for dynamically-created derived class objects.

❑ A native C++ class may be designated as a `friend` of another class. In this case, all the function members of the `friend` class may access all the members of the other class. If class `A` is a `friend` of `B`, class `B` is not a `friend` of `A` unless it has been declared as such.

❑ A virtual function in a native C++ base class can be specified as pure by placing = 0 at the end of the function declaration. The class then is an abstract class for which no objects can be created. In any derived class, all the pure virtual functions must be defined; if not, it, too, becomes an abstract class.

❑ A C++/CLI reference class can be derived from another reference classes. Value classes cannot be derived classes.

❑ An interface class declares a set of public functions that represent a specific capability that can be implemented by a reference class. An interface class can contain public functions, events, and properties. An interface can also define static data members, functions, events, and properties, and these are inherited in a class that implements the interface.

❑ An interface class can be derived from another interface class and the derived interface contains the members of both interfaces.

❑ A delegate is an object that encapsulates one or more pointers to functions that have the same return type and parameter list. Invoking a delegate calls all the functions pointed to by the delegate.

❑ An event member of a class can signal when the event occurs by calling one or more handler functions that have been registered with the event.

❑ A generic class is a parameterized type that is instantiated at run-time. The arguments you supply for type parameters when you instantiate a generic type can be value class types or reference class types.

❑   The `System::Collections::Generic` namespace contains generic collection classes that define typesafe collections of objects of any C++/CLI type.

❑   You can create a C++/CLI class library in a separate assembly and the class library resides in a `.dll` file.

You have now gone through all of the important language features of ISO/ANSI C++ and C++/CLI. It's important that you feel comfortable with the mechanisms for defining and deriving classes and the process of inheritance in both language versions. Windows programming with Visual C++ 2008 involves extensive use of all these concepts.

Exercises

You can download the source code for the examples in the book and the solutions to the following exercises from www.wrox.com.

1.   What's wrong with the following code?

```
class CBadClass
{
private:
    int len;
    char* p;
public:
    CBadClass(const char* str): p(str), len(strlen(p)) {}
    CBadClass(){}
};
```

2.   Suppose you have a class `CBird`, as follows, that you want to use as a base class for deriving a hierarchy of bird classes:

```
class CBird
{
protected:
    int wingSpan;
    int eggSize;
    int airSpeed;
    int altitude;
public:
    virtual void fly() { altitude = 100; }
};
```

Is it reasonable to create a `CHawk` by deriving from `CBird`? How about a `COstrich`? Justify your answers. Derive an avian hierarchy that can cope with both of these birds.

3.   Given the following class:

```
class CBase
{
protected:
    int m_anInt;
```

```
public:
    CBase(int n): m_anInt(n) { cout << "Base constructor\n"; }
    virtual void Print() const = 0;
};
```

What sort of class is CBase and why? Derive a class from CBase which sets its inherited integer value, m_anInt, when constructed, and prints it on request. Write a test program to verify that your class is correct.

4. A binary tree is a structure made up of nodes where each node contains a pointer to a "left" node and a pointer to a "right" node plus a data item, as shown in Figure 9-7.

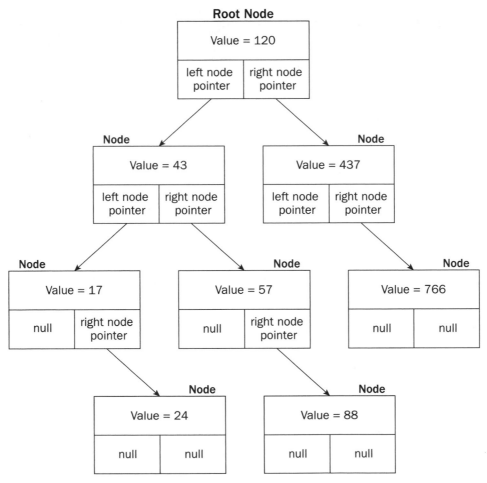

Figure 9-7

The tree starts with a root node, and this is the starting point for accessing the nodes in the tree. Either or both pointers in a node can be null. Figure 9-7 shows an ordered binary tree, which is a tree organized so that the value of each node is always greater than or equal to the value of the left node and less than or equal to the value of the right node.

Define a native C++ class to define an ordered binary tree that stores integer values. You also need to define a `Node` class, but that can be an inner class to the `BinaryTree` class. Write a program to test the operation of your `BinaryTree` class by storing an arbitrary sequence of integers in it and retrieving and outputting them in ascending sequence.

Hint: Don't be afraid to use recursion.

5. Implement Exercise 4 as a CLR program. If you did not manage to complete Exercise 4, look at the solution in the download and use that as a guide to doing this exercise.

6. Define a generic `BinaryTree` class for any type that implements the `IComparable` interface class and demonstrate its operation by using instances of the generic class to store and retrieve first a number of random integers, and then the elements of the following array:

```
array<String^>^ words = {L"Success", L"is", L"the", L"ability", L"to" ,
                         L"go" , L"from", L"one", L"failure", L"to",
                         L"another", L"with", L"no", L"loss", L"of",
                         L"enthusiasm"};
```

Write the values retrieved from the binary tree to the command line.

The Standard Template Library

At its name implies, the Standard Template Library (STL) is a library of standard class and function templates. You can use these templates to create a wide range of powerful general-purpose classes for organizing your data as well as functions for processing that data in various ways. The STL is defined by the standard for native C++ and is therefore always available with a conforming compiler. Because of its broad applicability, the STL can greatly simplify programming in many of your C++ applications.

Of course, the STL for native C++ does not work with C++/CLI class types but in Visual C++ 2008 you have an additional version of the STL available that contains templates and generic functions that you can instantiate with C++/CLI class types.

In this chapter you will learn:

- ❏ What capabilities are offered by the STL
- ❏ What containers are and how you create and use them
- ❏ What iterators are and how you use them with containers
- ❏ The types of algorithms that are available with the STL and how you can apply the more common ones
- ❏ What function objects are and how they are used with the STL
- ❏ How to use the STL version that supports C++/CLI class types

What Is the Standard Template Library?

The STL is a large collection of class and function templates that is provided with your native C++ compiler. I'll first explain in general terms the kinds of resources the STL provides and how they interact with one another before diving into the detail of working examples. The STL contains six kinds of components: containers, container adapters, iterators, algorithms, function objects, and function adapters. Because they are part of the standard library, the names of the STL components are all defined within the std namespace.

The STL is a very large library, some of which is highly specialized, and to cover the contents fully would require a book in its own right. In this chapter, I'll introduce the fundamentals of how you use the STL and describe the more commonly used capabilities. Before getting into containers in depth, I'll introduce you to the primary components, concepts and terminology you will find in the STL.

Containers

Containers are objects that you use to store and organize other objects. A class that implements a linked list is an example of a container. You create a container class from an STL template by supplying the type of the object that you intend to store. For example, `vector<T>` is a template for a container that is a linear array that automatically increases in size when necessary. `T` is the type parameter that specifies the type of objects to be stored. Here are a couple of statements that are examples of creating `vector<T>` containers:

```
vector<string> strings;    // Stores object of type string
vector<double> data;       // Stores values of type double
```

I chose the vector container as the example because it is probably used the most often. The first statement creates the container class, `strings`, that stores objects of type `string` while the second statement creates the `data` that stores values of type `double`.

You can store items of a fundamental type or of any class type in a container. If your type argument for an STL container template is a class type, the container can store objects of that type, or objects of any derived class type. Typically, containers store copies of the objects that you store in them and they allocate and manage the memory that the objects occupy automatically. When a container object is destroyed, the container takes care of deleting the objects it contains and freeing the memory they occupied. One advantage of using STL containers to store your objects is that it relieves you of the chore of managing the memory for them.

The templates for the STL container classes are defined in the standard headers shown in the following table.

Header File	Contents
`<vector>`	A `vector<T>` container represents an array that can increase in capacity automatically when required. You can only add new elements to the end of a vector container.
`<deque>`	A `deque<T>` container implements a double-ended queue. This is equivalent to a vector but with the additional capability for you to add elements to the beginning.
`<list>`	A `list<T>` container is a doubly-linked list.
`<map>`	A `map<K, T>` is an associative container that stores each object (of type T) with an associated key (of type K) that determines where the key/object pair is located. The value of each key in a map must be unique. This header also defines the `multimap<K,T>` container where the keys in the key/object pairs do not need to be unique.

Header File	Contents
<set>	A set<T> container is a map where each object serves as its own key. All objects in a set must be unique. A consequence of using an object as its own key is that you cannot change an object in a set; to change an object you must delete it and then insert the modified version. This header also defines the multiset<T> container, which is like a set container except that the entries do not need to be unique.
<bitset>	Defines the bitset<T> class template that represents a fixed number of bits. This is used typically to store flags that represent a set of states or conditions.

The containers in this table represent the complete set that is available with the STL and all the template names are defined within the std namespace. T is the template type parameter for the type of elements stored in a container and where keys are used, K is the type of key.

Microsoft Visual C++ also includes the headers <hash_map> and <hash_set> that define templates for the hash_map<K, T> and hash_set<K, T> containers. These are non-standard variations on the map<K, T> and set<K, T> containers and because they are not standard they are defined in the stdext namespace rather than std. The standard map and set containers use an ordering mechanism to locate entries whereas the non-standard hash_map and hash_set containers use a hashing mechanism.

Container Adapters

The STL also defines **container adapters**. A container adapter is a template class that wraps an existing STL container class to provide a different, and typically more restricted, capability. The container adapters are defined in the headers in the following table.

Header File	Contents
<queue>	A queue<T> container is defined by an adapter from a deque<T> container by default, but you could define it using a list<T> container. You can only access the first and last elements in a queue and you can only add elements at the back and remove them from the front. Thus a queue<T> container works more or less like the queue in your local coffee shop. This header also defines a priority_queue<T> container, which is a queue that orders the elements it contains so the largest element is always at the front. Only the element at the front can be accessed or removed. A priority queue is defined by an adapter from a vector<T> by default, but you could use a deque<T> as the base container.
<stack>	A stack container is defined by an adapter from a deque<T> container by default, but you could define it using a vector<T> or a list<T> container. A stack is a last-in first-out container so adding or removing elements always occurs at the top and you can only access the top element.

Iterators

Iterators are objects that behave like pointers and are very important for accessing the contents of all STL containers except for those defined by a container adapter; container adapters do not support iterators. You can obtain an iterator from a container that you can use to access the objects that you have previously stored. You can also create iterators that will allow input and output of objects or data items of a given type from or to a native C++ stream. Although basically all iterators behave like pointers, not all iterators provide the same functionality. However, they do share a base level of capability. Given two iterators, `iter1` and `iter2`, accessing the same set of objects, the comparison operations `iter1 == iter2`, `iter1 != iter2`, and the assignment `iter1 = iter2` are always possible, regardless of the types of `iter1` and `iter2`.

There are four different categories of iterators and each category supports a different range of operations, as shown in the following table. The operations described for each category are in addition to the three operations that I mentioned in the previous paragraph.

Iterator Category	Description

Input and output iterators	These iterators read or write a sequence of objects and may only be used once. To read or write a second time you must obtain a new iterator. You can perform the following operations on these iterators:
	`++iter` or `iter++`
	`*iter`
	For the dereferencing operation, only read access is allowed in the case of an input iterator and only write access for an output iterator.

Forward iterators	Forward iterators incorporate the capabilities of both input and output iterators so you can apply the operations shown above to them and you can use them for access and store operations. Forward iterators can also be reused to traverse a set of objects in a forward direction as many times as you want.
Bidirectional iterators	Bidirectional iterators provide the same capabilities as forward iterators and additionally allow the operations `--iter` and `iter--`. This means you can traverse backward through a sequence of objects as well as forward.

Random access iterators	Random access iterators have the same capabilities as bidirectional iterators but also allow the following operations:
	`iter+n` or `iter-n`
	`iter += n` or `iter -= n`
	`iter1 - iter2`
	`iter1 < iter2` or `iter1 > iter2`
	`iter1 <= iter2` or `iter1 >= iter2`
	`iter[n]`
	Being able to increment or decrement an iterator by an arbitrary value n allows random access to the set of objects. The last operation using the `[]` operator is equivalent to `*(iter + n)`.

Thus iterators in the four successive categories provide a progressively greater range of functionality. Where an algorithm requires an iterator with a given level of functionality, you can use any iterator that provides the required level of capability. For example, if a forward iterator is required, you must use at least a forward iterator; an input or an output operator will not do. On the other hand you could also use a bidirectional iterator or a random access iterator because they both have the capability provided by a forward iterator.

Note that when you obtain an iterator to access the contents of a container, the kind of iterator you get will depend on the sort of container you are using.

Algorithms

Algorithms are STL function templates that operate on a set of objects that are provided to them by an iterator. Because the objects are supplied by an iterator, the algorithm needs no knowledge of the source of the objects to be processed. The objects could be retrieved by the iterator from a container or even from a stream. Because iterators work like pointers, all STL template functions that accept an iterator as an argument will work equally well with a regular pointer.

As you'll see, you will frequently use containers, iterators, and algorithms in concert in the manner illustrated in Figure 10-1.

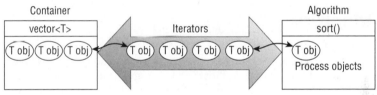

Figure 10-1

When you apply an algorithm to the contents of a container, you supply iterators that point to objects within the container. The algorithm uses these iterators to access objects within the container and to write them back when this is appropriate. For example, when you apply the sort() algorithm to the contents of a vector, you pass two iterators to the sort() function. One points to the first object, and the other points to the position that is one past the last element in the vector. The sort() function uses these iterators to access objects for comparison and to write the objects back to the container to establish the ordering. You see this working in an example later in this chapter.

Algorithms are defined in two standard header files, the <algorithm> header and the <numeric> header.

Function Objects

Function objects are objects of a class type that overloads the () operator, which means that the class implements the operator()() function. Function object types are defined in the STL as templates so you can create a function object where the overloaded () operator function works with your object type.

For example, the STL defines the template `less<T>`. If you instantiate the template as `less<myClass>` you have a type for function objects that implement `operator()()` to provide the less-than comparison for objects of type `myClass`.

Many algorithms make use of function objects to specify binary operations to be carried out, or to specify **predicates** that determine how or whether a particular operation is to be carried out. A predicate is a function that returns a value of type `bool` and because a function object is an object of a type that implements the `operator()()` member function to return a value of type `bool`, a function object is also a predicate. For example, suppose you have defined a class type `Comp` that implements the `operator()()` function to compare its two arguments and return a `bool` value. If you create an object `f` of type `Comp`, the expression `f(a,b)` returns a `bool` value that results from comparing a and b, and thus acts as a predicate.

Predicates come in two flavors, **binary predicates** that involve two operands, and **unary predicates** that require one operand. For example, comparisons such as less-than and equal-to and logical operations such as AND and OR are implemented as binary predicates that are members of function objects; logical negation, NOT, is implemented as a unary predicate member of a function object.

Function object templates are defined in the `<functional>` header and you can also define your own function objects when necessary. You'll see function objects in action with algorithms and some container class functions in this chapter.

Function Adapters

Function adapters are function templates the allow function objects to be combined to produce a more complex function object. A simple example is the `not1` function adapter. This takes an existing function object that provides a unary predicate and inverts it, so if the function object function returns `true`, the function that results from applying `not1` to it will be `false`. I won't be discussing function adapters in depth, not because they are terribly difficult to understand — they aren't; it's just that there's a limit to how much I can cram into a single chapter.

The Range of STL Containers

The STL provides templates for a variety of container classes that you can use in a wide range application contexts. **Sequence containers** are containers in which you store objects of a given type in a linear fashion, either as a dynamic array or as a list. **Associative containers** store objects based on a key that you supply with each object to be stored and the key is used to locate the object within the container. In a typical application you might be storing phone numbers in an associative container using names as the keys. This would enable you to retrieve a particular number from the container just by supplying the appropriate name.

I'll first introduce you to sequence containers, and then I'll delve into associative containers and what you can do with them.

Sequence Containers

The class templates for the three basic sequence containers are shown in the following table.

Template	Header File	Description
vector<T>	<vector>	Creates a class representing a dynamic array storing objects of type T
list<T>	<list>	Creates a class representing a linked list storing objects of type T
deque<T>	<deque>	Creates a class representing a double-ended queue storing objects of type T

Which template you choose to use in any particular instance will depend on the application. These three kinds of sequence containers are clearly differentiated by the operations they can perform efficiently, as Figure 10-2 shows.

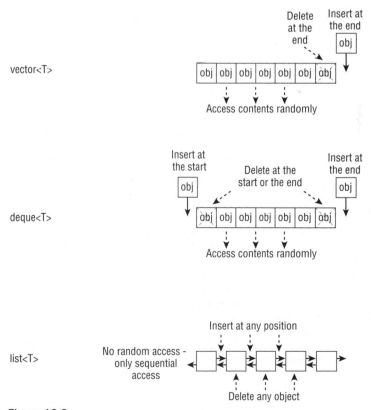

Figure 10-2

If you need random access to the contents of the container and you are happy to always add or delete objects at the end of a sequence, then vector<T> is the container template to choose. It is possible to add or delete objects randomly within a vector but the process will be very slow because all the objects past the insertion or deletion point will have to be moved. A deque<T> container is very similar to a vector<T> and supports the same operations, but it has the additional capability to add and delete at the beginning of the sequence. A list<T> container is a doubly-linked list, so adding and deleting at any position is efficient. The downside of a list is that there is no random access to the contents; the only way to access an object that is internal to the list is to traverse the contents from the beginning, or to run backward through the contents from the end.

Let's look at sequence containers in more detail and try some examples. I'll be introducing the use of some iterators, algorithms, and function objects along the way.

Creating Vector Containers

The simplest way to create a vector container is like this:

```
vector<int> mydata;
```

This creates a container that will store values of type int. The initial capacity to store elements is zero, so you will be allocating more memory right from the outset when you insert the first value. The push_back() function adds a new element to the end of a vector so to store a value in this vector you would write:

```
mydata.push_back(99);
```

The argument to the push_back() function is the item to be stored. This statement stores the value 99 in the vector so after executing this statement the vector contains one element.

Here's another way to create a vector to store integers:

```
vector<int> mydata(100);
```

This creates a vector that contains 100 elements that are all initialized to 0. If you add new elements to this vector, the memory allocated for storage in the vector will be increased automatically, so obviously it's a good idea to choose a reasonably accurate value for the number of integers you are likely to want to store. This vector already contains 100 elements and you can use it just like an array. For example, to store a value in the third element you can write:

```
mydata[2] = 999;
```

Of course, you can only use an index value to access elements within a vector that is within the range of elements that exist. You can't add new elements in this way though. To add a new element, you should use the push_back() function.

You can initialize the elements in a vector to a different value when you create it by using this statement:

```
vector<int> mydata(100, -1);
```

The second argument to the constructor is the initial value to be used, so all 100 elements in the vector will be set to -1.

If you don't want to create elements when you create the container, you can increase the capacity after you create it by calling its `reserve()` function:

```
vector<int> mydata;
mydata.reserve(100);
```

The argument to the `reserve()` function is the minimum number of elements to be accommodated. If the argument is less than the current capacity of the vector, then calling `reserve()` will have no effect. In this code fragment, calling `reserve()` causes the vector container to allocate sufficient memory for a total of 100 elements.

You can also create a vector with initial values for elements from an external array. For example:

```
double data[] = {1.5, 2.5, 3.5, 4.5, 5.5, 6.5, 7.5, 8.5, 9.5, 10.5};
vector<double> mydata(data, data+8);
```

Here the `data` array is created with 10 elements of type `double` with the initial values shown. The second statement creates a vector storing elements of type `double` with eight elements initially having the values corresponding to `data[0]` through `data[7]`. The arguments to the `vector<double>` constructor are pointers (and can also be iterators), where the first pointer points to the first initializing element in the array and the second points to one past the last initializing element. Thus the `mydata` vector will contain eight elements with initial values 1.5, 2.5, 3.5, 4.5, 5.5, 6.5, 7.5, and 8.5.

Because the constructor in the previous fragment can accept either pointer or iterator arguments, you can initialize a vector when you create it with values from another vector that contains elements of the same type. You just supply the constructor with an iterator pointing to the first element you want to use as an initializer, plus a second iterator pointing to one past the last element you want to use. Here's an example:

```
vector<double> values(mydata.begin(), mydata.end());
```

After executing this statement, the `values` vector will have elements that are duplicates of the `mydata` vector. As Figure 10-3 illustrates, the `begin()` function returns a random access iterator that points to the first element in the vector for which it is called and the `end()` function returns a random access iterator pointing to one past the last element. A sequence of elements is typically specified in the STL by two iterators, one pointing to the first element in the sequence and the other pointing to one past the last element in the sequence, so you'll see this time and time again.

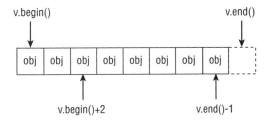

Iterators for a vector v

Figure 10-3

Because the `begin()` and `end()` functions for a vector container return random access iterators, you can modify what they point to when you use them. The type of the iterators that the `begin()` and `end()` function return is `vector<T>::iterator`, where `T` is the type of object stored in the vector.

Here's a statement that creates a vector that is initialized with the third through the seventh elements from the `mydata` vector:

```
vector<double> values(mydata.begin()+2, mydata.end()-1);
```

Adding 2 to the first iterator makes it point to the third element in `mydata`. Subtracting 1 from the second iterator makes it point to the last element in `mydata`; remember the second argument to the constructor is an iterator that points to a position that is *one past* the element to be used as the last initializer, so the object that the second iterator points to is not included in the set.

As I said earlier, it is pretty much standard practice in the STL to indicate a sequence of elements in a container by a begin iterator that points to the first element and an end iterator that points to one past the last element. This method allows you to iterate over all the elements in the sequence by incrementing the begin iterator until it equals the end iterator. This means that the iterators only need to support the equality operator to allow you to walk through the sequence.

Occasionally you may want to access the contents of a vector in reverse order. Calling the `rbegin()` function for a vector returns an iterator that points to the last element, and `rend()` points to one past the first element(that is, the position preceding the first element), as Figure 10-4 illustrates.

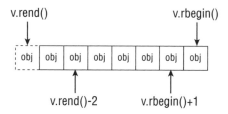

Reverse Iterators for a vector v

Figure 10-4

The iterators returned by `rbegin()` and `rend()` are called **reverse iterators** because they present the elements in reverse sequence. Reverse iterators are of type `vector<T>::reverse_iterator`. Figure 10-4 shows how adding a positive integer to the `rbegin()` iterator moves back through the sequence and subtracting an integer from `rend()` moves forward through the sequence.

Here's how you could create a vector containing the contents of another vector in reverse order:

```
double data[] = {1.5, 2.5, 3.5, 4.5, 5.5, 6.5, 7.5, 8.5, 9.5, 10.5};
vector<double> mydata(data, data+8);
vector<double> values(mydata.rbegin(), mydata.rend());
```

Because you are using reverse iterators as arguments to the constructor in the last statement, the `values` vector will contain the elements from `mydata` in reverse order.

The Capacity and Size of a Vector Container

It's about time I explained the difference between the *capacity* and the *size* of a vector container. The **capacity** is the maximum number of objects a container can accommodate currently without allocating more memory. The **size** is the number of objects actually stored in the container so the size cannot be greater than the capacity.

You can obtain both the size and capacity of a container, `data`, at any time by calling the `size()` and `capacity()` member functions. For example:

```
cout << endl << "The current capacity of the container is: " << data.capacity()
     << endl << "The current size of the container is: " << data.size() << endl;
```

Calling the `capacity()` function for a vector returns the current capacity and calling its `size()` function returns the current size, both values being returned as type `vector<T>::size_type`, which is an implementation-defined integer type that is defined within the `vector<T>` class template by a `typedef`. To create a variable to store the value returned from the `size()` or `capacity()` function you specify it to be of type `vector<T>::size_type`, where you replace `T` by the type of object stored in the container. The following fragment illustrates this:

```
vector<double> values;
vector<double>::size_type cap = values.capacity();
```

> *The Microsoft Visual C++ library implementation of STL defines the* `vector<T>::size_type` *type as* `size_t`. `size_t` *is an unsigned integer type that is also a type of the result of the* `sizeof` *operator and the value returned by the* `new` *operator.*

If the value returned by the `size()` function is zero, then clearly the vector contains no elements; thus you can use this as a test for an empty vector. You can also call the `empty()` function for a vector to test for this:

```
if(values.empty())
   cout << "No more elements in the vector."
```

The `empty()` function returns a value of type `bool` that is `true` when the vector is empty and `false` otherwise.

You are unlikely to need it very often but you can discover the maximum possible number of elements in a vector by calling its `max_size()` function. For example:

```
vector<string> strings;
cout << "Maximum length of strings vector: " << strings.max_size();
```

Executing this fragment produces the output:

```
Maximum length of strings vector: 153391689
```

The maximum length is returned by the `max_size()` function as a value in this case of type `vector<string>::size_type`. Note that the maximum length of a vector will depend on the type of element stored in the vector. If you try this out with a vector storing values of type `int`, you will get 1073741823 as the maximum length, and for a vector storing value of type `double` it is 536870911.

You can change the size of a vector by calling its `resize()` function, which can either increase or decrease the size of the vector. If you specify a new size that is less than the current size, sufficient elements will be deleted from the end of the vector to reduce it to its new size. If the new size is greater than the old, new elements will be added to the end of the vector to increase its length to the new size. Here's code illustrating this:

```
vector<int> values(5, 66);    // Contains 66 66 66 66 66
values.resize(7, 88);         // Contains 66 66 66 66 66 88 88
values.resize(10);            // Contains 66 66 66 66 66 88 88 0 0
values.resize(4);             // Contains 66 66 66 66
```

The first argument to `resize()` is the new size for the vector. The second argument, when it is present, is the value to be used for new elements that need to be added to make up the new size. If you are increasing the size and you don't specify a value to be used for new elements, the default value will be used. In the case of a vector storing objects of a class type, the default value will be the object produced by the no-arg constructor for the class.

You could explore the size and capacity of a vector through a working example.

Try It Out   Exploring the Size and Capacity of a Vector

In this example you will try out some of the ways you have seen for creating a vector, and you'll also see how the capacity changes as you add elements.

```cpp
// Ex10-01.cpp
// Exploring the size and capacity of a vector

#include <iostream>
#include <vector>
using std::cout;
using std::endl;
using std::vector;

// Template function to display the size and capacity of any vector
template<class T>
void listInfo(vector<T> &v)
{
  cout << "Container capacity: " << v.capacity()
       << " size: " << v.size() << endl;
}

int main()
{
  // Basic vector creation
  vector<double> data;
  listInfo(data);

  cout << endl << "After calling reserve(100):" << endl;
  data.reserve(100);
  listInfo(data);

  // Create a vector with 10 elements and initialize it
  vector<int> numbers(10,-1);
  cout << endl << "The initial values are:";
```

```
      for(vector<int>::size_type i = 0; i<numbers.size(); i++)
        cout << " " << numbers[i];

      // See how adding elements affects capacity increments
      vector<int>::size_type oldC = numbers.capacity();   // Old capacity
      vector<int>::size_type newC = oldC;                 // New capacity after adding element
      cout << endl << endl;
      listInfo(numbers);
      for(int i = 0; i<1000 ; i++)
      {
        numbers.push_back(2*i);
        newC = numbers.capacity();
        if(oldC < newC)
        {
          oldC = newC;
          listInfo(numbers);
        }
      }
      return 0;
    }
```

This example produces the following output:

```
Container capacity: 0 size: 0

After calling reserve(100):
Container capacity: 100 size: 0

The initial values are: -1 -1 -1 -1 -1 -1 -1 -1 -1 -1

Container capacity: 10 size: 10
Container capacity: 15 size: 11
Container capacity: 22 size: 16
Container capacity: 33 size: 23
Container capacity: 49 size: 34
Container capacity: 73 size: 50
Container capacity: 109 size: 74
Container capacity: 163 size: 110
Container capacity: 244 size: 164
Container capacity: 366 size: 245
Container capacity: 549 size: 367
Container capacity: 823 size: 550
Container capacity: 1234 size: 824
```

How It Works

The #include directive for the <vector> header adds the definition for the vector<T> template to the source file.

Following the using statement for the std namespace, you have a definition of the listInfo() function template:

```
template<class T>
void listInfo(vector<T> &v)
{
```

```
cout << "Container capacity: " << v.capacity()
     << " size: " << v.size() << endl;
}
```

This function outputs the current capacity and size of any vector container. You will often find it is convenient to write function templates when working with STL. The example shows how easy it is. The T parameter determines the type of argument the function expects. You can call this function with a vector container as the argument. Specifying the parameter as the reference type, vector<T>&, enables the code in the function body to access directly the container you pass as the argument to the function. If you specified the parameter as type vector<T>, then the argument would be copied each time the function is called and this could be a time-consuming process with a large vector container.

The first action in main() is to create a vector and output its size and capacity:

```
vector<double> data;
listInfo(data);
```

You can see from the output that the size and the capacity are zero for this container. Adding an element requires more space to be allocated.

Next you call the reserve() function for the container:

```
data.reserve(100);
```

You can see from the output that the capacity is now 100 and the size is zero. To put it another way, the container contains no elements but has memory allocated to accommodate up to 100 elements. Only when you add the 101st element will the capacity be increased automatically.

Next you create another container with this statement:

```
vector<int> numbers(10,-1);
```

This creates a container that contains 10 elements at the outset, each initialized with -1. To demonstrate this is indeed the case, you output the elements in the container with the following loop:

```
for(vector<int>::size_type i = 0; i<numbers.size(); i++)
  cout << " " << numbers[i];
```

The upper limit for the loop variable, i, is the value returned by the size() function for the container, the number of elements currently stored. As you see, within the loop you access the container elements in the same way as an ordinary array.

You could also use an iterator to access the elements. A loop to output the elements using an iterator looks like this:

```
for(vector<int>::iterator iter = numbers.begin(); iter < numbers.end(); iter++)
  cout << " " << *iter;
```

The loop variable is an iterator, iter, that you initialize to the iterator returned by the begin() function. This is incremented on each loop iteration and the loop ends when it reaches numbers.end(), which points to one past the last element. Note how you dereference the iterator just like a pointer to get at the value of the element.

The remaining statements in `main()` demonstrate how the capacity of a vector is increased as you add elements. The first two statements set up variables that store the current capacity and the new capacity after adding an element:

```
vector<int>::size_type oldC = numbers.capacity();    // Old capacity
vector<int>::size_type newC = oldC;                  // New capacity after adding element
```

After displaying the initial size and capacity, you execute the following loop:

```
for(int i = 0; i<1000 ; i++)
{
  numbers.push_back(2*i);
  newC = numbers.capacity();
  if(oldC < newC)
  {
    oldC = newC;
    listInfo(numbers);
  }
}
```

This loop calls the `push_back()` function for the `numbers` vector to add 1000 elements. We are only interested in seeing output when the capacity increases, so the `if` condition ensures that we only display the capacity and size when the capacity increases.

The output shows an interesting pattern in the way additional space is allocated in the container. As you would expect with the initial size and capacity at 10, the first capacity increase occurs when you add the 11th element. The increase in this case is half the capacity so the capacity increases to 15. The next capacity increase is when the size reaches 15 and the increase is to 22 so the increment is again half the capacity. This process continues with each capacity increase being half the current capacity. Thus you automatically get larger chunks of memory space allocated when required, the more elements the vector contains. On the one hand this mechanism ensures that once the initial memory allocation in a container is occupied, you don't cause more memory to be allocated every time you add a new element. On the other hand, this also implies that you should take care when reserving space for a large number of elements in a vector. If you set up a container that provides initially for 100,000 elements for example, exceeding this by one element will cause space for another 50,000 to be allocated. In this sort of situation you could check for reaching the capacity, and use `reserve()` to increase the available memory by a more appropriate and less extravagant amount.

Accessing the Elements in a Vector

You have already seen that you can access the elements in a vector by using the subscript operator, just as you would for an array. You can also use the `at()` function where the argument is the index position of the element you want to access. Here's how you could list the contents of the `numbers` vector of integer elements in the previous example:

```
for(vector<int>::size_type i = 0; i<numbers.size(); i++)
  cout << " " << numbers.at(i);
```

So how does the `at()` function differ from using the subscript operator, `[]`? Well, if you use a subscript with the subscript operator that is outside the valid range, the result is undefined. If you do the same with the `at()` function then an exception of type `out_of_range` will be thrown. If there's the potential for subscript values outside the legal range to arise in a program, it's generally better to use the `at()` function and catch the exception than allow the possibility for undefined results.

To access the first or last element in a vector container you can call the `front()` or `back()` function respectively:

```
cout << "The value of the first element is: " << numbers.front() << endl;
cout << "The value of the last element is: " << numbers.back() << endl;
```

Both functions come in two versions; one returns a reference to the object stored and the other returns a `const` reference to the object stored. The latter option enables you to explicitly prevent modification of the object:

```
const int& firstvalue = numbers.front();    // firstvalue cannot be changed
int& lastvalue = numbers.back();            // lastvalue can be changed
```

Storing the reference that is returned in a `const` variable automatically selects the version of the function that returns a `const` reference.

Inserting and Deleting Elements in a Vector

In addition to the `push_back()` function you have seen, a vector container supports the `pop_back()` operation that deletes the last element. Both operations execute in **constant time**, that is, the time to execute will be the same, regardless of the number of elements in the vector. The `pop_back()` function is very simple to use:

```
vec.pop_back();
```

This statement removes the last element from the vector, `vec`, and reduces the size by 1. If the vector contains no elements, then calling `pop_back()` has no effect.

You could remove all the elements in a vector by calling the `pop_back()` function repeatedly, but the `clear()` function does this much more simply:

```
vec.clear();
```

This statement removes all the elements from `vec` so the size will be zero. Of course, the capacity will be left unchanged.

You can call the `insert()` function to insert one or more new elements anywhere in a vector but this operation will execute in **linear time**, which means that the time will increase in proportion to the number of elements in the container. This is because inserting new elements involves moving the existing elements. The simplest version of the `insert()` function inserts a single new element at a specific position in the vector, where the first argument is an iterator specifying the position where the element is to be inserted and the second argument is the element to be inserted. For example:

```
vector<int> vec(5, 99);
vec.insert(vec.begin()+1, 88);
```

The first statement creates a vector with five integer elements all initialized to 99. The second statement inserts 88 after the first element so after executing this, the vector will contain:

```
99 88 99 99 99 99
```

You can also insert several identical elements, starting from a given position:

```
vec.insert(vec.begin()+2, 3, 77);
```

The first argument is an iterator specifying the position where the first element is to be inserted, the second argument is the number of elements to be inserted, and the third argument is the element to be inserted. After executing this statement, vec will contain:

```
99 88 77 77 77 99 99 99 99
```

You have yet another version of the insert() function that inserts a sequence of elements at a given position. The first argument is an iterator pointing to the position where the first element is to be inserted. The second and third arguments are input iterators specifying the range of elements to be inserted from some source. Here's an example:

```
vector<int> newvec(5, 22);
newvec.insert(newvec.begin()+1, vec.begin()+1, vec.begin()+5);
```

The first statement creates a vector with five integer elements initialized to 22. The second statement inserts four elements from vec starting with the second. After executing these statements, newvec will contain:

```
22 88 77 77 77 22 22 22 22
```

Don't forget that the second iterator in the interval specifies the position that is *one past* the last element, so the element it points to is not included.

The erase() function can delete one or more elements from any position within a vector, but this also is a linear time function and will typically be slow. Here's how you erase a single element at a given position:

```
newvec.erase(newvec.end()-2);
```

The argument is an iterator that points to the element to be erased, so this statement removes the second to last element from newvec.

To delete several elements, you supply two iterator arguments specifying the interval. For example:

```
newvec.erase(newvec.begin()+1, newvec.begin()+4);
```

This will delete the second, third, and fourth elements from newvec. The element that the second iterator argument points to is not included in the operation.

As I said, both the erase() and insert() operations are slow so you should use them sparingly when working with a vector. If you find you need to use them often in your application, a list<T> is likely to be a better choice of container.

The swap() function enables you to swap the contents of two vectors, provided of course the elements in the two vectors are of the same type. Here's a code fragment showing an example of how this works:

```
vector<int> first(5, 77);        // Contains 77 77 77 77 77
vector<int> second(8, -1);       // Contains -1 -1 -1 -1 -1 -1 -1 -1
first.swap(second);
```

After executing the last statement, the contents of the vectors first and second will have interchanged. Note that the capacities of the vectors are swapped as well as the contents and of course the size.

The assign() function enables you to replace the entire contents of a vector with another sequence, or to replace the contents with a given number of instances of an object. Here's how you could replace the contents of one vector with a sequence from another:

```
vector<double> values;
for(int i = 1 ; i <= 50 ; i++)
  values.push_back(2.5*i);
vector<double> newdata(5, 3.5);
newdata.assign(values.begin()+1, values.end()-1);
```

This code fragment creates the values vector and stores 50 elements that have the values 2.5, 5.0, 7.5,... 125.0. The newdata vector is created with five elements each having the value 3.5. The last statement calls the assign() function for newdata, which deletes all elements from newdata and then inserts copies of all the elements from values, except for the first and the last. You specify the new sequence to be inserted by two iterators, the first pointing to the first element to be inserted and the second pointing to one past the last element to be inserted. Because you specify the new elements to be inserted by two iterators, the source of the data can be from any sequence, not just a vector. The assign() function will also work with regular pointers so you could also insert elements from an array of double elements.

Here's how you use the assign() function to replace the contents of a vector with a sequence of instances of the same element:

```
newdata.assign(30, 99.5);
```

The first argument is the count of elements in the replacement sequence and the second argument is the element to be used. This statement will cause the contents of newdata to be deleted and replaced by 30 elements each having the value 99.5.

Storing Class Objects in a Vector

So far you have only seen vectors storing numerical values. You can store objects of any class type in a vector but the class must meet certain minimum criteria. Here's a minimum specification for a given class T to be compatible with a vector, or in fact any sequence container:

```
class T
{
  public:
  T();                           // default constructor
  T(const T& t);                 // Copy constructor
  ~T();                          // Destructor
  T& operator=(const T& t);      // Assignment operator
};
```

Of course, the compiler will supply default versions of these class members if you don't supply them so it's not difficult for a class to meet these requirements. The important thing to note is that they are required and are likely to be used, so when the default implementation that the compiler supplies will not suffice, you must provide your own implementation.

Let's try an example.

Try It Out   Storing Objects in a Vector

In this example you create `Person` objects that represent individuals by their name. Just to make it more interesting, I'm going to assume you have never heard of the `string` class, so you are stuck with using null-terminated strings to store names. This means you have to take care how you implement the class if you want to store objects in a `vector<Person>` container. In general such a class might have lots of different data members relating to a person, but I'll keep it simple with just their first and second names.

Here's the definition of the `Person` class:

```
// Person.h
// A class defining people by their names
#pragma once
#include <cstring>
#include <iostream>
using std::cout;
using std::endl;

class Person
{
  public:
  // Constructor, includes no-arg constructor
  Person(char* first = "John", char* second = "Doe")
  {
    size_t length = strlen(first)+1;
    firstname = new char[length];
    strcpy_s(firstname, length, first);
    length = strlen(second)+1;
    secondname = new char[length];
    strcpy_s(secondname, length, second);
  }

  // Copy constructor
  Person(const Person& p)
  {
    size_t length = strlen(p.firstname)+1;
    firstname = new char[length];
    strcpy_s(firstname, length, p.firstname);
    length = strlen(p.secondname)+1;
   secondname = new char[length];
    strcpy_s(secondname, length, p.secondname);
  }

  // Destructor
  ~Person()
  {
    delete[] firstname;
```

```
      delete[] secondname;
    }

    // Assignment operator
    Person& operator=(const Person& p)
    {
      // Deal with p = p assignment situation
      if(&p == this)
        return *this;

      delete[] firstname;
      delete[] secondname;
      size_t length = strlen(p.firstname)+1;
      firstname = new char[length];
      strcpy_s(firstname, length, p.firstname);
      length = strlen(p.secondname)+1;
      secondname = new char[length];
      strcpy_s(secondname, length, p.secondname);
      return *this;
    }

    // Less-than operator
    bool operator<(const Person& p) const
    {
      int result = strcmp(secondname, p.secondname);
      if(result < 0 || result ==  0 && strcmp(firstname, p.firstname) < 0)
        return true;
      return false;
    }

    // Output a person
    void showPerson() const
    {
      cout << firstname << " " << secondname << endl;
    }

    private:
    char* firstname;
    char* secondname;
};
```

The #pragma once directive is there to ensure that the header does not get included more than once into a program. Because the Person class allocates memory dynamically to store the first and second names of a person, you must implement the destructor to release the memory when an object is destroyed. You must also implement the assignment operator because this involves more memory allocation. Note the code at the beginning for dealing with the a = a assignment situation. Assigning an object to itself can arise in ways that are less than obvious, and can cause problems if you don't implement the operator=() function to take account of this.

The showPerson() function is a convenience function for outputting an entire name. It is declared as const to allow it to work with const and non-const Person objects. The operator<() function is there for use later.

The program to store `Person` objects in a vector looks like this:

```cpp
// Ex10-02.cpp
// Storing objects in a vector

#include <iostream>
#include <vector>
#include "Person.h"

using std::cin;
using std::cout;
using std::endl;
using std::vector;

int main()
{
  vector<Person> people;                      // Vector of Person objects
  const size_t maxlength = 50;
  char firstname[maxlength];
  char secondname[maxlength];

  // Input all the people
  while(true)
  {
    cout << "Enter a first name or press Enter to end: ";
    cin.getline(firstname, maxlength, '\n');
    if(strlen(firstname) == 0)
      break;
    cout << "Enter the second name: ";
    cin.getline(secondname, maxlength, '\n');
    people.push_back(Person(firstname, secondname));
  }

  // Output the contents of the vector
  cout << endl;
  vector<Person>::iterator iter = people.begin();
  while(iter != people.end())
    iter++->showPerson();

  return 0;
}
```

Here's an example of some output from this program:

```
Enter a first name or press Enter to end: Jane
Enter the second name: Fonda
Enter a first name or press Enter to end: Bill
Enter the second name: Cosby
Enter a first name or press Enter to end: Sally
Enter the second name: Field
Enter a first name or press Enter to end: Mae
Enter the second name: West
Enter a first name or press Enter to end: Oliver
```

```
Enter the second name: Hardy
Enter a first name or press Enter to end:

Jane Fonda
Bill Cosby
Sally Field
Mae West
Oliver Hardy
```

How It Works

You create a vector to store `Person` objects like this:

```
vector<Person> people;                   // Vector of Person objects
```

You then create two arrays of type `char[]` that you'll use as working storage when reading names from the standard input stream:

```
const size_t maxlength = 50;
char firstname[maxlength];
char secondname[maxlength];
```

Each array accommodates a name up to `maxlength` characters long, including the terminating null.

You read names from the standard input stream in an indefinite loop:

```
while(true)
{
  cout << "Enter a first name or press Enter to end: ";
  cin.getline(firstname, maxlength, '\n');
  if(strlen(firstname) == 0)
    break;
  cout << "Enter the second name: ";
  cin.getline(secondname, maxlength, '\n');
  people.push_back(Person(firstname, secondname));
}
```

You read each name using the `getline()` member function for `cin`. This reads characters until a new-line character is read, or until `maxlength-1` characters have been read. This ensures that you don't over-run the capacity of the input array because both arrays have `maxlength` elements, allowing for strings up to `maxlength-1` characters plus the terminating `NULL`. When an empty string is entered for the first name, the loop ends.

You create the `Person` object in the expression that is the argument to the `push_back()` function. This adds the objects to the end of the vector.

The last step is to output the contents of the vector:

```
cout << endl;
vector<Person>::iterator iter = people.begin();
while(iter != people.end())
  iter++->showPerson();
```

Here you use an iterator to output the elements of the vector. Within the body of the `while` loop, you output the element that the iterator points to and then you increment the iterator using the postfix increment operator. The loop continues as long as `iter` is not equal to the iterator returned by `end()`.

Sorting Vector Elements

The `sort()` function template that is defined in the `<algorithm>` header will sort a sequence of objects identified by two random access iterators that point the first and one past the last objects in the sequence. Note that random access iterators are essential; iterators with lesser capability will not suffice. The `sort()` function template uses the `<` operator to order the elements. Thus you can use the `sort()` template to sort the contents of any container that provides random access iterators as long as the objects it contains can be compared using the less-than operator.

In the previous example you implemented `operator<()` in the `Person` class, so you can sort a sequence of `Person` objects. Here's how you could sort the contents of the `vector<Person>` container:

```
sort(people.begin(), people.end());
```

This sorts the contents of the vector in ascending sequence. You can add an `#include` directive for `<algorithm>` and put the statement in `main()` before the output loop to see the sort in action. You'll also need a `using` declaration for `std::sort`.

Note that you can use the `sort()` template function to `sort()` arrays. The only requirement is that the `<` operator should work with the type of elements stored in the array. Here's a code fragment showing how you could use it to sort an array of integers:

```
const size_t max = 100;
int data[max];
cout << "Enter up to " << max << " non-zero integers. Enter 0 to end." << endl;
int value = 0;
size_t count = 0;
for(size_t i = 0 ; i<max ; i++)          // Read up to max integers
{
  cin >> value;                          // Read a value
  if(value == 0)                         // If it is zero,
    break;                               // We are done
  data[count++] = value;
}
sort(data, data+count);                  // Sort the integers
```

Note how the pointer marking the end of the sequence of elements that are to be sorted must still be one past the last element.

When you need to sort a sequence in descending order, you can use a version of the `sort()` algorithm that accepts a function object that is a binary predicate as the third argument to the function. The `<functional>` header defines a complete set of types for comparison predicates:

```
less<T>   less_equal<T>   equal<T>   greater_equal<T>   greater<T>
```

Each of these templates creates a class type for function objects that you can use with `sort()` and other algorithms. The `sort()` function used in the previous fragment uses a `less<int>` function object by default. To specify a different function object to be used as the sort criteria, you add it as a third argument, like this:

```
sort(data, data+count, greater<int>());       // Sort the integers
```

The expression that is the third argument to the function calls the constructor for the `greater<int>` type, so you are passing an object of this type to the `sort()` function. This statement will sort the contents of the `data` array in descending sequence. If you are trying these fragments out, don't forget that you need the `<functional>` header to be included for the function object and the greater name is defined in the `std` namespace.

Storing Pointers in a Vector

A vector container, like other containers, makes a copy of the objects you add to it. This has tremendous advantages in most circumstances but it could be very inconvenient in some situations. For example, if your objects are large, there could be considerable overhead in copying each object as you add it to the container. This is an occasion where you might be better off storing pointers to the objects in the container rather than the objects themselves, and managing the objects externally. You could create a new version of the `Ex10_02.cpp` example to store pointers to `Person` objects in a container.

Try It Out   Storing Pointers in a Vector

The `Person` class definition is exactly the same as before. Here's a revised version of the other source file:

```cpp
// Ex10_03.cpp
// Storing pointers to objects in a vector

#include <iostream>
#include <vector>
#include "Person.h"

using std::cin;
using std::cout;
using std::endl;
using std::vector;

int main()
{
  vector<Person*> people;                // Vector of Person objects
  const size_t maxlength = 50;
  char firstname[maxlength];
  char secondname[maxlength];
  while(true)
  {
    cout << "Enter a first name or press Enter to end: ";
    cin.getline(firstname, maxlength, '\n');
    if(strlen(firstname) == 0)
```

```
       break;
     cout << "Enter the second name: ";
     cin.getline(secondname, maxlength, '\n');
     people.push_back(new Person(firstname, secondname));
   }

   // Output the contents of the vector
   cout << endl;
   vector<Person*>::iterator iter = people.begin();
   while(iter != people.end())
     (*(iter++))->showPerson();

   // Release memory for the people
   iter = people.begin();
   while(iter != people.end())
     delete *(iter++);

   // Pointers in the vector are now invalid
   // so remove the contents
   people.clear();

   return 0;
 }
```

The output is essentially the same as before.

How It Works

Only the shaded lines of code have been changed. The first change is in the definition of the container:

```
    vector<Person*> people;                    // Vector of Person objects
```

The `vector<T>` template type parameter is now `Person*`, which is a pointer to a `Person` object.

Within the input loop, each `Person` object is now created on the heap and the address is passed to the `push_back()` function for the vector:

```
    people.push_back(new Person(firstname, secondname));
```

It is important to take care when storing addresses of objects in a container. If you create objects on the stack, these objects will be destroyed when the function exits and the pointers you have stored will be rendered invalid. With objects created on the heap using the `new` operator, the objects are only destroyed when you remove them using `delete`.

The iterator used to output the `Person` objects now has a different type:

```
    vector<Person*>::iterator iter = people.begin();
```

The way in which you output the `Person` object is also different:

```
    (*(iter++))->showPerson();
```

The iterator now points to a pointer, so you must dereference the iterator to get to the pointer and then use the pointer to call the `showPerson()` function for the `Person` object to produce the output. Note that the outer parentheses are essential because of operator precedence.

Because you created `Person` objects on the heap, you are responsible for deleting them:

```
iter = people.begin();
while(iter != people.end())
  delete *(iter++);
```

You obtain another random access iterator pointing to the first element in the vector and then use this in the loop to delete each of the `Person` objects. Of course, you have to dereference the iterator to get the address of the object to be deleted.

Finally, because all the objects have been deleted, the pointers in the vector are now not valid, so you empty the vector by calling its `clear()` function. This simply deletes everything stored in the container.

Double-Ended Queue Containers

The double-ended queue container template, `deque<T>`, is defined in the `<deque>` header. A double-ended queue container is very similar to a vector in that it can do everything a vector container can and includes the same function members, but you can also add and delete elements efficiently at the beginning of the sequence as well as at the end. You could replace the vector used in `Ex10_02.cpp` with a double-ended queue and it would work just as well:

```
deque<Person> people;              // Double-ended queue of Person objects
```

Of course, you would need to change the `#include` directive to include the `<deque>` header instead of `<vector>`.

The function to add an element to the front of the container is `push_front()` and you can delete the first element by calling the `pop_front()` function. Thus if you were using a `deque<Person>` container in `Ex10_02.cpp`, you could add elements at the front instead of the back:

```
people.push_front(Person(firstname, secondname));
```

The only difference in using this statement to add elements to the container would be that the order of the elements in the double-ended queue would be the reverse of what they would be in the vector.

The range of constructors available for a `deque<T>` container is the same as for `vector<T>`. Here are examples of each of them:

```
deque<string> strings;           // Create an empty container
deque<int> items(50);            // A container of 50 elements initialized to
default value
deque<double> values(5, 0.5);    // A container with 5 elements 0.5
deque<int> data(items.begin(), items.end());  // Initialized with a sequence
```

Although a double-ended queue is very similar to a vector and does everything a vector can do, as well as allowing you to add to the front of the sequence efficiently, it does have one disadvantage compared to a vector. Because of the additional capability it offers, the memory management for a double-ended queue is more complicated than for a vector, so it will be slightly slower. Unless you need the ability to add elements to the front of the container, a vector is a better choice. Let's see a double-ended queue in action.

Try It Out   Using a Double-Ended Queue

This example stores an arbitrary number of integers in a double-ended queue and then operates on them. Here's the code:

```cpp
// Ex10_04.cpp
// Using a double-ended queue

#include <iostream>
#include <deque>
#include <algorithm>
#include <numeric>

using std::cin;
using std::cout;
using std::endl;
using std::deque;
using std::sort;
using std::accumulate;

int main()
{
  deque<int> data;
  deque<int>::iterator iter;           // Stores an iterator
  deque<int>::reverse_iterator riter;  // Stores a reverse iteraotr

  // Read the data
  cout << "Enter a series of non-zero integers separated by spaces."
       << " Enter 0 to end." << endl;
  int value = 0;
  while(cin >> value, value != 0)
    data.push_front(value);

  // Output the data using an iterator
  cout << endl << "The values you entered are:" << endl;
  for(iter = data.begin() ; iter != data.end() ; iter++)
    cout << *iter << "  ";
  cout << endl;

  // Output the data using a reverse iterator
  cout << endl << "In reverse order the values you entered are:" << endl;
  for(riter = data.rbegin() ; riter != data.rend() ; riter++)
    cout << *riter << "  ";

  // Sort the data in descending sequence
```

```
      cout << endl;
      cout << endl << "In descending sequence the values you entered are:" << endl;
      sort(data.rbegin(), data.rend());
      for(iter = data.begin() ; iter != data.end() ; iter++)
        cout << *iter << "  ";
      cout << endl;

      // Calculate the sum of the elements
      cout << endl << "The sum of the elements in the queue is:"
           << accumulate(data.begin(), data.end(), 0)  << endl;

      return 0;
    }
```

Here is some sample output from this program:

```
Enter a series of non-zero integers separated by spaces. Enter 0 to end.
405 302 1 23 67 34 56 111 56 99 77 82 3 23 34 111 89 0

The values you entered are:
89  111  34  23  3  82  77  99  56  111  56  34  67  23  1  302  405

In reverse order the values you entered are:
405  302  1  23  67  34  56  111  56  99  77  82  3  23  34  111  89

In descending sequence the values you entered are:
405  302  111  111  99  89  82  77  67  56  56  34  34  23  23  3  1

The sum of the elements in the queue is:1573
```

How It Works

You create the double-ended queue container and two iterator variables at the beginning of `main()`:

```
deque<int> data;
deque<int>::iterator iter;              // Stores an iterator
deque<int>::reverse_iterator riter;     // Stores a reverse iterator
```

The `data` container is empty to start with. You will be using the `iter` variable for storing an iterator that accesses the queue elements in a forward direction and the `riter` variable for storing a reverse iterator. `iter` and `riter` are of different types but they are both random access iterators in the case of a `deque<T>` container. This means you can increment or decrement them or add or subtract integer values. The iterator types are defined within the container class so you always get the type of iterator that is suited to the organization of the container. For vector and double-ended queue containers you get random access iterators.

The input is read in a `while` loop:

```
int value = 0;
while(cin >> value, value != 0)
  data.push_front(value);
```

The `while` loop condition makes use of the comma operator to separate two expressions, one that reads an integer from `cin` into `value` and another that tests for the value read being non-zero. You saw in Chapter 2 that the value of a series of expressions separated by commas is the value of the rightmost expression, so the while loop continues as long as the expression value != 0 is true, and the value read is non-zero. Within the loop you store the value in the queue using the push_front() function.

The next loop lists the value contained in the queue:

```
cout << endl << "The values you entered are:" << endl;
for(iter = data.begin() ; iter != data.end() ; iter++)
   cout << *iter << "   ";
```

This uses iter as the loop control variable to output the values and the loop ends when iter is incremented to be equal to the iterator returned by the end() function. You could also write this as a while loop:

```
iter = data.begin();
while(iter != data.end())
   cout << *iter++ << "   ";
```

Here iter is incremented within the loop after the value it points to has been written to cout.

The next loop outputs the values in reverse order:

```
for(riter = data.rbegin() ; riter != data.rend() ; riter++)
   cout << *riter << "   ";
```

This uses a reverse iterator so the loop starts with the last element and ends when riter is incremented to be equal to the iterator returned by rend(). The rbegin() function returns an iterator pointing to the last elements and the rend() function returns an iterator pointing to one before the first element.

Next you sort the elements in descending sequence and output them:

```
sort(data.rbegin(), data.rend());
for(iter = data.begin() ; iter != data.end() ; iter++)
   cout << *iter << "   ";
```

The default operation of the sort() algorithm is to sort the sequence passed to it by the two random access iterator arguments in ascending sequence. Here you pass reverse iterators to the functions so it sees the elements in reverse order and so it sorts the reversed sequence in ascending order. The result is that the elements end up in descending sequence when seen in the normal forward order.

The last operation in main() is to output the sum of the elements:

```
cout << endl << "The sum of the elements in the queue is:"
     << accumulate(data.begin(), data.end(), 0)   << endl;
```

You could use a conventional loop to do this but here you make use of the accumulate() algorithm that is defined in the <numeric> header. This accumulates the sum of the sequence of elements identified by the first two iterator arguments. The third argument specifies an initial value for the sum and must be the same type as the elements in the sequence. Supplying an initial value ensures that you always get a sensible result, even if the sequence to be summed is empty. The accumulate() function returns the result of the operation. You can apply the accumulate() function to a sequence of values of any numeric type.

Using List Containers

The `List<T>` container template that is defined in the `<list>` header implements a doubly-linked list. The big advantage a list container has over a vector or a double-ended queue is that you can insert or delete elements anywhere in the sequence in constant time. The range of constructors for a list container is similar to that for a vector or double-ended queue. This statement creates an empty list:

```
list<string> names;
```

You can also create a list with a given number of default elements:

```
list<string> sayings(20);              // A list of 20 empty strings
```

Here's how you create a list containing a given number of elements that are identical:

```
list<double> values(50, 2.71828);
```

This creates a list of 50 values of type `double`.

Of course, you can also construct a list initialized with values from a sequence specified by two iterators:

```
list<double> samples(++values.begin(), --values.end());
```

This creates a list from the contents of the values list, omitting the first and last elements in values. Note that the iterators returned by the `begin()` and `end()` functions for a list are bidirectional iterators, so you do not have the same flexibility as with a vector or a deque container that supports random access iterators. You can only change the value of a bidirectional iterator using the increment or decrement operator.

Just like the other sequence containers, you can discover the number of elements in a list by calling its `size()` member function. You can also change the number of elements in a list by calling its `resize()` function. If the argument to `resize()` is less than the number of elements in the list, elements will be deleted from the end and if the argument is greater, elements will be added using the default constructor for the type of elements stored.

Adding Elements to a List

You add an element to the beginning or end of a list by calling `push_front()` or `push_back()`, just as you would for a double-ended queue. To add elements to the interior of a list, you use the `insert()` function, which comes in three versions. Using the first version you can insert a new element at a position specified by an iterator:

```
list<int> data(20, 1);                 // List of 20 elements value 1
data.insert(++data.begin(), 77);       // Insert 77 as the second element
```

The first argument to `insert()` is an iterator specified in the insertion position, and the second argument is the element to be inserted. The increment operator applied to the bidirectional iterator returned by `begin()` makes it point to the second element in the list. After executing this, the list contents will be:

```
1 77 1 1 1 1 1 1 1 1 1 1 1 1 1 1 1 1 1 1 1
```

You can see that the list now contains 21 elements and the elements from the insertion point on are simply displaced to the right.

You can also insert a number of copies of the same element at a given position:

```
list<int>::iterator iter = data.begin();
for(int i = 0 ; i<9 ; i++)
  ++iter;
data.insert(iter, 3, 88);    // Insert 3 copies of 88 starting at the 10th
```

The first argument to the `insert()` function here is an iterator specifying the position, the second argument is the number of elements to be inserted, and the third argument is the element to be inserted repeatedly. To get to the 10 element you increment the iterator nine times in the `for` loop. Thus this fragment inserts three copies of 88 in the list, starting at the tenth element. Now the contents of the list will be:

```
1 77 1 1 1 1 1 1 88 88 88 1 1 1 1 1 1 1 1 1 1 1 1
```

Now the list contains 24 elements.

Here's how you can insert a sequence of elements into a list:

```
vector<int> numbers(10, 5);               // Vector of 10 elements with value 5
data.insert(--(--data.end()), numbers.begin(), numbers.end());
```

The first argument to `insert()` is an iterator pointing to the second to last element position. The sequence to be inserted is specified by the second and third arguments to the `insert()` function, so this will insert all the elements from the vector into the list starting at the second to last element position. After executing this, the contents of the list will be:

```
1 77 1 1 1 1 1 1 88 88 88 1 1 1 1 1 1 1 1 1 1 5 5 5 5 5 5 5 5 5 5 1 1
```

Inserting the 10 elements from `numbers` in the second to last element position displaces the last two elements in the list to the right. The list now contains 34 elements.

Accessing Elements in a List

You can obtain a reference to the first or last element in a list by calling the `front()` or `back()` function for the list. To access elements interior to the list you must use an iterator and increment or decrement the iterator to get to the element you want. As you have seen, the `begin()` and `end()` functions return a bidirectional iterator pointing at the first element or one past the last element respectively. The `rbegin()` and `rend()` functions return bidirectional iterators and enable you to iterate through the elements in reverse sequence.

Let's try out some of what we have seen in an example.

Try It Out   **Working with a List**

In this example you read sentences from the keyboard and store them in a list. Here's the code:

```
// Ex10_05.cpp
// Working with a list
```

```cpp
#include <iostream>
#include <list>
#include <string>

using std::cin;
using std::cout;
using std::endl;
using std::list;
using std::string;

int main()
{
  list<string> text;
  list<string>::iterator iter;              // Stores an iterator

  // Read the data
  cout << "Enter a few lines of text. Just press Enter to end:"
       << endl;
  string sentence;
  while(getline(cin, sentence, '\n'), !sentence.empty())
    text.push_front(sentence);

  // Output the dat using an iterator
  cout << endl << "Here is the text you entered:" << endl;
  for(iter = text.begin() ; iter != text.end() ; iter++)
    cout << *iter << endl;

  // Sort the data in ascending sequence
  cout << endl << "In ascending sequence the sentences you entered are:" << endl;
  text.sort();
  for(iter = text.begin() ; iter != text.end() ; iter++)
    cout << *iter << endl;

  return 0;
}
```

Here is an example of some output from this program:

```
Enter a few lines of text. Just press Enter to end:
This sentance contains three erors.
This sentence is false.
People who live in glass houses might as well answer the door.
If all else fails, read the instructions.
Home is where the mortgage is.

Here is the text you entered:
Home is where the mortgage is.
If all else fails, read the instructions.
People who live in glass houses might as well answer the door.
This sentence is false.
This sentance contains three erors.

In ascending sequence the sentences you entered are:
Home is where the mortgage is.
```

```
If all else fails, read the instructions.
People who live in glass houses might as well answer the door.
This sentence contains three erors.
This sentence is false.
```

How It Works

You first create a list container to hold strings followed by an iterator variable for use in outputting the contents of the list:

```
list<string> text;
list<string>::iterator iter;              // Stores an iterator
```

You then read an arbitrary number of text inputs from the standard input stream, `cin`:

```
string sentence;
while(getline(cin, sentence, '\n'), !sentence.empty())
  text.push_front(sentence);
```

This uses the same idiom for input as the previous example. The second expression in the `while` loop condition determines when the loop ends, which will be when calling `empty()` for `sentence` returns `true`. You add each input to the list using the `push_front()` function but you could equally well use `push_back()`. The only difference would be that the order of elements in the list would be reversed.

You output the contents of the list in a loop:

```
for(iter = text.begin() ; iter != text.end() ; iter++)
  cout << *iter << endl;
```

This is exactly the same mechanism that you have used for a vector but remember: A list does not support random access to the elements so the iterators are bidirectional iterators, not random access iterators.

Lastly you sort the contents of the list and output it:

```
text.sort();
for(iter = text.begin() ; iter != text.end() ; iter++)
  cout << *iter << endl;
```

This uses the `sort()` member of the `list<string>` object to sort the contents. Because a `list<T>` container does not provide random access iterators, you cannot use the `sort()` function that is defined in the `<algorithm>` header. This is why the `list<T>` template defines its own `sort()` function member.

Other Operations on Lists

The `clear()` function deletes all the elements from a list. The `erase()` function allows you to delete either a single element specified by a single iterator, or a sequence of elements specified by a pair of iterators in the usual fashion — the first in the sequence and one past the last.

```
int data[] = {10, 22, 4, 56, 89, 77, 13, 9};
list<int> numbers(data, data+8);
```

```
numbers.erase(++numbers.begin());        // Remove the second element

// Remove all except the first and the last two
numbers.erase(++numbers.begin(), --(--numbers.end()));
```

Initially the list will contain all the values from the `data` array. The first `erase()` operation deletes the second element so the list will contain:

```
10 4 56 89 77 13 9
```

For the second `erase()` operation the first argument is the iterator returned by `begin()` incremented by 1 so it points to the second element. The second argument is the iterator returned by `end()` decremented twice, so it points to the second to last element. Of course, this is one past the end of the sequence so the element that this iterator points to is not included in the set to be deleted, so the list contents after this operation will be:

```
10 13 9
```

The `remove()` function removes the elements from a list that match a particular value. With the `numbers` list defined as in the previous fragment, you could remove all elements equal to 22 with the following statement:

```
numbers.remove(22);
```

The `assign()` function removes all the elements from a list and copies either a single object into the list a given number of times, or copies a sequence of objects specified by two iterators. Here's an example:

```
int data[] = {10, 22, 4, 56, 89, 77, 13, 9};
list<int> numbers(data, data+8);

numbers.assign(10, 99);        // Replace contents by 10 copies of 99

// Remove all except the first and the last two
numbers.assign(data+1, data+4); // Replace contents by 22 4 56
```

The `assign()` function comes in the two overloaded versions illustrated here. The arguments to the first are the count of the number of replacement elements, and the replacement element value. The arguments to the second version are two iterators or two pointers specifying a sequence in the way you have already seen.

The `unique()` function will eliminate adjacent duplicate elements from a list so if you sort the contents first, applying the function ensures that all elements are unique. Here's an example:

```
int data[] = {10, 22, 4, 10, 89, 22, 89, 10};
list<int> numbers(data, data+8);        // 10 22 4 10 89 22 89 10
numbers.sort();                         // 4 10 10 10 22 22 89 89
numbers.unique();                       // 4 10 22 89
```

The result of each operation is shown in the comments.

The `splice()` function allows you to remove all or part of one list and insert it in another. Obviously, both lists must store elements of the same type. Here's the simplest way you could use the `splice()` function:

```
int data[] = {1, 2, 3, 4, 5, 6, 7, 8};
list<int> numbers(data, data+3);              // 1 2 3
list<int> values(data+4, data+8);             // 5 6 7 8
numbers.splice(++numbers.begin(), values);    // 1 5 6 7 8 2 3
```

The first argument to the `splice()` function is an iterator specifying where the elements should be inserted and the second argument is the list that is the source of the elements to be inserted. This operation removes all the elements from the `values` list and inserts them immediately preceding the second element in the `numbers` list.

Here's another version of the `splice()` function that removes elements from a given position in a source list and inserts them at a given position in the destination list:

```
int data[] = {1, 2, 3, 4, 5, 6, 7, 8};
list<int> numbers(data, data+3);                        // 1 2 3
list<int> values(data+4, data+8);                       // 5 6 7 8
numbers.splice(numbers.begin(), values, --values.end());  // 8 1 2 3
```

In this version, the first two arguments to the `splice()` function are the same as the previous version of the function. The third argument is an iterator specifying the position of the first element to be selected from the source list; all elements from this position to the end are removed from the source and inserted in the destination list. After executing this code fragment, `values` will contain 5 6 7.

The third version of `splice()` requires four arguments and selects a range of elements from the source list:

```
int data[] = {1, 2, 3, 4, 5, 6, 7, 8};
list<int> numbers(data, data+3);              // 1 2 3
list<int> values(data+4, data+8);             // 5 6 7 8
numbers.splice(++numbers.begin(), values, ++values.begin(), --values.end());
                                              // 1 6 7 2 3
```

The first three arguments to the version of `splice()` are the same as the previous version and the last argument is one past the last element to be removed from the source, `values`. After executing this, `values` will contain 5 8.

The `merge()` function removes elements from the list that you supply as an argument and inserts them in the list for which the function is called. The function then sorts the contents of the extended list into ascending order by default, or some other order determined by a function object that you supply as a second argument to the `merge()` function. Both lists must be ordered appropriately before you call `merge()`; in other words the lists must be ordered in the way that you want the final combined list to be ordered. Here's a fragment showing how you might use it:

```
int data[] = {1, 2, 3, 4, 5, 6, 7, 8};
list<int> numbers(data, data+3);              // 1 2 3
list<int> values(data+1, data+8);             // 2 3 4 5 6 7 8
numbers.merge(values);                        // 1 2 2 3 3 4 5 6 7 8
```

This merges the contents of `values` into `numbers` so `values` will be empty after this operation. The `merge()` function that accepts a single argument orders the result in ascending sequence by default, and because the values in both lists are already ordered, you don't need to sort them. To merge the same lists in descending sequence, the code would be like this:

```
numbers.sort(greater<int>());                    // 3 2 1
numbers.sort(greater<int>());                    // 8 7 6 5 4 3 2
numbers.merge(values, greater<int>());           // 8 7 6 5 4 3 3 2 2 1
```

Here you use the `greater<int>()` function object that is defined in the `<functional>` header to specify that the lists should be sorted in descending sequence and they should be merged in the same sequence.

The `remove_if()` function removes elements from a list based on the result of applying a unary predicate; I'm sure you'll recall that a unary predicate is a function object that applies to a single argument and returns a `bool` value, `true` or `false`. If the result of applying the predicate to an element is `true`, then the element will be deleted from the list. Typically you would define your own predicate to do this. This involves defining your own class template for the function object that you want and the STL defines the `unary_function<T, R>` base template for use in this context. This template just defines types that will be inherited by your derived class that specifies your function object type. The base class template is defined as follows:

```
template<class _Arg, class _Result>
struct unary_function
{ // base class for unary functions
  typedef _Arg argument_type;
  typedef _Result result_type;
};
```

This defines `argument_type` and `result_type` as standardized types for use in your definition of the `operator()()` function. You must use this base template if you want to use your predicates with function adapters.

The way in which you can use the `remove_if()` function is best explained with a specific application, so let's try this in a working example.

Try It Out   Defining a Predicate for Filtering a List

Here's how you could define a template for a function object based on the helper template from the STL that you could use to remove negative values from a list:

```
// function_object.h
// Unary predicate to identify negative values
#pragma once
#include <functional>

template <class T> class is_negative: public std::unary_function<T, bool>
{
  public:
  result_type operator()(argument_type& value)
  {
    return value < 0;
  }
};
```

This predicate works with any numeric type. The base template is very useful in that it standardizes the representation of the argument and return types for the predicate, and this is required if you want your function object to be usable with function adapters. Function adapters allow function objects to be used in combination to provide more complex functions. You should be able to see how you could define unary predicates for filtering a list in other ways, selecting even or odd numbers for example, or multiples of a given number, or numbers falling within a given range.

If you are not concerned about the use of your predicate with function adapters, you could define the template very easily without the base class template:

```
// function_object.h
// Unary predicate to identify negative values
#pragma once

template <class T> class is_negative
{
  public:
  bool operator()(T& value)
  {
    return value<0;
  }
};
```

You don't need the `#include` directive for `<functional>` here because you are not using the base template. This is simple and perhaps easier to understand, but I included the original version just to show how you use the base template. You will want to do this if you intend to use your predicate in a more general context, in particular if you want to use it with function adapters. I'll create the example with the first version but you can use either version, or perhaps try both.

To make the example more interesting, I'll include function templates for inputting data to a list and for writing out the contents of a list. Here's the program to make use of your predicate:

```
// Ex10_06.cpp
// Using the remove_if() function for a list

#include <iostream>
#include <list>
#include "function_object.h"

using std::cin;
using std::cout;
using std::endl;
using std::list;
```

```
// Template function to list the contents of a list
template <class T>
void listlist(list<T>& data)
{
  for(list<T>::iterator iter = data.begin() ; iter != data.end() ; iter++)
    cout << *iter << "  ";
  cout << endl;
}
```

```
// Template function to read data from cin and store it in a list
```

```
template<class T>
void loadlist(list<T>& data)
{
  T value = 0;
  while(cin >> value , value != 0)  //Read non-zero values
    data.push_back(value);
}
```

```
int main()
{
  // Process integers
  list<int> numbers;
  cout << "Enter non-zero integers separated by spaces. Enter 0 to end."
       << endl;
  loadlist(numbers);
  cout << "The list contains:" << endl;
  listlist(numbers);
  numbers.remove_if(is_negative<int>());
  cout << "After applying the remove_if() function the list contains:"
       << endl;
  listlist(numbers);

  // Process floating-point values
  list<double> values;
  cout << endl
       << "Enter non-zero values separated by spaces. Enter 0 to end."
       << endl;
  loadlist(values);
  cout << "The list contains:" << endl;
  listlist(values);
  values.remove_if(is_negative<double>());
  cout << "After applying the remove_if() function the list contains:" << endl;
  listlist(values);

  return 0;
}
```

Here's a sample of output from this program:

```
Enter non-zero integers separated by spaces. Enter 0 to end.
23 -4 -5 66 67 89 -1 22 34 -34 78 62 -9 99 -19 0
The list contains:
23   -4   -5   66   67   89   -1   22   34   -34   78   62   -9   99   -19
After applying the remove_if() function the list contains:
23   66   67   89   22   34   78   62   99

Enter non-zero values separated by spaces. Enter 0 to end.
2.5 -3.1 5.5 100 -99 -.075 1.075 13 -12.1 13.2 0
The list contains:
2.5   -3.1   5.5   100   -99   -0.075   1.075   13   -12.1   13.2
After applying the remove_if() function the list contains:
2.5   5.5   100   1.075   13   13.2
```

How It Works

The output shows the predicate works for values of type int and type double. The remove_if() function applies the predicate to each element in a list in turn, and deletes the elements for which the predicate returns true.

The body of the loadlist<T>() template function that reads the input is:

```
T value = 0;
while(cin >> value , value != 0)   //Read non-zero values
   data.push_back(value);
```

The local variable value is defined as type T, the type parameter for the template, so this will be of whatever type you use to instantiate the function. The input is read in the while loop and values continue to be read until you enter zero, in which case the last expression in the while loop condition will be false, thus ending the loop.

The body of the listlist<T>() function template is also very straightforward:

```
for(list<T>::iterator iter = data.begin() ; iter != data.end() ; iter++)
   cout << *iter << "   ";
cout << endl;
```

This uses the type list<T>::iterator for the for loop control variable, which maps to the type required for the iterator for the list container that is passed as the argument. The output is produced by dereferencing the iterator in the way you have seen before.

If you wanted to try out the merge() function within this example, you could add the following code before the return statement in main():

```
// Another list to use in merge
list<double> morevalues;
cout << endl
     << "Enter non-zero values separated by spaces. Enter 0 to end."
     << endl;
loadlist(morevalues);
cout << "The list contains:" << endl;
listlist(morevalues);
values.remove_if(is_negative<double>());
cout << "After applying the remove_if() function the list contains:" << endl;
listlist(morevalues);

// Merge the last two lists
values.sort(greater<double>());
morevalues.sort(greater<double>());
values.merge(morevalues, greater<double>());
listlist(values);
```

Don't forget you need an #include directive for <functional> and a using directive for std::greater for this to compile.

Using Other Sequence Containers

The remaining sequence containers are implemented through container adapters that I introduced at the beginning of this chapter. I'll discuss each of them briefly and illustrate their operation with an example.

Queue Containers

A `queue<T>` container implements a first-in first-out storage mechanism through an adapter. You can only add to the end of the queue and remove from the front. Here's one way you can create a queue:

```
queue<string> names;
```

This creates a queue that can store elements of type `string`. By default the `queue<T>` adapter class uses a `deque<T>` container as the base, but you can specify a different sequence container as a base as long as it supports the operations `front()`, `back()`, `push_back()`, and `pop_front()`. These four functions are used to operate the queue. Thus a queue can be based on a list or a vector container. You specify the alternate container as a second template parameter. Here's how you would create a queue based on a list:

```
queue< string, list<string> > names;
```

The second type parameter to the adapter template specifies the underlying sequence container that is to be used. The queue adapter class acts as a wrapper for the underlying container class and essentially restricts the range of operations you can carry out to those described in the following table.

Function	Description
`back()`	Returns a reference to the element at the back of the queue. There are two versions of the function, one returning a `const` reference and the other returning a non-`const` reference. If the queue is empty, then the value returned is undefined.
`front()`	Returns a reference to the element at the front of the queue. There are two versions of the function, one returning a `const` reference and the other returning a non-`const` reference. If the queue is empty, then the value returned is undefined.
`push()`	Adds the element specified by the argument to the back of the queue.
`pop()`	Removes the element at the front of the queue.
`size()`	Returns the number of elements in the queue.
`empty()`	Returns `true` if the queue is empty and `false` otherwise.

Note that there are no functions in the table that make iterators available for a queue container. The only way to access the contents of a queue is via the `back()` or `front()` functions.

Try It Out   Using a Queue Container

In this example you read a succession of one or more sayings, store them in a queue, and then retrieve the sayings and output them. Here's the code:

```
// Ex10_07.cpp
// Exercising a queue container
```

```cpp
#include <iostream>
#include <queue>
#include <string>


using std::cin;
using std::cout;
using std::endl;
using std::queue;
using std::string;


int main()
{
  queue<string> sayings;
  string saying;
  cout << "Enter one or more sayings. Press Enter to end." << endl;
  while(true)
  {
    getline(cin, saying);
    if(saying.empty())
      break;
    sayings.push(saying);
  }

  cout << "There are " << sayings.size()
       << " sayings in the queue."
       << endl << endl;
  cout << "The sayings that you entered are:" << endl;
  while(!sayings.empty())
  {
    cout << sayings.front() << endl;
    sayings.pop();
  }

  return 0;
}
```

Here's an example of some output from this program:

```
Enter one or more sayings. Press Enter to end.
If at first you don't succeed, give up.
A preposition is something you should never end a sentence with.
The bigger they are, the harder they hit.
A rich man is just a poor man with money.
Wherever you go, there you are.
Common sense is not so common.

There are 6 sayings in the queue.

The sayings that you entered are:
If at first you don't succeed, give up.
A preposition is something you should never end a sentence with.
The bigger they are, the harder they hit.
A rich man is just a poor man with money.
```

```
Wherever you go, there you are.
Common sense is not so common.
```

How It Works

You first create a queue container that stores string objects:

```
queue<string> sayings;
```

You read sayings from the standard input stream and store them in the queue container in a `while` loop:

```
while(true)
{
  getline(cin, saying);
  if(saying.empty())
    break;
  sayings.push(saying);
}
```

This version of the `getline()` function reads text from `cin` into the `string` object, `saying`, until a new-line character is recognized. Newline is the default input termination character and when you want to override this, you specify the termination character as the third argument to `getline()`. The loop continues until the `empty()` function for saying in the `if` statement returns `true`, which indicates an empty line was entered. When the input in `saying` is not empty, you store it in the `sayings` queue container by calling its `push()` function.

When input is complete, you output the count of the number of sayings that were stored in the queue:

```
cout << "There are " << sayings.size()
     << " sayings in the queue."
     << endl << endl;
```

The `size()` function returns the number of elements in the queue.

You list the contents of the queue in another `while` loop:

```
while(!sayings.empty())
{
  cout << sayings.front() << endl;
  sayings.pop();
}
```

The `front()` function returns a reference to the object at the front of the queue but it remains there. Because you want to access each of the elements in the queue in turn, you have to call the `pop()` function after listing each element to remove it from the queue.

The process of listing the elements in the queue also deletes them, so after the loop ends the queue will be empty. What if you wanted to retain the elements in the queue? Well, one possibility is that you could put each saying back in the queue after you have listed it. Here's how you could do that:

```
for(int i = 0 ; i < sayings.size() ; i++)
{
```

```
        saying = sayings.front();
        cout << saying << endl;
        sayings.pop();
        sayings.push(saying);
    }
```

Here you make use of the value returned by `size()` to iterate over the number of sayings in the queue. After writing each saying to `cout`, you remove it from the queue by calling `pop()`, and then you return it to the back of the queue by calling `push()`. When the loop ends the queue will be left in its original state. Of course, if you don't want to remove the elements when you access them you could always use a different kind of container.

Priority Queue Containers

A `priority_queue<T>` container is a queue that always has the largest or highest priority element at the top. Here's one way to define a priority queue container:

```
    priority_queue<int> numbers;
```

The default criterion for determining the relative priority of elements as you add them to the queue is the standard `less<T>` function object template. You add an element to the priority queue using the `push()` function:

```
    numbers.push(99);                      // Add 99 to the queue
```

When you add an element to the queue, if the queue is not empty the function will use the `less<T>()` predicate to decide where to insert the new object. This will result in elements being ordered in ascending sequence from the back of the queue to the front. You cannot modify elements while they are in a priority queue as this could invalidate the ordering that has been established.

The complete set of operations for a priority queue is shown in the following table.

Function	Description
`top()`	Returns a `const` reference to the element at the front of the priority queue, which will be the largest or highest priority element in the container. If the priority queue is empty, then the value returned is undefined.
`push()`	Adds the element specified by the argument to the priority queue at a position determined by the predicate for the container, which by default is `less<T>`.
`pop()`	Removes the element at the front of the priority queue, which will be the largest or highest priority element in the container.
`size()`	Returns the number of elements in the priority queue.
`empty()`	Returns `true` if the priority queue is empty and `false` otherwise.

Note that there is a significant difference between the functions available for the priority queue and for the queue container. With a priority queue you have no access to the element at the back of the queue; only the element at the front is accessible.

By default, the base container used by the priority queue adapter class is vector<T>. You have the option of specifying a different sequence container as the base and an alternative function object for determining the priority of the elements. Here's how you could do that:

```
priority_queue<int, deque<int>, greater<int>> numbers;
```

This statement defines a priority queue based on a deque<int> container with elements being inserted using a function object of type greater<int>. The elements in this priority queue will be in descending sequence with the smallest element at the top. The three template parameters are the element type, the container to be used as a base, and the type for the predicate to be used for ordering the elements.

You could omit the third template parameter if you want the default predicate to apply, which will be less<int> in this case. If you want a different predicate but want to retain the default base container, you must explicitly specify it, like this:

```
priority_queue<int, vector<int>, greater<int>> numbers;
```

This specifies the default base container vector<int> and a new predicate type, greater<int> to be used to determine the ordering of elements.

Try It Out   Using a Priority Queue Container

In this example you store Person objects in the container, with the Person class defined this time to hold the names as type string:

```cpp
// Person.h
// A class defining a person
#pragma once
#include <iostream>
#include <string>
using std::cout;
using std::endl;
using std::string;

class Person
{
public:
  Person(string first, string second)
  {
    firstname = first;
    secondname = second;
  }

  // No-arg constructor
  Person(){}

  // Copy constructor
```

```
    Person(const Person& p)
    {
      firstname = p.firstname;
      secondname = p.secondname;
    }

    // Less-than operator
    bool operator<(const Person& p)const
    {
      if(secondname < p.secondname ||
        ((secondname == p.secondname) && (firstname < p.firstname)))
        return true;

      return false;
    }

    // Greater-than operator
    bool operator>(const Person& p)const
    {
      return p < *this;
    }

    // Output a person
    void showPerson() const
    {
      cout << firstname << " " << secondname << endl;
    }

private:
  string firstname;
  string secondname;
};
```

Note that the > operator is overloaded here. This will make it possible to put objects in a priority queue that is ordered in ascending or descending sequence.

Here's the program that stores Person objects in a priority queue:

```
// Ex10_08.cpp
// Exercising a priority queue container

#include <iostream>
#include <vector>
#include <queue>
#include <functional>
#include "Person.h"

using std::cin;
using std::cout;
using std::endl;
using std::vector;
using std::priority_queue;
using std::greater;
```

```
int main()
{
  priority_queue<Person, vector<Person>, greater<Person>> people;
  string first, second;;
  while(true)
  {
    cout << "Enter a first name or press Enter to end: " ;
    getline(cin, first);
    if(first.empty())
      break;

    cout << "Enter a second name: " ;
    getline(cin, second);
    people.push(Person(first, second));
  }

  cout << endl << "There are " << people.size()
       << " people in the queue."
       << endl << endl;

  cout << "The names that you entered are:" << endl;
  while(!people.empty())
  {
    people.top().showPerson();
    people.pop();
  }

  return 0;
}
```

Typical output from this example looks like this:

```
Enter a first name or press Enter to end: Oliver
Enter a second name: Hardy
Enter a first name or press Enter to end: Stan
Enter a second name: Laurel
Enter a first name or press Enter to end: Harold
Enter a second name: Lloyd
Enter a first name or press Enter to end: Mel
Enter a second name: Gibson
Enter a first name or press Enter to end: Brad
Enter a second name: Pitt
Enter a first name or press Enter to end:

There are 5 people in the queue.

The names that you entered are:
Mel Gibson
Oliver Hardy
Stan Laurel
Harold Lloyd
Brad Pitt
```

How It Works

The `Person` class is simpler than the earlier version because the names are stored as `string` objects and no dynamic memory allocation is necessary. You no longer need to define the assignment operator, as the default will be fine. Defining the < operator function is sufficient to allow `Person` objects to be stored in a default priority queue and the overloaded > operator will permit `Person` objects to be ordered using the `greater<Person>` predicate type.

You define the priority queue in `main()` like this:

```
priority_queue< Person, vector<Person>, greater<Person>> people;
```

Because you want to specify the third template type parameter, you must supply all three, even though the base container type is the default. Incidentally, don't confuse the *type argument* you are using in the template instantiation here, `greater<Person>`, with the *object*, `greater<Person>()`, that you might supply as an argument to the `sort()` algorithm.

Of course, the third parameter to the priority queue template that defines the predicate for ordering the objects does not have to be a template type. You could use your own function object type as long as it has a suitable implementation of `operator()()` in the class:

```
// function_object.h
#pragma once
#include <functional>
#include "Person.h"
using std::binary_function;

class PersonComp: binary_function<Person, Person, bool>
{
public:
  result_type operator()(const first_argument_type& p1,
                         const second_argument_type& p2) const
  {
    return p1 > p2;
  }
};
```

For function objects that work with the STL, a binary predicate must implement `operator()()` with two parameters, and if you want the predicate to work with function adapters, your function object type must have an instance of the `binary_function<Arg1Type, Arg2Type, ResultType>` template as a base. Although you will typically make both arguments to a binary predicate of the same type, the base class does not require this to be so, so when it is meaningful your predicates can apply to arguments of different types.

If you don't want to use your function objects with function adapters, you could define the type as:

```
// function_object.h
#pragma once
#include "Person.h"

class PersonComp
```

```
{
public:
  bool operator()(const Person& p1, const Person& p2) const
  {
    return p1 > p2;
  }
};
```

With this function object type, you could define the priority queue object as:

```
priority_queue< Person, vector<Person>, PersonComp> people;
```

You read names from the standard input stream in an indefinite `while` loop:

```
while(true)
{
  cout << "Enter a first name or press Enter to end: " ;
  getline(cin, first);
  if(first.empty())
    break;

  cout << "Enter a second name: " ;
  getline(cin, second);
  people.push(Person(first, second));
}
```

An empty first name will terminate the loop. After reading a second name, you create the `Person` object in the argument expression to the `push()` function that adds the object to the priority queue. It will be inserted at a position determined by a `greater<Person>()` predicate. This will result in the objects being ordered in the priority queue with the largest at the top. You can see from the output that the names are in ascending sequence.

After outputting the number of objects in the queue using the `size()` function, you output the contents of the queue in a `while` loop:

```
while(!people.empty())
{
  people.top().showPerson();
  people.pop();
}
```

The `top()` function returns a reference to the object at the front of the queue, and you use this reference to call the `showPerson()` function to output the name. You then call `pop()` to remove the element at the front of the queue; unless you do this, you can't access the next element.

When the loop ends the priority queue will be empty. There's no way to access all the elements and retain them in the queue. If you want to keep them you would have to put them somewhere else, perhaps in another priority queue.

Stack Containers

The `stack<T>` container adapter template is defined in the `<stack>` header and implements a pushdown stack based on a `deque<T>` container by default. A pushdown stack is a last-in first-out storage mechanism where only the object that was added most recently to the stack is accessible.

Here's how you can define a stack:

```
stack<Person> people;
```

This defines a stack to store `Person` objects.

The base container can be any sequence container that supports the operations `back()`, `push_back()`, and `pop_back()`. You could define a stack base on a list like this:

```
stack<string, list<string>> names;
```

The template type argument is the element type, as before, and the second is the container type to be used as a base for the stack.

There are only five operations available with a `stack<T>` container and they are shown in the following table.

Function	Description
`top()`	Returns a reference to the element at the top of the stack. If the stack is empty, then the value returned is undefined. You can assign the reference returned to a `const` or non-`const` reference and if it is assigned to the latter, you can modify the object in the stack.
`push()`	Adds the element specified by the argument to the top of the stack.
`pop()`	Removes the element at the top of the stack.
`size()`	Returns the number of elements in the stack.
`empty()`	Returns `true` if the stack is empty and `false` otherwise.

As with the other containers provided through container adapters, you cannot use iterators to access the contents of a stack.

Let's see a stack working in another example.

Try It Out   **Using a Stack Container**

This example stores `Person` objects in a stack. The `Person` class is the same as in the previous example, so I won't repeat the code here. Here's the program:

```
// Ex10_09.cpp
// Exercising a stack container
```

```cpp
#include <iostream>
#include <stack>
#include <list>
#include "Person.h"

using std::cin;
using std::cout;
using std::endl;
using std::stack;
using std::list;

int main()
{
  stack<Person, list<Person>> people;

  string first, second;
  while(true)
  {
    cout << "Enter a first name or press Enter to end: " ;
    getline(cin, first);
    if(first.empty())
      break;

    cout << "Enter a second name: " ;
    getline(cin, second);
    people.push(Person(first, second));
  }

  cout << endl << "There are " << people.size()
       << " people in the stack."
       << endl << endl;
  cout << "The names that you entered are:" << endl;
  while(!people.empty())
  {
    people.top().showPerson();
    people.pop();
  }

  return 0;
}
```

Here is an example of the output:

```
Enter a first name or press Enter to end: Gordon
Enter a second name: Brown
Enter a first name or press Enter to end: Harold
Enter a second name: Wilson
Enter a first name or press Enter to end: Margaret
Enter a second name: Thatcher
Enter a first name or press Enter to end: Winston
```

```
Enter a second name: Churchill
Enter a first name or press Enter to end: David
Enter a second name: Lloyd-George
Enter a first name or press Enter to end:

There are 5 people in the stack.

The names that you entered are:
David Lloyd-George
Winston Churchill
Margaret Thatcher
Harold Wilson
Gordon Brown
```

How It Works

The code in `main()` is more or less the same as in the previous example. Only the container definition is significantly different:

```
stack<Person, list<Person>> people;
```

The stack container stores `Person` objects and is based on a `list<T>` container in this instance. You could also use a `vector<T>` container and if you omit the second type parameter, the stack will use a `deque<T>` container as a base.

The output demonstrates that a stack is indeed a last-in first-out container as the order of names in the output is the reverse of the input.

Associative Containers

The most significant feature of the associative containers such as `map<K, T>` is that you can retrieve a particular object without searching. The location of an object of type `T` within an associative container is determined from a key of type `K` that you supply along with the object, so you can retrieve any object rapidly by just supplying the appropriate key. The key is actually a sort key that determines the order of the entries in the map.

For `set<T>` and `multiset<T>` containers, objects act as their own keys. You might be wondering what the use of a container is where before you can retrieve an object you have to have the object available. After all, if you already have the object, why would you need to retrieve it? The point of set and multiset containers is not so much to store objects for later retrieval, but to create an aggregation of objects that you can test to see whether or not a given object is already a member.

In this section I'll concentrate on map containers. The set and multiset containers are used somewhat less frequently and their operations are very similar to the map and multimap containers, so you should have little difficulty using these once you have learned how to apply the map containers.

Using Map Containers

The template for map containers is defined in the `<map>` header. When you create a `map<K, T>` container, you must supply type arguments for the type of key you will use, K, and the type of the object associated with a key, T. Here's an example:

```
map<Person, string> phonebook;
```

This defines an empty map container that stores entries that are key/object pairs where the keys are of type `Person` and the objects are of type `string`.

Note that although you use class objects here for both keys and objects to be stored in the map, the keys and associated objects in a map can also be of any fundamental type such as int, or double or char.

You can also create a map container that is initialized with a sequence of key/object pairs from another map container:

```
map<Person, string> phonebook(iter1, iter2);
```

`iter1` and `iter2` are a pair of iterators defining a series of key/object pairs from another container in the usual way, with `iter2` specifying a position one past the last pair to be included in the sequence. You obtain iterators to access the contents of a map by calling the `begin()` and `end()` functions, just as you would for a sequence container. The iterators for a map are bidirectional iterators.

The entries in a map are ordered based on a function object of type `less<Key>` by default, so they will be stored in ascending key sequence. You can change the type function object used for ordering entries in a map by supplying a third template type parameter. For example:

```
map<Person, string, greater<Person>> phonebook;
```

This map stores entries that are `Person`/`string` pairs, where `Person` is the key with an associated string object. The ordering of entries will be determined by a function object of type `greater<Person>`, so the entries will be in descending key sequence.

Storing Objects

The objects that you store in a map are always a key/object pair that are of a template type `pair<K, T>`, where K is the type of key and T is the type of object associated with the key. The `pair<K, T>` type is defined in the `<utility>` header, which is included into the `<map>` header, so if you are using a map the type is automatically available. You can define a pair object like this:

```
pair<Person, string> entry = pair<Person, string>(Person("Mel", "Gibson"),
                                                   "213 345 5678");
```

This creates the variable `entry` of type

```
pair<Person, string>
```

and initializes it to an object created from a `Person` object and a `string` object. I'm representing a phone number in a very simplistic way, just as a string, but of course it could be a more complicated class identifying the components of the number such as country code and area code. The `Person` class is the class you used in the previous example.

An instance of the pair<K, T> class template defines two constructors and the one you are using in the previous fragment defines an object from a key and its associated object. The other constructor is a copy constructor that allows you to construct a new pair from an existing one. You can access the elements in a pair through the members first and second, so in the example entry.first references the Person object and entry.second references the string object.

You can also use a helper function, make_pair(), that is defined in the <utility> header to create a pair object:

```
pair<Person, string> entry = make_pair(Person("Mel", "Gibson"),
                                        "213 345 5678");
```

Using the make_pair() function is a little less cluttered than using the explicit pair type. The make_pair() function is defined as a template function, so it automatically deduces the type for the pair from the argument types you supply.

All of the comparison operators are overloaded for pair objects so you can compare them with any of the operators <, <=, ==, !=, >=, and >.

It's sometimes convenient to use a typedef statement to abbreviate the pair<K, T> type you are using in a particular instance. For example:

```
map<Person, string> phonebook;
typedef pair<Person, string> Entry;
```

The first statement defines a map container that will store string objects using Person objects as keys. The second statement defines Entry as the type for the key/object pair. Having defined the Entry type, you can create objects of this type. For example:

```
Entry entry1 = Entry(Person("Jack", "Jones"), "213 567 1234");
```

This statement defines a pair of type pair<Person, string> using Person("Jack", "Jones") as the Person argument and "213 567 1234" as the string argument.

You can insert one or more pairs in a map using the insert() function. For example, here's how you insert a single object:

```
phonebook.insert(entry1);
```

This statement inserts the entry1 pair into the phonebook container as long as there is no other entry in the map that uses the same key. In fact this version of the insert() function returns a value that is also a pair, where the first object in the pair is an iterator and the second is a value of type bool. The bool value in the pair will be true if the insertion was made and false otherwise. The iterator value in the pair will point to the element if it was stored in the map, or the element that is already in the map if the insert failed. Therefore you can check if the object was stored like this:

```
pair<map<Person, string>::iterator, bool> checkpair;
checkpair = phonebook.insert(entry1);
if(checkpair.second)
  cout << "Insertion succeeded." << endl;
else
  cout << "Insertion failed." << endl;
```

The pair that the `insert()` function returns is stored in `checkpair`. The type for `checkpair` is a pair encapsulating an iterator for our map of type `map<Person, Number>::iterator`, which you could access as `checkpair.first`, and a value of type `bool`, which you access in the code as `checkpair.second`.

Dereferencing the iterator in the pair returned by the `insert()` function will give you access to the pair that is stored in the map and you can use the `first` and `second` members of that pair to access the key and object respectively. This can be a little tricky so let's see what it looks like for `checkpair` in the code above:

```
cout << "The key for the entry is:" << endl;
checkpair.first->first.showPerson();
```

The expression `checkpair.first` references the first member of the `checkpair` pair, which is an iterator, so you are accessing a pointer to the object in the map with this expression. The object in the map is another pair, so the expression `checkpair.first->first` accesses the first member of that pair, which is the `Person` object. You use this to call the `showPerson()` member to output the name. You could access the object in the pair in a similar way with the expression `checkpair.first->second`.

You have another version of the `insert()` function for inserting a series of pairs in a map. The pairs are defined by two iterator arguments and the series would typically be from another map container.

The `map<K,T>` template defines the `operator[]()` function, so you can also use the subscript operator to insert an object. Here's how you could insert the `entry1` object in the phonebook map:

```
phonebook[Person("Jack", "Jones")] = "213 567 1234";
```

The subscript value is the key to be used to store the object that appears on the right of the assignment operator. This is perhaps a somewhat more intuitive way to store objects in a map. The only disadvantage compared to the `insert()` function is that you lose the ability to discover whether the key was already in the map.

Accessing Objects

You can use the subscript operator to retrieve the object from a map that corresponds to a given key. For example:

```
string number = phonebook[Person("Jack", "Jones")];
```

This stores the object corresponding to the key

```
Person("Jack", "Jones")
```

in `number`. If the key is not in the map, then a pair entry will be inserted into the map for this key with the object as the default for the object type, so here the no-arg `Person` class constructor will be called to create the object for this key if the entry is not there.

Of course, you may not want a default object inserted when you attempt to retrieve an object corresponding to a given key. In this case you could use the `find()` function to check if there's an entry for a given key and then retrieve it:

```
string number;
Person key = Person("Jack", "Jones");
```

```
map<Person, string>::iterator iter = phonebook.find(key);

if(iter != phonebook.end())
{
  number = iter->second;
  cout << "The number is " << number << endl;
}
else
{
  cout << "No number for the key ";
  key.showPerson();
}
```

The find() function returns an iterator that points to the object corresponding to the key if the key is present in the map, or to one past the last entry in the map, which corresponds to the iterator returned by the end() function. Thus if iter is not equal to the iterator returned by end(), the entry is present and you can access the object through the second member of the pair. This fragment defines the iterator as type map<Person, Number>::iterator. If you want to prevent the object in the map from being modified, you could define the iterator as type map<Person, Number>::const_iterator.

Calling the count() function for a map with a key as the argument will return a count of the number of entries found corresponding to the key. For a map the value returned can only be 0 or 1 because each key in a map must be unique. A multimap container allows multiple entries for a given key, so in this case other values are possible for the return value from count().

Other Map Operations

The erase() function enables you to remove a single entry or a range of entries from a map. You have two versions of erase() that will remove a single entry. One version requires an iterator as the argument pointing to the entry to be erased, and the other requires a key corresponding to the entry to be erased. For example:

```
Person key = Person("Jack", "Jones");
map<Person, string>::size_type count = phonebook.erase(key);
if(count == 0)
  cout << "Entry was not found." << endl;
```

When you supply a key to the erase() function, it returns a count of the number of entries that were erased. With a map container, the value returned can only be 0 or 1. A multimap container can have several entries with the same key in which case the erase() function may return a value greater than 1.

You can also supply an iterator as an argument to erase():

```
Person key = Person("Jack", "Jones");
map<Person, string>::iterator iter = phonebook.find(key);
iter = phonebook.erase(iter);
if(iter == phonebook.end())
  cout << "End of the map reached." << endl;
```

In this case the erase() function returns an iterator that points to the entry that remains in the map beyond the entry that was erased, or a pointer to the ends of the map if no such element is present.

The following table shows the other operations available with a map container.

Function	Description
begin()	Returns a bidirectional iterator pointing to the first entry in the map.
end()	Returns a bidirectional iterator pointing to one past the last entry in the map.
rbegin()	Returns a reverse iterator pointing to the last entry in the map.
rend()	Returns a reverse iterator pointing to one past the first entry in the map.
lower_bound()	Accepts a key as an argument and returns an iterator pointing to the first entry with a key that is greater than or equal to (the lower bound of) the specified key. If the key is not present, the iterator pointing to one past the last entry will be returned.
upper_bound()	Accepts a key as an argument and returns an iterator pointing to the first entry with a key that is greater than (the upper bound of) the specified key. If the key is not present, the iterator pointing to one past the last entry will be returned.
equal_range()	Accepts a key as an argument and returns a pair object containing two iterators. The first member of the pair points to the lower bound of the specified key and the second member points to the upper bound of the specified key. If the key is not present, both iterators in the pair will point to one past the last entry in the map.
swap()	Interchanges the entries in the map you pass as the argument with the entries in the map for which the function is called.
clear()	Erases all entries in the map.
size()	Returns the number of elements in the map.
empty()	Returns true if the map is empty and false otherwise.

The lower_bound(), upper_bound(), and equal_range() functions are not very useful with a map container. However, they come into their own with a multimap container when you want to find all the elements with the same key.

Let's see a map in action.

Try It Out   Using a Map Container

In this example you use a map container to store phone numbers and provide a mechanism for finding a phone number for a person. You use a variation on the Person class in this example:

```
// Person.h
// A class defining a person
#pragma once
```

```
#include <iostream>
#include <string>
#include <functional>
using std::cout;
using std::endl;
using std::string;

class Person
{
public:
  Person(string first = "", string second = "")
  {
    firstname = first;
    secondname = second;
  }

  // Less-than operator
  bool operator<(const Person& p)const
  {
    if(secondname < p.secondname ||
      ((secondname == p.secondname) && (firstname < p.firstname)))
      return true;

    return false;
  }

  // Get the name
  string getName()const
  {
    return firstname + " " + secondname;
  }

private:
  string firstname;
  string secondname;
};
```

There are only a few minor changes from the previous version of the Person class. The no-arg constructor is now defined by providing default values for the constructor arguments. I have omitted the < operator function, the copy constructor, the assignment operator, and the showPerson() function. There is a new function, getName() that returns the complete name as a string object.

The source file containing main() and some helper functions looks like this:

```
// Ex10_10.cpp
// Using a map container

#include <iostream>
#include <cstdio>
#include <iomanip>
#include <string>
#include <map>
#include "Person.h"
```

```cpp
using std::cin;
using std::cout;
using std::endl;
using std::setw;
using std::ios;
using std::string;
using std::pair;
using std::map;
using std::make_pair;
```

```cpp
// Read a person from cin
Person getPerson()
{
  string first;
  string second;
  cout << "Enter a first name: " ;
  getline(cin, first);
  cout << "Enter a second name: " ;
  getline(cin, second);
  return Person(first, second);
}
```

```cpp
// Add a new entry to a phone book
void addEntry(map<Person, string>& book)
{
  pair<Person, string> entry;            // Stores a phone book entry
  string number;
  Person person = getPerson();

  cout << "Enter the phone number for "
    << person.getName() << ": ";
    getline(cin, number);
    entry = make_pair(person, number);
    pair<map<Person,string>::iterator, bool> pr = book.insert(entry);

    if(pr.second)
      cout << "Entry successful." << endl;
    else
    {
      cout << "Entry exists for " << person.getName()
           << ". The number is " << pr.first->second << endl;
    }
}
```

```cpp
// List the contents of a phone book
void listEntries(map<Person, string>& book)
{
  if(book.empty())
  {
    cout << "The phone book is empty." << endl;
    return;
  }
  map<Person, string>::iterator iter;
  cout << setiosflags(ios::left);              // Left justify output
  for(iter = book.begin() ; iter != book.end() ; iter++)
```

```
    {
      cout << setw(30) << iter->first.getName()
           << setw(12) << iter->second << endl;
    }
    cout << resetiosflags(ios::right);            // Right justify output
}
```

```
// Retrieve an entry from a phone book
void getEntry(map<Person, string>& book)
{
  Person person = getPerson();
  map<Person, string>::const_iterator iter = book.find(person);
  if(iter == book.end())
    cout << "No entry found for " << person.getName() << endl;
  else
    cout << "The number for " << person.getName()
         << " is " << iter->second << endl;
}
```

```
// Delete an entry from a phone book
void deleteEntry(map<Person, string>& book)
{
  Person person = getPerson();
  map<Person, string>::iterator iter = book.find(person);
  if(iter == book.end())
    cout << "No entry found for " << person.getName() << endl;
  else
  {
    book.erase(iter);
    cout << person.getName() << " erased." << endl;
  }
}
```

```
int main()
{
  map<Person, string> phonebook;
  char answer = 0;

  while(true)
  {
    cout << "Do you want to enter a phone book entry(Y or N): " ;
    cin >> answer;
    cin.ignore();                       // Ignore newline in buffer
    if(toupper(answer) == 'N')
      break;
    if(toupper(answer) != 'Y')
    {
      cout << "Invalid response. Try again." << endl;
      continue;
    }
    addEntry(phonebook);
  }

  // Query the phonebook
  while(true)
```

```
{
    cout << endl << "Choose from the following options:" << endl
        << "A  Add an entry   D Delete an entry   G  Get an entry" << endl
        << "L  List entries   Q  Quit" << endl;
    cin >> answer;
    cin.ignore();                      // Ignore newline in buffer

    switch(toupper(answer))
    {
      case 'A':
        addEntry(phonebook);
        break;
      case 'G':
        getEntry(phonebook);
        break;
      case 'D':
        deleteEntry(phonebook);
        break;
      case 'L':
        listEntries(phonebook);
        break;
      case 'Q':
        return 0;
      default:
        cout << "Invalid selection. Try again." << endl;
        break;
    }
  }
}
```

Here is some output from this program:

```
Do you want to enter a phone book entry(Y or N): y
Enter a first name: Jack
Enter a second name: Bateman
Enter the phone number for Jack Bateman: 312 455 6576
Entry successful.
Do you want to enter a phone book entry(Y or N): y
Enter a first name: Mary
Enter a second name: Jones
Enter the phone number for Mary Jones: 213 443 5671
Entry successful.
Do you want to enter a phone book entry(Y or N): y
Enter a first name: Jane
Enter a second name: Junket
Enter the phone number for Jane Junket: 413 222 8134
Entry successful.
Do you want to enter a phone book entry(Y or N): n

Choose from the following options:
A  Add an entry   D Delete an entry   G  Get an entry
L  List entries   Q  Quit
a
Enter a first name: Bill
Enter a second name: Smith
```

```
Enter the phone number for Bill Smith: 213 466 7688
Entry successful.

Choose from the following options:
A  Add an entry    D Delete an entry    G  Get an entry
L  List entries    Q  Quit
g
Enter a first name: Mary
Enter a second name: Miller
No entry found for Mary Miller

Choose from the following options:
A  Add an entry    D Delete an entry    G  Get an entry
L  List entries    Q  Quit
g
Enter a first name: Mary
Enter a second name: Jones
The number for Mary Jones is 213 443 5671

Choose from the following options:
A  Add an entry    D Delete an entry    G  Get an entry
L  List entries    Q  Quit
d
Enter a first name: Mary
Enter a second name: Jones
Mary Jones erased.

Choose from the following options:
A  Add an entry    D Delete an entry    G  Get an entry
L  List entries    Q  Quit
L
Jack Bateman               312 455 6576
Jane Junket                413 222 8134
Bill Smith                 213 466 7688

Choose from the following options:
A  Add an entry    D Delete an entry    G  Get an entry
L  List entries    Q  Quit
q
```

How It Works

You define a map container in main() like this:

```
map<Person, string> phonebook;
```

The object in an entry in the map is a string containing a phone number and the key is a Person object.

You load up the map initially in a while loop:

```
while(true)
{
  cout << "Do you want to enter a phone book entry(Y or N): " ;
  cin >> answer;
  cin.ignore();                    // Ignore newline in buffer
```

```
      if(toupper(answer) == 'N')
        break;
      if(toupper(answer) != 'Y')
      {
        cout << "Invalid response. Try again." << endl;
        continue;
      }
      addEntry(phonebook);
   }
```

You check whether an entry is to be read by reading a character from the standard input stream. Reading a character from `cin` leaves a newline character in the buffer and this can cause problems for subsequent input. Calling `ignore()` for `cin` ignores the next character so subsequent input will work properly. If `'n'` or `'N'` is entered, the loop is terminated. When `'y'` or `'Y'` is entered, an entry is created by calling the helper function `addEntry()` that is coded like this:

```
   void addEntry(map<Person, string>& book)
   {
     pair<Person, string> entry;              // Stores a phone book entry
     string number;
     Person person = getPerson();

     cout << "Enter the phone number for "
       << person.getName() << ": ";
       getline(cin, number);
       entry = make_pair(person, number);
       pair<map<Person,string>::iterator, bool> pr = book.insert(entry);

       if(pr.second)
         cout << "Entry successful." << endl;
       else
       {
         cout << "Entry exists for " << person.getName()
               << ". The number is " << pr.first->second << endl;
       }
   }
```

Note that the parameter for `addEntry()` is a reference. The function modifies the container that is passed as the argument, so the function must have access to the original object. In any event, even if only access to the container argument was needed, it is important not to allow potentially very large objects such as a map container to be passed by value because this can seriously degrade performance.

The process for adding an entry is essentially as you have seen in the previous section. The `getPerson()` helper function reads a first name and a second name and then returns a `Person` object that is created using the names. The `getName()` member of the `Person` class returns a name as a `string` object so you use this in the prompt for a number. Calling the `make_pair()` function returns a `pair<Person, string>` object that you store in `entry`. You then call `insert()` for the container object and store the object returned in `pr`. The `pr` object enables you to check that the entry was successfully inserted into the map by testing its `bool` member. The first member of `pr` provides access to the entry, whether it's an existing entry or the new entry, and you use this to output a message when insertion fails.

After initial input is complete, a `while` loop provides the mechanism for querying and modifying the phone book. The `switch` statement in the body of the loop decides the action to be taken based on the character that is entered and stored in answer. Querying the phone book is managed by the getEntry() function:

```
void getEntry(map<Person, string>& book)
{
  Person person = getPerson();
  map<Person, string>::const_iterator iter = book.find(person);
  if(iter == book.end())
    cout << "No entry found for " << person.getName() << endl;
  else
    cout << "The number for " << person.getName()
         << " is " << iter->second << endl;
}
```

A Person object is created from a name that is read from the standard input stream by calling the getPerson() function. The Person object is then used as the argument to the find() function for the map object. This returns an iterator that either points to the required entry, or points to one past the last entry in the map. If an entry is found, accessing the second member of the pair pointed to by the iterator provides the number corresponding to the Person object key.

The deleteEntry() function deletes an entry from the map. The process is similar to that used in the getEntry() function, the difference being that when an entry is found by the find() function, the erase() function is called to remove it. You could use another version of erase() to do this, in which case the code would be like this:

```
void deleteEntry(map<Person, string>& book)
{
  Person person = getPerson();
  if(book.erase(person))
    cout << person.getName() << " erased." << endl;
  else
    cout << "No entry found for " << person.getName() << endl;
}
```

The code turns out to be much simpler if you pass the key to the erase() function.

The listEntries() function lists the contents of a phone book:

```
void listEntries(map<Person, string>& book)
{
  if(book.empty())
  {
    cout << "The phone book is empty." << endl;
    return;
  }
  map<Person, string>::iterator iter;
  cout << setiosflags(ios::left);                 // Left justify output
  for(iter = book.begin() ; iter != book.end() ; iter++)
  {
    cout << setw(30) << iter->first.getName()
         << setw(12) << iter->second << endl;
  }
  cout << resetiosflags(ios::right);              // Right justify output
}
```

After an initial check for an empty map, the entries are listed in a `for` loop using an iterator. The output is left-justified by the `setiosflags` manipulator to produce tidy output. This remains in effect until `resetiosflags` manipulator is used to restore right-justification.

Using a Multimap Container

A multimap container works very much like the map container in that it supports the same range of functions except for the subscript operator, which you cannot use with a multimap. The principle difference between a map and a multimap is that you can have multiple entries with the same key in a multimap and this affects the way some of the functions behave. Obviously, with the possibility of several keys having the same value, overloading the `operator[]()` function would not make much sense for a multimap.

The `insert()` function flavors for a multimap are a little different from the function for a map. The simplest version of `insert()` that accepts a `pair<K, T>` object as an argument returns an iterator pointing to the entry that was inserted in the multimap. The equivalent function for a map returns a pair object because this provides an indication of when the key already exists in the map and the insertion is not possible; of course, this cannot arise with a multimap. A multimap also has a version of `insert()` with two arguments, the second being the pair to be inserted, the first being an iterator pointing to the position in the multimap to start searching for an insertion point. This gives you some control over where a pair will be inserted when the same key already exists. This version of `insert()` also returns an iterator pointing to the element that was inserted. The third version of `insert()` accepts two iterator arguments that specify a range of elements to be inserted from some other source.

When you pass a key to the `erase()` function for a multimap, it erases all entries with the same key and the value returned indicates how many entries were deleted. The significance of having another version of `erase()` available that accepts an iterator as an argument should now be apparent — it allows you to delete a single element.

The `find()` function can only find the first element with a given key in a multimap. You really need a way to find several elements with the same key and the `lower_bound()`, `upper_bound()`, and `equal_range()` functions provide you with a way to do this. For example, given a `phonebook` object that is type

```
multimap<Person, string>
```

rather than type `map<Person, string>`, you could list the phone numbers corresponding to a given key like this:

```
Person person = Person("Jack", "Jones");
multimap<Person, string>::iterator iter = phonebook.lower_bound(person);
if(iter == phonebook.end())
  cout << "The are no entries for " << person.getName() << endl;
else
{
  cout << "The following numbers are listed for " << person.getName() << ":" << endl;
  for(  ;  iter != phonebook.upper_bound(person) ; iter++)
     cout << iter->second << endl;
}
```

It's important to check the iterator returned by the `lower_bound()` function. If you don't, you could end up trying to reference an entry one beyond the last entry.

More on Iterators

The `<iterator>` header defines several templates for iterators for transferring data from a source to a destination. Stream iterators act as pointers to a stream for input or output and they enable you to transfer data between a stream and any source or destination that works with iterators, such as an algorithm. Inserter interators can transfer data into a basic sequence container. The `<iterator>` header defines two stream iterator templates, `istream_iterator<T>` for input streams and `ostream_iterator<T>` for output streams, where `T` is the type of object to be extracted from, or written to, the stream. The header also defines three inserter templates, `inserter<T>`, `back_inserter<T>` and `front_inserter<T>`, where `T` is the type of sequence container in which data is to be inserted.

Let's explore some of these iterators in a little more depth.

Using Input Stream Iterators

Here's an example of how you create an input stream iterator:

```
istream_iterator<int> numbersInput(cin);
```

This creates the iterator `numbersInput` of type `istream_iterator<int>` that can point to objects of type `int` in a stream. The argument to the constructor specifies the actual stream to which the iterator relates, so this is an iterator that can read integers from `cin`, the standard input stream.

The default `istream_iterator<T>` constructor creates an end-of-stream iterator, which will be the equivalent to the end iterator for a container that you have been obtaining by calling the `end()` function. Here's how you could create an end-of-stream iterator for `cin` complementing the `numbersInput` iterator:

```
istream_iterator<int> numbersEnd;
```

Now you have a pair of iterators that define a sequence of values of type `int` from `cin`. You could use these to load values from `cin` into a `vector<int>` container for example:

```
vector<int> numbers;
istream_iterator<int> numbersInput(cin), numbersEnd;
cout << "Enter integers separated by spaces then a letter to end:" << endl;
while(numbersInput != numbersEnd)
  numbers.pushback(*numbersIn++);
```

After defining the vector container to hold values of type `int`, you create two input stream iterators: `numbersIn` is an input stream iterator reading values of type `int` from `cin`, and `numbersEnd` is an end-of-stream iterator for the same input stream. The `while` loop continues as long as `numbersEnd` is not equal to the end-of-stream iterator, `numbersEnd`. When you execute this fragment, input continues until end-of-stream is recognized for `cin`, but what produces that condition? The end-of-stream condition will arise if you enter `Ctrl+Z` to close the input stream, or you enter an invalid character such as a letter.

Of course, you are not limited to using input stream iterators as loop control variables. You can use them to pass data to an algorithm such as the `accumulate()` that is defined in the `<numeric>` header:

```
vector<int> numbers;
istream_iterator<int> numbersInput(cin), numbersEnd;
cout << "Enter integers separated by spaces then a letter to end:" << endl;

cout << "The sum of the input values that you entered is "
     << accumulate(intvecRead, endStream, 0) << endl;
```

This fragment outputs the sum of however many integers you enter. You will recall that the arguments to the `accumulate()` algorithm are an iterator pointing to the first value in the sequence, an iterator pointing to one past the last value, and the initial value for the sum. Here you are transferring data directly from `cin` to the algorithm.

The `<sstream>` header defines the `basic_istringstream<char>` type that defines an object type that can access data from a stream buffer such as a `string` object. The header also defines the `istringstream` type as `basic_istringstream<char>`, which will be a stream of characters of type `char`. You can construct an `istringstream` object from a `string` object, which means you can read data from the `string` object just as you read from `cin`. Because an `istringstream<T>` object is a stream, you can pass it to an input iterator constructor and use the iterator to access the data in the underlying stream buffer. Here's an example of how you do that:

```
string data("2.4 2.5 3.6 2.1 6.7 6.8 94 95 1.1 1.4 32");
istringstream input(data);
istream_iterator<double> begin(input), end;
cout << "The sum of the values from the data string is "
     << accumulate(begin, end, 0.0) << endl;
```

You create the `istringstream` object, `input`, from the `string` object, `data`, so you can read from `data` as a stream. You create two stream iterators that can access `double` values in the `input` stream, and you use these to pass the contents of `data` to the `accumulate()` algorithm. Note that the type of the third argument to the `accumulate()` function determines the type of the result so you must specify this as a value of type `double` to get the sum produced correctly.

Let's try a working example.

Try It Out   Using an Input Stream Iterator

In this example you use a stream iterator to read text from the standard input stream and transfer it to a map container to produce a collocation for the text. Here's the code:

```
// Ex10_11.cpp
// A simple word collocation
#include <iostream>
#include <iomanip>
#include <string>
#include <map>
```

```
using std::cout;
using std::cin;
using std::endl;
using std::string;


int main()
{
  typedef std::map<string, int>::const_iterator Iter;

  std::map<string, int> words;              // Map to store words and word counts
  cout << "Enter some text and press Enter followed by Ctrl+Z to end:"
       << endl << endl;

  std::istream_iterator<string> begin(cin); // Stream iterator
  std::istream_iterator<string> end;        // End stream iterator

  while(begin != end )                      // Iterate over words in the stream
    words[*begin++]++;                      // Increment and store a word count

  // Output the words and their counts
  cout << endl << "Here are the word counts for the text you entered:" << endl;
  for(Iter iter = words.begin() ; iter != words.end() ; ++iter)
    cout << std::setw(5) << iter->second << " " << iter->first << endl;

  return 0;
}
```

Here's an example of some output from this program:

```
Enter some text and press Enter followed by Ctrl+Z to end:

Peter Piper picked a peck of pickled pepper
A peck of pickled pepper Peter Piper picked
If Peter Piper picked a peck of pickled pepper
Where's the peck of pickled pepper Peter Piper picked
^Z

Here are the word counts for the text you entered:
    1 A
    1 If
    4 Peter
    4 Piper
    1 Where's
    2 a
    4 of
    4 peck
    4 pepper
    4 picked
    4 pickled
    1 the
```

How It Works

You first define a type for a `const` iterator for the map container:

```
typedef std::map<string, int>::const_iterator Iter;
```

Using this `typedef` statement to define the `Iter` type will make the loop statement that outputs the contents of the map much more readable.

Next you define a map container to store the words and the word counts:

```
std::map<string, int> words;          // Map to store words and word counts
```

This container stores each word count of type `int` using the word of type `string` as the key. This will make it easy to accumulate the count for each word when you read from the input stream using stream iterators.

```
std::istream_iterator<string> begin(cin); // Stream iterator
std::istream_iterator<string> end;        // End stream iterator
```

The `begin` iterator is a stream iterator for the standard input stream and `end` is an end-of-stream iterator that you can use to detect when the end of the input is reached.

You read the words and accumulate the counts in a loop:

```
while(begin != end )                  // Iterate over words in the stream
  words[*begin++]++;                  // Increment and store a word count
```

This simple `while` loop does a great deal of work. The loop control expression will iterate over the words entered via the standard input stream until the end-of-stream state is reached. The stream iterator reads words from `cin` delimited by whitespace, just like the overloaded >> operator for `cin`. Within the loop you use the subscript operator for the map container to store a count with the word as the key; remember, the argument to the subscript operator for a map is the key. The expression `*begin` accesses a word and the expression `*begin++` increments the iterator after accessing the word.

The first time a word is read, it will not be in the map, so the expression `words[*begin++]` will store a new entry with the count having the default value 0, and increment the `begin` iterator to the next word, ready for the next loop iteration. The whole expression `words[*begin++]++` will increment the count for the entry, regardless of whether it is a new entry or not. Thus an existing entry will just get its count incremented whereas a new entry will be created and then its count incremented from 0 to 1.

Finally you output the count for each word in a `for` loop:

```
for(Iter iter = words.begin() ; iter != words.end() ; ++iter)
  cout << std::setw(5) << iter->second << " " << iter->first << endl;
```

This uses the iterator for the container in the way you have seen several times before. The loop control expressions are very much easier to read because of the `typedef` for `Iter`.

Using Inserter Iterators

An inserter iterator is an iterator that can add new elements to any of the sequence containers `vector<T>`, `deque<T>`, and `list<T>`. There are three templates that create inserter iterators:

❑ `back_inserter<T>` inserts elements at the end of a container of type `T`.

❑ `front_inserter<T>` inserts elements at the beginning of a container of type `T`.

❑ `inserter<T>` inserts elements starting at a specified position within a container of type `T`.

The constructors for the first two types of inserter iterators expect a single argument specifying the container in which elements are to be inserted. For example:

```
vector<int> numbers;
front_inserter<vector<int>> iter(numbers);
```

Here you create an inserter iterator that can insert data at the beginning of the `vector<int>` container `numbers`.

Inserting a value into the container is very simple:

```
*iter = 99;                    // Insert 99 at the front of the numbers container
```

The constructor for an `inserter<T>` iterator requires two arguments:

```
inserter<vector<int>> iter_anywhere(numbers, numbers.begin());
```

The second argument to the constructor is an iterator specifying where data is to be inserted — the start in the sequence in this instance. You can use this iterator in exactly the same way as the previous one. Here's how you could insert a series of values into a vector container using this iterator:

```
for(int i = 0 ; i<100 ; i++)
    *iter_anywhere = i + 1;
```

This loop inserts the values from 1 to 100 in the `numbers` container.

The inserter iterators can be used in conjunction with the `copy()` algorithm in a particularly useful way. Here's how you could read values from `cin` and transfer them to a `list<T>` container:

```
list<double> values;
cout << "Enter a series of values separated by spaces"
     << " followed by Ctrl+Z or a letter to end:" << endl;
istream_iterator<double> input(cin), input_end;
copy(input, input_end, back_inserter<list<double>>(values));
```

You first create a list container that stores `double` values. After a prompt for input, you create two input stream iterators for values of type `double`. The first iterator points to `cin` and the second iterator is an end-of-stream iterator created by the default constructor. You specify the input to the `copy()` function with the two iterators and the destination for the copy operation is a back inserter iterator that you create in the third argument to the `copy()` function. The back inserter iterator adds the data transferred by the copy operation to the list container, `values`. This is quite powerful stuff. If you ignore the prompt, in three statements you can read an arbitrary number of values from the standard input stream and transfer them to a list container.

Using Output Stream Iterators

Complementing the input stream iterator template, the `ostream_iterator<T>` template provides output stream iterators for writing objects of type `T` to an output stream. There are two constructors for an instance of the output stream iterator template. One creates an iterator that just transfers data to the destination stream:

```
ostream_iterator<int> out(cout);
```

The type argument, `int`, to the template specifies the type of data to be handled and the constructor argument, `cout`, specifies the stream that will be the destination for data so the `out` iterator can write value of type `int` to the standard output stream. Here's how you might use this iterator:

```
int data[] = {1, 2, 3, 4, 5, 6, 7, 8, 9};
vector<int> numbers(data, data+9);       // Contents 1 2 3 4 5 6 7 8 9
copy(numbers.begin(), numbers.end(), out);
```

The `copy()` algorithm that is defined in the `<algorithm>` header copies the sequence of objects specified by the first two iterator arguments to the output iterator specified by the third argument. Here the function copies the elements from the `numbers` vector to the `out` iterator, which will write the elements to `cout`. The result of executing this fragment will be:

```
123456789
```

As you can see, the values are written to the standard output stream with no spaces between. The second output stream iterator constructor can improve on this:

```
ostream_iterator<int>  out(cout, ", ");
```

The second argument to the constructor is a string to be used as a delimiter for output values. If you use this iterator as the third argument to the `copy()` function in the previous fragment, the output will be:

```
1, 2, 3, 4, 5, 6, 7, 8, 9,
```

The delimiter string that you specify as a second constructor argument is written to the stream following each value that is written out.

Let's see how an output stream iterator works in practice.

Try It Out   Using an Inserter Iterator

Suppose you want to read a series of integer values from `cin` and store them in a vector. You then want to output the values and their sum. Here's how you could do this with the STL:

```
// Ex10_12.cpp
// Using stream and inserter iterators
#include <iostream>
```

```
#include <numeric>
#include <vector>
using std::cout;
using std::cin;
using std::endl;
using std::vector;
using std::istream_iterator;
using std::ostream_iterator;
using std::back_inserter;
using std::accumulate;

int main()
{
  vector<int> numbers;
  cout << "Enter a series of integers separated by spaces"
       << " followed by Ctrl+Z or a letter:" << endl;

  istream_iterator<int> input(cin), input_end;
  ostream_iterator<int> out(cout, " ");

  copy(input, input_end, back_inserter<vector<int>>(numbers));

  cout << "You entered the following values:" << endl;
  copy(numbers.begin(), numbers.end(), out);

  cout << endl << "The sum of these values is "
       << accumulate(numbers.begin(), numbers.end(), 0) << endl;

  return 0;
}
```

Here's an example of some output:

```
Enter a series of integers separated by spaces followed by Ctrl+Z or a letter:
1 2 3 4 5 6 7 8 9 10 11 12 13 14 15 ^Z
You entered the following values:
1 2 3 4 5 6 7 8 9 10 11 12 13 14 15
The sum of these values is 120
```

How It Works

After creating the numbers vector to store integers and issuing a prompt for input, you create three stream iterators:

```
istream_iterator<int> input(cin), input_end;
ostream_iterator<int> out(cout, " ");
```

The first statement creates two input stream iterators for reading values of type int from the standard input stream, input and input_end, the latter being an end-of-stream iterator. The second statement creates an output stream iterator for transferring values of type int to the standard output stream with the delimiter following each output value being a single space.

Data is read from cin and transferred to the vector container using the copy() algorithm:

```
copy(input, input_end, back_inserter<vector<int>>(numbers));
```

You specify the source of data for the copy operation by the two input stream iterators, `input` and `input_end`, and the destination for the copy operation is a back inserter iterator for the `numbers` container. Thus the copy operation will transfer data values from `cin` to the `numbers` container via the back inserter.

You output the values that have been stored in the container using another copy operation:

```
copy(numbers.begin(), numbers.end(), out);
```

Here the source for the copy is specified by the `begin()` and `end()` iterators for the container, and the destination is the output stream iterator, `out`. This operation will therefore write the data from `numbers` to `cout` with the values separated by a space.

Finally you calculate the sum of the values in the `numbers` container in the output statement using the `accumulate()` algorithm:

```
cout << endl << "The sum of these values is "
     << accumulate(numbers.begin(), numbers.end(), 0) << endl;
```

You specify the range of values to be summed by the `begin()` and `end()` iterators for the container and the initial value for the sum is zero. If you wanted the average rather than the sum, this is easy too, being given by the expression:

```
accumulate(numbers.begin(), numbers.end(), 0)/numbers.size()
```

More on Function Objects

The `<functional>` header defines an extensive set of templates for creating function objects that you can use with algorithms and containers. I won't discuss them in detail but I'll summarize the most useful ones. The function objects for comparisons are shown in the following table.

Function Object Template	Description
`less<T>`	Creates a binary predicate representing the `<` operation between objects of type `T`. For example, `less<string>()` defines a function object for comparing objects of type `string`.
`less_equal<T>`	Creates a binary predicate representing the `<=` operation between objects of type `T`. For example, `less_equal<double>()` defines a function object for comparing objects of type `double`.
`equal<T>`	Creates a binary predicate representing the `==` operation between objects of type `T`.
`not_equal<T>`	Creates a binary predicate representing the `!=` operation between objects of type `T`.

Function Object Template	Description
greater_equal<T>	Creates a binary predicate representing the >= operation between objects of type T.
greater<T>	Creates a binary predicate representing the > operation between objects of type T.
not2<B>	Creates a binary predicate that is the negation of a binary predicate of type B. For example, not2(less<int>) creates a binary predicate for comparing objects of type int that returns true if the left operand is not less than the right operand. The template type parameter value B is deduced from the type of the constructor argument.

Here's how you could use the not2<B> template to define a binary predicate for use with the sort() algorithm:

```
sort(v.begin(), v.end(), not2(greater<string>()));
```

The argument to the not2 constructor is greater<string>(), which is a call to the constructor for the greater<string> class type, so the sort() function will sort using "not greater than" as the comparison between objects in the container, v.

The <functional> header also defines function objects for performing arithmetic operations on elements. You would typically use these to apply operations to sequences of numerical values using the transform() algorithm that is defined in the <algorithm> header. These function objects are described in the following table where the parameter T specifies the type of the operands.

Function Object Template	Description
plus<T>	Calculates the sum of two elements of type T.
minus<T>	Calculates the difference between two elements of type T by subtracting the second operand from the first.
multiplies<T>	Calculates the product of two elements of type T.
divides<T>	Divides the first operand of type T by the second operand of type T.
modulus<T>	Calculates the remainder after dividing the first operand of type T by the second.
negate<T>	Returns the negative of its operand of type T.

To make use of these you need to apply the transform() function, and I'll explain how this works in the next section.

More on Algorithms

The `<algorithm>` and `<numeric>` headers define a large number of algorithms. The algorithms in the `<numeric>` header are primarily devoted to processing arrays numerical values whereas those in the algorithm header are more general purpose and provide such things as the ability to search, sort, copy, and merge sequences of objects specified by iterators. There are far too many to discuss in detail in this introductory chapter, so I'll just introduce a few of the most useful algorithms from the `<algorithm>` header to give you a basic idea of how they can be used.

You have already seen the `sort()` and `copy()` algorithms from the `<algorithm>` header in action. Take a brief look at a few more of the more interesting functions in the `<algorithm>` header.

fill()

The `fill()` function is of this form:

```
fill(ForwardIterator begin, ForwardIterator end, const Type& value)
```

This fills the elements specified by the iterators `begin` and `end` with value. For example, given a vector `v` storing values of type `string` containing more than 10 elements, you could write:

```
fill(v.begin(), v.begin()+9, "invalid");
```

This would set the first 10 elements in `v` to the value specified by the last argument to `fill()`.

replace()

The `replace()` algorithm is of the form:

```
replace(ForwardIterator begin, ForwardIterator end,
                         const Type& oldValue, const Type& newValue)
```

This function examines each element in the range specified by `begin` and `end` and replaces each occurrence of `oldValue` by `newValue`. Given a vector `v` that stores `string` objects, you could replace occurrences of `"yes"` by `"no"` with the following statement:

```
replace(v.begin(), v.end(), "yes", "no");
```

Like all the algorithms that receive an interval defined by a couple of iterators, the `replace()` function will also work with pointers. For example:

```
char str[] =  "A nod is as good as a wink to a blind horse.";
replace(str, str+strlen(str), 'o', '*');
cout << str << endl;
```

This will replace every occurrence of `'o'` in the null-terminated string `str` by `'*'`, so the result of executing this fragment will be the output:

```
A n*d is as g**d as a wink t* a blind h*rse.
```

find()

The `find()` function is of the form:

```
find(InputIterator begin, InputIterator end, const Type& value)
```

This function searches the sequence specified by the first two arguments for the first occurrence of `value`. For example, given a vector `v` containing values of type `int`, you could write:

```
vector<int>::iterator iter = find(v.begin(), v.end(), 21);
```

Obviously by using `iter` as the starting point for a new search, you could use the `find()` algorithm repeatedly to find all occurrences of a given value. Perhaps like this:

```
vector<int>::iterator iter = v.begin();
int value = 21, count = 0;
while((iter = find(iter, v.end(), value)) != v.end())
{
  iter++;
  count++;
}
cout << "The vector contains " << count << " occurrences of " << value << endl;
```

This fragment searches the vector `v` for all occurrences of `value`. On the first loop iteration, the search starts at `v.begin()`. On subsequent iterations, the search starts at one past the previous position that was found. The loop will accumulate the total number of occurrences of value in `v`. You could also code the loop as a `for` loop:

```
for((iter = find(v.begin(), v.end(), value)); iter != v.end() ;
                        (iter = find(iter, v.end(), value))++, count++);
```

Now the find operation is in the third loop control expression and you increment `iter` after the result from the `find()` function is stored. In my view the `while` loop is a better solution because it's easier to understand.

transform()

The `transform()` function comes in two versions. The first version applies an operation specified by a unary function object to a set of elements specified by a pair of iterators, and is of the form:

```
transform(InputIterator begin, InputIterator end,
                        OutputIterator result, UnaryFunction f)
```

This version of `transform()` applies the unary function `f` to all elements in the range specified by the iterators `begin` and `end` and stores the results beginning at the position specified by the iterator `result`. The `result` iterator can be the same as `begin`, in which case the results will replace the original elements. The function returns an iterator that is one past the last result stored.

Here's an example:

```
double values[] = { 2.5, -3.5, 4.5, -5.5, 6.5, -7.5};
```

```
vector<double> data(values, values+6);
transform(data.begin(),data.end(),data.begin(), negate<double>());
```

The `transform()` function call applies a `negate<double>` function object to all the elements in the vector, `data`. The results are stored back in `data` and overwrite the original values; so after this operation the vector will contain:

```
-2.5, 3.5, -4.5, 5.5, -6.5, 7.5
```

Because the operation writes the results back to the `data` vector, the `transform()` function will return the iterator `data.end()`.

The second version of `transform()` applies a binary function with the operands coming from two ranges specified by iterators. The function is of the form:

```
transform(InputIterator1 begin1, InputIterator1 end1, InputIterator2 begin2,
                              OutputIterator result, BinaryFunction f)
```

The range specified by `begin1` and `end1` represents the set of left operands for the binary function `f` that is specified by the last argument. The range representing the right operands starts at the position specified by the `begin2` iterator; an end iterator does not need to be supplied for this range because there must be the same number of elements as in the range specified by `begin1` and `end1`. The results will be stored in the range starting at the `result` iterator position. The `result` iterator can be the same as `begin1` if you want the results stored back in that range but it must not be any other position between `begin1` and `end1`. Here's an example of how you might use this version of the `transform()` algorithm:

```
double values[] = { 2.5, -3.5, 4.5, -5.5, 6.5, -7.5};
vector<double> data(values, values+6);
vector<double> squares(data.size());
transform(data.begin(),data.end(),data.begin(),
                                    squares.begin(), multiplies<double>());
ostream_iterator<double> out(cout, " ");
copy(data.begin(), data.end(), out);
```

You initialize the `data` vector with the contents of the `values` array. You then create a vector `squares` to store the results of the `transform()` operation with the same number of elements as `data`. The `transform()` function uses the `multiplies<double>()` function object to multiply each element of `data` by itself. The results are stored in the `squares` vector. The last two statements use an output stream iterator to list the contents of `squares`, which will be:

```
6.25 12.25 20.25 30.25 42.25 56.25
```

The STL for C++/CLI Programs

The STL/CLR library is an implementation of the STL for use with C++/CLI programs and the CLR. The STL/CLR library covers all the capability that I have described for the STL for standard C++, so I won't go over the same ground again. I'll simply highlight some of the differences and illustrate how you use the STL/CLR with examples.

The STL/CLR library is contained within the `cliext` namespace so all STL names are qualified by `cliext` rather than `std`. There are `cliext` include subdirectories that are equivalents for each of the standard C++ STL headers, including those for container adapters, algorithms and function objects and the STL/CLR subdirectory name is the same in every case. Thus the C++/CLI equivalents to the templates defined in a standard STL header such as `<functional>` can be found in `<cliext/functional>`. So for example, if you want to use vector containers in your C++/CLI program you need an `#include` directive for `<cliext/vector>`, and to use the `queue<T>` adapter the include file is `<cliext/queue>`.

STL/CLR Containers

STL/CLR containers can store reference types, handles to reference types, and unboxed value types; they cannot store boxed value types. Most of the time, you will use STL/CLR containers with handles or value types. If you do choose to store reference types in a container, they will be passed by value, and the requirements for storing such objects in an STL/CLR container are essentially the same as for a native STL container. Any reference type stored in an STL/CLR container must at least implement a public copy constructor, a public assignment operator, and a public destructor. These requirements do not apply when you are storing value types or handles to reference types in an STL/CLR container.

Don't forget that the compiler does not supply default versions of the copy constructor and assignment operator for reference types so when they are needed, you must always define them in your `ref` classes. Just to remind you, for a type `T`, in a C++/CLI class these functions will be of the form:

```
T(const T% t)                          // Copy constructor
{
  // Function body...
}

T% operator=(const T% t)               // Assignement operator
{
  // Function body...
}

~T()                                   // Destructor
{
  // Function body...
}
```

Some container operations also require a no-arg constructor and the `operator==()` function to be defined. A no-arg constructor may be used when space for elements in a container need to be allocated when the container is storing objects rather than handles. If you are storing handles to reference types or value types in an associative container such as a set or a map, they must overload at least one comparison operator — the default requirement is for `operator<()`.

Using Sequence Containers

All the sequence containers provided by STL for native C++ are also available with the STL/CLR. The STL/CLR implements all the operations that the native STL containers support, so the differences tend to be notational arising from the use of C++/CLI types. Let's explore the differences through some examples.

Try It Out   **Storing Handles in a Vector**

First, define `Person` as a `ref` class type:

```cpp
// Person.h
// A class defining a person
#pragma once
using namespace System;

ref class Person
{
public:
 Person():firstname(""), secondname(""){}

 Person(String^ first, String^ second):firstname(first), secondname(second) {}

  // Destructor
  ~Person(){}

  // String representation of a person
  virtual String^ ToString() override
  {
    return firstname + L" " + secondname;
  }

private:
  String^ firstname;
  String^ secondname;
};
```

The class has two constructors including a no-arg constructor, and a destructor. You will be only storing handles to `Person` objects in a vector, so you don't need to implement a copy constructor or an assignment operator. The `ToString()` function here overrides the version inherited from class `Object` and provides the way to get a `String` representation of a `Person` object for output purposes.

You can define a `main()` program that will store `Person` object handles in a vector like this:

```cpp
// Ex10_13.cpp
// Storing handles in a vector

#include "Person.h"
#include <cliext/vector>

using namespace System;
using namespace cliext;

int main(array<System::String ^> ^args)
{
  vector<Person^>^ people = gcnew vector<Person^>();
  String^ first;                // Stores a first name
  String^ second;               // Stores a second name
  Person^ person;               // Stores a Person
```

```
    while(true)
    {
      Console::Write(L"Enter a first name or press Enter to end: ");
      first = Console::ReadLine();
      if(first->Length == 0)
        break;
      Console::Write(L"Enter a second name: ");
      second = Console::ReadLine();
      person = gcnew Person(first->Trim(),second->Trim());
      people->push_back(person);
    }

    // Output the contents of the vector
    Console::WriteLine(L"\nThe persons in the vector are:");
    for each(Person^ person in people)
      Console::WriteLine("{0}",person);
    return 0;
}
```

Here is a sample of output from this program:

```
Enter a first name or press Enter to end: Marilyn
Enter a second name: Monroe
Enter a first name or press Enter to end: Nicole
Enter a second name: Kidman
Enter a first name or press Enter to end: Judy
Enter a second name: Dench
Enter a first name or press Enter to end: Sally
Enter a second name: Field
Enter a first name or press Enter to end:

The persons in the vector are:
Marilyn Monroe
Nicole Kidman
Judy Dench
Sally Field
```

How It Works

You create the vector container on the CLR heap like this:

```
vector<Person^>^ people = gcnew vector<Person^>();
```

The template type argument is Person^, which is a handle to a Person object. The container is also created on the CLR heap so the people variable is a handle of type vector<Person^>^.

You create three handles for use as working storage in the input process:

```
String^ first;          // Stores a first name
String^ second;         // Stores a second name
Person^ person;         // Stores a Person
```

The first two refer to String objects and the third is a handle to a Person object.

You read names from the standard input stream and create `Person` objects in an indefinite `while` loop:

```
while(true)
{
  Console::Write(L"Enter a first name or press Enter to end: ");
  first = Console::ReadLine();
  if(first->Length == 0)
    break;
  Console::Write(L"Enter a second name: ");
  second = Console::ReadLine();
  person = gcnew Person(first->Trim(),second->Trim());
  people->push_back(person);
}
```

After prompting for the input, the `Console::ReadLine()` function reads a name from the standard input stream and stores it in `first`. If just the Enter key was pressed, the length of the string will be zero so you test for this to decide when to exit the loop. If the first name read is not of zero length, you read the second name. You then create a `Person` object on the CLR heap and store the handle in `person`. For each `String^` argument to the constructor, you call the `Trim()` function to remove any leading or trailing spaces. Calling the `push_back()` function for the `people` container stores the `person` handle in the vector.

The objects exist independently of the container, so if you were to discard the container (by assigning `nullptr` to `people` for example) it would not necessarily destroy the objects pointed to by the handles it contains. In our example, we do not retain any handles to the objects, so in this case destroying the container would result in the objects not being referenced anywhere so eventually the garbage collector would get around to destroying them and freeing the memory they occupy on the CLR heap.

After the input loop ends, you output the contents of a vector in a `for each` loop:

```
for each(Person^ person in people)
  Console::WriteLine("{0}",person);
```

The `for each` loop works directly with sequence containers so you can use this to iterate over all the handles stored in the `people` vector. The `Console::WriteLine()` function calls the `ToString()` function for each `Person` object to produce the string to be inserted in the first argument string.

It is not normal usage but let's look at another working example to explore how you can store `ref` class objects in a sequence container, rather than handles.

Try It Out   Storing Reference Class Objects in a Double-Ended Queue

You will use `Person` object again but this time you will sort the contents of the container before you generate the output. Here's the new version of the `Person` class:

```
// Person.h
// A class defining a person
#pragma once
```

```
using namespace System;

ref class Person
{
public:
 Person():firstname(""), secondname(""){}

 Person(String^ first, String^ second):firstname(first), secondname(second)
 {}

  // Copy constructors
 Person(const Person% p):firstname(p.firstname),secondname(p.secondname){}
 Person(Person^ p):firstname(p->firstname), secondname(p->secondname){}

  // Destructor
  ~Person(){}

  // Assignment operator
  Person% operator=(const Person% p)
  {
    if(this != %p)
    {
      firstname = p.firstname;
      secondname = p.secondname;
    }
    return *this;
  }

  // Less-than operator
  bool operator<(Person^ p)
  {
    if(String::Compare(secondname, p->secondname) < 0 ||
       (String::Compare(secondname, p->secondname)== 0 &&
        String::Compare(firstname, p->firstname) < 0))
     return true;
     return false;
  }

  // String representation of a person
  virtual String^ ToString() override
  {
    return firstname + L" " + secondname;
  }

private:
  String^ firstname;
  String^ secondname;
};
```

You now have two copy constructors for Person objects, one accepting a Person object as an argument and the other accepting a handle to a Person object. A sequence container requires both copy constructors if it is to compile. You also have the assignment operator for Person objects, which is also required by the container. The operator<() function is needed for the sort() algorithm.

Here's the program code that will utilize this version of the Person class:

```
// Ex10_14.cpp
// Storing ref class objects in a double-ended queue

#include "Person.h"
#include <cliext/deque>
#include <cliext/algorithm>

using namespace System;
using namespace cliext;

int main(array<System::String ^> ^args)
{

  deque<Person>^ people = gcnew deque<Person>();

  String^ first;              // Stores a first name
  String^ second;             // Stores a second name
  Person person;              // Stores a Person

  while(true)
  {
    Console::Write(L"Enter a first name or press Enter to end: ");
    first = Console::ReadLine();
    if(first->Length == 0)
      break;
    Console::Write(L"Enter a second name: ");
    second = Console::ReadLine();
    person = Person(first->Trim(),second->Trim());
    people->push_back(person);
  }

  sort(people->begin(), people->end());

  // Output the contents of the vector
  Console::WriteLine(L"\nThe persons in the vector are:");
  for each(Person^ p in people)
    Console::WriteLine("{0}",p);

  return 0;
}
```

Here is some output, similar to that of the previous example, except that the objects have been sorted in ascending sequence:

```
Enter a first name or press Enter to end: Brad
Enter a second name: Pitt
Enter a first name or press Enter to end: George
Enter a second name: Clooney
Enter a first name or press Enter to end: Mel
Enter a second name: Gibson
Enter a first name or press Enter to end: Clint
Enter a second name: Eastwood
Enter a first name or press Enter to end:
```

```
The persons in the vector are:
George Clooney
Clint Eastwood
Mel Gibson
Brad Pitt
```

How It Works

You create the double-ended queue container like this:

```
deque<Person>^ people = gcnew deque<Person>();
```

The type parameter to the deque<T> template is now Person, so you will be storing Person objects, not handles.

The storage for the element to be inserted into the container is now defined like this:

```
Person person;              // Stores a Person
```

You are now going to store Person objects, so the working storage is no longer a handle as in the previous example.

The input loop is the same as in the previous example except for the last two statements in the while loop:

```
person = Person(first->Trim(),second->Trim());
people->push_back(person);
```

You create a Person object using the same syntax as in native C++. Although you don't use the gcnew keyword here, the compiler will arrange for the object to be created on the CLR heap because ref class objects cannot be created on the stack.

After the input loop, you sort the elements in the container:

```
sort(people->begin(), people->end());
```

The sort() algorithm expects two iterators to specify the range of elements to be sorted and you obtain these by calling the begin() and end() functions for the container.

Finally you list the contents of the container in a for each loop:

```
for each(Person^ p in people)
  Console::WriteLine("{0}",p);
```

Note that you still use a handle as the loop variable. Even though the container stores the objects themselves, you access them through a handle in a for each loop.

Of course, you could use the subscript operator for the container to access the objects. In this case the output loop could be like this:

```
for(int i = 0 ; i<people->size() ; i++)
  Console::WriteLine("{0}", %people[i]);
```

The subscript operator returns a reference to an object in the container, so because the `Console::WriteLine()` function expects a handle, you have to use the `%` operator to obtain the address of the object.

You also have the possibility to use iterators:

```
deque<Person>::iterator iter;
for(iter = people->begin() ; iter < people->end() ; ++iter)
  Console::WriteLine("{0}", *iter);
```

The iterator type is defined in the `deque<Person>` class, as in native STL. The loop is very similar to a native STL iterator loop but when you dereference the iterator, you get a handle to the element to which the iterator points. This gives a clue as to why the `for each` loop iterates over handles — because it uses an iterator.

Just to complete the set, let's see a sequence container storing elements that are value types.

Try It Out   Storing Values Types in a List

This time you will use a list as the container and store values of type `double`. You will also try out the `sort()` member of the `list<T>` container. Here's the code:

```cpp
// Ex10_15.cpp
// Storing value class objects in a list

#include <cliext/list>

using namespace System;
using namespace cliext;

int main(array<System::String ^> ^args)
{
  array<double>^ values = {2.5, -4.5, 6.5, -2.5, 2.5, 7.5, 1.5, 3.5};
  list<double>^ data = gcnew list<double>();
  for(int i = 0 ; i<8 ; i++)
    data->push_back(values[i]);

  Console::WriteLine("The list contains: ");
  for each(double value in data)
    Console::Write("{0} ", value);
  Console::WriteLine();

  data->sort(greater<double>());
  Console::WriteLine("\nAfter sorting the list contains: ");
  for each(double value in data)
    Console::Write("{0} ", value);
  Console::WriteLine();

  return 0;
}
```

Here is the output from this example:

```
The list contains:
2.5 -4.5 6.5 -2.5 2.5 7.5 1.5 3.5

After sorting the list contains:
7.5 6.5 3.5 2.5 2.5 1.5 -2.5 -4.5
```

How It Works

You first create a handle to a list<T> object with this statement:

```
list<double>^ data = gcnew list<double>();
```

The elements to be stored are of type double, so the template type parameter is the same as for the native STL list.

The elements from the values array are stored in the data container in a loop:

```
for(int i = 0 ; i<8 ; i++)
   data->push_back(values[i]);
```

This is a straightforward loop that indexes through the values array and passes each element to the push_back() function for the list. Of course, you could also use a for each loop for this:

```
for each(double value in values)
   data->push_back(value);
```

You could also have initialized the list container with the contents of the values array:

```
list<double>^ data = gcnew list<double>(values);
```

Once the elements have been inserted in the list and the list contents have been written to the standard output stream, you sort the contents of the list using the sort() function that is defined in the list<double> class:

```
data->sort(greater<double>());
```

The sort() function will use the default function object, less<double>(), to sort the list unless you specify an alternative function object as the argument to the function. Here you specify greater<double>() as the function object to be used so the contents of the list are sorted in ascending sequence. Finally you output the contents of the list so you can confirm the sort does work as it should.

Using Associative Containers

All the associative containers in STL/CLR work in essentially the same way as the equivalent native STL containers but there are some important small differences, generally to do with how pairs are represented.

First, the type of an element that you store in a map of type

```
map<K, T>
```

in native STL is of type pair<K, T>, but in an STL/CLR map container it is of type
map<K,T>::value_type, which is a value type. This implies that you can no longer use the
make_pair() function to create a map entry in STL/CLR. Instead you use the static make_value()
function that is defined in the map<K, T> class.

Second, the insert() function that inserts a single element in a map<K, T> returns a value of type
pair<map<K, T>::iterator, bool> for a native STL container, whereas for a STL/CLR map<K, T>
container the insert() function returns an object of type

```
map<K, T>::pair_iter_bool
```

which is a reference type. An object of type map<K, T>::pair_iter_bool has two public fields, first
and second. first is a handle to an iterator of type

```
map<K, T>::iterator^
```

and second is of type bool. If second has the value true, then first points to the newly inserted element;
otherwise it points to an element that already exists in the map with the same key.

I'll take one example to illustrate how associative containers in the STL/CLR work, and reproduce
Ex10_12 as a C++/CLI program.

Try It Out   Implementing a Phone Book Using a Map

This example works in more or less the same way as the native STL example you saw earlier, Ex10_10.
First you must define a suitable version of the ref class Person that will represent keys in the map:

```cpp
// Person.h
// A class defining a person
#pragma once
using namespace System;

ref class Person
{
public:
 Person():firstname(L""), secondname(L""){}

 Person(String^ first, String^ second):
                firstname(first), secondname(second) {}

  // Destructor
  ~Person(){}

  // Less-than operator
  bool operator<(Person^ p)
  {
    if(String::Compare(secondname, p->secondname) < 0 ||
```

```
        (String::Compare(secondname, p->secondname)== 0 &&
          String::Compare(firstname, p->firstname) < 0))
      return true;
    return false;
  }

  // String representation of a person
  virtual String^ ToString() override
  {
    return firstname + L" " + secondname;
  }

private:
  String^ firstname;
  String^ secondname;
};
```

The `operator<()` member is essential because you will use `Person` objects as keys in the map and to store a key/object pair, the map has to be able to compare keys.

Here is the content of `Ex10_16.cpp`, including the same helper functions as the native STL version:

```
// Ex10_16.cpp
// Storing phone numbers in a map
#include "Person.h"
#include <cliext/map>

using namespace System;
using namespace cliext;
```

```
// Read a person from standard input
Person^ getPerson()
{
  String^ first;
  String^ second;
  Console::Write(L"Enter a first name: ") ;
  first = Console::ReadLine();
  Console::Write(L"Enter a second name: ") ;
  second = Console::ReadLine();
  return gcnew Person(first->Trim(), second->Trim());
}
```

```
// Add a new entry to a phone book
void addEntry(map<Person^, String^>^ book)
{
  map<Person^, String^>::value_type entry;         // Stores a phone book entry
  String^ number;
  Person^ person = getPerson();

  Console::Write(L"Enter the phone number for {0}: ", person);
  number = Console::ReadLine()->Trim();

  entry = book->make_value(person, number);
```

```
        map<Person^,String^>::pair_iter_bool pr = book->insert(entry);
      if(pr.second)
        Console::WriteLine(L"Entry successful.");
      else
        Console::WriteLine(L"Entry exists for {0}. The number is {1}",
                                          person, pr.first->second);
}
```

```
// List the contents of a phone book
void listEntries(map<Person^, String^>^ book)
{
  if(book->empty())
  {
    Console::WriteLine(L"The phone book is empty.");
    return;
  }
  map<Person^, String^>::iterator iter;
  for(iter = book->begin() ; iter != book->end() ; iter++)
    Console::WriteLine(L"{0, -30}{1,-12}",
                       iter->first, iter->second);
}
```

```
// Retrieve an entry from a phone book
void getEntry(map<Person^, String^>^ book)
{
  Person^ person = getPerson();
  map<Person^, String^>::const_iterator iter = book->find(person);
  if(iter == book->end())
    Console::WriteLine(L"No entry found for {0}", person);
  else
    Console::WriteLine(L"The number for {0} is {1}",
                                        person, iter->second);
}
```

```
// Delete an entry from a phone book
void deleteEntry(map<Person^, String^>^ book)
{
  Person^ person = getPerson();
  map<Person^, String^>::iterator iter = book->find(person);

  if(iter == book->end())
    Console::WriteLine(L"No entry found for {0}", person);
  else
  {
    book->erase(iter);
    Console::WriteLine(L"{0} erased.", person);
  }
}
```

```
int main(array<System::String ^> ^args)
{
  map<Person^, String^>^ phonebook = gcnew map<Person^, String^>();
  String^ answer;
```

```
    while(true)
    {
      Console::Write(L"Do you want to enter a phone book entry(Y or N): ") ;
      answer = Console::ReadLine()->Trim();
      if(Char::ToUpper(answer[0]) == L'N')
        break;
      addEntry(phonebook);
    }

    // Query the phonebook
    while(true)
    {
      Console::WriteLine(L"\nChoose from the following options:");
      Console::WriteLine(L"A  Add an entry    D Delete an entry    G  Get an entry");
      Console::WriteLine(L"L  List entries    Q  Quit");
      answer = Console::ReadLine()->Trim();

      switch(Char::ToUpper(answer[0]))
      {
        case L'A':
          addEntry(phonebook);
          break;
        case L'G':
          getEntry(phonebook);
          break;
        case L'D':
          deleteEntry(phonebook);
          break;
        case L'L':
          listEntries(phonebook);
          break;
        case L'Q':
          return 0;
        default:
          Console::WriteLine(L"Invalid selection. Try again.");
          break;
      }
    }

    return 0;
}
```

Here's a sample of output from this example:

```
Do you want to enter a phone book entry(Y or N): y
Enter a first name: Jack
Enter a second name: Bateman
Enter the phone number for Jack Bateman: 312 455 6576
Entry successful.
Do you want to enter a phone book entry(Y or N): y
Enter a first name: Mary
Enter a second name: Jones
Enter the phone number for Mary Jones: 213 443 5671
```

```
Entry successful.
Do you want to enter a phone book entry(Y or N): y
Enter a first name: Jane
Enter a second name: Junket
Enter the phone number for Jane Junket: 413 222 8134
Entry successful.
Do you want to enter a phone book entry(Y or N): n

Choose from the following options:
A  Add an entry    D Delete an entry    G  Get an entry
L  List entries    Q  Quit
a
Enter a first name: Bill
Enter a second name: Smith
Enter the phone number for Bill Smith: 213 466 7688
Entry successful.

Choose from the following options:
A  Add an entry    D Delete an entry    G  Get an entry
L  List entries    Q  Quit
g
Enter a first name: Mary
Enter a second name: Miller
No entry found for Mary Miller

Choose from the following options:
A  Add an entry    D Delete an entry    G  Get an entry
L  List entries    Q  Quit
g
Enter a first name: Mary
Enter a second name: Jones
The number for Mary Jones is 213 443 5671

Choose from the following options:
A  Add an entry    D Delete an entry    G  Get an entry
L  List entries    Q  Quit
d
Enter a first name: Mary
Enter a second name: Jones
Mary Jones erased.

Choose from the following options:
A  Add an entry    D Delete an entry    G  Get an entry
L  List entries    Q  Quit
L
Jack Bateman            312 455 6576
Jane Junket             413 222 8134
Bill Smith              213 466 7688

Choose from the following options:
A  Add an entry    D Delete an entry    G  Get an entry
L  List entries    Q  Quit
q
```

How It Works

The first action in `main()` is to define a suitable map object:

```
map<Person^, String^>^ phonebook = gcnew map<Person^, String^>();
```

This map stores an object that combines a handle to a `Person` object as the key and a handle to a `String` object as the associated object. Because this is an STL/CLR map, elements in the map are of type `map<Person^, String^>::value_type`; for a native STL map the elements would typically be of type `pair<Person, string>`.

Next you define somewhere to store an input response:

```
String^ answer;
```

The `Console::ReadLine()` function that you will use to obtain input from the standard input stream always reads a line of input as a `String` object, so it's convenient to store a response as type `String^`.

Within the `while` loop that loads the map with new entries, you obtain a response to the first prompt like this:

```
answer = Console::ReadLine()->Trim();
```

The `Console::ReadLine()` call reads a line of input as a `String` object and you call the `Trim()` function for the object returned to eliminate leading and railing spaces. The result is stored in `answer` and the first character will be the input response.

You check for `L'n'` or `L'N'` being entered as the response like this:

```
if(Char::ToUpper(answer[0]) == L'N')
  break;
```

This uses the `ToUpper()` function in the `Char` class to convert the first character in `answer` to uppercase before comparing it to `L'N'`. If the response is negative, you exit the loop. As it is coded, entering *any* response other than `L'n'` or `L'N'` is interpreted as `L'Y'`. To remove this anomaly you could add this `if` statement following the one above:

```
if(Char::ToUpper(answer[0]) != L'Y')
{
  Console::WriteLine(L"'{0}' response is not valid. Try again.", answer[0]);
  continue;
}
```

With this amendment, you output a message and go to the next iteration if an invalid response is entered.

If the response in `answer` is not in the negative, you call the `addEntry()` helper function to add a new entry to the map. The first statement in `addEntry()` defines a variable you will use to store a new map entry:

```
map<Person^, String^>::value_type entry;          // Stores a phone book entry
```

The `value_type` type is defined in the `map<K, T>` template and is the equivalent of a pair in native STL.

You obtain a handle to a new `Person` object by calling the `getPerson()` helper function. This uses `Console::ReadLine()` to read the names and creates the `Person` object on the CLR heap. The phone number corresponding to the `Person` object is read in the `getEntry()` function, and you call the `make_value()` function for the map with `person` and `number` as arguments to create the new map entry. You insert the new entry using this statement:

```
map<Person^,String^>::pair_iter_bool pr = book->insert(entry);
```

The `insert()` function returns an object of type `pair_iter_bool`, which is similar to the pair object returned by the native STL version of the function. The `first` field in the `pr` object is a handle to an iterator and the `second` field is a `bool` value that indicates whether or not the insert operation was successful. You use the `second` field in `pr` to output a suitable message, depending on how effective the insert operation was.

When the input loop ends, you prompt for operations on the map using a switch, as in the native version of the program. All the code for these operations is very similar to that in the native version. Note that the output in the `listEntries()` function could be coded like this:

```
for each(map<Person^, String^>::value_type entry in book)
    Console::WriteLine(L"{0, -30}{1,-12}", entry->first, entry->second);
```

This iterates over all the entries in the map using a `for each` loop. You access the key and object in each entry via the `first` and `second` fields.

Summary

This chapter introduced the capabilities of the STL in native C++ and how the same facilities are provided by STL/CLR for use in your C++/CLI programs. The important points discussed in this chapter are:

❑ The STL and STL/CLR capabilities include templates for containers, iterators, algorithms, and function objects.

❑ A container is a class object for storing and organizing other objects. Sequence containers store objects in a sequence, like an array. Associative containers store elements that are key/object pairs, where the key determines where the pair is stored in the container.

❑ Iterators are objects that behave like pointers. Iterators are used in pairs to define a set of objects by a semi-open interval, where the first iterator points to the first object in the series and the second iterator points to a position one past the last object in the series.

❑ Stream iterators are iterators that allow you to access or modify the contents of a stream.

❑ There are four categories of iterators: input and output iterators, forward iterators, bidirectional iterators, and random access iterators. Each successive category of iterator provides more functionality than the previous one, so input and output iterators provide the least functionality and random access iterators provide the most.

❑ Algorithms are template functions that operate on a sequence of objects specified by a pair of iterators.

❑ Function objects are objects of a type that overloads the () operator (by implementing the function operator()() in the class). The STL and STL/CLR define a wide range of standard iterators for use with containers and algorithms, and you can also write your own classes to define function objects.

My objective in this chapter was to introduce enough of the details of the STL and STL/CLR to enable you to explore the rest on your own. There's a great deal more there than I was able to discuss here, so I encourage you to browse the documentation.

Exercises

1. Write a native C++ program that will read some text from the standard input stream, possibly involving several lines of input, and store the letters from the text in a list<T> container. Sort the letters in ascending sequence and output them.

2. Use a priority_queue<T> container from the native STL to achieve the same result as Exercise 1.

3. Implement Exercise 2 as a C++/CLI program.

4. Modify Ex10_10.cpp so that it allows multiple phone numbers to be stored for a given name. The functionality in the program should reflect this, so the getEntry() function should display all numbers for a given name and the deleteEntry() function should delete a particular person/number combination.

5. Modify Ex10_16.cpp to use an STL/CLR multimap to support multiple phone numbers for a person in the phone book.

6. Write a native C++ program to implement a phone book capability that will allow a name to be entered to retrieve one or more numbers or a number to be entered to retrieve a name.

7. Implement the previous exercise solution as a C++/CLI program.

Debugging Techniques

If you have been doing the exercises in the previous chapters, you have most likely been battling with bugs in your code. In this chapter you will explore how the basic debugging capabilities built into Visual C++ 2008 can help with this. You will also investigate some additional tools that you can use to find and eliminate errors from your programs, and see some of the ways in which you can equip your programs with specific code to check for errors.

In this chapter, you will learn about:

❑ How to run your program under the control of the Visual C++ 2008 debugger

❑ How to step through your program a statement at a time

❑ How to monitor or change the values of variables in your programs

❑ How to monitor the value of an expression in your program

❑ The call stack

❑ Assertions and how to use them to check your code

❑ How to add debugging specific code to a program

❑ How to detect memory leaks in a native C++ program

❑ How to use the execution tracing facilities and generate debugging output in C++/CLI programs

Understanding Debugging

Bugs are errors in your program and **debugging** is the process of finding and eliminating them. You are undoubtedly aware by now that debugging is an integral part of the programming process — it goes with the territory as they say. The facts about bugs in your programs are rather depressing:

❑ Every program you write that is more than trivial will contain bugs that you need to try to expose, find, and eliminate if your program is to be reliable and effective. Note the three phases here — a program bug is not necessarily apparent; even when it is apparent you may not know where it is in your source code; and even when you know roughly where it is, it may not be easy to determine what exactly is causing the problem and thus eliminate it.

❑ Many programs that you write will contain bugs even after you think you have fully tested them.

❑ Program bugs can remain hidden in a program that is apparently operating correctly — sometimes for years. They generally become apparent at the most inconvenient moment.

❑ Programs beyond a certain size and complexity always contain bugs, no matter how much time and effort you expend testing them. (The measure of size and complexity that guarantees the presence of bugs is not precisely defined, but Visual C++ 2008 and your operating system certainly come into this category!)

It is unwise to dwell on this last point if you are of a nervous disposition, especially if you fly a lot or regularly are in the vicinity of any process dependent on computers for proper operation that can be damaging to your health in the event of failure.

Many potential bugs are eliminated during the compile and link phases, but there are still quite a few left even after you manage to produce an executable module for your program. Unfortunately, despite the fact that program bugs are as inevitable as death and taxes, debugging is not an exact science; however, you can still adopt a structured approach to eliminating bugs. There are four broad strategies you can adopt to make debugging as painless as possible:

❑ Don't re-invent the wheel. Understand and use the library facilities provided as part of Visual C++ 2008 (or other commercial software components you have access to) so that your program uses as much pre-tested code as possible. Note that while this will reduce the likelihood of bugs in your code, libraries, operating systems, and commercial software, components will still contain bugs in general, so your code can share those bugs.

❑ Develop and test your code incrementally. By testing each significant class and function individually, and gradually assembling separate code components after testing them, you can make the development process much easier, with fewer obscure bugs occurring along the way.

❑ Code defensively — which means writing code to guard against potential errors. For example, declare member functions of native C++ classes that don't modify an object as `const`. Use `const` parameters where appropriate. Don't use 'magic numbers' in your code — define `const` objects with the required values.

❑ Include debugging code that checks and validates data and conditions in your program from the outset. This is something you will look at in detail later in this chapter.

Because of the importance of ending up with programs that are as bug-free as is humanly possible, Visual C++ 2008 provides you with a powerful armory of tools for finding bugs. Before you get into the detailed mechanics, however, look a little closer at how bugs arise.

Program Bugs

Of course, the primary originator of bugs in your program is you and the mistakes you make. These mistakes range from simple typos — just pressing the wrong key — to getting the logic completely wrong. I, too, find it hard to believe that I can make such silly mistakes so often, but no one has yet managed to come up with a credible alternative as to how bugs get into your code — so it must be true! Humans are creatures of habit so you will probably find yourself making some mistakes time and time again. Frustratingly, many errors are glaringly obvious to others, but invisible to you — this is just your computer's way of teaching you a bit of humility. Broadly there are two kinds of errors you can make in your code that result in program bugs:

❑ **Syntactic errors** — These are errors that result from statements that are not of the correct form; for example, if you miss a semicolon from the end of a statement or use a colon where you should put a comma. You don't have to worry too much about syntactic errors. The compiler recognizes all syntactic errors, and you generally get a fairly good indication of what the error is so it's easy to fix.

❑ **Semantic errors** — These are errors where the code is syntactically correct, but it does not do what you intended. The compiler cannot know what you intended to achieve with your program, so it cannot detect semantic errors; however, you will often get an indication that something is wrong because the program terminates abnormally. The debugging facilities in Visual C++ 2008 are aimed at helping you find semantic errors. Semantic errors can be very subtle and difficult to find, for example, where the program occasionally produces the wrong results or crashes infrequently. Perhaps the most difficult of such bugs arise in multi-threaded programs where concurrent paths of execution are not managed properly.

Of course, there are bugs in the system environment that you are using (Visual C++ 2008 included) but this should be the last place you suspect when your program doesn't work. Even when you do conclude that it *must* be the compiler or the operating system, nine times out of ten you will be wrong. There are certainly bugs in Visual C++ 2008, however, and if you want to keep up with those identified to date, together with any fixes available, you can search the information provided on the Microsoft Web site related to Visual C++ (`http://msdn2.microsoft.com/en-us/visualc/default.aspx`), or better still, if you can afford a subscription to Microsoft Developer Network, you get quarterly updates on the latest bugs and fixes.

It can be helpful to make a checklist of bugs you find in your code for future reference. By examining new code that you write for the kinds of errors you have made in the past, you can often reduce the time needed to debug new projects.

From the nature of programming, bugs are virtually infinite in their variety, but there are some kinds that are particularly common. You may be well aware of most of these, but take a quick look at them anyway.

Common Bugs

A useful way of cataloguing bugs is to relate them to the symptoms they cause because this is how you experience them in the first instance. The following list of five common symptoms is by no means exhaustive, and you are certainly able to add to it as you gain programming experience:

Symptom	Possible Causes
Data corrupted	Failure to initialize variable Exceeding integer type range Invalid pointer Error in array index expression Loop condition error Error in size of dynamically allocated array Failing to implement class copy constructor, assignment operator, or destructor

Continued

Symptom	Possible Causes
Unhandled exceptions	Invalid pointer or reference Missing catch handler
Program hangs or crashes	Failure to initialize variable Infinite loop Invalid pointer Freeing the same free store memory twice Failure to implement, or error in, class destructor Failure to process unexpected user input properly
Stream input data incorrect	Reading using the extraction operator and the **getline()** function
Incorrect results	Typographical error: = instead of ==, or i instead of j etc. Failure to initialize a variable Exceeding the range of an integer type Invalid pointer Omitting break in a switch statement

Look at how many different kinds of errors can be caused by invalid pointers and the myriad symptoms that bad pointers can generate. This is possibly the most frequent cause of those bugs that are hard to find, so always double-check your pointer operations. If you are conscious of the ways in which bad pointers arise, you can avoid many of the pitfalls. The common ways in which bad pointers arise are:

❑ Failing to initialize a pointer when you declare it

❑ Failing to set a pointer to free store memory to null when you delete the space allocated

❑ Returning the address of a local variable from a function

❑ Failing to implement the copy constructor and assignment operator for classes that allocate free store memory

Even if you do all this, there will still be bugs in your code, so now look at the tools that Visual C++ 2008 provides to assist debugging.

Basic Debugging Operations

So far, although you have been creating debug versions of the program examples, you haven't been using the **debugger**. The debugger is a program that controls the execution of your program in such a way that you can step through the source code one line at a time, or run to a particular point in the program. At each point in your code where the debugger stops, you can inspect or even change the values of variables before continuing. You can also change the source code, recompile, and then restart the program from the beginning. You can even change the source code in the middle of stepping through a program. When you move to the next step after modifying the code, the debugger automatically recompiles before executing the next statement.

To understand the basic debug capabilities of Visual C++ 2008, you will use the debugger on a program that you are reasonably sure works. You can then just pull the levers to see how things operate. Take a simple example from back in Chapter 4 that uses pointers:

```cpp
// Ex4_05.cpp
// Exercising pointers
#include <iostream>
using namespace std;

int main()
{
  long* pnumber = NULL;                      // Pointer declaration & initialization
  long number1 = 55, number2 = 99;

  pnumber = &number1;                        // Store address in pointer
  *pnumber += 11;                            // Increment number1 by 11
  cout << endl
       << "number1 = " << number1
       << "   &number1 = " << hex << pnumber;

  pnumber = &number2;                        // Change pointer to address of number2
  number1 = *pnumber*10;                     // 10 times number2

  cout << endl
       << "number1 = " << dec << number1
       << "    pnumber = " << hex << pnumber
       << "    *pnumber = " << dec << *pnumber;

  cout << endl;
  return 0;
}
```

If you still have this example on your system, just open the project; otherwise, you need to download the code or enter it again.

When you write a program that doesn't behave as it should, the debugger enables you to inspect work through a program one step at a time to find out where and how it's going wrong, and to inspect the state of your program's data at any time during execution. You arrange to execute this example one statement at a time and to monitor the contents of the variables that you are interested in. In this case you want to look at pnumber, the contents of the location pointed to by pnumber (which is *pnumber), number1, and number2.

First you need to be sure that the build configuration for the example is set to Win32 Debug rather than Win32 Release (Win32 Debug is the default, unless you've changed it). The build configuration selects the set of project settings for the build operation on your program that you can see when you select the Project/Settings menu option. The current build configuration in effect is shown in the pair of adjacent drop-down lists on the Standard toolbar. To display or remove a particular toolbar you just right-click the toolbar and select or deselect a toolbar in the list. Make sure you check the box against Debug to display the debugging toolbar. It comes up automatically when the debugger is operating, but you should take a look at what it contains before you get to start the debugger. You can change the build configuration by extending the drop-down list and choosing the alternative. You can also use the Build > Configuration Manager... menu option. The Standard toolbar is shown in Figure 11-1.

Figure 11-1

You can find out what the toolbar buttons are for by letting the mouse cursor linger over a toolbar button. A tool tip for that button appears that identifies its function.

The Debug configuration in a project causes additional information to be included in your executable program when you compile it so that the debugging facilities can be used. This extra information is stored in the .pdb file that will be in the Debug folder for your project. The 'release' configuration omits this information as it represents overhead that you wouldn't want in a fully tested program. With the Professional version of Visual C++ 2008, the compiler also optimizes the code when compiling the release version of a program. Optimization is inhibited when the debug version is compiled because the optimization process can involve resequencing code to make it more efficient, or even omitting redundant code altogether. Because this destroys the one-to-one mapping between the source code and corresponding blocks of machine code, optimization makes stepping through a program potentially confusing to say the least.

The Debug toolbar is shown in Figure 11-2.

Figure 11-2

If you inspect the tooltips for the buttons on this toolbar, you get a preliminary idea of what they do — you will use some of them shortly. With the example from Chapter 4, you won't use all the debugging facilities available to you, but you will try out some of the more important features. After you are familiar with stepping through a program using the debugger, you explore more of the features with a program that has bugs.

You can start the debugger by clicking the leftmost button on the Debug toolbar, by selecting the Debug > Start Debugging menu item, or by pressing F5. I suggest that you use the toolbar for the example. The debugger has two primary modes of operation — it works through the code by single stepping (which is essentially executing one statement at a time), or runs to a particular point in the source code. The point in the source where the debugger is to stop is determined either by where you have placed the cursor or, more usefully, at a designated stopping point called a **breakpoint**. Check out how you define breakpoints.

Setting Breakpoints

A **breakpoint** is a point in your program where the debugger automatically suspends execution when in debugging mode. You can specify multiple breakpoints so that you can run your program, stopping at points of interest that you select along the way. At each breakpoint you can look at variables within the program and change them if they don't have the values they should. You are going to execute the Ex4_05 program one statement at a time, but with a large program this would be impractical. Usually, you will only want to look at a particular area of the program where you think there might be an error. Consequently, you would usually set breakpoints where you think the error is and run the program so that it halts at the first breakpoint. You can then single step from that point if you want, where a single step implies executing a single source code statement.

To set a breakpoint at the beginning of a line of source code, you simply click in the grayed-out column to the left of the line number for the statement where you want execution to stop. A red circular symbol called a glyph appears showing the presence of the breakpoint at that line and you can remove a breakpoint by double-clicking the glyph. Figure 11-3 shows the Editor pane with a couple of breakpoints set for Ex4_05.

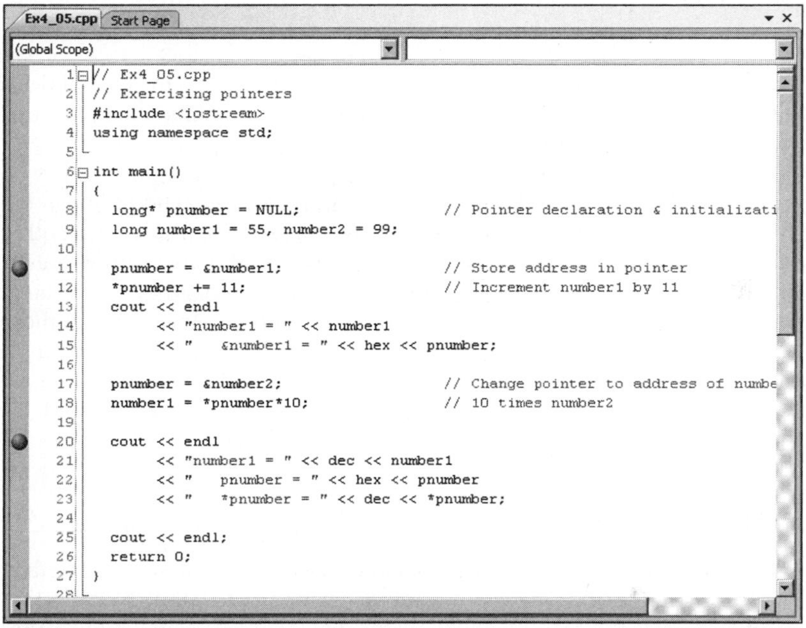

```
1 ⊟ // Ex4_05.cpp
2   // Exercising pointers
3   #include <iostream>
4   using namespace std;
5
6 ⊟ int main()
7   {
8     long* pnumber = NULL;              // Pointer declaration & initializati
9     long number1 = 55, number2 = 99;
10
11    pnumber = &number1;               // Store address in pointer
12    *pnumber += 11;                   // Increment number1 by 11
13    cout << endl
14        << "number1 = " << number1
15        << "    &number1 = " << hex << pnumber;
16
17    pnumber = &number2;               // Change pointer to address of numbe
18    number1 = *pnumber*10;            // 10 times number2
19
20    cout << endl
21        << "number1 = " << dec << number1
22        << "    pnumber = " << hex << pnumber
23        << "    *pnumber = " << dec << *pnumber;
24
25    cout << endl;
26    return 0;
27  }
28  
```

Figure 11-3

When debugging, you would normally set several breakpoints, each chosen to show when the variables that you think are causing a problem are changing. Execution stops *before* the statement indicated by the breakpoint is executed. Execution of the program can only break before a complete statement and not halfway through it. If you place a cursor in a line that doesn't contain any code (for example, the line above the second breakpoint in Figure 11-3), the breakpoint is set on that line, and the program stops at the beginning of the next executable line.

As I said, you can remove a breakpoint by double-clicking the red dot. You can also disable a breakpoint by right-clicking the line containing the breakpoint and selecting from the pop-up. You can remove all the breakpoints in the active project by selecting the Debug > Delete All Breakpoints menu item or by pressing Ctrl+Shift+F9. Note that this removes breakpoints from all files in the project, even if they're not currently open in the Editor pane. You can also disable all breakpoints by selecting the Debug > Disable All Breakpoints menu item.

Advanced Breakpoints

A more advanced way of specifying breakpoints is provided through a window you can display by pressing Alt+F9 or by selecting Breakpoints from the list displayed when you select the Windows button on the Debug toolbar — its at the right end. This window is shown in Figure 11-4.

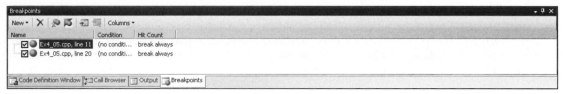

Figure 11-4

The Columns button on the toolbar enables you to add more columns to be displayed in the window. For example, you can display the source file name or the function name where the breakpoint is, or you can display what happens when the statement is reached.

You can set further options for a breakpoint by right-clicking the breakpoint line in the Breakpoints window and selecting from the pop-up. As well as setting a breakpoint at a location other than the beginning of a statement, you can set a breakpoint when a particular Boolean expression evaluates to true. This is a powerful tool but it does introduce very substantial overhead in a program, as the expression needs to be re-evaluated continuously. Consequently, execution is slow, even on the fastest machines. You can also arrange that execution only breaks when the hit count, which is when the number of the point has been reached, reaches a given value. This is most useful for code inside a loop where you won't want to break execution on every iteration. If you set any condition on a breakpoint, the glyph changes so that a + appears in the center.

Setting Tracepoints

A **tracepoint** is a special kind of breakpoint that has a custom action associated with it. You create a tracepoint by right-clicking the line where you want the tracepoint to be set and selecting the Breakpoint > When Hit menu item from the pop-up. You'll see the dialog window shown in Figure 11-5.

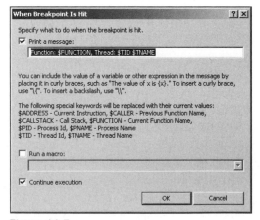

Figure 11-5

As you see, the tracepoint action can be to print a message and/or run a macro and you can choose whether execution stops or continues at the tracepoint. The presence of a tracepoint on a source code line where execution does not stop is indicated by a red diamond-shaped glyph. The dialog text explains how to specify the message to be printed. For instance, you could print the name of the current function and the value of pnumber by specifying the following in the text box:

```
$FUNCTION, The value of pnumber is {pnumber}
```

The output produced by this when the tracepoint is reached is displayed in the Output pane in the Visual Studio application window.

When you check the Run a macro: checkbox, you'll be able to choose from a long list of standard macros that are available.

Starting Debugging

There are five ways of starting your application in debug mode from the options on the Debug menu, shown in Figure 11-6.

Figure 11-6

1. The Start Debugging option (also available from a button on the Debug toolbar) simply executes a program up to the first breakpoint (if any) where execution will halt. After you've examined all you need to at a breakpoint, selecting the same menu item or toolbar button again will continue execution up to the next breakpoint. In this way, you can move through a program from breakpoint to breakpoint, and at each halt in execution have a look at critical variables, changing their values if you need to. If there are no breakpoints, starting the debugger in this way executes the entire program without stopping. Of course, just because you started debugging in this way doesn't mean that you have to continue using it; at each halt in execution, you can choose any of the possible ways of moving through your code.

2. The Start With Application Verifier option is for run-time verification of native C++ code. The Application Verifier is an advanced tool for identifying errors due to incorrect handle and critical section usage and corruption of the heap. I won't be discussing this in detail in this book.

3. The Attach to Process option on the Debug menu enables you to debug a program that is already running. This option displays a list of the processes that are running on your machine and you can select the process you want to debug. This is really for advanced users and you should avoid experimenting with it unless you are quite certain that you know what you are doing. You can easily lock up your machine or cause other problems if you interfere with critical operating system processes.

4. The Step Into menu item (also available as a button on the Debug toolbar) executes your program one statement at a time, stepping into every code block — which includes every function that is called. This would be something of a nuisance if you used it throughout the debugging process because, for example, it would also execute all the code in the library functions for stream output — you're not really interested in this as you didn't write these routines. Quite a few of the library functions are written in Assembler language — including some of those supporting stream input/output. Assembler language functions execute one machine instruction at a time, which can be rather time consuming as you might imagine.

5. The Step Over menu item (also available as a button on the Debug toolbar) simply executes the statements in your program one at a time and run all the code used by functions that might be called within a statement such as stream operations without stopping.

You have a sixth option for starting in debug mode that does not appear on the Debug menu. You can right-click any line of code and select Run to Cursor from the Context menu. This does precisely what it says — it runs the program up to the line where the cursor is and then breaks execution to allow you to inspect or change variables in the program. Whatever way you choose to start the debugging process, you can continue execution using any of the five options you have available from any intermediate breakpoint.

It's time to try it with the example. Start the program using the Step Into option, click the appropriate menu item or toolbar button, or press F11 to begin. After a short pause (assuming that you've already built the project), Visual C++ 2008 switches to debugging mode.

When the debugger starts, two tabbed windows appear below the Editor window. You can choose what is displayed at any time in either window by selecting one of the tabs. You can choose which windows appear when the debugger is started and they can be customized. The complete list of windows is shown on the Debug | Windows menu drop-down. The Autos window on the left shows current values for automatic variables in the context of the function that is currently executing. The Call Stack window on the right identifies the function calls currently in progress but the Output tab in the same window is probably more interesting in this example. In the Editor pane, you'll see that the opening brace of your `main()` function is highlighted by an arrow to indicate that this is the current point in the program's execution. This is shown in Figure 11-7.

You can also see the breakpoint at line 11 and the tracepoint at line 17. At this point in the execution of the program, you can't choose any variables to look at because none exist at present. Until a declaration of a variable has been executed, you cannot look at its value or change it.

To avoid having to step through all the code in the stream functions that deal with I/O, you'll use the Step Over facility to continue execution to the next breakpoint. This simply executes the statements in your `main()` function one at a time, and runs all the code used by the stream operations (or any other functions that might be called within a statement) without stopping.

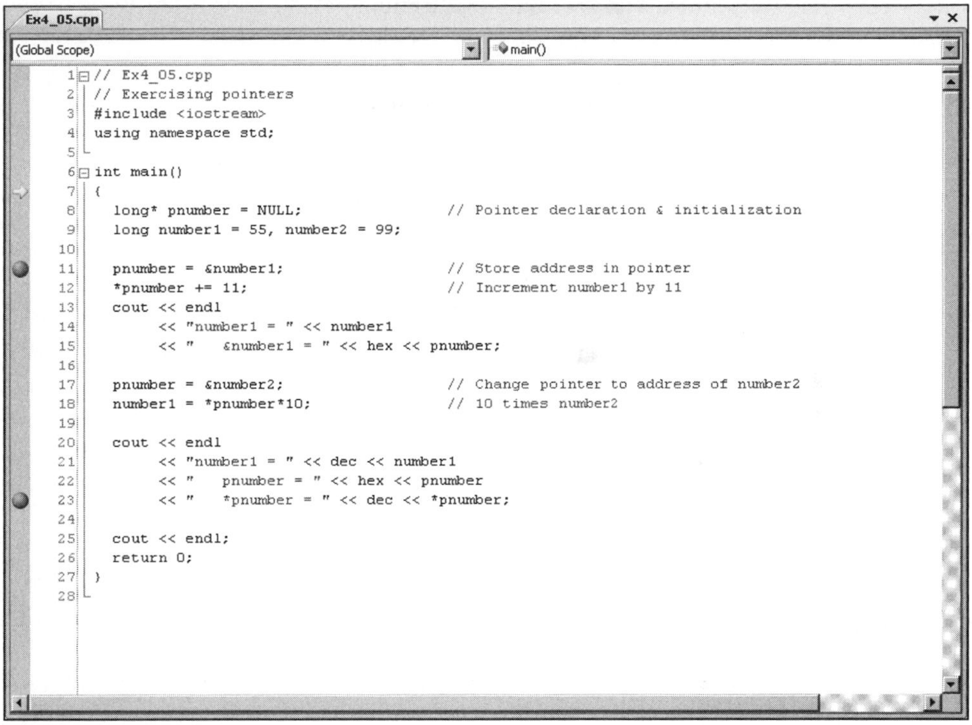

```
Ex4_05.cpp                                                                    ▼ ×
(Global Scope)                                    ▼    🔵 main()                 ▼
     1⊟ // Ex4_05.cpp
     2  // Exercising pointers
     3  #include <iostream>
     4  using namespace std;
     5  └
     6⊟ int main()
     7  {
     8    long* pnumber = NULL;                  // Pointer declaration & initialization
     9    long number1 = 55, number2 = 99;
    10
    11    pnumber = &number1;                    // Store address in pointer
    12    *pnumber += 11;                        // Increment number1 by 11
    13    cout << endl
    14        << "number1 = " << number1
    15        << "   &number1 = " << hex << pnumber;
    16
    17    pnumber = &number2;                    // Change pointer to address of number2
    18    number1 = *pnumber*10;                 // 10 times number2
    19
    20    cout << endl
    21        << "number1 = " << dec << number1
    22        << "    pnumber = " << hex << pnumber
    23        << "    *pnumber = " << dec << *pnumber;
    24
    25    cout << endl;
    26    return 0;
    27  }
    28  └
```

Figure 11-7

Inspecting Variable Values

Defining a variable that you want to inspect is referred to as **setting a watch** for the variable. Before you can set any watches, you must get some variables declared in the program. You can execute the declaration statements by invoking Step Over three times. Use the Step Over menu item, the toolbar icon, or press F10 three times so that the arrow now appears at the start of the line 11:

```
pnumber = &number1;              // Store address in pointer
```

If you look at the `Autos` window now, it should appear as shown in Figure 11-8 (although the value for `&number1` may be different on your system as it represents a memory location). Note that the values for `&number1` and `pnumber` are not equal to each other because the line in which `pnumber` is set to the address of `number1` (the line that the arrow is pointing at) hasn't yet been executed. You initialized `pnumber` as a **null pointer** in the first line of the function, which is why the address it contains is zero. If you had not initialized the pointer, it would contain a junk value that still could be zero on occasion, of course, because it contains whatever value was left by the last program to use these particular four bytes of memory.

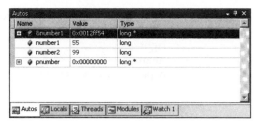

Figure 11-8

The Autos window has five tabs, including the Autos tab that is currently displayed, and the information they show is as follows:

❑ The Autos tab shows the automatic variables in use in the current statement and its immediate predecessor (in other words, the statement pointed to by the arrow in the Editor pane and the one before it).

❑ The Locals tab shows the values of the variables local to the current function. In general, new variables come into scope as you trace through a program and then go out of scope as you exit the block in which they are defined. In this case, this window always shows values for number1, number2 and pnumber because you have only one function, main(), consisting of a single code block.

❑ The Threads tab allows you to inspect and control threads in advanced applications.

❑ The Modules tab lists details of the code modules currently executing. If your application crashes, you can determine in which module the crash happened by comparing the address when the crash occurred with the range of addresses in the Address column on this tab.

❑ You can add variables to the Watch1 tab that you want to watch. Click a line in the window and type the variable name. You can also watch the value of a C++ expression that you enter in the same way as a variable. You can add up to three additional Watch windows via the Debug > Windows > Watch menu item.

Notice that pnumber has a plus sign to the left of its name in the Autos window. A plus sign appears for any variable for which additional information can be displayed, such as for an array, or a pointer, or a class object. In this case, you can expand the view for the pointer variables by clicking the plus sign. If you press F10 twice more and click the + adjacent to pnumber, the debugger displays the value stored at the memory address contained in the pointer, as shown in Figure 11-9.

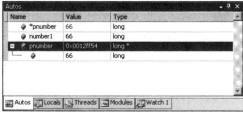

Figure 11-9

The Autos window automatically provides you with all the information you need, displaying both the memory address and the data value stored at that address. Integer values can be displayed as decimal or hexadecimal. To toggle between the two, right-click anywhere on the Autos tab and select from the pop-up menu. You can view the variables that are local to the current function by selecting the Locals tab. There are also other ways that you can inspect variables using the debugging facilities of Visual C++ 2008.

Viewing Variables in the Edit Window

If you need to look at the value of a single variable, and that variable is visible in the Text Editor window, the easiest way to look at its value is to position the cursor over the variable for a second. A tool tip pops up showing the current value of the variable. You can also look at more complicated expressions by highlighting them and resting the cursor over the highlighted area. Again, a tool tip pops up to display the value. Try highlighting the expression `*pnumber*10` a little lower down. Hovering the cursor over the highlighted expression results in the current value of the expression being displayed. Note that this won't work if the expression is not complete; if you miss the `*` that dereferences `pnumber` out of the highlighted text for instance, or you just highlight `*pnumber*`, the value won't be displayed.

Changing the Value of a Variable

The Watch windows also allow you to change the values of the variables you are watching. You would use this in situations where a value displayed is clearly wrong, perhaps because there are bugs in your program, or maybe all the code is not there yet. If you set the "correct" value, your program staggers on so that you can test out more of it and perhaps pick up a few more bugs. If your code involves a loop with a large number of iterations, say 30000, you could set the loop counter to 29995 to step through the last few to verify that the loop terminates correctly. It sure beats pressing F10 30,000 times! Another useful application of the ability to set values for variable during execution is to set values that cause errors. This enables you to check out the error handling code in your program, something almost impossible otherwise.

To change the value of a variable in a Watch window, double-click the variable value that is displayed, and type the new value. If the variable you want to change is an array element, you need to expand the array by clicking the + box alongside the array name and then changing the element value. To change the value for a variable displayed in hexadecimal notation, you can either enter a hexadecimal number, or enter a decimal value prefixed by 0n (zero followed by n), so you could enter a value as A9, or as 0n169. If you just enter 169 it is interpreted as a hexadecimal value. Naturally, you should be cautious about flinging new values into your program willy-nilly. Unless you are sure you know what effect your changes are going to have, you may end up with a certain amount of erratic program behavior, which is unlikely to get you closer to a working program.

You'll probably find it useful to run a few more of the examples you have seen in previous chapters in debug mode. It will enable you to get a good feel for how the debugger operates under various conditions. Monitoring variables and expressions is a considerable help in sorting out problems with your code, but there's a great deal more assistance available for seeking out and destroying bugs. Take a look at how you can add code to a program that provides more information about when and why things go wrong.

Adding Debugging Code

For a program involving a significant amount of code, you certainly need to add code that is aimed at highlighting bugs wherever possible and providing tracking output to help you pin down where the bugs are. You don't want to be in the business of single stepping through code before you have any idea of what bugs there are, or which part of the code is involved. Code that does this sort of thing is only required while you are testing a program. You won't need it after you believe the program is fully working, and you won't want to carry the overhead of executing it or the inconvenience of seeing all the output in a finished product. For this reason, code that you add for debugging only operates in the debug version of a program, not in the release version (provided you implement it in the right way, of course).

The output produced by debug code should provide clues as to what is causing a problem, and if you have done a good job of building debug code into your program, it will give you a good idea of which part of your program is in error. You can then use the debugger to find the precise nature and location of the bug, and fix it.

The first way you can check the behavior of your program that you will look at is provided by a C++ library function.

Using Assertions

The standard library header <cassert> declares the assert() function that you can use to check logical conditions within your program when a special preprocessor symbol, NDEBUG, is not defined. The function is declared as:

```
void assert(int expression);
```

The argument to the function specifies the condition to be checked, but the effect of the assert() function is suppressed if a special preprocessor symbol, NDEBUG, is defined. The symbol NDEBUG is automatically defined in the release version of a program, but not in the debug version. Thus an assertion checks its argument in the debug version of a program but does nothing in a release version. If you want to switch off assertions in the debug version of a program, you can define NDEBUG explicitly yourself using a #define directive. To be effective, you must place the #define directive for NDEBUG preceding the #include directive for the <cassert> header in the source file:

```
#define NDEBUG          // Switch off assertions in the code
#include <cassert>      // Declares assert()
```

If the expression passed as an argument to assert() is non-zero (i.e. true), the function does nothing. If the expression is 0 (false in other words) and NDEBUG are not defined, a diagnostic message is output showing the expression that failed, the source file name, and the line number in the source file where the failure occurred. After displaying the diagnostic message, the assert() function calls abort() to end the program. Here's an example of an assertion used in a function:

```
char* append(char* pStr, const char* pAddStr)
{
  // Verify non-null pointers
  assert(pStr != 0);
  assert(pAddStr != 0);

  // Code to append pAddStr to pStr...
}
```

Calling the `append()` function with a null pointer argument in a simple program produced the following diagnostic message on my machine:

```
Assertion failed: pStr != 0, file c:\beginning visual c++.net\examples\testassert\
testassert \ testassert.cpp, line 11
```

The assertion also displays a message box offering you the three options shown in Figure 11-10.

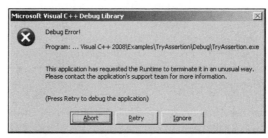

Figure 11-10

Clicking the Abort button ends the program immediately. The Retry button starts the Visual C++ 2008 debugger so you can step through the program to find out more about why the assertion failed. In principle, the Ignore button allows the program to continue in spite of the error, but this is usually an unwise choice as the results are likely to be unpredictable.

You can use any kind of logical expression as an argument to `assert()`. You can compare values, check pointers, validate object types, or whatever is a useful check on the correct operation of your code. Getting a message when some logical condition fails helps a little, but in general you will need considerably more assistance than that to detect and fix bugs. Now take a look at how you can add diagnostic code of a more general nature.

Adding Your Own Debugging Code

Using preprocessor directives, you can arrange to add any code you like to your program so that it is only compiled and executed in the debug version. Your debug code is omitted completely from the release version, so it does not affect the efficiency of the tested program at all. You could use the absence of the NDEBUG symbol as the control mechanism for the inclusion of debugging code; that's the symbol used to control the `assert()` function operation in the standard library, as discussed in the last section. Alternatively, for a better and more positive control mechanism, you can use another preprocessor symbol, _DEBUG, that is always defined automatically in Visual C++ in the debug version of a program, but is not defined in the release version. You simply enclose code that you only want compiled and executed when you are debugging between a preprocessor #ifdef/#endif pair of directives, with the test applied to the _DEBUG symbol, as follows:

```
#ifdef _DEBUG

  // Code for debugging purposes...

#endif // _DEBUG
```

The code between the `#ifdef` and the `#endif` is compiled only if the symbol `_DEBUG` is defined. This means that once your code is fully tested, you can produce the release version completely free of any overhead from your debugging code. The debug code can do anything that is helpful to you in the debugging process, from simply outputting a message to trace the sequence of execution (each function might record that it was called for example) to providing additional calculations to verify and validate data, or calling functions providing debug output.

Of course, you can have as many blocks of debug code like this in a source file as you want. You also have the possibility of using your own preprocessor symbols to provide more selectivity as to what debug code is included. One reason for doing this is if some of your debug code produced voluminous output, so you would only want to generate this when it was really necessary. Another is to provide granularity in your debug output, so you can pick and choose which output is produced on each run. But even in these instances it is still a good idea to use the `_DEBUG` symbol to provide overall control because this automatically ensures that the release version of a program is completely free of the overhead of debugging code.

Consider a simple case. Suppose you used two symbols of your own to control debug code: `MYDEBUG` that managed "normal" debugging code and `VOLUMEDEBUG` that you use to control code that produced a lot more output, and that you only wanted some of the time. You can arrange that these symbols are defined only if `_DEBUG` is defined:

```
#ifdef _DEBUG

#define MYDEBUG
#define VOLUMEDEBUG

#endif
```

To prevent volume debugging output you just need to comment out the definition of `VOLUMEDEBUG`, and neither symbol is defined if `_DEBUG` is not defined. Where your program has several source files, you will probably find it convenient to place your debug control symbols together in a header file and then `#include` the header into each file that contains debugging code.

Examine a simple example to see how adding debugging code to a program might work in practice.

Try It Out   Adding Code for Debugging

To explore these and some general debugging approaches, take an example of a program that, while simple, still contains quite a few bugs that you can find and eliminate. Thus you must regard all the code in the remainder of this chapter as suspect, particularly because it will not necessarily reflect good programming practice.

For experimenting with debugging operations, start by defining a class that represents a person's name and then proceed to test it in action. There is a lot wrong with this code, so resist the temptation to fix the obviously erroneous code here; the idea is to exercise the debugging operations to find them. However, in practice a great many bugs are very evident as soon as you run a program. You don't necessarily need the debugger or additional code to spot them.

Create an empty Win32 console application, Ex11_01. Next, add a header file, Name.h, to which you'll add the definition of the Name class. The class represents a name by two data members that are pointers to strings storing a person's first and second names. If you want to be able to declare arrays of Name objects you must provide a default constructor in addition to any other constructors. You want to be able to compare Name objects, so you should include overloaded operators in the class to do this. You also want to be able to retrieve the complete name as a single string for convenience. You can add a definition of the Name class to the Name.h file as follows:

```
// Name.h - Definition of the Name class
#pragma once

// Class defining a person's name
class Name
{
public:
  Name();                                      // Default constructor
  Name(const char* pFirst, const char* pSecond); // Constructor

  char* getName(char* pName) const;            // Get the complete name
  size_t getNameLength() const;                // Get the complete name length

  // Comparison operators for names
  bool operator<(const Name& name) const;
  bool operator==(const Name& name) const;
  bool operator>(const Name& name) const;

private:
  char* pFirstname;
  char* pSurname;
};
```

You can now add a Name.cpp file to the project to hold the definitions for the member functions of Name. The constructor definitions are shown here:

```
// Name.cpp - Implementation of the Name class
#include "Name.h"                    // Name class definitions
#include "DebugStuff.h"              // Debugging code control
#include <cstring>                   // For C-style string functions
#include <cassert>                   // For assertions
#include <iostream>
using namespace std;

// Default constructor
Name::Name()
{
#ifdef CONSTRUCTOR_TRACE
  // Trace constructor calls
  cerr << "\nDefault Name constructor called.";
#endif
  pFirstname = pSurname = "\0";
}

// Constructor
Name::Name(const char* pFirst, const char* pSecond):
                           pFirstname(pFirst), pSurname(pSecond)
{
```

```
  // Verify that arguments are not null
  assert(pFirst != 0);
  assert(pSecond != 0);

#ifdef CONSTRUCTOR_TRACE
  // Trace constructor calls
  cout << "\nName constructor called.";
#endif
}
```

Of course, you don't particularly want to have Name objects that have null pointers as members, so the default constructor assigns empty strings for the names. You have used your own debug control symbol, CONSTRUCTOR_TRACE, to control output that traces constructor calls. You can add the definition of this symbol to the DebugStuff.h header a little later. You could put anything at all as debug code here, such as displaying argument values, but it is usually best to keep it as simple as your debugging requirements allow; otherwise, your debug code may introduce further bugs. Here you just identify the constructor when it is called.

You have two assertions in the constructor to check for null pointers being passed as arguments. You could have combined these into one, but by using a separate assertion for each argument, you can identify which pointer is null (unless they both are, of course).

You might also want to check that the strings are not empty in an application by counting the characters prior to the terminating '\0' for instance. However, you should not use an assertion to flag this. This sort of thing could arise as a result of user input, so ordinary program checking code should be added to deal with errors that may arise in the normal course of events. It is important to recognize the difference between bugs (errors in the code) and error conditions that can be expected to arise during normal operation of a program. The constructor should never be passed a null pointer, but a zero length name could easily arise under normal operating conditions (from keyboard input, for example). In this case it would probably be better if the code reading the names were to check for this before calling the Name class constructor. You want errors that arise during normal use of a program to be handled within the release version of the code.

The getName() function requires the caller to supply the address of an array that accommodates the name:

```
  // Return a complete name as a string containing first name, space, surname
  // The argument must be the address of a char array sufficient to hold the name
char* Name::getName(char* pName) const
{
  assert(pName != 0);                                // Verify non-null argument

#ifdef FUNCTION_TRACE
  // Trace function calls
  cout << "\nName::getName() called.";
#endif

  strcpy(pName, pFirstname);                         // copy first name
  pName[strlen(pName)] = ' ';                         // Append a space

  // Append second name and return total
  return strcpy(pName+strlen(pName)+1, pSurname);
}
```

Here you have an assertion to check that the pointer argument passed is not null. Note that you have no way to check that the pointer is to an array with sufficient space to hold the entire name. You must rely on the calling function to do that. You also have debug code to trace when the function is called. Having a record of the complete sequence of calls up to the point where catastrophe strikes can sometimes provide valuable insights as to why and how the problem arose.

The `getNameLength()` member is a helper function that enables the user of a `Name` object to determine how much space must be allocated to accommodate a complete name:

```cpp
// Returns the total length of a name
size_t Name::getNameLength() const
{
#ifdef FUNCTION_TRACE
  // Trace function calls
  cout << "\nName::getNameLength() called.";
#endif
  return strlen(pFirstname)+strlen(pSurname);
}
```

A function that intends to call `getName()` is able use the value returned by `getNameLength()` to determine how much space is needed to accommodate a complete name. You also have trace code in this member function.

In the interests of developing the class incrementally, you can omit the definitions for the overloaded comparison operators. Definitions are only required for member functions that you actually use in your program, and in your initial test program you keep it very simple.

You can define the preprocessor symbols control whether or not the debug code is executed in the `DebugStuff.h` header:

```cpp
// DebugStuff.h - Debugging control
#pragma once

#ifdef _DEBUG

#define CONSTRUCTOR_TRACE        // Output constructor call trace
#define FUNCTION_TRACE           // Trace function calls

#endif
```

Your control symbols are defined only if `_DEBUG` is defined, so none of the debug code is included in a release version of the program.

You can now try out the `Name` class with the following `main()` function:

```cpp
// Ex11_01.cpp : Including debug code in a program

#include <iostream>
using namespace std;
#include "Name.h"
```

```
int main(int argc, char* argv[])
{
  Name myName("Ivor", "Horton");                      // Try a single object

  // Retrieve and store the name in a local char array
  char theName[10];
  cout << "\nThe name is " << myName.getName(theName);

  // Store the name in an array in the free store
  char* pName = new char[myName.getNameLength()+1];
  cout << "\nThe name is " << myName.getName(pName);

  cout << endl;
  return 0;
}
```

Now that all the code has been entered, double-checked, and is completely correct, all you have to do is run it to make sure. Hardly seems necessary.

How It Works

Well it doesn't — it doesn't even compile, does it? The major problem is the Name constructor. The parameters are const, as they should be, but the data members are not. You could declare the data members as const, but anyway, you should be copying the name strings, not just copying the pointers. Amend the constructor definition to:

```
// Constructor
Name::Name(const char* pFirst, const char* pSecond)
{
  // Verify that arguments are not null
  assert(pFirst != 0);
  assert(pSecond != 0);

#ifdef CONSTRUCTOR_TRACE
  // Trace constructor calls
  cout << "\nName constructor called.";
#endif
  pFirstname = new char[strlen(pFirst)+1];
  strcpy(pFirstname, pFirst);
  pFirstname = new char[strlen(pSecond)+1];
  strcpy(pSurname, pSecond);
}
```

Now you are copying the strings so you should be OK now, shouldn't you?

When you recompile the program there are some warnings about the strcpy() function being deprecated because it's much better to use strcpy_s() but strcpy() does work so ignore these in this exercise. However, when you rerun the program it fails almost immediately. You can see from the Console window that you got a message from the constructor, so you know roughly how far the execution went. Restart the program under the control of the debugger and you can see what happened.

Debugging a Program

When the debugger starts, you get a message box indicating you have an unhandled exception. In the debugger, you have a comprehensive range of facilities for stepping through your code and tracing the sequence of events. Click Break in the dialog that indicates there is an unhandled exception to halt execution. The program is at the point where the exception occurred and the code currently executing is in the Editor window. The exception is caused by referring to a memory location way outside the realm of the program, so a rogue pointer in our program is the immediate suspect.

The Call Stack

The call stack stores information about functions that have been called and are still executing because they have not returned yet. As you saw earlier, the Call Stack window shows the sequence of function calls outstanding at the current point in the program. Refer to Figure 11-11.

Figure 11-11

The sequence of function calls outstanding runs from the most recent call at the top, the library function strcat(), down to the Kernel32 calls at the bottom of the window in Figure 11-11. Each function was called directly or indirectly by the one below it, and none of those displayed have yet executed a return. The Kernel32 lines are all system routines that start executing prior to our main() function. Your interest is the role of your code in this, and you can see from the second line down in the window that the Name class constructor was still in execution (had not returned) when the exception was thrown. If you double-click on that line, the Editor window displays the code for that function, and indicates the line in the source code being executed when the problem arose, which in this case is:

```
strcpy(pSurname, pSecond);
```

This call caused the unhandled exception to be thrown — but why? The original problem is not necessarily here; it just became apparent here. This is typical of errors involving pointers. Take a look at the window showing the values in the variables in the context of the Name constructor that is presently displayed in the Editor pane. Figure 11-12 shows how it looks.

Figure 11-12

Because the context is a function that is a member of the Name class, the Autos window displays the this pointer that contains the address of the current object. The pSurname pointer contains a weird address, 0xcccccccc, and it has been flagged with <Bad Ptr>. The debugger recognizes that pSurname has got to be a rogue pointer and has marked it as such. If you look at pFirstname, this is also in a mess. At the point where you are in the code (copying the surname) the first name should already have been copied, but the contents are rubbish.

The culprit is in the preceding line. Hasty copying of code has resulted in allocating memory for pFirstname for a second time, instead of allocating space for pSurname. The copy is to a junk address, and this causes the exception to be thrown. Don't you wish you had checked what you did, properly? The line should be:

```
pSurname = new char[strlen(pSecond)+1];
```

It is typically the case that the code causing a bad pointer address is not the code where the error makes itself felt. In general it may be very far away. Just examining the pointer or pointers involved in the statement causing the error can often lead you directly to the problem, but sometimes it can involve a lot of searching. You can always add more debug code if you get really stuck.

Change the statement in the Editor window to what it should be and recompile the project with the change included. You can then restart the program inside the debugger after it has been recompiled by clicking the button on the Debug toolbar, but surprise, surprise you get another unhandled exception. This undoubtedly means more pointer trouble, and you can see from the output in the Console window that the last function call was to getNameLength():

```
Name constructor called.
Name::getName() called.
The name is Horton
Name::getNameLength() called.
```

The output for the name is definitely not right; however, you don't know where exactly the problem is. Restarting and stepping through the program once more should provide some clues.

Note that you can change the way numeric values are displayed in the Debugger windows. The default is to display values in hexadecimal format but you can change this to a decimal by right-clicking in a Debugger window and unchecking Hexadecimal Display. The change will apply to all Debugger windows.

Step Over to the Error

The getNameLength() function is currently displayed in the Editor pane and the debugger has indicated that the following line is where the problem arose:

```
return strlen(pFirstname)+strlen(pSurname)+1;
```

In the Call Stack window, you can see that the program is in the getNameLength() function member, which merely calls the strlen() library function to get the overall length of the name. The strlen() function is unlikely to be at fault, so this must mean there is something wrong with part of the object. The Autos window showing the variables in the context of this function shows that the current object has been corrupted, as you can see in Figure 11-13.

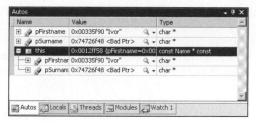

Figure 11-13

The current object is pointed to by this, and by clicking the plus symbol alongside this you can see the data members. It's the pSurname member that is the problem. The address it contains should refer to the string "Horton," but it clearly doesn't. Further, the debugger has flagged it as a bad pointer.

On the assumption that this kind of error does not originate at the point where you experience the effect, you can go back, restart the program, and single step through, looking for where the Name object gets messed up. You can select Step Over or press F10 to restart the application, and single step through the statements by repeatedly pressing F10. After executing the statement that defines the myName object, the Autos window for the main() function shows that it has been constructed successfully, as you can see in Figure 11-14.

Figure 11-14

Executing the next statement that outputs the name corrupts the object, myName. You can clearly see that this is the case from the Autos window for main() in Figure 11-15.

Figure 11-15

On the reasonable assumption that the stream output operations work OK, it must be your `getName()` member doing something it shouldn't. Restart the debugger once more, but this time use Step Into when execution reaches the output statement. When execution is at the first statement of the `getName()` function, you can step through the statements in the `getName()` function using Step Over. Watch the Context window as you progress through the function. You will see that everything is fine until you execute the statement:

```
strcpy(pName+strlen(pName)+1, pSurname);      // Append second name after the space
```

This statement causes the corruption of `pSurname` for the current object, pointed to by `this`. You can see this in the Autos window in Figure 11-16.

Figure 11-16

How can copying from the object to another array corrupt the object, especially because `pSurname` is passed as an argument for a `const` parameter? You need to look at the address stored in `pName` for a clue. Compare it with the address contained in the `this` pointer. The difference is only 20 bytes — they could hardly be closer really! The address calculation for the position in `pName` is incorrect, simply because you forgot that copying a space to overwrite the terminating `'\0'` in the `pName` array means that `strlen(pName)` can no longer calculate the correct length of `pName`. The whole problem is caused by the statement:

```
pName[strlen(pName)] = ' ';              // Append a space
```

This is overwriting the `'\0'` and thus making the subsequent call to `strlen()` produce an invalid result.

This code is unnecessarily messy anyway; using the library function `strcat()` to catenate a string is much better than using `strcpy()`, as it renders all this pointer modification unnecessary. You should rewrite the statement as:

```
strcat(pName, " ");              // Append a space
```

Of course, the subsequent statement also needs to be changed to:

```
return strcat(pName, pSurname);      // Append second name and return total
```

With these changes you can recompile and give it another go. The program appears to run satisfactorily as you can see from the output:

```
Name constructor called.
Name::getName() called.
```

```
The name is Ivor Horton
Name::getNameLength() called.
Name::getName() called.
The name is Ivor Horton
```

Getting the right output does not always mean that all is well, and it certainly isn't in this case. You get the message box displayed by the debug library shown in Figure 11-17 indicating that the stack is corrupted.

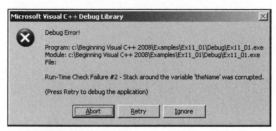

Figure 11-17

The following code shows where the problem lies:

```cpp
int main(int argc, char* argv[])
{
  Name myName("Ivor", "Horton");                    // Try a single object

  // Retrieve and store the name in a local char array
  char theName[10];
  cout << "\nThe name is " << myName.getName(theName);

  // Store the name in an array in the free store
  char* pName = new char[myName.getNameLength()];
  cout << "\nThe name is " << myName.getName(pName);

  cout << endl;
  return 0;
}
```

Both the shaded lines are in error. The first shaded line provides an array of 10 characters to store the name. In fact, 12 are required: 10 for the two names, one for the space, and one for '\0' at the end. The second shaded line should add 1 to the value returned by the getNameLength() function to allow for the '\0' at the end. Thus, the code in main() should be:

```cpp
int main(int argc, char* argv[])
{
  Name myName("Ivor", "Horton");                    // Try a single object

  // Retrieve and store the name in a local char array
  char theName[12];
  cout << "\nThe name is " << myName.getName(theName);

  // Store the name in an array in the free store
  char* pName = new char[myName.getNameLength()+1];
```

```
    cout << "\nThe name is " << myName.getName(pName);

    cout << endl;
    return 0;
}
```

There's a more serious problem in the definition `getNameLength()` member of the class. It omits to add 1 for the space between the first and second names, so the value returned is always one short. The definition should be:

```
int Name::getNameLength() const
{
#ifdef FUNCTION_TRACE
    // Trace function calls
    cout << "\nName::getNameLength() called.";
#endif
    return strlen(pFirstname)+strlen(pSurname)+1;
}
```

That's not the end of it by any means. You may have already spotted that your class still has serious errors, but press on with testing to see if they come out in the wash.

Testing the Extended Class

Based on the output, everything is working, so its time to add the definitions for the overloaded comparison operators to the `Name` class. I'll assume this is a new Win32 console project, Ex11_02. To implement the comparison operators for `Name` objects you can use the comparison functions declared in the `<cstring>` header. Start with the 'less than' operator:

```
// Less than operator
bool Name::operator<(const Name& name) const
{
  int result = strcmp(pSurname, name.pSurname);
  if(result < 0)
    return true;
  if(result == 0 && strcmp(pFirstname, name.pFirstname) < 0)
    return true;
  else
    return false;
}
```

You can now define the > operator very easily in terms of the < operator:

```
// Greater than operator
bool Name::operator>(const Name& name) const
{
  return name > *this;
}
```

For determining equal names you use the `strcmp()` function from the standard library again:

```
// Equal to operator
bool Name::operator==(const Name& name) const
{
  if(strcmp(pSurname, name.pSurname) == 0 &&
                                    strcmp(pFirstname, name.pFirstname) == 0)
    return true;
  else
    return false;
}
```

Now extend the test program. You can create an array of Name objects, initialize them in some arbitrary way, and then compare the elements of the array using your comparison operators for a Name object. Here's main() along with a function, init(), to initialize a Name array:

```
// Ex11_02.cpp : Extending the test operation

#include <iostream>
using namespace std;
#include "Name.h"
```

```
// Function to initialize an array of random names
void init(Name* names, int count)
{
  char* firstnames[] = { "Charles", "Mary", "Arthur", "Emily", "John"};
  int firstsize = sizeof (firstnames)/sizeof(firstnames[0]);
  char* secondnames[] = { "Dickens", "Shelley", "Miller", "Bronte", "Steinbeck"};
  int secondsize = sizeof (secondnames)/sizeof(secondnames[0]);
  char* first = firstnames[0];
  char* second = secondnames[0];

  for(int i = 0 ; i<count ; i++)
  {
    if(i%2)
      first = firstnames[i%firstsize];
    else
      second = secondnames[i%secondsize];

    names[i] = Name(first, second);
  }
}
```

```
int main(int argc, char* argv[])
{
  Name myName("Ivor", "Horton");                    // Try a single object

  // Retrieve and store the name in a local char array
  char theName[12];
  cout << "\nThe name is " << myName.getName(theName);

  // Store the name in an array in the free store
  char* pName = new char[myName.getNameLength()+1];
```

```
    cout << "\nThe name is " << myName.getName(pName);

    const int arraysize = 10;
    Name names[arraysize];                              // Try an array

    // Initialize names
    init(names, arraysize);

    // Try out comparisons
    char* phrase = 0;                                   // Stores a comparison phrase
    char* iName = 0;                                    // Stores a complete name
    char* jName = 0;                                    // Stores a complete name

    for(int i = 0; i < arraysize ; i++)                 // Compare each element
    {
      iName = new char[names[i].getNameLength()+1]; // Array to hold first name
      for(int j = i+1 ; j<arraysize ; j++)              // with all the others
      {
        if(names[i] < names[j])
          phrase = " less than ";
        else if(names[i] > names[j])
          phrase = " greater than ";
        else if(names[i] == names[j])    // Superfluous - but it calls operator==()
          phrase = " equal to ";

        jName = new char[names[j].getNameLength()+1]; // Array to hold second name
        cout << endl << names[i].getName(iName) << " is" << phrase
             << names[j].getName(jName);
      }
    }

    cout << endl;
    return 0;
}
```

The init() function picks successive combinations of first and second names from the array of names to initialize the array Name objects. Names repeat after 25 have been generated, but you need only 10 here.

Finding the Next Bug

If you start the program under the control of the debugger using the Start Debugging button on the Debug toolbar it fails again. The message box shown in Figure 11-18 is displayed.

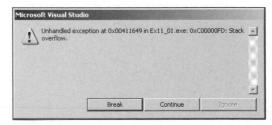

Figure 11-18

The message box indicates you have exceeded the capacity of the stack memory available and if you select the Break button the Call Stack window tells you what is wrong. You have successive calls of the `operator>()` function so it must be calling itself. If you look at the code, you can see why: a typo. The single line in the body of the function should be:

```
bool Name::operator>(const Name& name) const
{
  return name < *this;
}
```

You can fix that, recompile, and try again. This time it works correctly, but unfortunately the class is still defective. It has a memory leak that exhibits no symptoms here, but in another context could cause mayhem. Memory leaks are hard to detect ordinarily, but you can get some extra help from Visual C++ 2008.

Debugging Dynamic Memory

Allocating memory dynamically is a potent source of bugs and perhaps the most common bugs in this context are memory leaks. Just to remind you, a memory leak arises when you use the `new` operator to allocate memory, but you never use the `delete` operator to free it again when you are done with it. Apart from just forgetting to delete memory that you have allocated, you should particularly be aware that non-virtual destructors in a class hierarchy can also cause the problem because they can cause the wrong destructor to be called when an object is destroyed, as you have seen. Of course, when your program ends, all the memory is freed; however, while it is running, it remains allocated to your program. Memory leaks present no obvious symptoms much of the time, maybe never in some cases, but memory leaks are detrimental to the performance of your machine because memory is being occupied to no good purpose. Sometimes, it can result in a catastrophic failure of the program when all available memory has been allocated.

For checking your program's use of the free store, Visual C++ 2008 provides a range of diagnostic routines; these use a special debug version of the free store. These are declared in the header `crtdbg.h`. All calls to these routines are automatically removed from the release version of your program, so you don't need to worry about adding preprocessor controls for them.

Functions Checking the Free Store

Here's an overview of what's involved in checking free store operations and how memory leaks can be detected. The functions declared in `ctrdbg.h` check the free store using a record of its status stored in a structure of type `_CrtMemState`. This structure is relatively simple and is defined as:

```
typedef struct _CrtMemState
{
  struct _CrtMemBlockHeader* pBlockHeader; // Ptr to most recently allocated block
  unsigned long lCounts[_MAX_BLOCKS];      // Counter for each type of block
  unsigned long lSizes[_MAX_BLOCKS];// Total bytes allocated in each block type
  unsigned long lHighWaterCount;    // The most bytes allocated at a time up to now
  unsigned long lTotalCount;        // The total bytes allocated at present
} _CrtMemState;
```

You won't be concerned directly with the details of the state of the free store because you are using functions that present the information in a more readable form. There are quite a few functions involved in tracking free store operations but you will only look at the five most interesting ones. These provide you with the following capabilities:

- ❑ To record the state of the free store at any point
- ❑ To determine the difference between two states of the free store
- ❑ To output state information
- ❑ To output information about objects in the free store
- ❑ To detect memory leaks

Here are the declarations of these functions together with a brief description of what they do:

```
void _CrtMemCheckpoint(_CrtMemState* state);
```

This stores the current state of the free store in a `_CrtMemState` structure. The argument you pass to the function is a pointer to a `_CrtMemState` structure in which the state is to be recorded.

```
int _CrtMemDifference(_CrtMemState* stateDiff,
                      const _CrtMemState* oldState,
                      const _CrtMemState* newState);
```

This function compares the state specified by the third argument, with a previous state that you specify in the second argument. The difference is stored in a `_CrtMemState` structure that you specify in the first argument. If the states are different, the function returns a non-zero value (`true`); otherwise, 0 (`false`) is returned.

```
void _CrtMemDumpStatistics(const _CrtMemState* state);
```

This dumps information about the free store state specified by the argument to an output stream. The state structure pointed to by the argument can be a state that you recorded using `_CrtMemCheckpoint()` or the difference between two states produced by `_CrtMemDifference()`.

```
void _CrtMemDumpAllObjectsSince(const _CrtMemState* state);
```

This function dumps information on objects allocated in the free store, since the state of the free store specified by the argument; this has been recorded by an earlier call in your program to `_CrtMemCheckpoint()`. If you pass null to the function, it dumps information on all objects allocated since the start of execution of your program.

```
int _CrtDumpMemoryLeaks();
```

This is the function you need for the example as it checks for memory leaks and dumps information on any leak that is detected. You can call this function at any time, but a very useful mechanism can cause the function to be called automatically when your program ends. If you enable this mechanism, you get automatic detection of any memory leaks that occurred during program execution, so see how you can do that.

Controlling Free Store Debug Operations

You control free store debug operations by setting a flag, _crtDbgFlag, which is of type int. This flag incorporates five separate control bits, including one to enable automatic memory leak checking. You specify these control bits using the following identifiers:

_CRTDBG_ALLOC_MEM_DF	When this bit is on, it turns on debug allocation so the free store state can be tracked.
_CRTDBG_DELAY_FREE_MEM_DF	When this is on, it prevents memory from being freed by **delete**, so that you can determine what happens under low-memory conditions.
_CRTDBG_CHECK_ALWAYS_DF	When this is on, it causes the _CrtCheckMemory() function to be called automatically at every **new** and **delete** operation. This function verifies the integrity of the free store, checking, for example, that blocks have not been overwritten by storing values beyond the range of an array. A report is output if any defect is discovered. This slows execution but catches errors quickly.
_CRTDBG_CHECK_CRT_DF	When this is on, the memory used internally by the run-time library is tracked in debug operations.
_CRTDBG_LEAK_CHECK_DF	Causes leak checking to be performed at program exit by automatically calling _CrtDumpMemoryLeaks(). You only get output from this if your program has failed to free all the memory that it allocated.

By default, the _CRTDBG_ALLOC_MEM_DF bit is on, and all the others are off. You must use the bitwise operators to set and unset combinations of these bits. To set the _crtDbgFlag flag you pass a flag of type int to the _CrtDbgFlag() function that implements the combination of indicators that you require. This puts your flag into effect and returns the previous status of _CrtDbgFlag. One way to set the indicators you want is to first obtain the current status of the _crtDbgFlag flag. Do this by calling the _CrtSetDbgFlag() function with the argument _CRTDBG_REPORT_FLAG as follows:

```
int flag = _CrtSetDbgFlag(_CRTDBG_REPORT_FLAG);          // Get current flag
```

You can then set or unset the indicators by combining the identifiers for the individual indicators with this flag using bitwise operators. To set an indicator on, you OR the indicator identifier with the flag. For example, to set the automatic leak checking indicator on, in the flag, you could write:

```
flag |= _CRTDBG_LEAK_CHECK_DF;
```

To turn an indicator off, you must AND the negation of the identifier with the flag. For example, to turn off tracking of memory that is used internally by the library, you could write:

```
flag &= ~_CRTDBG_CHECK_CRT_DF;
```

To put your new flag into effect, you just call `_CrtSetDbgFlag()` with your flag as the argument:

```
_CrtSetDbgFlag(flag);
```

Alternatively, you can OR all the identifiers for the indicators that you want together, and pass the result as the argument to `_CrtSetDbgFlag()`. If you just want to leak check when the program exits, you could write:

```
_CrtSetDbgFlag(_CRTDBG_LEAK_CHECK_DF|_CRTDBG_ALLOC_MEM_DF);
```

If you need to set a particular combination of indicators, rather than setting or unsetting bits at various points in your program, this is the easiest way to do it. You are almost at the point where you can apply the dynamic memory debugging facilities to our example. You just need to look at how you determine where free store debugging output goes.

Free Store Debugging Output

The destination of the output from the free store debugging functions is not the standard output stream; by default it goes to the debug message window. If you want to see the output on `stdout` you must set this up. There are two functions involved in this: `_CrtSetReportMode()`, which sets the general destination for output, and `_CrtSetReportFile()`, which specifies a stream destination specifically. The `_CrtSetReportMode()` function is declared as:

```
int _CrtSetReportMode(int reportType, int reportMode);
```

There are three kinds of output produced by the free store debugging functions. Each call to the `_CrtSetReportMode()` function sets the destination specified by the second argument for the output type specified by the first argument. You specify the report type by one of the following identifiers:

`_CRT_WARN`	Warning messages of various kinds. The output when a memory leak is detected is a warning.
`_CRT_ERROR`	Catastrophic errors that report unrecoverable problems.
`_CRT_ASSERT`	Output from assertions (not output from the `assert()` function that I discussed earlier).

The `crtdbg.h` header defines two macros, `ASSERT` and `ASSERTE`, that work in much the same way as the `assert()` function in the standard library. The difference between these two macros is that `ASSERTE` reports the assertion expression when a failure occurs, whereas the `ASSERT` macro does not.

You specify the report mode by a combination of the following identifiers:

`_CRTDBG_MODE_DEBUG`	This is the default mode, which sends output to a debug string that you see in the Debug window when running under control of the debugger.
`_CRTDBG_MODE_FILE`	Output is to be directed to an output stream.

| _CRTDBG_MODE_WNDW | Output is presented in a message box. |
| _CRTDBG_REPORT_MODE | If you specify this, the _CrtSetReportMode() function just returns the current report mode. |

To specify more than one destination, you simply OR the identifiers using the | operator. You set the destination for each output type with a separate call of the _CrtSetReportMode() function. To direct the output when a leak is detected to a file stream, you can set the report mode with the following statement:

```
CrtSetReportMode(_CRT_WARN, _CRTDBG_MODE_FILE);
```

This just sets the destination generically as a file stream. You still need to call the _CrtSetReportFile() function to specify the destination specifically.

The _CrtSetReportFile() function is declared as:

```
_HFILE _CrtSetReportFile(int reportType, _HFILE reportFile);
```

The second argument here can either be a pointer to a file stream (of type _HFILE), which I will not go into further, or can be one of the following identifiers:

_CRTDBG_FILE_STDERR	Output is directed to the standard error stream, stderr.
_CRTDBG_FILE_STDOUT	Output is directed to the standard output stream, stdout.
_CRTDBG_REPORT_FILE	If you specify this argument, the _CrtSetReportFile() function will just return the current destination.

To set the leak detection output to the standard output stream, you can write:

```
_CrtSetReportFile(_CRT_WARN, _CRTDBG_FILE_STDOUT);
```

You now have enough knowledge of the free store debug routines to try out leak detection in your example.

Try It Out   Memory Leak Detection

Even though you have set the project settings to direct the standard output stream to a file, it would be a good idea to reduce the volume of output, so reduce the size of the names array to five elements. Here's the new version of main() for Ex11_02 to use the free store debug facilities in general and leak detection in particular:

```
int main(int argc, char* argv[])
{
    // Turn on free store debugging and leak-checking bits
    _CrtSetDbgFlag( _CRTDBG_LEAK_CHECK_DF|_CRTDBG_ALLOC_MEM_DF );

    // Direct warnings to stdout
```

```
  _CrtSetReportMode(_CRT_WARN, _CRTDBG_MODE_FILE);
  _CrtSetReportFile(_CRT_WARN, _CRTDBG_FILE_STDOUT);

Name myName("Ivor", "Horton");                    // Try a single object

// Retrieve and store the name in a local char array
char theName[12];
cout << "\nThe name is " << myName.getName(theName);

// Store the name in an array in the free store
char* pName = new char[myName.getNameLength()+1];
cout << "\nThe name is " << myName.getName(pName);

const int arraysize = 5;
Name names[arraysize];                            // Try an array

// Initialize names
init(names, arraysize);

// Try out comparisons
char* phrase = 0;                                 // Stores a comparison phrase
char* iName = 0;                                  // Stores a complete name
char* jName = 0;                                  // Stores a complete name

for(int i = 0; i < arraysize ; i++)               // Compare each element
{
  iName = new char[names[i].getNameLength()+1]; // Array to hold first name
  for(int j = i+1 ; j<arraysize ; j++)            // with all the others
  {
    if(names[i] < names[j])
      phrase = " less than ";
    else if(names[i] > names[j])
      phrase = " greater than ";
    else if(names[i] == names[j])    // Superfluous - but it calls operator==()
      phrase = " equal to ";
    jName = new char[names[j].getNameLength()+1]; // Array to hold second name
    cout << endl << names[i].getName(iName) << " is" << phrase
         << names[j].getName(jName);
  }
}
cout << endl;
return 0;
}
```

To reduce output further, you could switch off the trace output by commenting out the control symbols in the DebugStuff.h header:

```
// DebugStuff.h - Debugging control
#pragma once

#ifdef _DEBUG
```

```
//#define CONSTRUCTOR_TRACE          // Output constructor call trace
//#define FUNCTION_TRACE             // Trace function calls
#endif
```

You can recompile the example and run it again.

How It Works

It works just as expected. You get a report that your program does indeed have memory leaks, and you get a list of the objects in the free store at the end of the program. The output generated by the free store debug facility starts with:

```
Detected memory leaks!
Dumping objects ->
{143} normal block at 0x00355F08, 15 bytes long.
 Data: <              > CD CD CD CD CD CD CD CD CD CD CD CD CD CD CD
{142} normal block at 0x00355EC8, 15 bytes long.
 Data: <Emily Steinbeck> 45 6D 69 6C 79 20 53 74 65 69 6E 62 65 63 6B
{141} normal block at 0x00355E90, 12 bytes long.
 Data: <Emily Miller> 45 6D 69 6C 79 20 4D 69 6C 6C 65 72
...
```

and ends with:

```
...
{120} normal block at 0x003559D8, 8 bytes long.
 Data: <Dickens > 44 69 63 6B 65 6E 73 00
{119} normal block at 0x003559A0, 8 bytes long.
 Data: <Charles > 43 68 61 72 6C 65 73 00
{118} normal block at 0x00355968, 11 bytes long.
 Data: <Ivor Horton> 49 76 6F 72 20 48 6F 72 74 6F 6E
{117} normal block at 0x00355930, 7 bytes long.
 Data: <Horton > 48 6F 72 74 6F 6E 00
{116} normal block at 0x003558F8, 5 bytes long.
 Data: <Ivor > 49 76 6F 72 00
Object dump complete.
```

The objects reported as being left in the free store are presented with the most recently allocated first, and the earliest last. It is obvious from the output that the Name class is allocating memory for its data members, and never releasing it. The last three objects dumped correspond to the pName array allocated in main(), and the data members of the object, myName. The blocks for the complete names are allocated in main(), and they too are left lying about. The problem our class has is that we forgot the fundamental rules relating to classes that allocate memory dynamically; they should always define a destructor, a copy constructor, and the assignment operator. The class should be declared as:

```
class Name
{
  public:
    Name();                                      // Default constructor
    Name(const char* pFirst, const char* pSecond);   // Constructor
    Name(const Name& rName);                      // Copy constructor
```

```
      ~Name();                                      // Destructor

      char* getName(char* pName) const;        // Get the complete name
      int getNameLength() const;               // Get the complete name length

  // Comparison operators for names
    bool operator<(const Name& name) const;
    bool operator==(const Name& name) const;
    bool operator>(const Name& name) const;

    Name& operator=(const Name& rName);          // Assignment operator

  private:
    char* pFirstname;
    char* pSurname;
};
```

You can define the copy constructor as:

```
Name:: Name(const Name& rName)
{
  pFirstname = new char[strlen(rName.pFirstname)+1]; // Allocate space for 1st name
  strcpy(pFirstname, rName.pFirstname);              // and copy it.
  pSurname = new char[strlen(rName.pSurname)+1];     // Same for the surname...
  strcpy(pSurname, rName.pSurname);
}
```

The destructor just needs to release the memory for the two data members:

```
Name::~Name()
{
  delete[] pFirstname;
  delete[] pSurname;
}
```

In the assignment operator, you must make the usual provision for the left and right sides being identical:

```
Name& Name::operator=(const Name& rName)
{
  if(this == &rName)                         // If lhs equals rhs
    return *this;                            // just return the object

  delete[] pFirstname;
  pFirstname = new char[strlen(rName.pFirstname)+1]; // Allocate space for 1st name
  strcpy(pFirstname, rName.pFirstname);              // and copy it.
  delete[] pSurname;
  pSurname = new char[strlen(rName.pSurname)+1];     // Same for the surname...
  strcpy(pSurname, rName.pSurname);
  return *this;
}
```

You also should make the default constructor work properly. If the default constructor doesn't allocate memory in the free store, you have the possibility that the destructor will erroneously attempt to delete memory that was not allocated in the free store. You need to modify it to:

```
Name::Name()
{
#ifdef CONSTRUCTOR_TRACE
  // Trace constructor calls
  cout << "\nDefault Name constructor called.";
#endif

  // Allocate array of 1 for empty strings
  pFirstname = new char[1];
  pSurname = new char[1];

  pFirstname[0] = pSurname[0] = '\0';          // Store null character
}
```

If you add statements to `main()` to delete the memory that is allocate dynamically there, the program should run without any messages relating to memory leaks. In `main()` you need to add the following statement to the end of the inner loop that is controlled by `j`:

```
delete[] jName;
```

You also need to add the following statement to the end of the outer loop that is controlled by `i`:

```
delete[] iName;
```

Finally, you still have to release the memory for `pName` after the loops in `main()`:

```
delete[] pName;
```

Debugging C++/CLI Programs

Life is simpler with C++/CLI programming. None of the complications of corrupted pointers or memory leaks arise in programs written for the CLR, so this reduces the debugging problem substantially compared to native C++ at a stroke. You set breakpoints and tracepoints in a CLR program exactly the same way as you do for a native C++ code. You have a specific option that applies to C++/CLI code for preventing the debugger from stepping through library code. If you select the Tools > Options menu item a dialog is displayed, and if you select the Debugging/General set of options the dialog looks as shown in Figure 11-19.

Checking the option highlighted in Figure 11-19 ensures that the debugger only steps through your source statements and executes the library code normally.

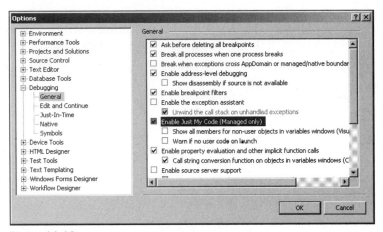

Figure 11-19

Using the Debug and Trace Classes

The `Debug` and `Trace` classes in the `System::Diagnostics` namespace are for tracing execution of a program for debugging purposes. The capabilities provided by the `Debug` and `Trace` classes are identical; the difference between them is that `Trace` functions are compiled into release builds, whereas `Debug` functions are not. Thus you can use `Debug` class functions when you are just debugging your code, and `Trace` class functions when you want to obtain `Trace` information in release versions of your code for performance monitoring or diagnostic and maintenance purposes. You also have control over whether the compile includes trace code in your program.

Because the functions and other members in the `Debug` and `Trace` classes are identical, I'll just describe the capability in terms of the `Debug` class.

Generating Output

You can produce output using the `Debug::WriteLine()` and `Debug::Write()` functions that write messages to an output destination; the difference between these two functions is that the `WriteLine()` function writes a newline character after the output whereas the `Write()` function does not. They both come in four overloaded versions; I'll use the `Write()` function as the example but `WriteLine()` versions have the same parameter lists:

Function	Description
`Debug::Write(String^ message)`	Writes `message` to the output destination.
`Debug::Write(String^ message, String^ category)`	Writes `categoryname` followed by `message` to the output destination. A category name is used to organize the output.

Function	Description
`Debug::Write(Object^ value)`	Writes the string returned by `value>ToString()` to the output destination.
`Debug::Write(Object^ value,` `          String^ category)`	Writes `categoryname` followed by the string returned by `value->ToString()` to the output destination.

The `WriteIf()` and `WriteLineIf()` are conditional versions of the `Write()` and `WriteLine()` functions in the `Debug` class:

Function	Description
`Debug::WriteIf(bool condition,` `          String^ message)`	Writes `message` to the output destination if `condition` is `true`; otherwise, no output is produced.

`Debug::WriteIf(bool condition,`
`          String^ message,`
`          String^ category)`
	Writes `category` followed by `message` to the output destination if `condition` is `true`; otherwise, no output is produced.

`Debug::WriteIf(bool condition,` `          Object^ value)`	Writes the string returned by `value>ToString()` to the output destination if `condition` is `true`; otherwise, no output is produced.

`Debug::WriteIf(bool condition,`
`          Object^ value,`
`          String^ category)`
	Writes `category` followed by the string returned by `value->ToString()` to the output destination if `condition` is `true`; otherwise, no output is produced.

As you see, the `WriteIf()` and `WriteLineIf()` functions have an extra parameter of type `bool` at the beginning of the parameter list for the corresponding `Write()` or `WriteLine()` function and the argument for this determines whether or not output occurs.

You can also write output using the `Debug::Print()` function that comes in two overloaded versions:

Function	Description
`Print(String^ message)`	This writes `message` to the output destination followed by a newline character.
`Print(String^ format,` `      ...array<Object^>^ args)`	This works in the same way as formatted output with the `Console::WriteLine()` function. The format string determines how the arguments that follow it are presented in the output.

Setting the Output Destination

By default the output messages are sent to the Output window in the IDE, but you can change this by using a **listener**, and a listener is an object that directs debug and trace output to one or more destinations. Here's how you can create a listener and direct debug output to the standard output stream:

```
TextWriterTraceListener^ listener = gcnew TextWriterTraceListener( Console::Out);
Debug::Listeners->Add(listener);
```

The first statement creates a `TextWriterTraceListener` object that directs the output to the standard output stream, which is returned by the static property, `Out`, in the `Console` class. (The `In` and `Error` properties in the `Console` class return the standard input stream and standard error stream respectively.) The `Listeners` property in the `Debug` class returns a collection of listeners for debug output so the statement adds the listener object to the collection. You could add other listeners that additionally directed output elsewhere (to a file perhaps).

Indenting the Output

You can control the indenting of the debug and trace messages. This is particularly useful in situations where functions are called at various depths. By indenting the output at the beginning of a function and removing the indent before leaving the function, the debug or trace output is easily identified and you'll be able to see the depth of function call from the amount of indentation of the output.

To increase the current indent level for output by one (one indent unit is four spaces by default), you call the static `Indent()` function in the `Debug` class like this:

```
Debug::Indent();                        // Increase indent level by 1
```

To reduce the current indent level by one you call the static `Unindent()` function:

```
Debug::Unindent();                      // Decrease indent level by 1
```

The current indent level is recorded in the static `IndentLevel` property in the `Debug` class so you can get or set the current indent level through this property. For example:

```
Debug::IndentLevel = 2*Debug::IndentLevel;
```

This statement doubles the current level of indentation for subsequent debug output.

The number of spaces in one indent unit is recorded in the static `IndentSize` property in the `Debug` class. You can retrieve the current indent size and change it to a different value. For example:

```
Console::WriteLine(L"Current indent unit = {0}", Debug::IndentSize);
Debug::IndentSize = 2;                   // Set indent unit to 2 spaces
```

The first statement simply outputs the indent size and the second statement sets it to a new value. Subsequent calls to `Indent()` increases the current indentation by the new size, which is two spaces.

Controlling Output

Trace switches provide you with a way to switch any of the debug or trace output on and off. You have two kinds of trace switches you can use:

❑ The `BooleanSwitch` reference class objects provide you with a way to switch segment of output on or off depending on the state of the switch.

❑ The `TraceSwitch` reference class objects provide you with a more sophisticated control mechanism because each `TraceSwitch` object has four properties that correspond to four control levels for output statements.

You could create a `BooleanSwitch` object to control output as a static class member like this:

```
public ref class MyClass
{
private:
  static BooleanSwitch^ errors =
                          gcnew BooleanSwitch(L"Error Switch", L"Controls error
output");

public:
  void DoIt()
  {
    // Code...

    if(errors->Enabled)
      Debug::WriteLine(L"Error in DoIt()");

    // More code...
  }
  // Rest of the class...
};
```

This shows the errors object as a static member of `MyClass`. The first argument to the `BooleanSwitch` constructor is the display name for the switch that is used to initialize the `DisplayName` property and the second argument sets the value of the `Description` property for the switch. There's another constructor that accepts a third argument of type `String^` that sets the `Value` property for the switch.

The `Enabled` property for a Boolean switch is of type `bool` and is `false` by default. To set it to `true`, you just set the property value accordingly:

```
errors->Enabled = true;
```

The `DoIt()` function in `MyClass` outputs the debug error message only when the `errors` switch is enabled.

The `TraceSwitch` reference class has two constructors that have the same parameters as the `BooleanSwitch` class constructors. You can create a `TraceSwitch` object like this:

```
TraceSwitch^ traceCtrl =
                    gcnew TraceSwitch(L"Update", L"Traces update operations");
```

The first argument to the constructor sets the value of the `DisplayName` property, and the second argument sets the value of the `Description` property.

The `Level` property for a `TraceSwitch` object is an enum class type, `TraceLevel`, and you can set this property to control trace output to any of the following values:

Value	Description
`TraceLevel::Off`	No trace output.
`TraceLevel::Info`	Output information, warning, and error messages.
`TraceLevel::Warning`	Output warning and error messages.
`TraceLevel::Error`	Output Error messages.
`TraceLevel::Verbose`	Output all messages.

The value you set determines the output produced. To get all messages, you set the property as follows:

```
traceCtrl->Level = TraceLevel::Verbose;
```

You determine whether a particular message should be issued by your trace and debug code by testing the state of one of four properties of type `bool` for the `TraceSwitch` object:

Property	Description
`TraceVerbose`	Returns the value `true` when all messages are to be output.
`TraceInfo`	Returns the value `true` when information messages are to be output.
`TraceWarning`	Returns the value `true` when warning messages are to be output.
`TraceError`	Returns the value `true` when error messages are to be output.

You can see from the significance of these property values that setting the `Level` property also sets the states of these properties. If you set the `Level` property to `TraceLevel::Warning` for instance, `TraceWarning` and `TraceError` is set to `true` and `TraceVerbose` and `TraceInfo` are set to `false`.

To decide whether to output a particular message, you just test the appropriate property:

```
if(traceCtrl->TraceWarning)
   Debug::WriteLine(L"This is your last warning!");
```

The message is output only if the `TraceWarning` property for `traceCtrl` is true.

Assertions

The `Debug` and `Trace` classes have static `Assert()` functions that provide a similar capability to the native C++ `assert()` function. The first argument to the `Debug::Assert()` function is a `bool` value or expression that causes the program to assert when the argument is `false`. The call stack is then displayed in a dialog as shown in Figure 11-20.

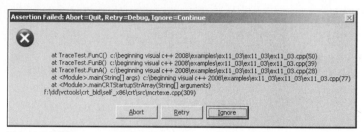

Figure 11-20

Figure 11-20 shows an assertion that is produced by the next example. When the program asserts the call stack presented in the dialog shows the line numbers in the code and the names of the functions that are executing at that point. Here there are four functions executing, including `main()`.

You have three courses of action after an assertion. Clicking the Abort button ends the program immediately; clicking the Ignore button allows the program to continue; and clicking the Retry button gives you the option of executing the program in debug mode.

You have three overloaded versions of the `Assert()` function available:

Function	Description
`Debug::Assert(bool condition)`	When `condition` is `false`, a dialog displays showing the call stack at that point.
`Debug::Assert(bool condition, String^ message)`	As above but with `message` displayed in the dialog above the call stack information.
`Debug::Assert(bool condition, String^ message, String^ details)`	As the preceding version but with `details` displayed additionally in the dialog.

Seeing it working is the best aid to understanding, so put together an example that demonstrates debug and trace code in action.

Try It Out   Using Debug and Trace

This example is just an exercise for some of the trace and debug functions I have described. Create a CLR console project and modify it to the following:

```cpp
// Ex11_03.cpp : main project file.
// CLR trace and debug output

#include "stdafx.h"

using namespace System;
```

```
using namespace System::Diagnostics;

public ref class TraceTest
{
public:
  TraceTest(int n):value(n){}

  property TraceLevel Level
  {
    void set(TraceLevel level) {sw->Level = level; }
    TraceLevel get(){return sw->Level; }
  }

  void FunA()
  {
    ++value;
    Trace::Indent();
    Trace::WriteLine(L"Starting FunA");
    if(sw->TraceInfo)
      Debug::WriteLine(L"FunA working...");
    FunB();
    Trace::WriteLine(L"Ending FunA");
    Trace::Unindent();
  }

  void FunB()
  {
    Trace::Indent();
    Trace::WriteLine(L"Starting FunB");
    if(sw->TraceWarning)
      Debug::WriteLine(L"FunB warning...");
    FunC();
    Trace::WriteLine(L"Ending FunB");
    Trace::Unindent();
  }

  void FunC()
  {
    Trace::Indent();
    Trace::WriteLine(L"Starting FunC");
    if(sw->TraceError)
      Debug::WriteLine(L"FunC error...");
    Debug::Assert(value < 4);
    Trace::WriteLine(L"Ending FunC");
    Trace::Unindent();
  }
private:
  int value;
  static TraceSwitch^ sw =
                       gcnew TraceSwitch(L"Trace Switch", L"Controls trace output");
};

int main(array<System::String ^> ^args)
{
```

```
      // Direct output to the command line
      TextWriterTraceListener^ listener = gcnew TextWriterTraceListener( Console::Out);
      Debug::Listeners->Add(listener);

      Debug::IndentSize = 2;                    // Set the indent size

      array<TraceLevel>^ levels = { TraceLevel::Off,      TraceLevel::Error,
                                    TraceLevel::Warning ,TraceLevel::Verbose};
      TraceTest^ obj = gcnew TraceTest(0);

      Console::WriteLine(L"Starting trace and debug test...");
      for each(TraceLevel level in levels)
      {
        obj->Level = level;                    // Set level for messages
        Console::WriteLine(L"\nTrace level is {0}", obj->Level);
        obj->FunA();
      }
   return 0;
}
```

This example results in an assertion dialog being displayed during execution. You can then choose to continue or abort execution or retry the program in debug mode by selecting the appropriate button in the dialog.

Depending on what you do when the program asserts, this example produces the following output:

```
Starting trace and debug test...

Trace level is Off
  Starting FunA
    Starting FunB
      Starting FunC
      Ending FunC
    Ending FunB
  Ending FunA

Trace level is Error
  Starting FunA
    Starting FunB
      Starting FunC
      FunC error...
      Ending FunC
    Ending FunB
  Ending FunA

Trace level is Warning
  Starting FunA
    Starting FunB
    FunB warning...
      Starting FunC
      FunC error...
      Ending FunC
    Ending FunB
```

```
      Ending FunA

  Trace level is Verbose
     Starting FunA
     FunA working...
        Starting FunB
        FunB warning...
           Starting FunC
           FunC error...
           Fail:
           Ending FunC
        Ending FunB
     Ending FunA
```

How It Works

The `TraceTest` class defines three instance functions `FunA()`, `FunB()`, and `FunC()`. Each function contains a call to the `Trace::Indent()` function to increase indentation for debug output and `Debug::WriteLine()` function calls to track when the function is entered and exited. The `Trace::Unindent()` function is called immediately before exiting each function to restore the indent level to what it was when the function was called.

The `TraceTest` class defines a private `TraceSwitch` member, `sw`, which controls what level of debug output is displayed. Each of the three member functions also calls the `Debug::WriteLine()` function to issue a debug message depending on the level set in the `sw` member of the class.

The `FunA()` function increments the value member of the class object each time it is called and the `FunC()` function asserts if `value` exceeds 3.

In `main()` you create a `TextWriterTraceListener` object that directs trace and debug output to the command line:

```
TextWriterTraceListener^ listener = gcnew TextWriterTraceListener( Console::Out);
```

You then add the `listener` object to the collection of listeners in the `Debug` class:

```
Debug::Listeners->Add(listener);
```

This causes debug and trace output to be directed to `Console::Out`, the standard output stream.

You create an array of `TraceLevel` objects that represent various control levels for debug and trace output:

```
array<TraceLevel>^ levels = { TraceLevel::Off,     TraceLevel::Error,
                              TraceLevel::Warning ,TraceLevel::Verbose};
```

After creating the `TraceLevel` object you set the trace levels for it in a `for each` loop:

```
for each(TraceLevel level in levels)
{
  obj->Level = level;                // Set level for messages
  Console::WriteLine(L"\nTrace level is {0}", obj->Level);
  obj->FunA();
}
```

The level is set through the `Level` property for `obj`. This sets the `Level` property in the `TraceSwitch` member, `sw`, which is used in the instances functions to control output.

From the output you can see that the indent you set affects output from the static `WriteLine()` function in both the `Debug` and `Trace` classes. You can also see how the level that you set in the `TraceSwitch` class member affects the output. When the value member of the `TraceTest` class object, `obj`, reaches 4, the `FunC()` function asserts. You can rerun the example and try out the effects of the three buttons on the assertion dialog.

Getting Trace Output in Windows Forms Applications

It's often useful to be able to output trace information from a Windows Forms application. There's a couple of barriers in the way of doing this: Firstly, the output can be voluminous, particularly if you want to trace the execution of functions that executed very frequently such as those dealing with mouse events, and secondly and more significantly, there is no console with a Windows Forms application to receive the output. You can get over this by adding some code to the constructor of the class encapsulating the form for the application, which reassigns output for `Console::Out` stream to a file. I won't explain every detail of the class objects involved and how this code works at this point but just offer it here as something you can plug into a Windows Forms application:

```
FileStream^ fs = gcnew FileStream(L"Trace.txt", FileMode::Create);
StreamWriter^ sw = gcnew StreamWriter(fs);
sw->Autoflush = true;
Console::SetOut(sw);
```

The first statement creates a stream that encapsulates the file `Trace.txt` that will be created in the current directory. You can specify a full path if you want; just set the first argument to the `FileStream` constructor as `L"C\Debug Output\MyTrace.txt"` for example. The next two statements set up an object that can write to the stream, `fs`, and make it flush data to the stream automatically. The last statement reassigns `Console::Out` to the `StreamWriter` object. To compile this code successfully you must add a `using` directive for the `System::IO` namespace to the header file containing the class definition for the form.

With this code in place you can put `Console` output statements anywhere in the code for the form to trace the execution sequence or to record data values. You can inspect the trace file with any simple text editor such as Notepad.

Summary

Debugging is a big topic and Visual C++ 2008 provides many debugging facilities beyond what I have discussed here. If you are comfortable with what I have covered in this chapter, you should have little trouble expanding your knowledge of the debug capabilities through the Visual C++ 2008 documentation. Searching on "debugging" should generate a rich list of further information.

The essential points introduced in this chapter were:

❑ You can use the `assert()` library function that is declared in the `<cassert>` header to check logical conditions in your native C++ program that should always be `true`.

❑ The preprocessor symbol, _NDEBUG, is automatically defined in the debug version of a native C++program. It is not defined in the release version.

❑ You can add your own debugging code by enclosing it between an #ifdef/#endif pair of directives testing for _NDEBUG. Your debug code is then included only in the debug version of the program.

❑ The crtdbg.h headers supplies declarations for functions to provide debugging of free store operations.

❑ By setting the _crtDbgFlag appropriately, you can enable automatic checking of your program for memory leaks.

❑ To direct output messages from the free store debugging functions, you call the _CrtSetReportMode() and _CrtSetReportFile() functions.

❑ Debugging operations using breakpoints and trace points in C++/CLI programs are exactly the same as in native C++ programs.

❑ The Debug and Assert classes defined in the System::Diagnostics namespace provide functions for tracing execution and generating debugging output in CLR programs.

❑ The static Assert() function in the Debug and Trace classes provides an assertion capability in CLR programs.

With the basics of debugging added to your knowledge of C++, you are ready for the big one: Windows programming!

Windows Programming Concepts

In this chapter, you take a look at the basic ideas that are involved in every Windows program in C++. You'll first develop a very simple example that uses the Windows operating system API directly. This will enable you to understand how a Windows application works behinds the scenes, which will be useful to you when you are developing applications using the more sophisticated facilities provided by Visual C++ 2008. You then see what you get when you create a Windows program using the Microsoft Foundation Classes, better known as the MFC. Finally, you'll create a basic program using Windows Forms that will execute with the CLR, so by the end of the chapter you'll have an idea of what each of the three approaches to developing a Windows application involves.

By the end of this chapter, you will have learned about:

- ❑ The basic structure of a window
- ❑ The Windows API and how it is used
- ❑ Windows messages and how you deal with them
- ❑ The notation that is commonly used in Windows programs
- ❑ The basic structure of a Windows program
- ❑ How you create an elementary program using the Windows API and how it works
- ❑ Microsoft Foundation Classes
- ❑ The basic elements of an MFC-based program
- ❑ Windows Forms
- ❑ The basic elements of a Windows Forms application

Windows Programming Basics

With Visual C++ 2008 you have three basic ways of creating an interactive Windows application:

❏ Using the **Windows API**. This is the fundamental interface that the Windows operating system provides for communications between itself and the applications that are executing under its control.

❏ Using the **Microsoft Foundation Classes**, better known as the **MFC**. This is a set of C++ classes that encapsulate the Windows API.

❏ Using **Windows Forms**. This is a forms-based development mechanism for creating applications that execute with the CLR.

In a way these three approaches form a progression from the most programming intensive to the least programming intensive. With the Windows API you are writing code throughout — all the elements that make up the GUI for your application must be created programmatically. With MFC applications there's some help with GUI build in that you can assemble controls on a dialog form graphically and just program the interactions with the user; however, you still are involved in a lot of coding. With a Windows Forms application you can build the complete GUI including the primary application window by assembling the controls that the user interacts with graphically. You just place the controls wherever you want them in a form window, and the code to create them is generated automatically. Using Windows Forms is by far the fastest and easiest mechanism for generating an application because the amount of code that you have to write is greatly reduced compared to the other two possibilities. The code for a Windows Forms application also gains all the benefits of executing with the CLR.

Using the MFC involves more programming effort than Windows Forms, but you have more control of how the GUI is created and you end up with a program that will execute natively on your PC. Because using the Windows API directly is the most laborious method for developing an application I won't go into this in detail. However, you will put together a basic Windows API application so you'll have an opportunity to understand the principles of the mechanism that all Windows applications use to work with the operating system under the covers. You'll explore the fundamentals involved in all three possibilities for Windows application development in this chapter and investigate using MFC and Windows Forms in more detail later in the book. Of course, it also is possible to develop applications in C++ that do not require the Windows operating system, and games programs often take this approach when the ultimate in graphics performance is required. Although this is itself an interesting topic, it would require a whole book to do it justice so I won't pursue this topic further.

Before you get into the examples in this chapter, I'll review the terminology that is used to describe an application window. You have already created a Windows program in Chapter 1 without writing a single line of code yourself and I'll use the window generated by this to illustrate the various elements that go to make up a window.

Elements of a Window

You will inevitably be familiar with most, if not all, of the principal elements of the user interface to a Windows program. However, I will go through them anyway just to be sure we have a common understanding of what the terms mean. The best way to understand what the elements of a window can be is to look at one. An annotated version of the window displayed by the example that you saw in Chapter 1 is shown in Figure 12-1.

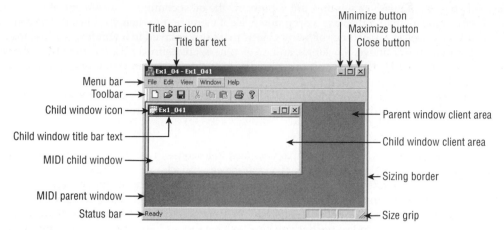

Figure 12-1

The example actually generated two windows. The larger window with the menu and the tool bars is the main, or **parent window**, and the smaller window is a **child window** of the parent. Although the child window can be closed without closing the parent window by double-clicking the title bar icon that is in the upper-left corner of the child window, closing the parent window automatically closes the child window as well. This is because the child window is owned by, and dependent upon, the parent window. In general, a parent window may have a number of child windows, as you'll see.

The most fundamental parts of a typical window are its **border**, the **title bar** that shows the name that you give to the window, the **title bar icon** that appears at the left end of the title bar, and the **client area**, which is the area in the center of the window not used by the title bar or borders. You can get all of these created for free in a Windows program. As you will see, all you have to do is provide some text for the title bar.

The border defines the boundary of a window and may be fixed or resizable. If the border is resizable, you can drag it to alter the size of the window. The window also may possess a size grip, which you can use to alter the size of a window while maintaining its aspect ratio — the ratio of the width to the height. When you define a window you can modify how the border behaves and appears if you want. Most windows will also have the maximize, minimize, and close buttons in the upper-right corner of the window. These allow the window to be increased to full screen size, reduced to an icon or closed.

When you click the title bar icon with the left mouse button, it provides a standard menu for altering or closing the window called the **system menu** or **control menu**. The system menu also appears when you right-click the title bar of a window. Although it's optional, it is a good idea always to include the title bar icon in any main windows that your program generates. Including the title bar icon provides you with a very convenient way of closing the program when things don't work during debugging.

The client area is the part of the window where you usually want your program to write text or graphics. You address the client area for this purpose in exactly the same way as the yard that you saw in Figure 7-1 in Chapter 7. The upper-left corner of the client area has the coordinates (0, 0), with x increasing from left to right, and y increasing from top to bottom.

The menu bar is optional in a window but is probably the most common way to control an application. Each menu in the menu bar displays a drop-down list of menu items when you click it. The contents of a menu and the physical appearance of many objects that are displayed in a window, such as the icons on the toolbar that appear above, the cursor, and many others, are defined by a **resource file**. You will see many more resource files when we get to write some more sophisticated Windows programs.

The toolbar provides a set of icons that usually act as alternatives to the menu options that you use most often. Because they give a pictorial clue to the function provided, they can often make a program easier and faster to use.

I'll mention a caveat about terminology that you need to be conscious of before I move on. Users tend to think of a window as the thing that appears on the screen with a border around it, and of course it is, but it is only one kind of window; however, in Windows a window is a generic term covering a whole range of entities. In fact almost any entity that is displayed is a window — for example, a dialog box is a window and each button is also a window. I will generally use terminology to refer to objects that describe what they are, buttons, dialogs, and so on, but you need to have tucked in the back of your mind that they are windows, too, because you can do things to them that you can do with a regular window — you can draw on a button for instance.

Windows Programs and the Operating System

When you write a Windows program, your program is subservient to the operating system and Windows is in control. Your program must not deal directly with the hardware and all communications with the outside must pass through Windows. When you use a Windows program you are interacting primarily with Windows, which then communicates with the application program on your behalf. Your Windows program is the tail, Windows is the dog, and your program wags only when Windows tells it to.

There are a number of reasons why this is so. First and foremost, because your program is potentially always sharing the computer with other programs that may be executing at the same time, Windows has to have primary control to manage the sharing of machine resources. If one application was allowed to have primary control in a Windows environment this would inevitably make programming more complicated because of the need to provide for the possibility of other programs, and information intended for other applications could be lost. A second reason for Windows being in control is that Windows embodies a standard user interface and needs to be in charge to enforce that standard. You can only display information on the screen using the tools that Windows provides, and then only when authorized.

Event-Driven Programs

You have already seen, in Chapter 1, that a Windows program is **event-driven**, so a Windows program essentially waits around for something to happen. A significant part of the code required for a Windows application is dedicated to processing events that are caused by external actions of the user, but activities that are not directly associated with your application can nonetheless require that bits of your program code are executed. For example, if the user drags the window of another application that is active alongside your program and this action uncovers part of the client area of the window devoted to your application, your application needs to redraw that part of the window.

Windows Messages

Events in a Windows application are occurrences such as the user clicking the mouse or pressing a key, or a timer reaching zero. The Windows operating system records each event in a **message** and places the message in a **message queue** for the program for which the message is intended. Thus a Windows message is simply a record of the data relating to an event, and the message queue for an application is just a sequence of such messages waiting to be processed by the application. By sending a message Windows can tell your program that something needs to be done, or that some information has become available, or that an event such as a mouse click has occurred. If your program is properly organized, it will respond in the appropriate way to the message. There are many different kinds of messages and they can occur very frequently — many times per second when the mouse is being dragged, for example.

A Windows program must contain a function specifically for handling these messages. The function is often called `WndProc()` or `WindowProc()`, although it doesn't have to have a particular name because Windows accesses the function through a pointer to a function that you supply. So the sending of a message to your program boils down to Windows calling a function that you provide, typically called `WindowProc()`, and passing any necessary data to your program by means of arguments to this function. Within your `WindowProc()` function, it is up to you to work out what the message is from the data supplied and what to do about it.

Fortunately, you don't need to write code to process every message. You can filter out those that are of interest in your program, deal with those in whatever way you want, and pass the rest back to Windows. You pass a message back to Windows by calling a standard function provided by Windows called `DefWindowProc()`, which provides default message processing.

The Windows API

All of the communications between any Windows application and Windows itself uses the Windows application programming interface, otherwise known as the **Windows API**. This consists of literally hundreds of functions that are provided as a standard with the Windows operating system that provides the means by which an application communicates with Windows, and vice versa. The Windows API was developed in the days when C was the primary language in use, long before the advent of C++, and for this reason structures rather than classes are frequently used for passing some kinds of data between Windows and your application program.

The Windows API covers all aspects of the communications between Windows and your application. Because there is such a large number of functions in the API, using them in the raw can be very difficult — just understanding what they all are is a task in itself. This is where Visual C++ 2008 makes the life of the application developer very much easier. Visual C++ 2008 packages the Windows API in a way that structures the API functions in an object-oriented manner, and provides an easier way to use the interface in C++ with more default functionality. This takes the form of the Microsoft Foundation Classes, MFC. Also, for applications targeting the CLR you have a facility called Windows Forms where the code necessary to create a GUI is all created automatically. All you have to do is supply the code necessary to handle the events in the way that your application requires. You'll be creating a Windows Forms application a little later in this chapter and you'll explore the use of Windows Forms in more detail in Chapter 23.

Visual C++ also provides Application Wizards that create basic applications of various kinds, including MFC and Windows Forms-based applications. The Application Wizard can generate a complete working application that includes all of the boilerplate code necessary for a basic Windows application, leaving you just to customize this for your particular purposes. The example in Chapter 1 illustrated how much functionality Visual C++ is capable of providing without any coding effort at all on your part. I will discuss this in much more detail when we get to write some more practical examples using the MFC Application Wizard.

Windows Data Types

Windows defines a significant number of data types that are used to specify function parameter types and return types in the Windows API. These Windows-specific types also propagate through to functions that are defined in MFC. Each of these Windows types will map to some C++ type, but because the mapping between Windows types and C++ types can change, you should always use the Windows type where this applies. For example, in the past the Windows type WORD has been defined in one version of Windows as type `unsigned short` and in another Windows version as type `unsigned int`. On 16-bit machines these types are equivalent, but on 32-bit machines they are decidedly different so anyone using the C++ type rather than the Windows type could run into problems.

You can find the complete list of Windows data types in the documentation but here are a few of the most common you are likely to meet:

BOOL or BOOLEAN	A Boolean variable can have the values TRUE or FALSE. Note that this is not the same as the C++ type **bool**, which can have the values true or false.
BYTE	An 8-bit byte.
CHAR	An 8-bit character.
DWORD	A 32-bit unsigned integer that corresponds to type **unsigned long** in C++.
HANDLE	A handle to an object — a handle being a 32-bit integer value that records the location of an object in memory.
HBRUSH	A handle to a brush, a brush being used to fill an area with color.
HCURSOR	A handle to a cursor.
HDC	Handle to a device context — a device context being an object that enables you to draw on a window.
HINSTANCE	Handle to an instance.
LPARAM	A message parameter.
LPCSTR	A pointer to a constant null-terminated string of 8-bit characters.

LPHANDLE	A pointer to a handle.
LRESULT	A signed value that results from processing a message.
WORD	A 16-bit unsigned integer so it corresponds to type unsigned short in C++.

I'll introduce any other Windows types we are using in examples as the need arises. All the types used by Windows, as well as the prototypes of the Windows API functions, are contained in the header file windows.h, so you need to include this header file when you put your basic Windows program together.

Notation in Windows Programs

In many Windows programs variable names have a prefix, which indicates what kind of value the variable holds and how it is used. There are quite a few prefixes and they are often used in combination. For example, the prefix lpfn signifies a long pointer to a function. A sample of the prefixes you might come across is:

Prefix	Meaning
b	a logical variable of type **BOOL**, equivalent to **int**
by	type unsigned char; a **byte**
c	type char
dw	type **DWORD**, which is **unsigned long**
fn	a function
h	a handle, used to reference something.
i	type **int**
l	type **long**
lp	**long** pointer
n	type **int**
p	a pointer
s	a string
sz	a zero terminated string
w	type **WORD**, which is **unsigned short**

This use of these prefixes is called **Hungarian notation**. It was introduced to minimize the possibility of misusing a variable by interpreting it differently from how it was defined or intended to be used. Such misinterpretation was easily done in the C language, a precursor of C++. With C++ and its stronger type checking you don't need to make such a special effort with your notation to avoid such problems. The compiler always flags an error for type inconsistencies in your program, and many of the kinds of bugs that plagued earlier C programs can't occur with C++.

On the other hand, Hungarian notation can still help to make programs easier to understand, particularly when you are dealing with a lot of variables of different types that are arguments to Windows API functions. Because Windows programs are still written in C, and of course because parameters for Windows API functions are still defined using Hungarian notation, the method is still used quite widely. You can find out more about Hungarian notation at `http://web.umr.edu/~cpp/common/hungarian.html`.

You can make up your own mind as to the extent to which you want to use Hungarian notation, as it is by no means obligatory. You may choose not to use it at all, but in any event, if you have an idea of how it works, you will find it easier to understand what the arguments to the Windows API functions are. There is a small caveat, however. As Windows has developed, the types of some of the API function arguments have changed slightly, but the variable names that are used remain the same. As a consequence, the prefix may not be quite correct in specifying the variable type.

The Structure of a Windows Program

For a minimal Windows program that just uses the Windows API, you will write two functions. These are a `WinMain()` function, where execution of the program begins and basic program initialization is carried out, and a `WindowProc()` function that is called by Windows to process messages for the application. The `WindowProc()` part of a Windows program is usually the larger portion because this is where most of the application-specific code is, responding to messages caused by user input of one kind or another.

Although these two functions make up a complete program, they are not directly connected. `WinMain()` does not call `WindowProc()`, Windows does. In fact, Windows also calls `WinMain()`. This is illustrated in Figure 12-2.

The function `WinMain()` communicates with Windows by calling some of the Windows API functions. The same applies to `WindowProc()`. The integrating factor in your Windows program is Windows itself, which links to both `WinMain()` and `WindowProc()`. You will take a look at what the pieces are that make up `WinMain()` and `WindowProc()` and then assemble the parts into a working example of a simple Windows program.

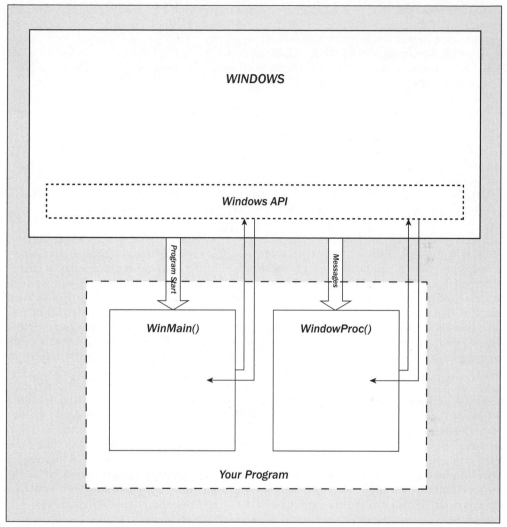

Figure 12-2

The WinMain() Function

The `WinMain()` function is the equivalent of the `main()` function in a console program. It's where execution starts and where the basic initialization for the rest of the program is carried out. To allow

Windows to pass data to it, `WinMain()` has four parameters and a return value of type `int`. Its proto-type is:

```
int WINAPI WinMain(HINSTANCE hInstance,
                   HINSTANCE hPrevInstance,
                   LPSTR lpCmdLine,
                   int nCmdShow
                   );
```

Following the return type specifier, `int`, you have a specification for the function, `WINAPI`, which is new to you. This is a Windows-defined macro that causes the function name and arguments to be handled in a special way, which happens to correspond to the way that a function is handled in the Pascal and Fortran languages. This is different from the way functions are normally handled in C++. The precise details are unimportant — this is simply the way Windows requires things to be, so you need to put the `WINAPI` macro name in front of the names of functions called by Windows.

The four arguments that are passed by Windows to your `WinMain()` function contain important data. The first argument, `hInstance`, is of type `HINSTANCE` which is a handle to an instance — an instance here being a running program. A **handle** is an integer value which identifies an object of some kind — in this case, the instance of the application. The actual integer value of a handle is not important. There can be several programs in execution under Windows at any given instant. This raises the possibility of several copies of the same application being active at once, and this needs to be recognized. Hence, the `hInstance` handle identifies a particular copy. If you start more than one copy of a program, each one has its own unique `hInstance` value. As you will see shortly, handles are also used to identify all sorts of other things. Of course, all handles in a particular context — application instance handles for example — need to be different from one another.

The next argument passed to your `WinMain()` function, `hPrevInstance`, is a legacy from the 16-bit versions of the Windows operating system. Under Windows 3.*x*, this parameter gave you the handle to the previous instance of the program, if there was one. If `hPrevInstance` was `NULL`, you knew that there was no previous instance of the program, so this must be the only copy of the program executing (at the moment, anyway). This information was necessary in many cases, because programs running under Windows 3.*x* share the same address space and multiple copies of a program executing simultaneously could cause complications. For this reason, programmers often limited their applications to only one running instance at a time and having the `hPrevInstance` argument passed to `WinMain()` allowed them to provide for this very easily by testing it in an `if` statement.

Under 32-bit versions of Windows the `hPrevInstance` parameter is completely irrelevant because each application runs in its own address space, and one application has no direct knowledge of the existence of another that is executing concurrently. This parameter is always `NULL`, even if another instance of an application is running.

The next argument, `lpCmdLine`, is a pointer to a string containing the command line that started the program. For instance, if you started it using the Run command from the Start button menu of Windows, the string contains everything that appears in the Open box. Having this pointer allows you to pick up any parameter values that may appear in the command line. The type `LPSTR` is another Windows type, specifying a 32-bit (long) pointer to a string.

The last argument, nCmdShow, determines how the window is to look when it is created. It could be displayed normally or it might need to be minimized; for example, the shortcut for the program might specify that the program should be minimized when it starts. This argument can take one of a fixed set of values that are defined by symbolic constants such as SW_SHOWNORMAL and SW_SHOWMINNOACTIVE. There are a number of other constants like these that define the way a window is to be displayed and they all begin SW_. Other examples are SW_HIDE or SW_SHOWMAXIMIZED. You don't usually need to examine the value of nCmdShow. You typically pass it directly to the Windows API function responsible for displaying your application window.

If you want to know what all the other constants are that specify how a window displays, you can find a complete list of the possible values if you search for WinMain in the MSDN Library. You can access the MSDN library online at http://msdn2.microsoft.com/en-us/library/default.aspx.

The function WinMain() in your Windows program needs to do four things:

❑ Tell Windows what kind of window the program requires

❑ Create the program window

❑ Initialize the program window

❑ Retrieve Windows messages intended for the program

Take a look at each of these in turn and then create a complete WinMain() function.

Specifying a Program Window

The first step in creating a window is to define just what sort of window it is that you want to create. Windows defines a special struct type called WNDCLASSEX to contain the data specifying a window. The data that is stored in an instance of the struct defines a window class, which determines the type of window. Do not confuse this with a C++ class — the MFC defines a class that represents a window but this is not the same this at all. You need to create a variable of type WNDCLASSEX, and give values to each of its members (just like filling in a form). After you've filled in the variables, you can pass it to Windows (via a function that you'll see later) to register the class. When that's been done, whenever you want to create a window of that class, you can tell Windows to look up the class that you've already registered.

The definition of the WNDCLASSEX structure is as follows:

```
struct WNDCLASSEX
{
  UINT cbSize;              // Size of this object in bytes
  UINT style;              // Window style
  WNDPROC lpfnWndProc;     // Pointer to message processing function
  int cbClsExtra;          // Extra byte after the window class
  int cbWndExtra;          // Extra bytes after the window instance
  HINSTANCE hInstance;     // The application instance handle
  HICON hIcon;             // The application icon
  HCURSOR hCursor;         // The window cursor
```

```
    HBRUSH hbrBackground;      // The brush defining the background color
    LPCTSTR lpszMenuName;      // A pointer to the name of the menu resource
    LPCTSTR lpszClassName;     // A pointer to the class name
    HICON hIconSm;             // A small icon associated with the window
};
```

You construct an object of type WNDCLASSEX in the way that you saw when I discussed structures, for example:

```
WNDCLASSEX WindowClass;                    // Create a window class object
```

All you need to do now is fill in values for the members of WindowClass.

Setting the value for the cbSize member of the struct is easy when you use the sizeof operator:

```
WindowClass.cbSize = sizeof(WNDCLASSEX);
```

The style member of the struct determines various aspects of the window's behavior, in particular, the conditions under which the window should be redrawn. You can select from a number of options for this member's value, each defined by a symbolic constant beginning CS_.

> *You'll find all the possible constant values for style if you search for WNDCLASSEX in the MSDN Library that you'll find at* http://msdn2.microsoft.com/en-us/library.

Where two or more options are required, the constants can be combined to produce a composite value using the bitwise OR operator, |. For example:

```
WindowClass.style = CS_HREDRAW | CS_VREDRAW;
```

The option CS_HREDRAW indicates to Windows that the window is to be redrawn if its horizontal width is altered, and CS_VREDRAW indicates that it is to be redrawn if the vertical height of the window is changed. In the preceding statement you have elected to have the window redrawn in either case. As a result, Windows sends a message to your program indicating that you should redraw the window whenever the width or height of the window is altered by the user. Each of the possible options for the window style is defined by a unique bit in a 32-bit word being set to 1. That's why the bitwise OR is used to combine them. These bits indicating a particular style are usually called **flags**. Flags are used very frequently, not only in Windows but also in C++ because they are an efficient way of representing and processing features that are either there or not or parameters that are either true or false.

The member lpfnWndProc stores a pointer to the function in your program that handles messages for the window you create. The prefix to the name signifies that this is a long pointer to a function. If you followed the herd and called the function to handle messages for the application WindowProc(), you would initialize this member with the statement:

```
WindowClass.lpfnWndProc = WindowProc;
```

The next two members, cbClsExtra and cbWndExtra, allow you to ask that extra space be provided internally to Windows for your own use. An example of this could be when you want to associate additional data with each instance of a window to assist in message handling for each window instance.

Normally you won't need extra space allocated for you, in which case you must set the cbClsExtra and cbWndExtra members to zero.

The hInstance member holds the handle for the current application instance, so you should set this to the hInstance value that was passed to WinMain() by Windows.

The members hIcon, hCursor, and hbrBackground are handles that in turn define the icon that represents the application when minimized, the cursor the window uses, and the background color of the client area of the window. (As you saw earlier, a handle is just a 32-bit integer used as an ID to represent something.) These are set using Windows API functions. For example:

```
WindowClass.hIcon = LoadIcon(0, IDI_APPLICATION);
WindowClass.hCursor = LoadCursor(0, IDC_ARROW);
WindowClass.hbrBackground =
                    static_cast<HBRUSH>(GetStockObject(GRAY_BRUSH));
```

All three members are set to standard Windows values by these function calls. The icon is a default provided by Windows and the cursor is the standard arrow cursor used by the majority of Windows applications. A brush is a Windows object used to fill an area, in this case the client area of the window. The function GetStockObject() returns a generic type for all stock objects, so you need to cast it to type HBRUSH. In the preceding example it returns a handle to the standard gray brush, and the background color for our window is thus set to gray. This function can also be used to obtain other standard objects for a window, such as fonts for example. You could also set the hIcon and hCursor members to null, in which case Windows would provide the default icon and cursor. If you set hbrBackground to null, your program is expected to paint the window background and messages are sent to your application whenever this becomes necessary.

The lpszMenuName member is set to the name of a resource defining the window menu, or to zero if there is no menu for the window. You will look into creating and using menu resources when you use the AppWizard.

The lpszClassName member of the struct stores the name that you supply to identify this particular class of window. You would usually use the name of the application for this. You need to keep track of this name because you will need it again when a window is created. This member would therefore be typically set with the statements:

```
static LPCTSTR szAppName = L"OFWin";      // Define window class name
WindowClass.lpszClassName = szAppName;    // Set class name
```

I have defined szAppName as a Unicode string here. In fact the LPCTSTR type is defined as const wchar_t* if UNICODE is defined for the application, or const char* if it is not. Thus, the definition for szAppName here assumes a Unicode application.

The last member is hIconSm, which identifies a small icon associated with the window class. If you specify this as null, Windows searches for a small icon related to the hIcon member and use that.

In fact, the WNDCLASSEX structure replaces another structure, WNDCLASS that was used for the same purpose. The old structure did not include the cbSize member that stores the size of the structure in bytes or the hIconSm member.

Creating a Program Window

After all the members of your WNDCLASSEX structure have been set to the values required, the next step is to tell Windows about it. You do this using the Windows API function RegisterClassEx(). Given that your structure is WindowClass, the statement to do this would be:

```
RegisterClassEx(&WindowClass);
```

Easy, isn't it? The address of the struct is passed to the function, and Windows extracts and squirrels away all the values that you have set in the structure members. This process is called **registering** the window class. Just to remind you, the term *class* here is used in the sense of classification and is not the same as the idea of a class in C++, so don't confuse the two. Each instance of the application must make sure that it registers the window classes that it needs. If you were using the obsolete WNDCLASS structure that I mentioned, you would have to use a different function here, RegisterClass().

After Windows knows the characteristics of the window that you want, and the function that is going to handle messages for it, you can go ahead and create it. You use the function CreateWindow() for this. The window class that you've already created determines the broad characteristics of a window, and further arguments to the function CreateWindow() add additional characteristics. Because an application may have several windows in general, the function CreateWindow() returns a handle to the window created that you can store to enable you to refer to that particular window later. There are many API calls that require you to specify the window handle as a parameter if you want to use them. You will look at a typical use of the CreateWindow() function at this point. This might be:

```
HWND hWnd;                                  // Window handle
...
hWnd = CreateWindow(
        szAppName,                          // the window class name
        "A Basic Window the Hard Way",      // The window title
        WS_OVERLAPPEDWINDOW,                // Window style as overlapped
        CW_USEDEFAULT,                      // Default screen position of upper left
        CW_USEDEFAULT,                      // corner of our window as x,y...
        CW_USEDEFAULT,                      // Default window size, width...
        CW_USEDEFAULT,                      // ...and height
        0,                                  // No parent window
        0,                                  // No menu
        hInstance,                          // Program Instance handle
        0                                   // No window creation data
    );
```

The variable hWnd of type HWND is a 32-bit integer handle to a window. You'll use this variable to record the value that the CreateWindow() function returns that identifies the window. The first argument that you pass to the function is the class name. This is used by Windows to identify the WNDCLASSEX struct that you passed to it previously, in the RegisterClassEx() function call, so that the information from this struct can be used in the window creation process.

The second argument to CreateWindow() defines the text that is to appear on the title bar. The third argument specifies the style that the window has after it is created. The option specified here,

WS_OVERLAPPEDWINDOW, actually combines several options. It defines the window as having the WS_OVERLAPPED, WS_CAPTION, WS_SYSMENU, WS_THICKFRAME, WS_MINIMIZEBOX and WS_MAXIMIZEBOX styles. This results in an overlapped window, which is a window intended to be the main application window, with a title bar and a thick frame, which has a title bar icon, system menu, and maximize and minimize buttons. A window that you specify as having a thick frame has borders that can be resized.

The next four arguments determine the position and size of the window on the screen. The first two are the screen coordinates of the upper-left corner of the window, and the second two define the width and height of the window. The value CW_USEDEFAULT indicates that you want Windows to assign the default position and size for the window. This tells Windows to arrange successive windows in cascading positions down the screen. CW_USEDEFAULT only applies to windows specified as WS_OVERLAPPED.

The next argument value is zero, indicating that the window being created is not a child window (a window that is dependent on a parent window). If you wanted it to be a child window, you would set this argument to the handle of the parent window. The next argument is also zero, indicating that no menu is required. You then specify the handle of the current instance of the program that was passed to the program by Windows. The last argument for window creation data is zero because you just want a simple window in the example. If you wanted to create a multiple-document interface (MDI) client window, the last argument would point to a structure related to this. You'll learn more about MDI windows later in the book.

> Note that the Windows API also includes a CreateWindowEx() function that you use to create a window with extended style information.

After calling the CreateWindow() function, the window now exists but is not yet displayed on the screen. You need to call another Windows API function to get it displayed:

```
ShowWindow(hWnd, nCmdShow);                // Display the window
```

Only two arguments are required here. The first identifies the window and is the handle returned by the function CreateWindow(). The second is the value nCmdShow that was passed to WinMain(), and that indicates how the window is to appear onscreen.

Initializing the Program Window

After calling the function ShowWindow(), the window appears onscreen but still has no application content, so you need to get your program to draw in the client area of the window. You could just put together some code to do this directly in the WinMain() function, but this would be most unsatisfactory: in this case, the contents of the client area are not considered to be permanent — if you want the client area contents to be retained, you can't afford to output what you want and forget about it. Any action on the part of the user that modifies the window in some way, such as dragging a border or dragging the whole window, typically requires that the window *and* its client area are redrawn.

When the client area needs to be redrawn for any reason, Windows sends a particular message to your program and your WindowProc() function needs to respond by reconstructing the client area of the window.

Therefore, the best way to get the client area drawn in the first instance is to put the code to draw the client area in the `WindowProc()` function and get Windows to send the message requesting that the client area be redrawn to your program. Whenever you know in your program that the window should be redrawn (when you change something, for example), you need to tell Windows to send a message back to get the window redrawn.

You can ask Windows to send your program a message to redraw the client area of the window by calling another Windows API function, `UpdateWindow()`. The statement to accomplish this is:

```
UpdateWindow(hWnd);                    // Cause window client area to be drawn
```

This function requires only one argument: the window handle `hWnd`, which identifies your particular program window. (In general there can be several windows in an application.) The result of the call is that Windows sends a message to your program requesting that the client area be redrawn.

Dealing with Windows Messages

The last task that `WinMain()` needs to address is dealing with the messages that Windows may have queued for your application. This may seem a bit odd because I said earlier that you needed the function `WindowProc()` to deal with messages, but let me explain a little further.

Queued and Non-Queued Messages

I oversimplified Windows messaging when I introduced the idea earlier. There are, in fact, two kinds of Windows messages:

There are **queued messages** that Windows places in a queue, and the `WinMain()` function must extract these messages from the queue for processing. The code in `WinMain()` that does this is called the **message loop**. Queued messages include those arising from user input from the keyboard, moving the mouse and clicking the mouse buttons. Messages from a timer and the Windows message to request that a window be redrawn are also queued.

There are **non-queued messages** that result in the `WindowProc()` function being called directly by Windows. A lot of the non-queued messages arise as a consequence of processing queued messages. What you are doing in the message loop in `WinMain()` is retrieving a message that Windows has queued for your application and then asking Windows to invoke your `WindowProc()` function to process it. Why can't Windows just call `WindowProc()` whenever necessary? Well, it could, but it just doesn't work this way. The reasons have to do with how Windows manages multiple applications executing simultaneously.

The Message Loop

As I said, retrieving messages from the message queue is done using a standard mechanism in Windows programming called the **message pump** or **message loop**. The code for this would be:

```
MSG msg;                                // Windows message structure
while(GetMessage(&msg, 0, 0, 0) == TRUE) // Get any messages
{
```

```
    TranslateMessage(&msg);              // Translate the message
    DispatchMessage(&msg);               // Dispatch the message
}
```

This involves three steps in dealing with each message:

❑   GetMessage() — retrieves a message from the queue

❑   TranslateMessage() — performs any conversion necessary on the message retrieved

❑   DispatchMessage() — causes Windows to call the WindowProc() function in your application
    to deal with the message

The operation of GetMessage() is important because it has a significant contribution to the way Windows
works with multiple applications so we should explore it in a little more detail.

The GetMessage() function retrieves a message queued for the application window and stores information about the message in the variable msg, pointed to by the first argument. The variable msg, which is a struct of type MSG, contains a number of different members that you are not accessing here. Still, for completeness, the definition of the structure looks like this:

```
struct MSG
{
    HWND    hwnd;         // Handle for the relevant window
    UINT    message;      // The message ID
    WPARAM  wParam;       // Message parameter (32-bits)
    LPARAM  lParam;       // Message parameter (32-bits)
    DWORD   time;         // The time when the message was queued
    POINT   pt;           // The mouse position
};
```

The wParam member is an example of a slightly misleading Hungarian notation prefix that I mentioned was now possible. You might assume that it was of type WORD (which is int), which used to be true in earlier Windows versions, but now it is of type WPARAM, which is a 32-bit integer value.

The exact contents of the wParam and lParam members are dependent on what kind of message it is. The message ID in the member message is an integer value and can be one of a set of values that are predefined in the header file, windows.h, as symbolic constants. Message IDs for general windows all start with WM_ and typical examples are WM_PAINT to redraw the screen and WM_QUIT to end the program. General windows messages cover a wide variety of events and include messages relating to mouse and menu events, keyboard input and window creation and management. The function GetMessage() always returns TRUE unless the message is WM_QUIT to end the program, in which case the value returned is FALSE, or unless an error occurs, in which case the return value is -1. Thus, the while loop continues until a quit message is generated to close the application or until an error condition arises. In either case, you need to end the program by passing the wParam value back to Windows in a return statement.

Note that there are prefixes other than WM for messages destined for other types of windows than a general window. The various types of message prefixes are listed in Appendix C.

The second argument in the call to `GetMessage()` is the handle of the window for which you want to get messages. This parameter can be used to retrieve messages for one window separately from another. If this argument is 0, as it is here, `GetMessage()` retrieves all messages for an application. This is an easy way of retrieving all messages for an application regardless of how many windows it has. It is also the safest way because you are sure of getting all the messages for your application. When the user of your Windows program closes the application window, for example, the window is closed before the `WM_QUIT` message is generated. Consequently, if you only retrieve messages by specifying a window handle to the `GetMessage()` function, you cannot retrieve the `WM_QUIT` message and your program is not able to terminate properly.

The last two arguments to `GetMessage()` are integers that hold minimum and maximum values for the message IDs you want to retrieve from the queue. This allows messages to be retrieved selectively. A range is usually specified by symbolic constants. Using `WM_MOUSEFIRST` and `WM_MOUSELAST` as these two arguments would select just mouse messages, for example. If both arguments are zero, as you have them here, all messages are retrieved.

Multitasking

If there are no messages queued, the `GetMessage()` function does not come back to your program. Windows allows execution to pass to another application and you only get a value returned from calling `GetMessage()` when a message appears in the queue. This mechanism was fundamental in enabling multiple applications to run under older versions of Windows and is referred to as **cooperative multitasking** because it depends on concurrent applications giving up their control of the processor from time to time. After your program calls `GetMessage()`, unless there is a message for your program, another application is executed and your program gets another opportunity to do something only if the other application releases the processor, perhaps by a call to `GetMessage()` when there are no messages queued for it, but this is not the only possibility.

With current versions of Windows, the operating system can interrupt an application after a period of time and transfer control to another application. This mechanism is called **pre-emptive multitasking** because an application can be interrupted in any event. With pre-emptive multitasking, however, you must still program the message loop in `WinMain()` using `GetMessage()` as before, and make provision for relinquishing control of the processor to Windows from time to time in a long running calculation (this is usually done using the `PeekMessage()` API function). If you don't do this, your application may be unable to respond to messages to repaint the application window when these arise. This can be for reasons that are quite independent of your application — when an overlapping window for another application is closed, for example.

The conceptual operation of the `GetMessage()` function is illustrated in Figure 12-3.

Within the `while` loop, the first function call to `TranslateMessage()` requests Windows to do some conversion work for keyboard related messages. Then the call to the function `DispatchMessage()` causes Windows to **dispatch** the message, or in other words, to call the `WindowProc()` function in your program to process the message. The return from `DispatchMessage()` does not occur until `WindowProc()` has finished processing the message. The `WM_QUIT` message indicates that the program should end, so this results in `FALSE` being returned to the application that stops the message loop.

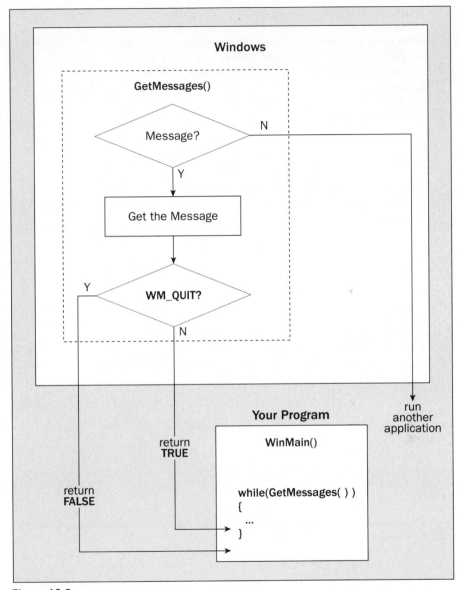

Figure 12-3

A Complete WinMain() Function

You have looked at all the bits that need to go into the function WinMain(). So now you can assemble them into a complete function:

```
// Listing OFWIN_1
int WINAPI WinMain(HINSTANCE hInstance, HINSTANCE hPrevInstance,
```

```
                        LPSTR lpCmdLine, int nCmdShow)
{
   WNDCLASSEX WindowClass;        // Structure to hold our window's attributes

   static LPCTSTR szAppName = L"OFWin";      // Define window class name
   HWND hWnd;                                // Window handle
   MSG msg;                                  // Windows message structure

   WindowClass.cbSize = sizeof(WNDCLASSEX);  // Set structure size

   // Redraw the window if the size changes
   WindowClass.style   = CS_HREDRAW | CS_VREDRAW;

   // Define the message handling function
   WindowClass.lpfnWndProc = WindowProc;

   WindowClass.cbClsExtra = 0;      // No extra bytes after the window class
   WindowClass.cbWndExtra = 0;      // structure or the window instance

   WindowClass.hInstance = hInstance;         // Application instance handle

   // Set default application icon
   WindowClass.hIcon = LoadIcon(0, IDI_APPLICATION);

   // Set window cursor to be the standard arrow
   WindowClass.hCursor = LoadCursor(0, IDC_ARROW);

   // Set gray brush for background color
   WindowClass.hbrBackground =
                      static_cast<HBRUSH>(GetStockObject(GRAY_BRUSH));

   WindowClass.lpszMenuName = 0;            // No menu
   WindowClass.lpszClassName = szAppName;   // Set class name
   WindowClass.hIconSm = 0;                 // Default small icon

   // Now register our window class
   RegisterClassEx(&WindowClass);

   // Now we can create the window
   hWnd = CreateWindow(
        szAppName,                         // the window class name
        L"A Basic Window the Hard Way",    // The window title
        WS_OVERLAPPEDWINDOW,               // Window style as overlapped
        CW_USEDEFAULT,           // Default screen position of  upper left
        CW_USEDEFAULT,           // corner of our window as x,y...
        CW_USEDEFAULT,           // Default window size
        CW_USEDEFAULT,           // ....
        0,                       // No parent window
        0,                       // No menu
        hInstance,               // Program Instance handle
        0                        // No window creation data
      );

   ShowWindow(hWnd, nCmdShow);      // Display the window
   UpdateWindow(hWnd);              // Cause window client area to be drawn
```

762

```
    // The message loop
    while(GetMessage(&msg, 0, 0, 0) == TRUE)    // Get any messages
    {
      TranslateMessage(&msg);                    // Translate the message
      DispatchMessage(&msg);                     // Dispatch the message
    }

    return static_cast<int>(msg.wParam);         // End, so return to Windows
  }
```

How It Works

After declaring the variables you need in the function, all the members of the WindowClass structure are initialized and the window is registered.

The next step is to call the CreateWindow() function to create the data for the physical appearance of the window, based on the arguments passed and the data established in the WindowClass structure that was previously passed to Windows using the RegisterClassEx() function. The call to ShowWindow() causes the window to be displayed according to the mode specified by nCmdShow, and the UpdateWindow() function signals that a message to draw the window client area should be generated.

Finally, the message loop continues to retrieve messages for the application until a WM_QUIT message is obtained, whereupon the GetMessage() function returns FALSE and the loop ends. The value of the wParam member of the msg structure is passed back to Windows in the return statement.

Message Processing Functions

The function WinMain() contained nothing that was application-specific beyond the general appearance of the application window. All of the code that makes the application behave in the way that you want is included in the message processing part of the program. This is the function WindowProc() that you identify to Windows in the WindowClass structure. Windows calls this function each time a message for your main application window is dispatched.

This example is simple, so you will be putting all the code to process messages in the one function, WindowProc(). More generally, though, the WindowProc() function is responsible for analyzing what a given message was and which window it was destined for and then calling one of a whole range of functions, each of which would be geared to handling a particular message in the context of the particular window concerned. However, the overall sequence of operations, and the way in which the function WindowProc() analyses an incoming message, is much the same in most application contexts.

The WindowProc() Function

The prototype of our WindowProc() function is:

```
LRESULT CALLBACK WindowProc(HWND hWnd, UINT message,
                            WPARAM wParam, LPARAM lParam);
```

The return type is LRESULT, which is a type defined by Windows and is normally equivalent to type long. Because the function is called by Windows through a pointer (you set the pointer up in WinMain() in the WNDCLASSEX structure), you need to qualify the function as CALLBACK. This is another specifier defined by

Windows that determines how the function arguments are handled. The four arguments that are passed provide information about the particular message causing the function to be called. The meaning of each of these arguments is described in the following table:

Argument	Meaning
HWND hWnd	A handle to the window in which the event causing the message occurred.
UINT message	The message ID, which is a 32-bit value indicating the type of message.
WPARAM wParam	A 32-bit value containing additional information depending on what sort of message it is.
LPARAM lParam	A 32-bit value containing additional information depending on what sort of message it is.

The window that the incoming message relates to is identified by the first argument, hWnd, which is passed to the function. In this case, you have only one window, so you can ignore it.

Messages are identified by the value message that is passed to WindowProc(). You can test this value against predefined symbolic constants, each of which relates to a particular message. They all begin with WM_, and typical examples are WM_PAINT, which corresponds to a request to redraw part of the client area of a window, and WM_LBUTTONDOWN, which indicates that the left mouse button was pressed. You can find the whole set of these by searching for WM_ in the MSDN Library.

Decoding a Windows Message

The process of decoding the message that Windows is sending is usually done using a switch statement in the WindowProc() function, based on the value of message. Selecting the message types that you want to process is then just a question of putting a case statement for each case in the switch. The typical structure of such a switch statement, with arbitrary cases included, is as follows:

```
switch(message)
{
  case WM_PAINT:
    // Code to deal with drawing the client area
    break;

  case WM_LBUTTONDOWN:
    // Code to deal with the left mouse button being pressed
    break;

  case WM_LBUTTONUP:
    // Code to deal with the left mouse button being released
    break;

  case WM_DESTROY:
    // Code to deal with a window being destroyed
    break;
```

```
    default:
       // Code to handle any other messages
  }
```

Every Windows program has something like this somewhere, although it may be hidden from sight in the Windows programs that you will write later using MFC. Each case corresponds to a particular value for the message ID and provides suitable processing for that message. Any messages that a program does not want to deal with individually are handled by the default statement, which should hand the messages back to Windows by calling `DefWindowProc()`. This is the Windows API function providing default message handling.

In a complex program dealing specifically with a wide range of possible Windows messages, this `switch` statement can become large and rather cumbersome. When you get to use the Application Wizard to generate a Windows application, you won't have to worry about this because it is all taken care of for you and you never see the `WindowProc()` function. All you need to do is to supply the code to process the particular messages in which you are interested.

Drawing the Window Client Area

Windows sends a `WM_PAINT` message to the program to signal that the client area of an application should be redrawn. So in your example, you need to draw the text in the window in response to the `WM_PAINT` message.

You can't go drawing in the window willy-nilly. Before you can write to the application window, you need to tell Windows that you want to do so, and get Windows' authority to go ahead. You do this by calling the Windows API function `BeginPaint()`, which should only be called in response to a `WM_PAINT` message. It is used as follows:

```
  HDC hDC;                              // A display context handle
  PAINTSTRUCT PaintSt;                  // Structure defining area to be redrawn

  hDC = BeginPaint(hWnd, &PaintSt);     // Prepare to draw in the window
```

The type `HDC` defines what is called a **display context**, or more generally a **device context**. A device context provides the link between the device-independent Windows API functions for outputting information to the screen or a printer, and the device drivers that support writing to the specific devices attached to your PC. You can also regard a device context as a token of authority that is handed to you on request by Windows and grants you permission to output some information. Without a device context, you simply can't generate any output.

The `BeginPaint()` function provides you with a display context as a return value and requires two arguments to be supplied. The window to which you want to write is identified by the window handle, `hWnd`, which you pass as the first argument. The second argument is the address of a `PAINTSTRUCT` variable `PaintSt`, in which Windows places information about the area to be redrawn in response to the `WM_PAINT` message. I will ignore the details of this because you are not going to use it. You will just redraw the whole of the client area. You can obtain the coordinates of the client area in a `RECT` structure with the statements:

```
  RECT aRect;                           // A working rectangle
  GetClientRect(hWnd, &aRect);
```

The `GetClientRect()` function supplies the coordinates of the upper-left and lower-right corners of the client area for the window specified by the first argument. These coordinates are stored in the RECT structure aRect, which is passed through the second argument as a pointer. You can then use this definition of the client area for your window when you write the text to the window using the `DrawText()` function. Because your window has a gray background, you should alter the background of the text to be transparent, to allow the gray to show through; otherwise, the text appears against a white background. You can do this with this API function call:

```
SetBkMode(hDC, TRANSPARENT);              // Set text background mode
```

The first argument identifies the device context and the second sets the background mode. The default option is OPAQUE.

You can now write the text with the statement:

```
DrawText(hDC,                         // Device context handle
         L"But, soft! What light through yonder window breaks?",
         -1,                          // Indicate null terminated string
         &aRect,                      // Rectangle in which text is to be drawn
         DT_SINGLELINE|               // Text format - single line
         DT_CENTER|                   //             - centered in the line
         DT_VCENTER                   //             - line centered in aRect
       );
```

The first argument to the `DrawText()` function is your certificate of authority to draw on the window, the display context hDC. The next argument is the text string that you want to output. You could equally well have defined this in a variable and passed the pointer to the text as the second argument in the function call. The next argument, with the value -1, signifies that your string is terminated with a null character. If it weren't, you would put the count of the number of characters in the string here. The fourth argument is a pointer to a RECT structure defining a rectangle in which you want to write the text. In this case it is the whole client area of the window defined in aRect. The last argument defines the format for the text in the rectangle. Here you have combined three specifications with a bitwise OR (|). The string is written as a single line with the text centered on the line and the line centered vertically within the rectangle. This places it nicely in the center of the window. There are also a number of other options, which include the possibility to place text at the top or the bottom of the rectangle, and to left or right justify it.

After you have written all that you want to display, you must tell Windows that you have finished drawing the client area. For every `BeginPaint()` function call, there must be a corresponding `EndPaint()` function call. Thus, to end processing the WM_PAINT message, you need the statement:

```
EndPaint(hWnd, &PaintSt);              // Terminate window redraw operation
```

The hWnd argument identifies your program window, and the second argument is the address of the PAINTSTRUCT structure that was filled in by the `BeginPaint()` function.

Ending the Program

You might assume that closing the window closes the application, but to get this behavior you actually have to add some more code. The reason that the application won't close by default when the window is closed is that you may need to do some clearing up. It is also possible that the application may have more than one window. When the user closes the window by double-clicking the title bar icon or clicking the

Close button, this causes a WM_DESTROY message to be generated. Therefore, to close the application, you need to process the WM_DESTROY message in the WindowProc() function. You do this by generating a WM_QUIT message with the following statement:

```
PostQuitMessage(0);
```

The argument here is an exit code. This Windows API function does exactly what its name suggests — it posts a WM_QUIT message in the message queue for your application. This results in the GetMessage() function in WinMain() returning FALSE and ending the message loop, so ending the program.

A Complete WindowProc() Function

You have covered all the elements necessary to make up the complete WindowProc() function for your example. The code for the function is as follows:

```
// Listing OFWIN_2
LRESULT WINAPI WindowProc(HWND hWnd, UINT message,
                          WPARAM wParam, LPARAM lParam)
{
  HDC hDC;                          // Display context handle
  PAINTSTRUCT PaintSt;              // Structure defining area to be drawn
  RECT aRect;                       // A working rectangle

  switch(message)                   // Process selected messages
  {
    case WM_PAINT:                          // Message is to redraw the window
      hDC = BeginPaint(hWnd, &PaintSt);// Prepare to draw the window

      // Get upper left and lower right of client area
      GetClientRect(hWnd, &aRect);

      SetBkMode(hDC, TRANSPARENT);     // Set text background mode

      // Now draw the text in the window client area
      DrawText(
              hDC,                  // Device context handle
              L"But, soft! What light through yonder window breaks?",
              -1,                   // Indicate null terminated string
              &aRect,               // Rectangle in which text is to be drawn
              DT_SINGLELINE|        // Text format - single line
              DT_CENTER|            //              - centered in the line
              DT_VCENTER);          //              - line centered in aRect

      EndPaint(hWnd, &PaintSt);     // Terminate window redraw operation
      return 0;

    case WM_DESTROY:                // Window is being destroyed
      PostQuitMessage(0);
      return 0;

    default:                        // Any other message - we don't
                                    // want to know, so call
                                    // default message processing
```

```
        return DefWindowProc(hWnd, message, wParam, lParam);
    }
}
```

How It Works

The entire function body is just a `switch` statement. A particular `case` is selected, based on the message ID that is passed to the function through the `message` parameter. Because this example is simple, you need to process only two different messages: `WM_PAINT` and `WM_DESTROY`. You hand all other messages back to Windows by calling the `DefWindowProc()` function in the `default` case for the `switch`. The arguments to `DefWindowProc()` are those that were passed to the function, so you are just passing them back as they are. Note the `return` statement at the end of processing each message type. For the messages you handle, a zero value is returned.

A Simple Windows Program

Because you have written `WinMain()` and `WindowProc()` to handle messages, you have enough to create a complete source file for a Windows program using just the Windows API. The complete source file simply consists of an `#include` directive for the `windows.h` header file, a prototype for the `WindowProc` function and the `WinMain` and `WindowProc` functions that you have already seen:

```
// Ex12_01.cpp   Native windows program to display text in a window
#include <windows.h>

LRESULT WINAPI WindowProc(HWND hWnd, UINT message,
                          WPARAM wParam, LPARAM lParam);

    // Insert code for WinMain() here (Listing OFWIN_1)

    // Insert code for WindowProc() here (Listing OFWIN_2)
```

Of course, you'll need to create a project for this program, but instead of choosing Win32 Console Application as you've done up to now, you should create this project using the Win32 Project template. You should elect to create it as an empty project and then add the Ex12_01.cpp file to hold the code.

Try It Out   A Simple Windows API Program

If you build and execute the example, it produces the window shown in Figure 12-4.

Note that the window has a number of properties provided by the operating system that require no programming effort on your part to manage. The boundaries of the window can be dragged to resize it, and the whole window can be moved about onscreen. The maximize and minimize buttons also work. Of course, all of these actions do affect the program. Every time you modify the position or size of the window, a `WM_PAINT` message is queued and your program has to redraw the client area, but all the work of drawing and modifying the window itself is done by Windows.

The system menu and Close button are also standard features of your window because of the options that you specified in the `WindowClass` structure. Again, Windows takes care of the management. The only additional effect on your program arising from this is the passing of a `WM_DESTROY` message if you close the window, as previously discussed.

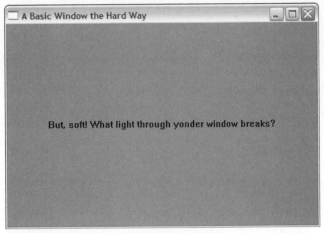

Figure 12-4

Windows Program Organization

In the previous example you saw an elementary Windows program that used the Windows API and displayed a short quote from the Bard. It's unlikely to win any awards, being completely free of any useful functionality, but it does serve to illustrate the two essential components of a Windows program: the WinMain() function that provides initialization and setup, and the WindowProc() function that services Windows messages. The relationship between these is illustrated in Figure 12-5.

It may not always be obvious in the code that you will see, but this structure is at the heart of *all* Windows programs, including programs written for the CLR. Understanding how Windows applications are organized can often be helpful when you are trying to determine why things are not working as they should be in an application. The WinMain() function is called by Windows at the start of execution of the program and the WindowProc() function, which you'll sometimes see with the name WndProc(), is called by the operating system whenever a message is to be passed to your application's window. In general there typically is a separate WindowProc() function in an application for each window in an application.

The WinMain() function does any initialization that's necessary and sets up the window or windows that are the primary interface to the user. It also contains the message loop for retrieving messages that are queued for the application.

The WindowProc() function handles all the messages for a given window that aren't queued, which includes those initiated in the message loop in WinMain(). WindowProc(), therefore, ends up handling both kinds of messages. This is because the code in the message loop sorts out what kind of message it has retrieved from the queue, and then dispatches it for processing by WindowProc(). WindowProc() is where you code your application-specific response to each Windows message, which should handle all the communications with the user by processing the Windows messages generated by user actions, such as moving or clicking the mouse or entering information at the keyboard.

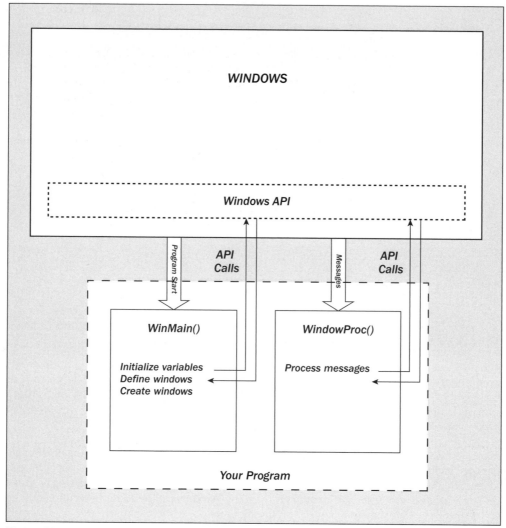

Figure 12-5

The queued messages are largely those caused by user input from either the mouse or the keyboard The non-queued messages for which Windows calls your `WindowProc()` function directly, are either messages that your program created, typically as a result of obtaining a message from the queue and then dispatching it, or messages that are concerned with window management — such as handling menus and scrollbars, or resizing the window.

The Microsoft Foundation Classes

The Microsoft Foundation Classes (**MFC**) are a set of predefined classes upon which Windows programming with Visual C++ is built. These classes represent an object-oriented approach to Windows programming that encapsulates the Windows API. MFC does not adhere strictly to the object-oriented principles of encapsulation and data hiding, principally because much of the MFC code was written before such principles were well established.

The process of writing a Windows program involves creating and using MFC objects, or objects of classes derived from MFC. In the main, you'll derive your own classes from MFC, with considerable assistance from the specialized tools in Visual C++ 2008 that make this easy. The objects of these MFC-based class types incorporate member functions for communicating with Windows, for processing Windows messages, and for sending messages to each other. These derived classes, of course, inherit all of the members of their base classes. These inherited functions do practically all of the general grunt work necessary for a Windows application to work. All you need to do is to add data and function members to customize the classes to provide the application-specific functionality that you need in your program. In doing this, you'll apply most of the techniques that you've been grappling with in the preceding chapters, particularly those involving class inheritance and virtual functions.

MFC Notation

All the classes in MFC have names beginning with **C**, such as CDocument or CView. If you use the same convention when defining your own classes, or when deriving them from those in the MFC library, your programs will be easier to follow. Data members of an MFC class are prefixed with m_. I'll also follow this convention in the examples that use MFC.

You'll find that MFC uses Hungarian notation for many variable names, particularly those that originate in the Windows API. As you recall, this involves using a prefix of p for a pointer, n for an int, l for long, h for a handle, and so on. The name m_lpCmdLine, for example, refers to a data member of a class (because of the m_ prefix) that is of type 'pointer to long'. This practice of explicitly showing the type of a variable in its name was important in the C environment because of the lack of type checking; because you could determine the type from the name, you had a fair chance of not using or interpreting its value incorrectly. The downside is that the variable names can become quite cumbersome, making the code look more complicated than it really is. Because C++ has strong type checking that picks up the sort of misuse that used to happen regularly in C, this kind of notation isn't essential, so I won't use it generally for variables in the examples in the book. I will, however, retain the p prefix for pointers and some of the other simple type denotations because this helps to make the code more readable.

How an MFC Program Is Structured

You know from Chapter 1 that you can produce a Windows program using the Application Wizard without writing a single line of code. Of course, this uses the MFC library, but it's quite possible to write a Windows program that uses MFC without using the Application wizard. If you first scratch the surface by constructing the minimum MFC-based program, you'll get a clearer idea of the fundamental elements involved.

The simplest program that you can produce using MFC is slightly less sophisticated than the example that you wrote earlier in this chapter using the raw Windows API. The example you'll produce here has a window, but no text displayed in it. This is sufficient to show the fundamentals, so try it out.

Try It Out   A Minimal MFC Application

Create a new project using the File > New > Project menu option, as you've done many times before. You won't use the Application wizard that creates the basic code here, so select the template for the project as Win32 Project and choose Windows Application and the Empty project options in the second dialog.

After the project is created, select `Project > Ex12_02 properties` from the main menu, and on the General sub-page from Configuration Properties, click the `Use of MFC` property to set its value to Use MFC in a Shared DLL.

With the project created you can create a new source file in the project as `Ex12_02.cpp`. So that you can see all the code for the program in one place, put the class definitions you need together with their implementations in this file. To achieve this, just add the code manually in the edit window — there isn't very much of it.

To begin with, add a statement to include the header file `afxwin.h`, as this contains the definitions for many MFC classes. This allows you to derive your own classes from MFC.

```
#include <afxwin.h>                    // For the class library
```

To produce the complete program, you'll only need to derive two classes from MFC: an **application class** and a **window class**. You won't even need to write a `WinMain()` function, as you did in the previous example in this chapter, because this is automatically provided by the MFC library behind the scenes. Take a look at how you define the two classes that you need.

The Application Class

The class CWinApp is fundamental to any Windows program written using MFC. An object of this class includes everything necessary for starting, initializing, running and closing the application. You need to produce the application to derive your own application class from CWinApp. You will define a specialized version of the class to suit your application needs. The code for this is as follows:

```
class COurApp: public CWinApp
{
   public:
      virtual BOOL InitInstance();
};
```

As you might expect for a simple example, there isn't a great deal of specialization necessary in this case. You've only included one member in the definition of the class: the `InitInstance()` function. This function is defined as a virtual function in the base class, so it's not a new function in your derived class; you are simply redefining the base class function for your application class. All the other data and function members that you need in the class you'll inherit from `CWinApp` unchanged.

The application class is endowed with quite a number of data members defined in the base, many of which correspond to variables used as arguments in Windows API functions. For example, the member `m_pszAppName` stores a pointer to a string that defines the name of the application. The member `m_nCmdShow` specifies how the application window is to be shown when the application starts up. You don't need to go into all the inherited data members now. You'll see how they are used as the need arises in developing application-specific code.

In deriving your own application class from `CWinApp`, you must override the virtual function `InitInstance()`. Your version is called by the version of `WinMain()` that's provided for you by MFC, and you'll include code in the function to create and display your application window. However, before you write `InitInstance()`, I should introduce you to a class in the MFC library that defines a window.

The Window Class

Your MFC application needs a window as the interface to the user, referred to as a **frame window**. You derive a window class for the application from the MFC class CFrameWnd, which is designed specifically for this purpose. Because the CFrameWnd class provides everything for creating and managing a window for your application, all you need to add to the derived window class is a constructor. This enables you to specify a title bar for the window to suit the application context:

```
class COurWnd: public CFrameWnd
{
  public:
    // Constructor
    COurWnd()
    {
      Create(0, L"Our Dumb MFC Application");
    }
};
```

The Create() function that you call in the constructor is inherited from the base class. It creates the window and attaches it to the COurWnd object that is being created. Note that the COurWnd object is not the same thing as the window that displayed by Windows — the class object and the physical window are distinct entities.

The first argument value for the Create() function, 0, specifies that you want to use the base class default attributes for the window — you'll recall that you needed to define window attributes in the previous example in this chapter that used the Windows API directly. The second argument specifies the window name that is used in the window title bar. You won't be surprised to learn that there are other parameters to the function Create(), but they all have default values which are quite satisfactory, so you can afford to ignore them here.

Completing the Program

Having defined a window class for the application, you can write the InitInstance() function in our COurApp class:

```
BOOL COurApp::InitInstance(void)
{
    // Construct a window object in the free store
    m_pMainWnd = new COurWnd;
    m_pMainWnd->ShowWindow(m_nCmdShow);        // ...and display it
    return TRUE;
}
```

This overrides the virtual function defined in the base class CWinApp, and as I said previously, it is called by the WinMain() function that's automatically supplied by the MFC library. The InitInstance() function constructs a main window object for the application in the free store by using the operator new. You store the address that is returned in the variable m_pMainWnd, which is an inherited member of your class COurApp. The effect of this is that the window object is owned by the application object. You don't even need to worry about freeing the memory for the object you have created — the supplied WinMain() function takes care of any cleanup necessary.

The only other item you need for a complete, albeit rather limited, program is to define an application object. An instance of our application class, COurApp, must exist before WinMain() is executed, so you must declare it at global scope with the statement:

```
COurApp AnApplication;      // Define an application object
```

The reason that this object needs to exist at global scope is that it is the application, and the application needs to exist before it can start executing. The WinMain() function that is provided by MFC calls the InitInstance() function member of the application object to construct the window object and, thus, implicitly assumes the application object already exists.

The Finished Product

Now that you've seen all the code, you can add it to the Ex12_02.cpp source file in the project. In a Windows program, the classes are usually defined in .h files, and the member functions that are not defined within the class definitions are defined in .cpp files. Your application is so short, though, that you may as well put it all in a single .cpp file. The merit of this is that you can view the whole lot together. The program code is structured as follows:

```
// Ex12_02.cpp
// An elementary MFC program
#include <afxwin.h>                         // For the class library

// Application class definition
class COurApp:public CWinApp
{
   public:
      virtual BOOL InitInstance();
};

// Window class definition
class COurWnd:public CFrameWnd
{
   public:
      // Constructor
      COurWnd()
      {
         Create(0, L"Our Dumb MFC Application");
      }
};

// Function to create an instance of the main application window
BOOL COurApp::InitInstance(void)
{
   // Construct a window object in the free store
   m_pMainWnd = new COurWnd;
   m_pMainWnd->ShowWindow(m_nCmdShow);      // ...and display it
   return TRUE;
}

// Application object definition at global scope
COurApp AnApplication;                              // Define an application object
```

774

That's all you need. It looks a bit odd because no `WinMain()` function appears, but as noted previously, there is a `WinMain()` function supplied by the MFC library.

How It Works

Now you're ready to roll, so build and run the application. Select the Build > Build Ex12_02.exe menu item, click the appropriate toolbar button, or just press `Ctrl+Shift+B` to build the solution. You should end up with a clean compile and link, in which case you can press `Ctrl+F5` to run it. Your minimum MFC program appears as shown in Figure 12-6.

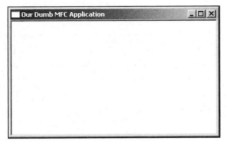

Figure 12-6

You can resize the window by dragging the border, move the whole thing around, and minimize or maximize it in the usual ways. The only other function that the program supports is "close," for which you can use the system menu, the Close button at the upper-right of the window, or just key `Alt+F4`. It doesn't look like much, but, considering that there are so few lines of code, it's quite impressive.

Using Windows Forms

A Windows form is an entity that represents a window of some kind. By a window I mean window in its most general sense, being an area on the screen that can be a button a dialog, a regular window, or any other kind of visible GUI component. A Windows form is encapsulated by the a subclass of the `System::Windows::Forms::Form` class, but you don't need to worry about this much initially, because all the code to create a form is created automatically. To see just how easy it's going to be, create a basic window using Windows Forms that has a standard menu.

Try It Out   **A Windows Forms Application**

Choose the `CLR` project type in the New Project dialog and select the Windows Forms Application as the template for the project. The New Project dialog window is shown in Figure 12-7.

Enter the project name as Ex12_03. When you click the OK button the Application Wizard generates the code for the Windows form application and displays the design window containing the form as it is displayed by the application. This is shown in Figure 12-8.

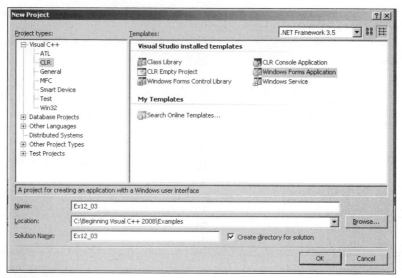

Figure 12-7

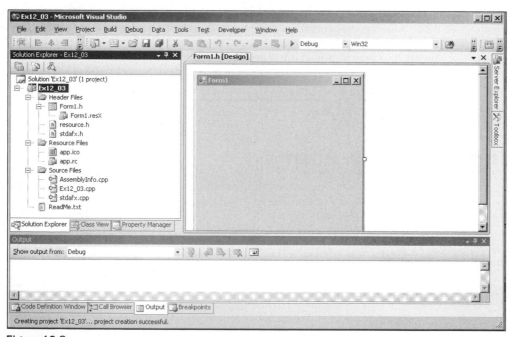

Figure 12-8

You can now make changes to the form in the design pane graphically, and the changes are automatically reflected in the code that creates the form. For a start, you can drag the bottom corner of the form with the mouse cursor to increase the size of the form window. You can also change the text in the title bar — right-click in the client area of the form and select Properties from the context menu. This displays the Properties window that allows you to change the properties for the form. From the list of properties to the right of the design pane, select Text, and then enter the new title bar text in the adjacent column showing the property value — I entered A Simple Form Window. When you press the key, the new text appears in the title bar of the form.

Just to see how easy it really is to add to the form window, display the Toolbox pane by selecting the tab on the right of the window if it is present, or by pressing Ctrl+Alt+X or by selecting Toolbox from the View menu. Find the MenuStrip option in the Menus and Toolbars list and drag it on to the form window in the Design tab pane. Right-click the MenuStrip1 that appears below the form window and select Insert Standard Items from the pop-up. You'll then have the menu in the form window populated with the standard File, Edit, Tools, Help menus, each complete with its drop-down list of menu items. The result of this operation is shown in Figure 12-9.

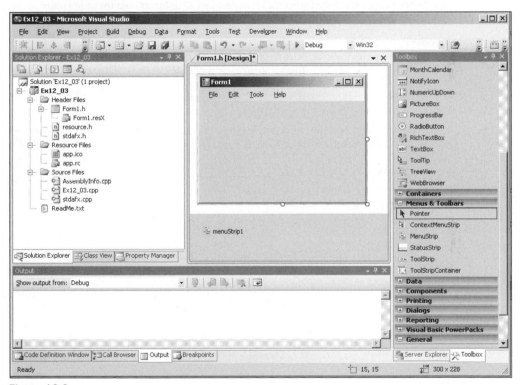

Figure 12-9

How It Works

If you build the project by pressing the Ctrl+Shift+B and then execute it by pressing Ctrl+F5, you'll see the form window displayed complete with its menus. Naturally the menu items don't do anything because you haven't added any code to deal with the events that result from clicking on them, but the icons at the right end of the title bar work so you can close the application. You'll look into how to develop a Windows Form application further, including handling events, later in the book.

Summary

In this chapter you've seen three different ways of creating an elementary Windows application with Visual C++ 2008 and you should now have a feel for the essential differences between these three approaches. In the remaining chapters of the book, you'll be exploring in more depth how you develop applications using the MFC and using Windows Forms.

The important points arising in the chapter include:

❑ The Windows API provides a standard programming interface by which an application communicates with the operating system.

❑ All Windows applications include a `WinMain()` function that is called by the operating system to begin execution of the application. The `WinMain()` function also includes code to retrieve messages from the operating system.

❑ The Windows operating system calls a particular function in an application to handle processing of specific messages. An application identifies the message processing function for each window in an application by calling a Windows API function.

❑ The MFC consists of a set of classes that encapsulate the Windows API and simplify programming using the Windows API.

❑ A Windows Forms application executes with the CLR. The windows in a Windows Forms application can be created graphically with all the required code being generated automatically.

Windows Programming with the Microsoft Foundation Classes

In this chapter, you start down the road of serious Windows application development using the MFC. You'll get an appreciation of what code the Application wizard generates for a Microsoft Foundation Class (MFC) program and what options you have for the features to be included in your code.

In this chapter, you will learn about:

- ❏ The basic elements of an MFC-based program
- ❏ How Single Document Interface (SDI) applications and Multiple Document Interface (MDI) applications differ
- ❏ How to use the MFC Application Wizard to generate SDI and MDI programs
- ❏ What files are generated by the MFC Application Wizard and what their contents are
- ❏ How an MFC Application Wizard-generated program is structured
- ❏ The key classes in an MFC Application Wizard-generated program, and how they are interconnected
- ❏ The general approach to customizing an MFC Application Wizard-generated program

You'll be expanding the programs that you generate in this chapter by adding features and code incrementally in subsequent chapters. You will eventually end up with a sizable, working Windows program that incorporates almost all the basic user interface programming techniques you will have learned along the way.

The Document/View Concept in MFC

When you write applications using MFC, it implies acceptance of a specific structure for your program, with application data being stored and processed in a particular way. This may sound restrictive, but it really isn't for the most part, and the benefits in speed and ease of implementation you gain far outweigh any conceivable disadvantages. The structure of an MFC program incorporates two application-oriented entities — a **document** and a **view** — so let's look at what they are and how they're used.

What Is a Document?

A **document** is the name given to the collection of data in your application with which the user interacts. Although the word *document* seems to imply something of a textual nature, a document isn't limited to text. It could be the data for a game, a geometric model, a text file, a collection of data on the distribution of orange trees in California or, indeed, anything you want. The term *document* is just a convenient label for the application data in your program, treated as a unit.

You won't be surprised to hear that a document in your program is defined as an object of a document class. Your document class is derived from the CDocument class in the MFC library, and you'll add your own data members to store items that your application requires, and member functions to support processing of that data. Your application is not limited to a single document type; you can define multiple document classes when there are several different kinds of document involved in your application.

Handling application data in this way enables standard mechanisms to be provided within MFC for managing a collection of application data as a unit and for storing and retrieving data contained in document objects to and from disk. These mechanisms are inherited by your document class from the base class defined in the MFC library, so you get a broad range of functionality built in to your application automatically, without having to write any code.

Document Interfaces

You have a choice as to whether your program deals with just one document at a time, or with several. The **Single Document Interface**, abbreviated as **SDI**, is supported by the MFC library for programs that only require one document to be open at a time. A program using this interface is referred to as an **SDI application**.

For programs needing several documents to be open at one time, you can use the **Multiple Document Interface**, which is usually referred to as **MDI**. With the MDI, as well as being able to open multiple documents of one type, your program can also be organized to handle documents of different types simultaneously with each document displayed in its own window. Of course, you need to supply the code to deal with processing whatever different kinds of documents you intend to support. With an MDI application, each document is displayed in a child window of the application window. You have an additional application variant called the **multiple top-level document architecture** where each document window is a child of the desktop.

What Is a View?

A **view** always relates to a particular document object. As you've seen, a document contains a set of application data in your program, and a view is an object that provides a mechanism for displaying some or all of the data stored in a document. It defines how the data is to be displayed in a window and how the user can interact with it. Similar to the way that you define a document, you'll define your own view class by deriving it from the MFC class CView. Note that a view object and the window in which it is displayed are distinct. The window in which a view appears is called a **frame window**. A view is actually displayed in its own window that exactly fills the client area of a frame window. Figure 13-1 illustrates a document with two views.

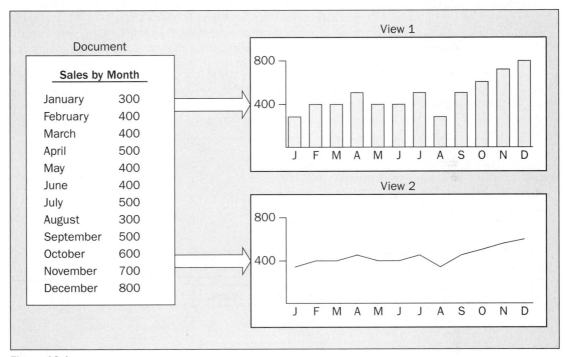

Figure 13-1

In the example in Figure 13-1, each view displays all the data that the document contains in a different form, although a view could display just part of the data in a document if that's what's required.

A document object can have as many view objects associated with it as you want. Each view object can provide a different presentation of the document data or a subset of the same data. If you were dealing with text, for example, different views could be displaying independent blocks of text from the same document. For a program handling graphical data, you could display all of the document data at different scales in separate windows, or in different formats, such as a textual representation of the elements that form the image. Figure 13-1 illustrates a document that contains numerical data — product sales data by month, where one view provides a bar chart representation of the sales performance and a second view shows the data in the form of a graph.

Linking a Document and Its Views

MFC incorporates a mechanism for integrating a document with its views, and each frame window with a currently active view. A document object automatically maintains a list of pointers to its associated views, and a view object has a data member holding a pointer to the document that it relates to.

Each frame window stores a pointer to the currently active view object. The coordination among a document, a view, and a frame window is established by another MFC class of objects called **document templates**.

Document Templates

A **document template** manages the document objects in your program, as well as the windows and views associated with each of them. There is one document template for each type of document that you have in your application. If you have two or more documents of the same type, you need only one document template to manage them. To be more specific about the role of a document template, a document template object creates document objects and frame window objects, and views of a document are created by a frame window object. The application object that is fundamental to every MFC application creates the document template object itself. Figure 13-2 shows a graphical representation of these interrelationships.

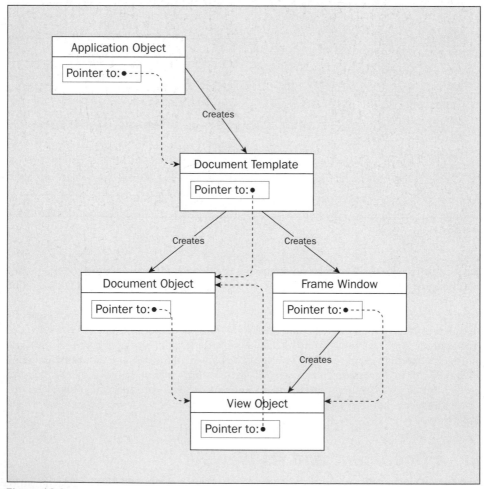

Figure 13-2

The diagram uses dashed arrows to show how pointers are used to relate objects. These pointers enable function members of one class object to access the **public** data or the function members in the interface of another object.

Document Template Classes

MFC has two classes for defining document templates. For SDI applications, the MFC library class CSingleDocTemplate is used. This is relatively straightforward because an SDI application has only one document and usually just one view. MDI applications are rather more complicated. They have multiple documents active at one time, so a different class, CMultiDocTemplate, is needed to define the document template. You'll see more of these classes as we progress into developing application code.

Your Application and MFC

Figure 13-3 shows the four basic classes that are going to appear in virtually all your MFC-based Windows applications:

- ❑ The application class CMyApp
- ❑ The frame window class CMyWnd
- ❑ The view class CMyView, which defines how data contained in CMyDoc is to be displayed in the client area of a window created by a CMyWnd object
- ❑ The document class CMyDoc defining a document to contain the application data

The actual names for these classes are specific to a particular application, but the derivation from MFC is much the same, although there can be alternative base classes, particularly with the view class. As you'll see a bit later, MFC provides several variations of the view class that provide a lot of functionality prepackaged for you, saving you lots of coding. You normally don't need to extend the class that defines a document template for your application, so the standard MFC class CSingleDocTemplate usually suffices in an SDI program. When you're creating an MDI program, your document template class is CMultiDocTemplate, which is also derived from CDocTemplate.

The arrows in the diagram point from a base class to a derived class. The MFC library classes shown here form quite a complex inheritance structure, but in fact these are just a very small part of the complete MFC structure. You need not be concerned about the details of the complete MFC hierarchy in the main, but it is important to have a general appreciation of it if you want to understand what the inherited members of your classes are. You will not see any of the definitions of the base classes in your program, but the inherited members of a derived class in your program are accumulated from the direct base class, as well as from each of the indirect base classes in the MFC hierarchy. To determine what members one of your program's classes has, you therefore need to know from which classes it inherits. After you know that, you can look up its members using the Help facility.

Another point you don't need to worry about is remembering which classes you need to have in your program and what base classes to use in their definition. As you'll see next, all of this is taken care of for you by Visual C++ 2008.

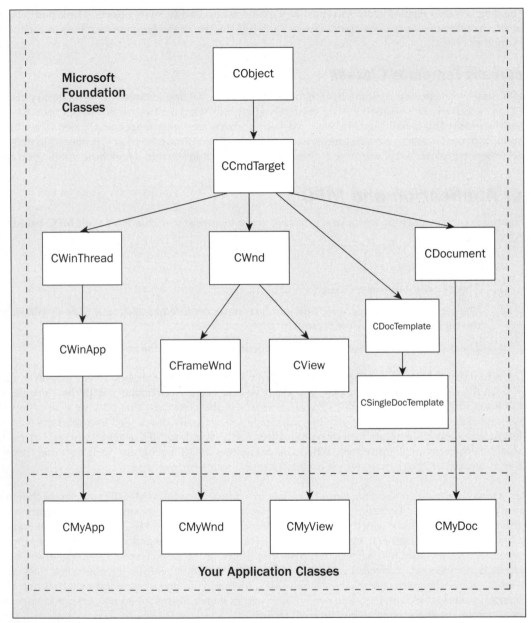

Figure 13-3

Creating MFC Applications

You use four primary tools in the development of your MFC-based Windows programs:

1. You use an **Application Wizard** for creating the basic application program code when you start. You use an Application Wizard whenever you create a project that results in code being automatically generated.

2. You use the project context menu in `ClassView` to add new classes and resources to your project. You display this context menu by right-clicking the project name in `ClassView` and using the `Add/Class` menu item to add a new class. Resources are things composed of non-executable data such as bitmaps, icons, menus, and dialog boxes. The `Add/Resource` menu item from the same context menu helps you to add a new resource.

3. You use the class context menu in `ClassView` for extending and customizing the existing classes in your programs. You use the `Add/Add Function` and `Add/Add Variable` menu items to do this.

4. You use a **Resource Editor** for creating or modifying such objects as menus and toolbars.

There are, in fact, several resource editors; the one used in any particular situation is selected depending on the kind of resource that you're editing. We'll look at editing resources in the next chapter, but for now let's jump in and create an MFC application.

The process for creating an MFC application is just as straightforward as that for creating a console program; there are just a few more choices along the way. As you have already seen, you start by creating a new project by selecting the `File > New > Project` menu item, or you can use the shortcut and press `Ctrl+Shift+N`. The New Project dialog box is displayed where you can then choose `MFC` as the project type and `MFC Application` as the template to be used. You also need to enter a name for the project that can be anything you want — I've used `TextEditor`, as shown in Figure 13-4. You won't be developing this particular example into a serious application so you can use any name you like.

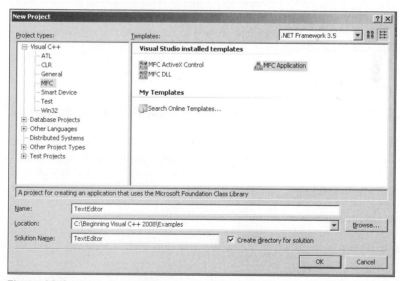

Figure 13-4

As you know, the name that you assign to the project — `TextEditor`, in this case — is used as the name of the folder that contains all the project files, but it is also used as a basis for creating the names for classes that the Application Wizard generates for your project. When you click OK in the New Project dialog window, you'll see the MFC Application Wizard dialog, where you can choose options for the application, as shown in Figure 13-5.

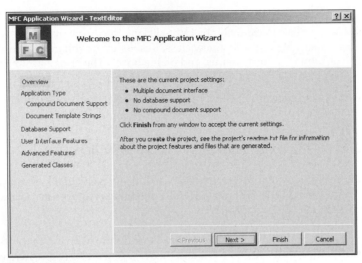

Figure 13-5

As you can see, the dialog explains the project settings that are currently in effect, and on the right of the dialog you have a range of options you can select. You can select any of these to have a look if you want — you can always get back to the base dialog box for the Application Wizard by selecting the Previous button. Selecting any of the options on the right presents you with a whole range of further choices, so there are a lot of options in total. I won't discuss all of them — I'll just outline the ones that you are most likely to be interested in and leave you to investigate the others. Initially, the Application Wizard allows you to choose an SDI application, an MDI application, or a dialog box-based application. Let's create an SDI application first of all and explore what some of the choices are as we go along.

Creating an SDI Application

Select the Application Type option from the list to the right of the dialog window.

The default option selected is Multiple documents, which selects the multiple document interface — MDI, and the appearance of an MDI application is shown top-left in the dialog window so that you'll know what to expect. Select the Single document option and the representation for the application that is shown top-left changes to a single window, as shown in Figure 13-6.

Consider some of the other options you have here for the application type:

Option	Description
Dialog based	The application window is a dialog window rather than a frame window.
Multiple top-level documents	Documents are displayed in child windows of the desktop rather than child windows of the application as they are with an MDI application.

Option	Description
Document/View architecture support	This option is selected by default so you get code built-in to support the document/view architecture. If you uncheck this option the support is not provided and it's up to you to implement whatever you want.
Resource language	The drop-down list box displays the choice of languages available that applies to resources such as menus and text strings in your application.
Use Unicode libraries	Support for Unicode is provided through Unicode versions of the MFC libraries; if you want to use them, you must check this option.

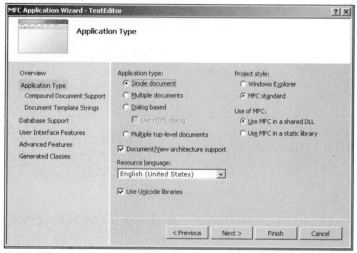

Figure 13-6

You should uncheck the Use Unicode libraries option that is checked by default. If you leave it checked, the application expects Unicode input and files are stored as Unicode characters. This makes them unreadable in programs that expect ASCII text.

You also can choose between Windows Explorer and MFC standard for the project style. The former implements the application window with the client area divided into two panes; the left pane displays data in the form of a tree and the right pane displays straight text.

You can also choose how MFC library code is used in your program. The default choice of using the MFC library as a shared DLL (Dynamic Link Library) means that your program links to MFC library routines at run time. This reduces the size of the executable file that you'll generate, but requires the MFC DLL to be on the machine that's running it. The two modules together (your application's .exe module and the MFC .dll) may be bigger than if you had statically linked the MFC library. If you opt for static linking, the MFC library routine is included in the executable module for your program when it is built. Statically linked applications run slightly faster than those that dynamically link to the MFC library so it's a tradeoff between memory usage and speed of execution. If you keep the default option of using MFC as a shared DLL, several programs running simultaneously using the dynamic link library can all share a single copy of the library in memory.

In the Document Template Strings dialog box, you can enter a file extension for files that the program creates. The extension .txt is a good choice for this example. You can also enter a Filter Name on this dialog box, which is the name of the filter that will appear in Open and Save As dialog boxes to filter the list of files so that only files with your file extension are displayed.

If you select User Interface Features from the list in the right pane of the MFC Application Wizard window you get a further set of options that can be included in your application:

Option	Description
Thick Frame	This enables you to resize the application window by dragging a border. It is selected by default.
Minimize box	This option is also selected by default and provides a minimize box at the top right of the application window.
Maximize box	This option is also selected by default and provides a maximize box at the top right of the application window.
Minimized	If you select this option the application starts with the window minimized so it appears as an icon.
Maximized	If you select this option the application starts with the window maximized.
Initial status bar	This option adds a status bar at the bottom of the application window containing indicators for CAPS LOCK, NUM LOCK, and SCROLL LOCK and a message line that displays help strings for menus and toolbar buttons. The option also adds menu commands to hide or show the status bar.
Split window	This option provides a splitter bar for each of the applications main views.
Standard docking toolbar	This option adds a toolbar to the application window that provides a standard range of buttons that are alternatives to using the standard menu items. A toolbar is provided by default. A docking toolbar can be dragged to the sides or the bottom of the application window, so you can put it wherever is most convenient. You'll see how to add buttons to the toolbar in Chapter 14.
Browser style toolbar	This adds an Internet Explorer-style toolbar to the application windows.

There are a couple of features under the Advanced Features set of options of which you need to be aware. One is `Printing and print preview`, which is selected by default, and the other is `Context-sensitive help`, which you get if you check the box. `Printing and print preview` adds the standard Page Setup, Print Preview, and Print items to the File menu and the Application Wizard also provides code to support these functions. Enabling the `Context-sensitive help` option results in a basic set of facilities to support context-sensitive help. You'll obviously need to add the specific contents of the help files if you want to use this feature.

If you select the Generated Classes option in the MFC Application Wizard dialog box, you'll see a list of the classes that the Application wizard generates in your program code, as shown in Figure 13-7.

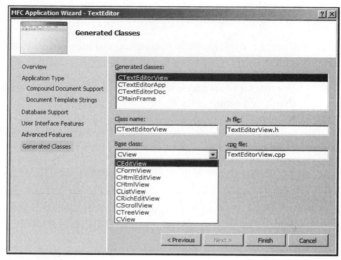

Figure 13-7

You can highlight any class in the list by clicking it and the boxes below show the name given to the class, the name of the header file in which the definition will be stored, the base class used, and the name of the file containing the implementation of member functions in the class. The class definition is always contained in a `.h` file, and the member function source code is always included in a `.cpp` file.

In the case of the class `CTextEditorDoc`, you can alter everything except the base class; however, if you select `CTextEditorApp` the only thing that you can alter is the class name. Try clicking the other classes in the list. For `CMainFrame` you can alter everything except the base class and for the `CTextEditorView` class shown in Figure 13-7 you can change the base class as well. Click the down arrow to display the list of other classes that you can have as a base class; the list appears in Figure 13-7. The capability built into your view class depends on which base class you select:

Base Class	View Class Capability
CEditView	Provides simple multiline text-editing capability, including find and replace and printing.

Continued

Base Class	View Class Capability
CFormView	Provides a view that is a form; a form is a dialog box that can contain controls for displaying data and for user input. This is essentially the same functionality as provided by a form in a Windows Forms application for the CLR that you will explore in Chapter 22.
CHtmlEditView	This class extends CHtmlView class and adds the ability to edit HTML pages.
CHtmlView	Provides a view in which Web pages and local HTML documents can be displayed.
CListView	Enables you to use the document-view architecture with list controls.
CRichEditView	Provides the capability to display and edit documents containing rich edit text.
CScrollView	Provides a view that automatically adds scrollbars when the data that is displayed requires them.
CTreeView	Provides the capability to use the document-view architecture with tree controls.
CView	Provides the basic capability for viewing a document.

Because you've called the application TextEditor, with the notion that it is able to edit text, choose CEditView to get basic editing capability provided automatically.

You can now click Finish to have the program files for a fully working base program generated by MFC Application wizard, using the options you've chosen.

The Output from the MFC Application Wizard

All the program files generated by the Application Wizard are stored in the TextEditor project folder, which is a subfolder to the solution folder with the same name. There are also resource files in the res subfolder to the project folder. The IDE provides several ways for you to view the information relating to your project:

Tab/Pane	Contents
Solution Explorer	Shows the files included in your project. The files are categorized in virtual folders with the names Header Files, Resource Files and Source Files.
Class View	Class View displays the classes you have in your project and their members. It also shows any global entities you have defined. The classes are shown in the upper pane and the lower pane displays the members for the class selected in the upper pane. By right-clicking entities in the Class View, you can display a menu that you can use to view the definition of the entity or where it is referenced.

Tab/Pane	Contents
Resource View	This displays the resources such as menu items and toolbar buttons used by your project. Right-clicking a resource displays a menu, enabling you to edit the resource or add new resources.
Property Manager	This displays the versions you can build for your project. The debug version includes extra facilities to make debugging your code easier. The release version results in a smaller executable, and you build this version when your code is fully tested for production use. By right-clicking a version — either Debug or Release — you can display a context menu where you can add a property sheet or display the properties currently set for that version. A property sheet enables you to set options for the compiler and linker.

You can switch to view any of these by selecting from the view menu or clicking on a tab label. If you right-click TextEditor in the Solution Explorer pane and select Properties from the pop-up, the project properties window is displayed, as shown in Figure 13-8.

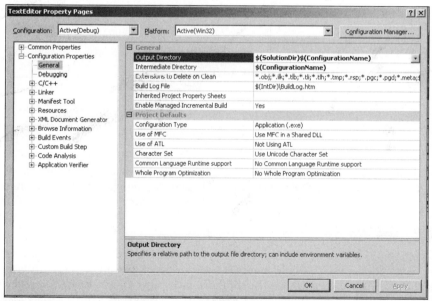

Figure 13-8

The left pane shows the property groups you can select to be displayed in the right pane. Currently the General group of properties is displayed and you can change the value for a property in the right pane by clicking it and selecting a new value from the drop-down list box to the right of the property name or in some cases by entering a new value.

At the top of the property pages window, you can see the current project configuration and the target platform when the project is built. You can change these by selecting from the drop-down list for each.

Viewing Project Files

If you select the Solution Explorer tab and expand the list by clicking the + for TextEditor files and then click the + for each of the Source Files, Header Files and Resource Files folders, you'll see the complete list of files for the project, as shown in Figure 13-9.

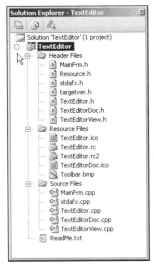

Figure 13-9

Figure 13-9 show the pane as a floating window to make the complete list of files visible at one time; you can arrange for any of the tabbed panes to be floating by clicking the down arrow at the top of the pane and selecting from the list of possible positions. As you can see, there are a total of 17 files in the project excluding ReadMe.txt. You can view the contents of any of the files simply by double-clicking the file-name. The contents of the file selected are displayed in the Editor window. Try it out with the ReadMe.txt file. You'll see that it contains a brief explanation of the contents of each of the files that make up the project. I won't repeat the descriptions of the files here, because they are very clearly summarized in ReadMe.txt.

Viewing Classes

The access to your project presented by the Class View tab is often much more convenient than that of Solution Explorer because classes are the basis for the organization of the application. When you want to look at the code, it's typically the definition of a class or the implementation of a member function you'll want to look at, and from Class View you can go directly to either. On occasions, however, Solution Explorer comes in handy. If you want to check the #include directives in a .cpp file, using Solution Explorer you can open the file you're interested in directly.

In the Class View pane, you can expand the TextEditor classes item to show the classes defined for the application. Clicking the name of any class shows the members of that class in the lower pane. In the Class View pane shown in Figure 13-10, the CTextEditorDoc class has been selected.

Figure 13-10 shows the Class View pane in its docked state. The icons code the various kinds of things that you can display and you will find a key to what each icon indicates if you look at the Class View documentation.

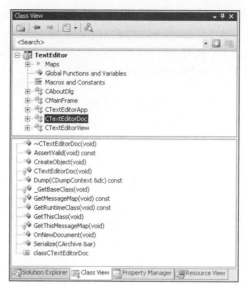

Figure 13-10

You can see that you have the four classes discussed earlier that are fundamental to an MFC application: CTextEditorApp for the application, CMainFrame for the application frame window, CTextEditorDoc for the document and CTextEditorView for the view. You also have a class CAboutDlg that defines objects that support the dialog box that appears when you select the menu item Help > About in the application. If you highlight Global Functions and Variables, you'll see that it contains two definitions: the application object theApp and indicators that is an array of indicators recording the status of caps lock, num lock and scroll lock that are displayed in the status bar.

To view the code for a class definition in the Editor pane you just double-click the class name in the tree in Class View. Similarly to view the code for a member function, double-click the function name. Note that you can drag the edges of any of the panes in an IDE window to view its contents or your code more easily. You can hide or show the Solution Explorer set of panes by clicking the Autohide button at the right end of the pane title bar.

The Class Definitions

I won't go into the classes in complete detail here — you'll just get a feel for how they look and I'll highlight a few important aspects. If you double-click the name of a class in the Class View, the code defining the class is displayed. Take a look at the application class, CTextEditorApp first. The definition for this class is shown here:

```
// TextEditor.h : main header file for the TextEditor application
//
#pragma once

#ifndef __AFXWIN_H__
  #error "include 'stdafx.h' before including this file for PCH"
#endif
```

```
#include "resource.h"        // main symbols


// CTextEditorApp:
// See TextEditor.cpp for the implementation of this class
//

class CTextEditorApp : public CWinApp
{
public:
  CTextEditorApp();


// Overrides
public:
  virtual BOOL InitInstance();

// Implementation
  afx_msg void OnAppAbout();
  DECLARE_MESSAGE_MAP()
};

extern CTextEditorApp theApp;
```

The `CTextEditorApp` class derived from `CWinApp` and includes a constructor, a virtual function `InitInstance()`, a function `OnAppAbout()`, and a macro `DECLARE_MESSAGE_MAP()`.

> *A macro is not C++ code. It's a name defined by a #define pre-processor directive that will be replaced by some text that will normally be C++ code, but could also be constants or symbols of some kind.*

The `DECLARE_MESSAGE_MAP()` macro is concerned with defining which Windows messages are handled by which function members of the class. The macro appears in the definition of any class that may process Windows messages. Of course, our application class inherits a lot of functions and data members from the base class, and you will be looking further into these as you expand the program examples. If you take a look at the beginning of the code for the class definition, you will notice that the `#pragma once` directive prevents the file being included more than once. Following that is a group of preprocessor directives that ensure that the `stdafx.h` file is included before this file.

The application frame window for our SDI program is created by an object of the class `CMainFrame`, which is defined by the code shown here:

```
class CMainFrame : public CFrameWnd
{

protected: // create from serialization only
  CMainFrame();
  DECLARE_DYNCREATE(CMainFrame)

// Attributes
public:

// Operations
```

```
public:

// Overrides
public:
  virtual BOOL PreCreateWindow(CREATESTRUCT& cs);

// Implementation
public:
  virtual ~CMainFrame();
#ifdef _DEBUG
  virtual void AssertValid() const;
  virtual void Dump(CDumpContext& dc) const;
#endif

protected:  // control bar embedded members
  CStatusBar  m_wndStatusBar;
  CToolBar    m_wndToolBar;

// Generated message map functions
protected:
  afx_msg int OnCreate(LPCREATESTRUCT lpCreateStruct);
  DECLARE_MESSAGE_MAP()
};
```

This class is derived from `CFrameWnd`, which provides most of the functionality required for our application frame window. The derived class includes two protected data members, `m_wndStatusBar` and `m_wndToolBar`, that are instances of the MFC classes `CStatusBar` and `CToolBar` respectively. These objects create and manage the status bar that appears at the bottom of the application window, and the toolbar that provides buttons to access standard menu functions.

The definition of the `CTextEditorDoc` class that was supplied by the MFC Application wizard is:

```
class CTextEditorDoc : public CDocument
{
protected: // create from serialization only
  CTextEditorDoc();
  DECLARE_DYNCREATE(CTextEditorDoc)

// Attributes
public:

// Operations
public:

// Overrides
  public:
  virtual BOOL OnNewDocument();
  virtual void Serialize(CArchive& ar);

// Implementation
public:
  virtual ~CTextEditorDoc();
#ifdef _DEBUG
```

```
    virtual void AssertValid() const;
    virtual void Dump(CDumpContext& dc) const;
#endif

protected:

// Generated message map functions
protected:
    DECLARE_MESSAGE_MAP()
};
```

As in the case of the previous classes, most of the meat comes from the base class and is therefore not apparent here. The macro DECLARE_DYNCREATE() that appears after the constructor (and was also used in the CMainFrame class) enables an object of the class to be created dynamically by synthesizing it from data read from a file. When you save an SDI document object, the frame window that contains the view is saved along with your data. This allows everything to be restored when you read it back. Reading and writing a document object to a file is supported by a process called **serialization**. You will see how to write your own documents to file using serialization and then reconstruct them from the file data in the examples we will develop.

The document class also includes the macro DECLARE_MESSAGE_MAP() in its definition to enable Windows messages to be handled by class member functions if necessary.

The view class in our SDI application is defined as:

```
class CTextEditorView : public CEditView
{
protected: // create from serialization only
    CTextEditorView();
    DECLARE_DYNCREATE(CTextEditorView)

// Attributes
public:
    CTextEditorDoc* GetDocument() const;

// Operations
public:

// Overrides
    public:
virtual BOOL PreCreateWindow(CREATESTRUCT& cs);
protected:
    virtual BOOL OnPreparePrinting(CPrintInfo* pInfo);
    virtual void OnBeginPrinting(CDC* pDC, CPrintInfo* pInfo);
    virtual void OnEndPrinting(CDC* pDC, CPrintInfo* pInfo);

// Implementation
public:
    virtual ~CTextEditorView();
#ifdef _DEBUG
    virtual void AssertValid() const;
```

```
    virtual void Dump(CDumpContext& dc) const;
#endif

protected:

// Generated message map functions
protected:
  DECLARE_MESSAGE_MAP()
};

#ifndef _DEBUG  // debug version in TextEditorView.cpp
inline CTextEditorDoc* CTextEditorView::GetDocument() const
   { return reinterpret_cast<CTextEditorDoc*>(m_pDocument); }
#endif
```

As you specified in the Application Wizard dialog box, the view class is derived from the class CEditView, which already includes basic text handling facilities. The GetDocument() function returns a pointer to the document object corresponding to the view, and you will be using this to access data in the document object when you add your own extensions to the view class.

Creating an Executable Module

To compile and link the program, click Build > Build Solution, press Ctrl+Shift+B, or click the Build icon in the toolbar.

There are two implementations of the CTextEditorView class member function GetDocument() in the code generated by Application wizard. The one in the .cpp file for the CEditView class is used for the debug version of the program. You will normally use this during program development because it provides validation of the pointer value stored for the document. (This is stored in the inherited data member m_pDocument in the view class.) The version that applies to the release version of your program you can find after the class definition in the TextEditorView.h file. This version is declared as inline and it does not validate the document pointer. The GetDocument() function just provides a link to the document object. You can call any of the functions in the interface to the document class using the pointer to the document that the function returns.

By default, you have debug capability included in your program. As well as the special version of GetDocument(), there are lots of checks in the MFC code that are included in this case. If you want to change this, you can use the drop-down list box in the Build toolbar to choose the release configuration, which doesn't contain all the debug code.

When compiling your program with debug switched on, the compiler doesn't detect uninitialized variables, so it can be helpful to do the occasional release build even while you are still testing your program.

Precompiled Header Files

The first time you compile and link a program, it will take some time. The second and subsequent times it should be quite a bit faster because of a feature of Visual C++ 2008 called **precompiled headers**. During the initial compilation, the compiler saves the output from compiling header files in a special file with the extension .pch. On subsequent builds, this file is reused if the source in the headers has not changed, thus saving the compilation time for the headers.

You can determine whether or not precompiled headers are used and control how they are handled through the Properties tab. Right-click TextEditor and select Properties from the menu that is displayed. If you expand the C/C++ node in the dialog box displayed, you can select Precompiled Headers to set this property.

Running the Program

To execute the program, press Ctrl+F5. Because you chose CEditView as the base class for the CTextEditorView class, the program is a fully functioning, simple text editor. You can enter text in the window, as shown in Figure 13-11.

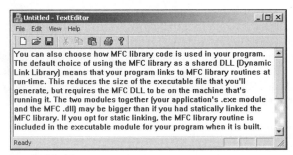

Figure 13-11

Note that the application has scroll bars for viewing text outside the visible area within the window, and of course you can resize the window by dragging the boundaries. All the items under all menus are fully operational so you can save and retrieve files, you can cut and paste text, and you can print the text in the window — and all that without writing a single line of code! As you move the cursor over the toolbar buttons or the menu options, prompts appear in the status bar describing the function that are invoked, and if you let the cursor linger on a toolbar button, a tooltip is displayed showing its purpose. (You'll learn about tooltips in more detail in Chapter 14.)

How the Program Works

As in the trivial MFC example you looked at earlier in this chapter, the application object is created at global scope in our SDI program. You can see this if you expand the Global Functions and Variables item in the Class View, and then double-click theApp. In the Editor window you'll see this statement:

```
CTextEditorApp theApp;
```

This declares the object theApp as an instance of our application class CTextEditorApp. The statement is in the file TextEditor.cpp, which also contains member function declarations for the application class, and the definition of the CAboutDlg class.

After the object theApp has been created, the MFC-supplied WinMain() function is called. This in turn calls two member functions of the theApp object. First it calls InitInstance(), which provides for any initialization of the application that is necessary, and then Run(), which provides initial handling for Windows messages. The WinMain() function does not appear explicitly in the project source code because it is supplied by the MFC class library and is called automatically when the application starts.

The InitInstance() Function

You can access the code for the `InitInstance()` function by double-clicking its entry in the Class View after highlighting the `CTextEditorApp` class — or if you're in a hurry, you can just look at the code immediately following the line defining the `theApp` object. The version created by the MFC Application wizard is as follows:

```
BOOL CTextEditorApp::InitInstance()
{
  // InitCommonControlsEx() is required on Windows XP if an application
  // manifest specifies use of ComCtl32.dll version 6 or later to enable
  // visual styles.  Otherwise, any window creation will fail.
  INITCOMMONCONTROLSEX InitCtrls;
  InitCtrls.dwSize = sizeof(InitCtrls);
  // Set this to include all the common control classes you want to use
  // in your application.
  InitCtrls.dwICC = ICC_WIN95_CLASSES;
  InitCommonControlsEx(&InitCtrls);

  CWinApp::InitInstance();

  // Initialize OLE libraries
  if (!AfxOleInit())
  {
    AfxMessageBox(IDP_OLE_INIT_FAILED);
    return FALSE;
  }
  AfxEnableControlContainer();
  // Standard initialization
  // If you are not using these features and wish to reduce the size
  // of your final executable, you should remove from the following
  // the specific initialization routines you do not need
  // Change the registry key under which our settings are stored
  // TODO: You should modify this string to be something appropriate
  // such as the name of your company or organization
  SetRegistryKey(_T("Local AppWizard-Generated Applications"));
  LoadStdProfileSettings(4);  // Load standard INI file options (including MRU)
  // Register the application's document templates.  Document templates
  //  serve as the connection between documents, frame windows and views
  CSingleDocTemplate* pDocTemplate;
  pDocTemplate = new CSingleDocTemplate(
    IDR_MAINFRAME,
    RUNTIME_CLASS(CTextEditorDoc),
    RUNTIME_CLASS(CMainFrame),        // main SDI frame window
    RUNTIME_CLASS(CTextEditorView));
  if (!pDocTemplate)
    return FALSE;
  AddDocTemplate(pDocTemplate);

  // Parse command line for standard shell commands, DDE, file open
  CCommandLineInfo cmdInfo;
  ParseCommandLine(cmdInfo);

  // Dispatch commands specified on the command line.  Will return FALSE if
```

```
      // app was launched with /RegServer, /Register, /Unregserver or /Unregister.
      if (!ProcessShellCommand(cmdInfo))
        return FALSE;

      // The one and only window has been initialized, so show and update it
      m_pMainWnd->ShowWindow(SW_SHOW);
      m_pMainWnd->UpdateWindow();
      // call DragAcceptFiles only if there's a suffix
      //  In an SDI app, this should occur after ProcessShellCommand
      return TRUE;
    }
```

The bits of the code that I want to mention at this point are shaded. The string passed to the `SetRegistryKey()` function is used to define a registry key under which program information is stored. You can change this to whatever you want. If I changed the argument to `"Horton"`, information about our program would be stored under the registry key

```
   HKEY_CURRENT_USER\Software\Horton\TextEditor\
```

All the application settings are stored under this key, including the list of files most recently used by the program. The call to the function `LoadStdProfileSettings()` loads the application settings that were saved last time around. Of course, the first time you run the program, there aren't any.

A document template object is created dynamically within `InitInstance()` by the statement:

```
      pDocTemplate = new CSingleDocTemplate(
          IDR_MAINFRAME,
          RUNTIME_CLASS(CTextEditorDoc),
          RUNTIME_CLASS(CMainFrame),        // main SDI frame window
          RUNTIME_CLASS(CTextEditorView));
```

The first parameter to the `CSingleDocTemplate` constructor is a symbol, `IDR_MAINFRAME`, which defines the menu and toolbar to be used with the document type. The following three parameters define the document, main frame window, and View Class objects that are to be bound together within the document template. Because you have an SDI application here, there is only one of each in the program, managed through one document template object. `RUNTIME_CLASS()` is a macro that enables the type of a class object to be determined at run time.

There's a lot of other stuff here for setting up the application instance that you need not worry about. You can add any initialization of your own that you need for the application to the `InitInstance()` function.

The Run() Function

The `CTextEditorApp` class inherits the `Run()` function in from the application base class `CWinApp`. Because the function is declared as **virtual**, you can replace the base class version of the function `Run()` with one of your own, but this is not usually necessary so you don't need to worry about it.

`Run()` acquires all the messages from Windows destined for the application and ensures that each message is passed to the function in the program designated to service it, if one exists. Therefore, this function continues executing as long as the application is running. It terminates when you close the application.

Thus, you can boil the operation of the application down to four steps:

1. Creating an application object, `theApp`

2. Executing `WinMain()`, which is supplied by MFC

3. `WinMain()` calling `InitInstance()`, which creates the document template, the main frame window, the document, and the view

4. `WinMain()` calling `Run()`, which executes the main message loop to acquire and dispatch Windows messages

Creating an MDI Application

Now let's create an MDI application using the MFC Application Wizard. Give it the project name **Sketcher** — and plan on keeping it, as you will be expanding it into a sketching program during subsequent chapters. You should have no trouble with this procedure because there are only three things that you need to do differently from the process that you have just gone through for the SDI application. You should leave the default option, MDI, rather than changing to the SDI option but still opt out of using Unicode libraries. Under the `Document Template Strings` set of options in the Application Wizard dialog box you should specify the file extension as `ske`. You should also leave the base class for the `CSketcherView` class as `CView` under the `Generated Classes` set of options.

You can see in the dialog box with `Generated Classes` selected that you get an extra class for your application compared to the `TextEditor` example, as Figure 13-12 shows.

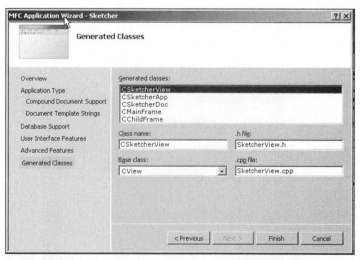

Figure 13-12

The extra class is `CChildFrame`, which is derived from the MFC class `CMDIChildWnd`. This class provides a frame window for a view of the document that appears *inside* the application window created by a `CMainFrame` object. With an SDI application there is a single document with a single view, so the view is displayed in the client area of the main frame window. In an MDI application, you can have multiple documents open, and each document can have multiple views. To accomplish this, each view of a document in the program has its own child frame window created by an object of the class CChildFrame. As you saw earlier, a view is displayed in what is actually a separate window, but one which exactly fills the client area of a frame window.

Running the Program

You can build the program in exactly the same way as the previous example. Then, if you execute it, you get the application window shown in Figure 13-13.

Figure 13-13

In addition to the main application window, you have a separate document window with the caption Sketch1. Sketch1 is the default name for the initial document, and it has the extension .ske if you save it. You can create additional views for the document by selecting the Window > New Window menu option. You can also create a new document by selecting File > New, so that there will be two active documents in the application. The situation with two documents active, each with two views open, is shown in Figure 13-14.

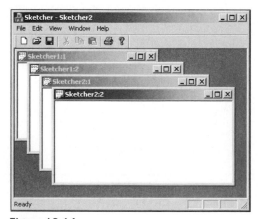

Figure 13-14

You can't yet actually create any data in the application because we haven't added any code to do that, but all the code for creating documents and views has already been included by the Application wizard.

Summary

In this chapter, you've been concerned mainly with the mechanics of using the MFC Application wizard. You have seen the basic components of the MFC programs the Application wizard generates for both SDI and MDI applications. All our MFC examples are created by the MFC Application wizard, so it's a good idea to keep the general structure and broad class relationships in mind. You probably won't feel too comfortable with the detail at this point, but don't worry about that now. You'll find that it becomes much clearer after you begin developing applications in the succeeding chapters.

The key points covered in this chapter are:

❑   The MFC Application wizard generates a complete, working, framework Windows application for you to customize to your requirements.

❑   The Application wizard can generate single document interface (SDI) applications that work with a single document and a single view, or multiple document interface (MDI) programs that can handle multiple documents with multiple views simultaneously.

❑   The four essential classes in an SDI application that are derived from the foundation classes are:

   ❑   The application class

   ❑   The frame window class

   ❑   The document class

   ❑   The view class

❑   A program can have only one application object. This is defined automatically by the Application wizard at global scope.

❑   A document class object stores application-specific data and a view class object displays the contents of a document object.

❑   A document template class object is used to tie together a document, a view, and a window. For an SDI application, a `CSingleDocTemplate` class does this, and for an MDI application, the `CDocTemplate` class is used. These are both foundation classes and application-specific versions do not normally need to be derived.

Exercises

It isn't possible to give programming examples for this chapter, because it really just introduced the basic mechanics of creating MFC applications. There aren't solutions to all the exercises because you will either see the answer for yourself on the screen, or be able to check your answer back with the text.

However, you can download the source code for the examples in the book and the solutions to other exercises from www.wrox.com.

1.   What is the relationship between a document and a view?

2.   What is the purpose of the document template in an MFC Windows program?

3.   Why do you need to be careful, and plan your program structure in advance, when using the Application Wizard?

4. Code up the simple text editor program. Build both debug and release versions, and examine the types and sizes of the files produced in each case.

5. Generate the text editor application several times, trying different window styles from the Advanced Options in Application Wizard.

Working with Menus and Toolbars

In the last chapter, you saw how a simple framework application generated by the MFC Application Wizard is made up and how the parts interrelate. In this chapter, you'll start customizing a Multiple Document Interface (MDI) framework application called Sketcher with a view to making it into a useful program. The first step in this process is to understand how menus are defined in Visual C++ 2008, and how functions are created to service the application-specific menu items that you add to your program. You'll also see how to add toolbar buttons to the application. By the end of this chapter, you'll have learned about:

❑   How an MFC-based program handles messages

❑   Menu resources, and how you can create and modify them

❑   Menu properties, and how you can create and modify them

❑   How to create a function to service the message generated when a menu item is selected

❑   How to add handlers to update menu properties

❑   How to add toolbar buttons and associate them with existing menu items

Communicating with Windows

As you saw in Chapter 12, Windows communicates with your program by sending messages to it. Most of the drudgery of message handling is taken care of by MFC, so you don't have to worry about providing a `WndProc()` function at all. MFC enables you to provide functions to handle the individual messages that you're interested in and to ignore the rest. These functions are referred to as message handlers or just handlers. Because your application is MFC-based, a message handler is always a member function of one of your application's classes.

The association between a particular message and the function in your program that is to service it is established by a message map — each class in your program that can handle Windows messages will have one. A message map for a class is simply a table of member functions that handle Windows messages. Each entry in the message map associates a function with a particular message; when a given message occurs, the corresponding function is called. Only the messages relevant to a class appear in the message map for the class.

A message map for a class is created automatically by the MFC Application Wizard when you create a project or by ClassWizard when you add a class that handles messages to your program. Additions to, and deletions from, a message map are mainly managed by ClassWizard, but there are circumstances where you need to modify the message map manually. The start of a message map in your code is indicated by a BEGIN_MESSAGE_MAP() macro, and the end is marked by an END_MESSAGE_MAP() macro. Let's look into how a message map operates using our Sketcher example.

Understanding Message Maps

A message map is established by the MFC Application Wizard for each of the main classes in your program. In the instance of an MDI program such as Sketcher, a message map is defined for each of CSketcherApp, CSketcherDoc, CSketcherView, CMainFrame, and CChildFrame. You can see the message map for a class in the .cpp file containing the implementation of the class. Of course, the functions that are included in the message map also need to be declared in the class definition, but they are identified here in a special way. Look at the definition for the CSketcherApp class shown here:

```
class CSketcherApp : public CWinApp
{
public:
  CSketcherApp();


// Overrides
public:
  virtual BOOL InitInstance();

// Implementation
  afx_msg void OnAppAbout();
  DECLARE_MESSAGE_MAP()
};
```

Only one message handler, OnAppAbout(), is declared in the CSketcherApp class. The word afx_msg at the beginning of the line declaring the OnAppAbout() function is just to distinguish a message handler from other member functions in the class. It is converted to white space by the preprocessor, so it has no effect when the program is compiled.

The macro DECLARE_MESSAGE_MAP() indicates that the class can contain function members that are message handlers. In fact, any class that you derive from the MFC class CCmdTarget can potentially have message handlers, so such classes will have this macro included as part of the class definition by the MFC Application Wizard or by the Add Class Wizard that you'll use to add a new class for a project, depending on which was responsible for creating it. Figure 14-1 shows the MFC classes derived from CCmdTarget that have been used in our examples so far.

The classes that have been used directly, or as a direct base for our own application classes, are shown shaded. Thus, the CSketcherApp class has CCmdTarget as an indirect base class and, therefore, are always included the DECLARE_MESSAGE_MAP() macro. All of the view (and other) classes derived from CWnd also have it.

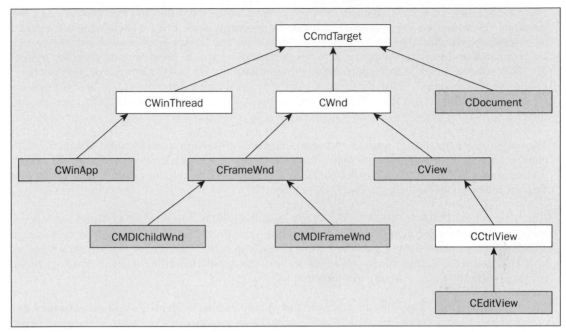

Figure 14-1

If you are adding your own members to a class directly, it's best to leave the DECLARE_MESSAGE_MAP()
macro as the last line in the class definition. If you do add members after DECLARE_MESSAGE_MAP(),
you'll also need to include an access specifier for them: public, protected, or private.

Message Handler Definitions

If a class definition *includes* the macro DECLARE_MESSAGE_MAP(), the class implementation must include
the macros BEGIN_MESSAGE_MAP() and END_MESSAGE_MAP(). If you look in Sketcher.cpp, you'll see the
following code as part of the implementation of CSketcherApp:

```
BEGIN_MESSAGE_MAP(CSketcherApp, CWinApp)
  ON_COMMAND(ID_APP_ABOUT, &CSketcherApp::OnAppAbout)
  // Standard file based document commands
  ON_COMMAND(ID_FILE_NEW, &CWinApp::OnFileNew)
  ON_COMMAND(ID_FILE_OPEN, &CWinApp::OnFileOpen)
  // Standard print setup command
  ON_COMMAND(ID_FILE_PRINT_SETUP, &CWinApp::OnFilePrintSetup)
END_MESSAGE_MAP()
```

This is a message map. The BEGIN_MESSAGE_MAP() and END_MESSAGE_MAP() macros define the boundaries of the message map, and each of the message handlers in the class appears between these macros. In
the preceding case, the code is only handling one category of message, the type of WM_COMMAND message
called a **command message**, which is generated when the user selects a menu option or enters an accelerator key. (If that seems clumsy, it's because there's another kind of WM_COMMAND message called a control notifications message, as you'll see later in this chapter.)

The message map knows which menu or key is pressed by the identifier (ID) that's included in the message. There are four ON_COMMAND macros in the preceding code, one for each of the command messages to be handled. The first argument to this macro is an ID that is associated with one particular command, and the ON_COMMAND macro ties the function name to the command specified by the ID. Thus, when a message corresponding to the identifier ID_APP_ABOUT is received, the function OnAppAbout() is called. Similarly, for a message corresponding to the ID_FILE_NEW identifier, the function OnFileNew() is called. This handler is actually defined in the base class, CWinApp, as are the two remaining handlers.

The BEGIN_MESSAGE_MAP() macro has two arguments. The first argument identifies the current class name for which the message map is defined and the second provides a connection to the base class for finding a message handler. If a handler isn't found in the class defining the message map, the message map for the base class is then searched.

Note that command IDs such as ID_APP_ABOUT are standard IDs defined in MFC. These correspond to messages from standard menu items and toolbar buttons. The ID_ prefix is used to identify a command associated with a menu item or a toolbar button, as you'll see when I discuss resources later. For example, ID_FILE_NEW is the ID that corresponds to the File > New menu item being selected, and ID_APP_ABOUT corresponds to the Help > About menu option.

There are more symbols besides WM_COMMAND that Windows uses to identify standard messages. Each of them is prefixed with WM_ for Windows Message. These symbols are defined in Winuser.h, which is included in Windows.h. If you want to look at them, you'll find Winuser.h in the include sub-folder to the VC folder containing your Visual C++ 2008 system.

There's a nice shortcut for viewing a .h file. If the name of the file appears in the Editor window, you can just right-click it, and select the menu item Open Document "Filename.h" from the pop-up menu. This works with standard library headers, too.

Windows messages often have additional data values that are used to refine the identification of a particular message specified by a given ID. The WM_COMMAND message, for instance, is sent for a whole range of commands, including those originating from selecting a menu item or a toolbar button.

Note that when you are adding message handlers manually you should not map a message (or in the case of command messages, a command ID) to more than one message handler in a class. If you do, it won't break anything, but the second message handler is never called. Normally you add message handlers through the properties window and, in this case, you will not be able to map a message to more than one message handler. If you want to see the properties window for a class, right-click a class name in Class View and select Properties from the pop-up menu. You add a message handler by selecting the Messages button at the top of the Properties window that is displayed (Figure 14-2). You can figure out which button is the Messages button by hovering the mouse cursor over each button until the tooltip displays.

Clicking the Messages button brings up a list of message IDs; however, before I go into what you do next, I need to explain a little more about the types of messages you may be handling.

Figure 14-2

Message Categories

There are three categories of messages that your program may be dealing with, and the category to which it belongs determines how a message is handled. The message categories are:

Message Category	Description
Windows messages	These are standard Windows messages that begin with the WM_ prefix, with the exception of WM_COMMAND messages that we shall come to in a moment. Examples of Windows messages are WM_PAINT, which indicates that you need to redraw the client area of a window, and WM_LBUTTONUP, which signals that the left mouse button has been released.
Control notification messages	These are WM_COMMAND messages sent from controls (such as a list box) to the window that created the control or from a child window to a parent window. Parameters associated with a WM_COMMAND message enable messages from the controls in your application to be differentiated.
Command messages	These are also WM_COMMAND messages that originate from the user interface elements, such as menu items and toolbar buttons. MFC defines unique identifiers for standard menu and toolbar command messages.

The standard Windows messages in the first category are identified by the WM_-prefixed IDs that Windows defines. You'll be writing handlers for some of these messages in the next chapter. The messages in the second category are a particular group of WM_COMMAND messages that you'll see in Chapter 17 when you work with dialog boxes. You'll deal with the last category, messages originating from menus and toolbars, in this chapter. In addition to the message IDs defined by MFC for the standard menus and toolbars, you can define your own message IDs for the menus and toolbar buttons that you add to your program. If you don't supply IDs for these items, MFC automatically generates IDs for you, based on the menu text.

Handling Messages in Your Program

You can't put a handler for a message anywhere you like. The permitted sites for a handler depend on what kind of message is to be processed. The first two categories of message that you saw above, that is, standard Windows messages and control notification messages, are always handled by objects of classes derived from CWnd. Frame window classes and view classes, for example, are derived from CWnd, so they can have member functions to handle Windows messages and control notification messages. Application classes, document classes, and document template classes are not derived from CWnd, so they can't handle these messages.

Using the properties window for a class to add a handler solves the headache of remembering where to place handlers, as it only offers you the IDs allowed for the class. For example, if you select CSketcherDoc as the class, you won't be offered any of the WM_ messages in the properties window for the class.

For standard Windows messages, the CWnd class provides default message handling. Thus, if your derived class doesn't include a handler for a standard Windows message, it is processed by the default handler defined in the base class. If you do provide a handler in your class, you'll sometimes still need to call the base class handler as well, so that the message is processed properly. When you're creating your own handler, a skeleton implementation of it is provided when you select the handler in the properties window for a class, and this includes a call to the base handler where necessary.

Handling command messages is much more flexible. You can put handlers for these in the application class, the document and document template classes, and of course in the window and view classes in your program. So, what happens when a command message is sent to your application, bearing in mind there are a lot of options as to where it is handled?

How Command Messages Are Processed

All command messages are sent to the main frame window for the application. The main frame window then tries to get the message handled by routing it in a specific sequence to the classes in your program. If one class can't process the message, it passes it on to the next.

For an SDI program, the sequence in which classes are offered an opportunity to handle a command message is:

1. The view object
2. The document object
3. The document template object
4. The main frame window object
5. The application object

The view object is given the opportunity to handle a command message first and, if no handler has been defined, the next class object has a chance to process it. If none of the classes has a handler defined, default Windows processing takes care of it, essentially throwing the message away.

For an MDI program, things are only a little more complicated. Although you have the possibility of multiple documents, each with multiple views, only the active view and its associated document are involved in the routing of a command message. The sequence for routing a command message in an MDI program is:

1. The active view object

2. The document object associated with the active view

3. The document template object for the active document

4. The frame window object for the active view

5. The main frame window object

6. The application object

It's possible to alter the sequence for routing messages, but this is so rarely necessary that I won't go into it in this book.

Extending the Sketcher Program

You're going to add code to the Sketcher program you created in the previous chapter to implement the functionality you need to create sketches. You'll provide code for drawing lines, circles, rectangles, and curves with various colors and line thicknesses, and for adding annotations to a sketch. The data for a sketch is stored in a document, and you'll also allow multiple views of the same document at different scales.

It will take several chapters to learn how to add everything that you need, but a good starting point would be to add menu items to deal with the types of elements that you want to be able to draw, and to select a color for drawing. You'll make both the element type and color selection persistent in the program, which means that having selected a color and an element type, both of these remain in effect until you change one or the other of them.

The steps that you'll work through to add menus to Sketcher are:

❑ Define the menu items to appear on the main menu bar and in each of the menus.

❑ Decide which of the classes in our application should handle the message for each menu item.

❑ Add message handling functions to the classes for the menu messages.

❑ Add functions to the classes to update the appearance of the menus to show the current selection in effect.

❑ Add a toolbar button complete with tooltips for each of the menu items.

Elements of a Menu

You'll be looking at two aspects of dealing with menus with the MFC: the creation and modification of the menu as it appears in your application and the processing necessary when a particular menu item is selected — the definition of a message handler for it. Let's look first at how you create new menu items.

Creating and Editing Menu Resources

Menus are defined external to the program code in a **resource** file and the specification of the menu is referred to as a **resource**. There are several other kinds of resources that you can include in your application; typical examples are dialogs, toolbars, and toolbar buttons. You'll be seeing more on these as you extend the Sketcher application.

Having a menu defined in a resource allows the physical appearance of the menu to be changed without affecting the code that processes menu events. For example, you could change your menu items from English to French or Norwegian or whatever without having to modify or recompile the program code. The code to handle the message created when the user selects a menu item doesn't need to be concerned with how the menu looks, only with the fact that it was selected. Of course, if you do add items to the menu, you'll need to add some code for each of them to ensure that they actually do something!

The Sketcher program already has a menu, which means that it already has a resource file. We can access the resource file contents for the Sketcher program by selecting the Resource View pane, or if you have the Solution Explorer pane displayed, you can double-click `Sketcher.rc`. This switches you to the Resource View, which displays the resources. If you expand the menu resource by clicking on the + symbol, you'll see that there are two menus defined, indicated by the identifiers `IDR_MAINFRAME` and `IDR_SketcherTYPE`. The first of these applies when there are no documents open in the application, and the second when you have one or more documents open. MFC uses the `IDR_` prefix to identify a resource that defines a complete menu for a window.

You're only going to be modifying the menu that has the identifier `IDR_SketcherTYPE`. You don't need to look at `IDR_MAINFRAME`, as your new menu items will only be relevant when a document is open. You can invoke a resource editor for the menu by double-clicking its menu ID in `Resource View`. If you do this for `IDR_SketcherTYPE`, the Editor pane appears as shown in Figure 14-3.

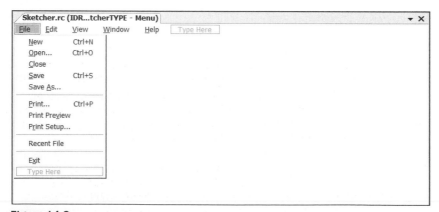

Figure 14-3

Adding a Menu Item to the Menu Bar

To add a new menu item, you can just click the menu box on the menu bar with the text "Type Here" to select it and then type in your menu name. If you insert the ampersand (&) in front of a letter in the menu item, the letter is identified as a shortcut key to invoke the menu from the keyboard. Type the first menu item as E&lement. This selects l as the shortcut letter, so you will be able invoke the menu item by typing Alt+l. You can't use E because it's already used by Edit. When you finish typing the name, you can double-click the new menu item to display its properties, as shown in Figure 14-4.

Figure 14-4

Properties are simply parameters that determine how the menu item will appear and behave. Figure 14-4 displays the properties for the menu item grouped by category. If you would rather have them displayed in alphabetical sequence, just click the second button from the left. Note that the Popup property is set as True by default; this is because the new menu item is at the top level on the menu bar so it would normally present a pop-up menu when it is selected. Clicking any property in the left column enables you to modify it in the right column. In this case you want to leave everything as it is so you can just close the Properties window. No ID is necessary for a pop-up menu item because selecting it just displays the menu beneath and there's no event for your code to handle. Note that you get a new blank menu box for the first item in the pop-up menu, as well as one on the main menu bar.

It would be better if the Element menu appeared between the View and Window menus, so place the cursor on the Element menu item and, keeping the left mouse button pressed, drag it to a position between the View and Window menu items, and release the left mouse button. After positioning the new Element menu item, the next step is to add items on the pop-up menu that corresponds to it.

Adding Items to the Element Menu

Select the first item (currently labeled "Type Here") in the `Element` pop-up menu by clicking it; then type `&Line` as the caption and press the Enter key. You can see the properties for this menu item by double-clicking it; the properties for this first item in the pop-up menu are shown in Figure 14-5.

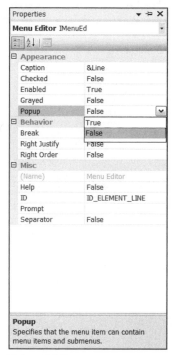

Figure 14-5

The properties modify the appearance of the menu item and also specify the ID of the message passed to your program when the menu item is selected. Here we have the ID already specified as `ID_ELEMENT_LINE`, but you could change it to something else if you want. Sometimes it's convenient to specify the ID yourself, such as when the generated ID is too long or its meaning is unclear. If you choose to define your own ID, you should use the MFC convention of prefixing it with `ID_` to indicate that it's a command ID for a menu item.

Because this item is part of a pop-up menu, the `Popup` property is `False` by default. You could make it another pop-up menu with a further list of items by setting the `Popup` property as `True`. As you see in Figure 14-5, you can display the possible values for the `Popup` property by selecting the down arrow. Don't you love the way pop-ups pop up all over the place?

You can enter a text string for the value of the `Prompt` property that appears in the status bar of your application when the menu item is highlighted. If you leave it blank, nothing is displayed in the status bar. I suggest you enter `Line` as the value for the `Prompt` property. Note how you get a brief indication of the purpose of the selected property at the bottom of the properties window. You want the default element selected in the application at start up to be a line, so you can set the `Checked` property value as `True` to get a check mark against the menu item to indicate when `Line` has been selected. We must remember to add code to update check marks for the menu items when a different selection is made. The `Break` property can alter the appearance of the pop-up by shifting the item into a new column. You don't need that here, so leave it as it is. Close the `Properties` window to save the values that you have set.

Modifying Existing Menu Items

If you think you may have made a mistake and want to change an existing menu item, or even if you just want to verify that you set the properties correctly, it's very easy to go back to an item. Just double-click the item you're interested in and the properties window for that item is displayed. You can then change the properties in any way that you want and close the window when you're done. If the item you want to access is in a pop-up menu that isn't displayed, just click the item on the menu bar to display the pop-up.

Completing the Menu

Now you can go through and create the remaining `Element` pop-up menu items that you need: `&Rectangle`, `&Circle`, and `Cur&ve`. Of course, all of these should have the `Checked` property left as `False`. You can't use `C` as the hotkey for the last item, as hotkeys must be unique and you've already assigned `C` to the menu item for a circle. You can accept the default IDs `ID_ELEMENT_RECTANGLE`, `ID_ELEMENT_CIRCLE`, and `ID_ELEMENT_CURVE` for these. You could also set the values for the `Prompt` property value as `Rectangle`, `Circle`, and `Curve` respectively.

You also need a `Color` menu on the menu bar, with pop-up menu items for `Black`, `Red`, `Green`, and `Blue`. You can create these, starting at the empty menu entry on the menu bar, using the same procedure that you just went through. Set `Black` as checked so that is the default color. You can use the default IDs (`ID_COLOR_BLACK`, etc.) as the IDs for the menu items. You can also add the status bar prompt for each as the value of the `Prompt` property. After you've finished, if you drag `Color` so that it's just to the right of `Element`, the menu should appear as shown in Figure 14-6.

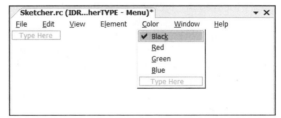

Figure 14-6

Note that you need to take care not to use the same letter more than once as a shortcut in the pop-up, or in the main menu, for that matter. There's no check made as you create new menu items, but if you right-click with the cursor on the menu bar when you've finished editing it, you'll get a pop-up that contains an item `Check Mnemonics`. Selecting this checks your menu for duplicate shortcut keys. It's a good idea to do this every time you edit a menu because it's easy to create duplicates by accident.

That completes extending the menu for elements and colors. Don't forget to save the file to make sure that the additions are safely stored away. Next, you need to decide in which classes you want to deal with messages from your menu items, and add member functions to handle each of the messages. For that you'll be using the Event Handler Wizard.

Adding Handlers for Menu Messages

To create an event handler for a menu item, right-click the item and select Add Event Handler from the pop-up that is displayed. If you try this with the Black menu item in the Color menu pop-up, you'll see the dialog shown in Figure 14-7.

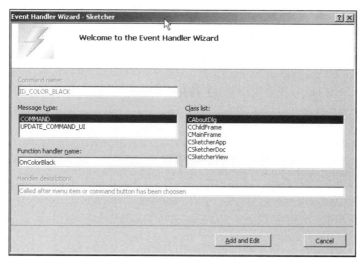

Figure 14-7

As you can see, the wizard has already chosen a name for the handler function. You could change it but OnColorBlack seems like a good name to me.

You obviously need to specify the message type as one of the choices shown in the dialog box. The Message type: box in the window in Figure 14-7 shows the two kinds of message that can arise for a particular menu ID. Each type of message serves a distinct purpose in dealing with a menu item.

Message Type	Description
COMMAND	This type of message is issued when a particular menu item has been selected. The handler should provide the action appropriate to the menu item being selected, for example, setting the current color in the document object or setting the element type.
UPDATE_COMMAND_UI	This is issued when the menu should be updated — checked or unchecked, for example — depending on its status. This message occurs before a pop-up menu is displayed so you can set the appearance of the menu item before the user sees it.

The way these work is quite simple. When you click a menu item in the Menu bar, an UPDATE_COMMAND_UI message is sent for each item in that menu before the menu is displayed. This provides the opportunity to do any necessary updating of the menu items' properties before the user sees it. When these messages are handled and any changes to the items' properties are completed, the menu is drawn. When you then click one of the items in the menu, a COMMAND message for that menu item is sent. I'll deal with the COMMAND messages now, and come back to the UPDATE_COMMAND_UI messages a little later in this chapter.

Because events for menu items result in command messages, you can choose to handle them in any of the classes that are currently defined in the Sketcher application. So how do you decide where you should process a message for a menu item?

Choosing a Class to Handle Menu Messages

Before you can decide which class should handle the messages for the menu items you've added, you need to decide what you want to do with the messages.

You want the element type and the element color to be modal — that is, whatever is set for the element type and element color should remain in effect until one or the other is changed. This allows you to create as many blue circles as you want, and when you want red circles, you just change the color. You have two basic possibilities for handling the setting of a color and the selection of an element type: setting them by view or by document. You could set them by view, in which case, if there's more than one view of a document, each view has its own color and element set. This means that you might draw a red circle in one view, switch to another view, and find that you're drawing a blue rectangle. This would be confusing and in conflict with how you would probably want them to work.

It would be better, therefore, to have the current color and element selection apply to a document. You can then switch from one view to another and continue drawing the same elements in the same color. There might be other differences between the views that you implement, such as the scale at which the document is displayed perhaps, but the drawing operation is consistent across multiple views.

This suggests that you should store the current color and element in the document object. These could then be accessed by any view object associated with the document object. Of course, if you had more than one document active, each document would have its own color and element type settings. It would therefore be sensible to handle the messages for your new menu items in the CSketcherDoc class and to store information about the current selections in an object of this class. I think you're ready to dive in and create a handler for the Black menu item.

Creating Menu Message Functions

Highlight the CSketcherDoc class name in the Event Handler Wizard dialog box by clicking it. You'll also need to click the COMMAND message type. You can then click the Add and Edit button. This closes the dialog box and the code for the handler you have created in the CSketcherDoc class is displayed in the edit window. The function looks like this:

```
void CSketcherDoc::OnColorBlack()
{
    // TODO: Add your command handler code here
}
```

The highlighted line is where you'll put your code that handles the event that results from the user selecting the Black menu item. The wizard also has updated the CSketcherDoc class definition:

```
class CSketcherDoc : public CDocument
{
protected: // create from serialization only
  CSketcherDoc();
  DECLARE_DYNCREATE(CSketcherDoc)

// Attributes
public:

// Operations
public:

// Overrides
  public:
  virtual BOOL OnNewDocument();
  virtual void Serialize(CArchive& ar);

// Implementation
public:
  virtual ~CSketcherDoc();
#ifdef _DEBUG
  virtual void AssertValid() const;
  virtual void Dump(CDumpContext& dc) const;
#endif

protected:

// Generated message map functions
protected:
  DECLARE_MESSAGE_MAP()
public:
  afx_msg void OnColorBlack();
};
```

The OnColorBlack() method has been added as a public member of the class and the afx_msg prefix marks it as a message handler.

You can now add COMMAND message handlers for the other color menu IDs and all the Element menu IDs in exactly the same way as this one. You can create each of the handler functions for the menu items with just four mouse clicks. Right-click the menu item, click the Add Event Handler menu item, click the CSketcherDoc class name in the dialog box for the Event Handler Wizard, and click the Add and Edit button for the dialog box.

The Event Handler Wizard should now have added the handlers to the CSketcherDoc class definition, which now looks like this:

```
class CSketcherDoc: public CDocument
{
...
```

```
protected:

// Generated message map functions
protected:
  DECLARE_MESSAGE_MAP()
public:
  afx_msg void OnColorBlack();
  afx_msg void OnColorRed();
  afx_msg void OnColorGreen();
  afx_msg void OnColorBlue();
  afx_msg void OnElementLine();
  afx_msg void OnElementRectangle();
  afx_msg void OnElementCircle();
  afx_msg void OnElementCurve();
};
```

A declaration has been added for each of the handlers that you've specified in the Event Handler Wizard dialog box. Each of the function declarations has been prefixed with afx_msg to indicate that it is a message handler.

The Event Handler Wizard also automatically updates the message map in your CSketcherDoc class implementation with the new message handlers. If you take a look in the file SketcherDoc.cpp, you'll see the message map as shown here:

```
BEGIN_MESSAGE_MAP(CSketcherDoc, CDocument)
  ON_COMMAND(ID_COLOR_BLACK, OnColorBlack)
  ON_COMMAND(ID_COLOR_RED, OnColorRed)
  ON_COMMAND(ID_COLOR_GREEN, OnColorGreen)
  ON_COMMAND(ID_COLOR_BLUE, OnColorBlue)
  ON_COMMAND(ID_ELEMENT_LINE, OnElementLine)
  ON_COMMAND(ID_ELEMENT_RECTANGLE, OnElementRectangle)
  ON_COMMAND(ID_ELEMENT_CIRCLE, OnElementCircle)
  ON_COMMAND(ID_ELEMENT_CURVE, OnElementCurve)
END_MESSAGE_MAP()
```

The Event Handler Wizard has added an ON_COMMAND() macro for each of the handlers that you have identified. This associates the handler name with the message ID, so, for example, the member function OnColorBlack() is called to service a COMMAND message for the menu item with the ID ID_COLOR_BLACK.

Each of the handlers generated by the Event Handler Wizard is just a skeleton. For example, take a look at the code provided for OnColorBlue(). This is also defined in the file SketcherDoc.cpp, so you can scroll down to find it, or go directly to it by switching to the Class View and double-clicking the function name after expanding the tree for the class CSketcherDoc (make sure that the file is saved first):

```
void CSketcherDoc::OnColorBlue()
{
    // TODO: Add your command handler code here
}
```

As you can see, the handler takes no arguments and returns nothing. It also does nothing at the moment, but this is hardly surprising, because the Event Handler Wizard has no way of knowing what you want to do with these messages!

Coding Menu Message Functions

Now consider what you should do with the COMMAND messages for our new menu items. I said earlier that you want to record the current element and color in the document, so you need to add a data member to the CSketcherDoc class for each of these.

Adding Members to Store Color and Element Mode

You could add the *data members* that you need to the CSketcherDoc class definition just by editing the class definition directly, but let's use the Add Member Variable Wizard to do it. Display the dialog box for the wizard by right-clicking the CSketcherDoc class name in the Class View and then selecting Add > Add Variable from the pop-up menu that appears. You then see the dialog box for the wizard, as shown in Figure 14-8.

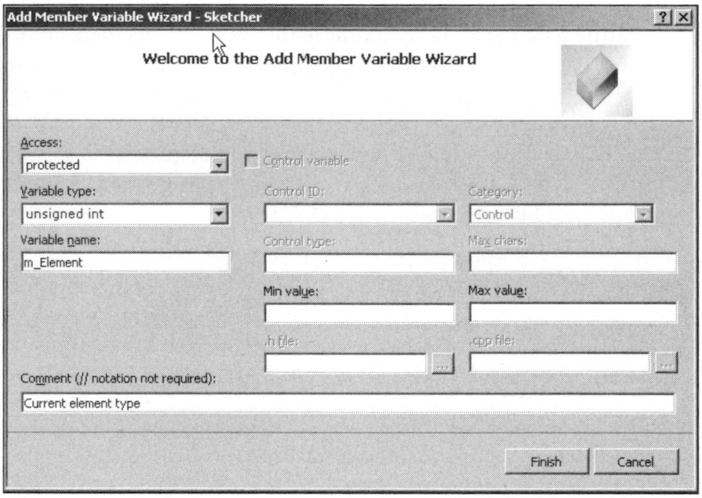

Figure 14-8

I've already entered the information in the dialog box for the m_Element variable that stores the current element type to be drawn. I have selected protected as the access because it should not be accessible directly from outside the class. I have also selected the type as unsigned int because you use a positive integer to identify each type of element. When you click the Finish button, the variable is added to the class definition in the CSketcherDoc.h file.

Add the CSketcherDoc class member to store the element color manually just to show that you can. Its name is m_Color and its type is COLORREF, which is a type defined by the Windows API for representing a color as a 32-bit integer. You can add the declaration for the m_Color member to the CSketcherDoc class like this:

```
class CSketcherDoc : public CDocument
{
...
// Generated message map functions
protected:
```

```
    DECLARE_MESSAGE_MAP()
public:
  afx_msg void OnColorBlack();
  afx_msg void OnColorRed();
  afx_msg void OnColorGreen();
  afx_msg void OnColorBlue();
  afx_msg void OnElementLine();
  afx_msg void OnElementRectangle();
  afx_msg void OnElementCircle();
  afx_msg void OnElementCurve();
protected:
  // Current element type
  unsigned int m_Element;
  COLORREF m_Color;              // Current drawing color
};
```

The m_Color member is also protected, as there's no reason to allow public access. You can always add functions to access or change the values of protected or private class members with the advantage that you then have complete control over what values can be set. Of course you could have used the Add Member Variable Wizard dialog as you did for m_Element; the difference is that you would type COLORREF in the Variable type box rather than select from the drop-down list.

Initializing the New Class Data Members

You need to decide how to represent an element type. You could just set m_Element to a unique numeric value, but this would introduce "magic numbers" into the program, the significance of which would be less than obvious to anyone else looking at the code. A better way would be to define a set of constants that you can use to set values for the member variable, m_Element. In this way, you can use a standard mnemonic to refer to a given type of element. You could define the element types with the following statements:

```
// Element type definitions
// Each type value must be unique
const unsigned int LINE = 101U;
const unsigned int RECTANGLE = 102U;
const unsigned int CIRCLE = 103U;
const unsigned int CURVE = 104U;
```

The constants initializing the element types are arbitrary unsigned integers. You can choose different values, if you like, as long as they are all distinct. If you want to add further types in the future, it will obviously be very easy to add definitions here.

For the color values, it would be a good idea if we used constant variables that are initialized with the values that Windows uses to define the color in question. You could do this with the following lines of code:

```
// Color values for drawing
const COLORREF BLACK = RGB(0,0,0);
const COLORREF RED = RGB(255,0,0);
const COLORREF GREEN = RGB(0,255,0);
const COLORREF BLUE = RGB(0,0,255);
```

Each constant is initialized by RGB(), which is a standard macro defined in the Wingdi.h, header file that is included as part of Windows.h. The three arguments to the macro define the red, green, and blue components of the color value respectively. Each argument must be an integer between 0 and 255, where these limits correspond to no color component and the maximum color component. RGB(0,0,0) corresponds to black because there are no components of red, green, or blue. RGB(255,0,0) creates a color value with a maximum red component, and no green or blue contribution. You can create other colors by combining red, green, and blue components.

You need somewhere to put these constants, so let's create a new header file and call it OurConstants.h. You can create a new file by right-clicking the Header Files folder in the Solution Explorer tab and selecting the Add > Add New Item menu option from the pop-up. Enter the header file name OurConstants in the dialog box that displays and then click the Open button. You'll then be able to enter the constant definitions in the Editor window as shown here.

```
//Definitions of constants

#pragma once

    // Element type definitions
    // Each type value must be unique
    const unsigned int LINE = 101U;
    const unsigned int RECTANGLE = 102U;
    const unsigned int CIRCLE = 103U;
    const unsigned int CURVE = 104U;
    /////////////////////////////////////

    // Color values for drawing
    const COLORREF BLACK = RGB(0,0,0);
    const COLORREF RED = RGB(255,0,0);
    const COLORREF GREEN = RGB(0,255,0);
    const COLORREF BLUE = RGB(0,0,255);
    /////////////////////////////////////
```

As you'll recall, the pre-processor directive #pragma once is there to ensure that the definitions cannot be included more than once in a file. The statements in the header file are included into a source file only by an #include directive if it hasn't been included previously. After the header has been included in a file, the statements will not be included again.

After saving the header file, you can add the following #include statement to the beginning of the file Sketcher.h:

```
#include "OurConstants.h"
```

Any .cpp file that has an #include directive for Sketcher.h has the constants available.

You can verify that the new constants are now part of the project by expanding Global Functions and Variables in the Class View. You'll see the names of the color and element types that have been added now appear along with the global variable theApp.

Modifying the Class Constructor

It's important to make sure that the data members you have added to the CSketcherDoc class are initialized appropriately when a document is created. You can add the code to do this to the class constructor as shown here:

```
CSketcherDoc::CSketcherDoc() : m_Element(LINE), m_Color(BLACK)
{
    // TODO: add one-time construction code here
}
```

The wizard already has arranged that the m_Element member will be initialized to 0 so change the initial value to LINE. You then need to add the initializer for the m_Color member with BLACK as the value so that everything is consistent with the initial check marks that you specified for the menus.

Now you're ready to add the code for the handler functions that you created for the Element and Color menu items. You can do this from the Class View. Click the name of the first handler function, OnColorBlack(). You just need to add one line to the function, so the code for it becomes:

```
void CSketcherDoc::OnColorBlack()
{
    m_Color = BLACK;           // Set the drawing color to black
}
```

The only job that the handler has to do is to set the appropriate color. In the interests of conciseness, the new line replaces the comment provided originally. You can go through and add one line to each of the Color menu handlers setting the appropriate color value.

The element menu handlers are much the same. The handler for the Element > Line menu item is:

```
void CSketcherDoc::OnElementLine()
{
    m_Element = LINE;          // Set element type as a line
}
```

With this model, it's not too difficult to write the other handlers for the Element menu. That's eight message handlers completed. You can now rebuild the example and see how it works.

Running the Extended Example

Assuming that there are no typos, the compiled and linked program should run without error. When you run the program, you should see the window shown in Figure 14-9.

The new menus are in place on the menu bar, and you can see that the items you have added to the menu are all there, and you should see the Prompt message in the status bar that you provided in the properties box when the mouse cursor is over a menu item. You could also verify that Alt+C and Alt+l work as well. The things that don't work are the check marks for the currently selected color and element, which remain firmly stuck to their initial defaults. Let's look at how you can fix that.

Figure 14-9

Adding Message Handlers to Update the User Interface

To set the check mark correctly for the new menus, you need to add the second kind of message handler, UPDATE_COMMAND_UI (signifying update command user interface), for each of the new menu items. This sort of message handler is specifically aimed at updating the menu item properties before the item is displayed.

Go back to viewing the Sketcher.rc file in the Editor window. Right-click the Black item in the Color menu and select Add Event Handler from the pop-up menu. You can then select UPDATE_COMMAND_UI as the message type and CSketcherDoc as the class as shown in Figure 14-10.

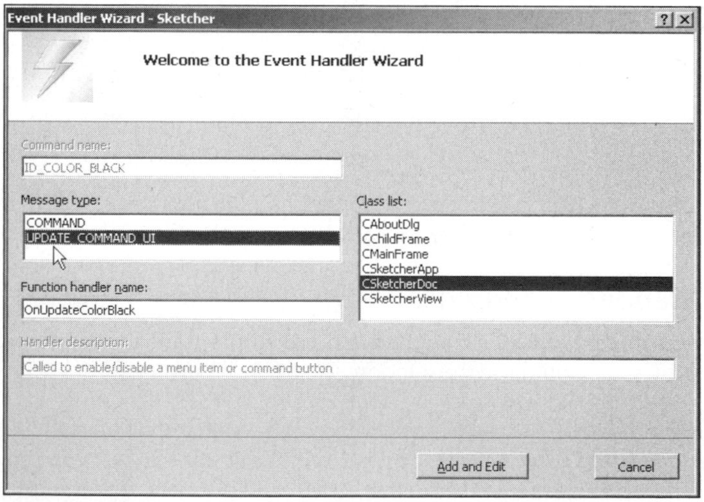

Figure 14-10

The name for the update function has been generated as `OnUpdateColorBlack()`. Because this seems a reasonable name for the function you want, click the Add and Edit button and have the Event Handler Wizard generate it. As well as generating the skeleton function definition in `SketcherDoc.cpp`, its declaration is added to the class definition. An entry for it is also made in the message map that looks like this:

```
ON_UPDATE_COMMAND_UI(ID_COLOR_BLACK, OnUpdateColorBlack)
```

This uses the `ON_UPDATE_COMMAND_UI()` macro that identifies the function you have just generated as the handler to deal with update messages corresponding to the ID shown. You could now enter the code for the new handler but I'll let you add command update handlers for each of the menu items for both the `Color` and `Element` menus first.

Coding a Command Update Handler

You can access the code for the `OnUpdateColorBlack()` handler in the `CSketcherDoc` class by selecting the function in Class View. This is the skeleton code for the function:

```
void CSketcherDoc::OnUpdateColorBlack(CCmdUI* pCmdUI)
{
    // TODO: Add your command update UI handler code here

}
```

The argument passed to the handler is a pointer to an object of the `CCmdUI` class type. This is an MFC class that is only used with update handlers, but it applies to toolbar buttons as well as menu items. The pointer points to an object that identifies the item that originated the update message so you use this to operate on the item to update how it appears before it is displayed. The `CCmdUI` class has five member functions that act on user interface items. The operations that each of these provides are as follows:

Function	Description
`ContinueRouting()`	Passes the message on to the next priority handler.
`Enable()`	Enables or disables the relevant interface item.
`SetCheck()`	Sets a check mark for the relevant interface item.
`SetRadio()`	Sets a button in a radio group on or off.
`SetText()`	Sets the text for the relevant interface item.

We'll use the third function, `SetCheck()`, as that seems to do what we want. The function is declared in the `CCmdUI` class as:

```
virtual void SetCheck(int nCheck = 1);
```

This function sets a menu item as checked if you pass 1 as the argument and set it unchecked if you pass 0 as the argument. The parameter has a default value of 1, so if you just want to set a check mark for a menu item regardless, you can call this function without specifying an argument.

In our case, you want to set a menu item as checked if it corresponds with the current color. You can, therefore, write the update handler for OnUpdateColorBlack() as:

```
void CSketcherDoc::OnUpdateColorBlack(CCmdUI* pCmdUI)
{
    // Set menu item Checked if the current color is black
    pCmdUI->SetCheck(m_Color==BLACK);
}
```

The statement you have added calls the SetCheck() function for the Color > Black menu item, and the argument expression m_Color==BLACK results in true if m_Color is BLACK, or false otherwise. The effect, therefore, is to check the menu item only if the current color stored in m_Color is BLACK, which is precisely what you want.

The update handlers for all the menu items in a menu are always called before the menu is displayed so you can code the other handlers in the same way to ensure that only the item corresponding to the current color (or the current element) is checked:

```
void CSketcherDoc::OnUpdateColorBlue(CCmdUI* pCmdUI)
{
    // Set menu item Checked if the current color is blue
    pCmdUI->SetCheck(m_Color==BLUE);
}

void CSketcherDoc::OnUpdateColorGreen(CCmdUI* pCmdUI)
{
    // Set menu item Checked if the current color is green
    pCmdUI->SetCheck(m_Color==GREEN);
}

void CSketcherDoc::OnUpdateColorRed(CCmdUI* pCmdUI)
{
    // Set menu item Checked if the current color is red
    pCmdUI->SetCheck(m_Color==RED);
}
```

A typical Element menu item update handler is coded as:

```
void CSketcherDoc::OnUpdateElementLine(CCmdUI* pCmdUI)
{
    // Set Checked if the current element is a line
    pCmdUI->SetCheck(m_Element==LINE);
}
```

You can now code all the other update handlers in a similar manner:

```
void CSketcherDoc::OnUpdateElementCurve(CCmdUI* pCmdUI)
{
```

```
    // Set Checked if the current element is a curve
    pCmdUI->SetCheck(m_Element==CURVE);
}

void CSketcherDoc::OnUpdateElementCircle(CCmdUI *pCmdUI)
{
    // Set Checked if the current element is a circle
    pCmdUI->SetCheck(m_Element==CIRCLE);
}

void CSketcherDoc::OnUpdateElementRectangle(CCmdUI* pCmdUI)
{
    // Set Checked if the current element is a rectangle
    pCmdUI->SetCheck(m_Element==RECTANGLE);
}
```

After you get the idea, it's easy, isn't it?

Exercising the Update Handlers

When you've added the code for all the update handlers, you can build and execute the Sketcher application again. Now, when you change a color or an element type selection, this is reflected in the menu, as shown in Figure 14-11.

Figure 14-11

You have completed all the code that you need for the menu items. Make sure that you have saved everything before embarking onto the next stage. These days, toolbars are a must in any Windows program of consequence, so the next step is to take a look at how you can add toolbar buttons to support our new menus.

Adding Toolbar Buttons

Select the Resource View and extend the toolbar resource. You'll see that it has the same ID as the main menu, IDR_MAINFRAME. If you double-click this ID, the Editor window appears as shown in Figure 14-12.

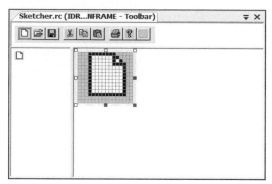

Figure 14-12

A toolbar button is a 16×15 array of pixels that contains a pictorial representation of the function it operates. You can see in Figure 14-12 that the resource editor provides an enlarged view of a toolbar button so that you can see and manipulate individual pixels. If you click the new button at the right end of the row as indicated, you'll be able to draw this button. Before starting the editing, drag the new button about half a button width to the right. It separates from its neighbor on the left to start a new block.

You should keep the toolbar button blocks in the same sequence as the items on the menu bar, so you'll create the element type selection buttons first. You'll be using the following editing buttons provided by the resource editor that appear in the toolbar for the Visual C++ 2008 application window.

❑   Pencil for drawing individual pixels

❑   Eraser for erasing individual pixels

❑   Fill an area with the current color

❑   Zoom the view of the button

❑   Draw a rectangle

❑   Draw an ellipse

❑   Draw a curve

If it is not already visible, you can display the window for selecting a color by right-clicking a toolbar button and selecting Show Colors Window from the pop-up. Make sure that the black color is selected and use the pencil tool to draw a diagonal line in the enlarged image of the new toolbar button. In fact, if you want it a bit bigger, you can use the Magnification Tool editing button to enlarge it up to eight times its actual size. If you make a mistake, you can change to the Erase Tool editing button, but you need to make sure that the color selected corresponds to the background color for the button you are editing. You can also erase individual pixels by clicking them using the right mouse button, but again you need to be sure that the background color is set correctly when you do this. To set the background color, just click the appropriate color using the right mouse button. After you're happy with what you've drawn, the next step is to edit the toolbar button properties.

Editing Toolbar Button Properties

Double-click your new button in the toolbar to bring up its properties window, as shown in Figure 14-13.

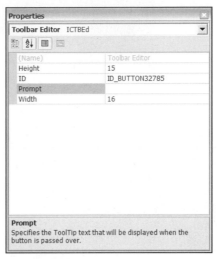

Figure 14-13

The properties box shows a default ID for the button, but you want to associate the button with the menu item Element > Line that we've already defined, so click ID and then click the down arrow to display alternative values. You can then select ID_ELEMENT_LINE from the drop-down box. If you click on Prompt you'll find that this also causes the same prompt to appear in the status bar because the prompt is recorded along with the ID. You can close the Properties window to complete the button definition.

You can now move on to designing the other three element buttons. You can use the rectangle editing button to draw a rectangle and the ellipse button to draw a circle. You can draw a curve using the pencil to set individual pixels, or use the curve button. You need to associate each button with the ID corresponding to the equivalent menu item that you defined earlier.

Now add the buttons for the colors. You should also drag the first button for selecting a color to the right so that it starts a new group of buttons. You could keep the color buttons very simple and just color the whole button with the color it selects. You can do this by selecting the appropriate foreground color, then selecting the "fill" editing button and clicking on the enlarged button image. Again you need to use ID_COLOR_BLACK, ID_COLOR_RED, and so on, as IDs for the buttons. The toolbar editing window should look like the one shown in Figure 14-14.

That's all you need for the moment, so save the resource file and give Sketcher another spin.

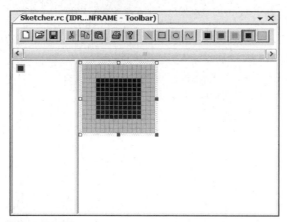

Figure 14-14

Exercising the Toolbar Buttons

Build the application once again and execute it. You should see the application window shown in Figure 14-15.

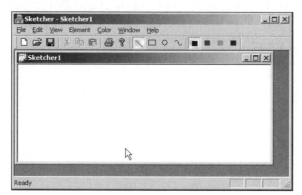

Figure 14-15

There are some amazing things happening here. The toolbar buttons that you added already reflect the default settings that you defined for the new menu items. If you let the cursor linger over one of the new buttons, the prompt for the button appears in the status bar. The new buttons work as a complete substitute for the menu items and any new selection made, using either the menu or the toolbar, is reflected by showing the toolbar button depressed, as well as the check against the menu item.

If you close the document view window, Sketcher1, you'll see that our toolbar buttons are automatically grayed and disabled. If you open a new document window, they are automatically enabled once again. You can also try dragging the toolbar with the cursor. You can move it to either side of the application window, or have it free-floating. You can also enable or disable it through the `View > Toolbar` menu option. You got all this without writing a single additional line of code!

Adding Tooltips

There's one further tweak that you can add to your toolbar buttons that is remarkably easy: adding tooltips. A tooltip is a small box that appears adjacent to the toolbar button when you let the cursor linger on the button. The tooltip contains a text string that is an additional clue as to the purpose of the toolbar button.

To add tooltips, select the Resource View tab and, after expanding the resource list, click the String Table folder and double-click the resource. This contains the IDs and prompt strings associated with menu items and toolbar buttons. You should see the IDs for the menus that you added earlier together with the prompt text for each under the caption heading. To add a tooltip, you just need to add \n (the newline character), followed by the tooltip text to the end of the caption text. For the prompt text you have already entered you can double-click text to enable editing of it and then add \n to the end of the prompt text in the caption column, so you could change the existing caption for the ID_ELEMENT_LINE ID from Line to Line\nSets line drawing mode, for example. Thus the caption text has two parts separated by \n, the first part being the prompt that appears in the status bar and the second is the tooltip text.

Add \n followed by a tooltip to the caption text for each of the IDs for the menu items in the Element and Color menus — not forgetting to start each tooltip text with \n. That's all you have to do. After saving the String Table resource, you can now rebuild the application and execute it. Placing the cursor over one of the new toolbar buttons causes the tooltip to be displayed after a second or two.

Menu and Toolbars in a C++/CLI Program

Of course, your C++/CLI programs can also have menus and toolbars. A good starting point for a windows-based C++/CLI program is to create a Windows Forms application. The Windows Forms technology is oriented toward the development of applications that use the vast array of standard controls that are provided, but there's no reason why you can't do drawing with a form-based application. There is much less programming for you to do with a Windows Forms application because you add the standard components for the GUI using the Windows Forms Designer capability and the code to generate and service the GUI components will be added automatically. Your programming activity will involve adding application-specific classes and customizing the behavior of the application by implementing event handlers.

Understanding Windows Forms

Windows Forms is a facility for creating Windows applications that execute with the CLR. A **form** is a window that is the basis for an application window or a dialog window to which you can add other controls that the user can interact with. Visual C++ 2008 comes with a standard set of more than 60 controls that you can use with a form. Because there is a very large number of controls, you'll get to grips only with a representative sample in this book, but that should give you enough of an idea of how they are used to explore the others for yourself. Many of the standard controls provide a straightforward interactive function, such as Button controls that represent buttons to be clicked or TextBox controls that allow text to be entered. Some of the standard controls are **containers**, which means that they are controls that can contain other controls. For example, a GroupBox control can contain other controls such as Button controls or TextBox controls, and the function of a GroupBox control is simply to group the controls together for some purpose and optionally provide a label for the group in the GUI. There are also a lot of third-party controls available. If you can't find the control you want in Visual C++, it is very likely that you can find a third party that produces it.

A form and the controls that you use with a form are represented by a C++/CLI class. Each class has a set of properties that determines the behavior and appearance of the control or form. For example, whether or not a control is visible in the application window and whether or not a control is enabled to allow user interaction are determined by the property values that are set. You can set a control's properties interactively when you assemble the GUI using the IDE. You can also set property values at run time using functions that you add to the program or via code that you add to existing functions through the code Editor pane. The classes also define functions that you call to perform operations on the control.

When you create a project for a Windows Forms application, an application window based on the Form class is created along with all the code to display the application window. After you create a Windows Forms project, there are four distinct operations involved in developing a Windows Forms application:

❑   You create the GUI interactively in the Form Design tab that is displayed in the Editor pane by selecting controls in the Toolbox window and placing them on the form. You can also create additional form windows.

❑   You modify the properties for the controls and the forms to suit your application needs in the Properties window.

❑   You can create click event handlers for a control by double-clicking the control on the Form Design tab. You can also set an existing function as the handler for an event for a control from its Properties window.

❑   You can modify and extend the classes that are created automatically from your interaction with the Form Design tab to meet the needs of your application.

You'll get a chance to see how it works in practice.

Understanding Windows Forms Applications

You first need to get an idea of how the default code for a Windows Forms application works. Create a new CLR project using the Windows Forms Application template and assign the name CLRSketcher to the project. The procedure is exactly the same as you used back in Chapter 12 when you created Ex12_03 so I won't repeat it here. The Design window for CLRSketcher will show the form as it is defined initially and you'll customize it to suit the development of a version of Sketcher for the CLR. It won't have the full capability of the MFC version but it will demonstrate how you implement the major features in a C++/CLI context. You'll continue to add functionality to this application over the next four chapters.

The Editor pane displays a graphical representation of the application window because with a Windows Forms application you build the GUI graphically. Even double-clicking Form1.h in the Solution Explorer pane does not display the code, but you can see it by right-clicking in the Editor window and selecting View Code from the context menu.

The code defines the Form1 class that represents the application window, and the first thing to note is that the code is defined in its own namespace:

```
namespace CLRSketcher
{
  using namespace System;
  using namespace System::ComponentModel;
```

```
    using namespace System::Collections;
    using namespace System::Windows::Forms;
    using namespace System::Data;
    using namespace System::Drawing;

    // rest of the code
}
```

When you compile the project, it creates a new assembly, and the code for this assembly is within the namespace CLRSketcher, which is the same as the project name. The namespace ensures that a type in another assembly that has the same name as a type in this assembly is differentiated because each type name is qualified by its own namespace name.

There are also six using directives for .NET library namespaces, and these cover the library functionality you are most likely to need in your application. These namespaces are:

Namespace	Contents
System	This namespace contains classes that define data types that are used in all CLR applications. It also contains classes for events and event handling, exceptions, and classes that support commonly used functions.
System::ComponentModel	This namespace contains classes that support the operation of GUI components in a CLR application.
System::Collections	This namespace contains collection classes for organizing data in various ways, and includes classes to define lists, queues, dictionaries (maps), and stacks.
System::Windows::Forms	This namespace contains the classes that support the use of Windows Forms in an application.
System::Data	This namespace contains classes that support ADO.NET, which is used for accessing and updating data sources. You'll learn more about accessing data sources in a CLR application in the next chapter.
System::Drawing	Defines classes that support basic graphical operations such as drawing on a form or a component.

The Form1 class is derived from the Form class that is defined in the System::Windows::Forms namespace. The Form class represents either an application window or a dialog window, and the Form1 class that defines the window for CLRSketcher inherits all the members of the Form class.

The section at the end of the Form1 class contains the definition of the InitializeComponent() function. This function is called by the constructor to set up the application window and any components that you add to the form. The comments indicate that you must not modify this section of code using the code editor, and this code is updated automatically as you alter the application window interactively. It's important when you do use Form Design that you do not ignore these comments and modify the automatically generated code yourself; if you do, things are certain to go wrong at some point. Of course, you can write all the code for a Windows Forms application from the ground up, but it is much quicker and less error-prone to use the Form Design capability to set up the GUI for your application interactively. This doesn't mean you shouldn't know how it works.

The code for the `InitializeComponent()` function initially looks like this:

```
void InitializeComponent(void)
{
   this->components = gcnew System::ComponentModel::Container();
   this->Size - System::Drawing::Size(300,300);
   this->Text = L"Form1";
   this->Padding = System::Windows::Forms::Padding(0);
   this->AutoScaleMode = System::Windows::Forms::AutoScaleMode::Font;
}
```

The `components` member of the `Form1` class is inherited from the base class, and its role is to keep track of components that you subsequently add to the form. The first statement stores a handle to a `Container` object in `components` and this object represents a collection that stores GUI components in a list. Each new component that you add to the form using the Form Design capability is added to this `Container` object.

Modifying the Properties of a Form

The remaining statements in the `InitializeComponent()` function set properties for `Form1`. You must not modify any of these directly in the code, but you can choose your own values for these through the Properties window for the form, so return to the `Form1.h` [Design] tab for the form in the Editor window and right-click it to display the Properties window shown in Figure 14-16.

Figure 14-16

Figure 14-16 shows the properties for the form in alphabetical sequence. You can also display the properties categorized by function by clicking the first button at the top of the window. It's worth browsing through the list of properties for the form to get an idea of the possibilities. Clicking any of the properties displays a description at the bottom of the window. Figure 14-16 shows the Properties window with the width increased to make the descriptions visible. You can select the cell in the right column to modify the property value. The properties that have a + to the left have multiple values and clicking the + displays the values so you can change them individually. You can also display the properties in alphabetical order by clicking a button. This is helpful when you know the name of the property you want to change, as it makes it easier to find it.

You can make the form a little larger by changing the value for the Size property in the Layout group to 500,350. You don't want to make it too large at this point because it will make it difficult to work with when you have several windows open in the IDE, so just size the form so it's easy to work with on your display. You could also change the Text property (which is in the Appearance category if you are looking at that organization for the properties) to CLR Sketcher. This changes the text in the title bar for the application window. If you go back to the Form1.h tab in the Editor window, you'll see that the code in the InitializeComponent() function has been altered to reflect the property changes you have made. As you'll see, the Properties window is a fundamental tool for implementing support for GUI components in a Forms-based application

Note that you can also arrange for the application window to be maximized when the program starts by setting the value for the WindowState property. With the default Normal setting, the window is the size you have specified, but you can set the property to Maximized or Minimized by selecting from the list of values for this property.

How the Application Starts

Execution of the application begins, as always, in the main() function, and this is defined in the CLRSketcher.cpp file as:

```
int main(array<System::String ^> ^args)
{
  // Enabling Windows XP visual effects before any controls are created
  Application::EnableVisualStyles();

  // Create the main window and run it
  Application::Run(gcnew Form1());
  return 0;
}
```

The main() function calls two static functions that are defined in the Application class that is defined in the System::Windows::Forms namespace. The static functions in the Application class are at the heart of every Windows Forms application. The EnableVisualStyles() function that is called first in main() enables visual styles for the application. The Run() function starts a Windows message loop for the application and makes the Form object that is passed as the argument visible. An application running with the CLR is still ultimately a Windows application, so it works with a message loop in the same way as all other Windows applications.

Adding a Menu to CLR Sketcher

The IDE provides you with a standard set of controls that you can add to your application interactively through the Design window. Press Ctrl+Alt+X or select from the View menu to display the Toolbox window. The window containing the list of available controls is displayed, as shown in Figure 14-17.

Figure 14-17

The first block in the Toolbox window is labelled All Windows Forms and lists all the controls available for use with a form. You can click the plus sign for the All Windows Forms tab if it is not already expanded. You can collapse this block by clicking the minus sign to the left of the block heading, and you'll see that the controls are also grouped by type in the list starting with the Common Controls block. You'll probably find it most convenient initially to use the group containing all the controls at the beginning of the list, but after you are familiar with what controls are available, you may find it easier to collapse the groups and just have one group expanded at one time.

A Menu Strip is a container for menu items, so add one to the form by dragging a MenuStrip from the Menus & Toolbars group in the Toolbox window to the form; the menu strip attaches itself to the top of the form below the title bar. You'll see a small arrow at the top right of the control. If you click this, a pop-up window appears, as shown in Figure 14-18.

Figure 14-18

The first item in the Menu Strip Tasks pop-up embeds the menu strip in a `ToolStripContainer` control that provides panels on all four sides of the form plus a central area in which you can place another control. The second item generates four standard menu items: `File Edit`, `Tools`, and `Help`, complete with menu item lists and as you'll see in a moment you can also do this without displaying this pop-up. The `RenderMode` allows you to choose the painting style for the menu strip, and you can leave this at the default selection. The `Dock` option enables you to choose which side of the form the menu strip is to be docked or you can elect to have it undocked. The `GripStyle` option determines whether the grip for dragging the menu around is visible or not. The Visual C++ 2008 menu strips have visible grips that allow you to move them around. Selecting the final `Edit Items` option displays a dialog box in which you can edit the properties for the menu strip or for any of its menu items.

If you right-click the menu strip and select Insert Standard Items from the pop-up, the standard menu items will be added; you'll only be implementing the `File` menu items but you can leave the others there if you want. Alternatively you can delete any of them by right-clicking the item and selecting Delete from the pop-up. I'll leave them in so they will appear in the subsequent figures.

To add the `Element` menu, click the box displaying "Type Here" and type `&Element`. You can then click the box that displays below `Element` and type `&Line` for the first submenu item. Continue to add the remaining submenu items by entering `&Rectangle`, `&Circle`, and `Cur&ve` in successive boxes in the drop-down menu. To shift the `Elements` menu to the left of the `Help` menu, select `Elements` on the menu strip and drag it to the left of `Help`. Next you can add the Color menu by typing `&Color` in the "Type Here" on the menu strip. You can then enter `Blac&k`, `&Red`, `&Green`, and `&Blue` successively in the menu slots below `Color` to create the drop-down menu. After dragging `Color` to the left of `Help`, your application window should look like Figure 14-19.

To check the default `Color/Black` menu item, right-click the menu item and select `Checked` from the pop-up. Do the same for the `Element/Line` menu item. All the code to create the menus is already in the application. You can see this if you select the Class View tab, select the + by CLRSketcher to extend the tree, and then click on the `Form1` class name. The code for the `Form1` class displays in a new tabbed window. Around line 44 you'll see the class members that reference the menu items and you'll see the code creating the objects that encapsulate the menu items in the body of the `InitializeComponent()` member of the `Form1` class. It's worth browsing the code in this function from time to time as you develop `CLRSketcher` because it will show you the code for creating GUI components as well as how delegates for events are created and registered. The code in the `Form1` class definition will grow considerably and look pretty daunting as you increase the capabilities of the application but you always can navigate through it relatively easily by using Class View.

Figure 14-19

You can add shortcut key combinations for menu items by setting the value of the ShortcutKeys property. Figure 14-20 shows this property for the Line menu item.

Select the modifier of modifiers by clicking the checkboxes and select the key from the drop-down list. Figure 14-20 shows Ctrl+Shift+L specified as the shortcut key combination. You can control whether or not the shortcut key combination is displayed in the menu by setting the value of the ShowShortcutKeys property appropriately.

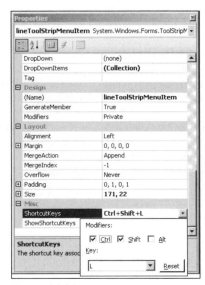

Figure 14-20

The next step is to add event handlers for the menu items.

Adding Event Handlers for Menu Items

Event handlers are delegates in a C++/CLI program, but you hardly need be aware of this in practice because all the functions that are delegates will be created automatically. Return to the Design tab by clicking on it. You can start by adding handlers for the items in the Element menu.

If it is not already visible, extend the Element drop-down menu on the form by clicking it, then right-click on the Line menu item and select Properties from the pop-up. Click on the events button in the Properties window (the one that looks like a lightning flash) and double-click the Click event at the top of the list. The IDE will switch to the code tab showing the delegate function for the menu item, which looks like this:

```
private: System::Void lineToolStripMenuItem_Click(System::Object^ sender,
                                    System::EventArgs^ e)

{

}
```

I have rearranged the code slightly to make it easier to read. This function will be called automatically when you click the Line menu item in the application. The first parameter identifies the source of the event, the menu item object in this case, and the second parameter provides information relating to the event. You'll learn more about EventArgs objects a little later in this chapter. This function has already been identified as the event handler for the menu item with the code:

```
this->lineToolStripMenuItem->Click += gcnew System::EventHandler(
                              this, &Form1::lineToolStripMenuItem_Click);
```

This is in the InitializeComponent() function and is located at about line 369 in the Form1.h listing on my system, but if you deleted the surplus standard menu items it will be a different line; you'll find it in the section labeled in comments as // lineToolStripMenuItem.

You can add event handlers for all the menu items in the Element and Color menus in the same way. If you switch back to the Design tab and you have not closed the Properties window, clicking on a new menu item will display the properties for that in the window. You can then double-click the Click property to generate the handler function. Note that the names of the handler functions are created by default, but if you want to change the name you can edit it in the value field to the right of the event name in the Properties window. The default names are quite satisfactory in this instance though.

Implementing Event Handlers

Following the model of the MFC version of Sketcher, you need a way to identify different element types in the CLR version. An enum class will do nicely for this. Add the following line of code in the Form1.h file following the using directives at the beginning of the file, and immediately before the comments preceding the Form1 class definition:

```
enum class ElementType {LINE, RECTANGLE, CIRCLE, CURVE};
```

This defines the four constants you need to specify the four types of element in Sketcher. As soon as you have entered this code, you see the new class appears in the Class View window as part of CLR Sketcher.

To identify the colors you can use objects of type System::Drawing::Color that represent colors. The System::Drawing namespace defines a wide range of types for use in drawing operations and you'll be using quite a number of them before CLRSketcher is finished. The Color structure defines a lot of standard colors, including Color::Black, Color::Red, Color::Green, and Color::Blue so you have everything you need.

The element type and the drawing color are modal, so you should add variables to the Form1 class to store the current element type and color. You can do this manually or use a code wizard to do it; let's try the latter. Right-click on Form1 in Class View and select Add /Add Variable... from the pop-up. Select the Access as private, double-click the default variable type and enter ElementType and type the variable name as elementType. You can also add a comment if you want, Current element type, and click Finish to add the variable to the class. Repeat the process for a private variable of type Color with the name color.

The new variables need to be initialized when the Form1 constructor is called so double-click on the constructor name, Form1(void), in the lower part of the Class View window (for the members of

Form1 to be displayed, Form1 must be selected in Class View). Modify the code for the constructor to the following:

```
Form1(void) : elementType(ElementType::LINE), color(Color::Black)
{
        InitializeComponent();
        //
        //TODO: Add the constructor code here
        //
}
```

The new variables are initialized in the first line. You should see IntelliSense prompts for possible values for the ElementType, and Color types as you type the initialization list. You now have enough in place to implement the menu event handlers. You can find the Line menu item handler toward the end of the code in Form1.h or double-click the Line menu item in the Design window to go directly to it. Modify the handler code to the following:

```
private: System::Void lineToolStripMenuItem_Click(
                                System::Object^ sender, System::EventArgs^ e)
{
  elementType = ElementType::LINE;
}
```

This just sets the current element type appropriately. You can do the same for the other three Element menu handlers. Simple, isn't it?

The first Color menu handler should be modified as follows:

```
private: System::Void blackToolStripMenuItem_Click(
System::Object^ sender, System::EventArgs^ e)
{
        color = Color::Black;
}
```

The other Color menu handlers should set the value of color appropriately to Color::Red, Color::Green, or Color::Blue.

Setting Menu Item Checks

At present, selecting element and color menu items sets the mode in the program but the checks shown on the menus remain stuck at the default. You don't have the COMMAND and COMMAND_UI message types with a CLR program that you have with the MFC, so you need a different approach to set the check mark against the element and color menu items that are in effect. You can handle messages for the Element and Color menu items on the menu strip when one or the other is selected and conveniently the handler for one of the messages is called before the corresponding drop-down menu is displayed. Right-click on the Element menu item in the Design window and select Properties from the pop-up. When you select the Events button in the Properties window, the window should look like Figure 14-21.

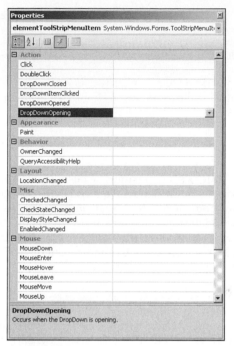

Figure 14-21

The Action group shows the events relating to when the menu item is clicked. Double-click the `DropDownOpening` event in the Action group to create a handler for it. This handler will be executed before the drop-down `Element` menu is displayed, so you can set the check mark in the function by modifying it like this:

```
private: System::Void elementToolStripMenuItem_DropDownOpening(
                               System::Object^ sender, System::EventArgs^ e)
{
    lineToolStripMenuItem->Checked = elementType == ElementType::LINE;
    rectangleToolStripMenuItem->Checked = elementType == ElementType::RECTANGLE;
    circleToolStripMenuItem->Checked = elementType == ElementType::CIRCLE;
    curveToolStripMenuItem->Checked = elementType == ElementType::CURVE;
}
```

The four lines of code you add set the `Checked` property for each of the menu items in the drop-down list. The `Checked` property will be set to `true` for the case where the value stored in `elementType` matches the element type set by the menu item and all the others will be `false`. The drop-down will then be displayed with the appropriate menu item checked.

You can create a `DropDownOpening` event handler for the `Color` menu item and implement it like this:

```
private: System::Void colorToolStripMenuItem_DropDownOpening(
                               System::Object^ sender, System::EventArgs^ e)
{
```

```
    blackToolStripMenuItem->Checked = color == Color::Black;
    redToolStripMenuItem->Checked = color == Color::Red;
    greenToolStripMenuItem->Checked = color == Color::Green;
    blueToolStripMenuItem->Checked = color == Color::Blue;
}
```

If you recompile `CLRSketcher` and execute it you should see the menu item checks working as they should.

Adding a Toolbar

You can add a toolbar with buttons corresponding to the `Element` and `Color` menu items. To add a toolbar to the application it's back to the Design window and the Toolbox. Toolbar buttons sit on a tool strip so drag a `ToolStrip` control from the Menus & Toolbars group in the Toolbox window on to the form; the tool strip will attach itself to the top of the form below the menu strip. You can add a set of standard toolbar buttons by right-clicking the tool strip and selecting Insert Standard Items from the pop-up. You get more than you need and because you will be adding eight more buttons, remove all but the four on the left that provide for a new document, open file, save file and print.

You will need bitmap images to display on the new toolbar buttons so it's a good idea to create these first. Select the Resource View tab and expand the tree in the window so the `app.rc` file name is visible. The `app.rc` file contains the icons and bitmaps that are used by the application so you will add the bitmaps to this file. Right-click on `app.rc` in the Resource View window and select `Add Resource...` from the pop-up. Select `Bitmap` in the dialog that displays and click on the New button. You will then see a window with a default 48×48 pixel image that you can edit and the Image Editor toolbar will be displayed for editing bitmap and icon images. You can undock this toolbar by dragging it off the tool strip if you want, in which case it looks like Figure 14-22.

Figure 14-22

The bitmap will be identified in the Resource View window with a default ID, `IDB_BITMAP1`. It will be convenient to change the ID and file name for the bitmap to something more meaningful, so right-click in the window displaying the bitmap image and select Properties from the pop-up. In the Properties window you can change the `Filename` property value to `line.bmp`, the `ID` property value to `IDB_LINE`, and the `Height` and `Width` values to 16 instead of 48. The new ID will enable you to identify the bitmap in Resource View in the event that you want to edit it. The new file name will make it easy to choose the correct bitmap for a given toolbar button.

If the Colors window is not visible, right-click in the window displaying the bitmap and select Show Colors Window from the pop-up. Right-clicking a color in the Colors window sets the background color and left-clicking a color sets the foreground color. When using the Image Editor tools, holding the left mouse button down when drawing in the bitmap uses the foreground color and holding the right button down draws in the background color. Use the Image Editor toolbar buttons to draw your own image to represent the `Line` menu item action. You can then save the file before adding the next bitmap. You can add three more bitmaps corresponding to the `Rectangle`, `Circle`, and `Curve` menu item actions to complete the element set. To add each of these you can right-click on the `Bitmap` folder name in the Resource View window and select `Insert Bitmap` from the pop-up. You should end up with four items in the Bitmap folder in Resource View, as shown in Figure 14-23.

Figure 14-23

Create four more bitmaps in `app.rc` for the color toolbar buttons. You can use the same principle for file names and IDs as you used for the element type bitmaps so the files will be `black.bmp`, `red.bmp`, `green.bmp` and `blue.bmp`, and the IDs will be `IDB_BLACK`, `IDB_RED`, `IDB_GREEN` and `IDB_BLUE`.

You can now return to the Design window to add the toolbar buttons. Click on the down arrow adjacent to the `Add ToolStripButton` icon on the tool strip to display the list shown in Figure 14-24.

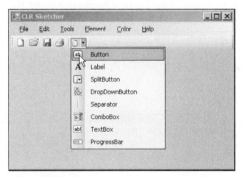

Figure 14-24

Select the Button item at the top of the list to add a button to the tool strip. You can then right-click the new button, select Set Image from the pop-up and select `line.bmp` from the dialog that displays; select the `Open` button in the dialog to set this image for the toolbar button.

Right-click on the new line button and display its properties. In the Properties window change the value of the `(Name)` property in the Design group to `toolStripLineButton`. You can also change the `ToolTipText` property to something helpful such as `Draw lines`.

Select the Events button to display the events for the button. You don't want to create a new handler for this button as the handler for the `Line` menu item will work perfectly well. Click on the down arrow in the value column for the `Click` event for the button to display the available handler functions, as shown in Figure 14-25.

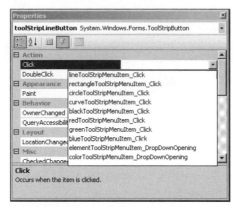

Figure 14-25

Select the `lineToolStripMenuItem_Click` handler from the list to register this function as the delegate for the `Click` event for the button. Repeat this process to create buttons to create the element toolbar buttons for drawing rectangles, circles, and curves and in each case set the `Click` event handler to be the corresponding menu item `Click` event handler.

Before you add the buttons for element colors, click on the down arrow at the side of the Add `ToolStripButton` icon on the toolbar and select Separator from the list; this inserts a separator to divide the element type button group from the colors group. You can now add the four buttons for colors with the `Click` event handler being the same as the handler for the corresponding menu item.

If you now recompile `CLRSketcher` and execute it, you should see your version of the application similar to the window shown in Figure 14-26.

Figure 14-26

Figure 14-26 shows the tooltip text for the red button and you should find that the menu items checks are all working regardless of whether you use the toolbar or the menus to select the element type and drawing color. You now have a CLR version of Sketcher that is essentially the same as the MFC version you developed earlier in this chapter. You won't retain exact correspondence between MFC and CLR versions of Sketcher in subsequent chapters but the main features will be in both.

Summary

In this chapter, you learned how MFC connects a message with a class member function to process it, and you wrote your first message handlers. Much of the work in writing a Windows program is writing message handlers, so it's important to have a good grasp of what happens in the process. When we get to consider other message handlers, you'll see that the process for adding them is just the same.

You have also extended the standard menu and the toolbar in the MFC Application Wizard-generated program, which provides a good base for the application code that you add in the next chapter. Although there's no functionality under the covers yet, the menu and toolbar operation looks very professional, courtesy of the Application Wizard-generated framework and the Event Handler Wizard.

You learned about creating menus and toolbars in a CLR version of the Sketcher program and how you handle events to provide equivalent function to the MFC version.

The important points that you've seen in this chapter are:

- ❑ MFC defines the message handlers for a class in a message map that appears in the `.cpp` file for the class.

- ❑ Command messages that arise from menus and toolbars can be handled in any class that's derived from `CCmdTarget`. These include the application class, the frame and child frame window classes, the document class, and the view class.

- ❑ Messages other than command messages can only be handled in a class derived from `CWnd`. This includes frame window and view classes, but not application or document classes.

- ❑ MFC has a predefined sequence for searching the classes in your program to find a message handler for a command message.

- ❑ You should always use the Event Handler Wizard to add message handlers to your program.

- ❑ The physical appearances of menus and toolbars are defined in resource files, which are edited by the built-in resource editor.

- ❑ Items in a menu that can result in command messages are identified by a symbolic constant with the prefix `ID`. These IDs are used to associate a handler with the message from the menu item.

- ❑ To associate a toolbar button with a particular menu item, you give it the same ID as that of the menu item.

- ❑ To add a tooltip for a toolbar button corresponding to a menu item, you add the tooltip text to the entry for the ID for the menu item in the caption column in the String Table resource. The tooltip text is separated from the menu prompt text by **\n**.

- ❑ You create menus and toolbars interactively in a CLR program through the Design window. Code is generated automatically to create menu items and toolbar buttons and display them on a form.

- ❑ You can create a delegate to handle a specific event for a control by double-clicking the event type in the Property window for the control. You can optionally select an existing delegate to handle the event. This is particularly relevant to handling toolbar button events that are equivalent to existing menu items events.

In the next chapter, you'll add the code necessary to both versions of Sketcher to draw elements in a view, and use the menus and toolbar buttons that you created here to select what to draw and in which color. This is where the Sketcher program begins to live up to its name.

Exercises

You can download the source code for the examples in the book and the solutions to the following exercises from www.wrox.com. You'll be developing both versions of Sketcher in subsequent chapters so you need to retain the state of the program at the end of each chapter. The exercises involve modifying the existing Sketcher versions but you can retain the original state quite easily by copying the entire contents of the project folder to another folder, Save Sketcher say. When you have finished the exercises on the original project, you can delete the contents of the project file (or save it somewhere else if you want to keep it) and copy the contents of the Save Sketcher folder back to the original project directory.

1. Add a menu item Ellipse to the Element pop-up.

2. Implement the command and command update handlers for it in the document class.

3. Add a toolbar button corresponding to the Ellipse menu item and add a tooltip for the button.

4. Modify the command update handlers for the color menu items so that the currently selected item is displayed in uppercase, and the others are displayed in lowercase.

5. Add an Ellipse menu item and toolbar button with a tooltip to CLR Sketcher.

Drawing in a Window

In this chapter, you will add some meat to the Sketcher application. You'll focus on understanding how you get graphical output displayed in the application window. By the end of this chapter, you'll be able to draw all but one of the elements for which you have added menu items. I'll leave the problem of how to store them in a document until the next chapter. In this chapter, you will learn about:

❑   What coordinate systems Windows provides for drawing in a window

❑   Device context and why it is necessary

❑   How and when your program draws in a window

❑   How to define handlers for mouse messages

❑   How to define your own shape classes

❑   How to program the mouse to draw your shapes in a window

❑   How to get your program to capture the mouse

Basics of Drawing in a Window

Before I go into drawing using MFC, it will be useful to get a better idea of what is happening under the covers of the Windows operating system when you are drawing in a window. Similar to any other operation under Windows, you write to a window on your display screen using Windows API functions. There's slightly more to it than that though; the way Windows works complicates the situation somewhat.

For a start, you can't just write to a window and forget it. There are many events that require that your application redraws the window — such as if the user resizes the window that you're drawing in, for instance, or if part of your window that was previously hidden is exposed by the user moving another window.

Fortunately, you don't need to worry about the details of such occurrences, because Windows actually manages all these events for you; however, it does mean that you can only write permanent data to a window when your application receives a specific Windows message requesting that you do so. It also means that you need to be able to reconstruct everything that you've drawn in the window at any time.

When all, or part, of a window needs to be redrawn, Windows sends a WM_PAINT message to your application. This is intercepted by MFC, which passes the message to a function member of one of your classes. I'll explain how you handle this a little later in this chapter.

The Window Client Area

A window doesn't have a fixed position onscreen, or even a fixed visible area, because a window can be dragged around using the mouse and resized by dragging its borders. How, then, do you know where to draw onscreen?

Fortunately, you don't. Because Windows provides you with a consistent way of drawing in a window, you don't have to worry about where it is onscreen; otherwise, drawing in a window would be inordinately complicated. Windows does this by maintaining a coordinate system for the client area of a window that is local to the window. It always uses the upper-left corner of the client area as its reference point. All points within the client area are defined relative to this point, as shown in Figure 15-1.

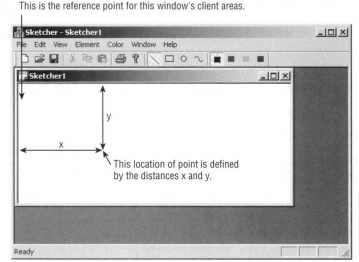

Figure 15-1

The horizontal and vertical distances of a point from the upper-left corner of the client area will always be the same, regardless of where the window is onscreen or how big it is. Of course, Windows needs to keep track of where the window is, and when you draw something at a point in the client area, it needs to figure out where that actually is onscreen.

The Windows Graphical Device Interface

The final constraint Windows imposes is that you don't actually write data to the screen in any direct sense. All output to your display screen is graphical, regardless of whether it is lines and circles, or text. Windows insists that you define this output using the **Graphical Device Interface (GDI)**. The GDI enables you to program graphical output independently of the hardware on which it is displayed, meaning that your program works on different machines with different display hardware. In addition to display screens, the Windows GDI also supports printers and plotters, so outputting data to a printer or a plotter involves essentially the same mechanisms as displaying information onscreen.

What Is a Device Context?

When you want to draw something on a graphical output device such as the display screen, you must use a **device context**. A device context is a data structure that's defined by Windows and contains information that allows Windows to translate your output requests, which are in the form of device-independent GDI function calls, into actions on the particular physical output device being used. A pointer to a device context is obtained by calling a Windows API function.

A device context provides you with a choice of coordinate systems called **mapping modes**, which are automatically converted to client coordinates. You can also alter many of the parameters that affect the output to a device context by calling GDI functions; such parameters are called **attributes**. Examples of attributes that you can change are the drawing color, the background color, the line thickness to be used when drawing, and the font for text output. There are also GDI functions that provide information about the physical device with which you're working such as the resolution and aspect ratio of a display.

Mapping Modes

Each **mapping mode** in a device context is identified by an ID, in a manner similar to what you saw with Windows messages. Each symbol has the prefix **MM_** to indicate that it defines a **m**apping **m**ode. The mapping modes provided by Windows are:

Mapping Mode	Description
MM_TEXT	A logical unit is one device pixel with positive x from left to right, and positive y from top to bottom of the window client area.
MM_LOENGLISH	A logical unit is 0.01 inches with positive x from left to right, and positive y from the top of the client area upward.
MM_HIENGLISH	A logical unit is 0.001 inches with the x and y directions as in MM_LOENGLISH.
MM_LOMETRIC	A logical unit is 0.1 millimeters with the x and y directions as in MM_LOENGLISH.
MM_HIMETRIC	A logical unit is 0.01 millimeters with the x and y directions as in MM_LOENGLISH.
MM_ISOTROPIC	A logical unit is of arbitrary length, but the same along both the x and y axes. The x and y directions are as in MM_LOENGLISH.
MM_ANISOTROPIC	This mode is similar to MM_ISOTROPIC, but allows the length of a logical unit on the x-axis to be different from that of a logical unit on the y-axis.
MM_TWIPS	A logical unit is a TWIP where a TWIP is 0.05 of a point and a point is $\frac{1}{2}$ of an inch. Thus a TWIP corresponds to $\frac{1}{1440}$ of an inch, which is $6.9*10^{-4}$ of an inch. (A point is a unit of measurement for fonts.) The x and y directions are as in MM_LOENGLISH.

You will not use all of these mapping modes with this book; however, the ones you will use form a good cross-section of those available, so you won't have any problem using the others when you need to.

MM_TEXT is the default mapping mode for a device context. If you need to use a different mapping mode, you have to take steps to change it. Note that the direction of the positive *y*-axis in the **MM_TEXT** mode is opposite to what you saw in high school coordinate geometry, as shown in Figure 15-2.

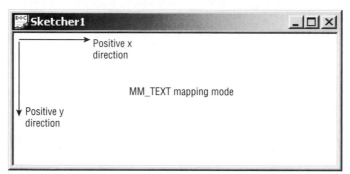

Figure 15-2

By default, the point at the upper-left corner of the client area has the coordinates (0, 0) in *every* mapping mode, although it's possible to move the origin away from the upper-left corner of the client area if you want to. For example, some applications that present data in graphical form move the origin to the center of the client area to make plotting of the data easier. With the origin at the upper-left corner in MM_TEXT mode, a point 50 pixels from the left border and 100 pixels down from the top of the client area will have the coordinates (50,100). Of course, because the units are pixels, the point will be nearer the upper-left corner of the client area if your monitor is set to use a resolution of 1280×1024 than if it's working with the resolution set as 1024×768. An object drawn in this mapping mode will be smaller at the 1280×1024 resolution than it would be at the 1024×768 resolution. Note that the DPI setting for your display affects presentation in all mapping modes. The default settings assume 96 DPI, so if the DPI for your display is set to a different value, this affects how things look. Coordinates are always 32-bit signed integers unless you are programming for the old Windows 95/98 operating systems, in which case they are limited to 16 bits. The maximum physical size of the total drawing varies with the physical length of a coordinate unit, which is determined by the mapping mode.

The directions of the *x* and *y* coordinate axes in MM_LOENGLISH and all the remaining mapping modes are the same as each other, but different from MM_TEXT. The coordinate axes for MM_LOENGLISH are shown in Figure 15-3. Although positive *y* is consistent with what you learned in high school (*y* values increase as you move up the screen), MM_LOENGLISH is still slightly odd because the origin is at the upper-left corner of the client area, so for points within the visible client area, *y* is always negative.

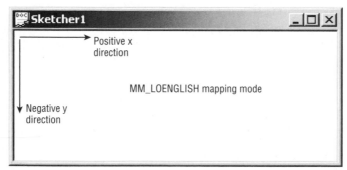

Figure 15-3

In the MM_LOENGLISH mapping mode, the units along the axes are 0.01 inches apiece, so a point at the position (50, -100) is half an inch from the left border and one inch down from the top of the client area. An object is the same size in the client area, regardless of the resolution of the monitor on which it is displayed. If you draw anything in the MM_LOENGLISH mode with negative x or positive y coordinates, it is outside the client area and therefore not visible because the reference point (0,0) is the upper-left corner by default. It's possible to move the position of the reference point though, by calling the Windows API function SetViewportOrg() (or the SetViewportOrg() member of the CDC MFC class encapsulating a device context that I'll discuss shortly).

The Drawing Mechanism in Visual C++

MFC encapsulates the Windows interface to your screen and printer and relieves you of the need to worry about much of the detail involved in programming graphical output. As you saw in the last chapter, the Application Wizard-generated program already contains a class derived from the MFC class CView that's specifically designed to display document data onscreen.

The View Class in Your Application

The MFC Application Wizard generated the class CSketcherView to display information from a document in the client area of a document window. The class definition includes overrides for several virtual functions, but the one of particular interest here is the function OnDraw(). This is called whenever the client area of the document window needs to be redrawn. It's the function that's called by the application framework when a WM_PAINT message is received in your program.

The OnDraw() Member Function

The implementation of the OnDraw() member function that's created by the MFC Application Wizard looks like this:

```
void CSketcherView::OnDraw(CDC* /*pDC*/)
{
   CSketcherDoc* pDoc = GetDocument();
   ASSERT_VALID(pDoc);
   if(!pDoc)
     return;

   // TODO: add draw code for native data here
}
```

A pointer to an object of the CDC class type is passed to the OnDraw() member of the view class. This object has member functions that call the Windows API functions and these allow you to draw in a device context. Note that the parameter name is commented out so you must uncomment the name or replace it with your own name before you can use the pointer.

Because you'll put all the code to draw the document in this function, the Application Wizard has included a declaration for the pointer pDoc and initialized it using the function GetDocument(), which returns the address of the document object related to the current view:

```
   CSketcherDoc* pDoc = GetDocument();
```

The GetDocument() function actually retrieves the pointer to the document from m_pDocument, an inherited data member of the view object. The function performs the important task of casting the pointer stored in this data member to the type corresponding to the document class in the application, CSketcherDoc. This is so that the compiler has access to the members of the document class that you've defined; otherwise, the compiler is able to access only the members of the base class. Thus, pDoc points to the document object in your application associated with the current view, and you will be using it to access the data that you've stored in the document object when you want to draw it.

The following line:

```
ASSERT_VALID(pDoc);
```

just makes sure that the pointer pDoc contains a valid address and the if statement that follows ensures that pDoc is not null.

The name of the parameter pDC for the OnDraw() function stands for "pointer to Device Context." The object of the CDC class pointed to by the pDC argument that's passed to the OnDraw() function is the key to drawing in a window. It provides a device context, plus the tools you need to write graphics and text to it, so you clearly need to look at it in more detail.

The CDC Class

You should do all the drawing in your program using members of the CDC class. All objects of this class and classes derived from it contain a device context and the member functions you need for sending graphics and text to your display and your printer. There are also member functions for retrieving information about the physical output device that you are using.

Because CDC class objects can provide almost everything you're likely to need by way of graphical output, there are a lot of member functions of this class — in fact, well over a hundred. Therefore, you'll only look at the ones you're going to use in the Sketcher program here in this chapter and go into others as you need them later on.

Note that MFC includes some more specialized classes for graphics output that are derived from CDC. For example, you be using objects of CClientDC because it is derived from CDC and contains all the members we will discuss at this point. The advantage that CClientDC has over CDC is that it always contains a device context that represents only the client area of a window, and this is precisely what you want in most circumstances.

Displaying Graphics

In a device context, you draw entities such as lines, circles, and text relative to a **current position**. A current position is a point in the client area that was set either by the previous entity that was drawn, or by calling a function to set it. For example, you could extend the OnDraw() function to set the current position as follows:

```
void CSketcherView::OnDraw(CDC* pDC)
{
    CSketcherDoc* pDoc = GetDocument();
    ASSERT_VALID(pDoc);
```

```
    if(!pDoc)
        return;

    pDC->MoveTo(50, 50);    // Set the current position as 50,50
}
```

The shaded line calls the `MoveTo()` function for the CDC object pointed to by pDC. This member function simply sets the current position to the *x* and *y* coordinates you specify as arguments. As you saw earlier, the default mapping mode is MM_TEXT, so the coordinates are in pixels and the current position will be set to a point 50 pixels from the inside left border of the window, and 50 pixels down from the top of the client area.

The CDC class overloads the `MoveTo()` function to provide flexibility over how you specify the position that you want to set as the current position. There are two versions of the function, declared in the CDC class as:

```
CPoint MoveTo(int x, int y);    // Move to position x,y
CPoint MoveTo(POINT aPoint);    // Move to position defined by aPoint
```

The first version accepts the *x* and *y* coordinates as separate arguments. The second accepts one argument of type POINT, which is a structure defined as:

```
typedef struct tagPOINT
{
    LONG x;
    LONG y;
} POINT;
```

The coordinates are members of the `struct` and are of type LONG (which is type defined in the Windows API corresponding to a 32-bit signed integer). You may prefer to use a class instead of a structure, in which case you can use objects of the class CPoint anywhere that a POINT object can be used. The class CPoint has data members x and y of type LONG, and using CPoint objects has the advantage that the class also defines member functions that operate on CPoint and POINT objects. This may seem weird because CPoint would seem to make POINT objects obsolete, but remember that the Windows API was built before MFC was around, and POINT objects are used in the Windows API and have to be dealt with sooner or later. CPoint objects are used in examples, so you'll have an opportunity to see some of the member functions in action.

The return value from the `MoveTo()` function is a CPoint object that specifies the current position as it was *before* the move. You might think this a little odd, but consider the situation where you want to move to a new position, draw something, and then move back. You may not know the current position before the move, and after the move occurs it would be lost so returning the position before the move makes sure it's available to you if you need it.

Drawing Lines

You can follow the call to `MoveTo()` in the `OnDraw()` function with a call to the function `LineTo()`, which draws a line in the client area from the current position to the point specified by the arguments to the `LineTo()` function, as illustrated in Figure 15-4.

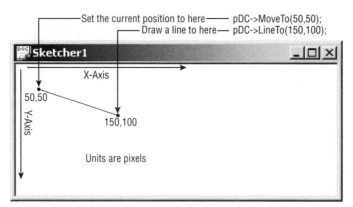

Figure 15-4

The CDC class also defines two versions of the LineTo() function that have the following prototypes:

```
BOOL LineTo(int x, int y);    // Draw a line to position x,y
BOOL LineTo(POINT aPoint);    // Draw a line to position defined by aPoint
```

This offers you the same flexibility in specifying the argument to the function as MoveTo(). You can use a CPoint object as an argument to the second version of the function. The function returns TRUE if the line was drawn and FALSE otherwise.

When the LineTo() function is executed, the current position is changed to the point specifying the end of the line. This allows you to draw a series of connected lines by just calling the LineTo() function for each line. Look at the following version of the OnDraw() function:

```
void CSketcherView::OnDraw(CDC* pDC)
{
   CSketcherDoc* pDoc = GetDocument();
   ASSERT_VALID(pDoc);
   if(!pDoc)
     return;

   pDC->MoveTo(50,50);          // Set the current position
   pDC->LineTo(50,200);         // Draw a vertical line down 150 units
   pDC->LineTo(150,200);        // Draw a horizontal line right 100 units
   pDC->LineTo(150,50);         // Draw a vertical line up 150 units
   pDC->LineTo(50,50);          // Draw a horizontal line left 100 units
}
```

If you plug this into the Sketcher program and execute it, it displays the document window shown in Figure 15-5.

The four calls to the LineTo() function draw the rectangle shown counterclockwise, starting with the upper-left corner. The first call uses the current position set by the MoveTo() function; the succeeding calls use the current position set by the previous LineTo() function call. You can use this to draw any figure consisting of a sequence of lines, each connected to the previous line. Of course, you are also free to use MoveTo() to change the current position at any time.

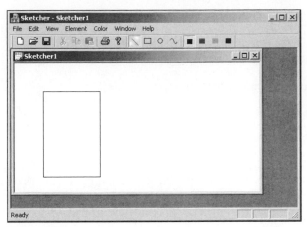

Figure 15-5

Drawing Circles

You have a choice of several function members in the CDC class for drawing circles, but they're all designed to draw ellipses. As you know from high school geometry, a circle is a special case of an ellipse, with the major and minor axes equal. You can, therefore, use the member function Ellipse() to draw a circle. Like other closed shapes supported by the CDC class, the Ellipse() function fills the interior of the shape with a color that you set. The interior color is determined by a **brush** that is selected into the device context. The current brush in the device context determines how any closed shape is filled.

MFC provides the CBrush class that you can use to define a brush. You can set the color of a CBrush object and also define a pattern to be produced when filling a closed shape. If you want to draw a closed shape that isn't filled, you can use a null brush, which leaves the interior of the shape empty. I'll come back to brushes a little later in this chapter.

Another way to draw circles that aren't filled is to use the Arc() function, which doesn't involve brushes. This has the advantage that you can draw any arc of an ellipse, rather than the complete curve. There are two versions of this function in the CDC class, declared as:

```
BOOL Arc(int x1, int y1, int x2, int y2, int x3, int y3, int x4, int y4);
BOOL Arc(LPCRECT lpRect, POINT StartPt, POINT EndPt);
```

In the first version, (x1,y1) and (x2,y2) define the upper-left and lower-right corners of a rectangle enclosing the complete curve. If you make these coordinates into the corners of a square, the curve drawn is a segment of a circle. The points (x3,y3) and (x4,y4) define the start and end points of the segment to be drawn. The segment is drawn counterclockwise. If you make (x4,y4) identical to (x3,y3), you'll generate a complete, apparently closed curve.

In the second version of Arc(), the enclosing rectangle is defined by a RECT object, and a pointer to this object is passed as the first argument. The function also accepts a pointer to an object of the class CRect, which has four public data members: left, top, right, and bottom. These correspond to the *x* and *y* coordinates of the upper-left and lower-right points of the rectangle respectively. The class also provides a range of function members that operate on CRect objects, and we shall be using some of these later.

The POINT objects StartPt and EndPt in the second version of Arc() define the start and end of the arc to be drawn.

Here's some code that exercises both versions of the Arc() function:

```
void CSketcherView::OnDraw(CDC* pDC)
{
  CSketcherDoc* pDoc = GetDocument();
  ASSERT_VALID(pDoc);
  if(!pDoc)
    return;

  pDC->Arc(50,50,150,150,100,50,150,100);  // Draw the 1st (large) circle

  // Define the bounding rectangle for the 2nd (smaller) circle
  CRect* pRect = new CRect(250,50,300,100);
  CPoint Start(275,100);                    // Arc start point
  CPoint End(250,75);                       // Arc end point
  pDC->Arc(pRect,Start, End);               // Draw the second circle
  delete pRect;
}
```

Note that you used a CRect class object instead of a RECT structure to define the bounding rectangle, and that you used CPoint class objects instead of POINT structures. You'll also be using CRect objects later, but they have some limitations, as you'll see. The Arc() function doesn't require a current position to be set, as the position and size of the arc are completely defined by the arguments you supply. The current position is unaffected by drawing an arc — it remains exactly wherever it was before the arc was drawn. Now try running Sketcher with this code in the OnDraw() function. You should get the results shown in Figure 15-6.

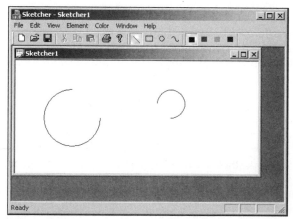

Figure 15-6

Try re-sizing the borders. The client area is automatically redrawn as you cover or uncover the arcs in the picture. Remember that screen resolution affects the scale of what is displayed. The lower the screen resolution you're using, the larger and further from the upper-left corner of the client area the arcs will be.

Drawing in Color

Everything that you've drawn so far has appeared on the screen in black. Drawing implies using a **pen object** that has a color and a thickness, and you've been using the default pen object that is provided in a device context. You're not obliged to do this, of course — you can create your own pen with a given thickness and color. MFC defines the class CPen to help you do this.

All closed curves that you draw are filled with the current brush in the device context. As mentioned earlier, you can define a brush as an instance of the class CBrush. Take a look at some of the features of CPen and CBrush objects.

Creating a Pen

The simplest way to create a pen object is first to declare an object of the CPen class:

```
CPen aPen;                      // Declare a pen object
```

This object now needs to be initialized with the properties you want. You do this using the class member function CreatePen(), which is declared in the CPen class as:

```
BOOL CreatePen (int aPenStyle, int aWidth, COLORREF aColor);
```

The function returns TRUE as long as the pen is successfully initialized and FALSE otherwise. The first argument defines the line style that you want to use when drawing. You must specify it with one of the following symbolic values:

Pen Style	Description
PS_SOLID	The pen draws a solid line.
PS_DASH	The pen draws a dashed line. This line style is valid only when the pen width is specified as 1.
PS_DOT	The pen draws a dotted line. This line style is valid only when the pen width is specified as 1.
PS_DASHDOT	The pen draws a line with alternating dashes and dots. This line style is valid only when the pen width is specified as 1.
PS_DASHDOTDOT	The pen draws a line with alternating dashes and double dots. This line style is valid only when the pen width is specified as 1.
PS_NULL	The pen doesn't draw anything.
PS_INSIDEFRAME	The pen draws a solid line, but unlike PS_SOLID, the points that specify the line occur on the edge of the pen rather than in the center, so that the drawn object never extends beyond the enclosing rectangle.

The second argument to the CreatePen() function defines the line width. If aWidth has the value 0, the line drawn is 1 pixel wide, regardless of the mapping mode in effect. For values of 1 or more, the pen width is in the units determined by the mapping mode. For example, a value of 2 for aWidth in MM_TEXT mode is 2 pixels; in MM_LOENGLISH mode the pen width is 0.02 inches.

The last argument specifies the color to be used when drawing with the pen, so you could initialize a pen with the statement:

```
aPen.CreatePen(PS_SOLID, 2, RGB(255,0,0));   // Create a red solid pen
```

Assuming that the mapping mode is MM_TEXT, this pen draws a solid red line that is 2 pixels wide.

Using a Pen

To use a pen, you must select it into the device context in which you are drawing. To do this, you use the CDC class member function SelectObject(). To select the pen you want to use, you call this function with a pointer to the pen object as an argument. The function returns a pointer to the previous pen object being used, so that you can save it and restore the old pen when you have finished drawing. A typical statement selecting a pen is:

```
CPen* pOldPen = pDC->SelectObject(&aPen);     // Select aPen as the pen
```

To restore the old pen when you're done, you simply call the function again, passing the pointer returned from the original call:

```
pDC->SelectObject(pOldPen);                    // Restore the old pen
```

You can see this in action if you amend the previous version of the OnDraw() function in the CSketcherView class to:

```
void CSketcherView::OnDraw(CDC* pDC)
{
    CSketcherDoc* pDoc = GetDocument();
    ASSERT_VALID(pDoc);
    if(!pDoc)
      return;

    // Declare a pen object and initialize it as
    // a red solid pen drawing a line 2 pixels wide
    CPen aPen;
    aPen.CreatePen(PS_SOLID, 2, RGB(255, 0, 0));

    CPen* pOldPen = pDC->SelectObject(&aPen); // Select aPen as the pen

    pDC->Arc(50,50,150,150,100,50,150,100);    // Draw the 1st circle

    // Define the bounding rectangle for the 2nd circle
    CRect* pRect = new CRect(250,50,300,100);
    CPoint Start(275,100);                      // Arc start point
    CPoint End(250,75);                         // Arc end point
    pDC->Arc(pRect,Start, End);                 // Draw the second circle
    delete pRect;

    pDC->SelectObject(pOldPen);                 // Restore the old pen
}
```

If you build and execute the Sketcher application with this version of the OnDraw() function, you get the same arcs drawn as before, but this time the lines will be thicker and they'll be red. You could usefully experiment with this example by trying different combinations of arguments to the CreatePen() function and seeing their effects. Note that we have ignored the value returned from the CreatePen() function, so you run the risk of the function failing and not detecting it in the program. It doesn't matter here, as the program is still trivial, but as you develop the program it becomes important to check for failures of this kind.

Creating a Brush

An object of the CBrush class encapsulates a Windows brush. You can define a brush to be solid, hatched, or patterned. A brush is actually an 8x8 block of pixels that's repeated over the region to be filled.

To define a brush with a solid color, you can specify the color when you create the brush object. For example,

```
CBrush aBrush(RGB(255,0,0));              // Define a red brush
```

This statement defines a red brush. The value passed to the constructor must be of type COLORREF, which is the type returned by the RGB() macro, so this is a good way to specify the color.

Another constructor is available to define a hatched brush. It requires two arguments to be specified, the first defining the type of hatching, and the second specifying the color, as before. The hatching argument can be any of the following symbolic constants:

Hatching Style	Description
HS_HORIZONTAL	Horizontal hatching
HS_VERTICAL	Vertical hatching
HS_BDIAGONAL	Downward hatching from left to right at 45 degrees
HS_FDIAGONAL	Upward hatching from left to right at 45 degrees
HS_CROSS	Horizontal and vertical crosshatching
HS_DIAGCROSS	Crosshatching at 45 degrees

So, to obtain a red, 45-degree crosshatched brush, you could define the CBrush object with the statement:

```
CBrush aBrush(HS_DIAGCROSS, RGB(255,0,0));
```

You can also initialize a CBrush object in a similar manner to that for a CPen object, by using the CreateSolidBrush() member function of the class for a solid brush, and the CreateHatchBrush() member for a hatched brush. They require the same arguments as the equivalent constructors. For example, you could create the same hatched brush as before, with the statements:

```
CBrush aBrush;                         // Define a brush object
aBrush.CreateHatchBrush(HS_DIAGCROSS, RGB(255,0,0));
```

Using a Brush

To use a brush, you select the brush into the device context by calling the `SelectObject()` member of the `CDC` class in a parallel fashion to that used for a pen. This member function is overloaded to support selecting brush objects into a device context. To select the brush defined previously, you would simply write:

```
pDC->SelectObject(aBrush);      // Select the brush into the device context
```

There are a number of standard brushes available. Each of the standard brushes is identified by a prede-fined symbolic constant, and there are seven that you can use. They are the following:

GRAY_BRUSH	LTGRAY_BRUSH	DKGRAY_BRUSH
BLACK_BRUSH	WHITE_BRUSH	
HOLLOW_BRUSH	NULL_BRUSH	

The names of these brushes are quite self-explanatory. To use one, you call the `SelectStockObject()` member of the `CDC` class, passing the symbolic name for the brush that you want to use as an argument. To select the null brush, which leaves the interior of a closed shape unfilled, you could write:

```
pDC->SelectStockObject(NULL_BRUSH);
```

Here, `pDC` is a pointer to a `CDC` object, as before. You can also use one of a range of standard pens through this function. The symbols for standard pens are `BLACK_PEN`, `NULL_PEN` (which doesn't draw anything), and `WHITE_PEN`. The `SelectStockObject()` function returns a pointer to the object being replaced in the device context. This enables you to save it for restoring later when you have finished drawing.

Because the function works with a variety of objects — you've seen pens and brushes in this chapter, but it also works with fonts — the type of the pointer returned is `CGdiObject*`. The `CGdiObject` class is a base class for all the graphic device interface object classes and thus a pointer to this class can be used to store a pointer to any object of these types. However, you need to cast the pointer value returned to the appropri-ate type so that you can select the old object back to restore it. This is because the `SelectObject()` func-tion you use to do this is overloaded for each of the kinds of object that can be selected. There's no version of `SelectObject()` that accepts a pointer to a `CGdiObject` as an argument, but there are versions that accept an argument of type `CBrush*`, `CPen*`, and pointers to other GDI objects.

The typical pattern of coding for using a stock brush and later restoring the old brush when you're done is:

```
CBrush* pOldBrush = (CBrush*)pDC->SelectStockObject(NULL_BRUSH);

// draw something...

pDC->SelectObject(pOldBrush);                 // Restore the old brush
```

You'll be using this in your example later in the chapter.

Drawing Graphics in Practice

You now know how to draw lines and arcs, so it's about time to consider how the user is going to define what they want drawn in Sketcher. In other words, you need to decide how the user interface is going to work.

Because the Sketcher program is to be a sketching tool, you don't want the user to worry about coordinates. The easiest mechanism for drawing is using just the mouse. To draw a line, for instance, the user could position the cursor and press the left mouse button where they wanted the line to start, and then define the end of the line by moving the cursor with the left button held down. It would be ideal if you could arrange that the line was continuously drawn as the cursor was moved with the left button down (this is known as "rubber-banding" to graphic designers). The line would be fixed when the left mouse button was released. This process is illustrated in Figure 15-7.

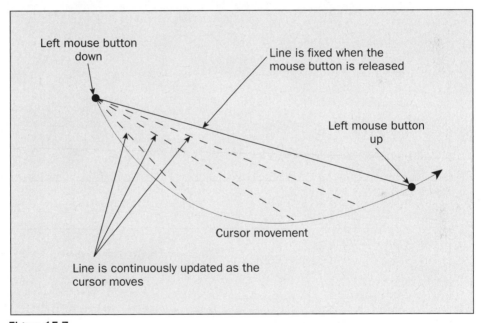

Figure 15-7

You could allow circles to be drawn in a similar fashion. The first press of the left mouse button would define the center and, as the cursor was moved with the button down, the program would track it. The circle would be continuously redrawn, with the current cursor position defining a point on the circumference of the circle. As with drawing a line, the circle would be fixed when the left mouse button was released. You can see this process illustrated in Figure 15-8.

You can draw a rectangle as easily as you draw a line, as illustrated in Figure 15-9.

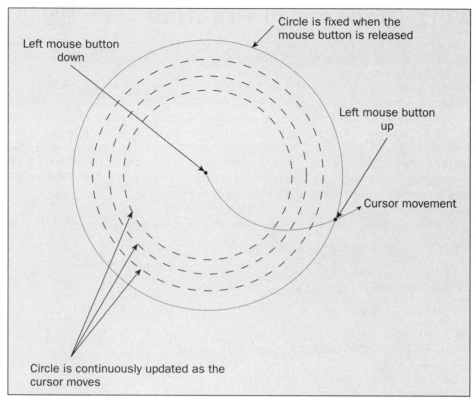

Figure 15-8

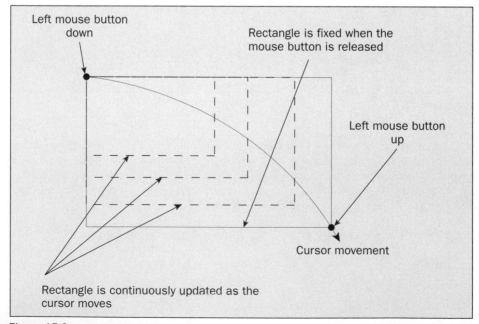

Figure 15-9

The first point is defined by the position of the cursor when the left mouse button is pressed. This is one corner of the rectangle. The position of the cursor when the mouse is moved with the left button held down defines the diagonal opposite corner of the rectangle. The rectangle actually stored is the last one defined when the left mouse button is released.

A curve is somewhat different. An arbitrary number of points may define a curve. The mechanism you'll use is illustrated in Figure 15-10.

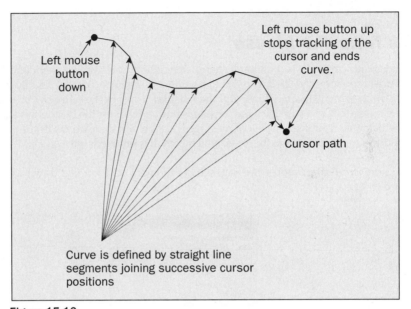

Figure 15-10

As with the other shapes, the first point is defined by the cursor position when the left mouse button is pressed. Successive positions recorded when the mouse is moved are connected by straight line segments to form the curve, so the mouse track defines the curve to be drawn.

Now that you know how the user is going to define an element, clearly the next step in understanding how to implement this is to get a grip on how the mouse is programmed.

Programming the Mouse

To be able to program the drawing of shapes in the way I have discussed, you need to know various things about the mouse:

❑ Pressing a mouse button signals the start of a drawing operation.

❑ The location of the cursor when the mouse button is pressed defines a reference point for the shape.

❑ A mouse movement after detecting that a mouse button has been pressed is a cue to draw a shape, and the cursor position provides a defining point for the shape.

❑ The cursor position at the time the mouse button is released signals that the final version of the shape should be drawn.

As you may have guessed, all this information is provided by Windows in the form of messages sent to your program. The implementation of the process for drawing lines and circles consists almost entirely of writing message handlers.

Messages from the Mouse

When the user of our program is drawing a shape, they will interact with a particular document view. The view class is, therefore, the obvious place to put the message handlers for the mouse. Right-click the CSketcherView class name in Class View and then display its properties window by selecting Properties from the context menu. If you then click the messages button (wait for the button tool tips to display if you don't know which it is), you'll see the list of message IDs. You will then see the list of message IDs for the standard Windows messages sent to the class, which have IDs prefixed with WM_.

You need to know about three mouse messages at the moment, so I scrolled down to bring them into view in Figure 15-11.

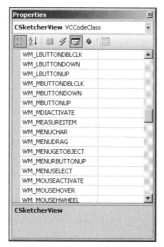

Figure 15-11

They are the following:

Message	Description
WM_LBUTTONDOWN	Message occurs when the left mouse button is pressed.
WM_LBUTTONUP	Message occurs when the left mouse button is released.
WM_MOUSEMOVE	Message occurs when the mouse is moved.

These messages are quite independent of one another and are being sent to the document views in your program even if you haven't supplied handlers for them. It's quite possible for a window to receive a WM_LBUTTONUP message without having previously received a WM_LBUTTONDOWN message. This can happen if the button is pressed with the cursor over another window and then moved to your view window before being released.

If you look at the list in the properties window you'll see there are other mouse messages that can occur. You can choose to process any or all of the messages, depending on your application requirements. Define in general terms what you want to do with the three messages that you're currently interested in, based on the process for drawing shapes that you saw earlier:

WM_LBUTTONDOWN

This starts the process of drawing an element. So you will:

1. Note that the element drawing process has started.
2. Record the current cursor position as the first point for defining an element.

WM_MOUSEMOVE

This is an intermediate stage where you want to create and draw a temporary version of the current element but only if the left mouse button is down, so:

1. Check that the left button is down.
2. If it is, delete any previous version of the current element that was drawn.
3. If it isn't, then exit.
4. Record the current cursor position as the second defining point for the current element.
5. Cause the current element to be drawn using the two defining points.

WM_LBUTTONUP

This indicates that the process for drawing an element is finished, so all you need to do is:

1. Store the final version of the element defined by the first point recorded, together with the position of the cursor when the button is released for the second point.
2. Record the end of the process of drawing an element.

Now generate handlers for these three mouse messages.

Mouse Message Handlers

You can create a handler for one of the mouse messages by clicking on the ID to select it and then selecting the down arrow in the adjacent column position; try selecting <add> OnLButtonUp for the ID_LBUTTONUP message, for example. Repeat the process for each of the messages WM_LBUTTONDOWN and WM_MOUSEMOVE. The functions generated in the CSketcherView class are OnLButtonDown(), OnLButtonUp() and OnMouseMove(). You don't get the option of changing the names of these functions because you're adding overrides for versions that are already defined in the base class for the CSketcherView class. Take a look at how you implement these handlers.

You can start by looking at the WM_LBUTTONDOWN message handler. This is the skeleton code that's generated:

```
void CSketcherView::OnLButtonDown(UINT nFlags, CPoint point)
{
    // TODO: Add your message handler code here and/or call default

    CView::OnLButtonDown(nFlags, point);
}
```

You can see that there is a call to the base class handler in the skeleton version. This ensures that the base handler is called if you don't add any code here. In this case you don't need to call the base class handler when you handle the message yourself, although you can if you want to. Whether you need to call the base class handler for a message depends on the circumstances.

Generally, the comment indicating where you should add your own code is a good guide. Where it suggests, as in the present instance, that calling the base class handler is optional, you can omit it when you add your own message handling code. Note that the position of the comment in relation to the call of the base class handler is also important, as sometimes you must call the base class message handler before your code, and other times afterwards. The comment indicates where your code should appear in relation to the base class message handler call.

The handler in your class is passed two arguments: nFlags, which is of type UINT and contains a number of status flags indicating whether various keys are down, and the CPoint object point, which defines the cursor position when the left mouse button was pressed. The UINT type is defined in the Windows API and corresponds to a 32-bit unsigned integer.

The value of nFlags that is passed to the function can be any combination of the following symbolic values:

Flag	Description
MK_CONTROL	Corresponds to the *Ctrl* key being pressed.
MK_LBUTTON	Corresponds to the left mouse button being down.
MK_MBUTTON	Corresponds to the middle mouse button being down.
MK_RBUTTON	Corresponds to the right mouse button being down.
MK_SHIFT	Corresponds to the *Shift* key being pressed.

Being able to detect if a key is down in the message handler enables you to support different actions for the message depending on what else you find. The value of nFlags may contain more than one of these indicators, each of which corresponds to a particular bit in the word, so you can test for a particular key using the bitwise AND operator. For example, to test for the Ctrl key being pressed, you could write:

```
if(nFlags & MK_CONTROL)
    // Do something...
```

The expression nFlags & MK_CONTROL will only have the value true if the nFlags variable has the bit defined by MK_CONTROL set. In this way, you can have different actions when the left mouse button is pressed, depending on whether or not the *Ctrl* key is also pressed. You use the bitwise AND operator here, so corresponding bits are ANDed together. Don't confuse this with the logical AND, &&, which would not do what you want here.

The arguments passed to the other two message handlers are the same as those for the OnLButtonDown() function; the code generated for them is:

```
void CSketcherView::OnLButtonUp(UINT nFlags, CPoint point)
{
  // TODO: Add your message handler code here and/or call default

  CView::OnLButtonUp(nFlags, point);
}
```

```
void CSketcherView::OnMouseMove(UINT nFlags, CPoint point)
{
  // TODO: Add your message handler code here and/or call default

  CView::OnMouseMove(nFlags, point);
}
```

Apart from the function names, the skeleton code is the same for each.

If you take a look at the end of the code for the CSketcherView class definition, you'll see that three function declarations have been added:

```
// Generated message map functions
protected:
  DECLARE_MESSAGE_MAP()
public:
  afx_msg void OnLButtonDown(UINT nFlags, CPoint point);
  afx_msg void OnLButtonUp(UINT nFlags, CPoint point);
  afx_msg void OnMouseMove(UINT nFlags, CPoint point);
};
```

These identify the functions that you added as message handlers.

Now that you have an understanding of the information passed to the message handlers you have created, you can start adding your own code to make them do what you want.

Drawing Using the Mouse

For the WM_LBUTTONDOWN message, you want to record the cursor position as the first point defining an element. You also want to record the position of the cursor after a mouse move. The obvious place to store these is in the CSketcherView class, so you can add data members to the class for these. Right-click the CSketcherView class name in Class View and select Add > Add Variable from the pop-up. You'll then be able to add details of the variable to be added to the class, as Figure 15-12 shows.

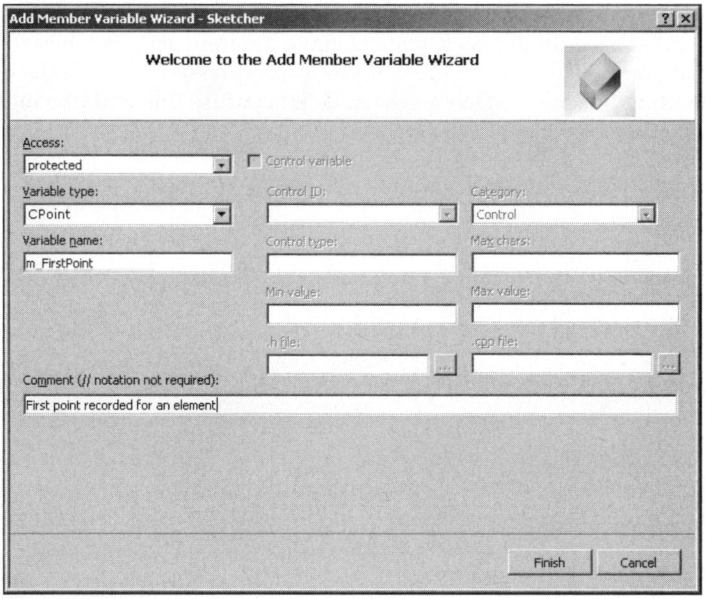

Figure 15-12

The drop-down list of types only includes fundamental types so to enter the type as CPoint you just high-light the type displayed by double-clicking it and then key in the type name you want. The new data member should be protected to prevent direct modification of it from outside the class. When you click the Finish button the variable will be created and an initial value will be set arbitrarily as 0 in the initialization list for the constructor. You'll need to amend the initial value to CPoint(0,0) so the code is:

```
// CSketcherView construction/destruction

CSketcherView::CSketcherView() :
        m_FirstPoint(CPoint(0,0))
{
    // TODO: add construction code here
}
```

This initializes the member to a CPoint object at position (0,0). You can now add m_SecondPoint as a protected member of type CPoint to the CSketcherView class that stores the next point for an element. You should also amend the initialization list for the constructor to initialize it to CPoint(0,0).

You can now implement the handler for the WM_LBUTTONDOWN message as:

```
void CSketcherView::OnLButtonDown(UINT nFlags, CPoint point)
{
    // TODO: Add your message handler code here and/or call default
    m_FirstPoint = point;                  // Record the cursor position
}
```

All it does is note the coordinates passed by the second argument. You can ignore the first argument in this situation altogether.

You can't complete WM_MOUSEMOVE message handler yet, but you can have a stab at writing the code for it in outline:

```
void CSketcherView::OnMouseMove(UINT nFlags, CPoint point)
{
    // TODO: Add your message handler code here and/or call default
    if(nFlags & MK_LBUTTON)                 // Verify the left button is down
    {
        m_SecondPoint = point;              // Save the current cursor position

        // Test for a previous temporary element
        {
            // We get to here if there was a previous mouse move
            // so add code to delete the old element
        }

        // Add code to create new element
        // and cause it to be drawn
    }
}
```

It's important to check that the left mouse button is down because you only want to handle the mouse move when this is the case. Without the check, you would be processing the event when the right button was down or when the mouse was moved with no buttons pressed.

The first thing that the handler does after verifying the left mouse button is down is to save the current cursor position. This is used as the second defining point for an element. The rest of the logic is clear in general terms, but you need to establish a few more things before you can complete the function. You have no means of defining an element — you'll want to define an element as an object of a class so some classes must be defined. You also need to devise a way to delete an element and get one drawn when you create a new one. A brief digression is called for.

Getting the Client Area Redrawn

Drawing or erasing elements involves redrawing all or part of the client area of a window. As you've already discovered, the client area gets drawn by the OnDraw() member function of the CSketcherView class, and this function is called when a WM_PAINT message is received by the Sketcher application. Along with the basic message to repaint the client area, Windows supplies information about the part of the client area that needs to be redrawn. This can save a lot of time when you're displaying complicated images because only the area specified actually needs to be redrawn, which may be a very small proportion of the total area.

You can tell Windows that a particular area should be redrawn by calling the InvalidateRect() function that is an inherited member of your view class. The function accepts two arguments, the first of which is a pointer to a RECT or CRect object that defines the rectangle in the client area to be redrawn. Passing null for this parameter causes the whole client area to be redrawn. The second parameter is a BOOL value, which is TRUE if the background to the rectangle is to be erased and FALSE otherwise. This argument has a default value of TRUE because you normally want the background erased before the rectangle is redrawn, so you can ignore it most of the time. BOOL is a Windows API type representing Boolean values and can be assigned the values TRUE or FALSE.

A typical situation in which you'd want to cause an area to be redrawn would be where something has changed that necessitates the contents of the area being recreated — moving a displayed entity might be an example. In this case, you want to erase the background to remove the old representation of what was displayed before you draw the new version. When you want to draw on top of an existing background, you just pass FALSE as the second argument to InvalidateRect().

Calling the InvalidateRect() function doesn't directly cause any part of the window to be redrawn; it just communicates to Windows the rectangle that you would like to have it redraw at some time. Windows maintains an update region — actually a rectangle — that identifies the area in a window that needs to be redrawn. The area specified in your call to InvalidateRect() is added to the current update region, so the new update region encloses the old region plus the new rectangle you have indicated as invalid. Eventually a WM_PAINT message is sent to the window, and the update region is passed to the window along with it. When processing of the WM_PAINT message is complete, the update region is reset to the empty state.

Thus, all you have to do to get a newly created shape drawn is:

1. Make sure that the OnDraw() function in your view includes the newly created item when it redraws the window.

2. Call InvalidateRect() with a pointer to the rectangle bounding the shape to be redrawn passed as the first argument.

Similarly, if you want a shape removed from the client area of a window, you need to do the following:

1. Remove the shape from the items that the OnDraw() function will draw.

2. Call InvalidateRect() with the first argument pointing to the rectangle bounding the shape that is to be removed.

Because the background to the rectangle specified is automatically erased, as long as the OnDraw() function doesn't draw the shape again, the shape disappears. Of course, this means that you need to be able to obtain the rectangle bounding any shape that you create, so you'll include a function to provide this as a member of the classes that define the elements that can be drawn by Sketcher.

Defining Classes for Elements

Thinking ahead a bit, you will need to store elements in a document in some way. You must also to be able to store the document in a file for retrieval subsequently if a sketch is to have any permanence. I'll deal with the details of file operations later on, but for now it's enough to know that the MFC class CObject includes the tools for us to do this, so you'll use CObject as a base class for the element classes.

You also have the problem that you don't know in advance what sequence of element types the user will create. The Sketcher program must be able to handle any sequence of elements. This suggests that using a base class pointer for selecting a particular element class function might simplify things a bit. For example, you don't need to know what an element is to draw it. As long as you are accessing the element through a base class pointer, you can always get an element to draw itself by using a virtual function. This is another example of the polymorphism I talked about when I discussed virtual functions. All you need to do to achieve this is to make sure that the classes defining specific elements share a common base class and that in this class you declare all the functions you want to be selected automatically at run time as **virtual**. This indicates that the element classes could be organized as shown in Figure 15-13.

The arrows in the diagram point toward the base class in each case. If you need to add another element type, all you need to do is derive another class from CElement. Because these classes are closely related, you'll be putting the definitions for all these classes in a single new .h file that you can call Elements.h. You can create the new CElement class by right-clicking Sketcher in Class View and selecting Add > Class from the pop-up. Select the class category as MFC and the template as MFC Class. When you click the Add button in the dialog, another dialog displays in which you can specify the class name, as shown in Figure 15-14.

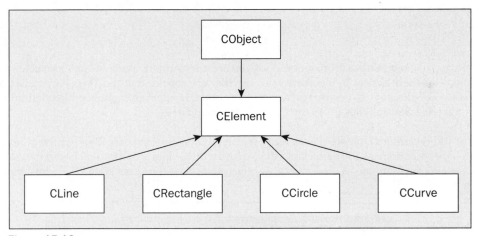

Figure 15-13

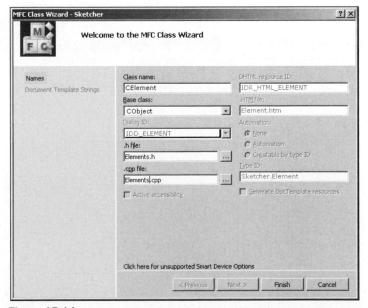

Figure 15-14

I have already filled in the class name as CElement and selected the base class to be CObject from the drop-down list. I have also adjusted the names of the source files to be Elements.h and Elements.cpp because eventually these files will contain definitions for the other element classes I need. When you click the Finish button, the code for the class definition is generated:

```
#pragma once


// CElement command target

class CElement : public CObject
{
public:
  CElement();  virtual ~CElement();
};
```

The only members that have been declared for you are a constructor and a virtual destructor and skeleton definitions for these appear in the Elements.cpp file. You can see that the Class Wizard has included a #pragma once directive to ensure that the contents of the header file cannot be included into a .cpp file more than once. Save all files to get the Class View tab updated.

You can add the other elements classes using essentially the same process. Because the other element classes have CElement as the base class rather than an MFC class, you should choose the class category to be C++ and the template as C++ class. For the CLine class the Class Wizard window should look as shown in Figure 15-15.

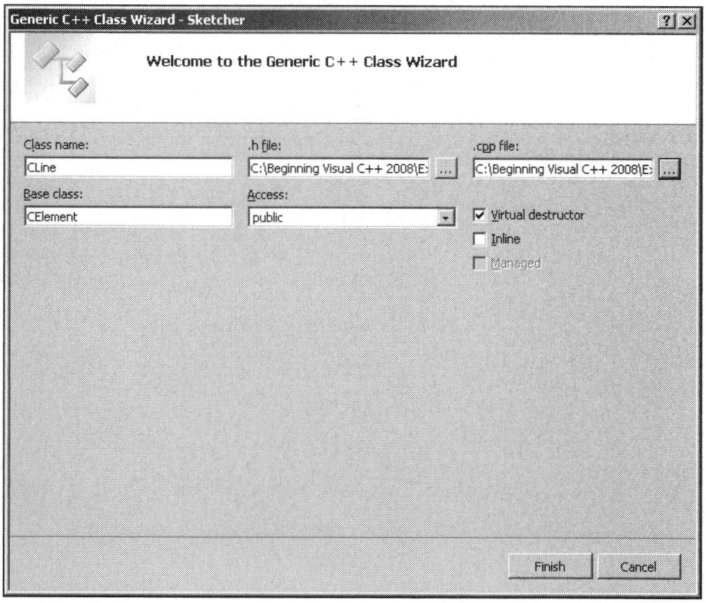

Figure 15-15

The Class Wizard supplies the name of the header files and .cpp file as Line.h and Line.cpp by default but you can change these to use different names for the files or use existing files. To have the CLine class code inserted in the files for the CElement class, just click the button alongside the file name and select the appropriate file to be used. I have already done this in Figure 15-14. You may need to erase the default file name that is supplied in the dialog and reselect the Sketcher directory to get the list of files displayed. You'll see a dialog displayed when you click the Finish button that asks you to confirm that you want to merge the new class into the existing header file. Just click the Yes button to confirm this and do the same for the dialog that appears relating to the Elements.cpp file. When you have created the CLine class definition, do the same for CRectangle, CCircle and CCurve. When you are done, you should see the definitions of all four subclasses of CElement in the Elements.h file, each with a constructor and a virtual destructor declared.

Storing a Temporary Element in the View

When I discussed how shapes would be drawn, it was evident that as the mouse was dragged after pressing the left mouse button, a series of temporary element objects would be created and drawn. Now that you know that the base class for all the shapes is CElement, you can add a pointer to the view class that you'll use to store the address of the temporary element. Right-click the CSketcherView class once more and select the Add > Add Variable option once again. The m_pTempElement should be of type CElement* and be protected like the previous two data members that you added earlier, as illustrated in Figure 15-16.

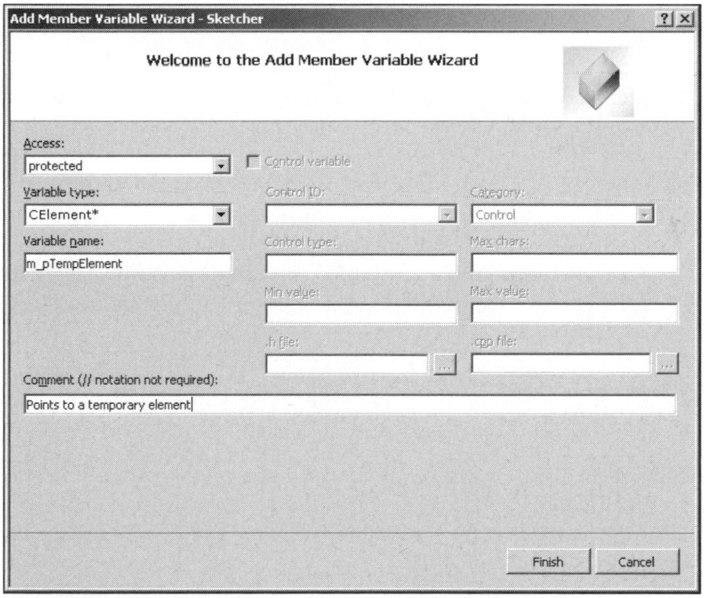

Figure 15-16

The Add Member Variable Wizard ensures that the new variable is initialized when the view object is constructed and the default value of NULL that is set will do nicely.

```
CSketcherView::CSketcherView()
:m_FirstPoint(CPoint(0,0))
, m_SecondPoint(CPoint(0,0))
, m_pTempElement(NULL)
{
   // TODO: add construction code here

}
```

You'll be able to use the m_pTempElement pointer in the WM_MOUSEMOVE message handler as a test for previous temporary elements because you'll arrange for it to be null when there are none.

If you check what has been added to the SketcherView.h header file, you'll see at the beginning there is the line:

```
#include "atltypes.h"
```

This has been inserted because the wizard has assumed the CElement type is an ATL type. You can delete this line as it is not required. For the CSketcherView class to compile correctly, you must add the following statement immediately following the #pragma once directive:

```
class CElement;                          // Forward class declaration
```

This just identifies the CElement identifier as the name of a class that is defined elsewhere so the compiler will process it as such.

Because you are creating CElement class objects in the view class member functions, and you refer to the CElement class in defining the data member that points to a temporary element, you should ensure that the definition of the CElement class is included before the CSketcherView class definition wherever SketcherView.h is included into a .cpp file. You can do this for CSketcherView by adding an #include directive for Elements.h to the SketcherView.cpp file before the #include directive for SketcherView.h:

```
#include "Elements.h"
#include "SketcherView.h"
```

Sketcher.cpp also has an #include directive for SketcherView.h, so you should add an #include for Elements.h to this file too.

The CElement Class

You can now start to fill out the element class definitions. You'll be doing this incrementally as you add more and more functionality to the Sketcher application — but what do you need right now? Some data items, such as color, are clearly common to all types of element so you can put those in the CElement class so that they are inherited in each of the derived classes; however, the other data members in the classes that define specific element properties will be quite disparate, so you'll declare these members in the particular derived class to which they belong.

Thus the CElement class contains only virtual functions that are replaced in the derived classes, plus data and function members that are the same in all the derived classes. The virtual functions are those that are selected automatically for a particular object through a pointer. You could use the Add Member Wizard you've used previously to do this, but modify the class manually for a change. For now, you can modify the CElement class to the following:

```
class CElement: public CObject
{
   protected:
      COLORREF m_Color;                       // Color of an element

   public:
      virtual ~CElement();
      virtual void Draw(CDC* pDC) {}   // Virtual draw operation

      CRect GetBoundRect();                   // Get the bounding rectangle for an element

   protected:
      CElement();                       // Here to prevent it being called
};
```

I have changed the access for the constructor from `public` to `protected` to prevent it from being called from outside the class. At the moment, the members to be inherited by the derived classes are a data member storing the color, m_Color, and a member function that calculates the rectangle bounding an element, GetBoundRect(). This function returns a value of type CRect that is the rectangle bounding the shape.

You also have a virtual Draw() function that is implemented in the derived classes to draw the particular object in question. The Draw() function needs a pointer to a CDC object passed to it to provide access to the drawing functions that you saw earlier that allow drawing in a device context.

You might be tempted to declare the Draw() member as a pure virtual function in the CElement class — after all, it can have no meaningful content in this class. This would also force its definition in any derived class. Normally you would do this, but the CElement class inherits a facility from CObject called **serialization** that you'll use later for storing objects in a file, and this requires that an instance of the CElement class can be created. A class with a pure virtual function member is an abstract class, and instances of an abstract class can't be created. If you want to use MFC's serialization capability for storing objects, your classes mustn't be abstract. You must also supply a no-arg constructor for a class to be serializable.

> *Note that serialization is a general term for writing objects to a file. Serialization in a C++/CLI application will work differently to serialization in the MFC.*

You might also be tempted to declare the GetBoundRect() function as returning a *pointer* to a CRect object — after all, you're going to pass a pointer to the InvalidateRect() member function in the view class; however, this could lead to problems. You'll be creating the CRect object as local to the function, so the pointer would be pointing to a nonexistent object on return from the GetBoundRect() function. You could get around this by creating the CRect object on the heap, but then you'd need to take care that it's deleted after use; otherwise, you'd be filling the heap with CRect objects — a new one for every call of GetBoundRect(). A further possibility is that you could store the bounding rectangle for an element as a class member and generate it when the element is created. This is a reasonable alternative, but if you changed an element subsequently, by moving it say, you would need to ensure the bounding rectangle was recalculated.

The CLine Class

You can amend the definition of the CLine class to:

```
class CLine: public CElement
{
   public:
      ~CLine(void);
      virtual void Draw(CDC* pDC);        // Function to display a line

      // Constructor for a line object
      CLine(CPoint Start, CPoint End, COLORREF aColor);

   protected:
      CPoint m_StartPoint;                // Start point of line
      CPoint m_EndPoint;                  // End point of line

      CLine(void);                        // Default constructor—should not be used
};
```

The data members that define a line are m_StartPoint and m_EndPoint, and these are both declared to be protected. The class has a public constructor that has parameters for the values that define a line, and the no-arg default constructor has been moved to the protected section of the class to prevent its use externally.

Implementing the CLine Class

You add the implementation of the member functions in the Elements.cpp that was created by the Class Wizard when you created the CElement class. The stdafx.h file was included in this file to make the definitions of the standard system header files available in the file. You may need to add #include directives for the files containing definitions for Application Wizard-generated classes if you use any in the code.

Of course, you'll have to add each of the member function definitions to this file manually because Class Wizard wasn't involved in defining the classes. You're now ready to add the constructor for the CLine class to the Elements.cpp file.

The CLine Class Constructor

The code for this is:

```
// CLine class constructor
CLine::CLine(CPoint Start, CPoint End, COLORREF aColor)
{
   m_StartPoint = Start;                 // Set line start point
   m_EndPoint = End;                     // Set line start point
   m_Color = aColor;                     // Set line color
}
```

You first store the start point in the m_StartPoint member that is inherited from the CElement class. Later you'll add code to allow an element to be moved and to enable a line to be moved by just changing the start point and the end point must be defined relative to the start point. You do this by subtracting the x and y coordinate values for Start from those for End. Both x and y are public members of the CPoint class so you can refer to them directly. Finally, you store the color in the m_Color member that is inherited from the CElement class.

Drawing a Line

The `Draw()` function for the `CLine` class isn't too difficult either, although you do need to take account of the color to be used when the line is drawn:

```
// Draw a CLine object
void CLine::Draw(CDC* pDC)
{
   // Create a pen for this object and
   // initialize it to the object color and line width of 1 pixel
   CPen aPen;
   if(!aPen.CreatePen(PS_SOLID, m_Pen, m_Color))
   {
      // Pen creation failed. Abort the program
      AfxMessageBox(_T("Pen creation failed drawing a line"), MB_OK);
      AfxAbort();
   }

   CPen* pOldPen = pDC->SelectObject(&aPen);   // Select the pen

   // Now draw the line
   pDC->MoveTo(m_StartPoint);
   pDC->LineTo(m_EndPoint);

   pDC->SelectObject(pOldPen);                 // Restore the old pen
}
```

You create a pen in the way you saw earlier, only this time you make sure that the creation works. In the unlikely event that it doesn't, the most likely cause is that you're running out of memory, which is a serious problem. This is almost invariably caused by an error in the program, so you have written the function to call `AfxMessageBox()`, which is a global function to display a message box, and then call `AfxAbort()` to terminate the program. The first argument to `AfxMessageBox()` specifies the message that is to appear, and the second specifies that it should have an `OK` button. You can get more information on either of these functions by placing the cursor within the function name in the editor window and then pressing F1.

After selecting the pen, you move the current position to the start of the line, defined in the inherited `m_StartPoint` data member, and then draw the line from this point to the end point. Finally, you restore the old pen in the device context and you are done. The `m_Pen` variable that is the second argument to the `CreatePen()` function does not exist yet; you'll add this to the `CElement` class a little later in this chapter.

Creating Bounding Rectangles

At first sight, obtaining the bounding rectangle for a shape looks trivial. For example, a line is always a diagonal of its enclosing rectangle, and a circle is *defined* by its enclosing rectangle, but there are a couple of slight complications. The shape must lie *completely* inside the rectangle; otherwise, part of the shape may not be drawn, so you must allow for the thickness of the line used to draw the shape when you create the bounding rectangle. Also, how you work out adjustments to the coordinates that define the bounding rectangle depends on the mapping mode, so you must take that into account, too.

Look at Figure 15-17, which relates to the method for obtaining the bounding rectangle for a line and a circle.

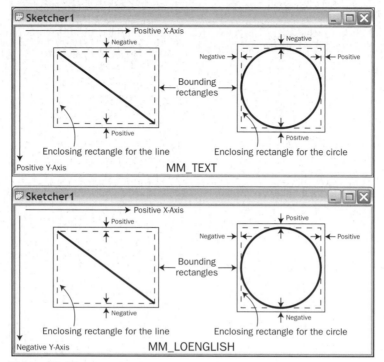

Figure 15-17

I have called the rectangle that is used to draw a shape the 'enclosing rectangle,' while the rectangle that takes into account the width of the pen I've called the 'bounding rectangle' to differentiate it. Figure 15-17 shows the shapes with their enclosing rectangles, and their bounding rectangles offset by the line thickness. This is obviously exaggerated here so you can see what's happening.

The differences in how you calculate the coordinates for the bounding rectangle in different mapping modes only concerns the y coordinate; calculation of the x coordinate is the same for all mapping modes. To get the corners of the bounding rectangle in the MM_TEXT mapping mode, subtract the line thickness from the y coordinate of the upper-left corner of the defining rectangle, and add it to the y coordinate of the lower-right corner. However, in MM_LOENGLISH (and all the other mapping modes), the y-axis increases in the opposite direction, so you need to *add* the line thickness to the y coordinate of the upper-left corner of the defining rectangle, and *subtract* it from the y coordinate of the lower-right corner. For all the mapping modes, you subtract the line thickness from the x coordinate of the upper-left corner of the defining rectangle, and add it to the x coordinate of the lower-right corner.

To implement the element types as consistently as possible in Sketcher, you could store an enclosing rectangle for each shape in a member in the base class. The enclosing rectangle needs to be calculated when a shape is constructed. The job of the GetBoundRect() function in the base class will then be to calculate the bounding rectangle by offsetting the enclosing rectangle by the pen width. You can amend the CElement class definition by adding two data members, as follows:

```
class CElement: public CObject
{
```

```
    protected:
        COLORREF m_Color;                  // Color of an element
        CRect m_EnclosingRect;             // Rectangle enclosing an element
        int m_Pen;                         // Pen width

    public:
        virtual ~CElement();               // Virtual destructor
        virtual void Draw(CDC* pDC) {}     // Virtual draw operation

        CRect GetBoundRect();        // Get the bounding rectangle for an element

    protected:
        CElement();                        // Here to prevent it being called
};
```

You can add these by right-clicking the class name and selecting Add Member Variable from the pop-up, or you can add the statements directly in the Editor window along with the comments.

You must also update the CLine constructor so that it has the correct pen width:

```
// CLine class constructor
CLine::CLine(CPoint Start, CPoint End, COLORREF aColor)
{
    m_StartPoint = Start;              // Set line start point
    m_EndPoint = End;                  // Set line start point
    m_Color = aColor;                  // Set line color
    m_Pen = 1;                         // Set pen width
}
```

You can now implement the GetBoundRect() member of the base class, assuming the MM_TEXT mapping mode:

```
// Get the bounding rectangle for an element
CRect CElement::GetBoundRect()
{
    CRect BoundingRect;                // Object to store bounding rectangle
    BoundingRect = m_EnclosingRect;    // Store the enclosing rectangle

    // Increase the rectangle by the pen width
    BoundingRect.InflateRect(m_Pen, m_Pen);
    return BoundingRect;               // Return the bounding rectangle
}
```

This returns the bounding rectangle for any derived class object. You define the bounding rectangle by modifying the coordinates of the enclosing rectangle stored in the base class data member so that it is enlarged all round by the pen width, using the InflateRect() method of the CRect class.

The CRect class provides an operator + for rectangles, which you could have used instead. For example, you could have written the statement before the return as:

```
BoundingRect = m_EnclosingRect + CRect(m_Pen, m_Pen, m_Pen, m_Pen);
```

Equally, you could have simply added (or subtracted) the pen width for each of the *x* and *y* values that make up the rectangle. You could have replaced the assignment with the following statements:

```
BoundingRect = m_EnclosingRect;
BoundingRect.top -= m_Pen;
BoundingRect.left -= m_Pen;
BoundingRect.bottom += m_Pen;
BoundingRect.right += m_Pen;
```

As a reminder, the individual data members of a CRect *object are* left *and* top *(storing the x and y coordinates of the upper-left corner) and* right *and* bottom *(storing the coordinates of the lower-right corner). These are all public members, so you can access them directly. A commonly made mistake, especially by me, is to write the coordinate pair as* (top, left) *instead of in the correct order* (left, top).

The hazard with both this and the InflateRect() option is that there is a built-in assumption that the mapping mode is MM_TEXT, which means that the positive *y*-axis is assumed to run from top to bottom. If you change the mapping mode, neither of these will work properly, although it's not immediately obvious that they won't.

Normalized Rectangles

The InflateRect() function works by subtracting the values that you give it from the top and left members of the rectangle and adding the values to the bottom and right. This means that you may find your rectangle actually decreasing in size if you don't make sure that the rectangle is **normalized**. A normalized rectangle has a left value that is less than or equal to the right value, and a top value that is less than or equal to the bottom value. You can make sure that a CRect object is normalized by calling the NormalizeRect() member of the object. Most of the CRect member functions require the object to be normalized for them to work as expected, so you need to make sure that when you store the enclosing rectangle in m_EnclosingRect, it is normalized.

Calculating the Enclosing Rectangle for a Line

All you need now is code in the constructor for a line to calculate the enclosing rectangle:

```
CLine::CLine(CPoint Start, CPoint End, COLORREF aColor)
{
    m_StartPoint = Start;                  // Set line start point
    m_EndPoint = End;                      // Set line end point
    m_Color = aColor;                      // Set line color
    m_Pen = 1;                             // Set pen width

    // Define the enclosing rectangle
    m_EnclosingRect = CRect(Start, End);
    m_EnclosingRect.NormalizeRect();
}
```

The arguments to the CRect constructor you are using here are the start and end points of the line. To ensure that the bounding rectangle has the top value less than the bottom value, regardless of the relative positions of the start and end points of the line, you call the NormalizeRect() member of the m_EnclosingRect object.

The CRectangle Class

Although you'll be defining a rectangle object by the same data that you use to define a line — a start point and an end point on a diagonal of the rectangle — you don't need to store the defining points. The enclosing rectangle in the data member inherited from the base class completely defines the shape, so you don't need any data members. You can therefore define the class like this:

```
// Class defining a rectangle object
class CRectangle: public CElement
{
   public:
      ~CRectangle(void);
      virtual void Draw(CDC* pDC);      // Function to display a rectangle

      // Constructor for a rectangle object
      CRectangle(CPoint Start, CPoint End, COLORREF aColor);

   protected:
      CRectangle(void);                 // Default constructor - should not be used
};
```

The no-arg constructor is now `protected` to prevent it from being used. The definition of the rectangle becomes very simple — just a constructor, the virtual `Draw()` function, plus the no-arg constructor in the `protected` section of the class.

The CRectangle Class Constructor

The code for the new `CRectangle` class constructor is somewhat similar to that for a `CLine` constructor:

```
// CRectangle class constructor
CRectangle:: CRectangle(CPoint Start, CPoint End, COLORREF aColor)
{
   m_Color = aColor;          // Set rectangle color
   m_Pen = 1;                 // Set pen width

   // Define the enclosing rectangle
   m_EnclosingRect = CRect(Start, End);
   m_EnclosingRect.NormalizeRect();
}
```

If you modified the `CRectangle` class definition manually, there is no skeleton definition for the constructor, so you just need to add the definition directly to `Elements.cpp`.

This is cheap code. Some minor alterations to a subset of the `CLine` constructor, fix the comments, and we have a new constructor for `CRectangle`. It just stores the color and pen width and computes the enclosing rectangle from the points passed as arguments.

Drawing a Rectangle

There is a member of the `CDC` class called `Rectangle()` that draws a rectangle. This function draws a closed figure and fills it with the current brush. You may think that this isn't quite what you want because you want to draw rectangles as outlines only, but by selecting a NULL_BRUSH that is exactly what you will draw. Just so you know, there's also a function PolyLine(), which draws shapes consisting of multiple line segments from an array of points, or you could have used LineTo() again, but the easiest approach is to use the Rectangle() function:

```
// Draw a CRectangle object
void CRectangle::Draw(CDC* pDC)
{
   // Create a pen for this object and
   // initialize it to the object color and line width of 1 pixel
   CPen aPen;
   if(!aPen.CreatePen(PS_SOLID, m_Pen, m_Color))
   {
      // Pen creation failed
      AfxMessageBox(_T("Pen creation failed drawing a rectangle"), MB_OK);
      AfxAbort();
   }

   // Select the pen
   CPen* pOldPen = pDC->SelectObject(&aPen);
   // Select the brush
   CBrush* pOldBrush = (CBrush*)pDC->SelectStockObject(NULL_BRUSH);

   // Now draw the rectangle
   pDC->Rectangle(m_EnclosingRect);

   pDC->SelectObject(pOldBrush);        // Restore the old brush
   pDC->SelectObject(pOldPen);          // Restore the old pen
}
```

After setting up the pen and the brush, you simply pass the whole rectangle directly to the Rectangle() function to get it drawn. All that remains to do is to clear up afterwards and restore the device context's old pen and brush.

The CCircle Class

The interface of the CCircle class is no different from that of the CRectangle class. You can define a circle solely by its enclosing rectangle, so the class definition is:

```
// Class defining a circle object
class CCircle: public CElement
{
   public:
      ~CCircle(void);
      virtual void Draw(CDC* pDC);       // Function to display a circle

      // Constructor for a circle object
      CCircle(CPoint Start, CPoint End, COLORREF aColor);

   protected:
      CCircle(void);                     // Default constructor - should not be used
};
```

You have defined a public constructor that creates a circle from two points, and makes the no-arg constructor as protected again. You have also added a declaration for the draw function to the class definition.

Implementing the CCircle Class

As discussed earlier, when you create a circle, the point where you press the left mouse button is the center, and after moving the cursor with the left button down, the point where you release the cursor is a point on the circumference of the final circle. The job of the constructor is to convert these points into the form used in the class to define a circle.

The CCircle Class Constructor

The point at which you release the left mouse button can be anywhere on the circumference, so the coordinates of the points specifying the enclosing rectangle need to be calculated, as illustrated in Figure 15-18.

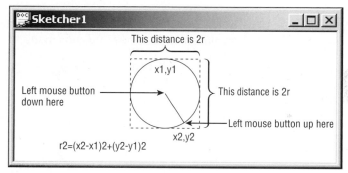

Figure 15-18

From Figure 15-18 you can see that you can calculate the coordinates of the upper-left and lower-right points of the enclosing rectangle relative to the center of the circle (x_1, y_1), which is the point you record when the left mouse button is pressed. Assuming that the mapping mode is MM_TEXT, for the upper-left point you just subtract the radius from each of the coordinates of the center. Similarly, the lower-right point is obtained by adding the radius to the x and y coordinates of the center. You can, therefore, code the constructor as:

```
// Constructor for a circle object
CCircle::CCircle(CPoint Start, CPoint End, COLORREF aColor)
{
   // First calculate the radius
   // We use floating point because that is required by
   // the library function (in math.h) for calculating a square root.
   long Radius = static_cast<long> (sqrt(
                   static_cast<double>((End.x-Start.x)*(End.x-Start.x)+
                                       (End.y-Start.y)*(End.y-Start.y))));

   // Now calculate the rectangle enclosing
   // the circle assuming the MM_TEXT mapping mode
   m_EnclosingRect = CRect(Start.x-Radius, Start.y-Radius,
                           Start.x+Radius, Start.y+Radius);

   m_Color = aColor;                  // Set the color for the circle
   m_Pen = 1;                         // Set pen width to 1
}
```

To use the `sqrt()` function, you must add the line to the beginning of the `Elements.cpp` file:

```
#include <cmath>
```

You can place this after the `#include` directive for `stdafx.h`.

The maximum coordinate values are 32 bits, and the `CPoint` members x and y are declared as `long`, so evaluating the argument to the `sqrt()` function can safely be carried out as an integer. The result of the square root calculation is of type `double`, so you cast it to `long` because you want to use it as an integer.

Drawing a Circle

You have already seen how to draw a circle using the `Arc()` function in the `CDC` class, so now use the `Ellipse()` function here. The implementation of the `Draw()` function in the `CCircle` class is:

```cpp
// Draw a circle
void CCircle::Draw(CDC* pDC)
{
   // Create a pen for this object and
   // initialize it to the object color and line width of 1 pixel
   CPen aPen;
   if(!aPen.CreatePen(PS_SOLID, m_Pen, m_Color))
   {
      // Pen creation failed
      AfxMessageBox(_T("Pen creation failed drawing a circle"), MB_OK);
      AfxAbort();
   }

   CPen* pOldPen = pDC->SelectObject(&aPen);   // Select the pen

   // Select a null brush
   CBrush* pOldBrush = (CBrush*)pDC->SelectStockObject(NULL_BRUSH);

   // Now draw the circle
   pDC->Ellipse(m_EnclosingRect);

   pDC->SelectObject(pOldPen);                 // Restore the old pen
   pDC->SelectObject(pOldBrush);               // Restore the old brush
}
```

After selecting a pen of the appropriate color and a null brush, the circle is drawn by calling the `Ellipse()` function. The only argument is a `CRect` object that encloses the circle you draw. This is another example of code that's almost for free because it's similar to the code you wrote earlier to draw a rectangle.

The CCurve Class

The `CCurve` class is different from the others in that it needs to be able to deal with a variable number of defining points. This necessitates maintaining a list of some kind and although you could use the STL template to define a list, this has the disadvantage that the list will not be serializable. Because you will look at how you can create lists that are serializable in the next chapter, I'll defer defining the detail of this class until then. For now, you can include a class definition that provides dummy member functions so you can compile and link code that contains calls to them. In `Elements.h`, you should have:

```
class CCurve: public CElement
{
    public:
        ~CCurve(void);
        virtual void Draw(CDC* pDC); // Function to display a curve

        // Constructor for a curve object
        CCurve(COLORREF aColor);

    protected:
        CCurve(void);                          // Default constructor - should not be used
};
```

And in `Elements.cpp`:

```
// Constructor for a curve object
CCurve::CCurve(COLORREF aColor)
{
    m_Color = aColor;
    m_EnclosingRect = CRect(0,0,0,0);
    m_Pen = 1;
}
```

```
// Draw a curve
void CCurve::Draw(CDC* pDC)
{
}
```

Neither the constructor nor the `Draw()` member function does anything useful yet, and you have no data members to define a curve. The constructor just sets the color, sets `m_EnclosingRect` to an empty rectangle, and sets the pen width. You'll expand the class into a working version in the next chapter.

Completing the Mouse Message Handlers

You can now come back to the `WM_MOUSEMOVE` message handler and fill out the detail. You can get to it through selecting `CSketcherView` in the Class View and double-clicking the handler name, `OnMouseMove()`.

This handler is concerned only with drawing a succession of temporary versions of an element as you move the cursor because the final element is created when you release the left mouse button. You can therefore treat the drawing of temporary elements to provide rubber-banding as being entirely local to this function, leaving the final version of the element that is created to be drawn by the `OnDraw()` function member of the view. This approach results in the drawing of the rubber-banded elements being reasonably efficient because it won't involve the `OnDraw()` function that ultimately is responsible for drawing the entire document.

You can do this best with the help of a member of the `CDC` class that is particularly effective in rubber-banding operations: `SetROP2()`.

Setting the Drawing Mode

The `SetROP2()` function sets the **drawing mode** for all subsequent output operations in the device context associated with a **CDC** object. The 'ROP' bit of the function name stands for **R**aster **OP**eration because the setting of drawing modes applies to raster displays. In case you're wondering, 'What's `SetROP1()` then?' — there isn't one. The function name represents 'Set Raster OPeration **to**', not 2!

The drawing mode determines how the color of the pen that you use for drawing is to combine with the background color to produce the color of the entity you are displaying. You specify the drawing mode with a single argument to the function that can be any of the following values:

Drawing Mode	Effect
R2_BLACK	All drawing is in black.
R2_WHITE	All drawing is in white.
R2_NOP	Drawing operations do nothing.
R2_NOT	Drawing is in the inverse of the screen color. This ensures the output is always visible because it prevents drawing in the same color as the background.
R2_COPYPEN	Drawing is in the pen color. This is the default drawing mode if you don't set it.
R2_NOTCOPYPEN	Drawing is in the inverse of the pen color.
R2_MERGEPENNOT	Drawing is in the color produced by ORing the pen color with the inverse of the background color.
R2_MASKPENNOT	Drawing is in the color produced by ANDing the pen color with the inverse of the background color.
R2_MERGENOTPEN	Drawing is in the color produced by ORing the background color with the inverse of the pen color.
R2_MASKNOTPEN	Drawing is in the color produced by ANDing the background color with the inverse of the pen color.
R2_MERGEPEN	Drawing is in the color produced by ORing the background color with the pen color.
R2_NOTMERGEPEN	Drawing is in the color that is the inverse of the R2_MERGEPEN color.
R2_MASKPEN	Drawing is in the color produced by ANDing the background color with the pen color.
R2_NOTMASKPEN	Drawing is in the color that is the inverse of the R2_MASKPEN color.
R2_XORPEN	Drawing is in the color produced by exclusive ORing the pen color and the background color.
R2_NOTXORPEN	Drawing is in the color that is the inverse of the R2_XORPEN color.

Each of these symbols is predefined and corresponds to a particular drawing mode. There are a lot of options here, but the one that can work some magic for us is the last of them, R2_NOTXORPEN.

When you set the mode as R2_NOTXORPEN, the first time you draw a particular shape on the default white background, it is drawn normally in the pen color you specify. If you draw the same shape again, over-writing the first, the shape disappears because the color that the shape is drawn in corresponds to that produced by exclusive ORing the pen color with itself. The drawing color that results from this is white. You can see this more clearly by working through an example.

White is formed from equal proportions of the "maximum" amounts of red, blue, and green. For simplicity, this can be represented as 1,1,1 — the three values represent the RGB components of the color. In the same scheme, red is defined as 1,0,0. These combine as follows:

	R	G	B
Background — white	1	1	1
Pen — red	1	0	0
XORed	0	1	1
NOT XOR — produces red	1	0	0

So, the first time you draw a red line on a white background, it comes out red as the last line above indicates. If you now draw the same line a second time, overwriting the existing line, the background pixels you are writing over are red. The resultant drawing color works out as follows:

	R	G	B
Background — red	1	0	0
Pen — red	1	0	0
XORed	0	0	0
NOT XOR — produces white	1	1	1

As the last line indicates the line comes out as white and because the rest of the background is white, the line disappears.

You need to take care to use the right background color here. You should be able to see that drawing with a white pen on a red background is not going to work too well, as the first time you draw something it is red, and therefore invisible. The second time it appears as white. If you draw on a black background, things appear and disappear, as on a white background, but they are not drawn in the pen color you choose.

Coding the OnMouseMove() Handler

Start by adding the code that creates the element after a mouse move message. Because you are going to draw the element from the handler function, you need to create an object for the device context. The most convenient class to use for this is CClientDC, which is derived from CDC. As I said earlier, the advantage of using this class rather than CDC is that it automatically takes care of creating the device context for you and destroying it when you are done. The device context that it creates corresponds to the client area of a window, which is exactly what you want. Add the following code to the outline handler that you defined earlier:

```cpp
void CSketcherView::OnMouseMove(UINT nFlags, CPoint point)
{
    // Define a Device Context object for the view
    CClientDC aDC(this);                    // DC is for this view
    aDC.SetROP2(R2_NOTXORPEN);              // Set the drawing mode
    if(nFlags & MK_LBUTTON)
    {
        m_SecondPoint = point;              // Save the current cursor position
        // Test for a previous temporary element
        {
            // We get to here if there was a previous mouse move
            // so add code to delete the old element
        }

        // Create a temporary element of the type and color that
        // is recorded in the document object, and draw it
        m_pTempElement = CreateElement();// Create a new element
        m_pTempElement->Draw(&aDC);         // Draw the element
    }
}
```

The first new line of code creates a local CClientDC object. The this pointer that you pass to the constructor identifies the current view object, so the CClientDC object has a device context that corresponds to the client area of the current view. As well as the characteristics I mentioned, this object has all the drawing functions you need because they are inherited from the CDC class. The first member function you use is SetROP2(), which sets the drawing mode to R2_NOTXORPEN.

To create a new element, you save the current cursor position in the data member m_SecondPoint, and then call a view member function CreateElement(). (You'll define the CreateElement() function as soon as you have finished this handler.) This function should create an element using the two points stored in the current view object, with the color and type specification stored in the document object, and return the address of the element. Save this in m_pTempElement.

Using the pointer to the new element, you call its Draw() member to get the object to draw itself. The address of the CClientDC object is passed as an argument. Because you defined the Draw() function as virtual in the base class, CElement, the function for whatever type of element m_pTempElement is pointing to is automatically selected. The new element is drawn normally with the R2_NOTXORPEN because you are drawing it for the first time on a white background.

You can use the pointer m_pTempElement as an indicator of whether a previous temporary element exists. The code for this part of the handler is:

```cpp
void CSketcherView::OnMouseMove(UINT nFlags, CPoint point)
{
    // Define a Device Context object for the view
```

```
        CClientDC aDC(this);               // DC is for this view
        aDC.SetROP2(R2_NOTXORPEN);         // Set the drawing mode
        if(nFlags&MK_LBUTTON)
        {
            m_SecondPoint = point;         // Save the current cursor position

            if(m_pTempElement)
            {
                // Redraw the old element so it disappears from the view
                m_pTempElement->Draw(&aDC);
                delete m_pTempElement;     // Delete the old element
                m_pTempElement = 0;        // Reset the pointer to 0
            }

            // Create a temporary element of the type and color that
            // is recorded in the document object, and draw it
            m_pTempElement = CreateElement();// Create a new element
            m_pTempElement->Draw(&aDC);    // Draw the element
        }
    }
```

A previous temporary element exists if the pointer m_pTempElement is not zero. You need to redraw the element to which it points to remove it from the client area of the view. You then delete the element and reset the pointer to zero. The new element is then created and drawn by the code that you added previously. This combination automatically rubber-bands the shape being created, so it appears to be attached to the cursor position as it moves. You must not forget to reset the pointer m_pTempElement back to 0 in the WM_LBUTTONUP message handler after you create the final version of the element.

Creating an Element

You should add the CreateElement() function as a protected member to the 'Operations' section of the CSketcherView class:

```
class CSketcherView: public CView
{

    // Rest of the class definition as before...

    // Operations
    public:

    protected:
        CElement* CreateElement(void);    // Create a new element on the heap

      // Rest of the class definition as before...

};
```

To do this you can either amend the class definition directly by adding the shaded line, or you can right-click on the class name, CSketcherView, in Class View, and select Add > Add Function from the context menu. This opens the dialog shown in Figure 15-19.

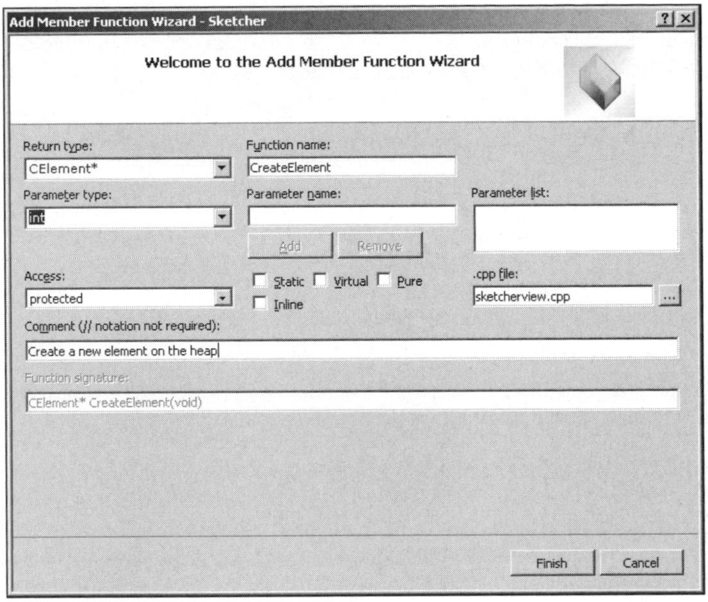

Figure 15-19

Add the specifications of the function, as shown, and click the Finish button. A declaration for the function member is added to the class definition and you are taken directly to a skeleton for the function in SketcherView.cpp. If you added the declaration to the class definition manually, you'll need to add the complete definition for the function to the .cpp file. This is:

```cpp
// Create an element of the current type
CElement* CSketcherView::CreateElement(void)
{
    // Get a pointer to the document for this view
    CSketcherDoc* pDoc = GetDocument();
    ASSERT_VALID(pDoc);                    // Verify the pointer is good

    // Now select the element using the type stored in the document
    switch(pDoc->GetElementType())
    {
    case RECTANGLE:
        return new CRectangle(m_FirstPoint, m_SecondPoint,
                                            pDoc->GetElementColor());

    case CIRCLE:
        return new CCircle(m_FirstPoint, m_SecondPoint,
                                        pDoc->GetElementColor());

    case CURVE:
        return new CCurve(pDoc->GetElementColor());

    case LINE:
        return new CLine(m_FirstPoint, m_SecondPoint,
                                        pDoc->GetElementColor());
```

```
        default:
            // Something's gone wrong
            AfxMessageBox(_T("Bad Element code"), MB_OK);
            AfxAbort();
            return NULL;
    }
}
```

The lines that aren't shaded are those that will have been supplied automatically if you added the function to the class using the Add > Add Function dialog. The first thing you do here is get a pointer to the document by calling GetDocument(), as you've seen before. For safety, you use the ASSERT_VALID() macro to ensure that a good pointer is returned. In the debug version of MFC that's used in the debug version of your application, this macro calls the AssertValid() member of the object, which is specified as the argument to the macro. This checks the validity of the current object, and if the pointer is NULL or the object is defective in some way, an error message is displayed. In the release version of MFC, the ASSERT_VALID() macro does nothing.

The switch statement selects the element to be created based on the type returned by a function in the document class, GetElementType(). Another function in the document class is used to obtain the current element color. You can add the definitions for both these functions directly to the CSketcherDoc class definition because they are very simple:

```
class CSketcherDoc: public CDocument
{

    // Rest of the class definition as before...

    // Operations
public:
        unsigned int GetElementType()      // Get the element type
            { return m_Element; }
        COLORREF GetElementColor()         // Get the element color
            { return m_Color; }

    // Rest of the class definition as before...

};
```

Each of the functions returns the value stored in the corresponding data member. Remember that putting a member function definition in the class definition is equivalent to a request to make the function inline; so as well as being simple, these should be fast.

Dealing with WM_LBUTTONUP Messages

The WM_LBUTTONUP message completes the process of creating an element. The job of the handler for this message is to pass the final version of the element that was created to the document object, and then clean up the view object data members. You can access and edit the code for this handler in the same way as you did for the previous one. Add the following lines to the function:

```
void CSketcherView::OnLButtonUp(UINT nFlags, CPoint point)
{
    // Make sure there is an element
    if(m_pTempElement)
```

```
    {
        // Call a document class function to store the element
        // pointed to by m_pTempElement in the document object

        delete m_pTempElement;        // This code is temporary
        m_pTempElement = 0;           // Reset the element pointer
    }
}
```

The if statement verifies that m_pTempElement is not zero before processing it. It's always possible that the user could press and release the left mouse button without moving the mouse, in which case no element would have been created. As long as there is an element, the pointer to the element is passed to the document object; you'll add the code for this in the next chapter. In the meantime, you just delete the element here so as not to pollute the heap. Finally, the m_pTempElement pointer is reset to 0, ready for the next time the user draws an element.

Exercising Sketcher

Before you can run the example with the mouse message handlers, you must update the OnDraw() function in the CSketcherView class implementation to get rid of any old code that you added earlier.

To make sure that the OnDraw() function is clean, go to Class View and double-click the function name to take you to its implementation in SketcherView.cpp. Delete any old code that you added, but leave in the first four lines that the wizard provided to get a pointer to the document object. You'll need this later to get to the elements when they're stored in the document. The code for the function should now be:

```
void CSketcherView::OnDraw(CDC* pDC)
{
    CSketcherDoc* pDoc = GetDocument();
    ASSERT_VALID(pDoc);
    if(!pDoc)
        return;
}
```

Because you have no elements in the document as yet, you don't need to add anything to this function at this point. When you start storing data in the document in the next chapter, you'll add code to draw the elements in response to a WM_PAINT message. Without it, the elements just disappear whenever you resize the view, as you'll see.

Running the Example

After making sure that you have saved all the source files, build the program. If you haven't made any mistakes entering the code, you'll get a clean compile and link, so you can execute the program. You can draw lines, circles and rectangles in any of the four colors the program supports. A typical window is shown in Figure 15-20.

Try experimenting with the user interface. Note that you can move the window around and that the shapes stay in the window as long as you don't move it so far that they're outside the borders of the application window. If you do, the elements do not reappear after you move it back. This is because the existing elements are never redrawn. When the client area is covered and uncovered, Windows sends a WM_PAINT message to the application that causes the OnDraw() member of the view object to be called. As you know, the OnDraw() function for the view doesn't do anything at present. This gets fixed when you use the document to store the elements.

Figure 15-20

When you resize the view window, the shapes disappear immediately, but when you move the whole view around, they remain (as long as they don't slide beyond the application window border). How come? Well, when you resize the window, Windows invalidates the whole client area and expects your application to redraw it in response to the WM_PAINT message. If you move the view around, Windows takes care of relocating the client area as it is. You can demonstrate this by moving the view so that a shape is partially obscured. When you slide it back, you still have a partial shape, with the bit that was obscured erased.

If you try drawing a shape while dragging the cursor outside the client view area, you'll notice some peculiar effects. Outside the view window, you lose track of the mouse, which tends to mess up the rubber-banding mechanism. What's going on?

Capturing Mouse Messages

The problem is caused by the fact that Windows is sending the mouse messages to the window under the cursor. As soon as the cursor leaves the client area of your application view window, the WM_MOUSEMOVE messages are being sent elsewhere. You can fix this by using some inherited members of the CSketcherView class.

The view class inherits a function, SetCapture(), which you can call to tell Windows that you want your view window to get *all* the mouse messages until such time as you say otherwise, by calling another inherited function in the view class, ReleaseCapture(). You can capture the mouse as soon as the left button is pressed by modifying the handler for the WM_LBUTTONDOWN message:

```
// Handler for left mouse button down message
void CSketcherView::OnLButtonDown(UINT nFlags, CPoint point)
{
```

```
        m_FirstPoint = point;              // Record the cursor position
        SetCapture();                      // Capture subsequent mouse messages
    }
```

Now you must call the `ReleaseCapture()` function in the WM_LBUTTONUP handler. If you don't do this, other programs cannot receive any mouse messages as long as your program continues to run. Of course, you should only release the mouse if you've captured it earlier. The `GetCapture()` function that the view class inherits returns a pointer to the window that has captured the mouse, and this gives you a way of telling whether or not you have captured mouse messages. You just need to add the following to the handler for WM_LBUTTONUP:

```
void CSketcherView::OnLButtonUp(UINT nFlags, CPoint point)
{
    if(this == GetCapture())
        ReleaseCapture();            // Stop capturing mouse messages

    // Make sure there is an element
    if(m_pTempElement)
    {
        // Call a document class function to store the element
        // pointed to by m_pTempElement in the document object

      delete m_pTempElement;    // This code is temporary
        m_pTempElement = 0;       // Reset the element pointer
    }
}
```

If the pointer returned by the `GetCapture()` function is equal to the pointer **this**, your view has captured the mouse, so you release it.

The final alteration you should make is to modify the WM_MOUSEMOVE handler so that it only deals with messages that have been captured by the view. You can do this with one small change:

```
void CSketcherView::OnMouseMove(UINT nFlags, CPoint point)
{
    // Define a Device Context object for the view
    CClientDC aDC(this);                  // DC is for this view
    aDC.SetROP2(R2_NOTXORPEN);            // Set the drawing mode
    if((nFlags & MK_LBUTTON) && (this == GetCapture()))
    {
        m_SecondPoint = point;            // Save the current cursor position

        if(m_pTempElement)
        {
            // Redraw the old element so it disappears from the view
            m_pTempElement->Draw(&aDC);
            delete m_pTempElement;        // Delete the old element
            m_pTempElement = 0;           // Reset the pointer to 0
        }

        // Create a temporary element of the type and color that
        // is recorded in the document object, and draw it
```

```
    m_pTempElement = CreateElement();// Create a new element
    m_pTempElement->Draw(&aDC);       // Draw the element
  }
}
```

The handler now processes only the message if the left button is down *and* the left button down handler for your view has been called, so that the mouse has been captured by your view window.

If you rebuild Sketcher with these additions, you'll find that the problems that arose earlier when the cursor was dragged off the client area no longer occur.

Drawing with the CLR

It's time to augment the CLRSketcher application from the previous chapter with some drawing capability. I won't discuss the principles of drawing shapes using the mouse again because they are essentially the same in both environments.

The MFC is a set of classes that wraps the Windows API, so inevitably most of the processes are very similar to the Windows API. Of course, the CLR is a virtual machine that insulates you from the host environment, so there is no need for the CLR to follow the patterns for handling events and drawing in a window that are in the Windows API. There are significant differences as you'll see, but it is not so far from the way that the MFC works that you will have any problems understanding it. Indeed, in a CLR program things are typically somewhat simpler.

Drawing on a Form

In a CLR program you have none of the complications of mapping modes when you are drawing on a form. The origin for drawing purposes is at the top left of the form with the positive *x*-axis running from left to right and the positive *y*-axis running from top to bottom. The classes that enable you to draw on a form are within the System::Drawing namespace and drawing on the form is carried out by a function in the Form1 class that handles the Paint event. Right-click on the form in the Design window for CLR Sketcher and select Properties from the pop-up. Select the Events button to display the events for the form and double-click the Paint event; it's the only event in the Appearance group in the Properties window. This generates the Form1_Paint() function that will be called in response to a Paint event that occurs when the form must be redrawn. You'll implement this method to draw a sketch in the next chapter.

One thing you can do at this point is to change the background color for the form. By default the background color is a shade of gray that is not ideal as a drawing background and it would be better a shade of white. Change the value of the BackColor property in the Properties window by selecting ControlLightLight from the drop-down list to the right. The form will now display with a nice white background to draw on.

Adding Mouse Event Handlers

As I said, the drawing principles in CLR Sketcher are essentially the same as in MFC Sketcher so you need handlers for the corresponding mouse events. If you scroll down the list of events in the Form1 Properties window you can find the Mouse group of events, as shown in Figure 15-21.

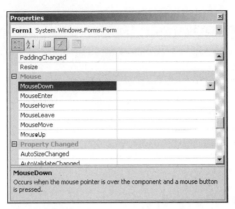

Figure 15-21

The ones that are of particular interest for drawing operations are the MouseDown, MouseMove, and MouseUp events. The MouseDown event occurs when a mouse button is pressed and you determine which mouse button from information passed to the event handler. Similarly, the MouseUp event occurs when any mouse button is released and the arguments passed to the handler for the event enable you to figure out which. You need handlers for these two events as well as the MouseMove event, so double-click each of these events in the Properties window to generate the event handler functions for them. The handler for the MouseDown event looks like this:

```
private: System::Void Form1_MouseDown(
System::Object^  sender, System::Windows::Forms::MouseEventArgs^  e)
{
}
```

The first parameter identifies the source of the event and the second parameter provides information about the event itself. The MouseEventArgs object that is passed to this handler function (in fact all of the mouse event handlers have a parameter of this type) contains several properties that provide information you can use in handling the event, and these are described in the following table.

Property Name	Description
Button	A property of enum type System::Windows::Forms::MouseButtons that identifies which mouse button was pressed. The MouseButtons enum defines the following possible values for the property: MouseButtons::Left: The left mouse. MouseButtons::Right: The right mouse. MouseButtons::None: No mouse button was pressed. MouseButtons::Middle: The middle mouse button. MouseButtons::XButton1: The first XButton. MouseButtons::XButton2: The second XButton.
Location	A property of type System::Drawing::Point that identifies the location of the mouse cursor. The X and Y properties of a Point object are the integer *x* and *y* coordinate values.

Property Name	Description
X	The *x* coordinate of the mouse cursor as a value of type int.
Y	The *y* coordinate of the mouse cursor as a value of type int.
Clicks	A count of the number of times the mouse button was pressed and released as a value of type int.
Delta	A signed count of the number of detents the mouse wheel has rotated as a value of type int.

Following the same logic as you used in the MFC Sketcher program, the MouseDown event handler needs to check that the left mouse button is pressed and record the current cursor position somewhere for use in the MouseMove handler. It also should record that drawing an element is in progress. To support this you can add two private data members to the Form1 class, a bool variable with the name drawing to record when drawing an element is in progress, and a variable of type Point with the name firstPoint to record the initial mouse cursor position. You can do this manually, or from Class View using the Add > Add Variable... capability. Make sure that the variables are initialized by the Form1 constructor, drawing to false and firstPoint to 0; the wizard should insert this automatically. The Point class is defined in the System::Drawing namespace, so you should add the following using directive at the end of the others in Form1.h:

```
using namespace System::Drawing;
```

You can now add the code for the MouseDown delegate like this:

```
private: System::Void Form1_MouseDown(
System::Object^  sender, System::Windows::Forms::MouseEventArgs^  e)
{
  if(e->Button == System::Windows::Forms::MouseButtons::Left)
  {
    drawing = true;
    firstPoint = e->Location;
  }
}
```

As long as the left mouse button is pressed, drawing an element has started so you set drawing to true. The Location property for the parameter e supplies the cursor location as a Point object so you can store it directly in firstPoint.

The MouseMove event handler will take care of creating elements for the sketch and the MouseUp event handler will finalize the process, but before you complete the code for these two mouse event handlers you need to take a little diversion to define the classes that encapsulate the elements you can draw.

Defining C++/CLI Element Classes

The pattern for the classes that define elements will be similar to those in the MFC version of Sketcher; an Element base class with the specific element types defined by classes derived from Element. Go to the Solution Explorer window, right-click on the Header Files folder and select Add > New Item...

from the pop-up. Use the dialog to add a header file with the name `Elements.h`. Add the code for `Element` base class definition to `Elements.h` like this:

```cpp
// Elements.h
// Defines element types
#pragma once

using namespace System;
using namespace System::Drawing;

namespace CLRSketcher
{

  public ref class Element abstract
  {
  protected:
    Point position;
    Color color;
    System::Drawing::Rectangle boundRect;

  public:
    virtual void Draw(Graphics^ g) abstract;
  };
}
```

You are using classes from the `System` and `System::Drawing` namespaces in the element class definitions so there are `using` directives for both. The code for the application is defined within the `CLRSketcher` namespace, so you put the definitions for the element classes in the same namespace. The `Element` class and its subclasses have to be ref classes because value classes cannot be derived classes. The `Element` class also must be defined as `abstract` because there is no implementation for the `Draw()` function. The `Draw()` function will be overridden in each of the derived classes to draw a specific type of element and you will call the function polymorphically, just as you did in MFC Sketcher.

The `position` member is of type `System::Drawing::Point`, which is a value type that defines a point object with two members `X` and `Y`. The `position`, `color`, and `boundRect` members will be inherited in the derived classes and will store the position of the element, the element color, and the bounding rectangle for the element. All elements will be drawn relative to the point `position`. For the moment you won't worry about the distinction between a bounding rectangle and an enclosing rectangle. Incidentally, the type name for the `boundRect` variable, `System::Drawing::Rectangle`, is fully qualified here because you will add a derived class with the name `Rectangle`; without the qualified name here, the compiler would assume you mean the `Rectangle` class in this header file, which is not what you want.

Defining a Line

Next you can add an initial definition for the `Line` class to `Elements.h`. Make sure you add this code before the closing brace for the `CLRSketcher` namespace block:

```cpp
public ref class Line : Element
{
  protected:
    Point end;

  public:
```

```
    // Constructor
    Line(Color color, Point start, Point end)
    {
      this->color = color;
      position = start;
      this->end = end;
      boundRect = System::Drawing::Rectangle(Math::Min(position.X, end.X),
                                          Math::Min(position.Y, end.Y),
                  Math::Abs(position.X - end.X), Math::Abs(position.Y - end.Y));

      // Provide for lines that are horizontal or vertical
      if(boundRect.Width < 2) boundRect.Width = 2;
      if(boundRect.Height < 2) boundRect.Height = 2;
    }

    // Function to draw a line
    virtual void Draw(Graphics^ g) override
    {
      // Code to draw a line...
    }
};
```

The constructor sets the value for the color member that is inherited from the base class. It also stores the start and end points of the line that are passed as arguments in the inherited `position` member and the end member respectively. The inherited `boundRect` member is initialized from the `position` and the end points. You have several ways to create a `System::Drawing::Rectangle` object. Here, the first two arguments to the `Rectangle` constructor are the coordinates of the top-left corner of the rectangle. The third and fourth arguments are the width and height of the rectangle. You use the `Min()` function from the `System::Math` class to obtain the minimum values of the coordinates of `position` and `end` and the `Abs()` function to obtain the absolute (positive) value for the difference between pairs of corresponding coordinates to get the width and height. The `Math` class defines several other static utility functions that are very handy when you want to carry out basic mathematical operations.

If a line is exactly horizontal or vertical, the bounding rectangle will have a width or height that is zero so the last two `if` statements in the constructor ensure that the rectangle always has a width and height greater than zero.

Defining a Color

`System::Drawing::Color` is a value class that encapsulates an ARGB color value. An ARGB color is a 32-bit value comprising four 8-bit components, an **a**lpha component that determines transparency and three primary color components, **r**ed, **g**reen and **b**lue. Each of the component values can be from 0 to 255 where an alpha of 0 is completely transparent and an alpha of 255 is completely opaque; an 8-bit color component value represents the intensity of that color where 0 is zero intensity (i.e., no color) and 255 is the maximum. A lot of the time you can make use of standard color constants that the `Color` class defines such as `Color::Blue` or `Color::Red`. If you look at the documentation for members of the `Color` class, you'll see the complete set.

Drawing Lines

The `Draw()` function will use the `System::Drawing::Graphics` object that is passed as the argument to draw the line in the appropriate color. The `Graphics` class defines a large number of functions that you use for drawing shapes, including those in the following table.

Function	Description
`DrawLine(Pen pen,` `        Point p1, Point p2)`	Draws a line from p1 to p2 using pen. A Pen object draws in a specific color and line thickness.

`DrawLine(Pen pen,`
`        int x1, int y1,`
`        int x2, int y2)`
	Draws a line from (x1,y1) to (x2,y2) using pen.

`DrawLines(Pen pen, Point[] pts)`	Draws a series of lines connecting the points in the pts array using pen.
`DrawRectangle(Pen pen,` `             Rectangle rect)`	Draws the rectangle rect using pen.

`DrawRectangle(Pen pen,`
`             int X, int Y,`
`             int width, int height)`
	Draws a rectangle at (x,y) using pen with the rectangle dimensions specified by width and height.

`DrawEllipse(Pen pen,` `            Rectangle rect)`	Draws the ellipse that is specified by the bounding rectangle rect using pen.

`DrawEllipse(Pen pen,`
`            int x, int y,`
`            int width, int height)`
	Draws an ellipse using pen. The ellipse is specified by the bounding rectangle at (x,y) with the dimensions width and height.

In each case the `Pen` parameter determines the color and style of line used to draw the shape so we'll explore the `Pen` class in a little more depth.

Defining a Pen for Drawing

The `System::Drawing::Pen` class represents a pen for drawing lines and curves. The simplest `Pen` object draws in a specified color with a default line width, for example:

```
Pen^ pen = gcnew Pen(Color::CornflowerBlue);
```

This defines a `Pen` object that you can use to draw in cornflower blue.

You can also define a `Pen` with a second argument to the constructor that defines the thickness of the line as a `float` value:

```
Pen^ pen = gcnew Pen(Color::Green, 2.0f);
```

This defines a `Pen` object that will draw green lines with a thickness of 2.0f. Note that the pen width is a public property so you can always set the width for a given `Pen` object explicitly:

```
pen->Width = 3.0f;
```

You could now conceivably complete the definition of the `Draw()` function in the `Line` class, like this:

```
virtual void Draw(Graphics^ g) override
```

```
    {
        g->DrawLine(gcnew Pen(color), position, end);
    }
```

This implementation of the function draws a line from `position` to `end` with a default line width of 1 and in the color specified by `color`. However, don't add this to CLR Sketcher yet as there's a better approach.

The default `Pen` object draws a continuous line of a default thickness of 1.0f but you can draw other types of line by setting properties for a `Pen` object; the following table shows `Pen` properties.

Pen Property	Description
Color	Gets or sets the color of the pen as a value of type `System::Drawing::Color`. For example, to set the drawing color for a `Pen` object, pen, to red, you set the property like this: `pen->Color = Color::Red;`
Width	Gets or sets the width of the line drawn by the pen as a value of type `float`.

DashPattern	Gets or sets an array of `float` values specifying a dash pattern for a line. The array values specify the lengths of alternating dashes and spaces in a line. For example:
	
	`array<float>^ pattern = { 5.0f, 2.0f, 4.0f, 3.0f};`
	`pen->DashPattern = pattern;`
	
	This defines a pattern that will be a dash of length 5 followed by a space of length 2 followed by a dash of length 4 followed by a space of length 3; the pattern repeats as often as necessary along a line.

DashOffset	Specifies the distance from the start of a line to the beginning of a dash pattern as a value of type `float`.

StartCap	Specifies the cap style for the start of a line. Cap styles are defined by the `System::Drawing::Drawing2D::LineCap` enumeration that defines the following possible values:
	
	`Flat, Square, Round, Triangle, NoAnchor, SquareAnchor, RoundAnchor, DiamondAnchor, ArrowAnchor, Custom, AnchorMask`
	
	For example, to draw lines with a round line cap at the start you set the property like this:
	
	`pen->StartCap =`
	`        System::Drawing::Drawing2D::LineCap::Round;`

EndCap	Specifies the cap style for the end of a line. The possible values for the cap style for the end of a line are the same as for `StartCap`.

When you are drawing with different line styles and colors, you have the option of creating a new `Pen` object for each drawing operation or using a single `Pen` object and changing the properties to provide the line that you want. It will be useful later to adopt the latter approach in CLR Sketcher, so add a protected `Pen` member to the `Element` base class:

```
Pen^ pen;
```

This will be inherited in each of the concrete derived classes and each derived class constructor will initialize the pen member appropriately. This will avoid having to create a new `Pen` object each time an element is drawn. Modify the `Line` class constructor like this:

```
Line(Color color, Point start, Point end)
{
  pen = gcnew Pen(color);
  this->color = color;
  position = start;
  this->end = end;
  boundRect = System::Drawing::Rectangle(Math::Min(position.X, end.X),
                                         Math::Min(position.Y, end.Y),
              Math::Abs(position.X - end.X), Math::Abs(position.Y - end.Y));
}
```

With the pen set up, you can now implement the `Draw()` function for the `Line` class:

```
virtual void Draw(Graphics^ g) override
{
  g->DrawLine(pen, position, end);
}
```

It's important to the performance of the application that the `Draw()` function does not carry excess overhead when it executes because it will be called many times, sometimes very frequently. Now the `Draw()` function doesn't create a new `Pen` object each time it is called. A positive side effect is that adding the ability to draw using different line styles would now be a piece of cake because all that's needed is to change the pen's properties.

Standard Pens

Sometimes you don't want full flexibility to change the properties of a `Pen` object you use. The `System::Drawing::Pens` class defines a large number of standard pens that draw a line of width 1 in a given color. For example, `Pens::Black` and `Pens::Beige` are standard pens that draw in black and beige respectively. Note that you cannot modify a standard pen — what you see is what you get. Consult the documentation for the `Pens` class for the full list of standard pen colors.

Defining a Rectangle

Add the definition of the class encapsulating CLR Sketcher rectangles to `Elements.h`:

```
public ref class Rectangle : Element
{
protected:
  int width;
  int height;
```

```
public:
  Rectangle(Color color, Point p1, Point p2)
  {
    pen = gcnew Pen(color);
    this->color = color;
    position = Point(Math::Min(p1.X, p2.X), Math::Min(p1.Y,p2.Y));
    width = Math::Abs(p1.X - p2.X);
    height = Math::Abs(p1.Y - p2.Y);
    boundRect = System::Drawing::Rectangle(position, Size(width, height));
  }

    virtual void Draw(Graphics^ g) override
  {
    g->DrawRectangle(pen, position.X, position.Y, width, height);
  }
};
```

A rectangle is defined by the top-left corner position and the width and height so you have defined class members to store these. As in the MFC version of Sketcher, you need to figure out the coordinates of the top-left corner of the rectangle from the points supplied to the constructor. Here you define the value of the inherited `boundRect` member of the class as a `System::Drawing::Rectangle` using a constructor that accepts a `Point` object specifying the top-left corner as the first argument. The second argument is a `System::Drawing::Size` object encapsulating the width and height of the rectangle. The `Draw()` function draws the rectangle on the form using the `DrawRectangle()` function for the `Graphics` object, g, which is passed to the `Draw()` function.

Defining a Circle

The definition of the `Circle` class in `Elements.h` is also very straightforward:

```
public ref class Circle : Element
{
protected:
  int width;
  int height;

public:
  Circle(Color color, Point center, Point circum)
  {
    pen = gcnew Pen(color);
    this->color = color;
    int radius = safe_cast<int>(Math::Sqrt(
                (center.X-circum.X)*(center.X-circum.X) +
                            (center.Y-circum.Y)*(center.Y-circum.Y)));
    position = Point(center.X - radius, center.Y - radius);
    width = height = 2*radius;
    boundRect = System::Drawing::Rectangle(position, Size(width, height));
  }

  virtual void Draw(Graphics^ g) override
  {
    g->DrawEllipse(pen, position.X, position.Y, width,height);
  }
};
```

The two points that are passed to the constructor are the center and a point on the circumference of the circle. The radius is the distance between these two points and the `Math::Sqrt()` function calculates this. You need the width and height of the rectangle enclosing the circle to draw it and the value of each of these is twice the radius. To draw the circle you use the `DrawEllipse()` function for the `Graphics` object, g.

A class to represent a curve is a little trickier as you will draw it as a series of line segments joining a set of points. As in the MFC version of Sketcher, you need a way to store an arbitrary number of points in a `Curve` object, so let's defer the problem for both versions of Sketcher and leave the `Curve` class definition to the next chapter.

Implementing the MouseMove Event Handler

The `MouseMove` event handler creates a temporary element object of the current type. Add a private member, `tempElement`, to the `Form1` class of type `Element^` to store the reference to the temporary element and initialize it to `nullptr` in the initialization list for the `Form1` constructor. This temporary element will be stored eventually in the sketch by the `MouseUp` event handler because the `MouseUp` event signals the end of the drawing process for an element but you'll deal with this in the next chapter. Don't forget to add an `#include` directive for the `Elements.h` header at the beginning of the `Form1.h` header file, otherwise the compiler will not recognize the `Element` type and the code won't compile.

You only want to create an element in the `MouseMove` event handler when the `drawing` member of the `Form1` class is `true` because this is how the `MouseDown` event handler records that drawing an element has started. Here's the code for implementing the `MouseMove` event handler that you added to the `Form1` class earlier:

```
private: System::Void Form1_MouseMove(System::Object^ sender,
System::Windows::Forms::MouseEventArgs^ e)
{
  if(drawing)
  {
    switch(elementType)
    {
      case ElementType::LINE:
        tempElement = gcnew Line(color, firstPoint, e->Location);
        break;
      case ElementType::RECTANGLE:
        tempElement = gcnew Rectangle(color, firstPoint, e->Location);
        break;
      case ElementType::CIRCLE:
        tempElement = gcnew Circle(color, firstPoint, e->Location);
        break;
      case ElementType::CURVE:
        // Code to create a Curve element...
        break;
    }
    Invalidate();
  }
}
```

If `drawing` is `false`, the handler does nothing. The `switch` statement determines which type of element is to be created from the `elementType` member of the `Form1` object. Creating lines, rectangles, and circles is very simple, just using the appropriate class constructor. You obtain the current mouse cursor position in the way that you used in the `MouseDown` event handler — by using the `Location` property for the `MouseEventArgs` object. You'll add the code to create a `Curve` element in the next chapter. Calling `Invalidate()` for the `Form1` object causes the form to be redrawn, which results in the `Paint` event handler for the form being called. Obviously this is where you will draw the entire sketch eventually and you'll implement that in the next chapter, too.

Implementing the MouseUp Event Handler

The task of the `MouseUp` event handler is to store the new element in the sketch, to reset `tempElement` back to `nullptr` and the `drawing` indicator back to `false`, and to redraw the sketch. Here's the code to do that:

```
private: System::Void Form1_MouseUp(System::Object^  sender,
System::Windows::Forms::MouseEventArgs^  e)
{
  if(!drawing)
    return;
  if(tempElement)
  {
    // Store the element in the sketch...
    tempElement = nullptr;
//  Invalidate();
  }
  drawing = false;
}
```

If `drawing` is `false`, you return immediately because the element drawing process has not started. The second `if` statement verifies that `tempElement` is not null before adding the element to the sketch. You might think that if you get to here, `tempElement` must exist but this is not so; apart from the fact that drawing a curve is not yet implemented, a user might press the left mouse button and release it immediately, in which case the `MouseMove` handler would not be invoked at all. Of course, you only need to call `Invalidate()` to redraw the form when you have added a new element to the sketch. The call to `Invalidate()` is commented out for the moment because there is no sketch at present and redrawing the form here would cause the temporary element to disappear as soon as you release the mouse button.

Implementing the Paint Event Handler for the Form

The `Paint` event delegate that you generated earlier has two parameters: the first parameter of type `Object^` identifies the source of the event and the second of type `System::Windows::Forms::PaintEventArgs` that provides information about the event, in particular, the `Graphics` property for this parameter provided the `Graphics` object that you use to draw on the form.

You call the `Invalidate()` function for the form in the `MouseUp` event handler to draw the sketch and in the `MouseMove` event handler to draw the temporary element. Therefore the `Paint` event handler must eventually do two things: It must draw the sketch and it must draw the temporary element, but only if there is one. Here's the code:

```
private: System::Void Form1_Paint(System::Object^  sender,
                              System::Windows::Forms::PaintEventArgs^  e)
{
    Graphics^ g = e->Graphics;
    // Code to draw the sketch...
    if(tempElement != nullptr)
        tempElement->Draw(g);
}
```

You initialize the local variable, g, with the value obtained from the Graphics property for the PaintEventArgs object, e. If tempElement is not nullptr, you call the Draw() function to display the element.

Summary

After completing this chapter, you should have a good grasp of how to write message handlers for the mouse, and how to organize drawing operations in your Windows programs. The important points covered in this chapter are:

❑ By default, Windows addresses the client area of a window using a client coordinate system with the origin in the upper-left corner of the client area. The positive x direction is from left to right, and the positive y direction is from top to bottom.

❑ You can only draw in the client area of a window by using a device context.

❑ A device context provides a range of logical coordinate systems called mapping modes for addressing the client area of a window.

❑ The default origin position for a mapping mode is the upper-left corner of the client area. The default mapping mode is MM_TEXT, which provides coordinates measured in pixels. The positive x-axis runs from left to right in this mode, and the positive y-axis from top to bottom.

❑ Your program should always draw the permanent contents of the client area of a window in response to a WM_PAINT message, although temporary entities can be drawn at other times. All the drawing for your application document should be controlled from the OnDraw() member function of a view class. This function is called when a WM_PAINT message is received by your application.

❑ You can identify the part of the client area you want to have redrawn by calling the InvalidateRect() function member of your view class. The area passed as an argument is added by Windows to the total area to be redrawn when the next WM_PAINT message is sent to your application.

❑ Windows sends standard messages to your application for mouse events. You can create handlers to deal with these messages by using ClassWizard.

❑ You can cause all mouse messages to be routed to your application by calling the SetCapture() function in your view class. You must release the mouse when you're finished with it by calling the ReleaseCapture() function. If you fail to do this, other applications are unable to receive mouse messages.

❑ You can implement rubber-banding when creating geometric entities by drawing them in the message handler for mouse movements.

❑ The `SetROP2()` member of the `CDC` class enables you to set drawing modes. Selecting the right drawing mode greatly simplifies rubber-banding operations.

❑ GUI elements for a CLR program can be created interactively using the Form Design capability. Controls can be dragged directly from the Toolbox window on to the form. Of course, you can also create GUI elements programmatically by adding suitable code manually.

❑ You customize GUI controls on a form by setting their properties.

❑ The Properties window for a GUI component also enables you to add event handler functions automatically.

❑ The `Graphics` class defines functions that enable you to draw on a form.

❑ The `Pen` class defines an object for drawing in a given color and line style.

Exercises

You can download the source code for the examples in the book and the solutions to the following exercises from www.wrox.com. Don't forget to back up the MFC Sketcher and CLRSketcher projects before you modify them for the exercises.

1. Add the menu item and Toolbar button to MFC Sketcher for an element of type ellipse, as in the exercises from Chapter 14, and define a class to support drawing ellipses defined by two points on opposite corners of their enclosing rectangle.

2. Which functions now need to be modified to support drawing an ellipse? Modify the program to draw an ellipse.

3. Which functions must you modify in the example from the previous exercise so that the first point defines the center of the ellipse, and the current cursor position defines a corner of the enclosing rectangle? Modify the example to work this way. (Hint — look up the `CPoint` class members in Help.)

4. Add a new menu pop-up to the `IDR_SketcherTYPE` menu for Pen Style, to allow solid, dashed, dotted, dash-dotted, and dash-dot-dotted lines to be specified.

5. Which parts of the program need to be modified to support the operation of the menu, and the drawing of elements in these line types?

6. Implement support for the new menu pop-up and drawing elements in any of the line types.

7. Modify `CLRSketcher` to support drawing an ellipse defined by two points on opposite corners of the enclosing rectangle. Add a toolbar button as well as a menu item to select ellipse mode.

8. Implement a `Line Style` menu in CLR Sketcher with menu items `Solid`, `Dashed`, and `Dotted`. Add toolbar buttons for the menu items with tooltips. Implement the capability in CLR Sketcher for drawing elements in any of the three line styles in the new menu. Create your own representation for the line styles by setting the `DashPattern` property for the pen appropriately.

Creating the Document and Improving the View

In this chapter, you'll look into the facilities offered by MFC for managing collections of data items; these are similar to the STL containers discussed in Chapter 10. You'll use the MFC collection classes to complete the class definition and implementation for the curve element that was left open in MFC Sketcher in the last chapter. You'll extend the MFC Sketcher to make the document view more flexible, introducing several new techniques in the process. You'll also extend the MFC and CLR versions of Sketcher to store elements in an object that encapsulates a complete sketch.

In this chapter, you'll learn about:

- ❑   MFC collections and what you can do with them
- ❑   How to use an MFC List collection and an STL/CLR vector container to store point data for a curve
- ❑   How to use an MFC List collection and an STL/CLR list container to store sketch data
- ❑   How to implement drawing a sketch in the MFC and CLR versions of Sketcher
- ❑   How to implement scrolling in a view in MFC Sketcher
- ❑   How to create a context menu at the cursor
- ❑   How to highlight the element nearest the cursor to provide feedback to the user for moving and deleting elements
- ❑   How to program the mouse to move and delete elements

The MFC Collection Classes

By the nature of Windows programming, you'll frequently need to handle collections of data items where you have no advance knowledge of how many items you will need to manage, or even what particular type they are going to be. This is clearly illustrated by the Sketcher application where the user can draw an arbitrary number of elements which can be lines, rectangles, circles and curves, and in any sequence. Of course, the STL that you learned about in Chapter 10 provides a wide range of container class templates that do the sort of thing you want to do in Sketcher to store a sketch but the STL containers have one limitation.

Serialization is a process for transferring objects to and from files that you'll learn about in Chapter 18 where you will implement the capability to store sketches in a file; unfortunately the STL containers are not supported by the serialization capability provided by the MFC. You could write your own code to write the contents of an STL container to a file, but using MFC serialization saves a lot of work, so there are considerable advantages to following that route.

MFC uses different terminology from the STL for container classes. MFC provides a group of what are called **collection classes** that provide similar capability to the STL containers — a **collection** being an aggregation of an arbitrary number of data items organized in a particular way. The major advantage offered by the MFC collection classes over STL containers is that MFC collection class objects are serializable as long as the objects they store are serializable.

Types of Collection

MFC provides you with a large number of collection classes for managing data. You'll use just a couple of them in Sketcher, but we'll explore the scope of the types of collections available. MFC supports three kinds of collections, differentiated by the way in which the data items are organized. The way a collection is organized is referred to as the **shape** of the collection. The three types of organization, or shape, are:

Shape	How information is organized
Array	An array in this context is just like the array you have seen in the C++ language. This is an ordered sequence of elements that is the equivalent of an STL sequence container.
List	This is a doubly linked list similar to an STL list container.
Map	A map is an unordered collection of data items that are key/object pairs and is equivalent to an STL map.

MFC collection classes provide two approaches to implementing each type of collection. One approach uses class templates and provides you with **type-safe** handling of data in a collection. Type-safe handling means that the data passed to a function member of the collection class is checked to ensure that it's of a type that can be processed by the function.

The other approach makes use of a range of concrete collection classes (rather than templates), but these perform no data checking. If you want your collection classes to be type-safe, you have to include code yourself to assure this. These latter classes were available in older versions of Visual C++ under Windows before the template collection classes were introduced and are still around for compatibility reasons. I'll concentrate on the template-based versions because these provide the best chance of avoiding errors in our application.

The Type-Safe Collection Classes

The template-based type-safe collection classes support collections of objects of any native C++ type, and collections of pointers to objects of any native C++ type. Collections of objects are supported by the template classes CArray, CList and CMap, and collections of pointers to objects are supported by the template classes CTypedPtrArray, CTypedPtrList and CTypedPtrMap. I won't go into the detail of all of these, just the two that you'll use in the Sketcher program. You'll use one to store objects and the other to store pointers to objects so you'll get a feel for both sorts of collection.

Collections of Objects

The template classes for defining collections of objects are all derived from the MFC class CObject. They are defined this way so that they inherit the properties of the CObject class, which includes file input and output operations for objects, generally referred to as serialization.

These template classes can store and manage any kind of object, including all the C++ basic data types, plus any classes or structures that you or anybody else might define. Because these classes store objects, whenever you add an element to a list, an array, or a map, the class template object needs to make a copy of your object. Consequently, any class type that you want to store in any of these collections must have a copy constructor. The copy constructor for your class is used to create a duplicate of the object that you want to store in the collection.

Take a look at the general properties of each of the template classes that provide type-safe management of objects. This is not an exhaustive treatment of all the member functions provided. Rather, it's intended to give you a sufficient flavor of how they work to enable you to decide if you want to use them or not. You can get information on all of the member functions by using Help to get to the template class definition.

The CArray Template Class

You can use this template to store any kind of object in an array and have the array automatically grow to accommodate more elements when necessary. An array collection is illustrated in Figure 16-1.

As with the STL vector<T> containers, elements in array collections are indexed from 0. The declaration of an array collection takes two template arguments. The first argument is the type of the object to be stored so if your array collection is to store objects of type CPoint for example, you specify CPoint as the first template argument. The second argument is the type used in member function calls. To avoid the overhead in copying objects when passed by value, the second argument is usually a reference, so an example of an array collection declaration to hold CPoint objects is:

```
CArray<CPoint, CPoint&> PointArray;
```

This defines the array collection class object, PointArray, that stores CPoint objects. When you call function members of this object, the argument is a reference, so to add a CPoint object, you would write

```
PointArray.Add(aPoint);
```

and the argument aPoint is passed as a reference.

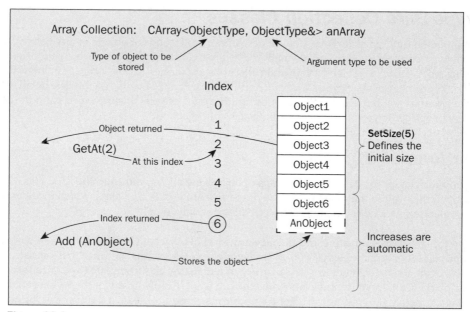

Figure 16-1

After you have declared an array collection, it's important to call the `SetSize()` member function to fix the initial number of elements that you require before you use it. It still works if you don't do this, but the initial allocation of elements and subsequent increments are small, resulting in inefficient operation and frequent reallocation of memory for the array. The initial number of elements that you should specify depends on the typical size of array you expect to need, and how variable the size is. If you expect that the minimum your program required is of the order of 400 to 500 elements, for example, but with expansion up to 700 or 800, an initial size of 600 is suitable.

To retrieve the contents of an element, you can use the `GetAt()` function, as shown in Figure 16-1. To store the third element of `PointArray` in a variable `aPoint`, you write:

```
aPoint = PointArray.GetAt(2);
```

The class also overloads the subscript operator ([]), so you could retrieve the third element of `PointArray` by using `PointArray[2]`. For example, if `aPoint` is a variable of type `CPoint`, you could write:

```
aPoint = PointArray[2];                    // Store a copy of the third element
```

For array collections that are not `const`, this notation can also be used instead of the `SetAt()` function to set the contents of an existing element. The following two statements are, therefore, equivalent:

```
PointArray.SetAt(3,NewPoint);              // Store NewObject in the 4th element
PointArray[3] = NewPoint;                  // Same as previous line of code
```

Here, `NewPoint` is an object of the type used to declare the array. In both cases, the element must already exist. You cannot extend the array by this means. To extend the array, you can use the `Add()` function shown in the diagram, which adds a new element to the array. There is also a function `Append()` to add an *array* of elements to the end of the array.

Helper Functions

Whenever you call the `SetSize()` function member of an array collection, a global function, `ConstructElements()`, is called to allocate memory for the number of elements you want to store in the array collection initially. This is called a **helper function** because it helps in the process of setting the size of the array collection. The default version of this function sets the contents of the allocated memory to zero and doesn't call a constructor for your object class, so you'll need to supply your own version of this helper function if this action isn't appropriate for your objects. This is the case if space for data members of objects of your class is allocated dynamically, or if there is other initialization required. `ConstructElements()` is also called by the member function `InsertAt()`, which inserts one or more elements at a particular index position within the array.

Members of the `CArray` collection class that remove elements call the helper function `DestructElements()`. The default version does nothing, so if your object construction allocates any memory on the heap, you must override this function to release the memory properly.

The `CList` collection template makes use of a helper function when searching the contents of a list for a particular object. I'll discuss this further in the next section. Another helper function, `SerializeElements()`, is used by the array, list, and map collection classes, and I'll discuss this when I explain how you can write a document to file.

The CList Template Class

Take a look at the list collection template in some detail because you'll apply it in your Sketcher program. The parameters to the `CList` collection class template are the same as those for the `CArray` template:

```
CList<ObjectType, ObjectType&> aList;
```

You need to supply two arguments to the template when you declare a list collection: the type of object to be stored, and the way an object is to be specified in function arguments. The example shows the second argument as a reference because this is used most frequently. It doesn't necessarily have to be a reference, though — you could use a pointer, or even the object type (so objects would be passed by value), but this would be slow.

You can use a list to manage a curve in the Sketcher program. You could declare a list collection to store the points specifying a curve object with the statement:

```
CList<CPoint, CPoint&> PointList;
```

This declares a list called `PointList` that stores `CPoint` objects that are passed to functions in the class by reference. You'll come back to this when you fill out more detail of the Sketcher program in this chapter.

Adding Elements to a List

You can add objects at the beginning or at the end of the list by using the `AddHead()` or `AddTail()` member functions, as shown in Figure 16-2.

Figure 16-2 shows backward and forward pointers for each list element that "'glue" the objects in the list together. These are internal links that you can't access in any direct way, but you can do just about anything you want by using the functions provided in the public interface to the class.

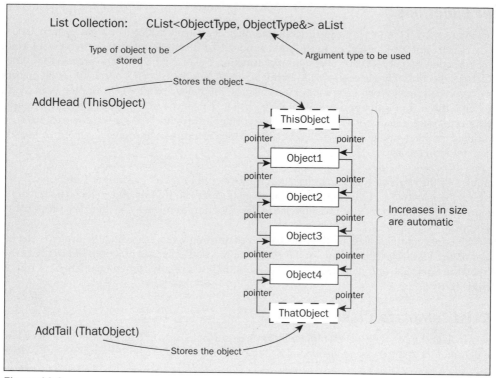

Figure 16-2

To add the object `aPoint` to the tail of the list `PointList`, you write:

```
PointList.AddTail(aPoint);                // Add an element to the end
```

As new elements are added, the size of the list increases automatically.

Both the `AddHead()` and `AddTail()` functions return a value of type `POSITION`, which specifies the position of the inserted object in the list. The way in which a variable of type `POSITION` is used is shown in Figure 16-3.

You can use a value of type `POSITION` to retrieve the object at a given position in the list by using the `GetNext()` function. Note that you can't perform arithmetic on values of type `POSITION` — you can only modify a position value through member functions of the list object. Furthermore, you can't set a position value to a specific numerical value. `POSITION` variables can only be set through member functions of the list object.

As well as returning the object, the `GetNext()` function increments the position variable passed to it so that it points to the next object in the list. You can, therefore, use repeated calls to `GetNext()` to step through a list element by element. The position variable is set to `NULL` if you use `GetNext()` to retrieve the last object from the list, so you can use this to control your loop operation. You should always make sure that you have a valid position value when you call member functions of a list object.

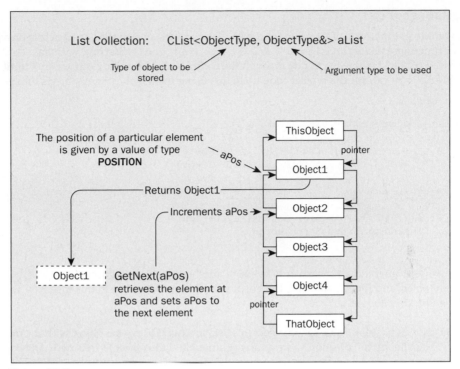

Figure 16-3

You can insert an element in a list at a specific position as long as you have a POSITION value. To insert the object ThePoint in the list PointList immediately *before* an element at the position aPosition, use the statement:

```
PointList.InsertBefore(aPosition, ThePoint);
```

The function InsertBefore() also returns the position of the new object. To insert an element after the object at a given position, the function InsertAfter() is provided. These functions are often used with a list containing geometric elements displayed. Elements are drawn on the screen in the sequence that you traverse the list. Elements that appear later in the list overlay elements positioned earlier, so the order of elements determines what overlays what. You can therefore determine which of the existing elements a new element overlays by entering it at an appropriate position in the list.

When you need to set an existing object in a list to a particular value, you can use the function SetAt(), as long as you know the position value for the object:

```
PointList.SetAt(aPosition, aPoint);
```

There is no return value for this function. You must ensure that the POSITION value you pass to the function is valid. An invalid value causes an error. You should, therefore, only pass a POSITION value to this function that was returned by one of the other member functions, and you must have verified that it isn't NULL.

Iterating through a List

If you want to get the POSITION value for the beginning or the end of the list, the class provides the member functions GetHeadPosition() and GetTailPosition(). Starting with the POSITION value for the head of the list, you can iterate through the complete list by calling GetNext() until the position value is NULL. You can see the typical code to do this using the list of CPoint objects that you declared earlier:

```
CPoint CurrentPoint(0,0);

// Get the position of the first list element
POSITION aPosition = PointList.GetHeadPosition();

while(aPosition)                          // Loop while aPosition is not NULL
{
    CurrentPoint = PointList.GetNext(aPosition);
    // Process the current object...
}
```

You can work through the list backwards by using another member function, GetPrev(), which retrieves the current object and then decrements the position indicator. Of course, in this case, you would start out by calling GetTailPosition().

After you know a position value for an object in a list, you can retrieve the object with the member function GetAt(). You specify the position value as an argument and the object is returned. An invalid position value causes an error.

Searching a List

You can find the position of an element that's stored in a list by using the member function Find():

```
POSITION aPosition = PointList.Find(ThePoint);
```

This searches for the object specified as an argument by calling a global template function CompareElements() to compare the objects in the list with the argument. This is the helper function I referred to earlier that aids the search process. The default implementation of this function compares the address of the argument with the address of each object in the list. This implies that if the search is to be successful, the argument must actually be an element in the list — not a copy. If the object is found in the list, the position of the element is returned. If it isn't found, NULL is returned. You can specify a second argument to define a position value where the search should begin.

If you want to search a list for an object that is *equal* to another object, you must implement your own version of CompareElements() that performs a proper comparison. The function template is of the form:

```
template<class TYPE, class ARG_TYPE> BOOL CompareElements(
                const TYPE* pElement1, const ARG_TYPE* pElement2);
```

where pElement1 and pElement2 are pointers to the objects to be compared. For the PointList collection class object, the prototype of the function generated by the template would be:

```
BOOL CompareElements(CPoint* pPoint1, CPoint* pPoint2);
```

To compare the `CPoint` objects, you could implement this as:

```
BOOL CompareElements(CPoint* pPoint1, CPoint* pPoint2)
   { return *pPoint1 == *pPoint2; }
```

This uses the `operator==()` function implemented in the `CPoint` class. In general you would need to implement the `operator==()` function for your own class in this context. You could then use it to implement the helper function `CompareElements()`.

You can also obtain the position of an element in a list by using an index value. The index works in the same way as for an array, with the first element being at index 0, the second at index 1, and so on. The function `FindIndex()` takes an index value of type `int` as an argument and returns a value of type `POSITION` for the object at the index position in the list. If you want to use an index value, you are likely to need to know how many objects there are in a list. The `GetCount()` function returns this for you:

```
int ObjectCount = PointList.GetCount();
```

Here, the integer count of the number of elements in the list is stored in the variable `ObjectCount`.

Deleting Objects from a List

You can delete the first element in a list using the member function `RemoveHead()`. This function will return the object that is the new head of the list. To remove the last object, you can use the function `RemoveTail()`. Both of these functions require that there should be at least one object in the list, so you should use the function `IsEmpty()` first, to verify that the list is not empty. For example:

```
if(!PointList.IsEmpty())
   PointList.RemoveHead();
```

The function `IsEmpty()` returns `TRUE` if the list is empty, and `FALSE` otherwise.

If you know the position value for an object that you want to delete from the list, you can do this directly:

```
PointList.RemoveAt(aPosition);
```

There's no return value from this function. It's your responsibility to ensure that the position value you pass as an argument is valid. If you want to delete the entire contents of a list, you use the member function `RemoveAll()`:

```
PointList.RemoveAll();
```

This function also frees the memory that was allocated for the elements in the list.

Helper Functions for a List

You have already seen how the `CompareElements()` helper function is used by the `Find()` function for a list. Both the `ConstructElements()` and `DestructElements()` global helper functions are also used by members of a `CList` template class. These are template functions that are declared using the object type you specify in your `CList` class declaration. The template prototypes for these functions are:

```
template< class TYPE > void ConstructElements(TYPE* pElements, int nCount);
template< class TYPE > void DestructElements(TYPE* pElements, int nCount);
```

To obtain the function that's specific to your list collection, just plug in the type for the objects you are storing. For example, the prototypes for the `PointList` class for these are:

```
void ConstructElements(CPoint* pPoint, int PointCount);
void DestructElements(CPoint* pPoint, int PointCount);
```

Note that the parameters here are pointers. I mentioned earlier that arguments to the `PointList` member functions would be references, but this doesn't apply to the helper functions. The parameters to both functions are the same: the first is a pointer to an array of `CPoint` objects, and the second is a count of the number of objects in the array.

The `ConstructElements()` function is called whenever you enter an object in the list, and the `DestructElements()` function is called when you remove an object. As for the `CArray` template class, you need to implement your versions of these functions if the default operation is not suitable for your object class.

The CMap Template Class

Because of the way they work, maps are particularly suited to applications where your objects obviously have a unique key associated with them, such as a customer class where each customer has an associated customer number or a name and address class where the name might be used as a key. The organization of a map is shown in Figure 16-4.

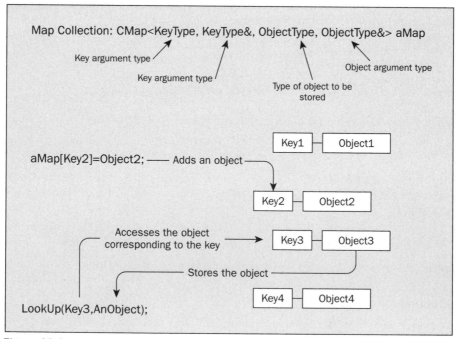

Figure 16-4

A map stores an object and key combination. The key is used to determine where in the block of memory allocated to the map the object is to be stored. The key, therefore, provides a means of going directly to an object stored, as long as the key is unique. The process of converting a key to an integer that can be used to calculate the address of an entry in a map is called **hashing**.

The hashing process applied to a key produces an integer called a **hash value**. This hash value is typically used as an offset to a base address to determine where to store the key and its associated object in the map. If the memory allocated to the map is at address **Base**, and each entry requires **Length** bytes, the entry producing the hash value **HashValue** is stored at **Base+HashValue*Length**.

The hashing process may not produce a unique hash value from a key, in which case an **element** — the key together with the associated object — is entered and linked to whatever element or elements were previously stored with the same hashed key value (often as a list). Of course, the fewer unique hash values generated, the less efficient the retrieval process from your map is because searching is required to retrieve elements that have the same hash value.

There are four arguments necessary when you declare a map:

```
CMap<LONG, LONG&, CPoint, CPoint&> PointMap;
```

The first two specify the key type and how it is passed as an argument. Usually, it is passed as a reference. The second pair of arguments specifies the object type and how the object is passed as an argument, as you have previously seen.

You can store an object in a map by using the `[]` operator, as shown in Figure 16-4. You can also use the `SetAt()` member function to store an object, where you supply the key value and the object as arguments. Note that you cannot use the `[]` operator on the right side of an assignment to retrieve an object, as this version of the operator is not implemented in the class.

To retrieve an object, use the `LookUp()` function shown in Figure 16-4. This retrieves the object corresponding to the key specified; the function returns TRUE if the object was found and FALSE otherwise. You can also iterate through all the objects in a map using a variable of type POSITION, although the sequence in which objects are retrieved is unrelated to the sequence in which they were added to the map. This is because objects are stored in a map in locations determined by the hash value, not by the sequence in which they were entered.

Helper Functions Used by CMap

As well as the helper functions that have been discussed in the context of arrays and lists, map collection classes also use a global function `HashKey()`, which is defined by this template:

```
template<class ARG_KEY>
   UINT HashKey(ARG_KEY key);
```

This function converts your key value to a hash value of type UINT, which is equivalent to `unsigned int`. The default version does this by simply shifting your key value right by 4 bit positions. You need to implement your own version of this function if the default operation isn't suited to your key type.

There are different techniques used for hashing that vary depending on the type of data being used as a key, and the number of elements you are likely to want to store in your map. The likely number of elements to be stored indicates the number of unique hash values you need. A common method for hashing a numeric key value is to compute the hash value as the value of the key modulo N, where N is the number of different values you want. For reasons it would take too long to explain here, N needs to be prime for this to work well. Didn't you just know that program to calculate primes from way back in Chapter 4 would turn out to be useful after all?

You can get an appreciation of the principles of the mechanism used here with a simple example. Suppose you expect to store up to 100 different entries in a map using a key value, Key. You could hash the key with the statement:

```
HashValue = Key%101;
```

This results in values for the HashValue between 0 and 100, which is exactly what you need to calculate the address for an entry. Assuming your map is stored at some location in memory, **Base**, and the memory required to store the object along with its key is **Length** bytes, then you can store an entry that produces the hash value **HashValue** at the location **Base+HashValue*Length**. With the hashing process mentioned previously, you can accommodate up to 101 entries at unique positions in the map.

Where a key is a character string, the hashing process is rather more complicated, particularly with long or variable length strings; however, a method commonly used involves using numerical values derived from characters in the string. This typically involves assigning a numerical value to each character, so if your string was lowercase letters plus spaces, you could assign each character a value between 0 and 26, with *space* as 0, *a* as 1, *b* as 2, and so on. The string can then be treated as the representation of a number to some base, 32 say. The numerical value for the string 'fred', for instance, is

$6*32^3+18*32^2+5*32^1+4*32^0$

and, assuming you expected to store 500 strings, you could calculate the hashed value of the key as:

$6*32^3+18*32^3+5*32^3+4*32^0 \bmod 503$

The value of 503 for N is the smallest prime greater than the likely number of entries. The base chosen to evaluate a hash value for a string is usually a power of 2 that corresponds to the minimum value that is greater than or equal to the number of possible different characters in a string. For long strings, this can generate very large numbers, so special techniques are used to compute the value modulo N. Detailed discussion of these techniques is beyond the scope of this book, but you can find numerous Web references by searching on "hashing."

The Typed Pointer Collections

The typed pointer collection class templates store pointers to objects, rather than objects themselves. This is the primary difference between these class templates and the template classes just discussed. Take a look at how the CTypedPtrList class template is used, because you'll use this as a basis for managing elements in your document class, CSketcherDoc.

The CTypedPtrList Template Class

You can declare a typed pointer list class with a statement of the form:

```
CTypedPtrList<BaseClass, Type*> ListName;
```

The first argument specifies a base class that must be one of two pointer list classes defined in MFC, either
CObList or CPtrList. Your choice depends on how your object class has been defined. Using the CObList
class creates a list supporting pointers to objects derived from CObject, while CPtrList supports lists of
void* pointers. Because the elements in the Sketcher example have CObject as a base class, I'll concentrate
on how CObList is used.

The second argument to the template is the type of the pointers to be stored in the list. In the example, this
is going to be CElement* because all your shapes have CElement as a base class and CElement is derived
from CObject. Thus, the declaration of a class for storing shapes is:

```
CTypedPtrList<CObList, CElement*> m_ElementList;
```

You could have used CObList* types to store the pointers to our elements, but then the list could contain
an object of any class that has CObject as a base. The declaration of m_ElementList ensures that only
pointers to objects of the class CElement can be stored. This provides a greatly increased level of security
in the program.

CTypePtrList Operations

The functions provided in the CTypedPtrList based classes are similar to those supported by CList,
except of course that all operations are with pointers to objects rather than with objects, so you need to
tabulate them. They fall into two groups: those that are defined in CTypedPtrList, and those that are
inherited from the base class — CObList in this case.

The functions defined in CTypedPtrList are:

Function	Description
GetHead()	Returns the pointer at the head of the list. You should use IsEmpty() to verify that the list is not empty before calling this function.
GetTail()	Returns the pointer at the tail of the list. You should use IsEmpty() to verify that the list is not empty before calling this function.
RemoveHead()	Removes the first pointer in the list. You should use IsEmpty() to verify that the list is not empty before calling this function.
RemoveTail()	Removes the last pointer in the list. You should use IsEmpty() to verify that the list is not empty before calling this function.

Continued

Function	Description
GetNext()	Returns the pointer at the position indicated by the variable of type POSITION passed as a reference argument. The variable is updated to indicate the next element in the list. When the end of the list is reached, the position variable is set to NULL. This function can be used to iterate forwards through all the pointers in the list.
GetPrev()	Returns the pointer at the position indicated by the variable of type POSITION passed as a reference argument. The variable is updated to indicate the previous element in the list. When the beginning of the list is reached, the position variable is set to NULL. This function can be used to iterate backwards through all the pointers in the list.
GetAt()	Returns the pointer stored at the position indicated by the variable of type POSITION passed as an argument, which isn't changed. Because the function returns a reference, as long as the list is not defined as const, this function can be used on the left of an assignment operator to modify a list entry.

The functions in CTypedPtrList inherited from CObList are:

Function	Description
AddHead()	Adds the pointer passed as an argument to the head of the list and returns a value of type POSITION that corresponds to the new element. There is another version of this function that can add another *list* to the head of the list.
AddTail()	Adds the pointer passed as an argument to the tail of the list and returns a value of type POSITION that corresponds to the new element. There is another version of this function that can add another *list* to the tail of the list.
RemoveAll()	Removes all the elements from the list. Note that this doesn't delete the objects pointed to by elements in the list. You need to take care of this yourself.
GetHeadPosition()	Returns the position of the element at the head of the list.
GetTailPosition()	Returns the position of the element at the tail of the list.
SetAt()	Stores the pointer specified by the second argument at the position in the list defined by the first argument. An invalid position value causes an error.
RemoveAt()	Removes the pointer from the position in the list specified by the argument of type POSITION. An invalid position value causes an error.

Function	Description
InsertBefore()	Inserts a new pointer specified by the second argument before the position specified by the first argument. The position of the new element is returned.
InsertAfter()	Inserts a new pointer specified by the second argument after the position specified by the first argument. The position of the new element is returned.
Find()	Searches for a pointer in the list that is identical to the pointer specified as an argument. Its position is returned if it is found. NULL is returned otherwise.
FindIndex()	Returns the position of a pointer in the list specified by a zero-based integer index argument.
GetCount()	Returns the number of elements in the list.
IsEmpty()	Returns TRUE if there are no elements in the list, and FALSE otherwise.

You'll see some of these member functions in action a little later in this chapter in the context of implementing the document class for the Sketcher program.

Using the CList Template Class

You can use of the CList collection template in the definition of the curve object in our Sketcher application. A curve is defined by two or more points, so storing these in a list would be a good method of handling them. You first need to define a CList collection class object as a member of the CCurve class. You'll use this collection to store points. You've already looked at the CList template class in some detail, so this should be easy.

The CList template class has two parameters, so the general form of declaring a collection class of this type is:

```
CList<YourObjectType, FunctionArgType> ClassName;
```

The first argument, YourObjectType, specifies the type of object that you want to store in the list. The second argument specifies the argument type to be used in function members of the collection class when referring to an object. This is usually specified as a reference to the object type to minimize copying of arguments in a function call. Declare a collection class object to suit your needs in the CCurve class as:

```
class CCurve: public CElement
{
  // Rest of the class definition...
```

```
protected:
  CCurve(void);                          // Default constructor - should not be used
  CList<CPoint, CPoint&> m_PointList;   // Type safe point list
};
```

You can either add this manually to the class definition or use the Add > Add Variable menu item that you've used before from Class View. I have omitted the rest of the class definition here because you're not concerned with it for now. The collection declaration is shaded. It declares the collection m_PointList that stores CPoint objects in the list, and its functions use reference arguments to CPoint objects.

The CPoint class doesn't allocate memory dynamically, so you won't need to implement ConstructElements() or DestructElements(), and because you don't need to use the Find() member function, you can forget about CompareElements() as well.

Drawing a Curve

Drawing a curve is different from drawing a line or a circle. With a line or a circle, as you move the cursor with the left button down, you are creating a succession of different line or circle elements that share a common reference point — the point where the left mouse button was pressed. This is not the case when you draw a curve, as shown in Figure 16-5.

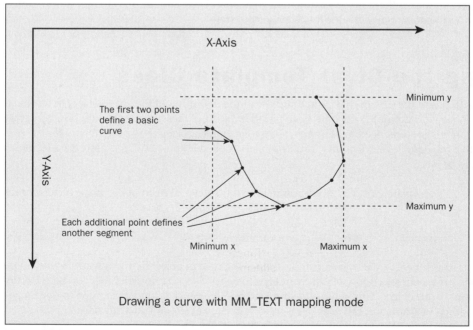

Figure 16-5

When you move the cursor while drawing a curve, you're not creating a sequence of new curves but rather extending the same curve, so each successive point adds another segment to the curve's definition. You therefore need to create a curve object as soon as you have the two points from the WM_LBUTTONDOWN message and the first WM_MOUSEMOVE message. Points defined with subsequent mouse move messages then define additional segments to the existing curve object. You'll need to add a function, AddSegment(), to the CCurve class to extend the curve once it has been created by the constructor.

A further point to consider is how you are to calculate the enclosing rectangle. This is defined by getting the minimum *x* and minimum *y* pair from all the defining points to establish the upper-left corner of the rectangle, and the maximum *x* and maximum *y* pair for the bottom right. This involves going through all the points in the list. You will, therefore, compute the enclosing rectangle incrementally in the AddSegment() function as points are added to the curve.

Defining the CCurve Class

With the constructor and the AddSegment() function added, the complete definition of the CCurve class is:

```
class CCurve: public CElement
{
public:
    ~CCurve(void);
    virtual void Draw(CDC* pDC);        // Function to display a curve

    // Constructor for a curve object
    CCurve(CPoint FirstPoint, CPoint SecondPoint, COLORREF aColor);

    void AddSegment(CPoint& aPoint);      //Add a segment to the curve

protected:
    CCurve(void);                         // Default constructor - should not be used
    CList<CPoint, CPoint&> m_PointList;  // Type safe point list

};
```

You should modify the definition of the class in Elements.h to correspond with the previous code. The constructor has the first two defining points and the color as parameters, so it only defines a curve with one segment. This is called in the CreateElement() function invoked by the OnMouseMove() function in the view class the first time a WM_MOUSEMOVE message is received for a curve, so don't forget to modify the definition of the CreateElement() function in CSketcherView to call the CCurve class constructor with the correct arguments. The statement using the CCurve constructor in the switch in the CreateElement() function should be changed to:

```
case CURVE:
    return new CCurve(m_FirstPoint, m_SecondPoint, pDoc->GetElementColor());
```

After the constructor has been called, all subsequent WM_MOUSEMOVE messages results in the AddSegment() function being called to add a segment to the existing curve, as shown in Figure 16-6:

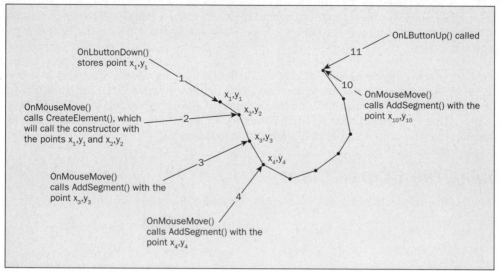

Figure 16-6

This shows the complete sequence of message handler calls for a curve comprised of nine segments. The sequence is indicated by the numbered arrows. The code for the OnMouseMove() function in CSketcherView needs to be updated as follows:

```
void CSketcherView::OnMouseMove(UINT nFlags, CPoint point)
{
    CClientDC aDC(this);                  // Device context for the current view
    if((nFlags&MK_LBUTTON)&&(this==GetCapture()))
    {
        m_SecondPoint = point;       // Save the current cursor position

        if(m_pTempElement)
        {
            if(CURVE == GetDocument()->GetElementType())    // Is it a curve?
            {   // We are drawing a curve
                // so add a segment to the existing curve
                static_cast<CCurve*>(m_pTempElement)->AddSegment(m_SecondPoint);
                m_pTempElement->Draw(&aDC);   // Now draw it
                return;                       // We are done
            }

            aDC.SetROP2(R2_NOTXORPEN);                  // Set drawing mode
            // Redraw the old element so it disappears from the view
            m_pTempElement->Draw(&aDC);
            delete m_pTempElement;                    // Delete the old element
            m_pTempElement = 0;                       // Reset the pointer to 0
        }
```

```
        // Create an element of the type and color
        // recorded in the document object
        m_pTempElement = CreateElement();
        m_pTempElement->Draw(&aDC);
    }
}
```

You have to treat an element of type CURVE as a special case after it has been created because on all subsequent calls of the OnMouseMove() handler, you want to call the AddSegment() function for the existing element, rather than construct a new one in place of the old. You don't want to set the drawing mode in this instance because you don't need to erase the previous curve each time. You take care of this by moving the call to SetROP2() to a position after the code processing a curve.

Adding the curve segment and drawing the extended curve is taken care of within the if statement you have added. Note that you must cast the m_pTempElement pointer to type CCurve* to use it to call AddSegment() for the old element because AddSegment() is not a virtual function. If you don't add the cast, you'll get an error because the compiler tries to resolve the call statically to a member of the CElement class.

Implementing the CCurve Class

Write the code for the constructor; this should be added to Elements.cpp in place of the temporary constructor that you used in the last chapter. It needs to store the two points passed as arguments in the CList data member, m_PointList:

```
CCurve::CCurve(CPoint FirstPoint,CPoint SecondPoint, COLORREF aColor)
{
    m_PointList.AddTail(FirstPoint);      // Add the 1st point to the list
    m_PointList.AddTail(SecondPoint);     // Add the 2nd point to the list
    m_Color = aColor;                     // Store the color
    m_Pen = 1;                            // Set the pen width

    // Construct the enclosing rectangle assuming MM_TEXT mode
    m_EnclosingRect = CRect(FirstPoint, SecondPoint);
    m_EnclosingRect.NormalizeRect();
}
```

The points are added to the list, m_PointList, by calling the AddTail() member of the CList template class. This function adds a copy of the point passed as an argument to the end of the list. The enclosing rectangle is defined in exactly the same way that that defined it for a line.

You can add the AddSegment() function to Elements.cpp next. This function is called when additional curve points are recorded, after the first version of a curve object has been created. This member function is very simple:

```
void CCurve::AddSegment(CPoint& aPoint)
{
    m_PointList.AddTail(aPoint);                      // Add the point to the end

    // Modify the enclosing rectangle for the new point
    m_EnclosingRect = CRect(min(aPoint.x, m_EnclosingRect.left),
```

```
                              min(aPoint.y, m_EnclosingRect.top),
                              max(aPoint.x, m_EnclosingRect.right),
                              max(aPoint.y, m_EnclosingRect.bottom));
   }
```

The `min()` and `max()` functions you use here are standard macros that are the equivalent of using the conditional operator for choosing the minimum or maximum of two values. The new point is added to the tail of the list in the same way as in the constructor. It's important that each new point is added to the list in a way that is consistent with the constructor because you'll draw the segments using the points in sequence, from the beginning to the end of the list. Each line segment is drawn from the end point of the previous line to the new point. If the points are not in the right sequence, the line segments won't be drawn correctly. After adding the new point, the enclosing rectangle for the curve is redefined, taking account of the new point.

The last member function you need to define for the interface to the `CCurve` class is `Draw()`:

```
void CCurve::Draw(CDC* pDC)
{
    // Create a pen for this object and
    // initialize it to the object color and line width of 1 pixel
    CPen aPen;
    if(!aPen.CreatePen(PS_SOLID, m_Pen, m_Color))
    {
        // Pen creation failed. Close the program
        AfxMessageBox(_T("Pen creation failed drawing a curve"), MB_OK);
        AfxAbort();
    }

    CPen* pOldPen = pDC->SelectObject(&aPen);   // Select the pen

    // Now draw the curve
    // Get the position in the list of the first element
    POSITION aPosition = m_PointList.GetHeadPosition();

    // As long as it's good, move to that point
    if(aPosition)
        pDC->MoveTo(m_PointList.GetNext(aPosition));

    // Draw a segment for each of the following points
    while(aPosition)
        pDC->LineTo(m_PointList.GetNext(aPosition));

    pDC->SelectObject(pOldPen);              // Restore the old pen
}
```

You draw the `CCurve` object by iterating through all the points in the list from the beginning, drawing each segment as you go. You get a `POSITION` value for the first element by using the function `GetHeadPosition()` and then use `MoveTo()` to set the first point as the current position in the device context. You then draw line segments in the `while` loop as long as `aPosition` is not `NULL`. The `GetNext()` function call that appears as the argument to the `LineTo()` function returns the current point and simultaneously increments `aPosition` to refer to the next point in the list.

Exercising the CCurve Class

With the changes I've just discussed added to the Sketcher program, you have implemented all the code necessary for the element shapes in your menu. You can now build the Sketcher program once more, and execute it. You should be able to create curves in all four colors. A typical application window is shown in Figure 16-7.

Figure 16-7

Of course, like the other elements you can draw, the curves are not persistent. As soon as you cause a `WM_PAINT` message to be sent to the application, by resizing the view for instance, they disappear. After you can store them in the document object for the application, though, they will be a bit more permanent, so take a look at that next.

Creating the Sketch Document

The document in the Sketcher application needs to be able to store a sketch consisting of an arbitrary collection of lines, rectangles, circles, and curves in any sequence, and an excellent vehicle for handling this is a list. Because all the element classes that you've defined include the capability for the objects to draw themselves, drawing the document is easily accomplished by stepping through the list.

Using a CTypedPtrList Template

You can declare a `CTypedPtrList` that stores pointers to instances of the shape classes as `CElement` pointers. You just need to add the list declaration as a new member in the `CSketcherDoc` class definition:

```
// SketcherDoc.h : interface of the CSketcherDoc class
//
```

```
#pragma once

class CSketcherDoc: public CDocument
{
protected: // create from serialization only
    CSketcherDoc();
    DECLARE_DYNCREATE(CSketcherDoc)

// Rest of the class as before...

protected:
    COLORREF m_Color;                            // Current drawing color
    unsigned int m_Element;                      // Current element type
    CTypedPtrList<CObList, CElement*> m_ElementList;  // Element list

// Rest of the class as before...

};
```

The CSketcherDoc class now refers to the CElement class and normally a forward declaration of the CElement class before the CSketcherDoc class definition would be enough for Sketcher to compile correctly, but not in this case. The compiler needs to know about the *base* class for the CElement class to compile the CTypedPtrList template instance correctly. This is only possible if the *definition* of the CElement class is available at this point. You have two ways to achieve this. You can make sure that every #include directive for the SketcherDoc.h header is preceded by an #include directive for CElement, or you can simply add an #include directive for Elements.h before the CSketcherDoc class definition. The latter course is the easiest and saves you from hunting for #include directives for SketcherDoc.h in the source files.

You'll also need a member function to add an element to the list and AddElement() is a good, if unoriginal, name for this. You create shape objects on the heap, so you can just pass a pointer to the function. Because all it does is add an element, you might just as well put the implementation in the class definition:

```
class CSketcherDoc: public CDocument
{

// Rest of the class as before...

// Operations
public:
    unsigned int GetElementType()           // Get the element type
        { return m_Element; }
    COLORREF GetElementColor()              // Get the element color
        { return m_Color; }
    void AddElement(CElement* pElement)     // Add an element to the list
        { m_ElementList.AddTail(pElement); }

// Rest of the class as before...

};
```

Adding an element to the list only requires one statement that calls the `AddTail()` member function. That's all you need to create the document, but you still have to consider what happens when a document is closed. You must ensure that the list of pointers and all the elements they point to are destroyed properly. To do this, you need to add code to the destructor for `CSketcherDoc` objects.

Implementing the Document Destructor

In the destructor, you'll first go through the list deleting the element pointed to by each entry. After that is complete, you must delete the pointers from the list. The code to do this is:

```
CSketcherDoc::~CSketcherDoc(void)
{
    // Get the position at the head of the list
    POSITION aPosition = m_ElementList.GetHeadPosition();

    // Now delete the element pointed to by each list entry
    while(aPosition)
        delete m_ElementList.GetNext(aPosition);

    m_ElementList.RemoveAll();    // Finally delete all pointers
}
```

You use the `GetHeadPosition()` function to obtain the position value for the entry at the head of the list, and initialize the variable `aPosition` with this value. You then use `aPosition` in the `while` loop to walk through the list and delete the object pointed to by each entry. The `GetNext()` function returns the current pointer entry and updates the `aPosition` variable to refer to the next entry. When the last entry is retrieved, `aPosition` is set to `NULL` by the `GetNext()` function and the loop ends. After you have deleted all the element objects pointed to by the pointers in the list, you can delete the pointers themselves. You delete the whole lot in one go by calling the `RemoveAll()` function for the list object.

You should add this code to the definition of the destructor in `SketcherDoc.cpp`. You can go directly to the code for the destructor through the Class View.

Drawing the Document

As the document owns the list of elements, and the list is protected, you can't use it directly from the view. The `OnDraw()` member of the view does need to be able to call the `Draw()` member for each of the elements in the list, though, so you need to consider how best to do this. Take a look at the options:

❑ You could make the list `public`, but this defeats the object of maintaining protected members of the document class because it exposes all the function members of the list object.

❑ You could add a member function to return a pointer to the list, but this effectively makes the list `public` and also incurs overhead in accessing it.

❑ You could add a `public` function to the document that calls the `Draw()` member for each element. You could then call this member from the `OnDraw()` function in the view. This wouldn't be a bad solution because it produces what you want and still maintains the privacy of the list. The only thing against it is that the function needs access to a device context, and this is really the domain of the view.

❑   You could make the OnDraw() function a friend of CSketcherDoc, but this exposes all of the
members of the class, which isn't desirable, particularly with a complex class.

❑   You could add a function to provide a POSITION value for the first list element, and a second
member to iterate through the list elements. This doesn't expose the list, but it makes the element pointers available.

The last option looks to be the best choice, so we will go with that. You can extend the document class
definition to:

```
class CSketcherDoc: public CDocument
{

// Rest of the class as before...

// Operations
public:
    unsigned int GetElementType()        // Get the element type
        { return m_Element; }
    COLORREF GetElementColor()           // Get the element color
        { return m_Color; }
    void AddElement(CElement* pElement) // Add an element to the list
        { m_ElementList.AddTail(pElement); }
    POSITION GetListHeadPosition()         // return list head POSITION value
        { return m_ElementList.GetHeadPosition(); }
    CElement* GetNext(POSITION& aPos)    // Return current element pointer
        { return m_ElementList.GetNext(aPos); }

// Rest of the class as before...

};
```

By using the two functions you have added to the document class, the OnDraw() function for the view
will be able to iterate through the list, calling the Draw() function for each element. The implementation
of OnDraw() to do this is:

```
void CSketcherView::OnDraw(CDC* pDC)
{
    CSketcherDoc* pDoc = GetDocument();
    ASSERT_VALID(pDoc);
    if(!pDoc)
      return;

    POSITION aPos = pDoc->GetListHeadPosition();
    while(aPos)                              // Loop while aPos is not null
    {
        pDoc->GetNext(aPos)->Draw(pDC);        // Draw the current element
    }
}
```

This implementation of the OnDraw() function always draws all the elements the document contains. The
statement in the while loop first gets a pointer to an element from the document with the expression
pDoc->GetNext(). The pointer that is returned is used to call the Draw() function for that element. The

statement works this way without parentheses because of the left to right associativity of the -> operator. The `while` loop plows through the list from beginning to end. You can do it better though, and make the program more efficient.

Frequently, when a `WM_PAINT` message is sent to your program, only part of the window needs to be redrawn. When Windows sends the `WM_PAINT` message to a window, it also defines an area in the client area of the window, and only this area needs to be redrawn. The `CDC` class provides a member function, `RectVisible()`, which checks whether a rectangle that you supply to it as an argument overlaps the area that Windows requires to be redrawn. You can use this to make sure you only draw the elements that are in the area Windows wants redrawn, thus improving the performance of the application:

```
void CSketcherView::OnDraw(CDC* pDC)
{
    CSketcherDoc* pDoc = GetDocument();
    ASSERT_VALID(pDoc);
    if(!pDoc)
      return;

    POSITION aPos = pDoc->GetListHeadPosition();
    CElement* pElement = 0;                 // Store for an element pointer
    while(aPos)                             // Loop while aPos is not null
    {
        pElement = pDoc->GetNext(aPos);    // Get the current element pointer
        // If the element is visible...
        if(pDC->RectVisible(pElement->GetBoundRect()))
            pElement->Draw(pDC);            // ...draw it
    }
}
```

You get the position for the first entry in the list and store it in `aPos`. You use the value stored in `aPos` to control the `while` loop that retrieves each pointer entry in turn so the loop continues until `aPos` is NULL. You retrieve the bounding rectangle for each element using the `GetBoundRect()` member of the object and pass it to the `RectVisible()` function in the `if` statement. As a result, only elements that overlap the area that Windows has identified as invalid are drawn. Drawing on the screen is a relatively expensive operation in terms of time, so checking for just the elements that need to be redrawn, rather than drawing everything each time, improves performance considerably.

Adding an Element to the Document

The last thing you need to do to have a working document in our program is to add the code to the `OnLButtonUp()` handler in the `CSketcherView` class to add the temporary element to the document:

```
void CSketcherView::OnLButtonUp(UINT nFlags, CPoint point)
{
    if(this == GetCapture())
      ReleaseCapture();          // Stop capturing mouse messages

    // If there is an element, add it to the document
    if(m_pTempElement)
    {
        GetDocument()->AddElement(m_pTempElement);
        InvalidateRect(0);           // Redraw the current window
```

```
            m_pTempElement = 0;          // Reset the element pointer
    }
}
```

Of course, you must check that there really is an element before you add it to the document. The user might just have clicked the left mouse button without moving the mouse. After adding the element to the list in the document, you call `InvalidateRect()` to get the client area for the current view redrawn. The argument of 0 invalidates the whole of the client area in the view. Because of the way the rubber-banding process works, some elements may not be displayed properly if you don't do this. If you draw a horizontal line, for instance, and then rubberband a rectangle with the same color so that its top or bottom edge overlaps the line, the overlapped bit of line disappears. This is because the edge being drawn is XORed with the line underneath, so you get the background color back. You also reset the pointer `m_pTempElement` to avoid confusion when another element is created.

Exercising the Document

After saving all the modified files, you can build the latest version of Sketcher and execute it. You'll now be able to produce art such as "the happy programmer" shown in Figure 16-8.

Figure 16-8

The program is now working more realistically. It stores a pointer to each element in the document object, so they're all automatically redrawn as necessary. The program also does a proper cleanup of the document data when it's deleted.

❏   There are still some limitations in the program that you can address. For instance: You can open another view window by using the `Window > New Window` menu option in the program. This capability is built in to an MDI application and opens a new view to an existing document, not a new document. If you draw in one window, however, the elements are not drawn in the other window. Elements never appear in windows other than the one where they were drawn, unless the area they occupy needs to be redrawn for some other reason.

❑ You can only draw in the client area you can see. It would be nice to be able to scroll the view and draw over a bigger area.

❑ Neither can you delete an element, so if you make a mistake, you either live with it or start over with a new document.

These are all quite serious deficiencies that, together, make the program fairly useless as it stands. You'll overcome all of them before the end of this chapter.

Improving the View

The first item that you can try to fix is the updating of all the document windows that are displayed when an element is drawn. The problem arises because only the view in which an element is drawn knows about the new element. Each view is acting independently of the others and there is no communication between them. You need to arrange for any view that adds an element to the document to let all the other views know about it, and they need to take the appropriate action.

Updating Multiple Views

The document class conveniently contains a function UpdateAllViews() to help with this particular problem. This function essentially provides a means for the document to send a message to all its views. You just need to call it from the OnLButtonUp() function in the CSketcherView class, whenever you have added a new element to the document:

```
void CSketcherView::OnLButtonUp(UINT nFlags, CPoint point)
{
   if(this == GetCapture())
      ReleaseCapture();                   // Stop capturing mouse messages

   // If there is an element, add it to the document
   if(m_pTempElement)
   {
      GetDocument()->AddElement(m_pTempElement);
      GetDocument()->UpdateAllViews(0,0,m_pTempElement);  // Tell all the views
      m_pTempElement = 0;                 // Reset the element pointer
   }
}
```

When the m_pTempElement pointer is not NULL, the specific action of the function has been extended to call the UpdateAllViews() member of your document class. This function communicates with the views by causing the OnUpdate() member function in each view to be called. The three arguments to UpdateAllViews() are described in Figure 16-9.

The first argument to the UpdateAllViews() function call is often the this pointer for the current view. This suppresses the call of the OnUpdate() function for the current view. This is a useful feature when the current view is already up to date. In the case of Sketcher, because you are rubber-banding you want to get the current view redrawn as well, so by specifying the first argument as 0 you get the OnUpdate() function called for all the views, including the current view. This removes the need to call InvalidateRect() as you did before.

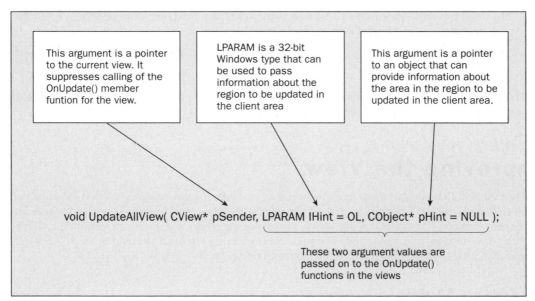

This argument is a pointer to the current view. It suppresses calling of the OnUpdate() member funtion for the view.

LPARAM is a 32-bit Windows type that can be used to pass information about the region to be updated in the client area

This argument is a pointer to an object that can provide information about the area in the region to be updated in the client area.

void UpdateAllView(CView* pSender, LPARAM lHint = OL, CObject* pHint = NULL);

These two argument values are passed on to the OnUpdate() functions in the views

Figure 16-9

You don't use the second argument to UpdateAllViews() here, but you do pass the pointer to the new element through the third argument. Passing a pointer to the new element allows the views to figure out which bit of their client area needs to be redrawn.

To catch the information passed to the UpdateAllViews() function, you add the OnUpdate() member function to the view class. You can do this from the Class wizard and looking at the properties for CSketcherView. As I'm sure you recall, you display the properties for a class by right-clicking the class name and selecting Properties from the pop-up. If you click the Overrides button in the Properties window, you'll be able to find OnUpdate in the list of functions you can override. Click the function name, then the <Add> OnUpdate option that shows in the drop-down list in the adjacent column. If you close the Properties window, you'll be able to edit the code for the OnUpdate() override you have added in the Editor pane. You only need to add the highlighted code below to the function definition:

```
void CSketcherView::OnUpdate(CView* pSender, LPARAM lHint, CObject* pHint)
{
    // Invalidate the area corresponding to the element pointed to
    // if there is one, otherwise invalidate the whole client area
    if(pHint)
        InvalidateRect(((CElement*)pHint)->GetBoundRect());
    else
        InvalidateRect(0);
}
```

Note that you must uncomment the parameter names in the generated version of the function; otherwise, it won't compile with the additional code here. The three arguments passed to the OnUpdate() function in the view class correspond to the arguments that you passed in the UpdateAllViews() function call. Thus, pHint contains the address of the new element. However, you can't assume that this is always the case. The OnUpdate() function is also called when a view is first created, but with a NULL pointer for the third argument. Therefore, the function checks that the pHint pointer isn't NULL and only then gets the bounding rectangle for the element passed as the third argument. It invalidates this area in the client area of the view by passing the rectangle to the InvalidateRect() function. This area is redrawn by the OnDraw() function in this view when the next WM_PAINT message is sent to the view. If the pHint pointer is NULL, the whole client area is invalidated.

You might be tempted to consider redrawing the new element in the OnUpdate() function. This isn't a good idea. You should only do permanent drawing in response to the Windows WM_PAINT message. This means that the OnDraw() function in the view should be the only place that's initiating any drawing operations for document data. This ensures that the view is drawn correctly whenever Windows deems it necessary.

If you build and execute Sketcher with the new modifications included, you should find that all the views are updated to reflect the contents of the document.

Scrolling Views

Adding scrolling to a view looks remarkably easy at first sight; the water is in fact deeper and murkier that it at first appears, but jump in anyway. The first step is to change the base class for CSketcherView from CView to CScrollView. This new base class has the scrolling functionality built in, so you can alter the definition of the CSketcherView class to:

```
class CSketcherView: public CScrollView
{
    // Class definition as before...
};
```

You must also modify two lines of code at the beginning of the SketcherView.cpp file, which refer to the base class for CSketcherView. You need to replace CView with CScrollView as the base class:

```
IMPLEMENT_DYNCREATE(CSketcherView, CScrollView)

BEGIN_MESSAGE_MAP(CSketcherView, CScrollView)
```

However, this is still not quite enough. The new version of the view class needs to know some things about the area you are drawing on, such as the size and how far the view is to be scrolled when you use the scroller. This information has to be supplied before the view is first drawn. You can put the code to do this in the OnInitialUpdate() function in the view class.

You supply the information that is required by calling a function that is inherited from the CScrollView class: SetScrollSizes(). The arguments to this function are explained in Figure 16-10.

Scrolling a distance of one line occurs when you click on the up or down arrow on the scroll bar; a page scroll occurs when you click on the scrollbar itself. You have an opportunity to change the mapping mode here. MM_LOENGLISH would be a good choice for the Sketcher application, but first get scrolling working with the MM_TEXT mapping mode because there are still some difficulties to be uncovered. (Mapping modes are introduced in Chapter 15.)

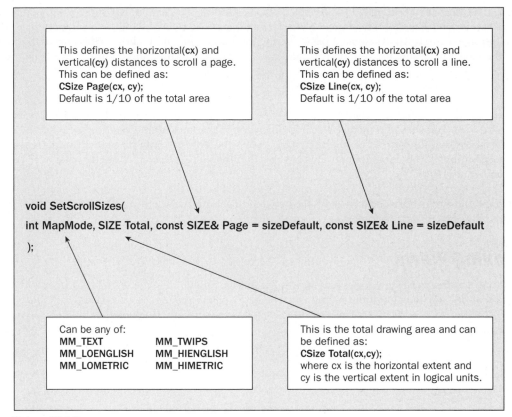

Figure 16-10

To add the code to call `SetScrollSizes()`, you need to override the default version of the `OnInitialUpdate()` function in the view. You access this in the same way as for the `OnUpdate()` function override — through the Properties window for the `CSketcherView` class. After you have added the override, just add the code to the function where indicated by the comment:

```
void CSketcherView::OnInitialUpdate()
{
    CScrollView::OnInitialUpdate();

    // Define document size
    CSize DocSize(20000,20000);

    // Set mapping mode and document size.
    SetScrollSizes(MM_TEXT,DocSize);
}
```

This maintains the mapping mode as `MM_TEXT` and defines the total extent that you can draw on as 20000 pixels in each direction.

This is enough to get the scrolling mechanism working after a fashion. Build the program and execute it with these additions, and you'll be able to draw a few elements and then scroll the view. However, although the window scrolls OK, if you try to draw more elements with the view scrolled, things don't work as they should. The elements appear in a different position from where you draw them and they're not displayed properly. What's going on?

Logical Coordinates and Client Coordinates

The problem is the coordinate systems that you're using — and that plural is deliberate. You've actually been using *two* coordinate systems in all the examples up to now, although you may not have noticed. As you saw in the previous chapter, when you call a function such as LineTo(), it assumes that the arguments passed are **logical coordinates**. The function is a member of the CDC class that defines a device context, and the device context has its own system of logical coordinates. The mapping mode, which is a property of the device context, determines what the unit of measurement is for the coordinates when you draw something.

The coordinate data that you receive along with the mouse messages, on the other hand, has nothing to do with the device context or the CDC object — and outside of a device context, logical coordinates don't apply. The points passed to the OnLButtonDown() and OnMouseMove() handlers have coordinates that are always in device units, that is, pixels, and are measured relative to the upper-left corner of the client area. These are referred to as **client coordinates**. Similarly, when you call InvalidateRect(), the rectangle is assumed to be defined in terms of client coordinates.

In MM_TEXT mode, the client coordinates and the logical coordinates in the device context are both in units of pixels, and so they're the same — *as long as you don't scroll the window*. In all the previous examples there was no scrolling, so everything worked without any problems. With the latest version of Sketcher, it all works fine until you scroll the view, whereupon the logical coordinates origin (the 0,0 point) is moved by the scrolling mechanism, so it's no longer in the same place as the client coordinates origin. The *units* for logical coordinates and client coordinates are the same here, but the *origins* for the two coordinates systems are different. This situation is illustrated in Figure 16-11.

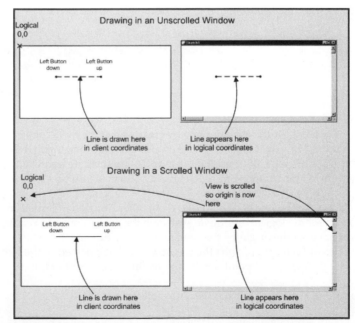

Figure 16-11

The left side shows the position in the client area where you draw, and the points that are the mouse positions defining the line. These are recorded in client coordinates. The right side shows where the line is actually drawn. Drawing is in logical coordinates, but you have been using client coordinate values. In the case of the scrolled window, the line appears displaced due to the logical origin being relocated.

This means that you are actually using the wrong values to define elements in the Sketcher program, and when you invalidate areas of the client area to get them redrawn, the rectangles passed to the function are also wrong — hence, the weird behavior of the program. With other mapping modes it gets worse, because not only are the units of measurement in the two coordinate systems different, but also the *y* axes may be in opposite directions!

Dealing with Client Coordinates

Consider what needs to be done to fix the problem. There are two things you may have to address:

❑ You need to convert the client coordinates that you got with mouse messages to logical coordinates before you can use them to create elements.

❑ You need to convert a bounding rectangle that you created in logical coordinates back to client coordinates if you want to use it in a call to InvalidateRect().

This amounts to making sure you always use logical coordinates when using device context functions, and always use client coordinates for other communications about the window. The functions you have to apply to do the conversions are associated with a device context, so you need to obtain a device context whenever you want to convert from logical to client coordinates, or vice versa. You can use the coordinate conversion functions of the CDC class inherited by CClientDC to do the work.

The new version of the OnLButtonDown() handler incorporating this is:

```
// Handler for left mouse button down message
void CSketcherView::OnLButtonDown(UINT nFlags, CPoint point)
{
    CClientDC aDC(this);                // Create a device context
    OnPrepareDC(&aDC);                  // Get origin adjusted
    aDC.DPtoLP(&point);                 // convert point to Logical
    m_FirstPoint = point;               // Record the cursor position
    SetCapture();                       // Capture subsequent mouse messages
}
```

You obtain a device context for the current view by creating a CClientDC object and passing the pointer this to the constructor. The advantage of CClientDC is that it automatically releases the device context when the object goes out of scope. It's important that device contexts are not retained, as there are a limited number available from Windows and you could run out of them. If you use CClientDC, you're always safe.

As you're using CScrollView, the OnPrepareDC() member function inherited from that class must be called to set the origin for the logical coordinate system in the device context to correspond with the scrolled position. After you have set the origin by this call, you use the function DPtoLP(), which converts from **Device Points to Logical Points**, to convert the point value that's passed to the handler to logical coordinates. You then store the converted point, ready for creating an element in the OnMouseMove() handler.

The new code for the OnMouseMove() handler is as follows:

```
void CSketcherView::OnMouseMove(UINT nFlags, CPoint point)
```

```
{
    CClientDC aDC(this);              // Device context for the current view
    OnPrepareDC(&aDC);                // Get origin adjusted

    if((nFlags&MK_LBUTTON)&&(this==GetCapture()))
    {
        aDC.DPtoLP(&point);          // convert point to Logical
        m_SecondPoint = point;        // Save the current cursor position

    // Rest of the function as before...
}
```

The code for the conversion of the point value passed to the handler is essentially the same as in the previous handler, and that's all you need here for the moment. The last function that you must change is easy to overlook: the OnUpdate() function in the view class. This needs to be modified to:

```
void CSketcherView::OnUpdate(CView* pSender, LPARAM lHint, CObject* pHint)
{
    // Invalidate the area corresponding to the element pointed to
    // if there is one, otherwise invalidate the whole client area
    if(pHint)
    {
        CClientDC aDC(this);          // Create a device context
        OnPrepareDC(&aDC);            // Get origin adjusted

        // Get the enclosing rectangle and convert to client coordinates
        CRect aRect=((CElement*)pHint)->GetBoundRect();
        aDC.LPtoDP(aRect);
        InvalidateRect(aRect);        // Get the area redrawn
    }
    else
        InvalidateRect(0);            // Invalidate the client area
}
```

The modification here creates a CClientDC object and uses the LPtoDP() function member to convert the rectangle for the area that's to be redrawn to client coordinates.

If you now compile and execute Sketcher with the modifications I have discussed and are lucky enough not to have introduced any typos, it will work correctly, regardless of the scroller position.

Using MM_LOENGLISH Mapping Mode

Now look into what you need to do to use the MM_LOENGLISH mapping mode. This provides drawings in logical units of 0.01 inches, and also ensures that the drawing size is consistent on displays at different resolutions. This makes the application much more satisfactory from the users' point of view.

You can set the mapping mode in the call to SetScrollSizes() made from the OnInitialUpdate() function in the view class. You also need to specify the total drawing area, so, if you define it as 3000 by 3000, this provides a drawing area of 30 inches by 30 inches, which should be adequate. The default scroll distances for a line and a page is satisfactory, so you don't need to specify those. You can use Class View to get to the OnInitialUpdate() function and then change it to the following:

```
void CSketcherView::OnInitialUpdate(void)
```

```
   {
      CScrollView::OnInitialUpdate();

      // Define document size as 30x30ins in MM_LOENGLISH
      CSize DocSize(3000,3000);

      // Set mapping mode and document size.
      SetScrollSizes(MM_LOENGLISH, DocSize);
   }
```

You just alter the arguments in the call to `SetScrollSizes()` for the mapping mode and document the size that you want. That's all that's necessary to enable the view to work in MM_LOENGLISH, but you still need to fix how you deal with rectangles.

Note that you are not limited to setting the mapping mode once and for all. You can change the mapping mode in a device context at any time and draw different parts of the image to be displayed using different mapping modes. A function `SetMapMode()` is used to do this, but I won't be going into this any further here. You can get your application working just using MM_LOENGLISH. Whenever you create a `CClientDC` object for the view and call `OnPrepareDC()`, the device context that it owns has the mapping mode you've set in the `OnInitialUpdate()` function.

The problem you have with rectangles is that the element classes all assume the mapping mode is MM_TEXT, and in MM_LOENGLISH the rectangles are upside down because of the reversal of the y-axis. When you apply `LPtoDP()` to a rectangle, it is assumed to be oriented properly with respect to the MM_LOENGLISH axes. Because yours are not, the function mirrors the rectangles in the x-axis. This creates a problem when you call `InvalidateRect()` to invalidate an area of a view because the mirrored rectangle in device coordinates is not recognized by Windows as being inside the visible client area.

You have two options for dealing with this. You can modify the element classes so that the enclosing rectangles are the right way up for MM_LOENGLISH, or you can re-normalize the rectangle that you intend to pass to the `InvalidateRect()` function. The latter is the easiest course because you only need to modify one member of the view class, `OnUpdate()`:

```
void CSketcherView::OnUpdate(CView* pSender, LPARAM lHint, CObject* pHint)
{
   // Invalidate the area corresponding to the element pointed to
   // if there is one, otherwise invalidate the whole client area
   if(pHint)
   {
      CClientDC aDC(this);            // Create a device context
      OnPrepareDC(&aDC);              // Get origin adjusted

      // Get the enclosing rectangle and convert to client coordinates
      CRect aRect=((CElement*)pHint)->GetBoundRect();
      aDC.LPtoDP(aRect);
      aRect.NormalizeRect();
      InvalidateRect(aRect);         // Get the area redrawn
   }
   else
      InvalidateRect(0);
}
```

That should do it for the program as it stands. If you rebuild Sketcher, you should have scrolling work-ing, with support for multiple views. You'll need to remember to re-normalize any rectangle that you convert to device coordinates for use with `InvalidateRect()` in the future. Any reverse conversions are also affected.

Deleting and Moving Shapes

Being able to delete shapes is a fundamental requirement in a drawing program. One question relating to this is how you're going to select the element you want to delete. Of course, after you decide how to select an element, this applies equally well if you want to move an element, so you can treat moving and deleting elements as related problems. But first consider how you're going to bring move and delete operations into the program.

A neat way of providing move and delete functions would be to have a pop-up **context menu** appear at the cursor position when you click the right mouse button. You could then put Move and Delete as items on the menu. A pop-up that works like this is a very handy facility that you can use in lots of different situations.

How should the pop-up be used? The standard way that context menus work is that the user moves the mouse over a particular object and right-clicks on it. This selects the object and pops up a menu contain-ing a list of items, which relate to actions that can be performed on that object. This means that different objects can have different menus. You can see this in action in Developer Studio itself. When you right-click on a class icon in Class View, you get a menu that's different from the one you get if you right-click on the icon for a member function. The menu that appears is sensitive to the context of the cursor, hence the term "context menu." You have two contexts to consider in Sketcher. You could right-click with the cursor over an element, and you could right-click when there is no element under the cursor.

So, how can you implement this functionality in the Sketcher application? You can do it simply by creating two menus: one for when you have an element under the cursor, and one for when you don't. You can check if there's an element under the cursor when the user presses the right mouse button. If there *is* an element under the cursor, you can highlight the element so that the user knows exactly which element the context pop-up is referring to.

Take a look at how you can create a pop-up at the cursor and, after that works, come back to how to implement the detail of the move and delete operations.

Implementing a Context Menu

The first step is to create a menu containing two pop-ups: one containing `Move` and `Delete` as items, the other a combination of items from the `Element` and `Color` menus. So, change to Resource View and expand the list of resources. Right-click on the `Menu` folder to bring up a context menu — another demonstration of what you are now trying to create in the Sketcher application. Select `Insert Menu` to create a new menu. This has a default ID `IDR_MENU1` assigned, but you can change this. Select the name of the new menu in the

Resource View and display the Properties window for the resource by pressing Alt+Enter (This is a short-cut to the View > Other Windows > Properties Window menu item). You can then edit the resource ID in the Properties window by clicking the value for the ID. You could change it to something more suitable, such as IDR_CURSOR_MENU, in the right column. Note that the name for a menu resource must start with IDR. Pressing the Enter key saves the new name.

You can now create two new items on the menu bar in the Editor pane. These can have any old captions because they won't actually be seen by the user. They represents the two context menus that you provide with Sketcher, so you can name them element and no element, according to the situation in which the context menu will be used. Now you can add the Move and Delete items to the element pop-up. The default IDs of ID_ELEMENT_MOVE and ID_ELEMENT_DELETE will do fine, but you could change them if you wanted to in the Properties window for each item. Figure 16-12 shows how the new element menu looks.

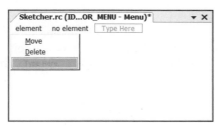

Figure 16-12

The second menu contains the list of available element types and colors, identical to the items on the Element and Color menus on the main menu bar, but here separated by a Separator. The IDs you use for these items must be the same as you applied to the IDR_SketcherTYPE menu. This is because the handler for a menu is associated with the menu ID. Menu items with the same ID use the same handlers, so the same handler is used for the Line menu item regardless of whether it's invoked from the main menu pop-up or from the context menu.

You have a shortcut that saves you having to create all these menu items one-by-one. If you display the IDR_SketcherTYPE menu and extend the Element menu, you can select all the menu items by clicking the first item and then by clicking the last item while holding down the Shift key. You can then right-click the selection and select Copy from the pop-up or simply press Ctrl+C. If you then return to the IDR_CURSOR_MENU and right-click the first item on the no-element menu, you can insert the complete contents of the Element menu by selecting Paste from the pop-up or by pressing Ctrl+V. The copied menu items will have the same IDs as the originals. To insert the separator, just right-click the empty menu item and select Insert Separator from the pop-up. Repeat the process for the Color menu items and you're done — almost. Putting the items from the Element and Color menus together has created a conflict — both Rectangle and Red share the same shortcut. Changing &Red to Re&d here will fix it, and it's a good idea to change it on in the IDRSketcherTYPE menu too for consistency. You do this by editing the Caption property for the menu item. The completed menu should look as shown in Figure 16-13.

Close the properties box and save the resource file. At the moment, all you have is the definition of the menu in a resource file. It isn't connected to the code in the Sketcher program. You now need to associate this menu and its ID, IDR_CURSOR_MENU, with the view class. You also must create command handlers for the menu items in the pop-up corresponding to the IDs ID_MOVE and ID_DELETE.

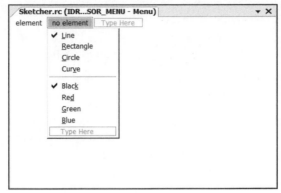

Figure 16-13

Associating a Menu with a Class

To associate the context menu with the view class in Sketcher, go to the Class View pane and display the Properties window for CSketcherView by right-clicking the class name and selecting Properties from the pop-up. If you click the Messages button in the Properties window, you'll be able to add a handler for the WM_CONTEXTMENU message by selecting <Add>OnContextMenu from the adjacent cell in the right column. You can then add the following code to the handler:

```
void CSketcherView::OnContextMenu(CWnd* pWnd, CPoint point)
{
  CMenu menu;
    menu.LoadMenu(IDR_CURSOR_MENU);              // Load the context menu
    CMenu* pPopup = menu.GetSubMenu(0);          // Get the first menu
    ASSERT(pPopup != NULL);                      // Ensure it's there

    // Display the popup menu
    pPopup->TrackPopupMenu(TPM_LEFTALIGN | TPM_RIGHTBUTTON, point.x, point.y, this);
}
```

For now, this handler arbitrarily displays the first of the two context menus. You still need to figure out how you'll determine whether or not the cursor is over an element to decide which menu to display, but we'll come back to that a little later. Calling the LoadMenu() method for the menu object loads the menu resource corresponding to the ID supplied as the argument and attaches it to the CMenu object menu. The GetSubMenu() function returns a pointer to the pop-up menu corresponding to the integer argument that specifies the position of the pop-up, with 0 being the first pop-up, 1 being the second, and so on. After you ensure the pointer returned by GetSubMenu() is not NULL, you display the pop-up by calling TrackPopupMenu().

The first argument to the `TrackPopupMenu()` function consists of two flags ORed together. One flag specifies how the pop-up menu should be positioned and can be any of the following values:

Flag	Description
TPM_CENTERALIGN	Centers the pop-up horizontally relative to the *x* coordinate supplied as the second argument to the function.
TPM_LEFTALIGN	Positions the pop-up so that the left side of the menu is aligned with the *x* coordinate supplied as the second argument to the function.
TPM_RIGHTALIGN	Positions the pop-up so that the right side of the menu is aligned with the *x* coordinate supplied as the second argument to the function.

The second flag specifies the mouse button and can be either of the following:

Flag	Description
TPM_LEFTBUTTON	Specifies that the pop-up tracks the left mouse button.
TPM_RIGHTBUTTON	Specifies that the pop-up tracks the right mouse button.

The next two arguments to the `TrackPopupMenu()` function specify the *x* and *y* coordinates of the pop-up menu on the screen respectively. The *y* coordinate determines to position of the top of the menu. The fourth argument specifies the window that owns the menu and that should receive all WM_COMMAND messages from the menu.

Now you can add the handlers for the items in the first pop-up menu. Return to the Resource View and double-click on IDR_CURSOR_MENU. Right-click the Move menu item and then select Add Event Handler from the pop-up. You can then specify the handler in the dialog for the Event Handler wizard, as shown in Figure 16-14.

It's a COMMAND handler and is to be created in the CSketcherView class. Click the Add and Edit button to create the handler function. You can follow the same procedure to create the hander for the Delete menu item.

You don't have to do anything for the second context menu, as you already have handlers written for them in the document class. These take care of the messages from the pop-up items automatically.

Choosing a Context Menu

At the moment, the `OnContextMenu()` handler only displays the first context pop-up, no matter where the right button is clicked in the view. This isn't really what you want it to do. The first context menu applies specifically to an element, whereas the second context menu applies in general. You want to display the first menu if there is an element under the cursor and to display the second menu if there isn't.

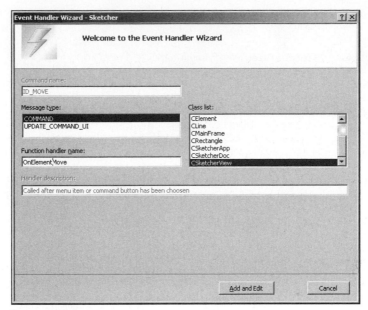

Figure 16-14

You need two things to fix this up: You need a mechanism to find out which (if any) element is at the current cursor position, and you need to save the address of this element somewhere so you can use it in the OnContextMenu() handler. You can deal with saving the address of the element first because this is the easier bit.

When you find out which element is under the cursor, you'll store its address in a data member, m_pSelected, of the view class. This is available to the right mouse button handler because that's in the same class. You can add the declaration for this variable to the protected section of the CSketcherView class:

```
class CSketcherView: public CScrollView
{
  // Rest of the class as before...

  protected:
    CPoint m_FirstPoint;        // First point recorded for an element
    CPoint m_SecondPoint;       // Second point recorded for an element
    CElement* m_pTempElement;   // Pointer to temporary element
    CElement* m_pSelected;      // Currently selected element

    // Rest of the class as before...
};
```

You can add this manually or alternatively, you can right-click the class name and select
Add > AddVariable from the pop-up to open the dialog for adding a data member. If you add

`m_pSelected` manually you'll also need to initialize this element in the class constructor, so add the following code:

```
CSketcherView::CSketcherView()
: m_FirstPoint(CPoint(0,0))
, m_SecondPoint(CPoint(0,0))
, m_pTempElement(NULL)
, m_pSelected(NULL)
{
    // TODO: add construction code here
}
```

You'll figure out how to decide when an element is under the cursor in a moment, but in the meantime you can use the `m_pSelected` member of the view in the implementation of the `OnContextMenu()` handler:

```
void CSketcherView::OnContextMenu(CWnd* pWnd, CPoint point)
{
    CMenu menu;
    menu.LoadMenu(IDR_CURSOR_MENU);
    CMenu* pPopup = menu.GetSubMenu(m_pSelected == 0 ? 1 : 0);
    ASSERT(pPopup != NULL);
    pPopup->TrackPopupMenu(TPM_LEFTALIGN | TPM_RIGHTBUTTON, point.x, point.y, this);
}
```

The expression `m_pSelected == 0 ? 1 : 0` results in 1 when the pointer is null and 0 otherwise; so you'll select the first pop-up menu containing Move and Delete when `m_pSelected` is not null and the second pop-up when it is.

Identifying a Selected Element

To keep track of which element is under the cursor you can add code to the `OnMouseMove()` handler in the `CSketcherView` class. This handler is called every time the mouse cursor moves, so all you have to do is add code to test whether there's an element under the current cursor position and set `m_pSelected` accordingly. The test whether a particular element is under the cursor is simple; if the cursor position is within the bounding rectangle for an element, that element is under the cursor. Here's how you can modify the `OnMouseMove()` handler to check if there's an element under the cursor:

```
void CSketcherView::OnMouseMove(UINT nFlags, CPoint point)
{
    // Define a Device Context object for the view
    CClientDC aDC(this);                 // DC is for this view
    OnPrepareDC(&aDC);                   // Get origin adjusted

    CSketcherDoc* pDoc=GetDocument();    // Get a pointer to the document
    CElement* pElement = 0;              // Store an element pointer
    CRect aRect(0,0,0,0);                // Store a rectangle
    POSITION aPos = pDoc->GetListHeadPosition();  // Get first element position
    m_pSelected = 0;
    while(aPos)                          // Iterate through the list
    {
        pElement = pDoc->GetNext(aPos);
        aRect = pElement->GetBoundRect();
        aDC.LPtoDP(aRect);               // Convert to device coordinates
```

```
      aRect.NormalizeRect();               // Renormalize the rectangle

      if(aRect.PtInRect(point))            // Is the current element under the cursor?
      {
        m_pSelected = pElement;
        break;
      }
    }

  if((nFlags&MK_LBUTTON)  && (this==GetCapture()))
  {
      aDC.DPtoLP(&point);                   // convert point to Logical
      m_SecondPoint = point;                // Save the current cursor position

      if(m_pTempElement)
      {
          if(CURVE == GetDocument()->GetElementType())    // Is it a curve?
          {  // We are drawing a curve
              // so add a segment to the existing curve
              static_cast<CCurve*>(m_pTempElement)->AddSegment(m_SecondPoint);
              m_pTempElement->Draw(&aDC);   // Now draw it
              return;                       // We are done
          }

          aDC.SetROP2(R2_NOTXORPEN);                      // Set drawing mode
          // Redraw the old element so it disappears from the view
          m_pTempElement->Draw(&aDC);
          delete m_pTempElement;            // Delete the old element
          m_pTempElement = 0;               // Reset the pointer to 0
      }

      // Create a temporary element of the type and color that
      // is recorded in the document object, and draw it
      m_pTempElement = CreateElement();// Create a new element
      m_pTempElement->Draw(&aDC);       // Draw the element
  }
}
```

The new code looks like a lot, but it is very simple. It tests whether the cursor lies within the bounding rectangle for each element in turn, and stores the address of the first element where this is the case in m_pSelected. If the cursor does not lie within any of the bounding rectangles, m_pSelected element contains 0. Note how you convert each bounding rectangle to device coordinates and renormalize before testing it. Without this the rectangle would be in the wrong place because the mapping mode is MM_LOENGLISH.

The code is now in a state where you can test the context menus.

Exercising the Pop-Ups

You have added all the code you need to make the pop-ups operate, so you can build and execute Sketcher to try it out. If there are no elements under the cursor, the second context pop-up appears, allowing you to change the element type and color. These options work because they generate exactly the same messages as the main menu options and because you have already written handlers for them.

If there is an element under the cursor, the first context menu will appear with Move and Delete on it. It won't do anything at the moment, as you've yet to implement the handlers for the messages it generates. Try right button clicks outside of the view window. Messages for these are not passed to the document view window in your application, so the pop-up is not displayed.

Note that the context menu to select elements and colors isn't quite right — they set the right type or color in the class but the check marks in the pop-up are not set properly. The document class handles the messages from the menu, but the UPDATE_COMMAND_UI messages don't apply to the context menu — they only work with the IDR_SketcherTYPE menu. Read on to see how you can fix that.

Checking the Context Menu Items

Checking the items in the no element menu has to be done in the OnContextMenu() function in the CSketcherView class before the context menu is displayed. The CMenu class has a function designed to do exactly what you want. Its prototype is:

```
UINT CheckMenuItem(UINT nIDCheckItem, UINT nCheck);
```

This function checks or unchecks any item in the context menu. The first parameter selects which entry in the context pop-up is to be checked or unchecked; the second parameter is a combination of two flags, one of which determines how the first parameter specifies which item is to be checked, and the other specifies whether the menu item is to be checked or unchecked. Because each flag is a single bit in a UINT value, you combine the two using the bitwise OR.

The flag to determine how the item is identified can be one of two possible values:

MF_BYPOSITION	The first parameter is an index where 0 specifies the first item, 1 the second, and so on.
MF_BYCOMMAND	The first parameter is a menu ID.

Use MF_BYCOMMAND so you won't have to worry about the sequence in which the menu items appear in the pop-up, or even in which submenu they appear.

The possible flag values to check or uncheck an item are MF_CHECKED and MF_UNCHECKED, respectively.

The code for checking or unchecking a menu item is essentially the same for all the menu items in the second context pop-up. See how you can set the check for the menu item Black correctly. The first argument to the CheckMenuItem() function will be the menu ID, ID_COLOR_BLACK. The second argument is MF_BYCOMMAND combined with either MF_CHECKED or MF_UNCHECKED, depending on the current color selected. You can obtain the current color from the document using the GetElementColor() function, with the following statement:

```
COLORREF Color = GetDocument()->GetElementColor();
```

You can use the `Color` variable to select the appropriate flag using the conditional operator, and then combine the result with the `MF_BYCOMMAND` flag to obtain the second argument to the `CheckMenuItem()` function, so the statement to set the check for the item is:

```
menu.CheckMenuItem(ID_COLOR_BLACK,
                    (BLACK==Color ? MF_CHECKED : MF_UNCHECKED) | MF_BYCOMMAND);
```

You don't need to specify the sub-menu here because the menu item is uniquely defined in the menu by its ID. You just need to change the ID and the color value in this statement to obtain the statement to set the flags for each of the other color menu items.

Checking the element menu items is essentially the same. To check the Line menu item you can write:

```
unsigned int ElementType = GetDocument()->GetElementType();
menu.CheckMenuItem(ID_ELEMENT_LINE,
                (LINE==ElementType ? MF_CHECKED : MF_UNCHECKED) | MF_BYCOMMAND);
```

The complete code for the `OnContextMenu()` handler is:

```
void CSketcherView::OnContextMenu(CWnd* pWnd, CPoint point)
{
    CMenu menu;
    menu.LoadMenu(IDR_CURSOR_MENU);

    // Set check marks if it's the no element menu
    if(m_pSelected == 0)
    {
        // Check color menu items
        COLORREF Color = GetDocument()->GetElementColor();
        menu.CheckMenuItem(ID_COLOR_BLACK,
            (BLACK==Color ? MF_CHECKED : MF_UNCHECKED) | MF_BYCOMMAND);
        menu.CheckMenuItem(ID_COLOR_RED,
            (RED==Color ? MF_CHECKED : MF_UNCHECKED) | MF_BYCOMMAND);
        menu.CheckMenuItem(ID_COLOR_GREEN,
            (GREEN==Color ? MF_CHECKED : MF_UNCHECKED) | MF_BYCOMMAND);
        menu.CheckMenuItem(ID_COLOR_BLUE,
            (BLUE==Color ? MF_CHECKED : MF_UNCHECKED) | MF_BYCOMMAND);

        // Check element menu items
        unsigned int ElementType = GetDocument()->GetElementType();
        menu.CheckMenuItem(ID_ELEMENT_LINE,
            (LINE==ElementType ? MF_CHECKED : MF_UNCHECKED) | MF_BYCOMMAND);
        menu.CheckMenuItem(ID_ELEMENT_RECTANGLE,
            (RECTANGLE==ElementType ? MF_CHECKED : MF_UNCHECKED) | MF_BYCOMMAND);
        menu.CheckMenuItem(ID_ELEMENT_CIRCLE,
            (CIRCLE==ElementType ? MF_CHECKED : MF_UNCHECKED) | MF_BYCOMMAND);
        menu.CheckMenuItem(ID_ELEMENT_CURVE,
            (CURVE==ElementType ? MF_CHECKED : MF_UNCHECKED) | MF_BYCOMMAND);
    }
```

```
        CMenu* pPopup = menu.GetSubMenu(m_pSelected == 0 ? 1 : 0);
        ASSERT(pPopup != NULL);
        pPopup->TrackPopupMenu(TPM_LEFTALIGN | TPM_RIGHTBUTTON, point.x, point.y, this);
    }
```

With this change, the context menu items should be checked correctly when you build and run Sketcher again.

Highlighting Elements

Ideally, the user will want to know which element is under the cursor *before* they right-click to get the context menu. When you want to delete an element, you want to know which element you are operating on. Equally, when you want to use the other context menu — to change color, for example — you need to be sure no element is under the cursor. To show precisely which element is under the cursor, you need to highlight it in some way before a right button click occurs.

You can do this in the `Draw()` member function for an element. All you need to do is pass an argument to the `Draw()` function to indicate when the element should be highlighted. If you pass the address of the currently-selected element that you save in the `m_pSelected` member of the view to the `Draw()` function, you will be able to compare it to the `this` pointer to see if it is the current element.

Highlights all work in the same way, so let's take the `CLine` member as an example. You can add similar code to each of the classes for the other element types. Before you start changing `CLine`, you must first amend the definition of the base class `CElement`:

```
class CElement : public CObject
{
    protected:
        COLORREF m_Color;              // Color of an element
        CRect m_EnclosingRect;         // Rectangle enclosing an element
        int m_Pen;                     // Pen width

    public:
        virtual ~CElement(void);
        // Virtual draw operation
        virtual void Draw(CDC* pDC,CElement* pElement=0) {}

        CRect GetBoundRect();          // Get the bounding rectangle for an element

    protected:
        CElement(void);                // Here to prevent it being called
};
```

The change is to add a second parameter to the virtual `Draw()` function. This is a pointer to an element. The reason for initializing the second parameter to zero is to allow the use of the function with just one argument; the second will be supplied as 0 by default.

You need to modify the declaration of the `Draw()` function in each of the classes derived from `CElement` in exactly the same way. For example, you should change the `CLine` class definition to:

```
class CLine :
    public CElement
```

```
{
public:
    ~CLine(void);
    // Function to display a line
    virtual void Draw(CDC* pDC, CElement* pElement=0);

    // Constructor for a line object
    CLine(CPoint Start, CPoint End, COLORREF aColor);

protected:
    CPoint m_StartPoint;            // Start point of line
    CPoint m_EndPoint;              // End point of line

    CLine(void);                    // Default constructor - should not be used
};
```

The implementation for each of the Draw() functions for the classes derived from CElement all need to be extended in the same way. The function for the CLine class is:

```
void CLine::Draw(CDC* pDC, CElement* pElement)
{
    // Create a pen for this object and
    // initialize it to the object color and line width of 1 pixel
    CPen aPen;
    COLORREF aColor = m_Color;           // Initialize with element color
    if(this == pElement)                 // This element selected?
        aColor = SELECT_COLOR;           // Set highlight color
    if(!aPen.CreatePen(PS_SOLID, m_Pen, aColor))
    {
        // Pen creation failed. Abort the program
        AfxMessageBox(_T("Pen creation failed drawing a line"), MB_OK);
        AfxAbort();
    }

    CPen* pOldPen = pDC->SelectObject(&aPen);  // Select the pen

    // Now draw the line
    pDC->MoveTo(m_StartPoint);
    pDC->LineTo(m_EndPoint);

    pDC->SelectObject(pOldPen);                // Restore the old pen
}
```

This is a very simple change. You set the new local variable aColor to the current color stored in m_Color, and the if statement will reset the value of aColor to SELECT_COLOR when pElement is equal to this — which is the case when the current element and the selected element are the same. You also need to add the definition for SELECT_COLOR to the OurConstants.h file:

```
//Definitions of constants

#pragma once

    // Element type definitions
    // Each type value must be unique
```

```
const unsigned int LINE = 101U;
const unsigned int RECTANGLE = 102U;
const unsigned int CIRCLE = 103U;
const unsigned int CURVE = 104U;
//////////////////////////////////

// Color values for drawing
const COLORREF BLACK = RGB(0,0,0);
const COLORREF RED = RGB(255,0,0);
const COLORREF GREEN = RGB(0,255,0);
const COLORREF BLUE = RGB(0,0,255);
const COLORREF SELECT_COLOR = RGB(255,0,180);
//////////////////////////////////
```

Now you should add an #include directive for OurConstants.h to the Elements.cpp file to make the definition of SELECT_COLOR available. You have nearly implemented the highlighting. The derived classes of the CElement class are now able to draw themselves as selected — you just need a mechanism to cause an element to *be* selected. So where should you do this? You determine which element, if any, is under the cursor in the OnMouseMove() handler in the CSketcherView class, so that's obviously the place to expedite the highlighting.

The amendments to the OnMouseMove() handler are:

```
void CSketcherView::OnMouseMove(UINT nFlags, CPoint point)
{
  // Define a Device Context object for the view
  CClientDC aDC(this);                   // DC is for this view
  OnPrepareDC(&aDC);                     // Get origin adjusted

  if((nFlags&MK_LBUTTON)  && (this==GetCapture()))
  {
    aDC.DPtoLP(&point);                  // convert point to Logical
    m_SecondPoint = point;               // Save the current cursor position

    if(m_pTempElement)
    {
      if(CURVE == GetDocument()->GetElementType())    // Is it a curve?
      {  // We are drawing a curve
         // so add a segment to the existing curve
         static_cast<CCurve*>(m_pTempElement)->AddSegment(m_SecondPoint);
         m_pTempElement->Draw(&aDC);    // Now draw it
         return;                         // We are done
      }

      aDC.SetROP2(R2_NOTXORPEN);         // Set drawing mode
      // Redraw the old element so it disappears from the view
      m_pTempElement->Draw(&aDC);
      delete m_pTempElement;             // Delete the old element
      m_pTempElement = 0;                // Reset the pointer to 0
    }

    // Create a temporary element of the type and color that
    // is recorded in the document object, and draw it
    m_pTempElement = CreateElement();  // Create a new element
```

```
        m_pTempElement->Draw(&aDC);          // Draw the element
  }
  else
  { // We are not drawing an element so do highlighting...
    CSketcherDoc* pDoc=GetDocument();    // Get a pointer to the document
    CElement* pElement = 0;              // Store an element pointer
    CRect aRect(0,0,0,0);                // Store a rectangle
    POSITION aPos = pDoc->GetListHeadPosition();  // Get first element posn
    CElement* pOldSelection = m_pSelected;        // Save old selected element
    m_pSelected = 0;
    while(aPos)                          // Iterate through the list
    {
      pElement = pDoc->GetNext(aPos);
      aRect = pElement->GetBoundRect();
      aDC.LPtoDP(aRect);
      aRect.NormalizeRect();

      // Select the first element that appears under the cursor
      if(aRect.PtInRect(point))
      {
        m_pSelected = pElement;
        break;
      }
    }
    if(m_pSelected == pOldSelection)     // If new selection is same as old
      return;                            // we are done

    // Unhighlight old selection if there is one
    if(pOldSelection != 0)               // Verify there is one
    {
      aRect = pOldSelection->GetBoundRect();
      aDC.LPtoDP(aRect);                 // Convert to device coords
      aRect.NormalizeRect();             // Normalize
      InvalidateRect(aRect, FALSE);      // Invalidate area
    }

    // Highlight new selection if there is one
    if(m_pSelected != 0)                 // Verify there is one
    {
      aRect = m_pSelected->GetBoundRect();
      aDC.LPtoDP(aRect);                 // Convert to device coords
      aRect.NormalizeRect();             // Normalize
      InvalidateRect(aRect, FALSE);      // Invalidate area
    }
  }
}
```

You only want to deal with highlighting elements when you are not in the process of creating a new element. All the highlighting code can thus be added in a new else clause for the main if. This involves moving the code you had previously to determine the element under the cursor to the new else clause and adding to it.

You must keep track of any previously highlighted element because if there's a new one, you must unhighlight the old one. To do this you save the value of m_pSelected in pOldSelection. You then search for an element under the cursor and if there is one, you store its address in m_pSelected.

If pOldSelection and m_pSelected are equal then either they both contain the address of the same element or they are both zero. If they are the same and non-zero, what was already highlighted should stay highlighted so there's nothing to be done. If they are both zero, nothing was highlighted and nothing needs to be highlighted so there's nothing to do in this case too. Either way you just return from the function. If they are different, you may have to do something with both.

If pOldSelection is not null then you must un-highlight the old element. The mechanism is the same as before — get the bounding rectangle in device coordinates and pass it to the InvalidateRect() function for the device context. You then check m_pSelected and if it is not null then you have to highlight the element whose address it contains. This again involves getting the bounding rectangle in device coordinates and pass it to the InvalidateRect() function.

Drawing Highlighted Elements

You still need to arrange that the highlighted element is actually drawn highlighted. Somewhere, the m_pSelected pointer must be passed to the draw function for each element. The only place to do this is in the OnDraw() function in the view:

```
void CSketcherView::OnDraw(CDC* pDC)
{
  CSketcherDoc* pDoc = GetDocument();
  ASSERT_VALID(pDoc);
  if(!pDoc)
    return;

  POSITION aPos = pDoc->GetListHeadPosition();
  CElement* pElement = 0;                // Store for an element pointer
  while(aPos)                            // Loop while aPos is not null
  {
    pElement = pDoc->GetNext(aPos);      // Get the current element pointer
    // If the element is visible...
    if(pDC->RectVisible(pElement->GetBoundRect()))
      pElement->Draw(pDC, m_pSelected);// ...draw it
  }
}
```

You only need to change one line. The Draw() function for an element has the second argument added to communicate the address of the element to be highlighted.

Exercising the Highlights

This is all that's required for the highlighting to work all the time. It wasn't trivial but on the other hand it wasn't terribly difficult either. You can build and execute Sketcher to try it out. Any time there is an element under the cursor, the element is drawn in magenta. This makes it obvious which element the context menu is going to act on before you right-click the mouse and means that you know in advance which context menu is displayed.

Servicing the Menu Messages

The next step is to provide code in the bodies of the handlers for the Move and Delete menu items that you added earlier. You can add the code for Delete first, as that's the simpler of the two.

Deleting an Element

The code that you need in the `OnElementDelete()` handler in the `CSketcherView` class to delete the currently selected element is simple:

```
void CSketcherView::OnElementDelete()
{
  if(m_pSelected)
  {
    CSketcherDoc* pDoc = GetDocument();// Get the document pointer
    pDoc->DeleteElement(m_pSelected);  // Delete the element
    pDoc->UpdateAllViews(0);           // Redraw all the views
    m_pSelected = 0;                   // Reset selected element ptr
  }
}
```

The code to delete an element is only executed if `m_pSelected` contains a valid address, indicating that there is an element to be deleted. You get a pointer to the document and call the function `DeleteElement()` for the document object; you'll add this member to the `CSketcherDoc` class in a moment. When the element has been removed from the document, you call `UpdateAllViews()` to get all the views redrawn without the deleted element. Finally, you set `m_pSelected` to zero to indicate that there isn't an element selected.

You can add a declaration for `DeleteElement()` as a `public` member of the `CSketcherDoc` class:

```
class CSketcherDoc : public CDocument
{
protected: // create from serialization only
  CSketcherDoc();
  DECLARE_DYNCREATE(CSketcherDoc)

// Attributes
public:

// Operations
public:
    void DeleteElement(CElement* pElement); // Delete an element
    unsigned int GetElementType()           // Get the element type
          { return m_Element; }

// Rest of the class as before...
};
```

It accepts a pointer to the element to be deleted as an argument and returns nothing. You can implement it in `SketcherDoc.cpp` as:

```
void CSketcherDoc::DeleteElement(CElement* pElement)
{
  if(pElement)
  {
    // If the element pointer is valid,
    // find the pointer in the list and delete it
    POSITION aPosition = m_ElementList.Find(pElement);
    m_ElementList.RemoveAt(aPosition);
```

```
        delete pElement;              // Delete the element from the heap
    }
}
```

You shouldn't have any trouble understanding how this works. After making sure that you have a non-null pointer, you find the POSITION value for the pointer in the list using the Find() member of the list object. You use this with the RemoveAt() member to delete the pointer from the list, then delete the element pointed to by the parameter pElement from the heap.

That's all you need to delete elements. You should now have a Sketcher program in which you can draw in multiple scrolled views, and delete any of the elements in your sketch from any of the views.

Moving an Element

Moving the selected element is a bit more involved. As the element must move along with the mouse cursor, you must add code to the OnMouseMove() method to account for this behavior. As this function is also used to draw elements, you need a mechanism for indicating when you're in "move" mode. The easiest way to do this is to have a flag in the view class, which you can call m_MoveMode. If you make it of type BOOL, you use the value TRUE for when move mode is on, and FALSE for when it's off. Of course, you could also define it as the fundamental type, bool, and the values are true and false.

You'll also have to keep track of the cursor during the move, so you can another data member in the view for this. You can call it m_CursorPos, and it will be of type CPoint. Another thing you should provide for is the possibility of aborting a move. To do this you must remember the first position of the cursor when the move operation started, so you can move the element back when necessary. This is another member of type CPoint, and it is called m_FirstPos. Add the three new members to the protected section of the view class:

```
class CSketcherView: public CScrollView
{
  // Rest of the class as before...

  protected:
    CPoint m_FirstPoint;        // First point recorded for an element
    CPoint m_SecondPoint;       // Second point recorded for an element
    CElement* m_pTempElement;   // Pointer to temporary element
    CElement* m_pSelected;      // Currently selected element
    BOOL m_MoveMode;            // Move element flag
    CPoint m_CursorPos;         // Cursor position
    CPoint m_FirstPos;          // Original position in a move

  // Rest of the class as before...
};
```

These must also be initialized in the constructor for CSketcherView so modify it to:

```
CSketcherView::CSketcherView()
: m_FirstPoint(CPoint(0,0))
, m_SecondPoint(CPoint(0,0))
, m_pTempElement(NULL)
, m_pSelected(NULL)
, m_MoveMode(FALSE)
, m_CursorPos(CPoint(0,0))
, m_FirstPos(CPoint(0,0))
```

```
{
  // TODO: add construction code here
}
```

The element move process starts when the Move menu item from the context menu is selected. Now you can add the code to the message handler for the Move menu item to set up the conditions necessary for the operation:

```
void CSketcherView::OnElementMove()
{
    CClientDC aDC(this);
    OnPrepareDC(&aDC);                   // Set up the device context
    GetCursorPos(&m_CursorPos);          // Get cursor position in screen coords
    ScreenToClient(&m_CursorPos);        // Convert to client coords
    aDC.DPtoLP(&m_CursorPos);            // Convert to logical
    m_FirstPos = m_CursorPos;            // Remember first position
    m_MoveMode = TRUE;                   // Start move mode
}
```

You are doing four things in this handler:

1. Getting the coordinate of the current position of the cursor because the move operation starts from this reference point.

2. Converting the cursor position to logical coordinates because your elements are defined in logical coordinates.

3. Remembering the initial cursor position in case the user wants to abort the move later.

4. Setting the move mode on as a flag for the OnMouseMove() handler to recognize.

The GetCursorPos() function is a Windows API function that stores the current cursor position in m_CursorPos. Note that you pass a pointer to this function. The cursor position is in screen coordinates (that is, coordinates relative to the upper-left corner of the screen). All operations with the cursor are in screen coordinates. You want the position in logical coordinates, so you must do the conversion in two steps. The ScreentoClient() function (which is an inherited member of the view class) converts from screen to client coordinates, and then you apply the DPtoLP() function member of the aDC object to the result to convert to logical coordinates.

After saving the initial cursor position in m_FirstPos, set m_MoveMode to TRUE so that the OnMouseMove() handler can deal with moving the element.

Now you have set the move mode flag, it's time to update the mouse move message handler to deal with moving an element.

Modifying the WM_MOUSEMOVE Handler

Moving an element only occurs when move mode is on and the cursor is being moved. Therefore, all you need to do in OnMouseMove() is to add code to handle moving an element in a block that only gets executed when m_MoveMode is TRUE. The new code to do this is as follows:

```
void CSketcherView::OnMouseMove(UINT nFlags, CPoint point)
{
    CClientDC aDC(this);                 // DC is for this view
```

```
OnPrepareDC(&aDC);                          // Get origin adjusted

   // If we are in move mode, move the selected element and return
   if(m_MoveMode)
   {
     aDC.DPtoLP(&point);                    // Convert to logical coordinatess
     MoveElement(aDC, point);               // Move the element
     return;
   }

      // Rest of the mouse move handler as before...
}
```

This addition doesn't need much explaining really, does it? The `if` statement verifies that you're in move mode and then calls a function `MoveElement()`, which does what is necessary for the move. All you have to do now is implement this function.

Add the declaration for `MoveElement()` as a `protected` member of the `CSketcherView` class by adding the following at the appropriate point in the class definition:

```
   void MoveElement(CClientDC& aDC, CPoint& point);   // Move an element
```

As always, you can also right-click the class name in Class View to do this, if you want to. The function needs access to the object encapsulating a device context for the view, `aDC`, and the current cursor position, `point`, so both of these are reference parameters. The implementation of the function in the `SketcherView.cpp` file is:

```
   void CSketcherView::MoveElement(CClientDC& aDC, CPoint& point)
   {
     CSize Distance = point - m_CursorPos;  // Get move distance
     m_CursorPos = point;                   // Set current point as 1st for next time

     // If there is an element, selected, move it
     if(m_pSelected)
     {
       aDC.SetROP2(R2_NOTXORPEN);
       m_pSelected->Draw(&aDC,m_pSelected); // Draw the element to erase it
       m_pSelected->Move(Distance);         // Now move the element
       m_pSelected->Draw(&aDC,m_pSelected); // Draw the moved element
     }
   }
```

The distance to move the element currently selected is stored locally as a `CSize` object, `Distance`. The `CSize` class is specifically designed to represent a relative coordinate position and has two public data members, `cx` and `cy`, which correspond to the x and y increments. These are calculated as the difference between the current cursor position, stored in `point`, and the previous cursor position saved in `m_CursorPos`. This uses the — operator, which is overloaded in the `CPoint` class. The version you are using here returns a `CSize` object, but there is also a version that returns a `CPoint` object. You can usually operate on `CSize` and `CPoint` objects combined. You save the current cursor position in `m_CursorPos` for use the next time this function is called, which occurs if there is a further mouse move message during the current move operation.

You are going to implement moving an element in the view using the R2_NOTXORPEN drawing mode, because it's easy and fast. This is exactly the same as what you have been using during the creation of an element. You redraw the selected element in its current color (the selected color) to reset it to the background color, and then call the function Move() to relocate the element by the distance specified by Distance. You'll add this function to the element classes in a moment. When the element has moved itself, you simply use the Draw() function once more to display it highlighted at the new position. The color of the element will revert to normal when the move operation ends, as the OnLButtonUp() handler will redraw all the windows normally by calling UpdateAllViews().

Getting the Elements to Move Themselves

Add the Move() function as a virtual member of the base class, CElement. Modify the class definition to:

```
class CElement:public CObject
{
  protected:
    COLORREF m_Color;                     // Color of an element
    CRect m_EnclosingRect;                // Rectangle enclosing an element
    int m_Pen;                            // Pen width

  public:
    virtual ~CElement(void);              // Virtual destructor

    // Virtual draw operation
    virtual void Draw(CDC* pDC, BOOL Select=FALSE){}
    virtual void Move(CSize& aSize){}  // Move an element
    CRect GetBoundRect();                 // Get the bounding rectangle for an element

  protected:
    CElement(void);                       // Here to prevent it being called
};
```

As discussed earlier in relation to the Draw() member, although an implementation of the Move() function here has no meaning, you can't make it a pure virtual function because of the requirements of serialization.

You can now add a declaration for the Move() function as a public member of each of the classes derived from CElement. It is the same in each:

```
// Function to move an element
virtual void Move(CSize& aSize);
```

Next you can implement the Move() function in the CLine class:

```
void CLine::Move(CSize& aSize)
{
  m_StartPoint += aSize;                  // Move the start point
  m_EndPoint += aSize;                    // and the end point
  m_EnclosingRect += aSize;               // Move the enclosing rectangle
}
```

This is easy because of the overloaded += operators in the CPoint and CRect classes. They all work with CSize objects, so you just add the relative distance specified by aSize to the start and end points for the line and to the enclosing rectangle.

Moving a CRectangle object is even easier:

```
void CRectangle::Move(CSize& aSize)
{
   m_EnclosingRect+= aSize;                // Move the rectangle
}
```

Because the rectangle is defined by the m_EnclosingRect member, that's all you need to move it.

The Move() member of the CCircle class is identical:

```
void CCircle::Move(CSize& aSize)
{
   m_EnclosingRect+= aSize;                // Move rectangle defining the circle
}
```

Moving a CCurve object is a little more complicated because it's defined by an arbitrary number of points. You can implement the function as follows:

```
void CCurve::Move(CSize& aSize)
{
   m_EnclosingRect += aSize;               // Move the rectangle

   // Get the 1st element position
   POSITION aPosition = m_PointList.GetHeadPosition();

   while(aPosition)
     m_PointList.GetNext(aPosition) += aSize; // Move each pt in the list
}
```

There's still not a lot to it. You first move the enclosing rectangle stored in m_EnclosingRect, using the overloaded += operator for CRect objects. You then iterate through all the points defining the curve, moving each one in turn with the overloaded += operator in CPoint.

Dropping the Element

All that remains now is to drop the element in position once the user has finished moving it, or to abort the whole move. To drop the element in its new position, the user clicks the left mouse button, so you can manage this operation in the OnLButtonDown() handler. To abort the operation, the user clicks the right mouse button — so you can add a handler for OnRButtonDown() to deal with this.

Take care of the left mouse button first. You'll have to provide for this as a special action when move mode is on. The changes are highlighted in the following:

```
void CSketcherView::OnLButtonDown(UINT nFlags, CPoint point)
{
   CClientDC aDC(this);                    // Create a device context
```

```
OnPrepareDC(&aDC);                      // Get origin adjusted
aDC.DPtoLP(&point);                     // convert point to Logical

   if(m_MoveMode)
   {
     // In moving mode, so drop the element
     m_MoveMode = FALSE;                // Kill move mode
     m_pSelected = 0;                   // De-select the element
     GetDocument()->UpdateAllViews(0);  // Redraw all the views
   }
   else
   {
     m_FirstPoint = point;              // Record the cursor position
     SetCapture();                      // Capture subsequent mouse messages
   }
}
```

The code is pretty simple. You first make sure that you're in move mode. If this is the case, you just set the move mode flag back to FALSE and then de-select the element. This is all that's required because you've been tracking the element with the mouse, so it's already in the right place. Finally, to tidy up all the views of the document, you call the document's UpdateAllViews() function, causing all the views to be redrawn.

Add a handler for the WM_RBUTTONDOWN message to CSketcherView using the Properties window for the class. The implementation for this must do two things: Move the element back to where it was and the turn off move mode. The code to do this is:

```
void CSketcherView::OnRButtonDown(UINT nFlags, CPoint point)
{
   if(m_MoveMode)
   {
     // In moving mode, so drop element back in original position
     CClientDC aDC(this);
     OnPrepareDC(&aDC);                  // Get origin adjusted
     MoveElement(aDC, m_FirstPos);       // Move element to orig position
     m_MoveMode = FALSE;                 // Kill move mode
     m_pSelected = 0;                    // De-select element
     GetDocument()->UpdateAllViews(0);   // Redraw all the views
     return;                             // We are done
   }
}
```

You first create a CClientDC object for use in the MoveElement() function. You then call the MoveElement() function to move the currently selected element the distance from the current cursor position to the original cursor position that we saved in m_FirstPos. After the element has been repositioned, you just turn off move mode, deselect the element, and get all the views redrawn.

Exercising the Application

Everything is now complete for the context pop-ups to work. If you build Sketcher, you can select the element type and color from one context menu, or if you are over an element, you can then move or delete that element from the other context menu.

Dealing with Masked Elements

There's still a limitation that you might want to get over. If the element you want to move or delete is enclosed by the rectangle of another element that is drawn after the element you want, you won't be able to highlight it because Sketcher always finds the outer element first. The outer element completely masks the element it encloses. This is a result of the sequence of elements in the list. You could fix this by adding a Send to Back item to the context menu that would move an element to the beginning of the list.

Add a separator and a menu item to the element drop-down in the IDR_CURSOR_MENU resource as shown in Figure 16-15.

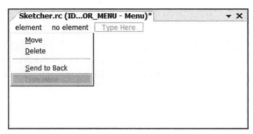

Figure 16-15

You can add a handler for the item to the view class through the Properties window for the CSketcherView class. It's best to handle it in the view because that's where you record the selected element. Select the Messages toolbar button in the Properties window for the class and double-click the message ID ID_ELEMENT_SENDTOBACK. You'll then be able to select COMMAND below and <Add>OnElementSendtoback in the right column. You can implement the handler as:

```
void CSketcherView:: OnElementSendtoback()
{
  GetDocument()->SendToBack(m_pSelected);   // Move element in list
}
```

You'll get the document to do the work by passing the currently selected element pointer to a public function SendToBack() that you implement in the CSketcherDoc class. Add it to the class definition with a void return type, and a parameter of type CElement*. You can implement this function as:

```
void CSketcherDoc::SendToBack(CElement* pElement)
{
  if(pElement)
  {
    // If the element pointer is valid,
    // find the pointer in the list and remove the element
    POSITION aPosition = m_ElementList.Find(pElement);
    m_ElementList.RemoveAt(aPosition);

    m_ElementList.AddTail(pElement);  // Put it back to the end of the list
  }
}
```

After you have the POSITION value corresponding to the element, you remove the element from the list by calling RemoveAt(). Of course, this does not delete the element from memory; it just removes the pointer to it from the list. You then add the element pointer back at the end of the list using the AddTail() function.

With the element moved to the end of the list, it cannot mask any of the others because you search from the beginning. You will always find one of the other elements first if the applicable bounding rectangle encloses the current cursor position. The Send to Back menu option is always able to resolve any element masking problem in the view.

Extending CLRSketcher

It's time to extend CLR Sketcher by implementing the class representing a curve element and adding a class encapsulating a complete sketch. You'll also implement element highlighting and a context menu with the ability to move and delete elements. You can adopt a different approach to drawing elements in this version of Sketcher that will make the move element operation easy to implement. Before you start extending CLR Sketcher and working with the element classes, let's explore another feature of the Graphics class that will be useful in the application.

Coordinate System Transformations

The Graphics class contains functions that can move, rotate, and scale the entire drawing coordinate system. This is a very powerful capability that you can use in the element drawing operations in Sketcher. The following table describes the most useful functions that transform the coordinate system.

Transform Function	Description
TranslateTransform(float dx, float dy)	Translate the coordinate system origin by dx in the x-direction and dy in the y-direction.
RotateTransform(float angle)	Rotates the coordinate system about the origin by angle degrees. A positive value for angle represents rotation from the x-axis toward the y-axis, a clockwise rotation in other words.
ScaleTransform(float scaleX, float scaleY)	Scales the x-axis by multiplying by scaleX and scales the y-axis by multiplying by scaleY.
ResetTransform()	Resets the current transform state for a Graphics object so no transforms are in effect.

You will be using the TranslateTransform() function in the element drawing operations. To draw an element you can translate the origin for the coordinate system to the position specified by the inherited position member of the Element class, draw the element relative to the origin, (0,0), and then restore the coordinate system back to its original state. This process is illustrated in Figure 16-16, which shows how you draw a circle.

The circle element is to be drawn at position (dx,dy)

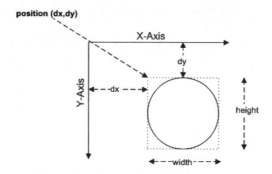

The Drawing Process

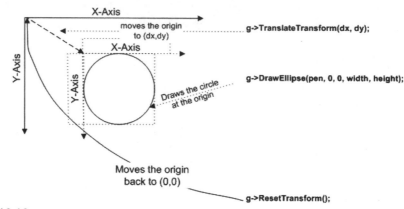

Figure 16-16

You can change the `Draw()` function in the `Circle` class to use the `TranslateTransform()` function:

```
virtual void Draw(Graphics^ g) override
{
    g->TranslateTransform(safe_cast<float>(position.X),
                          safe_cast<float>(position.Y));
    g->DrawEllipse(pen, 0, 0, width,height);
    g->ResetTransform();
}
```

The `TranslateTransform()` function requires arguments of type `float`, so you cast the coordinates to this type. This is not absolutely necessary but you will get warning messages from the compiler if you don't, so it is a good idea to always put the casts in.

Change the `Draw()` function in the `Line` class to the following:

```
virtual void Draw(Graphics^ g) override
{
  g->TranslateTransform(safe_cast<float>(position.X),
                        safe_cast<float>(position.Y));
  g->DrawLine(pen, 0, 0, end.X-position.X, end.Y-position.Y);
  g->ResetTransform();
}
```

Because you are drawing the line relative to the origin with the DrawLine() function, you must specify the end point relative to the origin. You subtract the coordinates of position from the coordinates of end to do this.

The Draw() function for the Rectangle class is very similar to that in the Circle class:

```
virtual void Draw(Graphics^ g) override
{
  g->TranslateTransform(safe_cast<float>(position.X),
                        safe_cast<float>(position.Y));
  g->DrawRectangle(pen, 0, 0, width, height);
  g->ResetTransform();
}
```

With the existing element classes updated, you are ready to tackle the Curve class.

Defining a Curve

A class that represents a curve needs to have a member that can store an arbitrary number of points that define the curve. An STL/CLR container looks to be a promising solution and a vector<Point> container is a good choice to store the points on a curve. Here's how the Curve class definition looks based on that:

```
public ref class Curve : Element
{
private:
  vector<Point>^ points;

public:
  Curve(Color color, Point p1, Point p2)
  {
    pen = gcnew Pen(color);
    this->color = color;
    points = gcnew vector<Point>();
    position = p1;
    points->push_back(Point(p2.X-position.X, p2.Y-position.Y));

    // Find the minimum and maximum coordinates
    int minX = p1.X < p2.X ? p1.X : p2.X;
    int minY = p1.Y < p2.Y ? p1.Y : p2.Y;
    int maxX = p1.X > p2.X ? p1.X : p2.X;
    int maxY = p1.Y > p2.Y ? p1.Y : p2.Y;
    int width = Math::Max(2, maxX - minX);
    int height = Math::Max(2, maxY - minY);
```

```
    boundRect = System::Drawing::Rectangle(minX, minY, width, height);
  }

  void Add(Point p)
  {
    points->push_back(Point(p.X-position.X, p.Y-position.Y));

    // Modify the bounding rectangle to accommodate the new point
    if(p.X < boundRect.X)
    {
      boundRect.Width = boundRect.Right - p.X;
      boundRect.X = p.X;
    }
    else if(p.X > boundRect.Right)
      boundRect.Width = p.X - boundRect.Left;

    if(p.Y < boundRect.Y)
    {
      boundRect.Height = boundRect.Bottom - p.Y;
      boundRect.Y = p.Y;
    }
    else if(p.Y > boundRect.Bottom)
      boundRect.Height = p.Y - boundRect.Top;
  }

virtual void Draw(Graphics^ g) override
{
g->TranslateTransform(safe_cast<float>(position.X), safe_cast<float>(position.Y));
Point previous = Point(0, 0);
for each(Point p in points)
{
g->DrawLine(pen, previous, p);
previous = p;
}
g->ResetTransform();
}
```

Don't forget to add an #include directive for the <cliext/vector> header to Elements.h. You will also need a using directive for the cliext namespace.

You create a Curve object initially from the first two points on the curve. The first point, p1, defines the position of the curve so you store it in position. Because you draw the curve relative to the origin, the second point must be specified relative to position so you store this in the points container. You add subsequent points to the vector<Point> container by calling the Add() member function after modifying the coordinates of each point so it is defined relative to position.

The constructor creates the initial bounding rectangle for the curve from the first two points by obtaining the minimum and maximum coordinate values and using these to determine the top left point coordinates and the width and height of the rectangle. A curve could be a vertical or horizontal line that would result in a zero width or height, so the width and height are always set to at least 2. The Add() function updates the object referenced by boundRect to accommodate the new point that it adds to the container. The Right property of a System::Drawing::Rectangle object corresponds to the sum of the x-coordinate for the top left position and the width and the Bottom property are the sum of the y-coordinate and the height;

these properties are set only. There are also `Left` and `Top` properties that are set only properties, and these correspond to the x-coordinate of the left edge and the y-coordinate of the top edge of the rectangle respectively. The `X`, `Y`, `Width`, and `Height` properties of a `System::Drawing::Rectangle` object are the x and y coordinates of the top-left corner and the width and height; you can get and set these properties.

You draw the curve in the `Draw()` member by setting the start point for the first line segment as 0,0 and iterating through the points in the `points` container. The `DrawLine()` member of the `Graphics` object draws the line, then you store the last point in previous so it becomes the first point for the next line segment.

To create a `Curve` object you must add some additional code to the `MouseMove` event handler in the `Form1` class:

```
private: System::Void Form1_MouseMove(System::Object^  sender,
System::Windows::Forms::MouseEventArgs^  e) {
  if(drawing)
  {
    switch(elementType)
    {
      case ElementType::LINE:
        tempElement = gcnew Line(color, firstPoint, e->Location);
        break;
      case ElementType::RECTANGLE:
        tempElement = gcnew Rectangle(color, firstPoint, e->Location);
        break;
      case ElementType::CIRCLE:
        tempElement = gcnew Circle(color, firstPoint, e->Location);
        break;
      case ElementType::CURVE:
        if(tempElement)
          safe_cast<Curve^>(tempElement)->Add(e->Location);
        else
          tempElement = gcnew Curve(color, firstPoint, e->Location);
        break;
    }
    Invalidate();
  }
}
```

If `tempElement` is not null, the `Curve` object already exists so you call the `Add()` function to add the new point to the curve. Note the cast of `tempElement` to type `Curve^` is necessary to allow the `Add()` member of the `Curve` class to be called. If `tempElement` is null, the `else` clause will execute to create the new `Curve` object from the `firstPoint` stored by the `MouseDown` event handler and the current point obtained from the `Location` property of the parameter e.

Next you need a class that encapsulates a sketch.

Defining a Sketch Class

Create a new header file with the name `Sketch.h` to hold the `Sketch` class using Solution Explorer; just right-click on the Header Files folder and select from the pop-up. A sketch is an arbitrary sequence of elements of any type that has `Element` as a base class. An STL/CLR container looks a good bet to store the elements in a sketch and this time you can use a `list<T>` container. To allow any type of element to be stored in the list you can define the container class as type `list<Element^>`. Specifying that the container stores references of type `Element^` will allow you to store references to objects of any type that is derived from `Element`.

Initially, the `Sketch` class will need a constructor, an `Add()` function that adds a new element to a sketch, and a `Draw()` function to draw a sketch. Here's what you need to put in `Sketch.h`:

```
// Sketch.h
// Defines a sketch
#pragma once
#include <cliext/list>
#include "Elements.h"

using namespace System;
using namespace cliext;

namespace CLRSketcher
{
 public ref class Sketch
  {
  private:
    list<Element^>^ elements;

  public:
    Sketch()
    {
    elements = gcnew list<Element^>();
    }

    void Add(Element^ element)
    {
      elements->push_back(element);
    }

    void Draw(Graphics^ g)
    {
      for each(Element^ element in elements)
        element->Draw(g);
    }
 };
 }
```

The `#include` directive for the `<cliext/list>` header is necessary to access the STL/CLR `list<T>` container template and the `#include` for the `Elements.h` header enables you to reference the `Element` base class. The `Sketch` class is defined within the `CLRSketcher` namespace so it can be referenced without qualification from anywhere within the `CLRSketcher` application. The `elements` container that the constructor creates stores the sketch. You add elements to a `Sketch` object by calling its `Add()` function, which calls the `push_back()` function for the `elements` container to store the new element. Drawing a sketch is very simple. The `Draw()` function for the `Sketch` object iterates over all the elements in the `elements` container and calls the `Draw()` function for each of them.

To make the current `Sketch` object a member of the `Form1` class, add a member of type `Sketch^` with the name `sketch` to the class. You can add the initialization for `sketch` to the `Form1` constructor:

```
Form1(void) : drawing(false), firstPoint(0),
              elementType(ElementType::LINE), color(Color::Black),
              tempElement(nullptr), sketch(gcnew Sketch())
{
  InitializeComponent();
  //
  //TODO: Add the constructor code here
  //
}
```

Don't forget to add an `#include` directive for the `Sketch.h` header at the beginning of the `Form1.h` header. Now you have the `Sketch` class defined, you can modify the `MouseUp` event handler in the `Form1` class to add elements to the sketch:

```
private: System::Void Form1_MouseUp(System::Object^ sender,
                             System::Windows::Forms::MouseEventArgs^ e)
{
  if(!drawing)
    return;
  if(tempElement)
  {
    sketch->Add(tempElement);
    tempElement = nullptr;
    Invalidate();
  }
  drawing = false;
}
```

The function calls the `Add()` function for the `sketch` object when `tempElement` is not `nullptr`. After resetting `tempElement` back to `nullptr` you call the `Invalidate()` function to redraw the form. The final piece of the jigsaw for creating a sketch is the implementation of the `Paint` event handler to draw the sketch.

Drawing the Sketch in the Paint Event Handler

Amazingly you only need one extra line of code to draw an entire sketch:

```
private: System::Void Form1_Paint(System::Object^ sender,
                             System::Windows::Forms::PaintEventArgs^ e)
{
  Graphics^ g = e->Graphics;
  sketch->Draw(g);
  if(tempElement != nullptr)
    tempElement->Draw(g);
}
```

You pass the `Graphics` object, `g`, to the `Draw()` function for the `sketch` object to draw the sketch. This will result in `g` being passed to the `Draw()` function for each element in the sketch to enable each element to draw itself. Finally, if `tempElement` is not `nullptr`, you call the `Draw()` function for that, too. With the `Paint()` event handler complete you should have a working version of CLR Sketcher capable of drawing sketches with the sort of quality shown in Figure 16-17.

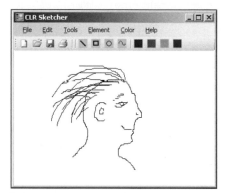

Figure 16-17

A little later in this chapter you will add the capability to pop a context menu to allow elements to be moved as in the MFC version of Sketcher, but first you need to get the element highlighting mechanism working.

Implementing Element Highlighting

You want to highlight an element when the mouse cursor is within the element's bounding rectangle, just like the MFC version of Sketcher. You will implement the mechanism to accomplish this in CLR Sketcher in a slightly different way.

The `MouseMove` event handler in the `Form1` is the prime mover in highlighting elements because it tracks the movement of the cursor, but highlighting should only occur when there is not a drawing operation in progress. The first thing you need to do before you can modify the `MouseMove` handler is to implement a way for an element to draw itself in a highlight color when it is under the cursor. Add `highlighted` as a public member of the `Element` class to record whether an element is highlighted or not. You can also add a protected member to the `Element` class to specify the highlight color for elements:

```
Color highlightColor;
```

Add a public constructor to the `Element` class to initialize the new members:

```
Element() : highlighted(false), highlightColor(Color::Magenta) {}
```

Now you can change the implementation of the `Draw()` function in each of the classes derived from `Element`. Here's how the function looks for the `Line` class:

```
virtual void Draw(Graphics^ g) override
{
  pen->Color = highlighted ? highlightColor : color;
  g->TranslateTransform(safe_cast<float>(position.X),
```

```
                                safe_cast<float>(position.Y));
        g->DrawLine(pen, 0, 0, end.X-position.X, end.Y-position.Y);
        g->ResetTransform();
    }
```

The extra statement sets the `Color` property for `pen` to `highlightColor` whenever `highlighted` is true, or to `color` otherwise. You can add the same statement to the `Draw()` function for the other element classes.

To highlight an element you must discover which element, if any, is under the cursor at any given time. It would be helpful if an element could tell you if a given point is within the bounding rectangle. This process will be the same for all types of element, so you can add a public function to the `Element` base class to implement this:

```
    bool Hit(Point p)
    {
      return boundRect.Contains(p);
    }
```

The `Contains()` member of the `System::Drawing::Rectangle` structure returns `true` if the `Point` argument lies within the rectangle and `false` otherwise. There are two other versions of this function: One accepts two arguments of type `int` that specify the x and y coordinates of a point and the other accepts an argument of type `System::Drawing::Rectangle` and returns `true` if the rectangle for which the function is called contains the rectangle passed as an argument.

You can now add a public function to the `Sketch` class to determine if any element in the sketch is under the cursor:

```
    Element^ HitElement(Point p)
    {
      for each(Element^ element in elements)
      {
        if(element->Hit(p))
          return element;
      }
      return nullptr;
    }
```

This function iterates over the elements in the sketch and returns a reference to the first element for which the `Hit()` function returns `true`. If the `Hit()` function does not return `true` for any of the elements in the sketch, the `HitElement()` function returns `nullptr`. This provides a simple way to detect whether or not there is an element under the cursor.

Add a protected member, `highlightedElement`, of type `Element^` to the `Form1` class to record the currently highlighted element and initialize it to `nullptr` in the `Form1` constructor. Now you can add code to the `MouseMove` handler to make the highlighting work:

```
    private: System::Void Form1_MouseMove(System::Object^  sender,
    System::Windows::Forms::MouseEventArgs^  e)
    {
      if(drawing)
```

```
  {
    switch(elementType)
    {
      case ElementType::LINE:
        tempElement = gcnew Line(color, firstPoint, e->Location);
        break;
      case ElementType::RECTANGLE:
        tempElement = gcnew Rectangle(color, firstPoint, e->Location);
        break;
      case ElementType::CIRCLE:
        tempElement = gcnew Circle(color, firstPoint, e->Location);
        break;
      case ElementType::CURVE:
        if(tempElement)
          safe_cast<Curve^>(tempElement)->Add(e->Location);
        else
          tempElement = gcnew Curve(color, firstPoint, e->Location);
        break;
    }
    Invalidate();
  }
  else
  {
    // Reset any existing highlighted element
    if(highlightedElement)
    {
      highlightedElement->highlighted = false;
      highlightedElement = nullptr;
    }
    // Find and set new highlighted element, if any
    if(highlightedElement = sketch->HitElement(e->Location))
    {
      highlightedElement->highlighted = true;
      Invalidate();
    }
  }
}
```

If drawing is false, you execute the highlighting code that is shaded. First you test for an existing highlighted element and if there is one, you reset it by setting the value of its highlighted member to false. You then set highlightedElement back to nullptr. To look for a new element to highlight, you call the HitElement() function for the sketch object with the current cursor location as the argument. You store the value returned by HitElement() in highlightedElement and if this is not null you set the highlighted member for the element to true and call Invalidate() to redraw the form.

The highlight code will execute repeatedly for every movement of the mouse cursor so it needs to be efficient. At the moment, the code redraws the entire sketch to highlight an element when in fact only the regions occupied by the unhighlighted element and the newly highlighted element need to be redrawn. The Invalidate() member of the System::Windows::Forms::Form class has an overloaded version that accepts an argument of type System::Drawing::Rectangle to add the rectangle specified by the argument to the currently invalidated region for the form. Thus you can call Invalidate() repeatedly to accumulate a composite of rectangles to be redrawn.

Calling `Invalidate()` with a rectangle argument does not redraw the form, but you can get the invalid region redrawn by calling the `Update()` function for the form. You must pass the *enclosing* rectangle for an element to `Invalidate()` rather than the bounding rectangle to get elements redrawn properly. At present, the element classes define the bounding rectangle but you can get the enclosing rectangle for an element quite easily by adding a public property to the `Element` class like this:

```
property System::Drawing::Rectangle Bound
{
  System::Drawing::Rectangle get()
  { return System::Drawing::Rectangle::Inflate(boundRect,1,1); }
}
```

The `Bound` property `get()` function calls the static `Inflate()` function in the `Rectangle` class to generate the enclosing rectangle. The `Inflate()` function increases the size of the rectangle that you supply as the first argument, and the second and third arguments specify the increases for the rectangle in the x and y directions respectively. By using the `Invalidate()` function with an enclosing rectangle argument you can improve the performance of the highlighting code:

```
else
{
  Element^ element = sketch->HitElement(e->Location);
  if(highlightedElement == element)
    return;

  if(highlightedElement)
  {
    Invalidate(highlightedElement->Bound);
    highlightedElement->highlighted = false;
    highlightedElement = nullptr;
  }

  if(element)
  {
    highlightedElement = element;
    highlightedElement->highlighted = true;
    Invalidate(highlightedElement->Bound);
  }
  Update();
}
```

If the `Hit()` member of the element classes returns a reference that is the same as the reference stored in `highlightedElement` you do nothing; the references can both be `nullptr` or both reference the same element, but in either case there's nothing to do. When the form display needs to be updated, the code only redraws the regions occupied by the two elements affected by a new element being highlighted. Overall the code will be faster than the previous version.

Of course, you can apply this technique to the code in the `MouseMove` handler that creates a temporary element, too:

```
if(drawing)
{
```

```
        if(tempElement)
          Invalidate(tempElement->Bound);   // The old element region
      switch(elementType)
      {
          // Code to create a temporary element as before...
      }
      Invalidate(tempElement->Bound);      // The new element region
      Update();
    }
```

The shaded `if` statement invalidates the region occupied by any existing temporary element and the two new lines at the end invalidate the region occupied by the new temporary element and redraw the total invalid region.

Creating Context Menus

You use the Design window to create context menus interactively by dragging a `ContextMenuStrip` control from the Toolbox window to the form. You need to display two different context menus, one for when there is an element under the cursor and one for when there isn't, and you can arrange for both possibilities using a single context menu strip. First drag a `ContextMenuStrip` control from the Toolbox window to the form in the Design window; this will have the default name `ContextMenuStrip1` but you can change this if you want. To make the context menu strip display when the form is right-clicked, display the Properties window for the form and set the `ContextMenuStrip` property in the Behavior group by selecting `ContextMenuStrip1` from the drop-down in the value column.

The drop-down for the context menu is empty at present and you are going to control what menu items it contains programmatically. When an element is under the cursor the element-specific menu items should display, and when there is no element under the cursor, menu items equivalent to those from the `Element` and `Color` menus should display. First add a `Send-To-Back` menu item, a `Delete` menu item, and a `Move` menu item to the drop-down for the context menu by typing the entries in the design window. Change the `(name)` properties for the items to `sendToBackContextMenuItem`, `deleteContextMenuItem`, and `moveContextMenuItem`. A menu item can only belong to one menu strip, so you need to add new ones matching those from the `Element` and `Color` menus.Add a separator and then add menu items `Line`, `Rectangle`, `Circle` and `Curve`, and `Black`, `Red`, `Green` and `Blue`. Change the `(name)` property for each in the same way as the others, to `lineContextMenuItem`, `rectangleContextMenuItem`, and so on. Also change the `(name)` property for the separator to `contextSeparator` so you can refer to it easily.

You need `Click` event handlers for all the menu items in the context menu, but the only new ones you need to create are for the `Move`, `Delete` and `Send-To-Back` items; you can set the handlers for all the other menu items to be the same as the corresponding items in the `Element` and `Color` menus.

You can control what displays in the drop-down for the context menu in the `Opening` event handler for the context menu strip because this event handler is called before the drop-down displays. Open the Properties window for the context menu strip, click the Events button and double-click the `Opening` event to add a handler. You are going to add a different set of menu items to the context menu strip depending on whether or not an element is under the cursor; so how can you determine if anything is under the cursor? Well, the `MouseMove` handler for the form has already taken care of it. All you need to do is check to see whether the reference contained in the `highlightElement` member of the form is `nullptr` or not.

You have added items to the drop-down for `contextMenuStrip1` to add the code to create the objects in the `Form1` class that encapsulate them, but you want to start with a clean slate for the drop-down menu when it is to display so you can set it up the way you want. In the `Opening` event handler you want to remove any existing menu items before you add back the specific menu items you want. A `ContextMenuStrip` object that encapsulates a context menu stores its drop-down menu items in an `Items` property that is of type `ToolStripItemsCollection^`. To remove existing items from the drop-down you simply call `Clear()` for the `Items` property. To add a menu item to the context menu you call the `Add()` function for the `Items` property with the menu item as the argument.

The implementation of the `Opening` handler for the context menu strip is as follows:

```
private: System::Void contextMenuStrip1_Opening(System::Object^ sender,
                                System::ComponentModel::CancelEventArgs^  e)
{
  contextMenuStrip1->Items->Clear();     // Remove existing items
  if(highlightedElement)
  {
    contextMenuStrip1->Items->Add(moveToolStripMenuItem);
    contextMenuStrip1->Items->Add(deleteToolStripMenuItem);
    contextMenuStrip1->Items->Add(sendToBackToolStripMenuItem);
  }
  else
  {
    contextMenuStrip1->Items->Add(lineToolStripMenuItem);
    contextMenuStrip1->Items->Add(rectangleToolStripMenuItem);
    contextMenuStrip1->Items->Add(circleToolStripMenuItem);
    contextMenuStrip1->Items->Add(curveToolStripMenuItem);
    contextMenuStrip1->Items->Add(contextSeparator);
    contextMenuStrip1->Items->Add(lineToolStripMenuItem);
    contextMenuStrip1->Items->Add(blackToolStripMenuItem);
    contextMenuStrip1->Items->Add(redToolStripMenuItem);
    contextMenuStrip1->Items->Add(greenToolStripMenuItem);
    contextMenuStrip1->Items->Add(blueToolStripMenuItem);

    // Set checks for the menu items
    lineContextMenuItem->Checked = elementType == ElementType::LINE;
    rectangleContextMenuItem->Checked = elementType == ElementType::RECTANGLE;
    circleContextMenuItem->Checked = elementType == ElementType::CIRCLE;
    curveContextMenuItem->Checked = elementType == ElementType::CURVE;
    blackContextMenuItem->Checked = color == Color::Black;
    redContextMenuItem->Checked = color == Color::Red;
    greenContextMenuItem->Checked = color == Color::Green;
    blueContextMenuItem->Checked = color == Color::Blue;
  }
}
```

After clearing the context menu, you add items depending on whether or not `highlightedElement` is null. You set the checks for the element and color menu items in the same way as you did for the main menu by setting the `Checked` property for each of the menu items.

All the element and color menu items in the context menu should now work, so try it out. All that remains is to implement the element-specific operations. Let's do the easiest one first.

Implementing the Element Delete Operation

To make it possible to delete an element from the sketch, you first must add a public function to the Sketch class definition that will delete an element:

```
Element^ Delete(Element^ element)
{
  elements->remove(element);
  return element;
}
```

The Delete() function calls remove() for the list<Element^> object to remove the element that you pass as the argument and returns the reference to the deleted element as a convenience.

You use the Delete() function in the implementation of the Click event handler for the Delete menu item:

```
private: System::Void deleteContextMenuItem_Click(System::Object^ sender,
                                                  System::EventArgs^ e)
{
  if(highlightedElement)
  {
    sketch->Delete(highlightedElement);
    Invalidate(highlightedElement->Bound);
    highlightedElement = nullptr;
    Update();
  }
}
```

As well as deleting the element from the sketch, the event handler also invalidates the region it occupies to remove it from the display and resets highlightedElement back to nullptr.

Implementing the Send-To-Back operation

The Send-To-Back operation works in the same way as in MFC Sketcher. You remove the highlighted element from the list in the Sketch object and add it to the end of the list. Here's the implementation of the handler function:

```
private: System::Void sendToBackContextMenuItem_Click(System::Object^ sender,
                                                      System::EventArgs^ e)
{
  if(highlightedElement)
  {
    sketch->Add(sketch->Delete(highlightedElement));
    highlightedElement->highlighted = false;
    Invalidate(highlightedElement->Bound);
    highlightedElement = nullptr;
    Update();
  }
}
```

You pass the reference returned by the Delete() member of the sketch to the Add() member to add the deleted element to the back of the list. You reset the highlighted member of the element to false and highlightedElement to nullptr before calling Invalidate() for the form to redraw the region occupied by the previously highlighted element.

Implementing the Element Move Operation

You'll move an element by dragging it with the left mouse button down. This implies that a move operation needs a different set of functions to be carried out by the mouse event handlers from normal so a move will have to be modal, as in the MFC version of Sketcher. You can identify possible modes by an enum class that you can add following the ElementType enum in Form1.h:

```
enum class Mode {Normal, Move,};
```

This just defines two modes but you could add more if you wanted to implement other modal operations. You can now add a private member of type Mode with the name mode to the Form1 class. Initialize the new variable to Mode::Normal in the Form1 constructor.

The only thing the Click event handler for the Move menu item has to do is set mode to Mode::Move:

```
private: System::Void moveContextMenuItem_Click(System::Object^  sender,
                                                System::EventArgs^  e)
{
    mode = Mode::Move;
}
```

The mouse event handlers for the form must take care of moving an element. Change the code for the MouseDown handler so it only sets drawing to true when mode is Mode::Normal:

```
private: System::Void Form1_MouseDown(System::Object^  sender,
                                      System::Windows::Forms::MouseEventArgs^  e)
{
    if(e->Button == System::Windows::Forms::MouseButtons::Left)
    {
        if(mode == Mode::Normal)
            drawing = true;
        firstPoint = e->Location;
    }
}
```

This sets drawing to true only when mode has the value Mode::Normal. If mode has a different value, only the point is stored for use in the MouseMove event handler. The MouseMove event handler will not create elements when drawing is false so this functionality is switched off for all modes except Mode::Normal. The MouseUp event handler will restore mode back to Mode::Normal when a move operation is complete.

Moving an Element

Because you now draw all elements relative to a given position, you can move an element just by changing the inherited position member to reflect the new position and adjust the location of the bounding rectangle in a similar way. You can add a public Move() function to the Element base class to take care of this:

```
void Move(int dx, int dy)
{
    position.Offset(dx, dy);
    boundRect.X += dx;
    boundRect.Y += dy;
}
```

Calling the `Offset()` function for the `Point` object, `position`, adds `dx` and `dy` to the coordinates stored in the object. To adjust the location of `boundRect`, you just add `dx` to the `Rectangle` object's `X` field and `dy` to its `Y` field.

The `MouseMove` event handler will expedite the moving process:

```
private: System::Void Form1_MouseMove(System::Object^  sender,
System::Windows::Forms::MouseEventArgs^  e) {
  if(drawing)
  {
    if(tempElement)
      Invalidate(tempElement->Bound);  // The old element region
    switch(elementType)
    {
       // Code to create a temporary element as before...
    }
    Invalidate(tempElement->Bound);    // The new element region
    Update();
  }
  else if(mode == Mode::Normal)
  {
     code to highlight the element under the cursor as before
  }
  else if(mode == Mode::Move &&
                    e->Button == System::Windows::Forms::MouseButtons::Left)
  {  // Move the highlighted element
    if(highlightedElement)
    {
      Invalidate(highlightedElement->Bound);    // Region before move
      highlightedElement->Move(e->X - firstPoint.X, e->Y - firstPoint.Y);
      firstPoint = e->Location;
      Invalidate(highlightedElement->Bound);    // Region after move
      Update();
    }
  }
}
```

This event handler now provides three different functions: It creates an element when `drawing` is `true`, it does element highlighting when `drawing` is `false` and `mode` is `Mode::Normal`, and it moves the currently highlighted element when `mode` is `Mode::Move` and the left mouse button is down.

The new `else if` clause executes only when `mode` has the value `Mode::Move` and the left button is down. Without the button test, moving would occur if you moved the cursor after clicking the menu item. This would happen without a `MouseDown` event occurring, which would create some confusion as `firstPoint` would not have been initialized. With the code as you have it here, the moving process is initiated when you click the menu item and release the left mouse button. You then press the left mouse button and drag the cursor to move the highlighted element.

If there is a highlighted element, you invalidate its bounding rectangle before moving the element the distance from `firstPoint` to the current cursor location. You then update `firstPoint` to the current cursor position ready for the next move increment and invalidate the new region the highlighted element occupies. You finally call `Update()` to redraw the invalid regions of the form.

The last part you must implement to complete the ability to move elements is in the MouseUp event handler:

```
private: System::Void Form1_MouseUp(System::Object^  sender,
System::Windows::Forms::MouseEventArgs^  e) {
  if(!drawing)
  {
    mode = Mode::Normal;
    return;
  }
  if(tempElement)
  {
    sketch->Add(tempElement);
    tempElement = nullptr;
    Invalidate();
  }
}
```

Releasing the left mouse button ends a move operation. The drawing variable is false when an element is being moved and the only thing the handler has to do is to reset mode back to Mode::Normal to end the move operation when this is the case.

With that done you should now have a version of CLR sketcher in which you can move and delete elements, as illustrated in Figure 16-18.

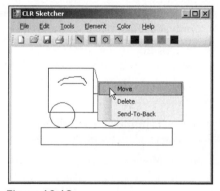

Figure 16-18

The Send-To-Back facility ensures that any element can always be highlighted to move or delete it; if an element will not highlight, just send-to-back any elements enclosing the element you want to move or delete. In Chapter 18 you implement the capability to save a sketch in a file.

Summary

In this chapter, you've seen how to apply MFC collection classes to the problems of managing objects and managing pointers to objects. Collections are a real asset in programming for Windows because the application data that you store in a document often originates in an unstructured and unpredictable way, and you need to be able traverse the data whenever a view needs to be updated.

You have also seen how to create document data and manage it in a pointer list in the document, and in the context of the Sketcher application, how the views and the document communicate with each other.

You have improved the view capability in Sketcher in several ways. You've added scrolling to the views using the MFC class `CScrollView`, and you've introduced a pop-up at the cursor for moving and deleting elements. You have also implemented an element highlighting feature to provide the user with feedback when moving or deleting elements.

CLR Sketcher has most of the features of MFC Sketcher including drawing operations and a context menu, but you implemented some things a little differently because the characteristics of the CLR are not the same as the MFC environment. The coding effort was considerably less than for MFC Sketcher because of the automatic code generation provided by the Forms Design capability. The downside of using Forms Design is that you can't control how the code is organized and the `Form1` class becomes rather unwieldy because of the sheer volume of code in the definition. However the Class View is a great help in navigating around the class definition.

You have covered quite a lot of ground in this chapter, and some of the important points you need to keep in mind are:

❑   The best choice of MFC collection class to manage your objects or pointers is one of the template-based collection classes because they provide type-safe operation in most cases.

❑   When you draw in a device context using the MFC, coordinates are in logical units that depend on the mapping mode set. Points in a window that are supplied along with Windows mouse messages are in client coordinates. The two coordinate systems are usually not the same.

❑   Coordinates that define the position of the cursor are in screen coordinates that are measured in pixels relative to the upper-left corner of the screen.

❑   Functions to convert between client coordinates and logical coordinates in a MFC application are available in the `CDC` class.

❑   Windows requests that a view is redrawn by sending a `WM_PAINT` message to your MFC application. This causes the `OnDraw()` member of the affected view to be called.

❑   You should always do any permanent drawing of a document in the `OnDraw()` member of the view class in your MFC application. This ensures that the window is drawn properly when required by Windows.

❑   You can make your `OnDraw()` implementation more efficient by calling the `RectVisible()` member of the `CDC` class to check whether an entity needs to be drawn.

❑   To get multiple views updated when you change the document contents, you can call the `UpdateAllViews()` member of the document object. This causes the `OnUpdate()` member of each view to be called.

❑   You can pass information to the `UpdateAllViews()` function to indicate which area in the view needs to be redrawn. This makes redrawing the views faster.

❑   You can display a context menu at the cursor position in an MFC application in response to a right mouse click. This menu is created as a normal pop-up.

❑   You create menu strips, context menus and toolbars in a Windows Forms application by dragging the appropriate component from the Toolbox window to the form in the Forms Designer window. You cause the context menu to be displayed on the form in response to right-clicking the mouse by setting the ContextMenuStrip property for the form.

❏   You create event handlers for a component in a Windows Forms application through the Properties window for the component. You can change the name of the event handler function that is created by changing the value of its (name) property.

❏   Implementing the DropDownOpening event handler for a menu item enables you to modify the drop-down before it displays.

Exercises

You can download the source code for the examples in the book and the solutions to the following exercises from www.wrox.com.

1.   Implement the CCurve class so that points are added to the head of the list instead of the tail.

2.   Implement the CCurve class in the Sketcher program using a typed pointer list, instead of a list of objects to represent a curve.

3.   Look up the CArray template collection class in Help, and use it to store points in the CCurve class in the Sketcher program.

4.   Add the capability in CLR Sketcher to change the color of an existing element. Make this available through the context menu.

Working with Dialogs and Controls

Dialogs and controls are basic tools for user communications in the Windows environment. In this chapter, you'll learn how to implement dialogs and controls by applying them to extend the Sketcher program. As you do so, you'll learn about:

- ❑ Dialogs and how you can create dialog resources
- ❑ Controls and how to add them to a dialog
- ❑ Basic varieties of controls available to you
- ❑ How to create a dialog class to manage a dialog
- ❑ How to program the creation of a dialog box and how to get information back from the controls in it
- ❑ Modal and modeless dialogs
- ❑ How to implement and use direct data exchange and validation with controls
- ❑ How to implement view scaling
- ❑ How you can add a status bar to an application

Understanding Dialogs

Of course, dialog boxes are not new to you. Most Windows programs of consequence use dialogs to manage some of their data input. You click a menu item and up pops a **dialog box** with various **controls** that you use for entering information. Just about everything that appears in a dialog box is a control. A dialog box is actually a window and, in fact, each of the controls in a dialog is also a specialized window. Come to think of it, most things you see on the screen under Windows are windows.

Although controls have a particular association with dialog boxes, you can also create and use them in other windows if you want to. A typical dialog box is illustrated in Figure 17-1.

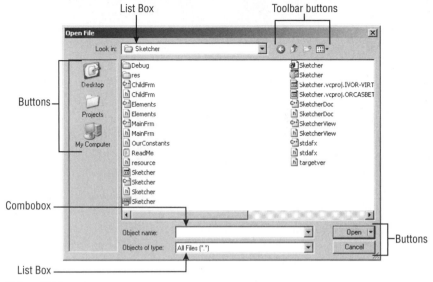

Figure 17-1

This is the `File > Open > File` dialog in Visual C++ 2008. The annotations show the variety of controls used that combine to provide an intuitive interface for selecting a file to be opened. This makes the dialog easy to use, even though there's a whole range of possibilities here.

There are two things needed to create and display a dialog box in an MFC program: the physical appearance of the dialog box, which is defined in a resource file, and a dialog class object used to manage the operation of the dialog and its controls. MFC provides a class called `CDialog` for you to use after you have defined your dialog resource.

Understanding Controls

There are many different controls available to you in Windows, and in most cases there's flexibility in how they look and operate. Most of them fall into one of the six categories shown in the following table.

Control Type	What They Do
Static Controls	These are used to provide titles or descriptive information.
Button Controls	Buttons provide a single-click input mechanism. There are basically three flavors of button controls, simple push buttons, radio buttons where only one may be in a selected state at any one time, and checkboxes where several may be in a selected state at one time.

Control Type	What They Do
Scrollbars	Scrollbars are typically used to scroll text or images either horizontally or vertically within another control.
List Boxes	These present a list of choices and one or more selections can be in effect at one time.
Edit Controls	Edit controls allow text input or editing of text that is displayed.
Combo boxes	Combo boxes present a list of choices from which you can select combined with the option of entering text yourself.

Figure 17-2 shows some examples of various types of controls.

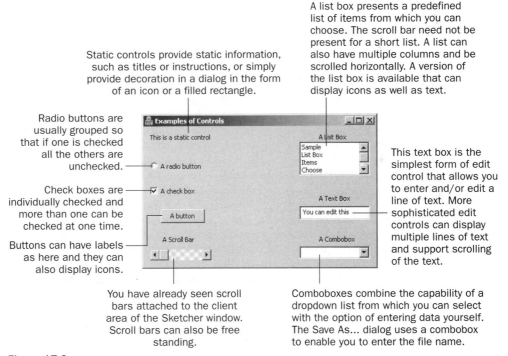

A list box presents a predefined list of items from which you can choose. The scroll bar need not be present for a short list. A list can also have multiple columns and be scrolled horizontally. A version of the list box is available that can display icons as well as text.

Static controls provide static information, such as titles or instructions, or simply provide decoration in a dialog in the form of an icon or a filled rectangle.

Radio buttons are usually grouped so that if one is checked all the others are unchecked.

This text box is the simplest form of edit control that allows you to enter and/or edit a line of text. More sophisticated edit controls can display multiple lines of text and support scrolling of the text.

Check boxes are individually checked and more than one can be checked at one time.

Buttons can have labels as here and they can also display icons.

You have already seen scroll bars attached to the client area of the Sketcher window. Scroll bars can also be free standing.

Comboboxes combine the capability of a dropdown list from which you can select with the option of entering data yourself. The Save As... dialog uses a combobox to enable you to enter the file name.

Figure 17-2

A control may or may not be associated with a class object. Static controls don't do anything directly, so an associated class object may seem superfluous; however, there's an MFC class, CStatic, that provides functions to enable you to alter the appearance of static controls. Button controls can also be handled by the dialog object in many cases, but again MFC does provide the CButton class for use in situations where you need a class object to manage a control. MFC also provides a full complement of classes to support the other controls. Because controls are windows, they are all derived from CWnd.

Common Controls

The set of standard controls that are supported by MFC and the Resource editor are called **common controls**. Common controls include all of the controls you have just seen, as well as other more complex controls such as the **animate control**, for example, which has the capability to play an AVI (**A**udio **V**ideo **I**nterleaved) file, and the **tree control** that can display a hierarchy of items in a tree.

Another useful control in the set of common controls is the **spin button**. You can use this to increment or decrement values in an associated edit control. To go into all of the possible controls that you might use is beyond the scope of this book, so I'll just take a few illustrative examples (including an example that uses a spin button) and implement them in the Sketcher program.

Creating a Dialog Resource

Here's a concrete example. You could add a dialog to Sketcher to provide a choice of pen widths for drawing elements. This ultimately involves modifying the current pen width in the document, as well as in the CElement class, and adding or modifying functions to deal with pen widths. You'll deal with all that, though, after you've got the dialog together.

Display the Resource View, expand the resource tree for Sketcher, and right-click the Dialog folder in the tree; then click Insert Dialog from the pop-up to add a new dialog resource to Sketcher. This results in the Dialog Resource editor swinging into action and displaying the dialog in the Editor pane along with the Toolbox showing a list of controls that you can add. The dialog has OK and Cancel button controls already in place. Adding more controls to the dialog is simplicity itself; you can just drag the control from the palette to the position where you want to place it in the dialog. Alternatively, you can click a control from the list to select it and then click in the dialog where you want the control to be positioned. When it appears you'll still be able to move it around to set its exact position, and you'll also be able to resize it by dragging handles on the boundaries.

The dialog has a default ID assigned that is IDD_DIALOG1, but it would be better to have an ID that was a bit more meaningful. You can edit the ID by right-clicking the dialog name in the Resource View pane and selecting Properties from the pop-up. You can also display the dialog's properties by right-clicking in the Dialog Editor pane and selecting from the pop-up. Change the ID to something that relates to the purpose of the dialog such as IDD_PENWIDTH_DLG. At the same time, you could also change the Caption property value to Set Pen Width.

Adding Controls to a Dialog Box

To provide a mechanism for entering a pen width, you can add controls to the basic dialog that's initially displayed until it looks like the one shown in Figure 17-3.

Figure 17-3 shows the grid that you can use to position controls. If the grid is not displayed, you can select the appropriate Toolbar button to display it; the Toolbar button toggles the grid on and off. Alternatively, you can display rules along the side and top of the dialog that you can use to create guide lines as shown in Figure 17-4.

You create a horizontal guide by clicking the appropriate rule. You can position a guide line by dragging the arrow for it along the rule and then using one or more guides when positioning a control.

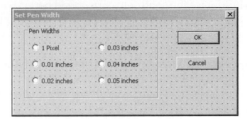

Figure 17-3

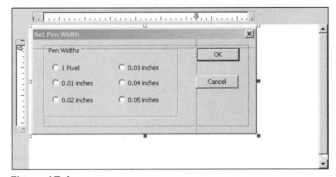

Figure 17-4

The dialog has six radio buttons that provide the pen width options. These are enclosed within a **group box** with the caption Pen Widths. The group box serves to enclose the radio buttons and make them operate as a group, where only one member of the group can be checked at any given time. Each radio button has an appropriate label to identify the pen width that is set when selected. There are also the default OK and Cancel buttons that close the dialog. Each of the controls in the dialog has its own set of properties that you can access and modify in the same way as for the dialog box itself.

The next step is to add the group box. As I said, the group box serves to associate the radio buttons in a group from an operational standpoint, and to provide a caption and a boundary for the group of buttons. Where you need more than one set of radio buttons, a means of grouping them is essential if they are to work properly. You can select the button corresponding to the group box from the common controls palette by clicking it; then click the approximate position in the dialog box where you want the center of the group box. This places a group box of default size on to the dialog. You can then drag the borders of the group box to enlarge it to accommodate the six radio buttons that you add. To set the caption for the group box, type the caption you want (in this, case type **Pen Widths**).

The last step is to add the radio buttons. Select the radio button control by clicking it and then clicking on the position in the dialog where you want to position a radio button within the group box. Do the same for all six radio buttons. For each button you can select it by clicking it; then type in the caption to change it. You can also drag the border of the button to set its size, if necessary. To display the Properties window for a control, select it by clicking it; then select Properties from the pop-up. You can change the ID for each radio button in the properties window for the control to correspond better with its purpose: IDC_PENWIDTH0 for the 1 pixel pen width, IDC_PENWIDTH1 for the 0.01 inch width pen, IDC_PENWIDTH2 for the 0.02 inch pen, and so on.

You can position individual controls by dragging them around with the mouse. You can also select a group of controls by selecting successive controls with the Shift key pressed, or by dragging the cursor with the left button pressed to create a rectangle enclosing them. To align a group of controls, select the appropriate button from the Dialog Editor toolbar shown in Figure 17-5.

Figure 17-5

The toolbar is shown in its undocked state — that is, dragged away from the toolbar area at the top of the window. If the toolbar is not visible, you can show it by right-clicking in the toolbar area and selecting it in the list of toolbars that is displayed. You also can align controls in the dialog by selecting from the Format menu.

Testing the Dialog

The dialog resource is now complete. You can test it by selecting the Toolbar button that appears at the left end of the toolbar in Figure 17-5 or by pressing Ctrl+T. This displays the dialog window with the basic operations of the controls available, so you can try clicking on the radio buttons. When you have a group of radio buttons, only one can be selected. As you select one, any other that was previously selected is reset. Click either of the OK or Cancel buttons or even the Close icon in the title bar for dialog to end the test. After you have saved the dialog resource, you're ready to add some code to support it.

Programming for a Dialog

There are two aspects to programming for a dialog: getting it displayed, and handling the effects of its controls. Before you can display the dialog corresponding to the resource you've just created, you must first define a dialog class for it. The Class Wizard helps with this.

Adding a Dialog Class

Right-click the dialog box that you just created in the Resource Editor pane and then select Add Class from the pop-up tool display the Class Wizard dialog. You'll define a new dialog class derived from the MFC class CDialog, so select that class name from the Base Class: drop-down list box. You can enter the class name as CPenDialog in the Class name: edit box. The Class Wizard dialog should look as shown in Figure 17-6.

Click the Finish button to create the new class.

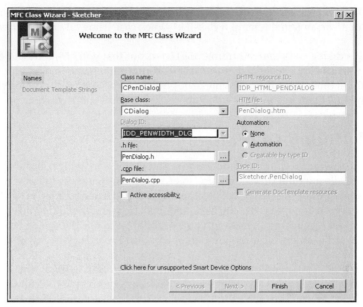

Figure 17-6

The CDialog class is a window class (derived from the MFC class CWnd) that's specifically for displaying and managing dialogs. The dialog resource that you have created automatically associates with an object of type CPenDialog because the IDD class member is initialized with the ID of the dialog resource:

```cpp
class CPenDialog : public CDialog
{
  DECLARE_DYNAMIC(CPenDialog)

public:
  CPenDialog(CWnd* pParent = NULL);   // standard constructor
  virtual ~CPenDialog();

// Dialog Data
  enum { IDD = IDD_PENWIDTH_DLG };

protected:
  virtual void DoDataExchange(CDataExchange* pDX);    // DDX/DDV support

  DECLARE_MESSAGE_MAP()
};
```

The highlighted statement defines IDD as a symbolic name for the dialog ID in the enumeration. Incidentally, using an enumeration is the *only* way you can get an initialized data member into a class definition. If you try putting an initial value for any regular data member declaration, it won't compile. You will get an error message about illegal use of pure syntax. It works here because an enum defines a symbolic name for a value of type int. Unfortunately, you can only define values of type int in this way. It's not strictly necessary here because the initialization for IDD could be done in the constructor, but this is how Class Wizard chooses to do it. This technique is more commonly used to define a symbol for the dimension of an array (a member of a class), in which case using an enumeration is your only option.

Having your own dialog class derived from CDialog means that you get all the functionality that that class provides. You can also customize the dialog class by adding data members and functions to suit your particular needs. You'll often want to handle messages from controls within the dialog class, although you can also choose to handle them in a view or a document class if this is more convenient.

Modal and Modeless Dialogs

There two different types of dialog, termed **modal** and **modeless** dialogs, and they work in completely different ways. While a modal dialog remains in effect, all operations in the other windows in the application are suspended until the dialog box is closed, usually by clicking an OK or Cancel button. With a modeless dialog, you can move the focus back and forth between the dialog box and other windows in your application just by clicking them, and you can continue to use the dialog box at any time until you close it. Class wizard is an example of a modal dialog; the Properties window is modeless.

A modeless dialog box is created by calling the Create() function defined in the CDialog class, but because you'll only be using modal dialogs in the Sketcher example, you'll call the DoModal() function for the dialog object, as you'll see shortly.

Displaying a Dialog

Where you put the code to display a dialog in your program depends on the application. In the Sketcher program, it is convenient to add a menu item that, when selected, results in the pen width dialog being displayed. You'll put this in the IDR_SketcherTYPE menu bar. As both the width and the color are associated with a pen, you can rename the Color menu as Pen. You do this just by double-clicking the Color menu item in the Resource Editor pane to open its Properties window and changing the value of the Caption property to &Pen. Closing the window puts the change into effect.

When you add the Width menu item to the Pen menu, you should separate it from the colors in the menu. You can add a separator after the last color menu item by right-clicking the empty menu item and selecting the Insert Separator menu item from the pop-up. You can then enter the new Width item as the next menu item after the separator. The menu item ends with an ellipsis (three periods) to indicate that it displays a dialog; this is a standard Windows convention. Double-click the menu to display the menu properties for modification, as shown in Figure 17-7.

Enter ID_PENWIDTH as the ID for the menu item, as shown in Figure 17-7. You can also add a status bar prompt for it and because you'll also add a toolbar button, you can include text for the tool tip as well. Remember, you just put the tooltip text following the status bar prompt text, separated from it by "\n". Here the value for the Prompt property is "Change pen width\nShow pen width options". The menu will look as shown in Figure 17-8.

To add the Toolbar button, open the toolbar resource by extending the Toolbar folder in the Resource View and double-clicking IDR_MAINFRAME. You can add a toolbar button to represent a pen width. The one shown in Figure 17-9 tries to represent a pen drawing a line.

To associate the new button with the menu item that you just added, open the properties box for the button and specify its ID as ID_PENWIDTH, the same as that for the menu item.

Figure 17-7

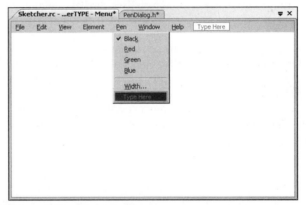

Figure 17-8

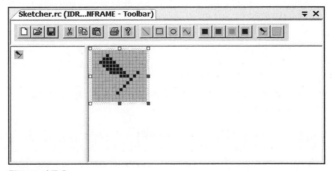

Figure 17-9

Code to Display the Dialog

The code to display the dialog goes in the handler for the Pen > Width menu item, so in which class should you implement this handler? The view class is a candidate for dealing with pen widths, but following the previous logic with colors and elements, it would be sensible to have the current pen width selection in the document, so the handler should go in the CSketcherDoc class. Right-click the Width menu item in the Resource View pane for the ID_SketcherTYPE menu and select Add Event Handler from the pop-up. You can then create a function for the COMMAND message handler corresponding to ID_PENWIDTH in the CSketcherDoc class. Now edit this handler and enter the following code:

```
// Handler for the pen width menu item
void CSketcherDoc::OnPenwidth()
{
    CPenDialog aDlg;                    // Create a local dialog object

    // Display the dialog as modal
    aDlg.DoModal();
}
```

There are just two statements in the handler at the moment. The first creates a dialog object that is automatically associated with your dialog resource. You then display the dialog by calling the DoModal() function for the aDlg object.

Because the handler declares a CPenDialog object, you must add a #include statement for PenDialog.h to the beginning of SketcherDoc.cpp (after the #include directives for stdafx.h and Sketcher.h); otherwise, you'll get compilation errors when you build the program. After you've done that, you can build Sketcher and try out the dialog. It should appear when you click the Toolbar button or the Pen > Width menu item. Of course, if the dialog is to do anything, you still have to add the code to support the operation of the controls; to close the dialog, you can use either of the buttons or the Close icon in the title bar.

Code to Close the Dialog

The OK and Cancel buttons (and the close icon on the title bar) already close the dialog. The handlers to deal with the BN_CLICKED event handlers for the OK and Cancel button controls have been implemented for you. However, it's useful to know how the action of closing the dialog is implemented in case you want to do more before the dialog is finally closed or if you are working with a modeless dialog.

The CDialog class defines the OnOK() method that is called when you click the default OK button, which has IDOK as its ID. This function closes the dialog and causes the DoModal() method to return the ID of the default OK button, IDOK. The OnCancel() function is called when you click the default Cancel button in the dialog and this closes the dialog and DoModal() returns the button ID, which is IDCANCEL. You can override either or both of these functions in your dialog class to do what you want. You just need to make sure you call the corresponding base class function at the end of your function implementation. You'll probably remember by now that you can add an override class by selecting the overrides button in the Properties window for the class.

For example, you could implement an override for the OnOK() function like this:

```
void CPenDialog::OnOK()
{
  // Your code for data validation or other actions...
```

```
    CDialog::OnOK();                          // Close the dialog
}
```

In a complicated dialog, you might want to verify that the options selected or the data that has been entered is valid. You could put code here to check the state of the dialog and fix up the data or even leave the dialog open if there are problems.

Calling the OnOK() function defined in the base class closes the dialog and causes the DoModal() function to return IDOK. Thus you can use the value returned from DoModal() to detect when the dialog was closed by clicking the OK button.

As I said, you can also override the OnCancel() function in a similar way if you need to do extra clean-up operations before the dialog closes. Be sure to call the base class method at the end of your function implementation.

When you are using a modeless dialog you must implement the OnOK() and OnCancel() function over-rides so that they call the inherited DestroyWindow() to terminate the dialog. In this case, you must not call the base class OnOK() or OnCancel() functions, because they do not destroy the dialog window, but merely render it invisible.

Supporting the Dialog Controls

For the Pen dialog, you'll store the selected pen width in a data member, m_PenWidth, of the CPenDialog class. You can either add the data member by right-clicking the CPenDialog class name and selecting from the context menu, or you can add it directly to the class definition as follows:

```
class CPenDialog : public CDialog
{
// Construction
public:
    CPenDialog(CWnd* pParent = NULL);    // standard constructor

// Dialog Data
    enum { IDD = IDD_PENWIDTH_DLG };

// Data stored in the dialog
public:
    int m_PenWidth;                      // Record the pen width

// Plus the rest of the class definition....

};
```

If you do use the context menu for the class to add m_PenWidth, be sure to add a comment to the class definition. This is a good habit to get into, even when the member name looks self-explanatory.

You'll use the m_PenWidth data member to set the radio button corresponding to the current pen width in the document as checked. You'll also arrange that the pen width selected in the dialog is stored in this member, so that you can retrieve it when the dialog closes. At this point you could arrange to initialize m_PenWidth to 0 in the class constructor.

Initializing the Controls

You can initialize the radio buttons by overriding the OnInitDialog() function that is defined in the base class, CDialog. This function is called in response to a WM_INITDIALOG message, which is sent during the execution of DoModal() just before the dialog box is displayed. You can add the function to the CPenDialog class by selecting OnInitDialog in the list of overrides in the Properties window for the CPenDialog class, as shown in Figure 17-10.

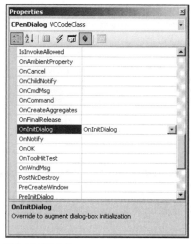

Figure 17-10

The implementation for the new version of OnInitDialog() is:

```
BOOL CPenDialog::OnInitDialog()
{
    CDialog::OnInitDialog();
```

```
    // Check the radio button corresponding to the pen width
    switch(m_PenWidth)
    {
    case 1:
        CheckDlgButton(IDC_PENWIDTH1,1);
        break;
    case 2:
        CheckDlgButton(IDC_PENWIDTH2,1);
        break;
    case 3:
        CheckDlgButton(IDC_PENWIDTH3,1);
        break;
    case 4:
        CheckDlgButton(IDC_PENWIDTH4,1);
        break;
```

```
      case 5:
        CheckDlgButton(IDC_PENWIDTH5,1);
        break;
      default:
        CheckDlgButton(IDC_PENWIDTH0,1);
    }
  return TRUE;   // return TRUE unless you set the focus to a control
                 // EXCEPTION: OCX Property Pages should return FALSE
}
```

You should leave the call to the base class function there because it does some essential setup for the dialog. The `switch` statement checks one of the radio buttons, depending on the value set in the `m_PenWidth` data member. This implies that you must arrange to set `m_PenWidth` to a suitable value before you execute `DoModal()` because the `DoModal()` function causes the `WM_INITDIALOG` message to be sent, resulting in your version of `OnInitDialog()` being called.

The `CheckDlgButton()` function is inherited indirectly from `CWnd` through `CDialog`. If the second argument is 1, it checks the button corresponding to the ID specified in the first argument. If the second argument is 0, the button is unchecked. This works with both checkboxes and radio buttons.

Handling Radio Button Messages

After the dialog box is displayed, every time you click on one of the radio buttons a message is generated and sent to the application. To deal with these messages, you can add handlers to the `CPenDialog` class. Right-click each of the radio buttons in turn and select Add Event Handler from the pop-up to create a handler for the `BN_CLICKED` message. Figure 17-11 shows the event handler dialog window for the button that has `IDC_PENWIDTH0` as its ID. Note that I have edited the name of the handler as the default name was a little cumbersome.

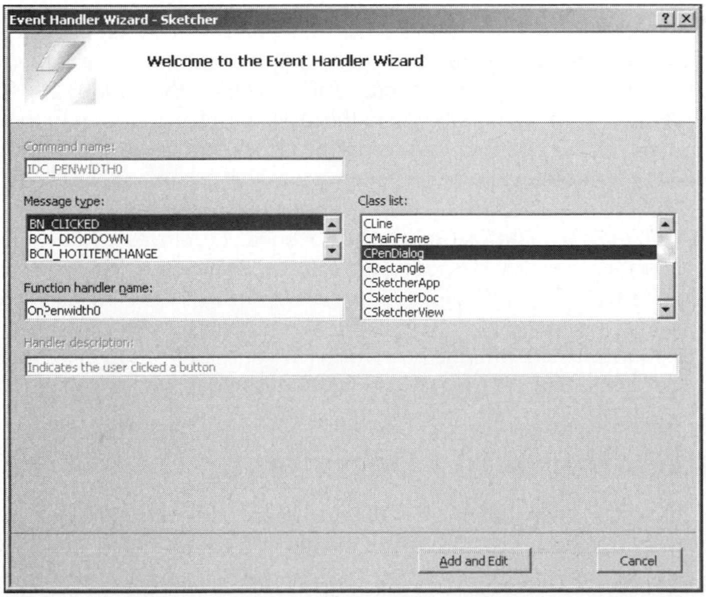

Figure 17-11

The implementations of the BN_CLICKED event handlers for all of these radio buttons are similar because they each just set the pen width in the dialog object. As an example, the handler for IDC_PENWIDTH0 is:

```
void CPenDialog::OnPenwidth0()
{
    m_PenWidth = 0;
}
```

You need to add the code for all six handlers to the CPenDialog class implementation, setting m_PenWidth to 1 in OnPenwidth1(), to 2 in OnPenwidth2(), and so on.

Completing Dialog Operations

You must now modify the OnPenwidth() handler in CSketcherDoc to make the dialog effective. Add the following code to the function:

```
// Handler for the pen width menu item
void CSketcherDoc::OnPenwidth()
{
    CPenDialog aDlg;        // Create a local dialog object

    // Set the pen width in the dialog to that stored in the document
    aDlg.m_PenWidth = m_PenWidth;

    // Display the dialog as modal
    // When closed with OK, get the pen width
    if(aDlg.DoModal() == IDOK)
       m_PenWidth = aDlg.m_PenWidth;
}
```

The m_PenWidth member of the aDlg object is passed a pen width stored in the m_PenWidth member of the document; you've still got to add this member to CSketcherDoc. The call of the DoModal() function now occurs in the condition of the if statement, which is true if the DoModal() function returns IDOK. In this case, you retrieve the pen width stored in the aDlg object and store it in the m_PenWidth member of the document. If the dialog box is closed using the Cancel button or the close icon, IDOK won't be returned by DoModal() and the value of m_PenWidth in the document is not changed.

Note that even though the dialog box is closed when DoModal() returns a value, the aDlg object still exists, so you can call its member functions without any problem. The aDlg object is destroyed automatically on return from OnPenwidth().

All that remains to do to support variable pen widths in your application is to update the affected classes: CSketcherDoc, CElement, and the four shape classes derived from CElement.

Adding Pen Widths to the Document

You need to add the m_PenWidth member to the document class, and the GetPenWidth() function to allow external access to the value stored. You should add the following shaded statements to the CSketcherDoc class definition:

```
class CSketcherDoc : public CDocument
```

```
{
// the rest as before...

protected:
// the rest as before...
   int m_PenWidth;                      // Current pen width

// Operations
public:
// the rest as before...
   int GetPenWidth()                    // Get the current pen width
      { return m_PenWidth; }

// the rest as before...
};
```

Because it's trivial, you can define the GetPenWidth() function in the definition of the class and gain the benefit of it being implicitly inline. You still need to add initialization for m_PenWidth to the constructor for CSketcherDoc, so modify the constructor in SketcherDoc.cpp by adding the shaded line:

```
CSketcherDoc::CSketcherDoc()
: m_Element(LINE), m_Color(BLACK)
 ,m_PenWidth(0)                         // 1 pixel pen
{
   // TODO: add one-time construction code here
}
```

Adding Pen Widths to the Elements

You have a little more to do to the CElement class and the shape classes that are derived from it. You already have a member m_Pen in CElement to store the width to be used when drawing an element, and you must extend each of the constructors for elements to accept a pen width as an argument, and set the member in the class accordingly. The GetBoundRect() function in CElement must be altered to deal with a pen width of zero. You can deal with the CElement class first. The new version of the GetBoundRect() function in the CElement class is:

```
// Get the bounding rectangle for an element
CRect CElement::GetBoundRect()
{
   CRect BoundingRect;                  // Object to store the bounding rectangle
   BoundingRect = m_EnclosingRect;      // Initialize with the enclosing rectangle

   //Increase bounding rectangle by the pen width
   int Offset = m_Pen == 0 ? 1 : m_Pen; // Width must be at least 1
   BoundingRect.InflateRect(Offset, Offset);
   return BoundingRect;
}
```

You use the local variable Offset to ensure that you pass the InflateRect() function a value of 1 if the pen width is zero (a pen width of 0 is always draw a line one pixel wide), and pass the actual pen width in all other cases.

Each of the constructors for CLine, CRectangle, CCircle and CCurve must be modified to accept a pen width as an argument, and to store it in the inherited m_Pen member of the class. The declaration for the constructor in each class definition needs to be modified to add the extra parameter. For example, in the CLine class, the constructor declaration becomes:

```
    CLine(CPoint Start, CPoint End, COLORREF aColor, int PenWidth);
```

and the constructor implementation should be modified to:

```
  CLine::CLine(CPoint Start, CPoint End, COLORREF aColor, int PenWidth)
   :m_EndPoint(CPoint(0,0))
  {
     m_StartPoint = Start;              // Set line start point
     m_EndPoint = End;                  // Set line end point
     m_Color = aColor;                  // Set line color
     m_Pen = PenWidth;                  // Set pen width

     // Define the enclosing rectangle
     m_EnclosingRect = CRect(Start, End);
     m_EnclosingRect.NormalizeRect();
  }
```

You should modify each of the class definitions and constructors for the shapes in the same way so that they each initialize m_Pen with the value passed as the last argument.

Creating Elements in the View

The last change you need to make is to the CreateElement() member of CSketcherView. Because you have added the pen width as an argument to the constructors for each of the shapes, you must update the calls to the constructors to reflect this. Change the definition of CSketcherView::CreateElement() to:

```
  CElement* CSketcherView::CreateElement()
  {
     // Get a pointer to the document for this view
     CSketcherDoc* pDoc = GetDocument();
     ASSERT_VALID(pDoc);                        // Verify the pointer is good

     // Now select the element using the type stored in the document
     switch(pDoc->GetElementType())
     {
       case RECTANGLE:
           return new CRectangle(m_FirstPoint, m_SecondPoint,
                       pDoc->GetElementColor(), pDoc->GetPenWidth());
       case CIRCLE:
           return new CCircle(m_FirstPoint, m_SecondPoint,
                       pDoc->GetElementColor(), pDoc->GetPenWidth());
       case CURVE:
           return new CCurve(m_FirstPoint, m_SecondPoint,
                       pDoc->GetElementColor(), pDoc->GetPenWidth());
       case LINE:                               // Always default to a line
           return new CLine(m_FirstPoint, m_SecondPoint,
                       pDoc->GetElementColor(), pDoc->GetPenWidth());
       default:                        // Something's gone wrong
           AfxMessageBox("Bad Element code", MB_OK);
```

```
            AfxAbort();
    }
}
```

Each constructor call now passes the pen width as an argument. This is retrieved from the document using the `GetPenWidth()` function that you added to the document class.

Exercising the Dialog

You can now build and run the latest version of Sketcher to see how the pen dialog works out. Selecting the `Pen > Width` menu option or the associated Toolbar button displays the dialog box so that you can select the pen width. The screen shown in Figure 17-12 is typical of what you might see when the Sketcher program is executing.

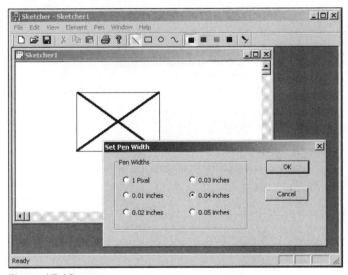

Figure 17-12

Note that the dialog box is a completely separate window. You can drag it around to position it where you want. You can even drag it outside the Sketcher application window.

Using a Spin Button Control

Now you can move on to looking at how the spin button can help in the Sketcher application. The spin button is particularly useful when you want to constrain an input within a given integer range. It's normally used in association with another control, called a **buddy control**, that displays the value that the spin button modifies. The associated control is usually an edit control, but it doesn't have to be.

It would be nice to be able to draw at different scales in Sketcher. If you had a way to change the drawing scale, you could scale up whenever you wanted to fill in the fine detail in your masterpiece and scale down again when working across the whole vista. You could apply the spin control to managing scaling in a document view. A drawing scale would be a view-specific property, and you would want the element drawing functions to take account of the current scale for a view. Altering the existing code to deal with view scaling requires rather more work than setting up the control, so first look at how you create a spin button and make it work.

Adding the Scale Menu Item and Toolbar Button

Begin by providing a means of displaying the scale dialog. Go to Resource View and open the IDR_SketcherTYPE menu. You are going to add a Scale menu item to the end of the View menu. Enter the caption for the unused menu item as Scale.... This item brings up the scale dialog, so you end the caption with an ellipsis (three periods) to indicate that it displays a dialog. Next you can add a separator preceding the new menu item by right-clicking it and selecting Insert Separator from the pop-up. You can then verify that the properties for the menu item are as shown in Figure 17-13.

The menu should now look as shown in Figure 17-14.

Figure 17-13

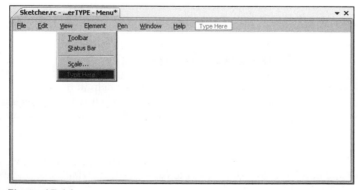

Figure 17-14

You can also add a Toolbar button for this menu item. All you need to do is make sure that the ID for the button is also set to ID_VIEW_SCALE.

Creating the Spin Button

You've got the menu item; you'd better have a dialog to go with it. In Resource View, add a new dialog by right-clicking the Dialog folder on the tree and selecting Insert Dialog from the pop-up. Change the ID to IDD_SCALE_DLG and the caption in the title bar to Set Drawing Scale.

Click the spin control in the palette and then click on the position in the dialog where you want it to be placed. Next, right-click the spin control to display its properties. Change its ID to something more meaningful than the default, such as IDC_SPIN_SCALE. Now take at look at the properties for the spin button. They are shown in Figure 17-15.

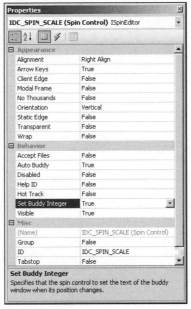

Figure 17-15

The Arrow Keys property is already set as True, enabling you to operate the spin button by using arrow keys on the keyboard. You should also set the value for the Set buddy integer property which specifies the buddy control value as an integer to True, and the Auto buddy which provides for automatic selection of the buddy control to True. The effect of this is that the control selected as the buddy is automatically the previous control defined in the dialog. At the moment, this is the Cancel button, which is not exactly ideal, but you'll see how to change this in a moment. The Alignment property determines how the spin button is displayed in relation to its buddy. You should set this to Right Align so that the spin button is attached to the right edge of its buddy control.

Next, add an edit control at the side of the spin button by selecting the edit control from the list in the Toolbox pane and clicking in the dialog where you want it positioned. Change the ID for the edit control to IDC_SCALE.

To make the contents of the edit control quite clear, you could add a static control just to the left of the edit control in the palette and enter **View Scale:** as the caption. You can select all three controls by clicking on them while holding down the Shift key. Pressing the F9 function key aligns the controls tidily, or you can use the Format menu.

The Controls' Tab Sequence

Controls in a dialog have what is called a **tab sequence**. This is the sequence in which the focus shifts from one control to the next, determined initially by the sequence in which controls are added to the dialog. You can see the tab sequence for the current dialog box by selecting `Format > Tab Order` from the main menu, or by pressing `Ctrl+D`. When I finished adding the controls, the dialog was annotated as shown on the left in Figure 17-16.

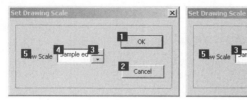

Original tab order for the controls   Tab order to make the Edit control the buddy for the Spin control

Figure 17-16

The tab order is indicated by the sequence of numbers in Figure 17-16. Because the Cancel button immediately precedes the spin button in sequence in the dialog on the left, the `Auto Buddy` property for the spin button selects it as the buddy control. You really want the edit control to precede the spin button in the tab sequence, so you need to select the controls by clicking on them in the sequence: OK button; Cancel button; edit control; spin button; and finally the static control so the tab order will be as shown in the dialog on the right in Figure 17-16. Now the edit control is selected as the buddy to the spin button.

Generating the Scale Dialog Class

After saving the resource file, you can right-click the dialog and select Add Class from the pop-up at the cursor. You'll then be able to define the new class associated with the dialog resource that you have created. You should name the class `CScaleDialog` and select the base class as `CDialog`. Clicking the Finish button adds the class to the Sketcher project.

You need to add a variable to the dialog class that stores the value returned from the edit control, so click the `CScaleDialog` class name in the Class View and select `Add > Add Variable` from the pop-up. The new data member of the class is a special kind, called a **control variable**, so first check the `Control variable` box in the window for the Add Member Variable wizard. Select `IDC_SCALE` as the ID from the Control ID: drop-down list and `Value` from the `Category:` list box. Enter the variable name as `m_Scale`. You'll be storing an integer scale value, so select `int` as the variable type. The Add Member Variable wizard displays edit boxes where you can enter maximum and minimum values for the variable `m_Scale`. For our application, a minimum of 1 and a maximum of 8 would be good values. Note that this constraint only applies to the edit box; the spin control is independent of it. Figure 17-17 shows how the window for the Add Member Wizard should look when you are done.

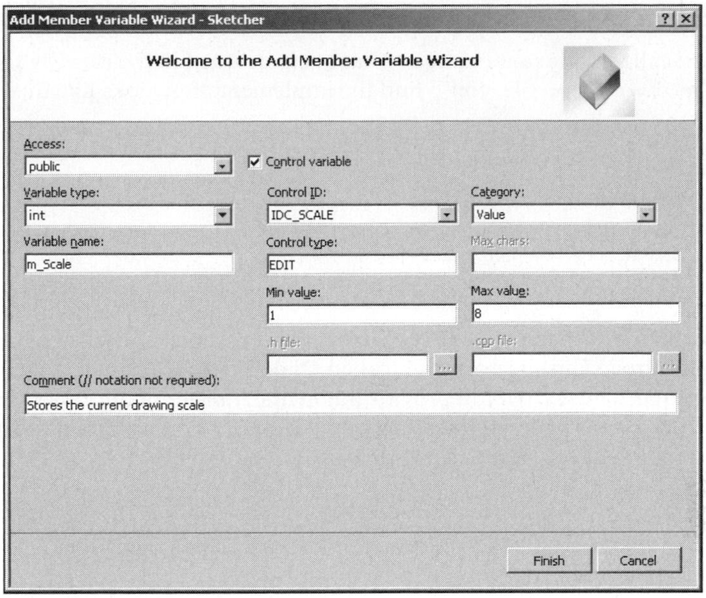

Figure 17-17

If you click the Finish button, the wizard takes care of entering the code necessary to support your new control variable. The class definition you'll end up with after the wizard has added the new member is as follows:

```cpp
class CScaleDialog : public CDialog
{
  DECLARE_DYNAMIC(CScaleDialog)

public:
  CScaleDialog(CWnd* pParent = NULL);   // standard constructor
  virtual ~CScaleDialog();

// Dialog Data
  enum { IDD = IDD_SCALE_DLG };

protected:
  virtual void DoDataExchange(CDataExchange* pDX);    // DDX/DDV support

  DECLARE_MESSAGE_MAP()
public:
  // Stores the current drawing scale
  int m_Scale;
};
```

The interesting bits of the class definition are shaded. The class is associated with the dialog resource through the enum statement initializing IDD with the ID of the resource. It contains the variable m_Scale, which is specified as a public member of the class, so you can set and retrieve its value in a CScaleDialog object directly. There's also some special code in the implementation of the class to deal with the new m_Scale member.

Dialog Data Exchange and Validation

A virtual function called DoDataExchange() has been included in the class by the Class Wizard. If you look in the ScaleDialog.cpp file, you'll find the implementation looks like this:

```
void CScaleDialog::DoDataExchange(CDataExchange* pDX)
{
    CDialog::DoDataExchange(pDX);
    DDX_Text(pDX, IDC_SCALE, m_Scale);
    DDV_MinMaxInt(pDX, m_Scale, 1, 8);
}
```

This function is called by the framework to carry out the exchange of data between variables in a dialog and the dialog's controls. This mechanism is called **Dialog Data Exchange**, usually abbreviated to **DDX**. This is a powerful mechanism that can provide automatic transfer of information between a dialog and its controls in most circumstances, thus saving you the effort of programming to get the data yourself, as you did with the radio buttons in the pen width dialog.

In the scale dialog, DDX handles data transfers between the edit control and the variable m_Scale in the CScaleDialog class. The variable pDX passed to the DoDataExchange() function controls the direction in which data is transferred. After calling the base class DoDataExchange() function, the DDX_Text() function is called, which actually moves data between the variable, m_Scale, and the edit control.

The call to the DDV_MinMaxInt() function verifies that the value transferred is within the limits specified. This mechanism is called **Dialog Data Validation**, or **DDV**. The DoDataExchange() function is called automatically before the dialog is displayed, to pass the value stored in m_Scale to the edit control. When the dialog is closed with the OK button, it is automatically called again to pass the value in the control back to the variable m_Scale in the dialog object. All this is taken care of for you. You need only to ensure that the right value is stored in m_Scale before the dialog box is displayed, and arrange to collect the result when the dialog box closes.

Initializing the Dialog

You'll use the OnInitDialog() function to initialize the dialog, just as you did for the pen width dialog. This time you'll use it to set up the spin control. You'll initialize the m_Scale member a little later when you create the dialog in the handler for a Scale menu item because it should be set to the value of the scale stored in the view. For now, add an override for the OnInitDialog() function to the CScaleDialog class, using the same mechanism that you used for the previous dialog, and add code to initialize the spin control as follows:

```
BOOL CScaleDialog::OnInitDialog()
{
    CDialog::OnInitDialog();

    // First get a pointer to the spin control
    CSpinButtonCtrl* pSpin;
    pSpin = (CSpinButtonCtrl*)GetDlgItem(IDC_SPIN_SCALE);

    // If you have not checked the auto buddy option in
    // the spin control's properties, set the buddy control here

    // Set the spin control range
```

```
        pSpin->SetRange(1, 8);

    return TRUE;  // return TRUE unless you set the focus to a control
                  // EXCEPTION: OCX Property Pages should return FALSE
}
```

There are only three lines of code to add, along with four lines of comments. The first line of code creates a pointer to an object of the MFC class `CSpinButtonCtrl`. This class is specifically for managing spin buttons, and is initialized in the next statement to point to the control in our dialog. The function `GetDlgItem()` is inherited from `CWnd` via `CDialog`, and it retrieves the address of any control from the ID you pass as the argument. As you saw earlier, a control is just a specialized window, so the pointer returned is of type `CWnd*`; you therefore have to cast it to the type appropriate to the particular control, which is `CSpinButtonCtrl*` in this case. The third statement that you've added sets the upper and lower limits for the spin button by calling the `SetRange()` member of the spin control object. Although you have set the range limits for the edit control, this doesn't affect the spin control directly. If you don't limit the values in the spin control here, you would be allowing the spin control to insert values in the edit control that were outside the limits, so there would be an error message from the edit control. You can demonstrate this by commenting out the statement that calls `SetRange()` here and trying out Sketcher without it.

If you want to set the buddy control using code rather than setting the value of `Auto buddy` in the spin button's properties to `True`, the `CSpinButtonCtrl` class has a function member to do this. You would need to add the statement

```
    pSpin->SetBuddy(GetDlgItem(IDC_SCALE));
```

at the point indicated by the comments.

Displaying the Spin Button

The dialog is to be displayed when the Scale menu option (or its associated toolbar button) is selected, so you need to add a COMMAND event handler to the `CSketcherView` class corresponding to the `ID_VIEW_SCALE` message through the Properties window for the class. You can then add code as follows:

```
    void CSketcherView::OnViewScale()
    {
      CScaleDialog aDlg;                  // Create a dialog object
      aDlg.m_Scale = m_Scale;            // Pass the view scale to the dialog
      if(aDlg.DoModal() == IDOK)
      {
        m_Scale = aDlg.m_Scale;          // Get the new scale
        InvalidateRect(0);               // Invalidate the whole window
      }
    }
```

You create the dialog as a modal dialog in the same way as for the pen width dialog. Before the dialog box is displayed by the `DoModal()` function call, you store the scale value provided by the `m_Scale` member of `CSketcherView` in the dialog member with the same name; this ensures that the control displays the current scale value when the dialog is displayed. If the dialog is closed with the OK button, you store the new scale from the `m_Scale` member of the dialog object in the view member with the same name.

Because you have changed the view scale, you need to get the view redrawn with the new scale value applied. The call to InvalidateRect() does this.

Of course, you must not forget to add the m_Scale data member to the definition of CSketcherView, so add the following line at the end of the other data members in the class definition:

```
int m_Scale;                          // Current view scale
```

You should also modify the CSketcherView constructor to initialize m_Scale to 1. This results in a view always starting out with a scale of one to one.

If you forget to do this, it's unlikely that your program will work properly.

Because you are referring the CScaleDialog class in the CSketcherView class implementation, you must add an #include directive for ScaleDialog.h to the beginning of the SketcherView.cpp file. That's all you need to get the scale dialog and its spin control operational. You can build and run Sketcher to give it a trial spin before you add the code to use a view scale factor in the drawing process.

Using the Scale Factor

Scaling with Windows usually involves using one of the scaleable mapping modes, MM_ISOTROPIC or MM_ANISOTROPIC. By using one or other of these mapping modes, you can get Windows to do most of the work. Unfortunately, it's not as simple as just changing the mapping mode, because neither of these mapping modes is supported by CScrollView. If you can get around that, however, you're home and dry. You'll use MM_ANISOTROPIC for reasons that you'll see in a moment, so let's first understand what's involved in using this mapping mode.

Scaleable Mapping Modes

As I've said, there are two mapping modes that allow the mapping between logical coordinates and device coordinates to be altered and these are the MM_ISOTROPIC and MM_ANISOTROPIC modes. The MM_ISOTROPIC mode has the property that Windows will force the scaling factor for both the *x* and *y* axes to be the same, which has the advantage that your circles will always be circles. The disadvantage is that you can't map a document to fit into a rectangle of a different shape. The MM_ANISOTROPIC mode, on the other hand, permits scaling of each axis independently. Because it's the more flexible mode of the two, you'll use MM_ANISOTROPIC for scaling operations in Sketcher.

The way in which logical coordinates are transformed to device coordinates is dependent on the following parameters, which you can set:

Parameter	Description
Window Origin	The logical coordinates of the upper-left corner of the window. This is set by calling the function CDC::SetWindowOrg().
Window Extent	The size of the window specified in logical coordinates. This is set by calling the function CDC::SetWindowExt().

Parameter	Description
Viewport Origin	The coordinates of the upper-left corner of the window in device coordinates (pixels). This is set by calling the function CDC::SetViewportOrg().
Viewport Extent	The size of the window in device coordinates (pixels). This is set by calling the function CDC::SetViewportExt().

The **viewport** referred to here has no physical significance by itself; it serves only as a parameter for defining how coordinates are transformed from logical coordinates to device coordinates.

Remember that:

❑ **Logical coordinates** (also referred to as **page coordinates**) are determined by the mapping mode. For example, the MM_LOENGLISH mapping mode has logical coordinates in units of 0.01 inches, with the origin in the upper-left corner of the client area, and the positive *y*-axis direction running from bottom to top. These are used by the device context drawing functions.

❑ **Device coordinates** (also referred to as **client coordinates** in a window) are measured in pixels in the case of a window, with the origin at the upper-left corner of the client area, and with the positive *y*-axis direction from top to bottom. These are used outside of a device context, for example for defining the position of the cursor in mouse message handlers.

❑ **Screen coordinates** are measured in pixels and have the origin at the upper-left corner of the screen, with the positive y-axis direction from top to bottom. These are used when getting or setting the cursor position.

The formulae used by Windows to convert from logical coordinates to device coordinates are:

$$xDevice = (xLogical - xWindowOrg) * \frac{xViewportExt}{xWindowExt} + xViewportOrg$$

$$yDevice = (yLogical - yWindowOrg) * \frac{yViewportExt}{yWindowExt} + yViewportOrg$$

With coordinate systems other than those provided by the MM_ISOTROPIC and MM_ANISOTROPIC mapping modes, the window extent and the viewport extent are fixed by the mapping mode and you can't change them. Calling the functions SetWindowExt() or SetViewportExt() in the CDC object to change them has no effect, although you can still move the position of (0,0) in your logical reference frame by calling SetWindowOrg() or SetViewportOrg(). However, for a given document size expressed by the window extent in logical coordinate units, you can adjust the scale at which elements are displayed by setting the viewport extent appropriately. By using and setting the window and viewport extents, you can get the scaling done automatically.

Setting the Document Size

You need to maintain the size of the document in logical units in the document object. You can add a protected data member, m_DocSize, to the CSketcherDoc class definition to store the size of the document:

```
CSize m_DocSize;                              // Document size
```

You will also want to access this data member from the view class, so add a `public` function to the `CSketcherDoc` class definition as follows:

```
    CSize GetDocSize()
      { return m_DocSize; }              // Retrieve the document size
```

You must initialize the `m_DocSize` member in the constructor for the document, so modify the implementation of `CSketcherDoc()` as follows:

```
CSkctchcrDoc::CSketcherDoc()
: m_Element(LINE)
, m_Color(BLACK)
,m_PenWidth(0)
,m_DocSize(CSize(3000,3000))
{
    // TODO: add one-time construction code here
}
```

You'll be using notional `MM_LOENGLISH` coordinates, so you can treat the logical units as 0.01 inches, and the value set gives you an area of 30 inches square to draw on.

Setting the Mapping Mode

You can set the mapping mode to `MM_ANISOTROPIC` in an override for the inherited `OnPrepareDC()` in the `CSketcherView` class. This function is always called for any `WM_PAINT` message, and you have arranged to call it when you draw temporary objects in the mouse message handlers; however, you have to do a little more than just set the mapping mode. You'll need to create the function override in `CSketcherView` before you can add the code. Just open the Properties window for the `CSketcherView` class and click the Overrides toolbar button. You can then add the override by selecting `OnPrepareDC` from the list and clicking on `<Add> OnPrepareDC` in the adjacent column. You then are able to type the code directly in the Editor pane. The implementation of `OnPrepareDC()` is:

```
void CSketcherView::OnPrepareDC(CDC* pDC, CPrintInfo* pInfo)
{
    CScrollView::OnPrepareDC(pDC, pInfo);
    CSketcherDoc* pDoc = GetDocument();
    pDC->SetMapMode(MM_ANISOTROPIC);      // Set the map mode
    CSize DocSize = pDoc->GetDocSize();   // Get the document size

    // y extent must be negative because we want MM_LOENGLISH
    DocSize.cy = -DocSize.cy;             // Change sign of y
    pDC->SetWindowExt(DocSize);           // Now set the window extent

    // Get the number of pixels per inch in x and y
    int xLogPixels = pDC->GetDeviceCaps(LOGPIXELSX);
    int yLogPixels = pDC->GetDeviceCaps(LOGPIXELSY);

    // Calculate the viewport extent in x and y
    long xExtent = static_cast<long>(DocSize.cx)*m_Scale*xLogPixels/100L;
    long yExtent = static_cast <long>(DocSize.cy)*m_Scale*yLogPixels/100L;
```

```
    pDC->SetViewportExt(static_cast<int>(xExtent),
                        static_cast<int>(-yExtent)); // Set viewport extent
}
```

The override of the base class function is unusual here in that you have left the call to `CScrollView::OnPrepareDC()` in and added the modifications after it rather than where the comment in the default code suggests. If the class was derived from `CView`, you would replace the call to the base class version because it does nothing, but in the case of `CScrollView` this isn't the case. You need the base class function to set some attributes before you set the mapping mode. Don't make the mistake of calling the base class function at the end of the override version though — if you do, scaling won't work.

After setting the mapping mode and obtaining the document extent, you set the window extent with the y extent negative. This is just to be consistent with the `MM_LOENGLISH` mode that you were using previously — remember that the origin is at the top, so y values in the client area are negative with this mapping mode.

The `CDC` member function `GetDeviceCaps()` supplies information about the device that the device context is associated with. You can get various kinds of information about the device, depending on the argument you pass to the function. In this case, the arguments `LOGPIXELSX` and `LOGPIXELSY` return the number of pixels per logical inch in the x and y directions. These values are equivalent to 100 units in your logical coordinates.

You use these values to calculate the x and y values for the viewport extent, which you store in the local variables `xExtent` and `yExtent`. The document extent along an axis in logical units divided by 100 gives the document extent in inches. If this is multiplied by the number of logical pixels per inch for the device, you get the equivalent number of pixels for the extent. If you then use this value as the viewport extent, you get the elements displayed at a scale of 1 to 1. If you simplify the equations for converting between device and logical coordinates by assuming the window origin and the viewport origin are both (0,0), they become:

$$xDevice = xLogical * \frac{xViewportExt}{xWindowExt}$$

$$yDevice = yLogical * \frac{yViewportExt}{yWindowExt}$$

If you multiply the viewport extent values by the scale (stored in `m_Scale`), the elements are drawn according to the value of `m_Scale`. This logic is exactly represented by the expressions for the x and y viewport extents in your code. The simplified equations with the scale included are:

$$xDevice = xLogical * \frac{xViewportExt * m\_Scale}{xWindowExt}$$

$$yDevice = yLogical * \frac{yViewportExt * m\_Scale}{yWindowExt}$$

You should be able to see from this that a given pair of device coordinates varies in proportion to the scale value. The coordinates at a scale of 3 are three times the coordinates at a scale of 1. Of course, as well as making elements larger, increasing the scale also moves them away from the origin.

That's all you need to scale the view. Unfortunately, at the moment the scrolling won't work with scaling, so you need to see what you can do about that.

Implementing Scrolling with Scaling

CScrollView just won't work with the MM_ANISOTROPIC mapping mode so clearly you must use another mapping mode to set up the scrollbars. The easiest way to do this is to use MM_TEXT, because in this case the logical coordinates are the same as the client coordinates — pixels, in other words. All you need to do, then, is to figure out how many pixels are equivalent to the logical document extent for the scale at which you are drawing, which is easier than you might think. You can add a function to CSketcherView to take care of the scrollbars and implement everything in there. Right-click the CSketcherView class name in Class View and add a public function ResetScrollSizes() with a void return type and no parameters. Add the code to the implementation, as follows:

```
void CSketcherView::ResetScrollSizes(void)
{
    CClientDC aDC(this);
    OnPrepareDC(&aDC);                          // Set up the device context
    CSize DocSize = GetDocument()->GetDocSize();  // Get the document size
    aDC.LPtoDP(&DocSize);                       // Get the size in pixels
    SetScrollSizes(MM_TEXT, DocSize);           // Set up the scrollbars
}
```

After creating a local CClientDC object for the view, you call OnPrepareDC() to set up the MM_ANISOTROPIC mapping mode. Because this takes account of the scaling, the LPtoDP() member of the aDC object converts the document size stored in the local variable DocSize to the correct number of pixels for the current logical document size and scale. The total document size in pixels defines how large the scrollbars must be in MM_TEXT mode — remember MM_TEXT logical coordinates are in pixels. You can then get the SetScrollSizes() member of CScrollView to set up the scrollbars based on this by specifying MM_TEXT as the mapping mode.

It may seem strange that you can change the mapping mode in this way, but it's important to keep in mind that the mapping mode is nothing more than a definition of how logical coordinates are to be converted to device coordinates. Whatever mode (and therefore coordinate conversion algorithm) you've set up applies to all subsequent device context functions until you change it, and you can change it whenever you want. When you set a new mode, subsequent device context function calls just use the conversion algorithm defined by the new mode. You figure how big the document is in pixels with MM_ANISOTROPIC because this is the only way you can get the scaling into the process, and then switch to MM_TEXT to set up the scrollbars because you need units for this in pixels for it to work properly. Simple really, when you know how.

Setting Up the Scrollbars

You must set up the scrollbars initially for the view in the OnInitialUpdate() member of CSketcherView. Change the previous implementation of the function to:

```
void CSketcherView::OnInitialUpdate()
{
    ResetScrollSizes();                    // Set up the scrollbars
    CScrollView::OnInitialUpdate();
}
```

All you do is call the `ResetScrollSizes()` function that you just added to the view. This takes care of everything — well, almost. The `CScrollView` object needs an initial extent to be set for `OnPrepareDC()` to work properly, so you need to add one statement to the `CSketcherView` constructor:

```
CSketcherView::CSketcherView()
: m_FirstPoint(CPoint(0,0))          // Set 1st recorded point to 0,0
, m_SecondPoint(CPoint(0,0))         // Set 2nd recorded point to 0,0
, m_pTempElement(NULL)               // Set temporary element pointer to 0
, m_pSelected(NULL)                  // No element selected initially
, m_MoveMode(FALSE)                  // Set move mode off
, m_CursorPos(CPoint(0,0))           // Initialize as zero
, m_FirstPos(CPoint(0,0))            // Initialize as zero
, m_Scale(1)                         // Set scale to 1:1
{
    SetScrollSizes(MM_TEXT, CSize(0,0));     // Set arbitrary scrollers
}
```

The additional statement just calls `SetScrollSizes()` with an arbitrary extent to get the scrollbars initialized before the view is drawn. When the view is drawn for the first time, the `ResetScrollSizes()` function call in `OnInitialUpdate()` sets up the scrollbars properly.

Of course, each time the view scale changes, you need to update the scrollbars before the view is redrawn. You can take care of this in the `OnViewScale()` handler in the `CSketcherView` class:

```
void CSketcherView::OnViewScale()
{
  CScaleDialog aDlg;                 // Create a dialog object
  aDlg.m_Scale = m_Scale;            // Pass the view scale to the dialog
  if(aDlg.DoModal() == IDOK)
  {
    m_Scale = aDlg.m_Scale;          // Get the new scale
    ResetScrollSizes();              // Adjust scrolling to the new scale
    InvalidateRect(0);               // Invalidate the whole window
  }
}
```

Using the `ResetScrollSizes()` function, taking care of the scrollbars isn't complicated. Everything is covered by the one additional line of code.

Now you can build the project and run the application. You'll see that the scrollbars work just as they should. Note that each view maintains its own scale factor, independently of the other views.

Working with Status Bars

With each view now being scaled independently, it becomes necessary to have some indication of what the current scale in a view is. A convenient way to do this would be to display the scale in the status bar that was created by default in the Sketcher application. By default the status bar appears at the bottom of the application window, below the horizontal scrollbar, although you can arrange for it to be at the top of the client area. The status bar is divided into segments called **panes**; the status bar in Sketcher has four panes. The one on the left contains the text Ready, and the other three are the recessed areas on the right that are used to record when CAPS lock, NUM lock, and SCROLL lock are in effect.

It's possible for you to write to the status bar that the Application Wizard supplied by default, but you need to get access to the m_wndStatusBar member of the CMainFrame object for the application as this represents it. As it's a protected member of the class, you must add a public member function to modify the status bar from outside the class. You could add the following public function member to the CMainFrame class to do this:

```
void CMainFrame::SetPaneText(int Pane, LPCTSTR Text)
{
    m_wndStatusBar.SetPaneText(Pane, Text);
}
```

The implementation goes in the .cpp file and you must add a declaration for the function to the class definition. The SetPaneText() function sets the text specified by the second parameter, Text, in the pane identified by the first parameter, Pane, in the status bar object represented by m_wndStatusBar. The status bar panes are indexed from the left, starting at 0. Now you can write to the status bar from anywhere outside the CMainFrame class using this function. For example:

```
CMainFrame* pFrame = (CMainFrame*)AfxGetApp()->m_pMainWnd;
pFrame->SetPaneText(0, "Goodbye cruel world");
```

This code fragment gets a pointer to the main window of the application and outputs the text string you see to the left-most pane in the status bar. This is fine, but the main application window is no place for a view scale. You may well have several views in Sketcher, so you really want to associate displaying the scale with each view. A better approach would be to give each child window its own status bar. The m_wndStatusBar in CMainFrame is an instance of the CStatusBar class. You can use the same class to implement your own status bars.

Adding a Status Bar to a Frame

The CStatusBar class defines a control bar with multiple panes in which you can display information. Objects of type CStatusBar can also provide the same functionality as the Windows common status bar control through a member function GetStatusBarCtrl(). There is an MFC class that specifically encapsulates each of the Windows common controls — the one for the common status bar control is CStatusBarCtrl. However, using this directly involves quite a bit of work to integrate it with the other MFC classes, as the raw Windows control doesn't connect to MFC. Using CStatusBar in our Sketcher program is easier and safer. The GetStatusBarCtrl() function returns a reference to a CStatusBarCtrl object that provides all the functionality of the common control, and the CStatusBar object takes care of the communications to the rest of the MFC.

The first step to utilizing it is to add a data member for the status bar to the definition of CChildFrame, which is the frame window for a view, so add the following declaration to the public section of the class:

```
CStatusBar m_StatusBar;                    // Status bar object
```

A little clarification may be required at this point. Status bars should be part of the frame, not part of the view. You don't want to be able to scroll the status bars or draw over them. They should just remain anchored to the bottom of the window. If you added a status bar to the view, it would appear inside the scrollbars and would be scrolled whenever you scrolled the view. Any drawing over the part of the view containing the status bar would cause the bar to be redrawn, leading to an annoying flicker. Having the status bar as part of the frame avoids these problems.

You should initialize the `m_StatusBar` data member just before the visible view window is displayed. So, using the Properties window for the `CChildFrame` class, add a function to the class that is called in response to the `WM_CREATE` message that is sent to the application when the window is to be created. Add the following code to the `OnCreate()` handler:

```
int CChildFrame::OnCreate(LPCREATESTRUCT lpCreateStruct)
{
  if(CMDIChildWnd::OnCreate(lpCreateStruct) == -1)
    return -1;

    // Create the status bar
    m_StatusBar.Create(this);

    // Work out the width of the text we want to display
    CRect textRect;
    CClientDC aDC(&m_StatusBar);
    aDC.SelectObject(m_StatusBar.GetFont());
    aDC.DrawText(_T("View Scale:99"), -1, textRect, DT_SINGLELINE|DT_CALCRECT);

    // Setup a part big enough to take the text
    int width = textRect.Width();
    m_StatusBar.GetStatusBarCtrl().SetParts(1, &width);

    // Initialize the text for the status bar
    m_StatusBar.GetStatusBarCtrl().SetText(_T("View Scale:1"), 0, 0);
    return 0;
}
```

The generated code isn't shaded. There's a call to the base class version of the `OnCreate()` function, which takes care of creating the definition of the view window. It's important not to delete this function call; otherwise, the window is not created.

The `Create()` function in the `CStatusBar` object creates the status bar. The `this` pointer for the current `CChildFrame` object is passed to the `Create()` function, setting up a connection between the status bar and the window that owns it. Take a look at what's happening in the code that you have added to the `OnCreate()` function.

Defining the Status Bar Parts

A `CStatusBar` object has an associated `CStatusBarCtrl` object with one or more **parts**. Parts and panes in the context of status bars are equivalent terms — `CStatusBar` refers to panes and `CStatusBarCtrl` refers to parts. You can display a separate item of information in each part.

You can define the number of parts and their widths by a call to the `SetParts()` member of the `CStatusBarCtrl` object. This function requires two arguments. The first argument is the number of parts in the status bar, and the second is an array specifying the right edge of each part in client coordinates. If you omit the call to `SetParts()`, the status bar has one part by default, which stretches across the whole bar; you could use this, but it looks untidy. A better approach is to size the part so that the text to be displayed fits nicely, and this is what you will do in Sketcher.

The first thing you do in the `OnCreate()` function is to create a temporary `CRect` object in which you'll store the enclosing rectangle for the text that you want to display. You then create a `CClientDC` object, which contains a device context with the same extent as the status bar. This is possible because the status bar, like all other controls, is just a window.

Next, the font used in the status bar (set up as part of the desktop properties) is selected into the device context by calling the `SelectObject()` function. The `GetFont()` member of `m_StatusBar` returns a pointer to a `CFont` object that represents the current font. Obviously, the particular font used determines how much space the text that you want to display takes up.

You call the `DrawText()` member of the `CClientDC` object to calculate the enclosing rectangle for the text you want to display. This function has four arguments:

❑   The text string you need drawn. You have passed a string containing the maximum number of characters you would ever want to display, `"View Scale:99"`.

❑   The count of the number of characters in the string. You have specified this as -1, which indicates you are supplying a null-terminated string. In this case the function works out the character count.

❑   Your rectangle, `textRect`. The enclosing rectangle for the text is stored here in logical coordinates.

❑   One or more flags controlling the operation of the function.

You have specified a combination of two flags; `DT_SINGLELINE` specifies that the text is to be on a single line, and `DT_CALCRECT` specifies that you want the function to calculate the size of the rectangle required to display the string and store it in the rectangle pointed to by the third argument. The `DrawText()` function is normally used to output text, but in this instance the `DT_CALCRECT` flag stops the function from actually drawing the string. There are a number of other flags that you can use with this function; you can find details about them by looking up this function with Help.

The next statement sets up the parts for the status bar:

```
m_StatusBar.GetStatusBarCtrl().SetParts(1, &width);
```

The expression `m_StatusBar.GetStatusBarCtrl()` returns a reference to the `CStatusBarCtrl` object that belongs to `m_StatusBar`. The reference returned is used to call the `SetParts()` function for the object. The first argument to `SetParts()` defines the number of parts for the status bar — which is 1 in this case. The second argument is typically the address of an array of type `int` containing the x coordinate of the right hand edge of each part in client coordinates. The array has one element for each part in the status bar. Because you have only one part, you pass the address of the single variable, `width`, which contains the width of the rectangle you stored in `textRect`. This is in client coordinates because the device context uses `MM_TEXT` by default.

Finally, you set the initial text in the status bar with a call to the `SetText()` member of `CStatusBarCtrl`. The first argument is the written text string, the second is the index position of the part that contains the text string, and the third argument specifies the appearance of the part on the screen. The third argument can be any of those shown in the following table.

Style Code	Appearance
0	The text has a border that appears recessed into the status bar.
SBT_NOBORDERS	The text is drawn without borders.
SBT_OWNERDRAW	The text is drawn by the parent window.
SBT_POPOUT	The text has a border that appears to stand out from the status bar.

In your code, you specify the text with a border so that it appears recessed into the status bar. You could try the other options to see how they look.

Updating the Status Bar

If you build and run the code now, the status bars appears, but they show only a scale factor of 1, no matter what scale factor is actually being used — not very useful. What you need to do is to add code somewhere that changes the text each time a different scale is chosen. This means modifying the `OnViewScale()` handler in `CSketcherView` to change the status bar for the frame. Only four additional lines of code are required:

```
void CSketcherView::OnViewScale()
{
  CScaleDialog aDlg;                    // Create a dialog object
  aDlg.m_Scale = m_Scale;               // Pass the view scale to the dialog
  if(aDlg.DoModal() == IDOK)
  {
    m_Scale = aDlg.m_Scale;             // Get the new scale

    // Get the frame window for this view
    CChildFrame* viewFrame = static_cast<CChildFrame*>(GetParentFrame());

    // Build the message string
    CString StatusMsg("View Scale:");
    StatusMsg += static_cast<char>('0' + m_Scale);

    // Write the string to the status bar
    viewFrame->m_StatusBar.GetStatusBarCtrl().SetText(StatusMsg, 0, 0);

    ResetScrollSizes();                 // Adjust scrolling to the new scale
    InvalidateRect(0);                  // Invalidate the whole window
  }
}
```

Because you refer to the `CChildFrame` object here, you must add an `#include` directive for `ChildFrm.h` to the beginning of `SketcherView.cpp` after the existing `#include` directives.

The first line calls the `GetParentFrame()` member of `CSketcherView` that's inherited from the `CScrollView` class. This returns a pointer to a `CFrameWnd` object to correspond to the frame window, so it has to be cast to `CChildFrame*` for it to be of any use to you.

The next two lines build the message that displays in the status bar. The `CString` class is used simply because it is more flexible than using a `char` array. I will discuss `CString` objects in greater depth a bit later when you add a new element type to Sketcher. You get the character for the scale value by adding the value of `m_Scale` (which will be from 1 to 8) to the character '0'. This generates a character from '1' to '8'.

Finally, you use the pointer to the child frame to get at the `m_StatusBar` member that you added earlier. You can then get its status bar control and use the `SetText()` member of the control to change the text that it displays. The rest of the `OnViewScale()` function remains unchanged.

That's all you need for the status bar. If you build Sketcher again, you should have multiple, scrolled windows, each at different scales, with the scale displayed in a status bar in each view.

Using a List Box

Of course, you don't have to use a spin button to set the scale. You could also use a list box, for example. The logic for handling a scale factor would be exactly the same, and only the dialog box and the code to extract the value for the scale factor from it would change. If you want to try this out without messing up the development of the Sketcher program, you can copy the complete Sketcher project to another folder and make the modifications to the copy. Deleting part of a Class Wizard managed program can be a bit messy, so it's useful experience for when you really need to do it.

Removing the Scale Dialog

You first need to delete the definition and implementation of `CScaleDialog` from the new Sketcher project, as well as the resource for the scale dialog. To do this, go to the Solution Explorer pane, select `ScaleDialog.cpp` and press Delete; then select `ScaleDialog.h` and press Delete to remove them from the project. In each instance you'll see a dialog that gives you the option of just removing the files from the project or permanently deleting the files; click on the Delete button in the dialog to do that unless you want to keep the code. Then go to Resource View, expand the Dialog folder, click on `IDD_SCALE_DLG` and press the Delete key to remove the dialog resource. Delete the `#include` directive for `ScaleDialog.h` from `SketcherView.cpp`. At this stage, all references to the original dialog class have been removed from the project. Are you all done yet? Almost. The IDs for the resources should have been deleted for you. To verify this, right-click `Sketcher.rc` in Resource View and select the `Resource Symbols` menu item from the pop-up; you can check that `IDC_SCALE` and `IDC_SPIN_SCALE` are no longer in the list. Of course, the `OnViewScale()` handler in the `CSketcherView` class still refers to `CScaleDialog`, so the Sketcher project won't compile yet. You'll fix that when you have added the list box control.

Select the `Build > Clean Solution` menu item to remove any intermediate files from the project that may contain references to `CScaleDialog`. After that's done, you can start by recreating the dialog resource for entering a scale value.

Creating a List Box Control

Right-click Dialog in Resource View and add a new dialog with a suitable ID and caption. You could use the same ID as before, IDD_SCALE_DLG.

Select the list box button in the list of controls and click on where you want the list box positioned in the dialog box. You can enlarge the list box and adjust its position in the dialog by dragging it appropriately. Right-click the list box and select Properties from the pop-up. You can set the ID to something suitable, such as IDC_SCALELIST as shown in Figure 17-18.

Figure 17-18

The Sort property will be True by default, so make sure you set it to False. This means that strings that you add to the list box are not automatically sorted. Instead, they're appended to the end of the list in the box, and are displayed in the sequence in which you enter them. Because you will be using the position in the list of the selected item to indicate the scale, it's important not to have the sequence changed. The list box has a vertical scrollbar for the list entries by default, and you can accept the defaults for the other properties. If you want to look into the effects of the other properties, you can click on each of them in turn to display text in the bottom of the Properties window explaining what the property does.

Now that the dialog is complete, you can save it and you're ready to create the class for the dialog.

Creating the Dialog Class

Right-click the dialog and select Add Class from the pop-up. Again, you'll be taken to the dialog to create a new class. Give the class an appropriate name, such as the one you used before, CScaleDialog, and select `CDialog` as the base class. If, when you click Finish, you get a message box displayed saying that `ScaleDialog.cpp` already exists, you forgot to explicitly delete the `.h` and `.cpp` files. Go back and do that now or rename the files if you want to keep them. Everything should then work as it's supposed to. After you've completed that, all you need to do is add a `public` control variable called `m_Scale` to the class, corresponding to the list box ID, `IDC_SCALELIST`. The type should be type `int` and the limits should be 0 and 7. Don't forget to set the `Category` as `Value`; otherwise, you won't be able to enter the limits. Because you have created it as a control variable, DDX is implemented for the `m_Scale` data member and you use the variable to store a zero-based index to one of the eight entries in the list box.

You need to initialize the list box in the `OnInitDialog()` handler `CScaleDialog`, so add an override for this function using the Properties window for the class. Add code as follows:

```
BOOL CScaleDialog::OnInitDialog()
{
  CDialog::OnInitDialog();

  CListBox* pListBox = static_cast<CListBox*>(GetDlgItem(IDC_SCALELIST));
  pListBox->AddString(_T("Scale 1"));
  pListBox->AddString(_T("Scale 2"));
  pListBox->AddString(_T("Scale 3"));
  pListBox->AddString(_T("Scale 4"));
  pListBox->AddString(_T("Scale 5"));
  pListBox->AddString(_T("Scale 6"));
  pListBox->AddString(_T("Scale 7"));
  pListBox->AddString(_T("Scale 8"));
  pListBox->SetCurSel(m_Scale-1);

  return TRUE;   // return TRUE unless you set the focus to a control
                 // EXCEPTION: OCX Property Pages should return FALSE
}
```

The first line that you have added obtains a pointer to the list box control by calling the `GetDlgItem()` member of the dialog class. This is inherited from the MFC class, `CWnd`. It returns a pointer of type `CWnd*`, so you cast this to the type `CListBox*`, which is a pointer to the MFC class defining a list box.

Using the pointer to the dialog's `CListBox` object, you then use the `AddString()` member repeatedly to add the lines defining the list of scale factors. These appear in the list box in the order that you enter them, so that the dialog is displayed as shown in Figure 17-19.

Each entry in the list is associated with a zero-based index value that is automatically stored in the `m_Scale` member of `CScaleDialog` through the DDX mechanism. Thus, if you select the third entry in the list, `m_Scale` is set to 2.

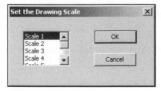

Figure 17-19

Displaying the Dialog

The dialog is displayed by the `OnViewScale()` handler that you added to `CSketcherView` in the previous version of Sketcher. You just need to amend this to deal with the new dialog using a list box. The code for it is as follows:

```
void CSketcherView::OnViewScale()
{
  CScaleDialog aDlg;                    // Create a dialog object
  aDlg.m_Scale = m_Scale;               // Pass the view scale to the dialog
  if(aDlg.DoModal() == IDOK)
  {
    m_Scale = 1 + aDlg.m_Scale;         // Get the new scale

    // Get the frame that wraps this view
    CChildFrame* viewFrame = static_cast<CChildFrame*>(GetParentFrame());

    // Build the message string
    CString StatusMsg("View Scale:");
    StatusMsg += static_cast<char>('1' + m_Scale - 1);
    // Set the status bar
    viewFrame->m_StatusBar.GetStatusBarCtrl().SetText(StatusMsg, 0, 0);

    ResetScrollSizes();                 // Adjust scrolling to the new scale
    InvalidateRect(0);                  // Invalidate the whole window
  }
}
```

Because the index value for the entry selected from the list is zero-based, you just need to add 1 to it to get the actual scale value to be stored in the view. The code to display this value in the view's status bar is exactly as before. The rest of the code to handle scale factors is already complete and requires no changes. After you've added back the `#include` directive for `ScaleDialog.h`, you can build and execute this version of Sketcher to see the list box in action.

Using an Edit Box Control

You could use an edit box control to add annotations in Sketcher. You'll need a new element type, `CText`, that corresponds to a text string, and an extra menu item to set a `TEXT` mode for creating elements. Because a text element needs only one reference point, you can create it in the `OnLButtonDown()` handler in the view class. You'll also need a new item in the `Element` menu to set `TEXT` mode. You'll add this text capability to Sketcher in the following sequence:

1. Create the dialog box resource and its associated class.

2. Add the new menu item.

3. Add the code to open the dialog for creating an element.

4. Add the support for a `CText` class.

Creating an Edit Box Resource

Create a new dialog resource in Resource View by right-clicking the Dialog folder and selecting Insert Dialog from the pop-up. Change the ID for the new dialog to `IDD_TEXT_DLG` and the caption text to **Enter Text**.

To add an edit box, select the edit box icon from the list of controls palette and then click the position in the dialog where you want to place it. You can adjust the size of the edit box by dragging its borders, and you can alter its position in the dialog by dragging the whole thing around. You can display the properties for the edit box by right-clicking it and selecting Properties from the pop-up. You could first change its ID to `IDC_EDITTEXT`, as shown in Figure 17-20.

Figure 17-20

Some of the properties for this control are of interest at this point. First, select the `Multiline` property. Setting the value for this as `True` creates a multiline edit box where the text you enter can span more than one line. This enables you to enter a long line of text and still remain visible in its entirety in the edit box.

The `Align text` property determines how the text is to be positioned in the multiline edit box. The value `Left` is fine here because you'll be displaying the text as a single line anyway, but you also have the options for `Center` and `Right`.

If you were to change the value for the Want return property to True, pressing Enter on the keyboard while entering the text in the control inserts a return character into the text string. This allows you to analyze the string if you wanted to break it into multiple lines for display. You don't want this effect, so leave the property value as False. In this state, pressing Enter has the effect of the default control (which is the OK button) being selected, so pressing Enter closes the dialog.

If you set the value of the Auto HScroll property as False, there is an automatic spill to the next line in the edit box when you reach the edge of the control while entering text. However, this is just for visibility in the edit box — it has no effect on the contents of the string. You could also change the value of the Auto VScroll property to True to allow text to continue beyond the number of lines that are visible in the control.

When you've finished setting the properties for the edit box, close its Properties window. Make sure that the edit box is first in the tab order by selecting the Format > Tab Order menu item or by pressing Ctrl+D. You can then test the dialog by selecting the Test Dialog menu item or by pressing Ctrl+T. The dialog is shown in Figure 17-21.

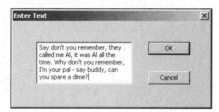

Figure 17-21

You can even enter text into the dialog in test mode to see how it works. Clicking the OK or Cancel button closes the dialog.

Creating the Dialog Class

After saving the dialog resource, you can create a suitable dialog class corresponding to the resource, which you could call CTextDialog. Right-click the dialog in Resource View and select Add Class from the pop-up to do this. The base class should be CDialog. Next you can add a control variable by right-clicking the class name in Class View and selecting Add > Add Variable from the pop-up. Select IDC_EDITTEXT as the control ID and the category as Value. Call the new variable m_TextString and leave its type as CString — you'll take a look at this class after you've finished the dialog class. You can also specify a maximum length for it in the Max chars: edit box, as shown in Figure 17-22.

A length of 100 is more than adequate for your needs. The variable that you have added here is automatically updated from the data entered into the control by the DDX mechanism. You can click Finish to create the variable in the CTextDialog class and close the Add Member Variable wizard.

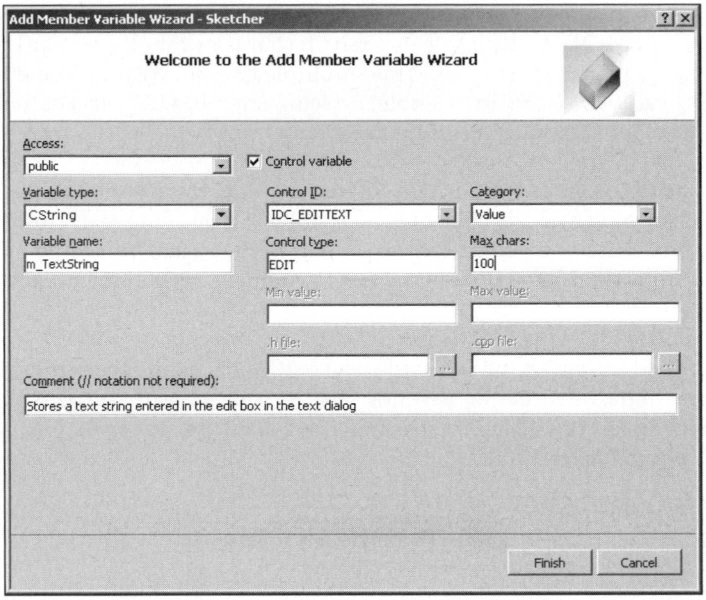

Figure 17-22

The CString Class

The CString class provides a very convenient and easy-to-use mechanism for handling strings that you can use just about anywhere a string is required. To be more precise, you can use a CString object in place of strings of type const char*, which is the usual type for a character string in native C++, or of type LPCTSTR, which is a type that comes up frequently in Windows API functions.

The CString class provides several overloaded operators, as shown in the following table, that make it easy to process strings.

Operator	Usage
=	Copies one string to another, as in: ```\nStr1 = Str2; // Copies contents of Str1 to Str2\nStr1 = "A normal string"; // Copies the RHS string to Str1\n```
+	Concatenates two or more strings, as in: ```\nStr1 = Str2 + Str3 + " more"; // Forms Str1 from 3 strings\n```
+=	Appends a string to an existing CString object.
==	Compares two strings for equality, as in: ```\nif(Str1 == Str2)\n // do something...\n```

Operator	Usage
<	Tests if one string is less than another.
<=	Tests if one string is less than or equal to another.
>	Tests if one string is greater than another.
>=	Tests if one string is greater than or equal to another.

The variables Str1 and Str2 in the table above are CString objects. CString objects automatically grow as necessary, such as when you add an additional string to the end of an existing object. For example, in the statements,

```
CString Str = "A fool and your money ";
Str += "are soon partners.";
```

the first statement declares and initializes the object Str. The second statement appends an additional string to Str, so the length of Str automatically increases.

Generally, you should avoid creating CString objects on the heap as far as possible. The memory management necessary for growing them means that operations will be slow.

Adding the Text Menu Item

Adding a new menu item should be easy by now. You just need to open the menu resource with the ID IDR_SketcherTYPE in Resource View by double-clicking it, and add a new menu item, Text, to the Element menu. The default ID, ID_ELEMENT_TEXT, that appears in the Properties window for the item is fine, so you can leave that as it is. You can add a prompt to be displayed on the status bar corresponding to the menu item, and because you'll also want to add an additional toolbar button corresponding to this menu item, you can add a tool tip to the end of the prompt line, using \n to separate the prompt and the tool tip.

Don't forget the context menu. You can copy the menu item from IDR_SketcherTYPE. Right-click the Text menu item and select Copy from the pop-up. Open the menu IDR_CURSOR_MENU, extend the no element menu, right-click the empty item at the bottom, and select Paste. All you then need to do is to drag the item to the appropriate position — above the separator — and save the resource file.

Add the toolbar button to the IDR_MAINFRAME toolbar and set its ID to the same as that for the menu item, ID_ELEMENT_TEXT. You can drag the new button so that it's positioned at the end of the block defining the other types of element. When you've saved the resources, you can add an event handler for the new menu item.

In the Class View pane, right-click CSketcherDoc and display its Properties window. Add a COMMAND handler for the ID_ELEMENT_TEXT ID and add code to it as follows:

```
void CSketcherDoc::OnElementText()
{
   m_Element = TEXT;
}
```

Only one line of code is necessary to set the element type in the document to TEXT.

You also need to add a function to check the menu item if it is the current mode, so add an UPDATE_COMMAND_UI handler corresponding to the ID_ELEMENT_TEXT ID, and implement the code for it as follows:

```
void CSketcherDoc::OnUpdateElementText(CCmdUI* pCmdUI)
{
   // Set checked if the current element is text
   pCmdUI->SetCheck(m_Element == TEXT);
}
```

This operates in the same way as the other Element pop-up menu items.

You must also add a line to the OurConstants.h header file:

```
   const unsigned int TEXT = 105U;
```

You can add this statement at the end of the other element type definitions in the header file. The next step is to define the CText class for an object of type TEXT.

Defining a Text Element

You can derive the class CText from the CElement class as follows:

```
// Class defining a text object
class CText: public CElement
{
   public:
     // Function to display a text element
     virtual void Draw(CDC* pDC, CElement* pElement=0);

     // Constructor for a text element
     CText(CPoint Start, CPoint End, CString aString, COLORREF aColor);
     virtual void Move(CSize& aSize);         // Move a text element

   protected:
     CPoint m_StartPoint;                     // position of a text element
     CString m_String;                        // Text to be displayed
     CText(){}                                // Default constructor
};
```

I added this manually, but I'll leave it to you to decide how you want to do this. This definition should go at the end of the Elements.h file following the other element types. This class definition declares the virtual Draw() and Move() functions, as the other element classes do. The data member m_String of type CString stores the text to be displayed, and m_StartPoint specifies the position of the string in the client area of a view.

Look at the constructor declaration in a little more detail. The CText constructor declaration defines four parameters that provide the following essential information:

Parameter	Defines
CPoint Start	The position of the text in logical coordinates.
CPoint End	The corner opposite Start that defines the rectangle enclosing the text.
CString aString	The text string to be displayed as a CString object.
COLORREF aColor	The color of the text.

The pen width doesn't apply to an item of text, because the appearance is determined by the font. Although you do not need to pass a pen width as an argument to the constructor, the constructor needs to initialize the m_PenWidth member inherited from the base class because it is used in the computation of the bounding rectangle for the text.

Implementing the CText Class

You have three functions to implement for the **CText** class:

❑   The constructor for a CText object.

❑   The virtual Draw() function to display it.

❑   The Move() function to support moving a text object by dragging it with the mouse.

I added these to the Elements.cpp file.

The CText Constructor

The constructor for a CText object needs to initialize the class and base class data members:

```
CText::CText(CPoint Start, CPoint End, CString aString, COLORREF aColor)
{
  m_Pen = 1;                        // Set the pen width
  m_Color = aColor;                 // Set the color for the text
  m_String = aString;               // Make a copy of the string
  m_StartPoint = Start;             // Start point for string

  m_EnclosingRect = CRect(Start, End);
  m_EnclosingRect.NormalizeRect();
}
```

This is all standard stuff, just like you've seen before for the other elements.

Drawing a CText Object

Drawing text in a device context is different to drawing a geometric figure. The implementation of the `Draw()` function for a `CText` object is as follows:

```
void CText::Draw(CDC* pDC, CElement* pElement)
{
  COLORREF Color(m_Color);                  // Initialize with element color

  if(this==pElement)
    Color = SELECT_COLOR;                   // Set selected color

  // Set the text color and output the text
  pDC->SetTextColor(Color);
  pDC->TextOut(m_StartPoint.x, m_StartPoint.y, m_String);
}
```

You don't need a pen to display text. You just need to specify the text color using the `SetTextColor()` function member of the `CDC` object and then use the `TextOut()` member to output the text string. This displays the string using the default font.

Because the `TextOut()` function doesn't use a pen, it isn't affected by setting the drawing mode of the device context. This means that the raster operations (ROP) method that you use to move the elements leaves temporary trails behind when applied to text. Remember that you used the `SetROP2()` function to specify the way in which the pen would logically combine with the background. By choosing `R2_NOTXORPEN` as the drawing mode, you could cause a previously drawn element to disappear by redrawing it — it would then revert to the background color and thus become invisible. Fonts aren't drawn using a pen, so it won't work with the text elements. You'll see how to fix this problem in the next chapter.

Moving a CText Object

The `Move()` function for a `CText` object is simple:

```
void CText::Move(CSize& aSize)
{
  m_StartPoint += aSize;                    // Move the start point
  m_EnclosingRect += aSize;                 // Move the rectangle
}
```

All you need to do is alter the point defining the position of the string, and the data member defining the enclosing rectangle, by the distance specified in the `aSize` parameter.

Creating a Text Element

After the element type has been set to `TEXT`, a text object should be created at the cursor position whenever you click the left mouse button and enter the text you want to display. You therefore need to open the dialog that permits text to be entered in the `OnLButtonDown()` handler. Add the following code to this handler in the `CSketcherView` class:

```
void CSketcherView::OnLButtonDown(UINT nFlags, CPoint point)
{
  CClientDC aDC(this);             // Create a device context
```

```
OnPrepareDC(&aDC);                   // Get origin adjusted
aDC.DPtoLP(&point);                  // convert point to Logical
// In moving mode, so drop the element
if(m_MoveMode)
{
  m_MoveMode = FALSE;                // Kill move mode
  m_pSelected = 0;                   // De-select element
  GetDocument()->UpdateAllViews(0);  // Redraw all the views
}
else
{
    CSketcherDoc* pDoc = GetDocument();// Get a document pointer
    if(pDoc->GetElementType() == TEXT)
    {
      CTextDialog aDlg;
      if(aDlg.DoModal() == IDOK)
      {
        // Exit OK so create a text element
        CSketcherDoc* pDoc = GetDocument();
        CSize TextExtent = aDC.GetTextExtent(aDlg.m_TextString);

        // Get bottom right of text rectangle - MM_LOENGLISH
        CPoint BottomRt(point.x+TextExtent.cx, point.y-TextExtent.cy);
        CText* pTextElement = new CText(point, BottomRt,
                         aDlg.m_TextString, pDoc->GetElementColor());

        // Add the element to the document
        pDoc->AddElement(pTextElement);

        // Get all views updated
        pDoc->UpdateAllViews(0,0,pTextElement);
      }
      return;
    }

    m_FirstPoint = point;              // Record the cursor position
    SetCapture();                      // Capture subsequent mouse messages
  }
}
```

The code to be added is shaded. It creates a CTextDialog object and then opens the dialog using the DoModal() function call. The m_TextString member of aDlg is automatically set to the string entered in the edit box, so you can use this data member to pass the string entered back to the CText constructor if the OK button is used to close the dialog. The color and pen width are obtained from the document using the GetElementColor() and GetPenWidth() members that you have used previously. The position of the text is the point value holding the cursor position that is passed to the handler.

You also need to calculate the opposite corner of the rectangle that bounds the text. Because the size of the rectangle for the block of text depends on the font used in a device context, you use the GetTextExtent() function in the CClientDC object, aDC, to initialize the CSize object, TextExtent, with the width and height of the text string in logical coordinates.

Calculating the rectangle for the text in this way is a bit of a cheat, which could cause a problem after you start saving documents in a file because it's conceivable that a document could be read back into an environment where the default font in a device context is larger than that in effect when the rectangle was calculated. This shouldn't arise very often, so no need to worry about it here, but as a hint — if you want to pursue it — you could use an object of the class CFont in the CText definition to define a specific font to be used. You could then use the characteristics of the font to calculate the enclosing rectangle for the text string.

You could also use CFont to change the font size so that the text is also zoomed when the scale factor is increased; however, you also need to devise a way to calculate the bounding rectangle based on the font size currently being used, which varies with the view scale.

The CText object is created on the heap because the list in the document only maintains pointers to the elements. You add the new element to the document by calling the AddElement() member of CSketcherDoc, with the pointer to the new text element as an argument. Finally, UpdateAllViews() is called with the first argument 0, which specifies that all views are to be updated.

For the program to compile successfully, you need to add a #include directive for TextDialog.h to the SketcherView.cpp file. You should now be able to produce annotated sketches using multiple scaled and scrolled views, such as the ones shown in Figure 17-23.

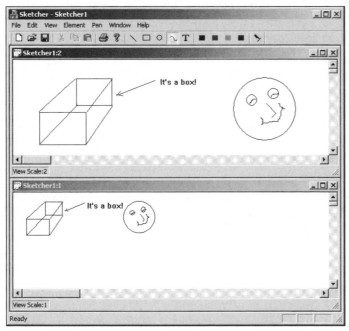

Figure 17-23

Dialogs and Controls in CLR Sketcher

There is a full range of dialogs and controls available for use in a CLR program but the procedure for adding them to an application is often different from what you have seen in the MFC version of Sketcher.

Extending CLR Sketcher will allow you to try out some of the ways in which you can use dialogs and controls in a Windows Forms application. You will not necessarily end up with a GUI for CLR Sketcher that you would want in practice because you will inevitably duplicate some functions in a way that is not needed in the application.

Adding a Dialog

It would be useful to add a dialog that you can use to enter pen widths to allow elements to be drawn with lines of different thicknesses. Your first thought as to how to do this is likely to be the Design window for the form and indeed, for some predefined dialogs this is the place to start. However, when you want to create your own dialog from the ground up, the starting point is Solution Explorer.

To add a dialog, you actually add a form to the project that you then modify to make it a dialog window. In Solution Explorer, right-click your project, click the Add menu item, then click New Item. In the dialog that displays, select the UI group in the left pane then select Windows Form in the right pane. Enter the name as PenDialog.cs and click the OK button. The .cs extension identifies that the dialog is for a C++/CLI program. A new Design window will display showing the dialog. In the Properties window for the dialog, change the FormBorderStyle property in the Appearance group to FixedDialog and set the ControlBox, MinimizeBox, and MaximizeBox properties in the Window Style group to false. Change the value of the Text property to Set Pen Width. You now have a modal dialog for setting the pen width so next you can add the controls you need to the dialog.

Customizing the Dialog

You'll use radio buttons to allow a pen width to be chosen and place them within a group box that serves to keep them in a group where only one radio button can be checked at one time. Drag a GroupBox control from the Containers group in the Toolbox window on to the dialog you have created. Change the value of the Text property for the group box to Select Pen Width and change the value of the (name) property to penWidthGroupBox. Adjust the size of the group box by dragging its border so it fits nicely within the dialog frame. Drag six RadioButton controls from the Toolbox window to the group box and arrange them in a rectangular configuration as you did in the MFC Sketcher program. You'll notice that alignment guides to help you position the controls display automatically for each RadioButton control after the first. Change the text properties for the radio button controls to Pen Width 1, Pen Width 2 through to Pen Width 6 and the corresponding (name) property values to penWidthButton1 through penWidthButton6. Change the value of the Checked property for penWidthButton1 to true.

Next you can add two buttons to the dialog and change their Text properties to OK and Cancel and the (name) properties to penWidthOK and penWidthCancel. Return to the dialog's property window and set the AcceptButton and CancelButton property values to penWidthOK and penWidthCancel by selecting from the list in the values column. Verify that the DialogResult property values for the buttons are OK and Cancel; this will cause the appropriate DialogResult value to be returned when the dialog is closed by clicking one or other button. You should now have a dialog in the Design window that looks similar to Figure 17-24.

The code for the dialog class is part of the project and is defined the PenDialog.h header file. However, there are no instances of the PenDialog class anywhere at the moment so to use the dialog you must create one. You will create a PenDialog object in the Form1 class so add an #include directive for PenDialog.h to Form1.h. Add a new private variable of type PenDialog^ to the Form1 class with the name penDialog and initialize it in the Form1 constructor to gcnew PenDialog().

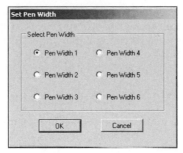

Figure 17-24

You need a way to get information about which radio button is checked from the `PenDialog` object. One way to do this is to add a public property to the class to make the information available. It can be a read-only property so you only need to implement `get()` for the property. The code that the Windows Form Designer generates is delimited by a `#pragma region` and a `#pragma endregion` directive and you should not modify this manually or add code in here. Add the following code to the `PenDialog` class definition immediately after the `#pragma endregion` directive:

```
public: property float PenWidth
{
  float get()
  {
    if(penWidthButton1->Checked)
      return 1.0f;
    if(penWidthButton2->Checked)
      return 2.0f;
    if(penWidthButton3->Checked)
      return 3.0f;
    if(penWidthButton4->Checked)
      return 4.0f;
    if(penWidthButton5->Checked)
      return 5.0f;
    return 6.0f;
  }
}
```

Now that the dialog is complete and you have a `Form1` member that references a dialog object, you need a mechanism to open the dialog. Another toolbar button on the `Form1` window is a good choice.

Displaying the Dialog

You need a bitmap to display on the new toolbar button. Switch to the Resource View and right-click the Bitmap folder and click Insert Bitmap. Set the `Height` and `Width` property values for the bitmap to 16, the `Filename` property value to `penwidth.bmp` and the `ID` to `IDB_PENWIDTH`. You can now create a bitmap of your choosing to represent a line width; I'll use a symbol looking like a pen drawing a line as in MFC Sketcher.

In the Design window for `Form1.h`, add a separator to the toolbar followed by a new toolbar button. Set the image for the new button to `penwidth.bmp`, then create a `Click` event handler for the toolbar button by double-clicking the `Click` event in its Properties window. Change the name of the handler function to penWidthButton_Click. You can add code to the new event handler to display the pen dialog:

```
private: System::Void penWidthButton _Click(
                                   System::Object^  sender, System::EventArgs^  e)
{
  if(penDialog->ShowDialog() == System::Windows::Forms::DialogResult::OK)
  {
    // Set the penwidth...
  }
}
```

Calling `ShowDialog()` for the `PenDialog` object displays the dialog. Because it is a modal dialog, it remains visible until a button is clicked to close it. The `ShowDialog()` function returns a value that is an enumerator from the `System::Windows::Forms::DialogResult` enumeration. This enumeration defines the following enumerator values:

```
None, OK, Cancel, Abort, Retry, Ignore, Yes, No
```

These provide for a variety of buttons being identified to close a dialog and you can set any of these values from the drop-down list of values for the `DialogResult` property of a button.

You must fully qualify the `DialogResult` type name here because the `Form1` class has an inherited member with the name `DialogResult`.

You need somewhere to record the current pen width in the `Form1` class, so add a private `penWidth` variable of type `float` to the class and initialize it to `1.0f` in the constructor. You can now replace the comment in the `Click` event handler above by:

```
penWidth = penDialog->PenWidth;
```

This will set the current pen width to the value returned by the `PenWidth` property for the dialog.

All that remains is to implement drawing elements with a given pen width.

Setting the Drawing Pen Width

This will involve modifying the constructor in each of the derived element classes. The modifications are essentially the same in each class, so I'll just show how the `Line` class constructor changes and you can do the rest. There's something else to consider, too. At present the `Bound` property that you defined in the `Element` base class returns a rectangle that is one pixel larger all round than the bounding rectangle for an element. Drawing with thicker lines will mess this up. The `Bound` property should take account of the pen width so add a private member of type `float` to the `Element` class with the name `penWidth` and update the definition of the `Bound` property to the following:

```
property System::Drawing::Rectangle Bound
{
  System::Drawing::Rectangle get()
  {
    int width = safe_cast<int>(penWidth);
    return System::Drawing::Rectangle::Inflate(boundRect,width,width);
```

```
        }
    }
```

The changes to the `Line` class constructor to allow for different pen widths are as follows:

```
        Line(Color color, Point start, Point end, float penWidth)
        {
          this->penWidth = penWidth;
          pen = gcnew Pen(color, penWidth);
          // Rest of the code as before...
        }
```

The only changes are to add an extra parameter to the `Line` constructor, to store the pen width in the inherited `penWidth` member, and to use the `Pen` constructor that accepts a second argument of type `float` that specifies the pen width. Make the same change to the constructors for the other element classes.

Because you have changed the parameter list for the element class constructors, you must change the `MouseMove` event handler that creates elements:

```
    private: System::Void Form1_MouseMove(System::Object^  sender,
    System::Windows::Forms::MouseEventArgs^  e) {
      if(drawing)
    {
      if(tempElement)
        Invalidate(tempElement->Bound);  // The old element region
      switch(elementType)
      {
        case ElementType::LINE:
          tempElement = gcnew Line(color, firstPoint, e->Location, penWidth);
          break;
        case ElementType::RECTANGLE:
          tempElement = gcnew Rectangle(color, firstPoint, e->Location, penWidth);
          break;
        case ElementType::CIRCLE:
          tempElement = gcnew Circle(color, firstPoint, e->Location, penWidth);
          break;
        case ElementType::CURVE:
          if(tempElement)
            safe_cast<Curve^>(tempElement)->Add(e->Location);
          else
            tempElement = gcnew Curve(color, firstPoint, e->Location, penWidth);
          break;
      }
      // Rest of the code as before...
    }
```

You should now have CLR Sketcher with pen widths fully working, as Figure 17-25 illustrates.

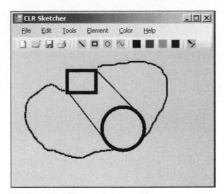

Figure 17-25

Using a Combo Box Control

You can add a combo box to the toolbar to provide an alternative means of entering a pen width. This is an option in the list that displays when you click on the down arrow for the toolbar item that adds new entries. You can customize this to do what you want.

Set the DropDownStyle property to DropDownList; the effect of this is to only allow values to be selected from the list. A value of DropDown allows any value to be typed in the combo box. Change the (name) to something more relevant such as penWidthComboBox. You want to add a specific set of items to be displayed in the combo box and the Items property holds these. Select the Items property, click on (Collection) in the value column and select the ellipsis at the right in the value column to open the String Collection Editor dialog. You can then enter strings, as shown in Figure 17-26.

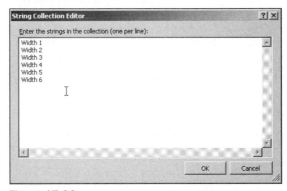

Figure 17-26

These are the entries that will be displayed in the drop-down for the combo box and they are indexed from 0 to 5.

Because the default size for the combo box is wider than you need, change the value of the Size property to 80,25. You can also change the FlatStyle property to System so it will display recessed. You can also set the ToolTipText property to Select pen width.

At present the combo box will not show anything when it is first displayed but you can fix that in the Form1 constructor. Add the following line of code to the constructor after the // TODO comment:

```
penWidthComboBox = SelectedIndex = 0;
```

The SelectedIndex property determines which of the entries in the Items collection is displayed in the combo box and because the entries in the combo box Items property collection are indexed from 0, this causes the first entry to be displayed initially. That will continue to be the entry displayed until you select a new entry from the combo box, so the combo box will always show the currently selected pen width.

You need to know when an entry from the combo box is selected so you can update the penWidth member of the Form1 class. An easy way to do this is to add a handler for the SelectedIndexChanged event for the ComboBox object so add this handler through the Properties window and implement it like this:

```
private: System::Void penWidthComboBox_SelectedIndexChanged(
                          System::Object^  sender, System::EventArgs^  e)
{
  penWidth = safe_cast<float>(penWidthComboBox->SelectedIndex + 1);
}
```

If you recompile CLR Sketcher and run it again, the combo box will allow you to select a new pen width but there's a problem. If you display the pen width dialog by clicking the toolbar button to change the pen width you'll see it shows a different pen width selected. Clearly they are operating independently of one another so you need to synchronize the two controls. When the pen width is changed by the combo box, the radio buttons in the pen dialog need to be updated and vice versa. You don't have a way to update the radio buttons, but adding a set() function for the PenWidth property in the PenDialog class will fix it:

```
public: property float PenWidth
{
  float get()
  {
    // Code as before...
  }

  void set(float penWidth)
  {
    if(penWidth = 1.0f)
      penWidthButton1->Checked = true;
    else if(penWidth == 2.0f)
      penWidthButton2->Checked = true;
    else if(penWidth == 3.0f)
      penWidthButton3->Checked = true;
    else if(penWidth == 4.0f)
      penWidthButton4->Checked = true;
    else if(penWidth == 5.0f)
      penWidthButton5->Checked = true;
    else if(penWidth == 6.0f)
      penWidthButton6->Checked = true;
  }
}
```

You only need one extra line in the `SelectedIndexChanged` event handler for the combo box:

```
private: System::Void penWidthComboBox_SelectedIndexChanged(
                                      System::Object^ sender, System::EventArgs^ e)
{
   penWidth = safe_cast<float>(penWidthComboBox->SelectedIndex + 1);
   penDialog->PenWidth = penWidth;
}
```

The handler function now sets the value of the `PenWidth` property for the `PenDialog` object to the current value of `penWidth`. This will cause the `Checked` property for the appropriate radio button to be set to `true`.

```
private: System::Void penWidthButton_Click(
                                      System::Object^ sender, System::EventArgs^ e)
{
   if(penDialog->ShowDialog() == System::Windows::Forms::DialogResult::OK)
   {
      penWidthComboBox->SelectedIndex = safe_cast<int>(penDialog->penWidth -1.0f);
      penWidthComboBox->Invalidate();
   }
}
```

You set the `SelectedIndex` property for `penWidthComboBox` according to the value returned by the `PenWidth` property for the `penDialog` object. You then call `Invalidate()` for the combo box to get it redrawn with the new value displayed. You no longer need to set the `penWidth` member of the `Form1` class in this handler because changing the `SelectedIndex` property for the combo box will result in a `SelectedIndexChanged` event and the handler for that will set the value of `penWidth`.

Creating Text Elements

Drawing text in CLR Sketcher will be similar to MFC Sketcher. Selecting a `Text` menu item or toolbar button will set `Text` as the element drawing mode and in this mode clicking anywhere of the form will display a modal dialog that allows some text to be entered; closing the dialog with the OK button will display the text at the cursor position. There are many ramifications to drawing text and in the interest of keeping the book to a modest weight, I'll limit this discussion to the basics.

Add a `TEXT` enumerator to the `ElementType` enum class, then add a `Text` menu item to the `Elements` menu and a corresponding toolbar button. Change the value of the `(name)` property for the menu item to `textToolStripMenuItem` and create a `Click` event handler for it. You can also add a value for the `ToolTipText` property for the menu item and the toolbar button. You can create a bitmap for the toolbar button to indicate text mode and select the `Click` event handler for the toolbar button to be the `Click` event handler for the menu item. You can implement the `Click` event handler like this:

```
private: System::Void textToolStripMenuItem_Click(
                                      System::Object^ sender, System::EventArgs^ e)
{
   elementType = ElementType::TEXT;
}
```

The function just sets `elementType` to the `ElementType` enumerator that represents text drawing mode.

Don't forget to add a Text menu item to the context menu, too.

Drawing Text

The `Graphics` class defines a `DrawString()` function for drawing text. There are several overloaded versions of this function, as described in the following table.

Function	Description

`DrawString(String^ str,`
`          Font^ font,`
`          Brush^ brush,`
`          PointF point)`
	Draws `str` at the position `point` using `font` with the color determined by `brush`. Type `Windows::Drawing::PointF` is a point represented by coordinates of type `float`. You can use a `Point` object as an argument in any of the functions for a `PointF` parameter.

`DrawString(String^ str,`
`          Font^ font,`
`          Brush^ brush,`
`          float X, float Y)`
	Draws `str` at the position `(X, Y)` using `font` with the color determined by `brush`. You can also use coordinate arguments of type `int` when you call this function.

`DrawString(String^ str,`
`          Font^ font,`
`          Brush^ brush,`
`          RectangleF rect)`
	Draws `str` within the rectangle `rect` using `font` with the color determined by `brush`. Type `Windows::Drawing::RectangleF` is a rectangle with its position width and height specified by values of type `float`. You can use a `Rectangle` object as an argument in any of the functions for a `RectangleF` parameter.

`DrawString(String^ str,`
`          Font^ font,`
`          Brush^ brush,`
`          PointF point,`
`          StringFormat^ format)`
	Draws `str` at the position `point` using `font` with the color determined by `brush` and the formatting of the string specified by `format`. A `StringFormat` object determines the alignment and other formatting properties for a string.

`DrawString(String^ str,`
`          Font^ font,`
`          Brush^ brush,`
`          float X, float Y,`
`          StringFormat^ format)`
	Draws `str` at the position `(X, Y)` using `font` with the color determined by `brush` and the formatting of the string specified by `format`.

`DrawString(String^ str,`
`          Font^ font,`
`          Brush^ brush,`
`          RectangleF rect,`
`          StringFormat^ format)`
	Draws `str` within the rectangle `rect` using `font` with the color determined by `brush` and the formatting of the string determined by `format`.

I'll briefly introduce fonts and brushes before returning to creating `Text` elements.

Creating Fonts

You specify the font to be used when you draw a string by a `System::Drawing::Font` object that defines the typeface, style, and size of the drawn characters. A `System::Drawing::FontFamily` defines a group of fonts with a given typeface such as `"Arial"` or `"Times New Roman"`. The `System::Drawing::FontStyle` enumeration defines possible font styles, which can be any of the following: `Regular`, `Bold`, `Italic`, `Underline`, `Strikeout`.

You can create create a `Font` object like this:

```
FontFamily^ family = gcnew FontFamily(L"Arial");
System::Drawing::Font^ font = gcnew System::Drawing::Font(family, 10,
                                     FontStyle::Bold,  GraphicsUnit::Point);
```

You create the `FontFamily` object by passing the name of the font to the constructor. The arguments to the `Font` constructor are the font family, the size of the font, the font style, and an enumerator from the `GraphicUnit` enumeration that defines the units for the font size. The possible values are: `World`, `Display`, `Pixel`, `Point`, `Inch`, `Document`, `Millimeter`.

Thus the code fragment defines a 10-point bold Arial font. Note that the `Font` type name is fully qualified in the fragment because a form object in a Windows Forms application inherits a property with the name Font from the `Form` base class. The `Font` property identifies the default font for the form and you pass this as the font argument to the `DrawString()` function.

Windows Forms applications support TrueType fonts primarily so it is best not to choose OpenType fonts. If you attempt to use a font that is not supported, or the font is not installed on your computer, the Microsoft Sans Serif font will be used.

Creating Brushes

A `System::Drawing::Brush` object determines the color used when drawing a string with a given font; it is also used to specify the color and texture used to fill a shape. You can't create a `Brush` object directly because `Brush` is an abstract class. You create brushes using the `SolidBrush`, the `TextureBrush`, and the `LinearGradientBrush` class types that are derived from `Brush`. A `SolidBrush` object is a brush of a single color, a `TextureBrush` object is a brush that uses an image to fill the interior of a shape and a `LinearGradientBrush` is a brush defining a color gradient blend usually between two colors but it is also possible to define blends between several colors. You will use a `SolidBrush` object to draw text, which you create like this:

```
SolidBrush^ brush = gcnew SolidBrush(Color::Red);
```

This creates a solid brush that will draw text in red.

Choosing a Font

You can store a reference to the current `Font` object to be used when creating `Text` elements by adding a variable of type `System::Drawing::Font^` and with the name `textFont` to the `Form1` class. Initialize textFont in the Form1 constructor to Font, which is a form property specifying the default font for the form. Be sure to do this in the body of the constructor following the // TODO: comment; if you attempt to initialize in the initialization list the program will fail because Font is not defined at this point.

You can add a toolbar button to allow the user to select a font for entering text, perhaps a button with a bitmap representation of F for font. Give the button a suitable value for the (name) property such as fontToolStripButton and add a Click event handler for it.

The Toolbox window has a standard dialog for choosing a font that will display all the fonts available on your system and allow selection of the font style and size. Select the Design window for Form1.h and drag a FontDialog control from the Toolbox window to the form. The Click event handler for the fontToolStripButton can display the font dialog:

```
private: System::Void fontToolStripButton_Click(
                               System::Object^  sender, System::EventArgs^  e)
{
    if(fontDialog1->ShowDialog() == System::Windows::Forms::DialogResult::OK)
       textFont = fontDialog1->Font;
}
```

You display the dialog by calling its ShowDialog() function, as you did for the pen dialog. If the function returns DialogResult::OK, then you know the dialog was closed using the OK button. In this case you retrieve the chosen font from the Font property for the dialog object and store it in the textFont variable in the Form1 class object. You can try this out if you want. The font dialog will look like Figure 17-27.

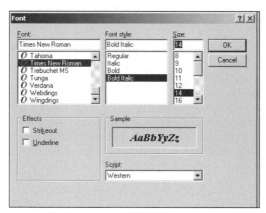

Figure 17-27

You need a class to represent a Text element, so let's define that next.

Defining the Text Element Class

The `TextElement` element type will have `Element` as a base class like the other element types so you can call the `Draw()` function polymorphically. Basic information about the location and color of the text element will be recorded in the members inherited from the base class, but you need to add extra members to store the text and information relating to the font. Here's the initial definition of the class:

```
public ref class TextElement : Element
{
  private:
    String^ text;
    SolidBrush^ brush;
    Font^ font;

  public:
    Text(Color color, Point p, String^ text, Font^ font)
    {
      this->color = color;
      brush = gcnew SolidBrush(color);
      position = p;
      penWidth = 1;
      this->text = text;
      this->font = font;
      int height = font->Height;
      int width = height*text->Length;
      boundRect = System::Drawing::Rectangle(position, Size(width, height));
    }

    virtual void Draw(Graphics^ g) override
    {
      brush->Color = highlighted ? highlightColor : color;
      g->TranslateTransform(safe_cast<float>(position.X),
                            safe_cast<float>(position.Y));
      g->DrawString(text, font, brush, position);
      g->ResetTransform();
    }
};
```

I chose the `TextElement` type name rather than just `Text` to avoid confusion with a member of the `Form` class with the name `Text`. A `TextElement` object has members to store the text string, and the font and the brush to be used to draw the text. Even though you don't use a `Pen` object in the `Text` class you must initialize the inherited `penWidth` member because it is used to create the enclosing rectangle for the element.

Determining the bounding rectangle for a text element introduces a slight complication in that it depends on the point size of the font and you have to figure out the width and height from the font size. The height is easy because the `font` object has a `Height` property that makes the height of the font available in pixels. This is the em height of the font (which is the height of the letter M), so you get a generous estimate of the width of the rectangle the string will occupy by multiplying the em height by the number of characters in the string.

Creating the Text Dialog

You'll want to enter text from the keyboard when you create a `TextElement` element, so you need a dialog to manage this. Go to the Solution Explorer window and add a new form to CLR Sketcher by right-clicking the project name, and clicking `Add > New Item...` from the menu. Enter the name as `TextDialog`. Change the `Text` property for the form to `Create Text Element` and change the properties to make it a dialog in the way you did for the `PenDialog`; this involves changing the `FormBorderStyle` property to `FixedDialog` and setting `MaximizeBox`, `MinimizeBox`, and `ControlBox` properties to `false`.

The next step is to add buttons to close the dialog. Add an `OK` button and a `Cancel` button to the text dialog with the `DialogResult` property values set appropriately. Change the `(name)` property values to `textOKButton` and `textCancelButton` respectively. Set the `AcceptButton` property value for `TextDialog` to `textOKButton` and the `CancelButton` property value to `textCancelButton`.

Using a Text Box

A `TextBox` control allows a single line or multiple lines of text to be entered, so it certainly covers what you want to do here. Add a `TextBox` to the text dialog by dragging it from the Toolbox window to the dialog in the Design window. By default a `TextBox` allows a single line of text to be entered and you can stick with that here. When you want to allow multiple lines of input, you click the down arrow to the right on the `TextBox` in the Design window and click the checkbox to enable `Multiline`. The `Text` property for the `TextBox` provides access to the input and makes it available as a `String` object.

Ideally you want the text dialog to open with the text box for entering the text having the focus. Then you can enter the text immediately after the dialog opens and press Enter to close it as if you selected the OK button. The control that has the focus initially is determined by the tab order of the controls on the dialog, which depends on the value for the `TabIndex` property for the controls. If you set the `TabIndex` property for the text box to 0 and the `OK` and `Cancel` buttons to 2 and 3, this will result in the text box having the focus when the dialog displays initially. The tab order also defines the sequence in which the focus changes when you press the Tab key. You can display the tab order for the controls in the Design window for the dialog by selecting `View > Tab Order` from the main menu; selecting the menu item again removes the display of the tab order.

The `TextBox1` control will store the string you enter but because this is a private member of the dialog object, it is not accessible directly. You must add a mechanism to retrieve the string from the dialog object. Another problem is that the `TextBox1` control will retain the text you enter and display it the next time the dialog is opened. You probably don't want this to occur, so you need a way to reset the `Text` property of `TextBox1`. You can add a public property to the `TextDialog` class that will deal with both difficulties. Add the following code to the `TextDialog` class definition following the `#pragma endregion` directive:

```
public: property String^ TextString
{
  String^ get() {return textBox1->Text; }
  void set(String^ text) { textBox1->Text = text; }
}
```

The `get()` function for the `TextString` property makes the string you enter available and the `set()` function enables you to reset it.

You need some extra data members in the Form1 class to help you create text elements. Add a member with the name text of type String^ to store the string for a TextElement element. Add an #include directive for TextDialog.h to Form1.h, then add a textDialog member of type TextDialog^. You can initialize it to gcnew TextDialog() in the initialization list for the Form1 class constructor.

Displaying the Dialog and Creating a Text Element

Creating an element that is text is different from the geometric elements and to understand the sequence of events in the code, let's describe the interactive process. Text element mode is in effect when you select the Text menu item or toolbar button. To create an element, you click at the position on the form where you want the top-left corner of the text string to be. This will display the text dialog and you type the text you want in the text box and press Enter to close the dialog. The MouseMove handler is not involved in the process at all. Clicking the mouse to define the position of the element embodies the whole process. This implies you must display the dialog and create the text element in the MouseDown event handler. Here's the code to do that:

```
private: System::Void Form1_MouseDown(System::Object^  sender,
System::Windows::Forms::MouseEventArgs^  e) {
  if(e->Button == System::Windows::Forms::MouseButtons::Left)
  {
    if(mode == Mode::Normal)
      drawing = true;
    firstPoint = e->Location;
    if(elementType == ElementType::TEXT && mode == Mode::Normal)
    {
      textDialog->TextString = L"";          // Reset the text box string
      if(textDialog->ShowDialog() == System::Windows::Forms::DialogResult::OK)
      {
        text = textDialog->TextString;
        tempElement = gcnew TextElement(color, firstPoint, text, textFont);
        sketch->Add(tempElement);
        Invalidate(tempElement->Bound);    // The text element region
        tempElement = nullptr;
        Update();
      }
      drawing = false;
    }
  }
}
```

You only create text elements when the elementType member of the form has the value ElementType::TEXT and mode is Mode::Normal; the second condition is essential to avoid displaying the dialog when you are in move mode. When the if condition is true, the first action is to reset the Text property for the TextBox1 control to an empty string by setting this as the value for the TextString property for the dialog. You then display the dialog by calling ShowDialog() in the if condition expression. If the ShowDialog() function returns DialogResult::OK, you retrieve the string from the dialog, create the TextElement object, and add it to the sketch. You then invalidate the region occupied by the new element and call Update() to display it. You also reset tempElement to nullptr when you are done with it. Finally you set drawing to false to prevent the MouseMove handler from attempting to create an element.

If you recompile Sketcher you should be able to create text elements using a font of your choice. Not only that, but you can move and delete them, too. Figure 17-28 shows Sketcher displaying text elements.

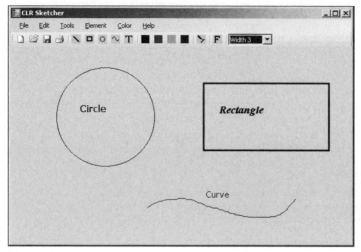

Figure 17-28

Summary

In this chapter, you've seen several different dialogs using a variety of controls. Although you haven't created dialogs involving several different controls at once, the mechanism for handling them is the same as you have seen because each control can operate independently of the others.

The most important points relating to MFC applications that you've seen in this chapter are:

❑ A dialog involves two components: a resource defining the dialog box and its controls, and a class that is used to display and manage the dialog.

❑ Information can be extracted from controls in a dialog using the DDX mechanism. The data can be validated using the DDV mechanism. To use DDX/DDV you need only to use the Add the Control Variable option for the Add Member Variable wizard to define variables in the dialog class associated with the controls.

❑ A modal dialog retains the focus in the application until the dialog box is closed. As long as a modal dialog is displayed, all other windows in an application are inactive.

❑ A modeless dialog allows the focus to switch from the dialog box to other windows in the application and back again. A modeless dialog can remain displayed as long as the application is executing, if required.

❑ Common Controls are a set of standard Windows controls that are supported by MFC and the resource editing capabilities of Developer Studio.

❑ Although controls are usually associated with a dialog, you can add controls to any window.

You also learned about the following points in the context of programming for the CLR:

❑ You add a form to a Windows Forms application using the Solutions Explorer pane; you right-click the project name and select Add > New Item... from the menu.

❑ You can convert a form into a modal dialog window by changing the value of the FormBorderStyle property to FixedDialog, and changing the values of the MaximizeBox, MinimizeBox, and ControlBox properties to false.

❑ You populate a dialog with controls by dragging them from the Toolbox window on to the dialog in the Design pane.

❑ You display a dialog by calling its ShowDialog() function.

❑ The value that you set for the DialogResult property for a button in a dialog determines the value returned by the ShowDialog() function when that button is used to close the dialog.

❑ The Toolbox has several complete standard dialogs available including a dialog for choosing a font.

❑ You can draw a string on a form by calling the DrawString() function for the Graphics object that encapsulates the drawing surface of a form. A Font object argument to the function determines the typeface, style, and size of the characters drawn and a Brush object argument determines the color.

Exercises

You can download the source code for the examples in the book and the solutions to the following exercises from www.wrox.com.

1. Implement the scale dialog in MFC Sketcher using radio buttons.

2. Implement the pen width dialog in MFC Sketcher using a list box.

3. Implement the pen width dialog in MFC Sketcher as a combo box with the drop list type selected on the Styles tab in the properties box. (The drop list type allows the user to select from a drop-down list but not to key alternative entries in the list.)

Storing and Printing Documents

With what you have accomplished so far in the Sketcher program, you can create a reasonably comprehensive document with views at various scales, but the information is transient because you have no means of saving a document. In this chapter, you'll remedy that by seeing how you can store a document on disk. You'll also investigate how you can output a document to a printer.

In this chapter, you'll learn about:

- ❏ Serialization and how it works
- ❏ How to make objects of a class serializable
- ❏ The role of a `CArchive` object in serialization
- ❏ How to implement serialization in your own classes
- ❏ How to implement serialization in the Sketcher application
- ❏ How printing works with MFC
- ❏ What view class functions you can use to support printing
- ❏ What a `CPrintInfo` object contains and how it's used in the printing process
- ❏ How to implement multipage printing in the Sketcher application

Understanding Serialization

A document in an MFC-based program is not a simple entity — it's a class object that can be very complicated. It typically contains a variety of objects, each of which may contain other objects, each of which may contain still more objects... and that structure may continue for a number of levels.

You want to be able to save a document in a file, but writing a class object to a file represents something of a problem because it isn't the same as a basic data item like an integer or a character string.

A basic data item consists of a known number of bytes, so to write it to a file only requires that the appropriate number of bytes be written. Conversely, if you know a value of type int was written to a file, to get it back you just read the appropriate number of bytes.

Writing objects is different. Even if you write away all the data members of an object, that's not enough to be able to get the original object back. Class objects contain function members as well as data members, and all the members, both data and functions, have access specifiers; therefore, to record objects in an external file, the information written to the file must contain complete specifications of all the class structures involved. The read process must also be clever enough to synthesize the original objects completely from the data in the file. MFC supports a mechanism called **serialization** to help you to implement input from and output to disk of your class objects with a minimum of time and trouble.

The basic idea behind serialization is that any class that's serializable must take care of storing and retrieving itself. This means that for your classes to be serializable — in the case of the Sketcher application, this will include the CElement class and the shape classes you have derived from it — they must be able to write themselves to a file. This implies that for a class to be serializable, all the class types that are used to declare data members of the class must be serializable too.

Serializing a Document

This all sounds rather tricky, but the basic capability for serializing your document was built into the application by the Application Wizard right at the outset. The handlers for the File > Save, File > Save As, and File > Open menu items all assume that you want serialization implemented for your document, and already contain the code to support it. Take a look at the parts of the definition and implementation of CSketcherDoc that relate to creating a document using serialization.

Serialization in the Document Class Definition

The code in the definition of CSketcherDoc that enables serialization of a document object is shown shaded in the following fragment:

```
class CSketcherDoc : public CDocument
{
protected: // create from serialization only
    CSketcherDoc();
    DECLARE_DYNCREATE(CSketcherDoc)

// Rest of the class...

// Overrides
    public:
    virtual BOOL OnNewDocument();
    virtual void Serialize(CArchive& ar);

// Rest of the class...

};
```

There are three things here that relate to serializing a document object:

1. The DECLARE_DYNCREATE() macro.

2. The Serialize() member function.

3. The default class constructor.

DECLARE_DYNCREATE() is a macro that enables objects of the CSketcherDoc class to be created dynamically by the application framework during the serialization input process. It's matched by a complementary macro, IMPLEMENT_DYNCREATE(), in the class implementation. These macros apply only to classes derived from CObject, but as you will see shortly, they aren't the only pair of macros that can be used in this context. For any class that you want to serialize, CObject must be a direct or indirect base because it adds the functionality that enables serialization to work. This is why the CElement class was derived from CObject. Almost all MFC classes are derived from CObject and, as such, are serializable.

> *The Hierarchy Chart in the Microsoft Foundation Class Reference for Visual C++ 2008 shows those classes, which aren't derived from* CObject. *Note that* CArchive *is in this list.*

The class definition also includes a declaration for a virtual function Serialize(). Every class that's serializable must include this function. It's called to perform both input and output serialization operations on the data members of the class. The object of type CArchive that's passed as an argument to this function determines whether the operation that is to occur is input or output. You'll explore this in more detail when considering the implementation of serialization for the document class.

Note that the class explicitly defines a default constructor. This is also essential for serialization to work because the default constructor is used by the framework to synthesize an object when reading from a file, and the synthesized object is then filled out with the data from the file to set the values of the data members of the object.

Serialization in the Document Class Implementation

There are two bits of the file containing the implementation of CSketcherDoc that relate to serialization. The first is the macro IMPLEMENT_DYNCREATE() that complements the DECLARE_DYNCREATE() macro:

```
// SketcherDoc.cpp : implementation of the CSketcherDoc class
//

#include "stdafx.h"
#include "Sketcher.h"
#include "PenDialog.h"

#include "SketcherDoc.h"

#ifdef _DEBUG
#define new DEBUG_NEW
#endif

// CSketcherDoc
```

```
IMPLEMENT_DYNCREATE(CSketcherDoc, CDocument)

// Message maps and the rest of the file...
```

All this macro does is define the base class for `CSketcherDoc` as `CDocument`. This is required for the proper dynamic creation of a `CSketcherDoc` object, including members inherited from the base class.

The Serialize() Function

The class implementation also includes the definition of the `Serialize()` function:

```
void CSketcherDoc::Serialize(CArchive& ar)
{
   if (ar.IsStoring())
   {
      // TODO: add storing code here
   }
   else
   {
      // TODO: add loading code here
   }
}
```

This function serializes the data members of the class. The argument passed to the function is a reference to an object of the `CArchive` class, `ar`. The `IsStoring()` member of this class object returns `TRUE` if the operation is to store data members in a file and `FALSE` if the operation is to read back data members from a previously stored document.

Because the Application Wizard has no knowledge of what data your document contains, the process of writing and reading this information is up to you, as indicated by the comments. To understand how this is done, look a little more closely at the `CArchive` class.

The CArchive Class

The `CArchive` class is the engine that drives the serialization mechanism. It provides an MFC-based equivalent of the stream operations in C++ that you used for reading from the keyboard and writing to the screen in the console program examples. An object of the MFC class `CArchive` provides a mechanism for streaming your objects out to a file, or recovering them again as an input stream, automatically reconstituting the objects of your class in the process.

A `CArchive` object has a `CFile` object associated with it which provides disk input/output capability for binary files, and provides the actual connection to the physical file. Within the serialization process, the `CFile` object takes care of all the specifics of the file input and output operations, and the `CArchive` object deals with the logic of structuring the object data to be written or reconstructing the objects from the information read. You need to worry about the details of the associated `CFile` object only if you are constructing your own `CArchive` object. With the document in Sketcher, the framework has already taken care of it and passes the `CArchive` object that it constructs, `ar`, to the `Serialize()` function in `CSketcherDoc`. You'll be able to use the same object in each of the `Serialize()` functions you add to the shape classes when you implement serialization for them.

The CArchive class overloads the extraction and insertion operators (>> and <<) for input and output operations respectively on objects of classes derived from CObject, plus a range of basic data types. These overloaded operators work with the object types and primitive types shown in the following table.

Type	Definition
bool	Boolean value, true or false
float	Standard single precision floating point
double	Standard double precision floating point
BYTE	8-bit unsigned integer
char	8-bit character
wchar_t	16-bit character
int and short	16-bit signed integer
LONG and long	32-bit signed integer
LONGLONG	64-bit signed integer
ULONGLONG	64-bit unsigned integer
WORD and unsigned int	16-bit unsigned integer
DWORD and unsigned int	32-bit unsigned integer
CObject*	Pointer to CObject
CString	A CString object defining a string
SIZE and CSize	An object defining a size as a **cx, cy** pair
POINT and CPoint	An object defining a point as an **x, y** pair
RECT and CRect	An object defining a rectangle by its upper-left and lower-right corners
CObject*	Pointer to CObject

For basic data types in your objects, you use the insertion and extraction operators to serialize the data. To read or write an object of a serializable class which you have derived from CObject, you can either call the Serialize() function for the object, or use the extraction or insertion operator. Whichever way you choose must be used consistently for both input and output, so you should not output an object using the insertion operator and then read it back using the Serialize() function, or vice versa.

Where you don't know the type of an object when you read it, as in the case of the pointers in the list of shapes in our document, for example, you must *only* use the `Serialize()` function. This brings the virtual function mechanism into play, so the appropriate `Serialize()` function for the type of object pointed to is determined at run time.

A `CArchive` object is constructed either for storing objects or for retrieving objects. The `CArchive` function `IsStoring()` returns `TRUE` if the object is for output, and `FALSE` if the object is for input. You saw this used in the `if` statement in the `Serialize()` member of the `CSketcherDoc` class.

There are many other member functions of the `CArchive` class which are concerned with the detailed mechanics of the serialization process, but you don't usually need to know about them to use serialization in your programs.

Functionality of CObject-Based Classes

There are three levels of functionality available in your classes when they're derived from the MFC class `CObject`. The level you get in your class is determined by which of three different macros you use in the definition of your class:

Macro	Functionality
`DECLARE_DYNAMIC()`	Support for runtime class information
`DECLARE_DYNCREATE()`	Support for runtime class information and dynamic object creation
`DECLARE_SERIAL()`	Support for runtime class information, dynamic object creation, and serialization of objects

Each of these macros requires that a complementary macro, named with the prefix `IMPLEMENT_` instead of `DECLARE_`, be placed in the file containing the class implementation. As the table indicates, the macros provide progressively more functionality, so I'll concentrate on the third macro, `DECLARE_SERIAL()`, because it provides everything that the preceding macros do and more. This is the macro you should use to enable serialization in your own classes. It requires that the macro `IMPLEMENT_SERIAL()` be added to the file containing the class implementation.

You may be wondering why the document class uses `DECLARE_DYNCREATE()` and not `DECLARE_SERIAL()`. The `DECLARE_DYNCREATE()` macro provides the capability for dynamic creation of the objects of the class in which it appears. The `DECLARE_SERIAL()` macro provides the capability for serialization of the class, plus the dynamic creation of objects of the class, so it incorporates the effects of `DECLARE_DYNCREATE()`. Your document class doesn't need serialization because the framework only has to synthesize the document object and then restore the values of its data members; however, the data members of a document *do* need to be serializable because this is the process used to store and retrieve them.

The Macros Adding Serialization to a Class

With the `DECLARE_SERIAL()` macro in the definition of your `CObject`-based class, you get access to the serialization support provided by `CObject`. This includes special `new` and `delete` operators that incorporate memory leak detection in debug mode. You don't need to do anything to use this because it works automatically.

The macro requires the class name to be specified as an argument, so for serialization of the CElement class, you would add the following line to the class definition:

```
DECLARE_SERIAL(CElement)
```

There's no semicolon required here because this is a macro, not a C++ statement.

It doesn't matter where you put the macro within the class definition, but if you always put it as the first line, you'll always be able to verify that it's there, even when the class definition involves a lot of lines of code.

The IMPLEMENT_SERIAL() macro, which you place in the implementation file for the class, requires three arguments to be specified. The first argument is the name of the class, the second is the name of the direct base class, and the third argument is an unsigned 32-bit integer identifying a **schema number**, or version number, for your program. This schema number allows the serialization process to guard against problems that can arise if you write objects with one version of a program and read them with another, in which the classes may be different.

For example, you could add the following line to the implementation of the CElement class:

```
IMPLEMENT_SERIAL(CElement, CObject, 1)
```

If you subsequently modified the class definition, you would change the schema number to something different, such as 2. If the program attempts to read data that was written with a different schema number from that in the currently active program, an exception is thrown. The best place for this macro is as the first line following the #include directives and any initial comments in the .cpp file.

Where CObject is an indirect base of a class, as in the case of the CLine class, for example, each class in the hierarchy must have the serialization macros added for serialization to work in the top level class. For serialization in CLine to work, the macros must also be added to CElement.

How Serialization Works

The overall process of serializing a document is illustrated in a simplified form in Figure 18-1.

The Serialize() function in the document object calls the Serialize() function (or uses an overloaded insertion operator) for each of its data members. Where a member is a class object, the Serialize() function for that object serializes each of its data members in turn until ultimately basic data types are written to the file. Because most classes in MFC ultimately derive from CObject, they contain serialization support, so you can almost always serialize objects of MFC classes.

The data that you'll deal with in the Serialize() member functions of your classes and the application document object are, in each case, just the data members. The structure of the classes that are involved and any other data necessary to reconstitute your original objects is automatically taken care of by the CArchive object.

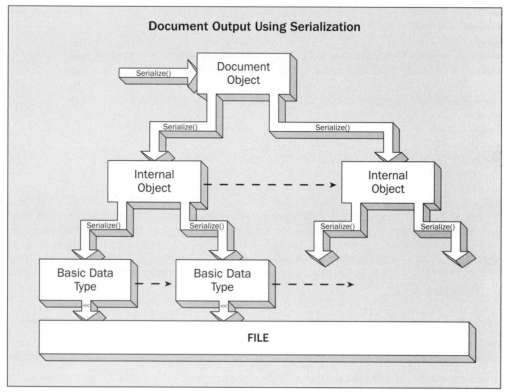

Figure 18-1

Where you derive multiple levels of classes from CObject, the Serialize() function in a class must call the Serialize() member of its direct base class to ensure that the direct base class data members are serialized. Note that serialization doesn't support multiple inheritance, so there can only be one base class for each class defined in a hierarchy.

How to Implement Serialization for a Class

From the previous discussion, I can summarize the steps that you need to take to add serialization to a class:

1. Make sure that the class is derived directly or indirectly from CObject.

2. Add the DECLARE_SERIAL() macro to the class definition (and to the direct base class if the direct base is not CObject).

3. Declare the Serialize() function as a member function of your class.

4. Add the IMPLEMENT_SERIAL() macro to the file containing the class implementation.

5. Implement the Serialize() function for your class.

Now take a look at how you can implement serialization for documents in the Sketcher program.

Applying Serialization

To implement serialization in the Sketcher application, you must implement the Serialize() function in CSketcherDoc so that it deals with all of the data members of that class. You need to add serialization to each of the classes which specify objects that may be included in a document. Before you start adding serialization to your application classes, you should make some small changes to the program to record when a user changes a sketch document. This isn't absolutely necessary, but it is highly desirable because it enables the program to guard against the document being closed without saving changes.

Recording Document Changes

There's already a mechanism for noting when a document changes; it uses an inherited member of CSketcherDoc, SetModifiedFlag(). By calling this function consistently whenever the document changes, you record the fact that the document has been altered in a data member of the document class object. This causes a prompt to be automatically displayed when you try to exit the application without saving the modified document. The argument to the SetModifiedFlag() function is a value of type BOOL, and the default value is TRUE. If you have occasion to specify that the document was unchanged, you can call this function with the argument FALSE, although circumstances where this is necessary are rare.

There are only three occasions when you alter a document object:

❑ When you call the AddElement() member of CSketcherDoc to add a new element.

❑ When you call the DeleteElement() member of CSketcherDoc to delete an element.

❑ When you move an element.

You can handle these three situations easily. All you need to do is add a call to SetModifiedFlag() to each of the functions involved in these operations. The definition of AddElement() appears in the CSketcherDoc class definition. You can extend this to:

```
void AddElement(CElement* pElement)     // Add an element to the list
{
  m_ElementList.AddTail(pElement);
  SetModifiedFlag();                    // Set the modified flag
}
```

You can get to the definition of DeleteElement() in CSketcherDoc by clicking the function name in the Class View pane. You should add one line to it, as follows:

```
void CSketcherDoc::DeleteElement(CElement* pElement)
{
  if(pElement)
  {
    // If the element pointer is valid,
    // find the pointer in the list and delete it
    SetModifiedFlag();                     // Set the modified flag
    POSITION aPosition = m_ElementList.Find(pElement);
    m_ElementList.RemoveAt(aPosition);
    delete pElement;                       // Delete the element from the heap
  }
}
```

Note that you must only set the flag if pElement is not null, so you can't just stick the function call anywhere.

In a view object, moving an element occurs in the MoveElement() member called by the handler for the WM_MOUSEMOVE message, but you only change the document when the left mouse button is pressed. If there's a right-button click, the element is put back to its original position, so you only need to add the call to the SetModifiedFlag() function for the document to the OnLButtonDown() function, as follows:

```
void CSketcherView::OnLButtonDown(UINT nFlags, CPoint point)
{
  CClientDC aDC(this);                   // Create a device context
  OnPrepareDC(&aDC);                     // Get origin adjusted
  aDC.DPtoLP(&point);                    // convert point to Logical

  if(m_MoveMode)
  {
    // In moving mode, so drop the element
    m_MoveMode = FALSE;                  // Kill move mode
    m_pSelected = 0;                     // De-select element
    GetDocument()->UpdateAllViews(0);   // Redraw all the views
    GetDocument()->SetModifiedFlag();   // Set the modified flag
  }
  // Rest of the function as before...
}
```

You call the inherited GetDocument() member of the view class to get access to a pointer to the document object and then use this pointer to call the SetModifiedFlag() function. You now have all the places where you change the document covered.

If you build and run Sketcher, and modify a document or add elements to it, you'll now get a prompt to save the document when you exit the program. Of course, the File > Save menu option doesn't do anything yet except clear the modified flag and save an empty file to disk. You must implement serialization to get the document written away to disk properly, and that's the next step.

Serializing the Document

The first step is the implementation of the Serialize() function for the CSketcherDoc class. Within this function, you must add code to serialize the data members of CSketcherDoc. The data members that you have declared in the class are as follows:

```
class CSketcherDoc : public CDocument
{
protected: // create from serialization only
  CSketcherDoc();
  DECLARE_DYNCREATE(CSketcherDoc)

// Attributes
public:
```

```
protected:
    COLORREF m_Color;                            // Current drawing color
    unsigned int m_Element;                      // Current element type
    CTypedPtrList<CObList, CElement*> m_ElementList; // Element list
    int m_PenWidth;                              // Current pen width
    CSize m_DocSize;                             // Document size

    // Rest of the class...
};
```

Note that you don't need to add any of the preceding code at this point as it's there already. All that's necessary is to insert the statements to store and retrieve these five data members in the `Serialize()` member of the class. You can do this with the following code:

```
void CSketcherDoc::Serialize(CArchive& ar)
{
    m_ElementList.Serialize(ar);          // Serialize the element list

    if (ar.IsStoring())
    {
        ar << m_Color                     // Store the current color
            << m_Element                  // the current element type,
            << m_PenWidth                 // and the current pen width
            << m_DocSize;                 // and the current document size
    }
    else
    {
        ar >> m_Color                     // Retrieve the current color
            >> m_Element                  // the current element type,
            >> m_PenWidth                 // and the current pen width
            >> m_DocSize;                 // and the current document size
    }
}
```

For four of the data members, you just use the extraction and insertion operators that are overloaded in the `CArchive` class. This works for the data member `m_Color`, even though its type is `COLORREF`, because type `COLORREF` is the same as type `long`. You can't use the extraction and insertion operators for `m_ElementList`, because its type isn't supported by the operators, but as long as the `CTypedPtrList` class is defined from the collection class template using `CObList`, as you have done in the declaration of `m_ElementList`, the class automatically supports serialization. You can, therefore, just call the `Serialize()` function for the object.

You don't need to place calls to the `Serialize()` member of the object `m_ElementList` in the `if-else` statement because the kind of operation performed is determined automatically by the `CArchive` argument, `ar`. The single statement calling the `Serialize()` member of `m_ElementList` takes care of both input and output.

That's all you need for serializing the document class data members, but serializing the element list, `m_ElementList`, causes the `Serialize()` functions for the element classes to be called to store and retrieve the elements themselves, so you also need to implement serialization for those classes.

Serializing the Element Classes

All the shape classes are serializable because you derived them from their base class CElement, which in turn is derived from CObject. The reason that you specified CObject as the base for CElement was solely to get support for serialization. You can now add support for serialization to each of the shape classes by adding the appropriate macros to the class definitions and implementations, and adding the code to the Serialize() function member of each class to serialize its data members. You can start with the base class, CElement, where you need to modify the class definition as follows:

```
class CElement: public CObject
{
DECLARE_SERIAL(CElement)

protected:
  COLORREF m_Color;                     // Color of an element
  CRect m_EnclosingRect;                // Rectangle enclosing an element
  int m_Pen;                            // Pen width

public:
  virtual ~CElement(){}                 // Virtual destructor

  // Virtual draw operation
  virtual void Draw(CDC* pDC, CElement* pElement=0){}
  virtual void Move(CSize& aSize){}     // Move an element
  CRect GetBoundRect();                 // Get the bounding rectangle for an element

  virtual void Serialize(CArchive& ar);// Serialize function for the class

protected:
  CElement(void);                       // Here to prevent it being called
};
```

You add the DECLARE_SERIAL() macro and a declaration for the virtual function Serialize().

You already have the default constructor that was created by the Application Wizard. You changed it to protected in the class, although it doesn't matter what its access specification is as long as it appears explicitly in the class definition. It can be public, protected, or private, and serialization still works. If you forget to include a default constructor in a class, though, you'll get an error message when the IMPLEMENT_SERIAL() macro is compiled.

You should add the DECLARE_SERIAL() macro to each of the derived classes CLine, CRectangle, CCircle, CCurve, and CText, with the relevant class name as the argument. You should also add a declaration for the Serialize() function as a public member of each class.

In the file Elements.cpp, you must add the following macro at the beginning:

```
IMPLEMENT_SERIAL(CElement, CObject, VERSION_NUMBER)
```

You can define the constant VERSION_NUMBER in the OurConstants.h file by adding the lines:

```
// Program version number for use in serialization
const UINT VERSION_NUMBER = 1;
```

You can then use the same constant when you add the macro for each of the other shape classes. For instance, for the CLine class you should add the line:

```
IMPLEMENT_SERIAL(CLine, CElement, VERSION_NUMBER)
```

and similarly for the other shape classes. When you modify any of the classes relating to the document, all you need to do is change the definition of VERSION_NUMBER in the OurConstants.h file, and the new version number applies in all your Serialize() functions. You can put all the IMPLEMENT_SERIAL() statements at the beginning of the file if you like. The complete set is:

```
IMPLEMENT_SERIAL(CElement, CObject, VERSION_NUMBER)
IMPLEMENT_SERIAL(CLine, CElement, VERSION_NUMBER)
IMPLEMENT_SERIAL(CRectangle, CElement, VERSION_NUMBER)
IMPLEMENT_SERIAL(CCircle, CElement, VERSION_NUMBER)
IMPLEMENT_SERIAL(CCurve, CElement, VERSION_NUMBER)
IMPLEMENT_SERIAL(CText, CElement, VERSION_NUMBER)
```

The Serialize() Functions for the Shape Classes

You can now implement the Serialize() member function for each of the shape classes. Start with the CElement class:

```
void CElement::Serialize(CArchive& ar)
{
  CObject::Serialize(ar);                 // Call the base class function

  if (ar.IsStoring())
   {
     ar << m_Color                        // Store the color,
         << m_EnclosingRect               // and the enclosing rectangle,
         << m_Pen;                        // and the pen width
   }
   else
   {
     ar >> m_Color                        // Retrieve the color,
         >> m_EnclosingRect               // and the enclosing rectangle,
         >> m_Pen;                        // and the pen width
   }
}
```

This function is of the same form as the one supplied for you in the CSketcherDoc class. All of the data members defined in CElement are supported by the overloaded extraction and insertion operators, and so everything is done using those operators. Note that you must call the Serialize() member for the CObject class to ensure that the inherited data members are serialized.

For the CLine class, you can code the function as:

```
void CLine::Serialize(CArchive& ar)
{
  CElement::Serialize(ar);                 // Call the base class function

  if (ar.IsStoring())
   {
```

```
      ar << m_StartPoint                  // Store the line start point,
         << m_EndPoint;                   // and the end point
  }
  else
  {
    ar >> m_StartPoint                    // Retrieve the line start point,
       >> m_EndPoint;                     // and the end point
  }
}
```

Again, the data members are all supported by the extraction and insertion operators of the CArchive object ar. You call the Serialize() member of the base class CElement to serialize its data members, and this calls the Serialize() member of CObject. You can see how the serialization process cascades through the class hierarchy.

The Serialize() function member of the CRectangle class is simple:

```
void CRectangle::Serialize(CArchive& ar)
{
  CElement::Serialize(ar);               // Call the base class function
}
```

This calls the direct base class function because the class has no additional data members.

The CCircle class doesn't have additional data members beyond those inherited from CElement either, so its Serialize() function also just calls the base class function:

```
void CCircle::Serialize(CArchive& ar)
{
  CElement::Serialize(ar);               // Call the base class function
}
```

For the CCurve class, you have surprisingly little work to do. You can code the Serialize() function as follows:

```
void CCurve::Serialize(CArchive& ar)
{
  CElement::Serialize(ar);               // Call the base class function
  m_PointList.Serialize(ar);             // Serialize the list of points
}
```

After calling the base class Serialize() function, you just call the Serialize() function for the CList object, m_PointList. Objects of any of the CList, CArray, and CMap classes can be serialized in this way because, once again, these classes are all derived from CObject.

The last class for which you need to add an implementation of Serialize() to Elements.cpp is CText:

```
void CText::Serialize(CArchive& ar)
{
```

```
    CElement::Serialize(ar);              // Call the base class function

    if (ar.IsStoring())
    {
      ar << m_StartPoint                   // Store the start point
         << m_String;                      // and the text string
    }
    else
    {
      ar >> m_StartPoint                   // Retrieve the start point
         >> m_String;                      // and the text string
    }
  }
```

After calling the base class function, you serialize the two data members using the insertion and extraction operators for ar. The CString class, although not derived from CObject, is still fully supported by CArchive with these overloaded operators.

Exercising Serialization

That's all you have to do to implement the storing and retrieving of documents in the Sketcher program! The save and restore menu options in the file menu are now fully operational without adding any more code. If you build and run Sketcher after incorporating the changes I've discussed in this chapter, you'll be able to save and restore files and be automatically prompted to save a modified document when you try to close it or exit from the program, as shown in Figure 18-2.

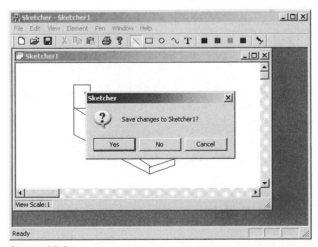

Figure 18-2

The prompting works because the SetModifiedFlag() calls that you added everywhere you update the document. If you click the Yes button in the screen shown in Figure 18-2, you'll see the File > Save As dialog box shown in Figure 18-3.

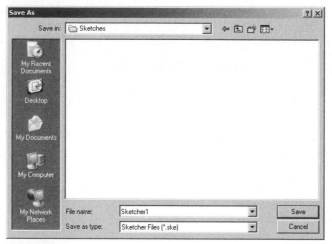

Figure 18-3

This is the standard dialog box for this menu item under Windows. It's all fully working, supported by code supplied by the framework. The file name for the document has been generated from that assigned when the document was first opened, and the file extension is automatically defined as .ske. The application now has full support for file operations on documents. Easy, wasn't it?

Moving Text

Now is a good time for me to digress briefly to go back and fix a problem that arose in the last chapter. Remember that whenever you try to move a text element, it leaves a trail behind it until the text is positioned on the document again. This is caused by the reliance on ROP drawing in the MoveElement() member of the view:

```
void CSketcherView::MoveElement(CClientDC& aDC, CPoint& point)
{
  CSize Distance = point - m_CursorPos;    // Get move distance
  m_CursorPos = point;                     // Set current point as 1st for next time

  // If there is an element, selected, move it
  if(m_pSelected)
  {
    aDC.SetROP2(R2_NOTXORPEN);
    m_pSelected->Draw(&aDC,m_pSelected); // Draw the element to erase it
    m_pSelected->Move(Distance);         // Now move the element
    m_pSelected->Draw(&aDC,m_pSelected); // Draw the moved element
  }
}
```

As previously mentioned, setting the drawing mode of the device context to R2_NOTXORPEN won't remove the trail left by moving the text. You could get around this by using a method of invalidating the rectangles that are affected by the moving elements so that they redraw themselves. This can cause some annoying flicker when an element is moving fast, however. A better solution is to use the invalidation method only for the text elements, and the original ROP method for all the other elements, but how do you know which class the selected element belongs to? This is surprisingly simple: you can use an `if` statement, as follows:

```
if (m_pSelected->IsKindOf(RUNTIME_CLASS(CText)))
{
  // Code here will only be executed if the selected element is of class CText
}
```

This uses the RUNTIME_CLASS macro to get a pointer to an object of type CRuntimeClass, then passes this pointer to the IsKindOf() member function of m_pSelected. This returns a non-zero result if m_pSelected is of class CText, and returns zero otherwise. The only proviso is that the class you're checking for must be declared using DECLARE_DYNCREATE or DECLARE_SERIAL macros, which is why I left this fix until now.

There is another way of determining the class type using a facility that is built in to ISO/ANSI C++. The typeid() operator returns a reference to an object of type type_info that encapsulates a pointer to the name of the runtime type of the object or expression that you place between the parentheses. Because you can compare type_info objects using the == operator (or the != operator), you could test whether m_pSelected is of type CText like this:

```
if (typeid(*m_pSelected) == typeid(CText))
{
  // Code here will only be executed if the selected element is of class CText
}
```

If you want to use a typeid() operator, you must add an #include directive for the <typeinfo> ISO/ANSI C++ header. Of course, there is no requirement for the types to be declared using the MFC macros noted for the previous method, although you must ensure that the /GR compiler option that enables runtime type information is specified.

The final code for MoveElement() using the MFC RUNTIME_CLASS macro is as follows:

```
void CSketcherView::MoveElement(CClientDC& aDC, CPoint& point)
{
  CSize Distance = point - m_CursorPos;   // Get move distance
  m_CursorPos = point;             // Set current point as 1st for next time

  // If there is an element, selected, move it
  if(m_pSelected)
  {
    // If the element is text use this method...
    if(m_pSelected->IsKindOf(RUNTIME_CLASS(CText)))
    {
      CRect OldRect=m_pSelected->GetBoundRect(); // Get old bound rect
      m_pSelected->Move(Distance);               // Move the element
      CRect NewRect=m_pSelected->GetBoundRect(); // Get new bound rect
      OldRect.UnionRect(&OldRect,&NewRect);      // Combine the bound rects
      aDC.LPtoDP(OldRect);                       // Convert to client coords
      OldRect.NormalizeRect();                   // Normalize combined area
      InvalidateRect(&OldRect);                  // Invalidate combined area
      UpdateWindow();                            // Redraw immediately
```

```
        m_pSelected->Draw(&aDC,m_pSelected);   // Draw highlighted

      return;
    }

    // ...otherwise, use this method
    aDC.SetROP2(R2_NOTXORPEN);
    m_pSelected->Draw(&aDC,m_pSelected);       // Draw the element to erase it
    m_pSelected->Move(Distance);               // Now move the element
    m_pSelected->Draw(&aDC,m_pSelected);       // Draw the moved element
  }
}
```

You can see that the code for invalidating the rectangles that you must use for moving the text is much less elegant than the ROP code that you use for all the other elements. It works, though, as you'll see for yourself if you make this modification and then build and run the application. If you would like to try the `typeid()` mechanism for testing the type, just change the condition in the `if` statement and add the `#include` directive for `<typeinfo>` to `SketcherView.cpp`.

Printing a Document

Now take a look at printing the document. You already have a basic printing capability implemented in the Sketcher program, courtesy of the Application Wizard and the framework. The `File > Print`, `File > Print Setup,` and `File > Print Preview` menu items all work. Selecting the `File > Print Preview` menu item displays a window showing the current Sketcher document on a page, as shown in Figure 18-4.

Figure 18-4

Whatever is in the current document is placed on a single sheet of paper at the current view scale. If the document's extent is beyond the boundary of the paper, the section of the document off the paper won't be printed. If you select the Print button, this page is sent to your printer.

As a basic capability which you get for free, it's quite impressive, but it's not adequate for most purposes. A typical document in our program may well not fit on a page, so you would either want to scale the document to fit, or perhaps more conveniently, print the whole document over as many pages as necessary. You can add your own print processing code to extend the capability of the facilities provided by the framework, but to implement this you first need to understand how printing has been implemented in MFC.

The Printing Process

Printing a document is controlled by the current view. The process is inevitably a bit messy because printing is inherently a messy business, and it potentially involves you in implementing your own versions of quite a number of inherited functions in your view class.

Figure 18-5 shows the logic of the process and the functions involved.

Figure 18-5 shows how the sequence of events is controlled by the framework and how printing a document involves calling five inherited members of your view class, which you may need to override. The CDC member functions shown on the left side of the diagram communicate with the printer device driver and are called automatically by the framework.

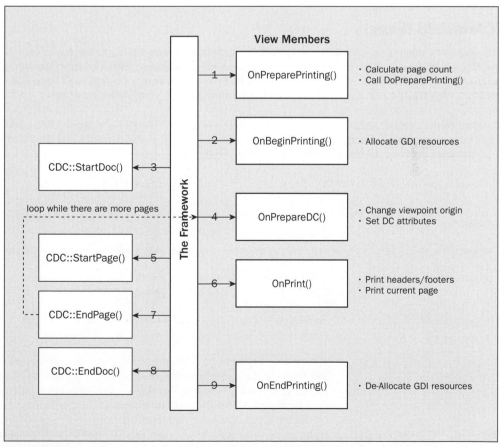

Figure 18-5

The typical role of each of the functions in the current view during a print operation is specified in the notes alongside it. The sequence in which they are called is indicated by the numbers on the arrows. In practice, you don't necessarily need to implement all of these functions, only those that you want to for your particular printing requirements. Typically, you'll want at least to implement your own versions of OnPreparePrinting(), OnPrepareDC(), and OnPrint(). You'll see an example of how these functions can be implemented in the context of the Sketcher program a little later in this chapter.

The output of data to a printer is done in the same way as outputting data to the display — through a device context. The GDI calls that you use to output text or graphics are device-independent, so they work just as well for a printer as they do for a display. The only difference is the device that the CDC object applies to.

The CDC functions in Figure 18-5 communicate with the device driver for the printer. If the document to be printed requires more than one printed page, the process loops back to call the OnPrepareDC() function for each successive new page, as determined by the EndPage() function.

All the functions in your view class that are involved in the printing process are passed a pointer to an object of type CPrintInfo as an argument. This object provides a link between all the functions that manage the printing process, so take a look at the CPrintInfo class in more detail.

The CPrintInfo Class

A CPrintInfo object has a fundamental role in the printing process because it stores information about the print job being executed and details of its status at any time. It also provides functions for accessing and manipulating this data. This object is the means by which information is passed from one view function to another during printing, and between the framework and your view functions.

An object of the CPrintInfo class is created whenever you select the File > Print or File > Print Preview menu options. After being used by each of the functions in the current view that are involved in the printing process, it's automatically deleted when the print operation ends.

All the data members of CPrintInfo are public. They are shown in the following table.

Member	Usage
m_pPD	A pointer to the CPrintDialog object that displays the Print dialog box.
m_bDirect	This is set to TRUE by the framework if the print operation is to bypass the Print dialog box; otherwise, FALSE.
m_bPreview	A member of type BOOL that has the value TRUE if File > Print Preview was selected; otherwise, FALSE.
m_bContinuePrinting	A member of type BOOL. If this is set to TRUE, the framework continues the printing loop shown in the diagram. If it's set to FALSE, the printing loop ends. You only need to set this variable if you don't pass a page count for the print operation to the CPrintInfo object (using the SetMaxPage() member function). In this case, you'll be responsible for signaling when you're finished by setting this variable to FALSE.

Member	Usage
m_nCurPage	A value of type UINT that stores the page number of the current page. Pages are usually numbered starting from 1.
m_nNumPreviewPages	A value of type UINT that specifies the number of pages displayed in the Print Preview window. This can be 1 or 2.
m_lpUserData	This is of type LPVOID and stores a pointer to an object that you create. This allows you to create an object to store additional information about the printing operation and associate it with the CPrintInfo object.
m_rectDraw	A CRect object that defines the usable area of the page in logical coordinates.
m_strPageDesc	A CString object containing a format string used by the framework to display page numbers during print preview.

A CPrintInfo object has the public member functions shown in the following table.

Function	Description
SetMinPage(UINT nMinPage)	The argument specifies the number of the first page of the document. There is no return value.
SetMaxPage(UINT nMaxPage)	The argument specifies the number of the last page of the document. There is no return value.
GetMinPage() const	Returns the number of the first page of the document as type UINT.
GetMaxPage() const	Returns the number of the last page of the document as type UINT.
GetFromPage() const	Returns the number of the first page of the document to be printed as type UINT. This value is set through the print dialog.
GetToPage() const	Returns the number of the last page of the document to be printed as type UINT. This value is set through the print dialog.

When you're printing a document consisting of several pages, you need to figure out how many printed pages the document occupies, and store this information in the CPrintInfo object to make it available to the framework. You can do this in your version of the OnPreparePrinting() member of the current view.

To set the number of the first page in the document, you need to call the function SetMinPage() in the CPrintInfo object, which accepts the page number as an argument of type UINT. There's no return value. To set the number of the last page in the document, you call the function SetMaxPage(), which also accepts the page number as an argument of type UINT and doesn't return a value. If you later want to retrieve these values, you can call the GetMinPage() and GetMaxPage() functions for the CPrintInfo object.

The page numbers that you supply are stored in the CPrintDialog object pointed to by the m_pPD member of CPrintInfo, and displayed in the dialog box that pops up when you select File > Print... from the menu. The user is then able to specify the numbers of the first and last pages that are printed, which you can retrieve by calling the GetFromPage() and GetToPage() members of the CPrintInfo object. In each case, the values returned are of type UINT. The dialog automatically verifies that the numbers of the first and last pages to be printed are within the range you supplied by specifying the minimum and maximum pages of the document.

You now know what functions you can implement in the view class to manage printing for yourself, with the framework doing most of the work. You also know what information is available through the CPrintInfo object passed to the functions concerned with printing. You'll get a much clearer understanding of the detailed mechanics of printing if you implement a basic multipage print capability for Sketcher documents.

Implementing Multipage Printing

You use the MM_LOENGLISH mapping mode in the Sketcher program to set things up and then switch to MM_ANISOTROPIC. This means that the shapes and the view extent are measured in terms of hundredths of an inch. Of course, with the unit of size a fixed physical measure, ideally you want to print objects at their actual size.

With the document size specified as 3000 by 3000 units, you can create documents up to 30 inches square, which spreads over quite a few sheets of paper if you fill the whole area. It requires a little more effort to work out the number of pages necessary to print a sketch than with a typical text document because in most instances, you'll need a two-dimensional array of pages to print a complete sketch document.

To avoid overcomplicating the problem, assume that you're printing a normal sheet of paper (either A4 size or 8 ½ by 11 inches) and in portrait orientation (which means the long edge is vertical). With either paper size, you'll print the document in a central portion of the paper measuring 6 inches by 9 inches. With these assumptions, you don't need to worry about the actual paper size; you just need to chop the document into 600 by 900 unit chunks. For a document larger than one page, you'll divide up the document as illustrated in the example in Figure 18-6.

As you can see, you'll be numbering the pages row-wise, so in this case pages 1 to 4 are in the first row and pages 5 to 8 are in the second.

Getting the Overall Document Size

To figure out how many pages a particular document occupies, you need to know how big the sketch is, and for this you want the rectangle that encloses everything in the document. You can do this easily by adding a function GetDocExtent() to the document class, CSketcherDoc. Add the following declaration to the public interface for CSketcherDoc:

```
CRect GetDocExtent();        // Get the bounding rectangle for the whole document
```

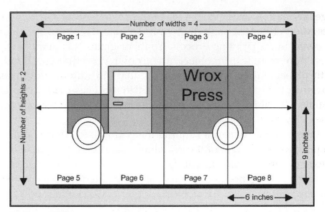

Figure 18-6

The implementation is no great problem. The code for it is:

```
// Get the rectangle enclosing the entire document
CRect CSketcherDoc::GetDocExtent()
{
  CRect DocExtent(0,0,1,1);              // Initial document extent
  CRect ElementBound(0,0,0,0);           // Space for element bounding rectangle

  POSITION aPosition = m_ElementList.GetHeadPosition();

  while(aPosition)                       // Loop through all the elements in the list
  {
    // Get the bounding rectangle for the element
    ElementBound=(m_ElementList.GetNext(aPosition))->GetBoundRect();

    // Make coordinates of document extent the outer limits
    DocExtent.UnionRect(DocExtent, ElementBound);
  }
  DocExtent.NormalizeRect();
  return DocExtent;
}
```

You can add this function definition to the `SketcherDoc.cpp` file, or simply add the code if you used the `Add > Add Function` capability from the pop-up in Class View. The process loops through every element in the document, using the `aPosition` variable to step through the list and getting the bounding rectangle for each element. The `UnionRect()` member of the `CRect` class calculates the smallest rectangle that contains the two rectangles passed as arguments, and puts that value in the `CRect` object for which the function is called. Therefore, `DocExtent` keeps increasing in size until all the elements are contained within it. Note that you initialize `DocExtent` with **(0,0,1,1)** because the `UnionRect()` function doesn't work properly with rectangles that have zero height or width.

Storing Print Data

The `OnPreparePrinting()` function in the view class is called by the application framework to enable you to initialize the printing process for your document. The basic initialization that's required is to provide information about how many pages are in the document for the print dialog that displays. You'll need to store information about the pages that your document requires so you can use it later in the other view functions involved in the printing process. You'll originate this in the OnPreparePrinting() member of the view class, too, store it in an object of your own class that you'll define for this purpose, and store a pointer to the object in the CPrintInfo object that the framework makes available. This approach is primarily to show you how this mechanism works; in most cases, you'll find it easier just to store the data in your view object, mainly because it makes the notation for referencing the data much simpler.

You'll need to store the number of pages running the width of the document, m_nWidths, and the number of rows of pages down the length of the document, m_nLengths. You'll also store the upper-left corner of the rectangle enclosing the document data as a CPoint object, m_DocRefPoint, because you'll use this when you work out the position of a page to be printed from its page number. You can store the file name for the document in a CString object, m_DocTitle, so that you can add it as a title to each page. The definition of the class to accommodate these is:

```
#pragma once

class CPrintData
{
  public:
    UINT m_nWidths;            // Page count for the width of the document
    UINT m_nLengths;           // Page count for the length of the document
    CPoint m_DocRefPoint;      // Top left corner of the document contents
    CString m_DocTitle;        // The name of the document
};
```

You can add a new header file with the name PrintData.h to the project by right-clicking the Header Files folder in the Solution Explorer pane and then selecting Add > New Item from the pop-up. You can now enter the class definition in the new file.

You don't need an implementation file for this class. The default constructor (which is automatically generated) is quite adequate here. Because an object of this class is only going to be used transiently, you don't need to use CObject as a base or to consider any other complication.

The printing process starts with a call to the view class member OnPreparePrinting(), so check out how you should implement that.

Preparing to Print

The Application Wizard added versions of OnPreparePrinting(), OnBeginPrinting(), and OnEndPrinting() to CSketcherView at the outset. The base code provided for OnPreparePrinting() calls DoPreparePrinting() in the return statement, as you can see:

```
BOOL CSketcherView::OnPreparePrinting(CPrintInfo* pInfo)
{
   // default preparation
   return DoPreparePrinting(pInfo);
}
```

The DoPreparePrinting() function displays the Print dialog box using information about the number of pages to be printed that's defined in the CPrintInfo object. Whenever possible, you should calculate the number of pages to be printed and store it in the CPrintInfo object before this call occurs. Of course, in many circumstances you may need information from the device context for the printer before you can do this — when you're printing a document where the number of pages is going to be affected by the size of font to be used, for example — in which case it won't be possible to get the page count before you call `OnPreparePrinting()`. In this case, you can compute the number of pages in the `OnBeginPrinting()` member, which receives a pointer to the device context as an argument. This function is called by the framework after `OnPreparePrinting()`, so the information entered in the Print dialog box is available. This means that you can also take account of the paper size selected by the user in the Print dialog box.

Assume that the page size is large enough to accommodate a 6 inch by 9 inch area to draw the document data, so you can calculate the number of pages in `OnPreparePrinting()`. The code for it is:

```
BOOL CSketcherView::OnPreparePrinting(CPrintInfo* pInfo)
{
    pInfo->m_lpUserData = new CPrintData;       // Create a print data object
    CSketcherDoc* pDoc = GetDocument();         // Get a document pointer

    // Get the whole document area
    CRect DocExtent = pDoc->GetDocExtent();

    // Save the reference point for the whole document
    ((CPrintData*)(pInfo->m_lpUserData))->m_DocRefPoint =
                                 CPoint(DocExtent.left, DocExtent.bottom);

    // Get the name of the document file and save it
    ((CPrintData*)(pInfo->m_lpUserData))->m_DocTitle = pDoc->GetTitle();

    // Calculate how many printed page widths of 600 units are required
    // to accommodate the width of the document
    ((CPrintData*)(pInfo->m_lpUserData))->m_nWidths =
          static_cast<UINT>(ceil((static_cast<double>(DocExtent.Width()))/600.0));

    // Calculate how many printed page lengths of 900 units are required
    // to accommodate the document length
    ((CPrintData*)(pInfo->m_lpUserData))->m_nLengths =
          static_cast<UINT>(ceil((static_cast<double>(DocExtent.Height()))/900.0));

    // Set the first page number as 1 and
    // set the last page number as the total number of pages
    pInfo->SetMinPage(1);
    pInfo->SetMaxPage((static_cast<CPrintData*>(pInfo->m_lpUserData))->m_nWidths *
                      (static_cast<CPrintData*>(pInfo->m_lpUserData))->m_nLengths);

    return DoPreparePrinting(pInfo);
}
```

You first create a `CPrintData` object on the heap and store its address in the pointer `m_lpUserData` in the `CPrintInfo` object passed to the function via the pointer `pInfo`. After getting a pointer to the document, you get the rectangle enclosing all of the elements in the document by calling the function `GetDocExtent()` that you added to the document class earlier in this chapter. You then store the corner of this rectangle in the `m_DocRefPoint` member of the `CPrintData` object and put the name of the file that contains the document in `m_DocTitle`.

Referencing the `CPrintData` object through the pointer in the `CPrintInfo` object is rather cumbersome. You get to the pointer with the expression `pInfo->m_lpUserData`, but because the pointer is of type `void`, you must add a cast to type `CPrintData*` to get to the `m_DocRefPoint` member of the object. The full expression to access the reference point for the document is:

```
(static_cast<CPrintData*>(pInfo->m_lpUserData))->m_DocRefPoint
```

You have to use this approach for all references to members of the `CPrintData` object, so any expressions using them are festooned with this notation. If you put the data in the view class, you only need to use the name of the data member. Don't forget to add an `#include` directive for `PrintData.h` to the `SketcherView.cpp` file.

The next two lines of code calculate the number of pages across the width of the document, and the number of pages required to cover the length. The number of pages to cover the width is computed by dividing the width of the document by the width of the print area of a page, which is 600 units or 6 inches, and rounding up to the next highest integer using the `ceil()` library function that is defined in the <cmath> header. An `#include` for this header file also needs to be added to `SketcherView.cpp`. For example, `ceil(2.1)` returns `3.0`, `ceil(2.9)` also returns `3.0`, and `ceil(-2.1)` returns `-2.0`. A similar calculation to that for the number of pages across the width of a document produces the number to cover the length. The product of these two values is the total number of pages to be printed, and this is the value that you'll supply for the maximum page number.

Cleaning Up After Printing

Because you created the `CPrintData` object on the heap, you must ensure that it's deleted when you're done with it. You do this by adding code to the `OnEndPrinting()` function:

```
void CSketcherView::OnEndPrinting(CDC* /*pDC*/, CPrintInfo* pInfo)
{
    // Delete our print data object
    delete static_cast<CPrintData*>(pInfo->m_lpUserData);
}
```

That's all that's necessary for this function in the Sketcher program, but in some cases you'll need to do more. Your one-time final cleanup should be done here. Make sure that you remove the comment delimiters (/* */) from the second parameter name; otherwise, your function won't compile. The default implementation comments out the parameter names because you may not need to refer to them in your code. Because you use the `pInfo` parameter, you must uncomment it; otherwise, the compiler reports it as undefined.

You don't need to add anything to the `OnBeginPrinting()` function in the Sketcher program, but you'd need to add code to allocate any GDI resources, such as pens, if they were required throughout the printing process. You would then delete these as part of the clean up process in `OnEndPrinting()`.

Preparing the Device Context

At the moment, the Sketcher program calls `OnPrepareDC()`, which sets up the mapping mode as `MM_ANISOTROPIC` to take account of the scaling factor. You must make some additional changes so that the device context is properly prepared in the case of printing:

```
void CSketcherView::OnPrepareDC(CDC* pDC, CPrintInfo* pInfo)
{
```

```
int Scale = m_Scale;                // Store the scale locally
if(pDC->IsPrinting())
  Scale = 1;                        // If we are printing, set scale to 1

CScrollView::OnPrepareDC(pDC, pInfo);
CSketcherDoc* pDoc = GetDocument();
pDC->SetMapMode(MM_ANISOTROPIC);    // Set the map mode
CSize DocSize = pDoc->GetDocSize(); // Get the document size

// y extent must be negative because we want MM_LOENGLISH
DocSize.cy = -DocSize.cy;           // Change sign of y
pDC->SetWindowExt(DocSize);         // Now set the window extent

// Get the number of pixels per inch in x and y
int xLogPixels = pDC->GetDeviceCaps(LOGPIXELSX);
int yLogPixels = pDC->GetDeviceCaps(LOGPIXELSY);

// Calculate the viewport extent in x and y
long xExtent = static_cast<long>(DocSize.cx)*Scale*xLogPixels/100L;
long yExtent = static_cast<long>(DocSize.cy)*Scale*yLogPixels/100L;

pDC->SetViewportExt(static_cast<int>(xExtent),
                    static_cast<int>(-yExtent)); // Set viewport extent
}
```

This function is called by the framework for output to the printer as well as to the screen. You should make sure that a scale of 1 is used to set the mapping from logical coordinates to device coordinates when you're printing. If you left everything as it was, the output would be at the current view scale, but you'd need to take account of the scale when calculating how many pages you needed, and how you set the origin for each page.

You can determine whether you have a printer device context or not by calling the IsPrinting() member of the current CDC object, which returns TRUE if you are printing. All you need to do when you have a printer device context is set the scale to 1. Of course, you must change the statements lower down which use the scale value, so that they use the local variable Scale rather than the m_Scale member of the view. The values returned by the calls to GetDeviceCaps() with the arguments LOGPIXELSX and LOGPIXELSY return the number of logical points per inch in the x and y directions for your printer when you're printing, and the equivalent values for your display when you're drawing to the screen, so this automatically adapts the viewport extent to suit the device to which you're sending the output.

Printing the Document

You can write the data to the printer device context in the OnPrint() function. This is called once for each page to be printed. You need to add an override for this function to CSketcherView, using the Properties window for the class. Select OnPrint from the list of overrides and then click <Add> OnPrint in the right column.

You can obtain the page number of the current page from the m_nCurPage member of the CPrintInfo object and use this value to work out the coordinates of the position in the document that corresponds to the upper-left corner of the current page. The way to do this is best understood using an example, so imagine that you are printing page seven of an eight-page document, as illustrated in Figure 18-7.

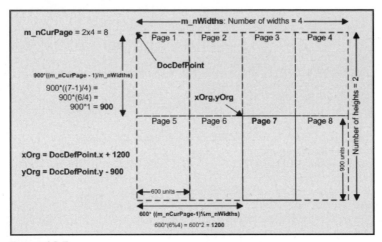

Figure 18-7

You can get an index to the horizontal position of the page by decrementing the page number by 1 and taking the remainder after dividing by the number of page widths required for the width of the printed area of the document. Multiplying the result by 600 produces the *x* coordinate of the upper-left corner of the page, relative to the upper-left corner of the rectangle enclosing the elements in the document. Similarly, you can determine the index to the vertical position of the document by dividing the current page number reduced by 1 by the number of page widths required for the horizontal width of the document. By multiplying the remainder by 900, you get the relative *y* coordinate of the upper-left corner of the page. You can express this in two statements as follows:

```
int xOrg = (static_cast<CPrintData*>(pInfo->m_lpUserData))->m_DocRefPoint.x +
            600*((pInfo->m_nCurPage - 1)%
                ((static_cast <CPrintData*>(pInfo->m_lpUserData))->m_nWidths));
int yOrg = (static_cast<CPrintData*>(pInfo->m_lpUserData))->m_DocRefPoint.y -
            900*((pInfo->m_nCurPage - 1)/
                ((static_cast <CPrintData*>(pInfo->m_lpUserData))->m_nWidths));
```

The statements look complicated, but that's mostly because of the need to access the information stored in the CPrintData object through the pointer in the CPrintInfo object.

It would be nice to print the file name of the document at the top of each page, but you want to be sure you don't print the document data over the file name. You also want to center the printed area on the page. You can do this by moving the origin of the coordinate system in the printer device context *after* you have printed the file name. This is illustrated in Figure 18-8.

Figure 18-8 illustrates the correspondence between the printed page area in the device context and the page to be printed in the reference frame of the document data. Remember that these are in logical coordinates — the equivalent of MM_LOENGLISH in Sketcher — so *y* is increasingly negative from top to bottom. The page shows the expressions for the offsets from the page origin for the 600 by 900 area where you are going to print the page. You want to print the information from the document in the dashed area shown on the page, so you need to map the xOrg, yOrg point in the document to the position shown in the printed page, which is displaced from the page origin by the offset values xOffset and yOffset.

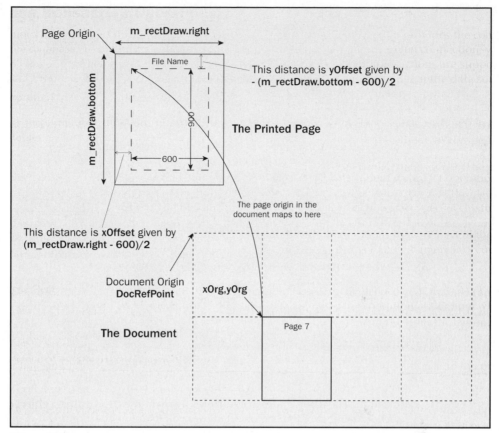

Figure 18-8

By default, the origin in the coordinate system that you use to define elements in the document is mapped to the origin of the device context, but you can change this. The CDC object provides a SetWindowOrg() function for this purpose. This enables you to define a point in the document's logical coordinate system that you want to correspond to the origin in the device context. It's important to save the old origin that's returned from the SetWindowOrg() function as a CPoint object. You must restore the old origin when you've finished drawing the current page; otherwise, the m_rectDraw member of the CPrintInfo object is not set up correctly when you come to print the next page.

The point in the document that you want to map to the origin of the page has the coordinates xOrgxOffset, yOrg+yOffset. This may not be easy to visualize, but remember that by setting the window origin, you're defining the point that maps to the viewport origin. If you think about it, you should see that the xOrg, yOrg point in the document is where you want it on the page.

The complete code for printing a page of the document is:

```
// Print a page of the document
void CSketcherView::OnPrint(CDC* pDC, CPrintInfo* pInfo)
{
    // Output the document file name
```

```
pDC->SetTextAlign(TA_CENTER);          // Center the following text
pDC->TextOut(pInfo->m_rectDraw.right/2, -20,
            (static_cast<CPrintData*>(pInfo->m_lpUserData))->m_DocTitle);
pDC->SetTextAlign(TA_LEFT);            // Left justify text

// Calculate the origin point for the current page
int xOrg = (static_cast<CPrintData*>(pInfo->m_lpUserData))->m_DocRefPoint.x +
            600*((pInfo->m_nCurPage - 1)%
                ((static_cast<CPrintData*>(pInfo->m_lpUserData))->m_nWidths));

int yOrg = (static_cast<CPrintData*>(pInfo->m_lpUserData))->m_DocRefPoint.y -
            900*((pInfo->m_nCurPage - 1)/
                ((static_cast<CPrintData*>(pInfo->m_lpUserData))->m_nWidths));

// Calculate offsets to center drawing area on page as positive values
int xOffset = (pInfo->m_rectDraw.right - 600)/2;
int yOffset = -(pInfo->m_rectDraw.bottom + 900)/2;

// Change window origin to correspond to current page & save old origin
CPoint OldOrg = pDC->SetWindowOrg(xOrg-xOffset, yOrg+yOffset);

// Define a clip rectangle the size of the printed area
pDC->IntersectClipRect(xOrg,yOrg,xOrg+600,yOrg-900);

OnDraw(pDC);                           // Draw the whole document
pDC->SelectClipRgn(NULL);              // Remove the clip rectangle
pDC->SetWindowOrg(OldOrg);             // Restore old window origin
}
```

The first step is to output the file name that you squirreled away in the CPrintInfo object. The SetTextAlign() function member of the CDC object allows you to define the alignment of subsequent text output in relation to the reference point you supply for the text string in the TextOut() function. The alignment is determined by the constant passed as an argument to the function. You have three possibilities for specifying the alignment of the text, as shown in the following table.

Constant	Alignment
TA_LEFT	The point is at the left of the bounding rectangle for the text, so the text is to the right of the point specified. This is default alignment.
TA_RIGHT	The point is at the right of the bounding rectangle for the text, so the text is to the left of the point specified.
TA_CENTER	The point is at the center of the bounding rectangle for the text.

You define the x coordinate of the file name on the page as half the page width, and the y coordinate as 20 units, which is 0.2 inches, from the top of the page. After outputting the name of the document file as centered text, you reset the text alignment to the default, TA_LEFT, for the text in the document.

The `SetTextAlign()` function also allows you to change the position of the text vertically by ORing a second flag with the justification flag. The second flag can be any of those shown in the following table.

Constant	Alignment
TA_TOP	Aligns the top of the rectangle bounding the text with the point defining the position of the text. This is the default.
TA_BOTTOM	Aligns the bottom of the rectangle bounding the text with the point defining the position of the text.
TA_BASELINE	Aligns the baseline of the font used for the text with the point defining the position of the text.

The next action in `OnPrint()` uses the method that I discussed for mapping an area of the document to the current page. You get the document drawn on the page by calling the `OnDraw()` function that is used to display the document in the view. This potentially draws the entire document, but you can restrict what appears on the page by defining a **clip rectangle**. A clip rectangle encloses a rectangular area in the device context within which output appears. Output is suppressed outside of the clip rectangle. It's also possible to define irregularly shaped areas for clipping called **regions**.

The initial default clipping area defined in the print device context is the page boundary. You define a clip rectangle which corresponds to the 600 by 900 area centered in the page. This ensures that you draw only in this area, and the file name is not to be overwritten.

After the current page has been drawn, you call `SetClipRgn()` with a `NULL` argument to remove the clip rectangle. If you don't do this, output of the document title is suppressed on all pages after the first because it lies outside the clip rectangle that would otherwise remain in effect in the print process until the next time `IntersectClipRect()` gets called.

Your final action is to call `SetWindowOrg()` again to restore the window origin to its original location, as discussed earlier in this chapter.

Getting a Printout of the Document

To get your first printed Sketcher document, you just need to build the project and execute the program (once you've fixed any typos). If you try `File > Print Preview`, you should get something similar to the window shown in Figure 18-9.

You get print preview functionality completely for free. The framework uses the code that you've supplied for the normal multipage printing operation to produce page images in the Print Preview window. What you see in the Print Preview window should be exactly the same as appears on the printed page.

Figure 18-9

Serialization and Printing in CLR Sketcher

Serialization is the process of writing objects to a stream, and deserialization is the reverse: reconstructing objects from a stream. The .NET Framework offers several different ways to serialize and deserialize your C++/CLI class objects. **XML serialization** serializes objects into an XML stream that conforms to a particular XML schema. You can also serialize objects into XML streams that conform to the Simple Object Access Protocol (SOAP) specification and this is referred to as **SOAP serialization**. A discussion of XML and SOAP is beyond the scope of this book, not because it's difficult — it isn't — but because to cover it adequately requires more pages than I can possibly include in this book. I'll therefore show you how to use the third and perhaps simplest form of serialization provided by the .NET Framework, **binary serialization**.

You'll also investigate how you can print sketches from CLR Sketcher. With the help given by the Form Designer, this is going to be easy.

Understanding Binary Serialization

Before you get into the specifics of serializing a sketch, let's get an overview of what's involved in binary serialization of your class objects. For binary serialization of your class objects to be possible, you have to make your classes serializable. You can make a ref class or value class serializable by marking it with the `Serializable` attribute, like this:

```
[Serializable]
public ref class MyClass
{
  // Class definition...
};
```

Of course, in practice there may be a little more to it. For serialization to work with `MyClass`, all the class fields must be serializable too, and often there are fields that are not serializable by default, or fields that it does not make sense to serialize because the data stored will not be valid when it is deserialized, or fields that you just don't want serialized for security reasons. In this case special measures are necessary to take care of the non-serializable class members.

Dealing with Fields That Are Not Serializable

Where a class has members that are not serializable, you can mark them with the `NonSerialized` attribute to prevent them from being serialized. For example:

```
[Serializable]
public ref class MyClass
{
  public:
  [NonSerialized]
   int value;
  // Rest of the class definition...
};
```

Here the serialization process will not attempt to serialize the `value` member of a `MyClass` object. For this to compile, you need a `using` declaration for the `System::Runtime::Serialization` namespace.

Although marking a data member as non-serializable avoids the possibility of the serialization process failing with types you cannot serialize, it does not solve the problem of serializing the objects unless the non-serialized data can be happily omitted when you come to reconstruct the object when it is deserialized. You will typically want to take some special action in relation to the non-serialized fields.

You use the `OnSerializing` attribute to mark a class function that you want to be called when the serialization of an object begins. This gives you an opportunity to do something about the non-serialized fields. For example:

```
[Serializable]
public ref class MyClass
{
  public:
  [NonSerialized]
   int value;
```

```
[OnSerializing]
void FixNonSerializedData(StreamingContext context)
{
    // Code to do the necessary...
}

// Rest of the class definition...
};
```

When a `MyClass` object is serialized, the `FixNonSerializedData()` function will be called for the object and the code in here will deal with the problem of `value` not being serialized, perhaps by allowing some other data to be serialized that will enable `value` to be reconstructed when the object is deserialized. The function that you mark with the `OnSerializing` attribute must have a `void` return type and a parameter of type `StreamingContext`. The `StreamingContext` object that is passed to the function when it is called is a struct containing information about the source and destination but you won't need to use this in CLR Sketcher.

You can also arrange for a member function to be called when an object is deserialized. You just have to mark the function with the `OnSerialized` attribute. For example:

```
[Serializable]
public ref class MyClass
{
    public:
    [NonSerialized]
    int value;

    [OnSerializing]
    void FixNonSerializedData(StreamingContext context)
    {
        // Code to do the necessary...
    }


    [OnSerialized]
    void ReconstructValue(StreamingContext context)
    {
        // Code to do the necessary...
    }

    // Rest of the class definition...
};
```

The `ReconstructValue()` function will be executed after the deserialization process is complete, so this function will have the responsibility for setting `value` appropriately. The function that you mark with the `OnSerialized` attribute must also have a `void` return type and a parameter of type `StreamingContext`.

To summarize, preparing a class to allow objects of that class type to be serialized involves the following five steps:

1. Mark the class to be serialized with the `Serializable` attribute.

2. Identify any data members that cannot or should not be serialized and mark them with NonSerialized attributes.

3. Add a public function with a return type of void and a single parameter of type StreamingContext to deal with the non-serializable fields when an object is serialized and mark the function with the OnSerializing attribute.

4. Add a public function with a return type of void and a single parameter of type StreamingContext to deal with the non-serialized fields when an object is deserialized and mark the function with the OnSerialized attribute.

5. Add a using declaration for the System::Runtime::Serialization namespace to the header file containing the class.

Serializing an Object

Serializing an object means writing it to a stream, so you first must define the stream that is the destination for the data defining the object. A stream is represented by a System::IO::Stream class, which is an abstract ref class type. A stream can be any source or destination for data that is a sequence of bytes; a file, a TCP/IP socket, and a pipe that allows data to be passed between two processes are all examples of streams.

You will usually want to serialize your objects to a file and the System::IO::File class contains static functions for creating objects that encapsulate files. You use the File::Open() function to create a new file or open an existing file for reading and/or writing. The Open() function returns a reference of type FileStream^ to an object that encapsulates the file. Because FileStream is a type that is derived from Stream, you can store the reference that the Open() function returns in a variable of type Stream^. The Open() function comes in three overloaded versions, and the version you will be using has the following form:

```
FileStream^ Open( String^ path, FileMode mode)
```

The path parameter is the path to the file that you want to open and can be a full path to the file, or just the file name. If you just specify an argument that is just a file name, the file will be assumed to be in the current directory.

The mode parameter controls whether the file is created if it does not exist, and whether the data can be overwritten if the file does exist. The mode argument can be any of the FileMode enumeration values described in the following table.

FileMode Enumerator	Description
CreateNew	Requests that a new file specified by path is created. If the file already exists, an exception of type System::IO::IOException is thrown. You use this when you are writing a new file.
Truncate	Requests that an existing file specified by path is opened and its contents discarded by truncating the size of the file to zero bytes. You use this when you are writing an existing file.

Continued

FileMode Enumerator	Description
Create	Specifies that if the file specified by path does not exist, it should be created and if the file does exist it should be overwritten. You use this when you are writing a file.
Open	Specifies that the existing file specified by `path` should be opened. If the file does not exist, an exception of type `System::IO::FileNotFoundException` is thrown. You use this when you are reading a file.
OpenOrCreate	Specifies that the file specified by path should be opened if it exists and created if it doesn't. You can use this to read or write a file, depending on the access argument.
Append	The file specified by path is opened if it exists and the file position set to the end of the file; if the file does not exist, it will be created. You use this to append data to an existing file or to write a new file.

Thus you could create a stream encapsulating a file in the current directory that you can write with the following statement:

```
Stream^ stream = File::Open(L"sketch.dat", FileMode::Create);
```

The file `sketch.dat` will be created in the current directory if it does not exist; if it exists the contents will be overwritten.

The static `OpenWrite()` function in the `File` class will open the existing file that you specify by the string argument with write access and return a `FileStream^` reference to the stream you use to write the file.

To serialize an object to a file encapsulated by a `FileStream` object that you have created, you use an object of type `System::Runtime::Serialization::Formatters::Binary::BinaryFormatter` that you create like this:

```
BinaryFormatter^ formatter = gcnew BinaryFormatter();
```

You need a `using` declaration for `System::Runtime::Serialization::Formatters::Binary` if this statement is to compile. The `formatter` object has a `Serialize()` function member that you use to serialize an object to a stream. The first argument to the function is a reference to the stream that is the destination for the data and the second argument is a reference to the object to be serialized to the stream. Thus you can write a `sketch` object to `stream` with the following statement:

```
formatter->Serialize(stream, sketch);
```

You read an object from a stream using the `Deserialize()` function for a `BinaryFormatter` object:

```
Sketch sketch = safe_cast<Sketch>(formatter->Deserialize(stream));
```

The argument to the `Deserialize()` function is a reference to the stream that is to be read. The function returns the object read from the stream as type `Object^` so you must cast it to the appropriate type.

Serializing a Sketch

You have to do two things to allow sketches to be serialized in the CLR Sketcher application: Make the Sketch class serializable and add code to enable the File menu items and toolbar buttons to support saving and retrieving sketches.

Making the Sketch Class Serializable

Add the Serializable attribute immediately before that Sketch class definition to specify that the class is serializable:

```
[Serializable]
 public ref class Sketch
{
  // Class definition as before...
};
```

Although this indicates that the class is serializable, in fact it is not. Serialization will fail because the STL/CLR container classes are not serializable by default. You must specify that the elements class member is not serializable, like this:

```
[Serializable]
 public ref class Sketch
{
  private:
    [NonSerialized]
    list<Element^>^ elements;

  // Rest of the class definition as before...
};
```

The class really is serializable now, but not in a useful way because none of the elements in the sketch will get written to the file. You must provide an alternative repository for the elements in the list<Element^> container that is serializable to get the sketch elements written to the file. Fortunately, a regular C++/CLI array is serializable and even more fortunately, the list container has a ToArray() function that returns the entire contents of the container as an array. You can therefore add a public function to the class with the OnSerializing attribute that will copy the contents of the elements container to an array and that you can arrange to be called before serialization begins. You can also add a public function with the OnSerialized attribute that will recreate the elements container when the array containing the elements is deserialized. Here are the changes to the Sketch class that will accommodate that:

```
[Serializable]
 public ref class Sketch
{
  private:
    [NonSerialized]
    list<Element^>^ elements;
    array<Element^>^ elementArray;

  public:
    Sketch(): elementArray(nullptr)
    {
    elements = gcnew list<Element^>();
    }
```

```
    [OnSerializing]
    void ListToArray(StreamingContext context)
    {
      elementArray = elements->to_array();
    }
```

```
    [OnDeserialized]
    void ArrayToList(StreamingContext context)
    {
      elements = gcnew list<Element^>(elementArray);
      elementArray = nullptr;
    }
```

```
  // Rest of the class definition as before...
};
```

You have a new private data member, elementArray, that holds all the elements in the sketch when it is serialized to a file. You initialize this to nullptr in the constructor. When a Sketch object is serialized, the ListToArray() function will be called first, and this function transfers the contents of the list container to the elementArray array before serialization of the object takes place. The Sketch object containing the elementArray object is then written to the file. When a sketch is read back from the file, the Sketch object is recreated containing the elementArray member, after which the ArrayToList() function is called to restore the contents of the elements container from the array. The array is no longer required, so you set it to nullptr in the function.

So far, so good but you are not quite there yet. For a sketch to be serializable, all the elements in the sketch must be serializable too, and there's the small problem of the Curve class that has an STL/CLR container as a member. First though, add the Serializable attribute to the Element class and all its subclasses.

You can pull the same trick with the container in the Curve class as you did with the Sketch class container, so amend the class definition to the following:

```
[Serializable]
  public ref class Curve : Element
  {
  private:
    [NonSerialized]
    vector<Point>^ points;
    array<Point>^ pointsArray;

  public:
    Curve(Color color, Point p1, Point p2, float penWidth) : pointsArray(nullptr)
    {
      this->penWidth = penWidth;
      pen = gcnew Pen(color, penWidth);
      this->color = color;
      points = gcnew vector<Point>();
      position = p1;
      points->push_back(Point(p2.X-position.X, p2.Y-position.Y));

      // Find the minimum and maximum coordinates
```

```
        int minX = p1.X < p2.X ? p1.X : p2.X;
        int minY = p1.Y < p2.Y ? p1.Y : p2.Y;
        int maxX = p1.X > p2.X ? p1.X : p2.X;
        int maxY = p1.Y > p2.Y ? p1.Y : p2.Y;
        int width = Math::Max(2, maxX - minX);
        int height = Math::Max(2, maxY - minY);
        boundRect = System::Drawing::Rectangle(minX, minY, width, height);
    }
```

```
    [OnSerializing]
    void VectorToArray(StreamingContext context)
    {
      pointsArray = points->to_array();
    }
```

```
    [OnDeserialized]
    void ArrayToVector(StreamingContext context)
    {
      points = gcnew vector<Point>(pointsArray);
      pointsArray = nullptr;
    }
```

```
    // Rest of the class definition as before...
};
```

The changes are very similar to those in the Sketch class. You have an array member to store the points defining the curve when serializing an object and two functions that take care of creating an array containing the points before serialization and restoring the points container after deserialization. Don't forget to add a using declaration for the System::Runtime::Serialization namespace to Sketch.h and Elements.h.

You are not out of the woods yet on serializing elements. If you try to serialize a sketch now, it will fail because objects of type Pen and Brush (and subclasses of these types) are not serializable. The Element class has a member of type Pen^ and the TextElement class has a member of type SolidBrush^ so neither of these classes is serializable at present. The first step to fixing this is to mark these members with the NonSerialized attribute. You can then add a public function to the Element class to restore the Pen object when an element is deserialized:

```
    [OnDeserialized]
    void CreatePen(StreamingContext context)
    {
      pen = gcnew Pen(color, penWidth);
    }
```

This function is called for the base class whenever an object of any of the derived class types is deserialized.

You can add a public function to the TextElement class to restore the SolidBrush object when a text element is deserialized:

```
    [OnDeserialized]
    void CreateBrush()
    {
```

```
        brush = gcnew SolidBrush(color);
    }
```

This recreates the brush when a `TextElement` object is deserialized. All the classes involved in serializing and deserializing a sketch should now be OK, so it's time to implement the event handlers for the menu items.

Implementing File Operations for a Sketch

The menu items and toolbar buttons for file operations are already in place in CLR Sketcher. If you double-click the `Click` event property in the Properties window for the `File > Save`, `File > Save As...` and `File > Open` menu items, you'll put the event handlers in place for all of them. Then just select the appropriate event handler from the drop-down list of values for the `Click` event for each of the toolbar buttons. All you have to do now is supply the code to make them do what you want.

Creating Dialogs for File Operations

The Toolbox has standard dialogs for opening and saving files and you can use both of these. Drag an `OpenFileDialog` and a `SaveFileDialog` from the Toolbox to the Design window for `Form1`. You can change the `(name)` property values to `saveFileDialog` and `openFileDialog`. Change the values for the `Title` properties for both dialogs to whatever you want displayed in the title bar. You can also change the `FileName` property in the `openFileDialog` to sketch; this is the default file name that will be displayed when the dialog is first used. It's a good idea to define a folder that will hold your sketches so create one now; you could use something like `C:\CLR Sketches`. You can specify the default directory as the value for the `InitialDirectory` property for both dialogs. Both dialogs have a `Filter` property that specifies the filters for the list of files that are displayed by the dialogs. You can set the value for the `Filter` property for both dialogs to `"CLR Sketches|*.ske| All files|*.*"`. The default value of 1 for the `FilterIndex` property determines that the first file filter applies by default. If you want the second file filter to apply, set the value for `FilterIndex` to 2. Verify that the values for the `ValidateNames` and `OverwritePrompt` properties for the `saveFileDialog` have default values of `true`; this results in the user being prompted when an existing sketch is about to be overwritten.

Saving a Sketch

You need a `BinaryFormatter` object to save a sketch and a good place to keep it is in the `Form1` class. Add a `using` declaration for the `System::Runtime::Serialization::Formatters::Binary` namespace to `Form1.h` and add a new private member, `formatter`, of type `BinaryFormatter^` to the `Form1` class. You can initialize it to `gcnew BinaryFormatter()` in the initialization list for the `Form1` class constructor.

Before you get into implementing the event handler for the `File > Save` menu item, let's consider what the logic is going to be. When you click the `File > Save` menu item, what happens depends on whether the current sketch has been saved before. If the sketch has never been saved, you want the file save dialog to be displayed; if the sketch has been saved previously, you just want to write the sketch to the file without displaying the dialog. To allow this to work, you need a way to record whether or not the sketch has been saved. One way to do this is to add a public member of type `bool` with the name `Saved` to the `Sketch` class. You can initialize it to `false` in the `Sketch` class constructor and set it to `true` the first time the sketch is saved.

Before you implement the `Click` event handler, add a `using` declaration for the `System.IO` namespace to the `Form1.h` header file. Add a private `String^` member, `sketchFilepath`, to the `Form1` class to store the file path for a sketch; initialize this to `nullptr` in the `Form1` constructor. You can add the following code to implement the `Click` event handler for save operations:

```
private: System::Void saveToolStripMenuItem_Click(
                              System::Object^ sender, System::EventArgs^ e)
{
  Stream^ stream;
  if(!sketch->Saved)
  { // Sketch not saved so display the dialog
    if(saveFileDialog->ShowDialog() == System::Windows::Forms::DialogResult::OK)
    {
      if((stream = File::Open(saveFileDialog->FileName, FileMode::Create))
                                                                != nullptr)
      {
        formatter->Serialize(stream, sketch);
        stream->Close();
        sketchFilepath = saveFileDialog->FileName;
        sketch->Saved = true;
      }
    }
  }
  else
  {  // Sketch saved previously so just save the sketch...
    stream = File::OpenWrite(sketchFilepath);
    formatter->Serialize(stream, sketch);
    stream->Close();
  }
}
```

There are two courses of action depending on whether or not the sketch has been saved previously.

If the sketch hasn't been saved before, you open the save dialog. If the OK button closes the dialog you call the static `Open()` function to create a `FileStream` object for the file using the file name provided by the `FileName` property for the dialog object. You serialize the sketch to the file by calling the `Serialize()` function for the `BinaryFormatter` object and close the stream. You save the file path for use next time around and set the `Saved` member of the `Sketch` object to true.

The `else` clause belonging to the first `if` statement specifies what happens when the sketch has been saved previously. You obtain a reference to a `FileStream` object that you can use to serialize the sketch by calling the static `OpenWrite()` function that is defined in the `File` class. You then serialize the sketch in the same way as before. Finally you call `Close()` for the stream to close the stream and release the resources.

Retrieving a Sketch from a File

The `Click` handler for the `File > Open` menu item deals with reading a sketch from a file. You can implement it like this:

```
private: System::Void openToolStripMenuItem_Click(
                              System::Object^ sender, System::EventArgs^ e)
{
  if(openFileDialog->ShowDialog() == System::Windows::Forms::DialogResult::OK)
```

```
      {
        Stream^ stream;
        if((stream = openFileDialog->OpenFile()) != nullptr)
        {
          sketch = safe_cast<Sketch^>(formatter->Deserialize(stream));
          stream->Close();
          sketch->Saved = true;
          sketchFilepath = openFileDialog->FileName;
          Invalidate();
        }
      }
    }
```

The `OpenFileDialog` class provides an `OpenFile()` function that returns a reference to the stream encapsulating the file selected in the dialog. You deserialize the sketch from the file by calling the `Deserialize()` function for the `formatter` object and close the stream. The sketch is obviously in a file so you set the `Saved` member of the sketch to `true`. You store the file name in `sketchFilepath` for use by subsequent save operations and call `Invalidate()` to get the form repainted to display the sketch you have just loaded.

Implementing the Save As Operation

For the Save As operation you always display a save dialog to allow a new file name to be entered. You can implement the `Click` event handler for the `File > Save As...` menu item like this:

```
private: System::Void saveAsToolStripMenuItem_Click(
                              System::Object^  sender, System::EventArgs^  e)
{
  if(saveFileDialog->ShowDialog() == System::Windows::Forms::DialogResult::OK)
  {
    Stream^ stream = File::Open(saveFileDialog->FileName, FileMode::Create);
    if(stream != nullptr)
    {
      formatter->Serialize(stream, sketch);
      stream->Close();
      sketchFilepath = saveFileDialog->FileName;
      sketch->Saved = true;
    }
  }
}
```

This is basically a simplified version of the save operation. You display the dialog; if the OK button closed the dialog you create a `Stream` object for the file that was selected and deserialize it. You then close the stream, save the file path information, and set the `Saved` member of the sketch object to `true`.

You now have a version of CLR Sketcher with saving and retrieving operational.

Printing a Sketch

You have a head start to printing a sketch because the Toolbox provides five components that support printing operations including a page setup dialog and print and print preview dialogs. To print a sketch you create an instance of the `PrintDocument` component, implement a `PrintPage` event handler for the `PrintDocument`, and call the `Print` function for the `PrintDocument` object to actually print the sketch. Of course, you also need to create `Click` event handlers for the menu items that are involved and display a few dialogs along the way, but let's start with the `PrintDocument` component.

Using the PrintDocument Component

Drag a `PrintDocument` component from the Toolbox window to the form in the Design window. This adds a `PrintDocument` member to the `Form1` class. If you display the Properties window for the `PrintDocument` object, you can change the value of its `(name)` property to `printDocument`. Click the `Events` button and double-click the `PrintPage` event to create a handler for it. The `PrintPageEventArgs^` parameter has a `Graphics` property that supplies a `Graphics` object that you can use to draw the sketch ready for printing, like this:

```
private: System::Void printDocument_PrintPage(
        System::Object^ sender, System::Drawing::Printing::PrintPageEventArgs^ e)
{
    sketch->Draw(e->Graphics);
}
```

It couldn't be much easier really, could it?

Implementing the Print Operation

You need a print dialog to allow the user to select the printer and initiate printing, so drag a `PrintDialog` component from the Toolbox window to the form and change the `(name)` property value to `printDialog`. To associate the `printDocument` object with the dialog, select `printDocument` as the value of the `Document` property from the drop-down in the value column. Add a `Click` event handler for the `File > Print` menu item, and set this handler as the handler for the toolbar button for printing. All you have to do now is add code to the handler to display the dialog to allow printing:

```
private: System::Void printToolStripMenuItem_Click(
                            System::Object^ sender, System::EventArgs^ e)
{
    if(printDialog->ShowDialog() == System::Windows::Forms::DialogResult::OK)
        printDocument->Print();
}
```

You display the dialog and if the value returned from `ShowDialog()` is `DialogResult::OK`, you call the `Print()` function for the `printDocument` object to print the sketch. That's it! You added two lines of code here plus one line of code in the `PrintPage` event handler and a basic printing capability for sketches is working.

Displaying the print dialog allows the user to choose the printer and change preferences for the print job before printing starts. Of course, you don't have to display the dialog to print the sketch. If you wanted to print the sketch immediately without displaying the dialog, you could just call the `Print()` function for the `PrintDocument` object.

Summary

In this chapter, you learned how to get a document stored on disk in a form that allows you to read it back and reconstruct its constituent objects using the serialization processes supported by MFC and the CLR. To implement serialization for MFC classes defining document data, you must:

1. Derive your class directly or indirectly from `CObject`.

2. Specify the `DECLARE_SERIAL()` macro in your class implementation.

3. Specify the `IMPLEMENT_SERIAL()` macro in your class definition.

4. Implement a default constructor in your class.

5. Declare the `Serialize()` function in your class.

6. Implement the `Serialize()` function in your class to serialize all the data members.

The serialization process uses a `CArchive` object to perform the input and output. You use the `CArchive` object passed to the `Serialize()` function to serialize the data members of the class.

To implement serialization for C++/CLI classes you must:

1. Mark the classes to be serialized with the `Serializable` attribute.

2. Identify any data members that cannot or should not be serialized and mark them with `NonSerialized` attributes.

3. Add a public function with a return type of `void` and a single parameter of type `StreamingContext` to each class that has non-serializable fields. Implement the function to deal with the non-serializable fields when an object is serialized and mark the function with the `OnSerializing` attribute.

4. Add a public function with a return type of `void` and a single parameter of type `StreamingContext` to each class that has non-serializable fields. Implement the function to deal with the non-serialized fields when an object is deserialized and mark the function with the `OnSerialized` attribute.

5. Add a `using` declaration for the `System::Runtime::Serialization` namespace to each header file containing classes you are making serializable.

You have also seen how MFC and the CLR support output to a printer. To add to the basic printing capability provided by default with the MFC, you can implement your own versions of the view class functions involved in printing a document. The principal roles of each of these functions are shown in the following table.

Function	Role
OnPreparePrinting()	Determine the number of pages in the document and call the DoPreparePrinting() member of the view.
OnBeginPrinting()	Allocate the resources required in the printer device context that are needed throughout the printing process, and determine the number of pages in the document, where this is dependent on information from the device context.
OnPrepareDC()	Set attributes in the printer device context as necessary.
OnPrint()	Print the document.
OnEndPrinting()	Delete any GDI resources created in OnBeginPrinting() and do any other necessary cleanup.

Information relating to the printing process is stored in an object of type CPrintInfo that's created by the framework. You can store additional information in the view, or in another object of your own. If you use your own class object, you can keep track of it by storing a pointer to it in the CPrintInfo object.

To implement printing in a Windows Forms application, add a PrintDocument component to the form and implement the handler for the PrintPage event to print the form. Add a PrintDialog component to the form and display it in the Click handler for the menu item/toolbar button that initiates printing. When the print dialog is closed using the OK button, call the Print() function for the PrintDocument object to print the form.

Exercises

You can download the source code for the examples in the book and the solutions to the following exercises from www.wrox.com.

1. Add some code to the OnPrint() function so that the page number is printed at the bottom of each page of the document in the form 'Page *n*'. If you use the features of the CString class, you can do this with just three extra lines!

2. As a further enhancement to the CText class, change the implementation so that scaling works properly. (Hint — look up the CreatePointFont() function in the online help.)

3. Modify CLR Sketcher so that it displays the sketch file name in the title bar for the application.

4. Modify CLR Sketcher to implement the File > New menu item. Don't forget to build in the logic so you don't discard an existing sketch that has not been saved in its present state. There is a little bit of work to this. (Hint: You will need to record in Sketch class when the sketch has been changed since it was last saved. Exploring the documentation for the System::Windows::MessageBox class will be helpful, too.)

19

Writing Your Own DLLs

Chapter 9 discussed how a C++/CLI class library is stored in a .dll file. Dynamic link libraries (DLLs) are also used extensively with native C++ applications. A complete discussion of DLLs in native C++ applications is outside the scope of a beginner's book, but they are important enough to justify including an introductory chapter on them. In this chapter, you will learn about:

❑   DLLs and how they work

❑   When you should consider implementing a DLL

❑   What varieties of DLL are possible and what they are used for

❑   How you can extend MFC using a DLL

❑   How to define what is accessible in a DLL

❑   How to access the contents of a DLL in your programs

Understanding DLLs

Almost all programming languages support libraries of standard code modules for commonly used functions. In native C++ you've been using lots of functions that are stored in standard libraries, such as the ceil() function that you used in the previous chapter, which is declared in the <cmath> header. The code for this function is stored in a library file with the extension .lib, and when the executable module for the Sketcher program was created, the linker retrieved the code for this standard function from the library file and integrated a copy of it into the .exe file for the Sketcher program. If you write another program and use the same function, it will also have its own copy of the ceil() function. The ceil() function is **statically linked** to each application and is an integral part of each executable module, as illustrated in Figure 19-1.

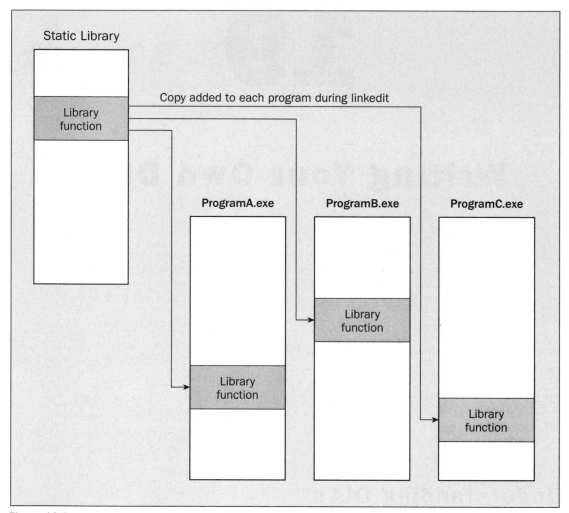

Figure 19-1

Although this is a very convenient way of using a standard function with minimal effort on your part, it does have its disadvantages as a way for several concurrently executing programs to make use of the same function in the Windows environment. A statically linked standard function being used by more than one program concurrently is duplicated in memory for each program using it. This may not seem to matter much for the `ceil()` function, but some functions — input and output, for instance — are invariably common to most programs and are likely to occupy sizable chunks of memory. Having these statically linked would be extremely inefficient.

Another consideration is that a standard function from a static library may be linked into hundreds of programs in your system, so identical copies of the code for them will be occupying disk space in the .exe file for each program. For these reasons, an additional library facility is supported by Windows for standard functions. It's called a **dynamic link library**, and it's usually abbreviated to **DLL**. This allows one copy of a function to be shared among several concurrently executing programs and avoids the need to incorporate a copy of the code for a library function into the executable module for a program that uses it.

How DLLs Work

A dynamic link library is a file containing a collection of modules that can be used by any number of different programs. The file usually has the extension .dll, but this isn't obligatory. When naming a DLL, you can assign any extension that you like, but this can affect how they're handled by Windows. Windows automatically loads dynamic link libraries that have the extension .dll. If they have some other extension, you will need to load them explicitly by adding code to do this to your program. Windows itself uses the extension .exe for some of its DLLs. You have likely seen the extensions .vbx (Visual Basic Extension) and .ocx (OLE Custom Extension), which are applied to DLLs containing specific kinds of controls.

You might imagine that you have a choice about whether or not you use dynamic link libraries in your program, but you don't. The Win32 API is used by every Windows program, and the API is implemented in a set of DLLs. DLLs are fundamental to Windows programming.

Connecting a function in a DLL to a program is achieved differently from the process used with a statically linked library, where the code is incorporated once and for all when the program is linked to generate the executable module. A function in a DLL is connected only to a program that uses it when the application is run, and this is done on each occasion the program is executed, as Figure 19-2 illustrates.

Figure 19-2 shows the sequence of events when three programs that use a function in a DLL are started successively and then all execute concurrently. No code from the DLL is included in the executable module of any of the programs. When one of the programs is executed, the program is loaded into memory, and if the DLL it uses isn't already present, it too is loaded separately. The appropriate links between the program and the DLL are then established. If, when a program is loaded, the DLL is already there, all that needs to be done is to link the program to the required function in the DLL.

Note particularly that when your program calls a function in a DLL, Windows will automatically load the DLL into memory. Any program subsequently loaded into memory that uses the same DLL can use any of the capabilities provided by the *same copy* of the DLL because Windows recognizes that the library is already in memory and just establishes the links between it and the program. Windows keeps track of how many programs are using each DLL that is resident in memory so that the library remains in memory as long as at least one program is still using it. When a DLL is no longer used by any executing program, Windows automatically deletes it from memory.

MFC is provided in the form of a number of DLLs that your program can link to dynamically, as well as a library that your program can link to statically. By default, the Application Wizard generates programs that link dynamically to the DLL form of MFC.

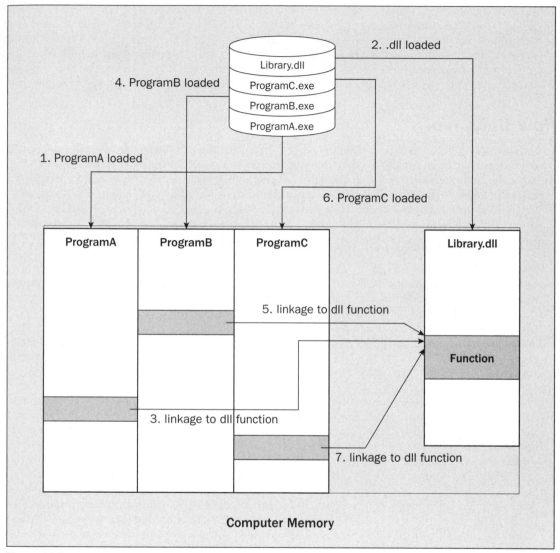

Figure 19-2

Having a function stored in a DLL introduces the possibility of changing the function without affecting the programs that use it. As long as the interface to the function in the DLL remains the same, the programs can use a new version of the function quite happily, without the need for recompiling or re-linking them. Unfortunately, this also has a downside: It's easy to end up using the wrong version of a DLL with a program. This can be a particular problem with applications that install DLLs in the Windows System folder. Some commercial applications arbitrarily write the DLLs associated with the program to this folder without regard to the possibility of a DLL with the same name being overwritten. This can interfere with other applications that you have already installed and, in the worst case, can render them inoperable.

Runtime Dynamic Linking

The DLL that you'll create in this chapter is automatically loaded into memory when the program that uses it is loaded into memory for execution. This is referred to as **load-time dynamic linking**, or **early binding**, because the links to the functions used are established as soon as the program and DLL have been loaded into memory. This kind of operation was illustrated in Figure 19-2; however, this isn't the only choice available. It's also possible to cause a DLL to be loaded after execution of a program has started. This is called **runtime dynamic linking** or **late binding**. The sequence of operations that occurs with this is illustrated in Figure 19-3.

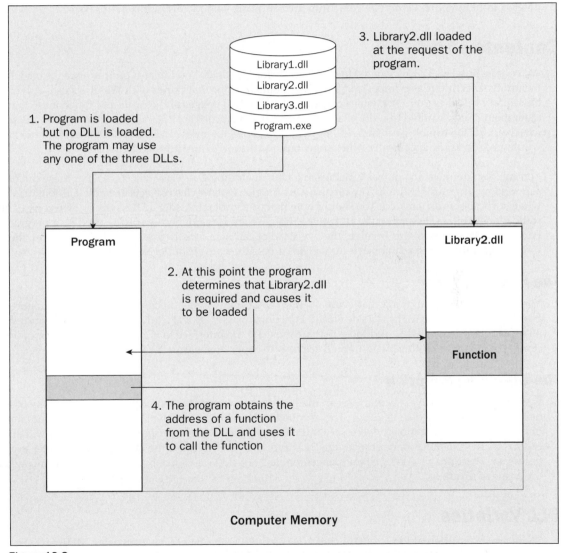

Figure 19-3

Runtime dynamic linking enables a program to defer linking of a DLL until it's certain that the functions in a DLL are required. This allows you to write a program that can choose to load one or more of a number of DLLs based upon input to the program so that only those functions that are necessary are actually loaded into memory. In some circumstances, this can drastically reduce the amount of memory required to run a program.

A program implemented to use runtime dynamic linking calls the Windows API function `LoadLibrary()` to load the DLL when it's required. The address of a function within the DLL can then be obtained using a function `GetProcAddress()`. When the program no longer has a need to use the DLL, it can detach itself from the DLL by calling the `FreeLibrary()` function. If no other program is using the DLL, it will be deleted from memory. I won't be going into further details of how this works in this book.

Contents of a DLL

A dynamic link library isn't limited to storing code for functions. You can also put resources into a DLL, including such things as bitmaps and fonts. The Solitaire game that comes with Windows uses a dynamic link library called `Cards.dll`, which contains all the bitmap images of the cards and functions to manipulate them. If you wanted to write your own card game, you could conceivably use this DLL as a base and save yourself the trouble of creating all the bitmaps needed to represent the cards. Of course, to use it, you would need to know specifically which functions and resources are included in the DLL.

You can also define static global variables in a DLL, including C++ class objects, so that these can be accessed by programs using it. The constructors for global static class objects are called automatically when such objects are created. You should note that each program using a DLL gets its own copy of any static global objects defined in the DLL, even though they may not necessarily be used by a program. For global class objects, this involves the overhead of calling a constructor for each. You should, therefore, avoid introducing such objects into a DLL unless they are absolutely essential.

The DLL Interface

You can't access just anything that's contained in a DLL. Only items specifically identified as **exported** from a DLL are visible to the outside world. Functions, classes, global static variables, and resources can all be exported from a DLL, and those that are make up the **interface** to it. Anything that isn't exported can't be accessed from the outside. You'll see how to export items from a DLL later in this chapter.

The DllMain() Function

Even though a DLL isn't executable as an independent program, it does contain a special variety of the `main()` function, called `DllMain()`. This is called by Windows when the DLL is first loaded into memory to allow the DLL to do any necessary initialization before its contents are used. Windows will also call `DllMain()` just before it removes the DLL from memory to enable the DLL to clean up after itself if necessary. There are also other circumstances where `DllMain()` is called, but these situations are outside the scope of this book.

DLL Varieties

There are three different kinds of DLL that you can build with Visual C++ 2008 using MFC: an MFC extension DLL, a regular DLL with MFC statically linked, and a regular DLL with MFC dynamically linked.

MFC Extension DLL

You build this kind of DLL whenever it's going to include classes derived from the MFC. Your derived classes in the DLL effectively extend the MFC. The MFC must be accessible in the environment where your DLL is used, so all the MFC classes are available together with your derived classes — hence the name "MFC extension DLL." However, deriving your own classes from the MFC isn't the only reason to use an MFC extension DLL. If you're writing a DLL that includes functions that pass pointers to MFC class objects to functions in a program using it or that receive such pointers from functions in the program, you must create it as an MFC extension DLL.

Accesses to classes in the MFC by an extension DLL are always resolved dynamically by linking to the shared version of MFC that is itself implemented in DLLs. An extension DLL is created using the shared DLL version of the MFC, so when you use an extension DLL, the shared version of MFC must be available. An MFC extension DLL can be used by a normal Application Wizard-generated application. It requires the option Use MFC in a Shared Dll to be selected under the General set of properties for the project, which you access through the `Project > Properties` menu option. This is the default selection with an Application Wizard-generated program. Because of the fundamental nature of the shared version of the MFC in an extension DLL, an MFC extension DLL can't be used by programs that are statically linked to MFC.

Regular DLL — Statically Linked to MFC

This is a DLL that uses MFC classes linked statically. Use of the DLL doesn't require MFC to be available in the environment in which it is used, because the code for all the classes it uses is incorporated into the DLL. This bulks up the size of the DLL, but the big advantage is that this kind of DLL can be used by any Win32 program, regardless of whether or not it uses MFC.

Regular DLL — Dynamically Linked to MFC

This is a DLL that uses dynamically linked classes from MFC but doesn't add classes of its own. This kind of DLL can be used by any Win32 program regardless of whether it uses MFC itself, but use of the DLL does require the MFC to be available in the environment.

You can use the Application Wizard to build all three types of DLL that use MFC. You can also create a project for a DLL that doesn't involve MFC at all, by creating a `Win32` project type using the `Win32 Project` template and selecting `DLL` in the application settings for the project.

Deciding What to Put in a DLL

How do you decide when you should use a DLL? In most cases, the use of a DLL provides a solution to a particular kind of programming problem, so if you have the problem, a DLL can be the answer. The common denominator is often sharing code among a number of programs, but there are other instances where a DLL provides advantages. The kinds of circumstance where putting code or resources in a DLL provides a very convenient and efficient approach include the following:

❑   You have a set of functions or resources on which you want to standardize and which you will use in several different programs. The DLL is a particularly good solution for managing these, especially if some of the programs using your standard facilities are likely to be executing concurrently.

❑ You have a complex application that involves several programs and a lot of code but that has sets of functions or resources that may be shared among several of the programs in the application. Using a DLL for common functionality or common resources enables you to manage and develop these with a great deal of independence from the program modules that use them and can simplify program maintenance.

❑ You have developed a set of standard application-oriented classes derived from MFC that you anticipate using in several programs. By packaging the implementation of these classes in an extension DLL, you can make using them in several programs very straightforward, and in the process provide the possibility of being able to improve the internals of the classes without affecting the applications that use them.

❑ You have developed a brilliant set of functions that provide an easy-to-use but amazingly powerful tool kit for an application area that just about everybody wants to dabble in. You can readily package your functions in a regular DLL and distribute them in this form.

There are also other circumstances where you may choose to use DLLs, such as when you want to be able to dynamically load and unload libraries, or to select different modules at run time. You could even use them to ease the development and updating of your applications generally.

The best way of understanding how to use a DLL is to create one and try it out. Let's do that now.

Writing DLLs

There are two aspects to writing a DLL that you'll look at: how you actually write a DLL and how you define what's to be accessible in the DLL to programs that use it. As a practical example of writing a DLL, you'll create an extension DLL to add a set of application classes to the MFC. You'll then extend this DLL by adding variables available to programs using it.

Writing and Using an Extension DLL

You can create an MFC extension DLL to contain the shape classes for the Sketcher application. Although this will not bring any major advantages to the program, it demonstrates how you can write an extension DLL without involving you in the overhead of entering a lot of new code.

The starting point is Application Wizard, so create a new project by pressing Ctrl+Shift+N and choosing the project type as MFC and the template as MFC DLL, as shown in Figure 19-4.

This selection identifies that you are creating a project for an MFC-based DLL with the name ExtDLLExample. Click the OK button and select Application Settings in the next window that is displayed. The window looks as shown in Figure 19-5.

Here, you can see three radio buttons corresponding to the three types of MFC-based DLL that I discussed earlier. You should choose the third option, as shown in the figure.

The two checkboxes below the first group of three radio buttons allow you to include code to support Automation and Windows Sockets in the DLL. These are both advanced capabilities within a Windows program, so you don't need either of them here. **Automation** provides the potential for hosting objects created and managed by one application inside another. **Windows Sockets** provides classes and functionality to enable your program to communicate over a network, but you won't be getting into this as it's beyond the scope of the book. You can click the Finish button and complete creation of the project.

When you first created the Sketcher application, you opted out of using Unicode. If the DLL is to work with Sketcher it must be consistent with this. Click the `Project > Properties...` menu item and select General in the Configuration Properties branch in the left pane of the dialog. Change the value of the Character Set option to "Use Multibyte Character Set" from the drop-down list in the value column.

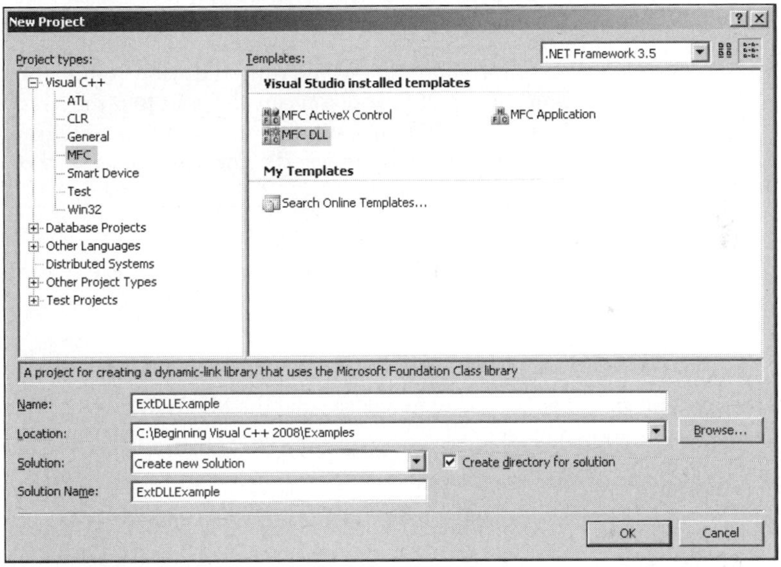

Figure 19-4

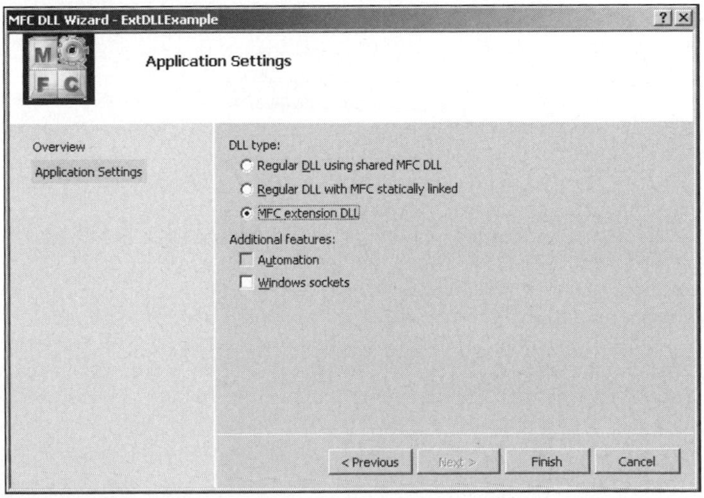

Figure 19-5

Now that the MFC DLL wizard has done its stuff, you can look into the code that has been generated on your behalf. If you look at the contents of the project in the Solution Explorer pane, you'll see that the MFC DLL wizard has generated several files, including a **.txt** file that contains a description of the other files. You can read what they're all for in the **.txt** file, but the two shown in the following table are the ones of immediate interest in implementing our DLL.

Filename	Contents
dllmain.cpp	This contains the function DllMain() and is the primary source file for the DLL.
ExtDLLExample.def	The information in this file is used during compilation. It contains the name of the DLL, and you can also add to it the definitions of those items in the DLL that are to be accessible to a program using the DLL. You'll use an alternative and somewhat easier way of identifying such items in the example.

When your DLL is loaded, the first thing that happens is that DllMain() is executed, so perhaps you should take a look at that first.

Understanding DllMain()

If you look at the contents of dllmain.cpp, you will see that the MFC DLL wizard has generated a version of DllMain() for you, as shown here:

```
extern "C" int APIENTRY
DllMain(HINSTANCE hInstance, DWORD dwReason, LPVOID lpReserved)
{
    // Remove this if you use lpReserved
    UNREFERENCED_PARAMETER(lpReserved);

    if (dwReason == DLL_PROCESS_ATTACH)
    {
        TRACE0("EXTDLLEXAMPLE.DLL Initializing!\n");

        // Extension DLL one-time initialization
        if (!AfxInitExtensionModule(ExtDLLExampleDLL, hInstance))
            return 0;

        // Insert this DLL into the resource chain
        // NOTE: If this Extension DLL is being implicitly linked to by
        //   an MFC Regular DLL (such as an ActiveX Control)
        //   instead of an MFC application, then you will want to
        //   remove this line from DllMain and put it in a separate
        //   function exported from this Extension DLL.  The Regular DLL
        //   that uses this Extension DLL should then explicitly call that
        //   function to initialize this Extension DLL.  Otherwise,
        //   the CDynLinkLibrary object will not be attached to the
        //   Regular DLL's resource chain, and serious problems will
```

```
        //  result.

        new CDynLinkLibrary(ExtDLLExampleDLL);
    }
    else if (dwReason == DLL_PROCESS_DETACH)
    {
        TRACE0("EXTDLLEXAMPLE.DLL Terminating!\n");
        // Terminate the library before destructors are called
        AfxTermExtensionModule(ExtDLLExampleDLL);
    }
    return 1;    // ok
}
```

There are three arguments passed to `DllMain()` when it is called. The first argument, `hInstance`, is a handle that has been created by Windows to identify the DLL. Every task under Windows has an instance handle which identifies it uniquely. The second argument, `dwReason`, indicates the reason why `DllMain()` is being called. You can see this argument being tested in the `if` statements in `DllMain()`. The first `if` tests for the value `DLL_PROCESS_ATTACH`, which indicates that a program is about to use the DLL, and the second `if` tests for the value `DLL_PROCESS_DETACH`, which indicates that a program has finished using the DLL. The third argument is a pointer that's reserved for use by Windows, so you can ignore it.

When the DLL is first used by a program, it's loaded into memory, and the `DllMain()` function is executed with the argument `dwReason` set to `DLL_PROCESS_ATTACH`. This results in the Windows API function `AfxInitExtensionModule()` being called to initialize the DLL and an object of the class `CDynLinkLibrary` created on the heap. Windows uses objects of this class to manage extension DLLs. If you need to add initialization of your own, you can add it to the end of this block. Any cleanup you require for your DLL can be added to the block for the second `if` statement.

Adding Classes to the Extension DLL

You'll use the DLL to contain the implementation of the Sketcher shape classes, so move the files `Elements.h` and `Elements.cpp` from the folder containing the source for Sketcher to the folder containing the DLL. Be sure that you *move* rather than copy the files. Because the DLL is going to supply the shape classes for Sketcher, you don't want to leave them in the source code for Sketcher.

You'll also need to remove `Elements.cpp` from the Sketcher project. To do this, open the Sketcher project, highlight `Elements.cpp` in the Solution Explorer pane by clicking the file, and then press Delete. If you don't do this, the compiler complains that it can't find the file when you try to compile the project. Follow the same procedure to get rid of `Elements.h` from the `Header Files` folder in the Solution Explorer pane.

The shape classes use the constants that you have defined in the file `OurConstants.h`, so *copy* this file from the Sketcher project folder to the folder containing the DLL. Note that the variable `VERSION_NUMBER` is used exclusively by the `IMPLEMENT_SERIAL()` macros in the shape classes, so you could delete it from the `OurConstants.h` file used in the Sketcher program.

You now need to add `Elements.cpp` containing the implementation of our shape classes to the extension DLL project, so open the `ExtDLLExample` project, select the menu option `Project > Add Existing Item` and choose the file `Elements.cpp` from the list box in the dialog box, as shown in Figure 19-6.

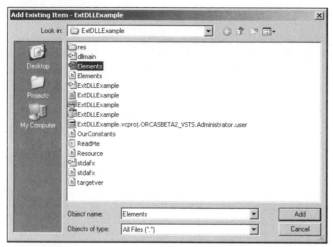

Figure 19-6

The project should also include the files containing the definitions of the shape classes and your constants, so repeat the process for `Elements.h` and `OurConstants.h` to add these to the project. You can add multiple files in a single step by holding down the Ctrl key while you select from the list of files in the Add Existing Item dialog box. You should eventually see all the files in the Solution Explorer pane and all the shape classes displayed in the Class View pane for the project.

Exporting Classes from the Extension DLL

The names of the classes defined in the DLL that are to be accessible in programs that use it must be identified in some way so that the appropriate links can be established between a program and the DLL. As you saw earlier, one way of doing this is by adding information to the `.def` file for the DLL. This involves adding what are called **decorated names** to the DLL and associating the decorated name with a unique identifying numeric value called an **ordinal**. A decorated name for an object is a name generated by the compiler, which adds an additional string to the name you gave to the object. This additional string provides information about the type of the object or, in the case of a function for example, information about the types of the parameters to the function. Among other things, it ensures that everything has a unique identifier and enables the linker to distinguish overloaded functions from each other.

Obtaining decorated names and assigning ordinals to export items from a DLL is a lot of work and isn't the best or the easiest approach with Windows. A much easier way to identify the classes that you want to export from the DLL is to modify the class definitions in `Elements.h` to include the keyword `AFX_EXT_CLASS` before each class name, as shown in the following for the `CLine` class:

```
// Class defining a line object
class AFX_EXT_CLASS CLine: public CElement
{
DECLARE_SERIAL(CLine)

public:
  virtual void Draw(CDC* pDC, CElement* pElement=0); // Function to display a line
```

```
    virtual void Move(CSize& aSize);                        // Function to move an element

    // Constructor for a line object
    CLine(CPoint Start, CPoint End, COLORREF aColor, int PenWidth);

    virtual void Serialize(CArchive& ar);// Serialize function for CLine

protected:
  CPoint m_StartPoint;                    // Start point of line
  CPoint m_EndPoint;                      // End point of line

  CLine(void);                            // Default constructor - should not be used
};
```

The AFX_EXT_CLASS keyword indicates that the class is to be exported from the DLL. This has the effect of making the complete class available to any program using the DLL and automatically allows access to any of the data and functions in the public interface of the class. The collection of things in a DLL that are accessible by a program using it is referred to as the **interface** to the DLL. The process of making an object part of the interface to a DLL is referred to as **exporting** the object.

You need to add the keyword AFX_EXT_CLASS to all of the other shape classes, including the base class CElement. Why is it necessary to export CElement from the DLL? After all, programs create only objects of the classes derived from CElement, and not objects of the class CElement itself. The reason is that you have declared public members of CElement which form part of the interface to the derived shape classes, and which are almost certainly going to be required by programs using the DLL. If you don't export the CElement class, functions such as GetBoundRect() will not be available.

The final modification needed is to add the directive:

```
    #include <afxtempl.h>
```

to stdafx.h in the DLL project so that the definition of CList is available.

You have done everything necessary to add the shape classes to the DLL. All that remains is for you compile and link the project to create the DLL.

Building a DLL

You build the DLL in exactly the same way as you build any other project — by using the Build > Build Solution menu option or selecting the corresponding toolbar button. The output produced is somewhat different, though. You can see the files that are produced in the debug subfolder of the project folder for a Debug build, or in the release subfolder for a Release build. The executable code for the DLL is contained in the file ExtDLLExample.dll. This file needs to be available to execute a program that uses the DLL. The file ExtDLLExample.lib is an import library file that contains the definitions of the items that are exported from the DLL, and it must be available to the linker when a program using the DLL is linked.

If you find the DLL build fails because Elements.cpp contains an #include directive for Sketcher.h, just remove it. On my system the Class Wizard added this #include directive when creating the code for the CElement class, but it is not required.

Using the Extension DLL in Sketcher

You now have no information in the Sketcher program on the shape classes because you moved the files containing the class definitions and implementations to the DLL project. However, the compiler still needs to know where the shape classes are coming from in order to compile the code for the program. The Sketcher program needs to include a header file that defines the classes that are to be imported from the DLL. It must also identify the classes as external to the project by using the AFX_EXT_CLASS macro in the class definitions in exactly the same way as for exporting the classes from the DLL. You can therefore just copy the file Elements.h from the DLL project to the folder containing the Sketcher source because it contains exactly what is required to import the classes into Sketcher. It would be a good idea to identify this file as specifying the imports from the DLL in the Sketcher source code. You could do this by changing its name to DllImports.h, in which case you'll need to change the #include directives that are already in the Sketcher program for Elements.h to refer to the new file name (these occur in Sketcher.cpp, SketcherDoc.h, and SketcherView.cpp). You should also add the DllImports.h file to the project by right-clicking the Header Files folder in the Solution Explorer pane and selecting Add > Existing Item from the context menu.

When you rebuild the Sketcher application, the linker needs to have the ExtDLLExample.lib file identified as a dependency for the project because this file contains information about the contents of the DLL. Right-click Sketcher in the Solution Explorer pane and select Properties from the pop-up. You can then expand the Linker folder and select Input in the left pane of the Properties window. You can then enter the name of the .lib file as an additional dependency as shown in Figure 19-7.

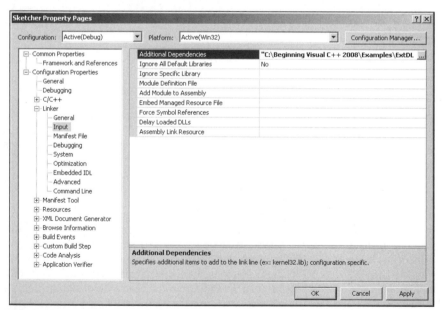

Figure 19-7

Figure 19-7 shows the entry for the debug version of Sketcher. The .lib file for the DLL is in the Debug folder within the DLL project folder. If you create a release version of Sketcher, you'll also need the release version of the DLL available to the linker and its .lib file, so you'll have to enter the fully qualified name of the .lib file for the release version of the DLL, corresponding to the release version of Sketcher. The file to which the properties apply is selected in the Configuration drop-down list box in the Properties window. You have only one external dependency, but you can enter several when this is necessary by clicking the button to the right of the text box for input. Because the full path to the .lib file has been entered here, the linker will know not only that ExtDLLExample.lib is an external dependency but also where it is.

> *Be aware that if the complete path to the .lib file contains spaces (as in the example here), you'll need to enclose it within quotation marks for the linker to recognize it correctly.*

You can now build the Sketcher application once more, and everything should compile and link as usual. However, if you try to execute the program, you see the message box shown in Figure 19-8.

Figure 19-8

This is one of the less cryptic error messages — it's fairly clear what's gone wrong. To enable Windows to load a DLL for a program, it's usual to place the DLL in your \WINNT\System folder. If it's not in this folder, Windows searches the folder containing the executable Sketcher.exe. If it isn't there you get the error message. Because you probably don't want to clutter up your \WINNT\System folder unnecessarily, you can copy ExtDllExample.dll from the debug folder of the DLL project to the debug folder for Sketcher. Sketcher should execute exactly as before, except that now it uses the shape classes in the DLL you have created.

Files Required to Use a DLL

From what you have just seen in the context of using the DLL you created in the Sketcher program, you can conclude that three files must be available to use a DLL in a program, as shown in the following table.

Extension	Contents
.h	Defines those items that are exported from a DLL and enables the compiler to deal properly with references to such items in the source code of a program using the DLL. The .h file needs to be added to the source code for the program using the DLL.
.lib	Defines the items exported by a DLL in a form, which enables the linker to deal with references to exported items when linking a program that uses a DLL.
.dll	Contains the executable code for the DLL, which is loaded by Windows when a program using the DLL is executed.

If you plan to distribute program code in the form of a DLL for use by other programmers, you need to distribute all three files in the package. For applications that already use the DLL, just the .dll is required along with the .exe file.

Exporting Variables and Functions from a DLL

You've seen how you can export classes from an extension DLL using the AFX_EXT_CLASS keyword. You can also export *objects* of classes that are defined in a DLL, as well as ordinary variables and functions. These can be exported from any kind of DLL by using the attribute dllexport to identify them. By using dllexport to identify class objects, variables, or functions that are to be exported from a DLL, you avoid getting involved in the complications of modifying the .def file and, as a consequence, you make defining the interface to the DLL a straightforward matter.

Don't be misled into thinking that the approach you're taking to exporting things from your DLL makes the .def file method redundant. The .def file approach is more complicated — which is why you're taking the easy way out — but it offers distinct advantages in many situations over the approach you're taking. This is particularly true in the context of products that are distributed widely, and are likely to be developed over time. One major plus is that a .def file enables you to define the ordinals that correspond to your exported functions. This allows you to add more exported functions later and assign new ordinals to them, so the ordinals for the original set of functions remain the same. This means that someone using a new version of the DLL with a program built to use the old version doesn't have to relink their application.

You must use the dllexport attribute in conjunction with the keyword _declspec when you identify an item to be exported. For example, the statement

```
_declspec(dllexport) double aValue = 1.5;
```

defines the variable aValue of type double with an initial value of 1.5 and identifies it as a variable that is to be available to programs using the DLL. To export a function from a DLL, you use the dllexport attribute in a similar manner. For example:

```
_declspec(dllexport) CString FindWinner(CString* Teams);
```

This statement exports the function FindWinner() from the DLL.

To avoid the slightly cumbersome notation for specifying the dllexport attribute, you can simplify it by using a preprocessor directive:

```
#define DllExport _declspec(dllexport)
```

With this definition, you can rewrite the two previous examples as:

```
DllExport double aValue = 1.5;
DllExport CString FindWinner(CString* Teams);
```

This notation is much more economical, as well as easier to read, so you may want to adopt this approach when coding your DLLs.

Obviously, only symbols that represent objects with global scope can be exported from a DLL. Variables and class objects that are local to a function in a DLL cease to exist when execution of a function is completed, in just the same way as in a function in a normal program. Attempting to export such symbols results in a compile-time error.

Importing Symbols into a Program

The `dllexport` attribute identifies the symbols in a DLL that form part of the interface. If you want to use these in a program, you must make sure that they are correspondingly identified as being imported from the DLL. This is done by using the `dllimport` keyword in declarations for the symbols to be imported in a `.h` file. You can simplify the notation by using the same technique you applied to the `dllexport` attribute. Define `DllImport` with the directive:

```
#define DllImport _declspec(dllimport)
```

You can now import the `aValue` variable and the `FindWinner()` function into a program with the declarations:

```
DllImport double aValue;
DllImport CString FindWinner(CString* Teams);
```

These statements would appear in a `.h` file that would be included into the `.cpp` files in the program that referenced these symbols.

Implementing the Export of Symbols from a DLL

You could extend the extension DLL for Sketcher to make the symbols defining shape types and colors available in the interface to it. You can then remove the definitions that you have in the Sketcher program and import the definitions of these symbols from the extension DLL.

You can modify the source code for the DLL first to add the symbols for shape element types and colors to its interface. To export the element types and colors, they must be global variables. As global variables, it would be better if they appeared in a `.cpp` file, rather than a `.h` file, so move the definitions of these out of the `OurConstants.h` file to the beginning of `Elements.cpp` in the DLL source. You can then apply the `dllexport` attribute to their definitions in the `Elements.cpp` file, as follows:

```
// Definitions of constants and identification of symbols to be exported

#define DllExport __declspec(dllexport)

// Element type definitions
// Each type value must be unique
DllExport extern const unsigned int LINE = 101U;
DllExport extern const unsigned int RECTANGLE = 102U;
DllExport extern const unsigned int CIRCLE = 103U;
DllExport extern const unsigned int CURVE = 104U;
DllExport extern const unsigned int TEXT = 105U;
////////////////////////////////////

// Color values for drawing
DllExport extern const COLORREF BLACK = RGB(0,0,0);
DllExport extern const COLORREF RED = RGB(255,0,0);
DllExport extern const COLORREF GREEN = RGB(0,255,0);
DllExport extern const COLORREF BLUE = RGB(0,0,255);
DllExport extern const COLORREF SELECT_COLOR = RGB(255,0,180);
////////////////////////////////////
```

Add these to the beginning of `Elements.cpp`, after the `#include` directives. You first define the symbol `DllExport` to simplify the specification of the variables to be exported, as you saw earlier. You then assign the attribute `dllexport` to each of the element types and colors.

Notice that the `extern` specifier has also been added to the definitions of these variables. The reason for this is the effect of the `const` modifier, which indicates to the compiler that the values are constants and shouldn't be modified in the program, which was what you wanted. However, by default the `const` keyword also specifies the variables as having internal linkage, so they are local to the file in which they appear. You want to export these variables to another program so you have to add the `extern` modifier to override the default linkage specification due to the `const` modifier and ensure that they have external linkage. Symbols that are assigned external linkage are global and so can be exported. Of course, if the variables didn't have the `const` modifier applied to them, you wouldn't need to add `extern` because they would be global automatically as long as they appeared at global scope.

The `OurConstants.h` file now contains only one definition:

```
// Definitions of constants
#pragma once

   // Define the program version number for use in serialization
   UINT VERSION_NUMBER = 1;
```

Of course, this is still required because it is used in the `IMPLEMENT_SERIAL()` macros in `Elements.cpp`. You can now build the DLL once again, so it's ready to use in the Sketcher program. Don't forget to copy the latest version of the `.dll` file to the Sketcher project `Debug` folder.

Using Exported Symbols

To make the symbols exported from the DLL available in the Sketcher program, you need to specify them as imported from the DLL. You can do this by adding the identification of the imported symbols to the file `DllImports.h`, which contains the definitions for the imported classes. In this way, you'll have one file specifying all the items imported from the DLL. The statements that appear in this file are as follows:

```
// Variables defined in the shape DLL ExtDLLExample.dll
#pragma once

#define DllImport __declspec( dllimport )

// Import element type declarations
// Each type value must be unique
DllImport extern const unsigned int LINE;
DllImport extern const unsigned int RECTANGLE;
DllImport extern const unsigned int CIRCLE;
DllImport extern const unsigned int CURVE;
DllImport extern const unsigned int TEXT;
/////////////////////////////////////

// Import color values for drawing
DllImport extern const COLORREF BLACK;
DllImport extern const COLORREF RED;
```

```
DllImport extern const COLORREF GREEN;
DllImport extern const COLORREF BLUE;
DllImport extern const COLORREF SELECT_COLOR;
//////////////////////////////////////

// Plus the definitions for the shape classes...
```

This defines and uses the `DllImport` symbol to simplify these declarations, in the way that you saw earlier. This means that the `OurConstants.h` file in the Sketcher project is now redundant, so you can delete it, along with the `#include` for it in `Sketcher.h` and `SketcherView.cpp`.

It looks as though you've done everything necessary to use the new version of the DLL with Sketcher, but you haven't. If you try to recompile Sketcher, you'll get error messages for the `switch` statement in the `CreateElement()` member of `CSketcherView`.

The values in the case statements must be constant, but although you have given the element type variables the attribute `const`, the compiler has no access to these values because they are defined in the DLL, not in the Sketcher program. The compiler, therefore, can't determine what these constant case values are, and flags an error. The simplest way round this problem is to replace the `switch` statement in the `CreateElement()` function by a series of `if` statements, as follows:

```
// Create an element of the current type
CElement* CSketcherView::CreateElement()
{
  // Get a pointer to the document for this view
  CSketcherDoc* pDoc = GetDocument();
  ASSERT_VALID(pDoc);                        // Verify the pointer is good

  // Now select the element using the type stored in the document
  unsigned int ElementType = pDoc->GetElementType();
  COLORREF ElementColor = pDoc->GetElementColor();
  int PenWidth = pDoc->GetPenWidth();
  if(ElementType == RECTANGLE)
    return new CRectangle(m_FirstPoint, m_SecondPoint, ElementColor, PenWidth);

  if(ElementType == CIRCLE)
    return new CCircle(m_FirstPoint, m_SecondPoint, ElementColor, PenWidth);

  if(ElementType == CURVE)
    return new CCurve(m_FirstPoint, m_SecondPoint, ElementColor, PenWidth);
  else
    // Always default to a line
    return new CLine(m_FirstPoint, m_SecondPoint, ElementColor, PenWidth);
}
```

You've added local variables to store the current element type and color and the pen width that are retrieved from the document object. The element type is tested against the element types imported from the DLL in the series of `if` statements. This does exactly the same job as the `switch` statement, but has no requirement for the element type constants to be known explicitly. If you now build Sketcher with these changes added, it executes using the DLL, using the exported symbols as well as the exported shape classes.

Summary

In this chapter, you've learned the basics of how to construct and use a dynamic link library. The most important points you have looked at in this context are:

❑ Dynamic link libraries provide a means of linking to standard functions dynamically when a program executes, rather than incorporating them into the executable module for a program.

❑ An Application Wizard-generated program links to a version of MFC stored in DLLs by default.

❑ A single copy of a DLL in memory can be used by several programs executing concurrently.

❑ An extension DLL is so called because it extends the set of classes in MFC. An extension DLL must be used if you want to export MFC-based classes or objects of MFC classes from a DLL. An extension DLL can also export ordinary functions and global variables.

❑ A regular DLL can be used if you want to export only ordinary functions or global variables that aren't instances of MFC classes.

❑ You can export classes from an extension DLL by using the keyword AFX_EXT_CLASS preceding the class name in the DLL.

❑ You can export ordinary functions and global variables from a DLL by assigning the dllexport attribute to them using the _declspec keyword.

❑ You can import the classes exported from an extension DLL by using the .h file from the DLL that contains the class definitions using the AFX_EXT_CLASS keyword.

❑ You can import ordinary functions and global variables that are exported from a DLL by assigning the dllimport attribute to their declarations in your program by using the _declspec keyword.

Exercises

You can download the source code for the examples in the book and the solutions to the following exercise from www.wrox.com.

1. This is the last time you'll be amending this version of the Sketcher program, so try this. Using the DLL we've just created, implement a Sketcher document viewer — in other words, a program that simply opens a document created by Sketcher and displays the whole thing in a window at once. You needn't worry about editing, scrolling, or printing, but you will have to work out the scaling required to make a big picture fit in a little window!

Connecting to Data Sources

In this chapter, I will show you to how you can interface to a database using Visual C++ and the MFC and access the data from it. This is by no means a comprehensive discussion of the possibilities, because a full discussion of database application development using Visual C++ would occupy a very substantial book in its own right. In this chapter, however, you will look at how you can read from a database, and in the next chapter you will explore the basics of how you can update a database. Of course, you can access data sources in CLR applications, and you'll look at this in Chapter 23.

In this chapter, you will learn about:

- ❑ SQL and how it is used
- ❑ How to retrieve data using the SQL SELECT operation
- ❑ What database services are supported by MFC
- ❑ What a recordset object is, and how it links to a relational database table
- ❑ How a recordset object can retrieve information from a database
- ❑ How a record view can display information from a recordset
- ❑ How to create a project for a database program
- ❑ How to add recordsets to your program
- ❑ How to handle multiple record views

Database Basics

This is not the place for a detailed dissertation on database technology, but I do need to make sure that we have a common understanding of database terminology. Databases come in a variety of flavors but the majority are **relational databases** these days. It is relational databases that I will be talking about throughout this chapter.

In a relational database, your data is organized into one or more **tables**. You can think of a database table as a spreadsheet table, made up of rows and columns. Each row contains information about a single item, and each column contains the information about the same characteristic from every item.

A **record** is equivalent to a row in the spreadsheet. Each record consists of elements of data that make up that record. These elements of data are known as **fields**. A field is a cell in the table identified by the column heading. The term *field* can also represent the whole column.

You can best see the structure of a table with the diagram shown in Figure 20-1.

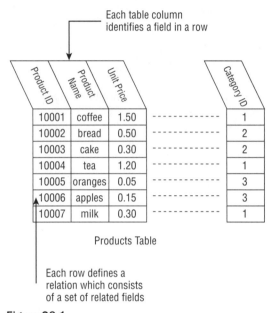

Each table column
identifies a field in a row

Products Table

Each row defines a
relation which consists
of a set of related fields

Figure 20-1

Here you can see that this table is being used to store information on a line of products. Unsurprisingly then, the table is called **Products Table**. Each record in the table, represented by a row in the diagram, contains the data for one product. The description of a product is separated into fields in the table, with each field storing information about one aspect of a product: Product Name, Unit Price, and so on.

Although the fields in this table store only relatively simple information (character strings or numeric values), the type of data you decide to put in a particular field can be virtually anything you want. You could store times, dates, pictures, or even binary objects in a database.

A table usually has at least one field that can be used to identify each record uniquely and in the example above the **Product ID** is a likely candidate. A field in a table that serves to identify each record within the table is called a **key**; a key that uniquely identifies each record in a table is referred to as a **primary key**. In some cases, a table may have no single field that uniquely identifies each record. In this circumstance, two or more key fields may be used, in which case the combination of fields represents the primary key.

The relational aspect of a database, and the importance of keys, comes into play when you store related information in separate tables. You define relationships between the tables, using keys, and use the relationships to find associated information stored in your database. Note that the tables themselves don't know about relationships, just as the table doesn't understand the bits of data stored in it. It is the program that accesses the data that must use the information in the tables to pull together related data, whether that program is Access, SQL Server, or your own program written in C++. These are known collectively as **relational database management systems** or **RDBMS**s.

A real-world, well-designed relational database usually consists of a large number of tables. Each table usually has only a few fields and many records. The reason for only having a few fields in each table is to increase query performance. Without going into the details of database optimization, have faith that it's much faster to query many tables with a few fields each than to query a single table with many fields.

I can extend the example shown in the previous diagram to illustrate a relational database with two tables: Products and Categories from the Northwind database as Figure 20-2 shows.

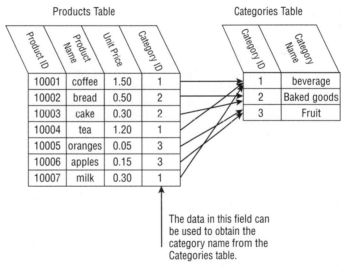

Figure 20-2

As you can see from the diagram, the **Category ID** field is used to relate the information stored in the two tables. Category ID uniquely identifies a category record in the Categories table, so it is a primary key for that table. In the Products Table, the Category ID field is used to relate a product record to a category, so the field is termed a **foreign key** for that table; foreign keys need not be unique and often aren't.

Relational databases can be created and manipulated in numerous ways. There are a large number of RDBMSs on the market that provide a wide range of facilities for creating and manipulating database information. Obviously, it's possible for you to add and delete records in a database table, and to update the fields in a record, although typically there are controls within the RDBMS to limit such activities, based on the authorization level of the user. As well as accessing information from a single table in a database, you can combine records from two or more tables into a new table, based on their relationships, and retrieve information from that. Combining tables in this way is called a **table join**. To program all these kinds of operations for a relational database, you can use a language known as **SQL**, which is supported by most RDBMSs and programming languages.

A Little SQL

SQL (often pronounced "sequel") stands for **S**tructured **Q**uery **L**anguage. It's a relatively simple language, designed specifically for accessing and modifying information in relational databases. It was originally developed at IBM in a mainframe environment, but is now used throughout the computing world. SQL doesn't actually exist as a software package by itself — it's usually hosted by some other environment, whether that's an RDBMS or as a library implemented for a programming language, such as Visual Basic.NET, Java or C++. The environment hosting SQL provides for mundane things such as regular I/O and talking to the operating system, while SQL is used to query the database.

MFC support for databases uses SQL to specify queries and other operations on database tables. These operations are provided by a set of specialized classes. You'll see how to use some of these in the example that you write later in this chapter.

SQL has statements to retrieve, sort, and update records from a table, to add and delete records and fields, to join tables and to compute totals, as well as a lot of other capabilities for creating and managing database tables. I won't be going into all the possible programming options available in SQL, but I'll discuss the details sufficiently to enable you to understand what's happening in the examples that you write, even though you may not have seen any SQL before.

When you use SQL in an MFC-based program, you won't need to write complete SQL statements for the most part because the framework takes care of assembling a complete statement and supplying it to the database engine you're using. Nevertheless, I'll discuss how typical SQL statements are written in their entirety, so that you get a feel for how the language statements are structured.

SQL statements are usually but not necessarily written with a terminating semicolon (just like C++ statements), and by convention keywords in the language are written in capital letters. Take a look at a few examples of SQL statements and see how they work.

Retrieving Data Using SQL

To retrieve data, you use the SELECT statement. In fact, it's surprising how much of what you want to do with a database is covered by the SELECT statement, which operates on one or more tables in your database. The result of executing a SELECT statement is always a **recordset**, a collection of data produced using the information from the tables you supply in the detail of the statement. The data in the recordset is organized in the form of a table, with named columns that are from the tables you specified in the SELECT statement, and rows or records that are selected, based on conditions specified in the SELECT statement. The recordset generated by a SELECT statement might have only one record, or might even be empty.

Perhaps the simplest retrieval operation on a database is to access all the records in a single table, so given that the database includes a table called Products, you can obtain all the records in this table with the following SQL statement:

```
SELECT * FROM Products;
```

The * indicates that you want all the fields in the database. The parameter following the keyword FROM defines the table from which the fields are to be selected. The records that are returned by the SELECT statement are not constrained in any way, so you'll get all of them. A little later you'll see how to constrain the records that are selected.

If you wanted all the records but needed to retrieve only specific fields in each record, you could specify these by using the field names separated by commas in place of the asterisk in the previous example. Here's an example of a statement that would do this:

```
SELECT ProductID,UnitPrice FROM Products;
```

This statement selects all the records from the `Products` table, but only the `ProductID` and `UnitPrice` fields for each record. This produces a table with just the two fields specified here.

The field names that I've used here don't contain spaces, but they could. Where a name contains spaces, standard SQL says that it has to be written between double quotes. If the fields had the names `Product ID` and `Unit Price`, you would write the SELECT statement as:

```
SELECT "Product ID","Unit Price" FROM Products;
```

Using double quotes with names, as I have done here, is a bit inconvenient in the C++ context, as you need to be able to pass SQL statements as strings. In C++, double quotes are already used as character string delimiters, so there would be confusion if you tried to enclose the names of database objects (tables or fields) in double quotes. For this reason, when you reference database table or field names that include spaces in the Visual C++ environment, you should enclose them within square brackets rather than double quotes. Thus, you would write the field names from the example as `[Product ID]` and `[Unit Price]`. You will see this notation in action in the database program that you'll write later in this chapter.

Choosing Records

Unlike fields, records in a table do not have names. The only way to choose particular records is by applying some condition or restriction on the contents of one or more of the fields in a record, so that only records meeting the condition are selected. This is done by adding a WHERE clause to the SELECT statement. The parameter following the WHERE keyword defines the condition to be used to select records.

You could select the records in the Products table that have a particular value for the `Category ID` field with the statement:

```
SELECT * FROM Products WHERE [Category ID] = 1;
```

This selects just those records where the `Category ID` field has the value 1, so from the table I illustrated earlier, you would get the records for coffee, tea, and milk. Note that a single equals sign is used to specify a check for equality in SQL, not == as you would use in C++.

You can use other comparison operators, such as <, >, <= and >=, to specify the condition in a WHERE clause. You can also combine logical expressions with AND and OR. To place a further restriction on the records selected in the last example, you could write:

```
SELECT * FROM Products WHERE [Category ID] = 1 AND [Unit Price] > 0.5;
```

In this case, the resulting table just contains two records because milk would be out as it's too cheap. Only records with a `Category ID` of 1 and a `Unit Price` value greater than 0.5 are selected by this statement.

Joining Tables Using SQL

You can also use the SELECT statement to join tables together, although it's a little more complicated than you might imagine. Suppose you have two tables: Products with three records and three fields, and Orders with three records and four fields. These are illustrated in Figure 20-3.

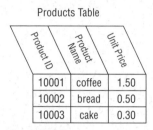

Products Table | Orders Table

Product ID	Product Name	Unit Price
10001	coffee	1.50
10002	bread	0.50
10003	cake	0.30

Order ID	Product ID	Customer ID	Quantity
20001	10002	VEAD	50
20002	10003	TOMS	40
20003	10002	VEAD	30

Figure 20-3

Here, you have a meager product set in the Products table, consisting of just coffee, bread, and cake, and you have three orders as shown in the Orders table — but you haven't managed to sell any coffee.

You could join these tables together with the SELECT statement:

```
SELECT * FROM Products,Orders;
```

This statement creates a recordset using the records from both the tables specified. The recordset has seven fields — three from the Products table and four from the Orders table — but how many records does it have? The answer is illustrated in Figure 20-4.

The recordset produced by the SELECT statement has nine records that are produced by combining each record from the Products table with every record from the Orders table, so all possible combinations are included. This may not be exactly what is required or what you expected. Arbitrarily including all combinations of records from one table with another is of limited value. The meaning of a record containing details of the bread product and an order for cake is hard to fathom. You could also end up with an incredibly big table in a real situation. If you combine a table containing 100 products with one containing 500 orders and you do not constrain the join operation, the resulting table will contain 50,000 records!

To get a useful join, you usually need to add a WHERE clause to the SELECT statement. With the tables we have been using, one condition that would make sense would be to only allow records where the Product ID from one table matched the same field in the other table. This would combine each record from the Products table with the records from the Orders table that related to that product. The statement to do this is:

```
SELECT * FROM Products,Orders
                    WHERE Products.[Product ID] = Orders.[Product ID];
```

Notice how a specific field for a particular table is identified here. You add the table name as a prefix and separate it from the field name with a period. This qualification of the field name is essential where the same field name is used in both tables. Without the table name, there's no way to know which of the two fields you mean. With this SELECT statement and the same table contents used previously, you'll get the recordset shown in Figure 20-5.

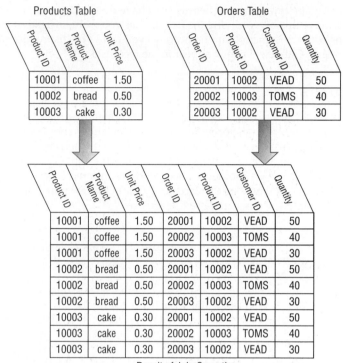

Figure 20-4

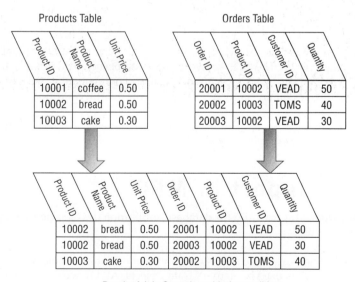

Result of Join Operation with the condition:
Products."Product ID" = Orders."Product ID"

Figure 20-5

Of course, this may still be unsatisfactory because you have two fields containing the Product ID, but you could easily remove this by specifying the field names you want, instead of the * in the SELECT statement. The columns with the same column name, however, would be distinguished by being qualified by the names of the original table when they appear in the recordset.

Sorting Records

When you retrieve data from a database using the SELECT statement, you will often want the records sorted in a particular order. With the previous example, the tables shown are already ordered, but in practice this is not necessarily the case. You might want to see the output of the last example sorted in a different way, depending on the circumstances. At one time, it might be convenient to have the records ordered by Customer ID, and on another occasion perhaps ordered by Quantity within Product ID. The ORDER BY clause added to the SELECT statement will do this for you. For example, you could refine the last SELECT statement by adding an ORDER BY clause:

```
SELECT * FROM Products,Orders
            WHERE Products.[Product ID] = Orders.[Product ID]
            ORDER BY [Customer ID];
```

The result of this is the same records that you obtained with the last example but with the records arranged so that the Customer ID field is in ascending sequence. Because the kind of data stored in a given field is known, the records are ordered according to the data type applicable to the field. In this case the order is alphabetical.

If you wanted to sort on two fields, Customer ID and Product ID say, and you wanted the records arranged in descending sequence, you would write:

```
SELECT * FROM Products,Orders
            WHERE Products.[Product ID] = Orders.[Product ID]
            ORDER BY [Customer ID] DESC, Products.[Product ID] DESC;
```

You must use the qualified name, Products.[Product ID], in the ORDER BY clause to avoid ambiguity, as you do in the WHERE clause. The DESC keyword at the end of each field in the ORDER BY statement specifies descending sequence for the sort operation. There is a complementary keyword, ASC, for ascending sequence, although this is usually omitted because it is the default condition.

This is by no means all there is to SQL or even all there is to the SELECT statement, but it's enough to get you through the database example that you will write.

Database Support in MFC

You have a choice when you use MFC for database application development, because two principle approaches are supported:

❑ **OLE DB:** Provides a way to access local and remote databases using COM, also referred to as ActiveX. OLE DB is used by ActiveX Data Objects (**ADO**), which provides an efficient way of accessing local and remote databases without the overhead implicit in the MFC.

❑ **ODBC: O**pen **DataB**ase **C**onnectivity, better known as **ODBC**, defines a standard function oriented interface for data access supported by a variety of database product vendors. I will be using ODBC to illustrate database application techniques in this chapter and the next.

To use OLE DB and ADO you need a good, deep knowledge of COM (ActiveX), so I will concentrate on ODBC, for which you just need some insight into SQL. When you are familiar with COM, ADO is well worth investigating if you want to get deep into database applications, as it is much more efficient than using ODBC.

ODBC is a system-independent interface to a database environment that requires an **ODBC driver** to be provided for each database system from which you want to manipulate data and there are ODBC drivers available for most databases. ODBC defines a set of function calls for database operations that are system-neutral, so using it is essentially function-call oriented. You can use a database with ODBC only if you have the DLL that contains the driver to work with that database application's file format. The purpose of the driver is to interface the standard set of system-independent calls for database operations that will be used in your program to the specifics of a particular database implementation.

MFC Classes Supporting ODBC

MFC support for ODBC is implemented through the five classes shown in the following table.

CDatabase	An object of this class represents a connection to your database. This connection must exist before you can carry out any operations on the database.
CRecordset	An object of a class derived from this class represents the result of an SQL SELECT operation — which is a set of records. The object makes one record from the set available at a time and provides functions for you to move backwards or forwards through the set.
CRecordView	An object of a class derived from this class is used to display current information from an associated recordset object. The view is essentially a dialog box, and the CRecordset object uses dialog data exchange (DDX) to access the data from the recordset.
CFieldExchange	This class provides for the exchange of data between the database and a recordset object. You would use this class directly only if you were implementing data exchange for custom data types.
CDBException	Objects of this class represent exceptions that occur within ODBC database operations.

You can best understand how database operations with MFC work by creating an example. I'll explain how you can apply the ODBC approach to accessing a sample database called Northwind Traders. The Northwind Traders database has the merit that it is easy to work with, but also contains a considerable variety of tables that are populated by realistic numbers of records. This gives you a lot of scope for experimentation, as well as providing some feel for how well your code will work in practice. It's easy to be lulled into a false sense of security by running your program against a test database where the numbers of tables and records within a table are trivial. It can be quite a surprise to find out how long transactions can take in a real-world context. One cautionary note about the Northwind database — you should not regard this as a good example of a database design, particularly with regard to security. It's very useful as a vehicle for understanding the mechanics of accessing a database though.

To develop and run the examples in this chapter and the next you need to have the Northwind Traders database installed; therefore, you'll need a database environment on your PC capable of supporting the

Northwind database. There are versions available at the time of writing for SQL Server Express, SQL Server 2000, and Microsoft Access. You can locate these by visiting www.microsoft.com/downloads/ details.aspx?FamilyID=06616212-0356-46A0-8DA2-EEBC53A68034. You'll find documentation on how to install the various versions available on the respective download page. The examples show the use of the Microsoft Access version of the Northwind Traders database, but the code is essentially the same whichever database system you are using.

If you don't have Microsoft Access installed but you still want to try the example in this chapter you can download a trial version by clicking Download a Free Trial at http://office.microsoft.com/ en-us/access/default.aspx.

Creating a Database Application

For the example, I'll show how to use three related tables in the Northwind database.

In the first step, you'll create a program to display records from the Products table in the database. You will then add code to allow you to examine all the orders for a given product using two other tables. Finally, you'll access the Customers table to enable the customer details for an order to be displayed. Before you can start with the code, you need to identify the database to the operating system.

Registering an ODBC Database

Before you can use an ODBC database, it needs to be registered. You do this through the Control Panel that you access from the Windows Start menu. In the Control Panel, select the Administrative Tools icon then select Data Sources (ODBC) from the list. You should see the dialog box shown in Figure 20-6.

This shows all the data sources that have been registered. You have the possibility of registering a database as a User DSN accessible only to you, as a System DSN accessible to all users on the machine, or as a File DSN that will be available generally, possibly over a network. I'll describe how you register the database as a User DSN.

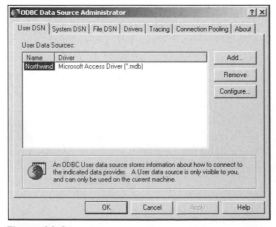

Figure 20-6

When you then click the Add button in the ODBC Data Source Administrator dialog, you will see the Create New Data Source dialog box shown in Figure 20-7.

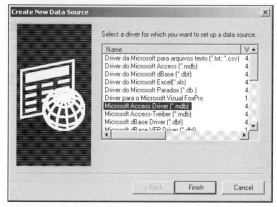

Figure 20-7

Here you must select from the list of ODBC drivers the one that you are going to use — Microsoft Access Driver (*.mdb) (or if you are using SQL Server, the driver for that). This should have been installed automatically with the typical setup when you installed Windows XP or Windows Vista. If you don't see the driver you want, you need to go back to Windows setup to install it. When you have selected the driver, click the Finish button. This takes you to yet another dialog box, as shown in Figure 20-8.

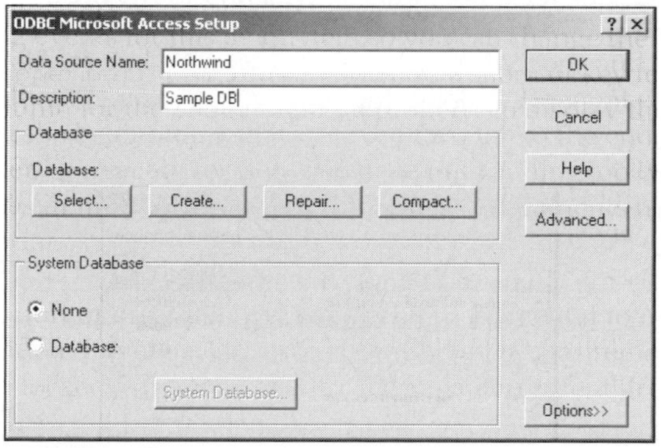

Figure 20-8

Enter the name of the database file as the Data Source Name, which is typically Northwind. You'll use this name to identify the database when you generate the application using an Application Wizard. You should now click the Select button to go to the final dialog box, which is the Select Database dialog, in which you can select the file in whichever directory it now sits. This last dialog to select the database is shown in Figure 20-9.

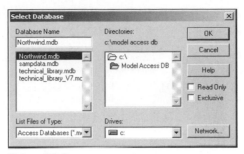

Figure 20-9

Finally, click three successive OK buttons, and you have registered the database. If this is not the same on your PC you will need to resort to `Help` for your operating system, or just experiment with the ODBC option on the Control Panel. The truth is in there.

When you have succeeded, you can now go ahead with your database application and, as ever, the starting point is the `New > Project` menu item in Visual C++ 2008, or you can just press `Ctrl+Shift+N`.

Generating an MFC ODBC Program

Create a new MFC project with the MFC Application template in the usual way and give it a suitable name, such as `DBSample`. After you click OK, select the Application Type set of options and choose the SDI interface for document support because that will be sufficient for your needs. The document is somewhat incidental to operations in a database application because most things are managed by recordset and record view objects. As you'll see, the main use of the document is to store recordset objects, so you won't need more than one document.

Select the Database Support set of options. You have a choice as to whether you include file support with the Database View option. File support refers to serializing the document, which is not normally necessary, because any database input and output that you require is taken care of using the recordset objects in your application. Choose the option without file support, as shown in Figure 20-10.

When you select either of the database options, the other checkboxes, radio buttons, and the Data Source button are activated. Select the ODBC radio button and then click the `Data Source` button to specify the database that your application is going to use. This displays the dialog box shown in Figure 20-11.

If the Northwind database was registered as a user database, it appears on the Machine Data Source tab, as in Figure 20-11. When you have selected the database and clicked the OK button, a Login dialog box for the database is displayed. You then can enter the login name and password to open the database. When you click the OK button, you'll see the dialog box shown in Figure 20-12 in which you have to select the database objects to which you need access.

Expand the `Tables` node in the dialog and click on the Products table. You could select as many of the tables as you want by clicking on each of the tables with the `Ctrl` key held down, but here you'll need only the Products table. Then click the OK button to close the dialog. You have now specified the operation for the recordset class that the Application Wizard generates as:

```
SELECT * FROM Products;
```

The use of * for all fields is determined by the framework. It just uses the table name or names you chose here to form the SQL operation that is applied for the recordset.

The MFC Application Wizard dialog box also shows a choice between Snapshot and Dynaset for the type of recordset your project uses. There is a significant difference between these options, so the next section looks at what they mean.

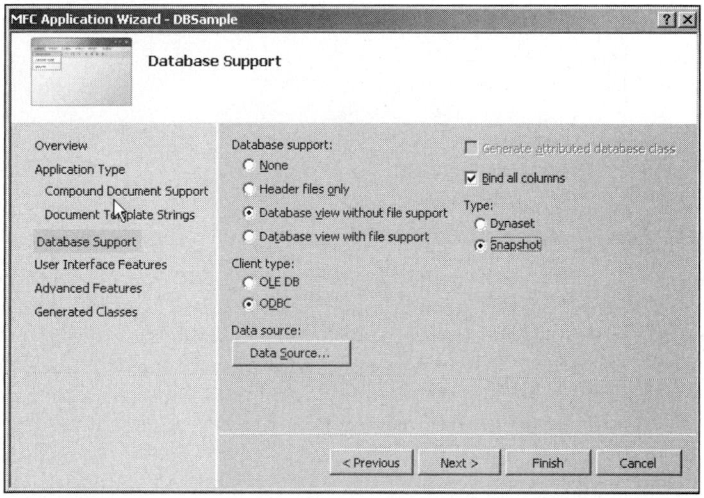

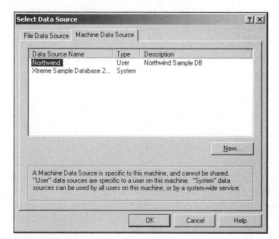

Figure 20-10

Figure 20-11

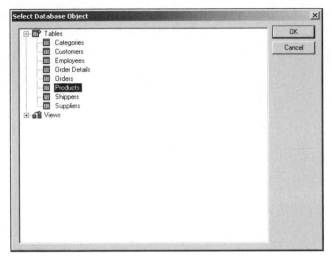

Figure 20-12

Snapshot versus Dynaset Recordsets

Your recordset object will provide you with the result of a SELECT operation on the database. In the case of a **snapshot** recordset, the query is executed once, and the result is stored in memory. Your recordset object can then make available to you any of the records in the table that result from the query, so a snapshot is essentially static in nature. Any changes that might occur in the database due to other users updating the database are not reflected in the data you obtained with your snapshot recordset. If you need to see changes that may have been made, you'll need to re-run the SELECT statement.

With the **dynaset** option, your recordset object automatically refreshes the current record from the database when you move from one record to another in the table generated by the query for the recordset. As a consequence, the record available in the recordset reflects the up-to-date status of the database when you accessed the record, not when you first opened the recordset. Be aware that the refresh occurs only when your recordset object accesses a record. If the data in the current record is modified by another user, this is not apparent in your recordset object unless you move to another record and then return to the original record. A dynaset recordset uses an index to the database tables involved to generate the contents of each record dynamically. Because you have no other users accessing the Northwind database, you can choose the Snapshot option for your example.

After Snapshot has been chosen, you can click the Generated Classes option to display the classes in your application. The dialog box is shown in Figure 20-13.

Here you can change the class names and the corresponding file names assigned by the wizard to something more suitable, if you want. I changed CDBSampleView class name to CProductView, the header file name from DBSampleView.h to ProductView.h and the source file name from DBSampleView.cpp to ProductView.cpp. In addition to the changes shown for the CDBSampleView and CProductView classes and the corresponding changes to the names of the .h and .cpp files for the class, you could also change the CDBSampleSet class name to CProductSet, and the associated .h and .cpp file names to be consistent with the class name. After that is done, click Finish and generate the project.

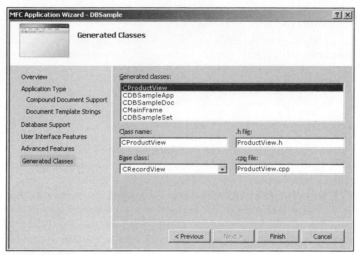

Figure 20-13

Understanding the Program Structure

The basic structure of the program is as you have seen before, with an application class CDBSampleApp, a frame window class CMainFrame, a document class CDBSampleDoc, and a view class CProductView. A document template object is responsible for creating and relating the frame window, document, and view objects. This is done in a standard manner in the InitInstance() member of the application object. The document class is standard, except that the MFC Application Wizard has added a data member, m_DBSampleSet, which is an object of the CProductSet class type. As a consequence, a recordset object is automatically created when the document object is created in the InitInstance() function member of the application object. The significant departures from a non-database program arise in the detail of the CRecordset class, and in the CRecordView class, so take a look at those.

Understanding Recordsets

You can look at the definition of the CProductSet class that the Application Wizard has generated piece-meal and see how each piece works. I'll show the bits under discussion as shaded in the code fragments.

Recordset Creation

The first segment of the class definition that is of interest is:

```
class CProductSet : public CRecordset
{
public:
    CProductSet(CDatabase* pDatabase = NULL);
    DECLARE_DYNAMIC(CProductSet)

// Plus more of the class definition...

// Overrides
```

```
      // Wizard generated virtual function overrides
      public:
      virtual CString GetDefaultConnect();      // Default connection string
      virtual CString GetDefaultSQL();          // default SQL for Recordset
      virtual void DoFieldExchange(CFieldExchange* pFX);// RFX support

   // Plus some more standard stuff


   };
```

The class has CRecordset as a base class and provides the functionality for retrieving data from the database. The constructor for the class accepts a pointer to a CDatabase object that is set to NULL as a default. The parameter to the constructor allows a CProductSet object to be created for a CDatabase object that already exists, which allows an existing connection to a database to be reused. Opening a connection to a database is a lengthy business, so it's advantageous to re-use a database connection when you can.

If no pointer is passed to the constructor, as is the case for the m_DBSampleSet member of the document class CDBSampleDoc, the framework automatically creates a CDatabase object for you and calls the GetDefaultConnect() function member of CProductSet to define the connection. The Application Wizard provides the following implementation of this function:

```
CString CProductSet::GetDefaultConnect()
{
   return _T(
   "DSN=Northwind;
   DBQ=C:\\Model Access DB\\Northwind.mdb;
   DriverId=25;
   FIL=MS Access;
   MaxBufferSize=2048;
   PageTimeout=5;
   UID=admin;");
}
```

The GetDefaultConnect() function is a pure virtual function in the base class, CRecordset, and so must always be implemented in a derived recordset class. The value returned from the function is a single string between double quotes but I have shown it spread over several lines to make the contents of the string more apparent. The implementation provided by Application Wizard returns the text string shown to the framework. This identifies the database with its name and path plus values for the other parameters you can see and enables the framework to create a CDatabase object that establishes the database connection automatically. The meaning of the arguments in the connection string is as shown in the following table.

Argument	Description
DSN	The data source name.
DBQ	The database qualifier, which in this case is the path to the Access database file.
DriverId	The ID of the ODBC driver for the database.
FIL	The database file type.

Argument	Description
MaxBufferSize	The maximum size of the buffer to be used for data transfer.
PageTimeout	The length of time in seconds to wait for a connection to the database. It is important to set this value to an adequate value to avoid connection failures when accessing a remote database.
UID	The user ID for accessing the database.

In practice, it's usually necessary to supply a password as well as a user ID before access to a database is permitted, and it's unwise to expose the password in the code in plain text form. For this reason the Application Wizard has inserted the following line preceding the definition of the GetDefaultConnect() function:

```
#error Security Issue: The connection string may contain a password
```

Compilation fails with this directive in the code, so you must comment it out or delete it to compile the program successfully.

You can make the framework pop up a dialog box for the user to select the database name from the list of registered database sources by writing the return statement in the GetDefaultConnect() function as:

```
    return _T("ODBC;");
```

You will also be prompted for a user ID and password when this is required for access to the database.

Querying the Database

The CProductSet class includes a data member for each field in the Products table. The Application Wizard obtains the field names from the database and uses these to name the corresponding data members of the class. They appear in the block of code following the Field/Param Data comment in the CProductSet class definition:

```
class CProductSet : public CRecordset
{
public:
    CProductSet(CDatabase* pDatabase = NULL);
    DECLARE_DYNAMIC(CProductSet)

// Field/Param Data
// The string types below (if present) reflect the actual data type of the
// database field - CStringA for ANSI datatypes and CStringW for Unicode
// datatypes. This is to prevent the ODBC driver from performing
// potentially unnecessary conversions.
// If you wish, you may change these members to
// CString types and the ODBC driver will perform all necessary
// conversions.
// (Note: You must use an ODBC driver version that is version 3.5 or
// greater to support both Unicode and these conversions).
```

```
    long m_ProductID;        // Number automatically assigned to new product.
    CStringW m_ProductName;
    long m_SupplierID;          // Same entry as in Suppliers table.
    long m_CategoryID;          // Same entry as in Categories table.
    CStringW m_QuantityPerUnit; // (e.g., 24-count case, 1-liter bottle).
    double m_UnitPrice;
    int m_UnitsInStock;
    int m_UnitsOnOrder;
    int m_ReorderLevel;         // Minimum units to maintain in stock.
    BOOL m_Discontinued;        // Yes means item is no longer available.

    // Overrides
    // Wizard generated virtual function overrides
    public:
    virtual CString GetDefaultConnect();   // Default connection string
    virtual CString GetDefaultSQL();        // default SQL for Recordset
    virtual void DoFieldExchange(CFieldExchange* pFX);   // RFX support

// Implementation
#ifdef _DEBUG
    virtual void AssertValid() const;
    virtual void Dump(CDumpContext& dc) const;
#endif

};
```

The type of each data member is set to correspond with the field type for the corresponding field in the Products table. You may not want all these fields in practice, but you shouldn't delete them willy-nilly in the class definition. As you will see shortly, they are referenced in other places, so you must ensure that all references to a field are deleted, too. A further caveat is that you must not delete primary keys. If you do, the recordset won't work, so you need to be sure which fields are primary keys before chopping out what you don't want.

Note that two of the fields have CStringW as the type. You haven't seen this before, but the CStringW class type just encapsulates a Unicode string rather than an ASCII string. It is more convenient when you are accessing the fields to use type CString, so change the type of the m_ProductName and m_QuantityPerUnit members to CString. This allows the strings to be handled as ASCII strings in the example. Clearly, if you are writing internationalized database applications, you would need to maintain any CStringW fields as such because they may contain characters that are not within the ASCII character set.

The SQL operation that applies to the recordset to populate these data members is specified in the GetDefaultSQL() function. The implementation that the Application Wizard has supplied for this is:

```
CString CProductSet::GetDefaultSQL()
{
    return _T("[Products]");
}
```

The string returned is obviously created based on the table that you selected during the creation of the project. The square brackets have been included to provide for the possibility of the table name containing spaces. If you had selected several tables in the project creation process, they would all be inserted here, separated by commas, with each table name enclosed within square brackets.

The GetDefaultSQL() function is called by the MFC framework when it constructs the SQL statement to be applied for the recordset. The framework slots the string returned by this function into a skeleton SQL statement with the form:

```
SELECT * FROM < String returned by GetDefaultSQL() >;
```

This looks simplistic, and indeed it is, but you can add WHERE and ORDER BY clauses to the operation, as you'll see later.

Data Transfer between the Database and the Recordset

The transfer of data from the database to the recordset, and vice versa, is accomplished by the DoFieldExchange() member of the CProductSet class. The implementation of this function is:

```
void CProductSet::DoFieldExchange(CFieldExchange* pFX)
{
  pFX->SetFieldType(CFieldExchange::outputColumn);
// Macros such as RFX_Text() and RFX_Int() are dependent on the
// type of the member variable, not the type of the field in the database.
// ODBC will try to automatically convert the column value to the requested
// type
  RFX_Long(pFX, _T("[ProductID]"), m_ProductID);
  RFX_Text(pFX, _T("[ProductName]"), m_ProductName);
  RFX_Long(pFX, _T("[SupplierID]"), m_SupplierID);
  RFX_Long(pFX, _T("[CategoryID]"), m_CategoryID);
  RFX_Text(pFX, _T("[QuantityPerUnit]"), m_QuantityPerUnit);
  RFX_Double(pFX, _T("[UnitPrice]"), m_UnitPrice);
  RFX_Int(pFX, _T("[UnitsInStock]"), m_UnitsInStock);
  RFX_Int(pFX, _T("[UnitsOnOrder]"), m_UnitsOnOrder);
  RFX_Int(pFX, _T("[ReorderLevel]"), m_ReorderLevel);
  RFX_Bool(pFX, _T("[Discontinued]"), m_Discontinued);
}
```

This function is called automatically by the MFC framework to store data in and retrieve data from the database. It works in a similar fashion to the DoDataExchange() function you have seen with dialog controls in that the pFX parameter determines whether the operation is a read or a write. Each time it's called, it moves a single record to or from the recordset object.

The first function called is SetFieldType(), which sets a mode for the RFX_() function calls that follow. In this case, the mode is specified as outputColumn, which indicates that data is to be exchanged between the database field and the corresponding argument specified in each of the following RFX_() function calls. (RFX here stands for Record Field Exchange.)

There is a whole range of RFX_() functions for various types of database fields. The function call for a particular field corresponds with the data type applicable to that field. The first argument to an RFX_() function call is the pFX object that determines the direction of data movement. The second argument is the table field name and the third is the data member that is to store that field for the current record.

Understanding the Record View

The purpose of the view class is to display information from the recordset object in the application window, so you need to understand how this works. The bits of the CProductView class definition that are of primary interest are shown shaded:

```cpp
class CProductView : public CRecordView
{
protected: // create from serialization only
    CProductView();
    DECLARE_DYNCREATE(CProductView)

public:
    enum{ IDD = IDD_DBSAMPLE_FORM };
    CProductSet* m_pSet;

// Attributes
public:
    CDBSampleDoc* GetDocument();

// Operations
public:

// Overrides
    public:
    virtual CRecordset* OnGetRecordset();
    virtual BOOL PreCreateWindow(CREATESTRUCT& cs);
    protected:
    virtual void DoDataExchange(CDataExchange* pDX);    // DDX/DDV support
    virtual void OnInitialUpdate(); // called first time after construct
    virtual BOOL OnPreparePrinting(CPrintInfo* pInfo);
    virtual void OnBeginPrinting(CDC* pDC, CPrintInfo* pInfo);
    virtual void OnEndPrinting(CDC* pDC, CPrintInfo* pInfo);

// Implementation
public:
    virtual ~CProductView();
#ifdef _DEBUG
    virtual void AssertValid() const;
    virtual void Dump(CDumpContext& dc) const;
#endif

protected:

// Generated message map functions
protected:
```

```
    DECLARE_MESSAGE_MAP()
};
```

The view class for a recordset always needs to be derived because the class has to be customized to display the particular fields from the recordset that you want. The base class, CRecordView, includes all the functionality required to manage communications with the recordset. All you need to do is tailor the record view class to suit your application. I'll get to that in a moment.

Note that the constructor is protected. This is because objects of this class are expected to be created from serialization, which is a default assumption for record view classes. When you add further record view classes to the application, you'll need to change the default access for their constructors to public because you'll be creating the views yourself.

In the first public block in the class, the enumeration adds the ID IDD_DBSAMPLE_FORM as a member of the class. This is the ID for a blank dialog that the Application Wizard has included in the program. You'll add controls to this dialog to display the database fields from the Products table that you want displayed. The dialog ID is passed to the base class, CRecordView, in the initialization list of the constructor for the view class:

```
CProductView::CProductView() : CRecordView(CProductView::IDD)
{
    m_pSet = NULL;
    // TODO: add construction code here
}
```

This action links the view class to the dialog box, which is necessary to enable the mechanism that transfers data between the recordset object and the view object to work.

There is also a pointer to a CProductSet object, m_pSet, in the class definition, which is initialized to NULL in the constructor. A more useful value for this pointer is set in the OnInitialUpdate() member of the class, which has been implemented as:

```
void CProductView::OnInitialUpdate()
{
    m_pSet = &GetDocument()->m_DBSampleSet;
    CRecordView::OnInitialUpdate();
}
```

This function is called when the record view object is created and sets the value of m_pSet to be the address of the m_DBSampleSet member of the document, thus tying the view to the product set object.

Figure 20-14 shows how data from the database ultimately gets to be displayed by the view.

The transfer of data between the data members in the CProductSet object that correspond to fields in the Products table and the controls in the dialog box associated with the CProductView object is managed by the DoDataExchange() member of CProductView. The code in this function to do this is not in place yet because you first need to add the controls to the dialog that are going to display the data and then link the controls to the recordset data members. You will do that next.

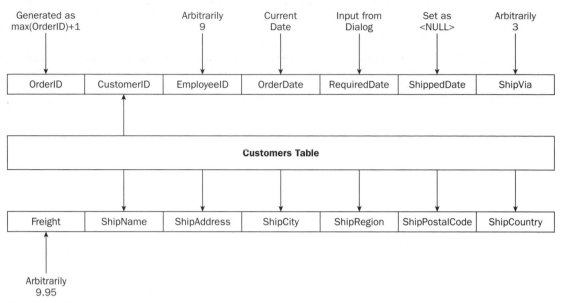

| OrderID | CustomerID | EmployeeID | OrderDate | RequiredDate | ShippedDate | ShipVia |

Generated as max(OrderID)+1 → OrderID

Arbitrarily 9 → EmployeeID

Current Date → OrderDate

Input from Dialog → RequiredDate

Set as <NULL> → ShippedDate

Arbitrarily 3 → ShipVia

Customers Table

| Freight | ShipName | ShipAddress | ShipCity | ShipRegion | ShipPostalCode | ShipCountry |

Arbitrarily 9.95 → Freight

Figure 20-14

Creating the View Dialog

The first step is to place the controls on the dialog box, so go to Resource View, expand the list of dialog resources, and double-click `Idd_Dbsample_Form`. You can delete the static text object with the TODO message from the dialog. If you right-click the dialog box, you can choose to view its properties, as shown in Figure 20-15.

If you scroll down through the properties you'll see that the `Style` property has been set to `Child` because the dialog box is going to be a child window and will fill the client area. The `Border` property has been set to `None` because if the dialog box is to fill the client area, it won't need a border.

You'll add a static text control to identify each field from the recordset that you want to display, plus an edit control to display it.

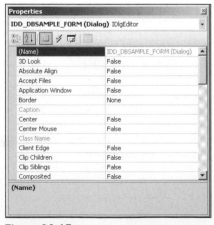

Figure 20-15

You can enlarge the dialog if necessary by dragging its borders. Then, place Static Text and Edit controls on the dialog as shown in Figure 20-16.

You can add the text to each static control by just typing it as soon as the control has been placed on the dialog. As you see, I have entered the text for each static control so that it corresponds to the field name in the database. It's a good idea to make sure that all the edit controls have sensible and different IDs, so right-click each of them in turn to display and modify their properties. Figure 20-17 shows the properties for the control corresponding to Product ID.

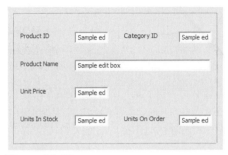

Figure 20-16

Figure 20-17

It's helpful to use the field name as part of the control ID as this indicates what the control displays. Figure 20-17 shows the ID for the first edit control in the title bar of the properties window after I have modified it. You can change the IDs for the other edit controls similarly. Because you are not intending to update the database in this example, you should make sure that the data displayed by each edit box cannot be modified from the keyboard. You can do that by setting the `Read Only` property for of each of the edit controls as `True`. The background to the edit boxes will then have a different color to signal that they cannot be altered, as shown in Figure 20-18.

You can add other fields to the dialog box, if you want. The one that is most important for the rest of our example is the `Product ID`, so you must include that. Save the dialog and then move on to the last step: linking the controls to the variables in the recordset class.

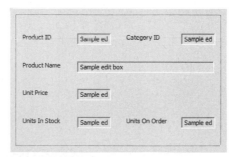

Figure 20-18

Linking the Controls to the Recordset

As you saw earlier in Figure 20-14, getting the data from the recordset displayed by the appropriate control is the job of the `DoDataExchange()` function in the `CProductView` class. The `m_pSet` member provides a means of accessing the members of the `CProductSet` object that contains the fields retrieved from the database, so linking the controls to the data members of `CProductSet` is easy. MFC defines a range of `DDX_Field` functions at global scope that are specifically for exchanging data between a view and a recordset (DDX stands for Dialog Data Exchange). In particular, the `DDX_FieldText()` function has overloaded versions that transfer a variety of types of data between a recordset field and an edit box in a `CRecordView` object. The types that can be exchanged by the `DDX_FieldText()` function are shown in the following table.

short	int	UINT	long	DWORD
float	double	CString	COleDateTime	COleCurrency

When you call the `DDX_FieldText()` function you must supply four arguments:

- ❏ A `CDataExchange` object that determines the direction of data transfer — whether the data is to be transferred to or from the recordset. You just supply the pointer that is passed as the argument to the `DoDataExchange()` function.
- ❏ The ID of the control that is the source or destination of the data.
- ❏ A reference to a field data member in the `CRecordset` object that is the source or destination of the data.
- ❏ A pointer to the `CRecordset` object with which data is to be exchanged.

So to implement the transfer of data between the recordset and the control for the Product ID field, insert the following call of the DDX_FieldText() function in the body of the DoDataExchange() function:

```
DDX_FieldText(pDX, IDC_PRODUCTID, m_pSet->m_ProductID, m_pSet);
```

The first argument is the pDX argument that is passed to the DoDataExchange() function. The second argument is the ID for the first edit control in the dialog box for the view, the third argument uses the m_pSet member of the CProductView class to access the m_ProductID member of the recordset object, and the last argument is the pointer to the recordset object.

You can therefore fill out the code for the DoDataExchange() function in the CProductView class like this:

```
void CProductView::DoDataExchange(CDataExchange* pDX)
{
    CRecordView::DoDataExchange(pDX);
    DDX_FieldText(pDX, IDC_PRODUCTID, m_pSet->m_ProductID, m_pSet);
    DDX_FieldText(pDX, IDC_PRODUCTNAME, m_pSet->m_ProductName, m_pSet);
    DDX_FieldText(pDX, IDC_UNITPRICE, m_pSet->m_UnitPrice, m_pSet);
    DDX_FieldText(pDX, IDC_UNITSINSTOCK, m_pSet->m_UnitsInStock, m_pSet);
    DDX_FieldText(pDX, IDC_CATEGORYID, m_pSet->m_CategoryID, m_pSet);
    DDX_FieldText(pDX, IDC_UNITSONORDER, m_pSet->m_UnitsOnOrder, m_pSet);
}
```

The programming mechanism for data transfer between the database and the dialog box owned by the CProductView object is illustrated in Figure 20-19.

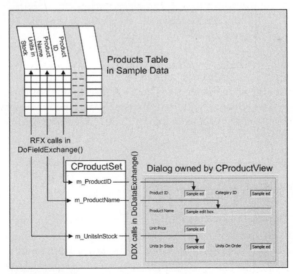

Figure 20-19

The recordset class and the record view class cooperate to enable data to be transferred between the database and the controls in the dialog box. The CProductSet class handles transfers between the database and its data members and CProductView deals with transfers between the data members of CProductSet and the controls in the dialog.

Exercising the Example

Believe it or not you can now run the example. Just build it in the normal way and then execute it. The application should display a window similar to the one shown in Figure 20-20.

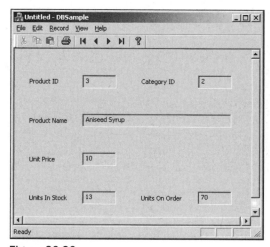

Figure 20-20

The CRecordView base class automatically implements toolbar buttons that step from one record in the recordset to the next or to the previous record. There are also toolbar buttons to move directly to the first or last record in the recordset. Of course, the products are displayed in a default sequence. It would be nice to have them sorted in categories and in product ID sequence within each category. Next, you'll see how you can do that.

Sorting a Recordset

As you saw earlier, the data is retrieved from the database by the recordset, using an SQL SELECT statement that is generated by the framework using the GetDefaultSQL() member. You can add an ORDER BY clause to the statement generated by setting a value in the m_strSort member of CProductSet, which is inherited from CRecordSet. This causes the output table from the query to be sorted, based on the string stored in m_strSort. You need to set only the m_strSort member to a string that contains the field name or names that you want to sort on; the framework provides the ORDER BY keywords. Where you have multiple names, you separate them by commas. But where should you add the code to do this?

The transfer of data between the database and the recordset occurs when the Open() member of the recordset object is called. In your program, the Open() function member of the recordset object is called by the `OnInitialUpdate()` member of the base class to the view class, `CRecordView`. You can, therefore, put the code for setting the sort specification in the `OnInitialUpdate()` member of the `CProductView` class, as follows:

```
void CProductView::OnInitialUpdate()
{
  m_pSet = &GetDocument()->m_productSet;
  m_pSet->m_strSort = "[CategoryID],[ProductID]";    // Set the sort fields
  CRecordView::OnInitialUpdate();
}
```

You just set `m_strSort` in the recordset to a string containing the name of the category ID field followed by the name of the `product ID` field. Square brackets are useful, even when there are no blanks in a name, because they differentiate strings containing these names from other strings, so you can immediately pick out the field names. They are, of course, optional if there are no blanks in the field name.

Modifying the Window Caption

There is one other thing you could add to this function at this point. The caption for the window would be better if it showed the name of the table being displayed. You can arrange for this to happen by adding code to set the title in the document object:

```
void CProductView::OnInitialUpdate()
{
  m_pSet = &GetDocument()->m_productSet;
  m_pSet >m_strSort = "[CategoryID],[ProductID]";    // Set the sort fields
  CRecordView::OnInitialUpdate();

  // Set the document title to the table name
  if (m_pSet->IsOpen())                              // Verify the recordset is open
  {
    CString strTitle = _T("Table Name");     // Set basic title string
    CString strTable = m_pSet->GetTableName();
    if(!strTable.IsEmpty())                          // Verify we have a table name
      strTitle += _T(": ") + strTable;       // and add to basic title
    GetDocument()->SetTitle(strTitle);       // Set the document title
  }
}
```

Note that the new code here must go after the call to the base class version of the `OnInitialUpdate()` function. After checking that the recordset is indeed open, you initialize a local `CString` object with a basic title string. You then get the name of the table from the recordset object by calling its `GetTableName()` member. In general, you should check that you do get a string returned from the `GetTableName()` function. Various conditions can arise that can prevent a table name from being set — for instance, there may be more than one table involved in the recordset. After appending a colon followed by the table name you have retrieved to the basic title in `strTitle`, you set the result as the document title by calling the document's `SetTitle()` member.

If you rebuild the application and run it again, it works as before but with a new window caption as Figure 20-21 shows. The product IDs are in ascending sequence within each category ID, with the category IDs in sequence, too.

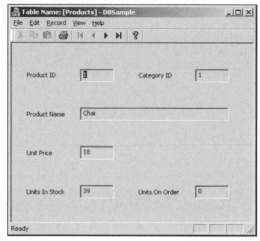

Figure 20-21

Using a Second Recordset Object

Now that you can view all the products in the database, a reasonable extension of the program would be to add the ability to view all the orders for any particular product. To do this, you'll add another record-set class to handle order information from the database and a complementary view class to display some of the fields from the recordset. You'll also add a button to the Products dialog to enable you to switch to the Orders dialog when you want to view the orders for the current product. This enables you to operate with the arrangement shown in Figure 20-22.

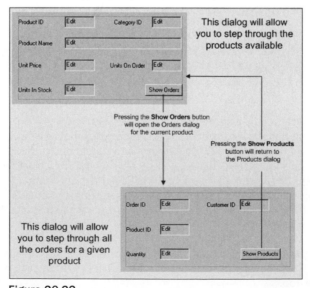

Figure 20-22

The Products dialog box is the starting position where you can step backwards and forwards through all the available products. Clicking the Show Orders button switches you to the dialog where you can view all the orders for the current product. You can return to the Products dialog box by clicking the Show Products button.

Adding a Recordset Class

You can start by adding the recordset class for the orders; right-click DBSample in Class View and select Add > Class from the pop-up. Select MFC from the set of Visual C++ categories and MFC ODBC Consumer as the template. When you click the Add button in the Add Class dialog box that is displayed, you'll see the MFC ODBC Consumer Wizard dialog box shown in Figure 20-23.

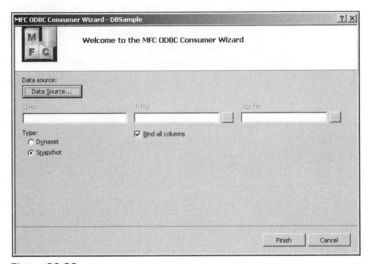

Figure 20-23

Select the type of consumer as Snapshot by selecting the radio button and then click the Data Sources button to go to the Select Data Source dialog box, where you'll be able to identify the data source; it should be on the Machine Data Source tab. When you have selected Northwind as the data source in the same way as you've seen previously, you'll see the Select Database Object dialog box as shown in Figure 20-24.

You'll select two tables to associate with the new recordset class that you're going to create, so hold the Ctrl key down and select the Orders and Order Details table names. You can then click the OK button to complete the selection process. This returns you to the MFC ODBC Consumer dialog box where you'll see the class name and file names have been entered. You can change the class name from COrderDetails_MULTI to COrderSet and the file names in a corresponding way, as shown in Figure 20-25.

Clicking on the Finish button completes the process and causes the COrderSet class to generate.

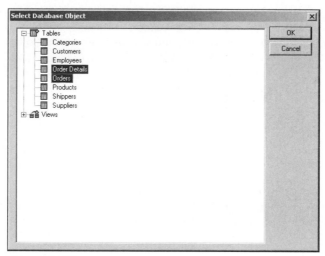

Figure 20-24

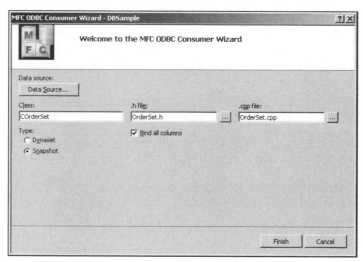

Figure 20-25

As you saw in the `CProductSet` class that was created as part of the initial project, the implementation of the `GetDefaultConnect()` function for the `COrderSet` class is preceded by an `#error` directive that prevents compilation from succeeding, so comment that out.

A data member has been created in the `COrderSet` class for every field in each of the tables. When you select two or more tables for a given recordset, it is always possible, indeed likely, that there are field names duplicated; the `OrderID` field appears in both tables, for example. To ensure the names corresponding to field data members are always differentiated, the field names are prefixed with the table name in each case. If you don't want to keep all these fields, you can delete or comment out any of them, but as I said earlier, you must take care not to delete any variables that are primary keys. When you delete a data member for a table field, you must also delete the initialization for it in the class constructor and the RFX_() call for it in the DoFieldExchange() member function. You must also change the initial value for the m_nFields member in the COrderSet constructor so that it reflects the number of fields left in the class. The data members that you need to keep for this example are as follows: m_OrdersOrderID, m_OrderDetailsOrderID, m_OrderDetailsProductID, m_OrderDetailsQuantity, and m_OrdersCustomerID. If you keep just these you should change the value assigned to m_nFields to 5. Change the members of type CStringW to type CString.

To hook the new recordset to the document, you need to add a data member to the definition of the CDBSampleDoc class, so right-click the class name in Class View and select Add > Add Variable from the pop-up. Specify the type as COrderSet and the variable name as m_OrderSet. You can leave it as a public member of the class. Click OK to finish adding the data member to the document. The compiler has to understand that COrderSet is a class before it begins compiling the CBSampleDoc class. If you take a look at the contents of the DBSampleDoc.h header file, you will see that an #include statement has already been added for you to the top of DBSampleDoc.h:

```
#pragma once
#include "ProductSet.h"
#include "orderset.h"
class CDBSampleDoc : public CDocument
{
 // Rest of class definition
}
```

Adding a View Class for the Recordset

At this point you might expect to be adding a class derived from CRecordView using the Add > Class menu item in the Class View context menu to display the data from the COrderSet object. This used to be possible in earlier versions of Visual C++, but unfortunately the Visual C++ 2008 product does not provide for this. The dialog box for adding a new class does not allow the possibility of selecting CRecordView as a base class at all, so you must always create classes that have CRecordView as a base manually.

You need to create another dialog resource before you create the view class so you have the ID for the resource that you can use in the definition of the view class.

Creating the Dialog Resource

Switch to Resource View, right-click the Dialog folder, and select Insert Dialog from the context menu. You can delete both of the default buttons from the dialog. Now change the ID and styles for the dialog, so right-click it and display its properties by selecting Properties from the pop-up. Change the ID property to IDD_ORDERS_FORM. You also need to change the Style property to Child and the Border property to None.

You're now ready to populate the dialog box with controls for the fields that you want to display from the Orders and Order Details tables. If you switch to Class View and select the COrderSet class name, you'll be able to see the names of the variables concerned while you are working on the dialog. Add controls to the dialog box as shown in Figure 20-26.

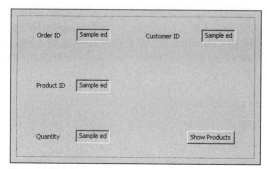

Figure 20-26

Here, there are four edit controls for the `OrderID`, `CustomerID`, `ProductID`, and `Quantity` fields from the tables associated with the `COrderSet` class, together with static controls to identify them. You can add controls to display a few more fields if you want, as long as you haven't deleted the class members. Don't forget to modify the IDs for the edit controls so that they are representative of the purpose of the control. You can use the table field names prefixed by the table name to match the data member names. Finally, you need to make the edit controls read-only by setting the `Read Only` property to `True` for each control. Alternatively, you can set them all to read-only in one go by selecting each of them with the `Ctrl` key held down and then setting the `Read Only` property to `True`.

The button control labeled `Show Products` is used to return to the Products table view, so modify the ID for this button to `IDC_PRODUCTS`. When you have arranged everything to your liking, save the dialog resource.

Creating the Record View Class

Create the `OrderView.h` file that will hold the `COrderView` class definition. To do this just right-click `DBSample` in Solution Explorer and select `Add > New Item` from the list. Choose the template to create a `.h` file and enter the file name as `OrderView`. After you have created the file, you can add the code for the class definition as:

```
#pragma once

class COrderSet;          // Declare the class name
class CDBSampleDoc;       // Declare the class name

// COrderView form view

class COrderView : public CRecordView
{
  DECLARE_DYNCREATE(COrderView)

protected:
  virtual ~COrderView(){}
  virtual void DoDataExchange(CDataExchange* pDX);     // DDX/DDV support
  virtual void OnInitialUpdate();

public:
  enum { IDD = IDD_ORDERS_FORM };
```

```
    COrderSet* m_pSet;

    // Inline function definition
    CDBSampleDoc* GetDocument() const
    {
      return reinterpret_cast<CDBSampleDoc*>(m_pDocument);
    }

    COrderSet* GetRecordset();
    virtual CRecordset* OnGetRecordset();
    COrderView();              // constructor now public


#ifdef _DEBUG
    virtual void AssertValid() const;
    virtual void Dump(CDumpContext& dc) const;
#endif
};
```

This code is based on the CProductView that was generated. The DECLARE_DYNCREATE macro enables objects of this class type to be created by the MFC framework at runtime. In general MFC document, view, and frame classes should define this macro. You will add the complementary IMPLEMENT_DYNCREATE macro to the .cpp file a little later. I have omitted the debug version of the GetDocument() because the CProductView class contains a version of the function that validates the document object. The inline version in the COrderView class definition just assumes the cast to CDBSampleDoc* will be OK. I have included declarations for AssertValid() and Dump() that is compiled only when debug mode is in effect, so definition has to be included in the .cpp file for the class. The enumeration defines the ID for the dialog and you will use this in the definition of the constructor. The m_pSet member will hold the address of the recordset object that supplies the data displayed by this view.

The implementation of the COrderView class goes in the OrderView.cpp file, so create that file within the project using the procedure you followed for the .h file. You can add the initial #include directive for the classes you will need to reference:

```
#include "stdafx.h"
#include "DBSample.h"
#include "OrderView.h"
#include "OrderSet.h"
#include "DBSampleDoc.h"
```

This is not the complete set — you'll be adding a couple more as you develop the class implementation.

You can add the macro to allow dynamic creation of COrderView objects next:

```
IMPLEMENT_DYNCREATE(COrderView, CRecordView)
```

The constructor just needs to initialize the m_pSet member to NULL:

```
COrderView::COrderView()
  : CRecordView(COrderView::IDD), m_pSet(NULL)
{
}
```

Here you call the base class constructor with the dialog ID that you defined in an enumeration in the class as the argument. This identifies the dialog that is associated with the view.

Now add definitions for the two functions that may be used when you execute in debug mode:

```
// COrderView diagnostics

#ifdef _DEBUG
void COrderView::AssertValid() const
{
  CRecordView::AssertValid();
}
```

```
void COrderView::Dump(CDumpContext& dc) const
{
  CRecordView::Dump(dc);
}
#endif //_DEBUG
```

The `DoDataExchange()` function links the controls in the dialog to the fields in the recordset. The definition of this function is:

```
void COrderView::DoDataExchange(CDataExchange* pDX)
{
  CRecordView::DoDataExchange(pDX);
  DDX_FieldText(pDX, IDC_ORDERDETAILS_ORDERID,
                      m_pSet->m_OrderDetailsOrderID, m_pSet);
  DDX_FieldText(pDX, IDC_ORDERS_CUSTOMERID,
                      m_pSet->m_OrdersCustomerID, m_pSet);
  DDX_FieldText(pDX, IDC_ORDERDETAILS_PRODUCTID,
                      m_pSet->m_OrderDetailsProductID, m_pSet);
  DDX_FieldText(pDX, IDC_ORDERDETAILS_QUANTITY,
                      m_pSet->m_OrderDetailsQuantity, m_pSet);
}
```

You use the `m_pSet` member to access the fields in the `COrderSet` object that are to be displayed. The second argument to each `DDX_FieldText()` method call identifies the control for the field identified by the third argument. As you saw when you explored the `CProductView` class, the first argument determines whether data is being transferred to or from the control. The last argument simply identifies the recordset that is involved in the process.

There are two functions to be defined that are involved in retrieving the recordset. You'll call the `GetRecordset()` function to obtain a pointer to the `COrderSet` object encapsulating the recordset. You can implement this as follows:

```
COrderSet* COrderView::GetRecordset()
{
  ASSERT(m_pSet != NULL);
  return m_pSet;
}
```

The `m_pSet` member contains a pointer to the recordset. The MFC `ASSERT` macro here aborts the program with a message if the expression between the parentheses evaluates to 0. Thus, this just verifies that the pointer to the COrderSet object is not NULL. The ASSERT macro has the advantage that it operates only in a debug version of the application. In a release version, it does nothing.

The OnGetRecordset() function is a pure virtual function in the base class, so you must define it here. You can implement it as.

```
CRecordset* COrderView::OnGetRecordset()
{
  return m_pSet;
}
```

This just returns the address in m_pSet in this case. Obviously, in a situation where you needed to recreate the recordset, the code would need to be more complicated.

You are not finished with the view class yet. The next step is to determine more precisely what the recordset for the orders contain.

Customizing the Recordset

As it stands, the SQL SELECT operation for a COrderSet object produces a table that will contain all combinations of records from the two tables involved. This could be a lot of records, so you must add the equivalent of a WHERE clause to the query to restrict the records selected to those that make sense. But there is another problem, too: when you switch from the Products table display, you don't want to look at just any old orders. You want to see precisely those orders for the product ID we were looking at, which amounts to selecting only those orders that have the same product ID as that contained in the current CProductSet record. This is also effected through a WHERE clause. In the MFC context, the WHERE clause for a SQL SELECT operation for a recordset is called a **filter**.

Adding a Filter to the Recordset

You add a filter to the query by assigning a string to the m_strFilter member of the recordset object. This member is inherited from the base class, CRecordSet. As with the ORDER BY clause, which you added by assigning a value to the m_strSort member of the recordset, the place to implement this is in the OnInitialUpdate() member of the record view class, just before the base class function is called.

You want to set two conditions in the filter. One is to restrict the records generated in the recordset to those where the OrderID field in the Orders table is equal to the field with the same name in the Order Details table. You can write this condition as:

```
[Orders].[OrderID] = [Order Details].[OrderID]
```

The other condition you want to apply is that, for the records meeting the first condition, you want only those with a ProductID field that is equal to the ProductID field in the current record in the recordset object displaying the Products table. This means that you need to have the ProductID field from the COrderSet object compared to a variable value. The variable in this operation is called a **parameter**, and the condition in the filter is written in a special way:

```
ProductID = ?
```

The question mark represents a parameter value for the filter, and the selected records are those where the ProductID field equals the parameter value. The value that is to replace the question mark is set in the `DoFieldExchange()` member of the recordset. You'll implement this in a moment, but first you'll complete the specification of the filter.

You can define the string for the filter variable that incorporates both the conditions that you need with the statement:

```
// Set the filter as Product ID field with equal Order IDs
m_pSet->m_strFilter =
    "[ProductID] = ? AND [Orders].[OrderID] = [Order Details].[OrderID]";
```

You'll incorporate this into the `OnInitialUpdate()` member of the `COrderView` class, but before that, you'll finish setting the parameter for the filter.

Defining the Filter Parameter

Add a data member to the `COrderSet` class to store the current value of the `ProductID` field from the `CProductSet` object. This member also actS as the parameter to substitute for the `?` in the filter for the `COrderSet` object. So, right-click the `COrderSet` class name in Class View and select Add > Add Variable from the pop-up. The variable type needs to be the same as that of the `m_ProductID` member of the `CProductSet` class, which is type `long`, and you can specify the name as `m_ProductIDparam`. You can also leave it as a `public` member. You need to initialize this data member in the constructor and also set the parameter count. The application framework requires the count of the number of parameters in your recordset to be set to reflect the number of parameters you are using; otherwise, it won't work correctly. Add the shaded code shown below to the `COrderSet` constructor definition:

```
COrderSet::COrderSet(CDatabase* pdb)  : CRecordset(pdb)
{
    m_OrderDetailsOrderID = 0;
    m_OrderDetailsProductID = 0;
    m_OrderDetailsQuantity = 0;
    m_OrdersOrderID = 0;
    m_OrdersCustomerID = L"";
    m_nFields = 5;
    m_ProductIDparam = 0L;      // Set initial parameter value
    m_nParams = 1;              // Set number of parameters
    m_nDefaultType = snapshot;
}
```

All of the unshaded code was supplied by Class wizard to initialize the data members corresponding to the fields in the recordset and to specify the type as `snapshot`. You should delete the initialization for the other fields in the recordset. The new code initializes the parameter to zero and sets the count of the number of parameters to 1. The `m_nParams` variable is inherited from the base class, `CRecordSet`. Because there is a parameter count, you can deduce that you can have more than one parameter in the filter for a recordset.

At this point you can also remove or comment out the members from the COrderSet class that store fields from the recordset that you won't need. Remove or comment out the fields that are not required from the class definition, just leaving the following:

```
long m_OrderDetailsOrderID;      // Same as Order ID in Orders table.
long m_OrderDetailsProductID;    // Same as Product ID in Products table.
int m_OrderDetailsQuantity;
```

```
long m_OrdersOrderID;              // Unique order number.
CString m_OrdersCustomerID;        // Same entry as in Customers table.
long m_ProductIDparam;
```

To identify the `m_ProductIDparam` variable in the class as a parameter to be substituted in the filter for the `COrderSet` object, you must also add some code to the `DoFieldExchange()` member of the class:

```
void COrderSet::DoFieldExchange(CFieldExchange* pFX)
{
  pFX->SetFieldType(CFieldExchange::outputColumn);
  RFX_Long(pFX, _T("[Order Details].[OrderID]"), m_OrderDetailsOrderID);
  RFX_Long(pFX, _T("[Order Details].[ProductID]"),
                                          m_OrderDetailsProductID);
  RFX_Int(pFX, _T("[Order Details].[Quantity]"),
                                          m_OrderDetailsQuantity);
  RFX_Long(pFX, _T("[Orders].[OrderID]"), m_OrdersOrderID);
  RFX_Text(pFX, _T("[Orders].[CustomerID]"), m_OrdersCustomerID);

  // Set the field type as parameter
  pFX->SetFieldType(CFieldExchange::param);
  RFX_Long(pFX,_T("ProductIDParam"), m_ProductIDparam);
}
```

The Class Wizard provided code to transfer data between the database and the field variables it has added to the class. There will be one `RFX_()` function call for each data member of the recordset. You can delete those that are not required in this application, leaving just those shown in the preceding code.

The first new line of code calls the `SetFieldType()` member of the `pFX` object to set the mode for the following `RFX_()` call to `param`. The effect of this is to cause the third argument in any succeeding `RFX_()` calls to be interpreted as a parameter that is to replace a `?` in the filter for the recordset. If you have more than one parameter, the parameters substitute for the question marks in the `m_strFilter` string in sequence from left to right, so it's important to ensure that the `RFX_()` calls are in the right order when there are several. With the mode set to `param`, the second argument in the `RFX_()` call is ignored, so you could put `NULL` here or some other string if you want.

Initializing the Record View

You can now implement the override for the `OnInitialUpdate()` function in the `COrderView` class. This function is called by the MFC framework before the view is initially displayed, so you can put code in this function to do any one-time initialization that you need. In this case you will specify the filter for the recordset. Here's the definition of the function to do this:

```
void COrderView::OnInitialUpdate()
{
  BeginWaitCursor();
  CDBSampleDoc* pDoc = static_cast<CDBSampleDoc*>(GetDocument());
  m_pSet = &pDoc->m_OrderSet;              // Get a pointer to the recordset

  // Use the DB that is open for products recordset
  m_pSet->m_pDatabase = pDoc->m_DBSampleSet.m_pDatabase;

  // Set the current product ID as parameter
```

```
        m_pSet->m_ProductIDparam = pDoc->m_DBSampleSet.m_ProductID;

        // Set the filter as product ID field
        m_pSet->m_strFilter =
          "[ProductID] = ? AND [Orders].[OrderID] = [Order Details].[OrderID]";

        CRecordView::OnInitialUpdate();
        EndWaitCursor();
    }
```

Add this function definition to `OrderView.cpp`. The version of the `COrderSet` class that was implemented by the Class wizard doesn't override the `GetDocument()` member because it isn't associated with the document class initially. As a result, you must cast the pointer from the base class `GetDocument()` member to a pointer to a `CDBSampleDoc` object. Alternatively, you could add an override version of `GetDocument()` to `COrderSet` to do the cast. Clearly, you need a pointer to the document object because you need to access the members of the object.

The `BeginWaitCursor()` call at the start of the `OnInitialUpdate()` function displays the hourglass cursor while this function is executing. The reason for this is that this function can take an appreciable time to execute, especially when multiple tables are involved. The processing of the query and the transfer of data to the recordset all takes place in here. The cursor is returned to normal by the `EndWaitCursor()` call at the end of the function.

The first thing that the code does is to set the `m_pDatabase` member of the `COrderSet` object to the same as that for the `CProductSet` object. If you don't do this, the framework re-opens the database when the orders recordset is opened. Because the database has already been opened for the products recordset, this wastes a lot of time.

Next, you set the value for the `m_ProductIDparam` parameter variable to the current value stored in the `m_ProductID` member of the products recordset. This value replaces the question mark in the filter when the orders recordset is opened, so select the records you want; then set the filter for the orders recordset to the string you saw earlier.

Accessing Multiple Table Views

Because you have implemented the program with the single document interface, the application has one document and one view. The availability of just one view might appear to be a problem, but it isn't in practice. You can arrange for the frame window object in the application to create an instance of the `COrderView` class and switch the current window to that when the orders recordset is to be displayed.

You'll need to keep track of what the current window is, which you can do by assigning a unique ID to each of the record view windows in the application. At the moment there are two views: the products view and the orders view. To define IDs for these, create a new file called `OurConstants.h` and add the following code to it:

```
// Definitions for our constants

#pragma once

// Arbitrary constants to identify record views
const unsigned int PRODUCT_VIEW = 1;
const unsigned int ORDER_VIEW = 2;
```

You can now use one of these constants to identify each view and to record the ID of the current view in the frame window object. To record the current view ID, add a `public` data member to the `CMainFrame` class of type `unsigned int` and give it the name `m_CurrentViewID`. After you have done that, you can initialize it in the constructor for `CMainFrame` by adding code as follows:

```
CMainFrame::CMainFrame()
  : m_CurrentViewID(PRODUCT_VIEW)
{
}
```

The application starts with the Product View initially, so you initialize `m_CurrentViewID` to be consistent with that. Now add an `#include` directive for `OurConstants.h` to the beginning of `MainFrm.cpp` so that the definition of `PRODUCT_VIEW` is accessible in the source file.

Switching Views

To enable the view switching mechanism, you add a `public` function member to the `CMainFrame` class with the name `SelectView()` with a parameter specifying a view ID. This function switches from the current view to whatever view is specified by the ID passed as an argument.

Right-click `CMainFrame` and select `Add > Add Function` from the pop-up to add a new public member to the class. You can enter the return type as `void` and the function name as `SelectView`. The parameter name can be `ViewID`, and the type is `unsigned int`. You can implement the function as follows:

```
void CMainFrame::SelectView(unsigned int ViewID)
{
  CView* pOldActiveView = GetActiveView();          // Get current view

  // Get pointer to new view if it exists
  // if it doesn't the pointer will be null
  CView* pNewActiveView = static_cast<CView*>(GetDlgItem(ViewID));

  // If this is 1st time around for the new view,
  // the new view won't exist, so we must create it
  if (pNewActiveView == NULL)
  {
    switch(ViewID)
    {
      case ORDER_VIEW:       // Create an Order view
        pNewActiveView = new COrderView;
        break;
      default:
        AfxMessageBox(L"Invalid View ID");
        return;
    }

    // Switching the views
    // Obtain the current view context to apply to the new view
    CCreateContext context;
    context.m_pCurrentDoc = pOldActiveView->GetDocument();
    pNewActiveView->Create(NULL, NULL, 0L, CFrameWnd::rectDefault,
                                        this, ViewID, &context);
    pNewActiveView->OnInitialUpdate();
  }
  SetActiveView(pNewActiveView);                     // Activate the new view
```

```
    pOldActiveView->ShowWindow(SW_HIDE);        // Hide the old view
    pNewActiveView->ShowWindow(SW_SHOW);        // Show the new view
    pOldActiveView->SetDlgCtrlID(m_CurrentViewID); // Set the old view ID
    pNewActiveView->SetDlgCtrlID(AFX_IDW_PANE_FIRST);
    m_CurrentViewID = ViewID;                   // Save the new view ID
    RecalcLayout();
  }
```

The operation of the function falls into three distinct parts:

1. Getting pointers to the current view and the new view

2. Creating the new view if it doesn't exist

3. Swapping to the new view in place of the current view

The address of the current active view is supplied by the GetActiveView() member of the CMainFrame object. To get a pointer to the new view, you call the GetDlgItem() member of the frame window object. If a view with the ID specified in the argument to the function exists, it returns the address of the view; otherwise, it returns NULL, and you need to create the new view.

After creating a view object, you define a CCreateContext object, context. A CCreateContext object is necessary only when you are creating a window for a view that is to be connected to a document. A CCreateContext object contains data members that can tie together a document, a frame window, and a view, and for MDI applications, a document template as well. When you switch between views, you will create a new window for the new view to be displayed. Each time you create a new view window, you use the CCreateContext object to establish a connection between the view and your document object. You need to store a pointer to the document object only in the m_pCurrentDoc member on context. In general, you may need to store additional data in the CCreateContext object before you create the view; it depends on the circumstances and what kind of window you are creating.

In the call to the Create() member of the view object that creates the window for the new view, you pass the context object as an argument. This establishes a proper relationship with your document and validates the document pointer. The argument this in the call to Create() specifies the current frame as the parent window, and the ViewID argument specifies the ID of the window. This ID enables the address of the window to be obtained with a subsequent call to the GetDlgItem() member of the parent window.

To make the new view the active view, you call the SetActiveView() member of CMainFrame. The new view then replaces the current active view. To remove the old view window, you call the ShowWindow() member of the view with the argument SW_HIDE using the pointer to the old view. To display the new view window, you call the same function with the argument SW_SHOW using the pointer to the new view.

```
    SetActiveView(pNewActiveView);              // Activate the new view
    pOldActiveView->ShowWindow(SW_HIDE);        // Hide the old view
    pNewActiveView->ShowWindow(SW_SHOW);        // Show the new view
    pOldActiveView->SetDlgCtrlID(m_CurrentViewID);// Set the old view ID
    pNewActiveView->SetDlgCtrlID(AFX_IDW_PANE_FIRST);
    m_CurrentViewID = ViewID;                   // Save the new view ID
```

You restore the ID of the old active view to the ID value that you have defined for it in the m_CurrentViewID member of the CMainFrame class that you added earlier. You also set the ID of the new view to AFX_IDW_PANE_FIRST to identify it as the first window for the application. This is necessary because the application has only one view, so the first view is the only view. Lastly, you save the ID for the new window in the m_CurrentViewID member, so it's available the next time the current view is replaced. The call to RecalculateLayout() causes the view to be redrawn when the new view is selected.

You must add a #include directive for the OrderView.h file to beginning of the MainFrm.cpp file so that the COrderView class definition is available here. After you save MainFrm.cpp, you can move on to adding a button control to the Products dialog to link to the Orders dialog. You'll then be able to add handlers for this button and its partner on the Orders dialog to call the SelectView() member of CMainFrame.

Enabling the Switching Operation

To implement the view switching mechanism, go back to Resource View and open the IDD_DBSAMPLE_FORM dialog. You need to add a button control to the dialog box, as shown in Figure 20-27:

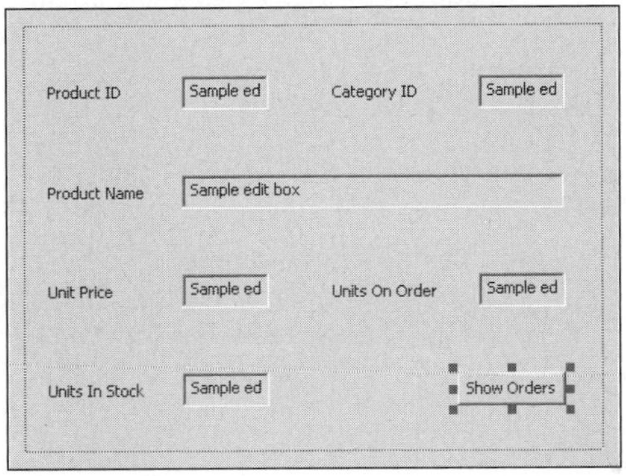

Figure 20-27

You can set the ID for the button to IDC_ORDERS, consistent with the naming for the other controls in the dialog box.

After saving the resource, you can create a handler for the button by right-clicking it and selecting Add Event Handler from the pop-up. Use the Event Handler Wizard dialog box to add the function OnOrders() to the CProductView class for the BN_CLICKED message type; this handler is called when the button is clicked. You need to add only one line of code to complete the handler:

```
void CProductView::OnOrders()
{
   static_cast<CMainFrame*>(GetParentFrame())->SelectView(ORDER_VIEW);
}
```

The GetParentFrame() member of the view object is inherited from CWnd, which is an indirect base class of CMainFrame. This function returns a pointer to the parent frame window, and you use it to call the SelectView() function that you have just added to the CMainFrame class. The ORDER_VIEW argument value causes the frame window to switch to the Orders dialog window. If this is the first time this has occurred, it will create the view object and the window. On the second and subsequent occasions that a switch to the orders view is selected, the existing orders view are re-used.

You must add the following #include directives to the beginning of the ProductView.cpp file:

```
#include "OurConstants.h"
#include "MainFrm.h"
```

The next task is to add the handler for the button that you previously placed on the IDD_ORDERS_FORM dialog. From the Editor window showing this dialog box, use the same process to add the OnProducts() handler to the COrderView class and add a single line of code to its implementation:

```
void COrderView::OnProducts()
{
    static_cast<CMainFrame*>(GetParentFrame())->SelectView(PRODUCT_VIEW);
}
```

This works in the same way as the previous button control handler. Again, you must add #include directives for the OurConstants.h and MainFrm.h files to the beginning of the OrderView.cpp file and then save it.

Handling View Activation

When you switch to a view that already exists, you need to ensure that the recordset is refreshed and that the dialog is re-initialized so that the correct information is displayed. When an existing view is activated or deactivated, the framework calls the OnActivateView() member of the class, so this is a good place to take care of refreshing the recordset and the dialog box. You can override this function in each of the view classes. You can do this by selecting the Overrides button in the Properties window for a view class and selecting OnActivateView from the list. Make sure you add the override to both view classes.

You can add the following code to complete the implementation of the OnActivateView() function override for the COrderView class:

```
void COrderView::OnActivateView(BOOL bActivate,
                        CView* pActivateView, CView* pDeactiveView)
{
    if(bActivate)
    {
        // Get a pointer to the document
        CDBSampleDoc* pDoc = GetDocument();

        // Get a pointer to the frame window
        CMainFrame* pMFrame = static_cast<CMainFrame*>(GetParentFrame());

        // If the last view was the product view, we must re-query
        // the recordset with the product ID from the product recordset
        if(pMFrame->m_CurrentViewID==PRODUCT_VIEW)
        {
            if(!m_pSet->IsOpen())           // Make sure the recordset is open
                return;
            // Set current product ID as parameter
            m_pSet->m_ProductIDparam = pDoc->m_DBSampleSet.m_ProductID;
            m_pSet->Requery();              // Get data from the DB

            // If we are past the EOF there are no records
```

```
    if(m_pSet->IsEOF())
      AfxMessageBox(L"No orders for the current product ID");
  }

  // Set the window caption
  CString strTitle = _T("Table Name: ");
  CString strTable = m_pSet->GetTableName();
  if(!strTable.IsEmpty())
    strTitle += strTable;
  else
    strTitle += _T("Orders - Multiple Tables");
  pDoc->SetTitle(strTitle);
  CRecordView::OnInitialUpdate();         // Update values in dialog
}
```

```
  CRecordView::OnActivateView(bActivate, pActivateView, pDeactiveView);
}
```

You execute the code only if the view is being activated, and when this is the case, the bActivate argument will be TRUE. After getting pointers to the document and the parent frame, you verify that the previous view was the Product View before re-querying the order set. This check is not necessary at present because the previous view is always the Product View, but when you add another view to the application, this will not always be true so you might as well put the code in now.

To re-query the database, you set the parameter member of COrderSet, m_ProductIDparam, to the current value of the m_ProductID member of the product recordset. This causes the orders for the current product to be selected. You don't need to set the m_strFilter member of the recordset here because that was set in the OnInitialUpdate() function when the CRecordView object was first created. The IsEOF() function member of the COrderSet object is inherited from CRecordSet and returns TRUE if the recordset is empty when it is re-queried.

Add the code for OnActivateView() function in the CProductView class as follows:

```
void CProductView::OnActivateView(BOOL bActivate,
                        CView* pActivateView, CView* pDeactiveView)
{
  if(bActivate)
  {
    // Update the window caption
    CString strTitle = _T("Table Name");
    CString strTable = m_pSet->GetTableName();
    strTitle += _T(": ") + strTable;
    GetDocument()->SetTitle(strTitle);
  }
  CRecordView::OnActivateView(bActivate, pActivateView, pDeactiveView);
}
```

In this case, all you need to do if the view has been activated is to update the window caption. Because the Product View is the driving view for the rest of the application, you always want to return the view to its state before it was deactivated. If you do nothing apart from updating the window caption, the view is displayed in its previous state.

Viewing Orders for a Product

You are now ready to try to build the executable module for the new version of the example. When you run the example, you should be able to see the orders for any product just by clicking the Orders button on the Products dialog box. A typical view of an order is shown in Figure 20-28.

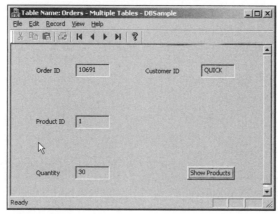

Figure 20-28

Clicking the `Show Products` button returns you to the Products dialog box, so you can browse further through the products. In this dialog, you can use the toolbar buttons to browse all the orders for the current product. The `Customer ID` is a bit cryptic. You could add one more view to display the details of the customer's name and address. It won't be too difficult, because you have built already the mechanism to switch between views.

Viewing Customer Details

The basic mechanism that you'll add will work through another button control on the Order dialog that switches to a new dialog for customer data. As well as controls to display customer data, you'll add two buttons to the customer dialog box: one to return to the Order View, and the other to return to the Product View. You'll need another view ID corresponding to the customer view, which you can add with the following line in the `OurConstants.h` file:

```
const unsigned int CUSTOMER_VIEW = 3;
```

Now you'll add the recordset for the customer details.

Adding the Customer Recordset

The process is exactly the same as you followed for the `COrderSet` class. Use the `Add > Class` menu item from the context menu in Class View and use the MFC ODBC Consumer template to define the `CCustomerSet` class, with `CRecordset` specified as the base class. Select the database as Northwind as before and select the `Customers` table for the recordset. You can select snapshot as the type of access to the table. The class should then be created with the data members shown as follows:

```
CStringW m_CustomerID;
CStringW m_CompanyName;
CStringW m_ContactName;
CStringW m_ContactTitle;
CStringW m_Address;
CStringW m_City;
CStringW m_Region;
CStringW m_PostalCode;
CStringW m_Country;
CStringW m_Phone;
CStringW m_Fax;
```

Don't forget to comment out the `#error` directive in the `CustomerSet.cpp` file. Change each of the `CStringW` types here to `CString` and then save the class file. At this point, you could add a `CCustomerSet` member to the document so that it is created when the document object is created. Right-click the `CDBSampleDoc` class name in Class View and add a variable of type `CCustomerSet` with the name `m_CustomerSet`. You can leave the access specifier as `public`.

You will find an `#include` directive for `CustomerSet.h` that has already been added to `DBSampleDoc.h`. After saving all the files you have modified, you can create the customer dialog resource.

Creating the Customer Dialog Resource

This process is also exactly the same as the one you went through for the Orders dialog. Change to Resource View and create a new dialog resource with the ID `IDD_CUSTOMER_FORM`, not forgetting to set the style to `Child` and the border to `None` in the `Properties` box for the dialog. After deleting the default buttons, add controls to the dialog box to correspond to the field names for the `Customers` table, as shown in Figure 20-29:

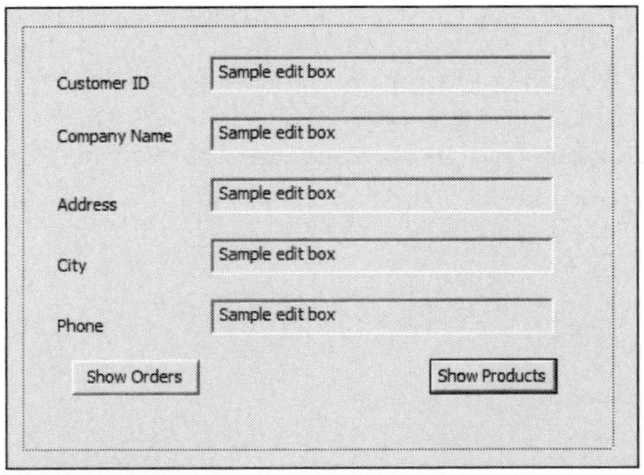

Figure 20-29

The two buttons enable you to switch to either the Orders dialog, which is how you got to this dialog, or directly back to the Products dialog. The size of the window for the application is determined by the size of the first dialog box displayed, so because the Customer dialog is a bit larger, resize the Products dialog box at least as large as this dialog box.

Specify the IDs for the controls using the field names as a basis. You can get help with this by expanding the list of members of CCustomerSet in Class View and keeping that visible while you work on the dialog. You can set the button IDs as IDC_ORDERS and IDC_PRODUCTS. After you save the dialog resource, you're ready to create the view class for the recordset.

Creating the Customer View Class

You'll create the view class for the customer recordset manually, just as you did for the COrderView class. Add CustomerView.h and CustomerView.cpp files to the project and insert the following code to define the class in the CustomerView.h file:

```
// CCustomerView record view
#pragma once

class CCustomerSet;
class CDBSampleDoc;

class CCustomerView : public CRecordView
{
   DECLARE_DYNCREATE(CCustomerView)

public:
   enum { IDD = IDD_CUSTOMER_FORM };
   CCustomerSet* m_pSet;


public:
   CCustomerView();
   CCustomerSet* GetRecordset();
   virtual CRecordset* OnGetRecordset();

   protected:
   virtual void DoDataExchange(CDataExchange* pDX);     // DDX/DDV support
   virtual void OnInitialUpdate();
   virtual void OnActivateView(BOOL bActivate, CView* pActivateView,
                                              CView* pDeactiveView);

// Implementation
protected:
   virtual ~CCustomerView(){}

#ifdef _DEBUG
   virtual void AssertValid() const;
   virtual void Dump(CDumpContext& dc) const;
#endif

};
```

The class has essentially the same members as the COrderView class.

You can add the following initial code to the `CustomerView.cpp`:

```cpp
// CCustomerView implementation
#include "stdafx.h"
#include "resource.h"

IMPLEMENT_DYNCREATE(CCustomerView, CRecordView)

CCustomerView::CCustomerView(): CRecordView(CCustomerView::IDD), m_pSet(NULL)
{
}

CCustomerSet* CCustomerView::GetRecordset()
  {
    ASSERT(m_pSet != NULL);
    return m_pSet;
  }

  CRecordset* CCustomerView::OnGetRecordset()
  {
    return m_pSet;
  }

  // COrderView diagnostics

#ifdef _DEBUG
void CCustomerView::AssertValid() const
{
  CRecordView::AssertValid();
}

void CCustomerView::Dump(CDumpContext& dc) const
{
  CRecordView::Dump(dc);
}
#endif //_DEBUG
```

This is the same boilerplate code as in the `COrderView` class, and the functions are defined here as in the earlier class. The first `#include` directive is for the precompiled headers, and the second provides the definitions for the resource IDs.

You can process the button controls in the `IDD_CUSTOMER_FORM` dialog box in the same way as you did previously to add the `OnOrders()` and `OnProducts()` functions to the `CCustomerView` class; right-click each button and select the Add Event Handler from the pop-up. The code for these is similar to the corresponding functions in the other views. The code you need to add to `OnOrders()` in the `CustomerView.cpp` file is:

```cpp
void CCustomerView::OnOrders()
{
  static_cast<CMainFrame*>(GetParentFrame())->SelectView(ORDER_VIEW);
}
```

You can add a similar line of code to the `OnProducts()` function:

```
void CCustomerView::OnProducts()
{
   static_cast<CMainFrame*>(GetParentFrame())->SelectView(PRODUCT_VIEW);
}
```

You now need to add code to specify a filter for the customer recordset so that you get only the customer details displayed that correspond to the customer ID field from the current order in the `COrderSet` object.

Adding a Filter

You can define the filter in the `OnInitialUpdate()` member of `CCustomerView`. Because you anticipate only one record being returned corresponding to each customer ID, you don't need to worry about sorting. The code for this function is as follows:

```
void CCustomerView::OnInitialUpdate()
{
  BeginWaitCursor();

  CDBSampleDoc* pDoc = static_cast<CDBSampleDoc*>(GetDocument());
  m_pSet = &pDoc->m_CustomerSet;        // Initialize the recordset pointer

  // Set the DB for the customer recordset
  m_pSet->m_pDatabase = pDoc->m_DBSampleSet.m_pDatabase;

  // Set the current customer ID as the filter parameter value
  m_pSet->m_CustomerIDparam = pDoc->m_OrderSet.m_OrdersCustomerID;
  m_pSet->m_strFilter ="CustomerID = ?";     // Filter on CustomerID field

  CRecordView::OnInitialUpdate();
  if (m_pSet->IsOpen())
  {
    CString strTitle = m_pSet->m_pDatabase->GetDatabaseName();
    CString strTable = m_pSet->GetTableName();
    if(!strTable.IsEmpty())
      strTitle += _T(":") + strTable;
    GetDocument()->SetTitle(strTitle);
  }
  EndWaitCursor();
}
```

After getting a pointer to the document, you store the address of the `CCustomerSet` object member of the document in the `m_pSet` member of the view. You know the database is already open, so you can set the database pointer in the customer recordset to that stored in the `CProductSet` object.

The parameter for the filter will be defined in the `m_CustomerIDparam` member of `CCustomerSet`. You'll add this member to the class in a moment. It's set to the current value of the `m_CustomerID` member of the `COrderSet` object owned by the document. You will define the filter in such a way that the customer recordset contains only the record with the same customer ID as that in the current order.

The `OnActivateView()` function handles activation of the customer view, and you can implement it in `CustomerView.cpp` as follows:

```cpp
void CCustomerView::OnActivateView(BOOL bActivate,
                           CView* pActivateView, CView* pDeactiveView)
{
  if(bActivate)
  {
    if(!m_pSet->IsOpen())
      return;
    CDBSampleDoc* pDoc = static_cast<CDBSampleDoc*>(GetDocument());

    // Set current customer ID as parameter
    m_pSet->m_CustomerIDparam = pDoc->m_OrderSet.m_OrdersCustomerID;
    m_pSet->Requery();               // Get data from the DB
    CRecordView::OnInitialUpdate();  // Redraw the dialog

    // Check for empty recordset
    if(m_pSet->IsEOF())
      AfxMessageBox(L"No customer details for the current customer ID");

    CString strTitle = _T("Table Name:");
    CString strTable = m_pSet->GetTableName();
    if(!strTable.IsEmpty())
      strTitle += strTable;
    else
      strTitle += _T("Multiple Tables");
    pDoc->SetTitle(strTitle);
  }
  CRecordView::OnActivateView(bActivate, pActivateView, pDeactiveView);
}
```

If this function is called because the view has been activated (rather than deactivated), `bActivate` has the value TRUE. In this case, you set the filter parameter from the order recordset and re-query the database.

The `m_CustomerIDparam` member for the `CCustomerSet` recordset object that is associated with this view object is set to the customer ID from the orders recordset object that is stored in the document. This will be the customer ID for the current order. The call to the `Requery()` function for the `CCustomerSet` object retrieves records from the database using the filter you have set up. The result is that the details for the customer for the current order are stored in the `CCustomerSet` object and then passed to the `CCustomerView` object for display in the dialog.

You will need to add the following `#include` statements to the beginning of the `CustomerView.cpp` file:

```cpp
#include "ProductSet.h"
#include "OrderSet.h"
#include "CustomerSet.h"
#include "DBSampleDoc.h"
#include "OurConstants.h"
#include "MainFrm.h"
```

The first three are required because of classes used in the definition of the document class. You need `DBSampleDoc.h` because of the `CDBSampleDoc` class reference in `OnInitialUpdate()`, and the remaining two `.h` files contain definitions that are referred to in the button handlers in the `CCustomerView` class.

Implementing the Filter Parameter

Add a `public` variable of type `CString` to the `CCustomerSet` class to correspond with the type of the `m_CustomerID` member of the recordset and give it the name `m_CustomerIDparam`. If you used the `Add > Add Variable` mechanism from Class View to do this, the new member will already be initialized in the constructor; otherwise, add the initialization as in the code that follows. You can set the parameter count in the `CCustomerSet` constructor as follows:

```
CCustomerSet::CCustomerSet(CDatabase* pdb)
: CRecordset(pdb)
, m_CustomerIDparam("")
{
  m_CustomerID = "";
  m_CompanyName = "";
  m_ContactName = "";
  m_ContactTitle = "";
  m_Address = "";
  m_City = "";
  m_Region = "";
  m_PostalCode = "";
  m_Country = "";
  m_Phone = "";
  m_Fax = "";
  m_nFields = 11;
  m_nParams = 1;                        // Number of parameters
  m_nDefaultType = snapshot;
}
```

The `m_CustomerIDparam` member is initialized to an empty string and the parameter count in `m_nParams` is set to 1.

To set up the `m_CustomerIDparam` parameter, you add statements to the `DoFieldExchange()` member, as before:

```
void CCustomerSet::DoFieldExchange(CFieldExchange* pFX)
{
  pFX->SetFieldType(CFieldExchange::outputColumn);
  RFX_Text(pFX, _T("[CustomerID]"), m_CustomerID);
  RFX_Text(pFX, _T("[CompanyName]"), m_CompanyName);
  RFX_Text(pFX, _T("[ContactName]"), m_ContactName);
  RFX_Text(pFX, _T("[ContactTitle]"), m_ContactTitle);
  RFX_Text(pFX, _T("[Address]"), m_Address);
  RFX_Text(pFX, _T("[City]"), m_City);
  RFX_Text(pFX, _T("[Region]"), m_Region);
  RFX_Text(pFX, _T("[PostalCode]"), m_PostalCode);
```

```
RFX_Text(pFX, _T("[Country]"), m_Country);
RFX_Text(pFX, _T("[Phone]"), m_Phone);
RFX_Text(pFX, _
pFX->SetFieldType(CFieldExchange::param);        // Set parameter mode
RFX_Text(pFX, _T("CustomerIDParam"), m_CustomerIDparam);
}
```

I have omitted comment lines from the beginning of this function to save space. After setting the `param` mode by calling the `SetFieldType()` member of the `pFX` object, you call the `RFX_Text()` function to pass the parameter value for substitution in the filter. You use `RFX_Text()` because the parameter variable is of type `CString`. There are various `RFX_()` functions supporting a range of parameter types.

After you have completed this modification, you can save the `CustomerSet.cpp` file.

Linking the Order Dialog to the Customer Dialog

To permit a switch to the Customer dialog, you require a button control on the `IDD_ORDERS_FORM` dialog, so open it in Resource View and add an extra button, as shown in Figure 20-30.

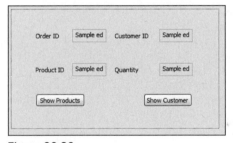

Figure 20-30

I have rearranged the original controls a little — you can arrange them to please yourself. You can define the ID for the new button control as `IDC_CUSTOMER`. After you save the dialog, you can add a handler for the button by right-clicking it and select `Add Event Handler` from the pop-up. The handler requires only one line of code to be added to it, as follows:

```
void COrderView::OnCustomer()
{
   static_cast<CMainFrame*>(GetParentFrame())->SelectView(CUSTOMER_VIEW);
}
```

This obtains the address of the frame window and uses it to call the `SelectView()` member of `CMainFrame` to switch to a customer view. The penultimate step to complete the program is to add the code to the `SelectView()` function that deals with the `CUSTOMER_VIEW` value being passed to it. This requires just three additional lines of code, as follows:

```
void CMainFrame::SelectView(UINT ViewID)
{
```

```
      CView* pOldActiveView = GetActiveView();        // Get current view

      // Get pointer to new view if it exists
      // if it doesn't the pointer will be null
      CView* pNewActiveView = static_cast<CView*>(GetDlgItem(ViewID));

      // If this is 1st time around for the new view,
      // the new view won't exist, so we must create it
      if (pNewActiveView == NULL)
      {
        switch(ViewID)
        {
          case ORDER_VIEW:       // Create an Order view
            pNewActiveView = new COrderView;
            break;
          case CUSTOMER_VIEW:    // Create a customer view
            pNewActiveView = new CCustomerView;
            break;
          default:
            AfxMessageBox("Invalid View ID");
            return;
        }

        // Switching the views
        // Obtain the current view context to apply to the new view
        CCreateContext context;
        context.m_pCurrentDoc = pOldActiveView->GetDocument();
        pNewActiveView->Create(NULL, NULL, 0L, CFrameWnd::rectDefault,
                                                this, ViewID, &context);
        pNewActiveView->OnInitialUpdate();
      }
      SetActiveView(pNewActiveView);                   // Activate the new view
      pOldActiveView->ShowWindow(SW_HIDE);             // Hide the old view
      pNewActiveView->ShowWindow(SW_SHOW);             // Show the new view
      pOldActiveView->SetDlgCtrlID(m_CurrentViewID);   // Set the old view ID
      pNewActiveView->SetDlgCtrlID(AFX_IDW_PANE_FIRST);
      m_CurrentViewID = ViewID;                        // Save the new view ID
      RecalcLayout();
    }
```

The only change necessary is the addition of a case statement in the switch to create a CCustomerView object when one doesn't exist. Each view object will be re-used next time around, so they get created only once. The code to switch between views works with any number of views, so if you want this function to handle more views, you just need to add another case in the switch for each new view that you want. Although you are creating view objects dynamically here, you don't need to worry about deleting them. Because they are associated with a document object, they are deleted by the framework when the application closes.

Because you reference the CCustomerView class in the SelectView() function, you must add an #include statement for the CustomerView.h file to the block at the beginning of MainFrm.cpp.

To complete the application you can add the implementation of the `DoDataExchange()` function for the `CCustomerView` class to `CustomerView.cpp`:

```
void CCustomerView::DoDataExchange(CDataExchange* pDX)
{
   CRecordView::DoDataExchange(pDX);
   DDX_FieldText(pDX, IDC_ADDRESS,
                        m_pSet->m_Address, m_pSet);
   DDX_FieldText(pDX, IDC_CITY,
                        m_pSet->m_City, m_pSet);
   DDX_FieldText(pDX, IDC_COMPANYNAME,
                        m_pSet->m_CompanyName, m_pSet);
   DDX_FieldText(pDX, IDC_PHONE,
                        m_pSet->m_Phone, m_pSet);
   DDX_FieldText(pDX, IDC_CUSTOMERID,
                        m_pSet->m_CustomerID, m_pSet);
}
```

This uses the DDX_ functions as before to transfer data from the edit controls to the members of the `CCustomerView` class. You must add an `#include` directive for the `CustomerSet.h` header file for this to compile correctly.

Exercising the Database Viewer

At this point, the program is complete. You can build the application and execute it. As before, the main view of the database is the products view. As before, clicking Orders takes you to the Orders view. The second button on this form should now be active, and clicking it takes you to the details of the customer for the current order, as Figure 20-31 illustrates.

The two buttons take you back to the Orders view or the Products view, respectively.

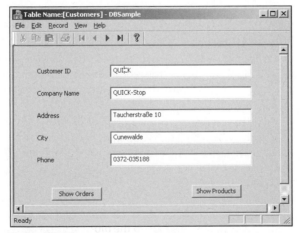

Figure 20-31

Summary

You should now be comfortable with the basics of how MFC links to your database using ODBC.

The key points you have seen in this chapter are:

- ❑ MFC provides OLE DB and ODBC support for accessing databases.
- ❑ To use a database with ODBC the database must be registered.
- ❑ A connection to a database is represented by a `CDatabase` or a `CDaoDatabase` object.
- ❑ A recordset object represents an SQL `SELECT` statement applied to a defined set of tables. Where necessary, the framework will automatically create a database object representing a connection to a database when a recordset object is created.
- ❑ A `WHERE` clause can be added for a recordset object through its `m_strFilter` data member.
- ❑ An `ORDER BY` clause can be defined for a recordset through its `m_strSort` data member.
- ❑ A record view object is used to display the contents of a recordset object.

Exercises

You can download the source code for the examples in the book and the solutions to the following exercises from www.wrox.com.

1. Using the **Products** table again, add a "stock control" dialog box to the application. This should be reachable through a button on the Products dialog box and must itself contain a button to go back to the Products dialog. The fields it should display are the product ID, product name, reorder level, unit price, and units in stock. Don't worry about filtering or sorting at the moment; just get the basic mechanism working.

2. Refine the preceding project so that the stock control dialog automatically displays information about the product that was being shown in the Products dialog box when the button was clicked.

3. Implement a system whereby the user of the database is warned in the stock control dialog about the present stock being near or below the reorder level. You'll have noticed by now that some of the stock reorder levels are set to zero; don't display a warning in those cases.

Updating Data Sources

In this chapter, you'll build on what you learned about accessing a database via ODBC (**O**pen **D**ata**B**ase **C**onnectivity) in the previous chapter, and try your hand at updating the Northwind Traders database through the same mechanism.

By the end of this chapter, you will have learned about:

❑   Database transactions

❑   How to update a database using recordset objects

❑   How data is transferred from a recordset to the database in an update operation

❑   How to update an existing row in a table

❑   How to add a new row to a table

Update Operations

When you are just writing code to view information from a database, the only issue is whether you are authorized to access the data. As long as the database has the right kind of access protection, the data in the database is safe. As soon as you start writing code to update a database, it's quite another kettle of fish. Because you are altering the contents of the database, such modifications could destroy the integrity of the database and make nonsense of the contents of a table, or even make it unusable. You always need to take great care to test your code properly with a test database before letting it loose on the real thing.

A database update typically involves modifying one or more fields in a row in an existing table, modifying an order quantity for instance, or adding a new row — a new order perhaps in the context of the Northwind database. You'll be developing examples of both of these, but first, consider the implications.

Most of the complications that can arise with database update operations become apparent in the context of multi-user databases. Without proper control of the update process, concurrent access by several users provides the potential for two kinds of problems. The first arises if one person is allowed to retrieve a record while an update operation is in progress on the same record. The person just reading the data can potentially end up with the old data prior to the update or even a mixture with some fields containing old data and some new. The second problem arises with concurrent update where one person starts updating a record while another update is already in progress on the same record. With a single record in a table involved in this, there is potential for an update to be lost. Where records from several tables are involved, the data in the database can end up in an inconsistent state. Before you look into how this can be handled, see how basic update operations on a recordset work.

CRecordset Update Operations

You saw in the previous chapter how the RFX_() function calls in the DoFieldExchange() member of the recordset object retrieved data from the selected fields in the table or tables in the database, and transferred it to the data members of the recordset object. The same functions are also used to update fields in a database table, or to add a completely new row.

As shown in the following table, there are five member functions of the CRecordset class that support update operations.

Edit()	Call this function to start updating an existing record. Throws a CDBException if the table cannot be updated, and throws a CMemoryException if an out of memory condition arises.
AddNew()	Call this function to start adding a completely new record. Throws a CDBException if a new record cannot be appended to the table.
Update()	Call this function to complete updating of an existing record or adding a new one. Throws a CDBException if a single record was not updated, or an error occurred.
Delete()	Delete the current record by creating and executing an SQL DELETE. Throws a CDBException if an error occurs — if the database is read-only for instance. After a Delete() operation, all the data members of the recordset will be set to null values — the equivalent of no value set. You must move to a new record before executing any other operation on the recordset object.
CancelUpdate()	Cancels any outstanding operation to modify an existing record, or to add a new one.

None of the functions have parameters. The first four functions here can throw exceptions, so you should put the call in a try block and add a catch block if you don't want your program to end abruptly when an error occurs.

To delete the current record for a recordset object, just call its Delete() member. You must then scroll the recordset to a new position before attempting to use any of the functions above because the values of the data members of the recordset object will be invalid after calling Delete().

Figure 21-1 illustrates the basic sequence of events in updating an existing record or adding a new one.

When you call `AddNew()` for a recordset to start adding a new record to a table, the function saves the current values of all the data members of the recordset object that correspond to field values in a buffer, and then sets the data members to `PSEUDO_NULL`. This is not zero or null as in a pointer. It is a value that indicates the data member has not been set. When you call `Update()` to complete adding a record, the original values of the data members of the recordset before `AddNew()` was called are restored. If you want the recordset to contain the values for the new record, you must call the `Requery()` member of the recordset object. This function returns `TRUE` (a value of the MFC type `BOOL`) if the operation was successful. You also call `Requery()` when you want to obtain a different view of the data where you will retrieve records using a different SQL command or a different filter for the records.

The transfer of data between the recordset data members and the database always uses the `DoFieldExchange()` member of the recordset object, so the `RFX_()` functions provide a dual capability — writing to the database as well as reading from it.

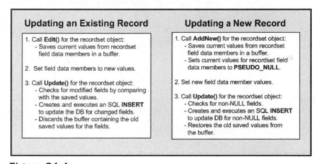

Figure 21-1

Checking that Operations are Legal

It is a good idea to confirm that the operation you intend to carry out is legal with your recordset object. It is all too easy to end up with a read-only recordset — just forgetting to reset the read-only attribute on the `Northwind.mdb` file will do it! If you try to update a table that is read-only, an exception is thrown that is entirely avoidable if you just verify that the operation is possible. Using exceptions to catch errors that aren't that unexpected is inefficient, and generally frowned upon. It's better to check beforehand when this is possible, as it is in this case. That way, your exception handling code is truly reserved for exceptional occurrences.

The `CanUpdate()` member of `CRecordset` returns `TRUE` if you can modify records in the table represented by the recordset object. When you want to add a new record, you can call the `CanAppend()` member of `CRecordset` beforehand to check. This returns `TRUE` if adding new records to the table is permitted.

Record Locking

Record locking prevents other users from accessing the locked record while a table row is being updated. The extent to which a record is locked during an update is determined by the locking mode set in the recordset object. There are two locking modes defined in `CRecordset`, referred to as **optimistic mode** and **pessimistic mode**.

`CRecordset::optimistic`	In optimistic locking mode, the record is only locked while the `Update()` member function is executing. This minimizes the time that the record in inaccessible to other users of the database. If an editing operation may take a long time, pessimistic locking is often not a practical solution because other users may need to access the database. The standard solution is to use optimistic locking and to introduce some sort of conflict resolution mechanism.
`CRecordset::pessimistic`	In pessimistic locking mode, the record is locked as soon as you call `Edit()`, and it remains locked and therefore inaccessible to other users until the completion of the call to `Update()` or until the update operation is aborted. This can obviously severely affect performance when updates are being prepared interactively; however, this mode is essential in many instances to ensure the integrity of the data is maintained.

The default mode for a recordset object is optimistic, so you have to set it only if you want pessimistic mode. To set this mode, you call the `SetLockingMode()` member of the recordset object with `CRecordset::pessimistic` as the argument. Of course, you can also reset it by calling the function with `CRecordset::optimistic` as the argument.

Transactions

The idea of a **transaction** in the database context is to enable operations to be safely undone when necessary. A transaction packages a well-defined series of one or more modifications to a database into a single operation so that at any point prior to the completion of the transaction everything can be reversed (or **rolled back**) if an error occurs. Clearly, if an update were to fail when it was partially completed, due to a hardware problem, for instance, it could have a disastrous effect on the integrity of the database. A transaction is not just an update to a single table. It can involve very complex operations on a database involving a series of modifications to multiple tables and may take an appreciable time to complete. In these situations, support for transactions is virtually a necessity if the integrity of the database is to be assured.

With transaction based operations, the database system manages the processing of the transaction and records recovery information so that anything that the transaction does to the data can be undone in the event of a problem part way through. Transaction events are recorded in a log file on disk, so even if the computer loses power, the system can recover by reading the entries in the log. By making your database operations based on transactions, you can protect the database against errors that might occur during processing. Typically, transaction processing locks records as necessary along the way and also ensures that any other database users accessing data that has been modified by the transaction will see the changes immediately.

Transactions are supported by most large commercial database systems on mainframe computers, and this is usually the case with database systems that run on a PC. The `CDatabase` class in MFC supports transactions, and as it happens, so does the Microsoft ODBC support for Access databases, so you can try out transaction processing with the Northwind database if you want.

CDatabase Transaction Operations

Transactions are managed through members of your CDatabase class object that provides the connection to the database. To determine whether transactions are supported for any given connection, you call the CanTransact() member of the CDatabase object. This returns TRUE if transactions are supported. Incidentally, there is also a CanUpdate() member of CDatabase that returns FALSE if the data source is read-only.

There are three member functions of CDatabase involved in transaction processing, as shown in the following table.

BeginTrans()	Starts a transaction on the database. All subsequent recordset operations are part of the transaction, until either CommitTrans() or Rollback() is called. The function returns TRUE if the transaction start was successful.
CommitTrans()	Commits the transaction so all recordset operations that are part of the transaction are expedited. The function returns FALSE if an error occurs, in which case the state of the data source is undefined.
Rollback()	Rolls back all the recordset operations executed since BeginTrans() was called, and restores the data source to the condition at the time when BeginTrans() was called.

The sequence of events in a transaction is very simple:

❑ Call BeginTrans() to start the transaction.

❑ Call Edit(), Update(), AddNew(), for your recordset as necessary.

❑ Call CommitTrans() to complete the transaction.

Outside of a transaction, Edit() or AddNew() operations on a recordset are executed when you call Update(). Within a transaction they are not executed until you call CommitTrans() for the CDatabase object. If you need to abort the transaction at any time after calling BeginTrans(), just call Rollback().

Complications can arise with the effect of CommitTrans() and Rollback() — the position in the recordset you are operating on can be lost for instance, so you may need to take some action in your program to recover the record pointer after completing or aborting a transaction. There are two members of CDatabase to help with this. After a CommitTrans() call you need to call the GetCursorCommitBehavior() member of CDatabase, and after calling Rollback() you need to call GetCursorRollbackBehavior(). Both of these functions return one of three values of type int, as shown in the following table, that indicate what you should do.

SQL_CB_PRESERVE	The recordset's connection to the data source is unaffected by the commit or rollback operation, so do nothing.
SQL_CB_CLOSE	You need to call Requery() for the recordset object to restore the current position in the recordset.
SQL_CB_DELETE	You must close the recordset by calling the Close() member of the object and then re-open the recordset if necessary.

There are further complications with using transactions in practice because the particular drivers you are using can affect when you must open the recordset. With some drivers you must open the recordset before you call `BeginTrans()`. With others, and the Microsoft Access ODBC drivers are a case in point, `Rollback()` will not work unless you open your recordset after you call `BeginTrans()`. You need to understand the particular drivers you intend to use before attempting to use transactions in your application.

A Simple Update Example

It's time to get some hands on experience with update operations in action starting with a very basic example. This omits most of what I have discussed so far in this chapter initially, but you will be building on this to apply some of what you have learned. You can create an application to update a database table with minimal effort using the MFC Application Wizard that you applied in the previous chapter. You'll be creating a program to allow updating of certain fields in the Order Details table.

Create a project called `DBSimpleUpdate` using the MFC Application template. Elect to go for the Database View without file support option with ODBC as the `Client type` option, as you did in the previous chapter. You are still going to use the Northwind database through ODBC, but this time you should choose dynaset as the recordset type. In a multiuser environment, a dynaset is automatically updated with any changes made to a record while it is accessed by your program. This ensures the data you have in your application is always up to date. For operations to modify an existing record or add new ones, you should choose dynaset as the recordset type.

Because you plan to update the database, you must map the recordset to a single database table. The database classes in MFC do not support updating of recordsets that involve joining two or more tables. Choose the Order Details table for the default recordset, as shown in Figure 21-2.

If you select multiple tables here, updating the recordset is inhibited because the recordset is automatically made read-only. The database classes support only read-only access to joins of multiple tables, not updating.

Figure 21-2

You can change the view and recordset class and associated file names to match the table you are dealing with, as illustrated by the window shown in Figure 21-3.

Now all you need to do is click the Finish button and then customize the dialog resource to do what you want.

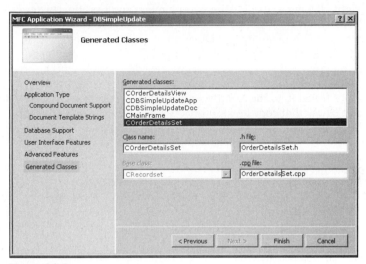

Figure 21-3

Customizing the Application

The Order Details table contains five columns — Order ID, Product ID, Unit Price, Quantity, and Discount. If you display Class View and look at the members of COrderDetailsSet, you will see the data members corresponding to these. You need a static text control and an edit control for each of these on the dialog corresponding to the recordset. I arranged them as shown in Figure 21-4, but you can arrange them how you like.

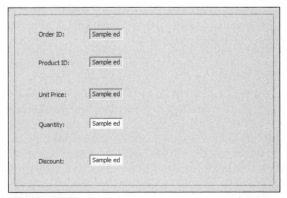

Figure 21-4

Assign IDs to the edit controls to match the field name as you did in the previous chapter — the last one is IDC_DISCOUNT, for example. The default style set for an edit control allows keyboard input, but on the assumption you want to limit which recordset fields can be altered, you should set the first three edit controls as read-only, using the styles tab in the Properties window. The value displayed in a read-only control can be set in the program, but a value cannot be entered in the control from the keyboard. You can set all these to read-only in a single step by selecting each of the three controls with the *Ctrl* key held down and then right-clicking to display the pop-up menu and selecting Properties. Whatever you then set in the Properties window is applied to all three. With the dialog arrangement shown, you will only be able to enter data for Quantity and Discount.

The only other thing you need to do is to associate the edit controls with a corresponding data member of the recordset, and as you saw in the previous chapter, you just add a DDX_ function call to the DoDataExchange() function in the recordset view class, COrderDetailsView, for each data field in the recordset. Here's how that code looks:

```
void COrderDetailsView::DoDataExchange(CDataExchange* pDX)
{
  CRecordView::DoDataExchange(pDX);
  DDX_FieldText(pDX, IDC_ORDERID, m_pSet->m_OrderID, m_pSet);
  DDX_FieldText(pDX, IDC_PRODUCTID, m_pSet->m_ProductID, m_pSet);
  DDX_FieldText(pDX, IDC_UNITPRICE, m_pSet->m_UnitPrice, m_pSet);
  DDX_FieldText(pDX, IDC_QUANTITY, m_pSet->m_Quantity, m_pSet);
  DDX_FieldText(pDX, IDC_DISCOUNT, m_pSet->m_Discount, m_pSet);
}
```

Having done that, you will have completed the program to update the Order Details table, believe it or not.

Try It Out   Updating a Database

This should compile right off the bat if you have set up the controls correctly and remembered to comment out the #error directive that appears before the definition of the GetDefaultConnect() function in the COrderDetailsSet class. This directive is there to ensure you consider security implications when connecting to the database. When the program executes, you will be able to move through the rows in the table using the toolbar buttons. If you enter data into the edit controls for the Quantity or Discount for an order, it is updated when you move backwards or forwards in the recordset. The application window is shown in Figure 21-5.

You can see here I have changed the quantity and discount values for the product with the ID 72 on the order with the ID 10248 to some unlikely values.

How It Works

When you click one of the toolbar buttons to move to another record, the OnMove() handler provided by the default base class, CRecordView, is called. This function writes out any changes that have been entered into the recordset before it moves to a new record in the recordset by calling the Move() member of the CRecordset class that is inherited in COrderDetailsSet. Remember there are two levels of data exchange going on here. The RFX_() functions called in the DoFieldExchange() member of the COrderDetailsSet class transfer data between a row in the recordset from the database and the data members of the class. The DDX_() functions called in the DoDataExchange() member of COrderDetailsView transfer data between the edit controls and the data members of COrderDetailsSet. When you change the value in an edit control, the new data is propagated through to the appropriate data member of the recordset object. When you move to the next recordset by clicking a toolbar button, the new data is written to the database by the `DoFieldExchange()` function.

This example is fine as far as it goes, but having data written to the database without any evident action on the part of the user is a bit disconcerting. You really should have a bit more control over what's going on. You can put together an example where the code requires the user to do something before expediting an update operation.

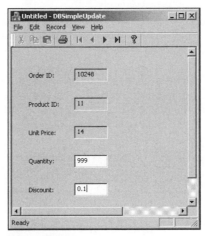

Figure 21-5

Managing the Update Process

You really want a positive action on the part of the user to enable an update rather than allowing it to happen by default. You could start making all the edit controls read-only, so by default data entry from the keyboard is inhibited for all the controls. You could then add an Edit Order button to the dialog box, which is intended to enable the appropriate edit controls to allow keyboard entry. This is shown in Figure 21-6.

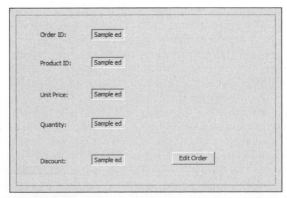

Figure 21-6

Here you will be implementing two notional modes in the program: read-only mode when updating is not possible, because the controls will be read-only, and edit mode when keyboard entry for selected controls are possible so the recordset can be updated. The idea is that when the user clicks the Edit Order button, the edit controls for fields you want to allow updating on are enabled for keyboard input, and you will enter your edit mode'. Add the button to the dialog box for your `DBSimpleUpdate` application. You can set the ID for the button as `IDC_EDITORDER`. You can also add a handler for the button to the `COrderDetailsView` class by right-clicking the button and selecting `Add Event Handler` from the pop-up. Shorten the name of the handler function to `OnEditorder()`.

Ideally, you should inhibit the use of the toolbar buttons or the Record menu items to move to another row in the table in update mode because you want a button click by the user to end the update operation, not move the current position of the recordset.

When the Edit Order button is clicked, the read-only status of the controls for quantity and discount should be removed, and there should be a button to be clicked when the update should take place. To accommodate all this, you want the dialog box in the application to look as in Figure 21-7 after an Edit Order button click.

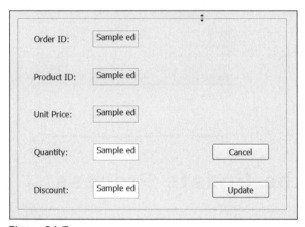

Figure 21-7

The edit controls for Quantity and Discount now allow data to be entered, the Edit Order button has a new label — Update — and there is a new button with the label Cancel that allows the operation to be aborted by the user, if necessary. In addition the toolbar buttons to move, the current record should be disabled when the Edit Order button is clicked. So, too, should be the menu items in the `Record` menu drop down. The program is now in "edit" mode.

You can add the `Cancel` button to the dialog box, but you don't want the button displayed initially so you should set the `Visible` property for the button to `False`. Set the `ID` property value to `IDC_CANCEL`. You will also need a handler for the `Cancel` button, so add one now to the `COrderDetailsView` class with the name `OnCancel()` in the same way as for the `Edit Order` button — you'll be filling in the code later.

The process for the update operation is that the user enters the data in the enabled fields on the dialog box and clicks the `Update` button to complete the update. The dialog box then returns to its original read-only mode state with all the edit controls read-only. The user clicks the Cancel button instead of Update if he or she does not want to proceed with the update operation.

To achieve this mechanism, and to manage the update process effectively, you will need to do several things after the Edit Order button is clicked:

❏ Change the text on the Edit Order button to "Update" so it now becomes the button to complete the update operation.

❏ Cause the Cancel button to appear on the dialog box — make it visible in other words.

❏ Record in the class that edit mode has been entered. This is necessary because you will use the same button for two purposes: flip-flopping the label between Edit Order and Update.

❏ Enable keyboard entry for the edit controls that show fields you want to allow updating on.

See how you can put the code together that will do what you want.

Implementing Update Mode

Let's start by providing for recording whether or not the application is in update mode. You can do that by adding an enum declaration to the COrderDetailsView class together with a variable of the enum type that reflect the current mode. Add the following two lines to the public section of the class:

```
enum Mode {READ_ONLY, UPDATE};     // Application modes
Mode m_Mode;                       // Records the current mode
```

The application is initially in READ_ONLY mode so you can initialize m_Mode in the constructor accordingly:

```
COrderDetailsView::COrderDetailsView()
  : CRecordView(COrderDetailsView::IDD)
  ,m_Mode(READ_ONLY)
{
  m_pSet = NULL;
  // TODO: add construction code here
}
```

You can do the switching of the button label and the program mode in the OnEditorder() handler that you added to the view class. In principle, a starting version of the function needs to implement capability something like this:

```
void COrderDetailsView::OnEditorder()
{
  if(m_Mode == UPDATE)
  { // When button was clicked we were in update

    // Disable input to edit controls
    // Change the Update button text to Edit Order
    // Make the Cancel button invisible
    // Enable Record menu items and toolbar buttons
    // Complete the update
    m_Mode = READ_ONLY;                    // Change to read-only mode
  }
  else
  { // When button was clicked we were in read-only mode
```

```
    // Enable input to edit controls
    // Change the Edit Order button text to Update
    // Make the Cancel button visible
    // Disable Record menu items and toolbar buttons
    // Start the update
    m_Mode = UPDATE;                    // Switch to update mode
  }
}
```

The mode switching code is already there. At the moment all the function does is switch the m_Mode member between READ_ONLY and UPDATE to record the current mode. The rest of the functionality that you require is simply described in comments. Next, investigate how to implement each of the comment lines in turn.

Enabling and Disabling Edit Controls

To modify the properties of a control, you need to call a function of some kind that relates to the control. This implies that you must have access to an object that represents the control. It's very easy to add a control variable to the view class; just right-click the control in the Design window for the dialog and select Add Variable from the pop-up menu. Figure 21-8 shows the dialog box that displays for the edit control showing the discount value.

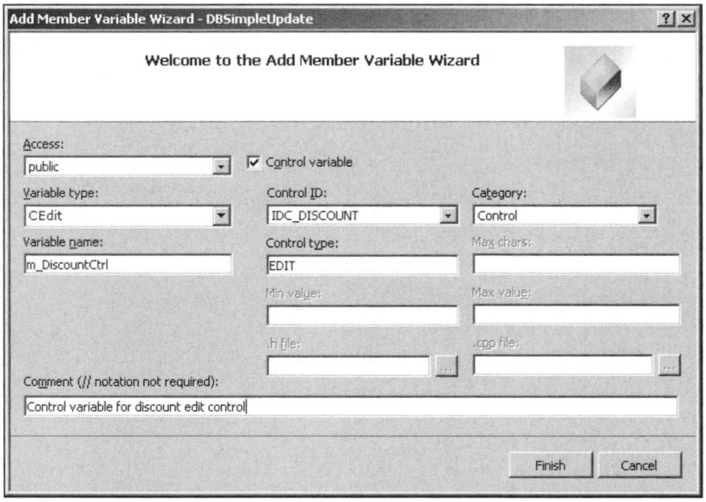

Figure 21-8

I have entered the variable name as m_DiscountCtrl. Because the variable relates to an edit control the variable is of type CEdit. Click Finish to add this variable to the View Class. Repeat this process for the edit control displaying the order quantity and give the variable the name m_QuantityCtrl.

With the two control variables added to the View Class you have access to the controls to update their styles, so you modify the OnEditorder() function as follows:

```
void COrderDetailsView::OnEditorder()
{
  if(m_Mode == UPDATE)
  { // When button was clicked we were in update

    // Disable input to edit controls
    m_QuantityCtrl.SetReadOnly();
    m_DiscountCtrl.SetReadOnly();

    // Change the Update button text to Edit Order
    // Make the Cancel button invisible
    // Enable Record menu items and toolbar buttons
    // Complete the update
    m_Mode = READ_ONLY;                  // Change to read-only mode
  }
  else
  { // When button was clicked we were in read-only mode

    // Enable input to edit controls
    m_QuantityCtrl.SetReadOnly(FALSE);
    m_DiscountCtrl.SetReadOnly(FALSE);

    // Change the Edit Order button text to Update
    // Make the Cancel button visible
    // Disable Record menu items and toolbar buttons
    // Start the update
    m_Mode = UPDATE;                     // Switch to update mode
  }
}
```

The SetReadOnly() member of the CEdit class has a parameter of type BOOL that has the default value TRUE. Thus calling the function with no argument implies the argument value is the default and the control read-only property is set to true. Passing a FALSE value to the function when you call it sets the read-only property to false. Incidentally, you could reduce the code in the function by removing the calls to SetReadOnly() in the if-else statement and adding two statements after the if statement:

```
m_QuantityCtrl.SetReadOnly(m_Mode == UPDATE);
m_DiscountCtrl.SetReadOnly(m_Mode == UPDATE);
```

The argument expression, m_Mode == UPDATE, is TRUE when m_Mode has the value UPDATE. This is FALSE otherwise, so these two calls to the SetReadOnly() function do the work of the original four. The downside is that it would not be quite as clear what was happening in the code.

Just to remind you — many of the MFC functions have parameters of type BOOL that can have values TRUE and FALSE because they were written before the availability of the bool type in C++. You can always use values of type `bool` as arguments for `BOOL` parameters if you want, but I prefer to stick to the `TRUE` and `FALSE` arguments values with type `BOOL` and only use `true` and `false` for variables of type `bool`.

Changing the Button Label

You can get at the object corresponding to the Edit Order button by adding a control data member, `m_EditOrderCtrl`, to the View Class in exactly the same way as you did for the edit controls. The variable is of type `CButton`, which is the MFC class that defines a button. You can use the variable to set the button label in the `OnEditorder()` member by calling the `SetWindowText()` member that is inherited in the `CButton` class from `CWnd`:

```
void COrderDetailsView::OnEditorder()
{
  if(m_Mode == UPDATE)
  { // When button was clicked we were in update
    // Disable input to edit controls
    m_QuantityCtrl.SetReadOnly();
    m_DiscountCtrl.SetReadOnly();

    // Change the Update button text to Edit Order
    m_EditOrderCtrl.SetWindowText(_T("Edit Order"));

    // Make the Cancel button invisible
    // Enable Record menu items and toolbar buttons
    // Complete the update
    m_Mode = READ_ONLY;                // Change to read-only mode
  }
  else
  { // When button was clicked we were in read-only mode

    // Enable input to edit controls
    m_QuantityCtrl.SetReadOnly(FALSE);
    m_DiscountCtrl.SetReadOnly(FALSE);

    // Change the Edit Order button text to Update
    m_EditOrderCtrl.SetWindowText(_T("Update"));

    // Make the Cancel button visible
    // Disable Record menu items and toolbar buttons
    // Start the update
    m_Mode = UPDATE;                   // Switch to update mode
  }
}
```

Each call of the `SetWindowText()` function sets the text displayed on the button to the string you supply as the argument to the function. The parameter type is `LPCTSTR` for which you can use a `CString` argument or a string constant of type `_T`.

Controlling the Visibility of the Cancel Button

To make the Cancel button visible or invisible, you need a control variable corresponding to that button available, so add a control variable with the name `m_CancelEditCtrl` just as you did for the Edit Order button. Because the CButton class is derived from CWnd, you can call the inherited ShowWindow() member of the CButton object to set the button as visible or invisible, as follows:

```
void COrderDetailsView::OnEditorder()
{
  if(m_Mode == UPDATE)
  { // When button was clicked we were in update
    // Disable input to edit controls
    m_QuantityCtrl.SetReadOnly();
    m_DiscountCtrl.SetReadOnly();

    // Change the Edit Order button text to Update
    m_EditOrderCtrl.SetWindowText(_T("Edit Order"));

    // Make the Cancel button invisible
    m_CancelEditCtrl.ShowWindow(SW_HIDE);

    // Enable Record menu items and toolbar buttons
    // Complete the update
    m_Mode = READ_ONLY;                    // Change to read-only mode
  }
  else
  { // When button was clicked we were in read-only mode

    // Enable input to edit controls
    m_QuantityCtrl.SetReadOnly(FALSE);
    m_DiscountCtrl.SetReadOnly(FALSE);

    // Change the Edit Order button text to Update
    m_EditOrderCtrl.SetWindowText(_T("Update"));

    // Make the Cancel button visible
    m_CancelEditCtrl.ShowWindow(SW_SHOW);

    // Disable Record menu items and toolbar buttons
    // Start the update
    m_Mode = UPDATE;                       // Switch to update mode
  }
}
```

The ShowWindow() function that the CButton class inherits from CWnd requires an argument of type int that must be one of a range of fixed values (see the documentation for the full set). You use the argument value SW_HIDE to make the button disappear if m_Mode has the value UPDATE, and SW_SHOW when the application is entering edit mode to make the button visible and activate it.

Disabling the Record Menu

You want to disable the menu items in the Record menu when the m_Mode member of the view has the value UPDATE. You won't do this in the OnEditorder() handler, though, because there is an easier and better way as you will now see, so you can remove the two comment lines in the if statement in the OnEditorder() handler that relate to this.

You can manage the state of the menu items and toolbar buttons by adding update handlers for them in the view class that are specifically for this purpose. Display the menu resource for the application by double-clicking the ID for the menu in Resource View. This is the menu resource in the DBSimpleUpdate.rc file with the ID IDR_MAINFRAME. Add a handler for the UPDATE_COMMAND_UI message for each of the menu items in the Record menu — starting with the First Record menu item. Extend the Record menu by clicking it and then right-click the First Record menu item in Resource View and select Add Event Handler from the pop-up menu. Figure 21-9 shows the Event Handler Wizard dialog box that is displayed as a result.

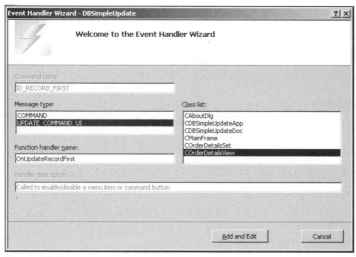

Figure 21-9

Select the COrderDetailsView class name from the class list, then select the message type as UPDATE_COMMAND_UI. The description at the bottom of the dialog box indicates the prime purpose of the UPDATE_COMMAND_UI handler — exactly what you need in this instance. Click the Add and Edit button in the dialog box to add the handler and repeat the process for the three other items in the Record menu.

The argument that is passed to the UPDATE_COMMAND_UI handler function is of type CCmdUI and the CCmdUI class has a member function, Enable(), that you can call to enable or disable the item. An argument value of TRUE enables the item, and a value of FALSE disables it. The default value for the parameter is TRUE so you can call the function with no argument value to enable the item. You want to disable the menu items and toolbar buttons when m_Mode has the value UPDATE, but the circumstances when you want to disable them are a little more complicated because of the behavior of the menu items and toolbar buttons before you started messing with them.

The program as generated by default already disables the menu items and toolbar buttons corresponding to the IDs ID_RECORD_FIRST and ID_RECORD_PREV when the current record is the first in the recordset. Similarly, when the current record is the last in the recordset, the ID_RECORD_NEXT and ID_RECORD_LAST items are disabled. You should maintain this behavior when m_Mode is READ_ONLY. The key to doing this is to use inherited functions in the View Class that test whether the current record is the first or the last.

You only need add one line of code to each of these handlers to do what you want. It's exactly the same line of code for OnUpdateRecordFirst() and OnUpdateRecordPrev(). For example:

```
void COrderDetailsView::OnUpdateRecordFirst(CCmdUI* pCmdUI)
{
  // Disable item if m_Mode is UPDATE
  // Enable item if m_Mode is READ_ONLY and it's not the 1st record
  pCmdUI->Enable((m_Mode == READ_ONLY) && !IsOnFirstRecord());
}
```

The IsOnFirstRecord() function returns TRUE if the view is on the first record in the recordset, and FALSE otherwise. This disables the items (the menu item and the corresponding toolbar button) if either m_Mode has the value UPDATE or the value returned by IsOnFirstRecord() member of COrderDetailsView is TRUE. The item is enabled if m_Mode has the value READ_ONLY and the value returned by the IsOnFirstRecord() function is FALSE. This handler affects both the menu item and the toolbar button because they both have the same ID, ID_RECORD_FIRST.

The handlers corresponding to ID_RECORD_NEXT and ID_RECORD_LAST also require the same line of code:

```
void COrderDetailsView::OnUpdateRecordLast(CCmdUI* pCmdUI)
{
  // Disable item if m_Mode is UPDATE
  // Enable item if m_Mode is READ_ONLY and it's not the 1st record
  pCmdUI->Enable((m_Mode == READ_ONLY) && !IsOnLastRecord());
}
```

This works in the same way as the previous handler.

Expediting the Update

The last piece you need is to actually carry out the update when the Update button is clicked. To update a record, the user first clicks the Edit Order button, so at this point you must call the Edit() member of the recordset object to start the process of modifying the recordset. When the Update button is clicked, you need to call the Update() member of the recordset object to get the new data written to the record in the database. You can implement it using the m_pSet member of the View Class like this:

```
void COrderDetailsView::OnEditorder()
{
  if(m_pSet->CanUpdate())
  {
    try
    {
      if(m_Mode == UPDATE)
      { // When button was clicked we were in update
        // Disable input to edit controls
        m_QuantityCtrl.SetReadOnly();
        m_DiscountCtrl.SetReadOnly();

        // Change the Update button text to Edit Order
        m_EditOrderCtrl.SetWindowText(_T("Edit Order"));
```

```
            // Make the Cancel button invisible
            m_CancelEditCtrl.ShowWindow(SW_HIDE);

            // Complete the update
            m_pSet->Update();
            m_Mode = READ_ONLY;                // Change to read-only mode
          }
        else
        { // When button was clicked we were in read-only mode

            // Enable input to edit controls
            m_QuantityCtrl.SetReadOnly(FALSE);
            m_DiscountCtrl.SetReadOnly(FALSE);

            // Change the Edit Order button text to Update
            m_EditOrderCtrl.SetWindowText(_T("Update"));

            // Make the Cancel button visible
            m_CancelEditCtrl.ShowWindow(SW_SHOW);

            // Start the update
            m_pSet->Edit();

            m_Mode = UPDATE;                   // Switch to update mode
          }
        }
      catch(CException* pEx)
      {
        pEx->ReportError();                    // Display the error message
      }
    }
  else
    AfxMessageBox(_T("Recordset is not updatable."));
}
```

As I discussed at the beginning of this chapter, the Edit() and Update() functions can throw an exception if an error occurs, so you put the calls within a try block along with the rest of the code. Clearly, if you cannot update the recordset, there is no purpose to any of the processing in the OnEditorder() function. If an exception is thrown, you call its ReportError() function to display an error message. The catch block exception parameter is a pointer to CException, so the catch block is executed for exceptions objects of type CException, or any class derived from CException. You need this to accommodate the CMemoryException that can be thrown by Edit(), as well as the CDBException that can be thrown by both Edit() and Update(). Note the use of the pointer as the catch block parameter. Recall that this is because these are MFC exceptions thrown using the THROW macro, not C++ exceptions thrown using the keyword throw. If they were the latter, you would use a reference as the catch block parameter type.

You also verify that the recordset is updateable by calling its CanUpdate() member. If this returns FALSE, you display an error message in a message box.

Implementing the Cancel Operation

The Cancel button should abort the update operation. All that is necessary to do this is to call the `CancelUpdate()` member of the `COrderDetailsSet` object. Of course, you have a little housekeeping to do, but this is exactly the same as if the `Update()` button was pressed, except that you don't call `Edit()`. Here's the code for the `OnCancel()` handler:

```
void COrderDetailsView::OnCancel()
{
   m_pSet->CancelUpdate();                       // Cancel the update operation
   m_EditOrderCtrl.SetWindowText(_T("Edit"));// Switch button text
   m_CancelEditCtrl.ShowWindow(SW_HIDE);         // Hide the Cancel button
   m_QuantityCtrl.SetReadOnly(TRUE);             // Set state of quantity edit control
   m_DiscountCtrl.SetReadOnly(TRUE);             // Set state of discount edit control
   m_Mode = READ_ONLY;                           // Switch the mode
}
```

The `CancelUpdate()` function ends the update operation and restores the recordset object's fields to what they were before `Edit()` was called. Because the Cancel button can only be clicked in edit mode, you can update the buttons and other controls in the same way as in the `OnEditorder()` handler. That's everything you need. You are ready for a trial run.

Try It Out   **Controlled Updating**

Assuming you have no typos in your code, when you compile and run the program, it should work as planned. You can only enter data in the Quantity and Discount edit controls after you have clicked the Edit button. Figure 21-10 shows an example of the update operation window.

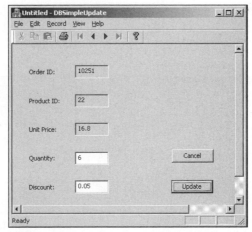

Figure 21-10

The buttons for moving to a new record are now disabled, as are the menu items for the Record menu. To complete the update after you have entered the new data, you click the Update button. This causes the new data to be written to the database, and the application returns to the normal state — all edit controls disabled and the buttons and menu restored to their original status.

Adding Rows to a Table

Next, extend the example to implement the capability to add a new order to the Northwind database. This provides insight into some of the practical problems and complexities you will face in this kind of operation.

An order itself is not a simple record in a table in the Northwind database. Two tables are involved in defining a new order. The basic order data is in the Orders table, where information about the customer is stored. For each order, there is one or more records in the Order Details table and one for each product in the order, the link to the record in the Orders table being the Order ID. The relationship between these tables is illustrated in Figure 21-11.

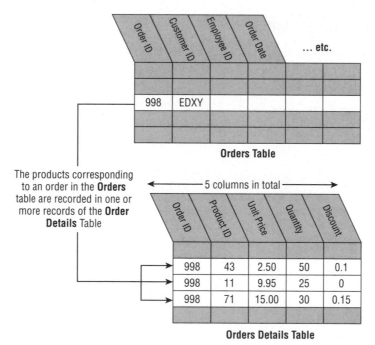

Figure 21-11

But there's more than these two tables involved in the process for adding a new order. When creating a new order you have to provide a way for the user to select a customer from the Customers table. The Orders table includes a field identifying the employee, which needs to be one of the employees recorded in the Employees table. After the information required for a new record in the Orders table has been established, one or more products obviously will need to be selected from those defined in the Products table. With all these tables involved, it's going to be a somewhat messy business. You can simplify it slightly by making the Employee ID field 1 by default. This avoids the need to deal with the Employees table in the example. You need to establish the overall logic first.

The Order Entry Process

You will be using two dialog forms in addition to the dialog form you already have that provides for viewing and editing the details of existing orders. One deals with the selection of the customer for the order, and setting the required delivery date, and the other takes care of entering the details of the products and quantities for the order. The dialog box to select the customer is associated with the Customers table in the database, and the dialog box for selecting products is associated with the Products table. Buttons on the dialog box enable the transition from one dialog box to another. The basic logic is shown in Figure 21-12.

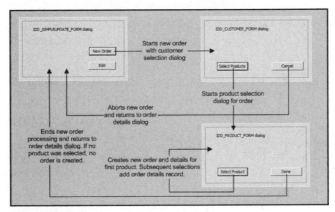

Figure 21-12

You will hold off creating a new record in the Orders table until you have the first Product Details record entered. That way you will avoid ending up with an order that doesn't order anything. Now you can put together the dialog resources you need and implement the code to support the operations.

Creating the Resources

You need an additional button on the dialog box that you have at present to initiate the process of creating a new order, so add a button with the label New Order, and with the ID IDC_NEWORDER and use the Format > Make Same Size > Both menu to make sure the new button is the same width and height as the Cancel button. After you have done this, you can place the new button coincident with the Cancel button if you want because only one is visible at any given time, with the New Order button being visible by default. On the other hand you could keep them distinct if you would prefer to avoid working with resources where one can mask another.

If you want the New Order button to appear on top when it is in the same position as the Cancel button, you need to make sure it follows the Cancel button in the tab order; you can check this by using the Format > Tab Order menu item. Figure 21-13 shows the revised IDD_SIMPLEUPDATE_FORM dialog form with the New Order button overlaying and therefore masking the Cancel button.

Figure 21-13

You can add a handler for the New Order button to COrderDetailsView by right-clicking the button and selecting Add Event Handler from the pop-up. You could shorten the default handler name to OnNewOrder() if you like. You may need to move the button before clicking it to get the handler for the right button. You will add the code for this handler later. Of course, you could have used the Cancel button here by changing its label and altering the effect of its handler depending on the state of the m_Mode member of COrderDetailsView, but with this approach you'll get to see how you can work with two buttons here.

You can create the two new dialog forms you need by right-clicking the Dialog folder in Resource View and selecting Insert Dialog from the pop-up. Assign the IDs as IDD_CUSTOMER_FORM and IDD_PRODUCT_FORM, respectively. They both need to have Child selected for the Style property and None selected in the Border property. You could also make all three dialog forms about the same size and a little larger than the original form.

Creating the Recordsets

Two recordset classes corresponding to the Customers and Products tables in the database are required. You add each of these in the same way; right-click on DBSimpleUpdate in Class View and select Add > Class from the pop-up and then choose MFC ODBC Consumer as the template. You can make the class names CCustomerSet and CProductSet set corresponding to the Customers and Products tables respectively and select the recordset type to be Snapshot in both instances. Change fields of type CStringW to type CString and don't forget to delete or comment out the #error directive that precedes the definition of the GetDefaultConnect() function in each class.

Creating the Recordset Views

You can now create record view classes that connect to the new dialogs, so add .h files and .cpp files to the project that will hold the code for the new CCustomerView and CProductView classes that you'll define; you use the Solution Explorer window for this. The CCustomerView class encapsulates a view of the CCustomerSet recordset and uses the IDD_CUSTOMER form dialog resource. The initial class definition is therefore:

```
// CustomerView.h : header file
```

```
#pragma once

class CCustomerSet;

class CCustomerView : public CRecordView
{
public:
  CCustomerView();
  virtual ~CCustomerView();

public:
  enum { IDD = IDD_CUSTOMER_FORM };// Form Data
  CCustomerSet* m_pSet;


// Operations
public:
  CCustomerSet* GetRecordset();

#ifdef _DEBUG
  virtual void AssertValid() const;
  virtual void Dump(CDumpContext& dc) const;
#endif

};
```

You can initialize the m_pSet member that stores the pointer to the recordset object in the constructor in the CustomerView.cpp file:

```
#include "stdafx.h"
#include "DBSimpleUpdate.h"            // Main header file for the application
#include "CustomerView.h"

// Constructor
CCustomerView::CCustomerView()
  : CRecordView(CCustomerView::IDD),
    m_pSet(NULL)
{
}
```

The constructor also establishes IDD_CUSTOMER_FORM as the dialog box for this view by passing its ID to the base class constructor. You need the #include directive for DBSimpleUpdate.h preceding the #include for CustomerView.h, as without it the symbol IDD_CUSTOMER_FORM would not be recognized during compilation. DBSimpleUpdate.h has an #include directive for Resource.h that contains the definitions for the IDs for the resources you have created.

Now add the definitions of the functions that are to be generated in debug mode to CustomerView.cpp:

```
// CCustomerView diagnostics

#ifdef _DEBUG
void CCustomerView::AssertValid() const
{
```

```
  CRecordView::AssertValid();
}
```

```
void CCustomerView::Dump(CDumpContext& dc) const
{
  CRecordView::Dump(dc);
}
#endif //_DEBUG
```

You probably won't need these, but it's good to have them defined — just in case something goes wrong.

You can now add overrides for the `DoDataExchange()`, `OnGetRecordset()`, and `OnInitialUpdate()` functions that are inherited from the base class. The example shows you how to customize these to work with the recordset in the way that you want. Right-click the `CCustomerView` class name in Class View and select Properties from the pop-up. Click the overrides toolbar button (wait for the tooltips for the buttons to display if you can't remember which button it is) and for each override select the function name in the left column and select the `<Add>` option in the cell to the right to add the function.

You can complete the implementation of the `OnGetRecordset()` function override right away:

```
CRecordset* CCustomerView::OnGetRecordset()
{
   if(m_pSet == NULL)                  // If we don't have the recordset address
   {
     m_pSet = new CCustomerSet(NULL);  // create a new one
     m_pSet->Open();                   // and open it
   }
    return m_pSet;                      // Return the recordset address
}
```

If `m_pSet` is NULL you create a recordset and open it before returning its address. If `m_pSet` is not NULL there is already a recordset created so you return the address that it contains. You must add an `#include` directive for `CCustomerSet.h` to the `.cpp` file because you refer to the `CCustomerSet` class name here.

You can now implement the `GetRecordset()` function to use this function:

```
CCustomerSet* CCustomerView::GetRecordset()
{
  return static_cast<CCustomerSet*>(OnGetRecordset());
}
```

The explicit cast is necessary here because the cast is down the class hierarchy from the base class to the derived class. You will be able to complete the detail of the other two overrides later.

Because you are creating the `CCustomerSet` object on the heap, you need to take care to delete it in the `CCustomerView` class destructor:

```
CCustomerView::~CCustomerView()
{
  if (m_pSet)
    delete m_pSet;
}
```

The `OnInitialUpdate()` function override in the `CCustomerView` class should be implemented as you have seen previously:

```
void CCustomerView::OnInitialUpdate()
{
  BeginWaitCursor();
  GetRecordset();
  CRecordView::OnInitialUpdate();
  if (m_pSet->IsOpen())
  {
    CString strTitle = m_pSet->m_pDatabase->GetDatabaseName();
    CString strTable = m_pSet->GetTableName();
    if(!strTable.IsEmpty())
      strTitle += _T(":") + strTable;
  GetDocument()->SetTitle(strTitle);
  }
  EndWaitCursor();
}
```

The definition of the `CProductView` class is much the same as the `CCustomerView` class, the primary difference being the dialog form associated with it:

```
// ProductView.h : header file
#pragma once

class CProductSet;

class CProductView : public CRecordView
{
public:
    CProductView();
  virtual ~CProductView();


public:
    enum { IDD = IDD_PRODUCT_FORM };        // Form Data
    CProductSet* m_pSet;


// Operations
public:
    CProductSet* GetRecordset();


// Implementation
protected:
#ifdef _DEBUG
    virtual void AssertValid() const;
    virtual void Dump(CDumpContext& dc) const;
#endif
};
```

Now you can add overrides for the `OnGetRecordset()`, `DoDataExchange()`, and `OnInitialUpdate()` functions using the method you used for the previous class and add the following directives to the beginning of the `ProductView.cpp` file:

```
#include "stdafx.h"
#include "DBSimpleUpdate.h"
#include "ProductView.h"
#include "ProductSet.h"
```

The constructor should initialize the `m_pSet` member and the destructor should delete the object pointed to by the `m_pSet` object because you'll create it on the heap. The constructor and destructor definitions are:

```
CProductView::CProductView()
  : CRecordView(CProductView::IDD),
    m_pSet(NULL)
{
}
```

```
CProductView::~CProductView()
{
  if (m_pSet)
    delete m_pSet;
}
```

The implementation of the `OnGetRecordset()` function is:

```
CRecordset* CProductView::OnGetRecordset()
{
  if(m_pSet == NULL)                  // If there is no recordset
  {
    m_pSet = new CProductSet(NULL);   // create one
    m_pSet->Open();                   // then open it
  }
  return m_pSet;                       // Return the address of the recordset
}
```

The implementation of the `GetRecordset()` function in the `CProductView` class is also essentially the same as for the `CCustomerView` class:

```
CProductSet* CProductView::GetRecordset()
{
  return static_cast<CProductSet*>(OnGetRecordset());
}
```

You can also add definitions for the diagnostic functions to be used in debug mode:

```
#ifdef _DEBUG
void CProductView::AssertValid() const
```

```
    {
      CRecordView::AssertValid();
    }

    void CProductView::Dump(CDumpContext& dc) const
    {
      CRecordView::Dump(dc);
    }
    #endif //_DEBUG
```

You'll return to the functions still to be implemented in CProductView a bit later in this chapter — in the meantime you are now ready to populate the dialog boxes with the controls you need.

Adding Controls to the Dialog Resources

Although you have only tied the IDD_CUSTOMER_FORM dialog box into the Customers table, within the process you need to provide all the information necessary to create a new record in the Orders table. The source of the data for each field of a new Orders record is shown in Figure 21-14.

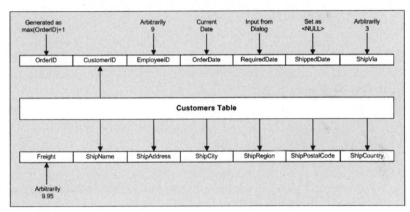

Figure 21-14

Half of the fields are drawn from the record in the Customers table that the user selects. Because you are creating a new order, you will need to synthesize a new unique order ID. To do this you can find the largest ID currently in use in the Orders table and then just add 1 to that value.

To select the customer, the user scrolls through the recordset until the required customer is displayed. You can then retrieve the data you need to construct the new Orders record from the recordset. You can display the current date in the dialog box as the order date, and you can provide a control for selecting the required ship date. The other fields you'll just assign arbitrary values to, so that you don't overcomplicate the example.

Of course, you don't need to display all the information from the Customers table in the dialog box — just the name is sufficient to identify the customer for selection purposes. You still need the data in the recordset though. You can place controls on the IDD_CUSTOMER_FORM dialog as shown in Figure 21-15.

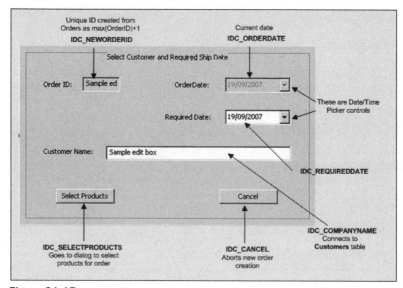

Figure 21-15

You can see from the diagram how the controls are to be used, and the IDs that you need to assign to them. The date/time picker controls allow a date or time to be entered or selected. Whether it selects a date or a time depends on the value you choose for the Format property. The controls here use Short Date format. The date is chosen by clicking the down arrow and choosing a date from the calendar that pops up. Note that the control showing the order date is not accessible by the user because the date value is just today's date. You set this state for the control by setting the Disabled property value to True. Note also that the edit controls for the order ID and customer name each have their Read Only property set to True to prevent modification of the values displayed.

You can add variables to the CCustomerView class to store values from the date/time picker controls. Right-click the order date edit control and select Add Variable from the pop-up. Figure 21-16 shows the dialog box.

You need to select the category as Value and the type as CTime because you want a variable that stores the value from the control rather than one that provides access to the control itself. You can give the member the name m_OrderDate. The Add Member Variable Wizard automatically adds initialization for the variable to the class constructor and adds a DDX_ function call to the DoDataExchange() function to effect data exchange between the variable and the control. You can add a variable with the name m_RequiredDate in a similar way for the other date/time picker control.

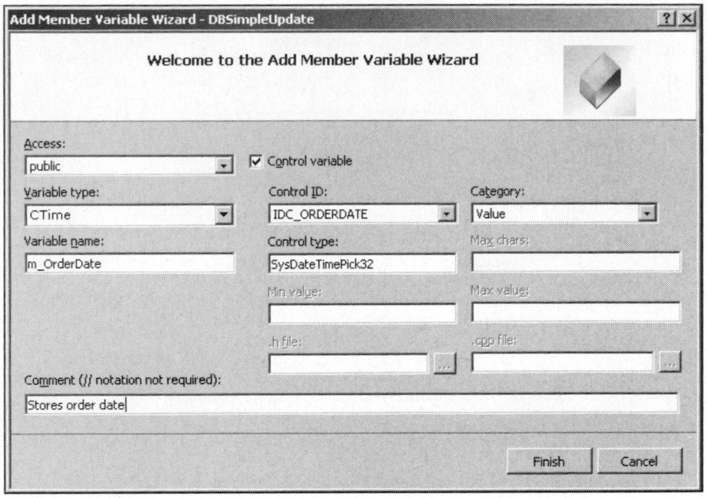

Figure 21-16

Although this view is associated with a recordset corresponding to the Customers table, in fact only the edit control showing the customer name needs to be connected to the `CCustomerSet` recordset as you are only displaying this field on the dialog box. You can add a `DDX_` function call for this to the `DoDataExchange()` function in the `CCustomerView` class:

```
void CCustomerView::DoDataExchange(CDataExchange* pDX)
{
  CRecordView::DoDataExchange(pDX);
  DDX_DateTimeCtrl(pDX, IDC_ORDERDATE, m_OrderDate);
  DDX_DateTimeCtrl(pDX, IDC_REQUIREDDATE, m_RequiredDate);
  DDX_FieldText(pDX, IDC_COMPANYNAME, m_pSet->m_CompanyName, m_pSet);
}
```

At this point you can also right-click each of the buttons and select Add Event Handler from the pop-up to add handlers to the `CCustomerView` class for them. You can short the default function names to `OnSelectproducts()` and `OnCancelorder()` if you want. You will fill in the code for these handlers and deal with the rest of the controls later.

The `IDD_PRODUCT_FORM` dialog selects the products to be ordered, after the customer has been selected. The application switches to this dialog box when the Select Products button is clicked on the customer selection dialog box. You need to show sufficient information on the dialog box to allow the product to be chosen, and you must provide for the quantity and discount to be entered. The dialog box with its controls is shown in Figure 21-17.

Note that the edit controls here are read-only except for the two for quantity and discount because these two values are the only ones the user needs to supply. You can connect the edit control for the product name to the recordset by adding a statement to the `DoDataExchange()` function in the `CProductView` class:

```
void CProductView::DoDataExchange(CDataExchange* pDX)
{
  CRecordView::DoDataExchange(pDX);
  DDX_FieldText(pDX, IDC_PRODUCTNAME, m_pSet->m_ProductName, m_pSet);
}
```

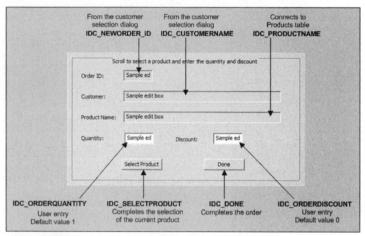

Figure 21-17

The `DDX_FieldText()` function call interchanges data between the `m_ProductSet` member of the `CProductSet` object and the control with the ID `IDD_PRODUCTNAME`.

Add `BN_CLICKED` event handlers for the `Select Product` and `Done` buttons to the `CProductView` using the same technique you used for the previous dialog resource; you can give them the names `OnSelectproduct()` and `OnDone()` to conform with the button labels.

The edit controls that display the order ID and the customer name must be initialized with values that originate in the previous dialog, so you need class variables to hold the values for these controls. Right-click each of these two controls in the `IDD_PRODUCT_FORM` dialog and select Add Variable from the pop-up. You should select the Value category for both variables and they can both be public. Select type `long` for the `m_OrderID` variable and type `CString` for the `m_CustomerName` variable.

The user enters values in the edit controls for quantity and discount, so you need variable for these too in the `CProductView` class; both of these are `Value` category, too. Add a variable of type `int` with the name `m_Quantity`, to store the quantity and a variable of type `float` with the name `m_Discount` for the discount value. You should now find that the variables are initialized in the constructor and the `DoDataExchange()` function looks like this:

```
void CProductView::DoDataExchange(CDataExchange* pDX)
{
  CRecordView::DoDataExchange(pDX);
  DDX_FieldText(pDX, IDC_PRODUCTNAME, m_pSet->m_ProductName, m_pSet);
  DDX_Text(pDX, IDC_NEWORDER, m_OrderID);
  DDX_Text(pDX, IDC_COMPANYNAME, m_CustomerName);
  DDX_Text(pDX, IDC_ORDERQUANTITY, m_Quantity);
  DDX_Text(pDX, IDC_ORDERDISCOUNT, m_Discount);
}
```

With the dialogs defined, you can implement the mechanism to switch between them.

Implementing Dialog Switching

You saw the basic logic for switching between dialogs in this program in Figure 21-12. A button click is the mechanism for switching from one dialog to the next, so the button handlers will contain code to cause the switch to happen. You can first define view IDs to identify each of the three dialogs, so add a header file, `ViewConstants.h`. This time you can try using an enum declaration to identify the views so the file should contain the following code:

```
// Definition of constants identifying the record views

#pragma once

enum ViewID{ ORDER_DETAILS, NEW_ORDER, SELECT_PRODUCT};
```

You need a variable of type `ViewID` in the `CMainFrame` class to record the ID of the current view, so add `m_CurrentViewID` by right-clicking on `CMainFrame` in Class View and selecting `Add > Add Variable` from the pop-up. You need to initialize this, so modify the `CMainFrame` constructor to:

```
CMainFrame::CMainFrame() : m_CurrentViewID(ORDER_DETAILS)
{
  // TODO: add member initialization code here
}
```

This identifies the view the application always starts with. An `#include` directive for `ViewConstants.h` was added automatically to the `MainFrm.h` file so the definitions for the view IDs are available here in the `MainFrm.cpp` file.

You can now add a member function, `SelectView()`, to `CMainFrame` that performs switching between dialogs. The return type is `void` and the single parameter is of type `ViewID` as the argument will be one of the view IDs defined in the `enum`. The implementation of `SelectView()` is like this:

```
// Enables switching between views. The argument specifies the new view
void CMainFrame::SelectView(ViewID viewID)
{
   CView* pOldActiveView = GetActiveView();      // Get current view

   // Get pointer to new view if it exists
   // if it doesn't the pointer will be null
   CView* pNewActiveView = static_cast<CView*>(GetDlgItem(viewID));

   // If this is first time around for the new view, the new view
   // won't exist, so we must create it
   // The Order Details view is always created first so we don't need
   // to provide for creating that.
   if (pNewActiveView == NULL)
   {
      switch(viewID)
      {
         case NEW_ORDER:                    // Create view to add new order
            pNewActiveView = new CCustomerView;
            break;
         case SELECT_PRODUCT:               // Create view to add product to order
```

```
                pNewActiveView = new CProductView;
                break;
            default:
                AfxMessageBox(_T("Invalid View ID"));
                return;
        }

        // Switching the views
        // Obtain the current view context to apply to the new view
        CCreateContext context;
        context.m_pCurrentDoc = pOldActiveView->GetDocument();
        pNewActiveView->Create(NULL, NULL, 0L, CFrameWnd::rectDefault,
                                             this, viewID, &context);

        pNewActiveView->OnInitialUpdate();
    }
    SetActiveView(pNewActiveView);                     // Activate the new view
    pOldActiveView->ShowWindow(SW_HIDE);               // Hide the old view
    pNewActiveView->ShowWindow(SW_SHOW);               // Show the new view
    pOldActiveView->SetDlgCtrlID(m_CurrentViewID);     // Set the old view ID
    pNewActiveView->SetDlgCtrlID(AFX_IDW_PANE_FIRST);
    m_CurrentViewID = viewID;                          // Save the new view ID
    RecalcLayout();
}
```

The code here refers to the `CCustomerView` and `CProductView` classes, so `#include` directives for `CustomerView.h` and `ProductView.h` are necessary in the source file.

Switching from the order details dialog to the dialog starting new order creation is done in the handler for `OnNeworder()` in the `COrderDetailsView` class:

```
void COrderDetailsView::OnNeworder()
{
    static_cast<CMainFrame*>(GetParentFrame())->SelectView(NEW_ORDER);
}
```

This gets a pointer to the parent frame for the view — the `CMainFrame` object for the application — and then uses that to call `SelectView()` to select the new order processing dialog. An `#include` directive for `MainFrm.h` is necessary in this source file to get at the definition of `CMainFrame`; `MAinFrm.h` has an `#include` directive for `ViewConstants.h` so `NEW_ORDER` is available here, too.

The Select Products button handler in the `CCustomerView` class switches to the dialog box for `CProductsView`:

```
void CCustomerView::OnSelectproducts()
{
    static_cast<CMainFrame*>(GetParentFrame())->SelectView(SELECT_PRODUCT);
}
```

The Cancel button handler in the same class just switches back to the previous view:

```
void CCustomerView::OnCancelorder()
{
```

```
    static_cast<CMainFrame*>(GetParentFrame())->SelectView(ORDER_DETAILS);
  }
```

Don't forget to add an `#include` directive for `MainFrm.h` in `CustomerView.cpp`.

The last switching operation to be implemented is in the `OnDone()` handler in the `CProductView` class:

```
void CProductView::OnDone()
{
  static_cast<CMainFrame*>(GetParentFrame())->SelectView(ORDER_DETAILS);
}
```

This switches back to the original application view that allows browsing and editing of order details. Of course, you could alternatively switch back to the `CCustomerView` dialog to provide a succession of order entries if you wanted to. Don't forget the `#include` directive for `MainFrm.h` once more.

The switching from the initial dialog box that allows you to browse order details to the dialog box for editing the details now has to control the visibility of the New Order button; otherwise, the Cancel button is hidden by the New Order button in the editing dialog. Add a control variable, `m_NewOrderCtrl`, in `COrderDetailsView` corresponding to the `IDC_NEWORDER` ID. Then you can amend the `OnEditorder()` handler to:

```
void COrderDetailsView::OnEditorder()
{
  if(m_pSet->CanUpdate())
  {
    try
    {
      if(m_Mode == UPDATE)
      { // When button was clicked we were in update
        // Disable input to edit controls
        m_QuantityCtrl.SetReadOnly();
        m_DiscountCtrl.SetReadOnly();

        // Change the Update button text to Edit Order
        m_EditOrderCtrl.SetWindowText(_T("Edit Order"));

        // Make the Cancel button invisible
        m_CancelEditCtrl.ShowWindow(SW_HIDE);

        // Show the new order button
        m_NewOrderCtrl.ShowWindow(SW_SHOW);

        // Complete the update
        m_pSet->Update();
        m_Mode = READ_ONLY;              // Change to read-only mode
      }
      else
      { // When button was clicked we were in read-only mode

        // Enable input to edit controls
        m_QuantityCtrl.SetReadOnly(FALSE);
```

```
                m_DiscountCtrl.SetReadOnly(FALSE);

                // Change the Edit Order button text to Update
                m_EditOrderCtrl.SetWindowText(_T("Update"));

                // Hide the new order button
                m_NewOrderCtrl.ShowWindow(SW_HIDE);

                // Make the Cancel button visible
                m_CancelEditCtrl.ShowWindow(SW_SHOW);

                // Start the update
                m_pSet->Edit();

                m_Mode = UPDATE;                    // Switch to update mode
            }
        }
        catch(CException* pEx)
        {
            pEx->ReportError();                    // Display the error message
        }
    }
    else
        AfxMessageBox(_T("Recordset is not updatable."));
}
```

Now you hide or show the New Order button, depending on whether the value stored in m_UpdateMode is READ_ONLY or UPDATE. You also must make the button visible in the OnCancel() handler:

```
void COrderDetailsView::OnCancel()
{
    m_pSet->CancelUpdate();                       // Cancel the update operation
    m_EditOrderCtrl.SetWindowText(_T("Edit"));    // Switch button text
    m_CancelEditCtrl.ShowWindow(SW_HIDE);         // Hide the Cancel button
    m_NewOrderCtrl.ShowWindow(SW_SHOW);           // Show the New Order button
    m_QuantityCtrl.SetReadOnly(TRUE);             // Set state of quantity edit control
    m_DiscountCtrl.SetReadOnly(TRUE);             // Set state of discount edit control
    m_UpdateMode = !m_UpdateMode;                 // Switch the mode
}
```

What you have done so far here is to implement the basic view switching mechanism. You will still need to come back and add code to deal with updating the database; however, this is a good point to try compiling and executing what you have to shake out any typos or other errors you might have added. After it works, you should find that you can scroll through the customers and the products. Make sure you check out all the switching paths.

Creating an Order ID

To create an ID for a new order, you need a recordset for the Orders table. Right-click DBSimpleUpdate in Class View and select the Add > Class menu item from the pop-up. Select MFC ODBC Consumer as the template and click the Add button; then select Northwind as the database and Orders as the table for the recordset. Choose Dynaset as the type because you reuse this recordset when you want to add a new order. Enter the class name as `COrderSet` and the corresponding files names as `OrderSet.h` and `OrderSet.cpp`. Click the Finish button to create the class. You can change the `CStringW` members of the new class to type `CString` and comment out the `#error` directive in the `OrderSet.cpp` class.

Storing the New Order ID

In this section I will go into operations with recordsets in a little more depth. You need to create a unique order ID whenever you start creating a new order in the `CCustomerView` class, so you need to think about where you can best do this and what the process should be. It really should be a `COrderSet` object's responsibility to create the new ID, even though the ID is displayed by one of the edit controls in the view represented by the `CCustomerView` object because the new ID is essentially dependent on the data in this recordset. A good approach would be to add a variable in the `CCustomerView` class that sets the value of the ID in the edit control that can be set using a function belonging to a `COrderSet` object.

Go to the Design window for the `IDD_CUSTOMER_FORM` dialog form and right-click the edit control for the order ID — the control has the ID `IDC_NEWORDERID`. Select Add Variable from the pop-up and then enter the name. Choose the variable type and category as shown in Figure 21-18.

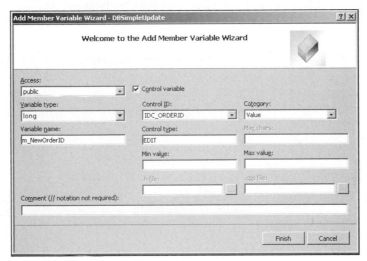

Figure 21-18

The type is `CString` by default, so make sure you set it to `long`. The `DDX_Text()` functions that transfer data to and from an edit control come in a number of flavors to accommodate the different data types shown in the drop-down list in the dialog box.

Creating the New Order ID

The `COrderSet` object belongs in the document object, so add a `public` data member to the `CDBSimpleUpdateDoc` class with the name `m_OrderSet` to go along with the `m_DBSimpleUpdateSet` member that was created by the Application Wizard. You do this as usual by right-clicking the class name in Class View and selecting `Add > Add Variable` from the pop-up. The `COrderSet` object is created automatically when the document object is created. With the object for the order set in the document, it is accessible in any of the view classes that need it.

You can add a new member function to the `COrderSet` class to generate the unique new order ID. Go to Class View and add the function, `CreateNewOrderID()`, with a `long` return type and no parameters.

The first thing the `CreateNewOrderID()` function needs to do is check whether the recordset is open:

```
long COrderSet::CreateNewOrderID()
{
  if(!IsOpen())
    Open(CRecordset::dynaset);

  // Rest of the function implementation...
}
```

The `IsOpen()` function that you call in the `if` statement returns `TRUE` if the recordset is open and `FALSE` otherwise. To open the recordset, you call the `Open()` member that is inherited from `CRecordset`. This runs an SQL query against the database with the recordset type specified by the first argument. You have the first argument specified as `CRecordset::dynaset`, which, as you might expect, opens the recordset as a dynaset. As it happens, this is unnecessary because if you omitted the argument, the default that you specified when you created the class — dynaset — would apply. However, this does provide a cue to mention the other options that you have for this argument, shown in the following table.

`CRecordset::snapshot`	Recordset is opened as snapshot — I discussed snapshot and dynaset in the previous chapter.
`CRecordset::forwardonly`	Recordset is opened as read-only and it can only be scrolled forward. (When a recordset is opened, it is positioned at the first record automatically.)
`CRecordset::dynamic`	Recordset is open with scrolling in both directions, and changes made by other users are reflected in the recordset fields.
`AFX_DB_USE_DEFAULT_TYPE`	Recordset is opened with the default recordset type stored in the inherited member, `m_nDefaultType`, which is initialized in the constructor.

There are two further parameters to `Open()` for which you have accepted default argument values. The second parameter is a pointer to a string that can be a table name, an SQL `SELECT` statement, a call of a predefined query procedure, or null, which is the default. If it is null, the string returned by `GetDefaultSQL()` is used. The third parameter is a bit mask that you can use to specify a myriad of options for the connection, including making it read-only, which means that you can't write to it at all, or making it append-only, which prohibits editing or deleting records. You will find more details on this in the documentation for this function.

With the recordset opened, you want to scan through all the records to find the largest value in the OrderID field. You can do that by adding the following code:

```
long COrderSet::CreateNewOrderID()
{
  if(!IsOpen())
    Open(CRecordset::dynaset);
```

```
  // Check for no records in recordset
  long newOrderID = 0;
  if(!(IsBOF() && IsEOF()))
  {                                      // We have records
    MoveFirst();                         // so go to the first
    while(!IsEOF())                      // Compare with all the others
    {
      // Save order ID if its larger
      if(newOrderID < m_OrderID)
          newOrderID = m_OrderID;

      MoveNext();                        // Go to next record
    }
  }
  return ++newOrderID;
}
```

The `IsBOF()` and `IsEOF()` members of the recordset class return `true` if you are beyond the beginning or end of the records in the recordset respectively, in which case no record is currently active so you should be using the fields. When a recordset is empty, both functions return `TRUE`. As long as there are records, you move to the first record by calling the `MoveFirst()` member function. There is also a `MoveLast()` member that goes to the last record in the recordset.

You create a local variable, `newOrderID`, with an initial value of 0 that eventually stores the maximum order ID in the table. The `while` loop moves through each of the records in the recordset using the `MoveNext()` member function, checking for a larger value for the `m_OrderID` member. Before calling any of the move members of a recordset, you must call either `IsEOF()` or `IsBOF()`, depending on which way you are going. If you call a move function when you are beyond the end or beginning of the recordset, the function throws an exception of type `CDBException`.

In addition to the move functions you have used here, a recordset object provides you with three others, shown in the following table.

`MoveLast()`	Moves to the last record in the recordset. You must not use this function (or `MoveFirst()`) with forward-only recordset, otherwise an exception of type `CDBEception` is thrown.
`MovePrev()`	Moves to the record preceding the current record in the recordset. If there isn't one, it moves to one position beyond the first record. After this the recordset fields are not valid and `IsBOF()` returns `true`.
`Move()`	This is used to move one or more records through a recordset. The first argument, of type `long`, specifies the number of rows to move. The second argument of type `WORD` determines the nature of the move operation. Four values for the second argument make the function equivalent to the other move functions we have seen. You will find more details on this in the Visual C++ documentation.

When the loop ends you have the maximum order ID stored in `newOrderID`, so you just need to increment it by 1 before returning it.

The last step is to get the value transferred to the control so it appears in the IDD_CUSTOMER_FORM dialog. A call to UpdateData() for the recordset view object with an argument of FALSE does this. This function is inherited in the record view class from CWnd. An argument of FALSE causes the data to be transferred from the data member of the View Class to the controls in the dialog. A value of TRUE causes data to be retrieved from the controls and stored in the data members. In both cases this is achieved by causing the DoDataExchange() member of view to be called by the framework.

Initiating ID Creation

The customer view needs a new order ID to be available when it is first displayed. Add a public member function, SetNewOrderID(), to the CCustomerView class and implement it as follows:

```
void CCustomerView::SetNewOrderID(void)
{
   // Get a new order ID from the COrderSet object in the document
   m_NewOrderID = static_cast<CDBSimpleUpdateDoc*>
                            (GetDocument())->m_OrderSet.CreateNewOrderID();
   UpdateData(FALSE);                              // Transfer data to controls
}
```

The pointer returned by the inherited GetDocument() function is of type CDocument. You want to use this to access the m_OrderSet member of the derived class so you must cast the pointer to type CDBSimpleUpdateDoc*. You then call the member function for the m_OrderSet member of the document class that returns the new order ID, and store the result in the m_NewOrderID member of the CCustomerView class. Calling the inherited UpdateData() member of the view transfers the data from the data members of the view to the controls. You must now add an #include directive for DBSimpleUpdateDoc.h to the source file because you refer to the CDBSimpleUpdateDoc class name.

Because you only ever create a single CCustomerView object and reuse it as necessary, you will want a new ID to be available each time you switch to that view. The SelectView() member of the CMainFrame object deals with switching between dialogs and this is also where a CCustomerView object gets created first time around. This is a good place to initiate the process for creating the new order ID. All you need to do is to add some code to call the SetNewOrderID() member if the view corresponds to the CCustomerView.

```
void CMainFrame::SelectView(ViewID viewID)
{
   CView* pOldActiveView = GetActiveView();      // Get current view

   // Get pointer to new view if it exists
   // if it doesn't the pointer will be null
   CView* pNewActiveView = static_cast<CView*>(GetDlgItem(viewID));

   // If this is first time around for the new view, the new view
   // won't exist, so we must create it
   // The Order Details view is always created first so we don't need
   // to provide for creating that.
   if (pNewActiveView == NULL)
   {
      switch(viewID)
      {
         case NEW_ORDER:                   // Create view to add new order
            pNewActiveView = new CCustomerView;
```

```
                break;
            case SELECT_PRODUCT:            // Create view to add product to order
              pNewActiveView = new CProductView;
              break;
             default:
              AfxMessageBox(_T("Invalid View ID"));
              return;
        }

        // Switching the views
        // Obtain the current view context to apply to the new view
        CCreateContext context;
        context.m_pCurrentDoc = pOldActiveView->GetDocument();
        pNewActiveView->Create(NULL, NULL, 0L, CFrameWnd::rectDefault,
                                            this, viewID, &context);
        pNewActiveView->OnInitialUpdate();
    }
    SetActiveView(pNewActiveView);               // Activate the new view
    if(viewID==NEW_ORDER)
      static_cast<CCustomerView*>(pNewActiveView)->SetNewOrderID();

    pOldActiveView->ShowWindow(SW_HIDE);         // Hide the old view
    pNewActiveView->ShowWindow(SW_SHOW);         // Show the new view
    pOldActiveView->SetDlgCtrlID(m_CurrentViewID); // Set the old view ID
    pNewActiveView->SetDlgCtrlID(AFX_IDW_PANE_FIRST);
    m_CurrentViewID = viewID;                    // Save the new view ID
    RecalcLayout();
  }
```

All you do is check the `viewID` value. If it is `NEW_ORDER` you call the `SetNewOrderID()` member of the new view object. Because `pNewActiveView` is of type `CView`, you must cast it to the actual view type to call the member function.

Storing the Order Data

You don't want to create a new entry in the Orders table until you have the first `Product Details` record for the order, so you need a way to pass the data accumulated in the `CCustomerView` object to the `CProductView` object. A simple way to do this is to define a new class to represent an order. It just needs to have a data member for each data value that you want to stash away. Except for the shipped date field that doesn't sensibly have a value in a new order, the data members are the same as the data members corresponding to the fields in the `COrderSet` class. Create a new header file, `Order.h`, in the project, and add the following code to it:

```
// Stores the data for a new order
#pragma once

class COrder
{
public:
  // Data members same as fields in COrderSet
  long m_OrderID;
  CString m_CustomerID;
```

```
    long m_EmployeeID;
    CTime m_OrderDate;
    CTime m_RequiredDate;
    long m_ShipVia;
    double m_Freight;
    CString m_ShipName;
    CString m_ShipAddress;
    CString m_ShipCity;
    CString m_ShipRegion;
    CString m_ShipPostalCode;
    CString m_ShipCountry;

    // Default constructor
    COrder():
        m_OrderID(0),                       // Will be set by CCustomerView object
        m_EmployeeID(1),                    // Arbitrary employee ID assigned
        m_ShipVia(3),                       // Arbitrary shipping company
        m_CustomerID(_T("")),    m_Freight(0.0),         m_ShipName(_T("")),
        m_ShipAddress(_T("")),   m_ShipCity(_T("")),   m_ShipRegion(_T("")),
        m_ShipPostalCode(_T("")), m_ShipCountry(_T(""))
    {
      SYSTEMTIME Now;
      GetLocalTime(&Now);                             // Get current time
      m_OrderDate = m_RequiredDate = CTime(Now); // Set time as today
    }
};
```

In general it is not good practice to make all the data members of a class public like this, but because the recordset classes generated by the Class Wizard all have public members, there is little to be gained by making them private in our class here.

If you add a data member, m_Order, of type COrder, to the CDBSimpleUpdateDoc class, you will be able to use this to pass the order data to the CProductView object. All you have to do is get the CCustomerView object to load up the data members when the Select Products button is pressed, ready to be picked up by the CProductView object. You can implement the button handler in CCustomerView like this:

```
void CCustomerView::OnSelectproducts()
{
  // Get a pointer to the document
  CDBSimpleUpdateDoc* pDoc = static_cast<CDBSimpleUpdateDoc*>(GetDocument());

  // Set up order field values from CCustomerSet object
  pDoc->m_Order.m_CustomerID = m_pSet->m_CustomerID;
  pDoc->m_Order.m_ShipAddress = m_pSet->m_Address;
  pDoc-> m_Order.m_ShipCity = m_pSet->m_City;
  pDoc-> m_Order.m_ShipCountry = m_pSet->m_Country;
  pDoc-> m_Order.m_ShipName = m_pSet->m_CompanyName;
  pDoc-> m_Order.m_ShipPostalCode = m_pSet->m_PostalCode;
  pDoc-> m_Order.m_ShipRegion = m_pSet->m_Region;


  // Set up order field values from CCustomerView dialog input
  pDoc-> m_Order.m_OrderID = m_NewOrderID;                // Generated new ID
```

```
    pDoc-> m_Order.m_OrderDate = m_OrderDate;        // From order date control
    pDoc-> m_Order.m_RequiredDate = m_RequiredDate;    // From required date control

    static_cast<CMainFrame*>(GetParentFrame())->SelectView(SELECT_PRODUCT);
}
```

This is straightforward stuff. You are just copying values from the recordset and record view objects to the `Order` object that is a member of the document object.

Setting Dates

There is a small problem with the date picker controls on the `CCustomerView` dialog: The variables corresponding to these, `m_OrderDate` and `m_RequiredDate`, are not initialized at the moment, so the controls do not display sensible values to start with. You want then to display the current date at the outset, so you should add some code to initialize them at the end of the `OnInitialUpdate()` member called when the view object is first created:

```
void CCustomerView::OnInitialUpdate()
{
  BeginWaitCursor();
  GetRecordset();
  CRecordView::OnInitialUpdate();
  if (m_pSet->IsOpen())
  {
    CString strTitle = m_pSet->m_pDatabase->GetDatabaseName();
    CString strTable = m_pSet->GetTableName();
    if(!strTable.IsEmpty())
      strTitle += _T(":") + strTable;
  GetDocument()->SetTitle(strTitle);
  }
  EndWaitCursor();

  // Initialize time values
  SYSTEMTIME Now;
  GetLocalTime(&Now);                             // Get current time
  m_OrderDate = m_RequiredDate = CTime(Now);      // Set time as today
}
```

Here you set both `CTime` variables to the current time, just as you did in the constructor for the `COrder` class.

Now the `CCustomerView` object is in good shape. It displays the right date and it squirrels away all the value for the fields in a row in the Orders table, so you are ready to tackle the production selection process.

Selecting Products for an Order

When the view for selecting a product is displayed, you want to have the variables for the controls that display the order ID and the customer name already set up with appropriate values. You get these values from the `Order` member of the document object. You can add a function to the `CProductView` class to do this. You can call it `InitializeView()` and the return type is `void`. You can call the function from the `SelectView()` member of the `CMainFrame` object for the application. That way you ensure that the controls are always initialized before the dialog box is displayed.

Before you implement `InitializeView()`, consider something else. The new Orders table record is added only when the Select Product button is clicked to add a product to the order for the first time. Subsequent button clicks should just add another product to the order, so you need a way to determine whether the Orders table has been appended to or not when the button is clicked. You can do this by adding a variable, `m_OrderAdded`, of type `bool` to `CProductView` that is `false` to start with and set to `true` by the Select Product button handler. So add this variable to the class. You can initialize it in the `InitializeView()` member that you can implement as follows:

```
void CProductView::InitializeView()
{
   // Get a pointer to the document
   CDBSimpleUpdateDoc* pDoc = static_cast<CDBSimpleUpdateDoc*>(GetDocument());

   m_OrderID = pDoc->m_Order.m_OrderID;
   m_CustomerName = pDoc->m_Order.m_ShipName;
   m_Quantity = 1;                              // Must order at least 1
   m_Discount = 0;                              // No default discount
   m_OrderAdded = false;                        // Order not added initially
   UpdateData(FALSE);                           // Transfer data to controls
}
```

This initializes the view class members for the order ID and customer name controls by copying values from the appropriate member of the `Order` member of the document. This function is also an opportunity to ensure that the controls for order quantity and discount start with suitable initial values. The order quantity for any product has to be at least 1, and the discount is 0 by default. Calling the inherited `UpdateData()` member with an argument value `FALSE` causes the data to be transferred from the class variables to the controls, as you saw previously. You need to add an `#include` directive for `DBSimpleUpdateDoc.h` to the beginning of the source file to make the document class definition available.

To put this into operation, you just need to call `InitializeView()` whenever you switch to the product selection dialog box. The obvious place to do this is in the `SelectView()` member of the `CMainFrame` class:

```
void CMainFrame::SelectView(ViewID viewID)
{
   CView* pOldActiveView = GetActiveView();      // Get current view

   // Get pointer to new view if it exists
   // if it doesn't the pointer will be null
   CView* pNewActiveView = static_cast<CView*>(GetDlgItem(viewID));

   // If this is first time around for the new view, the new view
   // won't exist, so we must create it
   // The Order Details view is always created first so we don't need
   // to provide for creating that.
   if (pNewActiveView == NULL)
   {
      switch(viewID)
      {
         case NEW_ORDER:                 // Create view to add new order
            pNewActiveView = new CCustomerView;
            break;
         case SELECT_PRODUCT:            // Create view to add product to order
```

```
                pNewActiveView = new CProductView;
                break;
            default:
                AfxMessageBox(_T("Invalid View ID"));
                return;
        }

        // Switching the views
        // Obtain the current view context to apply to the new view
        CCreateContext context;
        context.m_pCurrentDoc = pOldActiveView->GetDocument();
        pNewActiveView->Create(NULL, NULL, 0L, CFrameWnd::rectDefault,
                                                this, viewID, &context);
        pNewActiveView->OnInitialUpdate();
    }
    SetActiveView(pNewActiveView);                    // Activate the new view
    if(viewID==NEW_ORDER)
        static_cast<CCustomerView*>(pNewActiveView)->SetNewOrderID();
    else if(viewID == SELECT_PRODUCT)
        static_cast<CProductView*>(pNewActiveView)->InitializeView();

    pOldActiveView->ShowWindow(SW_HIDE);              // Hide the old view
    pNewActiveView->ShowWindow(SW_SHOW);              // Show the new view
    pOldActiveView->SetDlgCtrlID(m_CurrentViewID);    // Set the old view ID
    pNewActiveView->SetDlgCtrlID(AFX_IDW_PANE_FIRST);
    m_CurrentViewID = viewID;                         // Save the new view ID
    RecalcLayout();
}
```

When the `viewID` parameter has the value `SELECT_PRODUCT`, the `CProductView` class variables for the order ID and customer name controls will be initialized, as will the `bool` variable controlling the creation of a new record in the Orders table.

Adding a New Order

The final piece of the program that you have to put together is the code to add a new order. Adding an order is always done by the `OnSelectproducts()` member of `CProductView`. The effect of pressing the Select Products button depends on the value of the data member, `m_OrderAdded`. If it is `false`, the function should add a new record to the Orders table, as well as a new record to the Order Details table. If `m_OrderAdded` is `true`, only the Order Details table should have a new record added as this is another product for the same order. All the values you need for the new `Orders` record are stored in the `m_Order` member of the document. You just need to copy them to the members of the `COrderSet` object that is also a member of the document. The document object is in a strong position to deal with this, so add a member function, `AddOrder()` to `CDBSimpleUpdateDoc` with a `bool` return type, and implement it as:

```
bool CDBSimpleUpdateDoc::AddOrder()
{
    try
    {
        if(!m_OrderSet.IsOpen())                    // If recordset is not open
            m_OrderSet.Open();                      // open it
```

```
        if(m_OrderSet.CanAppend())                  // If we can add a record
        {                                            // then add it
          m_OrderSet.AddNew();                       // Start adding new record
          m_OrderSet.m_CustomerID = m_Order.m_CustomerID;
          m_OrderSet.m_EmployeeID = m_Order.m_EmployeeID;
          m_OrderSet.m_Freight = m_Order.m_Freight;
          m_OrderSet.m_OrderDate = m_Order.m_OrderDate;
          m_OrderSet.m_OrderID = m_Order.m_OrderID;
          m_OrderSet.m_RequiredDate = m_Order.m_RequiredDate;
          m_OrderSet.m_ShipAddress = m_Order.m_ShipAddress;
          m_OrderSet.m_ShipName = m_Order.m_ShipName;
          m_OrderSet.m_ShipPostalCode = m_Order.m_ShipPostalCode;
          m_OrderSet.m_ShipRegion = m_Order.m_ShipRegion;
          m_OrderSet.m_ShipVia = m_Order.m_ShipVia;

          // No value for the Shipped Date field
          m_OrderSet.SetFieldNull(&m_OrderSet.m_ShippedDate);

          m_OrderSet.Update();                       // Complete adding new record
          return true;                               // Return success
        }
        else
          AfxMessageBox(_T("Cannot append to Orders table"));
    }
    catch(CException* pEx)                            // Catch any exceptions
    {
      pEx->ReportError();                            // Display the error message
    }
    return false;                                    // Here we have failed
  }
```

You saw earlier in this chapter that the functions in a recordset object for adding and editing records can throw exceptions, so you put the code in a `try` block and catch any exceptions to avoid aborting the application if this happens.

After ensuring that the `COrderSet` recordset is open, you check that it allows records to be added by calling its `CanAppend()` member. Adding a new record involves three steps:

1. You first call the `AddNew()` member of the recordset. This starts the process and saves the current values of the data members in the recordset because you will be altering them and sets the values of the data members to null. This is nothing to do with null for pointers and it is not zero — null here implies no value has been set for a variable.

2. You set all the data members for the field values in the recordset to the values required in the record. This is quite straightforward. You just copy the values stored in the members of the `m_Order` object to the members of the recordset object. The `m_ShippedDate` member is null because you have not set a value for it here.

3. You call `Update()` to actually get the record written and this also restores the original values in the recordset object. It doesn't apply here, but if you were displaying the recordset that you were adding to, you would need to call the `Requery()` member of the recordset object to get the new record values displayed.

You can now put in the basic logic for the `OnSelectproduct()` handler for the `CProductView` class. You need to call `UpdateData()` for the view to get the data that was entered in the edit controls transferred to data members of the view object. Here's the outline code for the handler function:

```
void CProductView::OnSelectproduct()
{
  UpdateData(TRUE);                                    // Transfer data from controls

  // Get a pointer to the document
  CDBSimpleUpdateDoc* pDoc = static_cast<CDBSimpleUpdateDoc*>(GetDocument());

  if(!m_OrderAdded)                                     // If order not added
    m_OrderAdded = pDoc->AddOrder();                    // then try to add it
  if(m_OrderAdded)
    // Code to add new Order Details record...
}
```

After calling the `UpdateData()` for the `CProductView` object, you get a pointer to the document object. You need this to call the `AddOrder()` member of the document that will do the work. Next you check the `m_OrderAdded` member. You only want to add a record to `Orders` when this is `false`. The `AddOrder()` member of the document object returns a `bool` value that is `true` if the order was added successfully, and `false` for any failure. You use this value to set the `m_OrderAdded` member of `CProductView`, and as an indicator for whether you can continue to add order details. You don't need to display any message in the case of failure. The `AddOrder()` function has already done that.

The code to add a record to the Order Details table is also probably best handled by the document object, but the document class member function to do it needs access to four values from members of the `CProductView` and `CProductSet` classes — for the product ID, the order quantity, the unit price, and the applicable discount. The order ID is available in the document class from its `m_Order` member, so you don't need to worry about that. You can add a function, `AddOrderDetails()`, to `CDBSimpleUpdateDoc` to add a record to the Order Details table. The return type should be void and the function has four parameters the `ID` of type `long`, `price` of type `double`, `quantity` of type `int`, and `discount` of type `float`.

You can implement the function as follows:

```
void CDBSimpleUpdateDoc::AddOrderDetails(long ID, double price,
  int quantity, float discount)
{
  try
  {
    if(!m_DBSimpleUpdateSet.IsOpen())                   // If recordset is not open
      m_DBSimpleUpdateSet.Open();                       // open it

    m_DBSimpleUpdateSet.AddNew();                       // Start adding new record

    // Set Product Details recordset data member values
    m_DBSimpleUpdateSet.m_OrderID = m_Order.m_OrderID;
    m_DBSimpleUpdateSet.m_Quantity = quantity;
    m_DBSimpleUpdateSet.m_Discount = discount;
    m_DBSimpleUpdateSet.m_ProductID = ID;
    m_DBSimpleUpdateSet.m_UnitPrice = price;
```

```
        m_DBSimpleUpdateSet.Update();              // Complete adding new record
      }
    catch(CException* pEx)                      // Catch any exceptions
    {
      pEx->ReportError();                       // Display the error message
    }
  }
```

This sets up the values in the m_DBSimpleUpdateSet members and then updates the table in essentially the same way as for the Orders table. Again, you have to put the update code in a try block to catch any exceptions that might be thrown by AddNew() or Update().

You want to call this function every time the Select Product button handler in the CProductView class is called, so you can modify the handler to do this:

```
void CProductView::OnSelectproduct()
{
  UpdateData(TRUE);                           // Transfer data from controls

  // Get a pointer to the document
  CDBSimpleUpdateDoc* pDoc = static_cast<CDBSimpleUpdateDoc*>(GetDocument());

  if(!m_OrderAdded)                           // If order not added
    m_OrderAdded = pDoc->AddOrder();          // then try to add it
  if(m_OrderAdded)
  {
    pDoc->AddOrderDetails(m_pSet->m_ProductID,
                          m_pSet->m_UnitPrice,
                          m_Quantity,
                          m_Discount);
    // Now reset the values in the quantity and discount controls
    m_Quantity = 1;
    m_Discount = 0;
    UpdateData(FALSE);                        // Transfer data to controls
  }
}
```

You use the m_DBSimpleUpdateSet object to update the Order Details table. This was used by the original view in the application, and it is stored in the document object. You get the values for quantity and discount from the data members in the view object corresponding to the edit controls that provide for these values to be entered. The order ID value was set when the dialog was displayed so that it would be displayed for information only. The product ID and unit price values are retrieved from the CProductSet object associated with this view. After calling Update() to write the record, reset the values for quantity and discount back to their defaults.

Try It Out   **Adding New Orders**

After adding a number of other orders, as you might deduce from the order ID, I added the order shown in Figure 21-19.

Then I clicked the Select Product button, and selected the product, quantity, and discount shown in Figure 21-20.

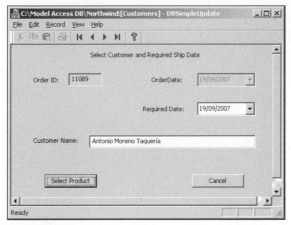

Figure 21-19

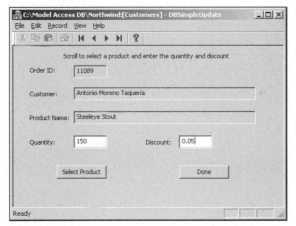

Figure 21-20

Clicking the Select Product button adds that product to the order for the customer and then allows the selection of another product. Each click of the Select Product button adds a new record to the Order Details table for the current order ID. When the order is complete, just click the Done button to end the process.

After you add an order, you can verify that it was added correctly by moving to the last order in the order details browsing view as Figure 21-21 shows.

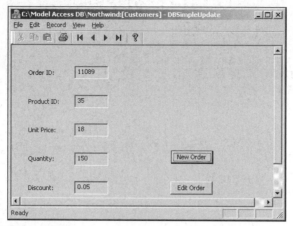

Figure 21-21

You may notice that the views don't reset to the beginning of the recordset when you finish an order entry operation. Try the first exercise at the end of the chapter to fix this for the customer recordset. You should not find this too difficult.

Summary

In this chapter you learned how elementary updating works using the ODBC support in MFC. The important points covered in this chapter include:

❑   Updating is only possible if a recordset corresponds to a single table. Recordsets corresponding to table joins cannot be updated.

❑   To start editing a record in a recordset you call the Edit() member of the recordset object.

❑   To start adding a new record to a recordset, you call the AddNew() member of the recordset object.

❑   To complete either modifying an existing record or adding a new one, you must call the Update() member of the recordset object.

❑   Before initializing an update of a recordset, you should always ensure that the recordset is open and that the update operation you intend to perform is legal.

❑   A transaction packages a series of database update operations so that the original state of that database can be restored in the event of an error.

Exercises

You can download the source code for the examples in the book and the solutions to the following exercises from www.wrox.com.

1. Modify the update application in this chapter so that the dialog box for adding a new order always displays the customers in alphabetical order, and the dialog box always displays the first customer each time it is displayed.

2. Modify the example to display the total value of a new order on the view to select products for the order (which corresponds to CProductView).

3. Extend the example in this chapter to enable the employee to be selected from the records in the Employees table.

4. Extend the example further to allow the shipped via field in an order to be chosen from the records in the Shippers table.

More on Windows Forms Applications

You already know quite a lot about the process of creating Windows Forms applications from CLR Sketcher. In this chapter, you will explore some more controls that you can use in the GUI for a Windows Forms application. You'll do this by assembling a single application incrementally throughout the chapter, so by the end of the chapter you'll have another Windows Forms program of a reasonable size.

In this chapter, you'll learn:

❑ How to use a wider variety of controls to build an application GUI

❑ How to display a Web page in an application

❑ How to work with control containers

❑ How to create and display message boxes

Creating the Application GUI

Create a new CLR project using the `Windows Forms Application` template and assign the name `Ex22_01` to the project. You are going to develop `Ex22_01` into a program to generate lottery entries. The program won't be an ideal design because it includes controls that duplicate some functions perhaps unnecessarily, but the benefit is that you get to try out various possibilities in a working application. I have chosen two lotteries with which I am familiar and for which the program generates entries; if these don't match the lottery that you favor, you should be able to adjust the example quite easily.

Let me make one point against entering a lottery — you would probably not choose the numbers 1 to 6 as your entry because it is extremely unlikely that such an entry would win. Of course, the truth is that it's just as likely as any other more random-looking set of numbers you might choose, but the numbers 1 to 6 have never come up as the winning entry in any lottery anywhere. So you can conclude that whatever you choose — you lose.

First, display the Properties window for the form and change the value of its Text property to A Winning Application. To display the controls that are available for use with the form, press Ctrl+Alt+X, or select the View > Toolbox menu item. Add a menu strip control to the top of the form by dragging a MenuStrip from the Toolbox window to the form. Add three menu items to the menu strip with the text &Play, &Limits, and &Help. The & precedes the character that is the accelerator character for the menu item, so Alt+P is the accelerator for the Play menu. The Editor window containing the form with the menu strip should now look as shown in Figure 22-1.

The Play menu won't have a submenu but will cause a Click event to fire when it is clicked. Because you'll be handling the event, it is convenient to give the menu item a name that is shorter than the default. You can access the properties by right-clicking the control in the form and selecting Properties from the context menu, but this time try clicking menuStrip1 below the form and select Edit Items from the context menu. It displays the Items Collection Editor dialog box shown in Figure 22-2.

If you select the name in the left pane in the dialog box corresponding to the Play menu, the properties for it are displayed in the right pane. You can then edit the (Name) property value to make it playMenuItem. Figure 22-2 shows the dialog box after the change has been made. The advantage of using this dialog box is that you can work through all the items on the menu strip adjusting the properties as necessary. You can also add new items to the menu strip or rearrange the menu sequence by moving items up or down using the buttons to the right of the left pane.

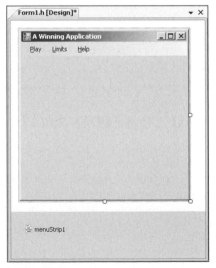

Figure 22-1

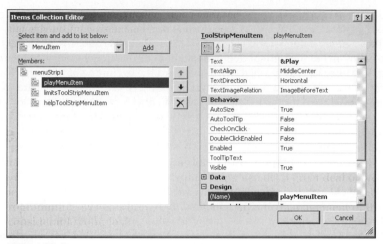

Figure 22-2

Adding Submenus

Add three menu items, Upper, Lower, and Reset, to the Limits menu and add an About menu item to the Help menu. You can add new menu items to a drop-down menu using the Items Collection Editor, too. You access this by right-clicking the top level menu item such as Limits and selecting `.EditDropDownItems...` from the pop-up. You just select the item you want to add from the drop-down list at the top, and click the Add button. Alternatively you can work through the Editor pane and interact directly with the menu strip as you did with the CLR Sketcher application. The properties for the new menu items need to be modified, so display the properties for the Upper menu first of all by right-clicking it and selecting Properties from the pop-up. You will be handling events for this menu item so you can change the default name property to something shorter, such as `upperMenuItem`. You can also add a shortcut key for the item by clicking the down arrow in the value column for the `ShortcutKeys` property to display the list shown in Figure 22-3.

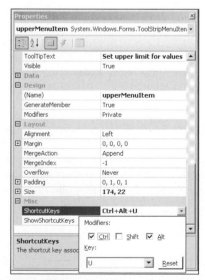

Figure 22-3

Select the modifier or modifiers by clicking one or more of the checkboxes and select the key from the drop-down list. I chose Ctrl+Alt+U as the shortcut for this menu item, as you can see. Figure 22-3 also shows that I have set the value for the ToolTipText property as "Set upper limit for values". As you know, hovering the mouse cursor over a menu item results in the tooltip being displayed after a brief delay. Setting the AutoToolTip property that is toward the beginning of the list to True makes the tooltip the same as the text on the menu item. Leaving the property value as False causes the ToolTipText property value to be chosen for the tooltip text. You can also control whether or not the shortcut key combination is displayed alongside the menu item text by setting the ShowShortcutKeys property value.

Clicking the Lower menu item causes its properties to be displayed in the Properties window. You can then change the (Name) property value to lowerMenuItem, the ShortcutKeys property value to Ctrl+Alt+L, and the ToolTipText property values to "Set lower limit for values". In the same way you can change the (Name) property for the Reset menu item to resetMenuItem, set the ShortCutKeys property value to Ctrl+Alt+R, and make the tooltip text "Reset limits to original values". You can also change the (Name) property value for the About menu item to aboutMenuItem and add tooltip text for that, too; an About menu item doesn't usually have a shortcut key combination defined. The Play menu item creates a complete new set of values for a lottery entry, so you could add tooltip text to indicate that, if you want.

Adding a Tab Control

A TabControl control provides multiple tabs that can each contain their own set of controls. You can use a tab control to provide for entries to more than one lottery in the application window client area. Display the Toolbox window (Ctrl+Alt+X) and select TabControl from the list — it's in the Containers group. Click in the client area of the form to add the tab control and then display its properties. All the controls listed under the Containers heading can contain other controls so they all provide a means of collecting together a set of controls into a group. Obviously with the tab control each tab can contain its own set of controls, and you can have as many tabs in the control as you want.

You want the tab control to always fill the client area of the window, and this is determined by the value of the Dock property that is in the Layout group of properties for the TabControl control. Figure 22-4 shows the Properties window for the tab control with the value cell for the Dock property expanded.

Clicking in the central area where the cursor currently appears in Figure 22-4 changes the Dock property value to Fill, which is what you want here. You can also dock the control to any of the four sides of the client area by clicking in one of the four areas around the edge of the pop-up or have it undocked by clicking in the area labelled None. The form in the Editor pane should now look like Figure 22-5.

The tab control has two tabs, but you can add another by clicking the arrow on the top edge of the control toward the right. Just click Add Tab from the pop-up. You'll need to change the text on each of the tabs to something more meaningful and change the (Name) property values too. Go to the Properties window for the TabControl control — right-clicking the control and selecting Properties from the pop-up displays the window if it is not already visible — then select the value field for the TabPages property and click the ellipsis that appears. The Tab Page Collection Editor dialog box shown in Figure 22-6 displays.

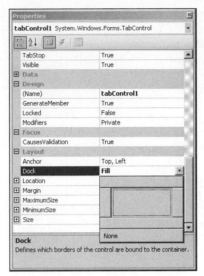

Figure 22-4

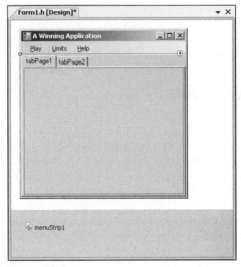

Figure 22-5

The text on the tab should reflect the lottery name to which the controls on this tab relate, so I changed the (Name) property value to lottoTab and the Text property value to Lotto, as shown in Figure 22-6. The (Name) property value is the name used in the Form1 class for the variable that references this tab, and the Text property value is the text on the tab.

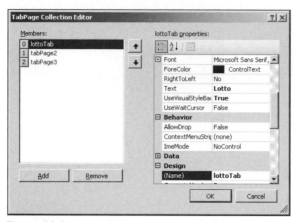

Figure 22-6

The tab labelled `tabPage2` is for an entry to a second lottery, which in my case is called Euromillions. Again, you can choose whatever lottery you prefer. Click `tabPage2` in the left pane to display the properties for it in the right pane; after you select the new tab you should see that the name in the left pane for `tabPage1` has been altered to `lottoTab` and the text on the first tab in the form has been updated. I set the `Text` property value for `tabPage2` as `Euromillions` and the `(Name)` property value as `euroTab`. You'll use the third tab to display a Web page for entering a lottery so change the `Text` property value for `tabPage3` to `Web Page` and the name property value to `webTab`. When you have completed that, you can click the OK button to close the dialog box.

Using GroupBox Controls

You can use a `GroupBox` control to collect other controls together in a group. A `GroupBox` control also delineates the group with a line boundary and allows you to label the group if you want. A Lotto lottery entry consists of six different numbers that are from 1 to 49 so you'll want to group together the controls that will display these numbers. Add a `GroupBox` control to the `Lotto` tab by clicking the control in the `Toolbox` window and then clicking in the `Lotto` tab. You can then modify the `Text`, `(Name)`, and `Dock` property values for the `GroupBox` to the values shown in Figure 22-7.

The `Text` property value indicates the range of possible values for the lottery entry that is displayed on this tab. The value for the `Dock` property makes the `GroupBox` control fill its container, which is the `Lotto` tab on the `Tab` control. The `(Name)` property value determines the name of the variable in the `Form1` class that identifies this control.

The lottery entry on the Euromillions tab involves two groups of values, one group of five different values from 1 to 50 and a second group of two different "star" values each from 1 to 9. Numbers in the first group can be the same as the two "star" values. Use yet another container in the Euromillions tab, so click on `SplitContainer` in the `Containers` group in the `Toolbox` window and click in the Euromillions tab to place it there. To select a tab, first click the tab label at the top of the tab control — this selects the tab control with the tab label you highlighted; you then click within the display area of the tab to select the highlighted tab within the control. The `Dock` property value for the `SplitContainer` control is `Fill` by default so the control should fill the tab. The control has two panes that can each contain further controls. You can drag the divider between the panes to adjust the relative sizes of the panes.

Figure 22-7

Display the Properties for the control and set the `Orientation` and `(Name)` properties, as shown in Figure 22-8.

The panes should now be separated by a horizontal divider, so drag this so that the lower pane is about half the height of the upper pane. Then set the `IsSplitterFixed` property for the control to have the value `True`, as shown in Figure 22-8. This fixes the divider at the position you have set. If you leave the `IsSplitterFixed` property value as `False`, you allow the divider to be dragged to any position by the user when the application is executing.

Figure 22-8

You can group the contents of each pane in the SplitContainer control using a GroupBox control, so add a GroupBox control to each of the panes. Set the Text, (Name), and Dock properties for the GroupBox control in the upper pane to have the values "Values 1 to 50", euroValues, and Fill, respectively, and set the Text, (Name), and Dock properties for the GroupBox control in the lower pane to have the values "Values 1 to 9," euroStars, and Fill, respectively. The Editor window should look like Figure 22-9.

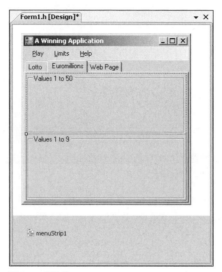

Figure 22-9

You have quite a hierarchy of controls now. The client area of the form contains a tab control and the Euromillions tab on the tab control contains a SplitContainer control and each of the panes in the SplitContainer control contains a GroupBox control. The next step is to add buttons to each of the GroupBox controls in the panes.

Using Button Controls

Button controls in the Common Controls group are regular buttons that typically appear in a dialog window. You'll use a button control to house each value in a lottery entry. For the Euromillions lottery you'll need seven buttons, five in the group box in the top pane with values from 1 to 50 and two in the group box in the bottom pane with values from 1 to 9.

Place five buttons in the group box in the upper pane on the Euromillions tab and add two more in the group box in the lower pane below to make an elegant arrangement. You can reposition any of the buttons by dragging it with the mouse whereupon you should see vertical and/or horizontal alignment guides displayed to help you align the control to the others. You can also use the Format > Horizontal Spacing > Make Equal menu item to make the spacing in a horizontal sequence of controls uniform. The other menu items in the Format menu are worth exploring; they provide for setting the vertical spacing, for aligning controls, for centering a selected group of controls in a form, and for adjusting the height and width of the controls. You can select any number of controls by clicking them while holding the Ctrl key down.

Figure 22-10 shows my arrangement for the buttons on the Euromillions tab.

You'll be generating values to display as the text on these buttons, so you need to change the properties for each of them. I suggest you make the values for the Text property on the upper five buttons the values 1, 2, 3, 4, and 5, and the values for the Text property on the two buttons in the lower pane 1 and 2. You can change the (Name) property for each button too. The buttons in the upper pane can have names euroValue1, euroValue2, through to euroValue5, and the two on the lower pane euroStar1 and euroStar1. While you're at it, you might like to change the BackColor property for each button that determines the background color. I chose the color Silver for the top five buttons and Gold for the bottom two — where both colors are from the Web palette. When you have completed that, the application window with the Euromillions tab selected should look as shown in Figure 22-11.

Now you can return to the Lotto tab by clicking it in the Editor window. You can then add buttons to that. The Lotto lottery is very simple: You just have to choose six different values from 1 to 49 for an entry. You therefore need to add six Button controls to the GroupBox that is already on the Lotto tab. After you have arranged the buttons to your satisfaction, change the text on the buttons so they show the default values 1 to 6 and change the (Name) property for the buttons to lottoValue1, lottoValue2, through to lottoValue6. You can also set the BackColor property value for the buttons to a color of your choice — I chose the SkyBlue from the Web color palette. If you compile and execute the application, it should look as shown in Figure 22-12.

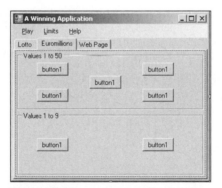

Figure 22-10

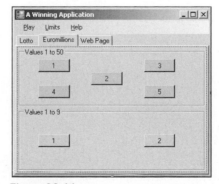

Figure 22-11

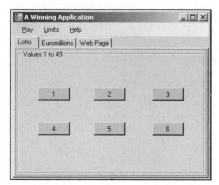

Figure 22-12

You can add a control to the Web Page tab next.

Using the WebBrowser Control

Displaying a Web page in the application is going to be much easier than you might have imagined because the WebBrowser control in the Common Controls group does all of the work. Click the Web Page tab in the form the Editor window; then click on WebBrowser in the Toolbox window, and click in the tab to place it there. You can display its properties by right-clicking it and selecting Properties from the pop-up. The Properties window for the control is shown in Figure 22-13.

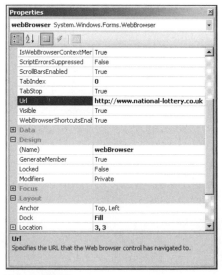

Figure 22-13

Figure 22-13 shows the properties after I have amended the (Name) property value to webBrowser, and set a value for the Url property as the URL for the Web page that the control should display; you can enter the URL for your local lottery organization here. If you verify that the Dock property value is Fill, that's all that's required to get the Web page displayed on the tab. Of course, the page displays only if your computer has an active Internet connection when you execute the program and the security settings for your browser do not prevent it from being displayed. If you recompile the program an execute it once more, the Web Page tab should look more or less like Figure 22-14.

Figure 22-14

If the Web page doesn't appear, it may be that your Internet connection is not active. Note how you get scrollbars by default in the WebBrowser control when they are necessary. You can also navigate by selecting active links in the Web page. If the Web page looks scrambled, it may be because you have strict Internet settings, in which case adding the Web site to your Trusted Sites zone may fix the problem.

You have almost — but not quite — finished the GUI for the application. It's time to review how the application is going to work in detail.

Operation of the Winning Application

Clicking the Play menu item displays a complete entry on the tab that is currently visible in the application window; thus you can apply the Play item to the Lotto tab or the Euromillions tab. The values for a lottery entry are displayed in ascending sequence. Switching to the Web Page tab displays the Web page where you can enter a lottery.

After an entry has been created, you might want to be able to change a particular value — because you have an irrational aversion to particular numbers, for instance, or because you don't believe numbers over 30 are for you. Clicking a button could cause a new number to be generated to replace the number on the button you clicked. Of course, the new number would have to be different from all the numbers in the current entry.

Another possibility is that you might want to choose a specific number that you regard to be lucky — a birthday or a birth month, for example, or the number of peas you left on your plate at lunch today. You could arrange for this possibility by adding a context menu that displays when you right-click on a particular button. A Choose menu item on the context menu could accommodate this. Dealing with the event arising from clicking the context menu item needs a little work because you'll have to provide for the entry of the data. The number that is entered also needs to be validated; the value must be within the permitted range, and it must not duplicate an existing value in the current group of buttons.

The Limits > Upper and Limits > Lower menu items allow a more constrained range of values to be used for generating an entry. There need to be checks here, too; the range must be inside the range that is permitted for a given lottery, and the range must be wide enough to allow the required number of different values to be generated.

Finally the Help > About menu item should display a message box displaying information about the application.

The first step in implementing the application so that it operates as described previously is to add a context menu for the buttons that display lottery entry values. That's surprisingly easy.

Adding a Context Menu

As you saw when developing CLR Sketcher, a context menu in a CLR Forms application is just another control. It's the ContextMenuStrip control that is in the Menus & Toolbars group of controls in the Toolbox window. Click the ContextMenuStrip control and then click in the grey area at the bottom of the Editor window to add the control to the application. The context menu displays in the form below the existing menu. If you click in the first menu, you can insert the item name. You can enter &Choose for the text for menu item, which makes Alt+C the accelerator for the item. It would be better to have a more meaningful name for the context menu, so open the Properties window for the ContextMenuStrip control and change its (Name) property value to buttonContextMenu. You could also change the value for the (Name) property for the Choose menu item to chooseValue.

You can now enable the buttonContextMenu control as the context menu for each of the buttons on the two lottery entry tabs. To do this, set the value of the ContextMenuStrip property for each button to the name of the ContextMenuStrip control, buttonContextMenu. The name appears in the drop-down list in the value cell for the property so you just click it to set the value. You can do this for all the buttons on a tab at once: Place the mouse cursor above and to the left of the group of buttons and drag the cursor so it's below and to the right of the buttons before releasing it. This selects all the buttons and you change the ContextMenuStrip property value in the Properties window for all the selected buttons.

Creating Event Handlers

The process of building the GUI graphically using the Form Design capability has automatically generated code for the controls you have added. There is now a member of the Form1 class for every control you have added to the form, and code to initialize these has been added to the InitializeComponent() function. If you look at the function, you'll see that it now contains a vast amount of code that sets properties for individual controls and assembles controls into their containers. Creating the GUI graphically is a breeze — you'll need a few more brain cells ticking over to move the application on from there.

To make the program work the way that you want, you must create event handler functions for the events you want the application to recognize and process, and implement these functions to make user interactions with the GUI do what you want. Although the code to handle the events cannot be generated automatically, the IDE can still help by generating the skeleton event handler functions and registering them with the event delegates.

You can view the events for a control by clicking the events button in the Properties window for the control. This displays all the possible events for the control and you set the name of the function that is to handle a particular event in the cell to the right of the event name. Of course, you identify handler functions only for the events you want to recognize and in most instances this is a very small proportion of the possible events for a control. You'll want to create handler functions for the Click event for the menu items for all the menu items and each of the buttons on the tabs. You did this in CLR Sketcher through the Properties window but there's also a shortcut for creating a handler function for a control to respond to a Click event; you just double-click the control in the Editor window and the code is created and displayed, and the function is registered as a handler for the event object. This creates a unique event handler for the control, but sometimes you'll want to make a single function handle events of a given type for more than one control. In this case, the Properties window route is the way to do it.

Event Handlers for Menu Items

You can start by creating an event handler function for the Play menu item. Double-clicking the menu item creates the following handler function code:

```
private: System::Void playMenuItem_Click(System::Object^  sender,
                                          System::EventArgs^  e)
{
}
```

This is a skeleton handler containing no code in the body of the function. Just to remind you of what you learned with CLR Sketcher, the first parameter is a handle referencing the control from which the event originated, and the second parameter provides information related to the event. The type of the first argument when a handler is called corresponds to the type of the control that originated the event, and this is ToolStripMenuItem^ in this case because the handler function is called when the Play menu item is clicked; the menu item handle is stored in the playMenuItem member of the Form1 class and you can check out its type in the class definition. Similarly, the actual type of the second argument to a Click event handler depends on the type of the control.

The handler function name that is generated by default is playMenuItem_Click. You must not change the function name in the code. In fact, I recommend you do not change *any* names in the code that is automatically generated; always do it through the Properties window. If you don't like the name that has been created for the event handler function, you can change it through the Click event property value in the Properties window for the control.

The name of the handler function has been registered with the event object by the following statement in the InitializeComponent() function:

```
this->playMenuItem->Click +=
          gcnew System::EventHandler(this, &Form1::playMenuItem_Click);
```

This statement adds the function name to the `Click` delegate in the `playMenuItem` object that is a member of the `Form1` class. You learned about delegates and how event handler functions are registered in Chapter 9.

Adding Members to the Form1 Class

Before you start implementing the handlers for the menu items, there are some additional fields that you'll need to store data relating to the constraints on the values for the lottery entries. You know how to add a new field to the `Form1` class; it's the way you have already used extensively to add members to a class. Switch to `Class View`, right-click the `Form1` class, and select `Add > Add Variable` from the context menu. Alternatively, you can just add the code manually, but be sure you don't intrude on the region of the class definition that is reserved for use by the Form Design operations. You'll need to add the following variables as private members:

```
private:
    int lottoValuesCount;            // Number of values in Lotto entry
    int euroValuesCount;             // Number of values in Euromillions entry
    int euroStarsCount;              // Number of stars in Euromillions entry
    int lottoLowerLimit;             // Minimum value allowed in Lotto
    int lottoUpperLimit;             // Maximum value allowed in Lotto
    int lottoUserMinimum;            // Lower lotto range limit from user
    int lottoUserMaximum;            // Upper lotto range limit from user

    int euroLowerLimit;              // Minimum value allowed in Euromillions
    int euroUpperLimit;              // Maximum value allowed in Euromillions
    int euroStarsLowerLimit;         // Minimum stars value allowed in Euromillions
    int euroStarsUpperLimit;         // Maximum stars value allowed in Euromillions
    int euroUserMinimum;             // Lower euro range limit from user
    int euroUserMaximum;             // Upper euro range limit from user
    int euroStarsUserMinimum;        // Lower euro stars range limit from user
    int euroStarsUserMaximum;        // Upper euro stars range limit from user
```

You also need to add a private field of type `Random` to the `Form1` class:

```
    Random^ random;                  // Generates pseudo-random numbers
```

An object of type `Random` can generate pseudo-random values of various types. You'll use this to generate the values for a lottery entry.

All of these fields must be initialized in the class constructor. Make sure the `Form1` constructor definition looks similar to this:

```
public ref class Form1 : public System::Windows::Forms::Form
{
public:
    Form1(void)
    : lottoValuesCount(6),
    euroValuesCount(5), euroStarsCount(2),
    lottoLowerLimit(1),lottoUpperLimit(49),
    lottoUserMinimum(lottoLowerLimit),lottoUserMaximum(lottoUpperLimit),
    euroLowerLimit(1), euroUpperLimit(50),
    euroStarsLowerLimit(1),euroStarsUpperLimit(9),
```

```
euroUserMinimum(euroLowerLimit),euroUserMaximum(euroUpperLimit),
euroStarsUserMinimum(euroStarsLowerLimit),euroStarsUserMaximum(euroStarsUpperLimit)
  {
    InitializeComponent();
    //
      random = gcnew Random;
    //
  }
```

That's all the new class data members you need for now, so back to event handling.

Handling the Play Menu Event

The `playMenuItem_Click()` handler should create a new set of values on the buttons for the tab that is currently visible. Recall earlier in this chapter that you set the `(Name)` property values for the tabs in the `TabControl` control as `lottoTab` and `euroTab`. If you look in the lower pane of the Class View window for the now extensive `Form1` class, you'll find two variables of type `TabPage^` with these names. Objects of type `TabPage` have a `Visible` property of type `bool` that has the value `true` if the page is visible and `false` if it is not. This is just what you need to implement the handler for the `Play` menu item.

The outline logic for the handler can use the values of the `Visible` property for the tab pages like this:

```
private: System::Void playMenuItem_Click(System::Object^  sender,
                                                    System::EventArgs^  e)
{
  if(lottoTab->Visible)
  {
    // Generate and set values for Lotto entry
  }
  else if(euroTab->Visible)
  {
    // Generate and set values for Euromillions entry
  }
}
```

If the `Visible` property for the `lottoTab` page is true, you create a new `Lotto` lottery entry, and if the `Visible` property for the `euroTab` page is true, you create a Euromillions lottery entry. Although both tabs cannot be visible at the same time, it's as well to test positively for both tab pages because a user might click the `Play` menu item when the Web Page tab is visible.

The process for generating a set of values for the two lotteries have some things in common. For lotto you must generate six different random integers in a given range. For Euromillions you must generate five different integers within a given range and then generate two different integers within another range. A helper function to generate an arbitrary number of integers within a given range would be useful. You could define such a function something like this:

```
void GetValues(array<int>^ values, int min, int max)
{
  // Fill the array with different random integers from min to max...
}
```

The `Length` property for the values array tells you how many values are to be generated. The calling function just needs to create an array of the appropriate size and pass it as the first argument to the `GetValues()` function. The second and third arguments specify the limits for the values to be generated.

Add the `GetValues()` function as a private member of the `Form1` class and complete the definition like this:

```
void GetValues(array<int>^ values, int min, int max)
{
  values[0] = random->Next(min, max+1);          // Generate first random value

  // Generate remaining random values
  for(int i = 1 ; i<values->Length ; i++)
  {
    for(;;)                                       // Loop until a valid value is found
    {
      // Generate random integer from min to max
      values[i] = random->Next(min, max+1);

      // Check that its different from previous values
      if(IsValid(values[i], values, i))          // Check against previous values...
        break;                                   // ...it is different so end loop
    }
  }
}
```

Any value within the range is fine for the first element. Subsequent values must be checked against the preceding values that have been generated, and the `IsValid()` function does this. Here's how you can implement this function:

```
// Check whether number is different from values array elements
// at index positions less than indexLimit
bool IsValid(int number, array<int>^ values, int indexLimit)
{
  for(int i = 0 ; i< indexLimit ; i++)
  {
    if(number == values[i])
      return false;
  }
  return true;
}
```

Add this function as a `private` member of the `Form1` class. It's operation is simple: it checks the first argument against the elements in the array specified by the second argument that have index values less than the third argument and returns `false` if the first argument is equal to any of the array elements; otherwise, it returns `true` to indicate the first argument is valid.

The indefinite `for` loop in the `GetValues()` function continues to execute and generate new random values until the `IsValid()` function returns `true`, whereupon the inner loop ends and the next iteration of the outer `for` loop executes to find the next unique value.

You can now use the `GetValues()` function in the implementation of the `Play` menu `Click` event handler:

```
private: System::Void playMenuItem_Click(System::Object^ sender,
                                         System::EventArgs^ e)
```

```
  {
    array<int>^ values;          // Variable to store a handle to array of integers
    if(lottoTab->Visible)
    {
      // Generate and set values for Lotto entry
      values = gcnew array<int>(lottoValuesCount);           // Create the array
      GetValues(values, lottoUserMinimum, lottoUserMaximum); // Generate values
      SetValues(values, lottoValues);
    }
    else if(euroTab->Visible)
    {
      // Generate and set values for Euromillions entry
      values = gcnew array<int>(euroValuesCount);
      GetValues(values, euroUserMinimum, euroUserMaximum);
      SetValues(values, euroValues);
      values = gcnew array<int>(euroStarsCount);
      GetValues(values, euroStarsUserMinimum, euroStarsUserMaximum);
      SetValues(values, euroStars);
    }
  }
```

The Lotto entry is created in three steps:

1. Create the array to hold the values.

2. Generate the values by calling the `GetValues()` function.

3. Set the values as text on the buttons by calling the `SetValues()` function.

The sequence of steps is repeated twice for the Euromillions lottery entry: once for the set of five values and again for the set of two stars.

You can make use of the fact that the buttons are contained within a `GroupBox` control when implementing the `SetValues()` function. The `Controls` property for a `GroupBox` object returns a collection on all the controls that have been added to the object. The collection that is returned by the `Controls` property for a `GroupBox` itself has a default indexed property that accesses the controls in the collection. The collection is first-in last-out like a stack, so index values for the property accesses the controls in the reverse sequence from the sequence in which you added them to the group box. You can implement the `SetValues()` function as a private member of the `Form1` class like this:

```
  // Set values as text on buttons in a GroupBox control
  void SetValues(array<int>^ values, GroupBox^ groupBox)
  {
    Array::Sort(values);                    // Sort values in ascending sequence
    int count = values->Length - 1;
    for(int i = 0 ; i<groupBox->Controls->Count ; i++)
      safe_cast<Button^>(groupBox->Controls[i])->Text = values[count-i].ToString();
  }
```

After sorting the array of values, you set the `count` variable as the index value for the last element in the array. The loop then stores the string representation of the values in the `Text` property for each `Button` control in reverse sequence. The expression `groupBox->Controls[i]` results in a handle of type `Control^` that references the control corresponding to index i in the collection, and you cast this to type `Button^` before accessing the `Text` property to set its value. The limitation of this approach is that the sequence in which you added buttons to the group box determines the sequence of buttons in the Controls collection. If this does not match the visible sequence of the buttons, the resulting button values will not appear in ascending sequence.

You don't have to implement the capability that the SetValues() function provides using the GroupBox object. All the buttons are explicit members of the Form1 class, so you could take the pedestrian approach and access each of them directly to set the value for the Text property. This will guarantee the button sequence is correct if you named them in sequence. You need at least two separate functions — one for the Lotto entry and one for the Euromillions entry, although the latter might more conveniently be split into two functions making three in all. Here's how the function to set values for the Lotto entry might look:

```
void SetNewValues(array<int>^ values)
{
  Array::Sort(values);
  lottoValue1->Text = values[0].ToString();
  lottoValue2->Text = values[1].ToString();
  lottoValue3->Text = values[2].ToString();
  lottoValue4->Text = values[3].ToString();
  lottoValue5->Text = values[4].ToString();
  lottoValue6->Text = values[5].ToString();
}
```

This function uses the handle to each button to set its Text property. Functions to set the Text property for the Euromillions entry could be implemented in essentially the same way. You would then need to modify the playMenuItem_Click() handler function to call these functions to set the values.

You can now recompile Ex22_01 to see if it all works. If you managed to enter all the code without typos, you should be able to generate a Lotto entry like the one shown in Figure 22-15.

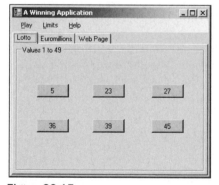

Figure 22-15

The numbers on the buttons appear in ascending sequence so they look neat and tidy. If they do not appear in sequence, it may be because you did not add the buttons to the GroupBox control in an orderly manner.

The program also produces an entry for the Euromillions lottery as in Figure 22-16.

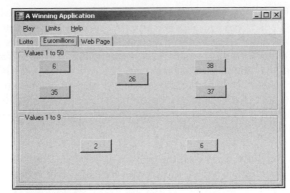

Figure 22-16

Now that the basic functionality is there, it's time to develop the application further.

Handling Events for the Limits Menu

There are three menu items on the Limits menu, and you'll need a handler for the Click event for each. Double-click each of the menu items in turn to generate the handler functions; this will also register each of them to handle the Click event.

The Click event handler for the Reset menu item is going to be the easiest to implement because all it has to do is set the user limits back to be the same as the limits imposed by the lottery that's currently visible. The Click event handlers for the other two menu items are going to involve rather more work. You will have to make provision for the limit values to be entered somehow, and the obvious way to do this is to display a dialog box when the menu item is clicked. Clearly, the next step in developing the application is to create a dialog box.

Creating a Dialog Box

The Toolbox window provides several standard dialog boxes; all of them are quite fancy but none of them are suitable in this instance. Because you need something very specific in this program, you must create the dialog box yourself. A dialog box is just a form with its FormBorderStyle property value set to FixedDialog, so you'll get a lot of help from the Form Designer in creating the dialog box.

Select Project > Add New Item on the main menu, or press Ctrl+Shift+A to display the Add New Item dialog. Select the UI from the Categories: list in the right pane and the template in the right pane as Windows Form and enter the name as LottoLimitsDialog. This is the dialog window you'll display when setting the upper or lower limits for the Lotto entry. You'll create another dialog form for the Euromillions lottery entry later on. When you click the Add button, a new form is added to the project and is displayed in the Editor window. The class type for the new dialog box is the name you supplied, LottoLimitsDialog.

Press F4 to display the Properties window for the new form. You can change the Text property value to "Set Limits for Lotto Values", and this text is displayed in the title bar of dialog window; you can adjust the width of the window by dragging the right side until the title bar text is visible. You can also set the value for the StartPosition property in the Layout group of properties to Center Parent so the dialog window displays at the center of the parent form that displays it — this is the application window in the example. Because this is going to be a dialog box and not an application window, set the FormBorderStyle property value to FixedDialog. The dialog window should not be minimized or maximized by the user when it is displayed, so set the MinimizeBox and MaximizeBox properties in the Window Style group to False to remove the capability. A dialog box should be closed through the buttons that you'll provide in the dialog window, so set the ControlBox property value to False to remove the control and system boxes from the title bar.

The next step is to add two buttons toward the bottom of the form; these are going to be the OK and Cancel buttons for the dialog box. Set the Text property value for the button to the left to be "OK" and the (Name) property to be lottoOK. You can also set the value for the DialogResult property in the Behavior group to OK. The values for the same properties for the right button should be "Cancel", lottoCancel, and Cancel, respectively. The effect of setting the DialogResult property value for the buttons is that the value of the DialogResult property for the dialog box is set to the value corresponding to the value for the DialogResult property for the button that was clicked to close the dialog box. This gives you the possibility of testing programmatically for which button was used to close the dialog and execute different code depending on whether it was the OK button or the Cancel button.

Now that you have added the buttons to the dialog box, you can return to the dialog properties and set the values for the AcceptButton and CancelButton properties in the Misc property group to lottoOK and lottoCancel, respectively. This has the effect that pressing the Enter key while the dialog box is displayed clicked the OK button, and pressing the Esc key clicks the Cancel button.

You have more than one control in the dialog box that you could use to permit a limit value to be entered. You can use a ListBox control to enable the user to select from a list of possible values, so you can try that here. You should add two Label controls to the dialog box form with two ListBox controls alongside, as shown in Figure 22-17.

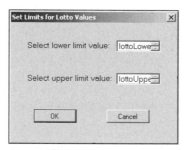

Figure 22-17

The (Name) property for the list boxes should be lottoLowerList and lottoUpperList for the top and bottom. As you see, I resized the ListBox controls to be the same height as the Label controls and a width sufficient to display a single limit value. I also changed the font Size property to 10 and the ScrollAlwaysVisible property to True. Make sure the SelectionMode property value is One for both list boxes, as you want to allow only one item to be selected from a list box at one time.

The GUI for the dialog box is complete, but to make it do what you want you are back in coding mode again. You can start with the code that populates the ListBox controls with limit values.

Adding a List to a ListBox

The list that a `ListBox` controls is a set of objects that are stored as handles of type `Object^`, so any kind of object can be stored in the list. In the example you want to store a set of integer limit values in each list box, and for the most part you are able to rely on autoboxing and unboxing to convert values of type `int` to and from objects of type `Int32` whenever necessary. The `Items` property for a `ListBox` object returns a reference to a collection of the objects in the list box; this collection has an `Add()` method that adds an object that you pass as the argument to the list. A `ListBox` object has a large number of properties including the `Enabled` property that has the value `true` when the user can interact with the list box and the value `false` when interaction is to be inhibited.

The basic process for loading up the list for a list box is the same for both `ListBox` controls, so you could code a private function member of the `LottoLimitsDialog` class that is generalized to add a range of integers to a list box:

```
void SetList(ListBox^ listBox, int min, int max, int selected)
{
  listBox->BeginUpdate();              // Suppress drawing the listbox

  for(int n = min ; n <= max ; n++)
    listBox->Items->Add(n);

  listBox->EndUpdate();                // Resume drawing the list box

  listBox->SelectedItem = Int32(selected);
}
```

The arguments to the `SetList()` function are the list box for which the list is to be added, the minimum and maximum integers in the range to be added, and the integer that is to be selected in the list box. The function adds integers from `min` to `max` inclusive to the list box using the `Add()` function for the collection object that is returned by the `Items` property for the `ListBox` object. It also sets the selected value as the item that is initially selected in the list when the list box is displayed by setting it as the value for the `SelectedItem` property for the list box.

When the user selects a limit in the dialog box, you'll need somewhere to put the value so that it can be accessed from a function belonging to the `Form1` object; the event handler for the menu items have responsibility for retrieving the limit value and storing it in the `Form1` object. One way to do this is to add a couple of private members to the `LottoLimitsDialog` class to store the upper and lower limit values and then add public properties to the class to make the values available externally. Adding the following code to the `LottoLimitsDialog` class definition does that:

```
private:
  int lowerLimit;                      // Lower limit from control
  int upperLimit;                      // upper limit from control

public:
  property int LowerLimit              // Property accessing lower limit
  {
    int get(){  return lowerLimit;  }

    void set(int limit)
    {
      lowerLimit = limit;
```

```
                    lottoLowerList->SelectedItem = Int32(limit);
                 }
             }
         }

         property int UpperLimit                // Property accessing upper limit
         {
           int get(){  return upperLimit;  }

           void set(int limit)
           {
             upperLimit = limit;
             lottoUpperList->SelectedItem = Int32(limit);
           }
         }
```

You need to be able to update the properties because the Click event handler for the Limits > Reset menu item changes the limits, and you want the ListBox objects to have whatever is the current upper or lower limit selected. As well as storing the value in the class object, you also update the ListBox objects to reflect the new limits.

You can now create two public member functions in the LottoLimitsDialog class that sets up the two ListBox controls:

```
         public:
             void SetLowerLimitsList(int min, int max, int selected)
             {
               SetList(lottoLowerList, min, max, selected);
               lowerLimit = selected;
             }
```

```
             void SetUpperLimitsList(int min, int max, int selected)
             {
               SetList(lottoUpperList, min, max, selected);
               upperLimit = selected;
             }
```

Each function uses the SetList() function to set the range of values in the corresponding ListBox object and then sets the selected value in the member for storing the limit.

Handling the Dialog Button Events

Add an event handler function for the Click event for the OK Button object, so return to the Design tab for the LottoLimitsDialog form and double-click the OK button to add the skeleton code.

You don't need to add a handler for the Click event for the Cancel button. The effect of clicking the button is to close the dialog box and no further action is required.

You can implement the handler for the Click event for the OK button like this:

```
         System::Void lottoOK_Click(System::Object^  sender, System::EventArgs^  e)
         {
             // If there's a currently selected upper limit item, save it
```

```
    if(lottoUpperList->SelectedItem != nullptr)
      upperLimit = safe_cast<Int32>(lottoUpperList->SelectedItem);

    // If there's a currently selected lower limit item, save it
    if(lottoLowerList->SelectedItem != nullptr)
      lowerLimit = safe_cast<Int32>(lottoLowerList->SelectedItem);
}
```

The function first stores the upper limit value from the `lottoUpperList` `ListBox` object in the member variable you added for that purpose. The `SelectedItem` property for a `ListBox` object makes the currently selected item available as a handle of type `Object^` and as a precaution the code verifies that the handle returned is not null. Before storing the selected item you must cast it to its actual type — type `Int32`. Auto-unboxing then takes care of converting the object to an integer. The handler next stores the lower limit value from the other `ListBox` object in the same way. When the handler finishes executing, the dialog box is closed automatically.

Controlling the State of the ListBox Objects

The same dialog object is used in the response to the `Click` events for both the `Limits > Upper` and `Limits > Lower` menu items, but you don't want to allow both list boxes to be changed in either case. For the `Upper` menu item event you'll want the selection of a lower limit to be inhibited, and for the `Lower` menu item you'll want the list box for the upper limit to be inhibited. You could add a couple of public function members to the `LottoLimitsDialog` class to make this possible. Here's the function to set the state of the `ListBox` objects for the `Upper` menu item:

```
void SetUpperEnabled()
{
  lottoUpperList->Enabled = true;   // Enable upper list box
  lottoLowerList->Enabled = false;  // Disable lower list box
}
```

You set the `Enabled` property for the `lottoUpperList` object to `true` to allow the user to interact with it. Setting the `Enabled` property for `lottoLowerList` to `false` makes it read-only.

For the `Lower` menu item you do the reverse:

```
void SetLowerEnabled()
{
  lottoUpperList->Enabled = false; // Disable upper list box
  lottoLowerList->Enabled = true;  // Enable lower list box
}
```

You have done a lot of work to get the dialog object to behave as you want in the application, but you don't yet have a dialog object. The application window object takes care of that.

Creating the Dialog Object

The `Form1` class constructor can create the dialog object. It can also initialize the `ListBox` objects in the dialog. Add a private member to the `Form1` class that stores the handle to the dialog box:

```
private: LottoLimitsDialog^ lottoLimitsDialog;
```

Add the following lines of code to the body of the `Form1` constructor:

```
lottoLimitsDialog = gcnew LottoLimitsDialog;
lottoLimitsDialog->SetLowerLimitsList(1, lottoUpperLimit-lottoValuesCount+1,
                                         lottoUserMinimum);
lottoLimitsDialog->SetUpperLimitsList(lottoValuesCount, lottoUpperLimit,
                                         lottoUserMaximum);
```

This code is very straightforward. The first statement creates the dialog object. The next two statements call the functions that initialize the lists in the `ListBox` objects. The maximum value in the `ListBox` object that sets the lower limit is calculated so that it permits the required number of values for an entry to be created. If the maximum value for a value is 49 and the number of values in an entry is 6, the maximum for the lower limit must be 44 — if it was any higher you could not create six different values. The same reasoning applies to the minimum value for the upper limit; it cannot be less than the number of values in an entry. The selected item for the list boxes are the `lottoUserMinimum` and `lottoUserMaximum` values.

Because you refer to the `LottoLimitsDialog` class name in the `Form1` class constructor, you'll need to add an `#include` directive for the class definition to `Form1.h`:

```
#include "LottoLimitsDialog.h"
```

Using the Dialog Box

You'll put the dialog box into operation in the code for the `Click` event handlers for the `Upper` and `Lower` menu items in the `Limits` menu. To display a dialog box as a modal dialog box, you call the `ShowDialog()` function for the dialog object. Optionally you can pass the handle to the parent form as the argument to the `ShowDialog()` function. You can implement the `Click` event handler functions like this:

```
System::Void lowerMenuItem_Click(System::Object^  sender, System::EventArgs^  e)
{
  if(lottoTab->Visible)
  {
    lottoLimitsDialog->SetLowerEnabled();
    ::DialogResult result = lottoLimitsDialog->ShowDialog(this);

    if(result == ::DialogResult::OK)
    {
      // Update user limits from dialog properties
      lottoUserMaximum = lottoLimitsDialog->UpperLimit;
      lottoUserMinimum = lottoLimitsDialog->LowerLimit;
    }
  }
}

System::Void upperMenuItem_Click(System::Object^  sender, System::EventArgs^  e)
{
  if(lottoTab->Visible)
  {
    lottoLimitsDialog->SetUpperEnabled();
    ::DialogResult result = lottoLimitsDialog->ShowDialog(this);
```

```
        if(result == ::DialogResult::OK)
        {
          // Update user limits from dialog properties
          lottoUserMaximum = lottoLimitsDialog->UpperLimit;
          lottoUserMinimum = lottoLimitsDialog->LowerLimit;
        }
    }
}
```

These two functions both work in the same way; they call the function to set the list box states and then display the dialog box as a modal dialog box by calling the ShowDialog() function for the dialog object. If you wanted to display the dialog box as a modeless dialog box, you call the Show() function for the dialog object instead.

When you call the ShowDialog() function, it does not return until the dialog box closes. This means that the code to update the limits is not executed until the new limits have been recorded in the dialog object by the Click event handler for the lottoOK button. When you display a dialog box as modeless by calling the Show() function, the function returns immediately. Thus if you need to be able to access data that might have been changed in the dialog box, you need another way to do it. Adding a handler function for the Closing event for the dialog form is one possibility; another would be to deal with transferring the data in the handler for the button that closes the dialog box.

The ShowDialog() function returns a value of the enumeration type DialogResult and you store this in the local variable, result. The return value from the ShowDialog() function indicates which button in the dialog was clicked, and if the value is the enumeration constant ::DialogResult::OK, it indicates that the OK button was clicked. Thus the code in each handler function updates only the lottoUserMaximum and LottoUserMinimum fields when the OK button was used to close the dialog.

Note the use of the :: operator in the type specification ::DialogResult and in the expression ::DialogResult::OK. The scope resolution operator is necessary preceding the DialogResult name to distinguish the name of the enumeration at global scope from the property with the same name that is a member of the Form1 class.

Of course, you could access the DialogResult property for the lottoLimitsDialog object directly, so you could write the if statement as:

```
        if(lottoLimitsDialog->DialogResult == ::DialogResult::OK)
        {
          // Update user limits from dialog properties
          lottoUserMaximum = lottoLimitsDialog->UpperLimit;
          lottoUserMinimum = lottoLimitsDialog->LowerLimit;
        }
```

The former version is better because it is obvious that you are checking the value returned by the ShowDialog() function.

At the moment, the Click event handler for the OK button does not validate the input values. It is currently quite possible to set the lower and upper limits to values that make it impossible to assign six unique values for the lottery entry. You can use the DialogResult property for the form to deal with the problem.

Validating the Input

The difference between the upper and lower limits that the user chooses must be greater than or equal to 5 if there are to be 6 unique values in a Lotto entry. You could modify the `Click` event handler for the `OK` button in the dialog class to check for this:

```
System::Void lottoOK_Click(System::Object^ sender, System::EventArgs^ e)
{
  int upper = 0;
  int lower = 0;
  // If there's a currently selected upper limit item, save it
  if(lottoUpperList->SelectedItem != nullptr)
    upper = safe_cast<Int32>(lottoUpperList->SelectedItem);

  // If there's a currently selected lower limit item, save it
  if(lottoLowerList->SelectedItem != nullptr)
    lower = safe_cast<Int32>(lottoLowerList->SelectedItem);

  if(upper - lower < 5)
  {
    MessageBox::Show(L"Upper limit: " + upper + L" Lower limit: " + lower +
             L"\nUpper limit must be at least 5 greater that the lower limit." +
             L"\nTry Again.",
             L"Limits Invalid",
             MessageBoxButtons::OK,
             MessageBoxIcon::Error);
    DialogResult = ::DialogResult::None;
  }
  else
  {
    upperLimit = upper;
    lowerLimit = lower;
  }
}
```

Now the function saves the values selected in the `ListBox` objects in the local variables `lower` and `upper`. If the values differ by less than 5, a message box is displayed and closing of the dialog box is inhibited by setting the value of the `DialogResult` property to `None`. The static `Show()` function in the `MessageBox` class displays a message box that is customized by the arguments to the function. This version of the `Show()` function used here accepts four arguments as shown in the following table.

Parameter Type	Description
`String^`	The text to be displayed in the message box.
`String^`	The text to appear in the title bar of the message box.
`MessageBoxButtons`	An enumeration constant specifying the buttons to appear in the message box. The `MessageBoxButtons` enumeration defines the following values: `OK, OKCancel, YesNo, YesNoCancel, RetryCancel, AbortRetryIgnore`

Parameter Type	Description
MessageBoxIcon	An enumeration constant specifying the icon to appear in the message box. The MessageBoxIcon enumeration defines the following values: Asterisk, Exclamation, Error, Hand, Information, None, Question, Stop, Warning

There are a significant number of overloaded versions of the static Show() function that range from the very simple with a single parameter of type String^ to the rather more complicated with up to 10 parameters.

If you compile and execute the example and set the limits inappropriately, you'll see a window similar to that shown in Figure 22-18.

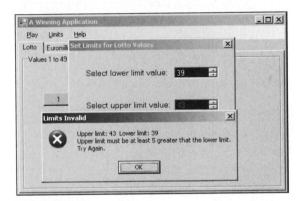

Figure 22-18

As you see, you automatically get a scrollbar for scrolling through the list of items in a list box. Note that scrolling to a given item does not select it. You must click on the item to select it before clicking the OK button. The circular red icon with the white cross was specified by the fourth argument to the Show() function, and the single OK button is the result of the third argument.

The Show() function that you call to display a message box returns a value of type DialogResult that indicates which button was used to close the message box. You can use this return value to decide what to do after the message box closes. In the lottoOK_Click() handler for the OK button in the limits dialog box, you could decide whether or not to close the limits dialog box using the value returned by the Show() function for the message box:

```
System::Void lottoOK_Click(System::Object^  sender, System::EventArgs^  e)
{
  int upper = 0;
  int lower = 0;
  // If there's a currently selected upper limit item, save it
  if(lottoUpperList->SelectedItem != nullptr)
    upper = safe_cast<Int32>(lottoUpperList->SelectedItem);

  // If there's a currently selected lower limit item, save it
```

```
  if(lottoLowerList->SelectedItem != nullptr)
    lower = safe_cast<Int32>(lottoLowerList->SelectedItem);

if(upper - lower < 5)
{
  ::DialogResult result =
  MessageBox::Show(L"Upper limit: " + upper + L"  Lower limit: " + lower +
              L"\nUpper limit must be at least 5 greater that the lower limit." +
              L"\nTry Again.",
              L"Limits Invalid",
              MessageBoxButtons::OKCancel,
              MessageBoxIcon::Error);
  if(result == ::DialogResult::OK)
    DialogResult = ::DialogResult::None;
  else
    DialogResult = ::DialogResult::Cancel;
}
else
{
  upperLimit = upper;
  lowerLimit = lower;
}
}
```

Because the third argument to the Show() function is MessageBoxButtons::OKCancel, the message box now has two buttons, as shown in Figure 22-19.

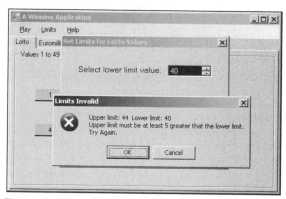

Figure 22-19

In the Click event handler for the OK button in the limits dialog box you store the return value from the Show() function in result. The type for result has to be specified using the scope resolution operator. Otherwise, it is interpreted by the compiler as the DialogResult property for the lottoLimitsDialog object, and the code does not compile. If result contains the value ::DialogResult::OK, you set the DialogResult property for the lottoLimitsDialog object to ::DialogResult::None, which prevents the dialog box from closing and allows the limit to be changed. Otherwise you set the DialogResult property for the dialog to ::Dialog::Cancel, which has the same effect as clicking the Cancel button for the dialog box so it closes.

Handling the Reset Menu Item Event

You can implement the event handler for the Reset menu item like this:

```
System::Void resetMenuItem_Click(System::Object^ sender, System::EventArgs^ e)
{
  if(lottoTab->Visible)
  {
    // Reset user limits for Lotto
    lottoUserMaximum = lottoUpperLimit;
    lottoUserMinimum = lottoLowerLimit;
    lottoLimitsDialog->UpperLimit = lottoUpperLimit;
    lottoLimitsDialog->LowerLimit = lottoLowerLimit;
  }
  else if(euroTab->Visible)
  {
    // Reset user limits for Euromillions
    euroUserMaximum = euroUpperLimit;
    euroUserMinimum = euroLowerLimit;
    euroStarsUserMaximum = euroStarsUpperLimit;
    euroStarsUserMinimum = euroStarsLowerLimit;

    // Code to update Euromillions limits dialog...
  }
}
```

This just resets the limits in the fields in the Form1 object and then updates the properties in the dialog object accordingly. You still have to add code to this function to deal with resetting the dialog box to which you have yet added the application that will handle the input for the Euromillions lottery limits.

You can now recompile the program and try resetting the limits for the Lotto entry after you have changed them. Selecting the Limits > Reset menu item resets both limits to their original values.

Adding the Second Dialog

The second dialog box for setting limits for the Euromillions lottery is going to be easy; it's the same process as for the first dialog box. Create a new form in the project by pressing Ctrl+Shift+A to display the Add New Item dialog box and select the UI category and the Windows Form template; the name should be EuroLimitsDialog. You can set property values for this dialog box in much the same way as for the previous dialog.

Form Property	Value to be Set
FormBorderStyle	FixedDialog
ControlBox	False
MinimizeBox	False
MaximizeBox	False
Text	Set Euromillions Limits

You can add OK and Cancel buttons to the dialog form next. Set the Text property values for the buttons to "OK" and "Cancel" and the (Name) property values to euroOK and euroCancel, respectively. You should also set the DialogResult property values to OK and Cancel. With the buttons defined, you can return to the properties for the dialog form and set the AcceptButton and CancelButton property values to euroOK and euroCancel, respectively. Set the value of the AcceptButton property for the form to be euroOK.

In the interests of getting experience of a wider range of controls, you'll forego consistency in the application, and you won't use ListBox controls to handle the input as you did in the first dialog box. In this dialog box you need to provide for the entry of upper and lower limits for the set of five values as well as the set of two stars. It won't make for a very elegant implementation, but to maximize the variety of controls you work with you'll use NumericUpDown controls for the former and ComboBox controls for the latter. You can add these controls together with associated Label controls to the dialog form with each group of controls placed within a GroupBox control, as illustrated in Figure 22-20. Obviously you'll need to add the GroupBox controls first and then place the other controls within them.

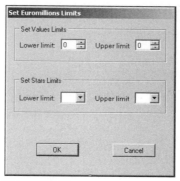

Figure 22-20

You can set the value of the Text property for each Label control as shown in Figure 22-20. The font size for the labels has been changed to 9 point. To identify the function of the controls within each group box, the value for the Text property for the upper group box has been set to "Set Values Limits" and that of the lower group box "Set Stars Limits." You won't be accessing the GroupBox objects in the code, so the (Name) property values for these are of no importance.

The values for the (Name) properties for the NumericUpDown controls in the upper group box should be set to lowerValuesLimits and upperValuesLimits. You can set the values that these controls display by setting values for the Maximum and Minimum properties. These values for the lowerValuesLimits control on the left should be 45 and 1 respectively, and the values for the Maximum and Minimum properties for the control to the right should be 49 and 5 respectively. You can set the value of the Value property for the upperValuesLimit control to 49; this is the value displayed initially in the control. If you also set the ReadOnly property value for each of the NumericUpDown controls to True, this prevents the entry of a value from the keyboard. You are using the NumericUpDown control very simply here. You can change the up down increment by setting the `Increment` property value. The `Increment` property is of type `Decimal` so you can set this to non-integral values, too.

You can set the values of the `(Name)` property for the `ComboBox` controls in the lower group box to `lowerStarsLimits` and `upperStarsLimits`. You can enter values to be displayed in a `ComboBox` quite easily. Click the small arrow at the top right of the leftmost `ComboBox` control to display the menu shown in Figure 22-21.

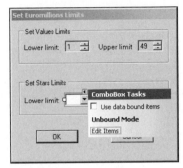

Figure 22-21

Select the `Edit Items` menu item at the bottom of the menu to display the dialog window for the `String Collection Editor` shown in Figure 22-22.

Figure 22-22 shows the values entered for the `ComboBox` control on the left. For the `ComboBox` control on the right you can enter the values from 2 to 9 inclusive.

The `ComboBox` is not ideal for this application because it allows text input as well as selection from a list; you want to have a limit value selected only from the list. The control gets its name, `ComboBox`, because it combines the function of a `ListBox` control that allows selection from a list with that of a `TextBox` control that provides for text input.

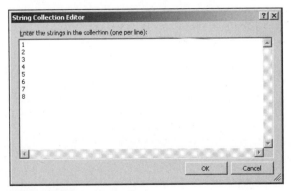

Figure 22-22

Getting the Data from the Dialog Controls

You'll get the limit values back from the controls in essentially the same way as you did for the dialog box for Lotto limits. You can add some new data members to the `EuroLimitsDialog` class to hold the user limit values first:

```
private:
  int lowerValuesLimit;
  int upperValuesLimit;
  int lowerStarsLimit;
  int upperStarsLimit;
```

To be on the safe side you had better initialize these members in the class constructor:

```
EuroLimitsDialog(void)
  :lowerValuesLimit(1)
  ,upperValuesLimit(50)
  ,lowerStarsLimit(1)
  ,upperStarsLimit(9)
{
  InitializeComponent();
  //
  //TODO: Add the constructor code here
  //
}
```

You'll also need some public properties defined in the dialog class to make the limits accessible from the application window object:

```
public:
  property int LowerValuesLimit
  {
    int get() {  return lowerValuesLimit;  }

    void set(int limit)
    {
      lowerValuesLimit = limit;
      lowerValuesLimits->Value = limit;          // Set as selected in NumericUpDown
    }
  }
  property int UpperValuesLimit
  {
    int get() {  return upperValuesLimit;  }

    void set(int limit)
    {
      upperValuesLimit = limit;
      upperValuesLimits->Value = limit;          // Set as selected in NumericUpDown
    }
  }
  property int LowerStarsLimit
  {
```

```
      int get() {  return lowerStarsLimit;  }

    void set(int limit)
    {
      lowerStarsLimit = limit;
      lowerStarsLimits->SelectedItem = limit;  // Set as selected in ComboBox
      lowerStarsLimits->SelectedIndex =        // Set index for selected item
                              lowerStarsLimits->FindString(limit.ToString());
    }
  }

  property int UpperStarsLimit
  {
    int get() {  return upperStarsLimit;  }

    void set(int limit)
    {
      upperStarsLimit = limit;
      upperStarsLimits->SelectedItem = limit;  // Set as selected in ComboBox
      upperStarsLimits->SelectedIndex =        // Set index for selected item
                              upperStarsLimits->FindString(limit.ToString());
    }
  }
```

The `get()` function for each property returns the value of the corresponding private member of the dialog class. The `set()` function sets the value of the data member and also updates the control in the dialog box so that the value set becomes the selected value. The `SelectedIndex` property value is the index to the selected item. You set this using the `FindString()` function for the `ComboBox` control that returns the index value for the first occurrence of the argument in the control's collection of items. The value at this position is displayed initially in the control.

Add a `Click` event handler for the `OK` button in the `EuroLimitsDialog` class by double-clicking the button in the Design window. You won't need to implement a handler for the `Cancel` button. You can implement the `OK` button handler like this:

```
System::Void euroOK_Click(System::Object^  sender, System::EventArgs^  e)
{
  ::DialogResult result;

  // get the limits for values
  int valuesLower = Decimal::ToInt32(lowerValuesLimits->Value);
  int valuesUpper = Decimal::ToInt32(upperValuesLimits->Value);
  if(valuesUpper - valuesLower < 4)                 // Check for an adequate range
  {
    result = MessageBox::Show(this,                 // Range insufficient so
            "Upper values limit: "+valuesUpper +  // display message box
            "  Lower values limit: "+ valuesLower+
            "\nUpper values limit must be at least 4 greater that the lower limit."+
            "\nTry Again.",
            "Limits Invalid",
            MessageBoxButtons::OKCancel,
            MessageBoxIcon::Error);
```

```
      if(result == ::DialogResult::OK)          // If message box OK clicked
        DialogResult = ::DialogResult::None;     // prevent dialog from closing
      else                                       // Messag box Cancel clicked
        DialogResult = ::DialogResult::Cancel;   // so close the dialog
      return;
    }


    // Get stars limits
    int starsLower = lowerStarsLimits->SelectedItem == nullptr ?
                     lowerStarsLimit :
                     Int32::Parse(lowerStarsLimits->SelectedItem->ToString());

    int starsUpper = upperStarsLimits->SelectedItem == nullptr ?
                     upperStarsLimit :
                     Int32::Parse(upperStarsLimits->SelectedItem->ToString());

    if(starsUpper - starsLower < 1)              // Check for an adequate range
    {
      result = MessageBox::Show(this,            // Range insufficient so
          "Upper stars limit: "+starsUpper +     // so display message box
          "  Lower stars limit: "+ starsLower+
          "\nUpper stars limit must be at least 1 greater that the lower limit."+
          "\nTry Again.",
          "Limits Invalid",
          MessageBoxButtons::OKCancel,
          MessageBoxIcon::Error);
      if(result == ::DialogResult::OK)           // If message box OK clicked
        DialogResult = ::DialogResult::None;     // prevent dialog from closing
      else                                       // Message box Cancel clicked
        DialogResult = ::DialogResult::Cancel;   // so close the dialog
    }
    // Store the new limits
    lowerValuesLimit = valuesLower;
    upperValuesLimit = valuesUpper;
    lowerStarsLimit = starsLower;
    upperStarsLimit = starsUpper;
  }
}
```

The Value property for a NumericUpDown control returns a value of type Decimal. To convert this to type Int32 you pass it as the argument to the static ToInt32() function in the Decimal class. The value that this function returns is automatically unboxed so that it can be stored in the variable of type int.

The value returned by the SelectedItem property for a ComboBox control is of type Object^, so to be on the safe side you check whether it is null. If it is null, you set the local variable to the current value recorded in the dialog object; if it isn't null, you store the value represented by the SelectedItem property. You can't store the value directly, but calling the ToString() function for the object produces a string representation of the object that you are then able to convert to type int using the static Parse() function in the Int32 class.

You will need a private member of the `Form1` class that stores a handle to the new dialog box:

```
private:
  EuroLimitsDialog^ euroLimitsDialog;     // Dialog to set Euromillions limits
```

You can add the following statements to the end of the code in the `Form1` class constructor to create the dialog object and update the properties for the stars limit values:

```
euroLimitsDialog = gcnew EuroLimitsDialog;
euroLimitsDialog->LowerStarsLimit = euroStarsLowerLimit;
euroLimitsDialog->UpperStarsLimit = euroStarsUpperLimit;
```

By setting the `LowerStarsLimit` and `UpperStarsLimit` properties for the dialog object, you ensure that the `ComboBox` controls show these values when the dialog box is initially displayed. If there is no selected item set for a `ComboBox` control, it displays nothing initially.

Don't forget to add the `#include` directive for the `EuroLimitsDialog` class definition to `Form1.h`:

```
#include "EuroLimitsDialog.h"
```

Disabling Input Controls

When the `Limits > Upper` menu item is clicked, you want to prevent the input for a lower limit being entered, and when the `Limits > Lower` menu item is selected, you want to prevent input for an upper limit value. You can add a couple of member functions to the `EuroLimitsDialog` class to make this possible:

```
public:
  // Disables controls for selecting upper limits
  void SetLowerEnabled(void)
  {
    upperValuesLimits->Enabled = false;
    upperStarsLimits->Enabled = false;
    lowerValuesLimits->Enabled = true;
    lowerStarsLimits->Enabled = true;
  }
```

```
  // Disables controls for selecting lower limits
  void SetUpperEnabled(void)
  {
    upperValuesLimits->Enabled = true;
    upperStarsLimits->Enabled = true;
    lowerValuesLimits->Enabled = false;
    lowerStarsLimits->Enabled = false;
  }
```

The value of the `Enabled` property for a control determines whether it is enabled. A `true` value enables the control, and a value of `false` disables it so the user cannot interact with it. The `SetLowerEnabled()` function disables the controls used to enter upper limits and enables those for entry of lower limits. The `SetUpperEnabled()` function does the reverse.

Updating the Limits Menu Item Handlers

The last step to complete the support for entering limits for the Euromillions lottery is to update the Click event handlers in the Form1 class for the items in the Limits menu. The handler for the Upper menu item should be modified as follows:

```
System::Void upperMenuItem_Click(System::Object^  sender, System::EventArgs^  e)
{
  ::DialogResult result;
  if(lottoTab->Visible)
  {
    lottoLimitsDialog->SetUpperEnabled();
    result = lottoLimitsDialog->ShowDialog(this);
    if(result == ::DialogResult::OK)
    {
      lottoUserMaximum = lottoLimitsDialog->UpperLimit;
      lottoUserMinimum = lottoLimitsDialog->LowerLimit;
    }
  }
  else if(euroTab->Visible)
  {
    euroLimitsDialog->SetUpperEnabled();
    result = euroLimitsDialog->ShowDialog(this);
    if(result == ::DialogResult::OK)
    {
      euroUserMaximum = euroLimitsDialog->UpperValuesLimit;
      euroUserMinimum = euroLimitsDialog->LowerValuesLimit;
      euroStarsUserMaximum = euroLimitsDialog->UpperStarsLimit;
      euroStarsUserMinimum = euroLimitsDialog->LowerStarsLimit;
    }
  }
}
```

The local variable result is used in both if statements, so it is now declared at the beginning of the function. After enabling the controls in the dialog box appropriately by calling the SetUpperEnabled() function for the dialog object, you display the dialog box as modal. If the user closes the dialog box by clicking the OK button, you store the results available through the properties of the dialog object.

The changes to the handler for the Click event for the Lower menu item are very similar:

```
System::Void lowerMenuItem_Click(System::Object^  sender, System::EventArgs^  e)
{
  ::DialogResult result;
  if(lottoTab->Visible)
  {
    lottoLimitsDialog->SetLowerEnabled();
    result = lottoLimitsDialog->ShowDialog(this);
    if(result == ::DialogResult::OK)
    {
      lottoUserMaximum = lottoLimitsDialog->UpperLimit;
      lottoUserMinimum = lottoLimitsDialog->LowerLimit;
    }
  }
}
```

```
        else if(euroTab->Visible)
        {
          euroLimitsDialog->SetLowerEnabled();
          result = euroLimitsDialog->ShowDialog(this);
          if(result == ::DialogResult::OK)
          {
            euroUserMaximum = euroLimitsDialog->UpperValuesLimit;
            euroUserMinimum = euroLimitsDialog->LowerValuesLimit;
            euroStarsUserMaximum = euroLimitsDialog->UpperStarsLimit;
            euroStarsUserMinimum = euroLimitsDialog->LowerStarsLimit;
          }
        }
      }
```

The logic here is the same as in the previous handler function.

Implementing the Help > About Menu Item

This is easy now that you know about the `MessageBox` class. You can just show a message box when the `Help > About` menu item is clicked:

```
System::Void aboutToolStripMenuItem_Click(System::Object^  sender,
                                          System::EventArgs^  e)
{
  MessageBox::Show(L"© Copyright Ivor Horton", L"About A Winning Application",
                MessageBoxButtons::OK, MessageBoxIcon::Exclamation);
}
```

When the the menu item is clicked, the handler function displays the message box shown in Figure 22-23.

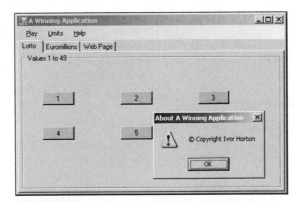

Figure 22-23

Handling a Button Click

Clicking a button should change the value on the button to a new random value. Of course, the value must be different from values on the other buttons as well as being different from the value for the button that was clicked. It would be a good idea to present the whole set in sorted order; this may result in the new value being on a different button, but that's likely to be better that not having the values in sequence.

The process for handling a button click is going to be the same for all the buttons, so you'll be able to economize on code by creating a generalized function to do the work. You can define a private function member of the `Form1` class that generates a new value for a given `Button` object from an array of buttons:

```
// Generates a new value for button different from current button values
void SetNewValue(Button^ button, array<Button^>^ buttons,
                                          int lowerLimit, int upperLimit)
{
  int index = 0;                          // Index of button in buttons

  // Array to store button values
  array<int>^ values = gcnew array<int>(buttons->Length);

  // Get values from buttons and find index for button
  for(int i = 0 ; i < values->Length ; i++)
  {
    values[i] = Int32::Parse(buttons[i]->Text);   // Get current button value

    // If current handle is same as button, save the index value
    if(button == buttons[i])
      index = i;
  }

  int newValue = 0;                       // Store the new button value
  // Check if it is different from the other button values
  for(;;)                                 // Loop until we get a good one
  {
    newValue = random->Next(lowerLimit, upperLimit);  // Generate a value
    if(IsValid(newValue, values, values->Length))     // If it's OK...
      break;                                          // ...end the loop
  }
  values[index] = newValue;               // Store the new value at index

  Array::Sort(values);                              // Sort the value
  for(int i = 0 ; i < values->Length ; i++)         // and set the values
    buttons[i]->Text = values[i].ToString();        // as text on the buttons
}
```

The first two function parameters are the button that is to have a new number and the array of buttons in the group to which the first button belongs. The next two parameters specify the lower and upper limits for the values. The current values of the buttons in the array are stored in the values array in the first loop. This loop also finds the index value in the `buttons` array for the `Button^` handle that is the first argument. You need this so you know which element of the `values` array is to be replaced by a new value.

The new value is created in the indefinite `for` loop. This is the same mechanism that you used to create the values for the button in the first instance. After you have a valid new value, you store it in the `values` array. You then sort the elements in the `values` array before storing them as the values for the `Text` properties for the buttons in the `buttons` array. You'll be able to use this function for dealing with the `Click` events for all of the buttons.

If you have not already done so, double-click the first button on the Lotto tab to generate a `Click` event handler function for it. You can edit the name of the handler function by opening the `Properties` tab for the button, selecting the `Events` button, and changing the value for the `Click` event. When you press Enter, the code is updated with the new name. I changed the value to `lottoValue_Click`.

You can amend the `Click` event handler to call the `SetNewValue()` function you have just added to the `Form1` class:

```
System::Void lottoValue_Click(System::Object^ sender, System::EventArgs^ e)
{
  Button^ button = safe_cast<Button^>(sender);

  // Create the array of button handles
  array<Button^>^ buttons = {lottoValue1, lottoValue2, lottoValue3,
                             lottoValue4, lottoValue5, lottoValue6};

  // Replace the value on button
  SetNewValue(button, buttons, lottoUserMinimum, lottoUserMaximum);
}
```

The availability of the `SetNewValue()` function makes this handler function very simple. The first statement stores the handle to the button that was clicked. The first parameter to the event handler is a handle to the object that originated the event, so all that's necessary is to cast it to the appropriate type. You then just assemble the handles for the buttons in an array and call the new function — job done!

You still have to deal with the `Click` event for the other buttons on the Lotto tab, but this doesn't require any more code. Open the `Properties` window for the second button and then click the `Events` button. If you click the `Click` event value, you'll see a list of the existing event handlers. If you select `lottoValue_Click` from the list, the event handler for the first button will be registered as the event handler for the second button, too.

You can repeat the process for the remaining four buttons on the Lotto tab so that the one event handler is called in response to the `Click` event for any of the buttons on the Lotto tab.

The `Click` event handlers for the buttons on the Euromillions tab are going to be very easy. Double-click the first of the five buttons in the `Values` group to create the event handler. Open the Properties window for the button and change the value for the `Click` event to `euroValue_Click`. You can then modify the code for the handler like this:

```
System::Void euroValue_Click(System::Object^ sender, System::EventArgs^ e)
{
  Button^ button = safe_cast<Button^>(sender);
  array<Button^>^ buttons = {euroValue1, euroValue2, euroValue3,
                             euroValue4, euroValue5 };
  SetNewValue(button, buttons, euroUserMinimum, euroUserMaximum);
}
```

This works exactly the same as the handler for the Lotto buttons. The array contains the handles to the five buttons in the values group, and the `SetNewValue()` function does the rest. If you open the `Properties` window for each of the remaining four buttons in the group, you can select this function to respond to the `Click` event for each of them. Be sure you select `euroValue_Click` and not `lottoValue_Click`!

Follow the same procedure for the Stars buttons on the Euromillions tab. You can implement the handler as:

```
System::Void euroStar_Click(System::Object^ sender, System::EventArgs^ e)
{
    Button^ button = safe_cast<Button^>(sender);
    array<Button^>^ buttons = { euroStar1, euroStar2 };
    SetNewValue(button, buttons, euroStarsUserMinimum, euroStarsUserMaximum);
}
```

Set the handler for the `Click` event for the second button to be `euro_StarClick` and you are done. If you recompile the example, you should be able to generate a new value for any button on either tab just by clicking it. The last piece to complete the example is to allow the user to enter a value for a button.

Responding to the Context Menu

Right-clicking a button brings up a context menu with a single menu item, `Choose`. When the user clicks this item, the program should display a dialog box that allowed a suitable value to be entered. Click the name of the context menu in the Design tab for `Form1` and then double-click the menu item to create the `Click` event handler.

The first problem is to determine which group of buttons was clicked to cause the event. Each group on buttons is in its own `GroupBox` control, and the `GroupBox` class has a `Controls` property that returns a reference to an object of type `Control::ControlCollection` that represents the collection of controls in the group box. The `Control::ControlCollection` class defines the `Contains()` function that returns `true` if the control that you pass as the argument is within the collection and `false` otherwise. Thus you have a way to determine to which group of buttons the button causing the `Click` event belongs. An outline implementation of the event handler looks like this:

```
System::Void chooseValue_Click(System::Object^ sender, System::EventArgs^ e)
{
    // Get the button that was clicked for the context menu, then...

    if(lottoValues->Controls->Contains(theButton))
    {
        // the button is from the lotto group...
    }
    else if(euroValues->Controls->Contains(theButton))
    {
        // The button is in the Values group...
    }
    else if(euroStars->Controls->Contains(theButton))
    {
        // The button is in the Stars group...
    }
}
```

That sorts out which group of buttons is involved, at least in principle. But there's still a bit of a problem — how do you find out which button was right-clicked to open the context menu?

The `chooseValue_Click()` handler is called when the `Choose` menu item is clicked, so the `sender` parameter for the handler identifies the menu item, not the button. You need a handler that responds to the original click on the button and you can create this by double-clicking `buttonContextMenu` in the Design pane for `Form1`. You can complete the code for the handler function that is created like this:

```
System::Void buttonContextMenu_Opening(System::Object^  sender,
                               System::ComponentModel::CancelEventArgs^  e)
{
    contextButton = safe_cast<Button^>(buttonContextMenu->SourceControl);
}
```

This casts the `sender` handle to type `Button^` and stores it in the `contextButton` member of the `Form1` class. Because in this case the event is for the context menu, the sender parameter identifies the component that was clicked to display it. Of course, you have yet to add the `contextButton` variable as a private member of the `Form1` class:

```
private:
    Button^ contextButton;              // Button that was right-clicked for context menu
```

All you need to do now is figure out what to do next.

The Logic for Dealing with the Choose Menu Item

The process for responding to the `Choose` item being clicked can be the same whichever group of buttons is involved, and it could work something like the following:

1. Display a dialog box to allow a value to be entered.
2. Check that the value is valid — that is, within range and different from the other buttons.
3. Display a message box if the value is not valid and allow the entry to be retired or the dialog operation to be cancelled.
4. If the value is valid, update the button that was right-clicked with the new value.

The first step in implementing this process is to create a new dialog form.

Creating the Dialog Form

Press `Ctrl+Shift+A` to display the `Add New Item` dialog box; then select `UI` as the category and `Windows Form` as the template. Enter the name as `UserValueDialog` and click the `Add` button. You can now open the `Properties` window for the form by pressing `F4` and setting the property values to make it a dialog box. Set the `ControlBox`, `MinimizeBox`, and `MaximizeBox` property values to `False`, and set the `Text` property to `"User Value Input"`. You should also set the `FormBorderStyle` property value to `FixedDialog`.

Add `OK` and `Cancel` buttons to the dialog form as well as a `Label` control and a `TextBox` control, as shown in Figure 22-24.

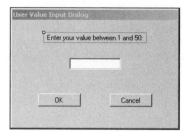

Figure 22-24

Set the `Text` and `(Name)` property values for the OK button to `OK`, and the value for the `DialogResult` property should be set to `OK`. The values for the `Text`, `(Name)`, and `DialogResult` properties for the Cancel button should be `Cancel`. Set the value of the `(Name)` property for the `TextBox` control to be `textBox` and the value for the `TextAlign` property as `Center`. The `(Name)` property for the `Label` control can be `label`, and the `Text` property can be anything you like because you'll change this in the code to suit the circumstances.

You can now display the properties for the dialog form once again and set the values for the `AcceptButton` and `CancelButton` properties to `OK` and `Cancel`, respectively.

Developing the Dialog Class

The value entered in the `TextBox` control must be available to the `Form1` object, so add a property to the `UserValueDialog` class to store it:

```
public:
   property int Value;
```

This is an example of a trivial scalar property so `get()` and `set()` functions are supplied by default.

The dialog object needs to know what the limits are for the value because the handler for the OK button in the dialog class is verifying that the value is legal. For the same reason, the dialog object needs to know what the current values on the buttons are to ensure they are not duplicated. You could add three further property members to the `UserValueDialog` class to store the data:

```
public:
   property int LowerLimit;
   property int UpperLimit;
   property array<int>^ Values;                 // Current button values
```

You won't want to leave spurious values lying around in the text box after it has been used, so add the following public function to the `UserValueDialog` class:

```
void ClearTextBox()
{
   textBox->Text = "";
}
```

The `Form1` object needs to be able to change the value of the `Text` property for the `label` control, depending on the limits in effect for button values when the dialog box is displayed; you can add a public member function to the `UserValidDialog` class to do this:

```
public:
  void SetLabelText(int lower, int upper)
  {
    label->Text = L"Enter your value between " + lower +L" and " + upper;
  }
```

You could conceivably pick up the limits from the properties in the dialog object, but this would require that the properties were always set first. By using parameters for the limits you remove this dependency.

You can create the dialog object in the `Form1` class constructor, but you'll need to add a private `Form1` class member to store the handle:

```
private: UserValueDialog^ userValueDialog;
```

You'll also need an `#include` directive for `UserValueDialog.h` in the `Form1.h` header file.

Adding the following line to the constructor creates the dialog object:

```
userValueDialog = gcnew UserValueDialog;
```

If you double-click the `OK` button in the `UserValueDialog` form, you'll create the `Click` event handler for the button. This function retrieves the value entered in the `TextBox` control, and checks that the value is within the limits and is different from the current set of values. If the value is not valid for any reason, the function displays a message box. Here's how you implement that:

```
System::Void OK_Click(System::Object^ sender, System::EventArgs^ e)
{
  ::DialogResult result;                      // Stores return value from Show()
  if(String::IsNullOrEmpty(textBox->Text))    // Chheck for null or empty string
  {
    result = MessageBox::Show(this,
                              L"No input - enter a value.",
                              L"Input Error",
                              MessageBoxButtons::RetryCancel,
                              MessageBoxIcon::Error);
    if(result == ::DialogResult::Retry)       // If Retry button clicked
      DialogResult = ::DialogResult::None;    // ...prevent dialog from closing...
    else                                      // ...otherwise...
      DialogResult = ::DialogResult::Cancel;  // ...close the dialog.
    return;
  }

  int value = Int32::Parse(textBox->Text);    // Get text box value
  bool valid = true;                          // Indicator for valid entry

  for each(int n in Values)                   // Check input against current values
```

```
      if(value == n)                          // If it's the same...
      {
        valid = false;                        // ...it is invalid.
        break;                                // Exit the loop
      }

    // Check limits and result of previous validity check
    if(!valid || value < LowerLimit || value > UpperLimit)
    {
      result = MessageBox::Show(this,
                                L"Input not valid." +
                                L"Value must  be from " + LowerLimit +
                                L" to " + UpperLimit +
                                L"\nand must be different from existing values.",
                                L"Input Error",
                                MessageBoxButtons::RetryCancel,
                                MessageBoxIcon::Error);
      if(result == ::DialogResult::Retry)
        DialogResult = ::DialogResult::None;
      else
        DialogResult = ::DialogResult::Cancel;
    }
    else
    Value = value;                            // Store the input in the property
}
```

A message box is displayed if the `Text` property for the text box is null or an empty string. The message box shows an error message and has `Retry` and `Cancel` buttons instead of OK and Cancel for a change. If `Retry` is clicked, the user wants another go at input so you prevent the dialog box from closing by setting its `DialogResult` property to `::DialogResult::None`. The only other possibility is that the user clicked `Cancel` in the message box, in which case you set the `DialogResult` property for the dialog object to `::DialogResult::Cancel`, which has the same effect as clicking the `Cancel` button for the dialog box.

The `Text` property for the `TextBox` control returns a handle of type `String^`. You convert this to an integer by passing the handle to the static `Parse()` function in the `Int32` class. You compare the value from the text box with the elements from the `values` array that represent the current set of button values. The new value should be different from all of these, so if you find one that is the same, you set `valid` to `false` and exit the loop.

The condition for the `if` statement following the `for each` loop checks the value against the limits and the current value of `valid` by ORing the conditions together. If any of the three expressions are `false`, the condition is `false`, and you display a message box. This works in the same way as the previous message box and displays an error message and `Retry` and `Cancel` buttons. If the value does indeed turn out to be valid you store it in the `Value` property for the dialog object ready for retrieval by the event handler in the `Form1` object that started the whole process off.

Handling the Click Event for the ChooseMenu

You are now going to complete the skeleton of the `chooseValue_Click()` handler function using the capabilities that you have added to the `UserValueDialog` class. The handle for the button that was right-clicked is already stored in the `contextButton` member because the `buttonContextMenu_Opening()` handler that you added earlier is executed first.

```cpp
System::Void chooseValue_Click(System::Object^  sender, System::EventArgs^  e)
{
   array<int>^ values;                 // Array to store current button values
   array<Button^>^ theButtons;         // Handle to aray of buttons

   // Check if the button is in the lottoValues group box
   if(lottoValues->Controls->Contains(contextButton))
   {
     // the button is from the lotto group...
     array<Button^>^ buttons = {lottoValue1, lottoValue2, lottoValue3,
                                lottoValue4, lottoValue5, lottoValue6};
     theButtons = buttons;             // Store array handle at outer scope
     values = GetButtonValues(buttons); // Get array of button values

     // Set up the dialog ready to be shown
     userValueDialog->Values = values = GetButtonValues(buttons);
     userValueDialog->LowerLimit = lottoUserMinimum;
     userValueDialog->UpperLimit = lottoUserMaximum;
     userValueDialog->SetLabelText(lottoUserMinimum, lottoUserMaximum);
     userValueDialog->ClearTextBox();
   }
   // Check if the button is in the euroValues group box
   else if(euroValues->Controls->Contains(contextButton))
   {
     // The button is in the Values group...
     array<Button^>^ buttons = {euroValue1, euroValue2, euroValue3,
                                euroValue4, euroValue5};
     theButtons = buttons;               // Store array handle at outer scope
     values = GetButtonValues(buttons); // Get array of button values

     // Set up the dialog ready to be shown
     userValueDialog->Values = values;
     userValueDialog->LowerLimit = euroUserMinimum;
     userValueDialog->UpperLimit = euroUserMaximum;
     userValueDialog->SetLabelText(euroUserMinimum, euroUserMaximum);
     userValueDialog->ClearTextBox();
   }
   // Check if the button is in the euroStars group box
   else if(euroStars->Controls->Contains(contextButton))
   {
     // The button is in the Stars group...
     array<Button^>^ buttons = { euroStar1, euroStar2 };
     theButtons = buttons;               // Store array handle at outer scope
     values = GetButtonValues(buttons); // Get array of button values

     // Set up the dialog ready to be shown
     userValueDialog->Values = values;
     userValueDialog->LowerLimit = euroStarsUserMinimum;
     userValueDialog->UpperLimit = euroStarsUserMaximum;
     userValueDialog->SetLabelText(euroStarsUserMinimum, euroStarsUserMaximum);
```

```
        userValueDialog->ClearTextBox();
    }
    // Display the dialog
    if(userValueDialog->ShowDialog(this) == ::DialogResult::OK)
    {
      // Determine which button value should be replaced
      for(int i = 0 ; i<theButtons->Length ; i++)
        if(contextButton == theButtons[i])
        {
          values[i] = userValueDialog->Value;
          break;
        }
      Array::Sort(values);                    // Sort the values

      // Set all the button values
      for(int i = 0 ; i<theButtons->Length ; i++)
        theButtons[i]->Text = values[i].ToString();
    }
}
```

You first define two array variables, one to hold the buttons, the other to hold the button values. You need to declare these here because these arrays are created within one or other of the `if` statement blocks and you'll want to access them outside the `if` blocks.

The first three `if` statements determine which group box contains the button that was right-clicked to open the context menu. The processes within the three `if` blocks are essentially the same, but the arrays created will be different. The array of buttons is created from the variables holding the handles to whichever set of buttons the `contextButton` belongs. The array handle is then stored in `theButtons` to make it accessible in the outer scope. You then call a function you have yet to add, `GetButtonValues()`, that returns an array containing the integer values from the buttons. Finally, in the `if` block you set the three properties for the dialog box object and call its `SetLabelText()` function to set the label text according to the applicable limits. The `contextButton` has to belong to one of the three group boxes as these are the only buttons that have the context menu available.

When one or other of the `if` blocks has executed, you display the dialog box by calling its `ShowDialog()` function in the condition for the fourth `if` statement. If the `ShowDialog()` function returns `::DialogResult::OK`, you execute the code in the `if` block. This first determines which button should have its value replaced by comparing the `contextButton` handle with the handles in the `theButtons` array. As soon as you find a match, you replace the corresponding element in the `values` array with the new `value` and exit the loop. After sorting the values, you update the `Text` property for each of the buttons in the `theButtons` array and you are done.

The implementation of the `GetButtonValues()` function in the `Form1` class looks like this:

```
// Creates an array of button values from an array of buttons
array<int>^ GetButtonValues(array<Button^>^ buttons)
{
  array<int>^ values = gcnew array<int>(buttons->Length);
  for(int i = 0 ; i<values->Length ; i++)
    values[i] = Int32::Parse(buttons[i]->Text);
  return values;
}
```

Here you create an array of integer values the same length as the array of button handles that is passed as the argument. You then populate the values array with the `int` equivalents of the string returned by the `Text` properties of the buttons, and return the handle to the values array.

After compiling the project once more, you should have a fully functional application. You can generate lottery entries for a variety of lotteries with the range of values constrained or not. You can also elect to generate new random individual values in an entry or choose your own. It has always worked but never won for me; of course, working is a measure of success.

Summary

In this chapter, you assembled a Windows Form application that uses the controls that you are most likely to need in the majority of programs. It should be apparent that Windows Forms programs are geared exclusively to using the Design capability. All the code for a class goes into the class definition, so with a very complex form the class is many lines of code. With a production application the code consists of a number of large classes that are rather unstructured, and difficult to modify and maintain at the code level. You should therefore always use the Design capability and the Properties window to expedite changes wherever you can and whenever you need to access the code, use Class View to find your way around.

The key points to keep in mind from this chapter include:

❑ An application window is a form, and a form is defined by a class derived from the `System::Form` class.

❑ A dialog window is a form that has its `FormBorderStyle` property value set to `FixedDialog`.

❑ A dialog box can be created as a modal dialog by calling its `ShowDialog()` function or as a modeless dialog by calling its `Show()` function.

❑ You can control whether or not a dialog box closes by setting the `DialogResult` property value for the dialog object.

❑ A `ComboBox` control combines the capabilities of a `ListBox` and a `TextBox` and allows selection of an item from a list or a new item to be entered from the keyboard.

❑ A `NumericUpDown` control allows the entry of numeric data by stepping through values within a given range with a given step increment.

❑ You can add the definition of a `Click` event handler for a control by double-clicking the control in the Form Design tab.

❑ You can specify an existing function to be a handler for a given event for a control through the Properties window. Clicking the `Events` button in the `Properties` window displays the list of events for a control.

❑ You should only change the names of automatically generated class members through the `Properties` window — not directly using the Code editor.

Exercises

You can download the source code for the examples in the book and the solutions to the following exercises from www.wrox.com.

1. Modify Ex22_01 so that it displays a dialog box that you created as a dialog form when the Help > About menu item is clicked.

2. Modify Ex22_01 so that the dialog box that displays for the Choose context menu item uses a ListBox control instead of the text box and displays the complete set of legal values that can be chosen.

3. Investigate the properties and functions available for the WebBrowser control and modify Ex22_01 to allow a URL to be entered through a TextBox so that the WebBrowser control displays the page at the URL that was entered.

Accessing Data Sources in a Windows Forms Application

In this chapter, you'll investigate how you can develop form-based applications that will display data from a variety of sources and specifically how you can create form-based programs to access an existing database. In this chapter, you will learn about:

❑   What kind of classes are involved in encapsulating a data source

❑   How you can use the `DataGridView` control to display your own data

❑   How you can customize the appearance of a `DataGridView` control

❑   What the function of the `BindingSource` component is and how you use it with a `DataGridView` control

❑   How you use a `BindingNavigator` control to navigate data from a source managed by a `BindingSource` control

❑   How you expedite updating of a database using a `BindingNavigator` control and a `BindingSource` component

Visual C++ 2008 provides a high degree of automation for creating Forms-based applications that access data sources but you will start by ignoring the automation and get a feel for how you can work with components programmatically. With this approach, you'll not only get a good insight into how things work; you'll also appreciate how much the automation is doing for you.

Working with Data Sources

A data source is any source of data for your application; relational databases, Web services that access data, and objects can all be data sources. When you are developing an application that will work with an existing data source, you will usually need to identify the data source within your project. You'll do this through the `Data Sources` window that is displayed when you select `Data > Show Data Sources` from the main menu or when you press `Shift+Alt+D`; note that this menu item is only available when you have a project created.

A data source is represented by a class object, so adding a data source to your project inevitably adds definitions for a number of classes. Take a brief look at what they are.

Data Source	A data source is defined by a class that is derived from the `DataSet` class that is defined in the `System::Data` namespace. This class encapsulates an in-memory cache of all the data from the database that is accessible in your project.
Database Tables	Each table in the database is defined by a nested class in the `DataSet` class that represents the database, and the class that defines a table is derived from the `System::Data::DataTable` class. The classes representing tables also define events that signal changes to the data in the table and properties, making each of the values of the current database record available. Each table in a data source is identified by a member in the `DataSet` class that is a handle to the corresponding `DataTable` object.
Table Columns	Each column in a given database table is identified by a member of the `DataTable` class that defines the table. The members representing columns are of type `System::Data::DataColumn` and define the characteristics of the column, such as the column name and the type of data in the column. These characteristics are collectively referred to as the **schema** for the column.
Table Rows	A row in a table is represented by an object of type `System::Data::DataRow`. A `DataRow` object contains the data in a row and has as many data items as there are columns in the `DataTable` object.

Clearly, with a database that involves several tables that each have a number of columns, you are going to see quite a lot of code generated to represent a data source; certainly, tens of thousands of lines of code are not uncommon in a practical context.

The classes I have identified in the previous table are solely to encapsulate data from a data source; they do not provide the mechanism for connecting to a data source such as a database and accessing the data within it. That capability is provided by a component class called a **table adapter** that will be generated automatically. A table adapter establishes a connection to a database and executes the commands or SQL statements that operate on the database. There is one table adapter class for each `DataTable` member in the `DataSet` object, so if your application is going to work with three tables from a database, there are three table adapter classes defined. A table adapter object populates a `DataTable` member of a `DataSet` object with data and can update the table in the database when required.

Accessing and Displaying Data

There are three components defined in the `System::Windows::Forms` namespace that are designed to be used together for accessing and displaying data in a Windows Forms application:

Component	Description
DataGridView	This control can display virtually any kind of data in a rectangular grid. You can use this control quite independently of the other two components.
BindingSource	This component is used to encapsulate data from a data source. The component can manage accessing and updating the data source, and can be used as the vehicle for displaying data in a `DataGridView` control.
BindingNavigator	This control provides a toolbar containing controls for navigating and manipulating data from a data source, typically a data source encapsulated in a `BindingSource` control.

The `BindingSource` component is not a control as it has no graphical representation that a user can interact with, but it's designed to complement and work with the `DataGridView` control and the `BindingNavigator` in database applications. The `BindingSource` component provides the communications with the data source necessary to execute queries and update commands, the `DataGridView` controls provides the user interface for viewing and entering the data and the `BindingNavigator` control provides a toolbar that simplifies data navigation. Using the `BindingNavigator` control is optional. If you prefer, you can change records programmatically yourself.

Although these three components are designed to work as a team, the `DataGridView` control is a particularly useful tool in its own right, as you can use it quite independently from the other two. It provides an astonishing range of capabilities for changing the visual appearance of the grid that displays the data. You'll explore some of the ways in which you can customize the `DataGridView` control before going into how you can use it combined with the `BindingSource` and `BindingNavigator` components.

> *Note that you can also use the* `SqlConnection`, `SqlDataAdapter`, *and* `DataSet` *controls for accessing a data source. If you want to use these controls, then you may need to add them to the ToolBox yourself. You do this by selecting* `Tools` > `Choose ToolBox Items` *from the main menu and checking the controls in the list that you want to have added to the ToolBox.*

Using a DataGridView Control

The `DataGridView` control enables you to display and modify a rectangular array of data from a wide range of data sources. You can also use the `DataGridView` control to display almost any kind of data that originates directly in a program. Under the covers it is a complex control that provides an enormous amount of flexibility, and you can take advantage of its many features through its many properties, functions, and events. At the same time, the `DataGridView` control can be remarkably easy to use. You can ignore the complexity of the internals and use it through the Form Design capability that takes care of all the basic detail for you. You'll see later in this chapter how you can produce a complete working program example to access the Northwind database with no programming at all on your part; the whole program will be generated through the Form Design capability and by setting properties for components used in the project.

The data in a `DataGridView` control is displayed in a rectangular array of cells that you can envisage as a collection of rows or as a collection of columns. Each column of cells has a header cell at the top that typically contains text that identifies it, and each row has a row header cell at the beginning, as shown in Figure 23-1.

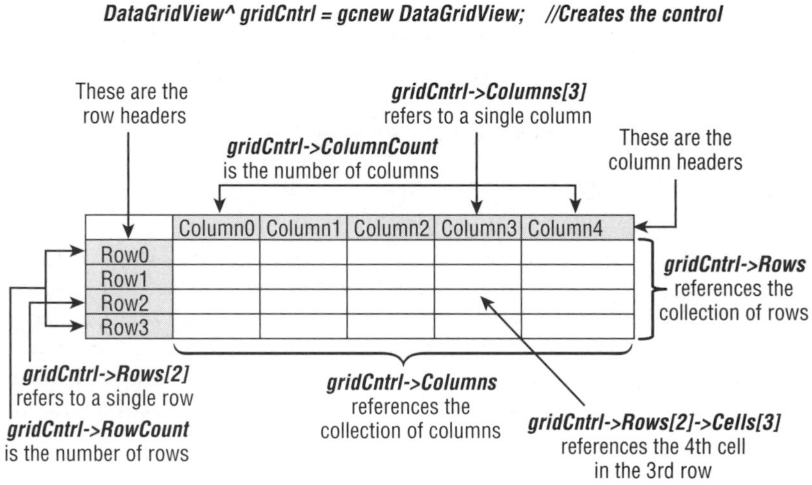

Figure 23-1

You reference rows and columns of cells through properties of the `DataGridView` control object. The `Rows` property returns a value of type `DataGridRowCollection` that is a collection of all the rows, and you refer to a particular row using an index, as illustrated in Figure 23-1. Similarly, the `Columns` property for the control returns a value of type `DataGridViewColumnCollection` that you can also index to reference a particular column. Rows and columns are indexed from zero. The `Cells` property for a `DataGridRowCollection` object represents a collection containing the cells in the row, and you can index the `Cells` property to access a specific cell in a row. Figure 23-1 shows an example of how you reference the fourth cell in the third row.

The number of rows is available as the value of the `RowCount` property for the control, and the `ColumnCount` property returns the number of columns. Initially, when the control is not bound to a data source, it will have no columns or rows. You can set the number of columns and or the number of rows by setting property values for the control, but when you use the control to display data from a data source, this is taken care of automatically.

You can use the `DataGridView` control in three different modes, as shown in the following table.

unbound mode	In unbound mode you transfer the data to the control yourself, typically using the `Add()` function for the `Rows` property for the control. You would use this mode for displaying relatively small amounts of data.

bound mode	In this mode you identify a source for the data that is to be displayed by setting a value for the `DataSource` property of the control.
virtual mode	In virtual mode you connect the control to a data cache in memory that you fill with data from a separate data source. You would use this mode to display data from a source where you want to manage data access in order to optimize performance.

In unbound mode, you can use the `DataGridView` control to display any data in your application that can be displayed in a grid. This makes it a very convenient tool for displaying data in many different kinds of applications. The next section looks into using the control in unbound mode in a little more depth.

Using a DataGridView Control in Unbound Mode

The data in `DataGridView` control is stored in a rectangular arrangement that is identified by the `Rows` and `Columns` properties for the control. In unbound mode you'll add the data to the control using the `Add()` function for the `Rows` property, but before you can add rows to the control, the columns need to be defined, at least to establish how many items are in a row. Setting the `ColumnCount` property for the control programmatically sets how many columns there are and determines that the control is to work in unbound mode. The following statements create a control that you reference using the handle `dataGridView` and then set the number of columns to 3:

```
DataGridView^ dataGridView = gcnew DataGridView;
dataGridView->ColumnCount = 3;          // Set number of columns
```

You can optionally label the columns in the control by specifying headers to identify the data in each column by setting the `Name` property for each column. Here's how that could be done:

```
dataGridView->Columns[0]->Name = L"Name";
dataGridView->Columns[1]->Name = L"Phone Number";
dataGridView->Columns[2]->Name = L"Address";
```

The `Columns` property for the control is an indexed property so you access individual columns using index values starting from 0. Thus these statements label the three columns in the `dataGridView` control. You can also set the column headers through the `Properties` window for the control, as you'll see in the next working example.

The value returned by the `Rows` property is a collection of type `DataGridViewRowCollection`, and this type is defined in the `System::Windows::Forms` namespace. The `Count` property for the collection returns the number of rows and there is also a default indexed property to return the row at a given index position. The collection of rows has a large number of functions; I won't go through them all here, but the following table shows a few of the most useful ones for adding and deleting rows.

`Add()`	Adds one or more rows to the collection.

Continued

1269

`Insert()`	Inserts one or more rows in the collection.
`Clear()`	Deletes all rows in the collection.
`AddCopy()`	Adds a copy of the row specified by the argument.
`InsertCopy()`	Inserts a copy of the row specified by the first argument at the position specified by the second argument.
`Remove()`	Removes the row specified by the argument, which is of type `DataGridViewRow^`.
`RemoveAt()`	Removes the row specified by the index value you supply as the argument.

The `Add()` function for the value returned by the `Rows` property comes in four overloaded versions that enable you to add a row of data to the control in a variety of ways.

`Add()`	Adds one new row to the collection.
`Add(int rowCount)`	Adds `rowCount` new rows to the collection. An exception of type `System::ArgumentOutOfRangeException` is thrown if `rowCount` is zero or negative.
`Add(DataGridViewRow^ row)`	Adds the row specified by the argument. A `DataGridViewRow` object contains the collection of cells in a row as well as the parameters that determine the appearance of the cells in the row.
`Add(... Object^ object)`	Adds a new row and populates the cells in the row with the objects specified by the arguments.

All versions of the `Add()` function return a value of type `int` that is the index of the last row that was added to the collection. If the `DataSource` property for the `DataGridView` control is not null, or the control has no columns, all versions of the `Add()` function throw an exception of type `System::InvalidOperationException`.

You could add rows to the `dataGridView` control that has three columns with the following statements:

```
dataGridView->Rows->Add(L"Fred Able", L"914 696 1200",
                                    L"1235 First Street, AnyTown");
dataGridView->Rows->Add(L"May East", L"914 696 1399",
                                    L"1246 First Street, AnyTown");
```

Each of these statements adds a new row to the collection and the three arguments to the `Add()` function correspond to the three columns in the control. The control must have sufficient columns to accommodate the number of items you add in a row. If you attempt to add more data items to a row than there are columns in the control, the excess items are ignored.

You will first try unbound mode in a working example where you set up the `DataGridView` control by setting its properties from the Form Design tab.

The DataGridView Control in Unbound Mode

This example displays a list of books where each book is specified by the ISBN, the title, the author, and the publisher. Create a new Windows Form project with the name Ex23_01. Add a DataGridView control to the form and click the arrow at the top-right of the control to display the pop-up menu shown in Figure 23-2.

If you click the bottom menu item, Dock in parent container, the control fills the client area of the form. The top menu item is for selecting a data source, but you are not going to specify a data source this time. If you click the AddColumn menu item, the dialog box shown in Figure 23-3 for entering columns to the control is displayed.

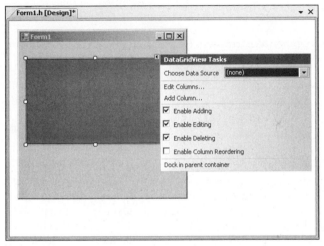

Figure 23-2

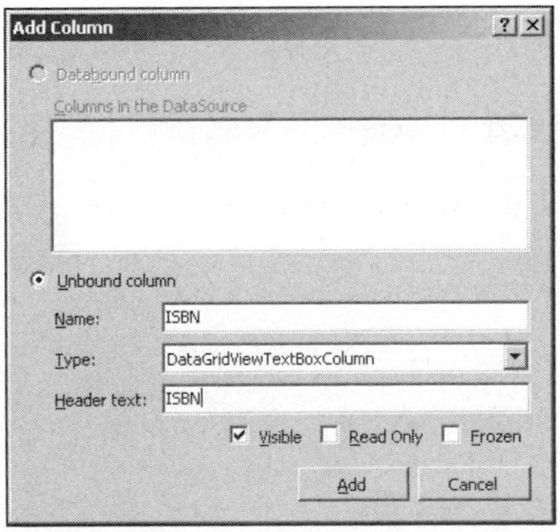

Figure 23-3

The Unbound column radio button is checked because there is no data source identified for the control, which is the way it should be for this example. The Name: entry is the value of the Name property for the column, and the `Header Text:` entry is the value of the `HeaderText` property, which corresponds to the text that is shown in the control as the column heading. If you extend the list box that is for selecting the `Type:` value, you'll see you have a range of choices for the type of column. Here you should leave it as the default choice — a `TextBox` column — because you'll be adding strings as the data to be displayed. The other column types in the list deal with provide for various controls in the cells representing the data:

`DataGridViewButtonColumn`	This type is used to display a button in each cell in the column.
`DataGridViewCheckBoxColumn`	This type is used when you want to store `bool` values (`System::Boolean` objects) or `System::Windows::Forms::CheckState` objects as checkboxes in the cells in the column.
`DataGridViewComboBoxColumn`	This type is used when you want to display a drop-down list in each cell in the column.
`DataGridViewImageColumn`	You select this type when each cell in the column is to display and image in each cell in the column.
`DataGridViewLinkColumn`	You use this type when each cell in the column is to display a link.

To add a column to the control, you enter values for the `Name:` and `Header Text:`, select the `Type:` from the list if you want other than the default type, and click the `Add` button. In this example, you can add columns with the names `ISBN`, `Title`, `Author`, and `Publisher`. The `Header Text:` entry can be the same as the name in each case. When you have entered the columns, click the `Close` button to close the dialog (the Close button is visible after you have added at least one column). All the columns should now be displayed in the control, so you can drag the right edge of the form so all four columns are visible.

You can edit the columns at any time by clicking the `Edit Columns` item in the pop-up menu; it displays the dialog box shown in Figure 23-4.

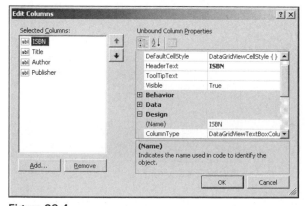

Figure 23-4

The `Edit Columns` dialog box enables you to resequence existing columns, to add new columns, or to delete columns; you can also edit any of the properties for a column.

Return to the Design tab and change the `Text` property for the form to `My Book List`. If you display the code for the form, you can modify the constructor to add data to the `DataGridView` control using the `Add()` function for the `Rows` property, like this:

```
Form1(void)
{
 InitializeComponent();
 //
 //TODO: Add the constructor code here
 // Create book data, one book per array
 array<String^>^ book1 = {L"0-09-174271-4", L"Wonderful Life",
                            L"Stephen Jay Gould", L"Hutchinson Radius"};
 array<String^>^ book2 = {L"0-09-977170-5", L"The Emperor's New Mind",
                            L"Roger Penrose", L"Vintage"};
 array<String^>^ book3 = {L"0-14-017996-8",L"Metamagical Themas",
                            L"Douglas R. Hofstadter", L"Penguin"};
 array<String^>^ book4 = {L"0-201-36080-2", L"The Meaning Of It All",
                            L"Richard P. Feynman", L"Addison-Wesley"};
 array<String^>^ book5 = {L"0-593-03449-X", L"The Walpole Orange",
                            L"Frank Muir", L"Bantam Press"};
 array<String^>^ book6 = {L"0-439-99358-X", L"The Amber Spyglass",
                            L"Philip Pullman", L"Scholastic Children's Books"};
 array<String^>^ book7 = {L"0-552-13461-9", L"Pyramids",
                            L"Terry Pratchett", L"Corgi Books"};
 array<String^>^ book8 = {L"0-7493-9739-X", L"Made In America",
                            L"Bill Bryson", L"Minerva"};

 // Create Array of books
 array<array<String^>^>^ books ={book1, book2, book3, book4,
                                   book5, book6, book7, book8};

 // Add all the books to the control
 for each(array<String^>^ book in books )
   dataGridView1->Rows->Add(book);
 //
}
```

There's an array of type `array<String^>` created for each book, and the handle to each array is stored in an array referenced by a variable of type `array<array<String^>^>^`. Each of the arrays of strings has four elements that contain data items that correspond to the columns in the `DataGridView` control, so each array defines a book.

For convenience, you assemble the handles to the arrays of strings into the `books` array. The type for `books` looks a little messy because of the ^ repetitions, but it is simply a handle to an array of elements where each element is of type `array<String^>^`. The `books` array enables you to set up all the data in the control in a single `for each` loop. The `Rows` property for the `DataGridView` object returns a handle of type `DataGridViewRowCollection^` that references the collection of rows in the control. Calling the `Add()` function for the object returned by the `Rows` property adds a complete row to the collection. Each element in the array that is passed as the argument corresponds to a column in the control, and the type of data element must correspond with the type you selected for the column. Here all the columns have the same type, so all the cells in a row can be passed in an array. If the columns were of different types, you could specify the item for each column by a separate argument to the Add() function, or you could use an array of elements of type Object^.

If you compile and execute the example by pressing Ctrl+F5, you should see the application window shown in Figure 23-5.

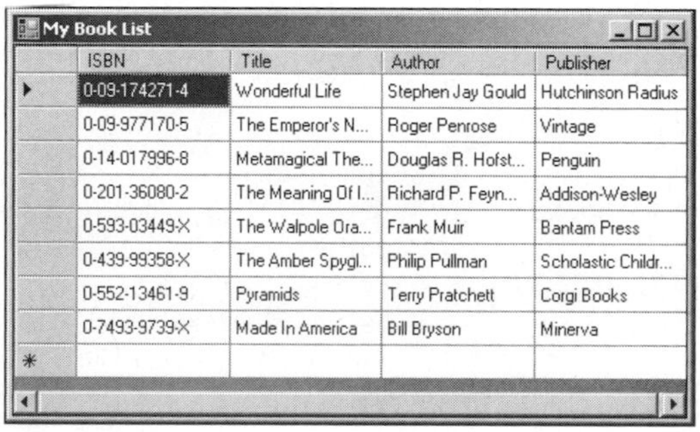

Figure 23-5

If you reduce the size of the application window by dragging the lower-right corner, you get scrollbars displayed automatically to enable you to scroll to see the rest of the control. If you increase the size of the window, eventually the scrollbars disappear.

It would be nice if the columns were wide enough to accommodate the maximum length of text they contain. Changing the value of the AutoSizeColumnsMode property in the Layout group fixes that. After you have closed the application, open the Properties window for the DataGridView control from the Form1[Design] tab in the Editor pane and change the AutoSizeColumnsMode property value to AllCells. If you recompile the program and run it again, you'll see that the application window is now as shown in Figure 23-6.

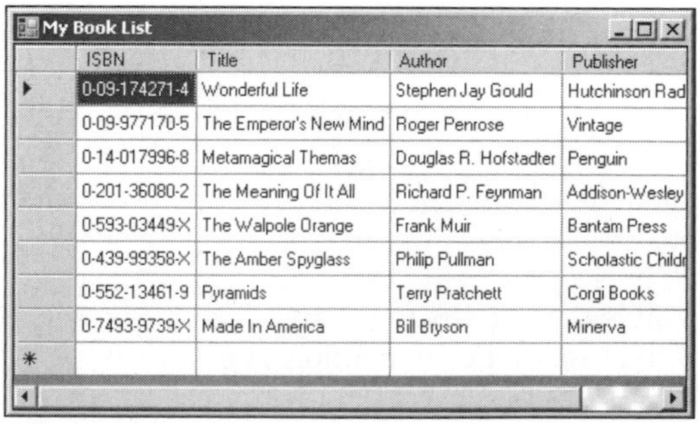

Figure 23-6

Each column has its width set so that it accommodates the longest string that the column contains. Overall, the resultant application window is not too bad, but you can do a lot more programmatically to personalize how it looks.

Customizing a DataGridView Control

As I said earlier in the chapter, the appearance of a `DataGridView` control is highly customizable. You will explore aspects of this using the control in unbound mode, but everything you'll learn in this context applies equally well to using the control in bound mode. The appearance of each of the cells in a `DataGridView` control is determined by an object of type `DataGridViewCellStyle` that has the properties shown in the following table.

Property	Description
BackColor	The value is a `System::Drawing::Color` object that determines the background color of a cell. The `Color` class defines a range of standard colors as static members. The default value is `Color::Empty`.
ForeColor	The value is a `Color` object that determines the foreground color of a cell. The default value is `Color::Empty`.
SelectionBackColor	The value is a `Color` object that determines the background color of a cell when it is selected. The default value is `Color::Empty`.
SelectionForeColor	The value is a `Color` object that determines the foreground color of a cell when it is selected. The default value is `Color::Empty`.
Font	The value is a `System::Drawing::Font` object that determines the font to be used to display text in the cell. The default value is null.

Alignment	The value determines the alignment of the contents of the cell. The values are defined by the `DataGridViewAlignment` enumeration so the value can be any of the following constants:
	
	`BottomCenter, BottomLeft, BottomRight,`
	`MiddleCenter, MiddleLeft, MiddleRight,`
	`TopCenter, TopLeft, TopRight, NotSet`
	
	The default value is `NotSet`.

WrapMode	The value determines whether the text in the cell is wrapped when it is too long to fit in the cell. The value is one of the constants defined by the `DataGridViewTriState` enumeration and can be: `True, False, NotSet` The default value is `NotSet`.

Continued

Property	Description
Padding	The value is an object of type System::Windows::Forms::Padding that determines the space between the cell contents and the edge of the cell. The Padding class constructor requires an argument of type int that is the padding measured in pixels. The default corresponds to no padding in the cell.
Format	The value is a format string that determines how the content of the string is formatted. This is the same kind of formatting as you have been using in the Console::WriteLine() function. The default value is an empty string.

This is not an exhaustive list of the properties of a DataGridViewCellStyle object, just those that relate to the appearance of a cell.

The way in which the appearance of a particular cell is determined is quite complicated because you have a number of different properties that you can set in a DataGridView control that all determine how a given cell or group of cells is displayed, and several of these can be in effect at any given time. For example, you can set property values that specify the appearance of a row of cells, or a column of cells, or all the cells in the control, and these can all be in effect concurrently. Clearly, because a row and column always intersect, all three of these possibilities apply to any given cell, so you have an apparent conflict.

Each cell in a DataGridView control is represented by a System::Windows::Forms::DataGridViewCell object, and the appearance of any given cell, including header cells, is determined by the value of its InheritedStyle property. The value of the InheritedStyle property for a cell is arrived at by looking at all the possible properties that return a value that is a DataGridViewCellStyle object that applies to the cell and then considering these properties in a priority sequence; the first property in the sequence that is found to be set is the one that takes effect. The determination of the value of the InheritedStyle property for header cells for rows and columns is handled differently from the InheritedStyle property for other cells, so I'll discuss them separately, starting with header cells.

Customizing Header Cells

The InheritedStyle property value for each header cell in the control is determined by considering the values of following properties in sequence:

❑ The Style property for the DataGridViewCell object that represents the cell.

❑ The ColumnHeadersDefaultCellStyle property or the RowHeadersDefaultCellStyle property for the control object.

❑ The DefaultCellStyle property for the control object.

So if the Style property value for the cell object has been set, the InheritedStyle property for the cell takes this value and determines the appearance of the cell. If not, the next candidate takes effect if the value for that has been set. If the second choice has not been set, the DefaultCellStyle property for the control is applied.

Don't forget that the value of the `InheritedStyle` property is an object of type `DataGridViewCellStyle`, which itself has properties that determine various aspects of the appearance of the cell. The process of going through the priority sequence applies to each of the properties of the `DataGridViewCellStyle` object, so overall there may be contributions from more than one of the properties in the priority sequence.

Customizing Non-Header Cells

The `InheritedStyle` property value for each non-header cell in the control (the non-header cells being the cells containing data) is determined from the following properties in the `DataGridView` object in sequence:

- ❏ The `Style` property for the `DataGridViewCell` object that represents the cell.

- ❏ The `DefaultCellStyle` property for the `DataGridViewRow` object that represents the row containing the cell. You would typically reference the `DataGridViewRow` object by indexing the `Rows` property for the control object.

- ❏ The `AlternatingRowsDefaultCellStyle` property for the control object; this applies only to cells in rows with odd index numbers.

- ❏ The `RowsDefaultCellStyle` property for the control object.

- ❏ The `DefaultCellStyle` property for the `DataGridViewColumn` object that contains the cell. You would typically access a `DataGridViewColumn` object by indexing the `Columns` property for the control object.

- ❏ The `DefaultCellStyle` property for the control object.

Potentially you could have a different `DataGridViewCellStyle` object for each cell, but for efficiency you need to keep the number of such objects to a minimum.

The next Try It Out explores some of these possibilities in an example where you set up the `DataGridView` object yourself.

Try It Out　　Setting the Appearance of the Control

Create a new CLR project using the Windows Forms template with the name `Ex23_02`. Add a `DataGridView` control to the form in the Design tab and change its `(Name)` property to `dataGridView`. This is the name of the handle in the class that references the control object. You can also change the `Text` property for the form to `"My Other Book List"`. For the rest of the example, you are going to be working with the code in the constructor.

The data that you display is similar to that in the previous example, but to extend the possibilities a little, you'll add a date entry at the beginning of each row specifying a book, so the cells in the first column will contain references to objects of type `System::DateTime`, and the remaining columns will be strings. The `DateTime` class defines an instant in time that you typically specify as a date plus the time of day. In the example, only the date is of interest, so you'll use a constructor that accepts only three arguments: the year, the month, and the day.

Setting Up the Data

The first step is to create the data to be displayed. Add the following code to the `Form1` constructor, after the call to `InitializeComponent()`:

```
// Create book data, one book per array
array<Object^>^ book1 = {gcnew DateTime(1999,11,5), L"0-09-174271-4",
    L"Wonderful Life", L"Stephen Jay Gould", L"Hutchinson Radius"};
array<Object^>^ book2 = {gcnew DateTime(2001,10,25), L"0-09-977170-5",
    L"The Emperor's New Mind", L"Roger Penrose", L"Vintage"};
array<Object^>^ book3 = {gcnew DateTime(1993,1,15), L"0-14-017996-8",
    L"Metamagical Themas", "Douglas R. Hofstadter", L"Penguin"};
array<Object^>^ book4 = {gcnew DateTime(1994,2,7), L"0-201-36080-2",
    L"The Meaning Of It All", L"Richard P. Feynman", L"Addison-Wesley"};
array<Object^>^ book5 = {gcnew DateTime(1995,11,6), L"0-593-03449-X",
    L"The Walpole Orange", "Frank Muir", L"Bantam Press"};
array<Object^>^ book6 = {gcnew DateTime(2004,7,16), L"0-439-99358-X",
    L"The Amber Spyglass", L"Philip Pullman", L"Scholastic Children's Books"};
array<Object^>^ book7 = {gcnew DateTime(2002,9,18), L"0-552-13461-9",
    L"Pyramids", L"Terry Pratchett", L"Corgi Books"};
array<Object^>^ book8 = {gcnew DateTime(1998,2,27), L"0-7493-9739-X",
    L"Made In America", L"Bill Bryson", L"Minerva"};

// Create Array of books
array<array<Object^>^>^ books = {book1, book2, book3, book4,
                                 book5, book6, book7, book8};
```

The basic mechanics of this are the same as in the previous example. The differences here are due to each book having an extra item of type `DateTime` in the specification, so the array elements are of type `Object^`. You'll recall that the `Object` class is a base class for every C++/CLI class so you can store a handle to an object of any class type in an element of type `Object^`.

You can add the following statement to the constructor next:

```
array<String^>^ headers = {L"Date", L"ISBN", L"Title", L"Author", L"Publisher"};
```

This creates an array containing the text that is to appear as column headers in the control. You can add these headers to the control by adding the following code to the constructor:

```
dataGridView->ColumnCount = headers->Length;          // Set number of columns
for(int i = 0 ; i<headers->Length ; i++)
  dataGridView->Columns[i]->Name = headers[i];
```

The first statement specifies the number of columns in the control by setting the value of the `ColumnCount` property; this also establishes the control in unbound mode. The `for` loop sets the `Name` property for each column object to the corresponding string in the `headers` array. The `Columns` property for the control returns a reference to the collection of columns, and you just index this to reference a particular column.

You can add the rows to the control in another loop:

```
for each(array<Object^>^ book in books)
  dataGridView->Rows->Add(book);
```

The `for each` loop selects each of the elements from the books array in turn add passes it to the `Add()` method for the reference returned by the `Rows` property for the control. Each element in the books array is an array of strings, and there are as many strings in the array as there are columns in the control.

The control has now been loaded with the data, so the number of rows and columns is determined and the contents of the column headers have been specified. You can now set about customizing the appearance of the control.

Setting Up the Control

You want the control to be docked in the client area of the form, and you can do this by setting the value of the `Dock` property:

```
dataGridView->Dock = DockStyle::Fill;
```

The `Dock` property must be set to one of the constants defined by the `DockStyle` enumeration; other possible values are `Top`, `Bottom`, `Left`, `Right`, or `None`, and these specify the sides of the control that are docked.

You can also relate the position of the control to the client area of the form by setting the `Anchor` property for the control. The value of `Anchor` property specifies the edges of the control that are to be attached to the client area of the form. The value is a bitwise combination of the constants defined by the `AnchorStyles` enumeration and can be any or all of `Top`, `Bottom`, `Left`, and `Right`. For example, to anchor the top and left sides of the control, you would specify the value as `AnchorStyles::Top & AnchorStyles::Left`. Setting the `Anchor` property fixes the position of the control plus its scrollbars within the container at a given size, so when you resize the application window the control and its scrollbars remain at a fixed size. If you set the `Dock` property as in the previous statement, resizing the application window exposes more or less of the control and the scrollbars adjust accordingly, so that is much better in this case.

You want the width of the columns to be adjusted to accommodate the data in the cells, and you can put this into effect by calling the `AutoResizeColumns()` function:

```
dataGridView->AutoResizeColumns();
```

This statement adjusts the width of all columns to accommodate the current contents, and this includes header cells. Note that this is effective at the time the function is called, so the contents need to be there when you call it. If the contents are changed subsequently, the column width is not adjusted. If you want the column widths to be adjusted whenever the contents of the cells change, you should also set the `AutoSizeColumnsMode` property for the control, like this:

```
dataGridView->AutoSizeColumnsMode = DataGridViewAutoSizeColumnsMode::AllCells;
```

The value must be one of the constants defined by the `DataGridViewAutoSizeColumnsMode` enumeration, and the other possible values are `ColumnHeader`, `AllCellsExceptHeader`, `DisplayedCells`, `DisplayedCellsExceptHeader`, `Fill`, and `None`. Of course, these are also the property values in the list for this property that displays on the Properties page for the `DataGridView` control.

It may be that you want to allow only the columns width for specific columns to be automatically adjusted when the contents change; in this case, you set a value for the `AutoSizeMode` property for the column object.

There are two further overloaded versions of the `AutoResizeColumns()` function. One accepts an argument of type `DataGridViewAutoSizeColumnsMode`, and the cells affected are determined by the value of the argument. The other overload is protected and, therefore, for use in functions in a derived class; it accepts an additional argument of type `bool` that indicates whether the cell height is to be considered in calculating a new width.

You can set the default background color of all cells in the control like this:

```
dataGridView->DefaultCellStyle->BackColor = Color::Pink;
```

This sets the background color as the standard color `Pink` that is defined as a static member of the `Color` class. The properties of the `DefaultCellStyle` property for the control object only determine what applies to a cell in the absence of any higher priority cell style being in effect.

You could also set the default foreground color for all cells:

```
dataGridView->DefaultCellStyle->ForeColor = Color::DarkBlue;
```

To identify when cells have been selected, you can specify selection colors for the foreground and background. Here's how you could define the background color when a cell is selected:

```
dataGridView->DefaultCellStyle->SelectionBackColor = Color::Green;
```

Of course, the point of setting property values programmatically is that it happens at run-time so you can set values depending on conditions and data values that you find when the application is running. Property values that you set through the Properties pane in the IDE are set once and for all — unless you have code that changes them subsequently.

That's enough for the control for now. You'll personalize the column headers next.

Setting Up the Column Headers

If you want to determine the appearance of the column headers yourself, you need to set the value of the `EnableHeadersVisualStyles` property for the control to `false`:

```
dataGridView->EnableHeadersVisualStyles = false;
```

The controls in a WindowsForms application are usually drawn according to the visual styles theme that is in effect, and this theme determines the appearance of the controls. If you are running the application under Windows XP, the controls are drawn according to the Windows XP theme; if you are using Windows Vista then controls will be drawn in the Vista style. When the `EnableHeadersVisualStyles` property value is `true`, the visual styles for the column headers will be set according to the visual styles theme in effect for the application, and the styles you set are ignored.

You'll be setting several properties for the appearance of the headers and an easy way to do this is to create a `DataGridViewCellStyle` object for which you can set the properties as you want them, and then make this object the one that determines the styles for the headers. You can create the `DataGridViewCellStyle` object like this:

```
DataGridViewCellStyle^ headerStyle = gcnew DataGridViewCellStyle;
```

It would be nice to have the header text in a larger font, and you can set the font by setting a value for the Font property:

```
headerStyle->Font = gcnew System::Drawing::Font("Times New Roman", 12,
                                                          FontStyle::Bold);
```

The header text is now in 12-point bold characters in the Times New Roman font.

You can also set the background and foreground colors for the header cells:

```
headerStyle->BackColor = Color::AliceBlue;
headerStyle->ForeColor = Color::BurlyWood;
```

The text is now drawn in the color BurlyWood against an AliceBlue background. If you prefer something different, the Color class offers you a lot of choices, and Intellisense should show the list as you complete typing the scope resolution operator.

To set the appearance of the header cells to correspond with the properties that you've set for the headerStyle object, you need to add the following statement:

```
dataGridView->ColumnHeadersDefaultCellStyle = headerStyle;
```

This sets the value of the ColumnHeadersDefaultCellStyle property for the control to be the headerStyle handle. This replaces the existing DataGridViewCellStyle object that was in effect for the headers.

There is one other thing you should do in relation to the column headers. The larger font requires the height of the cells to be adjusted to accommodate it. Calling the AutoResizeColumnHeadersHeight() function for the control adjusts the heights of the header cells to accommodate their current contents:

```
dataGridView->AutoResizeColumnHeadersHeight();
```

The height of all header cells is adjusted to fit the largest cell contents. If you just want the height of a particular column header to be adjusted, you can use the overloaded version of the function that accepts an argument specifying the index of the column to be adjusted.

If you don't want the row or column headers to be visible you can make them disappear by setting the value of the RowHeadersVisible property and/or ColumnHeadersVisible property for the control to false.

Formatting a Column

The first column contains handles to a DateTime object. As it is, the application simply calls the ToString() function for the objects to get something to display, but you can do better than that. You can set the Format property for the DefaultCellStyle property for the column, and this format specification is then used to display the contents of the cells:

```
dataGridView->Columns[0]->DefaultCellStyle->Format = L"y";
```

This sets the `Format` property to the string containing the `y` format specification for a `DateTime` object that presents the object in the short date form as month plus year. There are several other format specifiers for `DateTime` objects that you could use. For example, `D` displays the day as well as the month and year, and `f` and `F` displays the time as well as the date.

If you have added all that code to the `Form1` class constructor, it's time to don the sunglasses and give the example a whirl. If you compile and run it, you should see something like the application window shown in Figure 23-7.

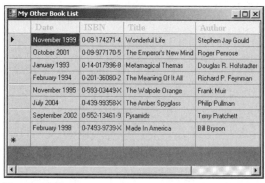

Figure 23-7

I have resized the width of the window in Figure 23-7 to show more of the columns. Unfortunately, in the book the application window appears in shades of grey but you should see it on your screen in glorious Technicolor.

If you click one of the row headers on the left of the control, you should see the row highlighted as shown in Figure 23-8.

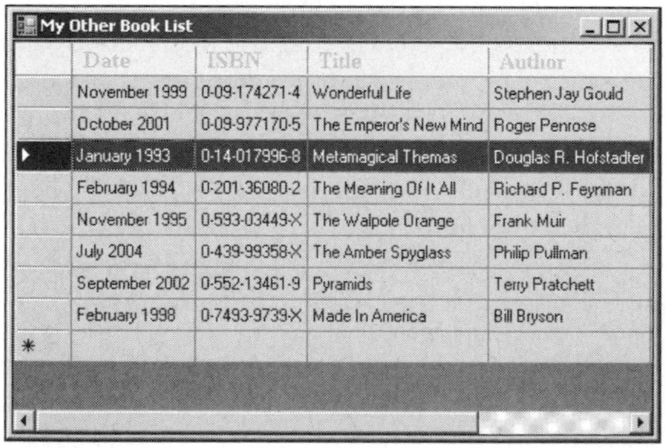

Figure 23-8

The background color in the cells in the row is the one you set for the `SelectionBackColor` property of the `DefaultCellStyle` property for the control. You can also select an individual cell by clicking it, and the background color of the cell changes to green.

The ability to sort the rows based on any given column is built into the `DataGridView` control. You could try clicking a column header and see the rows sorted by the column you select. If you click the column header a second time, the rows are ordered in the opposite sense. You could add a tooltip to each of the columns to explain the sort possibility. Adding this loop to the `Form1` class constructor does this:

```
for each(DataGridViewColumn^ column in dataGridView->Columns)
  column->ToolTipText = L"Click to\nsort rows";
```

The `Columns` property value is a collection of columns where each column is an object of type `DataGridViewColumn`. The loop iterates over each of the columns and sets the value of the `ToolTipText` property. Figure 23-9 shows the tooltip for one of the column headers.

These tooltips display only when the mouse cursor is over a column header cell. You can set a tooltip for any of the cells that display the data by setting the `ToolTipText` property for the cell object.

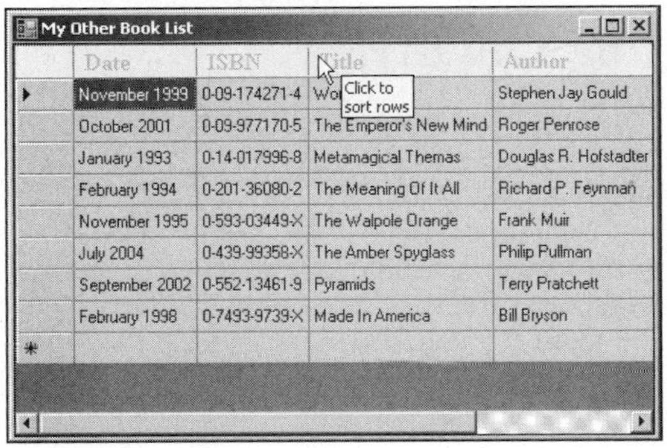

Figure 23-9

Customizing Alternate Rows

When you are displaying many rows that are similar in appearance, it can be difficult to see which row you are looking at. You can color alternate rows differently to help overcome the problem by setting a different color as the `BackColor` property for the `AlternatingRowsDefaultCellStyle` property for the control object:

```
dataGridView->AlternatingRowsDefaultCellStyle->BackColor = Color::Blue;
```

You will probably want to change the `ForeColor` property for the `AlternatingRowsDefaultCellStyle` property to get a reasonable contrast between the text and the background:

```
dataGridView->AlternatingRowsDefaultCellStyle->ForeColor = Color::White;
```

Now rows are displayed with colors alternating between pink and blue, as shown in Figure 23-10 (in shades of grey, of course, as there is no color in the book).

Now it's easy to separate the rows and the white text against a blue background is clear. You can still select a row by clicking a row header and see the selected row in green. Clicking in the cell at the left end of the column headers selects all the rows.

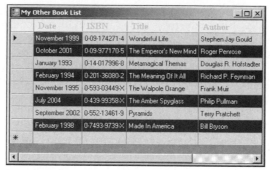

Figure 23-10

Dynamically Setting Cell Styles

You have several possibilities for changing the appearance of cells by handling events for the DataGridView control. The CellFormatting event for a DataGridView control fires when the contents of a cell need to be formatted ready to be displayed, so by adding a handler for this event you can adjust the appearance of any cell depending on what the contents are. I want now to explore how you could extend Ex23_02 to do this.

Suppose, for example, that in Ex23_02 you wanted to set the background color of cells in the Date column to red if the date is before the year 2000. Recall from the discussion of events in Chapter 9 that to register a handler for an event you add an instance of the delegate to the event. The delegate for the CellFormatting event is of type DataGridViewCellFormattingEventHandler, and it expects two parameters: the first parameter is of type Object^ and identifies the source of the event and the second parameter is a handle to an object of type DataGridViewCellFormattingEventArgs.

The second argument passed to a handler for the CellFormatting event provides additional information about the event through the properties shown in the following table.

Property	Description
Value	The value is a handle to the contents of the cell that is being formatted.
DesiredType	The value is a handle to an object of type Type that identifies the type of the contents off the cell being formatted.
CellStyle	Gets or sets the cell style of the cell that is associated with the formatting event so the value is a handle to an object of type DataGridViewCellStyle.
ColumnIndex	The value is the column index for the cell that is being formatted.
RowIndex	The value is the row index for the cell that is being formatted.
FormattingApplied	The value, true or false, indicates whether formatting of the cell contents has been applied.

These properties enable you to find out all you need to know about the cell being formatted — the row and column for the cell, the current style in effect, and the contents of the cell.

The first step in handling the `CellFormatting` event is to define a handler function for it. The handler code needs to be as short and efficient as possible because the function is called for every cell in the control whenever the cell needs to be formatted. You could add the following function to the `Form1` class that is a handler function for the `CellFormatting` event:

```
private:
void OnCellFormatting(Object^ sender, DataGridViewCellFormattingEventArgs^ e)
{
  // Check if it's the date column
  if(dataGridView->Columns[e->ColumnIndex]->Name == L"Date")
  {
    // If the cell content is not null and the year is less than 2000
    // Set the background to red
    if(e->Value != nullptr && safe_cast<DateTime^>(e->Value)->Year < 2000)
    {
      e->CellStyle->BackColor = Color::Red;
      e->FormattingApplied = false;            // We did not format the data
    }
  }
}
```

Don't forget, any code that you add manually to a form class definition must go after the `#pragma endregion` directive. You first check whether the current column is the `Date` column because you are interested only in modifying cells in that column. For cells in the `Date` column you check if the cell contents actually exist, and if there is a `DateTime` object present, that the year is less than 2000. In this case you set the `BackColor` property for the object returned by the `CellStyle` property to `Color::Red`. You set the `FormattingApplied` property to `false` to indicate that you have not formatted the contents. This is not strictly necessary because the value starts out as `false`. You would set it to `true` if you were taking care of formatting the contents in the handler and this would prevent subsequent formatting using the value of the `Format` property.

To register this function as a handler for the `CellFormatting` event, add the following statement to the end of the `Form1` class constructor:

```
dataGridView->CellFormatting +=
   gcnew DataGridViewCellFormattingEventHandler(this, &Form1::OnCellFormatting);
```

The first argument to the delegate is the handle to the object containing the handler function and is the current `Form1` object. The second argument is the address of the function that is the new handler for the event. If you recompile the example and execute it once again, you should see that all the cells in the `Date` column that contain a date prior to the year 2000 have the background color red.

The `DataGridView` control defines `CellMouseEnter` and `CellMouseLeave` events that fire when the mouse cursor enters or leaves a cell. You could implement handlers for these events to highlight the cell that the mouse cursor is over by changing its background color. You could set new background and foreground colors in the handler for the `CellMouseEnter` event and restore the original colors in the handler for the `CellMouseLeave` event. There are a few tricky aspects to this, so it's worth looking into specifically.

Try It Out Highlighting the Cell under the Mouse Cursor

This will be an extension to Ex23_02 including the latest addition of the CellFormatting event handler rather than a new example from scratch. You'll need to store the old background and foreground colors somewhere, so add the following private data members to the Form1 class:

```
// Stores for old cell colors in mouse enter event handler
// for restoring later in mouse leave event handler
private: Color oldCellBackColor;
private: Color oldCellForeColor;
```

You should initialize both of these to Color::Empty in the Form1 class constructor.

The first parameter to the delegate for either the CellMouseEnter or CellMouseLeave events is a handle to the object originating the event, which is the DataGridView control. The second parameter to both delegates is a handle to an object of type DataGridViewCellEventsArg that provides additional information about the event. This object has RowIndex and ColumnIndex properties, and the values of these properties enable you to locate the cell the mouse is entering or leaving; you can use the former to index the Rows property to select the row that contains the cell and the latter to index the Cells property to select the cell itself within the row. There's one thing to note — the value of the RowIndex property is -1 when the mouse cursor is in the column header row and the ColumnIndex property value is -1 when the mouse cursor is over one of the row headers. You'll need to check for these possibilities because attempting to use a negative index with the Rows property value causes an exception to be thrown, as does indexing the Cells property for a row with a negative value.

You can now define a private handler function in the Form1 class for the CellMouseEnter event like this:

```
private:
void OnCellMouseEnter(Object^ sender, DataGridViewCellEventArgs^ e)
{
  if(e->ColumnIndex >= 0 && e->RowIndex >= 0)      // Verify indexes non-negative
  {
    // Identify the cell we have entered
    DataGridViewCell^ cell =
                      dataGridView->Rows[e->RowIndex]->Cells[e->ColumnIndex];

    // Save any old colors that are set
    oldCellBackColor = cell->Style->BackColor;
    oldCellForeColor = cell->Style->ForeColor;

    // Set highlight colors
    cell->Style->BackColor = Color::White;
    cell->Style->ForeColor = Color::Black;
  }
}
```

After establishing that both index values are non-negative, you obtain the handle for the cell that the mouse cursor entered. You do this by first selecting the row by indexing the value of the Rows property for the control with the RowIndex property value for the parameter e; you then index the Cells property of the row using the ColumnIndex property of e to select the cell within the row.

After you have the cell handle, it's easy to save the values of the BackColor and ForeColor properties from the Style property of the cell and set new colors to display the cell as black text on a white background. The Style property may not have been set, in which case accessing the property value creates a new DataGridViewCellStyle object as the value that has BackColor and ForeColor property values as Color::Empty. If the Style property for the cell has been set, you'll get the object containing whatever properties have been set for it.

The handler function for the CellMouseEnter event has to restore the color back to what is was. You can implement this handler function like this:

```
private:
void OnCellMouseLeave(Object^ sender, DataGridViewCellEventArgs^ e)
{
  if(e->ColumnIndex >=0 && e->RowIndex >=0)
  {
    // Identify the cell we are leaving
    DataGridViewCell^ cell =
                      dataGridView->Rows[e->RowIndex]->Cells[e->ColumnIndex];

    // Restore the saved color values
    cell->Style->BackColor = oldCellBackColor;
    cell->Style->ForeColor = oldCellForeColor;

    // Reset save stores to no color
    oldCellForeColor = oldCellBackColor = Color::Empty;
  }
}
```

Again you check that the index values are non-negative before doing anything. After identifying the cell as in the previous handler, you restore the saved colors in the Style property for the cell. The way in which the foreground and background colors for a cell are determined is by the priority list you saw earlier. If the Style property had not been set for the cell, the values you restore are Color::Empty and this is ignored when the colors for the cells are determined. Thus, the original color applies. If the Style property had been defined with ForeColor and BackColor properties set, these are the values you restore, and they determine the cell formatting colors.

To register the function handlers, add the following statements to the end of the Form1 class constructor:

```
dataGridView->CellMouseEnter +=
            gcnew DataGridViewCellEventHandler(this, &Form1::OnCellMouseEnter);
dataGridView->CellMouseLeave +=
            gcnew DataGridViewCellEventHandler(this, &Form1::OnCellMouseLeave);
```

The same delegate applies to all cell events, so you register both handlers using the DataGridViewCellEventHandler delegate.

If you recompile the program a run it once again, you should see highlighting of cells in action, as illustrated in Figure 23-11.

Well, it certainly works — at least most of the time. However, the red cells in the Date column aren't highlighted, so what's going on?

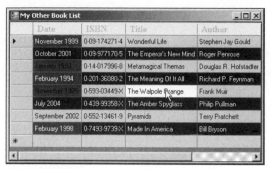

Figure 23-11

The sequence of events is at the root of the problem. The `CellFormatting` event is triggered after the `CellMouseEnter` event, so the handler function that sets the background color to red has the last word and overrides the effect of the handler for the `CellMouseEnter` event. What you want to happen is that the `CellFormatting` event handler should recognize that the cell is highlighted and do nothing when this is the case. You could provide for this by adding another member to the `Form1` class that stores the handle to the cell that is currently highlighted:

```
private: DataGridViewCell^ highlightedCell;        // The currently highlighted cell
```

You should also initialize this new member to `nullptr` in the `Form1` class constructor.

You now need to amend the handler for the `CellMouseEnter` event to store the handle for the highlighted cell in the new member:

```
void OnCellMouseEnter(Object^ sender, DataGridViewCellEventArgs^ e)
{
  if(e->ColumnIndex >= 0 && e->RowIndex >= 0)     // Verify indexes non-negative
  {
    // Identify the cell we have entered
    highlightedCell = dataGridView->Rows[e->RowIndex]->Cells[e->ColumnIndex];

    // Save any old colors that are set
    oldCellBackColor = highlightedCell->Style->BackColor;
    oldCellForeColor = highlightedCell->Style->ForeColor;

    // Set highlight colors
    highlightedCell->Style->BackColor = Color::White;
    highlightedCell->Style->ForeColor = Color::Black;
  }
}
```

You can change the implementation of the handler for the `CellMouseLeave` event to the following:

```
void OnCellMouseLeave(Object^ sender, DataGridViewCellEventArgs^ e)
{
```

```
    if(e->ColumnIndex >=0 && e->RowIndex >=0)
    {
      // Restore the saved color values
      highlightedCell->Style->BackColor = oldCellBackColor;
      highlightedCell->Style->ForeColor = oldCellForeColor;

      // Reset save stores to no color
      oldCellForeColor = oldCellBackColor = Color::Empty;

      highlightedCell = nullptr;          // Reset highlighted cell handle
    }
  }
```

You no longer need to determine the cell handle, as it's available in the `highlightedCell` member of the `Form1` class. You don't even need to check it, because a `CellMouseLeave` event must always be preceded by a `CellMouseEnter` event. You reset the handle of the highlighted cell to null because it's good practice to do so.

You can now amend the handler for the `CellFormatting` event:

```
void OnCellFormatting(Object^ sender, DataGridViewCellFormattingEventArgs^ e)
{
  // Check whether the cell is highlighted
  if(dataGridView->Rows[e->RowIndex]->Cells[e->ColumnIndex] == highlightedCell)
    return;

  // Check if it's the date column
  if(dataGridView->Columns[e->ColumnIndex]->Name == L"Date")
  {
    // If the cell content is not null and the year is less than 2000
    // Set the background to red
    if(e->Value != nullptr && safe_cast<DateTime^>(e->Value)->Year < 2000)
    {
      e->CellStyle->BackColor = Color::Red;
      e->FormattingApplied = false;      // We did not format the data
    }
  }
}
```

If you rebuild the example, you should now see that any of the cells can be highlighted by moving the mouse cursor over them.

You should now have a good idea of how you can implement an event handler for a `DataGridView` control. There are a multitude of other events, so you have huge scope for doing many more things dynamically to customize the control to your application needs.

Using Bound Mode

In bound mode, the source of the data that a `DataGridView` control displays is specified by the value of its `DataSource` property, which in general you can set to be any `ref class` object of a type that implements any of the interfaces shown in the following table.

Interface	Description
`System::Collections::IList`	A class that implements this interface represents a collection of objects that can be accessed through a single index. All C++/CLI one-dimensional arrays implement this interface, so a `DataGridView` object can use any one-dimensional array as the source of the data that is displayed. The `IList` interface inherits the members of the `ICollection` and `IEnumerable` interface classes that are defined in the `System::Collections` namespace.
`System::ComponentModel::IListSource`	A class that implements this interface makes the data available as a list that is an `IList` object. The list can contain objects that also implement the `IList` interface.
`System::ComponentModel::IBindingList`	This interface class extends the `IList` interface class to allow more complex data binding situations to be accommodated.
`System::ComponentModel::IBindingListView`	Adds sorting and filtering capabilities to the `IBindingList` interface. The `BindingSource` class that you'll meet a little later in this chapter defines a control that implements this interface.

You can obviously design your own classes so that they implement one or other of these interfaces, and then you'll be able to use them as a data source for a `DataGridView` control in bound mode. Most of the time, though, you'll want to access an existing data source without having to go to the trouble of creating your own classes to access the data in which case the `BindingSource` component is likely to be your first choice.

The BindingSource Component

You use the `BindingSource` component as an intermediary between controls on a form and a table in a data source. You have the option of binding the component to a `DataGridView` control that displays the contents of the table, or to a set of individual controls where each displays a column from the table. You can also add data programmatically to a `BindingSource` component, in which case it acts as the data source and behaves essentially as a list.

You'll first look at how you use a BindingSource component as the data source for a DataGridView control. There is a high degree of automation possible in creating a program that uses a BindingSource component, but to get an idea of how the component hooks up with the control, you'll assemble the components on the form manually in the first instance. To make a BindingSource component the data source for a DataGridView control, you set the value of the DataSource property for the control to be the handle that references the BindingSource component.

Note that at the time of writing a bug in Visual Studio 2008 prevents the creation of the next example, Ex23_03; this also affects the succeeding examples, Ex23_04 and Ex23_05. The symptoms of the bug are that the Data Source Configuration Wizard dialog that you use to associate a database with the DataGridView component in the application only displays the icon that you use to choose an object as the data source, so you have no possibility to choose a database.

The example can be created with Visual Studio 2005 and has been tested in that environment. The rest of screenshots shown in this chapter are also from Visual Studio 2005, but the screenshots from Visual Studio 2008 should be virtually identical. Hopefully by the time you are reading this, the bug will be fixed and will not be apparent in your version of Visual Studio 2008. If you do experience the bug, it is a good idea to see whether there are any updates for the product by selecting the Check for Updates menu item from the Help menu.

Try It Out   Using a BindingSource Component

Here you'll put together a simple program to view a database table. I'll describe the process assuming you are using the Northwind database that you used back when you were working with the MFC, but you can use any database you have available on your system.

Create a new Windows Forms project with the name Ex23_03 and change the Text property for the form to something helpful such as Using a Binding Source Component. Add a DataGridView control to the client area of the form and change its Name property to dataGridView. You can also set the Dock property value for the control to FILL. At the moment, the DataGridView control is unbound, so you need to add a data source to the project that you can bind to the control, and this process will create the BindingSource component along the way. Click the small arrow at the top right of the control to display its menu, click the arrow for the list box adjacent to the Choose Data Source menu item, and click the Add Project Data Source link. This displays the dialog box shown in Figure 23-12.

The same dialog box is displayed if you select the Data > Add New Data Source menu item from the main menu, but this only adds the data source to the project — it does not associate it with a control. As you see, you have a choice of two locations for the data source, but here you want to click the Database option. The second option allows you to specify an object that provides the data source defined either within the project or within some other assembly that you have created.

After selecting the Database option and clicking the Next button, you'll see the dialog box shown in Figure 23-13.

The existing data connections that you have set up appear in the drop-down list, and you can choose one of those. You can also click the New Connection button to set up a new connection to a data source. This displays the Add Connection dialog box shown in Figure 23-14.

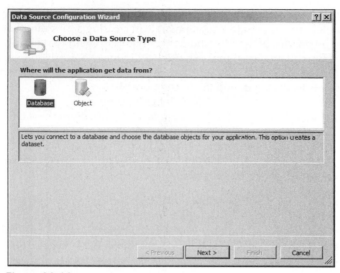

Figure 23-12

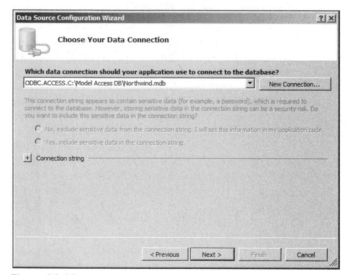

Figure 23-13

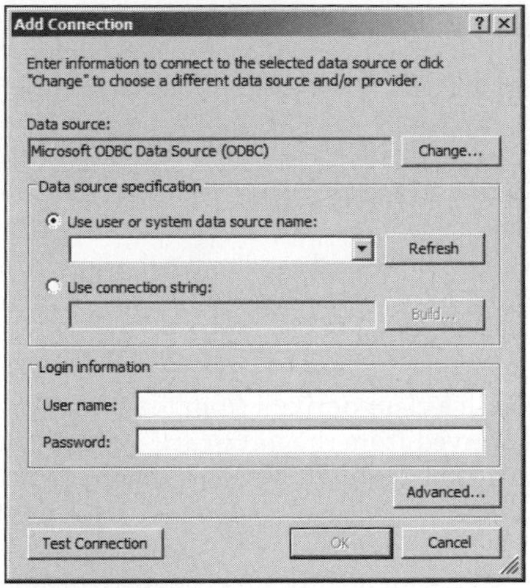

Figure 23-14

Here you can enter the data source specification as a name, or you can enter a connection string for the data source by clicking the second radio button. After you have entered any necessary login information, you can test that the connection really does work by clicking the Test Connection button. On my system, the ODBC source is preselected, but if you don't want the default that you see displayed, you can click the Change button to display the Change Data Source dialog box shown in Figure 23-15.

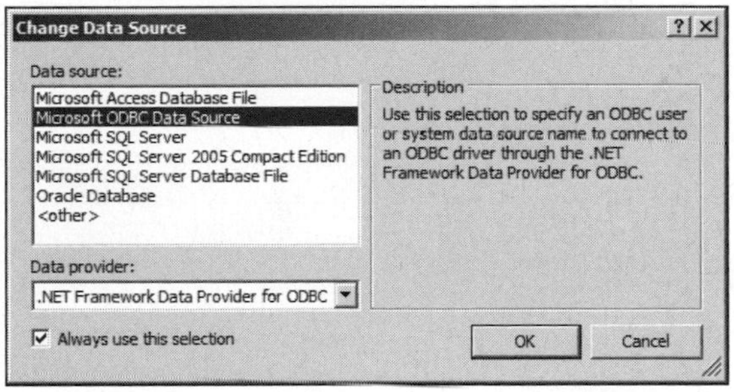

Figure 23-15

The dialog box displays the types of data sources that you have available, and you choose the type of data source that you want to work with and click the OK button. You'll then return to the dialog box shown in Figure 23-14 where you can complete the identification and verification of the data source before clicking the OK button to return to the dialog shown in Figure 23-13. When you click the Next button, you are likely to see a message box asking if you want to add the data source to the project; clicking the Yes button then displays the dialog box shown in Figure 23-16 where you can choose the objects in the database that you want to work with.

Here you can choose which database objects you want added to the project. You do this by expanding the tree so you can select the individual tables you want to work with, or even individual fields within a table. For this example, you can keep it simple and choose just the Customers table. You can also change the name of the dataset — I changed it to Customers. When you click the Finish button, the wizard creates the code that you need to access the database.

The database is encapsulated in a class derived from the DataSet class. Each database table that you select results in a class derived from the DataTable class being defined as an inner class to the DataSet class. There is also a table adapter class for each DataTable in the DataSet class that has the job of establishing the connection to the database and loading the data from the database table into the corresponding DataTable member of the DataSet object. This results in a considerable amount of code being generated; with just the Customers table in the Northwind database selected you get nearly 2000 lines of code. It also adds a BindingSource component to the project that provides the interface between the Customers table in the Northwind database and the DataGridView control. The Design tab in the editing window should look like Figure 23-17.

You can see that three objects have been added to the project as a result of adding the data source: the NorthWindDataSet object that encapsulates the database, the CustomersTableAdapter object that accesses the data in the Customers table in the database, and the CustomersBindingSource object that manages the communications between the database and the DataGridView control.

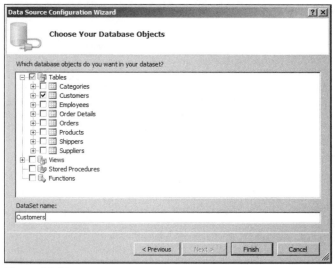

Figure 23-16

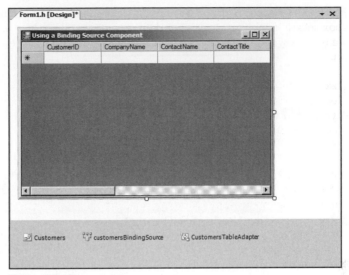

Figure 23-17

The application is now complete, and so far you have not written a single line of code. That's quite remarkable considering the amount of function you have in the program; however, when I ran the program, the column headers look a little cramped. I prefer the column widths to be set to accommodate the text in the rows, so I couldn't resist adding the following two lines of code to the `Form1` class constructor:

```
dataGridView->AutoSizeColumnsMode = DataGridViewAutoSizeColumnsMode::AllCells;
dataGridView->AutoResizeColumnHeadersHeight();
```

The application window now looks as shown in Figure 23-18.

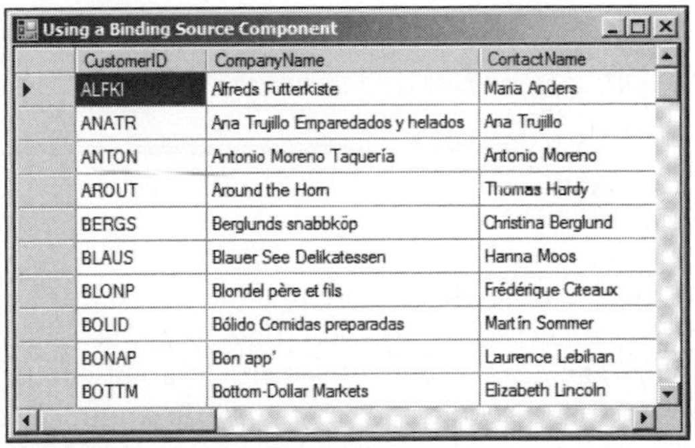

Figure 23-18

You can use the scrollbars to navigate the data and your mouse wheel should scroll the rows. The `BindingNavigator` control could improve things a bit, so next you'll see how to use that.

Using the BindingNavigator Control

The `BindingNavigator` control has been specifically designed to work with a `BindingSource` component. To use a `BindingNavigator` control to navigate the data from a data source could not be simpler; you just add the control to the form and set the value of the `BindingSource` property for the control to the variable encapsulating the `BindingSource` component. The next Try It Out extends `Ex23_03` to do that.

Try It Out   Using a BindingNavigator Control

Click the `BindingNavigator` control in the `Toolbox` window and then click in the client area of the form to add it to the project. If you open the `Properties` window for the control, you are able to set the value for the `BindingSource` property to `customersBindingSource`, which is the name of the handle to the `BindingSource` control that encapsulates the `Customers` table. That's it; you're done. If you recompile and rerun the application, you see that the application window now has a toolbar for navigating the data, as shown in Figure 23-19.

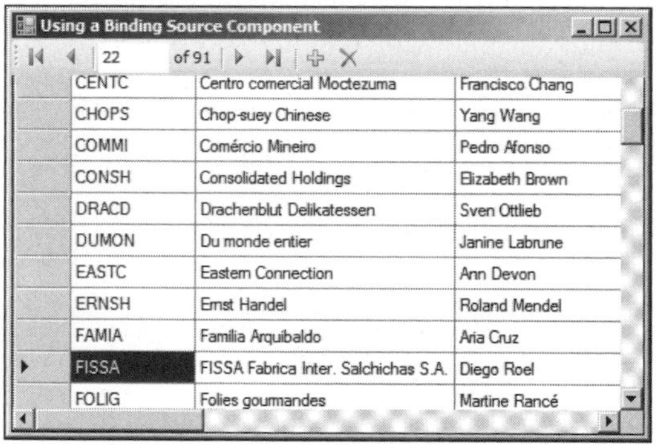

Figure 23-19

You can click the button arrows to progress forward and backward through the data records, and there are also buttons to go to the first or last records. If you type a record sequence number in the text box on the toolbar and press `Enter`, you'll go directly to that record. The ability to navigate through the records works in whatever sequence they are in. You could sort the records in country order by clicking the header for the `Country` column to sort the records, and you'll then be able to navigate through them in that sequence. The `BindingNavigator` control also provides buttons for adding a new record and deleting a record.

Each of the buttons provided by the `BindingNavigator` control connects to a member of the `BindingSource` object being navigated.

Toolbar Control	Action
Move First	Calls the MoveFirst() function for the BindingSource control object, which changes the current record for the underlying data source to be the first record.
Move Previous	Calls the MovePrevious() function for the BindingSource control object, which changes the current record for the underlying data source to be the previous record if there is one.
Current Position	Corresponds to the value of the Current property for the BindingSource object, which is the current record in the underlying data source.
Total Number of Items	Corresponds to the value of the Count property value for the BindingSource object, which corresponds to the number of records in the underlying data source.
Move Next	Calls the MoveNext() function for the BindingSource control object, which changes the current record for the underlying data source to be the next record if there is one.
Move Last	Calls the MoveLast() function for the BindingSource control object, which changes the current record for the underlying data source to be the last record.
Add New	Calls the AddNew() function for the BindingSource object. This has the effect of calling EndEdit() to execute any pending edit operations for the underlying data source and creates a new record in the list maintained by the BindingSource object. This does not update the underlying data source.
Delete	Calls the RemoveCurrent() function for the BindingSource object to remove the current record from the list. This does not modify the underlying data source.

Thus clicking a button on the navigator toolbar initiates an action in the BindingSource object that is managing the data source, but none of the default operations change the database that the BindingSource component is managing. To do that you must write some code.

Try It Out   Updating a Database

You are going to have to do something extra when the user clicks a button in the BindingNavigator control to add a new record or to delete a record. The way to do this is to implement a handler function to deal with a Click event for the buttons.

As you already know, you can add a `Click` event handler for a button by double-clicking the button in the `Design` tab, so add handler functions for the `Add New` and `Delete` buttons on the toolbar. When you click either button at the moment, everything has been put in place in the `BindingSource` component to allow the database to be updated. All you have to do is call the `Update()` function for the table adapter object for the table that is to be updated. This function throws an exception if things go wrong, so you must put the call in a `try` block and `catch` any exception that may be thrown. Here's how you can implement the handler function for the `Add New` button `Click` event:

```
System::Void bindingNavigatorAddNewItem_Click(System::Object^  sender,
                                              System::EventArgs^  e)
{
  try
  {
    CustomersTableAdapter->Update(Customers->_Customers);
  }
  catch (Exception^ ex)
  {
    MessageBox::Show(L"Update Failed!\n"+ex,
                 L"Database Record Update Error",
                 MessageBoxButtons::OK,
                 MessageBoxIcon::Error);
  }
}
```

The argument to the `Update()` function must be the name of the data table that contains the values that are to be written to the database, so in this case it's the `_Customers` member of the `Customers` object in the Form1 class. If things don't go as well as expected, you display a message box explaining the problem. The message box shows the text from the `Exception` object that was thrown, and this explains the cause of the problem.

The implementation of the `Click` event handler for the `Delete` button is almost identical:

```
private: System::Void bindingNavigatorDeleteItem_Click(System::Object^  sender,
                                              System::EventArgs^  e)
{
  try
  {
    CustomersTableAdapter->Update(Customers->_Customers);
  }
  catch (Exception^ ex)
  {
    MessageBox::Show(L"Delete Failed!\n"+ex,
                 L"Database Record Delete Error",
                 MessageBoxButtons::OK,
                 MessageBoxIcon::Error);
  }
}
```

The only difference is in the text in the message box. With these two handler functions in place, you should be able to add new customer records and delete existing records.

Binding to Individual Controls

You can also create a Windows Forms application that binds each column on a database table to a separate control; what's more, you'll find this easier and quicker than the previous example. Start by creating a new CLR project using the `Windows Forms Application` template with the name `Ex23_04`. The next step is to add a data source to the project, and again you will be working with a single table. Press `Shift+Alt+D` to display the `Data Sources` window and click `Add New Data Source`. You can use the Northwind database or a database of your choice, but keep in mind that you have a separate control on the form for each column in the table that you choose. To keep the number of controls manageable, for the Northwind database I suggest you select the `Order Details` table, as shown in Figure 23-20, because it has only five columns.

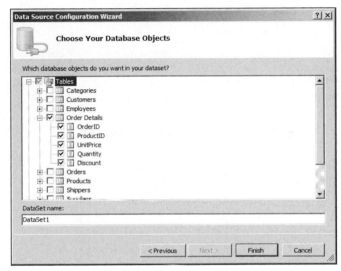

Figure 23-20

When you click the `Finish` button, the `Data Sources` window shows the Northwind database as the data source with just the `Order Details` table available. Click the `Order Details` table name to select it and then click the down arrow to the right to display the menu shown in Figure 23-21.

The top three menu items enable you to choose the controls to be used with the table when you add the data source to the form. If you click the `DataGridView` item from the menu, you are selecting that control as the one to be for displaying the table, whereas clicking on the `Details` item indicates you want one control per table column. If you click the `[None]` item, you are indicating you want no controls to be created when you add the data source to the form. The last menu item opens a dialog box for changing the default control for the table from the current default of `DataGridView` and for customizing the choice of controls. In this instance, you should just click `Details` because you want one control for each table column.

Figure 23-21

You now have to decide which control you want to use for each table column. You can extend the tree that shows the column names in the `Order Details` table name by clicking the + symbol to the left of the table name. If you then click the first column name to select it, you'll see that you can display a menu for that, too, by clicking the down arrow. The menu is shown in Figure 23-22.

Figure 23-22

You can choose any of the controls shown in the menu, but I suggest a `TextBox` control is most appropriate for the `OrderID` column. You need to repeat the process for each table column; you can choose a `NumericUpDown` control for the `Quantity` column and select a `TextBox` control for each of the others.

Note that selecting the Customize menu option in the Data Sources pane shown in Figure 23-22 displays the Options dialog box in which you can change the selection of controls available for displaying different types of data. You can also change the control to be selected by default when you drag an item from the Data Sources pane to a form. Figure 23-23 shows the Options dialog box.

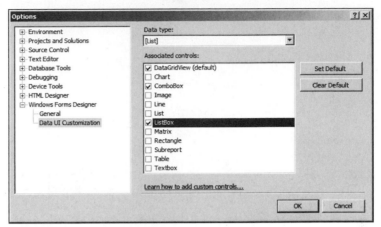

Figure 23-23

Figure 23-23 shows the controls associated with displaying a list, and there is a separate list of associated controls for each of the data types you can select. I have checked the ComboBox and ListBox controls in addition to the DataGridView default, so all three controls are options for displaying a list of data items. You can choose other data types in the drop-down list box at the top of the dialog box for which you want to modify the choice of controls available.

The final step to create the program is to drag the Order Details table from the Data Sources window to the client area of the form window. The Design tab in the Editor pane will then look similar to that shown in Figure 23-24.

I have changed the Text property for the form to make the text in the title bar a little more relevant, and I repositioned the controls slightly so they are better located within the client area. I also rearranged the items in the grey area at the bottom to make them all visible in the Design pane. You can see that five controls corresponding to the five table columns have been added automatically to the form as well as label controls to indicate which is which. There's a BindingNavigator control at the top of the client area for navigating the table data. Below the form you can see that the application has a BindingSource component that links the database to the controls, and the DataSet and table adapter classes are also identified.

If you press Ctrl+F5 to build and execute the program, you'll have a complete working program for viewing and editing the Order Details table in the Northwind database. There is a Save button that has been added to the BindingNavigator toolbar that you click to store any changes you make back in the database table. Figure 23-25 shows the application window.

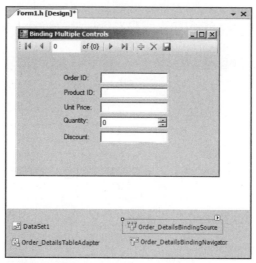

Figure 23-24

Figure 23-25

You could create a program that uses the `DataGridView` control to display a table in essentially the same way. If you want to try it, just create another project and add the data source as in the previous example. If you then immediately drag the table from the `Data Sources` window to the form, the application is complete. You need only set the `Text` property for the form for the title bar text and set the value of the `Dock` property for the `DataGridView` control before compiling and running the program.

Working with Multiple Tables

Creating an application that works with multiple tables is almost as easy as the previous example. In this example, you'll use a tab control to allow three different tables in the Northwind to be accessed. Create a new Forms project with the name `Ex23_05`, and press `Shift+Alt+D` to open the `Data Sources` window. Add the Northwind database to the project with the `Customers`, `Products`, and `Employees` tables checked.

Add a `TabControl` control from the `Containers` group in the `Toolbox` window to the form and set the `Dock` property value for the tab control to `Fill`. If you click the arrow at the top right of the control, you'll be able to add a third tab page to the control. You can move between the tabs on the `TabControl` control using the `Tab` key, or by clicking the tab page label twice; take care not to double-click the control or you'll generate handler functions for it. Move to the first tab page and set its `Text` property value to `Employees`. You can then set the `Text` property value for the other two tabs to `Customers` and `Products`.

You should also add a `Panel` control to each tab page with its `Dock` property value set to `Fill`. This is necessary to locate the `BindingNavigator` and `DataGridView` controls properly on the tab page. If you add them directly to the tab, setting the `DataGridView` `Dock` property to `Fill` with the `BindingNavigator` control docked to the top of the tab page, the column headers for the `DataGridView` control are hidden by the `BindingNavigator` control. This won't happen within a `Panel` container. You might also want to change the `Text` property value for the form to something relevant — I made it `"Accessing Multiple Tables"`.

You can now drag the `Customer` table from the `Data Sources` window to the panel on the tab page labeled `Customers`. A `DataGridView` control is added to the panel, and a `BindingNavigator` control appears at the top of the form. You'll want each tab page to have its own `BindingNavigator` control, so having it placed on the form is not convenient. You'll need to move it to the panel on the tab page. You can do this by first setting the `Dock` property value for the `BindingNavigator` control to `None` and then dragging the control on to panel on the `Customers` tab page.

After you have added the table to the `Customers` tab page, switch to the next tab before dragging the next table on to its panel from the `Data Sources` window. When you have added the appropriate table to the panels on the other two tab pages, they each contain a `DataGridView` control, but no `BindingNavigator` control — this was not added because you have one already from adding the `Customers` table. You could add `BindingNavigator` controls to these tab pages from the `Toolbox` window, but there's a shortcut you can use. Click the `BindingNavigator` control on the `Customers` tab page and press `Ctrl+C` to copy it to the Clipboard. Switch to one of the other tab pages, select its panel, and press `Ctrl+V` to copy the control from the Clipboard to the panel on the tab page. Switch to the third tab page, select its panel, and then press `Ctrl+V` once more to add a `BindingNavigator` control to the panel on that tab page. You can then set the `Dock` property value for each of the three `BindingNavigator` controls to `Top` and the `Dock` property value for each of the `DataGridView` controls to `Fill`.

The two `BindingNavigator` controls that are copies have their `BindingSource` property values set incorrectly, so select the value field for the property for each of these controls and select the correct `BindingSource` component from the drop-down list. You should select `EmployeesBindingSource` for the control on the `Employees` tab page, and `ProductsBindingSource` for the control on the `Products` tab page.

If you press `Ctrl+F5` to build and execute the example, you should see the application window shown in Figure 23-26.

This all works with no coding at all. I think you'll agree that this is an amazing capability for generating applications to access data sources.

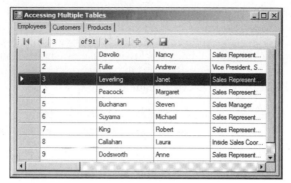

Figure 23-26

Summary

This has been a brief introduction to the capabilities you have for accessing data sources in a Windows Forms application. There's a great deal more you can do, but you should find that you now have a good idea of how you use the design capability to assemble controls on a form and how the controls involved in data access work together. You'll have few problems getting into other areas by yourself.

The key points you have learned about in this chapter include:

❑ A data source can be a relational database, a Web service, or an object.

❑ A class derived from the `System::Data::DataSet` class is used to encapsulate a data source, and a class derived from the `System::Data::DataTable` class table encapsulates a table in a data source.

❑ A row of data in a `DataTable` object is represented by an object of type `System::Data::DataRow`, and the schema for a column is described by an object of type `System::Data::DataColumn`.

❑ A connection to a data source and the commands to access the data are encapsulated in a component called a table adapter.

❑ You use a `DataGridView` control on a form to display data in the form of a rectangular grid.

❑ You can bind a `DataGridView` control to a data source to display the contents of a table. You can also use a `DataGridView` control in unbound mode to display data originating in your program.

❑ You can customize a `DataGridView` control to modify how rows, columns, headers, and individual cells are displayed.

❑ A `BindingSource` component provides an interface between a data source and controls on a form. A `BindingSource` component can link the columns in a table to individual controls on a form, or it can link the contents of a table to a `DataGridView` control.

❑ A `BindingNavigator` control provides a toolbar for navigating data that you access via a `BindingSource` component.

Exercises

You can download the source code for the examples in the book and the solutions to the following exercises from www.wrox.com.

1. Modify Ex23_04 so that the column headers are displayed in a 12-point italic font.

2. Modify Ex23_05 so the columns are wide enough to accommodate the text in each cell.

3. Modify Ex23_05 so that alternate rows of data on each tab page appear shaded.

4. Create a Windows Forms application that displays the Suppliers table from the Northwind database.

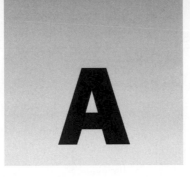

C++ Keywords

Keywords have been assigned special significance within the C++ language, so you must not use them as names within your programs. The Visual C++ 2008 compiler compiles programs written in ISO/ANSI C++ and programs written for the CLR that conform to the C++/CLI specification, so the compiler recognizes the set of keywords defined by ISO/ANSI C++ as well as the additional set of keywords defined by C++/CLI. However, when programming in native C++, you need be concerned only with the ISO/ANSI C++ keywords. When writing programs for the CLR, you need to be aware of both sets of keywords.

ISO/ANSI C++ Keywords

The ISO/ANSI C++ language specification defines the following keywords.

asm	do	if	return	try
auto	double	inline	short	typedef
bool	dynamic_cast	int	signed	typeid
break	else	long	sizeof	typename
case	enum	mutable	static	union
catch	explicit	namespace	static_cast	unsigned
char	export	new	struct	using
class	extern	operator	switch	virtual
const	false	private	template	void
const_cast	float	protected	this	volatile
continue	for	public	throw	wchar_t
default	friend	register	true	while
delete	goto	reinterpret_cast		

C++/CLI Keywords

The C++/CLI language specification defines the following keywords in addition to those defined for ISO/ANSI C++.

enum class	interface class	ref struct
enum struct	interface struct	value class
for each	nullptr	value struct
gcnew	ref class	

Note that the word pairs are keywords, not necessarily the individual words; for example, `for each` is a keyword, but `each` is not.

The C++/CLI language also defines a number of identifiers that are not keywords but have a context-sensitive meaning in some circumstances. These are shown in the following list.

abstract	in	override
delegate	initonly	property
event	internal	sealed
finally	literal	where
generic		

In principle you can still use these identifiers as names in your code because the context determines when they have special significance, but I recommend that you treat them as keywords and do not use them for other purposes. In that way you avoid any possibility for confusion on the part of someone else who may be reading your code.

ASCII Codes

The first 32 ASCII (American Standard Code for Information Interchange) characters provide control functions. In the following table, only the first 128 ASCII characters have been included. The remaining 128 characters include further special symbols and letters for national character sets, so there are many varieties of these to suit a wide range of language contexts.

Decimal	Hexadecimal	Character	Control
000	00	null	NUL
001	01	☺	SOH
002	02	●	STX
003	03	♥	ETX
004	04	♦	EOT
005	05	♣	ENQ
006	06	♠	ACK
007	07	•	BEL (Audible bell)
008	08		Backspace
009	09		HT
010	0A		LF (Line feed)
011	0B		VT (Vertical tab)
012	0C		FF (Form feed)
013	0D		CR (Carriage return)

Continued

Appendix B: ASCII Codes

Decimal	Hexadecimal	Character	Control
014	0E		SO
015	0F	¤	SI
016	10		DLE
017	11		DC1
018	12		DC2
019	13		DC3
020	14		DC4
021	15		NAK
022	16		SYN
023	17		ETB
024	18		CAN
025	19		EM
026	1A	→	SUB
027	1B	←	ESC (Escape)
028	1C	∟	FS
029	1D		GS
030	1E		RS
031	1F		US
032	20		space
033	21	!	
034	22	"	
035	23	#	

Decimal	Hexadecimal	Character	Control
036	24	$	
037	25	%	
038	26	&	
039	27	'	
040	28	(	
041	29	)	
042	2A	*	
043	2B	+	
044	2C	,	
045	2D	-	
046	2E	.	
047	2F	/	
048	30	0	
049	31	1	
050	32	2	
051	33	3	
052	34	4	
053	35	5	
054	36	6	
055	37	7	
056	38	8	
057	39	9	

Continued

Decimal	Hexadecimal	Character	Control
058	3A	:	
059	3B	;	
060	3C	<	
061	3D	=	
062	3E	>	
063	3F	?	
064	40	@	
065	41	A	
066	42	B	
067	43	C	
068	44	D	
069	45	E	
070	46	F	
071	47	G	
072	48	H	
073	49	I	
074	4A	J	
075	4B	K	
076	4C	L	
077	4D	M	
078	4E	N	
079	4F	O	

Decimal	Hexadecimal	Character	Control
080	50	P	
081	51	Q	
082	52	R	
083	53	S	
084	54	T	
085	55	U	
086	56	V	
087	57	W	
088	58	X	
089	59	Y	
090	5A	Z	
091	5B	[	
092	5C	\	
093	5D	]	
094	5E	^	
095	5F	_	
096	60	'	
097	61	a	
098	62	b	
099	63	c	
100	64	d	
101	65	e	

Continued

Appendix B: ASCII Codes

Decimal	Hexadecimal	Character	Control
102	66	f	
103	67	g	
104	68	h	
105	69	i	
106	6A	j	
107	6B	k	
108	6C	l	
109	6D	m	
110	6E	n	
111	6F	o	
112	70	p	
113	71	q	
114	72	r	
115	73	s	
116	74	t	
117	75	u	
118	76	v	
119	77	w	
120	78	x	
121	79	y	
122	7A	z	
123	7B	{	

Decimal	Hexadecimal	Character	Control
124	7C	|	
125	7D	}	
126	7E	~	
127	7F	delete	

The Unicode codes that have the same numerical code values as the ASCII codes in the table represent the same characters. You'll find comprehensive information on the Unicode character coding system at www.unicode.org.

Windows Message Types

The Windows operating system defines the type of system message that it sends to your application by a symbolic constant such as WM_PAINT. The symbolic constant is composed of two parts: a prefix, WM in this case, that identifies the type of window that can process the message, and the rest, PAINT in this case, that specifies what the window should do when the message is received. The following table shows the message prefixes and the corresponding target window category.

Message Prefix	Target Window Type
ABM	Application desktop toolbar control
BM	Button control
CB	Combo box control
CBEM	Extended combo box control
CDM	Common dialog box control
DBT	Device
DL	Drag list box control
DM	Default push button control
DTM	Date and time picker control
EM	Edit control
HDM	Header control
HKM	Hot key control

Continued

Message Prefix	Target Window Type
IPM	IP address control
LB	List box control
LVM	List view control
MCM	Month calendar control
PBM	Progress bar control
PGM	Pager control
PSM	Property sheet
RB	Rebar control
SB	Status bar control
SBM	Scroll bar control
STM	Static control
TB	Toolbar
TBM	Trackbar
TCM	Tab control
TTM	Tooltip control
TVM	Tree view control
UDM	Up-down control
WM	General window

The symbolic constants that identify system messages have values in the range 0 to WM_USER-1, so this range of values is reserved. An application can create messages for its own purposes and such messages can have identifiers with values in the range from WM_USER (that corresponds to the value 0x0400) to 0x7FFF.

Index

X